Lecture Notes in Computer Science 6397

Commenced Publication in 1973
Founding and Former Series Editors:
Gerhard Goos, Juris Hartmanis, and Jan van Leeuwen

Advanced Research in Computing and Software Science

Subline of Lectures Notes in Computer Science

Christian G. Fermüller Andrei Voronkov (Eds.)

Logic for Programming, Artificial Intelligence, and Reasoning

17th International Conference, LPAR-17
Yogyakarta, Indonesia, October 10-15, 2010
Proceedings

Springer

Volume Editors

Christian G. Fermüller
TU Wien
Institut für Computersprachen 185.2
Theory and Logic Group
Favoritenstraße 9-11
A-1040 Vienna, Austria
E-mail: chrisf@logic.at

Andrei Voronkov
University of Manchester
School of Computer Science
Kilburn Building
Oxford Road
Manchester, M13 9PL, UK
E-mail: andrei.voronkov@manchester.ac.uk

Library of Congress Control Number: 2010935496

CR Subject Classification (1998): F.3, I.2, D.2, F.4.1, D.3, H.4

LNCS Sublibrary: SL 1 – Theoretical Computer Science and General Issues

ISSN 0302-9743
ISBN-10 3-642-16241-X Springer Berlin Heidelberg New York
ISBN-13 978-3-642-16241-1 Springer Berlin Heidelberg New York

springer.com

Printed in Germany

Typesetting: Camera-ready by author, data conversion by Scientific Publishing Services, Chennai, India
Printed on acid-free paper SPIN: 06/3180 5 4 3 2 1 0

Preface

This volume contains the research papers presented at the 17th International Conference on Logic for Programming, Artificial Intelligence, and Reasoning (LPAR-17), held in Yogyakarta, Indonesia, October 10–15, 2010, accompanied by the 8th International Workshop on the Implementation of Logic (IWIL-8, organized by Eugenia Ternovska, Stephan Schulz, and Geoff Sutcliffe) and the 5th International Workshop on Analytic Proof Systems (APS-5, organized by Matthias Baaz and Christian Fermüller).

The call for papers attracted 133 abstract submissions of which 105 materialized into full submissions, each of which was assigned for reviewing to at least three Program Committee members; 41 papers were accepted after intense discussions. Once more the EasyChair system provided an ideal platform for submission, reviewing, discussions, and collecting final versions of accepted papers.

The program included three invited talks by Krishnendu Chatterjee, Joseph Halpern, and Michael Maher, as well as an invited tutorial by Norbert Preining. They are documented by the corresponding papers and abstract, respectively, in these proceedings, which this year appear for the first time in the ARCoSS subline of the *Lecture Notes in Computer Science.*

Apart from the authors, invited speakers, Program Committee members, and external reviewers, we would like to thank further people that made LPAR-17 a success: the General Chair, Steffen Hölldobler, and his team at the International Center for Computational Logic at TU Dresden; the Local Chairs, Taufiq Hidayat, Yudi Prayudi, and Reza Pulungan; the Publicity Chair, Geoff Sutcliffe; and the Workshop Chair, Laura Kovács. We also gratefully acknowledge financial support by the Kurt Gödel Society.

August 2010

Christian G. Fermüller
Andrei Voronkov

Conference Organization

Program Chairs

Christian Fermüller
Andrei Voronkov

Program Committee

Franz Baader
Matthias Baaz
Michael Backes
Gilles Barthe
Peter Baumgartner
Nikolaj Bjørner
Agata Ciabattoni
Alessandro Cimatti
Thierry Coquand
Nachum Dershowitz
Thomas Eiter
Javier Esparza
Thom Frühwirth
Lluís Godo
Georg Gottlob
Martin Grohe
John Harrison
Miki Hermann
Reiner Hähnle
Neil Immerman
Joxan Jaffar
Deepak Kapur
Claude Kirchner
Michael Kohlhase
Konstantin Korovin
Laura Kovacs
Aart Middeldorp
Dale Miller
Joachim Niehren
Michel Parigot
Frank Pfenning
Torsten Schaub
Natarajan Shankar
Geoff Sutcliffe
Wolfgang Thomas
Cesare Tinelli
Toby Walsh
Christoph Weidenbach
Frank Wolter

General Chair

Steffen Hölldobler

Local Chairs

Taufiq Hidayat
Yudi Prayudi
Reza Pulungan

Workshop Chair

Laura Kovács

Publicity Chair

Geoff Sutcliffe

External Reviewers

Andreas Abel
Babak Ahmadi
Martin Avanzini
Pavel Avgustinov
Chitta Baral
Hariolf Betz
Marc Bezem
Manuel Bodirsky
Julian Bradfield
Stéphane Bressan
Roberto Bruttomesso
Uwe Bubeck
Richard Bubel
Serena Cerrito
Kaustuv Chaudhuri
Taolue Chen
Jacek Chrząszcz
Frank Ciesinski
Hubert Comon-Lundh
Veronique Cortier
Juan Manuel Crespo
Pedro R. D'Argenio
Arnaud Durand
Bruno Dutertre
Roy Dyckhoff
Esra Erdem
Carsten Fuhs
Andrew Gacek
Peter Gacs
Vijay Ganesh
Paul Gastin
Martin Gebser
Birte Glimm
Guido Governatori
Alberto Griggio
Ashutosh Gupta
Yuri Gurevich
Dilian Gurov
Raúl Gutiérrez
Martin Henz
Matthias Horbach
Fulya Horozal
Clément Houtmann
Joe Hurd
Florent Jacquemard
Neil Jones
Roland Kaminski
Ioannis Kassios
George Katsirelos
Benjamin Kaufmann
Chantal Keller
Boris Konev
Martin Korp
Kersting Kristian
César Kunz
Roman Kuznets
Christoph Lange
Martin Lange
Christof Löding
Michel Ludwig
Michael Luttenberger
Stephen Magill
Stephan Merz
Georg Moser
Ben Moszkowski
Ralf Möller
Nina Narodytska
Jorge Navas
M.A. Hakim Newton
Dejan Nickovic
Vivek Nigam
Albert Oliveras
Federico Olmedo
Max Ostrowski
Friedrich Otto
Martin Otto
Joel Ouaknine
Pere Pardo
David Parker
Dirk Pattinson
David Pearce
Nicolas Peltier
Rafael Penaloza
Lee Pike
Luis Pinto
Frank Raiser
Christophe Ringeissen
Cody Roux
Luca Roversi
Pavel Rusnok
Vladislav Ryzhikov
Orkunt Sabuncu
Indranil Saha
Andrew Santosa
Christian Schallhart
Matthias Schmalz
Carsten Schuermann
Jan Schwinghammer
Frédéric Servais
Steven Shapiro
Laurent Simon
Christian Sternagel
Umberto Straccia
Aaron Stump
S.P. Suresh
Michael Thielscher
René Thiemann
Hans Tompits
Tarmo Uustalu
Jan Van den Bussche
Helmut Veith
Thomas Vetterlein
Razvan Voicu
Johannes Waldmann
Uwe Waldmann
Anduo Wang
Lena Wiese
Thomas Wilke
Sarah Winkler
Christoph Wintersteiger
Patrick Wischnewski
Stefan Woelfl
Stefan Woltran
Roland Yap
Fang Yu
Martin Zimmermann
Florian Zuleger

Table of Contents

The Complexity of Partial-Observation Parity Games

Krishnendu Chatterjee[1] and Laurent Doyen[2]

[1] IST Austria (Institute of Science and Technology Austria)
[2] LSV, ENS Cachan & CNRS, France

Abstract. We consider two-player zero-sum games on graphs. On the basis of the information available to the players these games can be classified as follows: (a) partial-observation (both players have partial view of the game); (b) one-sided partial-observation (one player has partial-observation and the other player has complete-observation); and (c) complete-observation (both players have complete view of the game). We survey the complexity results for the problem of deciding the winner in various classes of partial-observation games with ω-regular winning conditions specified as parity objectives. We present a reduction from the class of parity objectives that depend on sequence of states of the game to the sub-class of parity objectives that only depend on the sequence of observations. We also establish that partial-observation acyclic games are PSPACE-complete.

1 Introduction

Games on graphs. Games played on graphs provide the mathematical framework to analyze several important problems in computer science as well as mathematics. In particular, when the vertices and edges of a graph represent the states and transitions of a reactive system, then the synthesis problem (Church's problem) asks for the construction of a winning strategy in a game played on a graph [5,21,20,18]. Game-theoretic formulations have also proved useful for the verification [1], refinement [13], and compatibility checking [9] of reactive systems. Games played on graphs are dynamic games that proceed for an infinite number of rounds. In each round, the players choose moves which, together with the current state, determine the successor state. An outcome of the game, called a *play*, consists of the infinite sequence of states that are visited.

Strategies and objectives. A strategy for a player is a recipe that describes how the player chooses a move to extend a play. Strategies can be classified as follows: *pure* strategies, which always deterministically choose a move to extend the play, and *randomized* strategies, which may choose at a state a probability distribution over the available moves. Objectives are generally Borel measurable functions [17]: the objective for a player is a Borel set B in the Cantor topology on S^ω (where S is the set of states), and the player satisfies the objective iff the outcome of the game is a member of B. In verification, objectives are usually *ω-regular languages*. The ω-regular languages generalize the classical regular languages to infinite strings; they occur in the low levels of the Borel hierarchy (they lie in $\Sigma_3 \cap \Pi_3$) and they form a robust and expressive language for determining payoffs for commonly used specifications. We consider parity objectives and its sub-classes that are canonical forms to express objectives in verification.

C. Fermüller and A. Voronkov (Eds.): LPAR-17, LNCS 6397, pp. 1–14, 2010.

Classification of games. Games played on graphs can be classified according to the knowledge of the players about the state of the game. Accordingly, there are (a) *partial-observation* games, where each player only has a partial or incomplete view about the state and the moves of the other player; (b) *one-sided partial-observation* games, where one player has partial knowledge and the other player has complete knowledge about the state and moves of the other player; and (c) *complete-observation* games, where each player has complete knowledge of the game.

Analysis. The analysis of games can be classified as *qualitative* and *quantitative* analysis. The qualitative analysis consists of the following questions: given an objective and a state of the game, (a) can Player 1 ensure the objective with certainty against all strategies of Player 2 (*sure winning* problem); (b) can Player 1 ensure the objective with probability 1 against all strategies of Player 2 (*almost-sure winning* problem); and (c) can Player 1 ensure the objective with probability arbitrarily close to 1 against all strategies of Player 2 (*limit-sure winning* problem). Given an objective, a state of the game, and a rational threshold ν, the quantitative analysis problem asks whether the maximal probability with which Player 1 can ensure the objective against all Player 2 strategies is at least ν.

Organization. The paper is organized as follows: In Section 3 we show a new result that presents a reduction of general parity objectives that depend on state sequences to *visible* objectives that only depend on the sequence of observations (rather than the sequence of states). In Section 4 we survey the complexity of solving the three classes of partial-observation games with parity objectives and its sub-classes both for qualitative and quantitative analysis. In Section 5 we show that for the special case of *acyclic* games the qualitative analysis problem is PSPACE-complete both for one-sided partial-observation and partial-observation games. The PSPACE-completeness result for acyclic games is in contrast to general games where the complexities are EXPTIME-complete, 2EXPTIME-complete, and undecidable (depending on the objective and the specific qualitative analysis question).

2 Definitions

In this section we present the definition of partial-observation games and their sub-classes, and the notions of strategies and objectives. A *probability distribution* on a finite set A is a function $\kappa : A \to [0,1]$ such that $\sum_{a \in A} \kappa(a) = 1$. We denote by $\mathcal{D}(A)$ the set of probability distributions on A. We focus on partial-observation turn-based games, where at each round one of the players is in charge of choosing the next action.

Partial-observation games. A *partial-observation game* (or simply a *game*) is a tuple $G = \langle S_1 \cup S_2, A_1, A_2, \delta_1 \cup \delta_2, \mathcal{O}_1, \mathcal{O}_2 \rangle$ with the following components:

1. *(State space).* $S = S_1 \cup S_2$ is a finite set of states, where $S_1 \cap S_2 = \emptyset$ (i.e., S_1 and S_2 are disjoint), states in S_1 are Player 1 states, and states in S_2 are Player 2 states.
2. *(Actions).* A_i ($i = 1, 2$) is a finite set of actions for Player i.
3. *(Transition function).* For $i \in \{1, 2\}$, the transition function for Player i is the function $\delta_i : S_i \times A_i \to S_{3-i}$ that maps a state $s_i \in S_i$, and action $a_i \in A_i$ to the successor state $\delta_i(s_i, a_i) \in S_{3-i}$ (i.e., games are alternating).

4. *(Observations).* $\mathcal{O}_i \subseteq 2^{S_i}$ $(i = 1, 2)$ is a finite set of observations for Player i that partition the state space S_i. These partitions uniquely define functions $\mathsf{obs}_i : S_i \to \mathcal{O}_i$ $(i = 1, 2)$ that map each Player i state to its observation such that $s \in \mathsf{obs}_i(s)$ for all $s \in S_i$.

Special cases. We consider the following special cases of partial-observation games, obtained by restrictions in the observations:

- *(Observation restriction).* The games with *one-sided partial-observation* are the special case of games where $\mathcal{O}_2 = \{\{s\} \mid s \in S_2\}$ (Player 2 has complete observation), i.e., only Player 1 has partial-observation. The *games of complete-observation* are the special case of games where $\mathcal{O}_1 = \{\{s\} \mid s \in S_1\}$ and $\mathcal{O}_2 = \{\{s\} \mid s \in S_2\}$, i.e., every state is visible to each player and hence both players have complete observation. If a player has complete observation we omit the corresponding observation sets from the description of the game.

Classes of game graphs. We use the following abbreviations: Pa for partial-observation, Os for one-sided complete-observation, Co for complete-observation. For $\mathcal{C} \in \{\mathsf{Pa}, \mathsf{Os}, \mathsf{Co}\}$, we denote by $\mathcal{G}_\mathcal{C}$ the set of all $\mathcal{C}$ games. Note that the following strict inclusions hold: partial-observation (Pa) is more general than one-sided partial-observation (Os) and Os is more general than complete-observation (Co).

Plays. In a game, in each turn, for $i \in \{1, 2\}$, if the current state s is in S_i, then Player i chooses an action $a \in A_i$, and the successor state is $\delta_i(s, a)$. A *play* in G is an infinite sequence of states and actions $\rho = s_0 a_0 s_1 a_1 \dots$ such that for all $j \geq 0$, if $s_j \in S_i$, for $i \in \{1, 2\}$, then there exists $a_j \in A_i$ such that $\delta_i(s_j, a_j) = s_{j+1}$. The *prefix up to* s_n of the play ρ is denoted by $\rho(n)$, its *length* is $|\rho(n)| = n + 1$ and its *last element* is $\mathsf{Last}(\rho(n)) = s_n$. The set of plays in G is denoted by $\mathsf{Plays}(G)$, and the set of corresponding finite prefixes is denoted $\mathsf{Prefs}(G)$. For $i \in \{1, 2\}$, we denote by $\mathsf{Prefs}_i(G)$ the set of finite prefixes in G that end in a state in S_i. The *observation sequence* of $\rho = s_0 a_0 s_1 a_1 \dots$ for Player i $(i = 1, 2)$ is the unique infinite sequence of observations and actions of Player i, i.e., $\mathsf{obs}_i(\rho) \in (\mathcal{O}_i A_i)^\omega$ defined as follows: (i) if $s_0 \in S_i$, then $\mathsf{obs}_i(\rho) = o_0 a_0 o_2 a_2 o_4 \dots$ such that $s_j \in o_j$ for all even $j \geq 0$; (ii) if $s_0 \in S_{3-i}$, then $\mathsf{obs}_i(\rho) = o_1 a_1 o_3 a_3 o_5 \dots$ such that $s_j \in o_j$ for all odd $j \geq 1$. The observation sequence for finite sequences (prefix of plays) is defined analogously.

Strategies. A *pure strategy* in G for Player 1 is a function $\sigma : \mathsf{Prefs}_1(G) \to A_1$. A *randomized strategy* in G for Player 1 is a function $\sigma : \mathsf{Prefs}_1(G) \to \mathcal{D}(A_1)$. A (pure or randomized) strategy σ for Player 1 is *observation-based* if for all prefixes $\rho, \rho' \in \mathsf{Prefs}(G)$, if $\mathsf{obs}_1(\rho) = \mathsf{obs}_1(\rho')$, then $\sigma(\rho) = \sigma(\rho')$. We omit analogous definitions of strategies for Player 2. We denote by Σ_G, Σ_G^O, Σ_G^P, Π_G, Π_G^O and Π_G^P the set of all Player-1 strategies in G, the set of all observation-based Player-1 strategies, the set of all pure Player-1 strategies, the set of all Player-2 strategies in G, the set of all observation-based Player-2 strategies, and the set of all pure Player-2 strategies, respectively. Note that if Player 1 has complete observation, then $\Sigma_G^O = \Sigma_G$.

Objectives. An *objective* for Player 1 in G is a set $\phi \subseteq S^\omega$ of infinite sequences of states. A play $\rho \in \mathsf{Plays}(G)$ *satisfies* the objective ϕ, denoted $\rho \models \phi$, if $\rho \in \phi$. Objectives are generally Borel measurable: a Borel objective is a Borel set in the Cantor topology on S^ω [15]. We specifically consider ω-regular objectives specified as parity objectives (a canonical form to express all ω-regular objectives [25]). For a play $\rho = s_0 a_0 s_1 a_1 \dots$ we denote by ρ_k the k-th state s_k of the play and denote by $\mathrm{Inf}(\rho)$ the set of states that occur infinitely often in ρ, that is, $\mathrm{Inf}(\rho) = \{s \mid s_j = s \text{ for infinitely many } j\text{'s}\}$. We consider the following classes of objectives.

1. *Reachability and safety objectives.* Given a set $\mathcal{T} \subseteq S$ of target states, the *reachability* objective $\mathsf{Reach}(\mathcal{T})$ requires that a state in $\mathcal{T}$ be visited at least once, that is, $\mathsf{Reach}(\mathcal{T}) = \{\rho \mid \exists k \geq 0 \cdot \rho_k \in \mathcal{T}\}$. Dually, the *safety* objective $\mathsf{Safe}(\mathcal{T})$ requires that only states in $\mathcal{T}$ be visited. Formally, $\mathsf{Safe}(\mathcal{T}) = \{\rho \mid \forall k \geq 0 \cdot \rho_k \in \mathcal{T}\}$.
2. *Büchi and coBüchi objectives.* The *Büchi* objective $\mathsf{Buchi}(\mathcal{T})$ requires that a state in $\mathcal{T}$ be visited infinitely often, that is, $\mathsf{Buchi}(\mathcal{T}) = \{\rho \mid \mathrm{Inf}(\rho) \cap \mathcal{T} \neq \emptyset\}$. Dually, the *coBüchi* objective $\mathsf{coBuchi}(\mathcal{T})$ requires that only states in $\mathcal{T}$ be visited infinitely often. Formally, $\mathsf{coBuchi}(\mathcal{T}) = \{\rho \mid \mathrm{Inf}(\rho) \subseteq \mathcal{T}\}$.
3. *Parity objectives.* For $d \in \mathbb{N}$, let $p : S \to \{0, 1, \dots, d\}$ be a *priority function*, which maps each state to a nonnegative integer priority. The *parity* objective $\mathsf{Parity}(p)$ requires that the minimum priority that occurs infinitely often be even. Formally, $\mathsf{Parity}(p) = \{\rho \mid \min\{p(s) \mid s \in \mathrm{Inf}(\rho)\} \text{ is even}\}$. The Büchi and coBüchi objectives are the special cases of parity objectives with two priorities, $p : S \to \{0, 1\}$ and $p : S \to \{1, 2\}$, respectively.
4. *Visible objectives.* We say that an objective ϕ is *visible* for Player i if for all $\rho, \rho' \in S^\omega$, if $\rho \models \phi$ and $\mathsf{obs}_i(\rho) = \mathsf{obs}_i(\rho')$, then $\rho' \models \phi$. For example if the priority function maps observations to priorities (i.e., $p : \mathcal{O}_i \to \{0, 1, \dots, d\}$), then the parity objective is visible for Player i.

Outcomes. The *outcome* of two randomized strategies σ (for Player 1) and π (for Player 2) from a state s in G is the set of plays $\rho = s_0 s_1 \dots \in \mathsf{Plays}(G)$, with $s_0 = s$, where for all $j \geq 0$, if $s_j \in S_1$ (resp. $s_j \in S_2$), then there exists an action $a_j \in A_1$ (resp. $a_j \in A_2$), such that $\sigma(\rho(j))(a_j) > 0$ (resp. $\pi(\rho(j))(a_j) > 0$) and $\delta_1(s_j, a_j) = s_{j+1}$ (resp. $\delta_2(s_j, a_j) = s_{j+1}$). This set is denoted $\mathrm{Outcome}(G, s, \sigma, \pi)$. The outcome of two pure strategies is defined analogously by viewing pure strategies as randomized strategies that play their chosen action with probability one. The *outcome set* of the pure (resp. randomized) strategy σ for Player 1 in G is the set $\mathsf{Outcome}_1(G, s, \sigma)$ of plays ρ such that there exists a pure (resp. randomized) strategy π for Player 2 with $\rho \in \mathrm{Outcome}(G, s, \sigma, \pi)$. The outcome set $\mathsf{Outcome}_2(G, s, \pi)$ for Player 2 is defined symmetrically.

Sure winning, almost-sure winning, limit-sure winning and value function. An *event* is a measurable set of plays, and given strategies σ and π for the two players, the probabilities of events are uniquely defined [26]. For a Borel objective ϕ, we denote by $\mathrm{Pr}_s^{\sigma,\pi}(\phi)$ the probability that ϕ is satisfied by the play obtained from the starting state s when the strategies σ and π are used. Given a game G, an objective ϕ, and a state s, we consider the following winning modes: (1) an observation-based strategy σ for Player 1 is *sure winning* for the objective ϕ from s if $\mathrm{Outcome}(G, s, \sigma, \pi) \subseteq \phi$ for all observation-based strategies π for Player 2; (2) an observation-based strategy σ for Player 1 is *almost-sure winning* for the objective ϕ from s if $\mathrm{Pr}_s^{\sigma,\pi}(\phi) = 1$ for all observation-based strategies π for Player 2; and (3) a family $(\sigma_\varepsilon)_{\varepsilon > 0}$ of observation-based strategies for Player 1 is *limit-sure winning* for the objective ϕ from s if $\mathrm{Pr}_s^{\sigma_\varepsilon,\pi}(\phi) \geq 1 - \varepsilon$, for all $\varepsilon > 0$ and all observation-based strategies π for Player 2. The *value function* $\langle\langle 1 \rangle\rangle_{val}^{G} : S \to \mathbb{R}$ for objective ϕ for Player 1 assigns to every state the maximal probability with which Player 1 can guarantee the satisfaction of ϕ with an observation-based strategy, against all observation-based strategies for Player 2. Formally we have

$$\langle\langle 1 \rangle\rangle_{val}^{G}(\phi)(s) = \sup_{\sigma \in \Sigma_G^O} \inf_{\pi \in \Pi_G^O} \mathrm{Pr}_s^{\sigma,\pi}(\phi).$$

For $\varepsilon \geq 0$, an observation-based strategy is *ε-optimal* for ϕ from s if we have $\inf_{\pi \in \Pi_G^O} \mathrm{Pr}_s^{\sigma,\pi}(\phi) \geq \langle\langle 1 \rangle\rangle_{val}^{G}(\phi)(s) - \varepsilon$. An *optimal* strategy is a 0-optimal strategy. Given a rational value $0 \leq \nu \leq 1$ and a state s, the *value decision problem* asks whether the value of the game at s is at least ν. The qualitative analysis consists of the sure, almost-sure and limit-sure winning problems, and the quantitative analysis is the value decision problem.

3 Reduction of Objectives to Visible Objectives

The complexity lower bounds in this paper are given for visible objectives, while upper bounds are given for general objectives. In [23,7], algorithms based on a subset construction are given for visible objective, establishing upper bounds (namely EXPTIME) for visible objectives only.

We show that games with general parity objectives can be reduced to games with visible parity objective with an exponential blow-up. However, this blow-up has no impact on the complexity upper bounds because from a game G, the reduction constructs a game G' as the product of G with an exponentially large automaton M, such that the further subset construction of [7] applied to G' induces an exponential blow-up only with respect to G (the subset construction for G' has size $O(2^{|G|} \cdot |M|) = O(2^{|G|} \cdot 2^{|G|})$ which is simply exponential). This is because M is a deterministic automaton.

We give the idea of the construction. Assume that we have a game G with parity objective given by the priority function $p : S \to \{0, 1, \ldots, d\}$. We construct a game G' with visible objective as a product $G \times M$ where M is a finite automaton with parity condition that "synchronizes" with G on observations and actions of Player 1. We construct M as the complement of the automaton M' that we define as follows.

The automaton M' has state space S_1 and alphabet $\Sigma = \mathcal{O}_1 \times A_1$ that accepts the observations of the plays that are losing for Player 1. An observation sequence is losing if it is the observation of a losing play. The initial state of M' is the initial state of the game (we assume w.l.o.g that the game starts in a Player 1 state). The transitions of M' are $(s, (\mathsf{obs}_1(s), a), s'')$ for all $s, s'' \in S_1$ and $a \in A_1$ such that $\delta_1(s, a) = s'$ and $\delta_2(s', b) = s''$ for some $s' \in S_2$ and $b \in A_2$. The priority assigned to this transition is $1 + \min\{p(s), p(s')\}$. Note that M' has at most one run over each infinite word, and that a run in M' corresponds to a play in G. The language of M' is the set of infinite words over $\Sigma = \mathcal{O}_1 \times A_1$ that have a run in M' in which the least priority visited infinitely often is even, i.e. such that the least priority (according to p) visited infinitely often is odd (and thus the corresponding run violates the winning condition of the game G). By complementing M', we get an exponentially larger automaton M that accepts the winning observation sequences [24]. We can assume that M is deterministic and that the states rather than the transitions are labeled by priorities and letters. The game G' is obtained by a synchronized product of G and M in which Player 1 can see the state of M (i.e., the observation of a state (s, u) where s is a state of G and u is a state of M is $(\mathsf{obs}_1(s), u)$). The priority of a state (s, u) depends only on u and therefore defines a visible parity objective. Transitions in G and M are synchronized on the obervations and actions of Player 1.

Note that for reachability and safety objectives, there exists a reduction to a visible objective in polynomial time. First, we can assume that the target states T defining the objective are sink states (because once T is reached, the winner of the game is fixed). Second, we make the sink states visible, which makes the objective vissible, and does not change the winner of the game (observing the sink states is of no help since the game is over when this happens).

Theorem 1. *Given a game $G \in \mathcal{G}_{\mathsf{Os}}$ with parity objective, one can construct a game G' as a product of G with an exponentially large automaton M with a* visible *parity objective such that the following assertions hold:*

1. *G and G' have the same answer to the sure and the almost-sure winning problem;*
2. *the sure winning problem for G' can be solved in time exponential in the size of G; and*
3. *the almost-sure winning problem for G' can be solved in time exponential in the size of G for Büchi objectives.*

4 Complexity of Partial-Observation Parity Games

In this section we present a complete picture of the complexity results for the three different classes of partial-observation games, with different classes of parity objectives, both for qualitative and quantitative analysis.

4.1 Complexity of Sure Winning

We first show that for sure winning, pure strategies are sufficient for all partial-observation games.

Lemma 1 (Pure strategies suffice for sure winning). *For all games $G \in \mathcal{G}_{\mathsf{Pa}}$ and all objectives ϕ, if there is a sure winning strategy, then there is a pure sure winning strategy.*

Proof. Consider a randomized strategy σ for Player 1, let σ^P be the pure strategy such that for all $\rho \in \mathsf{Prefs}_1(G)$, the strategy $\sigma^P(\rho)$ chooses an action from $\mathrm{Supp}(\sigma(\rho))$. Then for all s we have $\mathsf{Outcome}_1(G, s, \sigma^P) \subseteq \mathsf{Outcome}_1(G, s, \sigma)$, and thus, if σ is sure winning, then so is σ^P. The result also holds for observation-based strategies. ∎

Spoiling strategies. To spoil a strategy of Player 1 (for sure-winning), Player 2 does not need the full memory of the history of the play, but only needs counting strategies [7]. We say that a pure strategy $\pi : \mathsf{Prefs}_2(G) \to A_2$ for Player 2 is *counting* if for all prefixes $\rho, \rho' \in \mathsf{Prefs}_2(G)$ such that $|\rho| = |\rho'|$ and $\mathsf{Last}(\rho) = \mathsf{Last}(\rho')$, we have $\pi(\rho) = \pi(\rho')$. Let Π_G^C be the set of counting strategies for Player 2. The memory needed by a counting strategy is only the number of turns that have been played. This type of strategy is sufficient to spoil the non-winning strategies of Player 1.

Lemma 2 (Counting spoiling strategies suffice). *Let G be a partial-observation game and ϕ be an objective. There exists a pure observation-based strategy $\sigma^o \in \Sigma_G^O$ such that for all $\pi^o \in \Pi_G^O$ we have* $\mathrm{Outcome}(G, s, \sigma^o, \pi^o) \in \phi$ *if and only if there exists a pure observation-based strategy $\sigma^o \in \Sigma_G^O$ such that for all counting strategies $\pi^c \in \Pi_G^C$ we have* $\mathrm{Outcome}(G, s, \sigma^o, \pi^c) \in \phi$.

Proof. We prove the equivalent statement that: for all pure observation-based strategies $\sigma^o \in \Sigma_G^O$ there exists $\pi^o \in \Pi_G^O$ such that $\mathrm{Outcome}(G, s, \sigma^o, \pi^o) \subsetneq \phi$ iff for all pure observation-based strategies $\sigma^o \in \Sigma_G^O$ there exists $\pi^c \in \Pi_G^C$ such that $\mathrm{Outcome}(G, s, \sigma^o, \pi^c) \subsetneq \phi$. The right implication ($\leftarrow$) is trivial. For the left implication ($\rightarrow$), let $\sigma^o \in \Sigma_G^O$ be an arbitrary pure observation-based strategy for Player 1 in G. Let $\pi^o \in \Pi_G^O$ be a strategy for Player 2 such that there exists $\rho^* \in \mathrm{Outcome}(G, s, \sigma^o, \pi^o)$ and $\rho^* \notin \phi$. Let $\rho^* = s_0 a_0 s_1 a_1 \ldots a_{n-1} s_n a_n \ldots$ and define a counting strategy π^c for Player 2 such that for all $\rho \in \mathsf{Prefs}_2(G)$ if $\mathsf{Last}(\rho) = s_{n-1}$ for $n = |\rho|$, then $\pi^c(\rho) = s_n$, and otherwise $\pi^c(\rho)$ is fixed arbitrarily. Clearly, π^c is a counting strategy and we have $\rho^* \in \mathrm{Outcome}(G, s, \sigma^o, \pi^o)$. Hence it follows that $\mathrm{Outcome}(G, s, \sigma^o, \pi^c) \subsetneq \phi$, and we obtain the desired result. ∎

Sure winning coincide for Pa **and** Os **games.** For all $\mathcal{O}_2$ partitions of a partial-observation game, a counting strategy is an observation-based strategy. From Lemma 1 it follows that pure strategies suffice for sure winning, and Lemma 2 shows that counting strategies suffice for spoiling pure strategies. Hence it follows that for spoiling strategies in sure winning games, the observation for Player 2 does not matter, and hence for sure winning, Pa and Os games coincide.

Lemma 3. *For a partial-observation game $G = \langle S_1 \cup S_2, A_1, A_2, \delta_1 \cup \delta_2, \mathcal{O}_1, \mathcal{O}_2 \rangle$ with an objective ϕ, consider the one-sided partial-observation game $G' = \langle S_1 \cup S_2, A_1, A_2, \delta_1 \cup \delta_2, \mathcal{O}_1, \mathcal{O}_2' \rangle$ such that $\mathcal{O}_2' = \{\{s\} \mid s \in S_2\}$. The answer to the sure winning questions in G and G' coincide for objective ϕ.*

Complexity of sure winning. The results for complete-observation games are as follows: (1) safety and reachability objectives can be solved in linear-time (this is alternating reachability in AND-OR graphs) [14]; (2) Büchi and coBüchi objectives can be solved in quadratic time [25]; and (3) parity objectives lie in NP $\cap$ coNP [10] and no polynomial time algorithm is known. The results for one-sided partial-observation games are as follows: (1) the EXPTIME-completeness for reachability objectives follows from the results of [22]; (2) the EXPTIME-completeness for safety objectives follows from the results of [4]; and (3) the EXPTIME-upper bound for all parity objective follows from the results of [7] and hence it follows that for all Büchi, coBüchi and parity objectives we have EXPTIME-complete bound. From Lemma 3 the results follow for partial-observation games. The results are summarized in the following theorem and shown in Table 1.

Table 1. Complexity of sure winning

	Complete-observation	One-sided	Partial-observation
Safety	Linear-time	EXPTIME-complete	EXPTIME-complete
Reachability	Linear-time	EXPTIME-complete	EXPTIME-complete
Büchi	Quadratic-time	EXPTIME-complete	EXPTIME-complete
coBüchi	Quadratic-time	EXPTIME-complete	EXPTIME-complete
Parity	NP ∩ coNP	EXPTIME-complete	EXPTIME-complete

Table 2. Complexity of almost-sure winning

	Complete-observation	One-sided	Partial-observation
Safety	Linear-time	EXPTIME-complete	EXPTIME-complete
Reachability	Linear-time	EXPTIME-complete	2EXPTIME-complete
Büchi	Quadratic-time	EXPTIME-complete	2EXPTIME-complete
coBüchi	Quadratic-time	Undecidable	Undecidable
Parity	NP ∩ coNP	Undecidable	Undecidable

Theorem 2 (Complexity of sure winning). *The following assertions hold:*

1. *The sure winning problem for complete-observation games (i) with reachability and safety objectives can be solved in linear time; (ii) with Büchi and coBüchi objectives can be solved in quadratic time; and (iii) with parity objectives is in NP ∩ coNP.*
2. *The sure winning problem for partial-observation and one-sided partial-observation games with reachability, safety, Büchi, coBüchi and parity objectives are EXPTIME-complete.*

4.2 Complexity of Almost-Sure Winning

In contrast to sure winning (Lemma 1), for almost-sure winning, randomized strategies are more powerful than pure strategies (for example see [7]) for one-sided partial-observation games. The celebrated determinacy result of Martin [16] shows that for complete-observation games either there is a sure winning strategy for Player 1, or there is a pure strategy for Player 2 that ensures against all Player 1 strategies the objective is not satisfied. It follows that for complete-observation games, the almost-sure, limit-sure winning, and value decision problems coincide with the sure winning problem. For safety objectives, the counter-examples are always finite prefixes, and it can be shown that for a given observation-based strategy for Player 1 if there is a strategy for Player 2 to produce a finite counter-example, then the finite counter-example is produced with some constant positive probability. It follows that for partial-observation games and one-sided partial-observation games with safety objectives, the almost-sure and the limit-sure winning problems coincide with the sure winning problem.

Lemma 4. *The following assertions hold:*

1. *For complete-observation games, the almost-sure, limit-sure winning, and value decision problems coincide with the sure winning problem.*

2. *For safety objectives, the almost-sure and the limit-sure winning problems coincide with the sure winning problem for partial-observation and one-sided partial-observation games.*

Complexity of almost-sure winning. In view of Lemma 4 the almost-sure winning analysis for complete-observation games with all classes of objectives follow from Theorem 2. Similarly due to Lemma 4 the results for partial-observation games and one-sided partial-observation games with safety objectives follow from Theorem 2. The EXPTIME-completeness for almost-sure winning with reachability and Büchi objectives for one-sided partial-observation games follows from [7]; and the 2EXPTIME-completeness for almost-sure winning with reachability and Büchi objectives for partial-observation games follows from [3,12]. The undecidability result for almost-sure winning for coBüchi objectives for one-sided partial-observation games is obtained as follows: (i) in [2] it was shown that for probabilistic automata with coBüchi conditions, the problem of deciding if there exists a word that is accepted with probability 1 is undecidable and from this it follows that for one-sided partial-observation games with probabilistic transitions, the problem of deciding the existence of a pure observation-based almost-sure winning strategy is undecidable; (ii) it was shown in [6] that probabilistic transitions can be removed from the game graph, and the problem remains undecidable under randomized observation-based strategies. The undecidability for the more general parity objectives, and partial-observation games follows. This gives us the results for almost-sure winning, and they are summarized in the theorem below (see also Table 2).

Theorem 3 (Complexity of almost-sure winning). *The following assertions hold:*

1. *The almost-sure winning problem for one-sided partial-observation games (i) with safety, reachability and Büchi objectives are EXPTIME-complete, and (ii) is undecidable for coBüchi and parity objectives.*
2. *The almost-sure winning problem for partial-observation games (i) with safety, reachability and Büchi objectives are 2EXPTIME-complete, and (ii) is undecidable for coBüchi and parity objectives.*

4.3 Complexity of Limit-Sure Winning and Value Decision Problems

The complexity results for limit-sure winning and value decision problems are as follows.

Complexity of limit-sure winning. In view of Lemma 4 the results for (i) limit-sure winning and value decision problem for complete-observation games with all classes of objectives, and (ii) for partial-observation games and one-sided partial-observation games with safety objectives with limit-sure winning, follow from Theorem 2. It follows from the results of [11] that the following question is undecidable for probabilistic automata with reachability condition: for all $\varepsilon > 0$ is there a word w_ε that is accepted with probability greater than $1 - \varepsilon$? It follows that for one-sided partial-information games with probabilistic transitions, the problem of deciding the existence of a family of pure observation-based limit-sure winning strategies is undecidable; and again

Table 3. Complexity of limit-sure winning

	Complete-observation	One-sided	Partial-observation
Safety	Linear-time	EXPTIME-complete	EXPTIME-complete
Reachability	Linear-time	Undecidable	Undecidable
Büchi	Quadratic-time	Undecidable	Undecidable
coBüchi	Quadratic-time	Undecidable	Undecidable
Parity	NP $\cap$ coNP	Undecidable	Undecidable

it follows from [6] that the problem is undecidable by removing probabilistic transitions from the game graph, and also for randomized observation-based strategies. Since (i) reachability objectives are special cases of Büchi, coBüchi and parity objectives, and (ii) one-sided partial-observation games are special cases of partial-observation games, the undecidability results for the more general cases follow. This gives us the results for limit-sure winning, and they are summarized in the theorem below (see also Table 3).

Theorem 4 (Complexity of limit-sure winning). *The following assertions hold:*

1. *The limit-sure winning problem for one-sided partial-observation games (i) with safety objectives are EXPTIME-complete, and (ii) with reachability, Büchi, coBüchi, and parity objectives are undecidable.*
2. *The limit-sure winning problem for partial-observation games (i) with safety objectives are EXPTIME-complete, and (ii) with reachability, Büchi, coBüchi, and parity objectives are undecidable.*

Complexity of the value decision problems. Since the limit-sure winning problem is a special case of the value decision problem (with $\nu = 1$), the undecidability results for all objectives other than safety objectives follow from Theorem 4. The undecidability of the value decision problem for probabilistic safety automata was shown in [8], and from [6] the undecidability follows for the value decision problem of one-sided partial-observation games with safety objectives. We summarize the results in Theorem 5 and Table 4.

Table 4. Complexity of value decision

	Complete-observation	One-sided	Partial-observation
Safety	Linear-time	Undecidable	Undecidable
Reachability	Linear-time	Undecidable	Undecidable
Büchi	Quadratic-time	Undecidable	Undecidable
coBüchi	Quadratic-time	Undecidable	Undecidable
Parity	NP $\cap$ coNP	Undecidable	Undecidable

Theorem 5 (Complexity of value decision problems). *The value decision problems for partial-observation and one-sided partial-observation games with safety, reachability, Büchi, coBüchi, and parity objectives are undecidable.*

5 The Complexity of Acyclic Games

We show that partial-observation games with reachability and safety objective played on acyclic graphs are PSPACE-complete. Note that for such games, the notion of sure-winning, almost-sure winning, and limit-sure winning coincide, and that randomized strategies are no more powerful than pure strategies.

A partial-observation game is *acyclic* if there are two distinguished sink states s_{acc} and s_{rej} (accepting and rejecting states) such that the transition relation is acyclic over $S \setminus \{s_{acc}, s_{rej}\}$. The objective is $\mathsf{Reach}(\{s_{acc}\})$ or equivalently $\mathsf{Safe}(S \setminus \{s_{rej}\})$. Clearly the winner of an acyclic game is known after at most $|S|$ rounds of playing. We claim that the qualitative analysis of acyclic partial-observation games (with reachability or safety objective) is PSPACE-complete. Since for acyclic games parity objectives reduce to safety or reachability objectives, the PSPACE-completeness follows for all parity objectives.

PSPACE upper bound. A PSPACE algorithm to solve acyclic games is as follows. Starting from $t_0 = \{s_0\}$, we choose an action $a \in A_1$ and we check that Player 1 is winning from each set $t_1 = \mathsf{Post}_a(t_0) \cap o_1$ for each $o_1 \in \mathcal{O}_1$ where $\mathsf{Post}_a(t) = \{s'' \mid \exists s \in t, b \in A_2 : \delta_2(\delta_1(s,a),b) = s''\}$. For each observation $o_1 \in \mathcal{O}_1$, we can reuse the space used by previous checks. Since the number of rounds is at most $|S_1|$, we can check if Player 1 is winning using a recursive procedure that tries out all choices of actions (the stack remains bounded by a polynomial in $|S_1|$).

PSPACE lower bound. We prove PSPACE-hardness using a reduction from QBF, which is the problem of evaluating a quantified boolean formula and is known to be PSPACE-complete [19]. A formula is defined over a finite set X of boolean variables, and is of the form $\varphi \equiv Q_1 x_1 \dots Q_n x_n \bigwedge_i c_i$, where $Q_k \in \{\exists, \forall\}$, $x_k \in X$ $(k = 1 \dots n)$ and each clause c_i is of the form $u_1 \vee u_2 \vee u_3$ and u_j are literals (i.e., either a variable or the negation of a variable). We assume without loss of generality that all variables occurring in φ are quantified. Given a formula φ, we construct an acyclic game G_φ and state s_I such that Player 1 has a sure winning strategy in G_φ from s_I if and only if the formula φ is true.

The idea of the construction is as follows. Let us call Player 1 the ∃player and Player 2 the ∀player. In the game G_φ, the ∀player chooses a valuation of the universally quantified variables, and the ∃player chooses a valuation of the existentially quantified variables. The choices are made in alternation, according to the structure of the formula. Moreover, the ∀player (secretly) chooses one clause that he will monitor. Since the ∃player does not know which clause is chosen by the ∀player, she has to ensure that all clauses are satisfied by her choice of valuation.

To be fair, when the ∃player is asked to choose a value for an existentially quantified variable x, the ∀player should have announced the value he has chosen for the variables that are quantified before x in the formula. We use observations to simulate this.

Note that, having chosen a clause, the ∀player has a unique clever choice of the value of the universally quantified variables (namely such that the corresponding literals in the clause are all false). Indeed, for any other choice, the clause would be satisfied no matter the ∃player's choice, and there would be nothing to check.

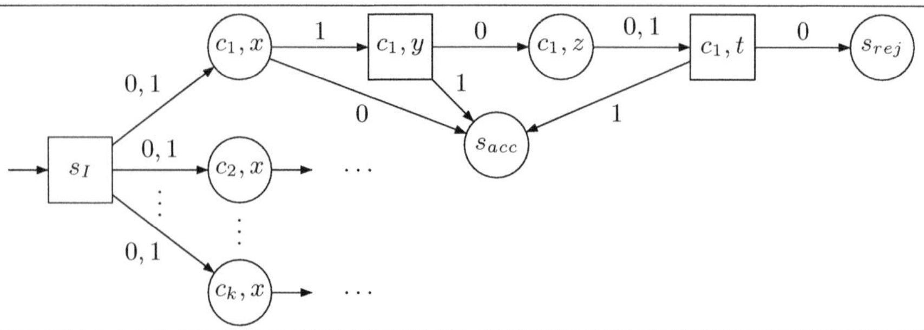

Fig. 1. Reduction of QBF to acyclic games for $\varphi = \exists x \, \forall y \, \exists z \, \forall t \; (x \vee \bar{y} \vee \bar{t}) \wedge \ldots$ Circles are states of $\exists$player, boxes are states of $\forall$player

The reduction is illustrated in Fig.1. We formally describe below the game G_φ. W.l.o.g. we assume that the quantifiers in φ are alternating, i.e. φ is of the form $\exists x_1 \forall x_2 \ldots \exists x_{2n-1} \forall x_{2n} \bigwedge_i c_i$. The set of actions in G_φ is $A_1 = A_2 = \{0, 1\}$ and the state space is $S_1 \cup S_2 \cup \{s_{acc}, s_{rej}\}$ where $S_1 = \{(c, x) \mid c \text{ is a clause in } \varphi \text{ and } x \text{ is an existentially quantified variable}\}$ and $S_2 = \{s_I\} \cup \{(c, x) \mid c \text{ is a clause in } \varphi \text{ and } x \text{ is a universally quantified variable}\}$. The transitions are as follows, for each clause c of φ:

- $(s_I, a, (c, x_1))$ for each $a \in \{0, 1\}$. Intuitively, Player 2 initially chooses which clause he will track;
- $((c, x_i), a, s_{acc})$ for all $1 \leq i \leq 2n$ if $a = 0$ and $\bar{x}_i \in c$, or if $a = 1$ and $x_i \in c$. Intuitively, the state s_{acc} is reached if the assignment to variable x_i makes the clause c true;
- $((c, x_i), a, (c, x_{i+1}))$ for all $1 \leq i \leq 2n$ if $a = 0$ and $\bar{x}_i \notin c$, or if $a = 1$ and $x_i \notin c$ (and we assume that (c, x_{2n+1}) denotes s_{rej}). Intuitively, the state s_{rej} is reached if no literal in c is set to true by the players.

The set of observations for Player 1 is $\mathcal{O}_1 = \{\mathsf{init}\} \cup \{x = 0 \mid x \in X\} \cup \{x = 1 \mid x \in X\}$, and the observation function is defined by $\mathsf{obs}_1(c, x_1) = \mathsf{init}$ for all clauses c in φ, and $\mathsf{obs}_1(c, x_i) = \begin{cases} x_i = 1 & \text{if } x_{i-1} \notin c \\ x_i = 0 & \text{otherwise} \end{cases}$ for all clauses c in φ, and all $1 < i \leq n$. Intuitively, the $\exists$player does not know which clause is monitored by the $\forall$player, but knows the value assigned by the $\forall$player to the universally quantified variables.

The correctness of this construction is established as follows. First, assume that $\exists$player has a sure winning strategy in G_φ. Since strategies are observation-based, the action choice after a prefix of a play $s_I a_0 (c, x_1) a_1 \ldots (c, x_k)$ is independent of c and depends only on the sequence of previous actions and observations which provide the value of variables $x_1, \ldots, x_{k-1}$ only. Therefore we can view the winning strategy as a function that assigns to each existentially quantified variable a value that depends on the value of the variables quantified earlier in the formula. This function is a witness for showing that φ holds, since the state s_{rej} is avoided.

Conversely, if φ holds, then there is a strategy to assign a value to the existentially quantified variables given the value of the variables quantified earlier in the formula, from which it is easy to construct a winning strategy in G_φ to reach s_{acc}.

Thus PSPACE-completeness follows for one-sided partial-observation games for sure winning. Since sure, almost-sure, and limit-sure winning coincide for acyclic games, and for sure winning partial-observation games coincide with one-sided partial-observation games (Lemma 3), the PSPACE-completeness for all the qualitative analysis problems follow.

Theorem 6 (Complexity of acyclic games). *The sure, almost-sure, and limit-sure winning problems for acyclic games of partial observation and one-sided partial observation with all parity objectives are PSPACE-complete.*

References

1. Alur, R., Henzinger, T.A., Kupferman, O.: Alternating-time temporal logic. Journal of the ACM 49, 672–713 (2002)
2. Baier, C., Bertrand, N., Größer, M.: On decision problems for probabilistic Büchi automata. In: Amadio, R.M. (ed.) FOSSACS 2008. LNCS, vol. 4962, pp. 287–301. Springer, Heidelberg (2008)
3. Bertrand, N., Genest, B., Gimbert, H.: Qualitative determinacy and decidability of stochastic games with signals. In: LICS, pp. 319–328. IEEE Computer Society, Los Alamitos (2009)
4. Berwanger, D., Doyen, L.: On the power of imperfect information. In: FSTTCS, Dagstuhl Seminar Proceedings 08004. Internationales Begegnungs- und Forschungszentrum fuer Informatik, IBFI (2008)
5. Büchi, J.R., Landweber, L.H.: Solving sequential conditions by finite-state strategies. Transactions of the AMS 138, 295–311 (1969)
6. Chatterjee, K., Doyen, L., Gimbert, H., Henzinger, T.A.: Randomness for free. In: Hlineny, P. (ed.) MFCS 2010. LNCS, vol. 6281, pp. 246–257. Springer, Heidelberg (2010)
7. Chatterjee, K., Doyen, L., Henzinger, T.A., Raskin, J.-F.: Algorithms for omega-regular games of incomplete information. Logical Methods in Computer Science 3(3:4) (2007)
8. Chatterjee, K., Henzinger, T.A.: Probabilistic automata on infinite words: Decidability and undecidability results. In: ATVA. Springer, Heidelberg (2010)
9. de Alfaro, L., Henzinger, T.A.: Interface theories for component-based design. In: Henzinger, T.A., Kirsch, C.M. (eds.) EMSOFT 2001. LNCS, vol. 2211, pp. 148–165. Springer, Heidelberg (2001)
10. Emerson, E.A., Jutla, C.: Tree automata, mu-calculus and determinacy. In: FOCS, pp. 368–377. IEEE, Los Alamitos (1991)
11. Gimbert, H., Oualhadj, Y.: Probabilistic automata on finite words: Decidable and undecidable problems. In: Gavoille, C. (ed.) ICALP 2010, Part II. LNCS, vol. 6199, pp. 527–538. Springer, Heidelberg (2010)
12. Gripon, V., Serre, O.: Qualitative concurrent stochastic games with imperfect information. In: Albers, S., Marchetti-Spaccamela, A., Matias, Y., Nikoletseas, S., Thomas, W. (eds.) ICALP 2009. LNCS, vol. 5556, pp. 200–211. Springer, Heidelberg (2009)
13. Henzinger, T.A., Kupferman, O., Rajamani, S.: Fair simulation. Information and Computation 173, 64–81 (2002)
14. Immerman, N.: Number of quantifiers is better than number of tape cells. Journal of Computer and System Sciences 22, 384–406 (1981)

15. Kechris, A.: Classical Descriptive Set Theory. Springer, Heidelberg (1995)
16. Martin, D.A.: Borel determinacy. Annals of Mathematics 102(2), 363–371 (1975)
17. Martin, D.A.: The determinacy of Blackwell games. The Journal of Symbolic Logic 63(4), 1565–1581 (1998)
18. McNaughton, R.: Infinite games played on finite graphs. Annals of Pure and Applied Logic 65, 149–184 (1993)
19. Papadimitriou, C.H.: Computational Complexity. Addison-Wesley, Reading (1993)
20. Pnueli, A., Rosner, R.: On the synthesis of a reactive module. In: POPL, pp. 179–190. ACM Press, New York (1989)
21. Ramadge, P.J., Wonham, W.M.: Supervisory control of a class of discrete-event processes. SIAM Journal of Control and Optimization 25(1), 206–230 (1987)
22. Reif, J.H.: Universal games of incomplete information. In: STOC, pp. 288–308. ACM Press, New York (1979)
23. Reif, J.H.: The complexity of two-player games of incomplete information. Journal of Computer and System Sciences 29(2), 274–301 (1984)
24. Safra, S.: On the complexity of ω-automata. In: FOCS, pp. 319–327. IEEE Computer Society Press, Los Alamitos (1988)
25. Thomas, W.: Languages, automata, and logic. In: Handbook of Formal Languages, ch. 7, vol. 3, Beyond Words, pp. 389–455. Springer, Heidelberg (1997)
26. Vardi, M.Y.: Automatic verification of probabilistic concurrent finite-state systems. In: FOCS, pp. 327–338. IEEE Computer Society Press, Los Alamitos (1985)

Awareness in Games, Awareness in Logic

Joseph Y. Halpern

Computer Science Department
Cornell University
Ithaca, NY 14853, USA
halpern@cs.cornell.edu

Standard game theory models implicitly assume that all significant aspects of a game (payoffs, moves available, etc.) are common knowledge among the players. There are well-known techniques going back to Harsanyi [4] for transforming a game where some aspects are not common knowledge to one where they are common knowledge. However, these techniques assume that players are at least *aware* of all possible moves in the game. But this is not always a reasonable assumption. For example, sleazy companies assume that consumers are not aware that they can lodge complaints if there are problems; in a war setting, having technology that an enemy is unaware of (and thus being able to make moves that the enemy is unaware of) can be critical; in financial markets, some investors may not be aware of certain investment strategies (complicated hedging strategies, for example, or tax-avoidance strategies).

In the first part of this talk, I discuss an approach for modeling lack of awareness in games, and what the appropriate solution concepts are in the presence of lack of awareness. In the second part of the talk, I consider logics for reasoning about awareness, and awareness of unawareness. This is done in a standard Kripke-style possible-worlds structure, using ideas that go back to [1]. However, there are new subtleties that arise; in particular, it turns out that we need to allow for different languages to be associated with different states of the world. Both parts of the talk are based on joint work with Leandro Rêgo [2,3].

There has been a great deal of work in the economics literature and computer science literature both on modeling awareness in games and on logics for reasoning about awareness. An excellent bibliography can be found at http://www.econ.ucdavis.edu/faculty/schipper/unaw.htm.

References

1. Fagin, R., Halpern, J.Y.: Belief, awareness, and limited reasoning. Artificial Intelligence 34, 39–76 (1988)
2. Halpern, J.Y., Rêgo, L.C.: Extensive games with possibly unaware players. In: Proc. Fifth International Joint Conference on Autonomous Agents and Multiagent Systems, pp. 744–751 (2006) full version available at arxiv.org/abs/0704.2014
3. Halpern, J.Y., Rêgo, L.C.: Reasoning about knowledge of unawareness revisited. In: Proc. Twelfth Conference on Theoretical Aspects of Rationality and Knowledge (TARK 2009), pp. 166–173 (2009)
4. Harsanyi, J.: Games with incomplete information played by 'Bayesian' players, parts I–III. Management Science 14, 159–182, 320–334, 486–502 (1968)

C. Fermüller and A. Voronkov (Eds.): LPAR-17, LNCS 6397, p. 15, 2010.

Human and Unhuman Commonsense Reasoning

Michael J. Maher

NICTA and University of NSW
Sydney, Australia
Michael.Maher@nicta.com.au

Abstract. Ford has introduced a non-monotonic logic, System **LS**, inspired by an empirical study of human non-monotonic reasoning. We define here a defeasible logic **FDL** based on Ford's logic, and in doing so identify some similarities and differences between Ford's logic and existing defeasible logics. Several technical results about **FDL** are established, including its inference strength in relation to other defeasible logics.

1 Introduction

From its earliest years, logic has been used both to model human reasoning and to express an idealization of human reasoning [1]. This work has focused largely on reasoning based on definitive, or certain statements. For example, in the classic syllogism there is no doubt that Socrates is a man, nor that, without exception, all men are mortal.

However, much of human language and reasoning involves statements that are not certain but rather are generalities that admit exceptions. The prototypical example is: "Birds fly". An effort to reason formally and sensibly with such statements, inspired by the human ability to reason with "common sense", has grown within Artificial Intelligence in the last 30 years. Human commonsense reasoning has been modelled and idealized in various ways, leading to the development and study of non-monotonic and defeasible reasoning.

There has been a proliferation of formalisms and a variety of semantics for them. Even a relatively simple formalism, non-monotonic inheritance networks (also known as inheritance networks with exceptions), has multiple interpretations based on clashing intuitions of researchers [28]. However, relatively little empirical study of human reasoning on such problems has been carried out.

Recent studies by Ford and Billington [13,11,12] of human reasoning on problems that can be formulated as inheritance with exceptions have identified reasoning principles that appear to underlie rational human reasoning about such problems. Out of these studies, Ford formulated a logic System **LS** [10] reflecting the idealized human reasoning that these principles represent.

This paper addresses the preliminary design of a defeasible logic **FDL** based on Ford's logic and the underlying principles she identified. The logic fits into the framework for defeasible logics described in [4].

[1] Interestingly, classical logic fails in some respects to model human reasoning or, to put it differently, humans often fail to reason in this ideal way [9,20], and attempts continue to model human language and reasoning in logics.

C. Fermüller and A. Voronkov (Eds.): LPAR-17, LNCS 6397, pp. 16–29, 2010.

In the next section, two defeasible reasoning formalisms are outlined: non-monotonic inheritance networks and defeasible logic. Then, in Section 3, Ford's logic **LS** and some intuitions that lie behind it are presented. Section 4 defines the defeasible logic **FDL** based on these ideas and Section 5 presents some properties of this logic.

2 Defeasible Reasoning

Defeasible reasoning concerns reasoning where a chain of reasoning can be defeated (that is, not considered the basis of an inference) by another chain of reasoning (or, perhaps, several chains of reasoning). Thus defeasible reasoning is very similar to argumentation. In this section we discuss two formalisms for defeasible reasoning: defeasible logic and non-monotonic inheritance networks.

2.1 Defeasible Logic

The defeasible logics considered here are those considered in [1,4,7], developed from the original formulation of Nute [26]. There are various analyses of the semantics of these logics [16,17,22,25] but here we will stick to a straightforward proof-theoretic view.

Defeasible logics have a comparatively simple syntax. The basic building blocks are literals (negated or unnegated atomic formulae) which may be arranged into rules. Rules consist of a single literal in the head, an arrow, and a collection of literals forming the body. Thus negation and arrows are the only syntactic operators, although we will find it convenient at times to view the bodies of rules to be constructed by a binary conjunction operator. We use $\neg$ as the negation symbol and $\sim$ for the complementary operation which maps an atom to its negation and vice versa.

There are three different kinds of arrows, distinguishing three different kinds of rules. The arrow $\rightarrow$ is used to denote definitive or *strict* rules: rules and inferences that are absolutely, certainly, always valid. For example, we might write

$$emu(X) \rightarrow bird(X)$$

denoting that we consider that every emu, without exception, is a bird.

The arrow $\Rightarrow$ denotes a *defeasible rule*: rules that can be taken to be valid a lot of the time, but for which there are exceptions. They correspond to statements in English that are modified by words such as "generally", "usually", "typically", "normally", "mostly", etc. For example,

$$bird(X) \Rightarrow flier(X)$$

denotes that birds are usually able to fly, while recognising that some birds, such as those covered in oil, might not fly.

The distinction between these two kinds of rules is common to several non-monotonic formalisms. The third rule, however is more unusual. It represents a reluctance or, stronger, an inability to allow some inferences. It cannot be used to make an inference based on its own form, and only describes situations where conflicting inferences are not allowed. The arrow is $\leadsto$ and the rule is called a *defeater*. For example,

$$heavy(X) \leadsto \neg flier(X)$$

denotes that while we might consider that birds, in general, can fly (according to the previous rule) we do not allow this inference when the bird is heavy. On the other hand, we cannot use this rule for inference so we cannot conclude that something cannot fly just because it is heavy.

Defeasible logic also includes a set of *facts*, that is, literals that specified to be true. For example, we might have facts $emu(tweety)$ and $heavy(tweety)$.

In addition, to resolve competing rules there is an acyclic binary relation among rules called the *superiority relation* and denoted by $>$. $r_2 > r_1$ expresses that whenever both rules apply but have conflicting conclusions r_2 should have priority over – or over-rule – r_1; we should not apply the inference associated with r_1 and apply that associated with r_2 (provided r_2 is not a defeater). For example,

$$\begin{array}{lll} r_1: & bird(X) & \Rightarrow flier(X) \\ r_2: & nest\_on\_ground(X), animal(X) & \Rightarrow \neg flier(X) \\ r_3: & bird(X) & \rightarrow animal(X) \end{array}$$

$$r_2 > r_1$$

describes a situation where usually birds fly, and usually animals that nest on the ground do not fly, and when we find a bird that nests on the ground we should conclude that it does not fly, since r_2 over-rides r_1.

Thus a *defeasible theory* is a triple $(F, R, >)$ where F is a set of facts, R is a set of rules, and $>$ is a superiority relation over R. Although rules are presented in a first-order style, we assume that they are grounded so that the proof theory operates over an essentially propositional language. A formal description of inference in a defeasible logic is, in general, more complicated than the above informal introduction suggests. We consider one deeply-studied defeasible logic **DL** [1] as an example. A proof is a sequence of tagged literals, where tags describe the strength of proof under consideration and whether the literal has been proved, or it has been established that the literal cannot be proved. For example, $+\Delta p$ denotes that p can be proved using only the strict rules and $-\Delta q$ denotes that all possibilities for proving q using only strict rules have been exhausted without proving q. Two other tags $+\partial$ and $-\partial$ refer to provability with respect to all rules.

The inference rules for Δ, formulated as conditions on proofs, are given in Figure 1. R_s refers to the strict rules of R, and $R_s[q]$ is the strict rules with head q. We will later use R_{sd} for the strict and defeasible rules of R, and R_{dd} for the defeasible rules and defeaters. $A(r)$ refers to the antecedent, or body, of rule r and $P(i+1)$ ($P[1..i]$) refers to the $i+1$'th tagged literal in the proof P (the initial segment of P of length i). The $+\Delta$ inference rule

$+\Delta$) If $P(i+1) = +\Delta q$ then either
  .1) $q \in F$; or
  .2) $\exists r \in R_s[q]\ \forall a \in A(r), +\Delta a \in P[1..i]$.
$-\Delta$) If $P(i+1) = -\Delta q$ then
  .1) $q \notin F$, and
  .2) $\forall r \in R_s[q]\ \exists a \in A(r), -\Delta a \in P[1..i]$.

Fig. 1. Inference rules for $+\Delta$ and $-\Delta$

is essentially *modus ponens* while the $-\Delta$ inference rule is the strong negation [4] of the $+\Delta$ rule. The Δ inference rules are sometimes referred to as the monotonic part of the defeasible logic, since defeasibility is not involved.

Notice that if D contains facts p and $\neg p$ then we have both $+\Delta p$ and $+\Delta\neg p$ as consequences of D.

The inference rules for ∂ are substantially more complicated (see Figure 2). They must take into account Δ inferences, all three kinds of rules and the superiority relation. Roughly speaking, $+\partial q$ can be derived if either p can be proved monotonically, or (1) there is a strict or defeasible rule for q, the body of which can be proved defeasibly; (2) $\sim q$ cannot be proved monotonically; and (3) every rule for $\sim q$ that is applicable is over-ruled by an applicable rule for q. This latter behaviour (3) is called team defeat: the rules for q, as a team, over-rule the rules for $\sim q$, even though possibly no individual rule for q over-rules all its competitors. For the simpler inferences where we require a single rule to over-ride all its competitors, the symbol ∂^* is used. Again, failure to prove $(-\partial)$ is the strong negation of $+\partial$.

Defeasible logics other than **DL** use different tags and inference rules. We will later refer to tags δ and $\int$, whose inference rules are defined in [17,7].

2.2 Non-monotonic Inheritance Networks

Inheritance hierarchies are used to represent a taxonomic-style division of classes into subclasses. Thus they can describe a situation where, say, the class of emus inherits

$+\partial$) If $P(i+1) = +\partial q$ then either
- .1) $+\Delta q \in P[1..i]$; or
- .2) The following three conditions all hold.
  - .1) $\exists r \in R_{sd}[q]\ \forall a \in A(r), +\partial a \in P[1..i]$, and
  - .2) $-\Delta{\sim}q \in P[1..i]$, and
  - .3) $\forall s \in R[{\sim}q]$ either
    - .1) $\exists a \in A(s), -\partial a \in P[1..i]$; or
    - .2) $\exists t \in R_{sd}[q]$ such that
      - .1) $\forall a \in A(t), +\partial a \in P[1..i]$, and
      - .2) $t > s$.

$-\partial$) If $P(i+1) = -\partial q$ then
- .1) $-\Delta q \in P[1..i]$, and
- .2) either
  - .1) $\forall r \in R_{sd}[q]\ \exists a \in A(r), -\partial a \in P[1..i]$; or
  - .2) $+\Delta{\sim}q \in P[1..i]$; or
  - .3) $\exists s \in R[{\sim}q]$ such that
    - .1) $\forall a \in A(s), +\partial a \in P[1..i]$, and
    - .2) $\forall t \in R_{sd}[q]$ either
      - .1) $\exists a \in A(t), -\partial a \in P[1..i]$; or
      - .2) not$(t > s)$.

Fig. 2. Inference rules for $+\partial$ and $-\partial$

All emus are birds
Usually, birds fly
Usually, emus do not fly

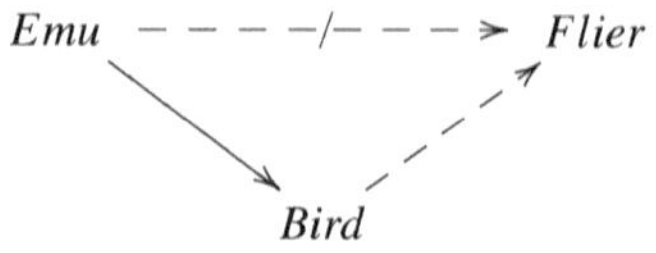

Fig. 3. Inheritance network for the Tweety problem

properties (such as having feathers) from the class of birds. Inheritance hierarchies can be represented by simple implications employing unary predicates. For example $emu(X) \rightarrow bird(X)$ represents that emu is a sub-class of bird.

However, emus are exceptional in the class of birds and to represent such situations where properties are generally – but not universally – inherited by subclasses, a weaker form of inheritance that admits exceptions is added.

An inheritance network can be described by a directed acyclic graph. Vertices of the graph represent properties (or classes) such as *emu* or *bird*. A solid arrow represents a strict (or definite, or certain) inference while a dashed arrow represents a defeasible inference. An arrow with a slash represents an exception: an inference of the negation of the target. For example, Figure 3 presents the well-known Tweety problem and an inheritance network representing it.

Inheritance hierarchies can be represented by simple implications employing unary predicates. For example $emu(X) \rightarrow bird(X)$ represents that emu is a sub-class of bird. For weaker inheritance statements we can use a defeasible implication. Thus $bird(X) \Rightarrow flier(X)$ represents that birds are generally fliers. Finally, exceptions can be expressed as implications to a negated literal. For example, $emu(X) \Rightarrow \neg flier(X)$. Facts state that constants are members of classes. For example, the fact $emu(tweety)$ expresses that Tweety is a member of the emu class.

Non-monotonic inheritance networks are one of the earliest formalisms for non-monotonic reasoning, and perhaps the earliest formalism involving defeasible reasoning. Early in the development of defeasible logic it was recognised that defeasible logic could be considered a generalization of non-monotonic inheritance networks [6]. Syntactically, inheritance networks are a very small subset of defeasible theories: only unary predicates are admitted, only one variable can be used in a rule, bodies of rules must contain exactly one atomic formula, and heads must contain exactly one literal.

As mentioned in the Introduction, there are many different semantics for non-monotonic inheritance networks. In the next section we will see a semantics for these networks inspired by empirical study of human reasoning.

3 Ford's Logic

Ford developed the logic **LS** from observation of human reasoning on inheritance problems and Gilio's analysis [14] of a probabilistic interpretation of system **P** [21].

Ford's logic is partly based on the recognition that chains of reasoning involving both strict and defeasible arrows may have different strengths. Consider the chain (1) below. If a typical A is a B, and every B is a C then it must be that all typical A's are C's, so we might be justified in drawing a defeasible arrow directly from A to C. In (2), however, every A is a B and a typical B is a C but we have no assurance that any A is a typical B. Thus following the chain from A to C makes an implicit and unsupported assumption that a typical A is typically a typical B. There is a similar problem in chain (3).

(1) $A \dashrightarrow B \longrightarrow C$

(2) $A \longrightarrow B \dashrightarrow C$

(3) $A \dashrightarrow B \dashrightarrow C$

This distinction between (1) and (2–3) was used by some of Ford's experimental subjects [13,11] and is also implicitly recognised in the research literature in the study of the Pennsylvania Dutch problem [19]. In terms of the inference rules discussed in [21], Ford identifies the weakness of (2) and (3) with the weakness of the Monotonicity and Transitivity rules.

LS is based on three tiers of defeasible inference, roughly characterized as follows [10]:

$\alpha \mid\!\sim_1 \beta$ *more than half of the α are β*
$\alpha \mid\!\sim_2 \beta$ *some α are β*
$\alpha \mid\!\sim_3 \beta$ *a relationship has been derived, but it is possible no α are β*

The index on $\mid\!\sim$ represents the "logical strength" of the relation, where smaller means stronger.

Thus, if we associate typicality/normality with more than half a population (which is in line with English usage), in chain (1) we feel justified in claiming $A \mid\!\sim_1 C$ while in chains (2) and (3) we can only claim $A \mid\!\sim_3 C$.

The intermediate tier of inference $\mid\!\sim_2$ is needed once conjunction is introduced. For example, it may be that A's are usually B's and A's are usually C's, but we cannot conclude that A's usually satisfy $B \wedge C$. This is because it might be that the the population of A's is largely polarized into individuals that are B's but not C's and individuals that are C's but not B's, with only a small proportion satisfying $B \wedge C$. On the other hand, if more than 75% of A's are B's and 75% of A's are C's then more than half of A's satisfy $B \wedge C$. Thus the use of the intermediate tier allows the logic to recognise the greater strength of the inference of $B \wedge C$ from A than the inference in (2) or (3) above.

The inference rules for **LS** are given in Figure 4. CM refers to Cautious Monotonicity. Throughout Ford's presentation of the logic, a collection of inheritance statements – both strict and defeasible – is assumed to exist as a parameter to the inference. Presumably, a statement $\models \alpha \rightarrow \beta$ refers to a consequence of the strict inheritance statements. Similarly, we presume that for every defeasible inheritance of α from β we can infer $\beta \mid\!\sim_1 \alpha$.

Ford leaves implicit inference rules that allow inferring $\alpha \mid\!\sim_{m+1} \beta$ from $\alpha \mid\!\sim_m \beta$ for $m = 1,2$. Without these, inference relation $\mid\!\sim_2$ is not contained in $\mid\!\sim_3$ as a result of (say)

Right Weakening $$\frac{\models \alpha \rightarrow \beta \qquad \gamma \mid\!\sim_n \alpha}{\gamma \mid\!\sim_n \beta}$$ S $$\frac{\alpha \wedge \beta \mid\!\sim_n \gamma}{\alpha \mid\!\sim_n \beta \rightarrow \gamma}$$

Left Logical Equivalence $$\frac{\models \alpha \leftrightarrow \beta \qquad \alpha \mid\!\sim_n \gamma}{\beta \mid\!\sim_n \gamma}$$

And (1) $$\frac{\alpha \mid\!\sim_1 \beta \qquad \alpha \mid\!\sim_1 \gamma}{\alpha \mid\!\sim_2 \beta \wedge \gamma}$$ CM (1) $$\frac{\alpha \mid\!\sim_1 \beta \qquad \alpha \mid\!\sim_1 \gamma}{\alpha \wedge \beta \mid\!\sim_2 \gamma}$$

And (2) $$\frac{\alpha \mid\!\sim_n \beta \qquad \alpha \mid\!\sim_m \gamma}{\alpha \mid\!\sim_3 \beta \wedge \gamma}$$ CM (2) $$\frac{\alpha \mid\!\sim_m \beta \qquad \alpha \mid\!\sim_n \gamma}{\alpha \wedge \beta \mid\!\sim_3 \gamma}$$

Cut (1) $$\frac{\alpha \wedge \beta \mid\!\sim_m \gamma \qquad \alpha \mid\!\sim_n \beta}{\alpha \mid\!\sim_2 \gamma}$$ Or (1) $$\frac{\alpha \mid\!\sim_m \gamma \qquad \beta \mid\!\sim_n \gamma}{\alpha \vee \beta \mid\!\sim_2 \gamma}$$

Cut (2) $$\frac{\alpha \wedge \beta \mid\!\sim_m \gamma \qquad \alpha \mid\!\sim_n \beta}{\alpha \mid\!\sim_3 \gamma}$$ Or (2) $$\frac{\alpha \mid\!\sim_m \gamma \qquad \beta \mid\!\sim_n \gamma}{\alpha \vee \beta \mid\!\sim_3 \gamma}$$

Monotonicity $$\frac{\models \alpha \rightarrow \beta \qquad \beta \mid\!\sim_n \gamma}{\alpha \mid\!\sim_3 \gamma}$$ Transitivity $$\frac{\alpha \mid\!\sim_m \beta \qquad \beta \mid\!\sim_n \gamma}{\alpha \mid\!\sim_3 \gamma}$$

Some inference rules have side-conditions: And (2) and CM (2) require $n \geq 2$ or $m \geq 2$; Cut (1) and Or (1) require $1 \leq n \leq 2$ and $1 \leq m \leq 2$; and Cut (2) and Or (2) require $n = 3$ or $m = 3$.

Fig. 4. Inference rules for **LS**

the restrictions on And(2). But it is clear that this presentation of inference rules like And is used to focus on the *strongest* inference that is permitted by the logic, and is not intended to exclude concluding $\alpha \mid\!\sim_3 \beta \wedge \gamma$ from $\alpha \mid\!\sim_1 \beta$ and $\alpha \mid\!\sim_1 \gamma$. Similarly, a Reflexivity axiom $\alpha \mid\!\sim_m \alpha$ could be added to **LS**.

When conflicting inferences can be derived in **LS**, say both $\alpha \mid\!\sim_i \beta$ and $\alpha \mid\!\sim_j \neg\beta$, the conclusion that is drawn is based on the logical strengths of the two statements. If $i < j$ then we conclude $\alpha \mid\!\sim \beta$ and if $i > j$ then we conclude $\alpha \mid\!\sim \neg\beta$. If $i = j$ we cannot draw any conclusion.

4 The Logic FDL

The defeasible logic derived from Ford's logic will be called **FDL**. There are several points of difference between Ford's logic **LS** and existing defeasible logics:

1. **LS** admits a broader syntax than defeasible logics, including the connectives $\vee$ and $\rightarrow$.
2. **LS** infers defeasible implications whereas defeasible logics infer tagged literals.

3. Defeasible logics may express priorities among rules using the superiority relation, which is not available in **LS**.
4. **LS** supports three tiers of defeasible inference, whereas most defeasible logics support only one.
5. **LS** takes a meta-theoretic approach to the resolution of conflicting conclusions: if we can derive $\alpha \mid\!\sim_1 \beta$ and $\alpha \mid\!\sim_2 \neg\beta$ then we conclude β defeasibly holds, based on the relative strength of the two inference relations. In contrast, in every defeasible logic investigated thus far, the resolution of conflicts is embedded in the inference rules. For example, in the inference rule for $+\partial$, condition 2.2 ensures that there is not a conflicting conclusion of greater strength.
6. **LS** does not express statements about literals that are not derivable, whereas defeasible logics provide inference rules for deriving such statements.

In **FDL** we will restrict the syntax of **LS** to the defeasible logic style to address the first two points. **FDL** will not use the superiority relation, but new tags $+\partial_1$, $+\partial_2$, and $+\partial_3$ are introduced in **FDL** to reflect the three tiers in **LS**. In place of the meta-logical balancing of logical strength in **LS** we will incorporate the resolution of conflicts within the inference rules, in the defeasible logic style. The end result is a defeasible logic that is guided by the principles of human commonsense reasoning identified by Ford but does not have the syntactic breadth of **LS**.

We now turn to the definition of **FDL** and motivation for some of the technical decisions.

Ford's logic, and the distinction between the three inference relations is partly based on the relative weakness of some paths, compared to others. This weakness relies on the loss of the presumption of typicality after the application of a rule. For example, although Tweety is an emu, and all emus are birds, the presumption that Tweety is a typical emu does not lead to a presumption that Tweety is a typical bird. Even if we were given, separately, the fact that Tweety is a bird, which would carry the presumption that Tweety is typical of birds, the existence of information that Tweety belongs to a subclass of birds should lead us at least to question – and perhaps to invalidate – the presumption.

Taking the latter approach, we must distinguish between facts that carry with them a presumption of typicality and facts that carry no such presumption. This distinction will be reflected in the tags we use. For facts that may or may not carry a presumption, we can use the Δ tags, while for facts that carry a presumption we introduce a new tag Φ. The inference rules for Φ are in Figure 5.

$+\Phi$) If $P(i+1) = +\Phi q$ then either	$-\Phi$) If $P(i+1) = -\Phi q$ then
.1) $q \in F$; and	.1) $q \notin F$, or
.2) $\forall r \in R_s[q]\ \exists a \in A(r), -\Delta a \in P[1..i]$.	.2) $\exists r \in R_s[q]\ \forall a \in A(r), +\Delta a \in P[1..i]$.

Fig. 5. Inference rules for $+\Phi$ and $-\Phi$

It is worthwhile noting that, as a result of this distinction, facts are not equivalent to strict rules with no antecedent, as is true in **DL**. Hence, a simplification of [1] which eliminates facts in **DL** is not valid for **FDL**.

To make matters simpler we will separate out inferring the status of conjunctions from inference involved in the application of a rule. We introduce tags on conjunctions for this purpose. Let p and q range over conjunctions of literals (including the trivial conjunction consisting of a single literal). The positive inference rules for conjunction are as follows.

$$\begin{array}{lll} \text{If } P(i+1) = +\Delta(p \wedge q) & \text{then} & +\Delta p \in P[1..i] \text{ and } +\Delta q \in P[1..i] \\ \text{If } P(i+1) = +\partial_1(p \wedge q) & \text{then} & +\Delta(p \wedge q) \in P[1..i] \\ \text{If } P(i+1) = +\partial_2(p \wedge q) & \text{then} & +\partial_1(p \wedge q) \in P[1..i] \text{ or} \\ & & (+\partial_1 p \in P[1..i] \text{ and } +\partial_1 q \in P[1..i]) \\ \text{If } P(i+1) = +\partial_3(p \wedge q) & \text{then} & +\partial_2(p \wedge q) \in P[1..i] \text{ or} \\ & & (+\partial_3 p \in P[1..i] \text{ and } +\partial_3 q \in P[1..i]) \end{array}$$

The negative inference rules are the strong negations of these rules.

The inference rules explicitly allow a conjunction to receive a tag if it has received a stronger tag. No conjunctions are tagged with $+\Phi$; this follows from the intended meaning of Φ to reflect that a fact $emu(tweety)$ expresses a presumption that Tweety is a typical emu. The first inference rule is simply a reflection of the conjunction implicitly used in the inference rule for $+\Delta$. The third inference rule reflects And(1) while the fourth reflects And(2). Following the And rules, a conjunction can have tag $+\partial_1$ only if the conjunction definitely holds (i.e. has tag $+\Delta$).

If we view conjunction as an operation on tags, it is commutative but not associative. For example, if $+\Delta p$, $+\Delta q$, and $+\partial_1 r$ then we can infer $+\partial_2((p \wedge q) \wedge r)$ but only infer $+\partial_3(p \wedge (q \wedge r))$. To extend conjunction to sets of literals we define the tag of the conjunction to be the strongest tag achievable by any grouping and ordering of the literals. This is equivalent to requiring that all Δ tagged literals are grouped together before applying binary conjunctions.

We now turn to the inference rules for tagged literals based on the application of rules. These rules are presented in Figure 6. As with the other tags we have used, the inference rule for $-\partial_i$ is the strong negation of the inference rules for $+\partial_i$, for each i.

There are several elements of the rules of interest. The conditions 1 in the inference rules ensure that there is a hierarchy of inference strength, from Δ to ∂_3. The conditions 2.1 for strict rules reflect Right Weakening in **LS**. Condition 2.1 for ∂_3 reflects Monotonicity and Transitivity.

In drawing conclusions with Ford's logic, a stronger inference overrides a conflicting weaker inference, although this occurs at the meta level. A similar behaviour is ensured in **FDL** from within the logic. Conditions 2.2 of the inference rules specify that to infer $+\partial_i q$ we must prove that $\sim q$ cannot be proved at a greater strength. Similarly, the combination of conditions 2.1 and 2.3 (and 2.4 for ∂_1) ensures that when we have competing inferences of equal strength no positive conclusion can be drawn.

For inheritance networks we can view the tags as encoding information about paths in the inheritance network. Φ represents the empty path, Δ paths consisting only of strict rules, ∂_1 paths of the form $\Rightarrow\rightarrow^*$, and ∂_3 represents all paths. The motivation for introducing $\mid\!\sim_2$ in **LS** was not related to paths and so its counterpart ∂_2 in **FDL** encodes no larger class of paths than ∂_1.

$+\partial_1$) If $P(i+1) = +\partial_1 q$ then either
.1) $+\Delta q \in P[1..i]$; or
.2) The following four conditions all hold.
.1) $\exists r \in R_s[q], +\partial_1 A(r) \in P[1..i]$ or
$\exists r \in R_d[q], +\Phi A(r) \in P[1..i]$, and
.2) $-\Delta{\sim}q \in P[1..i]$, and
.3) $\forall s \in R_s[{\sim}q], -\partial_1 A(s) \in P[1..i]$, and
.4) $\forall s \in R_{dd}[{\sim}q], -\Phi A(s) \in P[1..i]$

$+\partial_2$) If $P(i+1) = +\partial_2 q$ then either
.1) $+\partial_1 q \in P[1..i]$; or
.2) The following three conditions all hold.
.1) $\exists r \in R_s[q],\ +\partial_2 A(r) \in P[1..i]$, and
.2) $-\partial_1{\sim}q \in P[1..i]$, and
.3) $\forall s \in R_s[{\sim}q],\ -\partial_2 A(s) \in P[1..i]$
.4) $\forall s \in R_{dd}[{\sim}q],\ -\Phi A(s) \in P[1..i]$

$+\partial_3$) If $P(i+1) = +\partial_3 q$ then either
.1) $+\partial_2 q \in P[1..i]$; or
.2) The following three conditions all hold.
.1) $\exists r \in R_{sd}[q],\ +\partial_3 A(r) \in P[1..i]$, and
.2) $-\partial_2{\sim}q \in P[1..i]$, and
.3) $\forall s \in R[{\sim}q],\ -\partial_3 A(s) \in P[1..i]$

Fig. 6. Inference rules for $+\partial_i$ for $i = 1,2,3$

5 Properties of FDL

We now turn to investigate the properties of this logic. The fact that **FDL** can be seen as an instance of the framework for defeasible logics [4] greatly simplifies the establishment of these properties. The first property concerns the efficiency of inference in the logic. In line with other defeasible logics [23,7], inference can be performed in linear time. This is in contrast to many other non-monotonic logics, for which inference is NP-hard.

Proposition 1. *The set of all literals that can be inferred from a propositional* **FDL** *theory D can be computed in O(N) time, where N is the size of D.*

FDL is amenable to efficient implementation in the same way that other defeasible logics are [3,23,24].

Coherence of a defeasible logic refers to the property that tagged literals obtained by applying complementary tags to the same literal cannot both be inferred.

Definition 1. *A defeasible logic is* coherent *if, for every defeasible theory D in the logic, every tag d, and every literal q, we do not have both $D \vdash +dq$ and $D \vdash -dq$.*

It is this property that supports the intuition that $+d$ represents a form of provability while $-d$ represents finite failure to prove: we can never both prove and be unable to prove a proposition. As might be expected, **FDL** enjoys this property.

Proposition 2. **FDL** *is coherent.*

The monotonic part of a defeasible theory allows the inference of both a proposition and its negation. Thus defeasible logics may be inconsistent in the usual sense, independent of the defeasible inferences. Since the defeasible inferences are the main focus of defeasible logics, consistency for defeasible theories refers to a guarantee that the only contradictory information that is derived from a theory is already a consequence of the monotonic part of the theory alone.

Definition 2. *A defeasible logic is* relatively consistent *if, for every defeasible theory D in the logic, for every tag d, and every proposition q, we do not have $D \vdash +dq$ and $D \vdash +d\neg q$ unless $D \vdash +\Delta q$ and $D \vdash +\Delta\neg q$.*

Again, this is a property that holds for **FDL** In this sense, the logic is paraconsistent: beyond conflicting strict statements, no inconsistent inferences are made.

Proposition 3. **FDL** *is relatively consistent.*

Decisiveness insists that the proof theory determines the proof status of every tagged literal. It is a form of inverse of coherence. A logic is *decisive* for a defeasible theory D if, every tag d, and every literal q, either $D \vdash +dq$ or $D \vdash -dq$. A propositional defeasible theory D is acyclic if its dependency graph is acyclic. All non-monotonic inheritance networks form acyclic defeasible theories. The following result shows that, in particular, **FDL** is decisive on non-monotonic inheritance networks.

Proposition 4. *If the defeasible theory D is acyclic then* **FDL** *is decisive for D.*

Propositions 1–4 identify properties that **FDL** has in common with many other defeasible logics. We now look at inference strength, where we will see a difference between **FDL** and **DL**.

When comparing inference strength we use the following notation. Let d_1 and d_2 be tags. We write $d_1 \subseteq d_2$ to say that, for any defeasible theory D, $\{p \mid D \vdash +d_1 p\} \subseteq \{p \mid D \vdash +d_2 p\}$ and $\{p \mid D \vdash -d_1 p\} \supseteq \{p \mid D \vdash +d_2 p\}$. That is, we can derive p with d_2 any time we can derive p with d_1 and, conversely, we recognise that we cannot derive p with d_1 any time we recognise that we cannot derive p with d_2.

Almost immediately from the definitions we have a hierarchy of inference strength among the tags of **FDL**

Proposition 5

$$\Phi \subseteq \Delta \subseteq \partial_1 \subseteq \partial_2 \subseteq \partial_3$$

It is easy to see that these containments are *strict*, that is, for every $d \subseteq d'$, there is a defeasible theory D and literal q such that $D \vdash +dq$ but $D \not\vdash +d'q$ and/or $D \vdash -d'q$ but $D \not\vdash -dq$.

FDL does not involve a superiority relation. In comparing with other defeasible logics we consider only defeasible theories without a superiority relation. In that case, the logics with and without team defeat are equivalent. That is, $\partial = \partial^*$ and similarly $\delta = \delta^*$ and $\int = \int^*$. We now see that **FDL** and **DL** are incomparable in inference strength.

Proposition 6. *∂_1, ∂_3, and ∂_3 are incomparable to ∂. That is, $\partial_i \not\subseteq \partial$ and $\partial \not\subseteq \partial_i$, for $i = 1, \ldots, 3$,*

This result can be established using one simple defeasible theory. We will see that $\partial_1 \not\subseteq \partial$ and $\partial \not\subseteq \partial_3$. It follows immediately that $\partial_2 \not\subseteq \partial$ and $\partial_3 \not\subseteq \partial$ and, similarly, $\partial \not\subseteq \partial_1$ and $\partial \not\subseteq \partial_2$.

Consider a defeasible theory D consisting of facts p, r and s and rules

$$\begin{aligned} p &\Rightarrow q \\ r &\Rightarrow \neg q \\ s &\rightarrow r \\ q &\Rightarrow t \\ r &\Rightarrow \neg t \end{aligned}$$

Then $+\Delta p$ and $+\Delta r$, and $-\Delta t$. Consequently, in **DL** we have equal support for q and $\neg q$ and hence we derive $-\partial q$. As a result, we can derive $+\partial \neg t$.

On the other hand, in **FDL** we have $+\Phi p$ and $+\Phi s$ but $-\Phi r$. Hence, condition 2.1 for $+\partial_1 q$ and condition 2.4 are both satisfied. Furthermore, there is no strict rule for $\neg q$, so conditions 2.2 and 2.3 are satisfied. Thus we conclude $+\partial_1 q$. This establishes that $\partial_1 \not\subseteq \partial$.

Considering the status of $\neg t$ under **FDL**, we see that $-\partial_1 \neg t$ because condition 2.1 is satisfied. Consequently also $-\partial_2 \neg t$ by condition 2.1. Finally, by condition 2.3 of ∂_3 we must conclude $-\partial_3 \neg t$, since the antecedent of the rule for t is q and we know $+\partial_1 q$, and hence $+\partial_3 q$. This establishes that $\partial \not\subseteq \partial_3$.

Combining this result with results of [7] and some other results, we see the relationship between inference in **FDL** and inference in other defeasible logics.

Proposition 7. *Consider a defeasible theory D containing no superiority statements. Then the following containments hold.*

$$\begin{array}{ccccc} & & \partial_1 \subseteq \partial_2 \subseteq \partial_3 & & \\ & \rotatebox{45}{$\subseteq$} & & \rotatebox{-45}{$\subseteq$} & \\ \Phi \subseteq \Delta & & & & \int \\ & \rotatebox{-45}{$\subseteq$} & & \rotatebox{45}{$\subseteq$} & \\ & & \delta \subseteq \partial & & \end{array}$$

All of the containments in the above proposition are strict. Only the status of $\delta \subseteq \partial_3$ is not known.

6 Conclusion

We have seen a logic **FDL** that provides a model of human "common sense" reasoning. The logic is less expressive than Ford's System **LS** in that it does not support connectives $\vee$ and $\rightarrow$, but it has a low complexity and is amenable to efficient implementation.

It satisfies several desirable properties and we have seen its relationship to other defeasible logics. **FDL** in general makes different inferences than **DL** and other defeasible logics. There are even greater differences with logics and argumentation systems based on stable semantics, which tend to make more positive inferences than **DL**.

A computational model of human "common sense" reasoning is useful for any reasoning system that interacts with people. For these systems there is a danger that there is a mismatch between the logic it employs and the logic that people use or would accept as valid reasoning. For example, a formalization of regulations [5], business rules [18], or contracts [27,15] as defeasible rules might lead to differences in interpretation between the people who formulate the rules (and the people who must follow the rules) and systems that enforce the rules. Similarly, if a software agent's desired behaviour is described with defeasible rules by a naive user [8] then there is a danger that the implemented behaviour differs from the expected behaviour. Finally, for software agents that interact directly with people, an accurate model of human reasoning is useful, simply to understand the interaction properly.

There remains much more to do if we are to harmonise human and software reasoning. Although the design of **FDL** builds on **LS**, the formal relationship between the two logics has not been addressed. Clarifying this relationship will be necessary. However, there may be better models of human commonsense reasoning than **LS** and **FDL** and there is great scope for experimental and theoretical work on this subject.

Acknowledgments

My thanks to Marilyn Ford for discussions and several drafts of her work developing the logic **LS**, and to Grigoris Antoniou, David Billington, and Guido Governatori for their collaboration on defeasible logic over many years. And thanks to Guido for his comments on a rough draft.

NICTA is funded by the Australian Government as represented by the Department of Broadband, Communications and the Digital Economy and the Australian Research Council through the ICT Centre of Excellence program.

References

1. Antoniou, G., Billington, D., Governatori, G., Maher, M.J.: Representation results for defeasible logic. ACM Transactions on Computational Logic 2, 255–287 (2001)
2. Antoniou, G., Billington, D., Governatori, G., Maher, M.J.: Embedding Defeasible Logic into Logic Programming. Theory and Practice of Logic Programming 6, 703–735 (2006)
3. Antoniou, G., Billington, D., Governatori, G., Maher, M.J., Rock, A.: A family of defeasible reasoning logics and its implementation. In: Proc. 14th European Conference on Artificial Intelligence (ECAI 2000), pp. 459–463. IOS Press, Amsterdam (2000)
4. Antoniou, G., Billington, D., Governatori, G., Maher, M.J.: A Flexible Framework for Defeasible Logics. In: Proc. National Conference on Artificial Intelligence (AAAI 2000), pp. 405–410 (2000)
5. Antoniou, G., Billington, D., Maher, M.J.: On the analysis of regulations using defeasible rules. In: Proc. 32nd Hawaii International Conference on Systems Science (1999)
6. Billington, D., de Coster, K., Nute, D.: A Modular Translation from Defeasible Nets to Defeasible Logic. Journal of Experimental and Theoretical Artificial Intelligence 2, 151–177 (1990)

7. Billington, D., Antoniou, G., Governatori, G., Maher, M.J.: An Inclusion Theorem for Defeasible Logics. ACM Transactions on Computational Logic (to appear)
8. Dumas, M., Governatori, G., ter Hofstede, A., Oaks, P.: A formal approach to negotiating agents development. Electronic Commerce Research and Applications 1, 193–207 (2002)
9. Evans, J.S.B.T.: Bias in Human Reasoning. Erlbaum, Mahwah (1989)
10. Ford, M.: System LS: A three-tiered nonmonotonic reasoning system. Computational Intelligence 1, 89–107 (2004)
11. Ford, M.: Human nonmonotonic reasoning: The importance of seeing the logical strength of arguments. Synthese 146(1&2), 71–92 (2005)
12. Ford, M.: On using human nonmonotonic reasoning to inform artificial systems. Psychologica Belgica 45(1), 57–70 (2005)
13. Ford, M., Billington, D.: Strategies in human commonsense reasoning. Computational Intelligence 16, 446–468 (2000)
14. Gilio, A.: Probabilistic Reasoning Under Coherence in System P. Annals of Mathematics and Artificial Intelligence 34(1-3), 5–34 (2002)
15. Governatori, G.: Representing business contracts in RuleML. International Journal of Cooperative Information Systems 14, 181–216 (2005)
16. Governatori, G., Maher, M.J.: An Argumentation-Theoretic Characterization of Defeasible Logic. In: Proc. 14th European Conference on Artificial Intelligence (ECAI 2000), pp. 469–474. IOS Press, Amsterdam (2000)
17. Governatori, G., Maher, M.J., Antoniou, G., Billington, D.: Argumentation Semantics for Defeasible Logics. Journal of Logic and Computation 14, 675–702 (2004)
18. Grosof, B.N., Labrou, Y., Chan, H.Y.: A Declarative Approach to Business Rules in Contracts: Courteous Logic Programs in XML. In: Proc. 1st ACM Conference on Electronic Commerce (EC 1999). ACM Press, New York (1999)
19. Horty, J.F., Thomason, R.H.: Mixing Strict and Defeasible Inheritance. In: Proc. National Conference on Artificial Intelligence (AAAI 1988), pp. 427–432 (1988)
20. Johnson-Laird, P.N., Byrne, R.M.J.: Deduction. Erlbaum, Mahwah (1991)
21. Kraus, S., Lehmann, D., Magidor, M.: Nonmonotonic reasoning, preferential models and cumulative logics. Artificial Intelligence 44, 167–207 (1990)
22. Maher, M.J.: A Denotational Semantics for Defeasible Logic. In: Palamidessi, C., Moniz Pereira, L., Lloyd, J.W., Dahl, V., Furbach, U., Kerber, M., Lau, K.-K., Sagiv, Y., Stuckey, P.J. (eds.) CL 2000. LNCS (LNAI), vol. 1861, pp. 209–222. Springer, Heidelberg (2000)
23. Maher, M.J.: Propositional Defeasible Logic has Linear Complexity. Theory and Practice of Logic Programming 1, 691–711 (2001)
24. Maher, M.J., Rock, A., Antoniou, G., Billington, D., Miller, T.: Efficient Defeasible Reasoning Systems. International Journal on Artificial Intelligence Tools 10(4), 483–501 (2001)
25. Maher, M.J.: A Model-Theoretic Semantics for Defeasible Logic. In: Proc. Workshop on Paraconsistent Computational Logic, pp. 67–80 (2002)
26. Nute, D.: Defeasible Logic. In: Gabbay, D.M., Hogger, C.J., Robinson, J.A. (eds.) Handbook of Logic in Artificial Intelligence and Logic Programming, vol. 3, pp. 353–395. Oxford University Press, Oxford (1994)
27. Reeves, D.M., Grosof, B.N., Wellman, M.P., Chan, H.Y.: Towards a Declarative Language for Negotiating Executable Contracts. In: Proc. AAAI-99 Workshop on Artificial Intelligence in Electronic Commerce (AIEC 1999). AAAI Press/MIT Press (1999)
28. Touretzky, D.D., Horty, J.F., Thomason, R.H.: A Clash of Intuitions: The Current State of Nonmonotonic Multiple Inheritance Systems. In: Proc. 10th International Joint Conference on Artificial Intelligence (IJCAI 1987), pp. 476–482. Morgan Kaufmann, San Francisco (1987)

Gödel Logics – A Survey

Norbert Preining

Research Center of Integrated Science
Japan Advanced Institute of Science and Technology
Nomi-shi, Japan
preining@jaist.ac.jp

1 Introduction

The logics we present in this tutorial, Gödel logics, can be characterized in a rough-and-ready way as follows: The language is standard, defined at different levels: propositional, quantified-propositional, first-order. The logics are many-valued, and the sets of truth values considered are (closed) subsets of $[0, 1]$ which contain both 0 and 1. 1 is the 'designated value,' i.e., a formula is valid if it receives the value 1 in every interpretation. The truth functions of conjunction and disjunction are minimum and maximum, respectively, and in the first-order case quantifiers are defined by infimum and supremum over subsets of the set of truth values. The characteristic operator of Gödel logics, the Gödel conditional, is defined by $a \to b = 1$ if $a \leq b$ and $= b$ if $a > b$. Because the truth values are ordered (indeed, in many cases, densely ordered), the semantics of Gödel logics is suitable for formalizing *comparisons* with respect to degrees of truth. It is related in this respect to a more widely known many-valued logic, Łukasiewicz logic – although the truth function of the Łukasiewicz conditional is defined not just using comparison, but also addition. In contrast to Łukasiewicz logic, which might be considered a logic of *absolute* or *metric comparison*, Gödel logics are logics of *relative comparison*. This alone makes Gödel logics an interesting subject for logical investigations.

Yet Gödel logics are also closely related to intuitionistic logic: they are the logics of linearly-ordered Heyting algebras over $[0, 1]$. In the propositional case, infinite-valued Gödel logic can be axiomatized by the intuitionistic propositional calculus extended by the axiom schema $(A \to B) \vee (B \to A)$, a result by Dummett [17]. Because of that infinite-valued propositional Gödel logics is also called **LC**, or (Gödel-)Dummett-Logic. This connection extends also to Kripke semantics for intuitionistic logic: Gödel logics can also be characterized as logics of (classes of) linearly ordered and countable intuitionistic Kripke structures with constant domains [15].

Let us present an observation of Gaisi Takeuti concerning implication conditionals for many-valued logics, that spotlights why Gödel logics are gaining more and more interest, and why in some cases they behave well in contrast to other many-valued logics, namely that the truth function for the Gödel conditional can be 'deduced' from simple properties of the evaluation and the entailment relation.

C. Fermüller and A. Voronkov (Eds.): LPAR-17, LNCS 6397, pp. 30–51, 2010.

Lemma 1. *Suppose we have a standard language containing a 'conditional'* $\twoheadrightarrow$ *interpreted by a truth-function into* $[0,1]$*, and some standard entailment relation* $\models$*. Suppose further that*

1. *a conditional evaluates to* 1 *if the truth value of the antecedent is less or equal to the truth value of the consequent, i.e., if* $\mathcal{I}(A) \leq \mathcal{I}(B)$*, then* $\mathcal{I}(A \twoheadrightarrow B) = 1$*;*
2. *if* $\Gamma \models B$*, then* $\mathcal{I}(\Gamma) \leq \mathcal{I}(B)$*;*
3. *the deduction theorem holds, i.e.,* $\Gamma \cup \{A\} \models B \Leftrightarrow \Gamma \models A \twoheadrightarrow B$*.*

Then $\twoheadrightarrow$ *is the Gödel conditional.*

Proof. From (1), we have that $\mathcal{I}(A \twoheadrightarrow B) = 1$ if $\mathcal{I}(A) \leq \mathcal{I}(B)$. Since $\models$ is reflexive, $B \models B$. Since it is monotonic, $B, A \models B$. By the deduction theorem, $B \models A \twoheadrightarrow B$. By (2), $\mathcal{I}(B) \leq \mathcal{I}(A \twoheadrightarrow B)$. From $A \twoheadrightarrow B \models A \twoheadrightarrow B$ and the deduction theorem, we get $A \twoheadrightarrow B, A \models B$. By (2), $\min\{\mathcal{I}(A \twoheadrightarrow B), \mathcal{I}(A)\} \leq \mathcal{I}(B)$. Thus, if $\mathcal{I}(A) > \mathcal{I}(B)$, $\mathcal{I}(A \twoheadrightarrow B) \leq \mathcal{I}(B)$. □

Note that all usual conditionals (Gödel, Łukasiewicz, product conditionals) satisfy condition (1). So, in some sense, the Gödel conditional is the only many-valued conditional which validates both directions of the deduction theorem for $\models$. For instance, for the Łukasiewicz conditional $\to_{\text{Ł}}$ given by $\mathcal{I}(A \to_{\text{Ł}} B) = \min(1, 1 - \mathcal{I}(A) + \mathcal{I}(B))$ the right-to-left direction fails: $A \to_{\text{Ł}} B \models A \to_{\text{Ł}} B$, but $A \to_{\text{Ł}} B, A \not\models B$.

1.1 Syntax and Semantics for Propositional Gödel Logics

When considering propositional Gödel logics we fix a standard propositional language $\mathscr{L}^0$ with countably many propostional variables p_i, and the connectives $\wedge$, $\vee$, $\to$ and the constant $\bot$ (for 'false'); negation is introduced as an abbreviation: we let $\neg p \equiv (p \to \bot)$. For convenience, we also define $\top \equiv \bot \to \bot$. We will sometimes use the unary connective $\triangle$, introduced in [2]. Furthermore we will use $p \prec q$ as an abbreviation for $p \prec q \equiv (q \to p) \to q$.

Definition 2. *Let* $V \subseteq [0,1]$ *be some set of truth values which contains* 0 *and* 1*. A propositional Gödel valuation* $\mathcal{I}^0$ *(short valuation) based on* V *is a function from the set of propositional variables into* V *with* $\mathcal{I}^0(\bot) = 0$*. This valuation can be extended to a function mapping formulas from* $\mathrm{Frm}(\mathscr{L}^0)$ *into* V *as follows:*

$$\mathcal{I}^0(p \wedge q) = \min\{\mathcal{I}^0(p), \mathcal{I}^0(q)\} \qquad \mathcal{I}^0(p \vee q) = \max\{\mathcal{I}^0(p), \mathcal{I}^0(q)\}$$

$$\mathcal{I}^0(p \to q) = \begin{cases} \mathcal{I}^0(q) & \text{if } \mathcal{I}^0(p) > \mathcal{I}^0(q) \\ 1 & \text{if } \mathcal{I}^0(p) \leq \mathcal{I}^0(q). \end{cases} \qquad \mathcal{I}^0(\triangle p) = \begin{cases} 1 & \mathcal{I}^0(p) = 1 \\ 0 & \mathcal{I}^0(p) < 1 \end{cases}$$

A formula is called valid with respect to V *if it is mapped to* 1 *for all valuations based on* V*. The set of all formulas which are valid with respect to* V *will be called the propositional Gödel logic based on* V *and will be denoted by* $\mathbf{G}^0_V$*. The validity of a formula* p *with respect to* V *will be denoted by* $\models^0_V p$ *or* $\models_{\mathbf{G}^0_V} p$*.*

Remark 3. The extension of the valuation $\mathcal{I}^0$ to formulas provides the following truth functions:

$$\mathcal{I}^0(\neg p) = \begin{cases} 0 & \text{if } \mathcal{I}^0(p) > 0 \\ 1 & \text{otherwise} \end{cases}$$

$$\mathcal{I}^0(p \prec q) = \begin{cases} 1 & \text{if } \mathcal{I}^0(p) < \mathcal{I}^0(q) \text{ or } \mathcal{I}^0(p) = \mathcal{I}^0(q) = 1 \\ \mathcal{I}(q) & \text{otherwise} \end{cases}$$

Thus, the intuition behind $p \prec q$ is that p is strictly less than q, or both are equal to 1.

1.2 Syntax and Semantics for First-Order Gödel Logics

When considering first-order Gödel logics we fix a standard first-order language $\mathscr{L}$ with finitely or countably many predicate symbols P and finitely or countably many function symbols f for every finite arity k. In addition to the connectives of propositional Gödel logics the two quantifiers $\forall$ and $\exists$ are used.

Gödel logics are usually defined using the single truth value set $[0,1]$. For propositional logic, any choice of an infinite subset of $[0,1]$ leads to the same propositional logic (set of tautologies). In the first order case, where quantifiers will be interpreted as infima and suprema, a closed subset of $[0,1]$ is necessary.

The semantics of Gödel logics, with respect to a fixed closed subset of $[0,1]$ as set of truth values and a fixed language $\mathscr{L}$ of predicate logic, is defined using the extended language $\mathscr{L}^U$, where U is the universe of the interpretation $\mathcal{I}$. $\mathscr{L}^U$ is $\mathscr{L}$ extended with constant symbols for each element of U.

Definition 4 (Semantics of Gödel logic). *Let $\{0,1\} \subseteq V \subseteq [0,1]$ be closed. An* interpretation $\mathcal{I}$ into V, *or a* V-interpretation, *consists of*

1. *a nonempty set $U = U^{\mathcal{I}}$, the 'universe' of $\mathcal{I}$,*
2. *for each k-ary predicate symbol P, a function $P^{\mathcal{I}} \colon U^k \to V$,*
3. *for each k-ary function symbol f, a function $f^{\mathcal{I}} \colon U^k \to U$.*
4. *for each variable v, a value $v^{\mathcal{I}} \in U$.*

Given an interpretation $\mathcal{I}$, we can naturally define a value $t^{\mathcal{I}}$ for any term t and a truth value $\mathcal{I}(A)$ for any formula A of $\mathscr{L}^U$. For a term $t = f(u_1, \ldots, u_k)$ we define $\mathcal{I}(t) = f^{\mathcal{I}}(u_1^{\mathcal{I}}, \ldots, u_k^{\mathcal{I}})$. For atomic formulas $A \equiv P(t_1, \ldots, t_n)$, we define $\mathcal{I}(A) = P^{\mathcal{I}}(t_1^{\mathcal{I}}, \ldots, t_n^{\mathcal{I}})$. For composite formulas A we extend the truth definitions from the propositonal case for the new syntactic elements by:

$$\mathcal{I}(\forall x\, A(x)) = \inf\{\mathcal{I}(A(u)) : u \in U\}$$
$$\mathcal{I}(\exists x\, A(x)) = \sup\{\mathcal{I}(A(u)) : u \in U\}$$

(Here we use the fact that every Gödel set V is a closed *subset of $[0,1]$ in order to be able to interpret $\forall$ and $\exists$ as* inf *and* sup *in V.*

If $\mathcal{I}(A) = 1$, we say that $\mathcal{I}$ satisfies *A, and write $\mathcal{I} \models A$. If $\mathcal{I}(A) = 1$ for every V-interpretation $\mathcal{I}$, we say A is* valid *in $\mathbf{G}_V$ and write $\mathbf{G}_V \models A$.*

If Γ is a set of sentences, we define $\mathcal{I}(\Gamma) = \inf\{\mathcal{I}(A) : A \in \Gamma\}$.

Abusing notation slightly, we will often define interpretations simply be defining the truth values of atomic formulas in $\mathscr{L}^U$.

Definition 5. *If Γ is a set of formulas (possibly infinite), we say that Γ* entails *A* in *$\mathbf{G}_V$, $\Gamma \models_V A$ iff for all $\mathcal{I}$ into V, $\mathcal{I}(\Gamma) \leq \mathcal{I}(A)$.*

Γ 1-entails *A in $\mathbf{G}_V$, $\Gamma \Vdash_V A$, iff, for all $\mathcal{I}$ into V, whenever $\mathcal{I}(B) = 1$ for all $B \in \Gamma$, then $\mathcal{I}(A) = 1$.*

We will write $\Gamma \models A$ instead of $\Gamma \models_V A$ in case it is obvious which truth value set V is meant.

Definition 6. *For a Gödel set V we define the* first order Gödel logic *$\mathbf{G}_V$ as the set of all pairs (Γ, A) such that $\Gamma \models_V A$.*

One might wonder whether a different definition of the entailment relation in Gödel logic might give different results. But as the following proposition shows, the above two definitions yield the same result, allowing us to use the characterization of $\models$ or $\Vdash$ as convenient.

Proposition 7. *$\Pi \models_V A$ iff $\Pi \Vdash_V A$*

1.3 Axioms and Deduction Systems for Gödel Logics

In this section we introduce certain axioms and deduction systems for Gödel logics, and we will show completeness of these deduction systems subsequently.

We will denote by **IL** any sound and complete Hilbert-style axiomatization of Intuitionistic Logic. The following formulas will play an important rôle when axiomatizing Gödel logics

QS	$\forall x(C^{(x)} \vee A(x)) \rightarrow (C^{(x)} \vee \forall x A(x))$	LIN	$(A \rightarrow B) \vee (B \rightarrow A)$
ISO$_0$	$\forall x \neg\neg A(x) \rightarrow \neg\neg\forall x A(x)$	ISO$_1$	$\forall x \neg \triangle A(x) \rightarrow \neg \triangle \exists x A(x)$
FIN(n)	$(\top \rightarrow p_1) \vee (p_1 \rightarrow p_2) \vee \ldots \vee (p_{n-2} \rightarrow p_{n-1}) \vee (p_{n-1} \rightarrow \bot)$		

For the axiomatization of the $\triangle$-operator we use the following group of axioms, called $\triangle$-axioms:

$\Delta 1$	$\triangle A \vee \neg \triangle A$	$\Delta 2$	$\triangle(A \vee B) \rightarrow (\triangle A \vee \triangle B)$
$\Delta 3$	$\triangle A \rightarrow A$	$\Delta 4$	$\triangle A \rightarrow \triangle\triangle A$
$\Delta 5$	$\triangle(A \rightarrow B) \rightarrow (\triangle A \rightarrow \triangle B)$	$\Delta 6$	$\dfrac{A}{\triangle A}$

Definition 8. *If $\mathcal{A}$ is an axiom system, we denote by $\mathcal{A}^0$ the propositional part of $\mathcal{A}$, i.e. all the axioms which do not contain quantifiers. With $\mathcal{A}\Delta$ we denote the axiom system obtained from $\mathcal{A}$ by adding the axioms and rules* AXΔ*. With $\mathcal{A}_n$ we denote the axiom system obtained from $\mathcal{A}$ by adding the axiom* FIN(n)*. We denote by **H** the axiom system **IL** +* QS + LIN.

Example. $\mathbf{IL}^0$ is the same as **IPL**. $\mathbf{H}^0$ is the same as **LC**.

For all these axiom systems the general notion of deducability can be defined:

Definition 9. *If a formula/sequent Γ can be deduced from an axiom system $\mathcal{A}$ we denote this by $\vdash_{\mathcal{A}} \Gamma$.*

Theorem 10 (Soundness). *Suppose Γ contains only closed formulas, and all axioms of $\mathcal{A}$ are valid in $\mathbf{G}_V$. Then, if $\Gamma \vdash_{\mathcal{A}} A$ then $\Gamma \models_V A$. In particular, $\mathbf{H}$ is sound for $\models_V$ for any Gödel set V; $\mathbf{H}_n$ is sound for $\models_V$ if $|V| = n$; and $\mathbf{H}_0$ is sound for $\models_V$ if 0 is isolated in V.*

1.4 Topologic and Order

In the following we will recall some definitions and facts from topology and order theory which will be used later on in many places. All the following notations, lemmas, theorems are carried out within the framework of Polish spaces, which are separable, completely metrizable topological spaces. For our discussion it is only necessary to know that $\mathbb{R}$ and all its closed subsets are Polish spaces (hence, every Gödel set is a Polish space). For a detailed exposition see [22, 23].

Definition 11 (Limit point, perfect space, perfect set). *A* limit point *of a topological space is a point that is not isolated, i.e. for every open neighborhood U of x there is a point $y \in U$ with $y \neq x$. A space is* perfect *if all its points are limit points. A set $P \subseteq \mathbb{R}$ is* perfect *if it is closed and together with the topology induced from $\mathbb{R}$ is a perfect space.*

It is obvious that all (non-trivial) closed intervals are perfect sets, as well as all countable unions of (non-trivial) intervals. But all these sets generated from closed intervals have the property that they are 'everywhere dense,' i.e., contained in the closure of their inner component. There is a well-known example of a perfect set that is nowhere dense, the Cantor set $\mathbb{D}$, which can be defined as the set of all numbers in the unit interval which can be expressed in triadic notation only by digits 0 and 2. This set has a lot of interesting properties, the most important one for our purposes is that it is a perfect set:

Proposition 12. *The Cantor set is perfect.*

By embedding the Cauchy space into any perfect space one obtains

Proposition 13 ([22], Corollary 6.3). *If X is a nonempty perfect Polish space, then $|X| = 2^{\aleph_0}$. All nonempty perfect subsets of $[0, 1]$ have cardinality $2^{\aleph_0}$.*

It is possible to obtain the following characterization of perfect sets [30]:

Proposition 14 (Characterization of perfect sets in $\mathbb{R}$). *For any perfect subset of $\mathbb{R}$ there is a unique partition of the real line into countably many intervals such that the intersections of the perfect set with these intervals are either empty, the full interval or isomorphic to the Cantor set.*

So we see that intervals and Cantor sets are prototypical for perfect sets and the basic building blocks of more complex perfect sets.

Every Polish space can be partitioned into a perfect kernel and a countable rest. This is the well known Cantor-Bendixon Theorem:

Theorem 15 (Cantor-Bendixon). *Let X be a Polish space. Then X can be uniquely written as $X = P \cup C$, with P a perfect subset of X and C countable and open. The subset P is called the* perfect kernel *of X (denoted by X^∞).*

As a corollary we obtain that any uncountable Polish space contains a perfect set, and therefore, has cardinality $2^{\aleph_0}$.

2 Propositional Gödel Logics

As already mentioned Gödel introduced this family of logics on the propositional level to analyze Intuitionistic logic. This allows the approach to Gödel logics via restricting the possible accessibility relations of Kripke models of intuitionistic logic. Two somehow reasonable restrictions of the Kripke structures are the restriction to constant domains and the restriction that the Kripke worlds are linearly ordered and of order type ω. One can now ask what sentences are valid in this restricted class of Kripke models. This question has been settled by [17] for the propositional case by adding to a complete axiomatization of intuitionistic logic the axiom of linearity. The logic Dummett discussed, the logic of linearly ordered Kripke frames of order type ω, can also be viewed as $\mathbf{G}^0_\downarrow$ and therefore, as a subcase of Gödel logics. Although the proof of Dummett is only for weak completeness (as the entailment of the respective logic is not compact [12]), it is of importance since with respect to validity all the infinitely valued propositional Gödel logics coincide. Another interesting distinction between **LC**, which is $\mathbf{G}^0_\downarrow$, and other propositional Gödel logics is the fact that the entailment relation of **LC** is not compact, while the one corresponding to $\mathbf{G}^0_\mathbb{R}$ is.

2.1 Completeness of $\mathbf{H}^0$ for LC

Dummett [17] proved that a formula of propositional Gödel logic is valid in any infinite truth value set if it is valid in one infinite truth value set. Moreover, all the formulas valid in these sets are axiomatized by any axiomatization of intuitionistic propositional logic extended with the linearity axiom scheme $(p \to q) \vee (q \to p)$. It is interesting to note that p and q in the linearity scheme are propositional formulas. It is *not* enough to add this axiom for atomic p and q. For an axiom scheme only necessary for atomic formulas we have to use

$$((p \to q) \to p) \vee (p \to (p \to q))$$

to obtain completeness [11]. The proof given here is a simplified proof of the completeness of $\mathbf{H}^0$ taken from [21].

Definition 16. *An algebra $\mathbf{P} = \langle P, \cdot, +, \to, \mathbf{0}, \mathbf{1}\rangle$ is a* Heyting algebra *if the reduct $\langle P, \cdot, +, \mathbf{0}, \mathbf{1}\rangle$ is a lattice with least element $\mathbf{0}$, largest element $\mathbf{1}$ and $x \cdot y \leq z$ iff $x \leq (y \to z)$.*

Definition 17. *An L-*algebra *is a Heyting algebra in which*

$$(x \to y) + (y \to x) = \mathbf{1}$$

is valid for all x, y.

It is obvious that if we take L-algebras as our reference models for completeness, the proof of completeness is trivial. Generally, it is not very interesting to define algebras fitting to logics like a second skin, and then proving completeness with respect to this class (Ł-algebras, ...), without giving any connection to well known algebraic structures or already accepted reference models. In our case we want to show completeness with respect to the real interval $[0, 1]$ or one of its sub-orderings. More generally we aim at completeness with respect to chains, which are special Heyting algebras:

Definition 18. *A* chain *is a linearly ordered Heyting algebra.*

Chains are exactly what we are looking for as every chain (with cardinality less or equal to the continuum) is isomorphic to a sub-ordering of the $[0, 1]$ interval, and vice versa. Our aim is now to show completeness of the above axiomatization with respect to chains. Furthermore we will exhibit that the length of the chains for a specific formula can be bounded by the number of propositional variables in the formula. More precisely:

Theorem 19. *A formula α is provable in $\mathbf{H}^0 = \mathbf{LC}$ if and only if it is valid in all chains with at most $n + 2$ elements, where n is the number of propositional variables in α.*

Proof. As usual we define the relation $\alpha \leq^\circ \beta$ equivalent to $\vdash \alpha \to \beta$ and $\alpha \equiv \beta$ as $\alpha \leq^\circ \beta$ and $\beta \leq^\circ \alpha$. It is easy to verify that $\equiv$ is an equivalence relation. We denote $\alpha/\equiv$ with $|\alpha|$. It is also easy to show that with $|\alpha| + |\beta| = |\alpha \vee \beta|$, $|\alpha| \cdot |\beta| = |\alpha \wedge \beta|$, $|\alpha| \to |\beta| = |\alpha \to \beta|$ the set $\mathcal{F}/\equiv$ becomes a Heyting algebra, and due to the linearity axiom it is also an L-algebra. Furthermore note that $|\alpha| = \mathbf{1}$ if and only if α is provable in $\mathbf{H}^0$ ($\mathbf{1} = |p \to p|$, $|\alpha| = |p \to p|$ gives $\vdash (p \to p) \to \alpha$ which in turn gives $\vdash \alpha$).

If our aim would be completeness with respect to L-algebras the proof would be finished here, but we aim at completeness with respect to chains, therefore, we will take a close look at the structure of $\mathcal{F}/\equiv$ as L-algebra. Assume that a formula α is given, which is not provable, we want to give a chain where α is not valid. We already have an L-algebra where α is not valid, but how to obtain a chain?

We could use the general result from [21], Theorem 1.2, that a Heyting algebra is an L-algebra if and only if it is a subalgebra of a direct product of chains, but we will exhibit how to find explicitly a suitable chain. The idea is that the L-algebra $\mathcal{F}/\equiv$ describes all possible truth values for all possible orderings of the propositional variables in α. We want to make this more explicit:

Definition 20. *We denote with $\mathcal{C}(\bot, p_{i_1}, \ldots, p_{i_n}, \top)$ the chain with these elements and the ordering $\bot \leq p_{i_1} < \ldots < p_{i_n} \leq \top$. If $\mathcal{C}$ is a chain we denote with $|\alpha|_\mathcal{C}$ the evaluation of the formula in the chain $\mathcal{C}$.*

Lemma 21. *The L-algebra $\mathcal{F}/\equiv$ is a subalgebra of the following direct product of chains*

$$X = \prod_{i=1}^{n!} \mathcal{C}(\bot, \pi_i(p_1, \ldots, p_n), \top)$$

where π_i ranges over the set of permutations of n elements. We will denote $\mathcal{C}(\bot, \pi_i(p_1, \dots, p_n), \top)$ with $\mathcal{C}_i$.

Proof. Define $\phi : \mathcal{F}/\equiv \to X$ as follows: $\phi(|\alpha|) = (|\alpha|_{\mathcal{C}_1}, \dots, |\alpha|_{\mathcal{C}_{n!}})$. We have to show that ϕ is well defined, is a homomorphism and is injective. First assume that $\beta \in |\alpha|$ but $\phi(|\alpha|) \neq \phi(|\beta|)$, i.e. $(|\alpha|_{\mathcal{C}_1}, \dots, |\alpha|_{\mathcal{C}_{n!}}) \neq (|\beta|_{\mathcal{C}_1}, \dots, |\beta|_{\mathcal{C}_{n!}})$ but then there must be an i such that $|\alpha|_{\mathcal{C}_i} \neq |\beta|_{\mathcal{C}_i}$. Without loss of generality, assume that $|\alpha|_{\mathcal{C}_i} < |\beta|_{\mathcal{C}_i}$. From the fact that $|\alpha| = |\beta|$ we get $\vdash \beta \to \alpha$. From this we get that $|\beta \to \alpha|_{\mathcal{C}_i} < \mathbf{1}$ and from $\vdash \beta \to \alpha$ we get that $|\beta \to \alpha|_{\mathcal{C}_i} = \mathbf{1}$, which is a contradiction. This proves the well-definedness.

To show that ϕ is a homomorphism we have to prove that

$$\begin{aligned}
\phi(|\alpha| \cdot |\beta|) &= \phi(|\alpha|) \cdot \phi(|\beta|) \\
\phi(|\alpha| + |\beta|) &= \phi(|\alpha|) + \phi(|\beta|) \\
\phi(|\alpha| \to |\beta|) &= \phi(|\alpha|) \to \phi(|\beta|).
\end{aligned}$$

This is a straightforward computation using $|\alpha \wedge \beta|_{\mathcal{C}} = \phi(|\alpha|_{\mathcal{C}}) \cdot \phi(|\beta|_{\mathcal{C}})$.

Finally we have to prove that ϕ is injective. Assume that $\phi(|\alpha|) = \phi(|\beta|)$ and that $|\alpha| \neq |\beta|$. From the former we obtain that $|\alpha|_{\mathcal{C}_i} = |\beta|_{\mathcal{C}_i}$ for all $1 \leq i \leq n!$, which means that $\mathcal{I}_{\mathcal{C}_i}(\alpha) = \mathcal{I}_{\mathcal{C}_i}(\beta)$ for all $1 \leq i \leq n!$. On the other hand we know from the latter that there is an interpretation $\mathcal{I}$ such that $\mathcal{I}(\alpha) \neq \mathcal{I}(\beta)$. Without loss of generality assume that $\bot \leq \mathcal{I}(p_{i_1}) < \ldots < \mathcal{I}(p_{i_n}) \leq \top$. There is an index k such that the $\mathcal{C}_k$ is exactly the above ordering with $\mathcal{I}_{\mathcal{C}_k}(\alpha) \neq \mathcal{I}_{\mathcal{C}_k}(\beta)$, this is a contradiction.

This completes the proof that $\mathcal{F}/\equiv$ is a subalgebra of the given direct product of chains. □

Example. For $n = 2$ the chains are $\mathcal{C}(\bot, p, q, \top)$ and $\mathcal{C}(\bot, q, p, \top)$. The product of these two chains looks as given in Figure 1, p. 38. The labels below the nodes are the products, the formulas above the nodes are representatives for the class $\alpha/\equiv$.

Now the proof of Theorem 19 is trivial since, if $|\alpha| \neq \mathbf{1}$, there is a chain $\mathcal{C}_i$ where $|\alpha|_{\mathcal{C}_i} \neq \mathbf{1}$. □

This yields the following theorem:

Theorem 22. *A propositional formula is valid in any infinite chain iff it is derivable in* $\mathbf{LC} = \mathbf{H}^0$.

Going on to finite truth value set we can give the following theorem:

Theorem 23. *A formula is valid in any chain with at most n elements iff it is provable in* $\mathbf{LC}_n$.

As a simple consequence of these result the following corollaries settle the number of propositional Gödel logics and their relation:

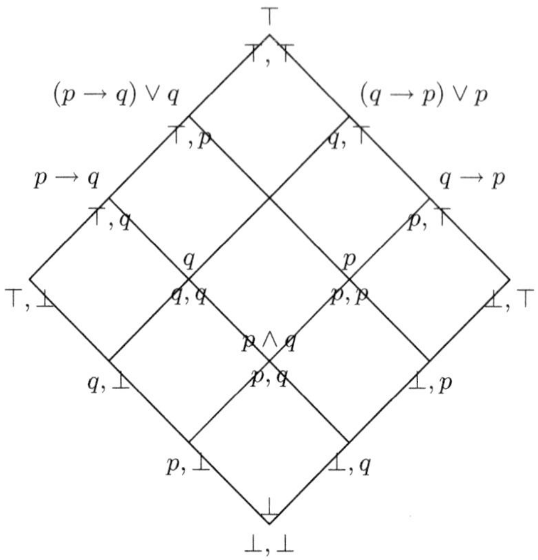

Fig. 1. L-algebra of $\mathcal{C}(\bot, p, q, \top) \times \mathcal{C}(\bot, q, p, \top)$. Labels below the nodes are the elements of the direct product, formulas above the node are representatives for the class $\alpha/\equiv$.

Corollary 24. *The propositional Gödel logics* $\mathbf{G}_n^0$ *and* $\mathbf{G}_{\mathbb{R}}^0$ *are all different, thus there are countable many different propositional Gödel logics, and*

$$\bigcap_{n \in \mathbb{N}} \mathbf{G}_n^0 = \mathbf{G}_{\mathbb{R}}^0$$

3 First Order Gödel Logics

Although standard first-order Gödel logic, the one based on the $[0,1]$-intervall, has been studied throughout the last decades as mentioned in the introduction again and again, the study of general Gödel logics based on arbitrary truth value sets started in the mid-nineties by [2, 6, 7] and the studies were continued over the last years. We give a detailed proof of the axiomatizability of standard Gödel logic, the on based on the full $[0,1]$ interval, and will only cite further results.

3.1 Preliminaries

We will be concerned below with the relationships between Gödel logics, here considered as entailment relations. Note that $\mathbf{G}_V \models A$ iff $(\emptyset, A) \in \mathbf{G}_V$, so in particular, showing that $\mathbf{G}_V \subseteq \mathbf{G}_W$ also shows that every valid formula of $\mathbf{G}_V$ is also valid in $\mathbf{G}_W$. On the other hand, to show that $\mathbf{G}_V \not\subseteq \mathbf{G}_W$ it suffices to show that for some A, $\mathbf{G}_V \models A$ but $\mathbf{G}_W \not\models A$.

Remark 25. Whether or not a formula A evaluates to 1 under an interpretation $\mathcal{I}$ depends only on the *relative ordering* of the truth values of the atomic formulas (in $\mathscr{L}^{\mathcal{I}}$), and not directly on the set V or on the specific values of the atomic formulas. If $V \subseteq W$ are both Gödel sets, and $\mathcal{I}$ is a V-interpretation, then $\mathcal{I}$ can be seen also as a W-interpretation, and the values $\mathcal{I}(A)$, computed recursively using (1)–(7), do not depend on whether we view $\mathcal{I}$ as a V-interpretation or a W-interpretation. Consequently, if $V \subseteq W$, there are more interpretations into W than into V. Hence, if $\Gamma \models_W A$ then also $\Gamma \models_V A$ and $\mathbf{G}_W \subseteq \mathbf{G}_V$.

This can be generalized to embeddings between Gödel sets other than inclusion. First, we make precise which formulas are involved in the computation of the truth-value of a formula A in an interpretation $\mathcal{I}$:

Definition 26. *The only subformula of an atomic formula A in $\mathscr{L}^U$ is A itself. The subformulas of $A \star B$ for $\star \in \{\to, \land, \lor\}$ are the subformulas of A and of B, together with $A \star B$ itself. The subformulas of $\forall x\, A(x)$ and $\exists x\, A(x)$ with respect to a universe U are all subformulas of all $A(u)$ for $u \in U$, together with $\forall x\, A(x)$ (or, $\exists x\, A(x)$, respectively) itself.*

The set of truth-values of subformulas of A under a given interpretation $\mathcal{I}$ is denoted by $\mathrm{Val}(\mathcal{I}, A) = \{\mathcal{I}(B) : B$ *subformula of A w.r.t.* $U^{\mathcal{I}}\} \cup \{0,1\}$. *If Γ is a set of formulas, then* $\mathrm{Val}(\mathcal{I}, \Gamma) = \bigcup\{\mathrm{Val}(\mathcal{I}, A) : A \in \Gamma\}$.

Lemma 27. *Let $\mathcal{I}$ be a V-interpretation, and let $h\colon \mathrm{Val}(\mathcal{I}, \Gamma) \to W$ be a mapping satisfying the following properties:*

1. *$h(0) = 0$, $h(1) = 1$;*
2. *h is strictly monotonic, i.e., if $a < b$, then $h(a) < h(b)$;*
3. *for every $X \subseteq \mathrm{Val}(\mathcal{I}, \Gamma)$, $h(\inf X) = \inf h(X)$ and $h(\sup X) = \sup h(X)$ (provided $\inf X, \sup X \in \mathrm{Val}(\mathcal{I}, \Gamma)$).*

Then the W-interpretation $\mathcal{I}_h$ with universe $U^{\mathcal{I}}$, $f^{\mathcal{I}_h} = f^{\mathcal{I}}$, and for atomic $B \in \mathscr{L}^{\mathcal{I}}$,

$$\mathcal{I}_h(B) = \begin{cases} h(\mathcal{I}(B)) & \text{if } \mathcal{I}(B) \in \operatorname{dom} h \\ 1 & \text{otherwise} \end{cases}$$

satisfies $\mathcal{I}_h(A) = h(\mathcal{I}(A))$ for all $A \in \Gamma$.

Proof. By induction on the complexity of A. If $A \equiv \bot$, the claim follows from (1). If A is atomic, it follows from the definition of $\mathcal{I}_h$. For the propositional connectives the claim follows from the strict monotonicity of h (2). For the quantifiers, it follows from property (3). □

Proposition 28 (Downward Löwenheim-Skolem). *For any interpretation $\mathcal{I}$ with $U^{\mathcal{I}}$ infinite, there is an interpretation $\mathcal{I}' \prec \mathcal{I}$ with a countable universe $U^{\mathcal{I}'}$.*

Lemma 29. *Let $\mathcal{I}$ be an interpretation into V, $w \in [0,1]$, and let $\mathcal{I}_w$ be defined by*

$$\mathcal{I}_w(B) = \begin{cases} \mathcal{I}(B) & \text{if } \mathcal{I}(B) < w \\ 1 & \text{otherwise} \end{cases}$$

for atomic formulas B in $\mathscr{L}^{\mathcal{I}}$. Then $\mathcal{I}_w$ is an interpretation into V. If $w \notin \mathrm{Val}(\mathcal{I}, A)$, then $\mathcal{I}_w(A) = \mathcal{I}(A)$ if $\mathcal{I}(A) < w$, and $\mathcal{I}_w(A) = 1$ otherwise.

Proof. By induction on the complexity of formulas A in $\mathscr{L}^{\mathcal{I}}$. The condition that $w \notin \mathrm{Val}(\mathcal{I}, A)$ is needed to prove the case of $A \equiv \exists x\, B(x)$, since if $\mathcal{I}(\exists x\, B(x)) = w$ and $\mathcal{I}(B(d)) < w$ for all d, we would have $\mathcal{I}_w(\exists x\, B(x)) = w$ and not $= 1$. □

The following lemma was originally proved in [25], where it was used to extend the proof of recursive axiomatizability of the 'standard' Gödel logic $\mathbf{G}_{\mathbb{R}}$ to Gödel logics with a truth value set containing a perfect set in the general case. The following simpler proof is inspired by [14]:

Lemma 30. *Suppose that* $M \subseteq [0,1]$ *is countable and* $P \subseteq [0,1]$ *is perfect. Then there is a strictly monotone continuous map* $h\colon M \to P$ *(i.e., infima and suprema already existing in* M *are preserved). Furthermore, if* $\inf M \in M$*, then one can choose* h *such that* $h(\inf M) = \inf P$.

Proof. See [10] □

Corollary 31. *A Gödel set* V *is uncountable iff it contains a non-trivial dense linear subordering.*

Proof. If: Every countable non-trivial dense linear order has order type η, $\mathbf{1}+\eta$, $\eta+\mathbf{1}$, or $\mathbf{1}+\eta+\mathbf{1}$ [26, Corollary 2.9], where η is the order type of $\mathbb{Q}$. The completion of any ordering of order type η has order type λ, the order type of $\mathbb{R}$ [26, Theorem 2.30], thus the truth value set must be uncountable. Only if: By Theorem 15, V^∞ is non-empty. Take $M = \mathbb{Q} \cap [0,1]$ and $P = V^\infty$ in Lemma 30. The image of M under h is a non-trivial dense linear subordering in V. □

Theorem 32. *Suppose* V *is a truth value set with non-empty perfect kernel* P*, and let* $W = V \cup [\inf P, 1]$*. Then* $\Gamma \models_V A$ *iff* $\Gamma \models_W A$*, i.e.,* $\mathbf{G}_V = \mathbf{G}_W$.

Proof. As $V \subseteq W$ we have $\mathbf{G}_W \subseteq \mathbf{G}_V$ (cf. Remark 25). Now assume that $\mathcal{I}$ is a W-interpretation which shows that $\Gamma \models_W A$ does *not* hold, i.e., $\mathcal{I}(\Gamma) > \mathcal{I}(A)$. By Proposition 28, we may assume that $U^{\mathcal{I}}$ is countable. The set $\mathrm{Val}(\mathcal{I}, \Gamma \cup A)$ has cardinality at most $\aleph_0$, thus there is a $w \in [0,1]$ such that $w \notin \mathrm{Val}(\mathcal{I}, \Gamma \cup A)$ and $\mathcal{I}(A) < w < 1$. By Lemma 29, $\mathcal{I}_w(A) < w < 1$. Now consider $M = \mathrm{Val}(\mathcal{I}_w, \Gamma \cup A)$: these are all the truth values from $W = V \cup [\inf P, 1]$ required to compute $\mathcal{I}_w(A)$ and $\mathcal{I}_w(B)$ for all $B \in \Gamma$. We have to find some way to map them to V so that the induced interpretation is a counterexample to $\Gamma \models_V A$.

Let $M_0 = M \cap [0, \inf P)$ and $M_1 = (M \cap [\inf P, w]) \cup \{\inf P\}$. By Lemma 30 there is a strictly monotone continuous (i.e. preserving all existing infima and suprema) map h from M_1 into P. Furthermore, we can choose h such that $h(\inf M_1) = \inf P$.

We define a function g from $\mathrm{Val}(\mathcal{I}_w, \Gamma \cup A)$ to V as follows:

$$g(x) = \begin{cases} x & 0 \le x \le \inf P \\ h(x) & \inf P \le x \le w \\ 1 & x = 1 \end{cases}$$

Note that there is no $x \in \mathrm{Val}(\mathcal{I}_w, \Gamma \cup A)$ with $w < x < 1$. This function has the following properties: $g(0) = 0$, $g(1) = 1$, g is strictly monotonic and preserves existing infima and suprema. Using Lemma 27 we obtain that $\mathcal{I}_g$ is a V-interpretation with $\mathcal{I}_g(C) = g(\mathcal{I}_w(C))$ for all $C \in \Gamma \cup A$, thus also $\mathcal{I}_g(\Gamma) > \mathcal{I}_g(A)$. □

3.2 Relationships between Gödel Logics

The relationships between finite and infinite valued *propositional* Gödel logics are well understood. Any choice of an infinite set of truth-values results in the same set of tautologies, viz., Dummett's **LC**. **LC** was originally defined using the set of truth-values $V_\downarrow$ (see below). Furthermore, we know that **LC** is the intersection of all finite-valued propositional Gödel logics (Corollary 24), and that it is axiomatized by intuitionistic propositional logic **IPL** plus the schema $(A \supset B) \vee (B \supset A)$. **IPL** is contained in all Gödel logics.

In the first-order case, the relationships are somewhat more interesting. First of all, let us note the following fact corresponding to the end of the previous paragraph:

Proposition 33. *Intuitionistic predicate logic* **IL** *is contained in all first-order Gödel logics.*

As a consequence of this proposition, we will be able to use any intuitionistically sound rule and intuitionistically valid formula when working in any of the Gödel logics.

We now establish some results regarding the relationships between various first-order Gödel logics. For this, it is useful to consider several 'prototypical' Gödel sets.

$$\begin{aligned} V_\mathbb{R} &= [0,1] \qquad V_0 = \{0\} \cup [1/2, 1] \\ V_\downarrow &= \{1/k : k \geq 1\} \cup \{0\} \\ V_\uparrow &= \{1 - 1/k : k \geq 1\} \cup \{1\} \\ V_n &= \{1 - 1/k : 1 \leq k \leq m - 1\} \cup \{1\} \end{aligned}$$

The corresponding Gödel logics are $\mathbf{G}_\mathbb{R}$, $\mathbf{G}_0$, $\mathbf{G}_\downarrow$, $\mathbf{G}_\uparrow$, and $\mathbf{G}_n$. $\mathbf{G}_\mathbb{R}$ is the *standard* Gödel logic.

The logic $\mathbf{G}_\downarrow$ also turns out to be closely related to some temporal logics [6,8]. $\mathbf{G}_\uparrow$ is the intersection of all finite-valued first-order Gödel logics as shown in Theorem 36.

Proposition 34. $\mathbf{G}_\mathbb{R} = \bigcap_V \mathbf{G}_V$, *where V ranges over all Gödel sets.*

Proof. If $\Gamma \models_V A$ for every Gödel set V, then it does so in particular for $V = [0, 1]$. Conversely, if $\Gamma \not\models_V A$ for a Gödel set V, there is a V-interpretation $\mathcal{I}$ with $\mathcal{I}(\Gamma) > \mathcal{I}(A)$. Since $\mathcal{I}$ is also a $[0, 1]$-interpretation, $\Gamma \not\models_\mathbb{R} A$. □

Proposition 35. *The following strict containment relationships hold: (1)* $\mathbf{G}_n \supsetneq \mathbf{G}_{n+1}$*, (2)* $\mathbf{G}_n \supsetneq \mathbf{G}_\uparrow \supsetneq \mathbf{G}_\mathbb{R}$*, (3)* $\mathbf{G}_n \supsetneq \mathbf{G}_\downarrow \supsetneq \mathbf{G}_\mathbb{R}$*, (4)* $\mathbf{G}_0 \supsetneq \mathbf{G}_\mathbb{R}$.

Proof. The only non-trivial part is proving that the containments are strict. For this note that $\textsc{fin}(n) \equiv (A_0 \supset A_1) \vee \ldots \vee (A_{n-1} \supset A_n)$ is valid in $\mathbf{G}_n$ but not in $\mathbf{G}_{n+1}$. Furthermore, let $C_\uparrow = \exists x(A(x) \supset \forall y\, A(y))$ and $C_\downarrow = \exists x(\exists y\, A(y) \supset A(x))$. $C_\downarrow$ is valid in all $\mathbf{G}_n$ and in $\mathbf{G}_\uparrow$ and $\mathbf{G}_\downarrow$; $C_\uparrow$ is valid in all $\mathbf{G}_n$ and in $\mathbf{G}_\uparrow$, but not in $\mathbf{G}_\downarrow$; neither is valid in $\mathbf{G}_0$ or $\mathbf{G}_\mathbb{R}$ ([8], Corollary 2.9).

$\mathbf{G}_0 \models \textsc{iso}_0$ but $\mathbf{G}_\mathbb{R} \not\models \textsc{iso}_0$. □

The formulas $C_\uparrow$ and $C_\downarrow$ are of some importance in the study of first-order infinite-valued Gödel logics. $C_\uparrow$ expresses the fact that the infimum of any subset of the set of truth values is contained in the subset (every infimum is a minimum), and $C_\downarrow$ states that every supremum (except possibly 1) is a maximum. The intuitionistically admissible quantifier shifting rules are given by the following implications and equivalences:

$$(\forall x\, A(x) \wedge B) \leftrightarrow \forall x(A(x) \wedge B) \tag{1}$$
$$(\exists x\, A(x) \wedge B) \leftrightarrow \exists x(A(x) \wedge B) \tag{2}$$
$$(\forall x\, A(x) \vee B) \supset \forall x(A(x) \vee B) \tag{3}$$
$$(\exists x\, A(x) \vee B) \leftrightarrow \exists x(A(x) \vee B) \tag{4}$$
$$(B \supset \forall x\, A(x)) \leftrightarrow \forall x(B \supset A(x)) \tag{5}$$
$$(B \supset \exists x\, A(x)) \subset \exists x(B \supset A(x)) \tag{6}$$
$$(\forall x\, A(x) \supset B) \subset \exists x(A(x) \supset B) \tag{7}$$
$$(\exists x\, A(x) \supset B) \leftrightarrow \forall x(A(x) \supset B) \tag{8}$$

The remaining three are:

$$(\forall x\, A(x) \vee B) \subset \forall x(A(x) \vee B) \tag{S_1}$$
$$(B \supset \exists x\, A(x)) \supset \exists x(B \supset A(x)) \tag{S_2}$$
$$(\forall x\, A(x) \supset B) \supset \exists x(A(x) \supset B) \tag{S_3}$$

Of these, S_1 is valid in any Gödel logic. S_2 and S_3 imply and are implied by $C_\downarrow$ and $C_\uparrow$, respectively (take $\exists y\, A(y)$ and $\forall y\, A(y)$, respectively, for B). S_2 and S_3 are, respectively, both valid in $\mathbf{G}_\uparrow$, invalid and valid in $\mathbf{G}_\downarrow$, and both invalid in $\mathbf{G}_\mathbb{R}$.

Note that since we defined $\neg A \equiv A \to \bot$, the quantifier shifts for $\to$ (7, 8, S_3) include the various directions of De Morgan's laws as special cases. Specifically, the only direction of De Morgan's laws which is not valid in all Gödel logics is the one corresponding to (S_3), i.e., $\neg\forall x\, A(x) \to \exists x \neg A(x)$. This formula is equivalent to $\textsc{iso}_0$. For, $\mathbf{G}_V \models \forall x \neg\neg A(x) \leftrightarrow \neg\exists\neg A(x)$ by (8). We get $\textsc{iso}_0$ using $\neg\exists x \neg A(x) \to \neg\neg\forall x\, A(x)$, which is an instance of (S_3).

We now also know that $\mathbf{G}_\uparrow \neq \mathbf{G}_\downarrow$. In fact, we have $\mathbf{G}_\downarrow \subsetneq \mathbf{G}_\uparrow$; this follows from the following theorem.

Theorem 36 ([10], Theorem 23)

$$\mathbf{G}_\uparrow = \bigcap_{n \geq 2} \mathbf{G}_n$$

Proof. The proof is a direct consequence of the following lemma.

Lemma 37. *If all infima in the truth value set are minima or A contains no universal quantifiers, and A evaluates to some $v < 1$ in $\mathcal{I}$, then A also evaluates to v in $\mathcal{I}_v$ where*

$$\mathcal{I}_v(P) = \begin{cases} 1 & \textit{if } \mathcal{I}(P) > v \\ \mathcal{I}(P) & \textit{otherwise} \end{cases}$$

for P atomic sub-formula of A.

Proof. We prove by induction on the complexity of formulas that any sub-formula F of A with $\mathcal{I}(F) \leq v$ has $\mathcal{I}'(F) = \mathcal{I}(F)$. This is clear for atomic sub-formulas. We distinguish cases according to the logical form of F:

$F \equiv D \wedge E$. If $\mathcal{I}(F) \leq v$, then, without loss of generality, assume $\mathcal{I}(F) = \mathcal{I}(D) \leq \mathcal{I}(E)$. By induction hypothesis, $\mathcal{I}'(D) = \mathcal{I}(D)$ and $\mathcal{I}'(E) \geq \mathcal{I}(E)$, so $\mathcal{I}'(F) = \mathcal{I}(F)$. If $\mathcal{I}(F) > v$, then $\mathcal{I}(D) > v$ and $\mathcal{I}(E) > v$, by induction hypothesis $\mathcal{I}'(D) = \mathcal{I}'(E) = 1$, thus, $\mathcal{I}'(F) = 1$.

$F \equiv D \vee E$. If $\mathcal{I}(F) \leq v$, then, without loss of generality, assume $\mathcal{I}(F) = \mathcal{I}(D) \geq \mathcal{I}(E)$. By induction hypothesis, $\mathcal{I}'(D) = \mathcal{I}(D)$ and $\mathcal{I}'(E) = \mathcal{I}(E)$, so $\mathcal{I}'(F) = \mathcal{I}(F)$. If $\mathcal{I}(F) > v$, then, again without loss of generality, $\mathcal{I}(F) = \mathcal{I}(D) > v$, by induction hypothesis $\mathcal{I}'(D) = 1$, thus, $\mathcal{I}'(F) = 1$.

$F \equiv D \supset E$. Since $v < 1$, we must have $\mathcal{I}(D) > \mathcal{I}(E) = \mathcal{I}(F)$. By induction hypothesis, $\mathcal{I}'(D) \geq \mathcal{I}(D)$ and $\mathcal{I}'(E) = \mathcal{I}(E)$, so $\mathcal{I}'(F) = \mathcal{I}(F)$. If $\mathcal{I}(F) > v$, then $\mathcal{I}(D) \geq \mathcal{I}(E) = \mathcal{I}(F) > v$, by induction hypothesis $\mathcal{I}'(D) = \mathcal{I}'(E) = \mathcal{I}'(F) = 1$.

$F \equiv \exists x D(x)$. First assume that $\mathcal{I}(F) \leq v$. Since $D(c)$ evaluates to a value less or equal to v in $\mathcal{I}$ and, by induction hypothesis, in $\mathcal{I}'$ also the supremum of these values is less or equal to v in $\mathcal{I}'$, thus $\mathcal{I}'(F) = \mathcal{I}(F)$. If $\mathcal{I}(F) > v$, then there is a c such that $\mathcal{I}(D(c)) > v$, by induction hypothesis $\mathcal{I}'(D(c)) = 1$, thus, $\mathcal{I}'(F) = 1$.

$F \equiv \forall x D(x)$. This is the crucial part. First assume that $\mathcal{I}(F) < v$. Then there is a witness c such that $\mathcal{I}(F) \leq \mathcal{I}(D(c)) < v$ and, by induction hypothesis, also $\mathcal{I}'(D(c)) < v$ and therefore, $\mathcal{I}'(F) = \mathcal{I}(F)$. For $\mathcal{I}(F) > v$ it is obvious that $\mathcal{I}'(F) = \mathcal{I}(F) = 1$. Finally assume that $\mathcal{I}(F) = v$. If this infimum would be proper, i.e. no minimum, then the value of all witnesses under $\mathcal{I}'$ would be 1, but the value of F under $\mathcal{I}'$ would be v, which would contradict the definition of the semantic of the $\forall$ quantifier. Since all infima are minima, there is a witness c such that $\mathcal{I}(D(c)) = v$ and therefore, also $\mathcal{I}'(D(c)) = v$ and thus $\mathcal{I}'(F) = \mathcal{I}(F)$.

Corollary 38. $\mathbf{G}_n \supsetneq \bigcap_n \mathbf{G}_n = \mathbf{G}_\uparrow \supsetneq \mathbf{G}_\downarrow \supsetneq \mathbf{G}_\mathbb{R}$

Note that also $\mathbf{G}_\uparrow \supsetneq \mathbf{G}_0 \supsetneq \mathbf{G}_\mathbb{R}$ by the above, and that neither $\mathbf{G}_0 \subseteq \mathbf{G}_\downarrow$ nor $\mathbf{G}_\downarrow \subseteq \mathbf{G}_0$ (counterexamples are $\textsc{iso}_0$ or $\neg\forall x\, A(x) \to \exists\neg A(x)$, and $C_\downarrow$, respectively).

As we will see later, the axioms $\textsc{fin}(n)$ axiomatize exactly the finite-valued Gödel logics. In these logics the quantifier shift axiom $\textsc{qs}$ is not necessary. Furthermore, all quantifier shift rules are valid in the finite valued logics. Since $\mathbf{G}_\uparrow$ is the intersection of all the finite ones, all quantifier shift rules are valid in $\mathbf{G}_\uparrow$. Moreover, any infinite-valued Gödel logic other than $\mathbf{G}_\uparrow$ is defined by some V which either contains an infimum which is not a minimum, or a supremum (other than 1) which is not a maximum. Hence, in V either $C_\uparrow$ or $C_\downarrow$ will be invalid, and therewith either S_3 or S_2. We have:

Corollary 39. *In $\mathbf{G}_V$ all quantifier shift rules are valid iff there is a strictly monotone and continuous embedding from V to $V_\uparrow$, i.e., V is either finite or order isomorphic to $V_\uparrow$.*

This means that it is in general not possible to transform formulas to equivalent prenex formulas in the usual way. Moreover, in general there is not even a recursive procedure for mapping formulas to equivalent, or even just validity-equivalent formulas in prenex form, since for some V, $\mathbf{G}_V$ is not r.e. whereas the corresponding prenex fragment is r.e.

3.3 Axiomatizability

The following table gives a complete characterization of axiomatizability of first-order Gödel logics:

V finite (n)	$\mathbf{H}_n$ complete for the logic
V countable	not recursively enumerable
$V^\infty \neq \emptyset$, $0 \in V^\infty$	$\mathbf{H}$ complete for the logic
$V^\infty \neq \emptyset$, 0 isolated	$\mathbf{H} + \text{ISO}_0$ complete for the logic
$V^\infty \neq \emptyset$, $0 \notin V^\infty$, 0 not isolated	not recursively enumerable
V finite (n)	$\mathbf{H}\Delta_n$ complete for the logic
$0, 1 \in V^\infty$	$\mathbf{H}\Delta$ complete for the logic
$0 \in V^\infty$, 1 isolated	$\mathbf{H}\Delta + \text{ISO}_1$ complete for the logic
0 isolated, $1 \in V^\infty$	$\mathbf{H}\Delta + \text{ISO}_0$ complete for the logic
$V^\infty \neq \emptyset$, 0, 1 isolated	$\mathbf{H}\Delta + \text{ISO}_0 + \text{ISO}_1$ complete
$V^\infty \neq \emptyset$, $1 \notin V^\infty$, 1 not isolated	not recursively enumerable

The results on being not recursively enumerable are based on Trakhtenbrodt's result on the classical first order logic of finite domains being undecidable and hence not recursively enumerable [10].

On the other hand, if V is uncountable, and 0 is contained in V^∞, then $\mathbf{G}_V$ is axiomatizable. Indeed, Theorem 32 showed that all such logics $\mathbf{G}_V$ coincide. Thus, it is only necessary to establish completeness of the axioms system $\mathbf{H}$ with respect to $\mathbf{G}_\mathbb{R}$. This result has been shown by several people over the years. We give here a generalization of the proof of [27]. Alternative proofs can be found in [20, 21, 29]. The proof of [21], however, does not give strong completeness, while the proof of [29] is specific to the Gödel set [0, 1]. Our proof is self-contained and applies to Gödel logics directly, making an extension of the result easier.

Theorem 40 ([27], [10] Theorem 37, Strong completeness). *If $\Gamma \models_\mathbb{R} A$, then $\Gamma \vdash_\mathbf{H} A$.*

Proof. Assume that $\Gamma \nvdash A$, we construct an interpretation $\mathcal{I}$ in which $\mathcal{I}(A) = 1$ for all $B \in \Gamma$ and $\mathcal{I}(A) < 1$. Let y_1, y_2, ... be a sequence of free variables which do not occur in $\Gamma \cup \triangle$, let $\mathcal{T}$ be the set of all terms in the language of $\Gamma \cup \Delta$ together with the new variables y_1, y_2, ..., and let $\mathcal{F} = \{F_1, F_2, \ldots\}$ be an enumeration of the formulas in this language in which y_i does not appear in F_1, ..., F_i and in which each formula appears infinitely often.

If Δ is a set of formulas, we write $\Gamma \Rightarrow \Delta$ if for some $A_1, \ldots, A_n \in \Gamma$, and some $B_1, \ldots, B_m \in \Delta$, $\vdash_\mathbf{H} (A_1 \wedge \ldots \wedge A_n) \to (B_1 \vee \ldots \vee B_m)$ (and $\not\Rightarrow$ if this is not the case). We define a sequence of sets of formulas Γ_n, Δ_n such that $\Gamma_n \not\Rightarrow \Delta_n$ by induction. First, $\Gamma_0 = \Gamma$ and $\Delta_0 = \{A\}$. By the assumption of the theorem, $\Gamma_0 \not\Rightarrow \Delta_0$.

If $\Gamma_n \Rightarrow \Delta_n \cup \{F_n\}$, then $\Gamma_{n+1} = \Gamma_n \cup \{F_n\}$ and $\Delta_{n+1} = \Delta_n$. In this case, $\Gamma_{n+1} \not\Rightarrow \Delta_{n+1}$, since otherwise we would have $\Gamma_n \Rightarrow \Delta_n \cup \{F_n\}$ and $\Gamma_n \cup \{F_n\} \Rightarrow \Delta_n$. But then, we'd have that $\Gamma_n \Rightarrow \Delta_n$, which contradicts the induction hypothesis (note that $\vdash_{\mathbf{H}} (A \to B \vee F) \to ((A \wedge F \to B) \to (A \to B)))$.

If $\Gamma_n \not\Rightarrow \Delta_n \cup \{F_n\}$, then $\Gamma_{n+1} = \Gamma_n$ and $\Delta_{n+1} = \Delta_n \cup \{F_n, B(y_n)\}$ if $F_n \equiv \forall x\, B(x)$, and $\Delta_{n+1} = \Delta_n \cup \{F_n\}$ otherwise. In the latter case, it is obvious that $\Gamma_{n+1} \not\Rightarrow \Delta_{n+1}$. In the former, observe that by $I10$ and QS, if $\Gamma_n \Rightarrow \Delta_n \cup \{\forall x\, B(x), B(y_n)\}$ then also $\Gamma_n \Rightarrow \Delta_n \cup \{\forall x\, B(x)\}$ (note that y_n does not occur in Γ_n or Δ_n).

Let $\Gamma^* = \bigcup_{i=0}^{\infty} \Gamma_i$ and $\Delta^* = \bigcup_{i=0}^{\infty} \Delta_i$. We have:

1. $\Gamma^* \not\Rightarrow \Delta^*$, for otherwise there would be a k so that $\Gamma_k \Rightarrow \Delta_k$.
2. $\Gamma \subseteq \Gamma^*$ and $\Delta \subseteq \Delta^*$ (by construction).
3. $\Gamma^* = \mathcal{F} \setminus \Delta^*$, since each F_n is either in Γ_{n+1} or Δ_{n+1}, and if for some n, $F_n \in \Gamma^* \cap \Delta^*$, there would be a k so that $F_n \in \Gamma_k \cap \Delta_k$, which is impossible since $\Gamma_k \not\Rightarrow \Delta_k$.
4. If $\Gamma^* \Rightarrow B_1 \vee \ldots \vee B_n$, then $B_i \in \Gamma^*$ for some i. For suppose not, then for $i = 1, \ldots, n$, $B_i \notin \Gamma^*$, and hence, by (3), $B_i \in \Delta^*$. But then $\Gamma^* \Rightarrow \Delta^*$, contradicting (1).
5. If $B(t) \in \Gamma^*$ for every $t \in \mathcal{T}$, then $\forall x\, B(x) \in \Gamma^*$. Otherwise, by (3), $\forall x\, B(x) \in \Delta^*$ and so there is some n so that $\forall x\, B(x) = F_n$ and Δ_{n+1} contains $\forall x\, B(x)$ and $B(y_n)$. But, again by (3), then $B(y_n) \notin \Gamma^*$.
6. Γ^* is closed under provable implication, since if $\Gamma^* \Rightarrow A$, then $A \notin \Delta^*$ and so, again by (3), $A \in \Gamma^*$. In particular, if $\vdash_{\mathbf{H}} A$, then $A \in \Gamma^*$.

Define relations $\leq^\circ$ and $\equiv$ on $\mathcal{F}$ by

$$B \leq^\circ C \Leftrightarrow B \to C \in \Gamma^* \quad \text{and} \quad B \equiv C \Leftrightarrow B \leq^\circ C \wedge C \leq^\circ B.$$

Then $\leq^\circ$ is reflexive and transitive, since for every B, $\vdash_{\mathbf{H}} B \to B$ and so $B \to B \in \Gamma^*$, and if $B \to C \in \Gamma^*$ and $C \to D \in \Gamma^*$ then $B \to D \in \Gamma^*$, since $B \to C, C \to D \Rightarrow B \to D$ (recall (6) above). Hence, $\equiv$ is an equivalence relation on $\mathcal{F}$. For every B in $\mathcal{F}$ we let $|B|$ be the equivalence class under $\equiv$ to which B belongs, and $\mathcal{F}/{\equiv}$ the set of all equivalence classes. Next we define the relation $\leq$ on $\mathcal{F}/{\equiv}$ by

$$|B| \leq |C| \Leftrightarrow B \leq^\circ C \Leftrightarrow B \to C \in \Gamma^*.$$

Obviously, $\leq$ is independent of the choice of representatives A, B.

Lemma 41. *$\langle \mathcal{F}/{\equiv}, \leq \rangle$ is a countably linearly ordered structure with distinct maximal element $|\top|$ and minimal element $|\bot|$.*

Proof. Since $\mathcal{F}$ is countably infinite, $\mathcal{F}/{\equiv}$ is countable. For every B and C, $\vdash_{\mathbf{H}} (B \to C) \vee (C \to B)$ by LIN, and so either $B \to C \in \Gamma^*$ or $C \to B \in \Gamma^*$ (by (4)), hence $\leq$ is linear. For every B, $\vdash_{\mathbf{H}} B \to \top$ and $\vdash_{\mathbf{H}} \bot \to B$, and so $B \to \top \in \Gamma^*$ and $\bot \to B \in \Gamma^*$, hence $|\top|$ and $|\bot|$ are the maximal and minimal elements, respectively. Pick any A in Δ^*. Since $\top \to \bot \Rightarrow A$, and $A \notin \Gamma^*$, $\top \to \bot \notin \Gamma^*$, so $|\top| \neq |\bot|$. □

We abbreviate $|\top|$ by $\mathbf{1}$ and $|\bot|$ by $\mathbf{0}$.

Lemma 42. *The following properties hold in* $\langle \mathcal{F}/{\equiv}, \leq \rangle$*:*

1. $|B| = \mathbf{1} \Leftrightarrow B \in \Gamma^*$.
2. $|B \wedge C| = \min\{|B|, |C|\}$.
3. $|B \vee C| = \max\{|B|, |C|\}$.
4. $|B \to C| = \mathbf{1}$ *if* $|B| \leq |C|$, $|B \to C| = |C|$ *otherwise.*
5. $|\neg B| = \mathbf{1}$ *if* $|B| = \mathbf{0}$*;* $|\neg B| = \mathbf{0}$ *otherwise.*
6. $|\exists x B(x)| = \sup\{|B(t)| : t \in \mathcal{T}\}$.
7. $|\forall x B(x)| = \inf\{|B(t)| : t \in \mathcal{T}\}$.

Proof. (1) If $|B| = \mathbf{1}$, then $\top \supset B \in \Gamma^*$, and hence $B \in \Gamma^*$. And if $B \in \Gamma^*$, then $\top \to B \in \Gamma^*$ since $B \Rightarrow \top \supset B$. So $|\top| \leq |B|$. It follows that $|\top| = |B|$ as also $|B| \leq |\top|$.

(2) From $\Rightarrow B \wedge C \to B$, $\Rightarrow B \wedge C \to C$ and $D \to B, D \to C \Rightarrow D \to B \wedge C$ for every D, it follows that $|B \wedge C| = \inf\{|B|, |C|\}$, from which (2) follows since $\leq$ is linear. (3) is proved analogously.

(4) If $|B| \leq |C|$, then $B \to C \in \Gamma^*$, and since $\top \in \Gamma^*$ as well, $|B \to C| = \mathbf{1}$. Now suppose that $|B| \not\leq |C|$. From $B \wedge (B \to C) \Rightarrow C$ it follows that $\min\{|B|, |B \to C|\} \leq |C|$. Because $|B| \not\leq |C|$, $\min\{|B|, |B \to C|\} \neq |B|$, hence $|B \to C| \leq |C|$. On the other hand, $\vdash C \to (B \to C)$, so $|C| \leq |B \to C|$.

(5) If $|B| = \mathbf{0}$, $\neg B = B \supset \bot \in \Gamma^*$, and hence $|\neg B| = \mathbf{1}$ by (1). Otherwise, $|B| \not\leq |\bot|$, and so by (4), $|\neg B| = |B \to \bot| = \mathbf{0}$.

(6) Since $\vdash_{\mathbf{H}} B(t) \to \exists x\, B(x)$, $|B(t)| \leq |\exists x\, B(x)|$ for every $t \in \mathcal{T}$. On the other hand, for every D without x free,

	$\lvert B(t)\rvert \leq \lvert D\rvert$	for every $t \in \mathcal{T}$
$\Leftrightarrow$	$B(t) \to D \in \Gamma^*$	for every $t \in \mathcal{T}$
$\Rightarrow$	$\forall x(B(x) \to D) \in \Gamma^*$	by property (5) of Γ^*
$\Rightarrow$	$\exists x\, B(x) \to D \in \Gamma^*$	since $\forall x(B(x) \to D) \Rightarrow \exists x\, B(x) \to D$
$\Leftrightarrow$	$\lvert\exists x\, B(x)\rvert \leq \lvert D\rvert$.	

(7) is proved analogously. □

$\langle \mathcal{F}/{\equiv}, \leq \rangle$ is countable, let $\mathbf{0} = a_0, \mathbf{1} = a_1, a_2, \ldots$ be an enumeration. Define $h(\mathbf{0}) = 0$, $h(\mathbf{1}) = 1$, and define $h(a_n)$ inductively for $n > 1$: Let $a_n^- = \max\{a_i : i < n \text{ and } a_i < a_n\}$ and $a_n^+ = \min\{a_i : i < n \text{ and } a_i > a_n\}$, and define $h(a_n) = (h(a_n^-) + h(a_n^+))/2$ (thus, $a_2^- = \mathbf{0}$ and $a_2^+ = \mathbf{1}$ as $\mathbf{0} = a_0 < a_2 < a_1 = \mathbf{1}$, hence $h(a_2) = \frac{1}{2}$). Then $h \colon \langle \mathcal{F}/{\equiv}, \leq \rangle \to \mathbb{Q} \cap [0,1]$ is a strictly monotone map which preserves infs and sups. By Lemma 30 there exists a **G**-embedding h' from $\mathbb{Q} \cap [0,1]$ into $\langle [0,1], \leq \rangle$ which is also strictly monotone and preserves infs and sups. Put $\mathcal{I}(B) = h'(h(|B|))$ for every atomic $B \in \mathcal{F}$ and we obtain a $V_{\mathbb{R}}$-interpretation.

Note that for every B, $\mathcal{I}(B) = 1$ iff $|B| = \mathbf{1}$ iff $B \in \Gamma^*$. Hence, we have $\mathcal{I}(B) = 1$ for all $B \in \Gamma$ while if $A \notin \Gamma^*$, then $\mathcal{I}(A) < 1$, so $\Gamma \not\models A$. Thus we have proven that on the assumption that if $\Gamma \nvdash A$, then $\Gamma \not\models A$. □

This completeness proof can be adapted to hypersequent calculi for Gödel logics (Section 4.3, [4,16]), even including the $\triangle$ projection operator [9].

As already mentioned we obtain from this completeness proof together with the soundness theorem (Theorem 10) and Theorem 32 the characterization of recursive axiomatizability:

Theorem 43 ([10], Theorem 40). *Let V be a Gödel set with 0 contained in the perfect kernel of V. Suppose that Γ is a set of closed formulas. Then $\Gamma \models_V A$ iff $\Gamma \vdash_{\mathbf{H}} A$.*

Corollary 44 (Deduction theorem for Gödel logics). *Suppose that Γ is a set of formulas, and A is a closed formula. Then $\Gamma, A \vdash_{\mathbf{H}} B$ iff $\Gamma \vdash_{\mathbf{H}} A \to B$.*

4 Further Topics

4.1 Relation to Kripke Frames

For propositional logic the truth value sets on which Gödel logics are based can be considered as linear Heyting algebras (or pseudo-Boolean algebras). By taking the prime filters of a Heyting algebra as the Kripke frame it is easy to see that the induced logics coincide [18,24]. This direct method does not work for first order logics as the structure of the prime filters does not coincide with the possible evaluations in the first order case.

[15] showed that the class of logics defined by countable linear Kripke frames on constant domains and the class of all Gödel logics coincide. More precisely, for every countable Kripke frame we will *construct* a truth value set such that the logic induced by the Kripke frame and the one induced by the truth value set coincide, and vice versa:

Theorem 45 ([15]). *For every countable linear Kripke frame K there is a Gödel set V_K such that $\mathbf{L}(K) = \mathbf{G}_{V_K}$.*

For every Gödel set V there is a countable linear Kripke frame K_V such that $\mathbf{G}_V = \mathbf{L}(K_V)$.

4.2 Number of Different Gödel Logics

In many areas there is a very common dichotomy: When counting various objects, logics, often there are either uncountably many or finitely many. The case that there are countably many is not that common. As an example take the class of modal logics, or intermediate logics. Considering Gödel logics, there is a common basic logic, the logic of the full interval, which is included in all other Gödel logics. There are still countably many extension principles but, surprisingly, in total only countably many different logics. This has been proven recently by formulating and solving a variant of a Fraïssé Conjecture [19] on the structure of countable linear orderings w.r.t. continuous embeddability.

The following table lists all known results on the number of different types of Gödel logics:

propositional logics	countably many (folklore, [17])
propositional entailments	uncountably many [12]
first order logics	countably many [14]
quantified propositional logics	uncountably many [11]

4.3 Proof Theory

The method of hypersequents for the axiomatization of non-classical logics was pioneered by Avron [1]. Hypersequent calculi are especially suitable for logics that are characterized semantically by linearly ordered structures, among them Gödel logics. Hypersequent calculi for first-order Gödel logics can be found in [4,13]. [16] extended hypersequent calculi for first-order Gödel logic by rules for $\triangle$ and studied their proof-theoretic properties.

Definition 46. *If Γ and Δ are finite multisets of formulas, and $|\Delta| \leq 1$, then $\Gamma \Rightarrow \Delta$ is a* sequent. *A finite multiset of sequents is a* hypersequent, *e.g.,* $\Gamma_1 \Rightarrow \Delta_1 \mid \dots \mid \Gamma_n \Rightarrow \Delta_n$.

Definition 47. *The hypersequent calculus* **HGIF** *is defined as follows:*
Axioms:

$$A \Rightarrow A \qquad \bot \Rightarrow$$

Internal and external structural rules:

$$\frac{G \mid \Gamma \Rightarrow \Delta}{G \mid A, \Gamma \Rightarrow \Delta}\, iw\Rightarrow \qquad \frac{G \mid \Gamma \Rightarrow}{G \mid \Gamma \Rightarrow A}\, \Rightarrow iw \qquad \frac{G \mid A, A, \Gamma \Rightarrow \Delta}{G \mid A, \Gamma \Rightarrow \Delta}\, ic\Rightarrow$$

$$\frac{G}{G \mid \Gamma \Rightarrow \Delta}\, ew \qquad \frac{G \mid \Gamma \Rightarrow \Delta \mid \Gamma \Rightarrow \Delta}{G \mid \Gamma \Rightarrow \Delta}\, ec$$

Logical rules:

$$\frac{G \mid \Gamma \Rightarrow A}{G \mid \neg A, \Gamma \Rightarrow}\, \neg\Rightarrow \qquad \frac{G \mid A, \Gamma \Rightarrow}{G \mid \Gamma \Rightarrow \neg A}\, \Rightarrow\neg$$

$$\frac{G \mid A, \Gamma \Rightarrow \Delta \quad G \mid B, \Gamma \Rightarrow \Delta}{G \mid A \vee B, \Gamma \Rightarrow \Delta}\, \vee\Rightarrow \qquad \frac{G \mid \Gamma \Rightarrow A \quad G \mid \Gamma \Rightarrow B}{G \mid \Gamma \Rightarrow A \wedge B}\, \Rightarrow\wedge$$

$$\frac{G \mid \Gamma \Rightarrow A}{G \mid \Gamma \Rightarrow A \vee B}\, \Rightarrow\vee_1 \qquad \frac{G \mid A, \Gamma \Rightarrow \Delta}{G \mid A \wedge B, \Gamma \Rightarrow \Delta}\, \wedge\Rightarrow_1$$

$$\frac{G \mid \Gamma \Rightarrow B}{G \mid \Gamma \Rightarrow A \vee B}\, \Rightarrow\vee_2 \qquad \frac{G \mid B, \Gamma \Rightarrow \Delta}{G \mid A \wedge B, \Gamma \Rightarrow \Delta}\, \wedge\Rightarrow_2$$

$$\frac{G \mid \Gamma_1 \Rightarrow A \quad G \mid B, \Gamma_2 \Rightarrow \Delta}{G \mid A \supset B, \Gamma_1, \Gamma_2 \Rightarrow \Delta}\, \supset\Rightarrow \qquad \frac{G \mid A, \Gamma \Rightarrow B}{G \mid \Gamma \Rightarrow A \supset B}\, \Rightarrow\supset$$

$$\frac{G \mid A(t), \Gamma \Rightarrow \Delta}{G \mid (\forall x)A(x), \Gamma \Rightarrow \Delta}\, \forall\Rightarrow \qquad \frac{G \mid \Gamma \Rightarrow A(a)}{G \mid \Gamma \Rightarrow (\forall x)A(x)}\, \Rightarrow\forall$$

$$\frac{G \mid A(a), \Gamma \Rightarrow \Delta}{G \mid (\exists x)A(x), \Gamma \Rightarrow \Delta}\, \exists\Rightarrow \qquad \frac{G \mid \Gamma \Rightarrow A(t)}{G \mid \Gamma \Rightarrow (\exists x)A(x)}\, \Rightarrow\exists$$

Rules for $\triangle$:

$$\frac{G \mid A, \Gamma \Rightarrow \Delta}{G \mid \triangle A, \Gamma \Rightarrow \Delta} \triangle\Rightarrow \qquad \frac{G \mid \triangle \Gamma \Rightarrow A}{G \mid \triangle \Gamma \Rightarrow \triangle A} \Rightarrow\triangle$$

$$\frac{G \mid \triangle \Gamma, \Gamma' \Rightarrow \Delta}{G \mid \triangle \Gamma \Rightarrow \mid \Gamma' \Rightarrow \Delta} \triangle cl$$

Cut and Communication:

$$\frac{G \mid \Gamma \Rightarrow A \quad G \mid A, \Pi \Rightarrow \Lambda}{G \mid \Gamma, \Pi \Rightarrow \Lambda} cut$$

$$\frac{G \mid \Gamma_1, \Gamma_2 \Rightarrow \Delta \quad G \mid \Gamma_1, \Gamma_2 \Rightarrow \Delta'}{G \mid \Gamma_1 \Rightarrow \Delta \mid \Gamma_2 \Rightarrow \Delta'} cm$$

The rules ($\Rightarrow\forall$) and ($\exists\Rightarrow$) are subject to eigenvariable conditions: the free variable a must not occur in the lower hypersequent.

Theorem 48 ([13]). **HIF** *is sound and complete for first-order Gödel logic.*

Theorem 49 (Cut-elimination, [3]). *If a hypersequent S is derivable in* **HIF** *then S is derivable in* **HIF** *without using the cut rule.*

As is well known, already Gentzen showed that in **LK** — as a consequence of cut-elimination — a separation between propositional and quantificational inferences can be achieved in deriving a prenex sequent (see, e.g., [28]). This result, that does not hold for **LJ**, was extended in [13] to Gödel logic, as follows:

Theorem 50 (Mid-hypersequent). *Any* **HIF***-derivation π of a prenex hypersequent H can be transformed into one in which no propositional rule is applied below any application of a quantifier rule.*

A corollaries to the above we obtain

Corollary 51. *The prenex fragment of standard first order Gödel logics has a Herbrand Theorem, and admit skolemization.*

For a semantic argument concerning the prenex fragment see [5].

References

1. Avron, A.: Hypersequents, logical consequence and intermediate logics for concurrency. Ann. Math. Artificial Intelligence 4, 225–248 (1991)
2. Baaz, M.: Infinite-valued Gödel logics with 0-1-projections and relativizations. In: Hájek, P. (ed.) Proc. Gödel 1996, Logic Foundations of Mathematics, Computer Science and Physics – Kurt Gödel's Legacy. Lecture Notes in Logic, vol. 6, pp. 23–33. Springer, Heidelberg (1996)
3. Baaz, M., Ciabattoni, A.: A Schütte-Tait style cut-elimination proof for first-order Gödel logic. In: Egly, U., Fermüller, C. (eds.) TABLEAUX 2002. LNCS (LNAI), vol. 2381, pp. 24–38. Springer, Heidelberg (2002)

4. Baaz, M., Ciabattoni, A., Fermüller, C.G.: Hypersequent calculi for Gödel logics—a survey. Journal of Logic and Computation 13, 835–861 (2003)
5. Baaz, M., Ciabattoni, A., Fermüller, C.G.: Herbrand's theorem for prenex Gödel logic and its consequences for theorem proving. In: Nieuwenhuis, R., Voronkov, A. (eds.) LPAR 2001. LNCS (LNAI), vol. 2250, pp. 201–216. Springer, Heidelberg (2001)
6. Baaz, M., Leitsch, A., Zach, R.: Completeness of a first-order temporal logic with time-gaps. Theoretetical Computer Science 160(1-2), 241–270 (1996)
7. Baaz, M., Leitsch, A., Zach, R.: Incompleteness of a first-order Gödel logic and some temporal logics of programs. In: Büning, H.K. (ed.) CSL 1995. LNCS, vol. 1092, pp. 1–15. Springer, Heidelberg (1996)
8. Baaz, M., Leitsch, A., Zach, R.: Incompleteness of an infinite-valued first-order Gödel logic and of some temporal logics of programs. In: Börger, E. (ed.) CSL 1995. LNCS, vol. 1092, pp. 1–15. Springer, Heidelberg (1996)
9. Baaz, M., Preining, N., Zach, R.: Completeness of a hypersequent calculus for some first-order Gödel logics with delta. In: Proceedings of 36th International Symposium on Multiple-valued Logic, Singapore. IEEE Press, Los Alamitos (May 2006)
10. Baaz, M., Preining, N., Zach, R.: First-order Gödel logics. Annals of Pure and Applied Logic 147, 23–47 (2007)
11. Baaz, M., Veith, H.: An axiomatization of quantified propositional Gödel logic using the Takeuti-Titani rule. In: Buss, S., Hájek, P., Pudlák, P. (eds.) Proceedings of the Logic Colloquium 1998, Prague. LNL, vol. 13, pp. 74–87. ASL (2000)
12. Baaz, M., Zach, R.: Compact propositional Gödel logics. In: Proceedings of 28th International Symposium on Multiple-valued Logic, Fukuoka, Japan, pp. 108–113. IEEE Press, Los Alamitos (May 1998)
13. Baaz, M., Zach, R.: Hypersequents and the proof theory of intuitionistic fuzzy logic. In: Clote, P.G., Schwichtenberg, H. (eds.) CSL 2000. LNCS, vol. 1862, pp. 187–201. Springer, Heidelberg (2000)
14. Beckmann, A., Goldstern, M., Preining, N.: Continuous Fraïssé conjecture. Order 25(4), 281–298 (2008)
15. Beckmann, A., Preining, N.: Linear Kripke frames and Gödel logics. Journal of Symbolic Logic 71(1), 26–44 (2007)
16. Ciabattoni, A.: A proof-theoretical investigation of global intuitionistic (fuzzy) logic. Archive of Mathematical Logic 44, 435–457 (2005)
17. Dummett, M.: A propositional logic with denumerable matrix. Journal of Symbolic Logic 24, 96–107 (1959)
18. Fitting, M.C.: Intuitionistic logic, model theory and forcing. Studies in Logic and the Foundation of Mathematics. North-Holland Publishing Company, Amsterdam (1969)
19. Fraïssé, R.: Sur la comparaison des types d'ordres. C. R. Acad. Sci. Paris 226, 1330–1331 (1948)
20. Hájek, P.: Metamathematics of Fuzzy Logic. Kluwer, Dordrecht (1998)
21. Horn, A.: Logic with truth values in a linearly ordered Heyting algebra. Journal of Symbolic Logic 34(3), 395–409 (1969)
22. Kechris, A.S.: Classical Descriptive Set Theory. Springer, Heidelberg (1995)
23. Moschovakis, Y.N.: Descriptive set theory. Studies in Logic and the Foundations of Mathematics, vol. 100. North-Holland, Amsterdam (1980)
24. Ono, H.: Kripke models and intermediate logics. Publ. Res. Inst. Math. Sci., Kyoto Univ. 6, 461–476 (1971)
25. Preining, N.: Complete Recursive Axiomatizability of Gödel Logics. PhD thesis, Vienna University of Technology, Austria (2003)

26. Rosenstein, J.G.: Linear Orderings. Academic Press, London (1982)
27. Takano, M.: Another proof of the strong completeness of the intuitionistic fuzzy logic. Tsukuba Journal of Mathematics 11(1), 101–105 (1987)
28. Takeuti, G.: Proof Theory, 2nd edn. North-Holland, Amsterdam (1987)
29. Takeuti, G., Titani, S.: Intuitionistic fuzzy logic and intuitionistic fuzzy set theory. Journal of Symbolic Logic 49, 851–866 (1984)
30. Winkler, R.: How much must an order theorist forget to become a topologist? In: Proc. of the Vienna Conference Contributions of General Algebra, Klagenfurt, Austria, vol. 12, pp. 420–433. Verlag Johannes Heyn (1999)

Tableau Calculus for the Logic of Comparative Similarity over Arbitrary Distance Spaces

Régis Alenda and Nicola Olivetti

LSIS - UMR CNRS 6168
Domaine Universitaire de Saint-Jérôme, Avenue Escadrille Normandie-Niemen, 13397 MARSEILLE CEDEX 20, France
regis.alenda@lsis.org, nicola.olivetti@univ-cezanne.fr

Abstract. The logic $\mathcal{CSL}$ (first introduced by Sheremet, Tishkovsky, Wolter and Zakharyaschev in 2005) allows one to reason about distance comparison and similarity comparison within a modal language. The logic can express assertions of the kind "A is closer/more similar to B than to C" and has a natural application to spatial reasoning, as well as to reasoning about concept similarity in ontologies. The semantics of $\mathcal{CSL}$ is defined in terms of models based on different classes of distance spaces and it generalizes the logic $\mathbf{S4}_u$ of topological spaces. In this paper we consider $\mathcal{CSL}$ defined over arbitrary distance spaces. The logic comprises a binary modality to represent comparative similarity and a unary modality to express the existence of the minimum of a set of distances. We first show that the semantics of $\mathcal{CSL}$ can be equivalently defined in terms of preferential models. As a consequence we obtain the finite model property of the logic with respect to its preferential semantic, a property that does not hold with respect to the original distance-space semantics. Next we present an analytic tableau calculus based on its preferential semantics. The calculus provides a decision procedure for the logic, its termination is obtained by imposing suitable blocking restrictions.

1 Introduction

In a series of papers [8,6,9,10], Sheremet, Tishkovsky, Wolter and Zakharyaschev have presented several modal logics to reason about distance comparisons and topological properties. The logic $\mathcal{QML}$, investigated in [10], is perhaps the most general one and provides a modal framework to capture several logics of topological and metric spaces. $\mathcal{QML}$ can be indeed considered as a kind of "'super logic"' to reason about distances and topological relations. The logic comprises a set of quantified distance modalities, where the quantifiers range on the reals. In this logic we can define sets like: "the set of objects w for which there is a positive real x such that all objects within distance x from w are in A"' (represented by $\exists x \forall^{\leq x} A$). This set corresponds to the *interior*, in a topological sense, of a set A. The logic $\mathcal{QML}$ covers a wide range of logics of metric spaces; some of these systems or fragments thereof have been used to provide suitable logics for spatial reasoning in AI (see [10]). For instance it includes the well-known

C. Fermüller and A. Voronkov (Eds.): LPAR-17, LNCS 6397, pp. 52–66, 2010.

logic $\mathbf{S4}_u$, which contains the mentioned interior operator $\Box A = \exists x(\forall^{\leq x} A)$ as well as the universal modality $\forall A = \forall x(\forall^{\leq x} A)$[1].

A striking result shown in [10] is that the logic $\mathcal{QML}$ can be reduced to a modal logic whose language abstracts away completely distance quantifiers and reals (although the reduction entails an exponential blowup). This logic, called $\mathcal{CSL}$, can be seen as a logic of qualitative distance comparison, or a logic of comparative similarity between objects. The logic $\mathcal{CSL}$ comprises only two primitive notions, whence modal operators: one to express distance comparisons, and one to express that the distance of an element to an (infinite) set is realized by some element of the set. The first modality is the (binary) operator $\leftleftarrows$: a formula $A \leftleftarrows B$ denotes the set of objects x that are closer to A than to B, that is to say such that $d(x, A) < d(x, B)$, where the distance $d(x, A)$ of an object x to a set A is defined as the *infimum* of the distances of x to any object in A. The latter one is the (unary) operator ⓡ, the so-called realization modality, ⓡA denotes the set of elements whose distance to A is *realized*, that is such that $d(x, A)$ is the *minimum* of the distances of x to every object in A. By means of its reduction to $\mathcal{CSL}$, the authors have obtained an axiomatization of $\mathcal{QML}$ over different classes of distance models[2] as well as an ExpTime-completeness result for decidability in all cases. Finally the authors have shown that $\mathcal{CSL}$ (whence $\mathcal{QML}$) interpreted over (subspaces of) the reals is undecidable.

The logic $\mathcal{CSL}$ without the realization operator, let us call it $\mathcal{CSL}^-$, has been previously investigated in itself: it has been proposed as a logic of qualitative similarity comparisons with possible applications in ontologies [9]. The logic $\mathcal{CSL}^-$ can express qualitative comparisons of the form: "Renault Clio is more similar to Peugeot 207 than to VW Golf". For a further example [8] the color "Reddish " may be defined as a color which is more similar to a prototypical "'Red"' than to any other color. In $\mathcal{CSL}^-$ the above examples can be encoded (using a description logic notation and nominals) by:

(1) $Reddish \equiv \{Red\} \leftleftarrows \{Green, \ldots, black\}$
(2) $Clio \sqsubseteq (Peugeot207 \leftleftarrows Ferrari430)$

In previous work, the analysis of $\mathcal{CSL}^-$ has concentrated on an important class of distance spaces models where the infimum of a set of distances is their minimum, the so-called minspaces. The minspace property entails the restriction to spaces where the distance function is discrete, a restriction that may by acceptable for qualitative reasoning about similarity comparisons, whereas it is not very reasonable for spatial reasoning. Observe that over minspaces, the distance from a point to any non-empty set of points is always realized so that the operator ⓡ collapse to the **S5**-existential modality which can be defined by ⓡ$A \equiv (A \leftleftarrows \bot)$, whence $\mathcal{CSL}$ and $\mathcal{CSL}^-$ are actually the same logic.

---

[1] More precisely in $\mathcal{QML}$ the real quantifier $\exists x$ (and its dual $\forall x$) can be applied to any boolean combination of formulas beginning with distance quantifiers like $\forall^{\leq x} A$ (we refer to [10] for the formal details).

[2] More precisely: arbitrary distance and symmetric distance models, metric space models, and distance models with triangular inequality.

When interpreted over minspaces, the logic $\mathcal{CSL}$ turns out to be strongly related to conditional logics, whose semantics is often expressed in terms of preferential structures; the latter being a set equipped by a family of binary relations indexed by the objects of the set, or a ternary relation. The relation $x \leq_y z$ can be interpreted intuitively as 'y is at least as similar/close to x than z'. Such a semantics was originally proposed by Lewis [7] to give a formal account of counterfactual conditionals and related notions. The relation $x \leq_y z$ satisfies some further properties, notably (i) it is a total preorder, (ii) minimal $\leq_x$ elements of a non-empty set always exist (limit assumption) and (iii) x is the *unique* smallest element wrt. $\leq_x$ (strong centering).

In [2] it is shown that the semantics of $\mathcal{CSL}$ over minspaces can be equivalently restated in terms or preferential structures. This correspondence has been used to find an axiomatization of $\mathcal{CSL}$ over minspaces and a decision procedure in the form of a tableau calculus. In this case the correspondence is clear, as a distance space is readily transformed into a preferential model by defining $x <_y z$ if $d(y, x) < d(y, z)$ (of course the truth conditions must be restated in a suitable way). More recently [3], the correspondence with the preferential semantics has been extended to $\mathcal{CSL}$ interpreted over *symmetric* minspace models [3], and a tableau-based decision procedure based on this correspondence has also been proposed.

Beyond the intrinsic theoretical interest, we believe that it is worthwhile to study the relations between the preferential semantic and the distance space semantic. The former, being closer to the semantics of traditional modal logics, allows a simpler analysis of logical properties (finite model property, complexity bounds, etc.) and it makes easier to develop proof systems.

In this paper we contribute to automated deduction of $\mathcal{CSL}$ and of $\mathcal{CSL}^-$ over arbitrary distance spaces (whence symmetric distance spaces [10]). The first question we answer: can we give a preferential semantics to $\mathcal{CSL}$ and to $\mathcal{CSL}^-$ over arbitrary distance spaces? In this case the simple correspondence mentioned above *cannot work*. However, rather unexpectedly, the answer is positive and simple for both $\mathcal{CSL}^-$ and $\mathcal{CSL}$. By a filtration technique, we show that the distance model semantics is equivalent to the preferential semantics, in the sense that the sets of valid formulas under the two semantics coincide. While for $\mathcal{CSL}^-$ no extra ingredient is required, for $\mathcal{CSL}$, preferential models are equipped by an additional binary accessibility relation needed interpret the ⓡ operator. Technically, we can observe that preferential model corresponding to arbitrary distance spaces do still satisfy limit assumption, but they do no longer satisfy strong centering (there might be several smallest elements with respect $\leq_x$).

As a byproduct of the correspondence between the two semantics, we obtain a finite model property for both $\mathcal{CSL}^-$ and $\mathcal{CSL}$ with respect to their preferential semantics, which also gives an alternative proof (with respect to [10]) of their decidability. Observe in contrast that the finite model property with respect to the distance base semantics does not hold, neither for $\mathcal{CSL}$, nor for $\mathcal{CSL}^-$.

We next define an analytic tableau calculus for checking satisfiability of $\mathcal{CSL}$ formulas based on the preferential semantics of this logic. The rules of the calculus encode directly the semantics of the logic over preferential models. Its termination is obtained by imposing a suitable *subset blocking* condition. To the best of our knowledge, the one presented is this paper is the first implementable decision procedure for this logic. In light of the encoding mentioned above, it gives also a decision procedure for $\mathcal{QML}$.

2 Syntax and Semantics

The language $\mathcal{L}_{\mathcal{CSL}}$ of $\mathcal{CSL}$ is generated from a (countable) set of propositional variables $V_1, V_2, \ldots \in \mathcal{V}_p$ by ordinary propositional connectives together with the two operators $\leftleftarrows$ and Ⓡ:

$$A, B ::= \perp \mid p_i \mid \neg A \mid A \sqcap B \mid A \leftleftarrows B \mid \text{Ⓡ}A \qquad (\text{where } p_i \in \mathcal{V}_p).$$

The language $\mathcal{L}_{\mathcal{CSL}^-}$ of the logic $\mathcal{CSL}^-$ is defined as the sub-language of $\mathcal{L}_{\mathcal{CSL}}$ comprising only the operators $\neg, \sqcap$ and $\leftleftarrows$.

The semantics of $\mathcal{CSL}$ introduced in [10] is based on distance spaces. A distance space is a pair (Δ, d) where Δ is a non-empty set, and $d : \Delta \times \Delta \to \mathbb{R}^{\geq 0}$ is a *distance function* satisfying the following condition[3]:

(ID) $$\forall x, y \in \Delta, \quad d(x, y) = 0 \text{ iff } x = y\ .$$

The distance between an object w and a non-empty subset X of Δ is defined by $d(w, X) = \inf\{d(w, x) \mid x \in X\}$. If $X = \varnothing$, then $d(w, X) = \infty$. If there exists a point $x \in X$ such that $d(w, X) = d(w, x)$, we say that the distance from w to X is *realized* (by the point x). In this case $d(w, X) = \min\{d(w, x) \mid x \in X\}$.

We next define $\mathcal{CSL}$-distance models as a kind of Kripke models based on distance spaces:

Definition 1 ($\mathcal{CSL}$-distance model). *A* $\mathcal{CSL}$-distance model $\mathcal{I}$ *is a triple* $\mathcal{I} = \langle \Delta^{\mathcal{I}}, d^{\mathcal{I}}, .^{\mathcal{I}} \rangle$ *where:*
- $(\Delta^{\mathcal{I}}, d^{\mathcal{I}})$ *is a distance space.*
- $.^{\mathcal{I}}$ *is the* evaluation function *defined as usual on propositional variables and boolean connectives, and as follows for* $\leftleftarrows$ *and* Ⓡ*:*

$$(A \leftleftarrows B)^{\mathcal{I}} \stackrel{\text{def}}{=} \{x \in \Delta^{\mathcal{I}} \mid d(x, A^{\mathcal{I}}) < d(x, B^{\mathcal{I}})\}.$$
$$(\text{Ⓡ}A)^{\mathcal{I}} \stackrel{\text{def}}{=} \{x \in \Delta^{\mathcal{I}} \mid d(x, A^{\mathcal{I}}) \textit{ is realized}\}.$$

As explained in introduction, we are interested in providing an alternative purely relational semantics, in terms of a preferential structure.

Definition 2. *A preferential space is a pair* $(\Delta, (\leq_w)_{w\in\Delta})$ *where* Δ *is a non-empty countable set and* $(\leq_w)_{w\in\Delta}$ *is a family of total pre-orders, each one satisfying the following properties:*

(limit assumption) *For all* $C \subseteq \Delta, C \neq \varnothing$ *implies* $\min_{\leq_w}(C) \neq \varnothing$.

(WKCT) *For all* $x, w \leq_w x$.

where $\min_{\leq_w}(X) = \{x \in X \mid \forall y((y \in X \textit{ and } y \leq_w x) \to x \leq_w y)\}$.

[3] To other properties of distance function are usually assumed: symmetry and triangular inequality; the logic is insensitive to the assumption of symmetry alone, whereas triangle inequality does matter [10]. However none of them will be considered here.

$$((A \leftleftarrows B) \sqcap (B \leftleftarrows C)) \to (A \leftleftarrows C) \qquad (\neg(A \leftleftarrows B) \sqcap \neg(B \leftleftarrows C)) \to \neg(A \leftleftarrows C)$$
$$\neg((A \sqcup B) \leftleftarrows A) \to \neg((A \sqcup B) \leftleftarrows B) \qquad \neg(\neg(A \to B) \leftleftarrows \bot) \to \neg(A \leftleftarrows B)$$
$$ⓡ(A \sqcup B) \to ⓡA \sqcup ⓡB \qquad (ⓡ(A \sqcup B) \sqcap (A \leftleftarrows B)) \to ⓡA$$
$$(ⓡA \sqcap \neg(B \leftleftarrows A)) \to ⓡ(A \sqcup B) \qquad \neg(\neg(A \leftrightarrow B) \leftleftarrows \bot) \to (ⓡA \leftrightarrow ⓡB)$$
$$(A \leftrightarrow ⓡA \sqcap \neg(\top \leftleftarrows A)) \qquad \top \leftleftarrows \bot$$
$$\neg ⓡ\bot \qquad (\neg(A \leftleftarrows \bot) \leftleftarrows \bot) \to \neg((A \leftleftarrows \bot) \leftleftarrows \bot)$$

Fig. 1. Axiomatization of $\mathcal{CSL}$ over arbitrary distance spaces [10]

We define $<_w$ as $x \leq_w y$ and $y \not\leq_w x$. We are now ready to restate the distance semantics in terms of preferential structures. We first consider the case of $\mathcal{CSL}^-$:

Definition 3 ($\mathcal{CSL}^-$ preferential model). *A $\mathcal{CSL}$-preferential $\mathcal{I}$ model is a triple $\langle \Delta^{\mathcal{I}}, (\leq_w^{\mathcal{I}})_{w \in \Delta^{\mathcal{I}}}, .^{\mathcal{I}} \rangle$ where:*
- *$(\Delta^{\mathcal{I}}, (\leq_w^{\mathcal{I}})_{w \in \Delta^{\mathcal{I}}})$ is a preferential space (Definition 2).*
- *$.^{\mathcal{I}}$ is the evaluation function defined as usual for propositional variables and boolean operators, and as follows for $\leftleftarrows$:*
$$(A \leftleftarrows B)^{\mathcal{I}} \stackrel{\text{def}}{=} \{w | \exists x \in A^{\mathcal{I}} \text{ such that } \forall y \in B^{\mathcal{I}}, x <_w^{\mathcal{I}} y\}$$

In order to interpret ⓡ, we need to introduce a further ingredient in preferential models: a binary relation denoted by ρ. The technical meaning of it, and its link with the preferential relations by the relation (RCT) will be clear after Theorem 6, which shows the correspondence between the distance semantics and the preferential one.

Definition 4 ($\mathcal{CSL}$ preferential model). *A $\mathcal{CSL}$-preferential $\mathcal{I}$ model is a four-tuple $\langle \Delta^{\mathcal{I}}, (\leq_w^{\mathcal{I}})_{w \in \Delta^{\mathcal{I}}}, \rho^{\mathcal{I}}, .^{\mathcal{I}} \rangle$ where:*
- *$\langle \Delta^{\mathcal{I}}, (\leq_w^{\mathcal{I}})_{w \in \Delta^{\mathcal{I}}}, .^{\mathcal{I}} \rangle$ is a $\mathcal{CSL}^-$-preferential model.*
- *$\rho^{\mathcal{I}}$ is a reflexive binary relation over Δ, and satisfies the following property:*

(RCT) $$(w, x) \in \rho^{\mathcal{I}} \wedge x \leq_w w \to x = w.$$

- *The interpretation of the ⓡ operator is defined as follows:*
$$(ⓡA)^{\mathcal{I}} \stackrel{\text{def}}{=} \{w | \exists x \in \min_{\leq_w}(A^{\mathcal{I}}) \text{ such that } (w, x) \in \rho^{\mathcal{I}}\}.$$

In the minspace case, we can directly transform a distance model into an equivalent preferential model based on the same domain by taking:

(1) $$x \leq_w y \text{ iff } d(w, x) \leq d(w, y).$$

The next example show that this correspondence is not possible for the general case.

Example 5. Consider the two (infinite) $\mathcal{CSL}$-distance models $\mathcal{I}$ and $\mathcal{J}$ defined on the same set $\Delta^{\mathcal{I}} = \Delta^{\mathcal{J}} = \{x, y_0, y_1, y_2, \ldots\}$. Let, for all $i \in \mathbb{N}$, $d^{\mathcal{I}}(x, y_i) = \frac{1}{1+i}$, $d^{\mathcal{J}}(x, y_i) = 1 + \frac{1}{1+i}$. For all the others cases, we let $d^{\mathcal{I}}(u, v) = d^{\mathcal{J}}(u, v)$. We let $p^{\mathcal{I}} = p^{\mathcal{J}} = \{x\}$ and $q^{\mathcal{I}} = q^{\mathcal{J}} = \{y_0, y_1, y_2, \ldots\}$. It is clear that $d^{\mathcal{I}}(x, p^{\mathcal{I}}) = 0$ while $d^{\mathcal{J}}(x, p^{\mathcal{J}}) = 1$, and thus $x \in (p \leftleftarrows q)^{\mathcal{J}}$ while $x \notin (p \leftleftarrows q)^{\mathcal{J}}$.

We now build two preferential models $\mathcal{I}'$ and $\mathcal{J}'$ based on the same set (i.e. we let $\Delta^{\mathcal{I}'} = \Delta^{\mathcal{J}'} = \Delta^{\mathcal{I}} = \Delta^{\mathcal{J}}$) using (1): $u \leq_w^{\mathcal{I}'} v$ iff $d^{\mathcal{I}}(w,u) \leq d^{\mathcal{I}}(w,v)$, and $u \leq_w^{\mathcal{J}'} v$ iff $d^{\mathcal{J}}(w,u) \leq d^{\mathcal{J}}(w,v)$. It is then easy to show that:

$$\text{For all } w, v, u \in \Delta^{\mathcal{I}'} = \Delta^{\mathcal{J}'}: u \leq_w^{\mathcal{I}'} v \text{ iff } u \leq_w^{\mathcal{J}'} v.$$

So that we have $\mathcal{I}' = \mathcal{J}'$. Therefore it is impossible to define preferential models as in Definition 3 for $\mathcal{CSL}^-$ over general distance spaces by means of the correspondence (1).

Nonetheless, we can show that the set of satisfiable formulas under the two semantics coincides.

Theorem 6. *A formula $C \in \mathcal{L}_{\mathcal{CSL}}$ is satisfiable in a $\mathcal{CSL}$-distance model iff it is satisfiable in a $\mathcal{CSL}$-preferential model.*

Proof (Theorem 6). As usual, $\mathsf{sub}(C)$ denotes the set of sub-formulas of C. Given a model $\mathcal{I}$ and an object $x \in \Delta^{\mathcal{I}}$, the type of x in $\mathcal{I}$ wrt. to a formula C is noted $\tau_C^{\mathcal{I}}(x)$ and defined as follows: $\tau_C^{\mathcal{I}}(x) \stackrel{\text{def}}{=} \{A | A \in \mathsf{sub}(C) \text{ and } x \in A^{\mathcal{I}}\}$.

Two objects x, y are C-equivalent in $\mathcal{I}$ (noted $x \sim_C^{\mathcal{I}} y$) if $\tau_C^{\mathcal{I}}(x) = \tau_C^{\mathcal{I}}(y)$. The equivalence class of x with respect to the relation $\sim_C^{\mathcal{I}}$ is denoted by $[x]_C^{\mathcal{I}}$.

When the context is clear, ie. when $\mathcal{I}$ and C are not ambiguous, we simply write $\tau(x)$, $x \sim y$, and $[x]$ instead of $\tau_C^{\mathcal{I}}(x)$, $x \sim_C^{\mathcal{I}}$ and $[x]_C^{\mathcal{I}}$.

($\Rightarrow$) Let a formula C be satisfiable in a $\mathcal{CSL}$-distance model $\mathcal{I}$. We construct a $\mathcal{CSL}$-preferential model based on the set of equivalences classes of objects of $\Delta^{\mathcal{I}}$ with respect to the relation $\sim$: $\Delta^{\mathcal{J}} = \{[x] | x \in \Delta^{\mathcal{I}}\}$.

To define the preferential relations, we use a choice function $f : \Delta^{\mathcal{J}} \to \Delta^{\mathcal{I}}$ which selects an arbitrary element from each equivalence class: $f([x]) \in [x]$. Note that by definition of the equivalence classes, for all formulas $D \in \mathsf{sub}(C)$, if $f([x]) \in D^{\mathcal{J}}$, then for all $x' \in [x]$, $x' \in D^{\mathcal{J}}$. We can now define the $\mathcal{CSL}$-preferential model $\mathcal{J}$ by taking:

- $[x] \leq_{[w]}^{\mathcal{J}} [y]$ iff $d^{\mathcal{I}}(f([w]), [x]) \leq d^{\mathcal{I}}(f([w]), [y])$.
- $([x], [y]) \in \rho^{\mathcal{J}}$ iff $d(f([x]), [y])$ is realized.
- $[x] \in p^{\mathcal{J}}$ iff $f([x]) \in p^{\mathcal{I}}$, for all propositional variable p.

It is easy to check that $\mathcal{J}$ satisfies all the properties of Definition 4. For (RCT), note that if $[x] \leq_{[w]}^{\mathcal{J}} [w]$, then $d^{\mathcal{I}}(f([w]), [x]) = 0$. Since $([w], [x]) \in \rho^{\mathcal{J}}$, the distance $d^{\mathcal{I}}(f([x]), [x])$ is realized, and thus, by (ID), $f([w]) \in [x]$. Therefore, $[w] = [x]$.

FACT 7. For all formulas $D \in \mathsf{sub}(C)$, $w \in D^{\mathcal{I}}$ iff $[w] \in D^{\mathcal{J}}$.

From Fact 7, and since $C \in \mathsf{sub}(C)$, we conclude that if $C^{\mathcal{I}} \neq \varnothing$, then $C^{\mathcal{J}} \neq \varnothing$.

($\Leftarrow$) Let $\mathcal{J} = \langle \Delta^{\mathcal{J}}, (\leq_w^{\mathcal{J}})_{w \in \Delta^{\mathcal{J}}}, \rho^{\mathcal{J}}, .^{\mathcal{J}} \rangle$ be a $\mathcal{CSL}$-preferential model. Since Δ is countable, we can represent each total preorder $\leq_w^{\mathcal{J}}$ by a *ranking function* $r_w : \Delta^{\mathcal{J}} \to \mathbb{R}$ such that $x \leq_w^{\mathcal{J}} y$ iff $r_w(x) \leq r_w(y)$. Since w is minimal for $\leq_w$, whence for r_w, we do not loose in generality by imposing $r_w(w) = 0$ (as a consequence, for all x, $r_w(x) \geq 0$). We now define the $\mathcal{CSL}$-distance model $\mathcal{I}$ as follows:

- $\Delta^{\mathcal{I}} = \Delta^{\mathcal{J}} \times \mathbb{N}$.
- For all $(x, i), (y, j) \in \Delta^{\mathcal{I}}$:

$$d^{\mathcal{I}}((x,i),(y,j)) = \begin{cases} 0 & \text{if } x = y \text{ and } i = j, \\ 1 & \text{if } x = y \text{ and } i \neq j, \\ r_x(y) & \text{if } x \neq y \text{ and } (x,y) \in \rho^{\mathcal{J}}, \\ r_x(y) + \frac{1}{j+1} & \text{if } x \neq y \text{ and } (x,y) \notin \rho^{\mathcal{J}}. \end{cases}$$

- For all $(x, i) \in \Delta^{\mathcal{I}}$, $(x, i) \in p^{\mathcal{I}}$ iff $x \in p^{\mathcal{J}}$, for any propositional variable p.

FACT 8. $\mathcal{I} = \langle \Delta^{\mathcal{I}}, d^{\mathcal{I}}, .^{\mathcal{I}} \rangle$ is a $\mathcal{CSL}$-distance model.

We denote by α_x the set $\{(x, i) | i \in \mathbb{N}\}$. By the definition of $d^{\mathcal{I}}$, we obtain:

FACT 9. For all $(x, i) \in \Delta^{\mathcal{I}}$ and for all $y \in \Delta^{\mathcal{J}}$, $d^{\mathcal{I}}((x, i), \alpha_y) = r_x(y)$.

We then conclude by the following fact:

FACT 10. For all formulas $D \in \mathsf{sub}(C)$, $w \in D^{\mathcal{J}}$ iff $\alpha_w \subseteq D^{\mathcal{I}}$. □

We can give a similar theorem for $\mathcal{CSL}^-$ by ignoring ρ in the proofs:

Theorem 11. *A formula $C \in \mathcal{L}_{\mathcal{CSL}^-}$ is satisfiable in a $\mathcal{CSL}$-distance model iff it is satisfiable in a $\mathcal{CSL}^-$-preferential model.*

Observe that the direction from distance models to preferential models makes use of a filtration construction. Moreover, if n is the length of the initial formula C, there cannot be more than 2^n different types; thus the preferential model $\mathcal{J}$ obtained by this construction is finite and we have $\mathsf{Card}(\Delta^{\mathcal{J}}) \leq 2^n$; therefore we obtain the following corollary:

Corollary 12. *If a $\mathcal{CSL}$-formula is satisfiable, then it is satisfiable in a finite $\mathcal{CSL}$-preferential model.*

Looking at the proof of Theorem 6 we see that ρ connects pairs of elements in the filtrated model, corresponding to sets of elements of the distance model whose distance is realized. Intuitively, the relation ρ reflects the realization relation of the original distance model in the filtrated model where elements are replaced by equivalence classes (set of elements). To make a connection with the minspace models ρ becomes universal and (RCT) becomes strong centering, namely:

$$x \leq_w w \rightarrow x = w.$$

This result may seem puzzling at the first sight; in the case of minspace models [2] the transformation between models is direct and we have that the minspace semantics is equivalent to the preferential semantics with limit assumption and strong centering. In particular, the limit assumption corresponds to the minspace property. In contrast, the above result shows that the limit assumption *does not* entail in itself the minspace property. To get the correspondence of Theorem 6, it is the strong centering property that has to be relaxed.

3 A Labeled Tableau Calculus

In this section we present a decision procedure for $\mathcal{CSL}$ over general distance spaces based on a labeled tableau calculus. Tableau rules act on sets of tableau formulas, defined next. These sets of formulas are denoted by $\Gamma, \Delta, \ldots$, and are called tableau sets. As usual, we use the notation Γ, Δ for the set union $\Gamma \cup \Delta$. Given an enumerable set Lab $= \{x_1, x_2, \ldots, x_n, \ldots\}$ of objects called *labels*, a tableau formula has the form i) $x : C$ where x is a label and C is a $\mathcal{CSL}$-formula. ii) $w \leq_w y$ or $x <_w y$ where w, x, y are labels. iii) $z : f(x, C)$ where x, y are labels and C is a $\mathcal{CSL}$-formula. iv) $\rho(x, y)$ or $\neg\rho(x, y)$ where x, y are labels.

As expected, labels represent the objects of the domain, so that i) states that $x \in C^{\mathcal{I}}$, and ii) encode the preferential relations. Note that the calculus uses both strict and non strict relations. The intuitive meaning of iii) is $z \in \min_{\leq_x}(C^{\mathcal{I}})$, and iv) encode the binary relation ρ.

A tableau derivation (or simply a derivation) for C (the input formula) is a tree whose root node is the tableau set $\{x : C\}$, and where successors of any node are obtained by the application of a *tableau rule*. A tableau rule has the form $\Gamma[X]/\Gamma_1 \mid \cdots \mid \Gamma_m$, where $\Gamma, \Gamma_1, \ldots, \Gamma_m$ are tableau sets. The meaning is that, given a tableau set Γ in a derivation, if $X \subseteq \Gamma$, then we can apply the rule to it and create m successors $\Gamma_1, \ldots, \Gamma_m$. The denominator can be the empty set, in which case the rule is a *closure rule* and is usually written $\Gamma[X]/\bot$. Closure rules detect tableau sets which contain a contradiction.

We give two calculi: one for the logic $\mathcal{CSL}^-$ whose rules are given in figure 2, and one for $\mathcal{CSL}$, obtained by adding the rules of figure 3. The rules are grounded on the preferential semantics. Observe that the rules (T1$\leftleftarrows$), (F1$\leftleftarrows$) and (Tf) comprise a case analysis in the form of analytic cut (the rule (Tf) is only needed in case of $(\neg)$ⓡ formulas.), which is needed for technical reasons (to ensure that the subset blocking will work properly). The semantic conditions for $(\neg) \leftleftarrows$ are captured by the rules (T2$\leftleftarrows$) and (T3$\leftleftarrows$) (resp. (F2$\leftleftarrows$) and (F3$\leftleftarrows$)). For instance the rule (F2$\leftleftarrows$) introduces an element $z \in \min_y(B^{\mathcal{I}})$, whenever A is non-empty and the rule (F3$\leftleftarrows$) states that no A-element y can be closer to x than z. The rule (Tf) states that x is w-minimal element for A (i.e. a minimal element of A for the relation $\leq_w$.). The rule (Tⓡ) create an x-minimal element z such that $(x, z) \in \rho$. The rules for $x : \neg$ⓡA are more complex: the rule (F1ⓡ) first perform an analytic cut on A. If no label satisfies A, then $x : \neg$ⓡA is trivially satisfied. If a label satisfy A, then the rule (F2ⓡ) creates an x-minimal element z for A. Note that if there is a y such that $y : A$ and $y \leq_x z$ are in the tableau set, then y is also an x-minimal element for A. The rules (F3ⓡ) states that in order to satisfy the formula $x : \neg$ⓡA, we must have $(x, y) \notin \rho$ for each x-minimal element y of A. In the (CTρ) rule, which encodes the RCT condition, we denote by $\Gamma_{s[x,y]}$ the tableau set obtained by replacing either y by x or x by y in every tableau formula of Γ.

A rule is *dynamic* if it introduces a new label, and *static* if it does not. Here, the dynamic rules are (T2$\leftleftarrows$), (F2$\leftleftarrows$), (Tⓡ) and (F2ⓡ). The others are static. Let us call *dynamic* formula of type $x : (\neg)(A \leftleftarrows B)$ or $x : (\neg)$ⓡA, that is the ones to which a dynamic rule can be applied.

$$(\neg\neg)\colon \frac{\Gamma[x : \neg\neg A]}{\Gamma,\, x : A} \qquad (\sqcup)\colon \frac{\Gamma[x : A \sqcup B]}{\Gamma,\, x : A \mid \Gamma,\, x : B} \qquad (\neg\sqcup)\colon \frac{\Gamma[x : \neg(A \sqcup B)]}{\Gamma,\, x : \neg A,\, x : \neg B}$$

$$(\sqcap)\colon \frac{\Gamma[x : A \sqcap B)]}{\Gamma,\, x : A,\, x : B} \qquad (\neg\sqcap)\colon \frac{\Gamma[x : \neg(A \sqcap B)]}{\Gamma,\, x : \neg A \mid \Gamma,\, x : \neg B}$$

$$(\mathsf{T1}\leftleftarrows)\colon \frac{\Gamma[x : A \leftleftarrows B,\, y : C]}{\Gamma,\, y : \neg B \mid \Gamma,\, y : B} \qquad (\mathsf{F1}\leftleftarrows)\colon \frac{\Gamma[x : \neg(A \leftleftarrows B),\, y : C]}{\Gamma,\, y : A \mid \Gamma,\, y : \neg A}$$

$$(\mathsf{T2}\leftleftarrows)\colon \frac{\Gamma[x : A \leftleftarrows B]}{\Gamma,\, z : f(x, A),\, z : A}(*) \qquad (\mathsf{F2}\leftleftarrows)\colon \frac{\Gamma[x : \neg(A \leftleftarrows B),\, y : A]}{\Gamma,\, z : f(x, B),\, z : B}(*)$$

$$(\mathsf{T3}\leftleftarrows)\colon \frac{\Gamma[x : A \leftleftarrows B,\, z : f(x, A),\, y : B]}{\Gamma,\, z <_x y} \qquad (\mathsf{F3}\leftleftarrows)\colon \frac{\Gamma[x : \neg(A \leftleftarrows B),\, z : f(x, B),\, y : A]}{\Gamma,\, z \leq_x y}$$

$$(\mathsf{cnt})\colon \frac{\Gamma[x : A,\, y : B]}{\Gamma,\, x \leq_x y,\, y \leq_y x} \qquad (\mathsf{asm})\colon \frac{\Gamma[x <_w y]}{\Gamma,\, x \leq_w y} \qquad (\mathsf{tr}\leq)\colon \frac{\Gamma[x \leq_w y,\, y \leq_w z]}{\Gamma,\, x \leq_w z}$$

$$(\mathsf{tr}<)\colon \frac{\Gamma[x <_w y,\, y <_w z]}{\Gamma,\, x <_w z} \qquad (\mathsf{r}\bot)\colon \frac{\Gamma[x <_w y,\, y \leq_w x]}{\bot} \qquad (\bot)\colon \frac{\Gamma[x : A,\, x : \neg A]}{\bot}$$

(*) z is a label not occurring in the current branch.

Fig. 2. Rules for tableau calculus $T_{\mathcal{CSL}^-}$ for $\mathcal{CSL}^-$

$$(\mathsf{T}\textcircled{r})\colon \frac{\Gamma[x : \textcircled{r}A]}{\Gamma,\, z : f(x, A),\, z : A,\, \rho(x, z)}(*) \qquad (\rho\bot)\colon \frac{\Gamma[\neg\rho(x, x)]}{\bot} \qquad (\mathsf{F2}\textcircled{r})\colon \frac{\Gamma[x : \neg\textcircled{r}A,\, y : A]}{\Gamma,\, z : f(x, A),\, z : A}(*)$$

$$(\mathsf{T}f)\colon \frac{\Gamma[x : f(w, A),\, w : (\neg)\textcircled{r}A,\, y : C]}{\Gamma,\, y : \neg A \mid \Gamma,\, y : A,\, x \leq_w y} \qquad (\mathsf{F3}\textcircled{r})\colon \frac{\Gamma[x : \neg\textcircled{r}A,\, z : f(x, A),\, y \leq_x z,\, y : A]}{\Gamma,\, \neg\rho(x, y)}$$

$$(\mathsf{CT}\rho)\colon \frac{\Gamma[\rho(x, y),\, y \leq_x x]}{\Gamma_{s[x,y]}} \qquad (\mathsf{F1}\textcircled{r})\colon \frac{\Gamma[x : \neg\textcircled{r}A,\, y : C]}{\Gamma,\, y : A \mid \Gamma,\, y : \neg A} \qquad (\neg\rho\bot)\colon \frac{\Gamma[\rho(x, y),\, \neg\rho(x, y)]}{\bot}$$

(*) z is a label not occurring in the current branch.

Fig. 3. Additional rules for the tableau calculus $T_{\mathcal{CSL}}$ for $\mathcal{CSL}$

This calculus does not provide a decision procedure, since the interplay between dynamic rules (introducing new labels) and static rules (adding new formulas to which the dynamic rules could be applied) can lead to infinite derivations. In order to make our calculus terminating, we introduce in Definition 13 some restrictions on the application of the rules. Note that to ensure termination we do not need any other assumption on the rule application strategy.

Given a derivation branch **B** and two labels x and y occurring in it, we say that x is older than y if x has been introduced before y in the branch[4]. Note that this older relation is *well founded*. We also define Lab_Γ as the set of all labels occurring in a tableau set Γ, and $\Pi_\Gamma(x) = \{A | A \in \mathcal{L}_{\mathcal{CSL}} \text{ and } x : A \in \Gamma\}$.

Definition 13 (Termination restrictions)

Irredundancy restriction 1. *Do not apply a static rule* $\Gamma/\Gamma_1 \mid \ldots \mid \Gamma_n$ *to a tableau set* Γ *if for some* $1 \leq i \leq n$, $\Gamma_i = \Gamma$.

2. *Do not apply the rule* $(\mathrm{T2}\leftleftarrows)$ *to some formula* $x : A \leftleftarrows B$ *in* Γ *if there exists some label* z *such that* $z : f(x, A)$ *and* $z : A$ *are in* Γ.

[4] From a practical point of view, the order of introduction of the labels can be stored locally within a tableau set and does not require to inspect a whole derivation branch.

3. *Do not apply the rule* (F2$\leftleftarrows$) *to some formulas* $x : \neg(A \leftleftarrows B), y : A$ *if there exists some label* z *such that* $z : f(x, B)$ *and* $z : B$ *are in* Γ.
4. *Do not apply the rule* (T$\circledR$) *to some formula* $x : \circledR A$ *if there exists some label* z *such that* $z : f(x, A)$*,* $z : A$*, and* $\rho(x, z)$ *are in* Γ.
5. *Do not apply the rule* (F2$\circledR$) *to some formulas* $x : \neg\circledR A, y : A$ *if there exists some label* z *such that* $z : f(x, B)$*,* $z : B$*, and* $\neg\rho(x, z)$ *are in* Γ.

Subset blocking. *Do not apply the rule* (T2$\leftleftarrows$) *to a formula* $x : A \leftleftarrows B$*, or the rule* (F2$\leftleftarrows$) *to some formulas* $x : \neg(A \leftleftarrows B), y : B$*, or the rule* (T$\circledR$) *to some formula* $x : \circledR A$*, or the rule* (F2$\circledR$) *to some formulas* $x : \neg\circledR A, y : A$ *if there exists some label* u *older than* x *and such that* $\Pi_\Gamma(x) \subseteq \Pi_\Gamma(u)$.

Substitution restriction. *When performing a substitution* $\Gamma_{s[x,y]}$ *in the rule* (CTρ)*, always replace the younger label by the older.*

The purpose of the termination restrictions is to prevent unnecessary applications of the rules that could lead to infinite derivations, as we prove in the next section. The subset blocking condition is similar to dynamic blocking [5].

A rule R is *applicable* to a tableau set Γ under termination restrictions if it respects all termination restrictions (Definition 13). A derivation is *under termination restrictions* if all rule applications respects the termination restrictions. From now on, we only consider derivations under termination restrictions.

Since termination restrictions prevent the application of some rules we have to define whenever a tableau is open or closed, thereby witnessing the satisfiability (or unsatisfiability) of the input formula.

Definition 14 (Finished/Closed/Open tableau sets, Finished/Closed/Open derivation). *A tableau set is* finished *if no rule is applicable to it. A tableau set* Γ *in a derivation is* closed *if a closure rule is applicable to it, and it is open otherwise. A derivation is* finished *if all its leaf nodes are either finished or closed; it is* closed *if all its leaf nodes are closed, and it is* open *if it contains a finished tableau set.*

In the next section, we prove the termination, soundness and completeness of the calculus for $\mathcal{CSL}$. Since the calculus $T_{\mathcal{CSL}^-}$ is a special case of $T_{\mathcal{CSL}}$, the corresponding property also holds.

Example 15. Let $C = A \sqcap \neg B \sqcap \circledR A \to (A \leftleftarrows B)$ is valid. In order to check whether C is valid, we try to build a closed tableau for $\neg C$ (meaning that $\neg C$ is unsatisfiable). One possible derivation is presented in figure 4.

On the contrary, we show that the formula $C' = A \sqcap \neg B \to (A \leftleftarrows B)$, which is an axiom in the minspace case [2], is not valid in the general distance case: an open derivation for $\neg C'$ is presented in figure 5, giving a counter-model for C'. By applying the construction of Theorem 6, we obtain a distance model $\mathcal{I}$ as follows: $\Delta^{\mathcal{I}} = \{x_i, y_i | i \in \mathbb{N}\}$; for all $i \in \mathbb{N}$, $x_i \in A^{\mathcal{I}}, x_i \notin B^{\mathcal{I}}$ and $y_i \in B^{\mathcal{I}}$; for all $i, j \in \mathbb{N}$, $d(x_i, y_j) = \frac{1}{1+j}$. Thus for all $i \in \mathbb{N}$, $d(x_i, B^{\mathcal{I}}) = 0$ and therefore x_i is in $(A \sqcap \neg B \sqcap \neg(A \leftleftarrows B))^{\mathcal{I}}$.

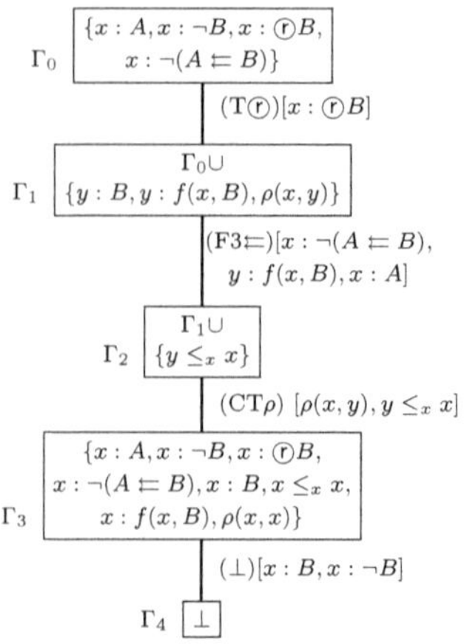

Fig. 4. Closed derivation for $A \sqcap \neg B \sqcap ⓡA \sqcap \neg(A \leftleftarrows B)$

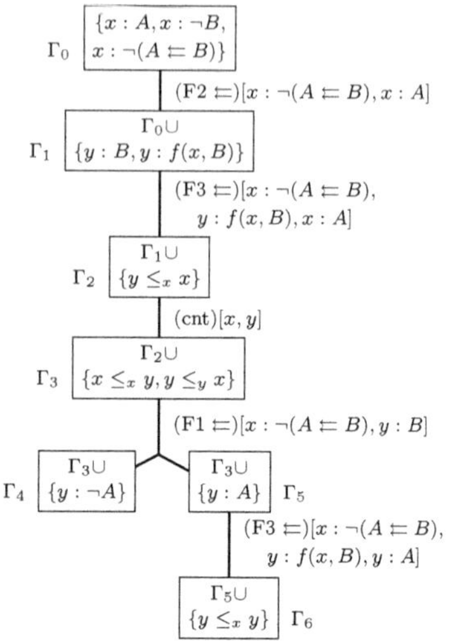

Fig. 5. Open derivation for $A \sqcap \neg B \sqcap \neg(A \leftleftarrows B)$

3.1 Termination

To prove termination we need some technical definitions. We define, for any tableau derivation T, $\Pi(T)$ as the set of all $\mathcal{CSL}$-formulas occurring in T:

$$\Pi(T) \stackrel{\text{def}}{=} \{A \mid A \in \mathcal{L}_{\mathcal{CSL}} \text{ and } x : A \in \Gamma \text{ for some } \Gamma \text{ from } T\}.$$

Given a node Γ in a branch $\mathbf{B}$, and x occurring in Γ or in any of its ancestors, we also define $\sigma^*(\Gamma, x) = x$ if x occurs in Γ, or $\sigma^*(\Gamma, x) = y$ where y is the label which finally replaces x in Γ along a sequence of (CTρ) substitutions applied on the path between Γ and its closest ancestor in which x occurs. Observe that this label y is unique, and is older than x (due to the centering restriction).

Proposition 16 (Monotonicity). *Let Γ be a tableau set in a derivation T, and Γ' be any descendant of Γ in T. Let $x : A$ be in Γ. Then: (i) $\Pi_\Gamma(x) \subseteq \Pi_{\Gamma'}(\sigma^*(\Gamma', x))$. (ii) if $x : A$ is blocked for a rule R in Γ by the irredundancy restriction, then also $\sigma^*(\Gamma', x) : A$ is blocked in Γ' for the rule R by the irredundancy restriction.*

Theorem 17. *Any derivation of $\mathcal{T}_{\mathcal{CSL}}$ under the termination restrictions is finite.*

Proof (Theorem 17). Let T be a derivation for C. By absurd, suppose that T contains an infinite branch $\mathbf{B} = (\Gamma_i)_{i \in \mathbb{N}}$. We can then prove the following:

Fact 18. There exists a dynamic formula D, a subsequence $(\Theta_n)_{n \in \mathbb{N}}$ of $\mathbf{B}$, and a sequence $(x_n)_{n \in \mathbb{N}}$ of labels such that: (i) For all n, $x_n : D \in \Gamma_n$. (ii) For all n, Θ_n is a node corresponding to the application of the corresponding dynamic dynamic rule to the formula $x_n : D$. (iii) There exists a label x^* such that x^* occurs in each Γ_n and for all n, $\Pi_{\Theta_n}(x_n) \subseteq \Pi_{\Theta_n}(x^*)$.

By the previous Facts, we have that (i) for all n, x_n must be older than x^*, as if it were younger no dynamic rule could be applied to $x_n : D$, due to the subset blocking. (ii) for all n, m, if $n \neq m$ then $x_n \neq x_m$, since the irredundancy restriction prevents multiple application of the same rule to the same formulas, due to Proposition 16. Therefore we have an infinite sequence of labels, all different and older than x^*, which is impossible as the relation older is well founded. □

A simple argument (see [3]) show that the size of any branch is exponentially bounded by the size of the initial formula C, so that $\mathcal{T}_{\mathcal{CSL}}$ runs in NEXPTIME.

3.2 Soundness

We first need the following definitions:

Definition 19 ($\mathcal{CSL}$-mapping). *Let Γ be a tableau set and $\mathcal{I}$ be a $\mathcal{CSL}$-preferential model. A $\mathcal{CSL}$-*mapping *m from Γ to $\mathcal{I}$ is a function $m : \mathrm{Lab}_\Gamma \rightarrow \Delta^\mathcal{I}$ such that: a) if $x \leq_w y \in \Gamma$ ($x <_w y \in \Gamma$), then $m(x) \leq^\mathcal{I}_{m(w)} m(y)$ ($m(x) <^\mathcal{I}_{m(w)} m(y)$). b) if $\rho(w,x) \in \Gamma$ ($\neg\rho(w,x) \in \Gamma$), then $(m(w), m(x)) \in \rho^\mathcal{I}$ ($(m(w), m(x)) \notin \rho^\mathcal{I}$).*

We say that a $\mathcal{CSL}$-mapping m is a min-mapping *if it satisfies the following additional property: if $z : f(w, A) \in \Gamma$, then $m(z) \in \min_{\leq_{m(w)}}(A^\mathcal{I})$.*

Definition 20 (Satisfiability). *A tableau set Γ is satisfiable in a $\mathcal{CSL}$-preferential model $\mathcal{I}$ under a $\mathcal{CSL}$-mapping m iff: if $x : A \in \Gamma$, then $m(x) \in A^\mathcal{I}$.*

A tableau set Γ is satisfiable if it is satisfiable in some model $\mathcal{I}$ under some $\mathcal{CSL}$-mapping[5] m.

As usual, we will prove the soundness of the calculus by showing that the rules preserve satisfiability of tableau sets.

Proposition 21 (Soundness of the rules). *Let Γ be a tableau set satisfiable under some min-mapping, and let $\Gamma/\Gamma_1 \mid \ldots \mid \Gamma_n$ be an instance of any rule. Then there is an i such that Γ_i is satisfiable under some min-mapping.*

Observe that if a $\mathcal{CSL}$-formula C is satisfiable, the tableau set $\{x : C\}$, which is the root of any derivation for C, is satisfiable under a min-mapping. Moreover a tableau set to which a closure rule can be applied is unsatisfiable. Therefore, by the previous proposition no derivation for a satisfiable formula C can be closed.

Theorem 22. *If C is a satisfiable $\mathcal{CSL}$-formula, then any tableau derivation for C is open.*

3.3 Completeness

As usual, we first define the saturation of a tableau set. Intuitively, a tableau set is saturated if it is saturated under applications of all rules.

Definition 23 (Saturated tableau set). *A tableau set Γ is saturated if it satisfies the following conditions: (i) Γ satisfies the usual boolean saturation conditions. (ii) if $x : A \leftleftarrows B$, or $x : \neg(B \leftleftarrows A)$, or $x :$ ⓡB, is in Γ, then for*

[5] Note that a min-mapping is also a $\mathcal{CSL}$-mapping.

all y, either $y : B$ *or* $y : \neg B$ *is in* Γ. *(iii) if* $x : A \leftleftarrows B \in \Gamma$, *then there exists a* z *such that* $z : A$ *and* $z : f(x, A)$ *are in* Γ, *and for all* y *such that* $y : B \in \Gamma$, $z <_x y$ *is in* Γ. *(iv) if* $x : \neg(A \leftleftarrows B) \in \Gamma$, *then either a)* $y : \neg A$ *is in* Γ *for all* y *occuring in* Γ, *or (b) there exists a* z *such that* $z : B$, $z : f(x, B)$ *are in* Γ, *and for all* y *such that* $y : A \in \Gamma$, $z \leq_x y$ *is in* Γ. *(v) if* $x : ⓡA \in \Gamma$, *then there exists a* z *such that* $z : f(x, A)$, $z : A$ *and* $\rho(x, z)$ *are in* Γ. *(vi) if* $x : \neg ⓡA \in \Gamma$, *then either (a)* $y : \neg A$ *is in* Γ *for all* y *occuring in* Γ, *or (b) there exists a* z *such that* $z : f(x, A)$, $z : A$ *are in* Γ, *and for all* y, *if* $y : A$ *and* $y \leq_x z$ *are in* Γ, *then* $\neg\rho(x, y)$ *is in* Γ. *(vii) if* $w : (\neg)ⓡA$ *and* $x : f(w, A)$ *are in* Γ, *then for all* y, *either* $y : \neg A$ *is in* Γ, *or* $y : A$ *and* $x \leq_w y$ *are in* Γ. *(viii) if* $x \leq_w w$ *and* $\rho(w, x)$ *are in* Γ, *then* $x = w$. *(ix) for all* x, y *occuring in* Γ, $x \leq_x y$ *and* $y \leq_y x$ *are in* Γ. *(x) if* $x <_w y \in \Gamma$, *then* $x \leq_w y$ *is in* Γ. *(xi) if* $x <_w y$ *and* $y <_w z$ *(resp.* $x \leq_w y$ *and* $y \leq_w z$*) are in* Γ, *then* $x <_w z$ *(resp.* $x \leq_w z$*) is in* Γ.

Lemma 24. *Any open and saturated tableau set is satisfiable.*

Proof (Lemma 24). As usual, we prove the lemma by building a canonical model $\mathcal{M}_C$ from an open saturated tableau set Γ. The main issue is that the preferential relations in Γ are not total preorders, and thus we need to complete them. Let $w \in \text{Lab}_\Gamma$. We first define a relation $=_w$ as follows: for all $x, y \in \text{Lab}_\Gamma$, $x =_w y$ iff $x \leq_w y$ and $y \leq_w x$ are in Γ (note that reflexivity of $=_w$ comes from saturation condition ix with $x = y$). Given a label $x \in \text{Lab}_\Gamma$, we denote by $[x]$ its equivalence class modulo $=_w$. The relation $\leq_w$ in Γ induces a relation $<^e_w$ over the equivalence classes: $[x] <^e_w [y]$ iff exists $x' \in [x]$ and $y' \in [y]$ such that $x' \leq_w y' \in \Gamma$. One can check that $<^e_w$ is a strict partial order (irreflexive, asymmetric, and transitive).

FACT 25. 1. If $x <_w y \in \Gamma$, then $[x] <^e_w [y]$.
2. If $x \leq_w y \in \Gamma$, and $y \leq_w x \notin \Gamma$, then $[x] <^e_w [y]$.

We denote by $<^*_w$ any linear extension of $<^e_w$. We are now ready to define the canonical model $\mathcal{M}_C$ as follows:

- $\Delta^{\mathcal{M}_C} = \text{Lab}_\Gamma$.
- For all $x, y \in \Delta^{\mathcal{M}_C}$, $x \leq^{\mathcal{M}_C}_w y$ iff either (i) $[x] = [y]$, or (ii) $[x] <^*_w [y]$.
- For all $x, y \in \Delta^{\mathcal{M}_C}$, $(x, y) \in \rho^{\mathcal{M}_C}$ iff $\rho(x, y) \in \Gamma$.
- For any propositional variable p, $p^{\mathcal{M}_C} = \{x | x : p \in \Gamma\}$.

It is easy to check that the relations $\leq^{\mathcal{M}_C}_w$ are total pre-orders, and that $\mathcal{M}_C$ satisfies the properties (WKCT) and (RCT) of Definition 4 (due to saturation condition ix and viii), so that $\mathcal{M}_C$ is a well-defined $\mathcal{CSL}$-preferential model.

FACT 26. Γ is satisfiable in $\mathcal{M}_C$ under the identity mapping $\text{id} : x \to x$. □

Due to the blocking conditions (subset blocking) it is not true that every open and finished tableau set is saturated; however we can show that we can always extend an open and finished tableau set to a saturated one.

Lemma 27. *If* Γ *is a finished tableau set, then there exists an open and saturated tableau set* Γ' *such that for every* $\mathcal{CSL}$*-formula* A *and every label* $x \in \text{Lab}_\Gamma$*: if* $x : A \in \Gamma$, *then* $x : A \in \Gamma'$.

Proof (Lemma 27). We say that a label w is blocked by a label u if u is older than w and $\Pi_\Gamma(w) \subseteq \Pi_\Gamma(u)$. To saturate Γ, we will apply the following procedure for every blocked label w, where u is the oldest label blocking w:

1. We delete every formula of the kind $x : f(w, A)$, $\rho(w, x)$, $\neg\rho(w, x)$, $x \leq_w y$, $x <_w y$, for every labels x, y and $\mathcal{CSL}$-formula A.
2. For every tableau formula $x : f(u, A)$, $\rho(u, x)$, $\neg\rho(u, x)$, $x \leq_u y$, $x <_w y$ (with x and y different from u and w) occurring in Γ, we add $x : f(w, A)$, $\rho(w, x)$, $\neg\rho(w, x)$, $x \leq_w y$, $x <_w y$ respectively.
3. For every formula $w : f(u, A)$ in Γ, we add $u : f(w, A)$.
4. For every formula $w \leq_u x$, $x \leq_u w$, $w <_u x$, $x <_u w$ in Γ (with $x \neq u$), we add $u \leq_w x$, $x \leq_w u$, $x <_w u$, $u <_w x$ (respectively).
5. If $u <_u w$, we add $w <_w u$.
6. We add $w \leq_w u$.
7. If $\rho(u, w)$ or $\neg\rho(u, w)$ is in Γ, we add $\rho(w, u)$ or $\neg\rho(w, u)$ (respectively).
8. We add $\rho(w, w)$.

We call Γ' the resulting tableau set. We then have the following fact.

FACT 28. Γ' is open and saturated. □

Since an open derivation contains a finished tableau set, by Lemmas 24 and 27, we finally obtain:

Theorem 29. *If there exist an open derivation for C, then C is satisfiable.*

4 Conclusion

In this work we have contributed to the study of automated deduction for the logic of comparative similarity $\mathcal{CSL}$ and its pure comparative fragment $\mathcal{CSL}^-$ interpreted arbitrary distance spaces. Our first result is that the distance space semantics is equivalent to preferential model semantics. As a consequence, we have obtained a proof of the finite model property for $\mathcal{CSL}$ with respect to its preferential semantics. Then we have presented a labeled tableau calculus which gives a practically implementable decision procedure for this logic. Our calculus gives a NExpTime decision procedure for satisfiability of $\mathcal{CSL}$ formulas, which however is not optimal in the light of the known ExpTime upper bound. Despite its non-optimality, we believe that the interest of a tableau calculus like the one we have presented lies in its pure declarative meaning: it is just a set of rules, independent from any algorithmic detail. Of course a battery of techniques might be applied to make it more efficient, first of all to control rules comprising analytic cut. To match the known ExpTime upper bound, we intend also to investigate whether our tableau method can be reformulated as a global caching algorithm [4], which usually provides optimal decision procedures.

In [2] a labeled tableau calculus for $\mathcal{CSL}^-$ over non symmetric minspaces is presented, implemented in a theorem prover [1]. This calculus is similar to the one introduced in this work for $\mathcal{CSL}^-$ as they are both based on the preferential semantics. However, it makes use of a family of modalities indexed on labels/objects and needs specific rules for handling them. Moreover termination is obtained by imposing more complex blocking restrictions. In [3], tableau calculi are provided for both $\mathcal{CSL}^-$ interpreted on both symmetric and non-symmetric minspaces. The calculus for $\mathcal{CSL}^-$ over non-symmetric minspaces is very similar to the one presented here in terms of rules; however the interpretation of the overall construction is significantly different: in $\mathcal{T}_{\mathcal{CSL}^-}$ a blocked finished tableau set provides a model of the right type, in contrast in the calculus presented in [3] a blocked finished tableau set is disregarded as it represents a potentially infinite model violating the minspace property. Finally, in [11], a tableau algorithm is proposed to handle a subset of $\mathcal{QML}$ comprising distance quantifiers of the form $\exists^{\leq a}$, where a is positive integer (together with an interior and a closure operator). The method proposed in [11] makes use of an elegant relational translation to handle distance quantifiers with fixed parameters. However, it is not clear if a similar method can be adapted to full $\mathcal{QML}$ and its modal counterpart $\mathcal{CSL}$.

In further research we shall investigate if we can extend the semantic characterization of $\mathcal{CSL}$ in terms of preferential models to other classes of models, notably based on metric spaces. These results could be the starting point to develop corresponding tableaux calculi.

References

1. Alenda, R., Olivetti, N., Pozzato, G.L.: Csl-lean: A theorem-prover for the logic of comparative concept similarity. ENTCS 262, 3–16 (2010)
2. Alenda, R., Olivetti, N., Schwind, C.: Comparative concept similarity over minspaces: Axiomatisation and tableaux calculus. In: Giese, M., Waaler, A. (eds.) TABLEAUX 2009. LNCS, vol. 5607, pp. 17–31. Springer, Heidelberg (2009)
3. Alenda, R., Olivetti, N., Schwind, C., Tishkovsky, D.: Tableau calculi for csl over minspaces. In: Proc. CSL 2010. LNCS. Springer, Heidelberg (to appear, 2010)
4. Goré, R., Nguyen, L.A.: Exptime tableaux with global caching for description logics with transitive roles, inverse roles and role hierarchies. In: Olivetti, N. (ed.) TABLEAUX 2007. LNCS (LNAI), vol. 4548, pp. 133–148. Springer, Heidelberg (2007)
5. Horrocks, I., Sattler, U.: A description logic with transitive and inverse roles and role hierarchies. J. Logic Computation 9(3), 385–410 (1999)
6. Kurucz, A., Wolter, F., Zakharyaschev, M.: Modal logics for metric spaces: Open problems. In: We Will Show Them!, vol. (2), pp. 193–108. College Publ. (2005)
7. Lewis, D.: Counterfactuals. Basil Blackwell Ltd., Malden (1973)
8. Sheremet, M., Tishkovsky, D., Wolter, F., Zakharyaschev, M.: Comparative similarity, tree automata, and diophantine equations. In: Sutcliffe, G., Voronkov, A. (eds.) LPAR 2005. LNCS (LNAI), vol. 3835, pp. 651–665. Springer, Heidelberg (2005)
9. Sheremet, M., Tishkovsky, D., Wolter, F., Zakharyaschev, M.: A logic for concepts and similarity. J. Log. Comput. 17(3), 415–452 (2007)
10. Sheremet, M., Wolter, F., Zakharyaschev, M.: A modal logic framework for reasoning about comparative distances and topology. Annals of Pure and Applied Logic 161(4), 534–559 (2010)
11. Wolter, F., Zakharyaschev, M.: Reasoning about distances. In: Proceedings of IJCAI 2003, pp. 1275–1280. Morgan Kaufmann, San Francisco (2003)

Extended Computation Tree Logic

Roland Axelsson[1], Matthew Hague[2], Stephan Kreutzer[2], Martin Lange[3], and Markus Latte[1]

[1] Department of Computer Science, Ludwig-Maximilians-Universität Munich
{roland.axelsson,markus.latte}@ifi.lmu.de
[2] Oxford University Computing Laboratory
{Matthew.Hague,stephan.kreutzer}@comlab.ox.ac.uk
[3] Department of Elect. Engineering and Computer Science, University of Kassel, Germany
martin.lange@uni-kassel.de

Abstract. We introduce a generic extension of the popular branching-time logic CTL which refines the temporal until and release operators with formal languages. For instance, a language may determine the moments along a path that an until property may be fulfilled. We consider several classes of languages leading to logics with different expressive power and complexity, whose importance is motivated by their use in model checking, synthesis, abstract interpretation, etc. We show that even with context-free languages on the until operator the logic still allows for polynomial time model-checking despite the significant increase in expressive power. This makes the logic a promising candidate for applications in verification. In addition, we analyse the complexity of satisfiability and compare the expressive power of these logics to CTL* and extensions of PDL.

1 Introduction

Computation Tree Logic (CTL) is one of the main logical formalisms for program specification and verification. It appeals because of its intuitive syntax and its very reasonable complexities: model checking is PTIME-complete [9] and satisfiability checking is EXPTIME-complete [12]. However, its expressive power is low.

CTL can be embedded into richer formalisms like CTL* [13] or the modal μ-calculus $\mathcal{L}_\mu$ [22]. This transition comes at a price. For CTL* the model checking problem increases to PSPACE-complete [30] and satisfiability to 2EXPTIME-complete [14,33]. Furthermore, CTL* cannot express regular properties like "something holds after an even number of steps". The modal μ-calculus is capable of doing so, and its complexities compare reasonably to CTL: satisfiability is also EXPTIME-complete, and model checking sits between PTIME and NP$\cap$coNP. However, it is much worse from a pragmatic perspective since its syntax is notoriously unintuitive.

Common to all these (and many other) formalisms is a restriction of their expressive power to at most regular properties. This follows since they can be embedded into (the bisimulation-invariant) fragment of monadic second-order logic on graphs. This restriction yields some nice properties — like the finite model property and decidability — but implies that these logics cannot be used for certain specification purposes.

For example, specifying the correctness of a communication protocol that uses a buffer requires a non-underflow property: an item cannot be removed when the buffer is

C. Fermüller and A. Voronkov (Eds.): LPAR-17, LNCS 6397, pp. 67–81, 2010.

empty. The specification language must therefore be able to track the buffer's size. If the buffer is unbounded, as is usual in software, this property is non-regular and a regular logic is unsuitable. If the buffer is bounded, the property is regular but depends on the actual buffer capacity, requiring a different formula for each size. This is unnatural for verification purposes. The formulas are also likely to be complex as they essentially have to hard-code numbers up to the buffer length. To express such properties naturally one has to step beyond regularity and consider logics of corresponding expressive power.

Also, consider program synthesis where, instead of verifying a program, one wants to automatically generate a correct program (skeleton) from the specification. This problem is very much linked to satisfiability checking, except, if a model exists, one is created and transformed into a program. This is known as controller synthesis and has been done mainly based on satisfiability checking for the modal μ-calculus [4]. The finite model property restricts the synthesization to finite state programs, i.e. hardware and controllers, etc. In order to automatically synthesize software (e.g. recursive functions) one has to consider non-regular logics.

Finally, consider the problem of verifying programs with infinite or very large state spaces. A standard technique is to abstract the large state space into a smaller one [10]. This usually results in spurious traces which then have to be excluded in universal path quantification on the small system. If the original system was infinite then the language of spurious traces is typically non-regular and, again, a logic of suitable expressive power is needed to increase precision [25].

In this paper we introduce a generic extension of CTL which provides a specification formalism for such purposes. We refine the usual until operator (and its dual, the release operator) with a formal language defining the moments at which the until property can be fulfilled. This leads to a family of logics parametrised by a class of formal languages. CTL is an ideal base logic because of its wide-spread use in actual verification applications. Since automata easily allow for an unambiguous measure of input size, we present the precise definition of our logics in terms of classes of automata instead of formal languages. However, we do not promote the use of automata in temporal formulas. For pragmatic considerations it may be sensible to allow more intuitive descriptions of formal languages such as Backus-Naur-Form or regular expressions.

As a main result we extend CTL using context-free languages, significantly increasing expressive power, while retaining polynomial time model-checking. Hence, we obtain a good balance between expressiveness — as non-regular properties become expressible — and low model-checking complexity, which makes this logic very promising for applications in verification. We also study model-checking for the new logics against infinite state systems represented by (visibly) pushdown automata, as they arise in software model-checking, and obtain tractability results for these. For satisfiability testing, equipping the path quantifiers with visibly pushdown languages retains decidability. However, the complexity increases from EXPTIME for CTL to 3EXPTIME for this new logic.

The paper is organised as follows. We formally introduce the logics and give an example demonstrating their expressive power in Section 2. Section 3 discusses related formalisms. Section 4 presents results on the expressive power of these logics, and Section 5 and 6 contain results on the complexities of satisfiability and model checking.

Finally, Section 7 concludes with remarks on further work. Due to space restrictions this paper contains no detailed proofs in its main part. A full version with all proof details is available online at `http://arxiv.org/abs/1006.3709`.

2 Extended Computation Tree Logic

Let $\mathcal{P} = \{p, q, \ldots\}$ be a countably infinite set of *propositions* and Σ be a finite set of *action names*. A *labeled transition system* (LTS) is a $\mathcal{T} = (\mathcal{S}, \rightarrow, \ell)$, where $\mathcal{S}$ is a set of states, $\rightarrow \subseteq \mathcal{S} \times \Sigma \times \mathcal{S}$ and $\ell : \mathcal{S} \rightarrow 2^{\mathcal{P}}$. We usually write $s \xrightarrow{a} t$ instead of $(s, a, t) \in \rightarrow$. A *path* is a maximal sequence of alternating states and actions $\pi = s_0, a_1, s_1, a_2, s_2, \ldots$, s.t. $s_i \xrightarrow{a_{i+1}} s_{i+1}$ for all $i \in \mathbb{N}$. We also write a path as $s_0 \xrightarrow{a_1} s_1 \xrightarrow{a_2} s_2 \ldots$. Maximality means that the path is either infinite or it ends in a state s_n s.t. there are no $a \in \Sigma$ and $t \in \mathcal{S}$ with $s_n \xrightarrow{a} t$. In the latter case, the domain $dom(\pi)$ of π is $\{0, \ldots, n\}$. And otherwise $dom(\pi){:=}\mathbb{N}$.

We focus on automata classes between deterministic finite automata (DFA) and nondeterministic pushdown automata (PDA), with the classes of nondeterministic finite automata (NFA), (non-)deterministic visibly pushdown automata (DVPA/VPA) [2] and deterministic pushdown automata (DPDA) in between. Beyond PDA one is often faced with undecidability. Note that some of these automata classes define the same class of languages. However, translations from nondeterministic to deterministic automata usually involve an exponential blow-up. For complexity estimations it is therefore advisable to consider such classes separately.

We call a class $\mathfrak{A}$ of automata *reasonable* if it contains automata recognising Σ and Σ^* and is closed under equivalences, i.e. if $\mathcal{A} \in \mathfrak{A}$ and $L(\mathcal{A}) = L(\mathcal{B})$ and $\mathcal{B}$ is of the same type then $\mathcal{B} \in \mathfrak{A}$. $L(\mathcal{A})$ denotes the language accepted by $\mathcal{A}$.

Let $\mathfrak{A}, \mathfrak{B}$ be two reasonable classes of finite-word automata over the alphabet Σ. Formulas of *Extended Computation Tree Logic over* $\mathfrak{A}$ *and* $\mathfrak{B}$ (CTL[$\mathfrak{A}$,$\mathfrak{B}$]) are given by the following grammar, where $\mathcal{A} \in \mathfrak{A}$, $\mathcal{B} \in \mathfrak{B}$ and $q \in \mathcal{P}$.

$$\varphi \;::=\; q \mid \varphi \vee \varphi \mid \neg\varphi \mid \mathtt{E}(\varphi \mathtt{U}^{\mathcal{A}} \varphi) \mid \mathtt{E}(\varphi \mathtt{R}^{\mathcal{B}} \varphi)$$

Formulas are interpreted over states of a transition system $\mathcal{T} = (\mathcal{S}, \rightarrow, \ell)$ in the following way.

- $\mathcal{T}, s \models q$ iff $q \in \ell(s)$
- $\mathcal{T}, s \models \varphi \vee \psi$ iff $\mathcal{T}, s \models \varphi$ or $\mathcal{T}, s \models \psi$
- $\mathcal{T}, s \models \neg\varphi$ iff $\mathcal{T}, s \not\models \varphi$
- $\mathcal{T}, s \models \mathtt{E}(\varphi \mathtt{U}^{\mathcal{A}} \psi)$ iff there exists a path $\pi = s_0, a_1, s_1, \ldots$ with $s_0 = s$ and $\exists n \in dom(\pi)$ s.t. $a_1 \ldots a_n \in L(\mathcal{A})$ and $\mathcal{T}, s_n \models \psi$ and $\forall i < n : \mathcal{T}, s_i \models \varphi$.
- $\mathcal{T}, s \models \mathtt{E}(\varphi \mathtt{R}^{\mathcal{A}} \psi)$ iff there exists a path $\pi = s_0, a_1, s_1, \ldots$ with $s_0 = s$ and for all $n \in dom(\pi)$: $a_1 \ldots a_n \notin L(\mathcal{A})$ or $\mathcal{T}, s_n \models \psi$ or $\exists i < n$ s.th. $\mathcal{T}, s_i \models \varphi$.

As usual, further syntactical constructs, like other boolean operators, are introduced as abbreviations. We define $\mathtt{A}(\varphi \mathtt{U}^{\mathcal{A}} \psi) := \neg\mathtt{E}(\neg\varphi \mathtt{R}^{\mathcal{A}} \neg\psi)$, $\mathtt{A}(\varphi \mathtt{R}^{\mathcal{A}} \psi) := \neg\mathtt{E}(\neg\varphi \mathtt{U}^{\mathcal{A}} \neg\psi)$, as well as $Q\mathtt{F}^{\mathcal{A}}\varphi := Q(\mathtt{tt}\mathtt{U}^{\mathcal{A}}\varphi)$, $Q\mathtt{G}^{\mathcal{A}}\varphi := Q(\mathtt{ff}\mathtt{R}^{\mathcal{A}}\varphi)$ for $Q \in \{\mathtt{E}, \mathtt{A}\}$. For presentation, we also use languages L instead of automata in the temporal operators. For instance,

$\texttt{EG}^L\varphi$ is $\texttt{EG}^{\mathcal{A}}\varphi$ for some $\mathcal{A}$ with $L(\mathcal{A}) = L$. This also allows us to easily define the original CTL operators: $Q\texttt{X}\varphi := Q\texttt{F}^{\Sigma}\varphi$, $Q(\varphi\texttt{U}\psi) := Q(\varphi\texttt{U}^{\Sigma^*}\psi)$, $Q(\varphi\texttt{R}\psi) := Q(\varphi\texttt{R}^{\Sigma^*}\psi)$, etc. The size of a formula φ is the number of its unique subformulas plus the sum of the sizes of all automata in φ, with the usual measure of size of an automaton.

The distinction between $\mathfrak{A}$ and $\mathfrak{B}$ is motivated by the complexity analysis. For instance, when model checking $\texttt{E}(\varphi\texttt{U}^{\mathcal{A}}\psi)$ the existential quantifications over system paths and runs of $\mathcal{A}$ commute and we can guess a path and an accepting run in a step-wise fashion. On the other hand, when checking $\texttt{E}(\varphi\texttt{R}^{\mathcal{A}}\psi)$ the existential quantification on paths and universal quantification on runs (by R — "on all prefixes ...") does not commute unless we determinise $\mathcal{A}$, which is not always possible or may lead to exponential costs.

However, $\mathfrak{A}$ and $\mathfrak{B}$ can also be the same and in this case we denote the logic by CTL[$\mathfrak{A}$]. Equally, by EF[$\mathfrak{A}$], resp. EG[$\mathfrak{B}$] we denote the fragments of CTL[$\mathfrak{A}$,$\mathfrak{B}$] built from atomic propositions, boolean operators and the temporal operators $\texttt{EF}^{\mathcal{A}}\varphi$, resp. $\texttt{EG}^{\mathcal{B}}\varphi$ only. Since the expressive power of the logic only depends on its class of *languages* rather than *automata*, we will write CTL[REG], CTL[VPL], CTL[CFL], etc. to denote the logic over regular, visibly pushdown, and context-free languages, represented by any type of automaton. We close this section with a CTL[VPL] example which demonstrates the buffer-underflow property discussed in the introduction.

Example. Consider a concurrent producer/consumer scenario over a shared buffer. If the buffer is empty, the consumer process requests a new resource and halts until the producer delivers a new one. Any parallel execution of these processes should obey a non-underflow property (NBU): at any moment, the number of produce actions is sufficient for the number of consumes.

If the buffer is realised in software it is reasonable to assume that it is unbounded, and thus, the NBU property becomes non-regular. Let $\Sigma = \{p, c, r\}$, where p stands for *production* of a buffer object, c for *consume* and r for *request*. Consider the VPL $L = \{w \in \Sigma^* \mid |w|_c = |w|_p \text{ and } |v|_c \leq |v|_p \text{ for all } v \preceq w\}$, where $\preceq$ denotes the prefix relation. We express the requirements in CTL[VPL].

1. $\texttt{AGEX}^p\texttt{tt}$: "at any time it is possible to produce an object"
2. $\texttt{AG}^L(\texttt{AX}^c\texttt{ff} \wedge \texttt{EX}^r\texttt{tt})$: "whenever the buffer is empty, it is impossible to consume and possible to request"
3. $\texttt{AG}^{\overline{L}}(\texttt{EX}^c\texttt{tt} \wedge \texttt{AX}^r\texttt{ff})$: "whenever the buffer is non-empty it is possible to consume and impossible to request"
4. $\texttt{EFEG}^{\overline{c^*}}\texttt{ff}$: "at some point there is a consume-only path"

Combining the first three properties yields a specification of the scenario described above and states that a *request* can only be made if the buffer is empty. For the third properly, recall that VPL are closed under complement [2]. Every satisfying model gives a raw implementation of the main characteristics of the system. Note that if it is always possible to *produce* and possible to *consume* iff the buffer is not empty, then a straight-forward model with self-loops p, c and r does not satisfy the specification. Instead, we require a model with infinitely many different p transitions. If we strengthen the specification by adding the fourth formula, it becomes unsatisfiable.

3 Related Formalisms

Several suggestions to integrate formal languages into temporal logics have been made so far. The goal is usually to extend the expressive power of a logic whilst retaining its intuitive syntax. The most classic example is Propositional Dynamic Logic (PDL) [17] which extends Modal Logic with regular expressions.

Similar extensions — sometimes using finite automata instead of regular expressions — of Temporal Logics have been investigated a long time ago. The main purpose has usually been the aim to increase the expressive power of seemingly weak specification formalisms in order to obtain at least ω-regular expressivity, but no efforts have been made at that point in order to go beyond that. This also explains why such extensions were mainly based on LTL [37,34,23,20], i.e. not leaving the world of linear-time formalisms.

The need for extensions beyond the use of pure temporal operators is also witnessed by the industry-standard *Property Specification Language* (PSL) [1] and its predecessor ForSpec [3]. However, ForSpec is a linear-time formalism and here we are concerned with branching-time. PSL does contain branching-time operators but they have been introduced for backwards-compatibility only.

On the other hand, some effort has been made with regards to extensions of branching-time logics like CTL [5,7,27]. These all refine the temporal operators of this logic with regular languages in some form.

Thus, while much effort has been put into regular extensions of standard temporal logics, little is known about extensions using richer classes of formal languages. We are only aware of extensions of PDL by context-free languages [19] or visibly pushdown languages [26]. The main yardstick for measuring the expressive power of CTL[$\mathfrak{A}$,$\mathfrak{B}$] will be therefore be PDL and one of its variants, namely PDL with the Δ-construct and tests, $\Delta\mathrm{PDL}^?[\mathfrak{A}]$, [17,31]. Note: for a class $\mathfrak{A}$ of automata, CTL[$\mathfrak{A}$] is a logic using such automata on finite words only, whereas $\Delta\mathrm{PDL}^?[\mathfrak{A}]$ uses those and their Büchi-variants on infinite words. In the following we will use some of the known results about $\Delta\mathrm{PDL}^?[\mathfrak{A}]$. For a detailed technical definition of its syntax and semantics, we refer to the literature on this logic [18].

There are also temporal logics which obtain higher expressive power through other means. These are usually extensions of $\mathcal{L}_\mu$ like the Modal Iteration Calculus [11] which uses inflationary fixpoint constructs or Higher-Order Fixpoint Logic [35] which uses higher-order predicate transformers. While most regular extensions of standard temporal logics like CTL and LTL can easily be embedded into $\mathcal{L}_\mu$, little is known about the relationship between richer extensions of these logics.

4 Expressivity and Model Theory

We write $\mathcal{L} \leq_f \mathcal{L}'$ with $f \in \{\mathsf{lin}, \mathsf{exp}\}$ to state that for every formula $\varphi \in \mathcal{L}$ there is an equivalent $\psi \in \mathcal{L}'$ with at most a linear or exponential (respectively) blow up in size. We use $\mathcal{L} \lneq_f \mathcal{L}'$ to denote that such a translation exists, but there are formulas of $\mathcal{L}'$ which are not equivalent to any formula in $\mathcal{L}$. Also, we write $\mathcal{L} \equiv_f \mathcal{L}'$ if $\mathcal{L} \leq_f \mathcal{L}'$ and $\mathcal{L}' \leq_f \mathcal{L}$. We will drop the index if a potential blow-up is of no concern.

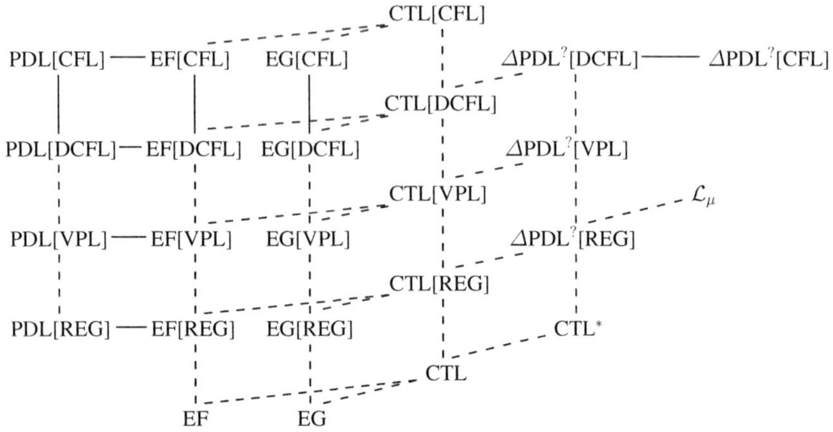

Fig. 1. The expressive power of Extended Computation Tree Logic

A detailed picture of the expressivity results regarding the most important CTL[$\mathfrak{A}$] logics is given in Fig. 1. A (dashed) line moving upwards indicates (strict) inclusion w.r.t. expressive power. A horizontal continuous line states expressive equivalence. The following proposition collects some simple observations.

Proposition 4.1. *1. For all* $\mathfrak{A}, \mathfrak{B}$*:* CTL $\lneqq_{\mathsf{lin}}$ CTL[$\mathfrak{A}$,$\mathfrak{B}$].
2. For all $\mathfrak{A}, \mathfrak{A}', \mathfrak{B}, \mathfrak{B}'$*: if* $\mathfrak{A} \leq \mathfrak{A}'$ *and* $\mathfrak{B} \leq \mathfrak{B}'$ *then* CTL[$\mathfrak{A}$,$\mathfrak{B}$] $\leq$ CTL[$\mathfrak{A}'$,$\mathfrak{B}'$].

CTL[$\mathfrak{A}$] extends PDL[$\mathfrak{A}$] since the latter is just a syntactic variation of the EF[$\mathfrak{A}$] fragment. On the other hand, CTL[$\mathfrak{A}$] can — in certain cases — be embedded into PDL[$\mathfrak{A}$]'s extension ΔPDL$^?$[$\mathfrak{A}$]. This, however, requires a transformation from automata on finite words to automata on infinite words which shows that these two formalisms are conceptually different.

Theorem 4.2. *1. For all* $\mathfrak{A}$*:* PDL[$\mathfrak{A}$] $\equiv_{\mathsf{lin}}$ EF[$\mathfrak{A}$].
2. For all $\mathfrak{A}, \mathfrak{B}$*:* EF[$\mathfrak{A}$] $\lneqq_{\mathsf{lin}}$ CTL[$\mathfrak{A}$,$\mathfrak{B}$].
3. For all $\mathfrak{A}, \mathfrak{B}$*:* CTL[$\mathfrak{A}$,$\mathfrak{B}$] $\leq_{\mathsf{lin}}$ ΔPDL$^?$[$\mathfrak{A} \cup \mathfrak{B}$]*, if* $\mathfrak{B}$ *is a class of deterministic automata.*
4. ΔPDL$^?$[PDA] $\equiv_{\mathsf{lin}}$ ΔPDL$^?$[DPDA].

Note that CFL does not admit deterministic automata. Hence, part 3 is not applicable in that case. If for some classes $\mathfrak{A}$,$\mathfrak{B}$ the inclusion in part 3 holds, then it must be strict. This is because fairness is not expressible in CTL[$\mathfrak{A}$] regardless of what $\mathfrak{A}$ is, as demonstrated by the following.

Theorem 4.3. *The* CTL**-formula* EGFq *expressing fairness is not equivalent to any* CTL[$\mathfrak{A}$, $\mathfrak{B}$] *formula, for any* $\mathfrak{A}$, $\mathfrak{B}$.

Fairness can be expressed by $\Delta\mathcal{A}_{\mathsf{fair}}$, where $\mathcal{A}_{\mathsf{fair}}$ is the standard Büchi automaton over some alphabet containing a test predicate q? that recognises the language of all infinite paths on which infinitely many states satisfy q.

Corollary 4.4. *1. For all* $\mathfrak{A}, \mathfrak{B}$*:* CTL* $\not\leq$ CTL[$\mathfrak{A}$,$\mathfrak{B}$].
2. *There are no* $\mathfrak{A}$,$\mathfrak{B}$ *such that any* CTL[$\mathfrak{A}$,$\mathfrak{B}$] *is equivalent to the* ΔPDL$^?$[REG] *formula* $\Delta\mathcal{A}_{\mathsf{fair}}$.

At least in the case of CFLs, the premise to part 3 of Thm. 4.2 cannot be dropped. Indeed, the formula $\mathtt{EG}^L p$ is not expressible as a ΔPDL$^?$[CFL]-formula where L is the language of palindromes.

Theorem 4.5. CTL[CFL] $\not\leq$ ΔPDL$^?$[CFL].

Finally, we provide some model-theoretic results which will also allow us to separate some of the logics with respect to expressive power. Not surprisingly, CTL[REG] has the finite model property which is a consequence of its embedding into the logic ΔPDL$^?$[REG]. It is not hard to bound the size of such a model given that ΔPDL$^?$[REG] has the small model property of exponential size.

Proposition 4.6. *Every satisfiable* CTL[REG] *formula has a finite model. In fact, every satisfiable* CTL[NFA,DFA], *resp.* CTL[NFA,NFA] *formula has a model of at most exponential, resp. double exponential size.*

We show now that the bound for CTL[NFA] cannot be improved.

Theorem 4.7. *There is a sequence of satisfiable* CTL[NFA]*-formulas* $(\psi_n)_{n\in\mathbb{N}}$ *such that the size of any model of* ψ_n *is at least doubly exponential in* $|\psi_n|$.

The next theorem provides information about the type of models we can expect. This is useful for synthesis purposes.

Theorem 4.8. *1. There is a satisfiable* CTL[VPL] *formula which does not have a finite model.*
2. *There is a satisfiable* CTL[DCFL] *formula which has no pushdown system as a model.*
3. *Every satisfiable* CTL[VPL] *formula has a visibly pushdown system as a model.*

Proof (Sketch of Part 3). The satisfiability problem for CTL[VPL] can be translated into that of a non-deterministic Büchi visibly pushdown tree automaton (VPTA). An unrolling of this automaton does not necessarily lead to the claimed visibly pushdown system. First, such a system might admit paths which violate the Büchi condition. And secondly, the lack of determinism combines successors of different transitions undesirably. However, Thm. 4.2 Part 3 states that CTL[VPL] can be translated into ΔPDL$^?$[VPL] whose satisfiability problem reduces to the emptiness problem for stair-parity VPTA [26]. There exists an exponential reduction from stair-parity VPTA to parity tree automata (PTA) which preserves satisfiability. The emptiness test is constructive in the sense that for every PTA accepting a non-empty language there exists a finite transition system which satisfies this PTA. This system can be translated back into a visibly pushdown system satisfying the given CTL[VPL]- or ΔPDL$^?$[VPL]-formula. Implementing this idea, however, requires some care and is technically involved. □

Putting Thm. 4.5, Prop. 4.6 and Thm. 4.8 together we obtain the following separations. Note that the first three inequalities of the corollary can also be obtained from language theoretical observations.

Corollary 4.9. CTL[REG] $\lneq$ CTL[VPL] $\lneq$ CTL[DCFL] $\lneq$ CTL[CFL].

5 Satisfiability

In this section we study the complexity of the satisfiability problem for a variety of CTL[$\mathfrak{A}$,$\mathfrak{B}$] logics. The presented lower and upper bounds, as shown in Fig. 2, also yield sharp bounds for EF[_] and CTL[_].

Theorem 5.1. *The satisfiability problems for* CTL[DPDA, _] *and for* CTL[_, DPDA] *are undecidable.*

Proof. Harel et al. [19] show that PDL over regular programs with the one additional language $L{:=}\{a^nba^n \mid n \in \mathbb{N}\}$ is undecidable. Since $L \in$ DCFL $\supseteq$ REG, the logic EF[DPDA] is undecidable and hence so is CTL[DPDA, _]. As for the second claim, the undecidable intersection problem of two DPDA, say $\mathcal{A}$ and $\mathcal{B}$, can be reduced to the satisfiability problem of the CTL[_, DPDA]-formula $\mathtt{AF}^{\mathcal{A}}\mathtt{AXff} \wedge \mathtt{AF}^{\mathcal{B}}\mathtt{AXff}$. Note that a single state with no outgoing transitions still has outgoing paths labeled with ϵ. This formula is therefore only satisfiable if $L(\mathcal{A}) \cap L(\mathcal{B}) \neq \emptyset$. □

Theorem 5.2. *The upper bounds for the satisfiability problem are as in Fig. 2.*

Proof. By Thm. 4.2(3), CTL[$\mathfrak{A}$, $\mathfrak{B}$] can be translated into ΔPDL$^?$[$\mathfrak{A} \cup \mathfrak{B}$] with a blow-up that is determined by the worst-case complexity of transforming an arbitrary $\mathfrak{A}$-automaton into a deterministic one. The claim follows using that REG $\subseteq$ VPL and that the satisfiability problem for ΔPDL$^?$[REG] is in EXPTIME [15] and for ΔPDL$^?$[VPL] is in 2EXPTIME [26]. □

The hardness results are more technically involved.

Theorem 5.3. *1.* CTL[DFA, NFA] *and* CTL[_, DVPA] *are 2EXPTIME-hard.*
2. CTL[DVPA, NFA] *and* CTL[_, DVPA $\cup$ NFA] *are 3EXPTIME-hard.*

Corollary 5.4. *The lower bounds for the satisfiability problem are as in Fig. 2.*

Proof. As CTL is EXPTIME-hard [12], so is CTL[_, _]. The 2EXPTIME lower bound for PDL[DVPA] [26] is also a lower bound for CTL[DVPA, _] due to Thm. 4.2. Finally, Thm. 5.3 and Prop. 4.1(2) complete the picture. □

In the remaining part of this section we sketch the proof of Thm. 5.3. For each of the four lower bounds, we reduce from the word problem of an alternating Turing machine T with an exponentially or doubly exponentially, resp., space bound. These problems are 2EXPTIME-hard and 3EXPTIME-hard [8], respectively.

A run of such a machine can be depicted as a tree. Every node stands for a configuration — that is, for simplicity, a bounded sequence of cells. An universal choice corresponds to a binary branching node, and an existential choice to an unary node. We aim to construct a CTL[_,_]-formula φ such that each of its tree-like models resembles a tree expressing a successful run of T on a given input. Thereto, the configurations are linearized — an edge becomes a chain of edges, in the intended model, and a node represents a single cell. The content of each cell is encoded as a proposition. However, the linearization separates neighboring cells of consecutive configurations. Between these cells, certain constraints have to hold. So, the actual challenge for the reduction is that φ

	DFA	NFA	DVPA	VPA	DPDA, PDA
DFA, NFA	EXPTIME	2EXPTIME	2EXPTIME	3EXPTIME	undec.
DVPA, VPA	2EXPTIME	3EXPTIME	2EXPTIME	3EXPTIME	undec.
DPDA, PDA	undec.	undec.	undec.	undec.	undec.

Fig. 2. The time complexities of checking satisfiability for a CTL[$\mathfrak{A}$,$\mathfrak{B}$] formula. Entries denote completeness results. The rows contain different values for $\mathfrak{A}$ as the results are independent of whether or not the automata from this class are deterministic.

must bridge this exponential or doubly exponential, resp., gap while be of a polynomial size in n, i.e. in the input size to T.

We sketch the construction for CTL[DFA, NFA]. The exponential space bound can be controlled by a binary counter. Hence, the constraint applies only to consecutive positions with the same counter value. To bridge between two such positions, we use a proof obligation of the form $\mathtt{AU}^{\mathcal{A}}$ for a NFA $\mathcal{A}$. In a tree model, we say that a node has a *proof obligation* for an AU-formula iff that formula is forced to hold at an ancestor but is not yet satisfied along the path to the said node. The key idea is that we can replace $\mathcal{A}$ by an equivalent automaton $\mathcal{D}$ without changing the models of φ. In our setting, $\mathcal{D}$ is the deterministic automaton resulting from the powerset-construction [28]. In other words, we simulate an exponentially sized automaton. Here, the mentioned obligation reflects the value of the counter and the expected content of a cell.

One of the building blocks of φ programs the obligation with the current value of the counter. Thereto, we encode the counter as a chain of labels in the model, say $(\mathtt{bit}_i^{b_i})_{1\leq i\leq n}$ where $b_i \in \mathbb{B}$ is the value of the ith bit. The automaton $\mathcal{A}$ contains states q_i^b for all $1 \leq i \leq n$ and $b \in \mathbb{B}$. Initially, it is ensured that $\mathcal{D}$ is in the state $\{q_i^b \mid 1 \leq i \leq n, b \in \mathbb{B}\}$. Informally, this set holds all possibilities for the values of each bit. In $\mathcal{A}$, any q_i^b has self-loops for any label except for $\mathtt{bit}_i^{\neg b}$. Hence, a traversal of a chain eliminates invalid bit assignments from the subset and brings $\mathcal{D}$ into the state $\{q_i^{b_i} \mid 1 \leq i \leq n\}$ which characterizes the counter for which the chain stands. Finally for matching, a similar construction separates proof obligations depending on whether or not they match the counter: unmatched obligations will be satisfied trivially, and matching ones are ensured to be satisfied only if the expected cell is the current one.

For the other parts involving DVPA, again, the constructed formula φ shall imitate a successful tree of T on the input. The space bound can be controlled by a counter with appropriate domain. The constraints between cells of consecutive configurations, however, are implemented differently. We use a deterministic VPA to push all cells along the whole branch of the run on the stack — configuration by configuration. At the end, we successively take the cells from the stack and branch. Along each branch, we use the counter to remove exponential or doubly exponential, resp., many elements from stack to access the cell at the same position in the previous configuration. So, as a main component of φ we use either $\mathtt{AU}^{\mathcal{A}}\mathtt{AXff}$ or $\mathtt{AG}^{\mathcal{A}}\mathtt{ff}$ for some VPA $\mathcal{A}$. In the case of a doubly exponential counter, the technique explained for CTL[DFA, NFA] can be applied. But this time, a proof obligation expresses a bit number and its value.

6 Model Checking

In this section we consider model-checking of CTL[$\mathfrak{A}$, $\mathfrak{B}$] against finite and infinite transition systems, obtained as the transition graphs of (visibly) pushdown automata. Note that undecidability is quickly obtained beyond that. For instance model checking the genuine CTL fragment EF is undecidable over the class of Petri nets, and for EG model checking becomes undecidable of the class of Very Basic Parallel Processes [16].

6.1 Finite State Systems

The following table summarises the complexities of model checking CTL[$\mathfrak{A}$,$\mathfrak{B}$] in finite transition systems in terms of completeness. Surprisingly, despite its greatly increased expressive power compared to CTL, CTL[PDA,DPDA] remains in PTIME. In general, it is the class $\mathfrak{B}$ which determines the complexity. The table therefore only contains one row ($\mathfrak{A}$) and several columns ($\mathfrak{B}$). Note that PDA covers everything down to DFA while DPDA covers DVPA and DFA.

	DPDA	NFA	VPA	PDA
PDA	PTIME	PSPACE	EXPTIME	undec.

Theorem 6.1. *Model checking of finite state systems against* CTL[PDA,DPDA] *is in* PTIME*,* CTL[PDA,VPA] *is in* EXPTIME*, and* CTL[PDA,NFA] *is in* PSPACE*.*

Proof (Sketch). To obtain a PTIME algorithm for CTL[PDA,DPDA] we observe that — as for plain CTL — we can model check a CTL[$\mathfrak{A}$,$\mathfrak{B}$] formula bottom-up for any $\mathfrak{A}$ and $\mathfrak{B}$. Starting with the atomic propositions one computes for all subformulas the set of satisfying states, then regards the subformula as a proposition. Hence, it suffices to give algorithms for $\mathtt{E}(x\mathtt{U}^{\mathcal{A}}y)$ and $\mathtt{E}(x\mathtt{R}^{\mathcal{B}}y)$ for propositions x and y.

We prove the case for $\mathtt{E}(x\mathtt{U}^{\mathcal{A}}y)$ by reduction to non-emptiness of PDA which is well-known to be solvable in PTIME. Let $\mathcal{T}{=}(\mathcal{S},\rightarrow,\ell)$ be an LTS and $\mathcal{A}{=}(Q,\Sigma,\Gamma,\delta,q_0,F)$. We construct for every $s\in\mathcal{S}$ a PDA $\mathcal{A}_{\mathcal{T}}{=}(Q\times\mathcal{S},\Sigma,\Gamma,\delta',(q_0,s),F')$, where

$$F'{:=}\{(q,s)\mid q\in F \text{ and } y\in\ell(s)\} \text{ and}$$
$$\delta'((q,s),a,\gamma){:=}\{(q',s')\mid q'\in\delta(q,a,\gamma) \text{ and } s\xrightarrow{a}s' \text{ and } x\in\ell(s)\}.$$

Clearly, if $\mathcal{L}(\mathcal{A}_{\mathcal{T}})\neq\emptyset$ then there exist simultaneously a word $w\in\mathcal{L}(\mathcal{A})$ and a path π in $\mathcal{T}$ starting at s and labeled with w, s.t. x holds everywhere along π except for the last state in which y holds. Note that this takes time $\mathcal{O}(|\mathcal{S}|\cdot|\mathcal{A}|\cdot|\mathcal{T}|)$.

The same upper bound can be achieved for ER-formulas. However, they require the automaton to be deterministic. This is due to the quantifier alternation in the release operator, as discussed in Sect. 2.

We show containment in PTIME by a reduction to the problem of model checking a fixed LTL formula on a PDS. Let $\mathcal{T}$ and $\mathcal{A}$ be defined as above except that $\mathcal{A}$ is deterministic. We construct a PDS $\mathcal{T}_{\mathcal{A}}=(Q\times\mathcal{S}\cup\{g,b\},\Gamma,\Delta,\ell')$, where ℓ' extends ℓ by $\ell'(b)=$ dead for a fresh proposition dead. Intuitively, g represents "good" and

b "bad" states, i.e. dead-end states, in which $\mathtt{E}(x\mathtt{R}^{\mathcal{A}}y)$ has been fulfilled or violated, respectively. Furthermore, Δ contains the following transition rules:

$$((q,s),\gamma) \hookrightarrow \begin{cases} (g,\epsilon) & \text{if } x \in \ell'(s) \text{ and } (q \in F \text{ implies } y \in \ell'(s)) \\ (b,\epsilon) & \text{if } q \in F \text{ and } y \notin \ell'(s) \\ ((q',s'),w) & \text{if none of the above match and there ex. } a \in \Sigma, \text{ s.t.} \\ & s \xrightarrow{a} s' \text{ and } (q',w) \in \delta(q,a,\gamma) \text{ for some } \gamma \in \Gamma, w \in \Gamma^* \end{cases}$$

Note that $|\mathcal{T}_{\mathcal{A}}| = \mathcal{O}(|\mathcal{T}| \cdot |\mathcal{A}|)$. Now consider the LTL formula $\mathtt{Fdead}$. It is not hard to show that $s \not\models_{\mathcal{T}} \mathtt{E}(x\mathtt{R}^{\mathcal{A}}y)$ iff $((q_0,s),\epsilon) \models_{\mathcal{T}_{\mathcal{A}}} \mathtt{Fdead}$. The fact that model checking a fixed LTL formula over a PDS is in PTIME [6] completes the proof.

To show that CTL[PDA,NFA] is in PSPACE we reduce $\mathtt{E}(x\mathtt{R}^{\mathcal{B}}y)$ to the problem of checking a fixed LTL formula against a determinisation of the NFA $\mathcal{B}$. This is a repeated reachability problem over the product of a Büchi automaton and a determinisation of the NFA. Since we can determinise by a subset construction, we can use Savitch's algorithm [29] and an on-the-fly computation of the edge relation. Because Savitch's algorithm requires logarithmic space over an exponential graph, the complete algorithm runs in PSPACE.

Using the fact that every VPA can be determinised at a possibly exponentially cost [2], we obtain an algorithm for CTL[PDA,VPA]. □

We now consider the lower bounds.

Theorem 6.2. *For fixed finite state transition systems of size 1, model checking for* EF[VPA] *is PTIME-hard,* EG[NFA] *is PSPACE-hard,* EG[VPA] *is EXPTIME-hard, and* EG[PDA] *is undecidable.*

Proof (Sketch). It is known that model checking CTL is PTIME-complete. Thus, the model checking problems for all logics between CTL and CTL[CFL] are PTIME-hard. However, for EF[VPL] it is already possible to strengthen the result and prove PTIME-hardness of the expression complexity, i.e. the complexity of model checking on a fixed transition system. The key ingredient is the fact that the emptiness problem for VPA is PTIME-hard.[1]

Model checking the fragment EG[$\mathfrak{A}$] is harder, namely PSPACE-hard for the class REG already. The proof is by a reduction from the n-tiling problem [32] resembling the halting problem of a nondeterministic linear-space bounded Turing Machine. Two aspects are worth noting. First, this result — as opposed to the one for the fragment EF[$\mathfrak{A}$] — heavily depends on the fact that $\mathfrak{A}$ is a class of nondeterministic automata. For $\mathfrak{A}$ = DFA for instance, there is no such lower bound unless PSPACE = PTIME. The other aspect is that the formulas constructed in this reduction are of the form $\mathtt{EG}^{\mathcal{A}}\mathtt{ff}$, no boolean operators, no multiple temporal operators, and no atomic propositions are needed.

The principle is that tilings can be represented by infinite words over the alphabet of all tiles. Unsuccessful tilings must have a finite prefix that cannot be extended to become successful. We construct an automaton $\mathcal{A}$ which recognises unsuccessful prefixes.

[1] This can be proved in just the same way as PTIME-hardness of the emptiness problem for PDA.

Every possible tiling is represented by a path in a one-state transition system with universal transition relation. This state satisfies the formula $\mathtt{EG}^{\mathcal{A}}\mathtt{ff}$ iff a successful tiling is possible.

However, if we increase the language class to CFL we are able to encode an undecidable tiling problem. The octant tiling problem asks for a successful tiling of the plane which has successively longer rows [32]. Since the length of the rows is unbounded, we need non-determinism and the unbounded memory of a PDA to recognise unsuccessful prefixes.

The situation is better for VPA. When used in EF-operators, visibly pushdown languages are not worse than regular languages, even for nondeterministic automata. This even extends to the whole of all context-free languages.

In EG-operators VPA increase the complexity of the model checking problem even further in comparison to NFA to EXPTIME. We reduce from the halting problem for alternating linear-space bounded Turing machines. An accepting computation of the machine can be considered a *finite* tree. We encode a depth-first search of the tree as a word and construct a VPA $\mathcal{A}$ accepting all the words that do not represent an accepting computation. As in previous proofs, one then takes a one-state transition system with universal transition relation and formula $\mathtt{EG}^{\mathcal{A}}\mathtt{ff}$. □

6.2 Visibly Pushdown Systems

We consider model checking over an infinite transition system represented by a visibly pushdown automaton. The following summarises the complexity results in terms of completeness.

	DFA,DVPA	NFA,VPA	DPDA
DFA . . . VPA	EXPTIME	2EXPTIME	undec.

Theorem 6.3. *Model checking visibly pushdown systems against* CTL[VPA,DVPA] *is in EXPTIME, whereas against* CTL[VPA,VPA] *it is in 2EXPTIME.*

Proof (sketch). To obtain the first result, we follow the game approach hinted at in Section 2 (hence the restriction to DVPA). We reduce the model checking problem to a Büchi game played over a PDS, which is essentially the product of the formula (including its automata) and the model. That is, for example, from a state $(s, \varphi_1 \wedge \varphi_2)$ the opponent can move to (s, φ_1) or (s, φ_2) — the strategy is to pick the subformula that is not satisfied. The stack alphabet is also a product of the model stack and the formula VPA stack. For a temporal operator augmented with a VPA, the formula VPA component is set to $\perp$ to mark its bottom of stack. Then the automaton is simulated step-wise with the model. At each step the appropriate player can decide whether to attempt to satisfy a subformula, or continue simulating a path and run. Since deciding these games is EXPTIME [36], we get the required result. The second result follows by determinisation of the VPA. □

Theorem 6.4. *Model checking visibly pushdown systems against* CTL[DFA] *is hard for EXPTIME,* EG[NFA] *is hard for 2EXPTIME, and* EF[DPDA] *and* EG[DPDA] *are undecidable.*

Proof (sketch). EXPTIME-hardness follows immediately from the EXPTIME-hardness of CTL over pushdown systems [21] and that CTL is insensitive to the transition labels.

2EXPTIME-hardness is similar to Bozzelli's 2EXPTIME-hardness for CTL* [24]. This is an intricate encoding of the runs of an alternating EXPSPACE Turing machine. The difficulty lies in checking the consistency of a guessed work tape of exponential length. We are able to replace the required CTL* subformula with a formula of the form $\mathtt{EG}^A$, giving us the result.

The undecidability results are via encodings of a two counter machine. Intuitively, the visibly pushdown system simulates the machine, keeping one counter in its stack. It outputs the operations on the second counter (appropriately marked to meet the visibly condition) and the DPDA checks for consistency. In this way we can simulate two counters. □

6.3 Pushdown Systems

For pushdown systems we have the following complexity-theoretic completeness results.

	DFA	NFA	DVPA
DFA/ NFA	EXPTIME	2EXPTIME	undec.

Theorem 6.5. *Model checking pushdown systems against* CTL[NFA,DFA] *is in EXPTIME, against* CTL[NFA,NFA] *it is in 2EXPTIME, against* EF[DVPA] *and* EG[DVPA] *it is undecidable.*

Proof (sketch). The decidability results are similar to the case of visibly pushdown systems; we simply drop the visibly restriction. The lower bounds which do not follow from the results on VPA can be obtained by a reduction from two counter machines. □

7 Conclusion and Further Work

To the best of our knowledge, this is the first work considering a parametric extension of CTL by arbitrary classes of formal languages characterising the complexities of satisfiability and model checking as well as the expressive power and model-theoretic properties of the resulting logics in accordance to the classes of languages. The results show that some of the logics, in particular CTL[VPL] may be useful in program verification because of the combination of an intuitive syntax with reasonably low complexities of the corresponding decision problems.

Some questions still remain to be answered. First, it is open whether the relationships are strict between logics which are connected by solid vertical lines in Fig. 1. Moreover, the presented separations are rather coarse. Hence, it is desirable to have a generic approach to separate logics, e.g. CTL[$\mathfrak{A}$] $\lneq$ CTL[$\mathfrak{B}$] whenever $\mathfrak{A}$ is a "reasonable" subset of $\mathfrak{B}$.

It is an obvious task for further work to consider CTL* or CTL$^+$ as the base for similar extensions, and to characterise the expressive power and the complexities of the resulting logics.

References

1. Inc. Accellera Organization. Formal semantics of Accellera property specification language. In: Appendix B (2004), `http://www.eda.org/vfv/docs/PSL-v1.1.pdf`
2. Alur, R., Madhusudan, P.: Visibly pushdown languages. In: Proc. 36th Ann. ACM Symp. on Theory of Computing, STOC 2004, pp. 202–211 (2004)
3. Armoni, R., Fix, L., Flaisher, A., Gerth, R., Ginsburg, B., Kanza, T., Landver, A., Mador-Haim, S., Singerman, E., Tiemeyer, A., Vardi, M.Y., Zbar, Y.: The ForSpec temporal logic: A new temporal property specification language. In: Katoen, J.-P., Stevens, P. (eds.) TACAS 2002. LNCS, vol. 2280, pp. 296–311. Springer, Heidelberg (2002)
4. Arnold, A., Vincent, A., Walukiewicz, I.: Games for synthesis of controllers with partial observation. Theor. Comput. Sci. 303(1), 7–34 (2003)
5. Beer, I., Ben-David, S., Landver, A.: On-the-fly model checking of RCTL formulas. In: Y. Vardi, M. (ed.) CAV 1998. LNCS, vol. 1427, pp. 184–194. Springer, Heidelberg (1998)
6. Bouajjani, A., Esparza, J., Maler, O.: Reachability analysis of pushdown automata: Application to model-checking. In: Mazurkiewicz, A., Winkowski, J. (eds.) CONCUR 1997. LNCS, vol. 1243, pp. 135–150. Springer, Heidelberg (1997)
7. Brázdil, T., Cerná, I.: Model checking of regCTL. Computers and Artificial Intelligence 25(1) (2006)
8. Chandra, A.K., Kozen, D.C., Stockmeyer, L.J.: Alternation. Journal of the ACM 28(1), 114–133 (1981)
9. Clarke, E.M., Emerson, E.A.: Synthesis of synchronization skeletons for branching time temporal logic. In: Kozen, D. (ed.) Logic of Programs 1981. LNCS, vol. 131, pp. 52–71. Springer, Heidelberg (1982)
10. Clarke, E.M., Grumberg, O., Jha, S., Lu, Y., Veith, H.: Counterexample-guided abstraction refinement for symbolic model checking. Journal of the ACM 50(5), 752–794 (2003)
11. Dawar, A., Grädel, E., Kreutzer, S.: Inflationary fixed points in modal logics. ACM Transactions on Computational Logic 5(2), 282–315 (2004)
12. Emerson, E.A., Halpern, J.Y.: Decision procedures and expressiveness in the temporal logic of branching time. Journal of Computer and System Sciences 30, 1–24 (1985)
13. Emerson, E.A., Halpern, J.Y.: "Sometimes" and "not never" revisited: On branching versus linear time temporal logic. Journal of the ACM 33(1), 151–178 (1986)
14. Emerson, E.A., Jutla, C.S.: The complexity of tree automata and logics of programs. SIAM Journal on Computing 29(1), 132–158 (2000)
15. Emerson, E.A., Jutla, C.S.: The complexity of tree automata and logics of programs. In: Annual IEEE Symposium on Foundations of Computer Science, pp. 328–337 (1988)
16. Esparza, J.: Decidability of model-checking for infinite-state concurrent systems. Acta Informatica 34, 85–107 (1997)
17. Fischer, M.J., Ladner, R.E.: Propositional dynamic logic of regular programs. Journal of Computer and System Sciences 18(2), 194–211 (1979)
18. Harel, D., Kozen, D., Tiuryn, J.: Dynamic Logic. MIT Press, Cambridge (2000)
19. Harel, D., Pnueli, A., Stavi, J.: Propositional dynamic logic of nonregular programs. Journal of Computer and System Sciences 26(2), 222–243 (1983)
20. Henriksen, J.G., Thiagarajan, P.S.: Dynamic linear time temporal logic. Annals of Pure and Applied Logic 96(1-3), 187–207 (1999)
21. Walukiewicz, I.: Model checking CTL properties of pushdown systems. In: Kapoor, S., Prasad, S. (eds.) FSTTCS 2000. LNCS, vol. 1974, pp. 127–138. Springer, Heidelberg (2000)
22. Kozen, D.: Results on the propositional μ-calculus. TCS 27, 333–354 (1983)
23. Kupferman, O., Piterman, N., Vardi, M.Y.: Extended temporal logic revisited. In: Larsen, K.G., Nielsen, M. (eds.) CONCUR 2001. LNCS, vol. 2154, pp. 519–535. Springer, Heidelberg (2001)

24. Bozzelli, L.: Complexity results on branching-time pushdown model checking. Theor. Comput. Sci. 379(1-2), 286–297 (2007)
25. Lange, M., Latte, M.: A CTL-based logic for program abstractions. In: de Queiroz, R. (ed.) WoLLIC 2010. LNCS (LNAI), vol. 6188, pp. 19–33. Springer, Heidelberg (2010)
26. Löding, C., Lutz, C., Serre, O.: Propositional dynamic logic with recursive programs. J. Log. Algebr. Program. 73(1-2), 51–69 (2007)
27. Mateescu, R., Monteiro, P.T., Dumas, E., de Jong, H.: Computation tree regular logic for genetic regulatory networks. In: Cha, S(S.), Choi, J.-Y., Kim, M., Lee, I., Viswanathan, M. (eds.) ATVA 2008. LNCS, vol. 5311, pp. 48–63. Springer, Heidelberg (2008)
28. Rabin, M.O., Scott, D.: Finite automata and their decision problems. IBM Journal 2(3), 115–125 (1959)
29. Savitch, W.J.: Relationships between nondeterministic and deterministic tape complexities. Journal of Computer and System Sciences 4, 177–192 (1970)
30. Sistla, A.P., Clarke, E.M.: The complexity of propositional linear temporal logics. Journal of the Association for Computing Machinery 32(3), 733–749 (1985)
31. Streett, R.S.: Propositional dynamic logic of looping and converse is elementarily decidable. Information and Control 54(1/2), 121–141 (1982)
32. van Emde Boas, P.: The convenience of tilings. In: Sorbi, A. (ed.) Complexity, Logic, and Recursion Theory. Lecture notes in pure and applied mathematics, vol. 187, pp. 331–363. Marcel Dekker, Inc., New York (1997)
33. Vardi, M.Y., Stockmeyer, L.: Improved upper and lower bounds for modal logics of programs. In: Proc. 17th Symp. on Theory of Computing, STOC 1985, Baltimore, USA, pp. 240–251. ACM, New York (1985)
34. Vardi, M.Y., Wolper, P.: Reasoning about infinite computations. Information and Computation 115(1), 1–37 (1994)
35. Viswanathan, M., Viswanathan, R.: A higher order modal fixed point logic. In: Gardner, P., Yoshida, N. (eds.) CONCUR 2004. LNCS, vol. 3170, pp. 512–528. Springer, Heidelberg (2004)
36. Walukiewicz, I.: Pushdown processes: Games and model-checking. Information and Computation 164(2), 234–263 (2001)
37. Wolper, P.: Temporal logic can be more expressive. In: SFCS 1981: Proceedings of the 22nd Annual Symposium on Foundations of Computer Science, Washington, DC, USA, pp. 340–348. IEEE Computer Society, Los Alamitos (1981)

Using Causal Relationships to Deal with the Ramification Problem in Action Formalisms Based on Description Logics

Franz Baader, Marcel Lippmann, and Hongkai Liu*

Theoretical Computer Science, TU Dresden
lastname@tcs.inf.tu-dresden.de

Abstract. In the reasoning about actions community, causal relationships have been proposed as a possible approach for solving the ramification problem, i.e., the problem of how to deal with indirect effects of actions. In this paper, we show that causal relationships can be added to action formalisms based on Description Logics (DLs) without destroying the decidability of the consistency and the projection problem. We investigate the complexity of these decision problems based on which DL is used as base logic for the action formalism.

1 Introduction

For action theories represented in the situation or fluent calculus [13,16], important inference problems such as the projection problem are in general undecidable since these calculi encompass full first-order logic (FOL). One possibility for avoiding this source of undecidability is to restrict the underlying logic from FOL to a decidable Description Logic [1]. The main argument for using DLs in this setting is that they offer considerable expressive power, going far beyond propositional logic, while reasoning is still decidable. An action formalism based on DLs was first introduced in [3], and it was shown that important reasoning problems such as the projection problem become decidable in this restricted formalism.

An action theory basically consists of three components: (i) a (possibly incomplete) description of the *initial state*; (ii) a description of the possible *actions*, which specifies the *pre-conditions* that need to be satisfied for an action to be applicable as well as the *post-conditions*, i.e., the changes to the current state that its application causes; and (iii) *domain constraints*, which formulate general knowledge about the functioning of the domain in which the actions are executed, and thus restrict the possible states. In a DL-based action formalism, the initial state is (incompletely) described by an ABox, pre-conditions are ABox assertions that must hold, post-conditions are ABox assertions that are added or removed, and domain constraints are specified using TBox axioms. Given a finite sequence of actions $\alpha_1 \ldots \alpha_n$, an incomplete description $\mathcal{A}_0$ of the initial state,

* Supported by DFG under grant BA 1122/13-1.

C. Fermüller and A. Voronkov (Eds.): LPAR-17, LNCS 6397, pp. 82–96, 2010.

and a formula φ specifying a (desired or unwanted) property of states, *projection* [13] is the inference problem that asks whether φ holds in all states that can be reached from a possible initial state (i.e., a state satisfying $\mathcal{A}_0$) by applying this sequence of actions. The formula φ may, for example, be the prerequisite of an action α to be applied after the last action of the sequence, or a condition used in the control structure of an agent's program. In [3], it was shown that the projection problem is decidable in action theories based on DLs between $\mathcal{ALC}$ and $\mathcal{ALCQIO}$. However, this paper did not deal with the so-called ramification problem [8,15].

The *ramification problem* is caused by the interaction of the post-conditions of an action with the domain constraints. To be more precise, when applying an action, it may not be enough to make only those changes to the current state that are explicitly required by its post-conditions (direct effects) since it might happen that the resulting state does not satisfy the domain constraints, in which case one needs to make additional changes in order to satisfy these constraints (indirect effects). For example, assume that we have a hiring action, which has the direct effect that the person that is hired is then an employee, and that we have a domain constraint that says that any employee must have a health insurance. If John does not have health insurance, then just applying the hiring action for John would result in a state that violates the health insurance domain constraint.

One approach for solving the ramification problem is trying to find a semantics for action theories that automatically deals with such indirect effects, i.e., somehow makes additional changes to the state in order to satisfy the domain constraints, while taking care that only "necessary" changes are made. An example of such an attempt is the possible models approach (PMA) [18,7]. However, without additional restrictions, the PMA and all the other approaches in this direction can lead to unintuitive results. It is not clear how to construct a general semantics that does not suffer from this problem. In our example, assume that there are only two insurance companies that offer health insurance: AOK and TK. In order to satisfy the health insurance domain constraint, John must get insured by one of them, but how should a general semantic framework be able to decide which one to pick.

A *second approach* is to avoid rather than solve the issues raised by the ramification problem. This is actually what is done in [3]: the domain constraints are given by an acyclic TBox and post-conditions of actions are restricted such that only primitive concepts and roles are changed. Since, w.r.t. an acyclic TBox, the interpretations of the primitive concepts and roles uniquely determine the interpretations of the defined concepts, it is then clear what indirect effects such a change has. The semantics obtained this way can be seen as an instance of the PMA. It is shown in [3] that the use of the PMA in a less restrictive setting (use of more general TBoxes as domain constraints or of non-primitive concepts in post-conditions) leads to unintuitive results.

A *third approach* is to let the user rather than a general semantic machinery decide which are the implicit effects of an action. In our example, assume that employers actually are required to enroll new employees with AOK in case they do not already have a health insurance. One can now try to extend the action formalism such that it allows the user to add such information to the action theory. For DL-based action formalisms, this approach was first used in [9], where the formalism for describing the actions is extended such that the user can make complex statements about the changes to the interpretations of concepts and roles that can be caused by a given action. It is shown in [9] that important inference problems such as the projection problem stay decidable in this setting, but that the consistency[1] problem for actions becomes undecidable. In the present paper, we realize this third approach in a different way, by adapting a method for addressing the ramification problem that has already been employed in the reasoning about actions community [8,15,17,6]. Instead of changing the formalism for defining actions, we introduce so-called *causal relationships* as an additional component of action theories. In our example, such a causal relationship would state that, whenever someone becomes a new employee, this person is then insured by AOK, unless (s)he already had a health insurance.

In this paper, we formally introduce DL-based action theories with causal relationships. The semantics we define for such theories is an adaptation of the one introduced in [17,6] in a more general setting, and it inherits the advantages and disadvantages of this approach. The main thrust of this work is not to invent a new solution of the ramification problem and discuss its appropriateness, but to show that adding a well-accepted existing solution from the reasoning about actions community [17,6] to DL-based action theories leaves important inference problems such as the consistency problem and the projection problem decidable. More precisely, we provide not only decidability results, but detailed results on the complexity of these two problems depending on which DL is used as base logic. With a few exceptions, these results show that adding causal relationships to DL-based action formalisms does not increase the complexity of these inference problems.

Using causal relationships has two advantages over the formalism for handling the ramification problem introduced in [9]. First, the formalism in [9] requires the user to deal with the ramification problem within every action description. In our formalism, causal relationships are defined independently of a specific action, stating general facts about causation. The semantics then takes care of how these relationships are translated into indirect effects of actions. A second, and more tangible, advantage is that, in our formalism, *consistency of actions* is decidable. Basically, an action is consistent if, whenever it is applicable in a state, there is a well-defined successor state that can be obtained by applying it. We believe that, in the context of the third approach, where the user is supposed to deal with the ramification problem (in our formalism by defining appropriate causal relationships), testing consistency helps the user to check whether (s)he got it right. For instance, consider our health insurance example. If the user does not specify any causal relationships, then the hiring action is inconsistent since its application may result in a state that does not satisfy the domain constraints,

[1] In [9], this is actually called strong consistency.

Table 1. Syntax and semantics of $\mathcal{ALCO}$

Name	Syntax	Semantics
negation	$\neg C$	$\Delta^{\mathcal{I}} \setminus C^{\mathcal{I}}$
conjunction	$C \sqcap D$	$C^{\mathcal{I}} \cap D^{\mathcal{I}}$
disjunction	$C \sqcup D$	$C^{\mathcal{I}} \cup D^{\mathcal{I}}$
nominal	$\{a\}$	$\{a^{\mathcal{I}}\}$
value restriction	$\forall r.C$	$\{x \mid \forall y.\ ((x,y) \in r^{\mathcal{I}} \rightarrow y \in C^{\mathcal{I}})\}$
existential restriction	$\exists r.C$	$\{x \mid \exists y.\ ((x,y) \in r^{\mathcal{I}} \wedge y \in C^{\mathcal{I}})\}$
general concept inclusion	$C \sqsubseteq D$	$C^{\mathcal{I}} \subseteq D^{\mathcal{I}}$
concept assertion	$C(a)$	$a^{\mathcal{I}} \in C^{\mathcal{I}}$
role assertion	$r(a,b)$	$(a^{\mathcal{I}}, b^{\mathcal{I}}) \in r^{\mathcal{I}}$
negated role assertion	$\neg r(a,b)$	$(a^{\mathcal{I}}, b^{\mathcal{I}}) \notin r^{\mathcal{I}}$

and thus is not well-defined. If (s)he adds the causal relationship mentioned above, then the action becomes consistent.

Due to space constraints, we cannot give complete proofs of all our results here. They can be found in the accompanying technical report [2].

2 DL-Based Action Formalisms and Causal Relationships

We assume that the reader is familiar with the basic notions from Description Logics, which can, for example, be found in [1]. In principle, our action formalism can be parameterized with any DL. In this paper, we restrict the detailed presentation to the DL $\mathcal{ALCO}$, and only list the results that we have obtained for other DLs in Section 5. The DL $\mathcal{ALCO}$ extends the smallest propositionally closed DL $\mathcal{ALC}$ with so-called nominals. In $\mathcal{ALC}$, one can build complex concept descriptions from atomic concepts (concept names) using the Boolean constructors ($\sqcap$, $\sqcup$, $\neg$) as well as value restrictions ($\forall r.C$) and existential restrictions ($\exists r.C$), where r is a role name. In $\mathcal{ALCO}$, one can additionally use individual names a to build nominal concepts $\{a\}$, which are interpreted as singleton sets.

An *ABox* is a finite set of *concept assertions* $C(a)$ and *role assertions* $r(a,b)$, and *negated role assertions* $\neg r(a,b)$, where C is a concept description, r is a role name, and a, b are individual names. An ABox is *simple* if all its concept assertions are of the form $A(a)$ or $\neg A(a)$, where A is a concept name. We will call the concept and (negated) role assertions that may occur in simple ABoxes *literals*. Literals of the form $A(a)$ and $r(a,b)$ ($\neg A(a)$ and $\neg r(a,b)$) are called *positive (negative)*. Given a literal L, its negation $\dot{\neg} L$ is $\neg L$ if L is positive, and it is L' if $L = \neg L'$ is negative. A *TBox* is a finite set of general concept inclusions (GCIs) of the form $C \sqsubseteq D$, where C, D are concept descriptions.

Example 2.1. Coming back to the health insurance example from the introduction, the following GCIs express that all employees must be insured by a health insurance company, and that AOK and TK are health insurance companies:

$$\mathsf{Employee} \sqsubseteq \exists \mathsf{insuredBy.HealthInsuranceCompany}$$
$$\{\mathsf{AOK}\} \sqcup \{\mathsf{TK}\} \sqsubseteq \mathsf{HealthInsuranceCompany}$$

The assertion $\neg\mathsf{Employee}(\mathsf{JOHN})$ says that John is not an employee.

The semantics of $\mathcal{ALCO}$ is defined in terms of an *interpretation* $\mathcal{I} = (\Delta^{\mathcal{I}}, \cdot^{\mathcal{I}})$, where $\Delta^{\mathcal{I}}$, the *domain*, is a non-empty set, and $\cdot^{\mathcal{I}}$, the *interpretation function*, maps each concept name A to a subset $A^{\mathcal{I}} \subseteq \Delta^{\mathcal{I}}$, each role name r to a binary relation $r^{\mathcal{I}} \subseteq \Delta^{\mathcal{I}} \times \Delta^{\mathcal{I}}$, and each individual name a to an element $a^{\mathcal{I}} \in \Delta^{\mathcal{I}}$. The extension of $\cdot^{\mathcal{I}}$ to complex concept descriptions is defined inductively, as shown in the semantics column of Table 1. The interpretation $\mathcal{I}$ *satisfies* a GCI or assertion φ (written $\mathcal{I} \models \varphi$) if the condition in the semantics column of Table 1 is satisfied. If $\mathcal{I}$ satisfies all the assertions of the ABox $\mathcal{A}$ (GCIs of the TBox $\mathcal{T}$), then we say that $\mathcal{I}$ is a *model* of $\mathcal{A}$ ($\mathcal{T}$), and write $\mathcal{I} \models \mathcal{A}$ ($\mathcal{I} \models \mathcal{T}$). The ABox $\mathcal{A}$ is *consistent* w.r.t. $\mathcal{T}$ if there exists an interpretation that is a model of $\mathcal{A}$ and $\mathcal{T}$. We say that the assertion φ (the TBox $\mathcal{T}'$) is a *logical consequence* of the ABox $\mathcal{A}$ and the TBox $\mathcal{T}$, denoted with $\mathcal{A} \cup \mathcal{T} \models \varphi$ ($\mathcal{A} \cup \mathcal{T} \models \mathcal{T}'$) iff every interpretation that is a model of $\mathcal{A}$ and $\mathcal{T}$ is also a model of φ ($\mathcal{T}'$).

The following definition recalls the notion of a DL action without occlusions, which has first been introduced in [3].[2] At the moment, we do not allow for occlusions in our framework since it is not yet clear how to handle them algorithmically in the presence of causal relationships.

Definition 2.2. *An* action *is a pair* $\alpha = (\mathsf{pre}, \mathsf{post})$, *where* pre *is a finite set of assertions, the* pre-conditions, *and* post *is a finite set of* conditional post-conditions *of the form* φ/ψ, *where* φ *is an assertion and* ψ *is a* literal. *Such an action is called* unconditional *if all its post-conditions are of the form* $true/\psi$, *where "true" stands for an assertion that is satisfied in every interpretation. We write such unconditional post-conditions simply as* ψ *rather than* $true/\psi$.

Basically, an action is applicable in an interpretation if its pre-conditions are satisfied. The conditional post-condition φ/ψ requires that ψ must hold after the application of the action if φ was satisfied before the application. According to the semantics of DL actions defined in [3], nothing should change that is not explicitly required to change by some post-condition. As already discussed in the introduction, this semantics is not appropriate if the domain constraints are given by a TBox containing arbitrary GCIs.

For examples, consider the TBox $\mathcal{T}$ consisting of the GCIs of Example 2.1 and the action $\mathsf{HireJohn} = (\emptyset, \{\mathsf{Employee}(\mathsf{JOHN})\})$, which has no pre-conditions and a single unconditional post-condition. Assume that $\mathcal{I}$ is a model of $\mathcal{T}$ with $\mathcal{I} \not\models \mathsf{Employee}(\mathsf{JOHN})$ and $\mathcal{I} \not\models \exists\mathsf{insuredBy.HealthInsuranceCompany}(\mathsf{JOHN})$ (obviously, such models exist). If we apply the semantics of DL actions introduced in [3], then $\mathcal{I}$ is transformed into an interpretation $\mathcal{I}'$, whose only difference to $\mathcal{I}$ is that now John is an employee, i.e., $\mathcal{I}' \models \mathsf{Employee}(\mathsf{JOHN})$. Since nothing else

[2] Intuitively, occlusions describe parts of the domain that can change arbitrarily when the action is applied. More details about occlusions can be found in [3] and in Section 7 of [2].

changes, we still have $\mathcal{I}' \not\models \exists \mathsf{insuredBy.HealthInsuranceCompany(JOHN)}$, which shows that $\mathcal{I}'$ is not a model of $\mathcal{T}$. Consequently, although the action HireJohn is applicable to $\mathcal{I}$ (since the empty set of pre-conditions does not impose any applicability condition), its application does not result in an interpretation satisfying the domain constraints in $\mathcal{T}$. We will call an action where this kind of problem can occur an *inconsistent action.* In our example, consistency can be achieved by complementing the action HireJohn with an appropriate causal relationship.

Definition 2.3. *A* causal relationship *is of the form* $\mathcal{A}_1 \longrightarrow_{\mathcal{B}} \mathcal{A}_2$, *where* $\mathcal{A}_1, \mathcal{A}_2$ *are simple ABoxes and* $\mathcal{B}$ *is an ABox.*

Such a causal relationship can be read as "$\mathcal{A}_1$ causes $\mathcal{A}_2$ if $\mathcal{B}$ holds." To be more precise, it says the following:[3] if $\mathcal{B}$ is satisfied *before*[4] the application of an action and $\mathcal{A}_1$ is *newly* satisfied by its application (i.e., was not satisfied before, but is satisfied after the application), then $\mathcal{A}_2$ must also be satisfied *after* the application. In our health insurance example, the causal relationship

$$\{\mathsf{Employee(JOHN)}\} \longrightarrow_{\{\neg\exists \mathsf{insuredBy.HealthInsuranceCompany(JOHN)}\}} \{\mathsf{insuredBy(JOHN, AOK)}\}$$

adds the following indirect effect to the direct effect of the HireJohn action: (i) if John becomes newly employed (i.e., was not an employee before) and did not have a health insurance before the application of the action, then he is newly insured with AOK after its application; (ii) if he becomes newly employed, but already has a health insurance, then he keeps his old health insurance and is *not* newly insured with AOK. In both cases, the GCIs of Example 2.1 stay satisfied.

In order to define the semantics of DL actions in the presence of causal relationships formally, we consider an action $\alpha = (\mathsf{pre}, \mathsf{post})$, a finite set of causal relationships CR, and an interpretation $\mathcal{I}$ to which the action is supposed to be applied. The actions and causal relationships introduced above can only effect changes to the membership of named individuals (pairs of named individuals) in atomic concepts (roles). Consequently, such *effects* can be described in an obvious way using literals. For this reason, we will sometimes call a simple ABox a *set of effects.*

Using the semantics of actions introduced in [3], the *set of direct effects* of α given $\mathcal{I}$ is defined as

$$\mathsf{Dir}(\alpha, \mathcal{I}) := \{\psi \mid \varphi/\psi \in \mathsf{post} \wedge \mathcal{I} \models \varphi\}.$$

Direct effects of an action may cause indirect effects specified by causal relationships, and these indirect effects may again cause indirect effects, etc. Thus, the overall effects of an action are obtained by iteratively adding indirect effects to the direct ones until no new indirect effects can be added.

[3] Actually, there are different ways of defining the meaning of causal relationships. Here, we follow the approach used in [17,6] rather than the one employed by [8,15].

[4] In the semantics of causal relationship introduced in [8,15], this "before" would need to be replaced by "after."

To be more precise, we start the iteration by defining $\mathcal{E}_0 := \mathsf{Dir}(\alpha, \mathcal{I})$. Assuming that $\mathcal{E}_i$ $(i \geq 0)$ is already defined, we define $\mathcal{E}_{i+1} := \mathcal{E}_i \cup \mathsf{Ind}_{i+1}$, where

$$\begin{aligned}\mathsf{Ind}_{i+1} := \{\psi \mid \exists \mathcal{A}_1 \longrightarrow_{\mathcal{B}} \mathcal{A}_2 \in \mathsf{CR} \text{ such that} \\ &(i)\ \psi \in \mathcal{A}_2,\ \ (ii)\ \mathcal{I} \models \mathcal{B},\ \ (iii)\ \mathcal{I} \not\models \mathcal{A}_1,\ \ \textit{and} \\ &(iv)\ \forall \varphi \in \mathcal{A}_1.\ (\varphi \in \mathcal{E}_i \vee (\mathcal{I} \models \varphi \wedge \dot{\neg}\varphi \notin \mathcal{E}_i))\}\ .\end{aligned}$$

Thus, we add the indirect effect ψ to our set of effects if (i) it is in the consequence set $\mathcal{A}_2$ of a causal relationship $\mathcal{A}_1 \longrightarrow_{\mathcal{B}} \mathcal{A}_2$ for which (ii) the condition $\mathcal{B}$ is satisfied in $\mathcal{I}$ (i.e., before applying the action), and (iii)+(iv) the trigger $\mathcal{A}_1$ is newly satisfied, i.e., (iii) $\mathcal{A}_1$ is not satisfied in $\mathcal{I}$, but (iv) it is satisfied according to the current effect set, i.e., every assertion $\varphi \in \mathcal{A}_1$ is a (direct or indirect) effect, or it is satisfied in $\mathcal{I}$ and this is not changed by an effect.

By definition, we have $\mathcal{E}_0 \subseteq \mathcal{E}_1 \subseteq \mathcal{E}_2 \cdots$. Since we only add literals that belong to the consequence set of a causal relationship in the finite set CR, there is an n such that $\mathcal{E}_n = \mathcal{E}_{n+1} = \mathcal{E}_{n+2} = \cdots$. We define

$$\mathcal{E}(\alpha, \mathcal{I}, \mathsf{CR}) := \mathcal{E}_n\ .$$

This set of literals represents the effects of applying the action α to the interpretation $\mathcal{I}$ w.r.t. the causal relationships in CR. It could happen, however, that this set is contradictory, and thus cannot lead to a well-defined successor interpretation: we say that $\mathcal{E}(\alpha, \mathcal{I}, \mathsf{CR})$ is *contradictory* if there is a literal L such that $\{L, \dot{\neg}L\} \subseteq \mathcal{E}(\alpha, \mathcal{I}, \mathsf{CR})$.

Now, we are ready to introduce our semantics of actions in the presence of causal relationships.

Definition 2.4. *Let α be an action,* CR *a finite set of causal relationships, $\mathcal{T}$ a TBox, and $\mathcal{I}$, $\mathcal{I}'$ two interpretations. We say that α* may transform $\mathcal{I}$ to $\mathcal{I}'$ w.r.t. $\mathcal{T}$ and CR *(denoted by $\mathcal{I} \Longrightarrow_{\alpha}^{\mathcal{T},\mathsf{CR}} \mathcal{I}'$) if*

- *$\Delta^{\mathcal{I}} = \Delta^{\mathcal{I}'}$ and $a^{\mathcal{I}} = a^{\mathcal{I}'}$ for every individual name a,*
- *$\mathcal{I} \models \mathcal{T}$ and $\mathcal{I}' \models \mathcal{T}$,*
- *$\mathcal{E}(\alpha, \mathcal{I}, \mathsf{CR})$ is not contradictory,*
- *for all concept names A we have $A^{\mathcal{I}'} = (A^{\mathcal{I}} \cup \{a^{\mathcal{I}} \mid A(a) \in \mathcal{E}(\alpha, \mathcal{I}, \mathsf{CR})\}) \setminus \{a^{\mathcal{I}} \mid \neg A(a) \in \mathcal{E}(\alpha, \mathcal{I}, \mathsf{CR})\}$, and*
- *for all role names r we have $r^{\mathcal{I}'} = (r^{\mathcal{I}} \cup \{(a^{\mathcal{I}}, b^{\mathcal{I}}) \mid r(a, b) \in \mathcal{E}(\alpha, \mathcal{I}, \mathsf{CR})\}) \setminus \{(a^{\mathcal{I}}, b^{\mathcal{I}}) \mid \neg r(a, b) \in \mathcal{E}(\alpha, \mathcal{I}, \mathsf{CR})\}$.*

The sequence of actions $\alpha_1, \ldots, \alpha_n$ may transform $\mathcal{I}$ to $\mathcal{I}'$ w.r.t. $\mathcal{T}$ and CR *(denoted by $\mathcal{I} \Longrightarrow_{\alpha_1,\ldots,\alpha_n}^{\mathcal{T},\mathsf{CR}} \mathcal{I}'$) iff there are interpretations $\mathcal{I}_0, \ldots, \mathcal{I}_n$ such that $\mathcal{I} = \mathcal{I}_0$, $\mathcal{I}_n = \mathcal{I}'$, and $\mathcal{I}_{i-1} \Longrightarrow_{\alpha_i}^{\mathcal{T},\mathsf{CR}} \mathcal{I}_i$ for all $i, 1 \leq i \leq n$.*

If $\mathcal{T}$ and CR are empty, then this semantics coincides with the one given in [3] for actions without occlusions. Note that our actions are *deterministic* in the sense that, for every model $\mathcal{I}$ of $\mathcal{T}$, there exists at most one interpretation $\mathcal{I}'$ such that $\mathcal{I} \Longrightarrow_{\alpha}^{\mathcal{T},\mathsf{CR}} \mathcal{I}'$. However, sometimes there may not exist any such interpretation $\mathcal{I}'$, either because $\mathcal{E}(\alpha, \mathcal{I}, \mathsf{CR})$ is contradictory, or because the new interpretation induced by $\mathcal{E}(\alpha, \mathcal{I}, \mathsf{CR})$ is not a model of $\mathcal{T}$. If this happens in the case where $\alpha = (\mathsf{pre}, \mathsf{post})$ is actually *applicable* to $\mathcal{I}$ (i.e., $\mathcal{I} \models \mathsf{pre}$), then this indicates a modeling error. In fact, the correct modeling of an action theory should ensure that, whenever an action is applicable, there is a well-defined successor state.

Definition 2.5. *The action α is* consistent *w.r.t. the TBox $\mathcal{T}$ and the finite set* CR *of causal relationships iff, for every model $\mathcal{I}$ of $\mathcal{T}$ with $\mathcal{I} \models \mathsf{pre}$, there exists an interpretation $\mathcal{I}'$ with $\mathcal{I} \Longrightarrow_{\alpha}^{\mathcal{T},\mathsf{CR}} \mathcal{I}'$.*

As argued above, the action $\mathsf{HireJohn}$ is not consistent w.r.t. the TBox consisting of the GCIs of Example 2.1 and the empty set of causal relationships, but it becomes consistent if we add the causal relationship introduced below Definition 2.3.

The projection problem is one of the most basic reasoning problems for action theories [13]. Given a (possibly incomplete) description of the initial world (interpretation), it asks whether a certain property is guaranteed to hold after the execution of a sequence of actions. Our formal definition of this problems is taken from [3], with the only difference that we use the "may transform" relation introduced in Definition 2.4, which takes causal relationships into account, instead of the one employed in [3].

Definition 2.6 (Projection problem). *Let $\alpha_1, \ldots, \alpha_n$ be a sequence of actions such that, for all $i, 1 \leq i \leq n$, the action α_i is consistent w.r.t. $\mathcal{T}$ and* CR. *The assertion φ is* a consequence of applying $\alpha_1, \ldots, \alpha_n$ to $\mathcal{A}$ w.r.t. $\mathcal{T}$ and CR *iff, for all $\mathcal{I}$ and $\mathcal{I}'$, if $\mathcal{I} \models \mathcal{A}$ and $\mathcal{I} \Longrightarrow_{\alpha_1,\ldots,\alpha_n}^{\mathcal{T},\mathsf{CR}} \mathcal{I}'$, then $\mathcal{I}' \models \varphi$.*

Note that we consider only consistent actions in our definition of the projection problem. In fact, if an action is inconsistent, then there is something wrong with the action theory, and this problem should be solved before starting to ask projection questions. Another interesting inference problem for action theories is *executability*: Are all pre-conditions guaranteed to be satisfied during the execution of a sequence of actions? As shown in [3], the projection and the executability problem can be reduced to each other in polynomial time. For this reason, we restrict our attention to the consistency and the projection problem.

3 Deciding Consistency

First, we develop a solution for the restricted case where the TBox is empty, and then we show how this solution can be extended to the general case.

3.1 Consistency w.r.t. the Empty TBox

We will show that, in this case, testing consistency of an action w.r.t. a set of causal relationships has the same complexity as the (in)consistency problem of an ABox. Given an action α and a finite set of causal relationships CR, we basically consider all the possible situations that the action could encounter when it is applied to an interpretation.

Definition 3.1. *Let* $\alpha = (\mathsf{pre}, \mathsf{post})$ *be an action and* CR *a finite set of causal relationships. The ABox* $\mathcal{A}(\alpha, \mathsf{CR})$ *is defined as follows:*

$$\mathcal{A}(\alpha, \mathsf{CR}) := \{\varphi, \neg\varphi \mid \varphi/\psi \in \mathsf{post} \text{ or } \varphi \in \mathcal{A}_1 \cup \mathcal{B} \text{ for some } \mathcal{A}_1 \longrightarrow_{\mathcal{B}} \mathcal{A}_2 \in \mathsf{CR}\}.$$

A diagram $\mathcal{D}$ for α and CR *is a maximal, consistent subset of* $\mathcal{A}(\alpha, \mathsf{CR})$. *We denote the set of all diagrams for* α *and* CR *by* $\mathfrak{D}(\alpha, \mathsf{CR})$.

For a given interpretation $\mathcal{I}$, there is exactly one diagram $\mathcal{D}$ such that $\mathcal{I} \models \mathcal{D}$. It is sufficient to know this diagram to determine what are the direct and indirect effects of applying α to $\mathcal{I}$ w.r.t. CR. Given a diagram $\mathcal{D}$, we will now define a set $\widehat{\mathcal{E}}(\alpha, \mathcal{D}, \mathsf{CR})$ such that $\widehat{\mathcal{E}}(\alpha, \mathcal{D}, \mathsf{CR}) = \mathcal{E}(\alpha, \mathcal{I}, \mathsf{CR})$ for every interpretation $\mathcal{I}$ with $\mathcal{I} \models \mathcal{D}$. The definition of the direct effects of an action can easily be adapted to the diagram case: $\widehat{\mathsf{Dir}}(\alpha, \mathcal{D}) := \{\psi \mid \varphi/\psi \in \mathsf{post} \wedge \varphi \in \mathcal{D}\}$.

The same is true for the sets $\mathcal{E}_i$. We start the iteration by defining $\widehat{\mathcal{E}}_0 := \widehat{\mathsf{Dir}}(\alpha, \mathcal{D})$. Assuming that $\widehat{\mathcal{E}}_i$ $(i \geq 0)$ is already defined, we define $\widehat{\mathcal{E}}_{i+1} := \widehat{\mathcal{E}}_i \cup \widehat{\mathsf{Ind}}_{i+1}$, where

$$\begin{aligned}\widehat{\mathsf{Ind}}_{i+1} := \{\psi \mid \exists \mathcal{A}_1 \longrightarrow_{\mathcal{B}} \mathcal{A}_2 \in \mathsf{CR} \text{ such that } & \\ (i)\ \psi \in \mathcal{A}_2,\ \ (ii)\ \mathcal{B} \subseteq \mathcal{D},\ \ (iii)\ \mathcal{A}_1 \not\subseteq \mathcal{D},\ \ \textit{and} & \\ (iv)\ \forall \varphi \in \mathcal{A}_1.\ (\varphi \in \widehat{\mathcal{E}}_i \vee (\varphi \in \mathcal{D} \wedge \dot\neg\varphi \notin \widehat{\mathcal{E}}_i))\} & \ .\end{aligned}$$

Again, there exists an $n \geq 0$ such that $\widehat{\mathcal{E}}_n = \widehat{\mathcal{E}}_{n+1} = \widehat{\mathcal{E}}_{n+2} = \cdots$, and we define $\widehat{\mathcal{E}}(\alpha, \mathcal{D}, \mathsf{CR}) := \widehat{\mathcal{E}}_n$. This set is *contradictory* if there is a literal L such that $\{L, \dot\neg L\} \subseteq \widehat{\mathcal{E}}(\alpha, \mathcal{D}, \mathsf{CR})$.

Checking which of the sets $\widehat{\mathcal{E}}(\alpha, \mathcal{D}, \mathsf{CR})$ for $\mathcal{D} \in \mathfrak{D}(\alpha, \mathsf{CR})$ are contradictory is sufficient for deciding the consistency problem in the case where the TBox is assumed to be empty. In fact, in this case the only reason for an interpretation not to have a successor interpretation w.r.t. α is that the set of effects is contradictory. Since we require the existence of a successor interpretation only for interpretations that satisfy the precondition set pre of α, it is enough to consider diagrams $\mathcal{D}$ that are consistent with pre.

Lemma 3.2. *The action* $\alpha = (\mathsf{pre}, \mathsf{post})$ *is consistent w.r.t.* CR iff $\widehat{\mathcal{E}}(\alpha, \mathcal{D}, \mathsf{CR})$ *is not contradictory for all* $\mathcal{D} \in \mathfrak{D}(\alpha, \mathsf{CR})$ *for which* $\mathcal{D} \cup \mathsf{pre}$ *is consistent.*

This lemma yields a PSPACE decision procedure for deciding consistency of an action w.r.t. a finite set of causal relationships. In order to check whether α is inconsistent, we first guess[5] a diagram $\mathcal{D} \in \mathfrak{D}(\alpha, \mathsf{CR})$, and then check whether $\mathcal{D} \cup \mathsf{pre}$ is consistent using the PSPACE decision procedure for ABox consistency in $\mathcal{ALCO}$ [14]. If $\mathcal{D} \cup \mathsf{pre}$ is consistent, we compute the set $\widehat{\mathcal{E}}(\alpha, \mathcal{D}, \mathsf{CR})$. This can be realized in polynomial time by performing the iteration used in the definition of $\widehat{\mathcal{E}}(\alpha, \mathcal{D}, \mathsf{CR})$. Checking whether this set is contradictory is obviously also possible in polynomial time.

[5] Recall that PSPACE = NPSPACE according to Savitch's theorem.

This PSPACE upper bound is optimal since the ABox inconsistency problem in $\mathcal{ALCO}$, which is known to be PSPACE-complete [14], can be reduced to our action consistency problem: for every ABox $\mathcal{A}$, we have that $\mathcal{A}$ is inconsistent iff $(\mathcal{A}, \{A(a), \neg A(a)\})$ is consistent w.r.t. the empty set of causal relationships, where A is an arbitrary concept name and a is an arbitrary individual name.

Theorem 3.3. *The problem of deciding consistency of an action w.r.t. a finite set of causal relationships is* PSPACE*-complete for* $\mathcal{ALCO}$.

3.2 The General Case

If $\mathcal{T}$ is not empty, then there is an additional possible reason for an action to be inconsistent: the successor interpretation induced by a non-contradictory set of effects may not be a model of $\mathcal{T}$. Thus, given a non-contradictory set of effects $\widehat{\mathcal{E}}(\alpha, \mathcal{D}, \mathsf{CR})$, we must check whether, for any model $\mathcal{I}$ of $\mathcal{T}$ and $\mathcal{D}$ that satisfies the preconditions of α, the interpretation $\mathcal{I}'$ obtained from $\mathcal{I}$ by applying the effects in $\widehat{\mathcal{E}}(\alpha, \mathcal{D}, \mathsf{CR})$ (see Definition 2.4) is a model of $\mathcal{T}$. To this purpose, we first define an unconditional action $\beta_{\alpha,\mathsf{CR},\mathcal{D}}$ that, applied to models of $\mathcal{D}$, has the same effect as α w.r.t. CR. Then, we adapt the approach for solving the projection problem introduced in [3] to the problem of checking whether $\beta_{\alpha,\mathsf{CR},\mathcal{D}}$ transforms models of $\mathcal{T}$ into models of $\mathcal{T}$.

Definition 3.4. *Let* $\alpha = (\mathsf{pre}, \mathsf{post})$ *be an action,* CR *a finite set of causal relationships, and* $\mathcal{D} \in \mathfrak{D}(\alpha, \mathsf{CR})$*. The action* $\beta_{\alpha,\mathsf{CR},\mathcal{D}}$ *has* $\mathsf{pre} \cup \mathcal{D}$ *as set of preconditions and* $\widehat{\mathcal{E}}(\alpha, \mathcal{D}, \mathsf{CR})$ *as set of (unconditional) post-conditions.*

The following lemma is an easy consequence of the definition of $\widehat{\mathcal{E}}(\alpha, \mathcal{D}, \mathsf{CR})$ and the semantics of actions (Definition 2.4).

Lemma 3.5. *For all* $\mathcal{D} \in \mathfrak{D}(\alpha, \mathsf{CR})$*, all models* $\mathcal{I}$ *of* $\mathcal{D}$*, and all interpretations* $\mathcal{I}'$*, we have* $\mathcal{I} \Longrightarrow_{\alpha}^{\emptyset,\mathsf{CR}} \mathcal{I}'$ *iff* $\mathcal{I} \Longrightarrow_{\beta_{\alpha,\mathsf{CR},\mathcal{D}}}^{\emptyset,\emptyset} \mathcal{I}'$.

The approach for solving the projection problem introduced in [3] considers a finite sequence of actions $\beta_1, \ldots, \beta_n$. In the present section, we are only interested in the special case where $n = 1$. However, since we will adopt this approach also in the next section, where we consider the case $n \geq 1$, we recall the relevant notions and results for the general case. In this approach, time-stamped copies $r^{(i)}$ $(0 \leq i \leq n)$ for all relevant role names and new time-stamped concept names $T_C^{(i)}$ $(0 \leq i \leq n)$ for all relevant concept descriptions are introduced. In our setting, the *relevant* role names (concept descriptions) will be the ones occurring in the input of the consistency or projection algorithm (see [2] for details). For every ABox assertion φ built using a relevant concept description C or a relevant role name r (called relevant assertion in the following) and every $i, 0 \leq i \leq n$, we can then define a time-stamped variant $\varphi^{(i)}$ as follows:

$$C(a)^{(i)} := T_C^{(i)}(a), \quad r(a,b)^{(i)} := r^{(i)}(a,b), \quad \neg r(a,b)^{(i)} := \neg r^{(i)}(a,b).$$

Given a set of relevant assertions $\mathcal{A}$, we define its time-stamped copy as $\mathcal{A}^{(i)} := \{\varphi^{(i)} \mid \varphi \in \mathcal{A}\}$. Given a set of GCIs $\mathcal{T}$ built from relevant concept descriptions, we define its time-stamped copy as $\mathcal{T}^{(i)} := \{T_C^{(i)} \sqsubseteq T_D^{(i)} \mid C \sqsubseteq D \in \mathcal{T}\}$.

Intuitively, given an initial interpretation $\mathcal{I}_0$, the application of β_1 to $\mathcal{I}_0$ yields a successor interpretation $\mathcal{I}_1$, the application of β_2 to $\mathcal{I}_1$ yields a successor interpretation $\mathcal{I}_2$, etc. Using the time-stamped copies of the relevant role names and concept descriptions, we can encode the sequence of interpretations $\mathcal{I}_0, \mathcal{I}_1, \ldots, \mathcal{I}_n$ into a single interpretation $\mathcal{J}$ such that the relevant assertion φ holds in $\mathcal{I}_i$ iff its time-stamped variant $\varphi^{(i)}$ holds in $\mathcal{J}$. In order to enforce that $\mathcal{J}$ really encodes a sequence of interpretations induced by the application of the action sequence $\beta_1, \ldots, \beta_n$, we require it to be a model of the (acyclic) TBox $\mathcal{T}_{\mathsf{red}}$ and the ABox $\mathcal{A}_{\mathsf{red}}$. Due to the space constraints, we cannot describe the construction of $\mathcal{T}_{\mathsf{red}}$ and $\mathcal{A}_{\mathsf{red}}$ here. This construction is very similar to the one introduced in [4], and it is described in detail in [2].[6] Here, we only recall the pertinent properties of $\mathcal{T}_{\mathsf{red}}$ and $\mathcal{A}_{\mathsf{red}}$ in the next lemma (whose proof is very similar to the one of Theorem 14 in [4]). It should be noted that our results actually do not depend on how the TBox $\mathcal{T}_{\mathsf{red}}$ and the ABox $\mathcal{A}_{\mathsf{red}}$ are exactly constructed. Any TBox and ABox satisfying the properties stated in the lemma can be used in our approach.

Lemma 3.6. *Let $\beta_1, \ldots, \beta_n$ be a sequence of $\mathcal{ALCO}$ actions, and $\mathcal{R}$ a set of relevant role names and concept descriptions such that $\mathcal{R}$ contains all the role names and concept descriptions occurring in $\beta_1, \ldots, \beta_n$. Then, there are an $\mathcal{ALCO}$ ABox $\mathcal{A}_{\mathsf{red}}$ and an (acyclic) $\mathcal{ALCO}$ TBox $\mathcal{T}_{\mathsf{red}}$ of size polynomial in the size of $\beta_1, \ldots, \beta_n$ and $\mathcal{R}$, such that the following properties (a) and (b) hold:*

(a) For all interpretations $\mathcal{I}_0, \ldots, \mathcal{I}_n$ such that $\mathcal{I}_i \Longrightarrow_{\beta_i}^{\emptyset,\emptyset} \mathcal{I}_{i+1}$ for every $i, 0 \leq i < n$, there exists an interpretation $\mathcal{J}$ such that $\mathcal{J} \models \mathcal{A}_{\mathsf{red}}$, $\mathcal{J} \models \mathcal{T}_{\mathsf{red}}$, and
  (i) for all $i, 0 \leq i \leq n$ and for all relevant assertions ψ: $\mathcal{I}_i \models \psi$ iff $\mathcal{J} \models \psi^{(i)}$;
  (ii) for all $i, 0 \leq i \leq n$ and all relevant concept descriptions C, we have $C^{\mathcal{I}_i} = (T_C^{(i)})^{\mathcal{J}}$.

(b) For all interpretations $\mathcal{J}$ such that $\mathcal{J} \models \mathcal{A}_{\mathsf{red}}$ and $\mathcal{J} \models \mathcal{T}_{\mathsf{red}}$, there exist interpretations $\mathcal{I}_0, \ldots, \mathcal{I}_n$ such that $\mathcal{I}_i \Longrightarrow_{\beta_i}^{\emptyset,\emptyset} \mathcal{I}_{i+1}$ for every $i, 0 \leq i < n$, and (i) and (ii) of (a) hold.

Now, we can come back to the consistency problem for actions. Let $\alpha = (\mathsf{pre}, \mathsf{post})$ be an action, CR a finite set of causal relationships, and $\mathcal{T}$ a TBox. The set $\mathcal{R}$ of relevant role names and concept descriptions consists of the ones occurring in α, CR, or $\mathcal{T}$. Given a diagram $\mathcal{D} \in \mathfrak{D}(\alpha, \mathsf{CR})$, we can compute the set $\widehat{\mathcal{E}}(\alpha, \mathcal{D}, \mathsf{CR})$, and check whether this set is non-contradictory. If this is the case, then we consider the action $\beta_{\alpha,\mathsf{CR},\mathcal{D}}$, and test whether an application of this action transforms models of $\mathcal{T}$ satisfying pre and $\mathcal{D}$ into models of $\mathcal{T}$. This test can be realized using the ABox $\mathcal{A}_{\mathsf{red}}$ and the (acyclic) TBox $\mathcal{T}_{\mathsf{red}}$ of Lemma 3.6.

Lemma 3.7. *The action α is consistent w.r.t. $\mathcal{T}$ and* CR iff *the following holds for all $\mathcal{D} \in \mathfrak{D}(\alpha, \mathsf{CR})$: if $\mathcal{D} \cup \mathsf{pre}$ is consistent w.r.t. $\mathcal{T}$, then*

[6] Note that this construction makes use of nominals.

– $\widehat{\mathcal{E}}(\alpha, \mathcal{D}, \mathsf{CR})$ *is non-contradictory, and*
– $\mathcal{A}_{\mathsf{red}} \cup \mathcal{T}_{\mathsf{red}} \cup \mathcal{D}^{(0)} \cup \mathsf{pre}^{(0)} \cup \mathcal{T}^{(0)} \models \mathcal{T}^{(1)}$, *where* $\mathcal{A}_{\mathsf{red}}$ *and* $\mathcal{T}_{\mathsf{red}}$ *are constructed using* $\beta_{\alpha,\mathsf{CR},\mathcal{D}}$ *and* $\mathcal{R}$.

This lemma shows that consistency of an action w.r.t. a TBox and a finite set of causal relationships can be tested by considering the exponentially many elements of $\mathfrak{D}(\alpha, \mathsf{CR})$. For each element $\mathcal{D} \in \mathfrak{D}(\alpha, \mathsf{CR})$, consistency of $\mathcal{D} \cup \mathsf{pre}$ w.r.t. $\mathcal{T}$ can be tested in exponential time since reasoning in $\mathcal{ALCO}$ w.r.t. (general) TBoxes is ExpTime-complete [5]. For a given diagram $\mathcal{D}$, the set $\widehat{\mathcal{E}}(\alpha, \mathcal{D}, \mathsf{CR})$ as well as $\beta_{\alpha,\mathsf{CR},\mathcal{D}}$ and $\mathcal{R}$ can be computed in polynomial time, and the same is true for the construction of the ABox $\mathcal{A}_{\mathsf{red}}$ and the TBox $\mathcal{T}_{\mathsf{red}}$ using $\beta_{\alpha,\mathsf{CR},\mathcal{D}}$ and $\mathcal{R}$. Checking whether $\widehat{\mathcal{E}}(\alpha, \mathcal{D}, \mathsf{CR})$ is contradictory or not can also be realized in polynomial time. Finally, testing whether $\mathcal{A}_{\mathsf{red}} \cup \mathcal{T}_{\mathsf{red}} \cup \mathcal{D}^{(0)} \cup \mathsf{pre}^{(0)} \cup \mathcal{T}^{(0)} \models \mathcal{T}^{(1)}$ is again a reasoning problem for $\mathcal{ALCO}$, which can be solved in exponential time. Overall, we have seen that Lemma 3.7 yields a consistency test that requires at most exponentially many calls to ExpTime reasoning procedures. This yields an ExpTime upper bound for the complexity of the consistency problem. ExpTime-hardness can be shown similarly to our proof of PSpace-hardness for the case with an empty TBox.

Theorem 3.8. *The problem of deciding consistency of an action w.r.t. a TBox and a finite set of causal relationships is* ExpTime*-complete for* $\mathcal{ALCO}$.

4 Deciding Projection

The projection problem considers a sequence of actions $\alpha_1, \ldots, \alpha_n$, together with a TBox $\mathcal{T}$, a finite set of causal relationships CR, an initial ABox $\mathcal{A}$, and an assertion φ. By definition, φ is a consequence of applying $\alpha_1, \ldots, \alpha_n$ to $\mathcal{A}$ w.r.t. $\mathcal{T}$ and CR iff, for all interpretations $\mathcal{I}_0, \ldots, \mathcal{I}_{n-1}, \mathcal{I}_n$, if $\mathcal{I}_0 \models \mathcal{A}$ and $\mathcal{I}_0 \Longrightarrow_{\alpha_1}^{\mathcal{T},\mathsf{CR}} \mathcal{I}_1 \Longrightarrow_{\alpha_2}^{\mathcal{T},\mathsf{CR}} \cdots \mathcal{I}_{n-1} \Longrightarrow_{\alpha_n}^{\mathcal{T},\mathsf{CR}} \mathcal{I}_n$, then $\mathcal{I}_n \models \varphi$.

Our solution of the projection problem w.r.t. $\mathcal{T}$ and CR uses the same ideas as the solution of the consistency sketched in Section 3. *First*, instead of considering interpretations $\mathcal{I}_0, \ldots, \mathcal{I}_{n-1}$, we consider diagrams $\mathcal{D}_0, \ldots, \mathcal{D}_{n-1}$, where $\mathcal{D}_i \in \mathfrak{D}(\alpha_{i+1}, \mathsf{CR})$ for $i = 0, \ldots, n-1$.[7] *Second*, we use the original sequence of actions $\alpha_1, \ldots, \alpha_n$ and the diagrams $\mathcal{D}_0, \ldots, \mathcal{D}_{n-1}$ to build the corresponding sequence of actions $\beta_{\alpha_1,\mathsf{CR},\mathcal{D}_0}, \ldots, \beta_{\alpha_n,\mathsf{CR},\mathcal{D}_{n-1}}$. Lemma 3.5 then tells us that, for all models $\mathcal{I}_{i-1}$ of $\mathcal{D}_{i-1}$ and all interpretations $\mathcal{I}_i$ we have $\mathcal{I}_{i-1} \Longrightarrow_{\alpha_i}^{\emptyset,\mathsf{CR}} \mathcal{I}_i$ iff $\mathcal{I}_{i-1} \Longrightarrow_{\beta_{\alpha_i,\mathsf{CR},\mathcal{D}_{i-1}}}^{\emptyset,\emptyset} \mathcal{I}_i$. *Third*, we use the sequence $\beta_{\alpha_1,\mathsf{CR},\mathcal{D}_0}, \ldots, \beta_{\alpha_n,\mathsf{CR},\mathcal{D}_{n-1}}$ and the set of relevant role names and concept descriptions $\mathcal{R}$ to construct an ABox $\mathcal{A}_{\mathsf{red}}$ and (acyclic) a TBox $\mathcal{T}_{\mathsf{red}}$ such that the properties (a) and (b) of Lemma 3.6 hold. These properties can be used to express that the initial interpretation $\mathcal{I}_0$ must be a model of $\mathcal{A}$ and that we only consider interpretations $\mathcal{I}_i$ that are models of $\mathcal{T}$. In addition, we can then check, whether all this implies that the

[7] Note that it is enough to consider diagrams $\mathcal{D}_0, \ldots, \mathcal{D}_{n-1}$ for $\mathcal{I}_0, \ldots, \mathcal{I}_{n-1}$ since no action is applied to $\mathcal{I}_n$.

final interpretation $\mathcal{I}_n$ is a model of φ. To be more precise, we can show that the following characterization of the projection problem holds:

Lemma 4.1. *Let $\alpha_1, \ldots, \alpha_n$ be a sequence of actions, $\mathcal{T}$ a TBox, CR a finite set of causal relationships, $\mathcal{A}$ an initial ABox, and φ an assertion. Then, φ is a consequence of applying $\alpha_1, \ldots, \alpha_n$ to $\mathcal{A}$ w.r.t. $\mathcal{T}$ and CR iff for all diagrams $\mathcal{D}_0, \ldots, \mathcal{D}_{n-1}$ such that $\mathcal{D}_i \in \mathfrak{D}(\alpha_{i+1}, \mathsf{CR})$ for $i = 0, \ldots, n-1$, we have*

$$\bigcup_{i=0}^{n-1} \mathcal{D}_i^{(i)} \cup \bigcup_{i=0}^{n} \mathcal{T}^{(i)} \cup \mathcal{A}^{(0)} \cup \mathcal{A}_{\mathsf{red}} \cup \mathcal{T}_{\mathsf{red}} \models \varphi^{(n)}, \tag{1}$$

where $\mathcal{A}_{\mathsf{red}}$ and $\mathcal{T}_{\mathsf{red}}$ are constructed from $\beta_{\alpha_1,\mathsf{CR},\mathcal{D}_0}, \ldots, \beta_{\alpha_n,\mathsf{CR},\mathcal{D}_{n-1}}$ and $\mathcal{R}$.

It is easy to see that this lemma yields an ExpTime decision procedure for the projection problem in $\mathcal{ALCO}$. In fact, one needs to consider exponentially many sequences of diagrams $\mathcal{D}_0, \ldots, \mathcal{D}_{n-1}$. For each such sequence, the actions $\beta_{\alpha_1,\mathsf{CR},\mathcal{D}_0}, \ldots, \beta_{\alpha_n,\mathsf{CR},\mathcal{D}_{n-1}}$, and thus also $\mathcal{A}_{\mathsf{red}}$ and $\mathcal{T}_{\mathsf{red}}$, can be constructed in polynomial time. Thus, the inference problem (1) is of polynomial size, and it can be solved in exponential time since reasoning in $\mathcal{ALCO}$ w.r.t. a (general) TBox is ExpTime-complete. ExpTime-hardness of the projection problem can easily be shown by a reduction of concept satisfiability w.r.t. a TBox in $\mathcal{ALCO}$.

Theorem 4.2. *The projection problem w.r.t. a TBox and a finite set of causal relationships for $\mathcal{ALCO}$ is* ExpTime*-complete.*

For the special case of an empty TBox, the decision procedure derived from Lemma 4.1 actually needs only polynomial space. In fact, the exponentially many sequences of diagrams $\mathcal{D}_0, \ldots, \mathcal{D}_{n-1}$ can be enumerated within polynomial space, and for $\mathcal{T} = \emptyset$, the inference problem (1) contains no GCIs since TBox $\mathcal{T}_{\mathsf{red}}$ is acyclic. Thus, it can be solved within PSpace. PSpace-hardness of the projection problem is again easy to show.

Corollary 4.3. *The projection problem w.r.t. the empty TBox and a finite set of causal relationships is* PSpace*-complete for $\mathcal{ALCO}$.*

5 Additional Results and Future Work

Our approach for deciding the consistency and the projection problem works not only for $\mathcal{ALCO}$, but also for all the other DLs considered in [3]. Basically, we can use the same algorithms. What differs from DL to DL is the complexity of the basic inference problems in the respective DL (extended with nominals). Except for two cases (consistency of actions in $\mathcal{ALCQI}$ and $\mathcal{ALCQIO}$ in the case where the TBox is non-empty), we get the matching hardness results by a reduction from such a basic inference problem. The complexity results obtained this way are listed in Table 2. They are proved in detail in [2]. The table shows that (with the two exceptions mentioned above) the projection problem and the consistency problem in DL-based action formalisms with causal relationships is not harder than reasoning in the underlying DL (extended with nominals).

Table 2. The complexity of the consistency and the projection problem. PSP is short for PSPACE-complete, EXP for EXPTIME-complete, cNE for co-NEXPTIME-complete, PNE for *in* $\text{PTIME}^{\text{NEXPTIME}}$.

	TBox?	$\mathcal{ALC}$	$\mathcal{ALCO}$	$\mathcal{ALCQ}$	$\mathcal{ALCI}$	$\mathcal{ALCQO}$	$\mathcal{ALCQI}$	$\mathcal{ALCIO}$	$\mathcal{ALCQIO}$
Consistency	$\mathcal{T} = \emptyset$	PSP	PSP	PSP	PSP	PSP	PSP	EXP	cNE
	$\mathcal{T} \neq \emptyset$	EXP	EXP	EXP	EXP	EXP	PNE	EXP	PNE
Projection	$\mathcal{T} = \emptyset$	PSP	PSP	PSP	EXP	PSP	cNE	EXP	cNE
	$\mathcal{T} \neq \emptyset$	EXP	EXP	EXP	EXP	EXP	cNE	EXP	cNE

Regarding future work, one interesting question is whether our approach for deciding the consistency and the projection problem can be extended to actions with occlusions. Note that such actions are non-deterministic, i.e., their application to an interpretation may yield several possible successor interpretations. Consequently, such an action may still be consistent although some of the successors interpretations are not models of the TBox. Thus, consistency can no longer be characterized by an analog of Lemma 3.7.

When defining our semantics for actions in the presence of causal relationships, we followed the approach used in [17,6] rather than the one employed by [8,15]. In our health insurance example, this was actually the appropriate semantics, but there may also be examples where it would be better to use the other semantics. Thus, it would be interesting to see whether our approach for deciding the consistency and the projection problem can be adapted to deal with the semantics of [8,15].

Instead of trying to decide the projection problem directly, one can also follow the progression approach: given an action and a (possibly incomplete) description of the current state, this approach tries to compute a description of the possible successor states. Projection then boils down to computing consequences of this successor description. For DL-based action theories, progression has been investigated in [10]. It would be interesting to see whether the results obtained there can be extended to the DL-based action theories with causal relationships considered in the present paper.

This paper follows the approach for obtaining decidability results for action theories introduced in [3], which is based on the idea of restricting the base logic to a decidable DL. In the literature, other ways of restricting the base logic to achieve this goal have been considered. For example, in [11] the authors consider so-called local effect actions[8] and restrict the base logic to so-called "proper$^+$ knowledge bases" [12]. They show that, in this setting, progression is efficiently computable, which implies that the projection problem is efficiently decidable. It would be interesting to see whether this result can be extended to actions theories with causal relationships.

[8] Note that our DL-based actions are local effect actions.

References

1. Baader, F., Calvanese, D., McGuinness, D.L., Nardi, D., Patel-Schneider, P.F. (eds.): The Description Logic Handbook: Theory, Implementation, and Applications. Cambridge University Press, Cambridge (2003)
2. Baader, F., Lippmann, M., Liu, H.: Adding causal relationships to DL-based action formalisms. LTCS-Report 10-01, Chair of Automata Theory, Technische Universität Dresden (2010), `http://lat.inf.tu-dresden.de/research/reports.html`
3. Baader, F., Lutz, C., Miličić, M., Sattler, U., Wolter, F.: Integrating description logics and action formalisms: First results. In: Proceedings of AAAI-2005 and IAAI-2005, pp. 572–577. AAAI Press/The MIT Press (2005) Short version of [4]
4. Baader, F., Miličić, M., Lutz, C., Sattler, U., Wolter, F.: Integrating description logics and action formalisms for reasoning about web services. LTCS-Report 05-02, Chair of Automata Theory, Technische Universität Dresden (2005), Long version of [3], `http://lat.inf.tu-dresden.de/research/reports.html`
5. De Giacomo, G.: Decidability of Class-Based Knowledge Representation Formalisms. PhD thesis, Università di Roma "La Sapienza" (1995)
6. Denecker, M., Theseider-Dupré, D., van Belleghem, K.: An inductive definition approach to ramifications. Linkoping Electronic Articles in Computer and Information Science 3(7), 1–43 (1998)
7. Herzig, A.: The PMA revisited. In: Proceedings of KR-1996, pp. 40–50 (1996)
8. Lin, F.: Embracing causality in specifying the indirect effects of actions. In: Proceedings of IJCAI-1995, pp. 1985–1993 (1995)
9. Liu, H., Lutz, C., Miličić, M., Wolter, F.: Reasoning about actions using description logics with general TBoxes. In: Fisher, M., van der Hoek, W., Konev, B., Lisitsa, A. (eds.) JELIA 2006. LNCS (LNAI), vol. 4160, pp. 266–279. Springer, Heidelberg (2006)
10. Liu, H., Lutz, C., Miličić, M., Wolter, F.: Updating description logic ABoxes. In: Proceedings of KR-2006, pp. 46–56. AAAI Press, Menlo Park (2006)
11. Liu, Y., Lakemeyer, G.: On first-order definability and computability of progression for local-effect actions and beyond. In: Proceedings of IJCAI-2009, pp. 860–866 (2009)
12. Liu, Y., Levesque, H.J.: Tractable reasoning in first-order knowledge bases with disjunctive information. In: Proceedings of AAAI-2005 and IAAI-2005, pp. 639–644. AAAI Press/The MIT Press (2005)
13. Reiter, R.: Knowledge in Action: Logical Foundations for Describing and Implementing Dynamical Systems. The MIT Press, Bradford Books (2001)
14. Schaerf, A.: Reasoning with individuals in concept languages. Data Knowledge Engineering 13(2), 141–176 (1994)
15. Thielscher, M.: Ramification and causality. AIJ 89(1–2), 317–364 (1997)
16. Thielscher, M.: Reasoning Robots: The Art and Science of Programming Robotic Agents. Applied Logic Series, vol. 33. Springer, Netherlands (2005)
17. van Belleghem, K., Denecker, M., Theseider-Dupré, D.: A constructive approach to the ramification problem. In: Proceedings of ESSLLI-1998, pp. 1–17 (1998)
18. Winslett, M.: Reasoning about action using a possible models approach. In: Proceedings of AAAI-1988, pp. 89–93 (1988)

SAT Encoding of Unification in $\mathcal{EL}$

Franz Baader and Barbara Morawska*

Theoretical Computer Science, TU Dresden, Germany
{baader,morawska}@tcs.inf.tu-dresden.de

Abstract. Unification in Description Logics has been proposed as a novel inference service that can, for example, be used to detect redundancies in ontologies. In a recent paper, we have shown that unification in $\mathcal{EL}$ is NP-complete, and thus of a complexity that is considerably lower than in other Description Logics of comparably restricted expressive power. In this paper, we introduce a new NP-algorithm for solving unification problems in $\mathcal{EL}$, which is based on a reduction to satisfiability in propositional logic (SAT). The advantage of this new algorithm is, on the one hand, that it allows us to employ highly optimized state-of-the-art SAT solvers when implementing an $\mathcal{EL}$-unification algorithm. On the other hand, this reduction provides us with a proof of the fact that $\mathcal{EL}$-unification is in NP that is much simpler than the one given in our previous paper on $\mathcal{EL}$-unification.

1 Introduction

Description logics (DLs) [3] are a well-investigated family of logic-based knowledge representation formalisms. They can be used to represent the relevant concepts of an application domain using concept terms, which are built from concept names and role names using certain concept constructors. The DL $\mathcal{EL}$ offers the constructors conjunction ($\sqcap$), existential restriction ($\exists r.C$), and the top concept ($\top$). This description logic has recently drawn considerable attention since, on the one hand, important inference problems such as the subsumption problem are polynomial in $\mathcal{EL}$ [1,2]. On the other hand, though quite inexpressive, $\mathcal{EL}$ can be used to define biomedical ontologies. For example, both the large medical ontology SNOMED CT and the Gene Ontology[1] can be expressed in $\mathcal{EL}$.

Unification in description logics has been proposed in [6] as a novel inference service that can, for example, be used to detect redundancies in ontologies. There, it was shown that, for the DL $\mathcal{FL}_0$, which differs from $\mathcal{EL}$ by offering value restrictions ($\forall r.C$) in place of existential restrictions, deciding unifiability is an ExpTime-complete problem. In [4], we were able to show that unification in $\mathcal{EL}$ is of considerably lower complexity: the decision problem is "only" NP-complete. However, the unification algorithm introduced in [4] to establish the NP upper bound is a brutal "guess and then test" NP-algorithm, and thus it is unlikely that a direct implementation of it will perform well in practice.

* Supported by DFG under grant BA 1122/14-1

[1] See http://www.ihtsdo.org/snomed-ct/ and http://www.geneontology.org/

C. Fermüller and A. Voronkov (Eds.): LPAR-17, LNCS 6397, pp. 97–111, 2010.

In this report, we present a new decision procedure for $\mathcal{EL}$-unification that takes a given $\mathcal{EL}$-unification problem Γ and translates it into a set of propositional clauses $C(\Gamma)$ such that (i) the size of $C(\Gamma)$ is polynomial in the size of Γ, and (ii) Γ is unifiable iff $C(\Gamma)$ is satisfiable. This allows us to use a highly-optimized SAT-solver such as MiniSat[2] to decide solvability of $\mathcal{EL}$-unification problems. Our SAT-translation is inspired by Kapur and Narendran's translation of ACIU-unification problems into satisfiability in propositional Horn logic (HornSAT) [9]. The connection between $\mathcal{EL}$-unification and ACIU-unification is due to the fact that (modulo equivalence) the conjunction constructor in $\mathcal{EL}$ is associative, commutative, and idempotent, and has the top concept $\top$ as a unit. Existential restrictions are similar to free unary functions symbols in ACIU, with the difference that existential restrictions are monotonic w.r.t. subsumption.

It should be noted that the proof of correctness of our translation into SAT does *not* depend on the results in [4]. Consequently, this translation provides us with a new proof of the fact that $\mathcal{EL}$-unification is in NP. This proof is much simpler than the original proof of this fact in [4].

2 Unification in $\mathcal{EL}$

Starting with a set N_{con} of concept names and a set N_{role} of role names, $\mathcal{EL}$-*concept terms* are built using the following concept constructors: the nullary constructor *top-concept* ($\top$), the binary constructor *conjunction* ($C \sqcap D$), and for every role name $r \in N_{role}$, the unary constructor *existential restriction* ($\exists r.C$). The semantics of $\mathcal{EL}$ is defined in the usual way, using the notion of an interpretation $\mathcal{I} = (\mathcal{D}_\mathcal{I}, \cdot^\mathcal{I})$, which consists of a nonempty domain $\mathcal{D}_\mathcal{I}$ and an interpretation function $\cdot^\mathcal{I}$ that assigns binary relations on $\mathcal{D}_\mathcal{I}$ to role names and subsets of $\mathcal{D}_\mathcal{I}$ to concept terms, as shown in the semantics column of Table 1.

Table 1. Syntax and semantics of $\mathcal{EL}$

Name	Syntax	Semantics
concept name	A	$A^\mathcal{I} \subseteq \mathcal{D}_\mathcal{I}$
role name	r	$r^\mathcal{I} \subseteq \mathcal{D}_\mathcal{I} \times \mathcal{D}_\mathcal{I}$
top-concept	$\top$	$\top^\mathcal{I} = \mathcal{D}_\mathcal{I}$
conjunction	$C \sqcap D$	$(C \sqcap D)^\mathcal{I} = C^\mathcal{I} \cap D^\mathcal{I}$
existential restriction	$\exists r.C$	$(\exists r.C)^\mathcal{I} = \{x \mid \exists y : (x,y) \in r^\mathcal{I} \wedge y \in C^\mathcal{I}\}$
subsumption	$C \sqsubseteq D$	$C^\mathcal{I} \subseteq D^\mathcal{I}$
equivalence	$C \equiv D$	$C^\mathcal{I} = D^\mathcal{I}$

The concept term C *is subsumed by* the concept term D (written $C \sqsubseteq D$) iff $C^\mathcal{I} \subseteq D^\mathcal{I}$ holds for all interpretations $\mathcal{I}$. We say that C *is equivalent to* D (written $C \equiv D$) iff $C \sqsubseteq D$ and $D \sqsubseteq C$, i.e., iff $C^\mathcal{I} = D^\mathcal{I}$ holds for all interpretations $\mathcal{I}$.

[2] http://minisat.se/

The following lemma provides us with a useful *characterization of subsumption in* $\mathcal{EL}$ [4].

Lemma 1. *Let* C, D *be* $\mathcal{EL}$*-concept terms such that*

$$C = A_1 \sqcap \ldots \sqcap A_k \sqcap \exists r_1.C_1 \sqcap \ldots \sqcap \exists r_m.C_m,$$
$$D = B_1 \sqcap \ldots \sqcap B_\ell \sqcap \exists s_1.D_1 \sqcap \ldots \sqcap \exists s_n.D_n,$$

where $A_1, \ldots, A_k, B_1, \ldots, B_\ell$ *are concept names. Then* $C \sqsubseteq D$ *iff*

- $\{B_1, \ldots, B_\ell\} \subseteq \{A_1, \ldots, A_k\}$ *and*
- *for every* $j, 1 \leq j \leq n$, *there exists* $i, 1 \leq i \leq m$, *s.t.* $r_i = s_j$ *and* $C_i \sqsubseteq D_j$.

When defining unification in $\mathcal{EL}$, we assume that the set of concepts names is partitioned into a set N_v of concept variables (which may be replaced by substitutions) and a set N_c of concept constants (which must not be replaced by substitutions). A *substitution* σ is a mapping from N_v into the set of all $\mathcal{EL}$-concept terms. This mapping is extended to concept terms in the usual way, i.e., by replacing all occurrences of variables in the term by their σ-images.

A substitution σ induces the following binary relation $>_\sigma$ on variables:

$$X >_\sigma Y \text{ iff there are } n \geq 1 \text{ role names } r_1, \ldots, r_n \in N_{role} \text{ such that}$$
$$\sigma(X) \sqsubseteq \sigma(\exists r_1. \cdots \exists r_n.Y).$$

The following lemma is an easy consequence of Lemma 1.

Lemma 2. *The relation* $>_\sigma$ *is a strict partial order.*

Unification tries to make concept terms equivalent by applying a substitution.

Definition 1. *An* $\mathcal{EL}$-unification problem *is of the form* $\Gamma = \{C_1 \equiv^? D_1, \ldots, C_n \equiv^? D_n\}$, *where* $C_1, D_1, \ldots C_n, D_n$ *are* $\mathcal{EL}$*-concept terms. The substitution* σ *is a* unifier *(or* solution*) of* Γ *iff* $\sigma(C_i) \equiv \sigma(D_i)$ *for* $i = 1, \ldots, n$. *In this case,* Γ *is called* solvable *or* unifiable.

Note that Lemma 2 implies that the variable X cannot unify with the concept term $\exists r_1. \cdots \exists r_n.X$ $(n \geq 1)$, i.e., the $\mathcal{EL}$-unification problem $\{X \equiv^? \exists r_1. \cdots \exists r_n.X\}$ does not have a solution. This means that an $\mathcal{EL}$-unification algorithm has to realize a kind of *occurs check*.

We will assume without loss of generality that our $\mathcal{EL}$-unification problems are flattened in the sense that they do not contain nested existential restrictions. To define this notion in more detail, we need to introduce the notion of an atom. An $\mathcal{EL}$-concept term is called an *atom* iff it is a concept name (i.e., concept constant or concept variable) or an existential restriction $\exists r.D$. A *non-variable atom* is an atom that is not a concept variable. The set of *atoms of an* $\mathcal{EL}$*-concept term* C consists of all the subterms of C that are atoms. For example, $A \sqcap \exists r.(B \sqcap \exists r.\top)$ has the atom set $\{A, \exists r.(B \sqcap \exists r.\top), B, \exists r.\top\}$.

Obviously, any $\mathcal{EL}$-concept term is (equivalent to) a conjunction of atoms, where the empty conjunction is $\top$. The following lemma is an easy consequence of Lemma 1.

Lemma 3. *Let C, D be $\mathcal{EL}$-concept terms such that $C = C_1 \sqcap \ldots \sqcap C_m$ and $D = D_1 \sqcap \ldots \sqcap D_n$, where $D_1, \ldots, D_n$ are atoms. Then $C \sqsubseteq D$ iff for every $j, 1 \leq j \leq n$, there exists an $i, 1 \leq i \leq m$, such that $C_i \sqsubseteq D_j$.*

In our reduction, we will restrict the attention (without loss of generality) to unification problems that are built from atoms without nested existential restrictions. To be more precise, concept names and existential restrictions $\exists r.D$ where D is a concept name are called *flat atoms*. An $\mathcal{EL}$-concept term is *flat* iff it is a conjunction of flat atoms (where the empty conjunction is $\top$). The $\mathcal{EL}$-unification problem Γ is *flat* iff it consists of equations between flat $\mathcal{EL}$-concept terms. By introducing new concept variables and eliminating $\top$, any $\mathcal{EL}$-unification problem Γ can be transformed in polynomial time into a flat $\mathcal{EL}$-unification problem Γ' such that Γ is solvable iff Γ' is solvable. Thus, we may assume without loss of generality that our input $\mathcal{EL}$-unification problems are flat. Given a flat $\mathcal{EL}$-unification problem $\Gamma = \{C_1 \equiv^? D_1, \ldots, C_n \equiv^? D_n\}$, we call the atoms of $C_1, D_1, \ldots, C_n, D_n$ the *atoms of* Γ.

3 The SAT Encoding

In the following, let Γ be a flat $\mathcal{EL}$-unification problem. We show how to translate Γ into a set of propositional clauses $C(\Gamma)$ such that (i) the size of $C(\Gamma)$ is polynomial in the size of Γ, and (ii) Γ is unifiable iff $C(\Gamma)$ is satisfiable. The main idea underlying this translation is that we want to guess, for every pair of atoms A, B of the flat unification problem Γ, whether or not A is subsumed by B after the application of the unifier σ to be computed. In addition, we need to guess a strict partial order $>$ on the variables of Γ, which corresponds to (a subset of) the strict partial order $>_\sigma$ induced by σ.

Thus, we use the following propositional variables:

- $[A \not\sqsubseteq B]$ for every pair A, B of atoms of Γ;
- $[X > Y]$ for every pair of variables occurring in Γ.

Note that we use non-subsumption rather than subsumption for the propositional variables of the first kind since this will allow us to translate the equations of the unification problem into Horn clauses (*à la* Kapur and Narendran [9]). However, we will have to "pay" for this since expressing transitivity of subsumption then requires the use of non-Horn clauses.

Given a flat $\mathcal{EL}$-unification problem Γ, the set $C(\Gamma)$ consists of the following clauses:

(1) Translation of the equations of Γ. For every equation $A_1 \sqcap \cdots \sqcap A_m \equiv^? B_1 \sqcap \cdots \sqcap B_n$ of Γ, we create the following Horn clauses, which express that any atom that occurs as a top-level conjunct on one side of an equivalence must subsume a top-level conjunct on the other side:[3]

[3] See Lemma 3.

1. For every non-variable atom $C \in \{A_1, \ldots, A_m\}$:
   $[B_1 \not\sqsubseteq C] \wedge \ldots \wedge [B_n \not\sqsubseteq C] \rightarrow$
2. For every non-variable atom $C \in \{B_1, \ldots, B_n\}$:
   $[A_1 \not\sqsubseteq C] \wedge \ldots \wedge [A_m \not\sqsubseteq C] \rightarrow$
3. For every non-variable atom C of Γ s.t. $C \notin \{A_1, \ldots, A_m, B_1, \ldots, B_n\}$:
   $[A_1 \not\sqsubseteq C] \wedge \ldots \wedge [A_m \not\sqsubseteq C] \rightarrow [B_j \not\sqsubseteq C]$ for $j = 1, \ldots, n$
   $[B_1 \not\sqsubseteq C] \wedge \ldots \wedge [B_n \not\sqsubseteq C] \rightarrow [A_i \not\sqsubseteq C]$ for $i = 1, \ldots, m$

(2) Translation of the relevant properties of subsumption in $\mathcal{EL}$.

1. For every pair of distinct concept constants A, B occurring in Γ, we say that A cannot be subsumed by B:
   $\rightarrow [A \not\sqsubseteq B]$
2. For every pair of distinct role names r, s and atoms $\exists r.A, \exists s.B$ of Γ, we say that $\exists r.A$ cannot be subsumed by $\exists s.B$:
   $\rightarrow [\exists r.A \not\sqsubseteq \exists s.B]$
3. For every pair $\exists r.A, \exists r.B$ of atoms of Γ, we say that $\exists r.A$ can only be subsumed by $\exists r.B$ if A is already subsumed by B:
   $[A \not\sqsubseteq B] \rightarrow [\exists r.A \not\sqsubseteq \exists r.B]$
4. For every concept constant A and every atom $\exists r.B$ of Γ, we say that A and $\exists r.B$ are not in a subsumption relationship
   $\rightarrow [A \not\sqsubseteq \exists r.B]$ and $\rightarrow [\exists r.B \not\sqsubseteq A]$
5. Transitivity of subsumption is expressed using the *non-Horn* clauses:
   $[C_1 \not\sqsubseteq C_3] \rightarrow [C_1 \not\sqsubseteq C_2] \vee [C_2 \not\sqsubseteq C_3]$ where C_1, C_2, C_3 are atoms of Γ.

Note that there are further properties that hold for subsumption in $\mathcal{EL}$ (e.g., the fact that $A \sqsubseteq B$ implies $\exists r.A \sqsubseteq \exists r.B$), but that are not needed to ensure soundness of our translation.

(3) Translation of the relevant properties of $>$.

1. Transitivity and irreflexivity of $>$ can be expressed using the Horn clauses:
   $[X{>}X] \rightarrow$ and $[X{>}Y] \wedge [Y{>}Z] \rightarrow [X{>}Z]$,
   where X, Y, Z are concept variables occurring in Γ.
2. The connection between this order and the order $>_\sigma$ is expressed using the *non-Horn* clauses:
   $\rightarrow [X{>}Y] \vee [X \not\sqsubseteq \exists r.Y]$,
   where X, Y are concept variables occurring in Γ and $\exists r.Y$ is an atom of Γ.

Since the number of atoms of Γ is linear in the size of Γ, it is easy to see that $C(\Gamma)$ is of size polynomial in the size of Γ, and that it can be computed in polynomial time. Note, however, that without additional optimizations, the polynomial can be quite big. If the size of Γ is n, then the number of atoms of Γ is in $O(n)$. The number of possible propositional variables is thus in $O(n^2)$. The size of $C(\Gamma)$ is dominated by the number of clauses expressing the transitivity of subsumption and the transitivity of the order on variables. Thus, the size of $C(\Gamma)$ is in $O((n^2)^3) = O(n^6)$.

Example 1. It is easy to see that the $\mathcal{EL}$-unification problem $\Gamma := \{X \sqcap \exists r.X \equiv^? X\}$ does not have a solution. The set of clauses $C(\Gamma)$ has the following elements:

(1) The only clause created in (1) is: $[X \not\sqsubseteq \exists r.X] \rightarrow$.
(2) Among the clauses introduced in (2) is the following:
   5. $[\exists r.X \not\sqsubseteq \exists r.X] \rightarrow [\exists r.X \not\sqsubseteq X] \vee [X \not\sqsubseteq \exists r.X]$
(3) The following clauses are created in (3):
   1. $[X > X] \rightarrow$
   2. $\rightarrow [X > X] \vee [X \not\sqsubseteq \exists r.X]$.

This set of clauses is unsatisfiable. In fact, $[X \not\sqsubseteq \exists r.X]$ needs to be assigned the truth value 0 because of (1). Consequently, (3)2. implies that $[X > X]$ needs to be assigned the truth value 1, which then falsifies (3)1.

The next example considers an equation where the right-hand side is the top concept, which is the empty conjunction of flat atoms.

Example 2. The $\mathcal{EL}$-unification problem $\Gamma := \{A \sqcap B \equiv^? \top\}$ has no solution.

In (1)1. we need to construct clauses for the atoms A and B on the left-hand side. Since the right-hand side of the equation is the empty conjunction (i.e., $n = 0$), the left-hand sides of the implications generated this way are empty, i.e., both atoms yield the implication $\rightarrow$, in which both the left-hand side and the right-hand side is empty. An empty left-hand side is read as true (1), whereas an empty right-hand side is read as false (0). Thus, this implication is unsatisfiable.

Theorem 1 (Soundness and completeness). *Let Γ be a flat $\mathcal{EL}$-unification problem. Then, Γ is solvable iff $C(\Gamma)$ is satisfiable.*

We prove this theorem in the next two subsections, one devoted to the proof of soundness and the other to the proof of completeness. After the formal proof, we will also explain the reduction on a more intuitive level. Since our translation into SAT is polynomial and SAT is in NP, Theorem 1 shows that $\mathcal{EL}$-unification is in NP. NP-hardness follows from the fact that $\mathcal{EL}$-matching is known to be NP-hard [10]: in fact, matching problems are special unification problems where the terms on the right-hand sides of the equations do not contain variables.

Corollary 1. *$\mathcal{EL}$-unification is NP-complete.*

3.1 Soundness

To prove soundness, we assume that $C(\Gamma)$ is satisfiable. We must show that this implies that Γ is solvable. In order to define a unifier of Γ, we take a propositional valuation τ that satisfies $C(\Gamma)$, and use τ to define an *assignment* of sets S_X of non-variable atoms of Γ to the variables X of Γ:

$$S_X := \{C \mid C \text{ non-variable atom of } \Gamma \text{ s.t. } \tau([X \not\sqsubseteq C]) = 0\}.$$

Given this assignment of sets of non-variable atoms to the variables in Γ, we say that the variable X *directly depends on* the variable Y if Y occurs in an atom of S_X. Let *depends on* be the transitive closure of *directly depends on*. We define the binary relation $>_d$ on variables as $X >_d Y$ iff X depends on Y.

Lemma 4. *Let X, Y be variables occurring in Γ.*

1. *If $X >_d Y$, then $\tau([X{>}Y]) = 1$.*
2. *The relation $>_d$ is irreflexive, i.e., $X \not>_d X$.*

Proof. (1) If X *directly depends on* the variable Y, then Y appears in a non-variable atom of S_X. This atom must be of the form $\exists r.Y$. By the construction of S_X, $\exists r.Y \in S_X$ can only be the case if $\tau([X \not\sqsubseteq \exists r.Y]) = 0$. Since $C(\Gamma)$ contains the clause $\to [X{>}Y] \vee [X \not\sqsubseteq \exists r.Y]$, this implies $\tau([X{>}Y]) = 1$.

Since the transitivity clauses introduced in (3)1. are satisfied by τ, we also have that $\tau([X{>}Y]) = 1$ whenever X *depends on* the variable Y.

(2) If X depends on itself, then $\tau([X{>}X]) = 1$ by the first part of this lemma. This is, however, impossible since τ satisfies the clause $[X{>}X] \to$. □

The second part of this lemma shows that the relation $>_d$, which is transitive by definition, is a strict partial order. We can now use the sets S_X to define a substitution σ along the strict partial order $>_d$:[4]

- If X is a minimal variable w.r.t. $>_d$, then $\sigma(X)$ is the conjunction of the elements of S_X, where the empty conjunction is $\top$.
- Assume that $\sigma(Y)$ is already defined for all variables Y such that $X >_d Y$, and let $S_X = \{D_1, \ldots, D_n\}$. We define $\sigma(X) := \sigma(D_1) \sqcap \ldots \sqcap \sigma(D_n)$, where again the empty conjunction (in case $n = 0$) is $\top$.

Note that the substitution σ defined this way is actually a *ground* substitution, i.e., for all variables X occurring in Γ we have that $\sigma(X)$ does not contain variables. In the following, we will say that this substitution is *induced by* the valuation τ. Before we can show that σ is a unifier of Γ, we must first prove the following lemma.

Lemma 5. *Let C_1, C_2 be atoms of Γ. If $\tau([C_1 \not\sqsubseteq C_2]) = 0$, then $\sigma(C_1) \sqsubseteq \sigma(C_2)$.*

Proof. Assume that $\tau([C_1 \not\sqsubseteq C_2]) = 0$. First, consider the case where C_1 is a variable. If C_2 is not a variable, then (by the construction of σ) $\tau([C_1 \not\sqsubseteq C_2]) = 0$ implies that $\sigma(C_2)$ is a conjunct of $\sigma(C_1)$, and hence $\sigma(C_1) \sqsubseteq \sigma(C_2)$. If C_2 is a variable, then $\tau([C_1 \not\sqsubseteq C_2]) = 0$, together with the transitivity clauses of (2)5., implies that every conjunct of $\sigma(C_2)$ is also a conjunct of $\sigma(C_1)$, which again yields $\sigma(C_1) \sqsubseteq \sigma(C_2)$. Second, consider the case where $\sigma(C_2) = \top$. Then $\sigma(C_1) \sqsubseteq \sigma(C_2)$ obviously holds.

Hence, it remains to prove the lemma for the cases when C_1 is not a variable (i.e., it is a concept constant or an existential restriction) and $\sigma(C_2)$ is not $\top$. We use induction on the role depth of $\sigma(C_1) \sqcap \sigma(C_2)$, where the role depth of an $\mathcal{EL}$-concept term is the maximal nesting of existential restrictions in this term. To be more precise, if D_1, D_2, C_1, C_2 are atoms of Γ, then we define $(D_1, D_2) \succ (C_1, C_2)$ iff the role depth of $\sigma(D_1) \sqcap \sigma(D_2)$ is greater than the role depth of $\sigma(C_1) \sqcap \sigma(C_2)$.

[4] $>_d$ is well-founded since Γ contains only finitely many variables.

We prove the lemma by induction on $\succ$. The base case for this induction is the case where $\sigma(C_1)$ and $\sigma(C_2)$ have role depth 0, i.e., both are conjunctions of concept constants. Since C_1 is not a variable, this implies that C_1 is a concept constant. The atom C_2 is either a concept constant or a concept variable. We consider these two cases:

- Let C_2 be a concept constant (and thus $C_2 = \sigma(C_2)$). Since $\tau([C_1 \not\sqsubseteq C_2]) = 0$ and the clauses introduced in (2)1. of the translation to SAT are satisfied by τ, we have $C_2 = C_1$, and thus $\sigma(C_1) \sqsubseteq \sigma(C_2)$.
- Assume that C_2 is a variable. Since the role depth of $\sigma(C_2)$ is 0 and $\sigma(C_2)$ is not $\top$, $\sigma(C_2)$ is a non-empty conjunction of concept constants, i.e., $\sigma(C_2) = B_1 \sqcap \cdots \sqcap B_n$ for $n \geq 1$ constants $B_1, \ldots, B_n$ such that $\tau([C_2 \not\sqsubseteq B_i]) = 0$ for $i = \{1, \ldots, n\}$. Then, since τ satisfies the transitivity clauses introduced in (2)5. of the translation to SAT, $\tau([C_1 \not\sqsubseteq B_i]) = 0$ for $i = \{1, \ldots, n\}$. Since τ satisfies the clauses introduced in (2)1. of the translation to SAT, B_i must be identical to C_1 for $i = \{1, \ldots, n\}$. Hence, $\sigma(C_2) = B_1 \sqcap \cdots \sqcap B_n \equiv C_1 = \sigma(C_1)$, which implies $\sigma(C_1) \sqsubseteq \sigma(C_2)$.

Now we assume by induction that the statement of the lemma holds for all pairs of atoms D_1, D_2 such that $(C_1, C_2) \succ (D_1, D_2)$. Notice that, if C_1 is a constant, then $\sigma(C_2)$ cannot contain an atom of the form $\exists r.D$ as a top-level conjunct. In fact, this could only be the case if either C_2 is an existential restriction, or C_2 is a variable and S_{C_2} contains an existential restriction. In the first case, $\tau([C_1 \not\sqsubseteq C_2]) = 0$ would then imply that one of the clauses introduced in (2)4. is not satisfied by τ. In the second case, τ would either need to violate one of the transitivity clauses introduced in (2)5. or one of the clauses introduced in (2)4. Thus, $\sigma(C_2)$ cannot contain an atom of the form $\exists r.D$ as a top-level conjunct. This implies that $\sigma(C_1) \sqcap \sigma(C_2)$ has role depth 0, which actually means that we are in the base case. Therefore, we can assume that C_1 is not a constant.

Since C_1 is not a variable, we have only one case to consider: C_1 is of the form $C_1 = \exists r.C$. Then, because of the clauses in (2)4. and the transitivity clauses in (2)5., $\sigma(C_2)$ cannot contain a constant as a conjunct. If C_2 is an existential restriction $C_2 = \exists s.D$, then $\tau([C_1 \not\sqsubseteq C_2]) = 0$, together with the clauses in (2)2. yields $r = s$. Consequently, $\tau([C_1 \not\sqsubseteq C_2]) = 0$, together with the clauses in (2)3., yields $\tau([C \not\sqsubseteq D] = 0$. By induction, this implies $\sigma(C) \sqsubseteq \sigma(D)$, and thus $\sigma(C_1) = \exists r.\sigma(C) \sqsubseteq \exists r.\sigma(D) = \sigma(C_2)$.

If C_2 is a variable, then (by the construction of σ and the clauses in (2)4.) $\sigma(C_2)$ must be a conjunction of atoms of the form $\exists r_1.\sigma(D_1), \ldots, \exists r_n.\sigma(D_n)$, where $\tau([C_2 \not\sqsubseteq \exists r_i.D_i]) = 0$ for $i = 1, \ldots, n$. The transitivity clauses in (2)5. yield $\tau([\exists r.C \not\sqsubseteq \exists r_1.D_1]) = \ldots = \tau([\exists r.C \not\sqsubseteq \exists r_n.D_n]) = 0$, and the clauses in (2)2. yield $r_1 = \cdots = r_n = r$. Using the clauses in (2)3., we thus obtain $\tau([C \not\sqsubseteq D_1]) = \ldots = \tau([C \not\sqsubseteq D_n]) = 0$. Induction yields $\sigma(C) \sqsubseteq \sigma(D_1), \ldots, \sigma(C) \sqsubseteq \sigma(D_n)$, which in turn implies $\sigma(C_1) = \exists r.\sigma(C) \sqsubseteq \exists r_1.\sigma(D_1) \sqcap \cdots \sqcap \exists r_n.\sigma(D_n) = \sigma(C_2)$. □

Now we can easily prove the soundness of the translation.

Proposition 1 (Soundness). *The substitution σ induced by a satisfying valuation of $C(\Gamma)$ is a unifier of Γ.*

Proof. We have to show, for each equation $A_1 \sqcap \ldots \sqcap A_m \equiv^? B_1 \sqcap \ldots \sqcap B_n$ in Γ, that $\sigma(A_1) \sqcap \ldots \sqcap \sigma(A_m) \equiv \sigma(B_1) \sqcap \ldots \sqcap \sigma(B_n)$. Both sides of this equivalence are conjunctions of ground atoms, i.e., $\sigma(A_1) \sqcap \ldots \sqcap \sigma(A_m) = E_1 \sqcap \ldots \sqcap E_l$ and $\sigma(B_1) \sqcap \ldots \sqcap \sigma(B_n) = F_1 \sqcap \ldots \sqcap F_k$. By Lemma 3, we can prove that the equivalence holds by showing that, for each F_i, there is an A_j such that $\sigma(A_j) \sqsubseteq F_i$, and for each E_j, there is a B_i such that $\sigma(B_i) \sqsubseteq E_j$. Here we show only the first part since the other one can be shown in the same way.

First, assume that $F_i = \sigma(B_\nu)$ for a non-variable atom $B_\nu \in \{B_1, \ldots, B_n\}$. Since the clauses introduced in (1)2. of the translation are satisfied by τ, there is an A_j such that $\tau([A_j \not\sqsubseteq B_\nu]) = 0$. By Lemma 5, this implies $\sigma(A_j) \sqsubseteq \sigma(B_\nu) = F_i$.

If there is no non-variable atom $B_\nu \in \{B_1, \ldots, B_n\}$ such that $\sigma(B_\nu) = F_i$, then there is a variable B_ν such that the atom F_i is a conjunct of $\sigma(B_\nu)$. By the construction of σ, we know that there is a non-variable atom C of Γ such that $F_i = \sigma(C)$ and $\tau([B_\nu \not\sqsubseteq C]) = 0$. By our assumption, C is not in $\{B_1, \ldots, B_n\}$. Since the clauses created in (1)3. are satisfied by τ, there is an A_j such that $\tau([A_j \not\sqsubseteq C]) = 0$. By Lemma 5, this implies $\sigma(A_j) \sqsubseteq \sigma(C) = F_i$. □

3.2 Completeness

To show *completeness*, assume that Γ is solvable, and let γ be a unifier Γ. We must show that there is a propositional valuation τ satisfying all the clauses in $C(\Gamma)$. We define the propositional valuation τ as follows:

- for all atoms C, D of Γ, we define $\tau([C \not\sqsubseteq D]) := 1$ if $\gamma(C) \not\sqsubseteq \gamma(D)$; and $\tau([C \not\sqsubseteq D]) := 0$ if $\gamma(C) \sqsubseteq \gamma(D)$.
- for all variables X, Y occurring in Γ, we define $\tau([X{>}Y]) := 1$ if $X >_\gamma Y$; and $\tau([X{>}Y]) := 0$ otherwise.

In the following, we call τ the valuation *induced by* γ. We show that τ satisfies all the clauses that are created by our translation:

(1) In (1) of the translation we create three types of Horn clauses for each equation $A_1 \sqcap \cdots \sqcap A_m \equiv^? B_1 \sqcap \cdots \sqcap B_n$.
  1. If $C \in \{A_1, \ldots, A_m\}$ is a non-variable atom, then $C(\Gamma)$ contains the clause $[B_1 \not\sqsubseteq C] \wedge \cdots \wedge [B_n \not\sqsubseteq C] \rightarrow$.

     The fact that C is a non-variable atom (i.e., a concept constant or an existential restriction) implies that $\gamma(C)$ is also a concept constant or an existential restriction. Since γ is a unifier of the equation, Lemma 3 implies there must be an atom B_i such that $\gamma(B_i) \sqsubseteq \gamma(C)$. Therefore $\tau([B_i \not\sqsubseteq C]) = 0$, and the clause is satisfied by τ.
  2. The clauses generated in (1)2. of the translation can be treated similarly.
  3. If C is a non-variable atom of Γ that does not belong to $\{A_1, \ldots, A_m, B_1, \ldots, B_n\}$, then $C(\Gamma)$ contains the clause $[A_1 \not\sqsubseteq C] \wedge \cdots \wedge [A_m \not\sqsubseteq C] \rightarrow [B_k \not\sqsubseteq C]$ for $k = 1, \ldots, n$. (The symmetric clauses also introduced in (1)3. can be treated similarly.)

     To show that this clause is satisfied by τ, assume that $\tau([B_k \not\sqsubseteq C]) = 0$, i.e., $\gamma(B_k) \sqsubseteq \gamma(C)$. We must show that this implies $\tau([A_j \not\sqsubseteq C]) = 0$ for some j.

Now, $\gamma(A_1) \sqcap \cdots \sqcap \gamma(A_m) \equiv \gamma(B_1) \sqcap \cdots \sqcap \gamma(B_n) \sqsubseteq \gamma(B_k) \sqsubseteq \gamma(C)$ implies that there is an A_j such that $\gamma(A_j) \sqsubseteq \gamma(C)$, by Lemma 3. Thus, or definition of τ yields $\tau([A_j \not\sqsubseteq C]) = 0$.

(2) Now we look at the clauses introduced in (2). Since two constants cannot be in a subsumption relationship, the clauses in (2)1. are satisfied by τ. Similarly, the clauses in (2)2. are satisfied by τ since no existential restriction can subsume another one built using a different role name. The clauses in (2)3. are satisfied because $\gamma(\exists r.A) \sqsubseteq \gamma(\exists r.B)$ implies $\gamma(A) \sqsubseteq \gamma(B)$, by Lemma 1. In a similar way we can show that all clauses in (2)4. and (2)5. are satisfied by our valuation τ. Indeed, these clauses just describe valid properties of the subsumption relation in $\mathcal{EL}$.

(3) The clauses introduced in (3) all describe valid properties of the strict partial order $>_\gamma$; hence they are satisfied by τ.

Proposition 2 (Completeness). *The valuation τ induced by a unifier of Γ satisfies $C(\Gamma)$.*

3.3 Some Comments Regarding the Reduction

We have shown above that our SAT reduction is sound and complete in the sense that the (flat) $\mathcal{EL}$-unification problem Γ is solvable iff its translation $C(\Gamma)$ into a SAT problem is satisfiable. This proof is, of course, a formal justification of our definition of this translation. Here, we want to explain some aspects of this translation on a more intuitive level.

Basically, the clauses generated in (1) enforce that "enough" subsumption relationships hold to have a unifier, i.e., solve each equation. What "enough" means is based on Lemma 3: once we have applied the unifier, every atom on one side of the (instantiated) equation must subsume an (instantiated) conjunct on the other side. Such an atom can either be an instance of a non-variable atom (i.e., an existential restriction or a concept constant) occurring on this side of the equation, or it is introduced by the instantiation of a variable. The first case is dealt with by the clauses in (1)1. and (1)2. whereas the second case is dealt with by (1)3. A valuation of the propositional variables of the form $[A \not\sqsubseteq B]$ guesses such subsumptions, and the clauses generated in (1) ensure that enough of them are guessed for solving all equations. However, it is not sufficient to guess enough subsumptions. We also must make sure that these subsumptions can really be made to hold by applying an appropriate substitution. This is the role of the clauses introduced in (2). Basically, they say that two existential restrictions can only subsume each other if they are built using the same role name, and their direct subterms subsume each other. Two concept constants subsume each other iff they are equal, and there cannot be a subsumption relation between a concept constant and an existential restriction. To ensure that all such consequences of the guessed subsumptions are really taken into account, transitivity of subsumption is needed. Otherwise, we would, for example, not detect the conflict caused by guessing that $[A \not\sqsubseteq X]$ and $[X \not\sqsubseteq B]$ should be evaluated to 0, i.e., that (for the unifier σ to be constructed) we have $\sigma(A) \sqsubseteq \sigma(X) \sqsubseteq \sigma(B)$ for distinct concept constants A, B. These kinds of conflicts correspond to what is called a *clash failure* in syntactic unification [8].

Example 3. To see the clauses generated in (1) and (2) of the translation at work, let us consider a simple example, where we assume that A, B are distinct concept constants and X, Y are distinct concept variables. Consider the equation

$$\exists r.X \equiv^? \exists r.Y, \tag{1}$$

which in (1)1. and (1)2. yields the clauses

$$[\exists r.Y \not\sqsubseteq \exists r.X] \rightarrow \quad \text{and} \quad [\exists r.X \not\sqsubseteq \exists r.Y] \rightarrow \tag{2}$$

These clauses state that, for any unifier σ of the equation (1) we must have $\sigma(\exists r.Y) \sqsubseteq \sigma(\exists r.X)$ and $\sigma(\exists r.X) \sqsubseteq \sigma(\exists r.Y)$. However, stating just these two clauses is not sufficient: we must also ensure that the assignments for the variables X and Y really realize these subsumptions. To see this, assume that we have the additional equation

$$X \sqcap Y \equiv^? A \sqcap B, \tag{3}$$

which yields the clauses

$$[X \not\sqsubseteq A] \wedge [Y \not\sqsubseteq A] \rightarrow \quad \text{and} \quad [X \not\sqsubseteq B] \wedge [Y \not\sqsubseteq B] \rightarrow \tag{4}$$

One possible way of satisfying these two clauses is to set

$$\tau([X \not\sqsubseteq A]) = 0 = \tau([Y \not\sqsubseteq B]) \quad \text{and} \quad \tau([X \not\sqsubseteq B]) = 1 = \tau([Y \not\sqsubseteq A]). \tag{5}$$

The substitution σ induced by this valuation replaces X by A and Y by B, and thus clearly does *not* satisfy the subsumptions $\sigma(\exists r.Y) \sqsubseteq \sigma(\exists r.X)$ and $\sigma(\exists r.X) \sqsubseteq \sigma(\exists r.Y)$. Choosing the incorrect valuation (5) is prevented by the clauses introduced in (2) of the translation. In fact, in (2)3. we introduce the clauses

$$[X \not\sqsubseteq Y] \rightarrow [\exists r.X \not\sqsubseteq \exists r.Y] \quad \text{and} \quad [Y \not\sqsubseteq X] \rightarrow [\exists r.Y \not\sqsubseteq \exists r.X] \tag{6}$$

Together with the clauses (2), these clauses can be used to deduce the clauses

$$[X \not\sqsubseteq Y] \rightarrow \quad \text{and} \quad [Y \not\sqsubseteq X] \rightarrow \tag{7}$$

Together with the transitivity clauses introduced in (2)5.:

$$[X \not\sqsubseteq B] \rightarrow [X \not\sqsubseteq Y] \vee [Y \not\sqsubseteq B] \quad \text{and} \quad [Y \not\sqsubseteq A] \rightarrow [Y \not\sqsubseteq X] \vee [X \not\sqsubseteq A] \tag{8}$$

the clauses (7) prevent the valuation (5).

This example illustrates, among other things, why the clauses introduced in (2)3. of the translation are needed. In fact, without the clauses (6), the incorrect valuation (5) could not have been prevented.

One may wonder why we only construct the implications in (2)3., but *not* the implications in the other direction:

$$[\exists r.A \not\sqsubseteq \exists r.B] \rightarrow [A \not\sqsubseteq B]$$

The reason is that these implications are not needed to ensure soundness.

Example 4. Consider the unification problem

$$\{X \equiv^? A,\;\; Y \equiv^? \exists r.X,\;\; Z \equiv^? \exists r.A\},$$

which produces the clauses $[X \not\sqsubseteq A] \rightarrow$, $[Y \not\sqsubseteq \exists r.X] \rightarrow$, $[Z \not\sqsubseteq \exists r.A] \rightarrow$.

The clause $[X \not\sqsubseteq A] \rightarrow$ states that, in any unifier σ of the first equation, we must have $\sigma(X) \sqsubseteq \sigma(A)$. Though this does imply that $\sigma(\exists r.X) \sqsubseteq \sigma(\exists r.A)$, there is no need to state this with the clause $[\exists r.X \not\sqsubseteq \exists r.A] \rightarrow$ since this subsumption is not needed to solve the equation. Thus, it actually does not hurt if a valuation evaluates $[\exists r.X \not\sqsubseteq \exists r.A]$ with 1. In fact, this decision does not influence the substitution for X that is computed from the valuation.

Expressed on a more technical level, the crucial tool for proving soundness is Lemma 5, which says that $\tau([C_1 \not\sqsubseteq C_2]) = 0$ implies $\sigma(C_1) \sqsubseteq \sigma(C_2)$ for the substitution σ induced by τ. This lemma does not state, and our proof of soundness does not need, the implication in the other direction. As illustrated in the above example, it may well be the case that $\sigma(C_1) \sqsubseteq \sigma(C_2)$ although the satisfying valuation τ evaluates $[C_1 \not\sqsubseteq C_2]$ to 1. The proof of Lemma 5 is by induction on the role depth, and thus reduces the problem of showing a subsumption relationship for terms of a higher role depth to the problem of showing subsumption relationships for terms of a lower role depth. This is exactly what the clauses in (2)3. allow us to do. The implications in the other direction are not required for this. They would be needed for proving the other direction of the lemma, but this is not necessary for proving soundness.

Until now, we have not mentioned the clauses generated in (3). Intuitively, they are there to detect what are called *occurs check failures* in the terminology of syntactic unification [8]. To be more precise, the variables of the form $[X{>}Y]$ together with the clauses generated in (3)1. are used to guess a strict partial order on the variables occurring in the unification problem. The clauses generated in (3)2. are used to enforce that only variables Y smaller than X can occur in the set S_X defined by a satisfying valuation. This makes it possible to use the sets S_X to define a substitution σ by induction on the strict partial order. Thus, this order realizes what is called a *constant restriction* in the literature on combining unification algorithms [7]. We have already seen the clauses generated in (3) at work in Example 1.

4 Connection to the Original "in NP" Proof

It should be noted that, in the present paper, we give a proof of the fact that $\mathcal{EL}$-unification is in NP that is independent of the proof in [4]. The only result from [4] that we have used is the characterization of subsumption (Lemma 1), which is an easy consequence of known results for $\mathcal{EL}$ [10]. In [4], the "in NP" result is basically shown as follows:

1. define a well-founded partial order $\succ$ on substitutions and use this to show that any solvable $\mathcal{EL}$-unification problem has a ground unifier that is minimal w.r.t. this order;

2. show that minimal ground unifiers are local in the sense that they are built from atoms of Γ;
3. use the locality of minimal ground unifiers to devise a "guess and then test" NP-algorithm for generating a minimal ground unifier.

The proof of 2., which shows that a non-local unifier cannot be minimal, is quite involved. Compared to that proof, the proof of soundness and completeness given in the present paper is much simpler.

In order to give a closer comparison between the approach used in [4] and the one employed in the present paper, let us recall some of the definitions and results from [4] in more detail:

Definition 2. *Let Γ be a flat $\mathcal{EL}$-unification problem, and γ be a ground unifier of Γ. Then γ is called* local *if, for each variable X in Γ, there are $n \geq 0$ non-variable atoms $D_1, \dots, D_n$ of Γ such that $\gamma(X) = \gamma(D_1) \sqcap \cdots \sqcap \gamma(D_n)$, where the empty conjunction is $\top$.*

The "guess and then test" algorithm in [4] crucially depends on the fact that any solvable $\mathcal{EL}$-unification problem has a local unifier. This result can be obtained as an easy consequence of our proof of soundness and completeness.

Corollary 2. *Let Γ be a flat $\mathcal{EL}$-unification problem that is solvable. Then Γ has a local unifier.*

Proof. Since Γ is solvable, our completeness result implies that $C(\Gamma)$ is satisfiable. Let τ be a valuation that satisfies $C(\Gamma)$, and let σ be the unifier of Γ induced by τ in our proof of soundness. Locality of σ is an immediate consequence of the definition of σ. □

This shows that one does not really need the notion of minimality, and the quite involved proof that minimal unifiers are local given in [4], to justify the completeness of the "guess and then test" algorithm from [4]. However, in [4] minimal unifiers are also used to show a stronger completeness result for the "guess and then test" algorithm: it is shown that (up to equivalence) every minimal ground unifier is computed by the algorithm. In the following, we show that this is also the case for the unification algorithm obtained through our reduction.

Definition 3. *Let σ and γ be substitutions, and Γ be an $\mathcal{EL}$-unification problem. We define*

- *$\gamma \succeq \sigma$ if, for each variable X in Γ, we have $\gamma(X) \sqsubseteq \sigma(X)$;*
- *$\gamma \equiv \sigma$ if $\gamma \succeq \sigma$ and $\sigma \succeq \gamma$, and $\gamma \succ \sigma$ if $\gamma \succeq \sigma$ and $\sigma \not\equiv \gamma$;*
- *γ is a* minimal *unifier of Γ if there is no unifier σ of Γ such that $\gamma \succ \sigma$.*

As a corollary to our soundness and completeness proof, we can show that any minimal ground unifier σ of Γ is computed by our reduction, in the sense that it is induced by a satisfying valuation of $C(\Gamma)$.

Corollary 3. *Let Γ be a flat $\mathcal{EL}$-unification problem. If γ is a minimal ground unifier of Γ, then there is a unifier σ, induced by a satisfying valuation τ of $C(\Gamma)$, such that $\sigma \equiv \gamma$.*

Proof. Let γ be a minimal ground unifier of Γ, and τ the satisfying valuation of $C(\Gamma)$ induced by γ. We show that the unifier σ of Γ induced by τ satisfies $\gamma \succeq \sigma$. Minimality of γ then implies $\gamma \equiv \sigma$.

We must show that, for each variable X occurring in Γ, we have $\gamma(X) \sqsubseteq \sigma(X)$. We prove this by well-founded induction on the strict partial order $>$ defined as $X > Y$ iff $\tau([X{>}Y]) = 1$.[5]

Let X be a minimal variable with respect to this order. Since τ satisfies the clauses in (3)2., the set S_X induced by τ (see the proof of soundness) contains only ground atoms. Let $S_X = \{C_1, \ldots, C_n\}$ for $n \geq 0$ ground atoms. If $n = 0$, then $\sigma(X) = \top$, and thus $\gamma(X) \sqsubseteq \sigma(X)$ is trivially satisfied. Otherwise, we have $\sigma(X) = \sigma(C_1) \sqcap \ldots \sqcap \sigma(C_n) = C_1 \sqcap \ldots \sqcap C_n$, and we know, for each $i \in \{1, \ldots, n\}$, that $\tau([X \not\sqsubseteq C_i]) = 0$ by the definition of S_X. Since τ is the valuation induced by the unifier γ, this implies that $\gamma(X) \sqsubseteq \gamma(C_i) = C_i$. Consequently, we have shown that $\gamma(X) \sqsubseteq C_1 \sqcap \ldots \sqcap C_n = \sigma(X)$.

Now we assume, by induction, that we have $\gamma(Y) \sqsubseteq \sigma(Y)$ for all variables Y such that $X > Y$. Let $S_X = \{C_1, \ldots, C_n\}$ for $n \geq 0$ non-variable atoms of Γ. If $n = 0$, then $\sigma(X) = \top$, and thus $\gamma(X) \sqsubseteq \sigma(X)$ is again trivially satisfied. Otherwise, we have $\sigma(X) = \sigma(C_1) \sqcap \cdots \sqcap \sigma(C_n)$, and we know, for each $i \in \{1, \ldots, n\}$, that $\tau([X \not\sqsubseteq C_i]) = 0$ by the definition of S_X. Since τ is the valuation induced by the unifier γ, this implies that $\gamma(X) \sqsubseteq \gamma(C_i)$. for each $i \in \{1, \ldots, n\}$. Since all variables occurring in $C_1, \ldots, C_n$ are smaller than X and since the concept constructors of $\mathcal{EL}$ are monotonic w.r.t. subsumption, we have by induction that $\gamma(C_i) \sqsubseteq \sigma(C_i)$ for each $i \in \{1, \ldots, n\}$. Consequently, we have $\gamma(X) \sqsubseteq \gamma(C_1) \sqcap \ldots \sqcap \gamma(C_n) \sqsubseteq \sigma(C_1) \sqcap \cdots \sqcap \sigma(C_n) = \sigma(X)$. □

Table 2. Experimental Results

Size	#InVars(#FlatVars)	#Atoms	#PropVars	#Clauses	OverallTime	MiniSatTime
10	2(5)	10	125	895	58 ms	0 ms
10	2(5)	11	146	1 184	79 ms	4 ms
22	2(10)	24	676	13 539	204 ms	4 ms
22	2(10)	25	725	15 254	202 ms	8 ms
22	2(10)	25	725	15 254	211 ms	8 ms
22	3(11)	26	797	17 358	222 ms	8 ms

5 Conclusion

The results presented in this paper are of interest both from a theoretical and a practical point of view. From the theoretical point of view, this paper gives a new proof of the fact that $\mathcal{EL}$-unification is in NP, which is considerably simpler

[5] The clauses in $C(\Gamma)$ make sure that this is indeed a strict partial order. It is trivially well-founded since Γ contains only finitely many variables.

than the original proof given in [4]. We have also shown that the stronger completeness result for the "guess and then test" NP algorithm of [4] (all minimal ground unifiers are computed) holds as well for the new algorithm presented in this paper. From the practical point of view, the translation into propositional satisfiability allows us to employ highly optimized state of the art SAT solvers when implementing an $\mathcal{EL}$-unification algorithm.

We have actually implemented the SAT translation described in this paper in Java, and have used MiniSat for the satisfiability check. Until now, we have not yet optimized the translation, and we have tested the algorithm only on relatively small (solvable) unification problems extracted from SNOMED CT. Table 1 shows the first experimental results obtained for these problems. The *first column* counts the size of the input problem (number of occurrences of concept and role names); the *second column* the number of concept variables before and after flattening; the *third column* the number of atoms in the flattened unification problem; the *fourth column* the number of propositional variables introduced by our translation; the *fifth column* the number of clauses introduced by our translation; the *sixth column* the overall run-time (in milliseconds) for deciding whether a unifier exists; and the *seventh column* the time (in milliseconds) needed by MiniSat for deciding the satisfiability of the generated clause set.

In [5] we have introduced a more goal-oriented variant of the brutal "guess and then test" algorithm of [4], which tries to transform a given flat unification problem into solved form. However, without any smart backtracking strategies, a first implementation of this algorithm cannot compete with the SAT translation presented in this paper.

References

1. Baader, F.: Terminological cycles in a description logic with existential restrictions. In: Proc. IJCAI 2003. Morgan Kaufmann, Los Altos (2003)
2. Baader, F., Brandt, S., Lutz, C.: Pushing the $\mathcal{EL}$ envelope. In: Proc. IJCAI 2005. Morgan Kaufmann, Los Altos (2005)
3. Baader, F., Calvanese, D., McGuinness, D., Nardi, D., Patel-Schneider, P.F. (eds.): The Description Logic Handbook: Theory, Implementation, and Applications. Cambridge University Press, Cambridge (2003)
4. Baader, F., Morawska, B.: Unification in the description logic $\mathcal{EL}$. In: Treinen, R. (ed.) RTA 2009. LNCS, vol. 5595, pp. 350–364. Springer, Heidelberg (2009)
5. Baader, F., Morawska, B.: Unification in the description logic $\mathcal{EL}$. In: Logical Methods in Computer Science (to appear, 2010)
6. Baader, F., Narendran, P.: Unification of concepts terms in description logics. J. of Symbolic Computation 31(3), 277–305 (2001)
7. Baader, F., Schulz, K.: Unification in the union of disjoint equational theories: Combining decision procedures. J. of Symbolic Computation 21(2), 211–243 (1996)
8. Baader, F., Snyder, W.: Unification theory. In: Handbook of Automated Reasoning, vol. I. Elsevier Science Publishers, Amsterdam (2001)
9. Kapur, D., Narendran, P.: Complexity of unification problems with associative-commutative operators. J. Automated Reasoning 9, 261–288 (1992)
10. Küsters, R. (ed.): Non-Standard Inferences in Description Logics. LNCS (LNAI), vol. 2100, p. 33. Springer, Heidelberg (2001)

Generating Combinatorial Test Cases by Efficient SAT Encodings Suitable for CDCL SAT Solvers

Mutsunori Banbara[1], Haruki Matsunaka[2],
Naoyuki Tamura[1], and Katsumi Inoue[3]

[1] Information Science and Technology Center, Kobe University, Japan
{banbara,tamura}@kobe-u.ac.jp
[2] Graduate School of System Informatics, Kobe University, Japan
matsunaka@stu.kobe-u.ac.jp
[3] National Institute of Informatics, Japan
ki@nii.ac.jp

Abstract. Generating test cases for combinatorial testing is to find a covering array in Combinatorial Designs. In this paper, we consider the problem of finding optimal covering arrays by SAT encoding. We present two encodings suitable for modern CDCL SAT solvers. One is based on the order encoding that is efficient in the sense that unit propagation achieves the bounds consistency in CSPs. Another one is based on a combination of the order encoding and Hnich's encoding. CDCL SAT solvers have an important role in the latest SAT technology. The effective use of them is essential for enhancing efficiency. In our experiments, we found solutions that can be competitive with the previously known results for the arrays of strength two to six with small to moderate size of components and symbols. Moreover, we succeeded either in proving the optimality of known bounds or in improving known lower bounds for some arrays.

1 Introduction

Propositional Satisfiability (SAT) is fundamental in solving many application problems in Artificial Intelligence and Computer Science: logic synthesis, planning, theorem proving, hardware/software verification, and Constraint Satisfaction Problems (CSPs). Remarkable improvements in the efficiency of SAT solvers have been made over the last decade. Such improvements encourage researchers to solve CSPs by encoding them into SAT (i.e. "SAT encoding"). A number of SAT encoding methods have been therefore proposed: *direct encoding* [1, 2], *support encoding* [3, 4], *multivalued encoding* [5], *log encoding* [6, 7], *order encoding* [8, 9], and *log-support encoding* [10].

Hardware/software testing plays an important role in enhancing the reliability of products. However, it has become one of the most expensive tasks in the product development process in recent years. *Combinatorial testing* is an effective black-box testing method to detect elusive failures of hardware/software. The basic idea is based on the observations that most failures are caused by

C. Fermüller and A. Voronkov (Eds.): LPAR-17, LNCS 6397, pp. 112–126, 2010.

interactions of multiple components. The number of test cases is therefore much smaller than exhaustive testing. Generating test cases for combinatorial testing is to find a *Covering Array* (*CA*) in Combinatorial Designs. A covering array provides a set of test cases, where each row of the array can be regarded as a set of component symbols for an individual test case.

Since the usefulness of covering arrays for combinatorial testing was shown, there has been a great deal of work for finding covering arrays with as small number of rows as possible [11–21]. From the perspective of SAT, Hnich *et al.* proposed a SAT encoding designed for incomplete SAT solvers based on stochastic local search algorithms [20, 21]. A non-clausal encoding on incomplete SAT solvers was studied in [22]. Myra B. Cohen *et al.* proposed algorithms that synergistically integrate SAT with greedy methods [23]. However, there is very little literature on SAT encoding of this problem suitable for modern *Conflict-Driven Clause Learning* (CDCL) SAT solvers.

In this paper, we consider the problem of finding optimal covering arrays by SAT encoding. We present two encodings suitable for modern CDCL SAT solvers. One is based on the order encoding which an award-winning SAT-based CSP solver Sugar [1] adopted. The order encoding is efficient in the sense that unit propagation keeps the *bounds consistency* in CSPs [24]. Another one is based on a combination of the order encoding and Hnich's encoding. It is designed to reduce the number of clauses required, compared with the order encoding. CDCL SAT solvers have an important role in the latest SAT technology. The effective use of them is essential for enhancing efficiency. Our two encodings are based on the idea of order encoding, and the practical effectiveness of a combination of the order encoding and CDCL SAT solvers has been shown by the fact that Sugar became an award-winning system in the Fourth International CSP Solver Competition for the past two years.

In our experiments, we found solutions that can be competitive with the previously known results obtained by orthogonal arrays, theoretical works, and several computational search methods for the arrays of strength two to six with small to moderate size of components and symbols. Moreover, we succeeded either in proving the optimality of known bounds or in improving known lower bounds for some arrays. Our results include a solution to an open problem listed in Handbook of Satisfiability [25] published in 2009.

The rest of this paper is organized as follows. Section 2 presents the basic definitions of covering arrays and related work, especially Hnich's constraint programming model. Section 3 presents Hnich's SAT encoding. Our encodings are presented in Section 4 and 5. Section 6 shows comparison results of different encodings. Section 7 shows experimental results of finding optimal covering arrays. The paper is concluded in Section 8.

2 Covering Arrays and Related Work

The following definitions are based on Colbourn [26].

[1] `http://bach.istc.kobe-u.ac.jp/sugar/`

1	2	3	4	5
0	**0**	0	0	0
0	**1**	1	2	2
0	**2**	2	1	1
1	**0**	1	1	1
1	**1**	0	1	2
1	**2**	1	2	0
1	2	2	0	2
2	**0**	2	2	2
2	**1**	1	0	1
2	1	2	1	0
2	**2**	0	2	1

Fig. 1. An optimal covering array of $CA(11; 2, 5, 3)$

(1,2)	(1,3)	(1,4)	(1,5)	(2,3)	(2,4)	(2,5)	(3,4)	(3,5)	(4,5)
0	0	0	0	0	0	0	0	0	0
1	1	2	2	4	5	5	5	5	8
2	2	1	1	8	7	7	7	7	4
3	4	4	4	1	1	1	4	4	4
4	3	4	5	3	4	5	1	2	5
5	4	5	3	7	8	6	5	3	6
5	5	3	5	8	6	8	6	8	2
6	8	8	8	2	2	2	8	8	8
7	7	6	7	4	3	4	3	4	1
7	8	7	6	5	4	3	7	6	3
8	6	8	7	6	8	7	2	1	7

Fig. 2. An alternative matrix of $CA(11; 2, 5, 3)$ shown in Fig. 1

Definition 1. A *covering array* $CA(b; t, k, g)$ is a $b \times k$ array (b rows and k columns) such that every $b \times t$ sub-array contains all t-tuples from g symbols at least once. The parameter t is the *strength* of the array, k is the number of components, and g is the number of symbols for each component.

Definition 2. The *covering array number* $CAN(t, k, g)$ is the smallest b for which a $CA(b; t, k, g)$ exists.

Definition 3. A covering array $CA(b; t, k, g)$ is *optimal* if $CAN(t, k, g) = b$.

For example, Fig. 1 shows an example of $CA(11; 2, 5, 3)$, a covering array of strength two ($t = 2$) with five components ($k = 5$) having three symbols ($g = 3$) each. It is an optimal covering array which has eleven rows ($b = 11$). We highlight the different 2-tuples from three symbols in the first 11×2 sub-array to show all possible 2-tuples occur at least once. This property holds for all sub-arrays.

In the case of $t = g = 2$, finding optimal covering arrays was solved in 1970s (see [27] for details). However, in general, the problem of finding optimal covering arrays is NP-complete [28]. To determine $CAN(t, k, g)$, the following basic properties are useful and will be used on Table 4 in Section 7.

Theorem 1 (Chateauneuf and Kreher [12] and Zhang [25]).

1. $g^t \leq CAN(t, k, g) \leq g^k$
2. $CAN(t, k-1, g) \leq CAN(t, k, g)$
3. $CAN(t, k, g-1) \leq CAN(t, k, g)$
4. $g \cdot CAN(t-1, k-1, g) \leq CAN(t, k, g)$

Table. 1 shows a list of current bounds on the covering array number $CAN(3, k, g)$ with small to moderate size of k and g. This table is based on Colbourn's CA tables [29] and the papers [12, 25]. The (k, g)-entry is either n when $CAN(t, k, g) = n$ or (n_ℓ, n_u) when $n_\ell \leq CAN(t, k, g) \leq n_u$.

In this paper, we define two kinds of problems to make our approach more understandable. For a given tuple $\langle t, k, g, b \rangle$, *CA decision problem* is the problem to decide whether a $CA(b; t, k, g)$ exists or not, and find it if exists. For a

Table 1. Current bounds on $CAN(3, k, g)$

$k \backslash g$	2	3	4	5	6	7	8
4	8	27	64	125	216	343	512
5	10	28,33	64	125	222,240	343	512
6	12	33	64	125	222,258	343	512
7	12	36,40	76,88	125,180	222,293	343	512
8	12	36,42	76,88	145,185	222,304	343	512
9	12	36,45	76,112	145,185	234,379	343,472	512
10	12	36,45	76,112	145,185	234,393	364,479	512
11	12	36,45	76,121	145,225	234,463	364,637	536,960
12	14,15	36,45	76,121	145,225	234,463	364,637	536,960
13	14,16	36,51	76,124	145,245	234,503	364,637	536,960
14	14,16	36,51	76,124	145,245	234,503	364,637	536,960
15	14,17	36,57	76,124	145,245	234,514	364,637	536,960
16	14,17	36,60	76,124	145,245	234,514	364,637	536,960

given tuple $\langle t, k, g \rangle$, *CA optimization problem* is the problem to find an optimal covering array $CA(b; t, k, g)$.

Hnich *et al.* proposed three different CSP representations for solving the CA decision problems: *naïve matrix model*, *alternative matrix model*, and *integrated matrix model* [20, 21]. In these models, the fact a CA exists is equivalent to its CSP representation being satisfiable. It can be easily applied to the CA optimization problems. The CSPs of CA decision problems with varying the value of b contain both satisfiable and unsatisfiable problems, and the optimal solution exists on the boundary. The integrated matrix model consists of two matrices and two kinds of constraints.

Original matrix is a $b \times k$ matrix of integer variables $x_{r,i}$ $(1 \le r \le b, 1 \le i \le k)$. The domain of each variable is $\{0, 1, 2, \ldots, g-1\}$. This matrix identifies a covering array itself.

Alternative matrix is a $b \times \binom{k}{t}$ matrix of integer variables $y_{r,i'}$ $(1 \le r \le b, 1 \le i' \le \binom{k}{t})$. Each column expresses one of the possible t-tuple of columns in the original matrix. Each variable expresses a t-tuple of variables in the original matrix (called *compound variables*). The domain of each variable is $\{0, 1, 2, \ldots, g^t - 1\}$.

Coverage constraints specify the condition that all possible t-tuples from g symbols must occur at least once for all $b \times t$ sub-arrays. In the alternative matrix, the coverage constraints can be expressed by using *Global Cardinality Constraints* (GCC) [30]. That is, for every column (i.e. every sub-array in the original matrix), one GCC is enforced to ensure that every number in the range 0 to $g^t - 1$ occurs at least once and at most $b - g^t + 1$ times.

Channelling constraints associate each compound variable in the alternative matrix with the t-tuples of corresponding variables in the original matrix. Let $1 \le c_1^{i'} \le c_2^{i'} \le \cdots \le c_t^{i'} \le k$ be t distinct columns in the original matrix, which correspond to the column i' in the alternative matrix. The channelling constraints can be intensionally expressed as $y_{r,i'} = \sum_{\ell=1}^{t} g^{t-\ell} x_{r,c_\ell^{i'}}$.

For example, the channelling constraints of $CA(11;2,5,3)$ can be intensionally expressed as $y_{r,(i,j)} = 3x_{r,i} + x_{r,j}$, or extensionally as follows:

$$(y_{r,(i,j)}, x_{r,i}, x_{r,j}) \in \{(0,0,0),(1,0,1),(2,0,2),(3,1,0),\\ (4,1,1),(5,1,2),(6,2,0),(7,2,1),(8,2,2)\}.$$

Fig. 2 shows an alternative matrix that corresponds to the array of $CA(11;2,5,3)$ shown in Fig. 1.

The integrated matrix model uses the idea of compound variables, and the coverage constraints can be elegantly expressed by the global constraints. In this paper, we solve the CA optimization problems by encoding this constraint model into SAT. Before showing our encodings, we present an existing encoding.

3 Hnich's SAT Encoding

Since we are working in SAT encoding, the integrated matrix model needs to be expressed as a propositional formula in Conjunctive Normal Form (CNF).

In Hnich's SAT encoding [20, 21], the propositional variables for $CA(b;t,k,g)$ are $p\,(x_{r,i} = v)$ and $p\,(y_{r,i'} = w)$ with $1 \le r \le b$, $1 \le i \le k$, $0 \le v \le g-1$, $1 \le i' \le \binom{k}{t}$, and $0 \le w \le g^t - 1$. The variable $p\,(x_{r,i} = v)$ and $p\,(y_{r,i'} = w)$ are intended to denote $x_{r,i} = v$ in the original matrix and $y_{r,i'} = w$ in the alternative matrix respectively. The formula for $CA(b;t,k,g)$ are defined to be

$$\bigvee_v p\,(x_{r,i} = v) \tag{1}$$

$$\neg p\,(x_{r,i} = v) \vee \neg p\,(x_{r,i} = v') \tag{2}$$

$$\bigvee_w p\,(y_{r,i'} = w) \tag{3}$$

$$\neg p\,(y_{r,i'} = w) \vee \neg p\,(y_{r,i'} = w') \tag{4}$$

$$\bigvee_r p\,(y_{r,i'} = w) \tag{5}$$

$$\neg p\,(y_{r,i'} = w) \vee p\,(x_{r,i} = v) \tag{6}$$

where $1 \le r \le b$, $1 \le i \le k$, $0 \le v < v' \le g-1$, $1 \le i' \le \binom{k}{t}$, and $0 \le w < w' \le g^t - 1$; the clauses (6) are defined for all r,i,i',v, and w such that $y_{r,i'} = w$ and $x_{r,i} = v$ are permitted by the channelling constraints between $y_{r,i'}$ and $x_{r,i}$.

The clauses (1,3) express the condition that each CSP variable is assigned to at least one domain value. The clauses (2,4) express the condition that each CSP variable is assigned to at most one domain value. The clauses (5) express the lower bound on the coverage constraints that every number in the range 0 to $g^t - 1$ occurs at least once in every column of the alternative matrix. There are no clauses for the upper bound on the coverage constraints since it is an implied constraint and can be omitted. The clauses (6) express the channelling constraints. Note that the clauses (1,3,4) can be omitted (see [20, 21] for details).

Hnich's SAT encoding, with the use of a stochastic local search algorithm, found many solutions that are competitive with the previously known results for the arrays of strength $2 \leq t \leq 4$ with small to moderate size of k and g. It also found an improved solution for a large array $CA(40; 3, 7, 3)$.

However, a good encoding for backtrack search is not necessarily the same as that for local search. We thus propose two encodings suitable for modern CDCL SAT solvers.

4 Order Encoding

4.1 Overview of Order Encoding

The order encoding [8, 9] is a method that encodes a finite linear CSP into SAT. In order encoding, we introduce one propositional variable $p\,(x \leq i)$ for each CSP variable x and each integer constant i ($\ell(x) - 1 \leq i \leq u(x)$), where $\ell(x)$ and $u(x)$ are the lower and upper bounds of x respectively[2]. The variable $p\,(x \leq i)$ is intended to indicate $x \leq i$. The key feature of this encoding is the natural representation of the order structure on integers.

For each CSP variable x, we require the following clauses as axioms expressing the bounds and the order relation, where $\ell(x) \leq i \leq u(x)$.

$$\neg p\,(x \leq \ell(x) - 1) \quad p\,(x \leq u(x)) \quad \neg p\,(x \leq i - 1) \lor p\,(x \leq i)$$

Constraints are encoded into clauses expressing conflict regions instead of conflict points. When all points $(x_1, \ldots, x_n)$ in the region $i_1 < x_1 \leq j_1, \ \ldots, \ i_n < x_n \leq j_n$ violate the constraint, the following clause is added.

$$p\,(x_1 \leq i_1) \lor \neg p\,(x_1 \leq j_1) \lor \cdots \lor p\,(x_n \leq i_n) \lor \neg p\,(x_n \leq j_n)$$

Any finite linear comparison $\sum_{i=1}^{n} a_i\, x_i \leq c$ can be encoded into the following CNF formula, where a_i's are non-zero integer constants, c is an integer constant, and x_i's are mutually distinct integer variables.

$$\bigwedge_{\sum_{i=1}^{n} b_i = c-n+1} \; \bigvee_{i} \, (a_i\, x_i \leq b_i)^{\#}$$

The parameters b_i's range over integers satisfying $\sum_{i=1}^{n} b_i = c - n + 1$ and $\ell(a_i x_i) - 1 \leq b_i \leq u(a_i x_i)$ for all i where functions ℓ and u give the lower and upper bounds of the given expression respectively. The translation $()^{\#}$ is defined as follows.

$$(a\, x \leq b)^{\#} \;\equiv\; \begin{cases} p\left(x \leq \left\lfloor \dfrac{b}{a} \right\rfloor\right) & (a > 0) \\ \neg p\left(x \leq \left\lceil \dfrac{b}{a} \right\rceil - 1\right) & (a < 0) \end{cases}$$

[2] The variables $p\,(x \leq \ell(x) - 1)$ and $p\,(x \leq u(x))$ are redundant because they are always false and true respectively. However, we use them for simplicity of explanation.

Let us consider an example of encoding $x+y \leq 7$ with $x, y \in \{2,3,4,5,6\}$. First, we introduce the following twelve variables.

$$\begin{array}{cccccc} p(x \leq 1) & p(x \leq 2) & p(x \leq 3) & p(x \leq 4) & p(x \leq 5) & p(x \leq 6) \\ p(y \leq 1) & p(y \leq 2) & p(y \leq 3) & p(y \leq 4) & p(y \leq 5) & p(y \leq 6) \end{array}$$

Second, we require the following fourteen axiom clauses for encoding the integer variables x and y.

$$\begin{array}{c} \neg p(x \leq 1) \qquad\qquad p(x \leq 6) \\ \neg p(x \leq 1) \vee p(x \leq 2) \quad \neg p(x \leq 2) \vee p(x \leq 3) \\ \neg p(x \leq 3) \vee p(x \leq 4) \quad \neg p(x \leq 4) \vee p(x \leq 5) \quad \neg p(x \leq 5) \vee p(x \leq 6) \\ \text{(Similar clauses for } y) \end{array}$$

Finally, the constraint $x+y \leq 7$ is encoded into the following five clauses.

$$\begin{array}{c} p(x \leq 1) \vee p(y \leq 5) \quad p(x \leq 2) \vee p(y \leq 4) \\ p(x \leq 3) \vee p(y \leq 3) \quad p(x \leq 4) \vee p(y \leq 2) \quad p(x \leq 5) \vee p(y \leq 1) \end{array}$$

4.2 An Order Encoding of CA

Now, we present an order encoding of the integrated matrix model. We introduce the variables $p(x_{r,i} \leq v)$ and $p(y_{r,i'} \leq w)$ with $1 \leq r \leq b$, $1 \leq i \leq k$, $-1 \leq v \leq g-1$, $1 \leq i' \leq \binom{k}{t}$, and $-1 \leq w \leq g^t - 1$. The formula for $CA(b;t,k,g)$ are defined as follows except for the channelling constraints:

$$\neg p(x_{r,i} \leq -1) \tag{7}$$

$$p(x_{r,i} \leq g-1) \tag{8}$$

$$\neg p(x_{r,i} \leq v-1) \vee p(x_{r,i} \leq v) \tag{9}$$

$$\neg p(y_{r,i'} \leq -1) \tag{10}$$

$$p(y_{r,i'} \leq g^t - 1) \tag{11}$$

$$\neg p(y_{r,i'} \leq w-1) \vee p(y_{r,i'} \leq w) \tag{12}$$

$$\bigvee_r (\neg p(y_{r,i'} \leq w-1) \wedge p(y_{r,i'} \leq w)) \tag{13}$$

where $1 \leq r \leq b$, $1 \leq i \leq k$, $0 \leq v \leq g-1$, $1 \leq i' \leq \binom{k}{t}$, and $0 \leq w \leq g^t - 1$.

The clauses (7,8,9) and (10,11,12) are axiom clauses expressing the bounds and the order relation of integer variables in the original and alternative matrices respectively. Obviously, the formula (13) is not clausal form. We thus translate it into equi-satisfiable CNF formula by using the well-known *Tseitin transformation* with introducing new additional b variables.

Each channelling constraint $y_{r,i'} = \sum_{\ell=1}^{t} g^{t-\ell} x_{r,c_\ell^{i'}}$ in the integrated matrix model is first replaced with the following conjunction of two linear comparisons:

$$\left(y_{r,i'} \leq \sum_{\ell=1}^{t} g^{t-\ell} x_{r,c_\ell^{i'}} \right) \wedge \left(y_{r,i'} \geq \sum_{\ell=1}^{t} g^{t-\ell} x_{r,c_\ell^{i'}} \right).$$

And then each linear comparison is encoded into SAT in the same way as $\sum_{i=1}^{n} a_i\, x_i \le c$, as described in previous subsection.

The drawback of this encoding is the number of clauses required for the coverage constraints. We need in total $O(b\binom{k}{t}g^t)$ clauses since additional $O(b)$ clauses are required for each of (13). To avoid this problem, we propose another encoding, called mixed encoding.

5 Mixed Encoding

The mixed encoding is based on a combination of the order encoding and Hnich's encoding. It is designed to slightly reduce the number of clauses required compared with the order encoding. The basic idea is that the original matrix is encoded by the order encoding, and the alternative matrix by Hnich's encoding.

In the mixed encoding, we introduce the variables $p\,(x_{r,i} \le v)$ and $p\,(y_{r,i'} = w)$ with $1 \le r \le b$, $1 \le i \le k$, $-1 \le v \le g-1$, $1 \le i' \le \binom{k}{t}$, and $0 \le w \le g^t - 1$. The formula for $CA(b; t, k, g)$ are defined as follows:

$$\neg p\,(x_{r,i} \le -1) \tag{14}$$

$$p\,(x_{r,i} \le g-1) \tag{15}$$

$$\neg p\,(x_{r,i} \le v-1) \vee p\,(x_{r,i} \le v) \tag{16}$$

$$\bigvee_{w} p\,(y_{r,i'} = w) \tag{17}$$

$$\neg p\,(y_{r,i'} = w) \vee \neg p\,(y_{r,i'} = w') \tag{18}$$

$$\bigvee_{r} p\,(y_{r,i'} = w) \tag{19}$$

$$\neg p\,(y_{r,i'} = w) \vee \neg p\,(x_{r,i} \le v-1) \tag{20}$$

$$\neg p\,(y_{r,i'} = w) \vee p\,(x_{r,i} \le v) \tag{21}$$

where $1 \le r \le b$, $1 \le i \le k$, $0 \le v \le g-1$, $1 \le i' \le \binom{k}{t}$, $0 \le w < w' \le g^t - 1$; the clauses (20,21) are defined for all r,i,i',v, and w such that $y_{r,i'} = w$ and $x_{r,i} = v$ (i.e. $x_{r,i} \ge v \wedge x_{r,i} \le v$) are permitted by the channelling constraints between $y_{r,i'}$ and $x_{r,i}$.

The clauses (14,15,16) are the same as (7,8,9) of our order encoding. The clauses (17,18,19) are the same as (3,4,5) of Hnich's encoding. The channelling constraints are expressed by the clauses (20,21) that are slightly modified to adjust the order encoding variables compared with (6) of Hnich's encoding.

In SAT encoding, it is often effective to keep the number of clauses relatively small with respect to the size of problems. In this sense, we can omit (18) since these clauses can be derived from (16,20,21) by the resolution principle. For example, in the case of $CA(11; 2, 5, 3)$, $\neg p\,(y_{r,(i,j)} = 0) \vee \neg p\,(y_{r,(i,j)} = 2)$ is derived from $\neg p\,(x_{r,j} \le 0) \vee p\,(x_{r,j} \le 1)$, $\neg p\,(y_{r,(i,j)} = 0) \vee p\,(x_{r,j} \le 0)$, and $\neg p\,(y_{r,(i,j)} = 2) \vee \neg p\,(x_{r,j} \le 1)$. We can also omit (17) since it can happen that some of the entries of the array are not needed in order to cover all t-tuples.

Table 2. Comparison of different encodings for $CA(b;t,k,g)$

	Hnich's encoding	Order encoding	Mixed encoding
Original matrix	$\{bk\} + bk\binom{g}{2}$	$bk(g-1)$	$bk(g-1)$
Alternative matrix	$\left\{b\binom{k}{t} + b\binom{k}{t}\binom{g^t}{2}\right\}$	$b\binom{k}{t}(g^t-1)$	$\left\{b\binom{k}{t} + b\binom{k}{t}\binom{g^t}{2}\right\}$
Coverage constraints	$\binom{k}{t}g^t$	$O(b\binom{k}{t}g^t)$	$\binom{k}{t}g^t$
Channelling constraints	$b\binom{k}{t}g^t t$	$O(b\binom{k}{t}g^t)$	$O(b\binom{k}{t}g^t t)$

Even if the clauses (17,18) may be omitted, we can still get a CSP solution by decoding a SAT solution. For any SAT solutions, the clauses (19) ensure that every number in the range 0 to g^t-1 occurs at least once in every column of the alternative matrix. For each of such occurrences, the corresponding entries of the original matrix (i.e. a t-tuple from g symbols) is derived from the clauses (20,21). The condition that each entry is assigned to exactly one domain value is ensured by the axiom clauses (14,15,16).

6 Comparison and Symmetry

We compare the number of clauses required for $CA(b;t,k,g)$ of three different encodings. Table 2 [3] shows the comparison results between Hnich's encoding, the order encoding, and the mixed encoding. The bracket "{}" means the bracketed number of clauses can be omitted. As a result, each encoding has strength and weakness. Without omitting any clauses, the order encoding is the best except for the coverage constraints. In contrast, for the reduced number of clauses, the mixed encoding is better than the order encoding except for the channelling constraints. The length of each clause for the channelling constraints is two in the mixed and Hnich's encodings, but $t+1$ in the order encoding.

On the other hand, it is common that symmetry breaking techniques can considerably reduce complete backtrack search. A covering array is highly symmetric, and we treat two kinds of symmetries in this paper.

One is the row and column symmetry [31]. For given a covering array, any row and/or column can be permuted with any other row and/or column. Hnich *et al.* reduce this symmetry by using *lexicographic ordering constraints* in their matrix models. In the integrated matrix model, they break the column symmetry by ordering adjacent pairs of columns of the original matrix lexicographically, and the row symmetry by ordering adjacent pairs of rows of either the original or the alternative matrix lexicographically. Alternatively, we can use an incomplete symmetry breaking method called *snake lex* [32].

Another one is the value symmetry. For given a covering array, the symbols in any column of the array can be swapped. Hnich *et al.* proposed two methods for breaking this symmetry. Let $f_{i,v}$ be the frequency of occurrences of the symbol v $(0 \le v \le g-1)$ in the column i $(1 \le i \le k)$ of the original matrix. They impose

[3] In our two encodings, the number of some redundant clauses including literals such as $p\,(x_{r,i} \le -1)$, $p\,(x_{r,i} \le g-1)$, $p\,(y_{r,i'} \le -1)$, and $p\,(y_{r,i'} \le g^t-1)$ are omitted.

the constraints such that $f_{i,0} \leq f_{i,1} \leq \ldots \leq f_{i,g-1}$ for all i. Alternatively, when $g = 2$, they constrain every symbol in the first (or the last) row of the original matrix to be 0 (or 1). Yan and Zhang proposed another method called LNH (*Least Number Heuristic*) for breaking this symmetry [33].

In our experiments, we use the same constraints as Hnich's methods for breaking two symmetries mentioned above. We note that applying these constraints does not lose any solutions.

7 Experiments

To evaluate the effectiveness of our encodings, we solve CA optimization problems (97 problems in total) of strength $2 \leq t \leq 6$ with small to moderate size of k and g. We then compare our two encodings with Hnich's encoding.

For each problem, we encode multiple CA decision problems of $CA(b; t, k, g)$ with varying the value of b into SAT. Such SAT-encoded problems contain both satisfiable and unsatisfiable problems and the optimal solution exists on the boundary. For every encoding, we add the clauses for breaking the row and column symmetry and value symmetry as discussed in the previous section. We omit the clause (17,18) in the mixed encoding and (3,4) in Hnich's encoding.

We use the MiniSat solver [34] as a high-performance CDCL SAT solver. More precisely, we use two implementations of the MiniSat solver: MiniSat 2.0 (simp) and the preview version of MiniSat 2.2 (simp). Main differences of MiniSat 2.2 (simp) are rapid restart, phase saving, blocking literals, and robust CNF-simplification.

First, Table 3 shows CPU time of the MiniSat solver in seconds for solving SAT-encoded $CA(b; t, k, g)$. We only shows our best lower and/or upper bounds of b for each CA optimization problem. We use the symbol "$*$" to indicate that the value of b is optimal. Each CPU time is better one of MiniSat 2.0 (simp) and MiniSat 2.2 (simp). We highlight the best time of different encodings for each problem. The column "Result" indicates whether it is satisfiable (`SAT`) or unsatisfiable (`UNSAT`). The columns "H.E.", "O.E.", and "M.E." indicate Hnich's encoding, the order encoding, and the mixed encoding respectively. All times were collected on a Linux machine with Intel Xeon 3.00GHz and 8GB memory. We set a timeout ($T.O$) for the MiniSat solver to 1800 seconds for each SAT-encoded $CA(b; t, k, g)$, except that the timeout of $CA(14; 3, 12, 2)$ is set to 12 hours.

Each of our encodings reproduced and re-proved 47 previously known optimal solutions, rather than 29 by Hnich's encoding. Moreover, our encodings found and proved the optimality of previously known upper bounds for $CAN(3, 12, 2)$ and $CAN(6, 8, 2)$. The previously known bound of $CAN(3, 12, 2)$ was $14 \leq CAN(3, 12, 2) \leq 15$. We found and proved $CAN(3, 12, 2) = 15$ since there is no solution to $CA(14; 3, 12, 2)$ as can be seen in Table 3. $CAN(3, 12, 2) = 15$ is the solution for an open problem listed in Handbook of Satisfiability [25][4]. We also improved on previously known lower bounds [12] for some arrays. Table 4 shows the summary of our newly obtained results to the best of our knowledge.

[4] We found and proved $CAN(3, 5, 3) = 33$. It is also the solution for an open problem listed in the same Handbook, but that was already closed in [19].

Table 3. Benchmark results of different encodings for $CA(b; t, k, g)$

t	k	g	b	Result	H.E.	O.E.	M.E.
2	3	3	**9***	SAT	**0.00**	0.01	**0.00**
2	4	3	**9***	SAT	0.01	**0.00**	0.01
2	5	3	10	UNSAT	0.59	**0.02**	**0.02**
2	5	3	**11***	SAT	0.03	0.03	**0.01**
2	6	3	11	UNSAT	7.55	**0.04**	0.05
2	6	3	**12***	SAT	0.03	**0.02**	0.03
2	7	3	**12***	SAT	**0.05**	0.38	0.32
2	8	3	13	SAT	**4.22**	1263.58	263.76
2	9	3	13	SAT	760.05	**228.39**	$T.O$
2	10	3	14	SAT	518.18	79.75	**14.60**
2	11	3	15	SAT	0.15	0.77	**0.13**
2	12	3	15	SAT	1.31	0.49	**0.21**
2	13	3	15	SAT	**16.40**	18.53	30.60
2	14	3	15	SAT	372.95	**192.93**	373.64
2	15	3	16	SAT	155.21	31.71	**30.80**
2	16	3	16	SAT	743.74	1674.69	**390.72**
2	3	4	**16***	SAT	0.02	**0.01**	**0.01**
2	4	4	**16***	SAT	0.04	0.04	**0.02**
2	5	4	**16***	SAT	0.05	0.05	**0.04**
2	6	4	18	UNSAT	$T.O$	**4.31**	9.90
2	6	4	**19***	SAT	21.28	**0.87**	3.14
2	7	4	19	UNSAT	$T.O$	177.23	**174.89**
2	7	4	22	SAT	71.18	20.71	**4.66**
2	8	4	23	SAT	550.61	22.89	**3.39**
2	9	4	24	SAT	$T.O$	**230.44**	469.66
2	10	4	25	SAT	$T.O$	440.30	**254.51**
2	11	4	26	SAT	$T.O$	$T.O$	**884.22**
2	3	5	**25***	SAT	0.08	**0.05**	0.06
2	4	5	**25***	SAT	0.26	0.18	**0.14**
2	5	5	**25***	SAT	0.47	0.46	**0.15**
2	6	5	**25***	SAT	3.21	**0.51**	0.76
2	7	5	29	SAT	$T.O$	394.38	**90.50**
2	8	5	36	SAT	$T.O$	**654.95**	$T.O$
2	9	5	38	SAT	$T.O$	914.78	**279.84**
2	10	5	41	SAT	$T.O$	$T.O$	**386.87**
2	11	5	42	SAT	$T.O$	**1330.56**	$T.O$
2	3	6	**36***	SAT	0.46	0.16	**0.14**
2	4	6	37	SAT	22.72	**4.19**	4.24
2	5	6	40	SAT	$T.O$	**627.67**	$T.O$
2	6	6	45	SAT	$T.O$	**614.53**	$T.O$
2	7	6	50	SAT	$T.O$	1765.78	**1110.20**
2	8	6	52	SAT	$T.O$	$T.O$	**1236.90**
2	9	6	57	SAT	$T.O$	$T.O$	**773.33**
2	10	6	62	SAT	$T.O$	$T.O$	**407.40**
2	11	6	63	SAT	$T.O$	$T.O$	**1287.25**
2	3	7	**49***	SAT	1.67	**0.64**	0.66
2	4	7	**49***	SAT	460.07	**98.10**	171.55
2	5	7	57	SAT	$T.O$	$T.O$	**570.96**
2	6	7	65	SAT	$T.O$	**1513.01**	$T.O$
2	7	7	68	SAT	$T.O$	$T.O$	**1446.27**
2	8	7	72	SAT	$T.O$	$T.O$	**1362.44**
2	9	7	81	SAT	$T.O$	$T.O$	**1098.09**
2	10	7	88	SAT	$T.O$	$T.O$	**442.81**
2	11	7	93	SAT	$T.O$	$T.O$	**449.59**

t	k	g	b	Result	H.E.	O.E.	M.E.
3	4	2	**8***	SAT	**0.00**	**0.00**	**0.00**
3	5	2	9	UNSAT	**0.01**	**0.01**	**0.01**
3	5	2	**10***	SAT	**0.00**	**0.00**	**0.00**
3	6	2	11	UNSAT	0.30	0.02	**0.01**
3	6	2	**12***	SAT	0.02	0.01	**0.00**
3	7	2	**12***	SAT	0.02	0.03	**0.01**
3	8	2	**12***	SAT	0.03	0.04	**0.01**
3	9	2	**12***	SAT	0.05	0.07	**0.03**
3	10	2	**12***	SAT	0.08	0.12	**0.05**
3	11	2	**12***	SAT	0.13	0.15	**0.05**
3	12	2	14	UNSAT	$T.O$	**5607.25**	6228.16
3	12	2	**15***	SAT	0.61	0.89	**0.44**
3	13	2	16	SAT	24.91	7.57	**4.24**
3	14	2	16	SAT	$T.O$	**15.09**	23.68
3	15	2	17	SAT	$T.O$	435.35	**1.97**
3	16	2	17	SAT	$T.O$	86.07	**14.93**
3	17	2	20	SAT	$T.O$	**62.40**	125.27
3	18	2	21	SAT	**2.46**	44.99	35.62
3	19	2	22	SAT	**1.54**	176.79	4.16
3	4	3	**27***	SAT	0.07	0.05	**0.04**
3	5	3	32	UNSAT	$T.O$	**16.07**	27.85
3	5	3	**33***	SAT	632.27	**2.81**	16.85
3	6	3	**33***	SAT	$T.O$	15.46	**12.44**
3	7	3	46	SAT	$T.O$	**1180.95**	$T.O$
3	8	3	52	SAT	**407.37**	1148.09	$T.O$
3	9	3	56	SAT	$T.O$	$T.O$	**202.78**
3	4	4	**64***	SAT	9.00	0.68	**0.56**
3	5	4	**64***	SAT	$T.O$	2.01	**1.35**
3	6	4	**64***	SAT	$T.O$	3.13	**1.54**
3	4	5	**125***	SAT	$T.O$	**6.13**	6.99
3	5	5	**125***	SAT	$T.O$	86.51	**54.96**
3	6	5	**125***	SAT	$T.O$	177.13	**59.09**
4	5	2	**16***	SAT	0.02	**0.01**	**0.01**
4	6	2	20	UNSAT	$T.O$	0.07	**0.05**
4	6	2	**21***	SAT	0.36	0.08	**0.03**
4	7	2	23	UNSAT	$T.O$	0.35	**0.32**
4	7	2	**24***	SAT	529.12	0.68	**0.37**
4	8	2	**24***	SAT	107.13	0.79	**0.63**
4	9	2	**24***	SAT	399.55	**1.13**	1.20
4	10	2	**24***	SAT	279.46	6.47	**0.96**
4	11	2	**24***	SAT	26.20	4.66	**1.92**
4	12	2	**24***	SAT	1573.40	11.28	**2.12**
4	13	2	36	SAT	$T.O$	**372.87**	734.72
4	5	3	**81***	SAT	840.28	**1.13**	1.52
4	5	4	**256***	SAT	$T.O$	105.37	**104.00**
5	6	2	**32***	SAT	4.66	0.13	**0.11**
5	7	2	41	UNSAT	$T.O$	1.53	**1.10**
5	7	2	**42***	SAT	849.79	1.41	**1.24**
5	8	2	52	SAT	$T.O$	**95.01**	134.37
5	9	2	49	UNSAT	$T.O$	**344.65**	521.59
5	9	2	54	SAT	$T.O$	1431.35	**1097.27**
5	10	2	60	SAT	$T.O$	**550.67**	$T.O$
5	6	3	**243***	SAT	$T.O$	**156.64**	197.40
6	7	2	**64***	SAT	922.29	**2.97**	3.42
6	8	2	84	UNSAT	$T.O$	86.91	**52.94**
6	8	2	**85***	SAT	$T.O$	76.28	**48.49**

Table 4. New results found and proved by our encodings. We note that $80 \leq CAN(3,8,4)$ and $15 \leq CAN(3,k,2)$ with $k \geq 13$ were proved by our experimental results $20 \leq CAN(2,7,4)$ and $CAN(3,12,2) = 15$ with the help of Theorem 1 of (4) and (2) respectively.

New results	Previously known results
$\mathbf{20} \leq CAN(2,7,4) \leq 21$	$19 \leq CAN(2,7,4) \leq 21$
$\mathbf{80} \leq CAN(3,8,4) \leq 88$	$76 \leq CAN(3,8,4) \leq 88$
$CAN(3,12,2) = \mathbf{15}$	$14 \leq CAN(3,12,2) \leq 15$
$\mathbf{15} \leq CAN(3,k,2)$ $(k \geq 13)$	$14 \leq CAN(3,k,2)$ $(k \geq 13)$
$\mathbf{50} \leq CAN(5,9,2) \leq 54$	$48 \leq CAN(5,9,2) \leq 54$
$CAN(6,8,2) = \mathbf{85}$	$84 \leq CAN(6,8,2) \leq 85$

Second, Table 5 shows the comparison results of different approaches on the best known upper bounds of $CAN(t,k,g)$. Our comparison includes our two encodings with MiniSat ("O.E. & M.E."), Hnich's encoding with a new variant of the walksat [21] ("HEW"), and the integrated matrix model with the ILOG solver [21] ("CSP"). We also include Colbourn's CA tables [29] ("CAT"). These tables include a list of current upper bounds on $CAN(t,k,g)$ for $(2 \leq t \leq 6)$. Their results have been obtained from orthogonal arrays, several theoretical works, and computational search methods such as greedy methods, tabu search, hill-climbing, simulated annealing, and so on. We highlight the best value of different approaches for each $CAN(t,k,g)$. The symbol "-" is used to indicate that the result is not available in published literature.

Our encodings with MiniSat were able to produce competitive bounds with those in Colbourn's CA tables for $CAN(t,k,g)$ of strength $2 \leq t \leq 6$ with small to moderate size of k and g. Although not able to match Hnich's encoding for some $CAN(2,k,g)$ and $CAN(3,k,3)$, our encodings were able to give a greater number of bounds than the integrated matrix model with ILOG and Hnich's encoding with walksat.

Finally, we discuss some details of our experimental results. Both of our encodings found and proved optimal solutions for the same number of problems (49 problems) including two open problems. The main difference between both encodings in Table 3 is that the mixed encoding gave approximate solutions for some arrays of strength two not solved in timeout by the order encoding. Compared to MiniSat 2.0 (simp), MiniSat 2.2 (simp) was better especially for the arrays of strength two. For example, our best approximate solutions for $CA(b;2,k,6)$ with $5 \leq k \leq 11$ and $CA(b;2,k,7)$ with $6 \leq k \leq 11$ were obtained by only MiniSat 2.2 (simp). As mentioned in Section 5, the clauses (17,18) can be omitted in the mixed encoding. In the case of $CA(15;3,12,2)$ with symmetry breaking, when we omit those clauses, the mixed encoding requires 77,442 clauses, but it requires 175,826 clauses when do not omit any clauses. For breaking the row and column symmetry, we applied *double lex* to the original matrix by encoding it into SAT. This greatly reduced the search space and execution time. Using snake lex [32] instead of double lex was less effective in our further experiments not presented in this paper.

Table 5. Comparison results of different approaches on the best known upper bounds of $CAN(t, k, g)$

t	k	g	O.E.& M.E.	HEW [21]	CAT [29]
2	3	3	**9**	**9**	**9**
2	4	3	**9**	**9**	**9**
2	5	3	**11**	**11**	**11**
2	6	3	**12**	**12**	**12**
2	7	3	**12**	**12**	**12**
2	8	3	**13**	14	**13**
2	9	3	**13**	**13**	**13**
2	10	3	**14**	**14**	**14**
2	11	3	**15**	**15**	**15**
2	12	3	**15**	–	**15**
2	13	3	**15**	–	**15**
2	14	3	**15**	–	**15**
2	15	3	16	–	**15**
2	16	3	16	–	**15**
2	3	4	**16**	**16**	**16**
2	4	4	**16**	**16**	**16**
2	5	4	**16**	**16**	**16**
2	6	4	**19**	**19**	**19**
2	7	4	22	**21**	**21**
2	8	4	23	23	**22**
2	9	4	24	24	**23**
2	10	4	25	25	**24**
2	11	4	26	25	**24**
2	3	5	**25**	**25**	**25**
2	4	5	**25**	**25**	**25**
2	5	5	**25**	**25**	**25**
2	6	5	**25**	**25**	**25**
2	7	5	**29**	**29**	**29**
2	8	5	36	34	**33**
2	9	5	38	**35**	**35**
2	10	5	41	38	**36**
2	11	5	42	39	**38**
2	3	6	**36**	**36**	**36**
2	4	6	**37**	**37**	**37**
2	5	6	40	**39**	**39**
2	6	6	45	42	**41**
2	7	6	50	45	**42**
2	8	6	52	48	**42**
2	9	6	57	51	**46**
2	10	6	62	53	**49**
2	11	6	63	55	**52**
2	3	7	**49**	**49**	**49**
2	4	7	**49**	**49**	**49**
2	5	7	57	52	**49**
2	6	7	65	58	**49**
2	7	7	68	61	**49**
2	8	7	72	63	**49**
2	9	7	81	66	**59**
2	10	7	88	71	**61**
2	11	7	93	73	**67**

t	k	g	O.E.& M.E.	CSP [21]	HEW [21]	CAT [29]
3	4	2	**8**	**8**	–	**8**
3	5	2	**10**	**10**	–	**10**
3	6	2	**12**	**12**	–	**12**
3	7	2	**12**	**12**	–	**12**
3	8	2	**12**	**12**	–	**12**
3	9	2	**12**	**12**	**12**	**12**
3	10	2	**12**	**12**	**12**	**12**
3	11	2	**12**	**12**	**12**	**12**
3	12	2	**15**	–	**15**	**15**
3	13	2	**16**	–	**16**	**16**
3	14	2	**16**	–	17	**16**
3	15	2	**17**	–	18	**17**
3	16	2	**17**	–	18	**17**
3	17	2	20	–	**18**	**18**
3	18	2	21	–	20	**18**
3	19	2	22	–	–	**18**
3	4	3	**27**	–	–	**27**
3	5	3	**33**	–	**33**	**33**
3	6	3	**33**	–	**33**	**33**
3	7	3	46	–	**40**	**40**
3	8	3	52	–	46	**42**
3	9	3	56	–	51	**45**
3	4	4	**64**	–	–	**64**
3	5	4	**64**	–	–	**64**
3	6	4	**64**	–	–	**64**
3	4	5	**125**	–	–	**125**
3	5	5	**125**	–	–	**125**
3	6	5	**125**	–	–	**125**
4	5	2	**16**	**16**	–	**16**
4	6	2	**21**	**21**	–	**21**
4	7	2	**24**	–	**24**	**24**
4	8	2	**24**	–	**24**	**24**
4	9	2	**24**	–	**24**	**24**
4	10	2	**24**	–	**24**	**24**
4	11	2	**24**	–	–	**24**
4	12	2	**24**	–	–	**24**
4	13	2	36	–	–	**32**
4	5	3	**81**	–	**81**	**81**
4	5	4	**256**	–	–	**256**
5	6	2	**32**	–	–	**32**
5	7	2	**42**	–	–	**42**
5	8	2	**52**	–	–	**52**
5	9	2	**54**	–	–	**54**
5	10	2	60	–	–	**56**
5	6	3	**243**	–	–	**243**
6	7	2	**64**	–	–	**64**
6	8	2	**85**	–	–	**85**

8 Conclusion

In this paper, we considered the problem of finding optimal covering arrays by SAT encoding. We presented two encodings suitable for modern CDCL SAT solvers. To evaluate the effectiveness of our encodings, we solved CA optimization problems (97 problems in total) of strength $2 \leq t \leq 6$ with small to moderate size of components k and symbols g. Each of our encodings found and proved 49 optimal solutions including two previously unknown results and also improved known lower bounds for some arrays, as shown in Table 4.

CDCL SAT solvers have an essential role in enhancing efficiency. We investigated a SAT-based approach to generate test cases for combinatorial testing. Our approach is based on an effective combination of the order encoding (or the mixed encoding) and CDCL SAT solvers. There are several future topics for making our approach scalable to large problems. Among them, it is very important to encode the upper bound of the coverage constraints into SAT with as small number of clauses as possible.

References

1. de Kleer, J.: A comparison of ATMS and CSP techniques. In: Proceedings of the 11th International Joint Conference on Artificial Intelligence (IJCAI 1989), pp. 290–296 (1989)
2. Walsh, T.: SAT v CSP. In: Dechter, R. (ed.) CP 2000. LNCS, vol. 1894, pp. 441–456. Springer, Heidelberg (2000)
3. Kasif, S.: On the parallel complexity of discrete relaxation in constraint satisfaction networks. Artificial Intelligence 45(3), 275–286 (1990)
4. Gent, I.P.: Arc consistency in SAT. In: Proceedings of the 15th European Conference on Artificial Intelligence (ECAI 2002), pp. 121–125 (2002)
5. Selman, B., Levesque, H.J., Mitchell, D.G.: A new method for solving hard satisfiability problems. In: Proceedings of the 10th National Conference on Artificial Intelligence (AAAI 1992), pp. 440–446 (1992)
6. Iwama, K., Miyazaki, S.: SAT-variable complexity of hard combinatorial problems. In: Proceedings of the IFIP 13th World Computer Congress, pp. 253–258 (1994)
7. Gelder, A.V.: Another look at graph coloring via propositional satisfiability. Discrete Applied Mathematics 156(2), 230–243 (2008)
8. Tamura, N., Taga, A., Kitagawa, S., Banbara, M.: Compiling finite linear CSP into SAT. In: Benhamou, F. (ed.) CP 2006. LNCS, vol. 4204, pp. 590–603. Springer, Heidelberg (2006)
9. Tamura, N., Taga, A., Kitagawa, S., Banbara, M.: Compiling finite linear CSP into SAT. Constraints 14(2), 254–272 (2009)
10. Gavanelli, M.: The log-support encoding of CSP into SAT. In: Bessière, C. (ed.) CP 2007. LNCS, vol. 4741, pp. 815–822. Springer, Heidelberg (2007)
11. Williams, A.W.: Determination of test configurations for pair-wise interaction coverage. In: Proceedings of 13th International Conference on Testing Communicating Systems (TestCom 2000), pp. 59–74 (2000)
12. Chateauneuf, M.A., Kreher, D.L.: On the state of strength-three covering arrays. Journal of Combinatorial Designs 10(4), 217–238 (2002)
13. Hartman, A., Raskin, L.: Problems and algorithms for covering arrays. Discrete Mathematics 284(1-3), 149–156 (2004)
14. Cohen, D.M., Dalal, S.R., Fredman, M.L., Patton, G.C.: The AETG system: An approach to testing based on combinatiorial design. IEEE Transactions on Software Engineering 23(7), 437–444 (1997)
15. Lei, Y., Tai, K.C.: In-parameter-order: A test generation strategy for pairwise testing. In: Proceedings of 3rd IEEE International Symposium on High-Assurance Systems Engineering (HASE 1998), pp. 254–261 (1998)

16. Nurmela, K.J.: Upper bounds for covering arrays by tabu search. Discrete Applied Mathematics 138(1-2), 143–152 (2004)
17. Cohen, M.B., Gibbons, P.B., Mugridge, W.B., Colbourn, C.J.: Constructing test suites for interaction testing. In: Proceedings of the 25th International Conference on Software Engineering (ICSE 2003), pp. 38–48 (2003)
18. Shiba, T., Tsuchiya, T., Kikuno, T.: Using artificial life techniques to generate test cases for combinatorial testing. In: Proceedings of 28th International Computer Software and Applications Conference (COMPSAC 2004), pp. 72–77 (2004)
19. Bulutoglu, D., Margot, F.: Classification of orthogonal arrays by integer programming. Journal of Statistical Planning and Inference 138, 654–666 (2008)
20. Hnich, B., Prestwich, S.D., Selensky, E.: Constraint-based approaches to the covering test problem. In: Faltings, B.V., Petcu, A., Fages, F., Rossi, F. (eds.) CSCLP 2004. LNCS (LNAI), vol. 3419, pp. 172–186. Springer, Heidelberg (2005)
21. Hnich, B., Prestwich, S.D., Selensky, E., Smith, B.M.: Constraint models for the covering test problem. Constraints 11(2-3), 199–219 (2006)
22. Lopez-Escogido, D., Torres-Jimenez, J., Rodriguez-Tello, E., Rangel-Valdez, N.: Strength two covering arrays construction using a sat representation. In: Gelbukh, A., Morales, E.F. (eds.) MICAI 2008. LNCS (LNAI), vol. 5317, pp. 44–53. Springer, Heidelberg (2008)
23. Cohen, M.B., Dwyer, M.B., Shi, J.: Constructing interaction test suites for highly-configurable systems in the presence of constraints: A greedy approach. IEEE Trans. Software Eng. 34(5), 633–650 (2008)
24. Drescher, C., Walsh, T.: A translational approach to constraint answer set solving. TPLP 10(4-6), 465–480 (2010)
25. Zhang, H.: Combinatorial designs by sat solvers. In: Handbook of Satisfiability, pp. 533–568. IOS Press, Amsterdam (2009)
26. Colbourn, C.J.: Strength two covering arrays: Existence tables and projection. Discrete Mathematics 308(5-6), 772–786 (2008)
27. Sloane, N.J.A.: Covering arrays and intersecting codes. Journal of Combinatorial Designs 1, 51–63 (1993)
28. Seroussi, G., Bshouty, N.H.: Vector sets for exhaustive testing of logic circuits. IEEE Transactions on Information Theory 34(3), 513–522 (1988)
29. Colbourn, C.J.: Covering array tables (2010), `http://www.public.asu.edu/~ccolbou/src/tabby/catable.html` (Last Accessed on April 26, 2010)
30. Régin, J.C.: Generalized arc consistency for global cardinality constraint. In: Proceedings of the 13th National Conference on Artificial Intelligence (AAAI 1996), vol. 1, pp. 209–215 (1996)
31. Flener, P., Frisch, A.M., Hnich, B., Kiziltan, Z., Miguel, I., Pearson, J., Walsh, T.: Breaking row and column symmetries in matrix models. In: Van Hentenryck, P. (ed.) CP 2002. LNCS, vol. 2470, pp. 462–476. Springer, Heidelberg (2002)
32. Grayland, A., Miguel, I., Roney-Dougal, C.M.: Snake lex: An alternative to double lex. In: Gent, I.P. (ed.) CP 2009. LNCS, vol. 5732, pp. 391–399. Springer, Heidelberg (2009)
33. Yan, J., Zhang, J.: A backtracking search tool for constructing combinatorial test suites. Journal of Systems and Software 81(10), 1681–1693 (2008)
34. Eén, N., Sörensson, N.: An extensible SAT-solver. In: Giunchiglia, E., Tacchella, A. (eds.) SAT 2003. LNCS, vol. 2919, pp. 502–518. Springer, Heidelberg (2004)

Generating Counterexamples for Structural Inductions by Exploiting Nonstandard Models*

Jasmin Christian Blanchette[1] and Koen Claessen[2]

[1] Institut für Informatik, Technische Universität München, Germany
[2] Dept. of CSE, Chalmers University of Technology, Gothenburg, Sweden

Abstract. Induction proofs often fail because the stated theorem is noninductive, in which case the user must strengthen the theorem or prove auxiliary properties before performing the induction step. (Counter)model finders are useful for detecting non-theorems, but they will not find any counterexamples for noninductive theorems. We explain how to apply a well-known concept from first-order logic, nonstandard models, to the detection of noninductive invariants. Our work was done in the context of the proof assistant Isabelle/HOL and the counterexample generator Nitpick.

1 Introduction

Much of theorem proving in higher-order logics, whether interactive or automatic, is concerned with induction proofs: rule induction over inductive predicates, structural induction over inductive datatypes (which includes mathematical induction over natural numbers as a special case), and recursion induction over well-founded recursive functions. Inductive properties are difficult to prove because the failure to perform an induction step can mean any of the following:

1. The property is not a theorem.
2. The property is a theorem but is too weak to support the induction step.
3. The property is a theorem and is inductive, although no proof has been found yet.

Depending on which of the above scenarios applies, the prover (human or machine) would take the appropriate course of action:

1. Repair the property's statement or its underlying specification so that it becomes a theorem.
2. Generalize the property and/or prove auxiliary properties.
3. Work harder on a proof.

How can we distinguish these three cases? Counterexample generators can often detect scenario 1, and automatic proof methods sometimes handle scenario 3, but what can we do when we have neither a proof nor a counterexample?

This paper introduces a method for detecting noninductive properties of datatypes (properties that cannot be proved without structural induction) using a model finder, inspired by previous work involving the second author to detect noninductive invariants of

* Research supported by the DFG grant Ni 491/11-1.

C. Fermüller and A. Voronkov (Eds.): LPAR-17, LNCS 6397, pp. 127–141, 2010.

state transition systems [8]. The basic idea is to weaken the higher-order axiomatization of datatypes to allow nonstandard models (Section 4). The existence of a nonstandard countermodel for a theorem means that it cannot be proved without structural induction. If the theorem is an induction step, we have identified scenario 2.

A concrete nonstandard model can also help the prover to figure out *how* the induction needs to be strengthened for the proof to go through, in the same way that a standard counterexample helps locate mistakes in a conjecture. Our examples (Sections 3 and 5) illustrate how this might be done.

We have implemented the approach in the counterexample generator Nitpick for the proof assistant Isabelle/HOL, which we employed for the examples and the evaluation (Section 6). When Nitpick finds no standard countermodel to an induction step, it asks permission to run again, this time looking for nonstandard countermodels.

2 Background

2.1 Isabelle/HOL

Isabelle [13] is a generic theorem prover whose built-in metalogic is an intuitionistic fragment of higher-order logic [7, 9]. The metalogical operators include implication, written $\varphi \Longrightarrow \psi$, and universal quantification, written $\bigwedge x.\ \varphi$. Isabelle's HOL object logic provides a more elaborate version of higher-order logic, complete with the familiar connectives and quantifiers ($\neg$, $\wedge$, $\vee$, $\longrightarrow$, $\longleftrightarrow$, $\forall$, $\exists$). Isabelle proofs are usually written in the human-readable Isar format inspired by Mizar [18]. This paper will show some proofs written in Isar. We do not expect readers to understand every detail of the proofs, and will explain any necessary Isar syntax in context.

The term language consists of simply-typed λ-terms augmented with constants and weak polymorphism. We adopt the convention that italicized Latin letters with optional subscripts denote variables, whereas longer names denote constants. Function application expects no parentheses around the argument list and no commas between the arguments, as in $f\ x\ y$. Syntactic sugar provides an infix syntax for common operators, such as $x = y$ and $x + y$. Variables may range over functions and predicates. Types are usually implicit but can be specified using a constraint $:: \tau$.

HOL's standard semantics interprets the Boolean type *bool* and the function space $\sigma \to \tau$. The function arrow associates to the right, reflecting the left-associativity of application. HOL identifies sets with unary predicates and provides syntactic sugar for set-theoretic notations. Additional types can be declared as uninterpreted types or as isomorphic to a subset of another type. Alternatively, inductive datatypes can be declared by specifying the constructors and the types of their arguments. For example, Isabelle's type α *list* of finite lists over the type variable α is declared as follows:

datatype α *list* = *Nil* | *Cons* α (α *list*) (**infixr** "·")

The type is generated freely from *Nil* :: α *list* and *Cons* :: $\alpha \to \alpha$ *list* $\to \alpha$ *list*. The **infixr** tag declares the infix syntax $x \cdot xs$ as an abbreviation for *Cons* $x\ xs$. Since lists are so common, Isabelle also supports the traditional notation $[x_1, \ldots, x_n]$.

Constants can be introduced axiomatically or definitionally. Isabelle also provides high-level definitional mechanisms for defining inductive sets and predicates as well as recursive functions. For example, the $hd :: \alpha\ list \to \alpha$ and $tl :: \alpha\ list \to \alpha\ list$ functions that return the head and tail of a list are specified by $hd\ (x \cdot xs) = x$ and $tl\ (x \cdot xs) = xs$.

2.2 Nitpick

Nitpick [5] is a counterexample generator for Isabelle/HOL based on Kodkod [17], a finite model finder for first-order relational logic that in turn relies on SAT solving. Given a conjecture, Nitpick determines which axioms and definitions are needed and searches for a standard set-theoretic model that satisfies the axioms and falsifies the conjecture.

The basic translation from HOL to Kodkod's relational logic is straightforward, but common HOL idioms such as inductive predicates, inductive datatypes, and recursive functions necessitate a translation scheme tailored for SAT solving. In particular, infinite datatypes are (soundly) approximated by finite subterm-closed subsets [4].

The following example shows Nitpick in action on a conjecture about list reversal:

theorem REV_CONS_REV: $rev\ (x \cdot rev\ xs) = x \cdot xs$
nitpick [*show_datatypes*]

Nitpick found a counterexample for $|\alpha| = 5$:

Free variables: $x = a_1 \quad xs = [a_2]$
Datatype: $\alpha\ list = \{[], [a_1], [a_1, a_2], [a_2], [a_2, a_1], \ldots\}$

(The output is shown in a slanted font to distinguish it from the user's proof text and interactive commands.) We see that it sufficed to consider the subset $\alpha\ list = \{[], [a_1], [a_1, a_2], [a_2], [a_2, a_1], \ldots\}$ of all lists over $\{a_1, \ldots, a_5\}$ to falsify the conjecture.

3 Introductory Examples

Our approach is best explained by demonstrating it on a few examples before looking at the technicalities. The first example focuses on rule induction: We define a set inductively and attempt to prove properties about it by following the introduction rules. Although rule induction is not our main topic, the example is instructive in its own right and serves as a stepping stone for the application of our method to structural induction proofs. The second example illustrates a failed structural induction on binary trees.

3.1 Rule Induction

Properties about inductively defined sets and predicates can be proved by rule induction. The following specification of the scoring of tennis games will serve as illustration:

datatype *player* = *Serv* | *Recv*
datatype *score* = *Points nat nat* (**infix** "$\diamond$") | *Adv player* | *Game player*

inductive_set *legal* :: *score list* $\rightarrow$ *bool* **where**
LOVE_ALL: $[0\diamond 0] \in \mathit{legal}$
SERV_15: $0\diamond n \cdot xs \in \mathit{legal} \Longrightarrow 15\diamond n \cdot 0\diamond n \cdot xs \in \mathit{legal}$
SERV_30: $15\diamond n \cdot xs \in \mathit{legal} \Longrightarrow 30\diamond n \cdot 15\diamond n \cdot xs \in \mathit{legal}$
$\vdots$
RECV_GAME: $n\diamond 40 \cdot xs \in \mathit{legal} \Longrightarrow n \neq 40 \Longrightarrow \mathit{Game\ Recv} \cdot n\diamond 40 \cdot xs \in \mathit{legal}$
DEUCE_ADV: $40\diamond 40 \cdot xs \in \mathit{legal} \Longrightarrow \mathit{Adv}\ p \cdot 40\diamond 40 \cdot xs \in \mathit{legal}$
ADV_DEUCE: $\mathit{Adv}\ p \cdot xs \in \mathit{legal} \Longrightarrow 40\diamond 40 \cdot \mathit{Adv}\ p \cdot xs \in \mathit{legal}$
ADV_GAME: $\mathit{Adv}\ p \cdot xs \in \mathit{legal} \Longrightarrow \mathit{Game}\ p \cdot \mathit{Adv}\ p \cdot xs \in \mathit{legal}$

A game is a trace $[s_n, \ldots, s_1]$ of successive scores listed in reverse order. The inductively defined set *legal* is the set of all legal (complete or incomplete) games, starting from the score $0\diamond 0$. For example, $[15\diamond 15, 15\diamond 0, 0\diamond 0]$ and $[\mathit{Game\ Recv}, 0\diamond 40, 0\diamond 30, 0\diamond 15, 0\diamond 0]$ are legal games, but $[15\diamond 0]$ is not.

By manually inspecting the rules, it is easy to persuade ourselves that no player can reach more than 40 points. Nitpick is also convinced:

theorem LE_40: $g \in \mathit{legal} \Longrightarrow a\diamond b \in g \longrightarrow \mathit{max}\ a\ b \leq 40$
nitpick

Nitpick found no counterexample.

(The symbol '$\in$' is overloaded to denote list membership as well as set membership.) Let us try to prove the above property by rule induction:

proof (*induct set*: *legal*)
case LOVE_ALL **thus** *?case* **by** *simp*

The first line of the proof script tells Isabelle that we want to perform a proof by rule induction over the set *legal*. The second line selects the proof obligation associated with the LOVE_ALL rule from *legal*'s definition and discharges it using the *simp* method, which performs equational reasoning.

case (SERV_15 *n xs*) **thus** *?case*

The next line selects the proof obligation associated with the SERV_15 rule. At this point, the induction hypothesis is

$$a\diamond b \in 0\diamond n \cdot xs \longrightarrow \mathit{max}\ a\ b \leq 40, \qquad (\mathcal{IH})$$

and we must prove

$$a\diamond b \in 15\diamond n \cdot 0\diamond n \cdot xs \longrightarrow \mathit{max}\ a\ b \leq 40. \qquad (\mathcal{G})$$

We may also assume

$$0\diamond n \cdot xs \in \mathit{legal}, \qquad (\mathcal{R})$$

since it occurs as a hypothesis in SERV_15. Observe that the hypothesis $\mathcal{R}$ involves *legal*, which is precisely the set on which we are performing rule induction. If we stated our theorem "strongly enough," it should be sufficient to use the induction hypothesis $\mathcal{IH}$ to prove the goal $\mathcal{G}$, without reasoning about *legal* directly. (There is certainly nothing wrong with reasoning about *legal*, but this would mean performing a nested induction proof or invoking a lemma that we would then prove by induction. We want to avoid this if we can.)

Can we prove $\mathcal{IH} \Longrightarrow \mathcal{G}$ without $\mathcal{R}$? None of Isabelle's automatic tactics appear to work, and if we tell Nitpick to ignore $\mathcal{R}$, it finds the following counterexample:

Free variables: $a = 15 \quad b = 41 \quad n = 41 \quad xs = []$

Indeed, the induction hypothesis is not applicable, because $15 \diamond 41 \notin [0 \diamond 41]$; and the goal is falsifiable, because $15 \diamond 41 \in [15 \diamond 41]$ and $max\ 15\ 41 \not\leq 40$. The counterexample disappears if we reintroduce $\mathcal{R}$, since $[0 \diamond 41]$ is not a legal game. This suggests that the stated theorem is correct, but that it is not general enough to support the induction step.

The countermodel tells us additional information that we can use to guide our search for a proof. First, notice that the counterexample falsifies $a \diamond b \in 0 \diamond n \cdot xs$, and so the induction hypothesis is useless. On closer inspection, instantiating a with 15 in the induction hypothesis is odd; it would make more sense to let a be 0. Then $\mathcal{IH}$ becomes $0 \diamond 41 \in [0 \diamond 41] \longrightarrow max\ 0\ 41 \leq 40$, which is false—and the countermodel disappears because $\mathcal{IH} \Longrightarrow \mathcal{G}$ is true. If we can eradicate all countermodels, it is likely that the formula will become provable.

This instantiation of a would have been possible if a had been universally quantified in $\mathcal{IH}$. This can be achieved by explicitly quantifying over a in the statement of the theorem. We do the same for b. The proof is now within the *auto* tactic's reach:

theorem LE_40: $g \in legal \Longrightarrow \forall a\ b.\ a \diamond b \in g \longrightarrow max\ a\ b \leq 40$
by (*induct set*: *legal*) *auto*

Explicit universal quantification is a standard proof heuristic [13, pp. 33–36]. An equally valid approach would have been to precisely characterize the possible scores in a legal game and then use that characterization to prove the desired property:

theorem ALL_LEGAL:
$g \in legal \Longrightarrow \forall s \in g.\ s \in \{m \diamond n \mid \{m, n\} \subseteq \{0, 15, 30, 40\}\}$
$\qquad \cup\ range\ Adv \cup range\ Game$
by (*induct set*: *legal*) *auto*

theorem LE_40: $g \in legal \Longrightarrow a \diamond b \in g \longrightarrow max\ a\ b \leq 40$
by (*frule* ALL_LEGAL [**THEN** BALL_E, **where** $x =$ "$a \diamond b$"]) *auto*

What can we learn from this example? In general, proofs by rule induction give rise to subgoals of the form $\mathcal{R} \wedge \mathcal{IH} \wedge \mathcal{SC} \Longrightarrow \mathcal{G}$, where $\mathcal{R}$ represents the recursive antecedents of the rule, $\mathcal{IH}$ represents the induction hypotheses, and $\mathcal{SC}$ is the rule's side condition. When we claim that an induction hypothesis is "strong enough," we usually mean that we can carry out the proof without invoking $\mathcal{R}$. If $\mathcal{IH} \wedge \mathcal{SC} \Longrightarrow \mathcal{G}$ admits a counterexample, the induction hypothesis is too weak: We must strengthen the formula we want to prove or exploit $\mathcal{R}$ in some way.

This issue arises whenever we perform induction proofs over inductively defined "legal" values or "reachable" states. In the next section, we will carry this idea over to structural induction.

3.2 Structural Induction

As an example, consider the following mini-formalization of full binary trees:

datatype α *btree* = *Lf* α | *Br* (α *btree*) (α *btree*)

fun *labels* :: α *btree* $\rightarrow \alpha \rightarrow$ *bool* **where**
labels (*Lf a*) = {*a*}
labels (*Br* t_1 t_2) = *labels* t_1 $\cup$ *labels* t_2

fun *swap* :: α *btree* $\rightarrow \alpha \rightarrow \alpha \rightarrow \alpha$ *btree* **where**
swap (*Lf c*) *a b* = *Lf* (if *c* = *a* then *b* else if *c* = *b* then *a* else *c*)
swap (*Br* t_1 t_2) *a b* = *Br* (*swap* t_1 *a b*) (*swap* t_2 *a b*)

A tree is either a labeled leaf (*Lf*) or an unlabeled inner node (*Br*) with a left and right child. The *labels* function returns the set of labels that occur on a tree's leaves, and *swap* simultaneously substitutes two labels for each other. Intuitively, if two labels *a* and *b* occur in a tree *t*, they should also occur in the tree obtained by swapping *a* and *b*:

theorem LABELS_SWAP: $\{a,b\} \subseteq$ *labels t* $\longrightarrow$ *labels* (*swap t a b*) = *labels t*

Nitpick cannot disprove this, so we proceed with structural induction on the tree *t*:

proof (*induct t*)
  case LF **thus** *?case* **by** *simp*
  case (BR t_1 t_2) **thus** *?case*

The induction hypotheses are

$$\{a,b\} \subseteq labels\ t_1 \longrightarrow labels\ (swap\ t_1\ a\ b) = labels\ t_1 \qquad (\mathcal{IH}_1)$$
$$\{a,b\} \subseteq labels\ t_2 \longrightarrow labels\ (swap\ t_2\ a\ b) = labels\ t_2 \qquad (\mathcal{IH}_2)$$

and the goal is

$$\{a,b\} \subseteq labels\ (Br\ t_1\ t_2) \longrightarrow labels\ (swap\ (Br\ t_1\ t_2)\ a\ b) = labels\ (Br\ t_1\ t_2). \qquad (\mathcal{G})$$

Nitpick cannot find any counterexample to $\mathcal{IH}_1 \wedge \mathcal{IH}_2 \Longrightarrow \mathcal{G}$, but thanks to the technique we present in this paper it now makes the following suggestion:

Hint: To check that the induction hypothesis is general enough, try this command: **nitpick** *[non_std, show_all].*

If we follow the hint, we get the output below.

Nitpick found a nonstandard counterexample for $|\alpha| = 3$:

Free variables: $a = a_1 \quad b = a_2 \quad t_1 = \xi_1 \quad t_2 = \xi_2$
Datatype: $\alpha\ btree = \{\xi_1 = Br\ \xi_1\ \xi_1,\ \xi_2 = Br\ \xi_2\ \xi_2,\ Br\ \xi_1\ \xi_2\}$
Constants: $labels = (\lambda x.\ ?)(\xi_1 \mapsto \{a_2, a_3\},\ \xi_2 \mapsto \{a_1\},$
$Br\ \xi_1\ \xi_2 \mapsto \{a_1, a_2, a_3\})$
$\lambda x.\ swap\ x\ a\ b = (\lambda x.\ ?)(\xi_1 \mapsto \xi_2,\ \xi_2 \mapsto \xi_2,\ Br\ \xi_1\ \xi_2 \mapsto \xi_2)$

The existence of a nonstandard model suggests that the induction hypothesis is not general enough or may even be wrong. See the Nitpick manual's "Inductive Properties" section for details.

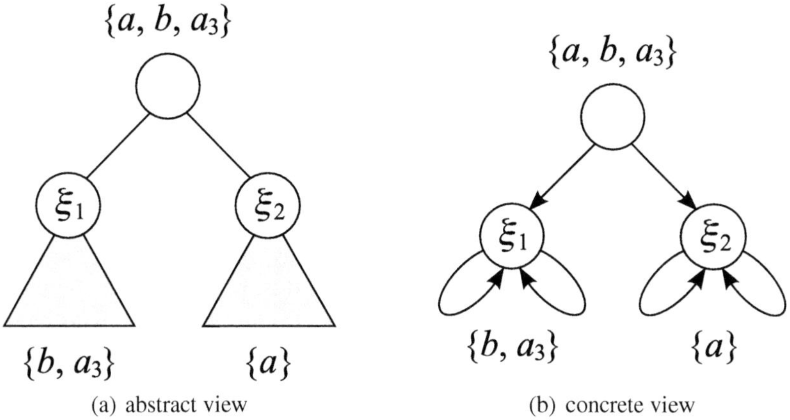

Fig. 1. A nonstandard tree

What is happening here? The *non_std* option told the tool to look for nonstandard models of binary trees, which means that new nonstandard trees ξ_1, ξ_2, ..., are now allowed in addition to the standard trees generated by *Lf* and *Br*. Unlike standard trees, these new trees contain cycles: The "Datatype" section of Nitpick's output tells us that $\xi_1 = Br\ \xi_1\ \xi_1$ and $\xi_2 = Br\ \xi_2\ \xi_2$. Although this may seem counterintuitive, every property of acyclic objects that can be proved without using induction also holds for cyclic objects. Hence, if Nitpick finds a counterexample with cyclic objects in it (a nonstandard countermodel), the property cannot be proved without using induction.

Here the tool found the nonstandard trees $t_1 = \xi_1$ and $t_2 = \xi_2$ such that $a \notin labels\ t_1$, $b \in labels\ t_1$, $a \in labels\ t_2$, and $b \notin labels\ t_2$. The situation is depicted in Figure 1. Because neither subtree contains both a and b, the induction hypothesis tells us nothing about the labels of $swap\ t_1\ a\ b$ and $swap\ t_2\ a\ b$. Thus, the model finder can assign arbitrary values to the results of *labels* and *swap* for the nonstandard trees, as long as the equations defining those functions are respected. The theorem is "falsified" because $labels\ (swap\ t_1\ a\ b) = \{b, a_3\}$ but $labels\ t_1 = \{a\}$. This could never happen for a standard tree t_1, but we need induction to prove this.

We can repair the proof of the theorem by ensuring that we always know what the labels of the subtrees are in the induction step, by also covering the cases where a and/or b is not in t:

theorem LABELS_SWAP:
labels (*swap t a b*) = (if $a \in labels\ t$ then
if $b \in labels\ t$ then *labels t* else (*labels t* $- \{a\}) \cup \{b\}$
else
if $b \in labels\ t$ then (*labels t* $- \{b\}) \cup \{a\}$ else *labels t*)

This time Nitpick will not find any nonstandard counterexample, and we can prove the induction step using the *auto* tactic.

4 The Approach

The previous section offered a black-box view of our approach to debugging structural induction steps. Let us now take a look inside the box.

4.1 Description

Our approach consists in weakening the datatype axioms so that the induction principle no longer holds. As a result, properties that can only be proved by induction are no longer valid and admit countermodels. To illustrate this, we restrict our attention to the type *nat* of natural numbers generated from $0 :: nat$ and $Suc :: nat \rightarrow nat$. It is axiomatized as follows [3]:

$$\begin{aligned} \text{DISTINCT: } & 0 \neq Suc\ n \\ \text{INJECT: } & Suc\ m = Suc\ n \longleftrightarrow m = n \\ \text{INDUCT: } & P\,0 \Longrightarrow \big(\textstyle\bigwedge n.\ P\,n \Longrightarrow P\,(Suc\ n)\big) \Longrightarrow P\,n \end{aligned}$$

When we declare a datatype, Isabelle constructs a set-theoretic definition for the type, derives characteristic theorems from the definition, and derives other useful theorems that follow from the characteristic theorems. From the user's point of view, the characteristic theorems axiomatize the datatype, and the underlying set-theoretic definition can be ignored. Accordingly, we will allow ourselves to write "axioms" instead of "characteristic theorems."[1]

The following theorem is a consequence of INDUCT:

$$\text{NCHOTOMY: } n = 0 \vee (\exists m.\ n = Suc\ m)$$

A well-known result from first-order logic is that if we consider only the DISTINCT and INJECT axioms and leave out INDUCT (which is second-order), nonstandard models of natural numbers are allowed alongside the standard model [15]. In these nonstandard models, we still have distinct values for 0, *Suc* 0, *Suc* (*Suc* 0), ..., but also additional values ("junk") that cannot be reached starting from 0 by applying *Suc* a finite number of times. For example, the domain

$$|\mathcal{M}| = \{0, 1, 2, \ldots\} \cup \{\tilde{0}, \tilde{1}, \tilde{2}, \ldots\} \cup \{a, b, c\}$$

with

$$\begin{array}{llll} 0^{\mathcal{M}} = 0 & Suc^{\mathcal{M}}(0) = 1 & Suc^{\mathcal{M}}(\tilde{0}) = \tilde{1} & Suc^{\mathcal{M}}(a) = a \\ & Suc^{\mathcal{M}}(1) = 2 & Suc^{\mathcal{M}}(\tilde{1}) = \tilde{2} & Suc^{\mathcal{M}}(b) = c \\ & \vdots & \vdots & Suc^{\mathcal{M}}(c) = b \end{array}$$

is a nonstandard model of natural numbers (Figure 2). If we introduce NCHOTOMY as an axiom, the above is no longer a model, because $\tilde{0}$ is neither zero nor the successor of some number. In contrast, $|\mathcal{M}'| = \{0, 1, 2, \ldots\} \cup \{a, b, c\}$ is a model, with $0^{\mathcal{M}'}$ and $Suc^{\mathcal{M}'}$ defined as for $\mathcal{M}$.

[1] Isabelle's definitional approach stands in contrast to the axiomatic approach adopted by PVS and other provers, where the datatype axioms' consistency must be trusted [14]. Here, we take a PVS view of Isabelle.

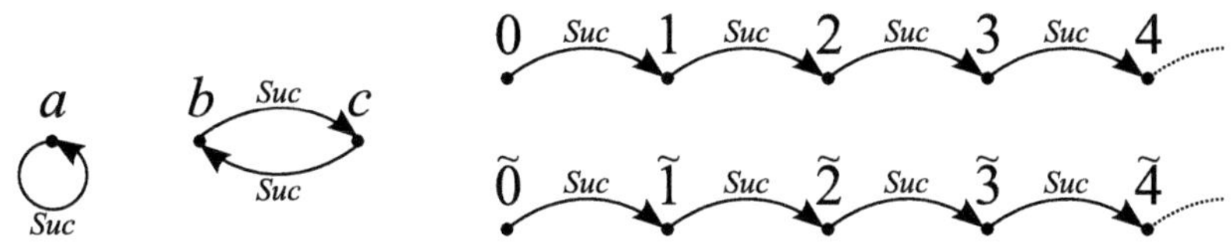

Fig. 2. A nonstandard model of the natural numbers

Our method relies on the following key observation: *If a property P is "general enough," the induction step $P\,n \Longrightarrow P\,(Suc\;n)$ can be proved without using the* INDUCT *axiom and hence it admits no countermodel even if we substitute* NCHOTOMY *for* INDUCT. It makes sense to add NCHOTOMY because users normally do not think of case distinction as a form of induction; NCHOTOMY is first-order and easy to apply.

The method was illustrated on natural numbers but is easy to generalize to all recursive datatypes. Self-recursive datatypes such as *α list* and *α btree* are handled in the same way. Mutually recursive datatypes share their INDUCT axiom, but each type has its own NCHOTOMY theorem; we simply replace INDUCT by the NCHOTOMY theorems.

4.2 Theoretical Properties

The soundness of our method follows directly from the definition.

Definition 1 (Nonstandard Models). Let $\bar{\tau}$ be some datatypes, $\mathcal{C}$ be a formula, and $\mathcal{A}$ the set of relevant axioms to $\mathcal{C}$. A *$\bar{\tau}$-nonstandard model* of $\mathcal{C}$ with respect to $\mathcal{A}$ is a model of $\tilde{\mathcal{A}} \vdash \mathcal{C}$, where $\tilde{\mathcal{A}}$ is constructed from $\mathcal{A}$ by replacing INDUCT with NCHOTOMY for all types $\bar{\tau}$.

Theorem 1 (Soundness). *If there exists a $\bar{\tau}$-nonstandard countermodel to $\mathcal{C}$, then $\mathcal{C}$ cannot be proved using only the* DISTINCT, INJECT, *and* NCHOTOMY *properties of $\bar{\tau}$.*

Proof. This follows directly from the definition of nonstandard models and the soundness of the proof system. □

The converse to Theorem 1, completeness, does not hold, because the HOL proof system is incomplete with respect to standard models, and because model finders such as Nitpick must necessarily miss some infinite models or be unsound.

4.3 Implementation

The implementation in Nitpick deviates from the above description, because it has its own axiomatization of datatypes based on selectors, directly encoded in Kodkod's relational logic [4]. The type *nat* would be axiomatized as follows:

DISJ:	no $zero \cap sucs$	UNIQ$_0$:	lone $zero$
EXHAUST:	$zero \cup sucs = nat$	UNIQ$_{Suc}$:	lone $prec^{-1}(n)$
SELECT$_{prec}$:	if $n \in sucs$ then one $prec(n)$ else no $prec(n)$	ACYCL:	$(n,n) \notin prec^{+}$.

In Kodkod's logic, terms denote relations; for example, $prec(n)$ denotes the set (or unary relation) of all m such that (n, m) belongs to the binary relation $prec$. Free variables denote singletons. The constraint $\textsf{no}\ r$ expresses that r is the empty relation, $\textsf{one}\ r$ expresses that r is a singleton, and $\textsf{lone}\ r \Longleftrightarrow \textsf{no}\ r \vee \textsf{one}\ r$.

Users can instruct Nitpick to generate nonstandard models by specifying the *non_std* option, in which case the ACYCL axiom is omitted. For finite model finding, the ACYCL axiom, together with EXHAUST, is equivalent to INDUCT, but it can be expressed comfortably in Kodkod's logic.

Cyclic objects are displayed as $\xi_1, \xi_2, \ldots$, and their internal structure is shown under the "Datatypes" heading. For the benefit of users who have not read the manual, Nitpick detects structural induction steps and gives a hint to the user, as we saw in Section 3.2.

5 A More Advanced Example

The next example is taken from the Isabelle tutorial [13, pp. 9–15]. We want to prove that reversing a list twice yields the original list:

theorem REV_REV: $rev\ (rev\ ys) = ys$

The rev function is defined in terms of the append operator (@). Their equational specifications follow:

$$rev\ [] = [] \qquad\qquad [] \mathbin{@} ys = ys$$
$$rev\ (x \cdot xs) = rev\ xs \mathbin{@} [x] \qquad\qquad (x \cdot xs) \mathbin{@} ys = x \cdot (xs \mathbin{@} ys).$$

The base case of the induction proof of REV_REV is easy to discharge using the *simp* method. For the induction step, we may assume

$$rev\ (rev\ zs) = zs \qquad (\mathcal{IH})$$

and the goal is

$$rev\ (rev\ (z \cdot zs)) = z \cdot zs. \qquad (\mathcal{G})$$

Applying *simp* rewrites the goal to

$$rev\ (rev\ zs \mathbin{@} [z]) = z \cdot zs \qquad (\mathcal{G}')$$

using the equational specification of *rev*. If we run Nitpick at this point, it does not find any standard countermodel, suggesting that $\mathcal{IH} \Longrightarrow \mathcal{G}'$ is valid. And if we instruct it to look for nonstandard countermodels, it quickly finds one:

Free variables: $z = a_1 \quad zs = \xi_1$
Datatype: $\alpha\ list = \{[],\ [a_1],\ \xi_1 = a_1 \cdot \xi_2,\ \xi_2 = a_1 \cdot \xi_1,\ \ldots\}$
Constants: $rev = (\lambda x.\ ?)([] \mapsto [],\ [a_1] \mapsto [a_1],\ \xi_1 \mapsto \xi_1,\ \xi_2 \mapsto \xi_1)$
$op\ @ = (\lambda x.\ ?)(([], []) \mapsto [],\ ([], [a_1]) \mapsto [a_1],\ ([], \xi_1) \mapsto \xi_1,$
$([], \xi_2) \mapsto \xi_2,\ ([a_1], []) \mapsto [a_1],\ ([a_1], \xi_1) \mapsto \xi_2,$
$([a_1], \xi_2) \mapsto \xi_1,\ (\xi_1, [a_1]) \mapsto \xi_1,\ (\xi_2, [a_1]) \mapsto \xi_2)$

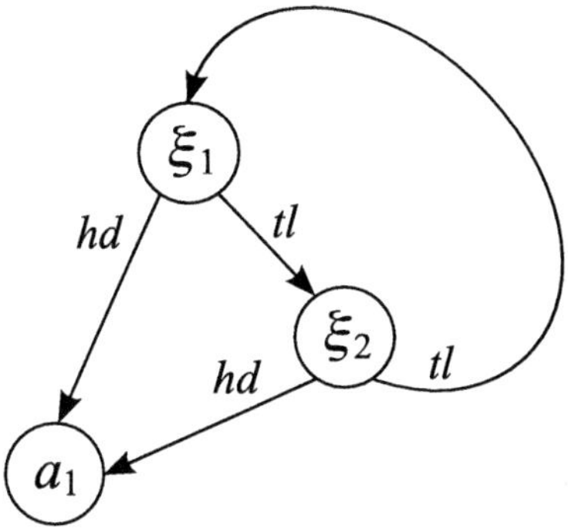

Fig. 3. Two nonstandard lists

The existence of the countermodel tells us that we must provide additional properties of *rev*, @, or both. It turns out the countermodel can provide some insight as to how to proceed. The model contains two distinct nonstandard lists, ξ_1 and ξ_2, that falsify the conjecture: $rev\ (rev\ \xi_2) = \xi_1$. The function table for @ contains the following information about them:

$$\xi_1 \mathbin{@} [a_1] = \xi_1 \qquad [a_1] \mathbin{@} \xi_1 = \xi_2$$
$$\xi_2 \mathbin{@} [a_1] = \xi_2 \qquad [a_1] \mathbin{@} \xi_2 = \xi_1.$$

The left column of the function table implies that both ξ_1 and ξ_2 represent infinite lists, because appending elements does not change them. The right column is depicted in Figure 3. Both lists ξ_1 and ξ_2 seem to only consist of the element a_1 repeated infinitely ($[a_1, a_1, \ldots]$), and yet $\xi_1 \neq \xi_2$.

A striking property of the function table of @ is that the left and right columns are not symmetric. For standard finite lists, appending and prepending an element should be symmetric. We can involve the function *rev* to make this relationship explicit: Appending an element and reversing the resulting list should construct the same list as reversing the list first and prepending the element. This clearly does not hold for the nonstandard model: $rev\ (\xi_1 \mathbin{@} [a_1]) = \xi_1$ but $[a_1] \mathbin{@} rev\ \xi_1 = \xi_2$.

We thus add and prove the following lemma.

theorem REV_SNOC: $rev\ (xs \mathbin{@} [x]) = [x] \mathbin{@} rev\ xs$
by (*induct xs*) *auto*

Equipped with this lemma, the induction step of $rev\ (rev\ ys) = ys$ is now straightforward to prove:

case (CONS *y ys*) **note** IH = *this*
have $rev\ (rev\ (y \cdot ys)) = rev\ (rev\ ys \mathbin{@} [y])$ **by** *simp*
moreover have $\ldots = y \cdot rev\ (rev\ ys)$ **using** REV_SNOC .
moreover have $\ldots = y \cdot ys$ **using** IH **by** *simp*
ultimately show *?case* **by** *simp*

Admittedly, some imagination is required to come up with the REV_SNOC lemma. However, it is the same kind of reasoning (building an intuition and then generalizing) that is needed to repair non-theorems on the basis of standard counterexamples.

6 Evaluation

Evaluating our method directly would require observing Isabelle users and estimating how much time they saved (or wasted) thanks to it. We chose instead to benchmark our core procedure: finding nonstandard models to properties that require structural induction. To achieve this, we took all the theories from the Archive of Formal Proofs [10] that are based on Isabelle's *HOL* theory and that contain at least 5 theorems proved by structural induction. We assumed that every theorem that was proved by structural induction needed it (but took out a few obviously needless inductions). For every theorem, we invoked Nitpick with the *non_std* option and a time limit of 30 seconds.

The table below summarizes the results per theory.

THEORY	FOUND	SUCCESS	THEORY	FOUND	SUCCESS
Comp.-Except.-Correctly	8/8	100.0%	*Prog.-Conflict-Analysis*	20/53	37.7%
Huffman	27/28	96.4%	*Simpl*	38/109	34.9%
FOL-Fitting	31/38	81.6%	*Completeness*	15/44	34.1%
POPLmark-deBruijn	90/112	80.4%	*CoreC++*	17/60	28.3%
RSAPSS	33/47	70.2%	*Group-Ring-Module*	41/151	27.2%
HotelKeyCards	16/23	69.6%	*SIFPL*	6/23	26.1%
Presburger-Automata	12/19	63.2%	*BinarySearchTree*	5/22	22.7%
SATSolverVerification	106/172	61.6%	*Functional-Automata*	9/41	22.0%
AVL-Trees	8/13	61.5%	*Fermat3_4*	2/12	16.7%
Collections	33/58	56.9%	*Recursion-Theory-I*	5/31	16.1%
FeatherweightJava	9/16	56.2%	*Cauchy*	1/9	11.1%
BytecodeLogicJmlTypes	10/18	55.6%	*Coinductive*	4/53	7.5%
Flyspeck-Tame	92/166	55.4%	*Lazy-Lists-II*	1/25	4.0%
Tree-Automata	32/64	50.0%	*MiniML*	0/98	0.0%
MuchAdoAboutTwo	4/8	50.0%	*Ordinal*	0/20	0.0%
Verified-Prover	4/8	50.0%	*Integration*	0/8	0.0%
VolpanoSmith	3/6	50.0%	*Topology*	0/5	0.0%
NormByEval	16/41	39.0%			

An entry m/n indicates that Nitpick found a nonstandard model for m of n theorems proved by induction. The last column expresses the same result as a percentage.

The success rates vary greatly from theory to theory. Nitpick performed best on theories involving lists, trees, and terms (*Compiling-Exceptions-Correctly*, *Huffman*, *POPLmark-deBruijn*). It performed poorly on theories involving arithmetic (*Cauchy*, *Integration*), complex set-theoretic constructions (*Lazy-List-II*, *Ordinal*), a large state space (*CoreC++*, *SIFPL*, *Recursion-Theory-I*), or nondefinitional axioms (*MiniML*). This is consistent with previous experience with Nitpick for finding standard models [5].

The main reason for the failures of our method is the inherent limitations of model finding in general, rather than our definition of nonstandard models. Our tool Nitpick is essentially a finite model finder, so only finite (fragments of) nonstandard models can be found. Nonstandard models are slightly easier to find than standard models because they have fewer axioms to fulfill, but they otherwise present the same challenges to Nitpick. Users who are determined to employ Nitpick can customize its behavior using various options, adapt their theories to avoid difficult idioms, or run it in an unsound mode that finds more genuine countermodels but also some spurious ones.

At first glance, the theory *BinarySearchTrees* seemed perfectly suited to our method, so we were surprised by the very low success rate. It turns out *BinarySearchTree* uses the type *int* to label its leaf nodes. In Isabelle, *int* is not defined as a datatype, and Nitpick handles it specially. Hence, proofs by induction on the structure or height of the trees could be avoided by applying an induction-like principle on *int*. Replacing *int* with *nat* for the labels increased the theory's score to 16/22 (72.7%).

7 Discussion and Related Work

Interpretation of Nonstandard Models. Our method presents the user with a countermodel whenever it detects that a property is noninductive. In some cases, the user must understand the cyclic structure of the nonstandard values ξ_i and see how they interfere with the induction step; in other cases, it is better to ignore the cyclic structures. Either way, it is usually difficult to isolate the relevant parts of the model and infer which properties were violated by the model and any other countermodel. The traditional approach of studying the form of the current goal to determine how to proceed always remains an alternative. Even then, the concrete nonstandard countermodel we compute provides added value, because we can use it to validate any assumption we want to add.

Inductiveness Modulo Theories. Arguably, users rarely want to know whether the step $\mathcal{IH} \Longrightarrow \mathcal{G}$ can be performed without induction; rather, they have already proved various theorems $\mathcal{T}$ and want to know whether $\mathcal{IH} \wedge \mathcal{T} \Longrightarrow \mathcal{G}$ can be proved without induction. The theorems $\mathcal{T}$ could be all the theorems available in Isabelle's database (numbering in the thousands), or perhaps those that are known to Isabelle's automatic proof methods. Some users may also want to specify the set $\mathcal{T}$ themselves.

The main difficulty here is that these theorems are generally free-form universally quantified formulas and would occur on the left-hand side of an implication: If any of the universal variables range over an infinite type, Nitpick gives up immediately and enters an unsound mode in which the quantifiers are artificially bounded. Counterexamples are then marked as "potential." Infinite universal quantification is problematic for any finite model finder. We have yet to try infinite (deductive) model finding [6] on this type of problem.

On the other hand, users can instantiate the relevant theorems and add them as assumptions. This requires guessing the proper instantiations for the theorem's universal variables. Nitpick can be quite helpful when trying different instantiations.

Possible Application to First-Order Proof Search. Isabelle includes a tool called Sledgehammer that translates the current HOL goal to first-order logic and dispatches it to automatic theorem provers (ATPs) [11, 12]. The tool heuristically selects theorems from Isabelle's database and encodes these along with the goal. Using nonstandard model finding, it should sometimes be possible to determine that no first-order proof of a goal exists and use this information to guide the theorem selection. Unfortunately, this suffers from the same limitations as "inductiveness modulo theories" described above.

Alternative Approach: A Junk Constructor. Our first attempt at detecting noninductive properties was also rooted in the world of nonstandard models, but instead of allowing cyclic values we added an extra constructor $Junk :: \sigma \rightarrow \tau$ to each datatype τ, where σ is a fresh type. The values constructed with *Junk* were displayed as $\xi_1, \xi_2, \ldots,$ to the user. For many examples the results are essentially the same as with the "cyclic value" approach, but the approaches behave differently for two classes of properties: (1) For properties that can be proved with case distinction alone, the "extra constructor" approach leads to spurious countermodels. (2) For properties that follow from the acyclicity of constructors, the "extra constructor" approach fails to exhibit counterexamples. An example of such a property is $Suc\ n \neq n$, which can only be falsified by a cyclic n.

The "extra constructor" approach also has its merits: It relieves the user from having to reason about cyclic structures, and it is easier to implement in counterexample generators such as Quickcheck [2] that translate HOL datatypes directly to ML datatypes.

More Related Work. There are two pieces of related work that have directly inspired the ideas behind this paper. The first is work by Claessen and Svensson on different kinds of counterexample generation in the context of reachability [8]; the rule induction example presented in Section 3.1 is a direct adaptation of their approach. The second inspiration is work by Ahrendt on counterexample generation in the context of specifications of datatypes [1]. Ahrendt finds finite (and thus "nonstandard") counterexamples by weakening the specifications, which would otherwise only admit infinite models. Ahrendt's work was not done in the context of induction, and his notion of nonstandard models is thus very different from ours.

There exists a lot of prior work on automating induction proofs. For example, using *rippling* [16], failed proof attempts are analyzed and may lead to candidates for generalized induction hypotheses or new lemmas. Work in this area has the same general aim as ours: providing useful feedback to provers (humans or machines) who get stuck in induction proofs. Our approach differs most notably with this work in that it provides definite feedback to the prover about the inadequacy of the used induction technique. When our method generates a counterexample, it is certain that more induction is needed to proceed with the proof, if the conjecture is provable at all. Another difference is that we focus on counterexamples rather than on failed proof attempts. However, our longer-term hope is to exploit the nonstandard counterexamples in an automatic induction prover. This remains future work.

8 Conclusion

We described a procedure for automatically detecting that a structural induction hypothesis is too weak to support the induction step when proving a theorem, and explained how we modified the model finder Nitpick for Isabelle/HOL to support it. The procedure is based on the concept of nonstandard models of datatypes. The tight integration with a model finder allows for precise feedback in the form of a concrete counterexample that indicates why the induction step fails.

Although our focus is on interactive theorem proving, our approach is also applicable to automatic inductive theorem provers. In particular, the nonstandard models produced by the method contain a wealth of information that could be used to guide the search for an induction proof. An exciting direction for future work would be to see how to exploit this information automatically.

Acknowledgment. We want to thank Tobias Nipkow for sponsoring this collaboration between Gothenburg and Munich, Sascha Böhme for helping with the implementation, and Alexander Krauss, Mark Summerfield, and the anonymous reviewers for suggesting textual improvements.

References

1. Ahrendt, W.: Deductive search for errors in free data type specifications using model generation. In: Voronkov, A. (ed.) CADE 2002. LNCS (LNAI), vol. 2392, pp. 211–225. Springer, Heidelberg (2002)
2. Berghofer, S., Nipkow, T.: Random testing in Isabelle/HOL. In: Cuellar, J., Liu, Z. (eds.) SEFM 2004, pp. 230–239. IEEE C.S., Los Alamitos (2004)
3. Berghofer, S., Wenzel, M.: Inductive datatypes in HOL—lessons learned in formal-logic engineering. In: Bertot, Y., Dowek, G., Hirschowitz, A., Paulin, C., Théry, L. (eds.) TPHOLs 1999. LNCS, vol. 1690, pp. 19–36. Springer, Heidelberg (1999)
4. Blanchette, J.C.: Relational analysis of (co)inductive predicates (co)inductive datatypes, and (co)recursive functions. In: Fraser, G., Gargantini, A. (eds.) TAP 2010. LNCS, vol. 6143, pp. 117–134. Springer, Heidelberg (2010)
5. Blanchette, J.C., Nipkow, T.: Nitpick: A counterexample generator for higher-order logic based on a relational model finder. In: Kaufmann, M., Paulson, L.C. (eds.) ITP 2010. LNCS, vol. 6172, pp. 131–146. Springer, Heidelberg (2010)
6. Caferra, R., Leitsch, A., Peltier, N.: Automated Model Building. Applied Logic, vol. 31. Springer, Heidelberg (2004)
7. Church, A.: A formulation of the simple theory of types. J. Symb. Log. 5, 56–68 (1940)
8. Claessen, K., Svensson, H.: Finding counter examples in induction proofs. In: Beckert, B., Hähnle, R. (eds.) TAP 2008. LNCS, vol. 4966, pp. 48–65. Springer, Heidelberg (2008)
9. Gordon, M.J.C., Melham, T.F. (eds.): Introduction to HOL: A Theorem Proving Environment for Higher Order Logic. Cambridge University Press, Cambridge (1993)
10. Klein, G., Nipkow, T., Paulson, L.: The archive of formal proofs, `http://afp.sf.net/`
11. Meng, J., Paulson, L.C.: Translating higher-order clauses to first-order clauses. J. Auto. Reas. 40(1), 35–60 (2008)
12. Meng, J., Paulson, L.C.: Lightweight relevance filtering for machine-generated resolution problems. J. Applied Logic 7(1), 41–57 (2009)
13. Nipkow, T., Paulson, L.C., Wenzel, M.: Isabelle/HOL. LNCS, vol. 2283. Springer, Heidelberg (2002)
14. Owre, S., Shankar, N.: Abstract datatypes in PVS. Technical report, SRI (1993)
15. Skolem, T.: Über die Nicht-charakterisierbarkeit der Zahlenreihe mittels endlich oder abzählbar unendlich vieler Aussagen mit ausschließlich Zahlenvariablen. Fundam. Math. 23, 150–161 (1934)
16. Stark, J., Ireland, A.: Invariant discovery via failed proof attempts. In: Flener, P. (ed.) LOPSTR 1998. LNCS, vol. 1559, pp. 271–288. Springer, Heidelberg (1999)
17. Torlak, E., Jackson, D.: Kodkod: A relational model finder. In: Grumberg, O., Huth, M. (eds.) TACAS 2007. LNCS, vol. 4424, pp. 632–647. Springer, Heidelberg (2007)
18. Wenzel, M., Wiedijk, F.: A comparison of the mathematical proof languages Mizar and Isar. J. Auto. Reas. 29(3–4), 389–411 (2002)

Characterising Space Complexity Classes via Knuth-Bendix Orders*

Guillaume Bonfante[1] and Georg Moser[2]

[1] INRIA-LORIA, Nancy, France
guillaume.bonfante@loria.fr
[2] Institute of Computer Science, University of Innsbruck, Austria
georg.moser@uibk.ac.at

Abstract. We study three different space complexity classes: LINSPACE, PSPACE, and ESPACE and give complete characterisations for these classes. We employ rewrite systems, whose termination can be shown by Knuth Bendix orders. To capture LINSPACE, we consider positively weighted Knuth Bendix orders. To capture PSPACE, we consider unary rewrite systems, compatible with a Knuth Bendix order, where we allow for padding of the input. And to capture ESPACE, we make use of a non-standard generalisation of the Knuth Bendix order.

1 Introduction

Term rewriting is a conceptually simple, but powerful abstract model of computation with applications in automated theorem proving, compiler optimisation, and declarative programming, to name a few. The *derivational complexity* of a term rewrite system (TRS for short) measures the complexity of a given TRS $\mathcal{R}$ by linking the maximal height of a given derivation over $\mathcal{R}$ to the size of the initial term. This notion was suggested by Hofbauer and Lautemann in [8]. Based on investigations of termination techniques, like simplification orders or the dependency pair method, a considerable number of results establish upper-bounds on the growth rate of the derivational complexity function. See for example [7,18,12,14,10,16,15] for a collection of results in this direction. We exemplary mention a result on the Knuth Bendix order (KBO for short). In [12] it is shown that KBO induced a tight 2-recursive upper bound on the derivational complexity. Note that this high upper bound on the complexity depends on the fact that we consider arbitrary TRSs. For unary TRS, Hofbauer has shown that the derivational complexity is bounded by an exponential function, cf. [6].

We are concerned here with a complementary point of view. The theme of our investigations is that of implicit characterisations of complexity classes: given a terminating TRS $\mathcal{R}$, can the information on the termination proof be applied to estimate the computational complexity of the functions computed by $\mathcal{R}$? For such investigations it is often possible to utilise results on the derivational complexity of a TRS. In particular in [4] the first author together with Cichon, Marion

* This research is partly supported by FWF (Austrian Science Fund) project P20133.

C. Fermüller and A. Voronkov (Eds.): LPAR-17, LNCS 6397, pp. 142–156, 2010.

and Touzet established for example complete characterisations of the complexity classes PTIME and ETIME, together with their nondeterministic analogues. These results were obtained by a fine analysis of polynomially terminating TRS. In a similar vein [13,5,1,2] establish the characterisations of various time and space complexity classes like LOGSPACE, PTIME, LINSPACE, and PSPACE. In this paper we focus on the space complexity classes LINSPACE, PSPACE, and ESPACE. In order to capture these classes we employ variants of KBO. More precisely we obtain the following results (all definitions will be given below):

- First, we completely capture LINSPACE through positively weighted KBOs on confluent TRS.
- Second, we completely capture PSPACE on unary TRS, compatible with KBO.
- Third, we completely capture ESPACE on unary TRS, compatible with enriched KBOs.

Moreover, we obtain similar characterisation of the nondeterministic analogues of these complexity classes, if the condition on confluence is dropped. Apart from the technical contribution these results are also of conceptional interest. On one hand they shows the versatility of KBO. On the other these results show how results on the derivational complexity of TRS (a measure on the *length* of derivations) are applicable to capture *space* complexity classes.

The paper is organised as follows. In Section 2 we recall basic notions form rewriting and the theory of computations. In Section 3 we define the notion of a relation computed by a rewrite systems, while in Section 4 we link this to the more standard notions of computation by a Turing machine. In Section 5, we recall the definition of KBO. Our main results are given in Section 6–8. Finally, we conclude in Section 9.

2 Preliminaries

We consider two ways of computing, the first one uses rewriting, the second one uses Turing machines. We assume familiarity with the basics of rewriting [3,17], and with the basics of the theory of computation [11]. In this section we recall the central definitions for these areas.

Let $\mathcal{V}$ denote a countably infinite set of variables and $\mathcal{F}$ a signature. A signature is called *unary* if $\mathcal{F}$ consists of constants and unary function symbols only. The set of terms over $\mathcal{F}$ and $\mathcal{V}$ is denoted as $\mathcal{T}(\mathcal{F},\mathcal{V})$. $\mathcal{V}\mathsf{ar}(t)$ denotes the set of variables occurring in a term t and $|t|_x$ denotes the number of occurrences of the variable x in t. A term t such that $\mathcal{V}\mathsf{ar}(t) = \varnothing$ is called *ground*. The *size* $|t|$ of a term is defined as the number of symbols in t.

A *term rewrite system* (*TRS* for short) $\mathcal{R}$ over $\mathcal{T}(\mathcal{F},\mathcal{V})$ is a *finite* set of rewrite rules $l \to r$, such that $l \notin \mathcal{V}$ and $\mathcal{V}\mathsf{ar}(l) \supseteq \mathcal{V}\mathsf{ar}(r)$. The induced rewrite relation is denoted by $\to_{\mathcal{R}}$. The transitive closure of $\to_{\mathcal{R}}$ is denoted by $\to_{\mathcal{R}}^{+}$, and its transitive and reflexive closure by $\to_{\mathcal{R}}^{*}$. A term $s \in \mathcal{T}(\mathcal{F},\mathcal{V})$ is called a *normal form* if there is no $t \in \mathcal{T}(\mathcal{F},\mathcal{V})$ such that $s \to_{\mathcal{R}} t$. We write $s \to_{\mathcal{R}}^{!} t$ if

$s \rightarrow^*_{\mathcal{R}} t$ and t is in normal forms with respect to $\rightarrow_{\mathcal{R}}$. If no confusion can arise from this, we simply write $\rightarrow$ ($\rightarrow^*$, $\rightarrow^+$) instead of $\rightarrow_{\mathcal{R}}$ ($\rightarrow^*_{\mathcal{R}}$, $\rightarrow^+_{\mathcal{R}}$). We call a TRS *terminating* if no infinite rewrite sequence exists. Let s and t be terms. If exactly n steps are performed to rewrite s to t we write $s \rightarrow^n t$. A TRS is called *confluent* if for all $s, t_1, t_2 \in \mathcal{T}(\mathcal{F}, \mathcal{V})$ with $s \rightarrow^* t_1$ and $s \rightarrow^* t_2$ there exists a term t_3 such that $t_1 \rightarrow^* t_3$ and $t_2 \rightarrow^* t_3$. A TRS $\mathcal{R}$ is said to be *unary* if $\mathcal{R}$ is based on a unary signature. The *derivation height* of a terminating term s (with respect to $\mathcal{R}$) is defined as $\mathsf{dh}(s) := \max\{n \mid \exists\, t \text{ such that } s \rightarrow^n_{\mathcal{R}} t\}$. The *derivational complexity function* (with respect to $\mathcal{R}$) is defined as follows: $\mathsf{dc}_{\mathcal{R}}(n) = \max\{\mathsf{dh}(t) \mid |t| \leqslant n\}$. A *proper order* is a transitive and irreflexive relation and a *preorder* is a transitive and reflexive relation. A proper order $\succ$ is *well-founded* if there is no infinite decreasing sequence $t_1 \succ t_2 \succ t_3 \cdots$.

Notation. Let $\mathcal{F}$ be a unary signature. In the sequel of the paper, we sometimes confuse the notation of elements of $\mathcal{T}(\mathcal{F}, \mathcal{V})$ as terms or strings. For example, for $\mathcal{F} = \{\mathsf{f}, \mathsf{g}, \bullet\}$, where f, g are unary and $\bullet$ is a constant, we may denote the ground term $\mathsf{f}(\mathsf{g}(\mathsf{f}(\bullet)))$ as the string fgf. We may even mix both representations, for example, we may write $\mathsf{f}(\mathsf{gg})$, instead of $\mathsf{f}(\mathsf{g}(\mathsf{g}(\bullet)))$. No confusion will arise from this.

We fix the representation of *Turing machines* (*TMs* for short). A *deterministic one-tape Turing machine* is a 9-tuple $\mathsf{M} = (Q, \Sigma, \Gamma, \triangleright, \sqcup, \delta, \mathrm{s}, \mathrm{t}, \mathrm{r})$ such that Q is a finite set of *states*, Σ is a finite *input alphabet*, Γ is a finite *tape alphabet*, $\Sigma \subseteq \Gamma$, $\sqcup \in \Gamma$ is the *blank symbol*, $\triangleright \in \Gamma$ is the *left endmarker*, $\delta\colon Q \times \Gamma \rightarrow Q \times \Gamma \times \{L, R\}$ is the *transition function*, and $\mathrm{s}, \mathrm{t}, \mathrm{r} \in Q$ are the *start state*, the *accept state*, and the *reject state*, respectively. (As usual, we demand $\mathrm{t} \neq \mathrm{r}$.) We assert that the left endmarker $\triangleright$ is never overwritten and the machine never moves off the left tape. Moreover, we require that once the machine enters an accept (reject) state, it must neither leave this state nor modify the tape. In order to define *nondeterministic* TMs, we replace the transition function δ by a relation Δ. We say a TM *halts* if it either reaches the accepting state t, or the rejecting state r.

A configuration of a TM M is given by a triple $(q, v\sqcup^\infty, n)$ with $q \in Q$ being the current state of the machine, $v \in \Gamma^*$ being the current content of the tape and n denotes the position of the head on the tape. (Here $\sqcup^\infty$ denotes an infinite number of blanks.) The *start configuration* on input $w \in \Sigma^*$ is defined as $(\mathrm{s}, \triangleright w \sqcup^\infty, 1)$. The *next configuration relation* of M is denoted as $\xrightarrow{\mathsf{M}}$.

Let $\xrightarrow{\mathsf{M}^*}$ denote the reflexive and transitive closure of the next configuration relation $\xrightarrow{\mathsf{M}}$. We say M *accepts* its input w if $(\mathrm{s}, \triangleright w \sqcup^\infty, 1) \xrightarrow{\mathsf{M}^*} (\mathrm{t}, v, n)$ for some $v \in \Gamma^*$, $n \in \mathbb{N}$. The language of M, that is the set of words it accepts, is denoted as $\mathsf{L}(\mathsf{M})$. We say M *decides* a language L if $L = \mathsf{L}(\mathsf{M})$ and M halts on all inputs. Furthermore M is said to *decide a binary relation* R if M decides the language $L = \{(w, v) \mid (w, v) \in R\}$. Finally, let R be a binary relation such that $R(w, v)$ can be decided by a (nondeterministic) TM. Then the *function problem* associated with R (denoted as F_R) is the problem to find a string v such that $R(w, v)$ holds, given the string w. Or reject, if no such v exists. For a complexity class $\mathcal{C}$, we write $\mathsf{F}\mathcal{C}$ to denote the function problems associated with this class.

We recall the definition of the complexity classes considered in the sequel. We say that a TM *runs in space* $S(n)$ or is $S(n)$ space-bounded, if on all but finitely many inputs w, no computation path uses more than $S(|w|)$ tape cells.

For any bounding function $S\colon \mathbb{N} \to \mathbb{N}$, such that $S(n) = \Omega(n)$, we define: $\mathsf{DSPACE}(S(n)) := \{\mathsf{L}(\mathsf{M}) \mid \mathsf{M}$ is a $S(n)$ space-bounded deterministic TM$\}$. The following definitions are well-known: $\mathsf{LINSPACE} := \bigcup_{k>0} \mathsf{DSPACE}(k \cdot n)$, $\mathsf{PSPACE} := \bigcup_{k>0} \mathsf{DSPACE}(n^k)$, $\mathsf{ESPACE} := \bigcup_{k>0} \mathsf{DSPACE}(2^{k \cdot n})$. NLINSPACE, NPSPACE, and NESPACE, respectively, denote the corresponding nondeterministic complexity classes. Recall the following equalities: PSPACE = NPSPACE, ESPACE = NESPACE, see [11].

3 Computation by Rewriting

In this section we introduce what is meant by the relation (or function) computed by a (confluent) TRS. We essentially follow the approach in [4].

Let Σ be a fixed finite alphabet and let ϵ denote the empty string. We define the signature $\mathcal{F}(\Sigma)$ *corresponding* to Σ as follows: for all $a \in \Sigma$ let $\alpha(a) \in \mathcal{F}(\Sigma)$ denote a unary function symbol. In addition $\mathcal{F}(\Sigma)$ contains a unique constant symbol $\bullet$. The mapping α is lifted to a function α between strings Σ^* and $\mathcal{T}(\mathcal{F}, \mathcal{V})$ as follows: (i) $\alpha(\epsilon) := \bullet$, (ii) $\alpha(av) := \alpha(a)(\alpha(v))$. The mapping α is called *translation from* Σ *to* $\mathcal{F}(\Sigma)$. The translation between $\mathcal{F}(\Sigma)$ and Σ, that is, the reversal of the mapping α, is defined analogously.

Definition 1. *Let Σ be an alphabet and let $\mathcal{F}(\Sigma)$ denote the signature corresponding to Σ. Suppose $\mathcal{R}$ is a terminating TRS over signature $\mathcal{F} \supseteq \mathcal{F}(\Sigma)$. Let* $\mathsf{No} \subseteq \mathcal{T}(\mathcal{F}, \mathcal{V})$ *be a finite set of* non-accepting *terms. A relation $R \subseteq \Sigma^* \times \Sigma^*$ is* computable *by $\mathcal{R}$ if there exists a function symbol $\mathsf{f} \in \mathcal{F}$ such that for all $w \in \Sigma^*$: $R(w, \mathsf{out}(t))$ if and only if $\mathsf{f}(\mathtt{inp}(w)) \rightarrow^!_{\mathcal{R}} t$ such that $t \notin \mathsf{No}$. Here* inp, out *denote translation from Σ and into Σ, respectively. To sum up, we say that R is computed by the 7-tuple $(\Sigma, \mathcal{F}, \mathtt{inp}, \mathtt{out}, \mathsf{f}, \mathcal{R}, \mathsf{No})$ or shorter by $\mathcal{R}$ when the other components are clear from the context.*

Suppose $\mathcal{R}$ is *confluent* and computes a relation R. For this case, we also say that $\mathcal{R}$ computes the (partial) *function* induced by the relation R. Note that the requirement $t \notin \mathsf{No}$ is a technical one and serves only to characterise an *accepting run* of a TRS $\mathcal{R}$. A typical example of its use would be to set $\mathsf{No} = \{\mathsf{undef}\}$ if the TRS contains a rule of the form $l \to \mathsf{undef}$ and undef is not part of the relation to be defined. If No is clear from context, we will not speak about it.

In the sequel of the section, we provide several examples of (unary) TRS together with the binary relation computed. Given a word w on some alphabet $\Sigma \cup \{b\}$, $\mathsf{rem}(b, w)$ denotes the word w where the letter b has been removed. We define: (i) $\mathsf{rem}(b, \epsilon) := \epsilon$, (ii) $\mathsf{rem}(b, bw) := \mathsf{rem}(b, w)$, (iii) $\mathsf{rem}(b, aw) := a\ \mathsf{rem}(b, w)$, if $a \neq b$. By extension, $\mathsf{rem}(\{b_1, \ldots, b_k\}, w) = \mathsf{rem}(b_1, \mathsf{rem}(b_2, \ldots, \mathsf{rem}(b_k, w) \cdots))$. Given a finite alphabet Σ and an extra letter $b \notin \Sigma$, the TRS $\mathcal{R}_{\leftarrow \mathsf{b}}$ defined in the next example, re-orders the symbols of a word by shifting the letter b on the left of the word. More precisely, $(\Sigma \cup \{b\}, \mathcal{F}(\Sigma \cup \{b\}), \mathtt{inp}, \mathtt{out}, \mathsf{f}_{\leftarrow \mathsf{b}}, \mathcal{R}_{\leftarrow \mathsf{b}}, \mathsf{No})$

computes the relation $S \subseteq (\Sigma \cup \{b\})^* \times (\Sigma \cup \{b\})^*$ containing all $(w, w') \in (\Sigma \cup \{b\})^* \times (\Sigma \cup \{b\})^*$ such that $w' = b^k \mathsf{rem}(b, w)$ with $k \geqslant 0$ and $|w| = |w'|$.

Example 2. Let $\mathtt{inp}(b) = \mathsf{b}$ and let $\mathcal{F} = \mathcal{F}(\Sigma) \cup \{\mathsf{b}, [\![_\mathsf{b},]\!]_\mathsf{b}, \mathsf{f}, \mathsf{f}_{\leftarrow \mathsf{b}}\}$, where all function symbols but $\bullet \in \mathcal{F}(\Sigma)$ are unary. Consider the TRS $\mathcal{R}_{\leftarrow \mathsf{b}}$ defined as follows:

$$
\begin{array}{lll}
\mathsf{f}_{\leftarrow \mathsf{b}}(x) \rightarrow [\![_\mathsf{b}(\mathsf{f}(x)) & g(\mathsf{b}(x)) \rightarrow \mathsf{b}(g(x)) & [\![_\mathsf{b}(\mathsf{b}(x)) \rightarrow \mathsf{b}([\![_\mathsf{b}(x)) \\
\mathsf{f}(h(x)) \rightarrow h(\mathsf{f}(x)) & g(]\!]_\mathsf{b}(x)) \rightarrow]\!]_\mathsf{b}(g(x)) & [\![_\mathsf{b}(]\!]_\mathsf{b}(x)) \rightarrow x \\
\mathsf{f}(\bullet) \rightarrow]\!]_\mathsf{b}(\bullet)\,, & &
\end{array}
$$

where $g \in \mathcal{F}(\Sigma)$, $h \in \mathcal{F}(\Sigma \cup \{b\})$. Let $\mathtt{inp} = \mathtt{out} : d \in \Sigma \cup \{b\} \mapsto d$ and $\mathsf{No} = \varnothing$. It is not difficult to see that the TRS $\mathcal{R}_{\leftarrow \mathsf{b}}$ is confluent.

Some comments about this system: $[\![_\mathsf{b},]\!]_\mathsf{b}$ serve respectively as the left and the right end markers of the symbol b. Along the computation, any occurrence of the symbol b is at the left of $]\!]_\mathsf{b}$ and any symbol $g \in \mathcal{F}(\Sigma)$ is at the right of $[\![_\mathsf{b}$. At any step of a derivation $\mathsf{f}_{\leftarrow \mathsf{b}}(\mathtt{inp}(w)) \rightarrow^+ t$, we have: (i) $\mathsf{rem}(\{[\![_\mathsf{b},]\!]_\mathsf{b}, \mathsf{f}\}, t) = w$, and (ii) either $t = b^k([\![_\mathsf{b}(v))$ for some $k \geqslant 0$ and some term v, or t does not contain $[\![_\mathsf{b}$ and t is the normal form with respect to $\mathcal{R}_{\leftarrow \mathsf{b}}$. That is, $t = b^k \mathsf{rem}(b, w)$ with k suitable such that $|t| = |w|$. Let $\#(b, w)$ denote the number of occurrence of b in w. Due to these two invariants, in the second clause, when $t = b^k([\![_\mathsf{b}(v))$, we can state that $k \leqslant \#(b, w)$. In other words, all along the computation, the prefix in front of $[\![_\mathsf{b}$ is a prefix of the normal form. Similar invariants and considerations can be applied to show that the TRS $\mathcal{R}_{\rightarrow \mathsf{b}}$, defined in the next example, operates as claimed.

Example 3. Let $\mathcal{F} = \mathcal{F}(\Sigma) \cup \{\mathsf{b}, [\![_\Sigma,]\!]_\Sigma, \mathsf{f}, \mathsf{f}_{\rightarrow \mathsf{b}}\}$. In an analogous way, the TRS $\mathcal{R}_{\rightarrow \mathsf{b}}$ shifts the symbols b to the right.

$$
\begin{array}{lll}
\mathsf{f}_{\rightarrow \mathsf{b}}(x) \rightarrow [\![_\Sigma(\mathsf{f}(x)) & \mathsf{b}(g(x)) \rightarrow g(\mathsf{b}(x)) & [\![_\Sigma(g(x)) \rightarrow g([\![_\Sigma(x)) \\
\mathsf{f}(h(x)) \rightarrow h(\mathsf{f}(x)) & \mathsf{b}(]\!]_\Sigma(x)) \rightarrow]\!]_\Sigma(\mathsf{b}(x)) & [\![_\Sigma(]\!]_\Sigma(x)) \rightarrow x \\
\mathsf{f}(\bullet) \rightarrow]\!]_\Sigma(\bullet)\,, & &
\end{array}
$$

where $g \in \mathcal{F}(\Sigma)$, $h \in \mathcal{F}(\Sigma \cup \{b\})$.

We end the section with a more liberal notion of computability by rewriting, computations up-to a *padding* function.

Definition 4. *Let $\Sigma, \mathcal{F}(\Sigma), \mathcal{R}$ and* No *be as in Definition 1. Furthermore, we suppose the signature $\mathcal{F} \supset \mathcal{F}(\Sigma)$ contains a fresh padding symbol, denoted by $\sqcap$. Let $F : \mathbb{N} \rightarrow \mathbb{N}$ be a function. A relation $R \subseteq \Sigma^* \times \Sigma^*$ is* computable by $\mathcal{R}$ *up-to the* padding function F*, if there exists a function symbol $\mathsf{f} \in \mathcal{F}$ such that for all $w \in \Sigma^*$: $R(w, \mathtt{out}(t))$ if and only if $\mathsf{f}(\mathtt{inp}(w) \sqcap^{F(|x|)}) \rightarrow^!_\mathcal{R} t$, such that $t \notin$* No. *Here* $\mathtt{inp}$, $\mathtt{out}$ *denote translations from Σ and into Σ as above.*

We say that a relation R is computable up-to F-padding, if it is computable by some $\mathcal{R}$ up-to the padding function F.

Example 5. Consider an alphabet Σ of unary symbols and a symbol $b \notin \Sigma$. On $(\Sigma \cup \{b\})^*$, we define a relation R as follows: $R(w, v)$ if and only if $v = b^{|w|}\ w$, such that w does not contain b. Consider the TRS $\mathcal{R}$, obtained by adding the following rules to the TRS $\mathcal{R}_{\leftarrow \mathsf{b}}$:

$$\begin{array}{lll} \mathsf{g}'(x) \to \mathsf{f}_{\leftarrow \mathsf{b}}(\mathsf{ver}(x)) & \mathsf{ver}(g(x)) \to g(\mathsf{ver}(x)) & h(\mathsf{undef}) \to \mathsf{undef} \\ \mathsf{ver}(\sqcap(x)) \to \mathsf{b}(\mathsf{ver}(x)) & \mathsf{ver}(\mathsf{b}(x)) \to \mathsf{undef} & \mathsf{ver}(\bullet) \to \bullet\ , \end{array}$$

where $g \in \mathcal{F}(\Sigma), h \in \mathcal{F} \setminus \{\bullet\}$. Then R is computable by $\mathcal{R}$ by padding up-to the polynomial $\lambda x.x$.

4 Turing Machines and Rewriting

In this section, we introduce a simulation of Turing machines by rewriting.

Let $\mathsf{M} = (Q, \Sigma, \Gamma, \rhd, \sqcup, \Delta, \mathrm{s}, \mathrm{t}, \mathrm{r})$ denote a (nondeterminstic) TM. We define the signature $\mathcal{F}(\mathsf{M})$ *corresponding* to M as follows. For each $a \in \Gamma$, there exists a unary function symbol $\mathsf{a} \in \mathcal{F}(\mathsf{M})$. Moreover define $Q(\mathcal{F}) := \{\mathsf{q}_\mathsf{a} \mid q \in Q \text{ and } a \in \Gamma\}$ and suppose $Q(\mathcal{F}) \subseteq \mathcal{F}(\mathsf{M})$. Finally we have $\bullet, 0, 1 \in \mathcal{F}(\mathsf{M})$.

It is well-known that TMs can be encoded as unary TRSs or even string rewrite systems, cf. [17]. In the following encoding, we make use of the fact that all here considered TMs are space bounded by some bounding function S. Thus we need only consider a finite part of the tape of M. In particular any configuration α of M becomes representable as a triple $(q, \rhd v \sqcup^m, \ell)$ for $m \in \mathbb{N}$. This is employed in the definition given belows. To represent the running time of M, we add a time point to the representation of the configuration. It is well-known that a halting machine working in space $S(n)$ runs in time $2^{k \cdot S(n)}$ for some $k > 0$ (see for example [11]). Thus, the running time can be represented in binary by a word of length $k \cdot S(n)$. Let w be a word of length $n = |w|$; we write w_i $(1 \leqslant i \leqslant n)$ to denote the ith letter in w.

Definition 6. *Let w be a word over Σ and let $n = |w|$. Suppose M is a (non-deterministic) TM running on input w in space $S(n)$ such that $S(n) = \Omega(n)$. Further let $\alpha = (q, \rhd v \sqcup^m, \ell)$ be a configuration of M at time t such that $|v| + m \leqslant S(n)$. Then α is represented as: $\gamma_{t,q,v,\ell} := t \rhd v_1 v_2 \dots v_{\ell-1} q_{v_\ell} v_{\ell+1} v_{\ell+2} \dots v_{|v|} \sqcup^m$. The time point t is represented as a string of length $k \cdot S(n)$, making use of the extra symbols $0, 1 \in \mathcal{F}(\mathsf{M})$.*

Lemma 7 (Step by step simulation of a TM). *Let S be a bounding function such that $S(n) = \Omega(n)$. Suppose we are given a nondeterminstic TM $\mathsf{M} = (Q, \Sigma, \Gamma, \rhd, \sqcup, \Delta, s, t, r)$ running with input w in space $S(|w|)$. Then there exists a unary TRS $\mathcal{R}$, simulating this machine step by step, starting with $\gamma_{t_0,s,w,1}$, where $t_0 = 0^{S(|w|)}$. More precisely: if $(p, w, m) \xrightarrow{\mathsf{M}} (q, v, n)$, then $\gamma_{t,p,w,m} \to^*_{\mathcal{R}} \gamma_{t+1,q,v,n}$ for $t \geqslant 0$.*

Proof. We add the extra symbol $0'$ to the signature to manage the clock (see the rules below). Let $\mathcal{F}$ be a signature that extends the signature $\mathcal{F}(\mathsf{M})$ so that $\{\mathsf{a}' \mid a \in \Gamma\} \cup \{0'\} \subseteq \mathcal{F}$.

Consider the following (schematic) TRS $\mathcal{R}_1$ over $\mathcal{F}$. Essentially $\mathcal{R}_1$ computes the binary successor and in addition marks letters. In conjunction with rules that express each transition of M it will be used to update the configuration.

$$\begin{array}{lll} \mathsf{0}(f(x)) \to \mathsf{1}(f'(x)) & \mathsf{1}(f(x)) \to \mathsf{0}'(f'(x)) & f'(g(x)) \to f(g'(x)) \\ \mathsf{0}(\mathsf{0}'(x)) \to \mathsf{1}(\mathsf{0}(x)) & \mathsf{1}(\mathsf{0}'(x)) \to \mathsf{0}'(\mathsf{0}(x)) \ , & \end{array}$$

where $f, g \in \mathcal{F}$ and f', g' denote marked copies of f, g, respectively. The next (schematic) rules represent the transition relation Δ of M.

$$\begin{array}{ll} \mathsf{a}'(\mathsf{p_b}(x)) \to \mathsf{q_a}(\mathsf{c}(x)) & \text{if } (q, c, L) \in \Delta(p, b) \\ \mathsf{a}'(\mathsf{p_b}(\mathsf{d}(x))) \to \mathsf{a}(\mathsf{c}(\mathsf{q_d}(x))) & \text{if } (q, c, R) \in \Delta(p, b) \end{array}$$

Here $\mathsf{a}, \mathsf{a}', \mathsf{c}, \mathsf{d} \in \mathcal{F}$. These rules are collected in the TRS $\mathcal{R}_2$. Finally, we define $\mathcal{R} := \mathcal{R}_1 \cup \mathcal{R}_2$. It is not difficult to see that $\mathcal{R}$ fulfils the conditions given in the lemma. Note that this simulation takes square time. More precisely, if M works in $T(n)$ (nondeterministic) steps, the derivation length of the rewriting system will be $\mathrm{O}(T(n)^2)$. □

5 The Knuth Bendix Order

In this section we recall the definition of the Knuth Bendix order. We follow the presentation in [3] closely.

Let $\succ$ be a proper order on signature $\mathcal{F}$, called *precedence*. A *weight function* for $\mathcal{F}$ is a pair (w, w_0) consisting of a function $\mathsf{w}\colon \mathcal{F} \to \mathbb{N}$ and a minimal weight $w_0 \in \mathbb{N}$, $w_0 > 0$ such that $\mathsf{w}(c) \geqslant w_0$ if c is a constant. A weight function (w, w_0) is called *admissible* for a precedence $\succ$ if the existence of $f \in \mathcal{F}$, such that f is unary and $\mathsf{w}(f) = 0$ entails that $f \succ g$ for all $g \in \mathcal{F}$, $g \neq f$. The symbol f is necessarily unique, it is qualified as *special*. We sometimes identify the pair (w, w_0) with the function $\mathsf{w}\colon \mathcal{F} \to \mathbb{N}$ and simply call the latter a weight function. The *weight* of a term t, denoted as $\mathsf{weight}(t)$ is defined inductively. Assume t is a variable, then set $\mathsf{weight}(t) := w_0$, otherwise if $t = f(t_1, \ldots, t_n)$, we define $\mathsf{weight}(t) := \mathsf{w}(f) + \mathsf{weight}(t_1) + \cdots + \mathsf{weight}(t_n)$.

Definition 8. *Let* $\succ$ *denote a precedence and* (w, w_0) *an admissible weight function. The* Knuth Bendix order *(*KBO *for short)* $\succ_{\mathsf{kbo}}$ *on* $\mathcal{T}(\mathcal{F}, \mathcal{V})$ *is inductively defined as follows: for all terms* s, t *we have* $s \succ_{\mathsf{kbo}} t$ *if* $|s|_x \geqslant |t|_x$ *for all* $x \in \mathcal{V}$ *and either*

1) $\mathsf{weight}(s) > \mathsf{weight}(t)$, *or*
2) $\mathsf{weight}(s) = \mathsf{weight}(t)$, *and one of the following alternatives holds:*
 (a) t *is a variable,* $s = f^n(t)$, *where* f *is the special symbol, and* $n > 0$,
 (b) $s = f(s_1, \ldots, s_n)$, $t = f(t_1, \ldots, t_n)$, *and there exists* $i \in \{i, \ldots, n\}$ *such that* $s_j = t_j$ *for all* $1 \leqslant j < i$ *and* $s_i \succ_{\mathsf{kbo}} t_i$, *or*
 (c) $s = f(s_1, \ldots, s_n)$, $t = g(t_1, \ldots, t_m)$, *and* $f \succ g$.

Let $\succcurlyeq_{\mathsf{kbo}}$ *denote the quasi-order induced by* $\succ_{\mathsf{kbo}}$.

We say a TRS $\mathcal{R}$ is *compatible* with a KBO $\succ_{\mathsf{kbo}}$ if $\mathcal{R} \subseteq \succ_{\mathsf{kbo}}$, that is for all rules $l \to r$: $l \succ_{\mathsf{kbo}} r$. It is well-known that KBO is a simplification order, in particular if $\mathcal{R}$ is compatible with $\succ_{\mathsf{kbo}}$, then $\mathcal{R}$ terminates. A KBO induced by a weight function $\mathsf{w}\colon \mathcal{F} \to \mathbb{N} \setminus \{0\}$ is said to be *positively weighted.*

Example 9. Recall Example 2. Let $\mathsf{w}(f) = 1$ for all symbols in the TRS $\mathcal{R}_{\leftarrow\mathsf{b}}$, with the exception of $\mathsf{f}_{\leftarrow\mathsf{b}}$, where we set $\mathsf{w}(\mathsf{f}_{\leftarrow\mathsf{b}}) = 3$. Consider a precedence $\succ$ defined as follows: $\mathsf{f} \succ [\![_{\mathsf{b}} \succ \mathcal{F}(\Sigma) \succ \mathsf{b} \succ]\!]_{\mathsf{b}} \succ \bullet$, where $[\![_{\mathsf{b}} \succ \mathcal{F}(\Sigma) \succ \mathsf{b}$ abbreviates that for any function symbol $g \in \mathcal{F}(\Sigma)$, $[\![_{\mathsf{b}} \succ g \succ \mathsf{b}$, and $\succ$ is defined arbitrary on $\mathcal{F}(\Sigma)$. It is easy to see that the KBO induced by the (admissible) weight function w and $\succ$ is compatible with $\mathcal{R}_{\leftarrow\mathsf{b}}$. Now, consider the TRS $\mathcal{R}_{\rightarrow\mathsf{b}}$ defined in Example 3. Let $\mathsf{w}(f) := 1$ for all symbols in the TRS $\mathcal{R}_{\leftarrow\mathsf{b}}$, with the exception of $\mathsf{f}_{\rightarrow\mathsf{b}}$, where we set $\mathsf{w}(\mathsf{f}_{\rightarrow\mathsf{b}}) := 3$. Consider a precedence $\succ$ defined as follows: we assert $\mathsf{f} \succ [\![_{\Sigma} \succ \mathsf{b}$, together with $\mathsf{b} \succ \mathcal{F}(\Sigma) \succ]\!]_{\Sigma} \succ \bullet$. Then $\mathcal{R}_{\rightarrow\mathsf{b}} \subseteq \succ_{\mathsf{kbo}}$, for the induced KBO $\succ_{\mathsf{kbo}}$.

The next example clarifies that the simulating TRS $\mathcal{R}$ defined in the proof of Lemma 7 is KBO terminating.

Example 10. Consider the TRS $\mathcal{R}$ over $\mathcal{F}$ defined in the proof of Lemma 7. Let $\mathsf{w}(f) := 1$ for all $f \in \mathcal{F}$. For the precedence $\succ$ we assert $\mathsf{0} \succ \mathsf{1} \succ \mathsf{0}'$ and for all $a, a' \in \mathcal{F}$ and all $q \in Q$ set $\mathsf{a}' \succ \mathsf{a}$, $\mathsf{a}' \succ \mathsf{q}_{\mathsf{b}}$, where $b \in \Sigma$. It is easy to see that $\mathcal{R}$ is compatible with the KBO induced by the given weight function and the precedence.

In the next sections, we discuss a variety of variants of KBO in order to classify their computational content precisely. For that we introduce the following technical definition. The *σ-size* of a term t measures the number of non-special non-constant function symbols occurring in t: (i) $|t|_\sigma := 0$, if t is a constant; (ii) $|t|_\sigma := |t'|_\sigma$, if $t = f(t')$, f special; (iii) $|t|_\sigma := 1 + \sum_1^n |t_i|_\sigma$, if $t = f(t_1, \ldots, t_n)$.

Lemma 11. *Let* w *denote a weight function and* weight *the induced weight function on terms. For all terms t, the following hold: (i)* $|t|_\sigma = \mathrm{O}(\mathsf{weight}(t))$ *and (ii)* $\mathsf{weight}(t) = \mathrm{O}(|t|)$.

In concluding this section, we show how a function f computed by a TM running in space $S(n)$, where S is at least linear, is computed (up to S) by a TRS $\mathcal{R}$, whose termination can be shown via KBO.

Suppose $S(n) = k \cdot n + l$ and let R be computed by the 7-tuple $(\Sigma, \mathcal{F} \cup \{\sqcap\}, \mathtt{inp}, \mathtt{out}, \mathsf{g}, \mathcal{R}, \mathsf{No})$ up-to the padding function $S(n)$. In the following we define the 7-tuple $(\Sigma, \mathcal{F}', \mathtt{inp}', \mathtt{out}, \mathsf{g}', \mathcal{R}', \mathsf{No})$.

Define $\mathcal{R}_{\rightarrow\sqcap}$ as in Example 3, so that the symbol b is specialised to the padding symbol $\sqcap \in \mathcal{F}$. Set $\mathcal{F}_0 = \{\mathsf{f}_{\rightarrow\sqcap}, \mathsf{f}, [\![_{\Sigma},]\!]_{\Sigma}\}$. Without loss of generality, we assert that $\mathcal{F}_0$ and $\mathcal{F}$ are disjoint. Let $\mathcal{F}_1 = \{\mathsf{g}', \mathsf{cpy}_3\}$ be disjoint with $\mathcal{F}$ and let $\overline{\Sigma}$ denote a copy of the alphabet Σ. Consider the auxiliary TRS $\mathcal{R}_{\mathsf{cpy}}$ over the signature $\mathcal{F}_1 \cup \mathcal{F}(\Sigma) \cup \mathcal{F}(\overline{\Sigma})$.

$$\mathsf{g}'(x) \to \mathsf{g}(\mathsf{f}_{\rightarrow\sqcap}(\mathsf{cpy}_3(x))) \quad \mathsf{cpy}_3(\bullet) \to \sqcap^l(\bullet) \quad \mathsf{cpy}_3(\overline{f}(x)) \to f(\sqcap^k(\mathsf{cpy}_3(x))) \ ,$$

where $f \in \mathcal{F}(\Sigma)$ and $\overline{f} \in \mathcal{F}(\overline{\Sigma})$ its copy. Define $\mathcal{F}' = (\mathcal{F} \setminus \{\sqcap\}) \cup \mathcal{F}_0 \cup \mathcal{F}_1 \cup \mathcal{F}(\overline{\Sigma})$ and let $\mathcal{R}'$ be defined over $\mathcal{F}'$ as follows: $\mathcal{R}' := \mathcal{R} \cup \mathcal{R}_{\rightarrow\sqcap} \cup \mathcal{R}_{\mathsf{cpy}}$. The translation $\mathtt{inp}'$ from Σ is defined as follows:

$$\mathtt{inp}' \colon a \in \Sigma \mapsto \overline{a} \in \mathcal{F}(\overline{\Sigma}) \ .$$

This completes the definition of the 7-tuple $(\Sigma, \mathcal{F}', \mathtt{inp}', \mathtt{out}, \mathsf{g}', \mathcal{R}', \mathsf{No})$.

Lemma 12. *Let R be computed by the 7-tuple $(\Sigma, \mathcal{F} \cup \{\sqcap\}, \mathtt{inp}, \mathtt{out}, \mathsf{g}, \mathcal{R}, \mathsf{No})$ up-to the padding function $\lambda x.k \cdot x + l$, using the padding symbol $\sqcap$. Then, R is also computed by the 7-tuple $(\Sigma, \mathcal{F}', \mathtt{inp}', \mathtt{out}, \mathsf{g}', \mathcal{R}', \mathsf{No})$ defined above. Moreover, if $\mathcal{R}$ is compatible with a positively weighted KBO, the same holds with respect to $\mathcal{R}'$.*

Theorem 13. *Let $R(w, v)$ be a binary relation, let $n = |w|$ and let M be a (nondeterministic) TM that solves the function problem associated with relation $R(w, v)$ in space $S(n) = \Omega(n)$ and time $2^{S(n)}$. Then the relation R is computable by $\mathcal{R}$ up-to S-padding using the padding symbol $\sqcap$. Moreover $\mathcal{R}$ is unary and compatible with a positively weighted KBO.*

Proof. In proof, we assume M is nondeterminstic and we utilise the step by step simulation of a nondeterminstic TM $\mathsf{M} = (Q, \Sigma, \Gamma, \triangleright, \sqcup, \Delta, \mathrm{s}, \mathrm{t}, \mathrm{r})$ as seen in Lemma 7. The main issue is to properly prepare the "data", that is, the initial configuration, so that one can apply the lemma. Let the TRS $\mathcal{R}_{\mathsf{M}}$ over the signature $\mathcal{F}$ be defined as in the proof of Lemma 7. Furthermore define $\mathcal{R}_{\leftarrow 0}$ as in Example 2, such that the symbol b is specialised to the clock symbol $\mathsf{0} \in \mathcal{F}$. Moreover consider the following auxiliary TRS $\mathcal{R}_{\mathsf{build}}$:

$$\begin{aligned} \mathsf{build}(x) &\rightarrow \triangleright'(\mathsf{f}_{\leftarrow 0}(\mathsf{cpy}_1(x))) & \mathsf{cpy}_1(f(x)) &\rightarrow f(\mathsf{cpy}_1(x)) \\ \mathsf{cpy}_1(\sqcap(x)) &\rightarrow \mathsf{0}(\sqcap(\mathsf{cpy}_1(x))) & \mathsf{cpy}_1(\bullet) &\rightarrow \bullet \\ \triangleright'(\mathsf{0}(x)) &\rightarrow \mathsf{0}(\triangleright'(x)) & \triangleright'(g(x)) &\rightarrow \triangleright(\mathrm{s}_{\mathsf{g}}(x)) \ , \end{aligned}$$

where $f, g \in \mathcal{F}(\Sigma)$. Finally, we set $\mathcal{R} := \mathcal{R}_{\mathsf{M}} \cup \mathcal{R}_{\leftarrow 0} \cup \mathcal{R}_{\mathsf{build}}$. It is not difficult to see that $\mathcal{R}$ computes the relation R up-to S-padding.

We extend the definitions of weight and precedence as given in Example 10 for $\mathcal{R}_{\mathsf{M}}$ and in Example 9 for $\mathcal{R}_{\leftarrow 0}$. Let $\mathcal{F}_{\mathsf{M}}$ denote the signature of $\mathcal{R}_{\mathsf{M}}$ and let $\mathsf{w}(f) := 1$ for all $f \in \mathcal{F}_{\mathsf{M}}$. Moreover, let $\mathcal{F}_0 = \{[\![_0,]\!]_0, \mathsf{f}, \mathsf{f}_{\leftarrow 0}\}$ and note that the signature of $\mathcal{R}_{\leftarrow 0}$ amounts to $\mathcal{F}(\Sigma) \cup \mathcal{F}_0 \cup \{\mathsf{0}\}$. Observe that $\mathcal{F}(\Sigma) \cup \{\mathsf{0}\}\} \subseteq \mathcal{F}_{\mathsf{M}}$, that is, those weights have already been assigned. Set $\mathsf{w}([\![_0) = \mathsf{w}(]\!]_0) = \mathsf{w}(\mathsf{f}) := 1$ and $\mathsf{w}(\mathsf{f}_{\leftarrow 0}) = 2$. Finally consider the new symbols in (the signature) of $\mathcal{R}_{\mathsf{build}}$ and set $\mathsf{w}(\sqcap) := 2$, $\mathsf{w}(\triangleright') = \mathsf{w}(\mathsf{cpy}_1) = 1$, and $\mathsf{w}(\mathsf{build}) := 4$. This completes the definition of w for the signature of $\mathcal{R}$. Moreover extend the precedence $\succ$ by $\mathsf{build} \succ \triangleright' \succ \mathsf{f}_{\leftarrow 0} \succ \mathsf{cpy}_1 \succ \mathcal{F}(\Sigma)$ and $\mathsf{cpy}_1 \succ \mathsf{0}$. It is not difficult to see that the KBO $\succ_{\mathsf{kbo}}$ thus induced is compatible with KBO; furthermore $\succ_{\mathsf{kbo}}$ is positively weighted. □

6 Characterising Linear Space via KBO

In this section, we show how to capture the complexity classes LINSPACE and its nondeterministic variant NLINSPACE with the help of a restriction of the Knuth-Bendix order.

Lemma 14. *Let $\mathcal{F}$ be a signature and* w *be a weight function over $\mathcal{F}$ such that for all $f \in \mathcal{F}$, $\mathsf{w}(f) > 0$. Then there exists a constant M such that for all terms t: $|t| \leqslant \mathsf{w}(t) \leqslant M \cdot |t|$.*

We specialise the definition of function problems given in Section 2 to the present context. Let $R(w, v)$ denote a binary relation that can be decided by a (nondeterministic) TM M. We say the function problem F_R associated with R can be solved in linear space, if it can be solved in space linear in $|w|$.

Theorem 15. *Let $\mathcal{R}$ be a TRS, let $\mathcal{R}$ be compatible with a positively weighted KBO, and let R denote the relation computed by $\mathcal{R}$. Then the function problem F_R can be solved on a (nondeterministic) TM in linear space. Moreover if $\mathcal{R}$ is confluent then the function computed by $\mathcal{R}$ can be computed in linear space on a deterministic TM.*

Proof. Assume R is computed by the 7-tuple $(\Sigma, \mathcal{F}, \mathtt{inp}, \mathtt{out}, \mathsf{f}, \mathcal{R}, \mathsf{No})$. Note that any rewrite step can be simulated (in linear space) on a TM. Indeed, pattern matching, binary subtraction, binary addition, character erasing, and character replacements can be done in linear space. The translation $\mathtt{out}$ provides a mapping from terms to the alphabet Σ. Thus it is easy to see how to define a suitable (nondeterministic) TM $\mathsf{M} = (Q, \Sigma, \Gamma, \triangleright, \sqcup, \Delta, \mathrm{s}, \mathrm{t}, \mathrm{r})$ such that any derivation over $\mathcal{R}$ can be simulated by M. Let s, t be terms such that $s \rightarrow^* t$. By definition of KBO, $\mathsf{weight}(s) \geqslant \mathsf{weight}(t)$ and thus due to Lemma 14 $\mathsf{weight}(t) = \mathrm{O}(|s|)$. Without loss of generality we can assume that the mapping $\mathtt{out}$ is linear in the size, that is, for any term t we have $|\mathtt{out}(t)| = \mathrm{O}(|t|)$. Thus the mentioned simulation can be performed by a TM running in space $\mathrm{O}(|\mathtt{out}(s)|)$. Hence the function problem F_R is computable by a TM in linear space. If in addition $\mathcal{R}$ is confluent, M is deterministic. □

Theorem 16. *Let* M *be a (nondeterministic) TM that solves in linear space the function problem associated with relation R. Then R is computable by a TRS $\mathcal{R}$ that is compatible with a positively weighted KBO. Moreover if* M *is deterministic, the TRS $\mathcal{R}$ is confluent.*

Proof. Without loss of generality we can assume that M runs in space $k \cdot n + l$ on input w, when $n = |w|$. Set $S(n) = k \cdot n + l$. By assumption M decides the relation R, hence it halts on any input. Thus we can assume M runs in time $2^{S(n)}$. Due to Theorem 13 there exists a TRS $\mathcal{R}'$ that computes the relation R up-to S-padding. Furthermore, as S is an affine function, Lemma 12 is applicable to transform $\mathcal{R}'$ to a TRS $\mathcal{R}$ that computes R (without padding). Moreover Theorem 13 and Lemma 12 guarantee that $\mathcal{R}$ is compatible with a positively weighted KBO. □

By Theorem 15 and 16 we obtain that positively weighted Knuth-Bendix orders characterises precisely the class of function problems $\mathsf{FNLINSPACE}$ on arbitrary TRS and the class $\mathsf{FLINSPACE}$ on confluent TRS. More precisely, if we restrict our attention to languages, positively weighted Knuth Bendix orders exactly captures ($\mathsf{LINSPACE}$) $\mathsf{NLINSPACE}$ on (confluent) TRSs.

7 Characterising Polynomial Space via KBO

In this section, we establish a complete characterisation of the complexity class PSPACE. For that it suffices to consider unary TRS. However, we have to make use of a more liberal use of padding function than in Section 6 above.

Our results rely on the insight that KBO induces exactly exponential derivational complexity on unary TRS. This is due to Hofbauer (compare [8,6]).

Proposition 17. *For all unary TRS $\mathcal{R}$ compatible with KBO $\mathsf{dc}_{\mathcal{R}}(n) = 2^{\mathrm{O}(n)}$ holds. Furthermore there exists a unary TRS $\mathcal{R}$ compatible with KBO such that $2^{\Omega(n)} = \mathsf{dc}_{\mathcal{R}}(n)$.*

Let $R(w, v)$ denote a binary relation that can be decided by a (nondeterministic) TM M. We say the function problem F_R associated with R can be solved in polynomial space, if it can be solved in space polynomial in $|w|$.

Theorem 18. *Let $\mathcal{R}$ be a unary TRS, let $\mathcal{R}$ be compatible with a KBO, and let R denote the relation computed by $\mathcal{R}$ up-to polynomial padding. Then the function problem F_R is solvable on a (nondeterministic) TM in polynomial space. Moreover if $\mathcal{R}$ is confluent then the function computed by $\mathcal{R}$ can be computed in polynomial space on a deterministic TM.*

Proof. Assume $R(w, v)$ is computed by the 7-tuple $(\Sigma, \mathcal{F}, \mathtt{inp}, \mathtt{out}, \mathsf{f}, \mathcal{R}, \mathsf{No})$ up-to the padding function P, where P is a polynomial. Without loss of generality we assume that the translations $\mathtt{inp}$, $\mathtt{out}$ are linear in size. Let s, t be terms. Consider a derivation $D\colon s \to^* t$, such that $\mathsf{dh}(s) = n$. Due to Proposition 17, there is a constant $c > 2$ such that $s \to^n t$ implies that $n \leqslant 2^{c\cdot(|s|+1)}$. Define $d = \max(2, \max(|r| : l \to r \in \mathcal{R}))$. By assumption $\mathcal{R}$ is compatible with a KBO. Hence $\mathcal{R}$ is non-duplicating. Thus each rewrite step increases the size by at most by d. We obtain:

$$|t| \leqslant |s| + d \cdot 2^{c\cdot(|s|+1)} \leqslant 2^{|s|+2} + 2^{c\cdot(|s|+1)+d} \leqslant 2^{(c+d+2)(|s|+1)} .$$

In the first inequality, we apply the definition of the constant d and in the third, we make use of the inequalities $2 \leqslant |s| + 2$ and $2 \leqslant d + c \cdot (|s| + 1)$. We set $e = c + d + 2$ and obtain $|t| \leqslant 2^{e\cdot(|s|+1)}$. Let i denote the special symbol. We decompose the term t as follows: $t = \mathsf{i}^{j_0} g_1 \mathsf{i}^{j_1} g_2 \mathsf{i}^{j_2} \cdots g_{i_m} \mathsf{i}^{j_m}$, where for all k: $g_k \in \mathcal{F} \setminus \{\mathsf{i}\}$ and thus m is precisely $|t|_\sigma$. By the above estimation on the size of t, we conclude that $j_k \leqslant 2^{e\cdot(|s|+1)}$ for all k $(0 \leqslant k \leqslant m)$. In order to simulate the derivation D on a TM we need to make sure that we can encode each term succinctly. For that we represent expressions i^{j_k} by $(j_k)_2$, where the latter denotes the binary representation of the number j_k. Hence we define $\ulcorner t \urcorner$ of t as follows: $\ulcorner t \urcorner := (j_0)_2 g_1 (j_1)_2 g_2 (j_2)_2 \cdots g_{i_m} (j_m)_2$. First, observe that $|(j_k)_2| \leqslant \log_2(2^{e\cdot(|s|+1)}) = e \cdot (|s| + 1)$. Second, due to Lemma 11, there exist constants ℓ, ℓ', such that $m = |t|_\sigma \leqslant \ell \cdot \mathsf{weight}(t) \leqslant \ell \cdot \mathsf{weight}(s) \leqslant \ell' \cdot |s|$. (Recall that we have $s \to^* t$). In summary, we obtain the following estimate for the size of $\ulcorner t \urcorner$:

$$\begin{aligned}|\ulcorner t \urcorner| &\leqslant m + (m + 1) \cdot (e \cdot (|s| + 1)) \\ &\leqslant (m + 1) \cdot (e \cdot (|s| + 2)) \leqslant (\ell' \cdot |s| + 1) \cdot (e \cdot (|s| + 2)) .\end{aligned}$$

Set $Q(n) := (\ell' \cdot n + 1) \cdot (e \cdot n + 2)$, which is a quadratic polynomial in n. Consider now some word w in the alphabet Σ. The initial term $\mathsf{f}(\mathtt{inp}(w) \sqcap^{P(|w|)})$ has size $P(|w|) + |w| + 2$, which is a polynomial in $|w|$. Applying the above equations we see that for all t such that $\mathsf{f}(\mathtt{inp}(w) \sqcap^{P(|x|)}) \to^* t$, the size of $\ulcorner t \urcorner$ is bounded by $Q(P(|w|) + |w| + 2)$, that is, polynomially bounded. As indicated above, each rewrite step can be simulated in linear space. Thus, any derivation $\mathsf{f}(\mathtt{inp}(w) \sqcap^{P(|w|)}) \to^* t$ can be simulated on a (nondeterministic) TM in space polynomial in $|w|$.

Hence the function problem F_R is computable by a TM in polynomial space. If in addition $\mathcal{R}$ is confluent, M can be assumed to be deterministic. □

Theorem 19. *Let* M *be a (nondeterministic) TM that solves in polynomial space the function problem associated with relation* R*. Then* R *is computable up-to polynomial padding by a unary TRS* $\mathcal{R}$ *such that* $\mathcal{R}$ *is compatible with a KBO. Moreover if* M *is deterministic, the TRS* $\mathcal{R}$ *is confluent.*

Proof. Observe that given such a machine M, there is a polynomial P such that M works in space $P(n)$ and time $2^{P(n)}$. Then the theorem follows by a straightforward application of Theorem 13. □

As a consequence of Theorem 18 and 19 we obtain that Knuth Bendix orders characterises precisely the class of function problems FPSPACE on unary TRS if computation up-to polynomial padding is considered. For languages, we conclude that KBO over unary TRS exactly captures PSPACE if polynomial padding is allowed. Observe that it is insignificant, whether the considered TRS is confluent or not.

8 Characterising Exponential Space via KBO

In this section, we establish a complete characterisation of the complexity class ESPACE.

Below we introduce a (non-standard) extension of Knuth Bendix orders. Recall the restriction to admissible weight functions in Definition 8. The following examples shows that we cannot dispense with this restriction (compare [9]).

Example 20. Let $\sqsupset$ denote the binary relation induced by Definition 8 induced by a non-admissible weight function and precedence $\succ$. Let $f, g \in \mathcal{F}$ such that $\mathsf{w}(f) = \mathsf{w}(g) = 0$ and $f \succ g$. Then $\sqsupset$ gives rise to the following infinite decent: $f(x) \sqsupset g(f(x)) \sqsupset g(g(f(x))) \sqsupset g(g(g(f(x)))) \ldots$

Let t be a term, let $f_1, \ldots, f_k \in \mathcal{F}$ denote function symbols of equal arity n. Suppose g is a fresh function symbol of arity n not in $\mathcal{F}$. We write $t[g \leftarrow f_1, \ldots, f_k]$ to denote the result of replacing all occurrences of f_i in t by g.

Definition 21. *Let* w *a (not necessarily admissible) weight function,* $\succ$ *a precedence and* $\succ_{\mathsf{kbo}}$ *be the order induced by* w *and* $\succ$ *according to Definition 8 but using only Cases 1, 2b, and 2c. Let* $f_1, \ldots, f_k \in \mathcal{F}$ *be unary symbols such that*

$\mathsf{w}(f_i) = 0$ *and let* $\mathsf{w}(g) = 0$ *for a fresh symbol* g. *Suppose* $g \succ h$ *for any* $h \in \mathcal{F} \setminus \{f_1, \ldots, f_k\}$. *Then* $\succ_{\mathsf{kbo}}$ *is said to be an* enriched Knuth Bendix order *if in addition for any terms* s *and* t, $s \succ_{\mathsf{kbo}} t$ *implies that* $s[g \leftarrow f_1, \ldots, f_k] \succcurlyeq_{\mathsf{kbo}} t[g \leftarrow f_1, \ldots, f_k]$ *(Property* (†)*). Here* $\succcurlyeq_{\mathsf{kbo}}$ *denote the quasi-order induced by* $\succ_{\mathsf{kbo}}$. *The equivalence relation induced by* $\succcurlyeq_{\mathsf{kbo}}$ *is denoted as* $\simeq_{\mathsf{kbo}}$.

It is easy to see that an enriched KBO $\succ_{\mathsf{kbo}}$ is closed under context and substitutions. For the later it is essential, that Case 2a in the standard definition of KBO is omitted. Moreover, the property (†) in Definition 21 guarantees that $\succ_{\mathsf{kbo}}$ is well-founded. Let $\mathcal{R}$ be a TRS. We say $\mathcal{R}$ is compatible with an enriched KBO $\succ_{\mathsf{kbo}}$. if $\mathcal{R} \subseteq \succ_{\mathsf{kbo}}$. Note that compatibility of $\mathcal{R}$ with an enriched KBO implies termination of $\mathcal{R}$.

Remark 22. It is perhaps important to emphasise that $\succ_{\mathsf{kbo}}$ does not admit the subterm property. Hence an enriched KBO is not a simplification order.

We obtain the following generalisation of Proposition 11 to enriched KBOs.

Lemma 23. *Let* $\mathcal{R}$ *be a TRS over a signature* $\mathcal{F}$ *that consists only of nullary or unary function symbols and let* $\mathcal{R}$ *be compatible to* $\succ_{\mathsf{kbo}}$ *as defined above. Then* $\mathsf{dc}_{\mathcal{R}}(n) = 2^{2^{\mathrm{O}(n)}}$. *Furthermore, the size of any term of a derivation is bounded by* $2^{\mathrm{O}(n)}$.

Let $R(w, v)$ denote a binary relation that can be decided by a (nondeterministic) TM M. We say the function problem F_R associated with R can be solved in exponential space, if it can be solved in space $2^{\mathrm{O}(|w|)}$. The next theorem follows directly from Lemma 23.

Theorem 24. *Let* $\mathcal{R}$ *be a unary TRS, let* $\mathcal{R}$ *be compatible with an enriched KBO, and let* R *denote the relation computed by* $\mathcal{R}$. *Then the function problem* F_R *associated with* R *is solvable on a (nondeterministic) TM in exponential space. Moreover if* $\mathcal{R}$ *is confluent then the function computed by* $\mathcal{R}$ *can be computed in polynomial space on a deterministic TM.*

Theorem 25. *Let* M *be a (nondeterministic) TM that solves the function problem* F_R *associated with relation* R *in exponential space. Then* R *is computable by a unary TRS* $\mathcal{R}$ *such that* $\mathcal{R}$ *is compatible with an enriched KBO. Moreover if* M *is deterministic, the TRS* $\mathcal{R}$ *is confluent.*

Proof. Let $S(n) = 2^{k \cdot n}$ denote the bounding function of M. In proof, we assume M is nondeterminstic and we utilise the step by step simulation of a nondeterminstic TM $\mathsf{M} = (Q, \Sigma, \Gamma, \rhd, \sqcup, \Delta, \mathrm{s}, \mathrm{t}, \mathrm{r})$ as seen in Lemma 7. In the following we define a 7-tuple $(\Sigma, \mathcal{F}, \mathtt{inp}', \mathtt{out}, \mathsf{h}, \mathcal{R}, \mathsf{No})$ that computes R. Essentially $\mathcal{R}$ will extend the simulating TRS $\mathcal{R}_{\mathsf{M}}$ as define in Lemma 7, but we need to prepare the input suitably. Let $\overline{\Sigma}$ denotes a (disjoint) copy of the alphabet Σ. We define two translations $\mathtt{inp}$, $\mathtt{inp}'$ from Σ to $\mathcal{F}(\Sigma)$ and $\mathcal{F}(\overline{\Sigma})$, respectively. Set $\mathtt{inp}\colon a \in \Sigma \mapsto a \in \mathcal{F}(\Sigma)$ and $\mathtt{inp}'\colon a \in \Sigma \mapsto \overline{a} \in \mathcal{F}(\overline{\Sigma})$. Consider the following auxiliary TRS $\mathcal{R}_{\mathsf{dec}}$ that implements the binary decrement, where $\top$, $\bot$ denotes 1 and 0, respectively.

$$\begin{aligned} \top(\bullet) &\to \bot(0 \sqcup (\bullet)) & \bot(\bullet) &\to \top'(0 \sqcup (\bullet)) \\ \bot(\top'(x)) &\to \top'(\top(x)) & \top(0(x)) &\to \bot(0 \sqcup (0(x))) \\ \bot(0(x)) &\to \top'(0 \sqcup (0(x))) & \top(\top'(x)) &\to \bot(\top(x)) \\ \mathsf{init}(0(x)) &\to 0(x) & \mathsf{init}(\top'(x)) &\to \mathsf{init}(x)\ . \end{aligned}$$

An inductive argument shows that $\mathsf{init}(\top^n(\bullet)) \to^* (0\sqcup)^{2^n-1}(\bullet)$ holds for all $n \geqslant 1$. Furthermore we make use of the following TRS $\mathcal{R}'_{\mathsf{cpy}}$:

$$\begin{aligned} \mathsf{cpy}_2(\bullet) &\to \bullet & \mathsf{cpy}_2(\overline{f}(x)) &\to f(\top^k(\mathsf{cpy}_2(x))) \\ \rhd'(0(x)) &\to 0(\rhd'(x)) & \rhd'(g(x)) &\to \rhd(\mathrm{s}_g(x)) \\ \mathsf{h}(x) &\to \rhd'(\mathsf{f}_{\leftarrow 0}(\mathsf{init}(\mathsf{f}_{\rightarrow\top}(\mathsf{cpy}_2(x))))) & \mathsf{init}(h(x)) &\to h(\mathsf{init}(x)) \end{aligned}$$

where $f \in \mathcal{F}(\Sigma)$, $\overline{f} \in \mathcal{F}(\overline{\Sigma})$ its copy, $g, h \in \mathcal{F}(\Sigma)$, and the symbols $\mathsf{f}_{\leftarrow 0}$, $\mathsf{f}_{\rightarrow\top}$ are defined as in Examples 2, 3. Let w be a word over Σ, let $n = |w|$, and let $\mathtt{inp}(w) = g_1 g_2 \cdots g_n$. Then it is not difficult to see that any derivation over $\mathcal{R}_{\mathsf{dec}} \cup \mathcal{R}'_{\mathsf{cpy}}$ has the following shape:

$$\begin{aligned} \mathsf{h}(\mathtt{inp}'(w)) &\to^* \rhd'(\mathsf{f}_{\leftarrow 0}(\mathtt{inp}(w)\mathsf{init}(\top^{k\cdot n}))) \\ &\to^* \rhd'(0^{2^{k\cdot n}-1}\mathtt{inp}(w)\sqcup^{2^{k\cdot n}-1})) \\ &\to^* 0^{2^{k\cdot n}-1} \rhd \mathrm{s}_{g_1} g_2 \cdots g_n \sqcup^{2^{k\cdot n}-1}\ . \end{aligned}$$

We set $\mathcal{R} := \mathcal{R}_{\mathsf{dec}} \cup \mathcal{R}'_{\mathsf{cpy}} \cup \mathcal{R}_{\mathsf{f}_{\rightarrow\top}} \cup \mathcal{R}_{\mathsf{f}_{\leftarrow 0}}$. It follows from Lemma 7 that the 7-tuple $(\Sigma, \mathcal{F}, \mathtt{inp}', \mathtt{out}, \mathsf{h}, \mathcal{R}, \mathsf{No})$ computes the relation R. Finally, it is not difficult to see how to define a suitable enriched KBO $\succ_{\mathsf{kbo}}$, such that $\mathcal{R} \subseteq \succ_{\mathsf{kbo}}$. □

As a consequence of Theorem 24 and 25 we obtain that enriched Knuth Bendix orders characterises precisely the class of function problems FESPACE on unary TRS. For languages, we conclude that enriched KBO over unary TRS exactly captures ESPACE. Observe that it is insignificant, whether the considered TRS is confluent or not.

9 Conclusion

In this paper we study three different space complexity classes: LINSPACE, PSPACE, and ESPACE, which are commonly believed to be distinct. We give complete characterisations of these classes exploiting TRSs, compatible with KBOs. To capture LINSPACE, we consider confluent, positively weighted KBOs. To capture PSPACE, we consider unary TRS, where we allow for padding of the input. And to capture ESPACE, we make use of enriched KBO. For all considered complexity classes, we show similar results for the corresponding nondeterministic classes. In this case the TRS $\mathcal{R}$ need no longer be confluent.

Furthermore we have also characterised the associated classes of function problems for the (nondeterministic) space complexity classes considered. This (technical) result is of some importance as it overcomes the problem that complexity classes are languages, while TRSs compute functions.

References

1. Avanzini, M., Moser, G.: Complexity Analysis by Rewriting. In: Garrigue, J., Hermenegildo, M.V. (eds.) FLOPS 2008. LNCS, vol. 4989, pp. 130–146. Springer, Heidelberg (2008)
2. Avanzini, M., Moser, G.: Dependency pairs and polynomial path orders. In: Treinen, R. (ed.) RTA 2009. LNCS, vol. 5595, pp. 48–62. Springer, Heidelberg (2009)
3. Baader, F., Nipkow, T.: Term Rewriting and All That. Cambridge University Press, Cambridge (1998)
4. Bonfante, G., Cichon, A., Marion, J.Y., Touzet, H.: Algorithms with polynomial interpretation termination proof. JFP 11(1), 33–53 (2001)
5. Bonfante, G., Marion, J.Y., Moyen, J.Y.: Quasi-interpretations and small space bounds. In: Giesl, J. (ed.) RTA 2005. LNCS, vol. 3467, pp. 150–164. Springer, Heidelberg (2005)
6. Hofbauer, D.: Termination Proofs and Derivation Lengths in Term Rewriting Systems. Ph.D. thesis, Technische Universität Berlin (1992)
7. Hofbauer, D.: Termination proofs with multiset path orderings imply primitive recursive derivation lengths. TCS 105(1), 129–140 (1992)
8. Hofbauer, D., Lautemann, C.: Termination Proofs and the Length of Derivation. In: Dershowitz, N. (ed.) RTA 1989. LNCS, vol. 355, pp. 167–177. Springer, Heidelberg (1989)
9. Knuth, D., Bendix, P.: Simple word problems in universal algebras. In: Leech, J. (ed.) Computational problems in abstract algebra. Pergamon, Oxford (1970)
10. Koprowski, A., Waldmann, J.: Arctic Termination ...Below Zero. In: Voronkov, A. (ed.) RTA 2008. LNCS, vol. 5117, pp. 202–216. Springer, Heidelberg (2008)
11. Kozen, D.: Theory of Computation. Springer, Heidelberg (2006)
12. Lepper, I.: Derivation lengths and order types of Knuth-Bendix orders. TCS 269, 433–450 (2001)
13. Marion, J.Y.: Analysing the Implicit Complexity of Programs. IC 183, 2–18 (2003)
14. Moser, G.: Derivational complexity of Knuth Bendix orders revisited. In: Hermann, M., Voronkov, A. (eds.) LPAR 2006. LNCS (LNAI), vol. 4246, pp. 75–89. Springer, Heidelberg (2006)
15. Moser, G., Schnabl, A.: The Derivational Complexity Induced by the Dependency Pair Method. In: Treinen, R. (ed.) RTA 2009. LNCS, vol. 5595, pp. 255–260. Springer, Heidelberg (2009)
16. Moser, G., Schnabl, A., Waldmann, J.: Complexity Analysis of Term Rewriting Based on Matrix and Context Dependent Interpretations. In: Proc. of 28th FST-TICS, pp. 304–315. Schloss Dagstuhl - Leibniz-Zentrum fuer Informatik, Germany (2008)
17. TeReSe: Term Rewriting Systems, Cambridge Tracks in Theoretical Computer Science, vol. 55. Cambridge University Press, Cambridge (2003)
18. Weiermann, A.: Termination proofs by lexicographic path orderings yield multiply recursive derivation lengths. Theoretical Computer Science 139(1), 355–362 (1995)

Focused Natural Deduction*

Taus Brock-Nannestad and Carsten Schürmann

IT University of Copenhagen
{tbro,carsten}@itu.dk

Abstract. Natural deduction for intuitionistic linear logic is known to be full of non-deterministic choices. In order to control these choices, we combine ideas from intercalation and focusing to arrive at the calculus of *focused natural deduction*. The calculus is shown to be sound and complete with respect to first-order intuitionistic linear natural deduction and the backward linear focusing calculus.

1 Introduction

The idea of focusing goes back to Andreoli [1] and gives an answer to the question on how to control non-determinism in proof search for the classical sequent calculus for fragments of linear logic. It removes the "bureaucracy" that arises due to the permutability of inference rules. Historically, the idea of focusing has influenced a great deal of research [2,3,5], all centered around sequent style systems. There is one area, however, which has been suspiciously neglected in all of this: natural deduction. In our view, there are two explanations.

First, for various reasons we don't want to get into here, most theorem proving systems are based on the sequent calculus. Therefore it is not surprising that most of the effort has gone into the study of sequent calculi as evidenced by results in uniform derivations [8] and of course focusing itself.

Second, it is possible to characterize the set of more "normalized" proofs for natural deduction in intuitionistic logic. Many such characterizations have been given in the past, for example, the intercalation calculus [9,10]. Backward chaining from the conclusion will only use introduction rules until only atomic formulas are leftover, and similarly, forward chaining will only use elimination rules.

Theorem provers for natural deduction, implementations of logical frameworks and bi-directional type checkers are all inspired by this idea of intercalation. One of its advantages is that the aforementioned "bureaucracy" never arises in part because the book-keeping regarding hypotheses is done externally and not within the formal system. In this paper we refine intercalation by ideas from focusing, resulting in a calculus with an even stricter notion of proof. This is useful when searching for and working with natural deduction derivations.

The hallmark characteristic of focusing is its two phases. First, invertible rules are applied eagerly, until both context and goal are non-invertible. This phase

* This work was in part supported by NABITT grant 2106-07-0019 of the Danish Strategic Research Council.

C. Fermüller and A. Voronkov (Eds.): LPAR-17, LNCS 6397, pp. 157–171, 2010.

is called the inversion or *asynchronous* phase. Second, a single formula taken from the context or the goal is selected and *focused* upon, applying a maximal sequence of non-invertible rules to this formula and its subformulas. This is known as the focusing or *synchronous* phase. The central idea of focusing is to polarize connectives into two groups. A connective is flagged *negative* when the respective introduction rule is invertible but the elimination rule(s) are not, and it is considered *positive* in the opposite case. Each connective of linear logic is either positive or negative, the polarity of atoms is uncommitted.

The main motivation for our work is to explore how proof theory, natural deduction in particular, can be used to explain concurrent systems. In that our goals are similar to those of the concurrent logical framework research project CLF [11]. Pragmatically speaking, in this paper, we remove all bureaucratic non-determinism from logical natural deduction derivations (as described by focusing), so that we can, in future work, use the remaining non-determinism to characterize concurrent systems. That the resulting focused natural deduction calculus is complete is perhaps the most important contribution of the paper.

Consider for example the judgment $a, a \multimap \mathbf{1} \Vdash \mathbf{1} \oplus b \Uparrow$, for which we would like to find a derivation in the intercalation calculus. The judgment should be read as find a *canonical* proof of $\mathbf{1} \oplus b$ from the linear assumptions a and $a \multimap \mathbf{1}$. As nothing is known about b, one might hope (at least intuitively) for one unique derivation. However, there are two, which we will next inspect in turn.

$$\dfrac{\dfrac{\dfrac{\dfrac{}{a \multimap \mathbf{1} \Vdash a \multimap \mathbf{1} \Downarrow}\,\text{hyp} \qquad \dfrac{\dfrac{}{a \Vdash a \Downarrow}\,\text{hyp}}{a \Vdash a \Uparrow}\,\Downarrow\Uparrow}{a, a \multimap \mathbf{1} \Vdash \mathbf{1} \Downarrow}\,\multimap\text{E} \qquad \dfrac{}{\cdot \Vdash \mathbf{1} \Uparrow}\,\mathbf{1}\text{I}}{a, a \multimap \mathbf{1} \Vdash \mathbf{1} \Uparrow}\,\mathbf{1}\text{E}}{a, a \multimap \mathbf{1} \Vdash \mathbf{1} \oplus b \Uparrow}\,\oplus\text{I}_1$$

The experienced eye might have already spotted, that this derivation is *negatively focused*, because the two upper rules in the left-most chain of inference rules hyp and $\multimap$E form a focus. However, it is not *positively focused*. The rule $\oplus\text{I}_1$ and the rule $\mathbf{1}$I ought to form a focus (both are positively polarized), but the $\mathbf{1}$E rule breaks it. This rule is the only inversion rule in this derivation, and hence it is *maximally inverted*.

$$\dfrac{\dfrac{\dfrac{}{a \multimap \mathbf{1} \Vdash a \multimap \mathbf{1} \Downarrow}\,\text{hyp} \qquad \dfrac{\dfrac{}{a \Vdash a \Downarrow}\,\text{hyp}}{a \Vdash a \Uparrow}\,\Downarrow\Uparrow}{a, a \multimap \mathbf{1} \Vdash \mathbf{1} \Downarrow}\,\multimap\text{E} \qquad \dfrac{\dfrac{}{\cdot \Vdash \mathbf{1} \Uparrow}\,\mathbf{1}\text{I}}{\cdot \Vdash \mathbf{1} \oplus b \Uparrow}\,\oplus\text{I}_1}{a, a \multimap \mathbf{1} \Vdash \mathbf{1} \oplus b \Uparrow}\,\mathbf{1}\text{E}$$

By permuting $\mathbf{1}$E and $\oplus\text{I}_1$ we can restore the focus, and again, the inversion phase of this derivation ($\mathbf{1}$E) is maximal. In summary, for intuitionistic linear logic, the intercalation calculus does not rule out as many derivations as it should.

In the remainder of this paper, we define and discuss the calculus of *focused natural deductions.* It is a simple, yet deep, generalization of the intercalation formulation. Among the two derivations above only the second one is derivable in focused natural deduction. The main idea behind this calculus is to distinguish negative from positive connectives and to make the related coercions explicit as connectives ${}^{\uparrow}P$ and ${}^{\downarrow}N$. We call these connectives *delay* connectives, because they effectively delay positive and negative focusing phases. To ensure maximal asynchronous phases, we use a generalization of the *patterns* introduced by Zeilberger in [12].

The paper is organized as follows. In Section 2 we introduce the focused natural deduction calculus. Next, we show soundness and completeness with respect to first-order intuitionistic linear natural deduction in Section 3 and with respect to the backward linear focusing calculus of Pfenning, Chaudhuri and Price [4] in Section 4. We conclude and assess results in Section 5.

2 Natural Deduction for Intuitionistic Linear Logic

First we give the definition of the intercalation calculus. The syntax of linear logic is standard.

$$A, B, C ::= a \mid A \otimes B \mid \mathbf{1} \mid A \oplus B \mid \mathbf{0} \mid \exists x.A \mid A \mathbin{\&} B \mid \top \mid A \multimap B \mid !A \mid \forall x.A$$

As for the judgment, we use a two zone formulation with a turnstile with double bars, $\Gamma; \Delta \Vdash A \Uparrow$, which reads as there is a canonical proof of A from intuitionistic assumptions Γ and linear assumptions Δ. Conversely, we define $\Gamma; \Delta \Vdash A \Downarrow$ for atomic derivation of A. The inference rules are standard and depicted in Figure 1.

2.1 Focused Natural Deduction

We split the connectives of linear logic into two disjoint groups based on their inversion properties. Connectives that are invertible on the right of the turnstile and non-invertible on the left become negative connectives. Conversely, connectives that are invertible on the left and non-invertible on the right become positive connectives. This gives us the following syntax of polarized formulas:

$$\begin{aligned} P, Q &::= a^{+} \mid P \otimes Q \mid \mathbf{1} \mid P \oplus Q \mid \mathbf{0} \mid \exists x.P \mid !N \mid {}^{\downarrow}N \\ N, M &::= a^{-} \mid N \mathbin{\&} M \mid \top \mid P \multimap N \mid \forall x.N \mid {}^{\uparrow}P \end{aligned}$$

We use P, Q for positive propositions, and N, M for negative propositions. We use A, B for propositions where the polarity does not matter. The syntax is similar to the ones presented in [2,7]. Additionally we use the following shorthand:

$$\gamma^{+} ::= {}^{\uparrow}P \mid a^{-}, \qquad \gamma^{-} ::= {}^{\downarrow}N \mid a^{+}$$

$$\frac{\Gamma;\Delta \Vdash a \Downarrow}{\Gamma;\Delta \Vdash a \Uparrow}\Downarrow\Uparrow \qquad \frac{}{\Gamma;A \Vdash A \Downarrow}\text{hyp} \qquad \frac{}{\Gamma,A;\cdot \Vdash A \Downarrow}\text{uhyp}$$

$$\frac{}{\Gamma;\cdot \Vdash \mathbf{1} \Uparrow}\mathbf{1}\text{I} \qquad \frac{\Gamma;\Delta_1 \Vdash \mathbf{1} \Downarrow \quad \Gamma;\Delta_2 \Vdash C \Uparrow}{\Gamma;\Delta_1,\Delta_2 \Vdash C \Uparrow}\mathbf{1}\text{E} \qquad \frac{}{\Gamma;\Delta \Vdash \top \Uparrow}\top\text{I} \qquad \frac{\Gamma;\Delta_1 \Vdash \mathbf{0} \Downarrow}{\Gamma;\Delta_1,\Delta_2 \Vdash C \Uparrow}\mathbf{0}\text{E}$$

$$\frac{\Gamma;\Delta_1 \Vdash A \Uparrow \quad \Gamma;\Delta_2 \Vdash B \Uparrow}{\Gamma;\Delta_1,\Delta_2 \Vdash A \otimes B \Uparrow}\otimes\text{I} \qquad \frac{\Gamma;\Delta_1 \Vdash A \otimes B \Downarrow \quad \Gamma;\Delta_2,A,B \Vdash C \Uparrow}{\Gamma;\Delta_1,\Delta_2 \Vdash C \Uparrow}\otimes\text{E}$$

$$\frac{\Gamma;\Delta \Vdash A_i \Uparrow}{\Gamma;\Delta \Vdash A_1 \oplus A_2 \Uparrow}\oplus\text{I}_i \qquad \frac{\Gamma;\Delta_1 \Vdash A \oplus B \Downarrow \quad \Gamma;\Delta_2,A \Vdash C \Uparrow \quad \Gamma;\Delta_2,B \Vdash C \Uparrow}{\Gamma;\Delta_1,\Delta_2 \Vdash C \Uparrow}\oplus\text{E}$$

$$\frac{\Gamma;\Delta \Vdash A \Uparrow \quad \Gamma;\Delta \Vdash B \Uparrow}{\Gamma;\Delta \Vdash A \,\&\, B \Uparrow}\&\text{I} \qquad \frac{\Gamma;\Delta \Vdash A_1 \,\&\, A_2 \Downarrow}{\Gamma;\Delta \Vdash A_i \Downarrow}\&\text{E}_i$$

$$\frac{\Gamma;\Delta \Vdash [a/x]A \Uparrow}{\Gamma;\Delta \Vdash \forall x.A \Uparrow}\forall\text{I}^a \qquad \frac{\Gamma;\Delta \Vdash \forall x.A \Downarrow}{\Gamma;\Delta \Vdash [t/x]A \Downarrow}\forall\text{E}$$

$$\frac{\Gamma;\Delta,A \Vdash B \Uparrow}{\Gamma;\Delta \Vdash A \multimap B \Uparrow}\multimap\text{I} \qquad \frac{\Gamma;\Delta_1 \Vdash A \multimap B \Downarrow \quad \Gamma;\Delta_2 \Vdash A \Uparrow}{\Gamma;\Delta_1,\Delta_2 \Vdash B \Downarrow}\multimap\text{E}$$

$$\frac{\Gamma;\cdot \Vdash A \Uparrow}{\Gamma;\cdot \Vdash !A \Uparrow}!\text{I} \qquad \frac{\Gamma;\Delta_1 \Vdash !A \Downarrow \quad \Gamma,A;\Delta_2 \Vdash C \Uparrow}{\Gamma;\Delta_1,\Delta_2 \Vdash C \Uparrow}!\text{E}$$

$$\frac{\Gamma;\Delta \Vdash [t/x]A \Uparrow}{\Gamma;\Delta \Vdash \exists x.A \Uparrow}\exists\text{I} \qquad \frac{\Gamma;\Delta_1 \Vdash \exists x.A \Downarrow \quad \Gamma;\Delta_2,[a/x]A \Vdash C \Uparrow}{\Gamma;\Delta_1,\Delta_2 \Vdash C \Uparrow}\exists\text{E}^a$$

Fig. 1. Linear natural deduction (in intercalation notation)

Patterns. We use the concept of patterns, as seen in [6,12], to capture the decomposition of formulas that takes place during the asynchronous phase of focusing. The previous notion of patterns is extended to work with unrestricted hypotheses and quantifiers.

Pattern judgments have the form $\Gamma;\Delta \vDash P$ and $\Gamma;\Delta \vDash N > \gamma^+$, the latter of which corresponds to decomposing N into γ^+ using only negative elimination rules. These judgments are derived using the inference rules given in Figure 2.

We require that the variable a in the judgments concerning the quantifiers satisfies the eigenvariable condition, and does not appear below the rule that mentions said variable.

Note that pattern derivations $\Gamma;\Delta \vDash P$ and $\Gamma;\Delta \vDash N > \gamma^+$ are entirely driven by the structure of P and N. In particular, this means that when we quantify over all patterns $\Gamma;\Delta \vDash P \multimap N > \gamma^+$ for a given formula $P \multimap N$, this is equivalent to quantifying over all patterns $\Gamma_1;\Delta_1 \vDash P$ and $\Gamma_2;\Delta_2 \vDash N > \gamma^+$.

A crucial part of the definition of this system, is that there are only finitely many patterns for any given polarized formula. For this reason, we treat the unrestricted context in the patterns as a multiset of formulas. This also means that we need to treat two patterns as equal if they only differ in the choice of eigenvariables in the pattern rules for the quantifiers. This is a reasonable decision, as the eigenvariable condition ensures that the variables are fresh, hence the actual names of the variables are irrelevant. With these conditions in place,

$$\frac{}{\cdot;\gamma^- \vDash \gamma^-} \qquad \frac{}{\cdot;\cdot \vDash \mathbf{1}} \qquad \frac{\Gamma_1;\Delta_1 \vDash P \quad \Gamma_2;\Delta_2 \vDash Q}{\Gamma_1,\Gamma_2;\Delta_1,\Delta_2 \vDash P \otimes Q}$$

$$\frac{\Gamma;\Delta \vDash P_i}{\Gamma;\Delta \vDash P_1 \oplus P_2} \qquad \frac{}{N;\cdot \vDash\, !N} \qquad \frac{\Gamma;\Delta \vDash [a/x]P}{\Gamma;\Delta \vDash \exists x.P}$$

$$\frac{}{\cdot;\cdot \vDash \gamma^+ > \gamma^+} \qquad \frac{\Gamma;\Delta \vDash N_i > \gamma^+}{\Gamma;\Delta \vDash N_1 \,\&\, N_2 > \gamma^+}$$

$$\frac{\Gamma_1;\Delta_1 \vDash P \quad \Gamma_2;\Delta_2 \vDash N > \gamma^+}{\Gamma_1,\Gamma_2;\Delta_1,\Delta_2 \vDash P \multimap N > \gamma^+} \qquad \frac{\Gamma;\Delta \vDash [a/x]N > \gamma^+}{\Gamma;\Delta \vDash \forall x.N > \gamma^+}$$

Fig. 2. Positive and negative pattern judgments

it is straightforward to prove that for any given formula, there are only finitely many patterns for said formula.

Inference rules. For the judgments in the polarized system, we use a turnstile with a single vertical bar. The inference rules can be seen in Figure 3.

The quantification used in the ${\uparrow}$E and ${\downarrow}$I rules is merely a notational convenience to ease the formulation of the rules. It is a shorthand for the finitely many premises corresponding to the patterns of the principal formula. Thus, the number of premises for these rules may vary depending on the principal formula. This does not, however, pose a problem when checking that a rule has been applied properly, as we can reconstruct the necessary subgoals from the formulas ${\uparrow}P$ and ${\downarrow}N$. As usual, we require that the eigenvariables introduced by the patterns must be fresh, i.e. may not occur further down in the derivation.

As an example, we show the only possible proof of the statement given in the introduction. We have chosen to polarize both atoms positively, and elided the empty intuitionistic context.

$$\frac{\dfrac{\dfrac{\dfrac{}{{\downarrow}(a \multimap {\uparrow}\mathbf{1}) \vdash {\downarrow}(a \multimap {\uparrow}\mathbf{1}) \Downarrow}\,\text{hyp}}{{\downarrow}(a \multimap {\uparrow}\mathbf{1}) \vdash a \multimap {\uparrow}\mathbf{1} \Downarrow}\,{\downarrow}\text{E} \qquad \dfrac{\dfrac{}{a \vdash a \Downarrow}\,\text{hyp}}{a \vdash a \Uparrow}\,{\Downarrow}{\Uparrow}}{a, {\downarrow}(a \multimap {\uparrow}\mathbf{1}) \vdash {\uparrow}\mathbf{1} \Downarrow}\,{\multimap}\text{E} \qquad \dfrac{\dfrac{\dfrac{}{\cdot \vdash \mathbf{1} \Uparrow}\,\mathbf{1}\text{I}}{\cdot \vdash \mathbf{1} \oplus b \Uparrow}\,\oplus\text{I}_1}{\cdot \vdash {\uparrow}(\mathbf{1} \oplus b) \Uparrow}\,{\uparrow}\text{I}}{a, {\downarrow}(a \multimap {\uparrow}\mathbf{1}) \vdash {\uparrow}(\mathbf{1} \oplus b) \Uparrow}\,{\uparrow}\text{E}$$

Note that the pattern judgment for $\mathbf{1}$ does not appear in this derivation. Indeed, the pattern judgments are only used to specify which premises should be present in a valid application of the ${\uparrow}$E and ${\downarrow}$I rules.

The use of patterns in the ${\uparrow}$E and ${\downarrow}$I rules collapses the positive and negative asynchronous phases into a single rule application. Thus we equate proofs that only differ in the order in which the negative introduction and positive elimination rules are applied. For instance, the assumption $(A \otimes B) \otimes (C \otimes D)$ can be eliminated two ways:

$$\frac{\Gamma;\Delta \vdash a \Downarrow}{\Gamma;\Delta \vdash a \Uparrow}\,\Downarrow\Uparrow \qquad \frac{}{\Gamma; P \vdash P \Downarrow}\,\text{hyp} \qquad \frac{}{\Gamma, N; \cdot \vdash N \Downarrow}\,\text{uhyp} \qquad \frac{}{\Gamma; \cdot \vdash \mathbf{1} \Uparrow}\,\mathbf{1}\text{I}$$

$$\frac{\Gamma;\Delta_1 \vdash P \Uparrow \qquad \Gamma;\Delta_2 \vdash Q \Uparrow}{\Gamma;\Delta_1,\Delta_2 \vdash P \otimes Q \Uparrow}\,\otimes\text{I} \qquad \frac{\Gamma;\Delta \vdash P_i \Uparrow}{\Gamma;\Delta \vdash P_1 \oplus P_2 \Uparrow}\,\oplus\text{I}_i \qquad \frac{\Gamma;\Delta \vdash [t/x]P \Uparrow}{\Gamma;\Delta \vdash \exists x.P \Uparrow}\,\exists\text{I}$$

$$\frac{\Gamma;\cdot \vdash {\downarrow}N \Uparrow}{\Gamma;\cdot \vdash !N \Uparrow}\,!\text{I} \qquad \frac{\Gamma;\Delta \vdash N_1 \mathbin{\&} N_2 \Downarrow}{\Gamma;\Delta \vdash N_i \Downarrow}\,\&\text{E}_i \qquad \frac{\Gamma;\Delta \vdash \forall x.N \Downarrow}{\Gamma;\Delta \vdash [t/x]N \Downarrow}\,\forall\text{E}$$

$$\frac{\Gamma;\Delta_1 \vdash P \multimap N \Downarrow \qquad \Gamma;\Delta_2 \vdash P \Uparrow}{\Gamma;\Delta_1,\Delta_2 \vdash N \Downarrow}\,\multimap\text{E}$$

$$\frac{\Gamma;\Delta \vdash P \Uparrow}{\Gamma;\Delta \vdash {\uparrow}P \Uparrow}\,{\uparrow}\text{I} \qquad \frac{\Gamma;\Delta_1 \vdash {\uparrow}P \Downarrow \qquad \begin{array}{c}\text{for all } \Gamma_P;\Delta_P \vDash P\\ \Gamma,\Gamma_P;\Delta_2,\Delta_P \vdash \gamma^+ \Uparrow\end{array}}{\Gamma_1;\Delta_1,\Delta_2 \vdash \gamma^+ \Downarrow}\,{\uparrow}\text{E}$$

$$\frac{\Gamma;\Delta \vdash {\downarrow}N \Downarrow}{\Gamma;\Delta \vdash N \Downarrow}\,{\downarrow}\text{E} \qquad \frac{\begin{array}{c}\text{for all } \Gamma_N;\Delta_N \vDash N > \gamma^+\\ \Gamma,\Gamma_N;\Delta,\Delta_N \vdash \gamma^+ \Uparrow\end{array}}{\Gamma;\Delta \vdash {\downarrow}N \Uparrow}\,{\downarrow}\text{I}$$

Fig. 3. Focused linear natural deduction

$$(A \otimes B) \otimes (C \otimes D) \rightsquigarrow A \otimes B, C \otimes D \rightsquigarrow A, B, C \otimes D \rightsquigarrow A, B, C, D$$
$$(A \otimes B) \otimes (C \otimes D) \rightsquigarrow A \otimes B, C \otimes D \rightsquigarrow A \otimes B, C, D \rightsquigarrow A, B, C, D$$

corresponding to which assumptions act as the principal formula for the $\otimes$E rule. By using patterns, this unnecessary distinction is avoided, as there is only one pattern for $(A \otimes B) \otimes (C \otimes D)$, specifically the pattern $\cdot; A, B, C, D$.

Note that the rules $\top$I and $\mathbf{0}$E are captured by the above rules, as there are no patterns of the form $\Gamma;\Delta \vDash \mathbf{0}$ and $\Gamma;\Delta \vDash \top > \gamma^+$.

The polarity restrictions on the hyp and uhyp rules are justified by noting that $\multimap$ is the internalized version of the linear hypothetical judgments. In particular, this means that the linear context can only contain positive formulas; any negative formulas must be in delayed form ${\downarrow}N$. Unrestricted formulas, on the other hand, are not delayed, as choosing whether or not to use an unrestricted resource is always a non-deterministic (hence synchronous) choice.

By inspecting the polarized rules, we may observe the following:

1. In a derivation of the judgment $\Gamma;\Delta \vdash A \Uparrow$ where A is positive (e.g. $A = P \otimes Q$), the final rule must be the positive introduction rule corresponding to A, or $\Downarrow\Uparrow$ if A is an atom. This follows from the fact that positive eliminations are only applicable when the succedent is negative.
2. The only rule applicable to the judgment $\Gamma;\Delta \vdash A \Downarrow$ where A is negative (e.g. $A = P \multimap N$), is the appropriate elimination rule for A, or $\Downarrow\Uparrow$ if A is an atom.

Based on the above observations, we define the following synchronous phases based on the polarity of the succedent and whether it is atomic or canonical.

$\Gamma; \Delta \vdash P \Uparrow$	Positive focusing, initiated by ${}^{\uparrow}$I
$\Gamma; \Delta \vdash N \Downarrow$	Negative focusing, initiated by ${}^{\downarrow}$E

By our use of patterns, we collapse the asynchronous phases, which would otherwise have corresponded to the judgments $\Gamma; \Delta \vdash P \Downarrow$ and $\Gamma; \Delta \vdash N \Uparrow$.

The positive focusing phase proceeds in a bottom-up fashion, and is initiated by using the ${}^{\uparrow}$I rule to remove the positive shift in front of the formula to be focused. The focused formula is then decomposed by a sequence of positive introduction rules. This phase ends when the succedent becomes negative or atomic.

The negative focusing phase proceeds in a top-down fashion, and is initiated by choosing a negative or delayed negative formula in either the linear or unrestricted context, and applying a sequence of negative elimination rules to the judgment $\Gamma; {}^{\downarrow}N \vdash {}^{\downarrow}N \Downarrow$ or $\Gamma, N; \cdot \vdash N \Downarrow$, given by either the hyp rule or the uhyp rule. The phase terminates when the succedent is either positive or atomic. In the former case, the subderivation must end in the ${}^{\uparrow}$E rule, and in the latter case in the $\Downarrow\Uparrow$ rule.

Note that because the positive elimination rules restrict the succedent of the conclusion to be of the form γ^{+}, it is not possible to apply the ${}^{\uparrow}$E rule inside a positive focusing phase. As negative focusing ends in positive elimination or coercion, it is not possible to perform negative focusing inside a positive focusing phase. Likewise, the negative focusing phase cannot be interrupted.

It is in this sense the above system is *maximally focused* — once a formula is chosen for focusing, it must be decomposed fully (i.e. keep the focus) before other formulas can be focused or otherwise eliminated.

3 Soundness and Completeness

A note on notation. To formulate the soundness and completeness theorems, we need to be able to talk about when the entire linear context is covered by some pattern. This is done using the judgment $\Gamma'; \Delta' \vDash \Delta$. The following inference rules define this judgment:

$$\frac{}{\cdot; \cdot \vDash \cdot} \qquad \frac{\Gamma'; \Delta' \vDash \Delta \quad \Gamma_P; \Delta_P \vDash P}{\Gamma', \Gamma_P; \Delta', \Delta_P \vDash \Delta, P}$$

We will tacitly use the fact that this judgment is well-behaved with regard to splitting the context Δ. In other words, that $\Gamma'; \Delta' \vDash \Delta_1, \Delta_2$ if and only if $\Gamma' = \Gamma'_1, \Gamma'_2$ and $\Delta' = \Delta'_1, \Delta'_2$ where $\Gamma'_i; \Delta'_i \vDash \Delta_i$ for $i = 1, 2$.

Soundness. To prove soundness, we define a function from polarized formulas to regular formulas. This is simply the function $(-)^e$ that erases all occurrences of the positive and negative shifts, i.e. $({}^{\uparrow}P)^e = P^e$ and $({}^{\downarrow}N)^e = N^e$, whilst $(P \multimap N)^e = P^e \multimap N^e$ and $(\forall x.N)^e = \forall x.N^e$ and so on.

Theorem 1 (Soundness of polarized derivations). *The following properties hold:*

1. *If* $\Gamma; \Delta \vdash A \Uparrow$ *then* $\Gamma^e; \Delta^e \Vdash A^e \Uparrow$.
2. *If* $\Gamma; \Delta \vdash A \Downarrow$ *then* $\Gamma^e; \Delta^e \Vdash A^e \Downarrow$.
3. *If for all* $\Gamma'; \Delta' \vDash \Omega$ *and* $\Gamma_A; \Delta_A \vDash A > \gamma^+$ *we have* $\Gamma, \Gamma', \Gamma_A; \Delta, \Delta', \Delta_A \vdash \gamma^+ \Uparrow$, *then* $\Gamma^e; \Delta^e, \Omega^e \Vdash A^e \Uparrow$.

Proof. The first two claims are proved by induction on the structure of the given derivations. In the case of the $^{\uparrow}$E and $^{\downarrow}$I rules, we reconstruct the asynchronous phases, hence the third hypothesis is needed.

We prove the third claim by an induction on the number of connectives in Ω and A. This is needed when reconstructing a tensor, as Ω will then grow in size. The base case for this induction is when all formulas in Ω are of the form γ^- and A is of the form γ^+. In this case, we appeal to the first induction hypothesis. We show a few representative cases here:

Case $A = P \multimap N$**:** By inversion on $\Gamma_A; \Delta_A \vDash A > \gamma^+$, we get $\Gamma_A = \Gamma_P, \Gamma_N$ and $\Delta_A = \Delta_P, \Delta_N$ such that $\Gamma_P; \Delta_P \vDash P$ and $\Gamma_N; \Delta_N \vDash N > \gamma^+$, hence $\Gamma', \Gamma_P; \Delta', \Delta_P \vDash \Omega, P$ and by the induction hypothesis $\Gamma^e; \Delta^e, \Omega^e, P^e \Vdash N^e \Uparrow$, hence by applying $\multimap$I we get the desired derivation of $\Gamma^e; \Delta^e, \Omega^e \Vdash (P \multimap N)^e \Uparrow$.

Case $\Omega = \Omega_1, P \otimes Q, \Omega_2$**:** By assumption, $\Gamma_1', \Gamma_{PQ}, \Gamma_2'; \Delta_1', \Delta_{PQ}, \Delta_2' \vDash \Omega_1, P \otimes Q, \Omega_2$, hence by inversion we have $\Gamma_{PQ} = \Gamma_P, \Gamma_Q$ and $\Delta_{PQ} = \Delta_P, \Delta_Q$ such that $\Gamma_P; \Delta_P \vDash P$ and $\Gamma_Q; \Delta_Q \vDash Q$. Then $\Gamma_1', \Gamma_P, \Gamma_Q, \Gamma_2'; \Delta_1', \Delta_P, \Delta_Q, \Delta_2' \vDash \Omega_1, P, Q, \Omega_2$, hence by the induction hypothesis $\Gamma^e; \Delta^e, \Omega_1^e, P^e, Q^e, \Omega_2^e \Vdash C^e \Uparrow$. Applying $\otimes$E to this judgment and the hypothesis judgment $\Gamma^e; (P \otimes Q)^e \Vdash P^e \otimes Q^e \Downarrow$, we get the desired derivation of $\Gamma^e; \Delta^e, \Omega_1^e, (P \otimes Q)^e, \Omega_2^e \Vdash C^e \Uparrow$. □

Polarizing formulae. To prove that the polarized system is complete with regard to the natural deduction calculus depicted in Figure 1, we first need to find a way of converting regular propositions into polarized propositions. To do this, we define the following two mutually recursive functions, $(-)^p$ and $(-)^n$, by structural induction on the syntax of unpolarized formulas.

$$
\begin{array}{ccc}
\mathbf{1}^p = \mathbf{1} & \mathbf{0}^p = \mathbf{0} & \top^n = \top \\
(A \otimes B)^p = A^p \otimes B^p & (A \oplus B)^p = A^p \oplus B^p & (!A)^p = !A^n \\
(A \,\&\, B)^n = A^n \,\&\, B^n & (A \multimap B)^n = A^p \multimap B^n & \\
(\exists x.A)^p = \exists x.A^p & (\forall x.A)^n = \forall x.A^n &
\end{array}
$$

The above definitions handle the cases where the polarity of the formula inside the parentheses matches the polarizing function that is applied, i.e. cases of the form N^n and P^p. All that remains is to handle the cases where the polarity does not match, which we do with the following definition:

$$
\begin{array}{ll}
A^n = {}^{\uparrow}A^p & \text{when } A \text{ is positive} \\
A^p = {}^{\downarrow}A^n & \text{when } A \text{ is negative}
\end{array}
$$

In the case of atoms we assume that there is some fixed assignment of polarity to atoms, and define $a^p = a$ for positive atoms and $a^n = a$ for negative atoms. Atoms with the wrong polarity, e.g. a^n for a positive atom a are handled by the P^n case above, i.e. $a^n = {\uparrow}a^p = {\uparrow}a$ for positive atoms, and conversely for the negative atoms.

In short, whenever a subformula of positive polarity appears in a place where negative polarity is expected, we add a positive shift to account for this fact, and vice versa. Thus, a formula such as $(a \,\&\, b) \multimap (c \otimes d)$ is mapped by $(-)^n$ to ${\downarrow}({\uparrow}a \& b) \multimap {\uparrow}(c \otimes {\downarrow}d)$, when a, c are positive, and b, d are negative. These functions are extended in the obvious way to contexts, in the sense that Δ^p means applying the function $(-)^p$ to each formula in Δ.

Of course, this is not the only way of polarizing a given formula, as we may always add redundant shifts ${\uparrow}{\downarrow}N$ and ${\downarrow}{\uparrow}P$ inside our formulas. The above procedure gives a *minimal polarization* in that there are no redundant negative or positive shifts. Note that $(A^p)^e = (A^n)^e = A$ for all unpolarized formulae A, and $(P^e)^p = P$ and $(N^e)^n = N$ for minimally polarized formulae P and N.

Completeness. Before we can prove completeness, we must prove a series of lemmas. First of all, we need the usual substitution properties.

Lemma 1 (Substituting properties for linear resources). *The following substitution properties hold:*

1. *If* $\Gamma; \Delta_1 \vdash N \Downarrow$ *and* $\Gamma; \Delta_2, {\downarrow}N \vdash C \Uparrow$ *then* $\Gamma; \Delta_1, \Delta_2 \vdash C \Uparrow$
2. *If* $\Gamma; \Delta_1 \vdash N \Downarrow$ *and* $\Gamma; \Delta_2, {\downarrow}N \vdash C \Downarrow$ *and the latter derivation is not an instance of the* hyp *rule then* $\Gamma; \Delta_1, \Delta_2 \vdash C \Downarrow$.

Proof. We proceed by mutual induction on the derivations of $\Gamma; \Delta_2, {\uparrow}N \vdash C \Downarrow$ and $\Gamma; \Delta_2, {\uparrow}N \vdash C \Uparrow$. In all cases, we proceed by applying the induction hypothesis to the premise which contains the formula ${\uparrow}N$, and then reapply the appropriate rule. This is possible if the premise is not a derivation of $\Gamma; {\downarrow}N \vdash {\downarrow}N \Downarrow$ using the hyp rule. This can only happen in the case of the ${\downarrow}$E rule, in which case, $C = N$ and Δ_2 is empty. Hence we may then apply the following reduction:

$$\dfrac{\dfrac{}{\Gamma; {\downarrow}N \vdash {\downarrow}N \Downarrow}\,\text{hyp}}{\Gamma; {\downarrow}N \vdash N \Downarrow}\,{\downarrow}\text{E} \quad \rightsquigarrow \quad \begin{array}{c} \vdots \\ \Gamma; \Delta_1 \vdash N \Downarrow \end{array}$$

□

Corollary 1. *If* $\Gamma; \Delta_1 \vdash A^n \Downarrow$ *and for all patterns* $\Gamma_A; \Delta_A \Vdash A^p$ *we have* $\Gamma, \Gamma_A; \Delta_2, \Delta_A \vdash \gamma^+ \Uparrow$ *then* $\Gamma; \Delta_1, \Delta_2 \vdash \gamma^+ \Uparrow$.

Proof. If A is positive, then $A^n = {\uparrow}A^p$, and the result follows by applying the ${\uparrow}$E rule. If A is negative, then $A^p = {\downarrow}A^n$, hence there is only one pattern for A^p, specifically $\cdot; {\downarrow}A^n \Vdash {\downarrow}A^n$ and the result follows from Lemma 1. □

For the synchronous rules, we need to capture the fact that we may push positive elimination rules below positive introduction rules. To formulate this, we introduce a new function $(-)^d$ that always produces a delayed formula. Thus, we define $A^d = {}^{\uparrow}A^p$ when A is positive, and $A^d = {}^{\downarrow}A^n$ when A is negative. We first note the following

Lemma 2. *If for all $\Gamma_A; \Delta_A \vDash A^n > \gamma^+$ we have $\Gamma, \Gamma_A; \Delta, \Delta_A \vdash \gamma^+ \Uparrow$, then $\Gamma; \Delta \vdash A^d \Uparrow$.*

Proof. By case analysis on the polarity of A. If A is positive then $A^n = {}^{\uparrow}A^p$, hence $\cdot; \cdot \vDash {}^{\uparrow}A^p > {}^{\uparrow}A^p$ is a pattern for A^n. Thus, $\Gamma; \Delta \vdash {}^{\uparrow}A^p \Uparrow$ as desired.

If A is negative, then $A^d = {}^{\downarrow}A^n$, hence by the rule ${}^{\downarrow}$I, we get the desired result. □

We are now able to prove that under certain circumstances we can change a positively polarized canonical premise to the corresponding delayed canonical premise.

Lemma 3. *For any admissible rule of the form*

$$\frac{\Gamma; \Delta \vdash A^p \Uparrow}{\Gamma; \Delta, \Delta' \vdash \gamma^+ \Uparrow}\,\Sigma$$

the following rule is admissible

$$\frac{\Gamma; \Delta \vdash A^d \Uparrow}{\Gamma; \Delta, \Delta' \vdash \gamma^+ \Uparrow}\,\Sigma^d$$

Proof. By case analysis on the polarity of A and induction on the derivation of $\Gamma; \Delta \vdash A^d \Uparrow$. If A is negative, $A^d = {}^{\downarrow}A^n = A^p$, hence the result follows immediately by applying Σ. If A is positive, $A^d = {}^{\uparrow}A^p$, hence the final rule of the derivation is either ${}^{\uparrow}$I or ${}^{\uparrow}$E. If the derivation ends in ${}^{\uparrow}$I, the result again by applying Σ to the premise of this rule. If the derivation ends in ${}^{\uparrow}$E, we apply the induction hypothesis to the second premise, and reapply the ${}^{\uparrow}$E rule. □

The above argument easily extends to admissible rules with multiple premises, hence we get the following

Corollary 2. *The following rules are admissible:*

$$\frac{\Gamma; \Delta_1 \vdash A^d \Uparrow \qquad \Gamma; \Delta_2 \vdash B^d \Uparrow}{\Gamma; \Delta_1, \Delta_2 \vdash (A \otimes B)^n \Uparrow}\,\otimes^d\mathrm{I} \qquad \frac{\Gamma; \Delta \vdash A_i^d \Uparrow}{\Gamma; \Delta \vdash (A_1 \oplus A_2)^n \Uparrow}\,\oplus_i^d\mathrm{I}$$

$$\frac{\Gamma; \Delta \vdash ([t/x]A)^d \Uparrow}{\Gamma; \Delta \vdash (\exists x.A)^n \Uparrow}\,\exists^d\mathrm{I}$$

Also, if $\Gamma; \Delta_1 \vdash A^d \Downarrow$ and for all $\Gamma_B; \Delta_B \vDash B^p$ we have $\Gamma, \Gamma_B; \Delta_2, \Delta_B \vdash \gamma^+ \Uparrow$, then $\Gamma; \Delta_1, \Delta_2, (A \multimap B)^p \vdash \gamma^+ \Uparrow$.

Proof. The first few rules are easy applications of the previous lemma to the positive introduction rules. The property holds by using the lemma on the following argument: If $\Gamma;\Delta_1 \vdash A^p \Uparrow$, then $\Gamma;\Delta_1,(A \multimap B)^p \vdash B^n \Uparrow$ by $\multimap$E, ${}^{\downarrow}$E and hyp on $(A \multimap B)^p$. With the additional assumption that $\Gamma,\Gamma_B;\Delta_2,\Delta_B \vdash \gamma^+$ for all patterns $\Gamma_B;\Delta_B \vDash B^p$, by applying Lemma 1, we get the desired result $\Gamma;\Delta_1,\Delta_2,(A \multimap B)^p \vdash \gamma^+ \Uparrow$. □

Before we formulate the completeness theorem, we have to decide which polarizing function to apply to the hypotheses and the conclusion. We would like translate a derivation of $\Gamma;\Delta \Vdash A \Uparrow$ into a derivation $\Gamma^x;\Delta^y \vdash A^z \Uparrow$, where each of x, y and z is one of the above functions. In the case of x and y, the nature of the uhyp and hyp rules force us to choose $x = n$ and $y = p$. If $z = p$, we should be able to derive $\cdot;(a \otimes b)^p \vdash a^p \otimes b^p \Uparrow$, as this is clearly derivable in the unpolarized system. In the polarized system, however, we are forced to enter a focusing phase prematurely requiring us to split a single element context into two parts. None of the resulting subgoals are provable. Therefore $z = n$. Thus, as far as the canonical judgments are concerned, the completeness theorem will take derivations of $\Gamma;\Delta \Vdash A \Uparrow$ to derivations of $\Gamma^n;\Delta^p \vdash A^n \Uparrow$.

As for atomic derivations, these cannot in general be transferred to atomic derivations in the focused system. The reader may verify this by checking that $\cdot;(a \otimes b),(a \otimes b) \multimap c \Vdash c \Downarrow$ is derivable in the unpolarized system, whereas $\cdot;(a \otimes b),{}^{\downarrow}((a \otimes b) \multimap c) \vdash c \Downarrow$ is not derivable in the polarized system. Thus, we need to generalize the induction hypothesis in the completeness theorem.

Theorem 2 (Completeness). *The following properties hold:*

1. *Given* $\Gamma;\Delta \Vdash A \Uparrow$ *and patterns* $\Gamma';\Delta' \vDash \Delta^p$ *and* $\Gamma_A;\Delta_A \vDash A^n > \gamma^+$, *then* $\Gamma^n,\Gamma',\Gamma_A;\Delta',\Delta_A \vdash \gamma^+ \Uparrow$.
2. *If* $\Gamma_1;\Delta_1 \Vdash A \Downarrow$ *and* $\Gamma';\Delta' \vDash \Delta_1^p$ *and for all* $\Gamma_A;\Delta_A \vDash A^p$, *then we have* $\Gamma_2,\Gamma_A;\Delta_2,\Delta_A \vdash \gamma^+ \Uparrow$ *then* $\Gamma_1^n,\Gamma_2,\Gamma';\Delta_1,\Delta_2,\Delta' \vdash \gamma^+ \Uparrow$.

Proof. By induction on the derivations of $\Gamma;\Delta \Vdash A \Uparrow$ and $\Gamma;\Delta \Vdash A \Downarrow$. We give a few representative cases.

Case $\otimes$**E:**

$$\dfrac{\overset{\mathcal{D}}{\Gamma;\Delta_1 \Vdash A \otimes B \Downarrow} \quad \overset{\mathcal{E}}{\Gamma;\Delta_2,A,B \Vdash C \Uparrow}}{\Gamma;\Delta_1,\Delta_2 \Vdash C \Uparrow}\otimes\text{E}$$

(1)	$\Gamma_1',\Gamma_2';\Delta_1',\Delta_2' \vDash \Delta_1^p,\Delta_2^p$	Assumption.
(2)	$\Gamma_C;\Delta_C \vDash C^n > \gamma^+$	Assumption.
(3)	$\Gamma_A,\Gamma_B;\Delta_A,\Delta_B \vDash A^p,B^p$	Assumption.
(4)	$\Gamma_2',\Gamma_A,\Gamma_B;\Delta_1',\Delta_2',\Delta_A,\Delta_B \vDash \Delta_2^p,A^p,B^p$	By (1) and (3).
(5)	$\Gamma^n,\Gamma_2',\Gamma_A,\Gamma_B,\Gamma_C;\Delta_2',\Delta_A,\Delta_B,\Delta_C \vdash \gamma^+ \Uparrow$	By i.h.1 on $\mathcal{E}$, (2), (4).
	$\Gamma_A,\Gamma_B;\Delta_A,\Delta_B \vDash A^p \otimes B^p$	By the pattern rule for $\otimes$.

$\Gamma_A, \Gamma_B; \Delta_A, \Delta_B \vDash (A \otimes B)^p$ By the defn. of $(-)^p$.

$\Gamma^n, \Gamma_1', \Gamma_2', \Gamma_C; \Delta_1', \Delta_2', \Delta_C \vdash \gamma^+ \Uparrow$ By i.h. 2 on $\mathcal{D}$ and (5).

Case $\multimap$ **I:**

$$\frac{\begin{array}{c}\mathcal{D}\\ \Gamma; \Delta, A \Vdash B \Uparrow\end{array}}{\Gamma; \Delta \Vdash A \multimap B \Uparrow} \multimap \mathrm{I}$$

(1) $\Gamma'; \Delta' \vDash \Delta^p$ Assumption.

$\Gamma_{AB}; \Delta_{AB} \vDash (A \multimap B)^n$ Assumption.

$\Gamma_{AB}; \Delta_{AB} \vDash A^p \multimap B^n$ By defn. of $(-)^n$.

(2) $\Gamma_{AB} = \Gamma_A, \Gamma_B$ and $\Delta_{AB} = \Delta_A, \Delta_B$ such that

(3) $\Gamma_A; \Delta_A \vDash A^p$,

$\Gamma_B; \Delta_B \vDash B^n > \gamma^+$ By inversion.

$\Gamma^n, \Gamma', \Gamma_A, \Gamma_B; \Delta', \Delta_A, \Delta_B \vdash \gamma^+ \Uparrow$ By i.h. 1 on $\mathcal{D}$, (1) and (3).

$\Gamma^n, \Gamma', \Gamma_{AB}; \Delta', \Delta_{AB} \vdash \gamma^+ \Uparrow$ By (2).

Case !I:

$$\frac{\begin{array}{c}\mathcal{D}\\ \Gamma; \cdot \Vdash A \Uparrow\end{array}}{\Gamma; \cdot \Vdash !A \Uparrow} !\mathrm{I}$$

$\Gamma'; \Delta' \vDash \cdot$ Assumption.

$\Gamma' = \Delta' = \cdot$ By inversion.

$\Gamma_A; \Delta_A \vDash (!A)^n > \gamma^+$ Assumption.

$\Gamma_A = \Delta_A = \cdot,\ \gamma^+ = {\uparrow}(!A^n)$ By inversion.

(1) $\Gamma_A'; \Delta_A' \vDash A^n > \gamma^+$ Assumption

$\Gamma^n, \Gamma_A'; \Delta_A' \vdash \gamma^+ \Uparrow$ By i.h. 1 on $\mathcal{D}$ and (1).

$\forall(\Gamma_A'; \Delta_A' \vDash A^n > \gamma^+) : \Gamma^n, \Gamma_A'; \Delta_A' \vdash \gamma^+ \Uparrow$ By discharging (1).

$\Gamma^n; \cdot \vdash {\downarrow}A^n \Uparrow$ By ${\downarrow}$I.

$\Gamma^n; \cdot \vdash !A^n$ By !I.

$\Gamma^n; \cdot \vdash {\uparrow}(!A^n)$ By ${\uparrow}$I.

Case $\otimes$ **I:**

$$\frac{\begin{array}{c}\mathcal{D}\\ \Gamma; \Delta_1 \Vdash A \Uparrow\end{array} \quad \begin{array}{c}\mathcal{E}\\ \Gamma; \Delta_2 \Vdash B \Uparrow\end{array}}{\Gamma; \Delta_1, \Delta_2 \Vdash A \otimes B \Uparrow} \otimes \mathrm{I}$$

$\Gamma_1', \Gamma_2'; \Delta_1', \Delta_2' \vDash \Delta_1^p, \Delta_2^p$ Assumption.

$\Gamma_{AB}; \Delta_{AB} \models (A \otimes B)^n > \gamma^+$	Assumption.
$\Gamma_{AB} = \Delta_{AB} = \cdot, \gamma^+ = (A \otimes B)^n$	By inversion.
$\Gamma^n, \Gamma_1'; \Delta_1' \vdash A^n \Uparrow$	By i.h. 1 on $\mathcal{D}$.
$\Gamma^n, \Gamma_2'; \Delta_2' \vdash B^n \Uparrow$	By i.h. 1 on $\mathcal{E}$.
$\Gamma^n, \Gamma_1', \Gamma_2'; \Delta_1', \Delta_2' \vdash (A \otimes B)^n \Uparrow$	By $\otimes^d$I. □

As the mapping of derivations that is implicit in the proof of the soundness theorem preserves (maximal) synchronous phases and reconstructs (maximal) asynchronous phases, one may prove the following corollary.

Corollary 3. *For any proof of a judgment $\Gamma; \Delta \Vdash A \Uparrow$ there exists a proof of the same judgment with maximal focusing and inversion phases.*

4 Relation to the Backward Linear Focusing Calculus

In this section we consider the connection between our system of focused linear natural deduction, and the backward linear focusing calculus of Pfenning, Chaudhuri and Price [4]. The main result of this section is a very direct soundness and completeness result between these two systems. The syntax of formulas in the sequent system is the same as the unpolarized system in Section 2. The same distinction between positive and negative connectives is made, but no shifts are present to move from positive to negative and vice versa. Additionally, the shorthand P^- and N^+ is used in a similar fashion to our γ^- and γ^+.

The judgments of their system have either two or three contexts of the following form: Γ is a context of unrestricted hypotheses, Δ is a linear context of hypotheses of the form N^+. A third context Ω which is both linear and ordered may also be present. This context may contain formulas of any polarity.

There are four different kinds of sequents:

$\Gamma; \Delta \gg A$	*right-focal* sequent with A under focus.
$\Gamma; \Delta; A \ll Q^-$	*left-focal* sequent with A under focus.
$\Gamma; \Delta; \Omega \Longrightarrow \cdot; Q^-$	
$\Gamma; \Delta; \Omega \Longrightarrow C; \cdot$	Active sequents

The focal sequents correspond to the synchronous phases where a positive or negative formula is decomposed maximally. Conversely, the active sequents correspond to the asynchronous phase where non-focal formulas in Ω and the formula C may be decomposed asynchronously. The goal $\cdot; Q^-$ signifies that Q^- has been inverted maximally, and is no longer active.

Theorem 3 (Soundness w.r.t. backward linear focusing calculus). *The following properties hold:*

1. *If $\Gamma; \Delta \vdash P \Uparrow$ then $\Gamma^e; \Delta^e \gg P^e$.*
2. *If $\Gamma; \Delta \vdash N \Downarrow$ and $\Gamma^e; \Delta'; N^e \ll Q^-$ then $\Gamma^e; \Delta^e, \Delta'; \cdot \Longrightarrow \cdot; Q^-$.*

3. *If* $\Gamma'; \Gamma_C; \Delta, \Delta', \Delta_C \vdash \gamma^+ \Uparrow$ *for all* $\Gamma'; \Delta' \models \Omega$ *and* $\Gamma_C; \Delta_C \models C > \gamma^+$*, then* $\Gamma^e; \Delta^e; \Omega^e \Longrightarrow C^e; \cdot$.
4. *If* $\Gamma; \Gamma'; \Delta, \Delta' \vdash \gamma^+ \Uparrow$ *for all* $\Gamma'; \Delta' \models \Omega$*, then* $\Gamma^e; \Delta^e; \Omega^e \Longrightarrow \cdot; (\gamma^+)^e$.

Theorem 4 (Completeness w.r.t. backward linear focusing calculus). *The following properties hold:*

1. *If* $\Gamma; \Delta \gg A$ *then* $\Gamma^n; \Delta^p \vdash A^p \Uparrow$.
2. *If* $\Gamma; \Delta; A \ll Q^-$ *and* $\Gamma^n; \Delta' \vdash A^n \Downarrow$ *then* $\Gamma^n; \Delta^p, \Delta' \vdash (Q^-)^n \Uparrow$.
3. *If* $\Gamma; \Delta; \Omega \Longrightarrow C; \cdot$ *then* $\Gamma^n, \Gamma', \Gamma_C; \Delta^p, \Delta', \Delta_C \vdash \gamma^+ \Uparrow$ *for all* $\Gamma'; \Delta' \models \Omega^p$ *and* $\Gamma_C; \Delta_C \models C^n > \gamma^+$.
4. *If* $\Gamma; \Delta; \Omega \Longrightarrow \cdot; Q^-$ *then* $\Gamma^n, \Gamma'; \Delta^p, \Delta' \vdash (Q^-)^n \Uparrow$ *for all* $\Gamma'; \Delta' \models \Omega^p$.

The proofs of the above theorems may be seen as a way of transferring proofs between the two systems, and its action may be summarized as follows:

- The soundness proof maps synchronous to synchronous phases, and reconstructs inversion phases from the principal formulas in the $^{\Uparrow}$E and $^{\Downarrow}$I rules.
- The completeness proof takes synchronous phases to synchronous phases, and collapses asynchronous phases into $^{\Uparrow}$E and $^{\Downarrow}$I rules.

In particular, this leads to the following

Corollary 4. *The mapping of proofs induced by the soundness theorem is injective on proofs of judgments of the form* $\Gamma; \Delta \vdash A \Uparrow$ *where* Γ*,* Δ *and* A *are minimally polarized.*

Consequently, if we consider proofs of minimally polarized judgments, the current system has the same number or fewer proofs of that judgment than the backward focused sequent calculus has proofs of the corresponding sequent.

5 Conclusion and Related Work

Using the concepts of focusing and patterns, we have presented a natural deduction formulation of first-order intuitionistic linear logic that ensures the maximality of both synchronous and asynchronous phases. This removes a large part of the bureaucracy and unnecessary choices that were present in the previous formulation.

In [4], completeness with regard to the unfocused linear sequent calculus is established by proving focused versions of cut admissibility and identity. Because of the four different kinds of sequents and the three contexts, the proof of cut admissibility consists of more than 20 different kinds of cuts, all connected in an intricate induction order. In contrast, the proofs of the soundness and completeness results we have established are relatively straightforward. This is in part because we only have two judgments, and also because the intercalation formulation of linear natural deduction is already negatively focused.

From Corollary 4, it follows that our system, when restricted to minimally polarized formulas, has the same number or fewer proofs than the backward linear focusing calculus. This is only the case if we consider minimally polarized formulas, however. In particular this opens the possibility of using different polarization strategies to capture different classes of proofs.

In our formulation, we have chosen to use patterns only as a means of ensuring maximal asynchronous phases. It is possible to extend the use of patterns to the synchronous phases as well, but there are several reasons why we have chosen not to do this. The first and most compelling reason is that it is not necessary to ensure maximal synchronous phases. The restrictions on the succedent of the ${}^{\uparrow}\mathrm{E}$ rule suffices to ensure the maximality of the synchronous phases. Second, the use of patterns for the asynchronous phase extends easily to the case of quantifiers because the actual choice of eigenvariables does not matter — only freshness is important. Interpreting the pattern rules for quantifiers in a synchronous setting, we would need to substitute appropriately chosen *terms* for these variables, to capture the behavior of the $\forall$E and $\exists$I rules. This would complicate the system considerably.

References

1. Andreoli, J.: Logic programming with focusing proofs in linear logic. Journal of Logic and Computation 2(3), 297 (1992)
2. Chaudhuri, K.: Focusing strategies in the sequent calculus of synthetic connectives. In: Cervesato, I., Veith, H., Voronkov, A. (eds.) LPAR 2008. LNCS (LNAI), vol. 5330, pp. 467–481. Springer, Heidelberg (2008)
3. Chaudhuri, K., Miller, D., Saurin, A.: Canonical sequent proofs via multi-focusing. In: Fifth International Conference on Theoretical Computer Science, vol. 273, pp. 383–396. Springer, Heidelberg (2008)
4. Chaudhuri, K., Pfenning, F., Price, G.: A logical characterization of forward and backward chaining in the inverse method. Journal of Automated Reasoning 40(2), 133–177 (2008)
5. Krishnaswami, N.R.: Focusing on pattern matching. In: Proceedings of the 36th annual ACM SIGPLAN-SIGACT symposium on Principles of programming languages, pp. 366–378. ACM, New York (2009)
6. Licata, D.R., Zeilberger, N., Harper, R.: Focusing on binding and computation. In: LICS, pp. 241–252. IEEE Computer Society, Los Alamitos (2008)
7. McLaughlin, S., Pfenning, F.: Efficient intuitionistic theorem proving with the polarized inverse method. In: Proceedings of the 22nd International Conference on Automated Deduction, p. 244. Springer, Heidelberg (2009)
8. Miller, D., Nadathur, G., Pfenning, F., Scedrov, A.: Uniform proofs as a foundation for logic programming. Ann. Pure Appl. Logic 51(1-2), 125–157 (1991)
9. Prawitz, D.: Natural Deduction. Almquist & Wiksell, Stockholm (1965)
10. Sieg, W., Byrnes, J.: Normal natural deduction proofs (in classical logic). Studia Logica 60(1), 67–106 (1998)
11. Watkins, K., Cervesato, I., Pfenning, F., Walker, D.: A concurrent logical framework: The propositional fragment. In: Berardi, S., Coppo, M., Damiani, F. (eds.) TYPES 2003. LNCS, vol. 3085, pp. 355–377. Springer, Heidelberg (2004)
12. Zeilberger, N.: Focusing and higher-order abstract syntax. In: Necula, G.C., Wadler, P. (eds.) POPL, pp. 359–369. ACM, New York (2008)

How to Universally Close the Existential Rule

Kai Brünnler

Institut für angewandte Mathematik und Informatik
Universität Bern, Neubrückstr. 10, CH – 3012 Bern, Switzerland
http://www.iam.unibe.ch/~kai/

Abstract. This paper introduces a nested sequent system for predicate logic. The system features a structural universal quantifier and a universally closed existential rule. One nice consequence of this is that proofs of sentences cannot contain free variables. Another nice consequence is that the assumption of a non-empty domain is isolated in a single inference rule. This rule can be removed or added at will, leading to a system for free logic or classical predicate logic, respectively. The system for free logic is interesting because it has no need for an existence predicate. We see syntactic cut-elimination and completeness results for these two systems as well as two standard applications: Herbrand's Theorem and interpolation.

1 Introduction

The mismatch. Traditional analytic proof systems like Gentzen's sequent calculus often cannot capture non-classical logics. Various formalisms have been designed to overcome this problem. The most prominent ones seem to be hypersequents [1], the display calculus [3], labelled systems [18], the calculus of structures [12], and nested sequents [5,6]. All these formalisms work by enriching the structural level of proofs. We can thus see the problem of the traditional sequent calculus as a *mismatch* between the logic and the structural level of proofs, and we can see these formalisms as ways of repairing it. See also the note [11] by Guglielmi for an exposition of this mismatch.

The mismatch in predicate logic. Our proposition here is that the mismatch even affects sequent systems for classical predicate logic. Technically, there is obviously no match between structural and logical connectives, in particular there is no structural counterpart for quantification. The question is whether that is a problem. It turns out that it is if we either want to extend the logic, such as to modal predicate logic, or to slightly weaken the logic, such as by admitting models with an empty domain.

It is a well-known problem in modal predicate logic that combining a traditional sequent system for modal logic with one for predicate logic results in a system which forces the provability of the converse Barcan formula. The existential (right) rule is responsible for that. As it happens, the same existential rule forces the provability of the formula $\forall xA \supset \exists xA$ and thus restricts us to non-empty domains.

C. Fermüller and A. Voronkov (Eds.): LPAR-17, LNCS 6397, pp. 172–186, 2010.

Repairing the mismatch. We now take a quick look at Hilbert-style axiom systems, because there these two problems also occur, but have an elegant solution. The analogue of the existential rule, and equally problematic, is the axiom of instantiation. It typically has the form:

$$\forall x A \supset A[x := y] \quad ,$$

where it suffices to have a variable y instead of an arbitrary term because we have no function symbols. This axiom can be universally closed as follows:

$$\forall y(\forall x A \supset A[x := y]) \quad .$$

And indeed, this closed form of instantiation leads to an axiomatisation for modal predicate logic which does not force the converse Barcan formula and is thus modular in the sense that we can add or remove the converse Barcan formula at will. It also leads to an axiomatisation for predicate logic which does not force non-empty domains, so we can add or remove the non-emptyness requirement at will. This trick of universally closing the instantiation axiom is attributed to Kripke in the context of modal predicate logic in [8] and to Lambert in the context of free logic in [4]. The purpose of the present work is essentially to bring this trick to cut-free systems.

Nested sequents. To that end, we use nested sequents. Compared to usual sequents, nested sequents simply add more structural counterparts for logical connectives. In modal logic, for example, in addition to having the comma (on the right) as a structural counterpart for disjunction, one also has a structural connective for the modality. Since in the present work we are concerned with predicate logic, we have a structural counterpart for universal quantification.

The first use of nested sequents under that name seems to be by Kashima in [13] for tense logics. However, the concept is very natural, and it has been used independently many times in different places. The earliest references I am aware of are from the seventies, by Dunn [7] and by Mints [14], on proof systems for relevance logics. More recent uses for modal logics can be found in the work by the author [5], by Goré, Tiu and Postniece [10], by Dyckhoff and Sadrzadeh [16], or by Poggiolesi [15].

Why repair the mismatch? For now, repairing the mismatch gives us a proof system in which the assumption of a non-empty domain is isolated in a single inference rule. This rule can be removed or added at will, leading to a system for free logic or classical predicate logic, respectively. This is of course not possible in the standard sequent calculus. The system for free logic is interesting because it does not rely on a so-called existence predicate, contrary to traditional sequent systems for free logic. This allows for a syntactic proof of an interpolation theorem, which is slightly stronger than what can be (easily) obtained from the traditional systems: the existence predicate does not occur in the interpolant. However, this is just for now. I think that repairing the mismatch becomes more fruitful the further we move away from classical logic. I am currently working on proof systems for modal predicate logic, in which both the Barcan and converse Barcan formula can be added in a modular fashion. I also think that nested sequents can provide proof systems for logics which currently do not seem to have cut-free systems such as (first-order) Gödel-logic without constant domains, see for example [2].

Outline. The outline of this paper is as follows. In Section 2 we introduce our two nested sequent systems: System Q for predicate logic and a subsystem of it, called System FQ, for free logic. In Section 3 we show some basic properties such as invertibility and some admissible rules. Section 4 relates System Q to a traditional system for predicate logic, and Section 5 relates System FQ to traditional proof systems for free logic. In Section 6 we prove cut-elimination. Finally, in Section 7 we show two simple consequences of cut-admissibility: Herbrand's Theorem and interpolation.

2 The Sequent Systems

Formulas. We assume given an infinite set of predicate symbols for each arity $n \geq 0$ and an infinite set of variables. Predicate symbols are denoted by P, variables by x, y, z. A *proposition*, denoted by p, is an expression $P(x_1, \ldots, x_n)$ where P is a predicate symbol of arity n and $x_1, \ldots, x_n$ are variables. *Formulas*, denoted by A, B, C, D are given by the grammar

$$A ::= p \mid \bar{p} \mid (A \vee A) \mid (A \wedge A) \mid \exists x A \mid \forall x A \quad .$$

Propositions p and their *negations* $\bar{p}$ are called *atoms*. Given a formula A, its *negation* $\bar{A}$ is defined as usual using the double negation law and the De Morgan laws, $A \supset B$ is defined as $\bar{A} \vee B$ and both $\top$ and $\bot$ are respectively defined as $p \vee \bar{p}$ and $p \wedge \bar{p}$ for some proposition p. The binary connectives are left-associative, and we drop parentheses whenever possible, so for example $A \vee B \vee C$ denotes $((A \vee B) \vee C)$.

Nested sequents. A *nested sequent* is defined inductively as one of the following: 1) a finite multiset of formulas, 2) the singleton multiset containing the expression $\forall x[\Gamma]$ where Γ is a nested sequent, or 3) the multiset union of two nested sequents. The expression $\forall x[\ ]$ in $\forall x[\Gamma]$ is called the *structural universal quantifier*: the intention is that it relates to the universal quantifier just like comma relates to disjunction. It binds variables in the same way as usual quantifiers, these variables are then called *structurally bound*. We will often save brackets and write $\forall x \Gamma$ instead of $\forall x[\Gamma]$ and $\forall xy\Gamma$ instead of $\forall x \forall y \Gamma$ if it does not lead to confusion. In the following, a *sequent* is a nested sequent. Sequents are denoted by Γ and Δ. We adopt the usual notational conventions for sequents, in particular the comma in the expression Γ, Δ is multiset union. A sequent Γ is always of the form

$$A_1, \ldots, A_m, \forall x_1[\Delta_1], \ldots, \forall x_n[\Delta_n] \quad .$$

The *corresponding formula* $\underline{\Gamma}_{\mathsf{F}}$ of the above sequent is

$$A_1 \vee \ldots \vee A_m \vee \forall x_1 \underline{\Delta_1}_{\mathsf{F}} \vee \ldots \vee \forall x_n \underline{\Delta_n}_{\mathsf{F}} \quad ,$$

where an empty disjunction is $\bot$ and both the shown formulas and the shown variables are ordered according to some fixed total order.

Structural α-equivalence. Two sequents are *structurally α-equivalent* if they are equal up to the naming of structurally bound variables. This is a weaker equivalence than the usual notion of α-equivalence, which identifies formulas and sequents up to the naming of all bound variables. In particular, given different variables x and y, the sequents $\forall x[A]$ and $\forall y[A[x := y]]$ are structurally α-equivalent while the sequents $\forall x A$ and $\forall y A[x := y]$ are not. Our inference rules will apply modulo structural α-equivalence.

Sequent contexts. Informally, a context is a sequent with holes. We will mostly encounter sequents with just one hole. A *unary context* is a sequent with exactly one occurrence of the symbol $\{\ \}$, the *hole*, which does not occur inside formulas. Such contexts are denoted by $\Gamma\{\ \}$, $\Delta\{\ \}$, and so on. The hole is also called the *empty context*. The sequent $\Gamma\{\Delta\}$ is obtained by replacing $\{\ \}$ inside $\Gamma\{\ \}$ by Δ. For example, if $\Gamma\{\ \} = A, \forall x[B, \{\ \}]$ and $\Delta = C, D$ then $\Gamma\{\Delta\} = A, \forall x[B, C, D]$. More generally, a *context* is a sequent with $n \geq 0$ occurrences of $\{\ \}$, which do not occur inside formulas, and which are linearly ordered. A context with n holes is denoted by $\Gamma\underbrace{\{\ \}\ldots\{\ \}}_{n-\text{times}}$.

Holes can be filled with sequents, or contexts, in general. For example, if $\Gamma\{\ \}\{\ \} = A, \forall x[B, \{\ \}], \{\ \}$ and $\Delta\{\ \} = C, \{\ \}$ then

$$\Gamma\{\Delta\{\ \}\}\{\ \} = A, \forall x[B, C, \{\ \}], \{\ \} \quad ,$$

where in all contexts the holes are ordered from left to right as shown.

Inference rules, derivations, and proofs. *Inference rules* are of the form

$$\rho\,\frac{\Gamma_1\ \ldots\ \Gamma_n}{\Gamma} \quad ,$$

where the $\Gamma_{(i)}$ are schematic sequents and ρ is the *name* of the rule. We sometimes write ρ^n to denote n instances of ρ and ρ^* to denote an unspecified number of instances of ρ. A *system*, denoted by $\mathcal{S}$, is a set of inference rules. A *derivation* in a system $\mathcal{S}$ is a finite tree which is built in the usual way from instances of inference rules from $\mathcal{S}$, which are applied modulo structural α-equivalence. The sequent at the root is the *conclusion* and the sequents at the leaves are the *premises* of the derivation. An *axiom* is a rule without premises. A *proof* of a sequent Γ in a system is a derivation in this system with conclusion Γ where each premise is an instances of an axiom. Derivations are denoted by $\mathcal{D}$ and proofs are denoted by $\mathcal{P}$. A derivation $\mathcal{D}$ in system $\mathcal{S}$ with premises $\Gamma_1 \ldots \Gamma_n$ and conclusion Γ and a proof $\mathcal{P}$ in system $\mathcal{S}$ of Γ are respectively denoted as

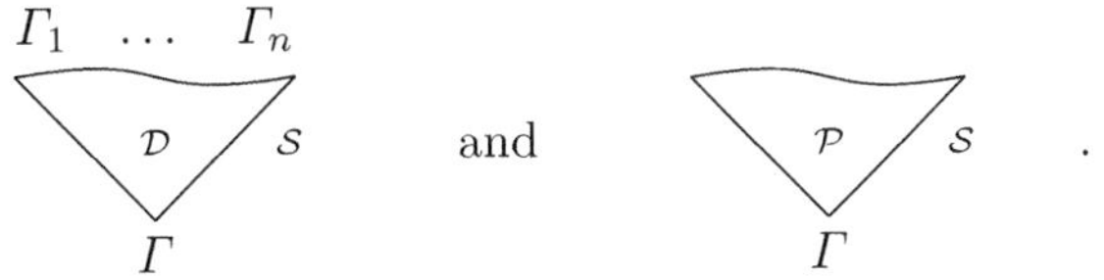

$$\text{id}\,\frac{}{\Gamma\{p,\bar{p}\}} \qquad \wedge\,\frac{\Gamma\{A\} \quad \Gamma\{B\}}{\Gamma\{A \wedge B\}} \qquad \vee\,\frac{\Gamma\{A,B\}}{\Gamma\{A \vee B\}}$$

$$\forall\,\frac{\Gamma\{\forall x[A]\}}{\Gamma\{\forall x A\}} \qquad \text{scp}\,\frac{\forall x[\Gamma\{\Delta\}]}{\Gamma\{\forall x[\Delta]\}} \text{ where } x \text{ does not occur in } \Gamma\{\ \}$$

$$\exists c_1\,\frac{\Gamma\{\exists x A, A[x:=y]\}}{\Gamma\{\exists x A\}} \text{ where } \Gamma\{\ \} \text{ binds } y \qquad \exists c_2\,\frac{\Gamma\{\exists x A, \forall x[A]\}}{\Gamma\{\exists x A\}}$$

Fig. 1. System Q

$$\begin{array}{ll}
\text{id} & \overline{\forall xz[\forall y[\overline{P}(z), P(y), \overline{P(x)}, P(z)]]} \\
\text{scp} & \overline{\forall xz[\,\forall y[\overline{P(z)}, P(y)]\,, \overline{P(x)}, P(z)]} \\
\vee,\forall & \overline{\forall xz[\,\forall y(P(z) \supset P(y))\,, \overline{P(x)}, P(z)]} \\
\exists_1 & \overline{\forall x\, z\,[\exists x \forall y(P(x) \supset P(y))\,, \overline{P(x)}, P(\,z\,)]} \\
= & \overline{\forall x\, y\,[\exists x \forall y(P(x) \supset P(y)), \overline{P(x)}, P(y)\,]} \\
\text{scp}^2 & \overline{\exists x \forall y(P(x) \supset P(y)), \forall x[\,\forall y[\overline{P(x)}, P(y)]]} \\
\vee,\forall & \overline{\exists x \forall y(P(x) \supset P(y)), \forall x[\forall y(P(x) \supset P(y))\,]} \\
\exists c_2 & \overline{\exists x \forall y(P(x) \supset P(y))}
\end{array}$$

Fig. 2. A proof of the drinker's formula

Systems Q and FQ. We say that a unary context *binds* y if it is of the form $\Gamma_1\{\forall y[\Gamma_2\{\ \}]\}$. Figure 1 shows *System Q*, the set of rules {id, $\wedge$, $\vee$, $\forall$, scp, $\exists c_1$, $\exists c_2$}. The id-rule is also called the *identity axiom* and the scp-rule is also called the *scope rule*. Notice how the existential rule is closed, and how the system thus has the *free variable property*: all free variables that occur in a proof occur in its conclusion. The $\exists c_2$-rule postulates that the domain is non-empty. Removing it from System Q gives us *System FQ*, our system for free logic.

Provisos modulo renaming. Note that, since rules apply modulo structural α-equivalence, so do their provisos. In particular, the following is a valid instance of the scp-rule:

$$\text{scp}\,\frac{\forall x[P(x), \forall x Q(x)]}{\forall x[P(x)], \forall x Q(x)} \quad .$$

A proof of the drinker's formula. Figure 2 shows a proof of the drinker's formula: there is a man such that when he drinks, everyone drinks. The proof makes use of the $\exists_1$-rule, which is just the $\exists c_1$-rule without built-in contraction and will be shown to be admissible in the next section. The notation scp^2 denotes two instances of the scope rule and the notation $\vee, \forall$ denotes an instance of the $\vee$-rule followed by an instance of the $\forall$-rule. Note also that implication is a defined connective.

The drinker's formula is not provable in System FQ. Notice also that this is very easy to see: the $\exists c_1$-rule does not apply because of its proviso and thus no rule at all is applicable to the formula.

System Q is complete for sentences only. System Q does not prove all valid sequents. In particular it is easy to see that it does not prove the valid sequent $\exists x P(x), \overline{P(y)}$. It only proves its universal closure $\forall y[\exists x P(x), \overline{P(y)}]$. This is by design: the non-closed sequent is not valid in varying domain semantics for modal predicate logic. Note that, thanks to the free variable property, restricting ourselves to sentences is less problematic than in the usual sequent calculus.

Why structural α-equivalence? Without α-renaming our system would not be complete even for sentences. The closed valid sequent $\forall y[\exists x \exists y P(x), \overline{P(y)}]$ would not be provable. Of course this situation is well-known. Many systems handle it by treating formulas modulo α-equivalence. In System Q it is sufficient to allow for structural α-renaming. The intention here is that a connective should be free while its corresponding structural connective is subject to some equations. We have disjunction and its corresponding comma (with associativity and commutativity) and similarly we have the universal quantifier and its corresponding structural universal quantifier (with α-renaming).

3 Admissible Rules and Invertibility

Figure 3 show some rules which are admissible for System Q. Their names are: *general identity*, *weakening*, *contraction*, *instantiation*, *generalisation*, *permutation*, *vacuous quantification*, *cut*, *first existential* and *second existential*. To show their admissibility we first need some definitions of standard notions.

Cut rank. The *depth* of a formula A, denoted $depth(A)$, is defined as usual, the depth of possibly negated propositions being zero. Given an instance of the *cut-rule* as shown in Figure 3, its *cut formula* is A and its *cut rank* is one plus the depth of its cut formula. For $r \geq 0$ we define the cut_r*-rule* which is cut with at most rank r. The *cut rank* of a derivation is the supremum of the cut ranks of its cuts.

Admissibility and derivability. An inference rule ρ is *(depth-preserving) admissible* for a system $\mathcal{S}$ if for each proof in $\mathcal{S} \cup \{\rho\}$ there is a proof in $\mathcal{S}$ with the same conclusion (and with at most the same depth). An inference rule ρ is *derivable* for a system $\mathcal{S}$ if for each instance of ρ there is a derivation $\mathcal{D}$ in $\mathcal{S}$ with the same conclusion and the same set of premises. A rule is *cut-rank (and depth-) preserving admissible* for a system $\mathcal{S}$ if for all $r \geq 0$ the rule is (depth-preserving) admissible for $\mathcal{S} + \mathsf{cut}_r$.

Invertibility. For each rule ρ there is its *inverse*, denoted by ρ^{-1}, which is obtained by exchanging premise and conclusion. The inverse of a two-premise-rule allows each premise as a conclusion. An inference rule ρ is *(depth-preserving) invertible* for a system $\mathcal{S}$ if ρ^{-1} is (depth-preserving) admissible for $\mathcal{S}$. An

$$\text{gid}\,\frac{}{\Gamma\{A,\bar{A}\}} \qquad \text{wk}\,\frac{\Gamma\{\varnothing\}}{\Gamma\{\Delta\}} \qquad \text{ctr}\,\frac{\Gamma\{\Delta,\Delta\}}{\Gamma\{\Delta\}} \qquad \text{ins}\,\frac{\Gamma\{\forall x[\Delta]\}}{\Gamma\{\Delta[x:=y]\}}\ \text{where } \Gamma\{\ \} \text{ binds } y$$

$$\text{gen}\,\frac{\Gamma}{\forall x[\Gamma]} \qquad \text{per}\,\frac{\Gamma\{\forall x[\forall y[\Delta]]\}}{\Gamma\{\forall y[\forall x[\Delta]]\}} \qquad \text{vac}\,\frac{\Gamma\{\forall x[\Delta]\}}{\Gamma\{\Delta\}}\ \text{where } x \text{ does not occur in } \Delta$$

$$\text{cut}\,\frac{\Gamma\{A\} \quad \Gamma\{\bar{A}\}}{\Gamma\{\varnothing\}} \qquad \exists_1\,\frac{\Gamma\{A[x:=y]\}}{\Gamma\{\exists x A\}}\ \text{where } \Gamma\{\ \} \text{ binds } y \qquad \exists_2\,\frac{\Gamma\{\forall x[A]\}}{\Gamma\{\exists x A\}}$$

Fig. 3. Admissible rules

inference rule ρ is *cut-rank (and depth-) preserving invertible* for a system $\mathcal{S}$ if ρ^{-1} is cut-rank (and depth-) preserving admissible for $\mathcal{S}$.

We are now ready to state our lemma on admissibility and invertibility. Its proof is a lengthy but unproblematic list of rule permutations, which has been left out for space reasons.

Lemma 1 (Admissibility and Invertibility).
(i) For each system $\mathcal{S} \in \{\mathsf{FQ}, \mathsf{Q}\}$, each rule of $\mathcal{S}$ is cut-rank and depth-preserving invertible for $\mathcal{S}$.
(ii) For each system $\mathcal{S} \in \{\mathsf{FQ}, \mathsf{Q}\}$, each of the first six rules from Figure 3 is cut-rank and depth-preserving admissible for $\mathcal{S}$.
(iii) The vacuous quantification rule is depth-preserving admissible for System Q.

Note that the vacuous quantification rule is not admissible for System FQ: the sequent $\forall x[\exists y(p \vee \bar{p})]$ is provable, but not the sequent $\exists y(p \vee \bar{p})$.

By the $\forall$- and $\vee$-rules and their invertibility we get the following corollary.

Corollary 2. *Each system from $\{\mathsf{FQ}, \mathsf{Q}\}$ proves a sequent iff it proves its corresponding formula.*

By weakening admissibility we also get the following corollary.

Corollary 3. *The $\exists_1$-rule is admissible for each system from $\{\mathsf{FQ}, \mathsf{Q}\}$. The $\exists_2$-rule is admissible for System* Q.

4 Relation between System Q and the Usual Sequent Calculus

We now see how to embed System Q into a standard sequent system and vice versa. The specific standard system we use is a variant of System GS1 from [17]. We call this variant *System* LK1 and the only difference between LK1 and GS1 is that LK1 does not treat formulas modulo α-equivalence. Instead it requires that free and bound variables come from disjoint sets, just like in Gentzen's original System LK [9]. So an $\mathsf{LK1}$-*sequent* is a multiset of formulas for which the set of free variables and the set of bound variables are disjoint.

We denote sets of variables by $\vec{x}$ and write $\vec{x}, y$ for $\vec{x} \cup \{y\}$. Given a set of variables $\vec{x}$, the corresponding sequence of structural universal quantifiers is written as $\forall\vec{x}[\ ]$, where variables are ordered according to the fixed total order. The *universal closure* of a sequent Γ is the sequent $\forall\vec{x}[\Gamma]$ where $\vec{x}$ is the set of free variables of Γ.

Theorem 4 (Embedding System $\mathsf{LK1}$ into System Q). *If System $\mathsf{LK1}$ proves an $\mathsf{LK1}$-sequent then System Q proves its universal closure.*

Proof. We proceed by induction on the depth of the given proof in $\mathsf{LK1}$. The identity axiom and the rules for disjunction and conjunction are trivial, so we just show the cases for the quantifier rules. For the universal rule there are two cases. Here is the first, where x occurs free in A (and thus y occurs free in the premise of the $\forall$-rule). Note that the proviso of the scope rule and of the renaming below it are fulfilled because of the proviso of the $\forall$-rule:

$$\forall\,\frac{\Gamma, A[x := y]}{\Gamma, \forall x A}\ \text{where } y \text{ does not occur in conclusion} \quad \rightsquigarrow \quad \forall\,\cfrac{=\,\cfrac{\mathsf{scp}\,\cfrac{\mathsf{per}^*\,\cfrac{\forall\vec{x}, y[\Gamma, A[x := y]]}{\forall y \forall\vec{x}[\Gamma, A[x := y]]}}{\forall\vec{x}[\Gamma, \forall y[A[x := y]]]}}{\forall\vec{x}[\Gamma, \forall x[A]]}}{\forall\vec{x}[\Gamma, \forall x A]} \quad .$$

In the second case, where x does not occur free in A, the translation is almost the same, just the instances of the permutation rule are replaced by an instance of generalisation.

For the existential rule, there are three cases. Here is the first, where y is free in the conclusion:

$$\exists\,\frac{\Gamma, A[x := y]}{\Gamma, \exists x A} \quad \rightsquigarrow \quad \exists_1\,\frac{\forall\vec{x}, y[\Gamma, A[x := y]]}{\forall\vec{x}, y[\Gamma, \exists x A]} \quad .$$

The second case, where y is free in the premise of the $\exists$-rule but not in the conclusion is as follows. Note that here the proviso in the scope rule is fulfilled because free and bound variables are disjoint in $\mathsf{LK1}$-proofs:

$$\exists\,\frac{\Gamma, A[x := y]}{\Gamma, \exists x A} \quad \rightsquigarrow \quad \exists_2\,\cfrac{=\,\cfrac{\mathsf{scp}\,\cfrac{\mathsf{per}^*\,\cfrac{\forall\vec{x}, y[\Gamma, A[x := y]]}{\forall y \forall\vec{x}[\Gamma, A[x := y]]}}{\forall\vec{x}[\Gamma, \forall y[A[x := y]]]}}{\forall\vec{x}[\Gamma, \forall x[A]]}}{\forall\vec{x}[\Gamma, \exists x A]} \quad .$$

The third case, where y is neither free in premise nor conclusion is similar to the second case, with the instances of permutation replaced by one instance of generalisation. □

We now see the reverse direction, that is, we embed System Q into System LK1. We first need some definitions. Define *formula contexts* in analogy to sequent contexts. Let a *restricted formula context* be one where the hole occurs in the scope of at most disjunction and universal quantification. The *glue rules* are shown in Figure 4, where $F\{\ \}$ is a restricted formula context. They are just a technical device useful for embedding System Q into System LK1.

Lemma 5 (Glue for LK1). *The glue rules are admissible for System* LK1.

Proof. By an induction on the depth of $F\{\ \}$ and using invertibility of the $\forall$-rule and of a G3-style $\vee$-rule, we can reduce the admissibility of each glue rule to the admissibility of its restriction to an empty formula context $F\{\ \}$. The admissibility of the restricted glue rules is easy to see. □

Theorem 6. *If System* Q *proves a sequent, then System* LK1 *proves its corresponding formula.*

Proof. Since by the previous lemma the $\{\mathsf{g_c}, \mathsf{g_a}, \mathsf{g}_\alpha\}$-rules are admissible for LK1 we assume in the following equiprovability of sequents that only differ modulo commutativity and associativity of disjunction and renaming of universally bound variables. We proceed by induction on the depth of the given proof in System Q. The propositional rules are just translated to the corresponding glue rules which are admissible for LK1 by the previous lemma. The case for the scope rule is as follows:

$$
\begin{array}{c}\mathcal{P}\ \ \mathsf{Q}\\ \mathsf{scp}\,\dfrac{\forall x\Gamma\{\Delta\}}{\Gamma\{\forall x\Delta\}}\end{array}
\ \text{where } x \text{ does not occur in } \Gamma\{\ \}
\quad\leadsto\quad
\begin{array}{c}IH(\mathcal{P})\ \ \mathsf{LK1}\\ \forall^{-1}\,\dfrac{\forall x\Gamma\{\Delta\}}{\Gamma\{\Delta\}[x:=y]}\\ =\,\dfrac{}{\Gamma\{\Delta[x:=y]\}}\\ \mathsf{g}_\forall\,\dfrac{}{\Gamma\{\forall x\Delta\}}\end{array}\quad,
$$

where on the right y is a fresh variable, the equality is justified by the proviso of the scope rule, and we have just written sequents to denote their corresponding formulas. The case for the $\exists\mathsf{c}_1$ is handled easily by splitting it into an instance of $\exists_1$ and contraction and using the corresponding glue rules. The case for the $\exists\mathsf{c}_2$-rule is also handled splitting it into $\exists_2$ and contraction, and translating $\exists_2$ as follows:

$$
\begin{array}{c}\mathcal{P}\ \ \mathsf{Q}\\ \exists_2\,\dfrac{\Gamma\{\forall x[A]\}}{\Gamma\{\exists xA\}}\end{array}
\quad\leadsto\quad
\begin{array}{c}\mathcal{P}\ \ \mathsf{Q}\\ \mathsf{ins}\,\dfrac{\Gamma\{\forall x[A]\}}{\Gamma\{A\}}\\ \mathsf{IH}\,\dfrac{}{\underline{\Gamma\{A\}}_{\mathsf{F}}}\\ \mathsf{g}_\exists\,\dfrac{}{\underline{\Gamma\{\exists xA\}}_{\mathsf{F}}}\end{array}\quad,
$$

$$\mathsf{g_c}\ \frac{\Gamma, F\{A \vee B\}}{\Gamma, F\{B \vee A\}} \qquad \mathsf{g_a}\ \frac{\Gamma, F\{(A \vee B) \vee C\}}{\Gamma, F\{A \vee (B \vee C)\}} \qquad \mathsf{g_\alpha}\ \frac{\Gamma, F\{\forall x A\}}{\Gamma, F\{\forall y A[x := y]\}}$$

$$\mathsf{g_{id}}\ \frac{}{\Gamma, F\{p \vee \bar{p}\}} \qquad \mathsf{g_\wedge}\ \frac{\Gamma, F\{A\} \quad \Gamma, F\{B\}}{\Gamma, F\{A \wedge B\}} \qquad \mathsf{g_{ctr}}\ \frac{\Gamma, F\{A \vee A\}}{\Gamma, F\{A\}}$$

$$\mathsf{g_\forall}\ \frac{\Gamma, F\{A[x := y]\}}{\Gamma, F\{\forall x A\}}\ \text{where } y \text{ does not occur in the conclusion} \qquad \mathsf{g_\exists}\ \frac{\Gamma, F\{A[x := y]\}}{\Gamma, F\{\exists x A\}}$$

Fig. 4. Some glue for embedding System Q into System LK1

(Tautology)	a propositional tautology
(Distributivity)	$\forall x(A \supset B) \supset (\forall x A \supset \forall x B)$
(Vacuous)	$A \supset \forall x A$ where x does not occur free in A
(Instantiation)	$\forall y(\forall x A \supset A[x := y])$
(Permutation)	$\forall x \forall y A \supset \forall y \forall x A$

Fig. 5. Axioms of System FQC

where on the right ins is depth-preserving admissible for Q and IH denotes applying the induction hypothesis to the proof above. □

By soundness and completeness of LK1 our embeddings give us soundness and completeness for System Q.

Theorem 7 (System Q is sound and complete). *System* Q *proves a sentence iff it is valid (for the standard notion of validity in classical predicate logic).*

5 Relation between System FQ and Free Logic

We will now see that System FQ is sound and complete with respect to free logic. For completeness we embed a Hilbert-style system for free logic into System FQ + cut and then use cut elimination for System FQ, which is proved in the next section. The specific Hilbert-system we use is *System FQC* from Bencivenga [4], which consists of modus ponens and all generalisations of instances of the axioms shown in Figure 5. As usual, a *generalisation* of a formula is obtained by prefixing it with any sequence of universal quantifiers.

It is easy to see that the axioms of FQC are provable in System FQ and that modus pones is admissible for System FQ+cut, so we have the following theorem.

Theorem 8 (Embedding System FQC into System FQ + cut). *If a formula is provable in System* FQC *then it is provable in System* FQ + cut.

To show soundness of System FQ we embed it into a sequent system for free logic, a variant of a system from Bencivenga [4]. *System FLK1* is System LK1 with the quantifier rules replaced by the ones shown in Figure 6, where E, the *existence predicate*, is a fixed unary predicate symbol, which is not used in formulas.

The proof of the following lemma is standard.

Lemma 9 (Invertibility for FLK1). *All rules of System FLK1 are depth-preserving invertible for System FLK1.*

The *free glue rules* are shown in Figure 7, where $F\{\ \}$ is a restricted formula context. The proof of the following lemma follows the lines of the corresponding proof for LK1 and makes use of the invertibility of rules in FLK1.

Lemma 10 (Glue for FLK1). *The rules* $\{\mathsf{g_c}, \mathsf{g_a}, \mathsf{g}_\alpha, \mathsf{g_{id}}, \mathsf{g}_\wedge, \mathsf{g_{ctr}}\}$ *and the free glue rules are admissible for System FLK1.*

We can now embed FQ into FLK1.

Theorem 11 (Embedding System FQ into System FLK1). *If System FQ proves a sequent, then System FLK1 proves its corresponding formula.*

Proof. The proof is similar to the embedding of System Q into System LK1. The difference is in the translation of the scope rule and the $\exists\mathsf{c}_1$-rule, and, of course, the fact that we do not need to translate the $\exists\mathsf{c}_2$-rule. Here is the case for the scope rule:

$$\mathsf{scp}\,\frac{\forall x\Gamma\{\Delta\}}{\Gamma\{\forall x\Delta\}}\ \ \text{where } x \text{ does not occur in } \Gamma\{\ \} \qquad\rightsquigarrow\qquad \mathsf{g}_{\forall_\mathsf{F}}\,\dfrac{=\,\dfrac{\forall_\mathsf{F}^{-1}\,\dfrac{\forall x\Gamma\{\Delta\}}{\Gamma\{\Delta\}[x:=y],\overline{E(y)}}}{\Gamma\{\Delta[x:=y]\},\overline{E(y)}}}{\Gamma\{\forall x\Delta\}}\ ,$$

where on the right y is a fresh variable, the equality is justified by the proviso of the scope rule, and we have just written sequents to denote their corresponding formulas.

For simplicity we just show $\exists_1$ since $\exists\mathsf{c}_1$ is derivable for $\exists_1$ and contraction:

$$\exists_1\,\frac{\Gamma\{A[x:=y]\}}{\Gamma\{\exists xA\}}\ \ \text{where } \Gamma\{\ \} \text{ binds } y \qquad\rightsquigarrow\qquad \mathsf{g}_{\exists_\mathsf{F}}\,\dfrac{\Gamma\{A[x:=y]\} \qquad \forall_\mathsf{F}^*,\vee^*,\mathsf{wk}^*\,\dfrac{\forall_\mathsf{F}\,\dfrac{\mathsf{id}\,\dfrac{}{E(z),\overline{E(z)}}}{\forall yE(y)}}{\Gamma\{E(y)\}}}{\Gamma\{\exists xA\}}\ ,$$

□

By soundness of FLK1 and completeness of FQC with respect to free logic, our embeddings, and cut-elimination for FQ we obtain soundness and completeness for System FQ with respect to free logic.

Theorem 12 (System FQ is sound and complete). *System FQ proves a formula iff it is a theorem of free logic.*

$$\forall_{\mathsf{F}}\ \frac{\Gamma, A[x := y], \overline{E(y)}}{\Gamma, \forall x A}\ \text{where } y \text{ does not occur in the conclusion} \qquad \exists_{\mathsf{F}}\ \frac{\Gamma, A[x := y] \quad \Gamma, E(y)}{\Gamma, \exists x A}$$

Fig. 6. Quantifier rules of System FLK1

$$\mathsf{g}\forall_{\mathsf{F}}\ \frac{\Gamma, F\{A[x := y]\}, \overline{E(y)}}{\Gamma, F\{\forall x A\}}\ \text{where } y \text{ does not occur in the conclusion} \qquad \mathsf{g}\exists_{\mathsf{F}}\ \frac{\Gamma, F\{A[x := y]\} \quad \Gamma, F\{E(y)\}}{\Gamma, F\{\exists x A\}}$$

Fig. 7. Glue for FLK1

6 Syntactic Cut-Elimination

We now turn to cut-elimination. As usual, the reduction lemma is the centerpiece of the cut elimination argument.

Lemma 13 (Reduction Lemma). *Let $\mathcal{S} \in \{\mathsf{FQ}, \mathsf{Q} + \mathsf{vac}\}$. If there is a proof as shown on the left, then there is a proof as shown on the right:*

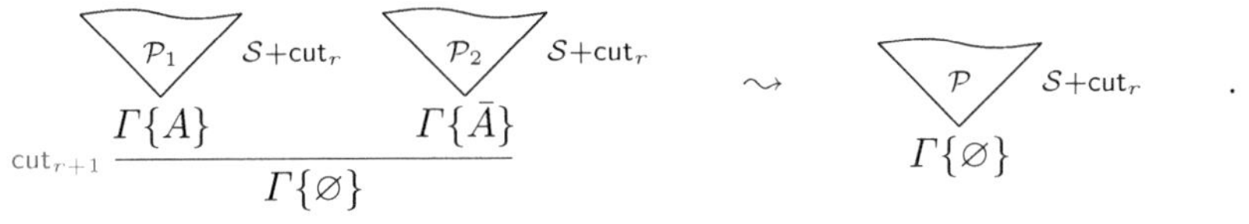

Proof. We first prove the lemma for System FQ. We proceed as usual, by an induction on the sum of the depths of $\mathcal{P}_1$ and $\mathcal{P}_2$ and by a case analysis on their lowermost rules. All passive cases (that is, those where the lowermost rule does not apply to the cut-formula) are handled using invertibility, and using contraction admissibility in the passive conjunction case. Note that scope can only be passive. The active cases for the axiom and the propositional connectives are as usual. We now look at the only interesting case, namely $\forall$ vs. $\exists \mathsf{c}_1$, which is handled as follows:

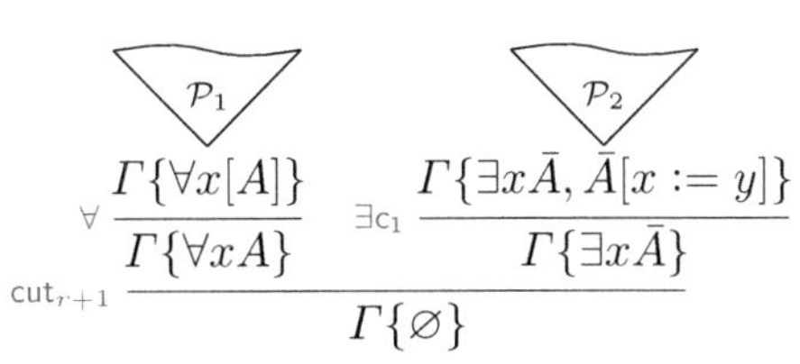

$$\leadsto\quad \mathsf{cut}\,\dfrac{\mathsf{ins}\,\dfrac{\overset{\mathcal{P}_1}{\Gamma\{\forall x[A]\}}}{\Gamma\{A[x:=y]\}} \qquad \mathsf{cut}\,\dfrac{\forall\,\dfrac{\mathsf{wk}\,\dfrac{\overset{\mathcal{P}_1}{\Gamma\{\forall x[A]\}}}{\Gamma\{\bar{A}[x:=y],\forall x[A]\}}}{\Gamma\{\bar{A}[x:=y],\forall xA\}} \quad \overset{\mathcal{P}_2}{\Gamma\{\exists x\bar{A},\bar{A}[x:=y]\}}}{\Gamma\{\bar{A}[x:=y]\}}}{\Gamma\{\emptyset\}}\ ,$$

where the proviso of the ins-rule is fulfilled because of the proviso of the $\exists c_1$-rule. This concludes the proof for System FQ. The proof for System Q + vac is the same, but with the additional case $\forall$ vs. $\exists c_2$:

$$\mathsf{cut}_{r+1}\,\dfrac{\forall\,\dfrac{\overset{\mathcal{P}_1}{\Gamma\{\forall x[A]\}}}{\Gamma\{\forall xA\}} \qquad \exists c_2\,\dfrac{\overset{\mathcal{P}_2}{\Gamma\{\exists x\bar{A},\forall x[\bar{A}]\}}}{\Gamma\{\exists x\bar{A}\}}}{\Gamma\{\emptyset\}}$$

$$\leadsto\quad \mathsf{vac}\,\dfrac{\mathsf{cut}\,\dfrac{\overset{\mathcal{P}_1}{\Gamma\{\forall x[A]\}} \qquad \mathsf{cut}\,\dfrac{\forall\,\dfrac{\mathsf{wk}\,\dfrac{\overset{\mathcal{P}_1}{\Gamma\{\forall x[A]\}}}{\Gamma\{\forall x[A],\forall x[\bar{A}]\}}}{\Gamma\{\forall xA,\forall x[\bar{A}]\}} \quad \overset{\mathcal{P}_2}{\Gamma\{\exists x\bar{A},\forall x[\bar{A}]\}}}{\Gamma\{\forall x[\bar{A}]\}}}{\Gamma\{\forall x[\emptyset]\}}}{\Gamma\{\emptyset\}}$$

□

Cut-elimination for System FQ now follows from a routine induction on the cut-rank of the given proof with a subinduction on the depth of the proof, using the reduction lemma in the case of a maximal-rank cut. To get cut-elimination for System Q we first prove it for System Q + vac, in the same way as we did for FQ, and then use the admissibility of the vac-rule. So we have the following theorem.

Theorem 14 (Cut-Elimination). *Let $\mathcal{S} \in \{\mathsf{FQ}, \mathsf{Q}\}$. If a sequent is provable in System $\mathcal{S}$ + cut then it is provable in System $\mathcal{S}$.*

7 Herbrand's Theorem and Interpolation

We now see two simple applications of our cut-free system: Herbrand's Theorem and interpolation, both for classical predicate logic and free logic. The point here is of course not that these results are new, the point is that our cut-free systems are useful enough to easily provide them. That said, in the case of free logic the syntactic proof of interpolation seems to be new: it is not easy to see how to get it from System FLK1 without allowing the existence predicate to occur in the interpolant.

Theorem 15 (Mid-Sequent Theorem). *Let* $\mathcal{S} \in \{\mathsf{FQ}, \mathsf{Q}\}$ *and let* Γ *contain only prenex formulas. If there is a proof of* Γ *in System* $\mathcal{S}$ *then there is a sequent* Γ' *provable in* $\{\mathsf{id}, \wedge, \vee\}$ *and a derivation from* Γ' *to* Γ *in* $\mathcal{S} - \{\mathsf{id}, \wedge, \vee\}$.

Proof. We first establish the claim that each rule in $\{\forall, \mathsf{scp}, \exists\mathsf{c}_1, \exists\mathsf{c}_2\}$ is depth-preserving invertible for System $\{\mathsf{id}, \wedge, \vee\}$.

To prove the decomposition theorem we now proceed by induction on the depth of the given proof and a case analysis on the lowermost rule. Consider the case when that is the $\wedge$-rule, which is the only interesting case. We first decompose the left subproof by induction hypothesis. Then we permute all the quantifier rules we obtained down below the $\wedge$-rule, using invertibility to compensate on its right premise. Note that the depth of the right subproof is preserved. Now we decompose the right subproof by induction hypothesis. Then we permute all the quantifier rules that we obtained down below the $\wedge$-rule, using the claim to compensate on its left premise. We have now obtained a proof of the desired form. □

The mid-sequent Γ' may still contain formulas with quantifiers as well as structural universal quantifiers. However, since its proof contains only propositional rules, both can be easily removed. So we have the following corollary.

Corollary 16 (Herbrand's Theorem). *Let* $\mathcal{S} \in \{\mathsf{FQ}, \mathsf{Q}\}$ *and let* A *be a prenex formula which is provable in System* $\mathcal{S}$*. Then there is a sequent which 1) consists only of substitution instances of the matrix of* A *and 2) is propositionally provable.*

We also easily obtain the following interpolation theorem, by a standard induction on the depth of the given proof.

Theorem 17 (Interpolation). *Let* $\mathcal{S} \in \{\mathsf{FQ}, \mathsf{Q}\}$*. If* $\mathcal{S}$ *proves the sequent* $\forall\vec{z}[\Gamma, \Delta]$ *then there is a formula* C*, called* interpolant*, such that 1) each predicate symbol and each free variable in* C *occurs both in* Γ *and in* Δ*, and 2) system* $\mathcal{S}$ *proves both the sequent* $\forall\vec{z}[\Gamma, C]$ *and the sequent* $\forall\vec{z}[\bar{C}, \Delta]$.

References

1. Avron, A.: The method of hypersequents in the proof theory of propositional non-classical logics. In: Hodges, W., Hyland, M., Steinhorn, C., Truss, J. (eds.) Logic: from foundations to applications. Proc. Logic Colloquium, Keele, UK, 1993, pp. 1–32. Oxford University Press, New York (1996)
2. Baaz, M., Ciabattoni, A., Fermüller, C.G.: Hypersequent calculi for Gödel logics: a survey. Journal of Logic and Computation 13, 1–27 (2003)

3. Belnap Jr., N.D.: Display logic. Journal of Philosophical Logic 11, 375–417 (1982)
4. Bencivenga, E.: Free logics. In: Gabbay, D., Guenthner, F. (eds.) Handbook of Philosophical Logic: Volume III: Alternatives to Classical Logic, pp. 373–426. Reidel, Dordrecht (1986)
5. Brünnler, K.: Deep sequent systems for modal logic. Archive for Mathematical Logic 48(6), 551–577 (2009), `http://www.iam.unibe.ch/~kai/Papers/2009dssml.pdf`
6. Brünnler, K., Straßburger, L.: Modular sequent systems for modal logic. In: Giese, M., Waaler, A. (eds.) TABLEAUX 2009. LNCS, vol. 5607, pp. 152–166. Springer, Heidelberg (2009)
7. Michael Dunn, J.: A 'Gentzen' system for positive relevant implication. The Journal of Symbolic Logic 38, 356–357 (1974) (Abstract)
8. Fitting, M., Mendelsohn, R.L.: First-order Modal Logic. Synthese library, vol. 277. Kluwer, Dordrecht (1998)
9. Gentzen, G.: Investigations into logical deduction. In: Szabo, M.E. (ed.) The Collected Papers of Gerhard Gentzen, pp. 68–131. North-Holland Publishing Co., Amsterdam (1969)
10. Goré, R., Postniece, L., Tiu, A.: Taming displayed tense logics using nested sequents with deep inference. In: Giese, M., Waaler, A. (eds.) TABLEAUX 2009. LNCS, vol. 5607, pp. 189–204. Springer, Heidelberg (2009)
11. Guglielmi, A.: Mismatch (2003), `http://cs.bath.ac.uk/ag/p/AG9.pdf`
12. Guglielmi, A.: A system of interaction and structure. ACM Transactions on Computational Logic 8(1), 1–64 (2007)
13. Kashima, R.: Cut-free sequent calculi for some tense logics. Studia Logica 53, 119–135 (1994)
14. Mints, G.: Cut-elimination theorem in relevant logics. The Journal of Soviet Mathematics 6, 422–428 (1976)
15. Poggiolesi, F.: The tree-hypersequent method for modal propositional logic. In: Malinowski, J., Makinson, D., Wansing, H. (eds.) Towards Mathematical Philosophy. Trends in Logic, pp. 9–30. Springer, Heidelberg (2009)
16. Sadrzadeh, M., Dyckhoff, R.: Positive logic with adjoint modalities: Proof theory, semantics and reasoning about information. Review of Symbolic Logic (to appear, 2010)
17. Troelstra, A.S., Schwichtenberg, H.: Basic Proof Theory. Cambridge University Press, Cambridge (1996)
18. Viganò, L.: Labelled Non-Classical Logics. Kluwer Academic Publishers, Dordrecht (2000)

On the Complexity of the Bernays-Schönfinkel Class with Datalog

Witold Charatonik and Piotr Witkowski

Institute of Computer Science
University of Wrocław
{wch,pwit}@ii.uni.wroc.pl

Abstract. The Bernays-Schönfinkel class with Datalog is a 2-variable fragment of the Bernays-Schönfinkel class extended with least fixed points expressible by certain monadic Datalog programs. It was used in a bounded model checking procedure for programs manipulating dynamically allocated pointer structures, where the bounded model checking problem was reduced to the satisfiability of formulas in this logic. The best known upper bound on the complexity of the satisfiability problem for this logic was 2NEXPTIME.

In this paper we extend the Bernays-Schönfinkel class with Datalog to a more expressive logic — a fragment of two-variable logic with counting quantifiers extended with the same kind of fixed points. We prove that both satisfiability and entailment for the new logic are decidable in NEXPTIME and we give a matching lower bound for the original logic, which establishes NEXPTIME-completeness of the satisfiability and entailment problems for both of them. Our algorithm is based on a translation to 2-variable logic with counting quantifiers.

1 Introduction

Automated verification of programs manipulating dynamically allocated pointer structures is a challenging task. The reachable state space of such programs is infinite and the verification problem is undecidable. Moreover, to reason about sets of nodes reachable from a program variable one often wants to be able to compute transitive closure or least fixed points of some operators. Unfortunately, even quite simple logics like two-variable fragments of first-order logic or even two-variable fragments of the Bernays-Schönfinkel class extended with either transitive closure or least fixed points quickly become undecidable [7,9].

In [4] the authors proposed a bounded model checking procedure for imperative programs that manipulate dynamically allocated pointer structures on the heap. Although in this procedure an explicit bound is assumed on the length of the program execution, the size of the initial data structure is not bounded. Therefore, such programs form infinite and infinitely branching transition systems. The procedure is based on the following four observations. First, error conditions like dereference of a dangling pointer, are expressible in the two-variable fragment of the Bernays-Schönfinkel class with equality. Second, the fragment is closed under weakest preconditions wrt. finite paths. Third, data structures like trees, lists (singly or doubly linked, or even circular) are expressible in a fragment of monadic Datalog. Finally, the combination of the Bernays-Schönfinkel

C. Fermüller and A. Voronkov (Eds.): LPAR-17, LNCS 6397, pp. 187–201, 2010.

fragment with Datalog fragment is decidable. The bounded model checking problem for pointer programs is then reduced to the satisfiability of formulas in the Bernays-Schönfinkel class with Datalog. The authors gave an algorithm solving the satisfiability problem in 2NEXPTIME.

In this paper, we improve the logic from [4] in terms of both expressibility and complexity. The two-variable fragment of the Bernays-Schönfinkel class (BS_2 for short) is simply a fragment of first-order logic restricted to two universally quantified variables. In the new logic, we are able to use both universal and existential quantifiers and additionally we may use counting in quantifiers. Moreover, the logic in [4] has additional semantic restrictions, some of which we are able to drop here. This gives us an increase of expressibility.

We give an algorithm for testing satisfiability of our logic that runs in NEXPTIME. The algorithm is based on a translation to 2-variable logic with counting quantifiers. Since our logic subsumes the the Bernays-Schönfinkel class with Datalog (further called BS_2+Datalog), we improve the previous complexity upper bound. We also give a matching lower bound and establish NEXPTIME-completeness of both logics. Finally, we also solve the entailment problem, which was left open in [4] and has further consequences for the applicability of the logic in verification.

The paper is organized as follows. The main results on satisfiability and entailment are proved in Section 3. Section 4 gives the corresponding lower bound. In Section 5 we show that dropping one of the restrictions on sharing data that forbids us to model directed acyclic graphs leads to a very complex logic. The main part of the paper is finished with the discussion on related and future work. For missing proofs we refer the reader to full version of the paper [5].

2 Preliminaries

Let Σ_E (extensional database vocabulary) be a vocabulary containing relational symbols of arity at most 2 and functional symbols of arity 0 (that is, constants). Let Σ_I (intensional database vocabulary) be a relational vocabulary containing only unary symbols and let Σ_P be a set containing some of Σ_E binary predicates. Assume in addition that a countably infinite set of variables V is available. Σ_E is a vocabulary of some (to be precised later) two-variable logic formula, Σ_I defines symbols that occur in heads of clauses from Datalog programs and Σ_P — binary symbols used in their bodies. Following [4], we are interested in *monadic tree-automaton like* Datalog programs, which are Datalog programs whose clauses are similar to transitions in edge-labeled tree automata.

Definition 1. *A monadic tree-automaton like Datalog program over Σ_I,Σ_E and Σ_P is a conjunction of clauses of the form*

$$p(u) \leftarrow B, r_1(u, v_1), q_1(v_1), \ldots, r_l(u, v_l), q_l(v_l)$$

where

- *B is a conjunction of Σ_E-literals containing constants and possibly the variable u,*
- *$p, q_1, \ldots, q_l$ are Σ_I-predicates,*

- $r_1, \ldots, r_l$ *are distinct* Σ_P*-predicates,*
- $l \geq 0$ *and* $u, v_1, \ldots, v_l$ *are distinct variables from* V.

Monadic tree-automaton like Datalog programs are further called (monadic, t.a. like) Datalog programs for short.

Example 1. A binary tree with *left* and *right* pointers, whose leaves point to constant *NULL* is defined by Datalog program

$$tree(x) \leftarrow x = NULL; \; tree(x) \leftarrow left(x,y), tree(y), right(x,z), tree(z).$$

Let P be a monadic Datalog program. Given a Σ_E-structure M, the *least extension* of M wrt. P is the least $(\Sigma_E \cup \Sigma_I)$-structure that is a model of the clause set P. More formally, we have the following definition.

Definition 2 (Least extension). *Let* M *be a relational structure over* Σ_E *and let* P *be a monadic Datalog program over* Σ_I,Σ_P *and* Σ_E *whose variables come from* V. *Let* $F^M = \{p(e) \mid p(\cdot) \in \Sigma_I \wedge e \in M\}$. *The direct consequence operator* T_P^M *is a function from* $2^{F^M} \to 2^{F^M}$ *defined as follows.*

$$T_P^M(I) = I \cup \{p(e) \mid \exists [p(x) \leftarrow body] \in P. \exists \Theta \in V \to M. \;\; \Theta(x) = e \wedge M \cup I \models (body\Theta)\}$$

Let $T_P^M = \bigcup_{i=1}^{\infty} (T_P^M)^i(\emptyset)$. *Then the least extension of* M *with respect to* P *is a structure* M_P *over* $\Sigma_E \cup \Sigma_I$, *such that* $M_P = M \cup T_P^M$.

Definition 3 (Sliced Datalog program). *A monadic tree-automaton like Datalog program* P *over* Σ_I, Σ_E *and* Σ_P *is called* sliced *if, for some natural* k, $P = \bigwedge_{i=1}^{k} P_i$ *where*

- *each* P_i *is a monadic tree-automaton like Datalog program over vocabularies* Σ_I^i, Σ_P^i *and* Σ_E,
- $\Sigma_I^i \cap \Sigma_I^j = \emptyset$ *and* $\Sigma_P^i \cap \Sigma_P^j = \emptyset$ *for* $i \neq j$, $1 \leq i, j \leq k$,
- $\bigcup_{i=1}^{k} \Sigma_I^i = \Sigma_I$ *and* $\bigcup_{i=1}^{k} \Sigma_P^i = \Sigma_P$.

We sometimes write $\{P_1, \ldots, P_k\}$ instead of $\bigwedge_{i=1}^{k} P_i$. In the following, we will use sliced programs in two ways. The first is to control if some data structures are allowed or are forbidden to share substructures (see the bounded-sharing restriction below). The second way is to solve the entailment problem, where we have to assure that the structures defined by the two formulas may interfere.

The two-variable fragment of the Bernays-Schönfinkel class (BS_2 for short) is the set of all formulas of the form $\forall x \forall y \, \phi$, where ϕ is a quantifier-free first-order formula over Σ_E. We specify reachability predicates via sliced Datalog programs.

Definition 4 (BS_2 + Datalog)**.** *A formula of the Bernays-Schönfinkel class with Datalog is a conjunction* $\phi \wedge P \wedge Q$ *where*

- ϕ *is a* BS_2 *formula over* Σ_E,
- $P = \{P_1, \ldots, P_k\}$ *is a sliced monadic tree-automaton like Datalog program*
- Q *is a conjunction (called a query) of constant positive atoms* $\bigwedge_i p_i(c_i)$ *(where* $p_i \in \Sigma_I$ *and* $c_i \in \Sigma_E$*) and* BS_2 *formulas over* $\Sigma_E \cup \Sigma_I$ *with only negative occurrences of atoms* $p_i(x)$ *(where* $p_i \in \Sigma_I$ *and* x *is a variable).*

Example 2. A tree rooted in a constant *root* whose nodes have a backward link r to *root* is specified by the BS_2+Datalog formula $\phi \wedge P \wedge Q$, where Q is $tree(root) \wedge \forall x\; tree(x) \rightarrow (x = NULL \vee r(x, root))$, P is the Datalog program from Example 1 (with only one slice) and ϕ is simply *true*.

For a given Σ_E-formula ϕ and a query Q, we say that Σ_E-structure M *satisfies* $\phi \wedge P \wedge Q$, denoted by $M \models \phi \wedge P \wedge Q$, if M_P is a model of $\phi \wedge Q$, where M_P is the least extension of M wrt. P. However, this still does not define the semantics of the Bernays-Schönfinkel class with Datalog. The logic was designed to model heaps of pointer programs, therefore we are not interested in general satisfiability of formulas in this class, but we impose two additional restrictions on models.

Functionality. We require that all binary relations are functional, i. e., for all predicates r in Σ_E, the structure M (and thus also M_P must be a model of $\forall u, v_1, v_2 (r(u, v_1) \wedge r(u, v_2) \rightarrow v_1 = v_2)$. This ensures that every pointer at any given moment points to at most one heap cell.

Bounded-Sharing. We require that the binary relations occurring in each slice P_i of the Datalog program $P = \{P_1, \ldots, P_k\}$ represent pointers in data structures that do not share memory with other data structures defined by P_i. That is, the structure M_P must be a model of all sentences of the form $\forall u_1, u_2, v\; (s_1(u_1, v) \wedge s_1(u_2, v) \wedge u_1 \neq u_2 \rightarrow const(v))$ and $\forall u_1, u_2, v(s_1(u_1, v) \wedge s_2(u_2, v) \rightarrow const(v))$, where s_1 and s_2 are two distinct predicates occurring in Σ_P^i and $const(v)$ is a shorthand for the disjunction $\bigvee_{c \in \Sigma_E} v = c$. Note that the bounded-sharing restriction is not imposed on all binary predicates but just on the ones occurring in the Datalog program P.

As an example consider two programs defining lists

$$list_1(x) \leftarrow x = NULL;\;\; list_1(x) \leftarrow next_1(x, y), list_1(y).$$
$$list_2(x) \leftarrow x = NULL;\;\; list_2(x) \leftarrow next_2(x, y), list_2(y).$$

together with a formula $\forall x\; \neg next_1(NULL, x) \wedge \neg next_2(NULL, x)$. If the two programs are in the same slice then, with the exception of constants, they are not allowed to have common nodes. On the other hand, if they are in different slices, they may freely share nodes.

The functionality and bounded-sharing restrictions are expressible in the Bernays-Schönfinkel class with equality, but they require more than two variables, so we cannot add them to the formula ϕ. Each Datalog slice P_i can define multiple structures. Constant elements are intended to model nodes pointed to by program variables. Such nodes are allowed to be pointed to by elements of different structures, even from the same slice.

Definition 5 (Semantics of the Bernays-Schönfinkel class with Datalog). *Let $\varphi = \phi \wedge P \wedge Q$ and M be a finite structure over Σ_E such that*

- *Structure M_P, that is the least extension of M wrt. P, obeys functionality and bounded-sharing restrictions,*
- $M_P \models \phi \wedge Q$,

Then M is said to satisfy φ, in symbols $M \models \varphi$.

Remark 1. Contrary to our definition of Σ_E, in [4] the vocabulary of ϕ does not contain unary relational symbols. One can however get rid of them by introducing additional constant (say d) and replacing each occurrence of an atom $r(x)$ by $r'(x, d)$, where r' is a fresh binary symbol. Thus presence of unary symbols in Σ_E incurs no increase in asymptotic complexity of the satisfiability problem. Furthermore, in [4] queries Q are limited to be conjunctions of constant positive atoms, only one-sliced Datalog programs are allowed and admissible models obey additional semantic restriction called intersection-freeness. We removed here this last restriction since it is expressible as a query $\bigwedge_{p(\cdot)\in\Sigma_I} \bigwedge_{q(\cdot)\in\Sigma_I, q\neq p} \forall v(p(v) \wedge q(v) \rightarrow const(v))$. These extensions do not however increase the asymptotic complexity of satisfiability and entailment problems compared to [4]. Lower bound proof from section 4 holds as is for the logic defined in [4].

Definition 6 (Derivation). *Let M be a structure over the signature Σ_E satisfying the bounded-sharing restriction, let P be a monadic sliced t.a. like Datalog program, let $p \in \Sigma_I$ and $e \in M$. A* derivation *$deriv(p(e))$ is a tree labeled with atoms of the form $q(a)$ with $q \in \Sigma_I$ and $a \in M$ such that*

- *the root of $deriv(p(e))$ is labeled with $p(e)$,*
- *if a leaf of $deriv(p(e))$ is labeled with $q(a)$ then there exists a clause $[q(x) \leftarrow B] \in P$ and a valuation Θ such that $\Theta(x) = a$ and $M \models B\Theta$,*
- *for every inner node of $deriv(p(e))$ labeled with $q(a)$ there exists a clause $[q(u) \leftarrow B \wedge \bigwedge_{i=1}^{k}(r_i(u, v_i) \wedge q_i(v_i))] \in P$ and a valuation Θ, such that $\Theta(u) = a$, $M \models B\Theta \wedge \bigwedge_{i=1}^{k} r_i(a, \Theta(v_i))$ and the children of $q(a)$ are roots of derivations $deriv(q_i(\Theta(v_i)))$ for all $1 \leq i \leq k$.*

Note that since vocabularies of different slices are disjoint, the whole tree $deriv(p(e))$ contains only symbols from one slice.

A constant atom is an atom of the form $p(c)$ where c is an element interpreting a constant symbol. A constant derivation is a derivation of a constant atom. A minimal derivation is a derivation whose all subderivations have the minimal possible height. Unless otherwise specified, all derivations we consider are minimal.

Remark 2. Without loss of generality we assume that all leaves in derivations are constant atoms, that is, for all clauses of the form $p(u) \leftarrow B$ in P there exists a constant $c \in \Sigma_E$ such that $u = c$ is a conjunct in B. If $p(u) \leftarrow B$ does not satisfy this requirement, then it is replaced by $p(u) \leftarrow B, c(u, y), c(y)$ and $c(x) \leftarrow x = c$, where c, $c(\cdot)$ and $c(\cdot, \cdot)$ are fresh constant, fresh unary Σ_I-predicate and fresh binary Σ_P-predicate, respectively. By the definition of vocabularies $c(\cdot, \cdot)$ is then also a fresh Σ_E-predicate.

Definition 7 ($p(e)$-tree). *A $p(e)$-tree is a maximal subtree of a derivation $deriv(p(e))$ with root labeled $p(e)$ and no inner nodes labeled with constant atoms.*

By remark 2 leaves of each finite derivation are labeled by constant atoms, so are leaves of any $p(e)$-tree. The least extension (Definition 2) gives a model-theoretic semantics of Datalog programs over Σ_E-structures; derivations (Definition 6) gives a proof-theoretic semantics. By a simple inductive proof it is not difficult to see that they are equivalent.

Proposition 1. *Let M be a finite structure satisfying the bounded-sharing restriction. There exists a finite derivation of $p(e)$ if and only if $p(e) \in T_M^P$.*

3 NEXPTIME Upper Bound

In this section we prove that the satisfiability and entailment problems for the Bernays-Schönfinkel class with Datalog are decidable in NEXPTIME. This is done by a satisfiability (respectively, entailment) preserving polynomial translation from the Bernays-Schönfinkel class with Datalog to the two-variable logic with counting quantifiers.

The two variable logic with counting (C^2) is a fragment of first order logic containing formulas whose all subformulas have at most two free variables, but these formulas may contain counting quantifiers $\exists^{\leq k}$, $\exists^{\geq k}$, $\exists^{=k}$. Decidability of the satisfiability problem was discovered independently in [8] and [16]. First NEXPTIME results for C^2, under unary encoding of counts, were obtained in [16,17] and under binary coding in [18]. While C^2 does not enjoy the finite model property it is natural to ask for finite satisfiability. This question was positively answered in [8], NEXPTIME complexity was established by [18] even under the binary encoding. The (finite) satisfiability of C^2 is NEXPTIME-hard as a consequence of NEXPTIME-hardness of the two variable fragment of first-order logic.

Our translation is done in two steps. First we translate the input formula to an intermediate logic C^2_r + Datalog + bsr (restricted C^2 with Datalog and bounded-sharing restriction), and then we translate the resulting formula to C^2. The reason to introduce this intermediate logic is that it is more expressive than the Bernays-Schönfinkel class with Datalog and may be of its own interest. In this logic the Bernays-Schönfinkel part of the formula (that is, the ϕ conjunct in a formula of the form $\phi \wedge P \wedge Q$) is relaxed to use arbitrary quantifiers (not only the $\forall$ quantifier), even with counting; the query Q is incorporated into the conjunct ϕ and relaxed to be arbitrary formula with constant atoms and restricted occurrences of non-constant Σ_I-atoms. This is a good step forward in ability to express more complicated verification conditions of pointer programs. Moreover, we skip one out of two semantic restrictions on models, namely functionality which is expressible in C^2. The bounded-sharing restriction could not be dropped — it is the restriction that allows to keep the complexity of Datalog programs under control. In Section 5 we show that the complexity of unrestricted C^2_r with Datalog is much worse than NEXPTIME.

Let ϕ be a C^2 formula over $\Sigma_E \cup \Sigma_I$ and let ϕ' be its negation normal form. We say that a Σ_I-atom $p(x)$ has a restricted occurrence in ϕ if either $p(x)$ occurs positively in ϕ' and only in the scope of existential quantifiers or $p(x)$ occurs negatively in ϕ' and only in the scope of universal quantifiers. For example $p(x)$ has a restricted occurrence in formulas $\forall x\ p(x) \rightarrow \psi$, $\forall x\ (p(x) \wedge q(x)) \rightarrow \psi$, $\exists x\ p(x) \wedge \psi$ or $\exists x\ p(x) \wedge q(x) \wedge \psi$, where ψ is some C^2 formula with one free variable x and $q(\cdot)$ is some Σ_I-predicate. The occurrence of the atom $p(x)$ in the formula $\forall y \exists x\ p(x) \wedge \psi$ is not restricted, because $p(x)$ occurs here positively and in the scope of a universal quantifier.

Definition 8 (Syntax of C^2_r + Datalog + bsr). *A formula of* C^2_r + Datalog + bsr *is a conjunction of the form* $\phi \wedge P$ *such that*

- ϕ *is a formula of the two-variable logic with counting quantifiers over the signature* $\Sigma_E \cup \Sigma_I$,
- *all* Σ_I*-literals occurring in* ϕ *are either constant literals or have only restricted occurrences in* ϕ*, and*
- P *is a sliced monadic tree-automaton like Datalog program.*

Definition 9 (Semantics of C_r^2 + Datalog + bsr). *Let $\varphi = \phi \wedge P$ be a formula of C_r^2 +* Datalog + bsr *and let M be a finite structure over Σ_E such that the structure M_P, that is the least extension of M wrt. P, obeys bounded-sharing restriction, and $M_P \models \phi$. Then M is said to satisfy φ, in symbols $M \models \varphi$.*

The following proposition reduces the satisfiability problem for BS_2 + Datalog to the satisfiability for C_r^2 + Datalog + bsr.

Proposition 2. *For every formula $\varphi = \phi \wedge P \wedge Q$ in the Bernays-Schönfinkel class with Datalog there exists an equivalent formula ψ of C_r^2 +* Datalog + bsr *of size polynomial in the size of φ.*

Proof. Let ψ be the conjunction of the following formulas

1. $\phi \wedge Q$,
2. $\bigwedge_{r(\cdot,\cdot)\in\Sigma_E} \forall u \exists^{\leq 1} v\; r(u,v)$,
3. P.

Then ψ is a formula of C_r^2 + Datalog + bsr, because ϕ is a BS_2 formula and all Σ_I–atoms in $\phi \wedge Q$ are either constant atoms or have only restricted occurrences. Furthermore, the conjunct number 2 expresses the functionality restriction, so ψ is equivalent to φ. □

We say that a formula φ entails a formula φ' (in symbols $\varphi \models \varphi'$) if for all structures M we have that $M \models \varphi$ implies $M \models \varphi'$. Below we show that the entailment problem of BS_2 + Datalog is reducible to the satisfiability of C_r^2 + Datalog + bsr. We start with an observation that names of predicates defined by Datalog programs may be arbitrarily changed. By a renaming function we mean here any bijection between different vocabularies.

Lemma 1. *Let $\varphi = \phi \wedge P \wedge Q$ be a BS_2 +* Datalog *formula, where P is a sliced Datalog program over Σ_I and Σ_P. Let φ_{ren} be a formula φ where Σ_I-predicates were arbitrarily renamed. Then $M \models \varphi$ if and only if $M \models \varphi_{ren}$.*

Proposition 3 (entailment). *For all formulas $\varphi = \phi \wedge P \wedge Q$ and $\varphi' = \phi' \wedge P' \wedge Q'$ in the BS_2 +* Datalog *class there exists a formula ψ of C_r^2 +* Datalog + bsr *of size polynomial in the size of φ and φ', such that $\varphi \models \varphi'$ if and only if ψ is unsatisfiable.*

Proof. Let Σ_I,Σ_P be vocabularies of sliced monadic t.a. like Datalog program P, let $\Sigma_{I'}$,$\Sigma_{P'}$ be vocabularies of P'. By previous lemma it may be w.l.o.g assumed, that $\Sigma_I \cap \Sigma_{I'} = \emptyset$. Furthermore if $r(\cdot,\cdot) \in \Sigma_P \cap \Sigma_{P'}$ then replacing each occurrence of $r(\cdot,\cdot)$ in P by a fresh predicate $r'(\cdot,\cdot)$ and adding a conjunct $\forall x \forall y\; r(x,y) \iff r'(x,y)$ to ϕ decreases cardinality of $\Sigma_P \cap \Sigma_{P'}$ while preserving entailment. By iteratively applying this procedure it can be ensured, that also $\Sigma_P \cap \Sigma_{P'} = \emptyset$. Let $P = \{P_1,\ldots,P_k\}$ and $P' = \{P_1^{'},\ldots,P_l^{'}\}$. It follows that $\{P_1,\ldots,P_k,P_1^{'},\ldots,P_l^{'}\}$ is also a sliced monadic Datalog program. Formula ψ is defined to be $(\phi \wedge Q \wedge \neg(\phi' \wedge Q)) \wedge \{P_1,\ldots,P_k,P_1^{'},\ldots,P_l^{'}\}$. Notice also, that by the definition of BS_2 + Datalog formulas, all Σ_I–atoms in $\neg(\phi' \wedge Q')$ are either constant atoms or have restricted occurrences, so ψ is a correct C_r^2 + Datalog + bsr formula. We now prove, that $\varphi \models \varphi'$ if and only if ψ is unsatisfiable. Let Σ be a dictionary of formulas ϕ and ϕ' (in particular $\Sigma_P \cup \Sigma_{P'} \subseteq \Sigma$). Let M be an arbitrary structure over Σ. Then $M \models \phi \wedge P \wedge Q$ if and only if the least extension of M wrt. P models $\phi \wedge P$, that is, $M_P \models \phi \wedge Q$. Since $\Sigma_P \cap \Sigma_{P'} = \emptyset$, this is equivalent to $M_{P\wedge P'} \models \phi \wedge Q$. Similarly, $M \models \phi' \wedge P' \wedge Q'$ is equivalent to $M_{P\wedge P'} \models \phi' \wedge Q'$. Therefore, by definition of entailment, $\phi \wedge P \wedge Q \not\models \phi' \wedge P' \wedge Q'$ if and only if there exists a structure M, such that $M_{P\wedge P'} \models \phi \wedge Q$ and $M_{P\wedge P'} \not\models \phi' \wedge Q'$, that is, if $(\phi \wedge Q \wedge \neg(\phi' \wedge Q)) \wedge (P \wedge P')$ is satisfiable. □

We now give a polynomial translation from satisfiability of C^2_r + Datalog + bsr to finite satisfiability of C^2. We start by removing positive occurrences of non-constant Σ_I–atoms.

Proposition 4. *Let $\varphi = \phi \wedge P$ be a C^2_r +* Datalog + bsr *formula. Then there exists C^2_r +* Datalog + bsr *formula $\varphi' = \phi' \wedge P$, such that φ' is satisfiable if and only if φ is satisfiable and no atom of the form $p(x)$ (for a variable x and $p(\cdot) \in \Sigma_I$) occurs positively in ϕ'.*

Proof. Assume w.l.o.g. that ϕ is in negation normal form. By the definition of C^2_r + Datalog + bsr, each positive occurrence of an atom $p(x)$ is in the scope of $\exists$ quantifiers only. In particular, the variable x is existentially quantified, so it can be skolemized. This process replaces x by a fresh constant. By iteration a required formula ϕ' can be obtained. □

Definition 10 (Translation from C^2_r + Datalog + bsr **to C^2).** *Let $\varphi = \phi \wedge P$ be a formula of C^2_r +* Datalog + bsr *over the vocabulary $\Sigma_E \cup \Sigma_I$, such that no atom of the form $p(x)$ ($p(\cdot) \in \Sigma_I$ and x is a variable) occurs positively in ϕ. Let Σ_P be the set of binary relations from $P = \{P_1, \ldots, P_k\}$ and let Σ be a vocabulary containing $\Sigma_E \cup \Sigma_I$ and predicates $const(\cdot)$, $\{p(c)\text{-}node_q(\cdot), p(c)\text{-}edge_q(\cdot,\cdot), p(c)\text{-}leaf_q(\cdot) \mid p, q \in \Sigma_I, c \in \Sigma_E\}$. The translation $\tau(\varphi)$ of φ to C^2 over Σ is the conjunction of the following formulas.*

1. ϕ
2. $\forall x\, const(x) \leftrightarrow \bigvee_{c\in\Sigma_E} x = c$
3. $$\bigwedge_{i=1}^{k} \forall v\, (\neg const(v) \rightarrow \exists^{\leq 1} u(\bigvee_{r(\cdot,\cdot)\in\Sigma_P^i} r(u,v)))$$
   where $\Sigma_P^1, \ldots, \Sigma_P^k$ are vocabularies of binary symbols used by clauses from slices $P_1, \ldots, P_k$ respectively,
4. $$\bigwedge_{i=1}^{k} \bigwedge_{r(\cdot,\cdot)\in\Sigma_P^i} \bigwedge_{s(\cdot,\cdot)\in\Sigma_P^i, s\neq r} \forall u \forall v\, (r(u,v) \wedge s(u,v) \rightarrow const(v))$$
5. $$\forall u\; p(u) \leftarrow \bigwedge_{i=1}^{l} \exists v (r_i(u,v) \wedge q_i(v)) \wedge B(u)$$
   for all Datalog clauses $p(u) \leftarrow B(u), r_1(u,v_1), q_1(v_1), \ldots, r_l(u,v_l), q_l(v_l)$ from P,

6.

$$(q(c) \rightarrow \bigvee_{j=1}^{m} (\bigwedge_{i=1}^{l_j} \exists v(r_i^j(c,v) \wedge q_i^j(v) \wedge p(c)\text{-}edge_{q^j}(c,v)) \wedge B^j(c)))$$

and

$$\forall u\ (q(u) \wedge \neg const(u) \wedge p(c)\text{-}node_q(u) \rightarrow \bigvee_{j=1}^{m} (\bigwedge_{i=1}^{l_j} \exists v(r_i^j(u,v) \wedge q_i^j(v) \wedge p(c)\text{-}edge_{q^j}(u,v)) \wedge B^j(u)))$$

for all $q \in \Sigma_I$, *all* $c \in \Sigma_E$ *and all* $p \in \Sigma_I$ *where* $\{q(u) \leftarrow B^j(u) \wedge \bigwedge_{i=1}^{l_j}(r_i^j(u,v_i) \wedge q_i^j(v_i))\}_{j=1}^m$ *is the set of all clauses from P defining the predicate q,*

7.

$$\forall x \forall y\ p(c)\text{-}edge_q(x,y) \wedge \neg const(y) \rightarrow p(c)\text{-}node_q(y)$$

for all $p(\cdot), q(\cdot) \in \Sigma_I$ *and all* $c \in \Sigma_E$

8.

$$\forall x\ p(c)\text{-}edge_q(x,d) \rightarrow p(c)\text{-}leaf_q(d)$$

for all $p(\cdot), q(\cdot) \in \Sigma_I$ *and all* $c, d \in \Sigma_E$,

9.

$$p(c)\text{-}leaf_q(d) \wedge q(d)\text{-}leaf_r(e) \rightarrow p(c)\text{-}leaf_r(e)$$

for all $p(\cdot), q(\cdot), r(\cdot) \in \Sigma_I$ *and all* $c, d, e \in \Sigma_E$

10.

$$\neg p(c)\text{-}leaf_p(c)$$

for all $p(\cdot) \in \Sigma_I$ *and all* $c \in \Sigma_E$.

The intuition behind this translation is the following. First, observe that the conjuncts 3 and 4 express the bounded-sharing restriction. Then we want to rewrite Datalog clauses to implications (conjunct 5), but we need also the reverse directions of these implications — this is done with conjunct 6, separately for elements interpreting and not interpreting constants. Now we are almost done, but this construction possibly leads to cyclic structures (that would correspond to infinite derivations). Thanks to the bounded-sharing restriction it is possible to forbid cycles containing constant elements, which is enough for correctness since only formulas from C_r are allowed. Let $M \models \tau(\varphi)$. Then for any given $p(c)$, such that $M \models p(c)$, the set $\{p(c)\text{-}node_q(e) \mid q \in \Sigma_I \wedge M \models p(c)\text{-}node_q(e)\}$ forms a superset of non-constant nodes of a $p(c) - tree$, the set $\{p(c)\text{-}edge_q(e_1,e_2) \mid q \in \Sigma_I \wedge M \models p(c)\text{-}edge_q(e_1,e_2)\}$ a superset of its edges and finally the set $\{p(c)\text{-}leaf_q(d) \mid q \in \Sigma_I \wedge M \models p(c)\text{-}leaf_q(d)\}$ is a superset of its leaves. This is enforced by conjuncts 6–8. Irreflexivity (conjunct 10) of transitive closure (conjunct 9) of "being a leaf of" relation assures inexistence of cycles. More formally, we have the following proposition.

Proposition 5. *Let* $\varphi = \phi \wedge P$ *be a* C_r^2 + Datalog + bsr *formula. Then* φ *is satisfiable if and only if the* C^2 *formula* $\tau(\varphi)$ *is finitely satisfiable.*

Observe that the size of $\tau(\varphi)$ is polynomial in the size of φ, which together with Proposition 4 gives us the following corollary.

Corollary 1. *The satisfiability problem for* C_r^2 + Datalog + bsr *is in NEXPTIME.*

Together with Proposition 2 and Proposition 3 this gives us our main theorem.

Theorem 1. *The satisfiability and entailment problems for the Bernays-Schönfinkel class with Datalog are in NEXPTIME.*

4 NEXPTIME Lower Bound

In this section we show that the satisfiability problem for the Bernays-Schönfinkel class with Datalog is NEXPTIME-hard. This is done by a reduction from the following version of a tiling problem, which is known [6] to be NEXPTIME-complete.

Definition 11 (Tiling problem).
Instance: *a tuple* $\langle T, H, V, k\rangle$ *where* T *is a finite set of tile colors,* $H, V \subseteq T \times T$ *are binary relations and* k *is a positive integer encoded in binary (on* $\lceil \log k \rceil$ *bits).*
Question: *does there exist a tiling of* $k \times k$ *square by* 1×1 *tiles such that colors of each pair of horizontally adjacent tiles satisfy the relation* H *and colors of each pair of vertically adjacent tiles satisfy* V*?*

If the question in the tiling problem has a positive answer then we say that the instance $\langle T, H, V, k\rangle$ has a solution or that there exists a good tiling for this instance. In the following, for a given instance $\langle T, H, V, k\rangle$ we define a formula φ of the Bernays-Schönfinkel class with Datalog such that φ is satisfiable if and only if there exists an appropriate tiling.

The idea is that any model of the formula describes a good tiling and any such tiling defines a model of φ. The size of the formula is polynomial in $|T| + |H| + |V| + \lceil \log k \rceil$. Using simple Datalog program and simulating two counters by BS_2 formulas it is enforced that any model of φ has $k \times k$ square as a substructure. Is is then enough to constrain pairs of adjacent nodes according to H and V. Conversely any good tiling can be labelled by Σ_E predicates to form model of φ. A detailed description can be found in the full version of the paper.

The constructed monadic Datalog program has only one slice and its query Q is simply a constant Σ_I-atom. There are also no two distinct Σ_I-predicates. Hence, this reduction also establishes NEXPTIME lower bound for the satisfiability and entailment problems for the logic defined in [4].

Theorem 2. *The satisfiability problem for the Bernays-Schönfinkel class with Datalog is NEXPTIME-hard.*

5 Hardness of C_r^2 + Datalog

In Section 3 we have shown that the logic C_r^2 + Datalog + bsr is decidable in NEXPTIME. In this section we show that if we skip the bounded-sharing restriction then the obtained logic C_r^2 + Datalog becomes much harder. Dropping this restriction is quite tempting, because it would allow to reason about data structures that do share substructures, like DAG representations of trees. Here we prove that with the possibility to share structure, the logic becomes powerful enough to express vector addition systems (VAS). The reduction in Section 3 relied on the fact that in order to conform with the least fixed point semantics of Datalog we have to keep cycles on the heap under control, and with the bounded-sharing restriction we have to worry only about cycles with occurrences of constants. Without this restriction we would have to additionally handle cycles that avoid constants, which is out of scope of the C^2 logic.

Vector addition systems [15] is a very simple formalism equivalent to Petri Nets. It is known that its reachability problem is decidable [10,14,12] and EXPSPACE-hard [13], but precise complexity is not known, and after almost 40 years of research it is even not known if the problem is elementary. Below we give an exponential reduction from the reachability problem for VAS to the satisfiability problem for C^2_r + Datalog. Although we believe that C^2_r + Datalog is decidable, it is very unlikely that it has an elementary decision algorithm since existence of such an algorithm implies existence of an elementary algorithm for VAS reachability.

Now we recall definitions from [15]. An n-dimensional vector addition system is an ordered pair $\langle \boldsymbol{v}, W\rangle$ where $\boldsymbol{v}$ is an n-tuple of non-negative integers and W is a finite set of n-tuples of integers. Given two n-tuples $\boldsymbol{x} = \langle x_1, \ldots, x_n\rangle$ and $\boldsymbol{y} = \langle y_1, \ldots, y_n\rangle$ we write $\boldsymbol{x} \leq \boldsymbol{y}$ if $x_i \leq y_i$ for all $i = 1, \ldots, n$ and we define $\boldsymbol{x}+\boldsymbol{y}$ to be the tuple $\langle x_1+y_1, \ldots, x_n+y_n\rangle$. The reachability problem for VAS is the problem whether for a given VAS $\langle \boldsymbol{v}, W\rangle$ there exists a finite sequence $\boldsymbol{w}_1, \ldots, \boldsymbol{w}_m$ such that

- $\boldsymbol{w}_i \in W$ for all $i = 1, \ldots, m$,
- $\boldsymbol{v} + \boldsymbol{w}_1 + \ldots + \boldsymbol{w}_i \geq \boldsymbol{0}$ for all $i = 1, \ldots, m$, and
- $\boldsymbol{v} + \boldsymbol{w}_1 + \ldots + \boldsymbol{w}_m = \boldsymbol{0}$

where $\boldsymbol{0}$ is the n-tuple $\langle 0, \ldots, 0\rangle$.

To reduce the VAS reachability problem to the satisfiability in C^2_r + Datalog we first represent solutions to the reachability problem as directed acyclic graphs and then write a formula that describes such graphs.

Definition 12 (Transition sequence dag). *Let $\langle \boldsymbol{v}, W\rangle$ be an n-dimensional VAS. A transition sequence dag for $\langle \boldsymbol{v}, W\rangle$ is a directed acyclic multigraph G such that*

- *nodes of G are $n_0, n_1, \ldots, n_m$ for some positive integer m,*
- *node n_0 corresponds to vector $\boldsymbol{v}$, each node n_i for $i = 1, \ldots, m$ corresponds to some vector in W,*
- *edges of G are colored with colors numbered from 1 to n (the dimension of the VAS)*
- *if an edge of G starts in n_i and ends in n_j then $i < j$,*
- *if $\boldsymbol{v} = \langle v_1, \ldots, v_n\rangle$ then for all $i = 1, \ldots, n$ there are v_i edges of color i starting in n_0,*
- *if a node n corresponds to a vector $\boldsymbol{w} = \langle w_1, \ldots, w_n\rangle$ and $w_i \geq 0$ then there are w_i edges of color i starting in n, and there are no edges of color i ending in n,*
- *if a node n corresponds to a vector $\boldsymbol{w} = \langle w_1, \ldots, w_n\rangle$ and $w_i \leq 0$ then there are w_i edges of color i ending in n, and there are no edges of color i starting in n.*

Figure 1 shows an example of a transition sequence dag for the vector addition system $\langle\langle 4, 4\rangle, \{\langle -1, -2\rangle, \langle -1, 2\rangle\}\rangle$. Edges of color 1 are drawn with solid arrows while edges of

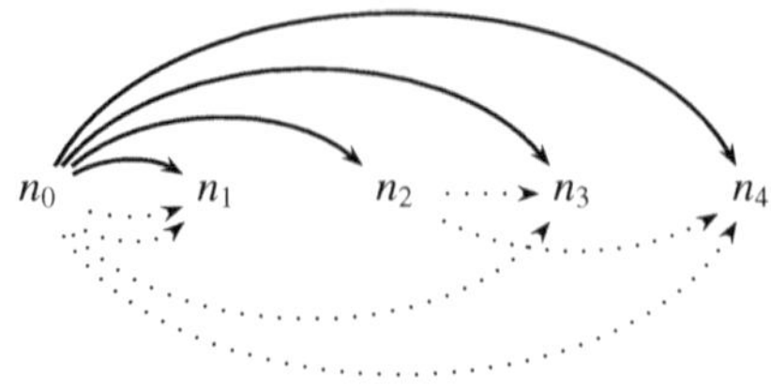

Fig. 1. Transition sequence dag for the vector addition system $\langle\langle 4,4\rangle, \{\langle -1,-2\rangle, \langle -1,2\rangle\}\rangle$

color 2 are drawn with dotted arrows. Nodes n_1, n_3 and n_4 correspond to vector $\langle -1,-2\rangle$; node n_2 corresponds to vector $\langle -1,2\rangle$.

It is not difficult to see that the following lemma holds.

Lemma 2. *The reachability problem for a vector addition system* $\langle \mathbf{v}, W\rangle$ *has a solution if and only if there exists a transition sequence dag for* $\langle \mathbf{v}, W\rangle$.

Now we are ready to give the reduction. Let $\langle \mathbf{v}, W\rangle$ be an n-dimensional vector addition system. We construct a C^2_r + Datalog formula $\varphi = \phi \wedge P$ as follows. The vocabulary Σ_E is $\{e_i(\cdot,\cdot) \mid 1 \le i \le n\} \cup \{e_{i,j}(\cdot,\cdot) \mid 1 \le i \le n \wedge 1 \le j \le \max_j\} \cup \{tosink(\cdot,\cdot), src, sink\}$. We use the predicate e_i for edges of color i. Additionally, to capture multiple edges of the same color starting in the same node we shall use touches of colors: the predicate $e_{i,j}$ is used for touch j of color i. Here j ranges from 1 to the maximum number occurring in a vector in $W \cup \{v\}$ as i-th component, denoted $\max_i$. The constant *src* is used to model the starting node of a transition sequence dag. To have exactly one ending node we introduce additional *sink* node and connect all nodes of outdegree 0 to it.

The vocabulary Σ_I is $\{node^{\mathbf{w}}(\cdot) \mid \mathbf{w} \in W\} \cup \{color_i(\cdot) \mid 1 \le i \le n\} \cup \{start(\cdot), end(\cdot)\}$.

First we give Datalog program P. It consists of the following clauses.

1. $$start(x) \leftarrow x = src \wedge \bigwedge_{i=1}^{n} \bigwedge_{j=1}^{v_i} e_{i,j}(x, y_{i,j}) \wedge color_i(y_{i,j})$$
   where $\mathbf{v} = \langle v_1, \ldots, v_n\rangle$,
2. $color_i(x) \leftarrow e_i(x,y), node^{\mathbf{w}}(y)$ for all $\mathbf{w} \in W$,
3. $$node^{\mathbf{w}}(x) \leftarrow x \ne src \wedge \bigwedge_{k:w_k>0} \bigwedge_{j=1}^{w_k} e_{k,j}(x, y_{k,j}) \wedge color_k(y_{k,j})$$
   for all $\mathbf{w} \in W$ such that $\{k \mid w_k > 0\} \ne \emptyset$
4. $$node^{\mathbf{w}}(x) \leftarrow x \ne src \wedge tosink(x,y), end(y)$$
   for all $\mathbf{w} \in W$ such that $\{k \mid w_k > 0\} = \emptyset$
5. $end(x) \leftarrow x = sink$.

To define the formula ϕ we use two macro-definitions: *forbid-out*(x, S) is an abbreviation for $\forall y\ (\bigwedge_{r(\cdot,\cdot)\in S} \neg r(x,y))$ and *forbid-in*(S, x) is $\forall y\ (\bigwedge_{r(\cdot,\cdot)\in S} \neg r(y,x))$. Then ϕ is defined as the conjunction of

1. Functionality restriction and intersection freeness (expressed as in the proof of Proposition 2 in Section 3 and as in Remark 1 in Section 2 respectively),
2.
$$\forall x\ node^{\boldsymbol{w}}(x) \rightarrow forbid\text{-}out(x, \Sigma_E \setminus \{e_{i,j}(\cdot,\cdot) \mid w_i > 0 \wedge j \leq w_i\}),$$
$$\forall x\ node^{\boldsymbol{w}}(x) \rightarrow forbid\text{-}in(\Sigma_E \setminus \{e_i(\cdot,\cdot) \mid w_i < 0\}, x)$$
$$\forall x\ node^{\boldsymbol{w}}(x) \rightarrow (\bigwedge_{i:w_i<0} (\exists^{=-w_i} y\ e_i(y,x)))$$
for all $\boldsymbol{w} \in W$
3. $\forall y\ color_i(y) \rightarrow \exists^{=1} x\ (\bigvee_{j=1}^{\max_i} (e_{i,j}(x,y) \wedge forbid\text{-}in(\Sigma_E \setminus \{e_{i,j}\}, y)))$ and $\forall y\ color_i(x) \rightarrow forbid\text{-}out(x, \Sigma_E \setminus \{e_i\})$
4. $\forall y\ end(y) \rightarrow forbid\text{-}out(x, \Sigma_E) \wedge forbid\text{-}in(\Sigma_E \setminus \{tosink\}, y)$
5. $\forall x\ start(x) \rightarrow forbid\text{-}in(\Sigma_E, x) \wedge forbid\text{-}out(x, \Sigma_E \setminus \{e_{i,j}(\cdot,\cdot) \mid v_i > 0 \wedge j \leq v_i\})$ where $\boldsymbol{v} = \langle v_1, \ldots, v_n \rangle$
6. $start(src)$.

Proposition 6. *Let $\langle \boldsymbol{v}, W\rangle$ be an n-dimensional vector addition system and let φ be the C_r^2 +* Datalog *formula constructed above. The reachability problem for $\langle \boldsymbol{v}, W\rangle$ has a solution if and only if φ is satisfiable.*

Proof (sketch). ($\Rightarrow$) Assume that $\langle \boldsymbol{v}, W\rangle$ has a solution. Let G be a transition sequence dag for $\langle \boldsymbol{v}, W\rangle$. For every edge $e = \langle n_i, n_j\rangle$ of color k in G introduce an intermediate node n_e; label the node n_e and the edge $\langle n_e, n_j\rangle$ with color k; if e was the l-th edge of color k starting in the node n_i then label the edge $\langle n_i, n_e\rangle$ with touch l of color k. Remove e from G. Add a new node *sink* to the graph and connect all nodes that have no successors in G to it via edges labeled *tosink*. Label node n_0 by constant *src*. Compute the least extension of the constructed structure wrt P. The obtained graph is a model of φ.

($\Leftarrow$) Take a model of φ. By clauses 3 and 4 each element labeled $node^{\boldsymbol{w}}$ has at least required by the vector $\boldsymbol{w}$ number of successors of each color, by conjuncts 2 in ϕ it has exactly required number of successors and predecessors. Clause 2 of P together with conjuncts 3 of ϕ ensures that all elements labeled $color_i$ are intermediate elements on edges of color i. By removing these intermediate elements and the element interpreting the *sink* constant we obtain some graph G. Since G comes from a model of a Datalog program, it is acyclic. A topological sorting of this graph shows that it is a transition sequence dag for $\langle \boldsymbol{v}, W\rangle$, so $\langle \boldsymbol{v}, W\rangle$ has a solution. □

6 Related Work

We refer the reader to [4] for a discussion of relations between our approach and work based on abstract interpretation and shape analysis, fragments of first-order logic with transitive closure or least fixed point, reachability logic, monadic second order logic, graph logics based on C^2, separation logic and bounded model checking. More recent work includes [1,19,11,2,3]. The last three papers focus on reasoning about lists and cannot express properties like reachability in a tree between a pair of program variables. In [1] the authors are able to analyze trees without sharing by simulating them by a set of converging lists. They then apply abstraction refinement framework and verify a finite-state over-approximation of the input program. In contrast, we allow bounded sharing and in our bounded-model-checking application we check properties of an under-approximation (due to a bounded execution of a program) of an infinite-state system. It seems that in terms of expressibility the logic most related to ours is the one from [19]. The exact difference in expressive power needs to be investigated, but the two logics differ in terms of complexity and underlying decision procedures. The satisfiability problem for the logic in [19] has NEXPTIME lower bound and elementary upper bound and it is based on a translation to monadic second-order logic on trees (the authors say that they have another doubly-exponential procedure, but it is not published).

7 Conclusion and Future Work

We extended the work from [4] on bounded model checking of imperative programs that manipulate dynamically allocated pointer structures on the heap. We improved the complexity of this method and increased the expressibility of the logic. We solved the entailment problem which opens the possibilities to use the logic not only in bounded model checking but also in verification.

Our algorithms are based on a translation to two-variable logic with counting quantifiers (C^2). One may ask why we do not use directly this logic. The most important reason is that in Datalog it is relatively easy to express common data structures; the semantics based on least fixed points allows to control in a simple way (a)cyclicity of these structures. Trying to express it in C^2 leads to formulas like our translation, which is of course too complicated to be used. Foe example, the translation of the specification of a tree from Example 1 heavily depends on the context (in particular, used variables) of the source program and may have hundreds of conjuncts.

There are several possibilities for future work. An obvious one is to implement the method. Another one is investigation of applications in verification. Still another one is further extension of the expressibility. Although we have relaxed some restrictions from [4] (now we are able to express lists that may share some nodes or that are forbidden to share nodes), we are still not able to express DAG representations of trees. In a separate work (not published) we have developed a direct algorithm (not based on a translation to C^2) for satisfiability of the Bernays-Schönfinkel class with Datalog; we believe that it will be more suitable for implementation and that it will allow us to express quantitative properties like a tree being balanced.

References

1. Balaban, I., Pnueli, A., Zuck, L.D.: Shape analysis of single-parent heaps. In: Cook, B., Podelski, A. (eds.) VMCAI 2007. LNCS, vol. 4349, pp. 91–105. Springer, Heidelberg (2007)
2. Bansal, K., Brochenin, R., Lozes, E.: Beyond shapes: Lists with ordered data. In: Castagna, G. (ed.) ESOP 2009. LNCS, vol. 5502, pp. 425–439. Springer, Heidelberg (2009)
3. Bouajjani, A., Drăgoi, C., Enea, C., Sighireanu, M.: A logic-based framework for reasoning about composite data structures. In: Bravetti, M., Zavattaro, G. (eds.) CONCUR 2009 - Concurrency Theory. LNCS, vol. 5710, pp. 178–195. Springer, Heidelberg (2009)

4. Charatonik, W., Georgieva, L., Maier, P.: Bounded model checking of pointer programs. In: Ong, L. (ed.) CSL 2005. LNCS, vol. 3634, pp. 397–412. Springer, Heidelberg (2005)
5. Charatonik, W., Witkowski, P.: On the complexity of the Bernays-Schönfinkel class with datalog. Full version, http://www.ii.uni.wroc.pl/~pwit/BSD-full.pdf
6. Fürer, M.: The computational complexity of the unconstrained limited domino problem (with implications for logical decision problems). In: Proceedings of the Symposium "Rekursive Kombinatorik" on Logic and Machines: Decision Problems and Complexity, London, UK, pp. 312–319. Springer, London (1984)
7. Grädel, E., Otto, M., Rosen, E.: Undecidability results on two-variable logics. In: Reischuk, R., Morvan, M. (eds.) STACS 1997. LNCS, vol. 1200, pp. 249–260. Springer, Heidelberg (1997)
8. Graedel, E., Otto, M., Rosen, E.: Two-variable logic with counting is decidable. In: LICS 1997: Proceedings of the 12th Annual IEEE Symposium on Logic in Computer Science, Washington, DC, USA, p. 306. IEEE Computer Society, Los Alamitos (1997)
9. Immerman, N., Rabinovich, A., Reps, T., Sagiv, M., Yorsh, G.: The boundary between decidability and undecidability for transitive-closure logics. In: Marcinkowski, J., Tarlecki, A. (eds.) CSL 2004. LNCS, vol. 3210, pp. 160–174. Springer, Heidelberg (2004)
10. Kosaraju, S.R.: Decidability of reachability in vector addition systems (preliminary version). In: Proceedings of the Fourteenth Annual ACM Symposium on Theory of Computing, pp. 267–281 (1982)
11. Lahiri, S., Qadeer, S.: Back to the future: revisiting precise program verification using smt solvers. In: POPL 2008: Proceedings of the 35th annual ACM SIGPLAN-SIGACT symposium on Principles of programming languages, pp. 171–182. ACM Press, New York (2008)
12. Leroux, J.: The general vector addition system reachability problem by presburger inductive invariants. In: Proceedings of the 24th Annual IEEE Symposium on Logic in Computer Science, pp. 4–13 (2009)
13. Lipton, R.J.: The Reachability Problem Requires Exponential Space, Technical Report 62, Yale University, Department of Computer Science (January 1976)
14. Mayr, E.W.: An algorithm for the general petri net reachability problem. SIAM J. Comput. 13(3), 441–460 (1984)
15. Nas, B.O.: Reachability problems in vector addition systems. The American Mathematical Monthly 80(3), 292–295 (1973)
16. Pacholski, L., Szwast, W., Tendera, L.: Complexity of two-variable logic with counting. In: LICS 1997: Proceedings of the 12th Annual IEEE Symposium on Logic in Computer Science, Washington, DC, USA, p. 318. IEEE Computer Society, Los Alamitos (1997)
17. Pacholski, L., Szwast, W., Tendera, L.: Complexity results for first-order two-variable logic with counting. SIAM J. Comput. 29(4), 1083–1117 (2000)
18. Pratt-Hartmann, I.: Complexity of the two-variable fragment with counting quantifiers. J. of Logic, Lang. and Inf. 14(3), 369–395 (2005)
19. Yorsh, G., Rabinovich, A., Sagiv, M., Meyer, A., Bouajjani, A.: A logic of reachable patterns in linked data-structures. Journal of Logic and Algebraic Programming 73(1-2), 111–142 (2007)

Magically Constraining the Inverse Method Using Dynamic Polarity Assignment

Kaustuv Chaudhuri

INRIA Saclay, France
kaustuv.chaudhuri@inria.fr

Abstract. Given a logic program that is terminating and mode-correct in an idealised Prolog interpreter (i.e., in a top-down logic programming engine), a bottom-up logic programming engine can be used to compute exactly the same set of answers as the top-down engine for a given mode-correct query by rewriting the program and the query using the Magic Sets Transformation (MST). In previous work, we have shown that focusing can logically characterise the standard notion of bottom-up logic programming if atomic formulas are statically given a certain polarity assignment. In an analogous manner, dynamically assigning polarities can characterise the effect of MST without needing to transform the program or the query. This gives us a new proof of the completeness of MST in purely logical terms, by using the general completeness theorem for focusing. As the dynamic assignment is done in a general logic, the essence of MST can potentially be generalised to larger fragments of logic.

1 Introduction

It is now well established that two operational "dialects" of logic programming—top-down (also known as backward chaining or goal-directed) in the style of Prolog, and bottom-up (or forward chaining or program-directed) in the style of hyperresolution—can be expressed in the uniform lexicon of polarity and focusing in the cut-free sequent calculus for a general logic such as intuitionistic logic [8]. The difference in these diametrically opposite styles of logic programming amounts to a static and global *polarity assignment* to the atomic formulas. Such a *logical characterisation* allows a general theorem proving strategy for the sequent calculus, which might be backward (goal sequent to axioms) as in tableau methods or forward (axioms to goal sequent) like in the inverse method, to implement either forward or backward chaining (or any combination) for logic programs by selecting the polarities for the atoms appropriately. Focused inverse method provers have been built for linear logic [4], intuitionistic logic [16], bunched logic [10] and several modal logics [11] in recent years.

The crucial ingredient for the characterisation is that polarities and focusing are sufficiently general that all static polarity assignments are complete [8,1]. The two assignments may be freely mixed for different atoms, which will produce hybrid strategies. The proofs are very different: in a standard example with Fibonacci numbers, one assignment admits exponentially sized derivations, while the other has only the linear proofs. Even more importantly, the search space for proofs is wildly different for different assignments. Which static assignment to pick is not always obvious and very difficult to perform automatically, as was noted in the experiments in [8,16].

C. Fermüller and A. Voronkov (Eds.): LPAR-17, LNCS 6397, pp. 202–216, 2010.

In this paper, we propose to look at *dynamic polarity assignment* as a means to do better than static assignment for certain well-known classes of problems. To our knowledge, dynamic assignment of polarities has been investigated only once before [17]; however, the notion of assignment there is a means of incorporating tables into proof objects using new atomic cut rules with asymmetric assignments to the cut atoms. Our proposal, in contrast, retains the *same* inference rules as ordinary focusing, but dynamically specialises them based on polarity assignments performed at runtime; this lets us reuse the strong proof-theoretic results about focusing. Note that "dynamic polarity assignment" is not a particular algorithm but a general class of approaches for controlling search behaviour. It is useful to think of it by analogy with ordering strategies in resolution theorem proving.

In particular, we give a dynamic assignment strategy that implements the effect of the so-called *magic sets transformation* [3,19,15], which is a program transformation that constrains forward chaining to have the same set of answers as backward chaining. It is difficult to show that the transformation has this intended property. Moreover, since it is a global transformation on the program, that might even (in the general case) depend on the query, it is not modular and compositional. Our proposal reconstructs magic sets and not only avoids the transformation but also gives a characterises them in the common lexicon of focusing and polarities. That is, the magic sets approach is just a special case of dynamic polarity assignment, in much the same way as forward and backward chaining for Horn clauses are just special cases of static polarity assignment.

We limit our attention in this paper to the focused inverse method [4] as the particular general search strategy for the sequent calculus. Intuitively (but not precisely; see sec. 3), this method "compiles" a clause into an inference rule as follows:

$$\texttt{sum (s X) Y (s Z) :- sum X Y Z.} \quad \longrightarrow \quad \frac{\vdash \texttt{sum}\ x\ y\ z}{\vdash \texttt{sum}\ (\texttt{s}\ x)\ y\ (\texttt{s}\ z)}$$

When this inference rule is read from premise to conclusion, the interpretation is of forward chaining on the corresponding clause. Such rules can be repeatedly applied to produce an infinite number of new sequents differing only in the number of ss, which prevents *saturation* even for queries with a finite backward chaining search space. With such clauses, forward chaining cannot appeal to *negation by failure*, unlike backward chaining. We show how to use dynamic polarity assignment to instead produce a new side condition on such inference rules: the conclusion ($\texttt{sum}\ (\texttt{s}\ x)\ y\ (\texttt{s}\ z)$) must be negatively polarised for the rule to be applicable. The atoms are polarised negatively by carefully selecting only those atoms that are in the *base* of the logic program.

One important feature of this re-examination of the magic sets approach is that, because it is performed in a more general setting, we can potentially generalise it to larger fragments of logic such as the uniform fragment. As it does not change the underlying proof system, it can potentially co-exist with other strategies. For example, if the dynamic assignment algorithm gets stuck, the remaining atoms can be polarised in some other fashion and the inverse method resumed without losing completeness.

The rest of this paper is organised as follows. In sec. 2 the magic sets transformation is sketched by way of example. Section 3 then summarises the design of the focused inverse method and static polarity assignment. Section 4 introduces dynamic polarity assignment and shows how to use it to implement the magic sets restriction (sec. 4.2).

Finally, sec. 5 discusses the conclusions and scope of future work on dynamic polarity assignment.

2 Magic Sets Transformation

This section contains a quick overview of the *magic sets transformation* for logic programs. We use the "core" version presented in [15], which is less general than some other designs in the literature [3,19] but also easier to explain and reason about. The logic programs we will consider are made up of Horn clauses and satisfy a global *well-modedness* criterion.

Definition 1 (abstract syntax of Horn clauses). *A* Horn clause *is an iterated implication of atomic formulas that is implicitly universally closed over all its variables. That is, Horn clauses $(C, D, \ldots)$ satisfy the following grammar:*

$$C, D, \ldots ::= a\,\vec{t} \;\big|\; a\,\vec{t} \rightarrow C \qquad\qquad t, s, \ldots ::= x \;\big|\; f\,\vec{t}$$

where a ranges over predicate symbols, f over function symbols, and x over variables. The notation $\vec{t}$ stands for a list, possibly empty, of terms.

Note that the clause `a :- b, ..., z` in a Prolog-like concrete syntax would be written as `z` $\rightarrow \cdots \rightarrow$ `b` $\rightarrow$ `a` in the above abstract syntax that is, the order of the clauses in the body is reversed. Many extensions of this definition of Horn clauses exist in the literature, but they are all generally equivalent to this fragment. A *logic program* is an unordered collection of Horn clauses where each predicate and function symbol has a unique arity. (We do not consider particular orderings of the clauses because we are not interested in the operational semantics of a particular logic programming language.)

Definition 2 (moding). *Every predicate symbol of arity n can be assigned a* mode, *which is a string of length n composed of the characters* `i` *and* `o`, *which are mnemonics for "input" and "output" respectively. A mode assignment to all predicates in a logic program is called a* moding. *The* inputs *of a predicate with respect to a mode are those arguments corresponding to the occurrences of* `i` *in the mode; likewise, the* outputs *are the arguments corresponding to* `o` *in the mode.*

Definition 3 (well-modedness). *All the following are with respect to a given moding:*

- *A goal query is* well-moded *iff its inputs are ground.*
- *A clause $a_1\,\vec{t_1} \rightarrow \cdots \rightarrow a_n\,\vec{t_n} \rightarrow b\,\vec{s}$ is* well-moded *iff for all $i \in 1..n$, the variables in the inputs of $a_i\,\vec{t_i}$ are contained in the union of the variables in the outputs of $a_j\,\vec{t_j}$ for $i < j \leq n$ and of the variables in the inputs of $b\,\vec{s}$.*
- *A logic program is* well-moded *iff every clause in it is well-moded.*

The definition of well-modedness for non-unit clauses intuitively states that, in a right-to-left reading of the clause, the inputs of an atomic formula must be defined by the outputs of earlier atomic formulas and the inputs of the head. Given a well-moded program and query, every derivation of an instance of the query from the program will be ground (for the proof, see [2]).

Consider the motivating example from [15]: computing the sum of the elements of a list of natural numbers. The clauses of the program are as follows in Prolog style.

```
(* mode lsum = io *)
lsum [] 0.
lsum (X :: Y) K :- lsum Y J, sum X J K. (* mode sum = iio *)
sum 0 X X.
sum (s X) Y (s Z) :- sum X Y Z.
```

This program is well-moded because the outputs flow into the inputs from left to right in the body of the clauses. A query such as `?- lsum [1, 2, 3] X` is well-moded because the input is ground, while a query such as `?- lsum X 20` is not well-moded.

To prove a well-moded query, the *backward chaining* or *top-down logic programming* approach matches the goal with the heads of the clauses in the program, and for each successful match, replaces the goal with the matched instance of the body of the clause as new subgoals. A well-moded program is said to be *terminating* if there are no infinite backward chaining derivations for a well-moded query.

The *forward chaining* or *bottom-up logic programming* strategy starts from the unit clauses in the program, matches the body of a clause with these clauses, and adds the most general instance of the matched head as a new clause. This is iterated until (a generalisation of) the goal query is derived. This direction is not quite as obviously goal-directed as backward chaining, but it has many fundamental merits. It builds a database of computed facts that are all mutually non-interfering, and therefore requires no backtracking or global, stateful updates. Moreover, facts and therefore derivations are implicitly shared, so the loop detection issue that plagues backward chaining does not apply here.

However, forward chaining suffers from the obvious problem that it over-approximates the query, performing a lot of wasteful search. Fortunately, it is possible to constrain forward chaining for a given program and query such that the algorithm will *saturate*, *i.e.*, reach a state where no new facts can be generated, iff the query terminates in backward chaining. This is achieved by rewriting the program and the query so that the forward algorithm approximates backward search.

The common element of the approaches to constrain forward chaining is the notion of a *magic set*, which is an abstract representation of the *base* of the program [15]. We shall illustrate it here with the example above. For each predicate a, a new magic predicate a' is added that has the same arity as the input arity of the original predicate. Then, each clause of the program is transformed to depend on the magic predicate applied to the inputs of the head. That is, we obtain the following rewritten clauses:

```
lsum [] 0 :- lsum' [].
lsum (X :: Y) K :- lsum' (X :: Y), lsum Y J, sum X J K.
sum 0 X X :- sum' 0 X.
sum (s X) Y (s Z) :- sum' (s X) Y, sum X Y Z.
```

As there are no longer any unit clauses, forward chaining cannot begin without some additional input. This is provided in the form of the magic version of the goal query as a new unit clause: `lsum' [1, 2, 3]`. Finally, clauses are added for the magic predicates to propagate information about the base. For each non-unit clause, there is one propagation rule for each predicate in the body of the clause. In this example, they are:

```
lsum' Y :- lsum' (X :: Y).
sum' X J :- lsum' (X :: Y), lsum Y J.
sum' X Y :- sum' (s X) Y.
```

Forward chaining on this transformed program will compute the same instances of the query as backward chaining on the original program and query.

The correctness of this *magic sets transformation* is generally quite difficult to prove. One of the most readable proofs was provided by Mascellani *et al* [15]; that paper also contains a fully formal definition of the transformation and a number of other examples. However, all transformational approaches suffer from the same problems outlined in the introduction: they are not modular and compositional. In the rest of the paper we will give a different explanation of the magic sets transformation that does not suffer from these problems, and is moreover manifestly correct because of general proof theoretic properties of focused sequent calculi.

3 The Focused Inverse Method

In this section we review the focused inverse method for intuitionistic logic. Most of the material of this section has already appeared in in [4,8,16,9] and in references therefrom. Like other recent accounts of intuitionistic focusing [16,6], we adopt a polarised syntax for formulas. Intuitively, *positive* formulas (*i.e.*, formulas of the positive *polarity*) are those formulas whose left sequent rules are invertible and *negative* formulas are those whose right rules are invertible. Every polarised logical connective is unambiguously in one of these two classes. In order to prevent an overlap, we also *assign* the atomic formulas individually to one of the two classes. Any polarity assignment for the atoms is complete [8].

Definition 4 (syntax). *We follow this grammar:*

$$P, Q ::= p \mid P \otimes Q \mid \mathbf{1} \mid P \oplus Q \mid \mathbf{0} \mid \exists x.\, P \mid {\downarrow}N \qquad N, M ::= n \mid N \mathbin{\&} M \mid \top \mid P \multimap N \mid \forall x.\, N \mid {\uparrow}P$$
$$p ::= \langle a\,\vec{t}, +\rangle \qquad n ::= \langle a\,\vec{t}, -\rangle \qquad P^- ::= P \mid n \qquad N^+ ::= N \mid p$$

- Formulas *($A, B, \ldots$) are either* positive *($P, Q, \ldots$) or* negative *($N, M, \ldots$).*
- Atomic formulas *(or* atoms*) ($p, q, n, m, \ldots$) are also polarised. Each atom consists of an atomic predicate ($a, b, \ldots$) applied to a (possibly empty) list of terms, and a* polarity. *We shall generally abuse notation and write $\langle a\,\vec{t}, \pm\rangle$ as $a^{\pm}\,\vec{t}$, even though it is the atom and not the predicate that carries the polarity.*
- Left passive formulas *($N^+, M^+, \ldots$) and* right passive formulas *($P^-, Q^+, \ldots$) are used to simplify the presentation of rules.*

We use connectives from polarised linear logic instead of the more usual intuitionistic connectives to make the polarities explicit. The polarity *switching* connectives $\downarrow$ and $\uparrow$ are only bureaucratic and do not change the truth value of their operands. Both $\otimes$ and & have the same truth value as the usual intuitionistic conjunction $\wedge$—that is, $A \otimes B \equiv A \mathbin{\&} B$ if we ignore polarities and omit the switching connectives $\downarrow$ and $\uparrow$—just different inference rules. In other formulations of polarised intuitionistic logic these two polarisations of conjunction are sometimes written as $\wedge^+$ or $\wedge^-$ [14], but we prefer the familiar notation from linear logic. Likewise, $\oplus$ has the same truth value as $\vee$ and $\multimap$ the same truth value as $\rightarrow$.

The inference system for this logic will be given in the form of focused sequent calculus rules [1,16]. We have the following kinds of sequents:

$$\Gamma \vdash [P] \quad \text{right-focus on } P \qquad \Gamma\ ;\ [N] \vdash Q^- \quad \text{left-focus on } N$$

$$\underbrace{\Gamma\ ;\ \Omega \vdash \begin{cases} N\ ;\ \cdot \\ \cdot\ ;\ Q^- \end{cases}}_{\gamma} \quad \text{left-active on } \Omega \text{ and right-active on } N$$

where: $\Gamma ::= \cdot \mid \Gamma, N^-$ is called the *passive context* and $\Omega ::= \cdot \mid \Omega, P$ is the *active context*. Both contexts are interpreted as multisets (admits only exchange). We adopt the usual convention of denoting multiset union with commas. It will turn out that the passive context is also a set, but this is an admissible principle and does not depend on primitive weakening and contraction rules. Note therefore that Γ_1, Γ_2 is not the same as $\Gamma_1 \cup \Gamma_2$; if the latter interpretation is needed, it will be written explicitly.

(active)

$$\frac{\Gamma\ ;\ \Omega \vdash \cdot\ ;\ n}{\Gamma\ ;\ \Omega \vdash n\ ;\ \cdot}\ \text{NR} \qquad \frac{\Gamma\ ;\ \Omega \vdash \cdot\ ;\ P}{\Gamma\ ;\ \Omega \vdash {\uparrow}P\ ;\ \cdot}\ {\uparrow}\text{R} \qquad \frac{\Gamma\ ;\ \Omega \vdash N\ ;\ \cdot \quad \Gamma\ ;\ \Omega \vdash M\ ;\ \cdot}{\Gamma\ ;\ \Omega \vdash N \,\&\, M\ ;\ \cdot}\ \&\text{R}$$

$$\frac{}{\Gamma\ ;\ \Omega \vdash \top\ ;\ \cdot}\ \top\text{R} \qquad \frac{\Gamma\ ;\ \Omega, P \vdash N\ ;\ \cdot}{\Gamma\ ;\ \Omega \vdash P \multimap N\ ;\ \cdot}\ {\multimap}\text{R} \qquad \frac{\Gamma\ ;\ \Omega \vdash N[a/x]\ ;\ \cdot}{\Gamma\ ;\ \Omega \vdash \forall x.\, N\ ;\ \cdot}\ \forall\text{R}^a$$

$$\frac{\Gamma, p\,\vec{t}\ ;\ \Omega \vdash \gamma}{\Gamma\ ;\ \Omega, p\,\vec{t} \vdash \gamma}\ \text{PL} \qquad \frac{\Gamma, N\ ;\ \Omega \vdash \gamma}{\Gamma\ ;\ \Omega, {\downarrow}N \vdash \gamma}\ {\downarrow}\text{L} \qquad \frac{\Gamma\ ;\ \Omega, P, Q \vdash \gamma}{\Gamma\ ;\ \Omega, P \otimes Q \vdash \gamma}\ \otimes\text{L} \qquad \frac{\Gamma\ ;\ \Omega \vdash \gamma}{\Gamma\ ;\ \Omega, \mathbf{1} \vdash \gamma}\ \mathbf{1}\text{L}$$

$$\frac{\Gamma\ ;\ \Omega, P \vdash \gamma \quad \Gamma\ ;\ \Omega, Q \vdash \gamma}{\Gamma\ ;\ \Omega, P \oplus Q \vdash \gamma}\ \oplus\text{L} \qquad \frac{}{\Gamma\ ;\ \Omega, \mathbf{0} \vdash \gamma}\ \mathbf{0}\text{L} \qquad \frac{\Gamma\ ;\ \Omega, N[a/x] \vdash \gamma}{\Gamma\ ;\ \Omega, \exists x.\, N \vdash \gamma}\ \exists\text{L}^a$$

(right focus)

$$\frac{}{\Gamma, p \vdash [p]}\ \text{PR} \qquad \frac{\Gamma\ ;\ \cdot \vdash N\ ;\ \cdot}{\Gamma \vdash [{\downarrow}N]}\ {\downarrow}\text{R}$$

$$\frac{\Gamma \vdash [P] \quad \Gamma \vdash [Q]}{\Gamma \vdash [P \otimes Q]}\ \otimes\text{R} \qquad \frac{}{\Gamma \vdash [\mathbf{1}]}\ \mathbf{1}\text{R} \qquad \frac{\Gamma \vdash [P_i]}{\Gamma \vdash [P_1 \oplus P_2]}\ \oplus\text{R}_i \qquad \frac{\Gamma\ ;\ [P[t/x]]}{\Gamma \vdash [\exists x.\, P]}\ \exists\text{R}$$

(left focus)

$$\frac{}{\Gamma\ ;\ [n] \vdash n}\ \text{NL} \qquad \frac{\Gamma\ ;\ P \vdash \cdot\ ;\ Q^-}{\Gamma\ ;\ [{\uparrow}P] \vdash Q^-}\ {\uparrow}\text{L}$$

$$\frac{\Gamma\ ;\ [N_i] \vdash Q^-}{\Gamma\ ;\ [N_1 \,\&\, N_2] \vdash Q^-}\ \&\text{L}_i \qquad \frac{\Gamma \vdash [P] \quad \Gamma\ ;\ [N] \vdash Q^-}{\Gamma\ ;\ [P \multimap N] \vdash Q^-}\ {\multimap}\text{L} \qquad \frac{\Gamma\ ;\ [N[t/x]] \vdash Q^-}{\Gamma\ ;\ [\forall x.\, N] \vdash Q^-}\ \forall\text{L}$$

(decision)

$$\frac{\Gamma \vdash [P]}{\Gamma\ ;\ \cdot \vdash \cdot\ ;\ P}\ \text{DR} \qquad \frac{\Gamma, N\ ;\ [N] \vdash Q^-}{\Gamma, N\ ;\ \cdot \vdash \cdot\ ;\ Q^-}\ \text{DL}$$

Fig. 1. Focused sequent calculus for polarised first-order intuitionistic logic. In the rules $\exists\text{L}^a$ and $\forall\text{R}^a$ the *parameter* a is not free in the conclusion.

The focused sequent calculus will be presented in a stylistic variant of Andreoli's original formulation [1]. The full set of rules is in fig. 1. It has an intensional reading in terms of *phases*. At the boundaries of phases are sequents of the form $\Gamma\,;\,\cdot \vdash \cdot\,;\,Q^-$, which are known as *neutral sequents*. Proofs of neutral sequents proceed (reading from conclusion to premises) as follows:

1. *Decision*: a *focus* is selected from a neutral sequent, either from the passive context or from the right. This focused formula is moved to its corresponding focused zone using one of the rules DL or DR (D = "decision", and R/L = "right"/"left"). The left rule copies the focused formula.
2. *Focused phase*: for a left or a right focused sequent, left or right focus rules are applied to the formula under focus. These focused rules are all non-invertible in the (unfocused) sequent calculus—that is, they can fail to apply—and therefore depend on essential choices made in the proof. This is familiar from focusing for linear logic [1,8].
3. *Active phase*: once the switch rules $\downarrow$R and $\uparrow$L are applied, the sequents become active and active rules are applied. The order of the active rules is immaterial as all orderings will produce the same list of neutral sequent premises. In Andreoli's system the irrelevant non-determinism in the order of these rules was removed by treating the active context Ω as ordered; however, we do not fix any particular ordering.

The soundness of this calculus with respect to an unfocused sequent calculus, such as Gentzen's LJ, is obvious. For completeness, we refer the interested reader to a number of published proofs in the literature [8,13,18,12].

The purpose of starting with a polarised syntax and a focused calculus is that we are able to look at derived inference rules for neutral sequents as the basic unit of *steps*. For instance, one of the derived inference rules for the formula $N \triangleq p \oplus q \multimap m \mathbin{\&} (\downarrow l \multimap n)$ in the passive context is given in fig. 2. The instance of PR above forces p to be in the passive context because that is the only rule that can be applied to contruct a sequent of the form $\Delta \vdash [p]$. Likewise, the NL rule forces the right hand side of the conclusion sequent to be the same as the left focused atom n. Finally, the DL rule requires N to already be present in the passive context.

As we observe, focusing *compiles* formulas such as N above, which may be clauses in a program, into (derived) inference rules. Focusing can also produce new *facts*, which

$$\dfrac{\dfrac{\dfrac{}{\Gamma, N, p \vdash [p]}\,\text{PR}}{\Gamma, N, p \vdash [p \oplus q]} \qquad \dfrac{\dfrac{\dfrac{\dfrac{\Gamma, N, p\,;\,\cdot \vdash \cdot\,;\,l}{\Gamma, N, p\,;\,\cdot \vdash l\,;\,\cdot}}{\Gamma, N, p \vdash [\downarrow l]} \qquad \dfrac{}{\Gamma, N, p\,;\,[n] \vdash n}\,\text{NL}}{\Gamma, N, p\,;\,[\downarrow l \multimap n] \vdash n}}{\Gamma, N, p\,;\,[m \mathbin{\&} (\downarrow l \multimap n)] \vdash n}\,\&\text{L}_2}{\dfrac{\Gamma, N, p\,;\,[N] \vdash n}{\Gamma, N, p\,;\,\cdot \vdash \cdot\,;\,n}\,\text{DL}} \qquad \text{i.e.,} \qquad \dfrac{\Gamma, N, p\,;\,\cdot \vdash \cdot\,;\,l}{\Gamma, N, p\,;\,\cdot \vdash \cdot\,;\,n}$$

Fig. 2. One derived inference rule for N

are neutral sequents that have no open premises after applying a derived inference rule. An example would be the case for the derivation above where, instead of $\&L_2$ we were to use $\&L_1$. In this case we would obtain the fact $\Gamma, N, p\ ;\ \cdot \vdash \cdot\ ;\ m$. If the goal were of this form, we would be done.

This property of focusing can be exploited to give a purely proof-theoretic explanation for certain *dialects* of proofs. For Horn clauses, consider the case where all the atoms are negative, *i.e.*clauses are of the form $\forall \vec{x}\,.\,{\downarrow} m_1 \multimap \cdots \multimap {\downarrow} m_j \multimap n$. If clause were named N, then its derived inference rule is:

$$\frac{\Gamma, N\ ;\ \cdot \vdash \cdot\ ;\ m_1[\vec{t}/\vec{x}] \quad \cdots \quad \Gamma, N\ ;\ \cdot \vdash \cdot\ ;\ m_j[\vec{t}/\vec{x}]}{\Gamma, N\ ;\ \cdot \vdash \cdot\ ;\ n[\vec{t}/\vec{x}]}$$

Since the context is the same in all premises and the conclusion, we need only look at the right hand side. If we read the rule from conclusion to premises, then this rule implements back-chaining from an instance of the head of this Horn clause to the corresponding instances of the body of the clause, where the neutral sequents represent the current list of sub-goals. Thus, the general top-down logic programming strategy (or backward chaining) consists of performing goal-directed focused proof search on Horn clauses with negative atoms. If the atoms were all assigned positive polarity instead, then the same goal-directed focused proof search would perform a kind of bottom-up logic programming (or forward chaining). Static polarity assignment for the atoms is therefore a *logical characterisation* of forward and backward chaining strategies. Indeed, if the atoms were not uniformly given the same polarities, then the focused proofs would be a mixture of forward and backward chaining.

3.1 Forward Reasoning and the Inverse Method

An important property of the (cut-free) sequent calculus of fig. 1 is that there is a structural cut-elimination algorithm [8]; as a consequence, the calculus enjoys the subformula property. Indeed, it is possible to state the subformula property in a very strong form that also respects the *sign* of the subformula (*i.e.*, whether it is principal on the left or the right of the sequent) and the *parametricity* of instances (*i.e.*, the subformulas of a right $\forall$ or a left $\exists$ can be restricted to generic instances). We omit a detailed definition and proof here because it is a standard result; see *e.g.* [7] for the definition.

With the strong subformula property, we can restrict the rules of fig. 1 to subformulas of a given fixed *goal sequent*. It then becomes possibile to apply the inference rules in a forward manner, from premises to conclusion. The inputs of such a forward reasoning strategy would be the facts that correspond to focusing on the passive formulas and operands of the switch connectives in the goal sequent, subject to the subformula restriction. That is, the initial sequents (in the rules PR and NL) correspond to atomic formulas that are both a left and a right signed subformula of the goal sequent. From these initial sequents we apply the (subformula-restricted) inference rules forward until we derive (a generalisation of) the goal sequent. In order to implement the calculus, the axiomatic rules such as **1**R are refined to omit the passive context; the additive rules are turned into multiplicative rules and an explicit rule of *factoring* added; and the calculus is lifted to free variables with identity replaced with unifiability, and only most general instances are considered. This core "recipe" is outlined in the *Handbook* article on the inverse method [9] and is not repeated here.

One optimisation not mentioned in [9] but implemented in many inverse method provers [4,16] is *globalisation*: the forward version of the DL rule is specialized into the following two forms:

$$\frac{\Gamma\,;\,[N] \vdash Q^- \quad N \notin \Gamma_0}{\Gamma, N\,;\,\cdot \vdash \cdot\,;\,Q^-}\,\text{DLF}_1 \qquad \frac{\Gamma\,;\,[N] \vdash Q^- \quad N \in \Gamma_0}{\Gamma\,;\,\cdot \vdash \cdot\,;\,Q^-}\,\text{DLF}_2$$

where Γ_0 is the passive context of the goal sequent. This context is present in every sequent in the backward proof, so there is no need to mention it explicitly in the forward direction. For logic programs, Γ_0 will contain the clauses of the program and it is not important to distinguish between two computed sequents that differ only in the used clauses of the program.

Let us revisit the static polarity assignment question in the forward direction. The forward derived rule for the Horn clause $\forall \vec{x}\,.\,{\downarrow}m_1 \multimap \cdots \multimap {\downarrow}m_j \multimap n \in \Gamma_0$, after lifting to free variables, is:

$$\frac{\Gamma_1\,;\,\cdot \vdash \cdot\,;\,m_1' \quad \cdots \quad \Gamma_j\,;\,\cdot \vdash \cdot\,;\,m_j' \quad \theta = \text{mgu}(\langle m_1,\ldots,m_j\rangle, \langle m_1',\ldots,m_j'\rangle)}{(\Gamma_1,\ldots,\Gamma_n\,;\,\cdot \vdash \cdot\,;\,n)[\theta]}$$

For unit clauses, which provide the initial sequents, the passive context Γ is empty (because there are no premises remaining after globalisation). Therefore, all neutral sequents computed by forward reasoning will have empty passive contexts, giving us the rule:

$$\frac{\cdot\,;\,\cdot \vdash \cdot\,;\,m_1' \quad \cdots \quad \cdot\,;\,\cdot \vdash \cdot\,;\,m_j' \quad \theta = \text{mgu}(\langle m_1,\ldots,m_j\rangle, \langle m_1',\ldots,m_j'\rangle)}{(\cdot\,;\,\cdot \vdash \cdot\,;\,n)[\theta]}$$

Thus, this derived inference rule implements forward chaining for this clause. This situation is dual to the backward reading of the rules of fig. 1 where a static negative assignment to the atoms implemented backward chaining. As expected, a static positive polarity assignment to the atoms implements backward chaining in the forward calculus. The technical details of operational adequacy can be found in [8].

4 Dynamic Polarity Assignment

The previous section demonstrates that we can implement forward chaining (or bottom up logic programming) using the vocabulary of focusing and polarity assignment. For the rest of this paper we shall limit or attention to forward reasoning as the global strategy, with negative polarity assignment for the atoms as our means of implementing forward chaining.

Obviously the benefit of polarity assignment is that completeness is a trivial consequence of the completeness of focusing with respect to any arbitrary, even heterogeneous, polarity assignment for the atoms. Moreover, the completeness of the inverse method merely requires that the rule application strategy be fair. This minimal requirement of fairness does not force us to assign the polarity of all atoms statically, as long as we can guarantee that every atom that is relevant to the proof is eventually assigned a polarity (and that the rest of the inverse method engine is fair). Can we do better than static assignment with dynamic assignment? This section will answer this question affirmatively.

4.1 The Mechanism of Dynamic Polarity Assignment

Let us write unpolarised atoms (*i.e.*, atoms that haven't been assigned a polarity) simply in the form $a\,\vec{t}$, and allow them to be used as both positive and negative formulas in the syntax. That is, we extend the syntax as follows:

$$P, Q, \ldots ::= a\,\vec{t} \mid p \mid P \otimes Q \mid \mathbf{1} \mid P \oplus Q \mid \mathbf{0} \mid \exists x.\, P \mid {\downarrow} N$$
$$N, M, \ldots ::= a\,\vec{t} \mid n \mid N \,\&\, M \mid \top \mid P \multimap N \mid \forall x.\, N \mid {\uparrow} P$$

For example, A Horn clause with unpolarised atoms have the syntax $\forall \vec{x}.\, a_1\,\vec{t_1} \multimap \cdots \multimap a_j\,\vec{t_j} \multimap b\,\vec{s}$ where the $\vec{x}$ are the variables that occur in the terms $\vec{t_1}, \ldots, \vec{t_j}, \vec{s}$.

Consider a variant of the focused inverse method where we allow two kinds of sequents as premises for inference rules: neutral sequents, as before, and sequents that have a focus on an unpolarised atom which we call *proto sequents*. An inference rule with proto sequent premises will be called a *proto rule*.

Definition 5. Environments *($\mathcal{E}, \mathcal{F}, \ldots$) are given by the following grammar:*

$$\mathcal{E}, \ldots ::= \mathcal{P} \mid \mathcal{Q}$$
$$\mathcal{P}, \mathcal{Q}, \ldots ::= \Box \mid \mathcal{P} \otimes Q \mid P \otimes \mathcal{Q} \mid \mathcal{P} \oplus Q \mid P \oplus \mathcal{Q} \mid \exists x.\, \mathcal{P} \mid {\downarrow} \mathcal{N}$$
$$\mathcal{N}, \mathcal{M}, \ldots ::= \Box \mid \mathcal{N} \,\&\, M \mid N \,\&\, \mathcal{M} \mid \mathcal{P} \multimap N \mid P \multimap \mathcal{N} \mid \forall x.\, \mathcal{N} \mid {\uparrow} \mathcal{P}$$

We write $\mathcal{E}(A)$ for the formula formed by replacing the $\Box$ in $\mathcal{E}$ with A, assuming it is syntactically valid. An environment $\mathcal{E}$ is called positive *(resp.* negative*) if $\mathcal{E}(p)$ (resp. $\mathcal{E}(n)$) is syntactically valid for any positive atom p (resp. negative atom n).*

Definition 6 (polarity assignment). *We write $A[a\,\vec{t} \leftarrow +]$ (resp. $A[a\,\vec{t} \leftarrow -]$) to stand for the positive (resp. negative) polarity assignment to the unpolarised atom $a\,\vec{t}$ in the formula A. It has the following recursive definition:*

- *If the unpolarised atom $a\,\vec{t}$ does not occur in A, then $A[a\,\vec{t} \leftarrow \pm] = A$.*
- *If $A = \mathcal{E}(a\,\vec{t})$ and $\mathcal{E}$ is positive, then*

$$A[a\,\vec{t} \leftarrow +] = (\mathcal{E}(a^+\,\vec{t}))[a\,\vec{t} \leftarrow +]$$
$$A[a\,\vec{t} \leftarrow -] = (\mathcal{E}({\downarrow} a^-\,\vec{t}))[a\,\vec{t} \leftarrow -]$$

- *If $A = \mathcal{E}(a\,\vec{t})$ and $\mathcal{E}$ is negative, then*

$$A[a\,\vec{t} \leftarrow +] = (\mathcal{E}({\uparrow} a^+\,\vec{t}))[a\,\vec{t} \leftarrow +]$$
$$A[a\,\vec{t} \leftarrow -] = (\mathcal{E}(a^-\,\vec{t}))[a\,\vec{t} \leftarrow -]$$

This definition is extended in the natural way to contexts, (proto) sequents, and (proto) rules.

Polarity assignment on proto rules generally has the effect of instantiating certain schematic meta-variables. For instance, consider the following proto-rule that corresponds to a left focus on the unpolarised Horn clause $C \triangleq \forall x, y.\, a\ x \multimap b\ y \multimap c\ x\ y$:

$$\frac{\Gamma, C \vdash [a\ s] \quad \Gamma, C \vdash [b\ t] \quad \Gamma, C\ ;\ [c\ s\ t] \vdash Q^-}{\Gamma, C\ ;\ \cdot \vdash \cdot\ ;\ Q^-}$$

All the premises of this rule are proto sequents. Suppose we assign a positive polarity to $a\ s$; this will change the proto rule to:

$$\frac{\Gamma, C \vdash [a^+ s] \quad \Gamma, C \vdash [b\ t] \quad \Gamma, C\ ;\ [c\ s\ t] \vdash Q^-}{\Gamma, C\ ;\ \cdot \vdash \cdot\ ;\ Q^-}$$

(where C' is $C[a\ s \leftarrow +]$). This proto rule actually corresponds to:

$$\frac{\Gamma, C', a^+ s \vdash [b\ t] \quad \Gamma, C', a^+ s\ ;\ [c\ s\ t] \vdash Q^-}{\Gamma, C', a^+ s\ ;\ \cdot \vdash \cdot\ ;\ Q^-}$$

because the only way to proceed further on the first premise is with the PR rule. This instantiates Γ with $\Gamma, a^+ s$. If we now assign a negative polarity to $c\ s\ t$, we would obtain the rule:

$$\frac{\Gamma, C'', a^+ s \vdash [b\ t]}{\Gamma, C'', a^+ s\ ;\ \cdot \vdash \cdot\ ;\ c^- s\ t}$$

(where $C'' = C'[c\ s\ t \leftarrow -]$) which instantiates Q^- to $c^- s\ t$. Finally, if we assign a negative polarity to $b\ t$, we would obtain the ordinary (non-proto) inference rule with neutral premise and conclusion:

$$\frac{\Gamma, C''', a^+ s\ ;\ \cdot \vdash \cdot\ ;\ b^- t}{\Gamma, C''', a^+ s\ ;\ \cdot \vdash \cdot\ ;\ c^- s\ t}$$

(where $C''' = C''[b\ t \leftarrow -]$).

4.2 Implementing Magic Sets with Dynamic Polarity Assignment

This sub-section contains the main algorithm of this paper – a dynamic polarity assignment strategy that implements magic sets in the inverse method. The key feature of the algorithm is that it involves no global rewriting of the program clauses, so soundness is a trivial property. Completeness is obtained by showing that the algorithm together with the inverse method performs fairly on well-moded logic programs and queries.

The algorithm consists of dynamically assigning negative polarity to unpolarised atoms. Initially, all atoms in the program are unpolarised and the atom in the goal query is negatively polarised. It maintains the following lists:

- *Seeds*, which is a collection of the negatively polarised atoms;
- *Facts*, which is a list of computed facts which are ordinary neutral sequents;
- *Rules*, which is a list of partially applied, possibly proto, rules.

Whenever a fact is examined by the inner loop of the inverse method, new facts and partially applied (possibly proto) rules are generated. After the inner loop ends (*i.e.*, after all subsumption checks and indexing), the following *seeding step* is repeatedly performed until quiescence.

Definition 7 (seeding step). *For every right-focused proto-sequent in the premise of every proto rule, if the focused atom is mode correct—that is, if the input arguments of the atom are ground—then all instances of that atom for arbitrary outputs are assigned a negative polarity. These new negatively polarised atoms are added to the Seeds.*

For example, if the unpolarised atom sum 3 4 $(f(x))$ has a right focus in a proto rule and sum has mode iio, then all atoms of the form sum 3 4 _ are assigned negative polarity. The seeding step will generate new facts or partially applied rules, which are then handled as usual by the inverse method.

4.3 Example

Let us revisit the example of sec. 2. Let Π_0 be the collection of unpolarised Horn clauses representing the program, *i.e.*:

$$\begin{aligned}\Pi_0 = {} & \mathtt{lsum}\ []\ 0, && (C_1)\\ & \forall x,y,j,k.\ \mathtt{lsum}\ y\ j \multimap \mathtt{sum}\ x\ j\ k \multimap \mathtt{lsum}\ (x :: y)\ k, && (C_2)\\ & \forall x.\ \mathtt{sum}\ 0\ x\ x, && (C_3)\\ & \forall x,y,z.\ \mathtt{sum}\ x\ y\ z \multimap \mathtt{sum}\ (\mathtt{s}\ x)\ y\ (\mathtt{s}\ z) && (C_4)\end{aligned}$$

As before, let the modes be io for lsum and iio for sum. The above program is terminating and mode-correct for this moding. Consider the query lsum $[1,2,3]\ X$, i.e., we are proving the goal sequent:

$$\underbrace{\Pi_0, \forall x.\ \mathtt{lsum}\ [1,2,3]\ x \multimap \mathtt{g}}_{\Gamma_0}\ ;\ \cdot \vdash \cdot\ ;\ \mathtt{g}$$

Since there are no switched subformulas, the only available rules will be for clauses in Γ_0 and the goal g. Using the subformula restriction and globalisation, we would then obtain the following derived proto rules:

$$\frac{\Gamma\ ;\ [\mathtt{lsum}\ []\ 0] \vdash Q^-}{\Gamma\ ;\ \cdot \vdash \cdot\ ;\ Q^-}(C_1) \qquad \frac{\Gamma_1\ ;\ [\mathtt{lsum}\ (x :: y)\ k] \vdash Q^- \quad \Gamma_2 \vdash [\mathtt{lsum}\ y\ j] \quad \Gamma_3 \vdash [\mathtt{sum}\ x\ j\ k]}{\Gamma_1, \Gamma_2, \Gamma_3\ ;\ \cdot \vdash \cdot\ ;\ Q^-}(C_2)$$

$$\frac{\Gamma\ ;\ [\mathtt{sum}\ 0\ x\ x] \vdash Q^-}{\Gamma\ ;\ \cdot \vdash \cdot\ ;\ Q^-}(C_3) \qquad \frac{\Gamma_1\ ;\ [\mathtt{sum}\ (\mathtt{s}\ x)\ y\ (\mathtt{s}\ z)] \vdash Q^- \quad \Gamma_2 \vdash [\mathtt{sum}\ x\ y\ z]}{\Gamma_1, \Gamma_2\ ;\ \cdot \vdash \cdot\ ;\ Q^-}(C_4)$$

$$\frac{\Gamma_1\ ;\ [\mathtt{g}] \vdash Q^- \quad \Gamma_2 \vdash [\mathtt{lsum}\ [1,2,3]\ x]}{\Gamma_1, \Gamma_2\ ;\ \cdot \vdash \cdot\ ;\ Q^-}(\mathtt{g})$$

There are no initial sequents, so we perform some seeding steps. The initial polarity assignment is negative for the goal g; this produces the following instance of (g):

$$\frac{\Gamma_2 \vdash [\mathtt{lsum}\ [1,2,3]\ x]}{\Gamma\ ;\ \cdot \vdash \cdot\ ;\ \mathtt{g}^-}(\mathtt{g}')$$

Now we have a right focus on a well-moded unpolarised atom, *viz.* lsum $[1,2,3]\ x$, so we add $\mathtt{lsum}^-\ [1,2,3]\ \_$ to the *Seeds*. This produces two instances of the proto rule (C_2) depending on the two ways in which the seed can match the proto premises.

$$\frac{\Gamma_1 \vdash [\texttt{lsum}\ [2,3]\ j] \quad \Gamma_2 \vdash [\texttt{sum}\ 1\ j\ k]}{\Gamma_1, \Gamma_2\ ;\ \cdot \vdash \cdot\ ;\ \texttt{lsum}^-\ [1,2,3]\ k}\,(C_{21})$$

$$\frac{\Gamma_1\ ;\ [\texttt{lsum}\ (x :: [1,2,3])\ k] \vdash Q^- \quad \Gamma_2\ ;\ \cdot \vdash \cdot\ ;\ \texttt{lsum}^-\ [1,2,3]\ j \quad \Gamma_3 \vdash [\texttt{sum}\ x\ j\ k]}{\Gamma_1, \Gamma_2, \Gamma_3\ ;\ \cdot \vdash \cdot\ ;\ Q^-}\,(C_{22})$$

The first premise in (C_{21}) is well-moded and will produce further seeds. However, (C_{22}) produces no seeds as there are no proto premises with a right focus on a well-moded unpolarised atom. Continuing the seeding steps for (C_{21}) we produce the following new useful proto rules:

$$\frac{\Gamma_1 \vdash [\texttt{lsum}\ [2]\ j] \quad \Gamma_2 \vdash [\texttt{sum}\ 2\ j\ k]}{\Gamma_1, \Gamma_2\ ;\ \cdot \vdash \cdot\ ;\ \texttt{lsum}^-\ [2,3]\ k}\,(C_{211}) \qquad \frac{\Gamma_1 \vdash [\texttt{lsum}\ []\ j] \quad \Gamma_2 \vdash [\texttt{sum}\ 3\ j\ k]}{\Gamma_1, \Gamma_2\ ;\ \cdot \vdash \cdot\ ;\ \texttt{lsum}^-\ [3]\ k}\,(C_{2111})$$

The rule (C_{2111}) produces a seed $\texttt{lsum}^-\ []\ \_$ that matches the premise of (C_1) to produce our first fact: $\cdot\ ;\ \cdot \vdash \cdot\ ;\ \texttt{lsum}^-\ []\ 0$. This can now be applied in the premise of (C_{2111}) by the inverse method loop to produce the following partially applied instance:

$$\frac{\Gamma \vdash [\texttt{sum}\ 3\ 0\ k]}{\Gamma\ ;\ \cdot \vdash \cdot\ ;\ \texttt{lsum}^-\ [3]\ k}\,(C_5)$$

This finally gives us our first seed for sum, *viz.* $\texttt{sum}^-\ 3\ 0\ \_$. This seed will, in turn produce seeds $\texttt{sum}^-\ 2\ 0\ \_$, $\texttt{sum}^-\ 1\ 0\ \_$, and $\texttt{sum}^-\ 0\ 0\ \_$ from instances of the rule (C_4). The last of these seeds will instantiate (C_3) to give our second fact, $\cdot\ ;\ \cdot \vdash \cdot\ ;\ \texttt{sum}^-\ 0\ 0\ 0$. The inverse method will then be able to use this rule to partially apply the instances of the (C_3) rule to produce, eventually, $\cdot\ ;\ \cdot \vdash \cdot\ ;\ \texttt{sum}^-\ 3\ 0\ 3$, which can be matched to (the instance of) (C_5) to give our second derived fact about lsum, *viz.* $\cdot\ ;\ \cdot \vdash \cdot\ ;\ \texttt{lsum}^-\ [3]\ 3$. These steps repeat twice more until we eventually derive $\cdot\ ;\ \cdot \vdash \cdot\ ;\ \texttt{lsum}^-[1,2,3]\ 6$, which finally lets us derive the goal sequent using (the instance of) (g).

4.4 Correctness

Crucially, no further inferences are possible in the example of the previous section. There will never be any facts generated about $\texttt{lsum}^-\ [5,1,2,3,4]\ x$, for instance, because there is never a seed of that form. Thus, as long as there is a well-founded measure on the seeds that is strictly decreasing for every new seed, this implementation of the inverse method will saturate.

Lemma 8 (seeding lemma). *All atoms occurring to the right of sequents in the Facts list are instances of atoms in the Seeds.*

Proof. Since the only polarity assignment is to assign an unpolarised atom the negative polarity, the only effect it has on proto inference rules is to finish left-focused proto sequent premises with NL, and turn right-focused proto sequent premises into neutral sequent premises. Finishing the left-focused premises has the side effect of instantiating the right hand side with the newly negatively polarised atom. If there are no neutral premises as a result of this assignment, then the newly generated fact satisfies the required criterion. Otherwise, when the conclusion is eventually generated by applying the rule in the inverse method, the right hand side will be an instance of the negatively polarised atom. □

The main result of this paper is a simple corollary.

Corollary 9 (saturation). *Given a well-moded logic program that terminates on all well-moded queries—i.e., all derivations of a well-moded query are finite—the inverse method with the dynamic polarity assignment algorithm of sec. 4.1 saturates for all well-moded queries.*

Proof (Sketch). Instead of giving a fully formal proof, which is doable in the style of [15], we give only the intuition for the proof. Note that if the logic program is terminating for all well-moded queries, then there is a bounded measure $|\ |$ that is strictly decreasing from head to body of all clauses in the program. We use this measure to build a measure on the *Seeds* collection as follows:

- For each atom in *Seeds*, pick the element with the smallest $|\ |$-measure.
- For each atom not in *Seeds*, pick greatest lower bound of the $|\ |$-measure.
- Pick a strict but arbitrary ordering of all the predicate symbols and arrange the measures selected in the previous two steps in a tuple according to this ordering. This tuple will be the measure of *Seeds*.

It is easy to see that this measure on *Seeds* has a lower bound according to the lexicographic ordering. Therefore, all we need to show is that this measure is decreasing on *Seeds* for every seeding step and then we can use lem. 8 to guarantee saturation. But this is easily shown because the $|\ |$-measure decreases when going from the conclusion to the premises of every derived inference rule for the clauses of the logic program (see the example in sec. 4.3). □

The completeness of the dynamic polarity assignment algorithm follows from the completeness of focusing with (arbitrary) polarity assignment, the completeness of the inverse method given a fair strategy, and the observation that *Seeds* contains a superset of all predicates that can appear as subgoals in a top-down search of the given logic program.

5 Conclusion

We have shown how to implement the magic sets constraint on a focused forward search strategy by dynamically assigning polarities to unpolarised atoms. As one immediate consequence, our forward engine can respond with the same answer set as traditional back-chaining for well-moded and terminating programs. The notion of dynamic polarity assignment is novel to this work and the last word on it is far from written. The obvious next step is to see how it generalises to fragments larger than Horn theories. More fundamentally, while fairness in the inverse method gives a general external criterion for completeness, an internal criterion for judging when a given dynamic polarity assignment strategy will be complete is currently missing.

Acknowledgement. We thank Brigitte Pientka for several useful discussions about magic sets and polarity assignment.

References

1. Andreoli, J.-M.: Logic programming with focusing proofs in linear logic. J. of Logic and Computation 2(3), 297–347 (1992)
2. Apt, K.R., Marchiori, E.: Reasoning about prolog programs from modes through types to assertions. Formal Aspects of Computing 6(A), 743–764 (1994)
3. Beeri, C., Ramakrishnan, R.: On the power of magic. J. of Logic Programming 10(1/2/3&4), 255–299 (1991)
4. Chaudhuri, K.: The Focused Inverse Method for Linear Logic. PhD thesis, Carnegie Mellon University, Technical report CMU-CS-06-162 (2006)
5. Chaudhuri, K.: Focusing strategies in the sequent calculus of synthetic connectives. In: Cervesato, I., Veith, H., Voronkov, A. (eds.) LPAR 2008. LNCS (LNAI), vol. 5330, pp. 467–481. Springer, Heidelberg (2008)
6. Chaudhuri, K.: Classical and intuitionistic subexponential logics are equally expressive. In: Veith, H. (ed.) CSL 2010. LNCS, vol. 6247, pp. 185–199. Springer, Heidelberg (2010)
7. Chaudhuri, K., Pfenning, F.: A focusing inverse method theorem prover for first-order linear logic. In: Nieuwenhuis, R. (ed.) CADE 2005. LNCS (LNAI), vol. 3632, pp. 69–83. Springer, Heidelberg (2005)
8. Chaudhuri, K., Pfenning, F., Price, G.: A logical characterization of forward and backward chaining in the inverse method. J. of Automated Reasoning 40(2-3), 133–177 (2008)
9. Degtyarev, A., Voronkov, A.: The inverse method. In: Handbook of Automated Reasoning, pp. 179–272. Elsevier and MIT Press (2001)
10. Donnelly, K., Gibson, T., Krishnaswami, N., Magill, S., Park, S.: The inverse method for the logic of bunched implications. In: Baader, F., Voronkov, A. (eds.) LPAR 2004. LNCS (LNAI), vol. 3452, pp. 466–480. Springer, Heidelberg (2005)
11. Heilala, S., Pientka, B.: Bidirectional decision procedures for the intuitionistic propositional modal logic IS4. In: Pfenning, F. (ed.) CADE 2007. LNCS (LNAI), vol. 4603, pp. 116–131. Springer, Heidelberg (2007)
12. Howe, J.M.: Proof Search Issues in Some Non-Classical Logics. PhD thesis, U. of St Andrews, Research Report CS/99/1 (1998)
13. Liang, C., Miller, D.: Focusing and polarization in linear, intuitionistic, and classical logics. Theoretical Computer Science 410(46), 4747–4768 (2009)
14. Liang, C., Miller, D.: A unified sequent calculus for focused proofs. In: LICS 24, pp. 355–364 (2009)
15. Mascellani, P., Pedreschi, D.: The declarative side of magic. In: Kakas, A.C., Sadri, F. (eds.) Computational Logic: Logic Programming and Beyond. LNCS (LNAI), vol. 2408, pp. 83–108. Springer, Heidelberg (2002)
16. McLaughlin, S., Pfenning, F.: Imogen: Focusing the polarized focused inverse method for intuitionistic propositional logic. In: Cervesato, I., Veith, H., Voronkov, A. (eds.) LPAR 2008. LNCS (LNAI), vol. 5330, pp. 174–181. Springer, Heidelberg (2008)
17. Miller, D., Nigam, V.: Incorporating tables into proofs. In: Duparc, J., Henzinger, T.A. (eds.) CSL 2007. LNCS, vol. 4646, pp. 466–480. Springer, Heidelberg (2007)
18. Miller, D., Saurin, A.: From proofs to focused proofs: a modular proof of focalization in linear logic. In: Duparc, J., Henzinger, T.A. (eds.) CSL 2007. LNCS, vol. 4646, pp. 405–419. Springer, Heidelberg (2007)
19. Ullman, J.D.: Principles of Database and Knowledge-base Systems, Volume II: The New Techniques. In: Principles of Computer Science. Computer Science Press, Rockville (1989)

Lazy Abstraction for Size-Change Termination*

Michael Codish[1], Carsten Fuhs[2], Jürgen Giesl[2], and Peter Schneider-Kamp[3]

[1] Department of Computer Science, Ben-Gurion University, Israel
[2] LuFG Informatik 2, RWTH Aachen University, Germany
[3] IMADA, University of Southern Denmark, Odense, Denmark

Abstract. Size-change termination is a widely used means of proving termination where source programs are first abstracted to size-change graphs which are then analyzed to determine if they satisfy the size-change termination property. Here, the choice of the abstraction is crucial to the success of the method, and it is an open problem how to choose an abstraction such that no critical loss of precision occurs. This paper shows how to couple the search for a suitable abstraction and the test for size-change termination via an encoding to a single SAT instance. In this way, the problem of choosing the right abstraction is solved en passant by a SAT solver. We show that for the setting of term rewriting, the integration of this approach into the dependency pair framework works smoothly and gives rise to a new class of *size-change* reduction pairs. We implemented size-change reduction pairs in the termination prover AProVE and evaluated their usefulness in extensive experiments.

1 Introduction

Proving termination is a fundamental problem in verification. The challenge of termination analysis is to design a program abstraction that captures the properties needed to prove termination as often as possible, while providing a decidable sufficient criterion for termination. The size-change termination method (SCT) [21] is one such technique where programs are abstracted to *size-change graphs* which describe how the sizes of program data are affected by the transitions made in a computation. Size is measured by a well-founded base order. A set of size-change graphs has the *SCT property* iff for every path through any infinite concatenation of these graphs, a value would descend infinitely often w.r.t. the base order. This contradicts the well-foundedness of the base order, which implies termination of the original program. Lee et al. prove in [21] that the problem to determine if a set of size-change graphs has the SCT property is PSPACE-complete. The size-change termination method has been successfully applied in a variety of different application areas [2,7,19,25,28,29].

Another approach emerges from the term rewriting community where termination proofs are performed by identifying suitable orders on terms and showing that every transition in a computation leads to a reduction w.r.t. the order. This

* Supported by the G.I.F. grant 966-116.6, the DFG grant GI 274/5-3, and the Danish Natural Science Research Council.

C. Fermüller and A. Voronkov (Eds.): LPAR-17, LNCS 6397, pp. 217–232, 2010.

approach provides a decidable sufficient termination criterion for a given class of orders and can be considered as a program abstraction because terms are viewed modulo the order. Tools based on these techniques have been successfully applied to prove termination automatically for a wide range of different programming languages (e.g., Prolog [23,27], Haskell [17], and Java Bytecode [24]).

A major bottleneck when applying SCT is due to the fact that it is a 2-phase process: First, a suitable program abstraction must be found, and then, the resulting size-change graphs are checked for termination. It is an open problem how to choose an abstraction such that no critical loss of precision occurs. Thus, our aim is to couple the search for a suitable abstraction with the test for size-change termination. To this end we model the search for an abstraction as the search for an order on terms (like in term rewriting). Then we can encode both the abstraction and the test for the SCT property into a single SAT instance.

Using a SAT-based search for orders to prove termination is well established by now. For instance [8,9,13,26,30] describe encodings for RPO, polynomial orders, or KBO. However, there is one major obstacle when using SAT for SCT. SCT is PSPACE-complete and hence (unless NP = PSPACE), there is no polynomial-size encoding of SCT to SAT. Thus, we focus on a subset of SCT which is in NP and can therefore be effectively encoded to SAT. This subset, called SCNP, is introduced by Ben-Amram and Codish in [5] where experimental evidence indicates that the restriction to this subset of SCT hardly makes any difference in practice. We illustrate our approach in the context of term rewrite systems (TRSs). The basic idea is to give a SAT encoding for the following question:

> For a given TRS (and a class of base orders such as RPO), is there a base order such that the resulting size-change graphs have the SCT property?

In [29], Thiemann and Giesl also apply the SCT method to TRSs and show how to couple it with the *dependency pair* (DP) method [1]. However, they take the 2-phase approach, first (manually) choosing a base order, and then checking if the induced size-change graphs satisfy the SCT property. Otherwise, one might try a different order. The implementation of [29] in the tool AProVE [15] only uses the (weak) embedding order in combination with argument filters [1] as base order. It performs a naive search which enumerates all argument filters. The new approach in this paper leads to a significantly more powerful implementation.

Using SCNP instead of SCT has an additional benefit. SCNP can be directly simulated by a new class of orders which can be used for *reduction pairs* in the DP framework. Thus, the techniques (or "processors") of the DP framework do not have to be modified at all for the combination with SCNP. This makes the integration of the size-change method with DPs much smoother than in [29] and it also allows to use this integration directly in arbitrary (future) extensions of the DP framework. The orders simulating SCNP are novel in the rewriting area.

The paper is structured as follows: Sect. 2 and 3 briefly present the DP framework and the SCT method for DPs. Sect. 4 adapts the SCNP approach to term rewriting. Sect. 5 shows how to encode the search for a base order which satisfies the SCNP property into a single SAT problem. Sect. 6 presents our experimental evaluation in the AProVE tool [15]. We conclude in Sect. 7.

2 Term Rewrite Systems and Dependency Pairs

We assume familiarity with term rewriting [3] and briefly introduce the main ideas of the DP method. The basic idea is (i) to describe all (finitely many) paths in the program from one function call to the next by special rewrite rules, called *dependency pairs.* Then (ii) one has to prove that these paths cannot follow each other infinitely often in a computation.

To represent a path from a function call of f with arguments $s_1, \ldots, s_n$ to a function call of g with arguments $t_1, \ldots, t_m$, we extend the signature by two new *tuple symbols* F and G. Then a function call is represented by a *tuple term*, i.e., by a term rooted by a tuple symbol, but where no tuple symbols occur below the root. The DP for this path is the rule $F(s_1, \ldots, s_n) \to G(t_1, \ldots, t_m)$.

The DP framework operates on *DP problems* $(\mathcal{P}, \mathcal{R})$, which are pairs of two TRSs. Here, for all $s \to t \in \mathcal{P}$, both s and t are tuple terms, whereas for all $l \to r \in \mathcal{R}$, both l and r are *base terms*, i.e., they do not contain tuple symbols. In the *initial* DP problem $(\mathcal{P}, \mathcal{R})$, $\mathcal{P}$ contains all DPs and $\mathcal{R}$ contains all rules of the TRS. Then, to show that this problem does not allow infinite chains of function calls, there is a large number of *processors* for analyzing and simplifying such DP problems. We refer to [1,14,16,18] for further details on the DP framework.

The most common processor for simplifying DP problems is the reduction pair processor. In a *reduction pair* $(\succsim, \succ)$, $\succsim$ is a stable monotonic[1] quasi-order comparing either two tuple terms or two base terms. Moreover, $\succ$ is a stable well-founded order on terms, where $\succsim$ and $\succ$ are compatible (i.e., $\succ \circ \succsim \subseteq \succ$ and $\succsim \circ \succ \subseteq \succ$). Given such a reduction pair and a DP problem $(\mathcal{P}, \mathcal{R})$, if we can show a weak decrease (i.e., a decrease w.r.t. $\succsim$) for all rules from $\mathcal{R}$ and all DPs from $\mathcal{P}$, we can delete all those DPs from $\mathcal{P}$ that are strictly decreasing (i.e., that decrease w.r.t. $\succ$). In other words, we are asking the following question:

> For a given DP problem $(\mathcal{P}, \mathcal{R})$, is there a reduction pair that orients all rules of $\mathcal{R}$ and $\mathcal{P}$ weakly and at least one of the rules of $\mathcal{P}$ strictly?

If we can delete all DPs by repeatedly applying this processor, then the initial DP problem does not allow infinite chains of function calls. Consequently, there is no infinite reduction with the original TRS $\mathcal{R}$, i.e., $\mathcal{R}$ is terminating.

3 Size-Change Termination and Dependency Pairs

Size-change termination [21] is a program abstraction where termination is decidable. As mentioned in the introduction, an abstract program is a finite set of size-change graphs which describe, in terms of size-change, the possible transitions between consecutive function calls in the original program.

Size-change termination and the DP framework have some similarities: (i) size-change graphs provide a representation of the paths from one function call to the next, and (ii) in a second stage we show that these graphs do not allow infinite descent. So these steps correspond to steps (i) and (ii) in the DP method.

The main difference between SCT and the DP method is the stage when the undecidable termination problem is abstracted to a decidable one. For SCT, we

[1] If monotonicity of $\succsim$ is not required, we speak of a *non-monotonic* reduction pair.

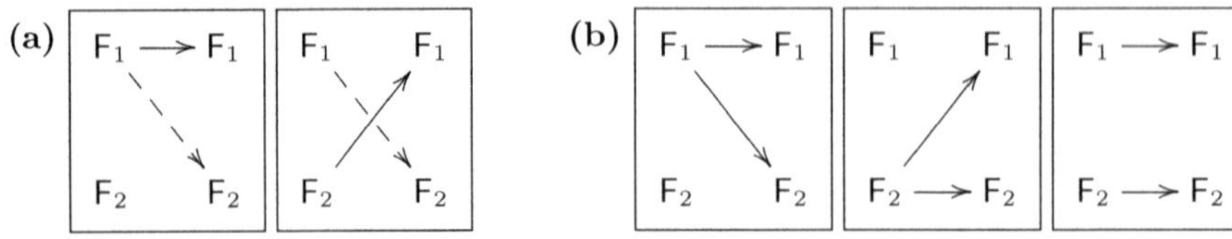

Fig. 1. Size-change graphs from Ex. 2

use a base order to obtain the finite representation of the paths by size-change graphs. For DPs, no such abstraction is performed and, indeed, the termination of a DP problem is undecidable. Here, the abstraction step is only the second stage where typically a decidable class of base orders is used.

The SCT method can be used with any base order. It only requires the information which arguments of a function call become (strictly or weakly) smaller w.r.t. the base order. To prove termination, the base order has to be well-founded. For the adaptation to TRSs we will use a reduction pair $(\succsim, \succ)$ for this purpose and introduce the notion of a size-change graph directly for dependency pairs.

If the TRS has a DP $F(s_1, \ldots, s_n) \to G(t_1, \ldots, t_m)$, then the corresponding size-change graph has nodes $\{F_1, \ldots, F_n, G_1, \ldots, G_m\}$ representing the argument positions of F and G. The labeled edges in the size-change graph indicate whether there is a strict or weak decrease between these arguments.

Definition 1 (size-change graphs). *Let $(\succsim, \succ)$ be a (possibly non-monotonic) reduction pair on base terms, and let $F(s_1, \ldots, s_n) \to G(t_1, \ldots, t_m)$ be a DP. The* size-change graph *resulting from this DP and from $(\succsim, \succ)$ is the graph (V_s, V_t, E) with source vertices $V_s = \{F_1, \ldots, F_n\}$, target vertices $V_t = \{G_1, \ldots, G_m\}$, and labeled edges $E = \{(F_i, G_j, \succ) \mid s_i \succ t_j\} \cup \{(F_i, G_j, \succsim) \mid s_i \succsim t_j\}$.*

Size-change graphs are depicted as in Fig. 1. Each graph consists of source vertices, on the left, target vertices, on the right, and edges drawn as full and dashed arrows to indicate strict and weak decrease (i.e., corresponding to "$\succ$" and "$\succsim$", respectively). We introduce the main ideas underlying SCT by example.

Example 2. Consider the TRS $\{(1), (2)\}$. It has the DPs (3) and (4).

$$\mathsf{f}(\mathsf{s}(x), y) \to \mathsf{f}(x, \mathsf{s}(x)) \quad (1) \qquad\qquad \mathsf{F}(\mathsf{s}(x), y) \to \mathsf{F}(x, \mathsf{s}(x)) \quad (3)$$

$$\mathsf{f}(x, \mathsf{s}(y)) \to \mathsf{f}(y, x) \quad (2) \qquad\qquad \mathsf{F}(x, \mathsf{s}(y)) \to \mathsf{F}(y, x) \quad (4)$$

We use a reduction pair based on the embedding order where $\mathsf{s}(x) \succ x$, $\mathsf{s}(y) \succ y$, $\mathsf{s}(x) \succsim \mathsf{s}(x)$, $\mathsf{s}(y) \succsim \mathsf{s}(y)$. Then we get the size-change graphs in Fig. 1(**a**). Between consecutive function calls, the first argument decreases in size or becomes smaller than the original second argument. In both cases, the second argument weakly decreases compared to the original first argument. By repeated composition of the size-change graphs, we obtain the three "idempotent" graphs in Fig. 1(**b**). All of them exhibit *in situ decrease* (at F_1 in the first graph, at F_2 in the second graph, and at both F_1 and F_2 in the third graph). This means that the original size-change graphs from Fig. 1(**a**) *satisfy the SCT property.*

Earlier work [29] shows how to combine SCT with term rewriting. Let $\mathcal{R}$ be a TRS and $(\succsim, \succ)$ a reduction pair such that if $s \succ t$ (or $s \succsim t$), then t contains no defined symbols of $\mathcal{R}$, i.e., no root symbols of left-hand sides of rules from $\mathcal{R}$.[2] Let $\mathcal{G}$ be the set of size-change graphs resulting from all DPs with $(\succsim, \succ)$. In [29] the authors prove that if $\mathcal{G}$ satisfies SCT then $\mathcal{R}$ is innermost terminating.

Example 3. If one restricts the reduction pair in Ex. 2 to just terms without defined symbols, then one still obtains the same size-change graphs. Since these graphs satisfy the SCT property, one can conclude that the TRS is indeed innermost terminating. Note that to show termination without SCT, an order like RPO would fail (since the first rule requires a lexicographic comparison and the second requires a multiset comparison). While termination could be proved by polynomial orders, as in [29] one could unite these rules with the rules for the Ackermann function. Then SCT with the embedding order would still work, whereas a direct application of RPO or polynomial orders fails.

So our example illustrates a major strength of SCT. A proof of termination is obtained by using just a *simple* base order and by considering each idempotent graph in the closure under composition afterwards. In contrast, without SCT, one would need more complex termination arguments.

In [29] the authors show that when constructing the size-change graphs from the DPs, one can even use *arbitrary* reduction pairs as base orders, provided that all rules of the TRS are weakly decreasing. In other words, this previous work essentially addresses the following question for any DP problem $(\mathcal{P}, \mathcal{R})$:

> For a given base order where $\mathcal{R}$ is weakly decreasing, do all idempotent size-change graphs, under composition closure, exhibit in situ decrease?

Note that in [29], the base order is always given and the only way to search for a base order automatically would be a hopeless generate-and-test approach.

4 Approximating SCT in NP

In [5] the authors identify a subset of SCT, called SCNP, that is powerful enough for practical use and is in NP. For SCNP just as for SCT, programs are abstracted to sets of size-change graphs. But instead of checking SCT by the closure under composition, one identifies a suitable ranking function to certify the termination of programs described by the set of graphs. Ranking functions map "program states" to elements of a well-founded domain and one has to show that they (strictly) decrease on all program transitions described by the size-change graphs.

In the rewriting context, program states are terms. Here, instead of a ranking function one can use an arbitrary stable well-founded order $\sqsupset$. Let (V_s, V_t, E) be a size-change graph with source vertices $V_s = \{F_1, \ldots, F_n\}$, target vertices $V_t = \{G_1, \ldots, G_m\}$, and let $(\succsim, \succ)$ be the reduction pair on base terms which was used for the construction of the graph. Now the goal is to extend the order $\succ$ to a well-founded order $\sqsupset$ which can also compare tuple terms and which *satisfies*

[2] Strictly speaking, this is not a reduction pair, since it is only stable under substitutions which do not introduce defined symbols.

the size-change graph (i.e., $F(s_1, \ldots, s_n) \sqsupset G(t_1, \ldots, t_m)$). Similarly, we say that $\sqsupset$ satisfies a *set* of size-change graphs iff it satisfies all the graphs in the set.

If the size-change graphs describe the transitions of a program, then the existence of a corresponding ranking function obviously implies termination of the program. As in [29], to ensure that the size-change graphs really describe the transitions of the TRS correctly, one has to impose suitable restrictions on the reduction pair (e.g., by demanding that all rules of the TRS are weakly decreasing w.r.t. $\succsim$). Then one can indeed conclude termination of the TRS.

In [22], a class of ranking functions is identified which can simulate SCT. So if a set of size-change graphs has the SCT property, then there is a ranking function of that class satisfying these size-change graphs. However, this class is typically exponential in size [22]. To obtain a subset of SCT in NP, [5] considers a restricted class of ranking functions. A set of size-change graphs has the *SCNP* property iff it is satisfied by a ranking function from this restricted class.

Our goal is to adapt this class of ranking functions to term rewriting. The main motivation is to facilitate the *simultaneous* search for a ranking function on the size-change graphs and for the base order which is used to derive the size-change graphs from a TRS. It means that we are searching both for a program abstraction to size-change graphs, and also for the ranking function which proves that these graphs have the SCNP (and hence also the SCT) property.

This is different from [5], where the concrete structure of the program has already been abstracted away to size-change graphs that must be given as inputs. It is also different from the earlier adaption of SCT to term rewriting in [29], where the base order was fixed. As shown by the experiments with [29] in Sect. 6, fixing the base order for the size-change graphs leads to severe limitations in power.

The following example illustrates the SCNP property and presents a ranking function (resp. a well-founded order $\sqsupset$) satisfying a set of size-change graphs.

Example 4. Consider the TRS from Ex. 2 and its size-change graphs in Fig. 1**(a)**. Here, the base order is the reduction pair $(\succsim, \succ)$ resulting from the embedding order. We now extend $\succ$ to an order $\sqsupset$ which can also compare tuple terms and which satisfies the size-change graphs in this example. To compare tuple terms $\mathsf{F}(s_1, s_2)$ and $\mathsf{F}(t_1, t_2)$, we first map them to the multisets $\{\, \langle s_1, 1\rangle, \langle s_2, 0\rangle \,\}$ and $\{\, \langle t_1, 1\rangle, \langle t_2, 0\rangle \,\}$ of *tagged* terms (where a tagged term is a pair of a term and a number). Now a multiset S of tagged terms is greater than a multiset T iff for every $\langle t, m\rangle \in T$ there is an $\langle s, n\rangle \in S$ where $s \succ t$ or both $s \succsim t$ and $n > m$.

For the first graph, we have $s_1 \succ t_1$ and $s_1 \succsim t_2$ and hence the multiset $\{\, \langle s_1, 1\rangle, \langle s_2, 0\rangle \,\}$ is greater than $\{\, \langle t_1, 1\rangle, \langle t_2, 0\rangle \,\}$. For the second graph, $s_1 \succsim t_2$ and $s_2 \succ t_1$ also implies that the multiset $\{\, \langle s_1, 1\rangle, \langle s_2, 0\rangle \,\}$ is greater than $\{\, \langle t_1, 1\rangle, \langle t_2, 0\rangle \,\}$. Thus, if we define our well-founded order $\sqsupset$ in this way, then it indeed satisfies both size-change graphs of the example. Since this order $\sqsupset$ belongs to the class of ranking functions defined in [5], this shows that the size-change graphs in Fig. 1**(a)** have the SCNP property.

In term rewriting, size-change graphs correspond to DPs and the arcs of the size-change graphs are built by only comparing the arguments of the DPs (which are *base terms*). The ranking function then corresponds to a well-founded order on tuple terms. We now reformulate the class of ranking functions of [5] in the term rewriting context by defining *SCNP reduction pairs*. The advantage of this reformulation is that it allows us to integrate the SCNP approach directly into the DP framework and that it allows a SAT encoding of both the search for suitable base orders and of the test for the SCNP property. In [5], the class of ranking functions for SCNP is defined incrementally. We follow this, but adapt the definitions of [5] to the term rewriting setting and prove that the resulting orders always constitute reduction pairs. More precisely, we proceed as follows:

step one: $(\succsim, \succ)$ is an arbitrary reduction pair on base terms that we start with (e.g., based on RPO and argument filters or on polynomial orders). The main observation that can be drawn from the SCNP approach is that it is helpful to compare base terms and tuple terms in a different way. Thus, our goal is to extend $(\succsim, \succ)$ appropriately to a reduction pair $(\sqsupseteq, \sqsupset)$ that can also compare tuple terms. By defining $(\sqsupseteq, \sqsupset)$ in the same way as the ranking functions of [5], it can simulate the SCNP approach.
step two: $(\succsim^{\mathbb{N}}, \succ^{\mathbb{N}})$ is a reduction pair on *tagged* base terms, i.e., on pairs $\langle t, n\rangle$, where t is a base term and $n \in \mathbb{N}$. Essentially, $(\succsim^{\mathbb{N}}, \succ^{\mathbb{N}})$ is a lexicographic combination of the reduction pair $(\succsim, \succ)$ with the usual order on $\mathbb{N}$.
step three: $(\succsim^{\mathbb{N},\mu}, \succ^{\mathbb{N},\mu})$ extends $(\succsim^{\mathbb{N}}, \succ^{\mathbb{N}})$ to compare *multisets* of tagged base terms. The *status* μ determines how $(\succsim^{\mathbb{N}}, \succ^{\mathbb{N}})$ is extended to multisets.
step four: $(\succsim^{\mu,\ell}, \succ^{\mu,\ell})$ is a full reduction pair (i.e., it is the reduction pair $(\sqsupseteq, \sqsupset)$ we were looking for). The *level mapping* ℓ determines which arguments of a tuple term are selected and tagged, resulting in a multiset of tagged base terms. On tuple terms, $(\succsim^{\mu,\ell}, \succ^{\mu,\ell})$ behaves according to $(\succsim^{\mathbb{N},\mu}, \succ^{\mathbb{N},\mu})$ on the multisets as determined by ℓ, and on base terms, it behaves like $(\succsim, \succ)$.

Thus, we start with extending a reduction pair $(\succsim, \succ)$ on base terms to a reduction pair $(\succsim^{\mathbb{N}}, \succ^{\mathbb{N}})$ on tagged base terms. We compare tagged terms lexicographically by $(\succsim, \succ)$ and by the standard orders $\geq$ and $>$ on numbers.

Definition 5 (comparing tagged terms). *Let $(\succsim, \succ)$ be a reduction pair on terms. We define the corresponding reduction pair $(\succsim^{\mathbb{N}}, \succ^{\mathbb{N}})$ on tagged terms:*

- $\langle t_1, n_1\rangle \succsim^{\mathbb{N}} \langle t_2, n_2\rangle \quad \Leftrightarrow \quad t_1 \succ t_2 \ \vee \ (t_1 \succsim t_2 \wedge n_1 \geq n_2).$
- $\langle t_1, n_1\rangle \succ^{\mathbb{N}} \langle t_2, n_2\rangle \quad \Leftrightarrow \quad t_1 \succ t_2 \ \vee \ (t_1 \succsim t_2 \wedge n_1 > n_2).$

The motivation for tagged terms is that we will use different tags (i.e., numbers) for the different argument positions of a function symbol. For instance, when comparing the terms $s = \mathsf{F}(\mathsf{s}(x), y)$ and $t = \mathsf{F}(x, \mathsf{s}(x))$ as in Ex. 4, one can assign the tags 1 and 0 to the first and second argument position of F, respectively. Then, if $(\succsim, \succ)$ is the reduction pair based on the embedding order, we have $\langle \mathsf{s}(x), 1\rangle \succ^{\mathbb{N}} \langle x, 1\rangle$ and $\langle \mathsf{s}(x), 1\rangle \succ^{\mathbb{N}} \langle \mathsf{s}(x), 0\rangle$. In other words, the first argument of s is greater than both the first and the second argument of t.

The following lemma states that if $(\succsim, \succ)$ is a reduction pair on terms, then $(\succsim^{\mathbb{N}}, \succ^{\mathbb{N}})$ is a reduction pair on tagged terms (where we do not require monotonicity, since monotonicity is not defined for tagged terms). This lemma will be needed for our main theorem (Thm. 12) which proves that the reduction pair defined to simulate SCNP is really a reduction pair.

Lemma 6 (reduction pairs on tagged terms). *Let* $(\succsim, \succ)$ *be a reduction pair. Then* $(\succsim^{\mathbb{N}}, \succ^{\mathbb{N}})$ *is a non-monotonic reduction pair on tagged terms.*[3]

The next step is to introduce a "reduction pair" $(\succsim^{\mathbb{N},\mu}, \succ^{\mathbb{N},\mu})$ on multisets of tagged base terms, where μ is a status which determines how $(\succsim^{\mathbb{N}}, \succ^{\mathbb{N}})$ is extended to multisets. Of course, there are many possibilities for such an extension. In Def. 7, we present the four extensions which correspond to the ranking functions defining SCNP in [5]. The main difference to the definitions in [5] is that we do not restrict ourselves to *total* base orders. Hence, the notions of maximum and minimum of a multiset of terms are not defined in the same way as in [5].

Definition 7 (multiset extensions of reduction pairs). *Let* $(\succsim, \succ)$ *be a reduction pair on (tagged) terms. We define an extended reduction pair* $(\succsim^{\mu}, \succ^{\mu})$ *on multisets of (tagged) terms, for* $\mu \in \{max, min, ms, dms\}$. *Let* S *and* T *be multisets of (tagged) terms.*

1. (max order) $S \succsim^{max} T$ *holds iff* $\forall t \in T.\ \exists s \in S.\ s \succsim t$.
   $S \succ^{max} T$ *holds iff* $S \neq \varnothing$ *and* $\forall t \in T.\ \exists s \in S.\ s \succ t$.
2. (min order) $S \succsim^{min} T$ *holds iff* $\forall s \in S.\ \exists t \in T.\ s \succsim t$.
   $S \succ^{min} T$ *holds iff* $T \neq \varnothing$ *and* $\forall s \in S.\ \exists t \in T.\ s \succ t$.
3. (multiset order [10]) $S \succ^{ms} T$ *holds iff* $S = S_{\text{strict}} \uplus \{ s_1, \ldots, s_k \}$, $T = T_{\text{strict}} \uplus \{ t_1, \ldots, t_k \}$, $S_{\text{strict}} \succ^{max} T_{\text{strict}}$, *and* $s_i \succsim t_i$ *for* $1 \le i \le k$.
   $S \succsim^{ms} T$ *holds iff* $S = S_{\text{strict}} \uplus \{ s_1, \ldots, s_k \}$, $T = T_{\text{strict}} \uplus \{ t_1, \ldots, t_k \}$, *either* $S_{\text{strict}} \succ^{max} T_{\text{strict}}$ *or* $S_{\text{strict}} = T_{\text{strict}} = \varnothing$, *and* $s_i \succsim t_i$ *for* $1 \le i \le k$.
4. (dual multiset order [4]) $S \succ^{dms} T$ *holds iff* $S = S_{\text{strict}} \uplus \{ s_1, \ldots, s_k \}$, $T = T_{\text{strict}} \uplus \{ t_1, \ldots, t_k \}$, $S_{\text{strict}} \succ^{min} T_{\text{strict}}$, *and* $s_i \succsim t_i$ *for* $1 \le i \le k$.
   $S \succsim^{dms} T$ *holds iff* $S = S_{\text{strict}} \uplus \{ s_1, \ldots, s_k \}$, $T = T_{\text{strict}} \uplus \{ t_1, \ldots, t_k \}$, *either* $S_{\text{strict}} \succ^{min} T_{\text{strict}}$ *or* $S_{\text{strict}} = T_{\text{strict}} = \varnothing$, *and* $s_i \succsim t_i$ *for* $1 \le i \le k$.

Here $\succ^{ms}$ is to the standard multiset extension of an order $\succ$ as used, e.g., for the classical definition of RPO. However, our use of tagged terms as elements of the multiset introduces a lexicographic aspect that is missing in RPO.

Example 8. Consider again the TRS from Ex. 2 with the reduction pair based on the embedding order. We have $\{\mathsf{s}(x), y\} \succsim^{max} \{x, \mathsf{s}(x)\}$, since for both terms in $\{x, \mathsf{s}(x)\}$ there is an element in $\{\mathsf{s}(x), y\}$ which is weakly greater (w.r.t. $\succsim$). Similarly, $\{x, \mathsf{s}(y)\} \succsim^{max} \{y, x\}$. However, $\{x, \mathsf{s}(y)\} \not\succ^{max} \{y, x\}$, since not every element from $\{y, x\}$ has a strictly greater one in $\{x, \mathsf{s}(y)\}$. We also have $\{x, \mathsf{s}(y)\} \succsim^{min} \{y, x\}$, but $\{\mathsf{s}(x), y\} \not\succsim^{min} \{x, \mathsf{s}(x)\}$, since for y in $\{\mathsf{s}(x), y\}$, there is no term in $\{x, \mathsf{s}(x)\}$ which is weakly smaller.

We have $\{\mathsf{s}(x), y\} \not\succ^{ms} \{x, \mathsf{s}(x)\}$, since even if we take $\{\mathsf{s}(x)\} \succ^{max} \{x\}$, we still do not have $y \succsim \mathsf{s}(x)$. Moreover, also $\{\mathsf{s}(x), y\} \not\succsim^{ms} \{x, \mathsf{s}(x)\}$. Otherwise, for every element of $\{x, \mathsf{s}(x)\}$ there would have to be a *different* weakly greater element in $\{\mathsf{s}(x), y\}$. In contrast, we have $\{x, \mathsf{s}(y)\} \succ^{ms} \{y, x\}$. The element $\mathsf{s}(y)$ is replaced by the strictly smaller element y and for the remaining element x on the right-hand side there is a weakly greater one on the left-hand side. Similarly, we also have $\{\mathsf{s}(x), y\} \not\succsim^{dms} \{x, \mathsf{s}(x)\}$ and$\{x, \mathsf{s}(y)\} \succ^{dms} \{y, x\}$.

[3] All proofs can be found in [6].

So there is no μ such that the multiset of arguments strictly decreases in some DP and weakly decreases in the other DP. We can only achieve a weak decrease for all DPs. To obtain a strict decrease in such cases, one can add tags.

We want to define a reduction pair $(\succsim^{\mu,\ell}, \succ^{\mu,\ell})$ which is like $(\succsim^{\mathbb{N},\mu}, \succ^{\mathbb{N},\mu})$ on tuple terms and like $(\succsim, \succ)$ on base terms. Here, we use a *level mapping* ℓ to map tuple terms $F(s_1, \ldots, s_n)$ to multisets of tagged base terms.

Definition 9 (level mapping). *For each tuple symbol F of arity n, let $\pi(F) \subseteq \{1, \ldots, n\} \times \mathbb{N}$ such that for each $1 \leq j \leq n$ there is at most one $m \in \mathbb{N}$ with $\langle j, m \rangle \in \pi(F)$. Then $\ell(F(s_1, \ldots, s_n)) = \{ \langle s_i, n_i \rangle \mid \langle i, n_i \rangle \in \pi(F) \}$.*

Example 10. Consider again the TRS from Ex. 2 with the reduction pair based on the embedding order. Let π be a status function with $\pi(\mathsf{F}) = \{ \langle 1, 1 \rangle, \langle 2, 0 \rangle \}$. So π selects both arguments of terms rooted with F for comparison and associates the tag 1 with the first argument and the tag 0 with the second argument. This means that it puts "more weight" on the first than on the second argument. The level mapping ℓ defined by π transforms the tuple terms from the DPs of our TRS into the following multisets of tagged terms:

$$\ell(\mathsf{F}(\mathsf{s}(x), y)) = \{ \langle \mathsf{s}(x), 1 \rangle, \langle y, 0 \rangle \} \qquad \ell(\mathsf{F}(x, \mathsf{s}(x))) = \{ \langle x, 1 \rangle, \langle \mathsf{s}(x), 0 \rangle \}$$
$$\ell(\mathsf{F}(x, \mathsf{s}(y))) = \{ \langle x, 1 \rangle, \langle \mathsf{s}(y), 0 \rangle \} \qquad \ell(\mathsf{F}(y, x)) = \{ \langle y, 1 \rangle, \langle x, 0 \rangle \}$$

Now we observe that for the multisets of the tagged terms above, we have

$$\ell(\mathsf{F}(\mathsf{s}(x), y)) \succ^{\mathbb{N},max} \ell(\mathsf{F}(x, \mathsf{s}(x))) \qquad \ell(\mathsf{F}(x, \mathsf{s}(y))) \succ^{\mathbb{N},max} \ell(\mathsf{F}(y, x))$$

So due to the tagging now we can find an order such that both DPs are strictly decreasing. This order corresponds to the ranking function given in Ex. 4.

Finally we define the class of reduction pairs which corresponds to the class of ranking functions considered for SCNP in [5].

Definition 11 (SCNP reduction pair). *Let $(\succsim, \succ)$ be a reduction pair on base terms and let ℓ be a level mapping. For $\mu \in \{max, min, ms, dms\}$, we define the* SCNP reduction pair $(\succsim^{\mu,\ell}, \succ^{\mu,\ell})$. *For base terms l, r we define $l \underset{(\sim)}{\succ}^{\mu,\ell} r \Leftrightarrow l \underset{(\sim)}{\succ} r$ and for tuple terms s and t we define $s \underset{(\sim)}{\succ}^{\mu,\ell} t \Leftrightarrow \ell(s) \underset{(\sim)}{\succ}^{\mathbb{N},\mu} \ell(t)$.*

So we have $s \succ^{max,\ell} t$ for the DPs $s \to t$ in Ex. 2 and the level mapping ℓ in Ex. 10. Thm. 12 states that SCNP reduction pairs actually *are* reduction pairs.

Theorem 12. *For $\mu \in \{max, min, ms, dms\}$, $(\succsim^{\mu,\ell}, \succ^{\mu,\ell})$ is a reduction pair.*

We now automate the SCNP criterion of [5]. For a DP problem $(\mathcal{P}, \mathcal{R})$ with the DPs $\mathcal{P}$ and the TRS $\mathcal{R}$, we have to find a suitable base order $(\succsim, \succ)$ to construct the size-change graphs $\mathcal{G}$ corresponding to the DPs in $\mathcal{P}$. So every graph (V_s, V_t, E) from $\mathcal{G}$ with source vertices $V_s = \{F_1, \ldots, F_n\}$ and target vertices $V_t = \{G_1, \ldots, G_m\}$ corresponds to a DP $F(s_1, \ldots, s_n) \to G(t_1, \ldots, t_m)$. Moreover, we have an edge $(F_i, G_j, \succ) \in E$ iff $s_i \succ t_j$ and $(F_i, G_j, \succsim) \in E$ iff $s_i \succsim t_j$.

In our example, if we use the reduction pair $(\succsim, \succ)$ based on the embedding order, then $\mathcal{G}$ are the size-change graphs from Fig. 1(**a**). For instance, the first size-change graph results from the DP (3).

For SCNP, we have to extend $\succ$ to a well-founded order $\sqsupset$ which can also compare tuple terms and which satisfies all size-change graphs in $\mathcal{G}$. For $\sqsupset$, we could take any order $\succ^{\mu,\ell}$ from an SCNP reduction pair $(\succsim^{\mu,\ell}, \succ^{\mu,\ell})$. To show that $\sqsupset$ satisfies the size-change graphs from $\mathcal{G}$, one then has to prove $F(s_1,\ldots,s_n) \succ^{\mu,\ell} G(t_1,\ldots,t_m)$ for every DP $F(s_1,\ldots,s_n) \to G(t_1,\ldots,t_m)$. Moreover, to ensure that the size-change graphs correctly describe the transitions of the TRS-program $\mathcal{R}$, one also has to require that all rules of the TRS $\mathcal{R}$ are weakly decreasing w.r.t. $\succsim$ (cf. the remarks at the beginning of Sect. 4). Of course, as in [29], this requirement can be weakened (e.g., by only regarding *usable* rules) when proving *innermost* termination.

As in [5], we define $\sqsupset$ as a lexicographic combination of several orders of the form $\succ^{\mu,\ell}$. We define the lexicographic combination of two reduction pairs as $(\succsim_1, \succ_1) \times (\succsim_2, \succ_2) = (\succsim_{1\times 2}, \succ_{1\times 2})$. Here, $s \succsim_{1\times 2} t$ holds iff both $s \succsim_1 t$ and $s \succsim_2 t$. Moreover, $s \succ_{1\times 2} t$ holds iff $s \succ_1 t$ or both $s \succsim_1 t$ and $s \succ_2 t$. It is clear that $(\succsim_{1\times 2}, \succ_{1\times 2})$ is again a reduction pair.

A suitable well-founded order $\sqsupset$ is now constructed automatically as follows. The pair of orders $(\sqsupseteq, \sqsupset)$ is initialized by defining $\sqsupseteq$ to be the relation where only $t \sqsupseteq t$ holds for two tuple or base terms t and where $\sqsupset$ is the empty relation. As long as the set of size-change graphs $\mathcal{G}$ is not empty, a status μ and a level mapping ℓ are synthesized such that $(\succsim^{\mu,\ell}, \succ^{\mu,\ell})$ orients all DPs weakly and at least one DP strictly. In other words, the corresponding ranking function satisfies one size-change graph and "weakly satisfies" the others. Then the strictly oriented DPs (resp. the strictly satisfied size-change graphs) are removed, and $(\sqsupseteq, \sqsupset) := (\sqsupseteq, \sqsupset) \times (\succsim^{\mu,\ell}, \succ^{\mu,\ell})$ is updated. In this way, the SCNP approach can be simulated by a repeated application of the *reduction pair processor* in the DP framework, using the special class of SCNP reduction pairs.

So in our example, we could first look for a μ_1 and ℓ_1 where the first DP (3) decreases strictly (w.r.t. $\succ^{\mu_1,\ell_1}$) and the second decreases weakly (w.r.t. $\succsim^{\mu_1,\ell_1}$). Then we would remove the first DP and could now search for a μ_2 and ℓ_2 such that the remaining second DP (4) decreases strictly (w.r.t. $\succ^{\mu_2,\ell_2}$). The resulting reduction pair would be $(\sqsupseteq, \sqsupset) = (\succsim^{\mu_1,\ell_1}, \succ^{\mu_1,\ell_1}) \times (\succsim^{\mu_2,\ell_2}, \succ^{\mu_2,\ell_2})$.

While in [5], the set of size-change graphs remains fixed throughout the whole termination proof, the DP framework allows to use a lexicographic combination of SCNP reduction pairs which are constructed from *different* reduction pairs $(\succsim, \succ)$ on base terms. In other words, after a base order and a ranking function satisfying one size-change graph and weakly satisfying all others have been found, the satisfied size-change graph (resp. the corresponding DP) is removed, and one can synthesize a possibly different ranking function and also a *possibly different base order* for the remaining DPs (i.e., different abstractions to different size-change graphs can be used in one and the same termination proof).

Example 13. We add a third rule to the TRS from Ex. 2: $\mathsf{f}(\mathsf{c}(x), y) \to \mathsf{f}(x, \mathsf{s}(x))$. Now no SCNP reduction pair based only on the embedding order can orient all DPs strictly at the same time anymore, even if one permits combinations with arbitrary argument filters. However, we can first apply an SCNP reduction pair that sets all tags to 0 and uses the embedding order together with an argument filter to collapse the symbol s to its argument. Then the DP for the newly added rule is oriented strictly and all other DPs are oriented weakly. After removing the new DP, the SCNP reduction pair that we already used for the DPs of Ex. 2 again orients all DPs strictly. Note that the base order for this second SCNP reduction pair is the embedding order without argument filters, i.e., it differs from the base order used in the first SCNP reduction pair.

By representing the SCNP method via SCNP reduction pairs, we can now benefit from the flexibility of the DP framework. Thus, we can use other termination methods in addition to SCNP. More precisely, as usual in the DP framework, we can apply arbitrary processors one after another in a modular way. This allows us to interleave arbitrary other termination techniques with termination proof steps based on size-change termination, whereas in [29], size-change proofs could only be used as a final step in a termination proof.

5 Automation by SAT Encoding

Recently, the search problem for many common base orders has been reduced successfully to SAT problems [8,9,13,26,30]. In this section, we build on this earlier work and use these encodings as components for a SAT encoding of SCNP reduction pairs. The corresponding decision problem is stated as follows:

> For a DP problem $(\mathcal{P}, \mathcal{R})$ and a given class of base orders, is there a status μ, a level mapping ℓ, and a concrete base reduction pair $(\succsim, \succ)$ such that the SCNP reduction pair $(\succsim^{\mu,\ell}, \succ^{\mu,\ell})$ orients all rules of $\mathcal{R}$ and $\mathcal{P}$ weakly and at least one of $\mathcal{P}$ strictly?

We assume a given *base SAT encoding* $[\![.]\!]_{base}$ which maps base term constraints of the form $s \underset{(\sim)}{\succ} t$ to propositional formulas. Every satisfying assignment for the formula $[\![s \underset{(\sim)}{\succ} t]\!]_{base}$ corresponds to a particular order where $s \underset{(\sim)}{\succ} t$ holds.

We also assume a given encoding for partial orders (on tags), cf. [9]. The function $[\![.]\!]_{po}$ maps partial order constraints of the form $n_1 \geq n_2$ or $n_1 > n_2$ where n_1 and n_2 represent natural numbers (in some fixed number of bits) to corresponding propositional formulas on the bit representations for the numbers.

For brevity, we only show the encoding for SCNP reduction pairs $(\succsim^{\mu,\ell}, \succ^{\mu,\ell})$ where $\mu = max$. The encodings for the other cases are similar: The encoding for the min comparison is completely analogous. To encode (dual) multiset comparison one can adapt previous approaches to encode multiset orders [26].

First, for each tuple symbol F of arity n, we introduce natural number variables denoted tag_i^F for $1 \leq i \leq n$. These encode the tags associated with the argument positions of F by representing them in a fixed number of bits. In our case, it suffices to consider tag values which are less than the sum of the arities of the tuple symbols. In this way, every argument position of every tuple symbol could get a different tag, i.e., this suffices to represent all possible level mappings.

Now consider a size-change graph corresponding to a DP $\delta = s \to t$ with $s = F(s_1, \ldots, s_n)$ and $t = G(t_1, \ldots, t_m)$. The edges of the size-change graph are determined by the base order, which is not fixed. For any $1 \leq i \leq n$ and $1 \leq j \leq m$, we define a propositional formula $weak^{\delta}_{i,j}$ which is *true* iff $\langle s, tag^F_i \rangle \succsim^{\mathbb{N}} \langle t, tag^G_j \rangle$. Similarly, $strict^{\delta}_{i,j}$ is *true* iff $\langle s, tag^F_i \rangle \succ^{\mathbb{N}} \langle t, tag^G_j \rangle$. The definition of $weak^{\delta}_{i,j}$ and $strict^{\delta}_{i,j}$ corresponds directly to Def. 5. It is based on the encodings $[\![.]\!]_{base}$ and $[\![.]\!]_{po}$ for the base order and for the tags, respectively.

$$weak^{\delta}_{i,j} = [\![s_i \succ t_j]\!]_{base} \ \vee \ ([\![s_i \succsim t_j]\!]_{base} \wedge [\![tag^F_i \geq tag^G_j]\!]_{po})$$
$$strict^{\delta}_{i,j} = [\![s_i \succ t_j]\!]_{base} \ \vee \ ([\![s_i \succsim t_j]\!]_{base} \wedge [\![tag^F_i > tag^G_j]\!]_{po})$$

To facilitate the search for level mappings, for each tuple symbol F of arity n we introduce propositional variables reg^F_i for $1 \leq i \leq n$. Here, reg^F_i is *true* iff the i-th argument position of F is regarded for comparison. The formulas $[\![s \succsim^{max,\ell} t]\!]$ and $[\![s \succ^{max,\ell} t]\!]$ then encode that the DP $s \to t$ can be oriented weakly or strictly, respectively. By this encoding, one can simultaneously search for a base order that gives rise to the edges in the size-change graph and for a level mapping that satisfies this size-change graph.

$$[\![s \succsim^{max,\ell} t]\!] = \bigwedge_{1 \leq j \leq m} (reg^G_j \to \bigvee_{1 \leq i \leq n} (reg^F_i \wedge weak^{\delta}_{i,j}))$$
$$[\![s \succ^{max,\ell} t]\!] = \bigwedge_{1 \leq j \leq m} (reg^G_j \to \bigvee_{1 \leq i \leq n} (reg^F_i \wedge strict^{\delta}_{i,j})) \ \wedge \ \bigvee_{1 \leq i \leq n} reg^F_i$$

For any DP problem $(\mathcal{P}, \mathcal{R})$ we can now generate a propositional formula which ensures that the corresponding SCNP reduction pair orients all rules from $\mathcal{R}$ and $\mathcal{P}$ weakly and at least one rule from $\mathcal{P}$ strictly:

$$\bigwedge_{l \to r \in \mathcal{R}} [\![l \succsim r]\!]_{base} \quad \wedge \quad \bigwedge_{s \to t \in \mathcal{P}} [\![s \succsim^{max,\ell} t]\!] \quad \wedge \quad \bigvee_{s \to t \in \mathcal{P}} [\![s \succ^{max,\ell} t]\!]$$

Similar to [8,30], our approach is easily extended to refinements of the DP method where one only regards the *usable* rules of $\mathcal{R}$ and where these usable rules can also depend on the (explicit or implicit) argument filter of the order.

6 Implementation and Experiments

We implemented our contributions in the automated termination prover AProVE [15]. To assess their impact, we compared three configurations of AProVE. In the first, we use SCNP reduction pairs in the reduction pair processor of the DP framework. This configuration is parameterized by the choice whether we allow just max comparisons of multisets or all four multiset extensions from Def. 7. Moreover, the configuration is also parameterized by the choice whether we use classical size-change graphs or *extended* size-change graphs as in [29]. In an extended size-change graph, to compare $s = F(s_1, \ldots, s_n)$ with $t = G(t_1, \ldots, t_m)$, the source and target vertices $\{s_1, \ldots, s_n\}$ and $\{t_1, \ldots, t_m\}$ are extended by additional vertices s and t, respectively. Now an edge from s to t_j indicates that the whole term s is greater (or equal) to t_j, etc. So these additional vertices

Table 1. Comparison of SCNP reduction pairs to SCT and direct reduction pairs

order		SCNP fast	SCNP max	SCNP all	reduction pairs	SCT [29]
EMB	proved	346	346	**347**	325	341
	runtime	**2882.6**	3306.4	3628.5	2891.3	10065.4
LPO	proved	500	**530**	527	505	385
	runtime	**3093.7**	5985.5	7739.2	3698.4	10015.5
RPO	proved	501	**531**	**531**	527	385
	runtime	**3222.2**	6384.1	8118.0	4027.5	10053.4
POLO	proved	477	**514**	**514**	511	378
	runtime	3153.6	5273.6	7124.4	**2941.7**	9974.0

also allow us to compare the whole terms s and t. By adding these vertices, size-change termination incorporates the standard comparison of terms as well.

In the second configuration, we use the base orders directly in the reduction pair processor (i.e., here we disregard SCNP reduction pairs). In the third configuration, we use the implementation of the SCT method as described in [29]. For a fair comparison, we updated that old implementation from the DP *approach* to the modular DP *framework* and used SAT encodings for the base orders. (While this approach only uses the embedding order and argument filters as the base order for the construction of size-change graphs, it uses more complex orders (containing the base order) to weakly orient the rules from the TRS.)

We considered all 1381 examples from the standard TRS category of the *Termination Problem Data Base* (TPDB version 7.0.2) as used in the *International Termination Competition* 2009.[4] The experiments were run on a 2.66 GHz Intel Core 2 Quad and we used a time limit of 60 seconds per example. We applied SAT4J [20] to transform propositional formulas to conjunctive normal form and the SAT solver MiniSAT2 [11] to check the satisfiability of the resulting formulas.

Table 1 compares the power and runtimes of the three configurations depending on the base order. The column "*order*" indicates the base order: embedding order with argument filters (EMB), lexicographic path order with arbitrary permutations and argument filters (LPO), recursive path order with argument filters (RPO), and linear polynomial interpretations with coefficients from $\{0, 1\}$ (POLO). For the first configuration, we used three different settings: full SCNP reduction pairs with extended size-change graphs ("SCNP all"), SCNP reduction pairs restricted to max-comparisons with extended size-change graphs ("SCNP max"), and SCNP reduction pairs restricted to max comparisons and non-extended size-change graphs ("SCNP fast"). The second and third configuration are called "reduction pairs" and "SCT [29]", respectively. For each experiment, we give the number of TRSs which could be proved terminating ("proved") and the analysis time in seconds for running AProVE on all 1381 TRSs ("runtime"). The "best" numbers are always printed in **bold**. For further details on the experiments, we refer to `http://aprove.informatik.rwth-aachen.de/eval/SCNP`. The table allows the following observations:

[4] `http://www.termination-portal.org/wiki/Termination_Competition/`

(1) Our SCNP reduction pairs are *much more powerful and significantly faster* than the implementation of [29]. By integrating the search for the base order with SCNP, our new implementation can use a much larger class of base orders and thus, SCNP reduction pairs can prove significantly more examples. The reason for the relatively low speed of [29] is that this approach iterates through argument filters and then generates and analyzes size-change graphs for each of these argument filters. (So the low speed is not due to the repeated composition of size-change graphs in the SCT criterion.)

(2) Our new implementation of SCNP reduction pairs is *more powerful* than using the reduction pairs directly. Note that when using extended size-change graphs, *every* reduction pair can be simulated by an SCNP reduction pair.

(3) SCNP reduction pairs *add significant power when used for simple orders* like EMB and LPO. The difference is less dramatic for RPO and POLO. Intuitively, the reason is that SCNP allows for multiset comparisons which are lacking in EMB and LPO, while RPO contains multiset comparisons and POLO can often simulate them. Nevertheless, SCNP also adds some power to RPO and POLO, e.g., by extending them by a concept like "maximum". This even holds for more powerful base orders like matrix orders [12]. In [6], we present a TRS where all existing termination tools fail, but where termination can easily be proved automatically by an SCNP reduction pair with a matrix base order.

7 Conclusion

We show that the practically relevant part of size-change termination (SCNP) can be formulated as a reduction pair. Thus, SCNP can be applied in the DP framework, which is used in virtually all termination tools for term rewriting.

Moreover, by combining the search for the base order and for the SCNP level mapping into one search problem, we can automatically find the right base order for constructing size-change graphs. Thus, we now generate program abstractions automatically such that termination of the abstracted programs can be shown.

The implementation in AProVE confirms the usefulness of our contribution. Our experiments indicate that the automation of our technique is more powerful than both the direct use of reduction pairs and the SCT adaptation from [29].

References

1. Arts, T., Giesl, J.: Termination of term rewriting using dependency pairs. Theoretical Computer Science 236, 133–178 (2000)
2. Avery, J.: Size-change termination and bound analysis. In: Hagiya, M., Wadler, P. (eds.) FLOPS 2006. LNCS, vol. 3945, pp. 192–207. Springer, Heidelberg (2006)
3. Baader, F., Nipkow, T.: Term Rewriting and All That, Cambridge (1998)
4. Ben-Amram, A.M., Lee, C.S.: Size-change termination in polynomial time. ACM Transactions on Programming Languages and Systems 29(1) (2007)
5. Ben-Amram, A.M., Codish, M.: A SAT-based approach to size change termination with global ranking functions. In: Ramakrishnan, C.R., Rehof, J. (eds.) TACAS 2008. LNCS, vol. 4963, pp. 218–232. Springer, Heidelberg (2008)

6. Codish, M., Fuhs, C., Giesl, J., Schneider-Kamp, P.: Lazy abstraction for size-change termination. Technical Report AIB-2010-14, RWTH Aachen University (2010), http://aib.informatik.rwth-aachen.de
7. Codish, M., Taboch, C.: A semantic basis for termination analysis of logic programs. Journal of Logic Programming 41(1), 103–123 (1999)
8. Codish, M., Schneider-Kamp, P., Lagoon, V., Thiemann, R., Giesl, J.: SAT solving for argument filterings. In: Hermann, M., Voronkov, A. (eds.) LPAR 2006. LNCS (LNAI), vol. 4246, pp. 30–44. Springer, Heidelberg (2006)
9. Codish, M., Lagoon, V., Stuckey, P.: Solving partial order constraints for LPO termination. J. Satisfiability, Boolean Modeling and Computation 5, 193–215 (2008)
10. Dershowitz, N., Manna, Z.: Proving termination with multiset orderings. Communications of the ACM 22(8), 465–476 (1979)
11. Eén, N., Sörensson, N.: MiniSAT, http://minisat.se
12. Endrullis, J., Waldmann, J., Zantema, H.: Matrix interpretations for proving termination of term rewriting. J. Automated Reasoning 40(2-3), 195–220 (2008)
13. Fuhs, C., Giesl, J., Middeldorp, A., Thiemann, R., Schneider-Kamp, P., Zankl, H.: SAT solving for termination analysis with polynomial interpretations. In: Marques-Silva, J., Sakallah, K.A. (eds.) SAT 2007. LNCS, vol. 4501, pp. 340–354. Springer, Heidelberg (2007)
14. Giesl, J., Thiemann, R., Schneider-Kamp, P.: The dependency pair framework: Combining techniques for automated termination proofs. In: Baader, F., Voronkov, A. (eds.) LPAR 2004. LNCS (LNAI), vol. 3542, pp. 301–331. Springer, Heidelberg (2005)
15. Giesl, J., Schneider-Kamp, P., Thiemann, R.: AProVE 1.2: Automatic termination proofs in the dependency pair framework. In: Furbach, U., Shankar, N. (eds.) IJCAR 2006. LNCS (LNAI), vol. 4130, pp. 281–286. Springer, Heidelberg (2006)
16. Giesl, J., Thiemann, R., Schneider-Kamp, P., Falke, S.: Mechanizing and improving dependency pairs. Journal of Automated Reasoning 37(3), 155–203 (2006)
17. Giesl, J., Raffelsieper, M., Schneider-Kamp, P., Swiderski, S., Thiemann, R.: Automated termination proofs for Haskell by term rewriting. ACM Transactions on Programming Languages and Systems (to appear, 2010); Preliminary version appeared in Pfenning, F. (ed.) RTA 2006. LNCS, vol. 4098, pp. 297–312. Springer, Heidelberg (2006)
18. Hirokawa, N., Middeldorp, A.: Automating the dependency pair method. Information and Computation 199(1,2), 172–199 (2005)
19. Jones, N.D., Bohr, N.: Termination analysis of the untyped lambda calculus. In: van Oostrom, V. (ed.) RTA 2004. LNCS, vol. 3091, pp. 1–23. Springer, Heidelberg (2004)
20. Le Berre, D., Parrain, A.: SAT4J, http://www.sat4j.org
21. Lee, C.S., Jones, N.D., Ben-Amram, A.M.: The size-change principle for program termination. In: Proc. POPL 2001, pp. 81–92 (2001)
22. Lee, C.S.: Ranking functions for size-change termination. ACM Transactions on Programming Languages and Systems 31(3), 1–42 (2009)
23. Nguyen, M.T., De Schreye, D., Giesl, J., Schneider-Kamp, P.: Polytool: Polynomial interpretations as a basis for termination analysis of logic programs. In: Theory and Practice of Logic Programming (to appear, 2010)
24. Otto, C., Brockschmidt, M., von Essen, C., Giesl, J.: Automated termination analysis of Java Bytecode by term rewriting. In: Proc. RTA 2010. LIPIcs, vol. 6, pp. 259–276 (2010)
25. Podelski, A., Rybalchenko, A.: Transition Invariants. In: Proc. 19th LICS, pp. 32–41. IEEE, Los Alamitos (2004)

26. Schneider-Kamp, P., Thiemann, R., Annov, E., Codish, M., Giesl, J.: Proving termination using recursive path orders and SAT solving. In: Konev, B., Wolter, F. (eds.) FroCos 2007. LNCS (LNAI), vol. 4720, pp. 267–282. Springer, Heidelberg (2007)
27. Schneider-Kamp, P., Giesl, J., Serebrenik, A., Thiemann, R.: Automated termination proofs for logic programs by term rewriting. ACM Transactions on Computational Logic 11(1), 1–52 (2009)
28. Sereni, D., Jones, N.D.: Termination analysis of higher-order functional programs. In: Yi, K. (ed.) APLAS 2005. LNCS, vol. 3780, pp. 281–297. Springer, Heidelberg (2005)
29. Thiemann, R., Giesl, J.: The size-change principle and dependency pairs for termination of term rewriting. Applicable Algebra in Engineering, Communication and Computing 16(4), 229–270 (2005)
30. Zankl, H., Hirokawa, N., Middeldorp, A.: KBO orientability. Journal of Automated Reasoning 43(2), 173–201 (2009)

A Syntactical Approach to Qualitative Constraint Networks Merging

Jean-François Condotta, Souhila Kaci, Pierre Marquis, and Nicolas Schwind

Université Lille-Nord de France, Artois, F-62307 Lens
CRIL, F-62307 Lens
CNRS UMR 8188, F-62307 Lens
{condotta,kaci,marquis,schwind}@cril.univ-artois.fr

Abstract. We address the problem of merging qualitative constraint networks (QCNs) representing agents local preferences or beliefs on the relative position of spatial or temporal entities. Two classes of merging operators which, given a set of input QCNs defined on the same qualitative formalism, return a set of qualitative configurations representing a global view of these QCNs, are pointed out. These operators are based on local distances and aggregation functions. In contrast to QCN merging operators recently proposed in the literature, they take account for each constraint from the input QCNs within the merging process. Doing so, inconsistent QCNs do not need to be discarded at start, hence agents reporting locally consistent, yet globally inconsistent pieces of information (due to limited rationality) can be taken into consideration.

1 Introduction

Qualitative representation of time and space arises in many domains of Artificial Intelligence such as language processing, computer vision, planning. One needs to take advantage of a qualitative formalism when the available information about a set of spatial or temporal entities is expressed in terms of non-numerical relationships between these entities (e.g., when information comes primarily from natural language sentence). Starting from Allen's formalism [1] basically used to represent relative positions of temporal intervals, many other qualitative formalisms have been put forward in the literature these last three decades [24,19,15,2,8,20]. Besides temporal and spatial aspects, these formalisms also constitute powerful representation settings for a number of applications of Artificial Intelligence, such as reasoning about preferences [9] or multiple taxonomies [23].

When we are asked to express a set of preferred or believed relationships between entities, we are generally more willing to provide local relations about a small number of entities from which the underlying set of preferred or possible configurations about the whole set of entities can be deduced. Consider for example a student, William, who expresses his preferences on the schedule of four courses (Operating Systems, Algebra, Analysis, Programming). William prefers to learn Analysis after Algebra. Assume William would also like to learn Programming after Analysis and wants to start learning Programming before Algebra finishes. Then no schedule can satisfy all his preferences, since satisfying

C. Fermüller and A. Voronkov (Eds.): LPAR-17, LNCS 6397, pp. 233–247, 2010.

two of his wishes implies the third one to be discarded. Obviously, conflicts can also arise in the case when several students are asked to express their preferences on a common schedule.

In this paper we address the problem where several agents express their preferences / beliefs on relative positions of (spatial or temporal) entities. This information is represented, for each agent, by means of a qualitative constraint network (QCN). A procedure for merging QCN has been proposed in [6], directly adapted from a "model-based" method for merging propositional knowledge bases [13,14]. This procedure is generic in the sense that it does not depend on a specific qualitative formalism. It consists in defining a merging operator which associates with a finite set of QCNs a set of consistent (spatial or temporal) information representing a global view of the input QCNs. While this method represents a starting point in the problem of merging QCNs, it has however some limitations. First, a QCN to be merged is reduced to its global possible configurations; therefore inconsistent QCNs are discarded. As we will show in the paper, even if a QCN is inconsistent, it may however contain relevant information which deserves to be considered in the merging process. Secondly, this approach is expensive from a computational point of view as it requires the computation of all possible configurations about the whole set of entities. This paper aims at overcoming the above limitations. We propose a syntactical approach for merging QCNs in which each constraint from the input QCNs participates in the merging process. We define two classes of QCN merging operators, where each operator associates with a finite set of QCNs defined on the same qualitative formalism and the same set of entities a set of consistent qualitative configurations representing a global view of the input set of QCNs. Each operator is based on distances between relations of the underlying qualitative formalism and on two aggregation functions.

The rest of the paper is organized as follows. The next section recalls necessary preliminaries on qualitative constraint networks, distances between relations of a qualitative formalim and aggregation functions. In Section 3, we address the problem of dealing with conflicting QCNs. We introduce a running example and give some postulates that QCN merging operators are expected to satisfy. In Section 4, we define the two proposed classes of QCN merging operators and discuss their logical properties. We give some hints to choose a QCN merging operator in Section 5, and also give some comparisons with related works. We conclude in the last section and present some perspectives for further research. For space reasons, proofs are not provided; they are available in the longer version of the paper, http://www.cril.univ-artois.fr/~marquis/lpar2010longversion.pdf.

2 Preliminaries

2.1 Qualitative Formalisms and Qualitative Constraint Networks

A qualitative formalism considers a finite set B of basic binary relations defined on a domain D. The elements of D represent the considered (spatial or temporal) entities. Each basic relation $b \in$ B represents a particular relative position between two elements of D. The set B is required to be a *partition scheme* [16], i.e., it satisfies the following properties: (i) B forms a partition of $\mathsf{D} \times \mathsf{D}$, namely any pair of $\mathsf{D} \times \mathsf{D}$ satisfies one and only one basic relation of B; (ii) the identity relation on D, denoted by eq, belongs to B; lastly, (iii) if b is a basic relation of B, then its converse, denoted by b^{-1}, also belongs to B.

For illustration we consider a well-known qualitative formalism introduced by Allen, called Interval Algebra [1]. This formalism considers a set $\mathsf{B}_{\mathsf{int}}$ of thirteen basic relations defined on the domain of non-punctual (durative) intervals over the rational numbers: $\mathsf{D}_{\mathsf{int}} = \{(x^-, x^+) \in \mathbb{Q} \times \mathbb{Q} : x^- < x^+\}$. An interval typically represents a temporal entity. The basic relations of $\mathsf{B}_{\mathsf{int}} = \{eq, p, pi, m, mi, o, oi, s, si, d, di, f, fi\}$ are depicted in Figure 1. Each one of them represents a particular situation between two intervals. For example, the relation $m = \{((x^-, x^+), (y^-, y^+)) \in \mathsf{D}_{\mathsf{int}} \times \mathsf{D}_{\mathsf{int}} : x^+ = y^-\}$ represents the case where the upper bound of the first interval and the lower bound of the second one coincide.

Relation	Symbol	Inverse	Illustration
precedes	p	pi	
meets	m	mi	
overlaps	o	oi	
starts	s	si	
during	d	di	
finishes	f	fi	
equals	eq	eq	

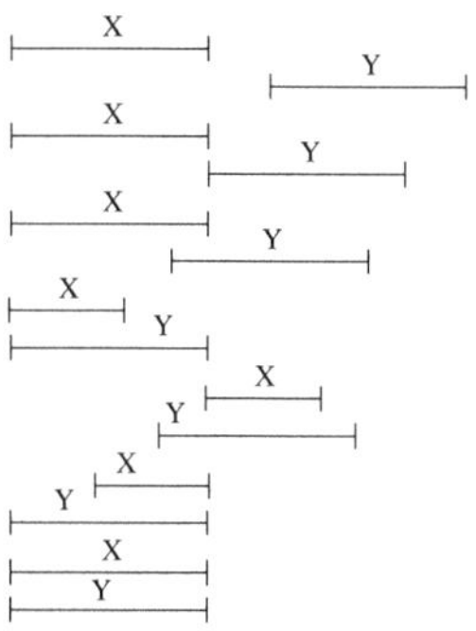

Fig. 1. The basic relations of Interval Algebra

Given a set B of basic relations, a *complex relation* is the union of basic relations and is represented by the set of the basic relations it contains. In the following we omit the qualifier "complex". For instance, considering Interval Algebra, the set $\{m, d\}$ represents the union of the basic relations m and d. The set of all relations is denoted by 2^{B}.

Pieces of information about the relative positions of a set of (spatial or temporal) entities can be represented by means of qualitative constraint networks (QCNs for short). Formally, a QCN (on B) is defined as follows:

Definition 1 (Qualitative constraint network). *A* QCN N *is a pair* (V, C) *where:*

- $V = \{v_1, \ldots, v_n\}$ *is a finite set of variables representing the entities,*
- C *is a mapping which associates with each pair of variables* (v_i, v_j) *a relation* $N[i, j]$ *of* 2^{B}. C *is such that* $N[i, i] = \{eq\}$ *and* $N[i, j] = N[j, i]^{-1}$ *for every pair of variables* $v_i, v_j \in V$.

Given a QCN $N = (V, C)$, a *consistent instantiation* of N over $V' \subseteq V$ is a mapping α from V' to D such that for every pair $(v_i, v_j) \in V' \times V'$, $(\alpha(v_i), \alpha(v_j))$ satisfies $N[i, j]$, i.e., there exists a basic relation $b \in N[i, j]$ such that $(\alpha(v_i), \alpha(v_j)) \in b$ for every $v_i, v_j \in V'$. A *solution* of N is a consistent instantiation of N over V. N is *consistent* iff it admits a solution. A *sub-network* N' of N is a QCN (V, C') such that $N'[i, j] \subseteq N[i, j]$, for every pair of variables v_i, v_j. A *scenario* σ is a QCN such that each constraint is defined by a singleton relation of 2^{B}, i.e., a relation containing exactly one basic relation. Let σ be a scenario, the basic relation specifying the constraint between two variables v_i and v_j is denoted by σ_{ij}. A scenario σ of N is a sub-network of N. In the rest of this paper, $\langle N \rangle$ denotes the set of scenarios of N and $[N]$ the set of its consistent scenarios. Two QCNs N and N' are said to be *equivalent*, denoted by $N \equiv N'$, iff $[N] = [N']$. N^V_{All} denotes the QCN on V such that for each pair of variables (v_i, v_j), $N^V_{All}[i, j] = \{eq\}$ if $v_i = v_j$, $N^V_{All}[i, j] = \mathsf{B}$ otherwise. N^V_{All} represents the complete lack of information about the relative positions of the variables.

Figures 2(a), 2(b) and 2(c) represent respectively a QCN N of Interval Algebra defined on the set $V = \{v_1, v_2, v_3, v_4\}$, an inconsistent scenario σ of N and a consistent scenario σ' of N. A solution α of σ' is represented in Figure 2(d). In order to alleviate the figures, for each pair of variables (v_i, v_j), we do not represent the constraint $N[i, j]$ when $N[i, j] = \mathsf{B}$, when $N[j, i]$ is represented or when $i = j$.

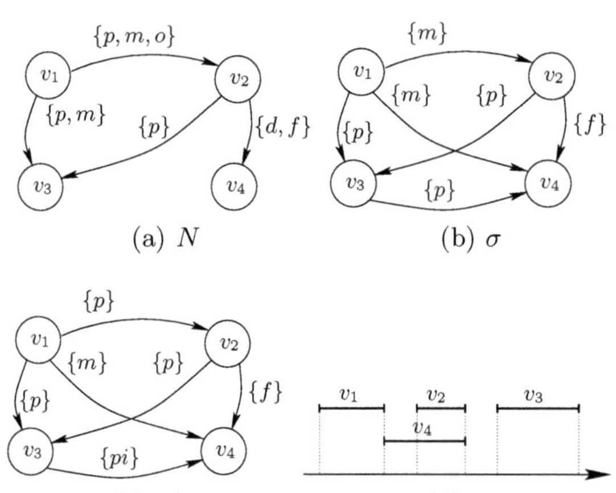

Fig. 2. A QCN N, an inconsistent scenario σ of N, a consistent scenario σ' of N and a solution α of σ'

2.2 Basic Distances and Aggregation Functions

In the following, we consider two classes of QCN merging operators parameterized by a distance between basic relations of B called *basic distance*, and by aggregation functions.

Basic distances. A basic distance associates with a pair of basic relations of B a positive number representing their degree of closeness [6].

Definition 2 (Basic distance). *A basic distance* d_{B} *is a pseudo-distance, i.e., a mapping from* $\mathsf{B} \times \mathsf{B}$ *to* $\mathbb{R}_0^+$ *such that* $\forall b, b' \in \mathsf{B}$, *we have:*

$$\begin{cases} d_{\mathsf{B}}(b, b') = d_{\mathsf{B}}(b', b) & \textit{(symmetry)} \\ d_{\mathsf{B}}(b, b') = 0 \textit{ iff } b = b' & \textit{(identity of indiscernibles)} \\ d_{\mathsf{B}}(b, b') = d_{\mathsf{B}}(b^{-1}, (b')^{-1}). \end{cases}$$

For instance, the drastic distance d_D is equal to 1 for every pair of distinct basic relations, 0 otherwise.

In the context of qualitative algebras, two distinct basic relations can be more or less close from each other. This intuition takes its source in works of Freksa [7] who defined different notions of conceptual neighborhood between basic relations of Interval Algebra. By generalizing his definition, it is natural to state that two basic relations $b, b' \in \mathsf{B}$ are conceptually neighbors if a continuous transformation on the elements of the domain leads to two entities which satisfy the basic relation b and also directly satisfy the basic relation b' without satisfying any other basic relation. A conceptual neighborhood defines a binary relation on elements of B. This relation can be represented by an undirected connected graph in which every vertice is an element of B. In such a graph, called *conceptual neighborhood graph*, two vertices connected by an edge are conceptual neighbors. For example, in a context where a continuous transformation between two intervals corresponds to moving only one of the four possible bounds, we get the conceptual neighborhood graph $\mathsf{GB}_{\mathsf{int}}$ depicted in Figure 3.

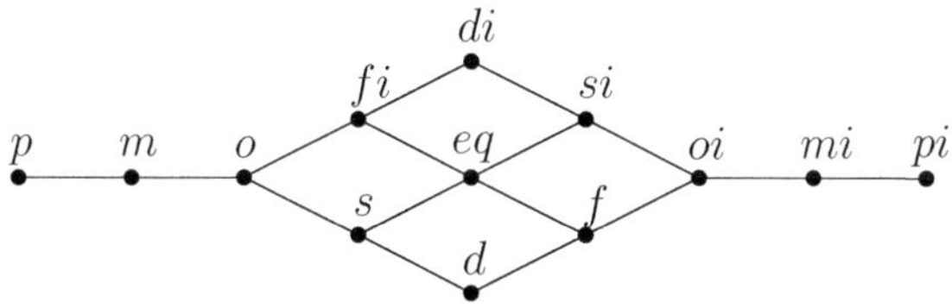

Fig. 3. The conceptual neighborhood graph $\mathsf{GB}_{\mathsf{int}}$ of Interval Algebra

Using conceptual neighborhood graphs a specific basic distance has been defined in the context of QCNs in [6]. The so-called *conceptual neighborhood distance* is formally defined as follows:

Definition 3 (Conceptual neighborhood distance). *Let* GB *be a conceptual neighborhood graph on* B. *The conceptual neighborhood distance* $d_{\mathsf{GB}}(a, b)$ *between two basic relations* $a, b \in \mathsf{B}$ *is the length of the shortest chain leading from* a *to* b *in* GB.

In the following examples, we will use the conceptual neighborhood distance $d_{\mathsf{GB}_{\mathsf{int}}}$ defined from the graph $\mathsf{GB}_{\mathsf{int}}$. For instance, $d_{\mathsf{GB}_{\mathsf{int}}}(m, di) = 4$. Notice that $d_{\mathsf{GB}_{\mathsf{int}}}$ is a basic distance in the sense of Definition 2.

Aggregation functions. An aggregation function [18,11,12] typically combines in a given manner several numerical values into a single one.

Definition 4 (Aggregation function). *An aggregation function f associates with a vector of non-negative real numbers a non-negative real number verifying the following properties:*

$$\begin{cases} \textit{if } x_1 \leq x'_1, \ldots, x_p \leq x'_p, \\ \qquad\qquad \textit{then } f(x_1, \ldots, x_p) \leq f(x'_1, \ldots, x'_p) \ \textit{(non-decreasingness)} \\ x_1 = \cdots = x_p = 0 \ \ \textit{iff} \ \ f(x_1, \ldots, x_p) = 0 \qquad \textit{(minimality).} \end{cases}$$

Many aggregation functions have been considered so far in various contexts. For instance, $\sum$ (sum), Max (maximum), $Leximax$[1] are often considered in the belief merging setting [17,21,13,11,14]. We give some additional properties on aggregation functions.

Definition 5 (Properties on aggregation functions). *Let f and g be two aggregation functions.*

- *f is* symmetric *iff for every permutation τ from $\mathbb{R}_0^p$ to $\mathbb{R}_0^p$, p being a positive integer, $f(x_1, \ldots, x_p) = f(\tau(x_1), \ldots, \tau(x_p))$.*
- *f is* associative *iff*
$$f(f(x_1, \ldots, x_p), f(y_1, \ldots, y_{p'})) = f(x_1, \ldots, x_p, y_1, \ldots, y_{p'}).$$
- *f is* strictly non-decreasing *iff if $x_1 \leq x'_1, \ldots, x_p \leq x'_p$ and $\exists i \in \{1, \ldots, p\}$, $x_i < x'_i$, then $f(x_1, \ldots, x_p) < f(x'_1, \ldots, x'_p)$.*
- *f* commutes with *g (or f and g are* commuting aggregation functions*) iff $f(g(x_{1,1}, \ldots, x_{1,q}), \ldots, g(x_{p,1}, \ldots, x_{p,q})) = g(f(x_{1,1}, \ldots, x_{p,1}), \ldots, f(x_{1,q}, \ldots, x_{p,q}))$.*

For example, the aggregation function $\sum$ is symmetric and associative, hence it commutes with itself, as well as the aggregation function Max. Symmetry means that the order of the aggregated values does not affect the result, associativity means that the aggregation of values can be factorized into partial aggregations. In the following, aggregation functions are supposed to be symmetric, i.e., they aggregate multi-sets of numbers instead of vectors of numbers. In [22], the authors focus on commuting aggregation functions since such functions play a significant role in any two-step merging process for which the result should not depend on the order of the aggregation processes. In the end of Section 4.2 we stress the influence of commuting aggregation functions in our merging procedures.

---

[1] Stricto sensu the $Leximax$ function returns the input vector sorted decreasingly w.r.t the standard lexicographic ordering; it turns out that we can associate to $Leximax$ an aggregation function in the sense of Definition 4, leading to the same vector ordering as $Leximax$ (see [11], Definition 5.1); for this reason, slightly abusing words, we also call this function "$Leximax$".

3 The Merging Issue

3.1 Problem and Example

Let $V = \{v_1, \ldots, v_n\}$ be a set of variables and $\mathcal{N} = \{N^1, \ldots, N^m\}$ be a multiset of QCNs defined over V. $\mathcal{N}$ is called a *profile*. Every input QCN $N^k \in \mathcal{N}$ stems from a particular agent k providing her own preferences or beliefs about the relative configurations over V. Every constraint $N^k[i, j]$ corresponds to the set of basic relations that agent k considers as possibly satisfied by (v_i, v_j). In such a setting, two kinds of inconsistency are likely to appear. On the one hand, a QCN N^k may be inconsistent since the agent expresses local preferences over pairs of variables. Therefore an inconsistency may arise without the agent being necessarily aware of that. On the other hand, the multiplicity of sources makes that the underlying QCNs are generally conflicting when combined. For example, in case of preferences representation, a single conflict of interest between two agents about the same pair of variables is sufficient to introduce inconsistency.

Consider a group of three students expressing their preferences about the schedule of fours common courses: Operating Systems (OS), Algebra, Analysis and Programming. Every student of the group provides a set of binary relations between these courses. The variables we consider here are four temporal entities v_1, v_2, v_3, v_4 that respectively correspond to OS, Algebra, Analysis, Programming and that form the set V. We consider Interval Algebra to model qualitative relations between these courses. For exemple, the first student prefers to start learning OS before the beginning of Algebra and to finish studying OS before the end of Algebra. This can be expressed by the relation $v_1 \; \{p, m, o\} \; v_2$. The three students provide the QCNs N^1, N^2, N^3 depicted in Figure 4 and forming the profile $\mathcal{N}$. Notice that the conflict occurring in the example sketched in the introduction is represented in the QCN N^3, indeed there does not exist any consistent instantiation of N^3 over $\{v_2, v_3, v_4\}$.

3.2 Rationality Postulates for QCN Merging Operators

Given a profile $\mathcal{N} = \{N^1, \ldots, N^m\}$ defined on V representing local preferences or beliefs of a set of agents, we want to get as result of the merging operation a non-empty set of *consistent* information representing $\mathcal{N}$ in a global way. Formally, this calls for a notion of merging operator. In [5] a set of rationality postulates has been proposed for QCN merging operators. These postulates are

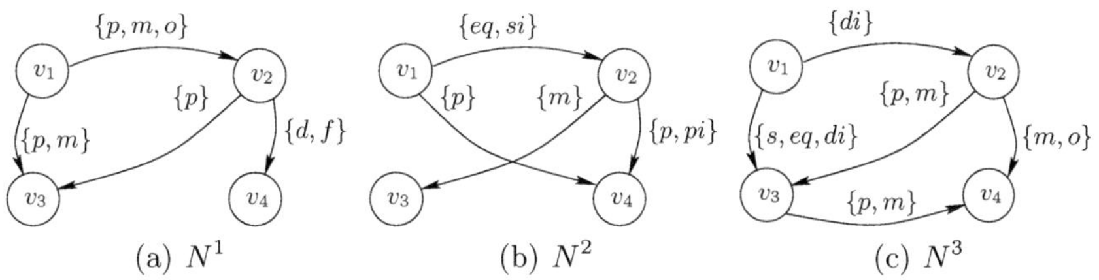

Fig. 4. Three QCNs N^1, N^2 and N^3 to be merged

the direct counterparts in the QCN setting of the postulates from [13] characterizing merging operators for propositional logic. We separate these postulates into two classes: the first one defines the QCN merging operators, the second one provides additional properties that QCN merging operators should satisfy to exhibit a rational behaviour.

Definition 6 (QCN **merging operator**). *An operator Δ is a mapping which associates with a profile $\mathcal{N}$ a set $\Delta(\mathcal{N})$ of consistent scenarios. Let $\mathcal{N}$ be a profile. Δ is a* QCN *merging operator iff it satisfies the following postulates:*

(N1) $\Delta(\mathcal{N}) \neq \emptyset$.
(N2) If $\bigcap\{[N^k] \mid N^k \in \mathcal{N}\} \neq \emptyset$, *then* $\Delta(\mathcal{N}) = \bigcap\{[N^k] \mid N^k \in \mathcal{N}\}$.

(N1) ensures that the result of the merging is non-trivial; (N2) requires $\Delta(\mathcal{N})$ to be the set of consistent scenarios shared by all $N^k \in \mathcal{N}$, when this set is non-empty.

Before giving the additional postulates, we need to define the notion of equivalence between profiles. Two profiles $\mathcal{N}$ and $\mathcal{N}'$ are said to be *equivalent*, denoted by $\mathcal{N} \equiv \mathcal{N}'$, iff there exists a one-to-one correspondence f between $\mathcal{N}$ and $\mathcal{N}'$ such that $\forall N^k \in \mathcal{N}$, $f(N^k) \equiv N^k$. We use $\sqcup$ to denote the union operator for multisets.

Definition 7 (postulates (N3) - (N6)). *Let $\mathcal{N}, \mathcal{N}_1$ and $\mathcal{N}_2$ be three profiles, and let N, N' be two consistent* QCNs.

(N3) If $\mathcal{N}_1 \equiv \mathcal{N}_2$, *then* $\Delta(\mathcal{N}_1) = \Delta(\mathcal{N}_2)$.
(N4) If $\Delta(\{N, N'\}) \cap [N] \neq \emptyset$, *then* $\Delta(\{N, N'\}) \cap [N'] \neq \emptyset$.
(N5) $\Delta(\mathcal{N}_1) \cap \Delta(\mathcal{N}_2) \subseteq \Delta(\mathcal{N}_1 \sqcup \mathcal{N}_2)$.
(N6) If $\Delta(\mathcal{N}_1) \cap \Delta(\mathcal{N}_2) \neq \emptyset$, *then* $\Delta(\mathcal{N}_1 \sqcup \mathcal{N}_2) \subseteq \Delta(\mathcal{N}_1) \cap \Delta(\mathcal{N}_2)$.

(N3) is the syntax-irrelevance principle for QCNs. It states that if two profiles are equivalent, then merging independently each profile should lead to the same result. (N4) is an equity postulate, it requires the QCN merging operator not to exploit any hidden preference between two QCNs to be merged. (N5) and (N6) together ensure that when merging independently two profiles leads both results to share a non-empty set of consistent scenarios, let us say E, then merging the joint profiles should return E as result.

4 Two Classes of QCN Merging Operators

In this section, we define two classes of QCN merging operators. Operators from the first and second class are respectively denoted by Δ_1 and Δ_2. These operators associate with a profile $\mathcal{N}$ a set of consistent scenarios that are the "closest" ones to $\mathcal{N}$ in terms of "distance". The difference between Δ_1 and Δ_2 is inherent to the definition of such a distance.

For $i \in \{1, 2\}$, a QCN merging operator Δ_i is characterized by a triple $(d_{\mathsf{B}}, f_i, g_i)$ where d_{B} is a basic distance on B and f_i and g_i are two symmetric aggregation functions. Δ_i is then denoted by $\Delta_i^{d_{\mathsf{B}}, f_i, g_i}$. The set of consistent scenarios $\Delta_i^{d_{\mathsf{B}}, f_i, g_i}(\mathcal{N})$ is the result of a two-step process.

4.1 Δ_1 Operators

The first step consists in computing a *local distance* d_{f_1} between every consistent scenario on V, i.e., every element of $[N_{All}^V]$ and each QCN of the profile $\mathcal{N}$. For this purpose, the basic distance d_B and the aggregation function f_1 are used to define the distance d_{f_1} between two scenarios σ and σ' of N_{All}^V, as follows:

$$d_{f_1}(\sigma, \sigma') = f_1\{d_\mathsf{B}(\sigma_{ij}, \sigma'_{ij}) \mid v_i, v_j \in V, i < j\}.$$

Therefore the distance between two scenarios results from the aggregation of distances at the constraints level. The definition of d_{f_1} is extended in order to compute a distance between a consistent scenario σ of N_{All}^V and a QCN N^k of $\mathcal{N}$ as follows:

$$d_{f_1}(\sigma, N^k) = \min\{d_{f_1}(\sigma, \sigma') \mid \sigma' \in \langle N^k \rangle\}.$$

Therefore the distance between a scenario σ and a QCN N^k is the minimal distance (w.r.t. d_{f_1}) between σ and a scenario of N^k.

The choice of the aggregation function f_1 depends on the context. For example, $f_1 = Max$ is appropriate when only the greatest distance over all constraints between a scenario and a QCN is important, whatever their number. However, by instantiating $f_1 = \sum$, the distances d_B over all constraints are summed up, thus all of them are taken into account.

Example (continued). For the sake of conciseness, we represent a scenario as the list of its constraints following the lexicographical order over (v_i, v_j), $i < j$. For instance, the consistent scenario σ_1 depicted in Figure 5(a) is specified by the list $(\{fi\}, \{m\}, \{p\}, \{m\}, \{p\}, \{m\})$. Let σ'' be the (inconsistent) scenario of N^1 (see Figure 4(a)) defined by $(\{o\}, \{m\}, \{p\}, \{p\}, \{d\}, \{m\})$. We use here the basic distance $d_{\mathsf{GB}_\mathsf{int}}$ and will do so for the next examples. We consider $f_1 = \sum$. Then we have:

$$\begin{aligned} d_{\sum}(\sigma_1, N^1) &= \min\{d_{\sum}(\sigma_1, \sigma') \mid \sigma' \in \langle N^1 \rangle\} = d_{\sum}(\sigma_1, \sigma'') \\ &= \textstyle\sum\{d_{\mathsf{GB}_\mathsf{int}}(fi, o), d_{\mathsf{GB}_\mathsf{int}}(m, m), d_{\mathsf{GB}_\mathsf{int}}(p, p), \\ &\qquad d_{\mathsf{GB}_\mathsf{int}}(m, p), d_{\mathsf{GB}_\mathsf{int}}(p, d), d_{\mathsf{GB}_\mathsf{int}}(m, m)\} \\ &= 1 + 0 + 0 + 1 + 4 + 0 = 6. \end{aligned}$$

Similarly we get $d_{\sum}(\sigma_1, N^2) = 1$ and $d_{\sum}(\sigma_1, N^3) = 4$.

The second step of the merging process consists in taking advantage of the aggregation function g_1 to aggregate the local distances $d_{f_1}(\sigma, N^k)$ for every QCN $N^k \in \mathcal{N}$; the resulting value can be viewed as a *global distance* d_{g_1} between σ and the profile $\mathcal{N}$. This distance is defined as follows:

$$d_{g_1}(\sigma, \mathcal{N}) = g_1\{d_{f_1}(\sigma, N^k) \mid N^k \in \mathcal{N}\}.$$

For the arbitration function $g_1 = Max$, the global distance represents a consensual value w.r.t. all sources [21]; with $g_1 = \sum$, it reflects the majority point of view of the sources [17].

Example (continued). Consider here $g_1 = Max$. We have :

$$d_{Max}(\sigma_1, \mathcal{N}) = \max\{d_{\sum}(\sigma_1, N^k) \mid N^k \in \mathcal{N}\} = \max\{6, 1, 4\} = 6.$$

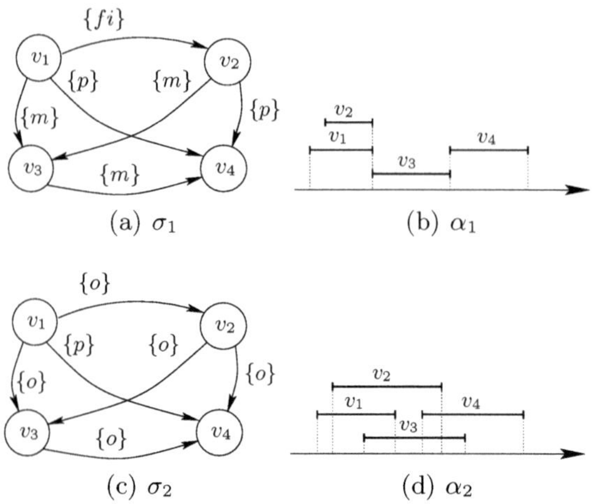

Fig. 5. Two consistent scenarios σ_1 and σ_2 of N_{All}^V, and two consistent instantiations α_1 and α_2 of σ_1 and σ_2

The set $\Delta_1^{d_{\mathsf{B}},f_1,g_1}(\mathcal{N})$ is the set of the consistent scenarios of N_{All}^V having a minimal global distance d_{g_1}. Formally,

$$\Delta_1^{d_{\mathsf{B}},f_1,g_1}(\mathcal{N}) = \{\sigma \in [N_{All}^V] \mid \nexists \sigma' \in [N_{All}^V], d_{g_1}(\sigma',\mathcal{N}) < d_{g_1}(\sigma,\mathcal{N})\}.$$

Example (continued). Consider the consistent scenario σ_2 depicted in Figure 5(c). We can compute its global distance similarly as for σ_1. We then have $d_{Max}(\sigma_2,\mathcal{N}) = 5$. Since $d_{Max}(\sigma_2,\mathcal{N}) < d_{Max}(\sigma_1,\mathcal{N})$, we can conclude that the consistent scenario σ_1 does not belong to the set $\Delta_1^{d_{\mathsf{GB}_{\mathsf{int}}},\Sigma,Max}(\mathcal{N})$.

Proposition 1. $\Delta_1^{d_{\mathsf{B}},f_1,g_1}$ *is a* QCN *merging operator in the sense of Definition 6, i.e., it satisfies postulates (N1) and (N2). Moreover, if* g_1 *is an associative aggregation function, then* $\Delta_1^{d_{\mathsf{B}},f_1,g_1}$ *satisfies (N5), and if* g_1 *is an associative and strictly non-decreasing aggregation function, then* $\Delta_1^{d_{\mathsf{B}},f_1,g_1}$ *satisfies (N6). It does not satisfy (N3) and (N4).*

4.2 Δ_2 Operators

An operator from the Δ_2 family is defined in two steps as follows. The first step consists in computing a *local distance* d_{f_2} between every basic relation of B and the multiset $\mathcal{N}[i,j] = \{N^k[i,j] \mid N^k \in \mathcal{N}\}$, for every pair (v_i, v_j), $i < j$. The definition of the basic distance d_{B} between two basic relations of B is extended to the basic distance between a basic relation $b \in \mathsf{B}$ and a relation $R \in 2^{\mathsf{B}}$, $R \neq \emptyset$. It corresponds to the minimal basic distance between b and every basic relation of R. Formally we write:

$$d_{\mathsf{B}}(b,R) = \min\{d_{\mathsf{B}}(b,b') \mid b' \in R\}.$$

The aggregation function f_2 is used to compute the local distance between every basic relation of B and the multiset of constraints $\mathcal{N}[i,j] = \{N^k[i,j] \mid N^k \in \mathcal{N}\}$ as follows:

$$d_{f_2}(b, \mathcal{N}[i,j]) = f_2\{d_{\mathsf{B}}(b, N^k[i,j]) \mid N^k[i,j] \in \mathcal{N}[i,j]\}.$$

The choice of f_2 is motivated in the same way as that of g_1 for Δ_1 operators. Depending on the context, we opt for a majority function $\sum$ [17], or for an arbitration function Max [21]. Here the aggregation step relates the constraints $N^k[i,j]$ of the QCNs $N^k \in \mathcal{N}$, for a given pair of variables (v_i, v_j), $i < j$.

Example (continued). Consider the multiset $\mathcal{N}[1,2] = \{\{p,m,o\},\{eq,si\},\{di\}\}$ (see Figure 4). We consider $d_{\mathsf{GB}_{\mathsf{int}}}$ as the basic distance and $f_2 = Max$. The distance between the basic relation fi and the multiset $\mathcal{N}[1,2]$ is defined as follows:

$$\begin{aligned} d_{Max}(fi, \mathcal{N}[1,2]) &= \max\{d_{\mathsf{GB}_{\mathsf{int}}}(fi,\{p,m,o\}), \\ &\qquad d_{\mathsf{GB}_{\mathsf{int}}}(fi,\{eq,si\}), d_{\mathsf{GB}_{\mathsf{int}}}(fi,\{di\})\} \\ &= \max\{d_{\mathsf{GB}_{\mathsf{int}}}(fi,o), d_{\mathsf{GB}_{\mathsf{int}}}(fi,eq), d_{\mathsf{GB}_{\mathsf{int}}}(fi,di)\} \\ &= \max\{1,1,1\} = 1. \end{aligned}$$

The second step consists in aggregating the local distances computed in the previous step for all pairs (v_i, v_j), $i < j$, in order to compute a *global distance* d_{g_2} between a scenario σ of N^V_{All} and the profile $\mathcal{N}$. This distance is computed using the aggregation function g_2 as follows:

$$d_{g_2}(\sigma, \mathcal{N}) = g_2\{d_{f_2}(\sigma_{ij}, \mathcal{N}[i,j]) \mid v_i, v_j \in V, i < j\}.$$

The choice of g_2 is motivated in the same way as the aggregation function f_1 for Δ_1 operators.

Example (continued). Consider again the consistent scenario σ_1 (see Figure 5(a)) and choose $g_2 = \sum$. We get:

$$\begin{aligned} d_{\sum}(\sigma_1, \mathcal{N}) &= \textstyle\sum\{d_{Max}(\sigma_1(1,2), \mathcal{N}[1,2]), \ldots, d_{Max}(\sigma_1(3,4), \mathcal{N}[3,4])\} \\ &= 1+2+0+1+4+0 = 8. \end{aligned}$$

Similarly to Δ_1 operators, the result of the merging process over the profile $\mathcal{N}$ using $\Delta_2^{d_{\mathsf{B}}, f_2, g_2}$ corresponds to the set of consistent scenarios of N^V_{All} that minimize the global distance d_{g_2}. Formally,

$$\Delta_2^{d_{\mathsf{B}}, f_2, g_2}(\mathcal{N}) = \{\sigma \in [N^V_{All}] \mid \nexists \sigma' \in [N^V_{All}], d_{g_2}(\sigma', \mathcal{N}) < d_{g_2}(\sigma, \mathcal{N})\}.$$

Example (continued). Consider again the consistent scenario σ_2 depicted in Figure 5(c). Its global distance to $\mathcal{N}$, computed similarly to the one of σ_1, is $d_{\sum}(\sigma_2, \mathcal{N}) = 8$. Notice that the consistent scenarios σ_1 and σ_2 have the same global distance to $\mathcal{N}$. We can then conclude that $\sigma_1 \in \Delta_2^{d_{\mathsf{GB}_{\mathsf{int}}}, Max, \sum}(\mathcal{N})$ iff $\sigma_2 \in \Delta_2^{d_{\mathsf{GB}_{\mathsf{int}}}, Max, \sum}(\mathcal{N})$.

One can prove that Δ_2 operators typically satisfies less expected postulates than the Δ_1 ones:

Proposition 2. *$\Delta_2^{d_B,f_2,g_2}$ is a* QCN *merging operator in the sense of Definition 6, i.e., it satisfies the postulates (N1) and (N2). The postulates (N3) - (N6) are not satisfied.*

That Δ_1 and Δ_2 are syntactical operators is reflected by the fact that they do not satisfy the syntax-independence postulate (N3) (see Propositions 1 and 2). Similarly in [10] several syntax-sensitive propositional merging operators have been investigated, none of them satisfying the counterpart of (N3) in the propositional setting. We give some conditions under which Δ_1 and Δ_2 operators are equivalent.

Proposition 3. *If $f_1 = g_2$, $f_2 = g_1$ and f_1 and f_2 are commuting aggregation functions, then $\Delta_1^{d_B,f_1,g_1}(\mathcal{N}) = \Delta_2^{d_B,f_2,g_2}(\mathcal{N})$.*

Consequently, when $f_1 = g_2$, $f_2 = g_1$ and for instance when $(f_1, f_2) \in \{(\sum, \sum), (Max, Max)\}$, then choosing a Δ_1 operator rather than a Δ_2 one (or conversely) has no impact on the result. However, $\sum$ and Max are not commuting aggregation functions, so for such choices using Δ_1 or Δ_2 can lead to different results.

4.3 Computational Complexity

Beyond logical postulates, complexity considerations can be used as choice criteria for a QCN merging operator. Clearly enough, the merging result may be of exponential size in the worst case, just like representation of the merging result in the propositional case [3,11,12]. As discussed in [6], a set of consistent scenarios cannot always be represented by a single QCN. In [6] a basic construction of a QCN N_S is given from a set S of consistent scenarios leading to $S = [N_S]$ when possible. Nevertheless, computing explicitly the merging result (as a set of consistent scenarios in our setting, as a propositional formula in the propositional framework) is not mandatory to reason with [3,11,12]; often it is enough to be able to determine whether a given scenario belongs to it. This is why we focus on the following MEMBERSHIP problem (MS for short): given $i \in \{1, 2\}$, d_B a basic distance, f_i, g_i two aggregation functions, $\mathcal{N}$ a profile and σ_* a scenario, does σ_* belong to $\Delta_i^{d_B,f_i,g_i}(\mathcal{N})$? The following proposition provides an upper bound of complexity for the MS problem.

Proposition 4. *If f_i, g_i are computed in polynomial time, then* MS $\in$ **coNP**.

Interestingly, usual aggregation functions like $\sum$ or Max can be computed in polynomial time. For the merging procedure proposed in [6], MS is likely harder, i.e., falls to a complexity class above **coNP** in the polynomial hierarchy. Indeed for both Δ_1 and Δ_2 operators, the global distance between a scenario and a profile is computed in polynomial time. In comparison, for the merging operator proposed in [6], computing the global distance between a scenario and a profile requires the computation of all consistent scenarios of every QCN of the profile, which are exponentially many in the worst case.

5 Comparison between Δ_1, Δ_2 and Related Works

5.1 When to Choose a Δ_1 Operator

Given a profile $\mathcal{N}$, opting for an operator Δ_1 is appropriate when the sources are independent of one another, i.e., when information provided by each QCN of the profile should be treated independently. Indeed the first aggregation step is "local" to a particular QCN, while the second one is an "inter-source" aggregation. In this respect, Δ_1 operators are close to QCN merging operators Θ proposed in [6] and propositional merging operators $\mathbf{DA}^2$ studied in [11,12]. In [6] the QCN merging operators Θ consider like Δ_1 operators a profile $\mathcal{N}$ as input and return a set of consistent scenarios following a similar two-step process, with only $f_1 = \sum$. However, while Δ_1 operators consider the sets of scenarios of the QCNs of $\mathcal{N}$ in the computation of the local distance d_{f_1}, Θ operators consider the sets of their *consistent* scenarios. Doing so, neither inconsistent QCNs of $\mathcal{N}$ are taken into account by Θ operators, nor the basic relations of the constraints of the QCNs which do not participate in any consistent scenario of this QCN. In [11,12] the authors define a class $\mathbf{DA}^2$ of propositional knowledge bases merging operators, based on a distance between interpretations and two aggregation functions. A profile corresponds in this case to a multiset of knowledge bases, each one expressed as a finite set of propositional formulas. A first step consists in computing a local distance between an interpretation ω and a knowledge base K through the aggregation of the distances between ω and every propositional formula of K. A second step then consists in aggregating the local distances to combine all knowledge bases of the profile. In the context of QCN merging, the Δ_1 operators typically follow the same merging principle.

5.2 When to Choose a Δ_2 Operator

Δ_2 operators are suited to the context when a global decision should be made *a priori* for every pair of variables (v_i, v_j). In this case every pair of variables is considered as a "criterion' or "topic" on which a mutual agreement has to be found as a first step. The second step then can be viewed as a relaxation of the independence criteria which are combined in order to find consistent global configurations. Δ_2 operators consider a local distance d_{f_2} which coincides with the one proposed in [4]. In this work, the authors use this local distance d_{f_2} to define a *constraint merging operator*. Such an operator associates with a multiset $\mathcal{R}$ of relations the set of basic relations for which the distance d_{f_2} to $\mathcal{R}$ is minimal. In this framework, a QCN merging operator, denoted by Ω, associates with a profile $\mathcal{N}$ a single QCN $\Omega(\mathcal{N})$. Similarly to Δ_2 operators, Ω operators take into consideration inconsistent QCNs and consider every basic relation of all constraints of the input QCNs as a relevant piece of information in the merging process. However, Ω operators require to be given a fixed total ordering $<_V$ on the pairs of variables (v_i, v_j). Following this ordering, the constraint of the QCN $\Omega(\mathcal{N})$ bearing on (v_i, v_j) is affected using the constraint merging operator on the constraints of the QCNs of $\mathcal{N}$ bearing on (v_i, v_j). At each step, $\Omega(\mathcal{N})$ is kept consistent. Though the computation of $\Omega(\mathcal{N})$ is efficient, the choice of $<_V$ leads to specific results, while Δ_2 operators - which do not require $<_V$ to be specified - do not suffer from this drawback.

6 Conclusion

In this paper, we have defined two classes Δ_1 and Δ_2 of operators for merging qualitative constraint networks (QCNs) defined on the same qualitative formalism. We have studied their logical properties and we have also considered the problem of deciding whether a given scenario belongs to the result of the merging. From a methodology point of view, we have addressed the problem of choosing such a merging operator. Compared with previous merging operators, Δ_1 and Δ_2 operators achieve a good compromise to QCN merging. Indeed, (i) they take into account fine-grained information provided by the input sources in the sense that each constraint from the input QCNs participates in the merging process (in particular inconsistent scenarios are not excluded); (ii) the computational complexity of query answering for those operators is not very high; (iii) they are QCN merging operators since rationality postulates (N1) and (N2) hold. Interestingly, our operators do not trivialize when applied to a single inconsistent QCN; as such, they can also be viewed as consistency restoring operators.

As a matter for further research, we plan to investigate in depth the complexity issues for all classes of operators defined so far.

References

1. Allen, J.-F.: An interval-based representation of temporal knowledge. In: Proc. of IJCAI 1981, pp. 221–226 (1981)
2. Balbiani, P., Condotta, J.-F., Fariñas del Cerro, L.: A new tractable subclass of the rectangle algebra. In: Proc. of IJCAI 1999, pp. 442–447 (1999)
3. Cadoli, M., Donini, F.M., Liberatore, P., Schaerf, M.: The size of a revised knowledge base. Artificial Intelligence 115(1), 25–64 (1999)
4. Condotta, J.-F., Kaci, S., Marquis, P., Schwind, N.: Merging qualitative constraint networks in a piecewise fashion. In: Proc. of ICTAI 2009, pp. 605–608 (2009)
5. Condotta, J.-F., Kaci, S., Marquis, P., Schwind, N.: Merging qualitative constraints networks using propositional logic. In: Sossai, C., Chemello, G. (eds.) ECSQARU 2009. LNCS, vol. 5590, pp. 347–358. Springer, Heidelberg (2009)
6. Condotta, J.-F., Kaci, S., Schwind, N.: A Framework for Merging Qualitative Constraints Networks. In: Proc. of FLAIRS 2008, pp. 586–591 (2008)
7. Freksa, C.: Temporal reasoning based on semi-intervals. Artificial Intelligence 54(1), 199–227 (1992)
8. Gerevini, A., Renz, J.: Combining topological and size information for spatial reasoning. Artificial Intelligence 137(1-2), 1–42 (2002)
9. Kaci, S., Piette, C.: Looking for the best and the worst. In: Colloque sur l'Optimisation et les Systèmes d'Information, COSI (2009)
10. Konieczny, S.: On the difference between merging knowledge bases and combining them. In: Proc. of KR 2000, pp. 135–144 (2000)

11. Konieczny, S., Lang, J., Marquis, P.: Distance-based merging: a general framework and some complexity results. In: Proc. of KR 2002, pp. 97–108 (2002)
12. Konieczny, S., Lang, J., Marquis, P.: $\mathbf{DA}^2$ merging operators. Artificial Intelligence 157(1-2), 49–79 (2004)
13. Konieczny, S., Pino Pérez, R.: On the logic of merging. In: Proc. of KR 1998, pp. 488–498 (1998)
14. Konieczny, S., Pino Prez, R.: Merging information under constraints: a logical framework. Journal of Logic and Computation 12(5), 773–808 (2002)
15. Ligozat, G.: Reasoning about cardinal directions. Journal of Visual Languages and Computing 9(1), 23–44 (1998)
16. Ligozat, G., Renz, J.: What Is a Qualitative Calculus? A General Framework. In: Zhang, C., W. Guesgen, H., Yeap, W.-K. (eds.) PRICAI 2004. LNCS (LNAI), vol. 3157, pp. 53–64. Springer, Heidelberg (2004)
17. Lin, J.: Integration of weighted knowledge bases. Artificial Intelligence 83(2), 363–378 (1996)
18. Marichal, J.-L.: Aggregation Operators for Multicriteria Decision Aid. PhD thesis, Institute of Mathematics, University of Liège, Liège, Belgium (1998)
19. Randell, D.-A., Cui, Z., Cohn, A.: A spatial logic based on regions and connection. In: Proc. of KR 1992, pp. 165–176 (1992)
20. Renz, J., Mitra, D.: Qualitative direction calculi with arbitrary granularity. In: Zhang, C., W. Guesgen, H., Yeap, W.-K. (eds.) PRICAI 2004. LNCS (LNAI), vol. 3157, pp. 65–74. Springer, Heidelberg (2004)
21. Revesz, P.Z.: On the Semantics of Arbitration. Journal of Algebra and Computation 7(2), 133–160 (1997)
22. Saminger-Platz, S., Mesiar, R., Dubois, D.: Aggregation operators and commuting. IEEE T. Fuzzy Systems 15(6), 1032–1045 (2007)
23. Thau, D., Bowers, S., Ludäscher, B.: Merging taxonomies under RCC-5 algebraic articulations. In: Proc. of ONISW 2008, pp. 47–54 (2008)
24. van Beek, P.: Reasoning about qualitative temporal information. In: Proc. of AAAI 1990, pp. 728–734 (1990)

On the Satisfiability of Two-Variable Logic over Data Words

Claire David, Leonid Libkin, and Tony Tan

School of Informatics, University of Edinburgh

Abstract. Data trees and data words have been studied extensively in connection with XML reasoning. These are trees or words that, in addition to labels from a finite alphabet, carry labels from an infinite alphabet (data). While in general logics such as MSO or FO are undecidable for such extensions, decidablity results for their fragments have been obtained recently, most notably for the two-variable fragments of FO and existential MSO. The proofs, however, are very long and nontrivial, and some of them come with no complexity guarantees. Here we give a much simplified proof of the decidability of two-variable logics for data words with the successor and data-equality predicates. In addition, the new proof provides several new fragments of lower complexity. The proof mixes database-inspired constraints with encodings in Presburger arithmetic.

1 Introduction

The classical theory of automata and formal languages deals primarily with finite alphabets. Nonetheless, there are several models of formal languages, regular or context free, that permit an infinite alphabet, e.g., [4,7,15,18,25,26]. Most of the models, however, lack the usual nice decidability properties of automata over finite alphabets, unless strongs restrictions are imposed.

Recently the subject of languages over infinite alphabets received much attention due to its connection with the problems of reasoning about XML [3,5,6,9,10]. The structure of XML documents is usually modeled by labeled unranked trees [16,22,28], and thus standard automata techniques can be used to reason about the structure of XML documents. However, XML documents carry *data*, which is typically modeled as labeling nodes by letters from a different, infinite alphabet.

Thus, one needs to look for *decidable formalisms* in the presence of a second, infinite alphabet. Such formalisms are hard to come by, and tend to be of very high complexity. Nonetheless, some significant progress has been made recently [5]. Namely, it was shown that the restriction of first-order logic to its two-variable fragment, FO^2, remains decidable over trees with labels coming from an infinite alphabet (we refer to them as *data trees*). This is the best possible restriction in terms of the number of variables: the three-variable fragment FO^3 is undecidable [5].

C. Fermüller and A. Voronkov (Eds.): LPAR-17, LNCS 6397, pp. 248–262, 2010.

The result is true even if the sentence is preceded by a sequence of existential monadic second-order quantifiers, i.e., for logic $\exists$MSO^2. The proof of this decidability result, however, was very nontrivial relying on a complicated automaton model, and gave no insight into the complexity of fragments nor the possibility of extending it to more expressive logics.

However, we do want to have tools to reason about languages over infinite alphabets, so there is a search for easier tools. One direction is to look for restrictions, both in terms of structures and logics [3,11]. As for restrictions, the most natural idea appears to be to look for tools over *words*, rather than trees. This has been done in [6,9], which provided decidable formalisms for *data words*, i.e., words labeled by both a finite and an infinite alphabet. In fact, [6] showed that the two-variable logic is decidable. Specifically, it showed that in the presence of both ordering and successor relations on the domain, the logic $\exists$MSO^2 is decidable; no upper bound on the complexity is known, however. The proof, however, is again highly nontrivial and not particularly modular.

Our *main goal* is to give a much simpler and completely self-contained proof of the decidability of satisfiability of the two-variable logic over data words. We do it for the case when the successor relation is available on the domain (as with the successor relation, the logic $\exists$MSO^2 can already define all regular languages). The proof relies on two key ideas: reducing the problem to resoning about some specific constraints (similar to those used in database theory [2]), and using tools based on Presburger arithmetic to reason about those.

Organization. In Section 2 we give the key definitions of data words and logics on them and state the main result. In Section 3 we provide additional definitions and notations. In Section 4 we provide the machinery needed for the main proof. In Section 5 we present the proof of the decidability result. In conclusion, we analyse the complexity of the our decision procedures.

2 Data Words and the Main Result

2.1 Data Words

Let Σ be a finite alphabet and $\mathfrak{D}$ be an infinite set of data values. To be concrete, we assume that $\mathfrak{D}$ contains $\mathbb{N}$, the set of natural numbers. A data word is simply an element of $(\Sigma \times \mathfrak{D})^*$. We usually write $w = \binom{a_1}{d_1} \cdots \binom{a_n}{d_n}$ for data words, where $a_i \in \Sigma$ and $d_i \in \mathfrak{D}$. We define the Σ projection of w as $\mathsf{Proj}(w) = a_1 \cdots a_n$.

An a-position is a position labeled with the symbol a. The set of data values found in a-positions of a data word w is denoted by $V_w(a)$, while the number of a-positions in w is denoted by $\#_w(a)$.

The following notion is used throughout the paper. For a set $S \subseteq \Sigma$,

$$[S]_w = \bigcap_{a \in S} V_w(a) \cap \bigcap_{b \notin S} \overline{V_w(b)}.$$

That is, $[S]_w$ is the set of data values that are found in a-positions for all $a \in S$ but are not found in any b-position for $b \notin S$. Note that the sets $[S]_w$'s are disjoint, and that $V_w(a) = \bigcup_{a \in S} [S]_w$ for each $a \in \Sigma$.

We say that a data word is *locally different*, if every position has a different data value than its left- and right-neighbors.

2.2 Logics over Data Words

For the purpose of logical definability, we view data words of length n as structures

$$w = \langle \{1,\ldots,n\}, +1, \{a(\cdot)\}_{a\in\Sigma}, \sim\rangle, \qquad (1)$$

where $\{1,\ldots,n\}$ is the domain of positions, $+1$ is the successor relation (i.e., $+1(i,j)$ iff $i+1=j$), the $a(\cdot)$'s are the labeling predicates, and $i \sim j$ holds iff positions i and j have the same data value.

We let FO stand for first-order logic, MSO for monadic second-order logic (which extends FO with quantification over sets of positions), and $\exists$MSO for existential monadic second order logic, i.e., sentences of the form $\exists X_1 \ldots \exists X_m\ \psi$, where ψ is an FO formula over the vocabulary extended with the unary predicates $X_1,\ldots,X_m$. We let FO^2 stand for FO with two variables, i.e., the set of FO formulae that only use two variables x and y. The set of all sentences of the form $\exists X_1 \ldots \exists X_m\ \psi$, where ψ is an FO^2 formula is denoted by $\exists\text{MSO}^2$.

To emphasize that we are talking about a logic over data words we write $(+1,\sim)$ after the logic: e.g., $\text{FO}^2(+1,\sim)$ and $\exists\text{MSO}^2(\sim,+1)$. Note that $\exists\text{MSO}^2(+1)$ is equivalent in expressive power to MSO over the usual (not data) words, i.e., it defines precisely the regular languages [27].

It was shown in [6] that $\exists\text{MSO}^2(+1,<,\sim)$ is decidable over data words. In terms of complexity, the satisfiability of this logic is shown to be at least as hard as reachability in Petri nets. Without the $+1$ relation, the complexity drops to NEXPTIME-complete; however, without $+1$ the logic is not sufficiently expressive to capture regular relations on the data-free part of the word.

Our main goal is to give a transparent and self-contained proof of the following:

Theorem 1. *The satisfiability problem is decidable for* $\exists\text{MSO}^2(\sim,+1)$ *over data words. Moreover, the complexity of the decision procedure is elementary.*

The result itself can already be infered from the decidability proof of the logic with local navigation over data trees given in [5], which yields a 4-exponential complexity bound. However this proof does not give any hints in understanding the difficulty of the problem. Our proof yields a 5-exponential bound.

Neither of these bounds are of course even remotely practical. The primary goal of these results is to delineate the boundary of decidability, so that later we could search for efficient subclasses of decidable classes of formulae. And for such a search, it is crucial to have simple and well-defined tools for proving decidability; providing such tools is precisely our goal here. Indeed a few fragments of lower complexity are already provided here. Furthermore, in [10] a fragment whose satisfiability is decidable in NP is obtained. [1] With our proof we gain some insight on how the complexity "moves up continuously" from NP to 5-exponential.

---

[1] This fragment is context free languages with the constraints on the data values of the forms: $\forall x \forall y\ a(x) \wedge a(y) \wedge x \sim y \rightarrow x = y$, and $\forall x \exists y\ a(x) \rightarrow b(y) \wedge x \sim y$.

3 Additional Notations

3.1 Disjunctive Constraints for Data Words

We consider two types of constraints on data words, which are slight generalizations of keys and inclusion constraints used in relational databases [2]. They are defined as the following logical sentences.

1. A *disjunctive key* constraint (dk) is a sentence of the form:

$$\forall x \, \forall y \, \Big(\big(\bigvee_{a \in \Sigma'} a(x) \wedge \bigvee_{a \in \Sigma'} a(y) \wedge x \sim y \big) \rightarrow x = y \Big),$$

   where $\Sigma' \subseteq \Sigma$. We denote such sentence by $V(\Sigma') \mapsto \Sigma'$.
2. A *disjunctive inclusion constraint* (dic) is as sentence of the form:

$$\forall x \, \exists y \, \Big(\bigvee_{a \in \Sigma_1} a(x) \rightarrow \bigvee_{b \in \Sigma_2} b(y) \wedge x \sim y \Big),$$

   where $\Sigma_1, \Sigma_2 \subseteq \Sigma$. We denote such sentence by $V(\Sigma_1) \subseteq V(\Sigma_2)$.

For a set $\mathcal{C}$ of dk's and dic's, the data word w satisfies $\mathcal{C}$, written as $w \models \mathcal{C}$, if w satisfies all sentences in $\mathcal{C}$.

In [10] the constraints considered are when all the cardinalities $|\Sigma'|$, $|\Sigma_1|$, $|\Sigma_2|$ are one, which are simply known as key and inclusion constraint.

3.2 Existential Presburger Formulae

Atomic Presburger formulae are of the form: $x_1 + x_2 + \cdots x_n \leq y_1 + \cdots + y_m$, or $x_1 + \cdots x_n \leq K$, or $x_1 + \cdots x_n \geq K$, for some constant $K \in \mathbb{N}$. *Existential Presburger formulae* are Presburger formulae of the form $\exists \bar{x} \; \varphi$, where φ is a Boolean combination of atomic Presburger formulae.

We shall be using Presburger formulae defining Parikh images of words. Let $\Sigma = \{a_1, \ldots, a_k\}$, and let $v \in \Sigma^*$. By $\mathsf{Parikh}(v)$ we mean the *Parikh image* of v, i.e., $(\#_v(a_1), \ldots, \#_v(a_k))$, i.e., k-tuple of integers $(n_1, \ldots, n_k)$ so that n_i is the number of occurrences of a_i in v.

With alphabet letters, we associate variables $x_{a_1}, \ldots, x_{a_k}$. Given a Presburger formula $\varphi(x_{a_1}, \ldots, x_{a_k})$, we say that a word $v \in \Sigma^*$ satisfies it, written as $v \models \varphi(x_{a_1}, \ldots, x_{a_k})$ if and only if $\varphi(\mathsf{Parikh}(v))$ holds. It is well-known that for every regular language L, one can construct an existential Presburger formula $\varphi_L(x_{a_1}, \ldots, x_{a_k})$ so that a word v satisfies it iff it belongs to L [21]; moreover, the formula can be constructed in polynomial time [24].

3.3 Presburger Automata

A *Presburger automaton* is a pair $(\mathcal{A}, \varphi)$, where $\mathcal{A}$ is a finite state automaton and φ is an existential Presburger formula. A word w is accepted by $(\mathcal{A}, \varphi)$, denoted by $\mathcal{L}(\mathcal{A}, \varphi)$, if $w \in \mathcal{L}(\mathcal{A})$ (the language of $\mathcal{A}$) and $\varphi(\mathsf{Parikh}(w))$ holds.

Theorem 2. *[24] The emptiness problem for presburger automata is decidable in* NP.

3.4 Profile Automata for Data Words

Given a data word $w = \binom{a_1}{d_1} \cdots \binom{a_n}{d_n}$, the *profile word* of w, denoted by $\mathsf{Profile}(w)$, is the word

$$\mathsf{Profile}(w) = (a_1, L_1, R_1), \ldots, (a_n, L_n, R_n) \in (\Sigma \times \{*, \top, \bot\} \times \{*, \top, \bot\})^*$$

such that for each position $i = 1, \ldots, n$, the values of L_i and R_i are either $\top$, or $\bot$, or $*$. If $L_i = \top$ and $i > 1$, it means that the position on the left, $i - 1$, has the same data value as position i; otherwise $L_i = \bot$. If $i = 1$ (i.e., there is no position on the left), then $L_i = *$. The meaning of the R_i's is similar with respect to positions on the right of i.

Definition 1. *A* profile automaton $\mathcal{A}$ *is a finite state automaton over the alphabet* $\Sigma \times \{*, \top, \bot\} \times \{*, \top, \bot\}$. *It defines a set* $\mathcal{L}_{data}(\mathcal{A})$ *of data words as follows:* $w \in \mathcal{L}_{data}(\mathcal{A})$ *if and only if* $\mathcal{A}$ *accepts* $\mathsf{Profile}(w)$ *in the standard sense.*

A profile automaton $\mathcal{A}$ and a set $\mathcal{C}$ of disjunctive constraints define a set of data words as follows.

$$\mathcal{L}(\mathcal{A}, \mathcal{C}) = \{w \mid w \in \mathcal{L}_{data}(\mathcal{A}) \text{ and } w \models \mathcal{C}\}.$$

3.5 A Normal Form for $\exists\mathrm{MSO}^2(\sim, +1)$

Decidability proofs for two-variable logics typically follow this pattern: first, in an easy step, a syntact normal form is established; then the hard part is combinatorial, where decidability is proved for that normal form (by establishing the finite-model property, or by automata techniques, for example).

A normal form for $\exists\mathrm{MSO}^2(\sim, +1)$ was already given in [5], and we shall use it with just a small modification. In [5] it was shown that every $\exists\mathrm{MSO}^2(\sim, +1)$ formula over data words is equivalent to a formula

$$\exists X_1 \ldots \exists X_k (\chi \wedge \bigwedge_i \varphi_i \wedge \bigwedge_j \psi_j)$$

where

1. χ describes the behavior of a profile automaton (i.e., it can be viewed as an $\mathrm{FO}^2(+1)$ formula over the extended alphabet $\Sigma \times \{*, \top, \bot\} \times \{*, \top, \bot\}$);
2. each φ_i is of the form $\forall x \forall y (\alpha(x) \wedge \alpha(y) \wedge x \sim y \rightarrow x = y)$, where α is a conjunction of labeling predicates, X_k's, and their negations; and
3. each ψ_j is of the form $\forall x \exists y\ \alpha(x) \rightarrow (x \sim y \wedge \alpha'(y))$, with α, α' as in item 2.

The number of the unary predicates X's is single exponential in the size of the original input sentence.

If we extend the alphabet to $\Sigma \times 2^k$ so that each label also specifies the family of the X_i's the node belongs to, then formulae in items 2 and 3 can be encoded by disjunctive constraints: formulae in item 2 become dk's $V(\Sigma') \mapsto \Sigma'$, and formulae in item 3 become dic's $V(\Sigma_1) \subseteq V(\Sigma_2)$, where $\Sigma', \Sigma_1, \Sigma_2 \subseteq \Sigma \times 2^k$.

Indeed, consider, for example, the constraint $\forall x \forall y(\alpha(x) \wedge \alpha(y) \wedge x \sim y \rightarrow x = y)$. Let Σ' be the set of all symbols $(a, \bar{b}) \in \Sigma \times 2^k$ consistent with α. That is, a is the labeling symbol used in α (if α uses one) or an arbitrary letter (if α does not use a labeling predicate), and the Boolean vector $\bar{b}$ has 1 in positions of the X_is used positively in α and 0 in positions of X_j's used negatively in α. Then the original constraint is equivalent to $V(\Sigma') \mapsto \Sigma'$. The transformation of type-2 constraints into dic's is the same. The details of this straightforward construction can be found in the Appendix in [1].

Hence, [5] and the above, imply the following. Let SAT-PROFILE be the problem:

PROBLEM:	SAT-PROFILE
INPUT:	a profile automaton $\mathcal{A}$ and a collection $\mathcal{C}$ of disjunctive constraints
QUESTION:	is there a data word $w \in \mathcal{L}_{data}(\mathcal{A})$ such that $w \models \mathcal{C}$?

Then:

Lemma 1. *Given an $\exists\mathrm{MSO}^2(\sim, +1)$ sentence φ, one can construct, in triple exponential time, an instance $(\mathcal{A}, \mathcal{C})$ of* SAT-PROFILE *over a new alphabet Σ so that* SAT-PROFILE$(\mathcal{A}, \mathcal{C})$ *returns true iff φ is satisfiable. However, the size of $(\mathcal{A}, \mathcal{C})$ and Σ is double exponential in the size of φ.*

Thus, our main goal now is to prove:

Theorem 3. SAT-PROFILE *is decidable with elementary complexity.*

The main result, Theorem 1, is an immediate consequence of Theorem 3 and Lemma 1.

4 Some Preliminary Results

Proposition 1. *For every data word w, the following holds.*

1. *$w \models V(\Sigma') \mapsto \Sigma'$ if and only if $\#_w(a) = |V_w(a)|$ for each $a \in \Sigma'$ and $[S]_w = \emptyset$, whenever $|S \cap \Sigma'| \geq 2$.*
2. *$w \models V(\Sigma_1) \subseteq V(\Sigma_2)$ if and only if $[S]_w = \emptyset$, for all S such that $S \cap \Sigma_1 \neq \emptyset$ and $S \cap \Sigma_2 = \emptyset$.*

Proof. Part 1 is trivial. For part 2, note that $\bigcup_{a \in \Sigma_1} V_w(a) \subseteq \bigcup_{b \in \Sigma_2} V_w(b)$ if and only if $\left(\bigcup_{a \in \Sigma_1} V_w(a)\right) \cap \bigcap_{b \in \Sigma_2} \overline{V_w(b)} = \emptyset$, which, of course, is equivalent to $[S]_w = \emptyset$, whenever $S \cap \Sigma_1 \neq \emptyset$ and $S \cap \Sigma_2 = \emptyset$. □

Lemma 2. *For every set $\mathcal{C}$ of disjunctive constraints, one can construct, in single-exponential time, a Presburger formula $\varphi_{\mathcal{C}}(x_{a_1}, \ldots, x_{a_k})$ such that for every data word w, we have $w \models \mathcal{C}$ if and only if $\varphi_{\mathcal{C}}(\mathsf{Parikh}(\mathsf{Proj}(w)))$ holds.*

Proof. Let $S_1, \ldots, S_m$ be the enumeration of non-empty subsets of Σ, where $m = 2^{|\Sigma|} - 1$. The formula $\varphi_{\mathcal{C}}$ is of the form $\exists z_{S_1} \cdots \exists z_{S_m}\ \psi$, where ψ is the conjunction of the following quantifier-free formulas:

P1. $x_a \geq \sum_{S \ni a} z_S$, for every $a \in \Sigma$;
P2. if $V(\Sigma') \mapsto \Sigma' \in \mathcal{C}$, we have the conjunction:

$$\bigwedge_{|S \cap \Sigma'| \geq 2} z_S = 0 \quad \wedge \quad \bigwedge_{a \in \Sigma'} x_a = \sum_{a \in S} z_S$$

P3. if $V(\Sigma_1) \subseteq \Sigma_2 \in \mathcal{C}$, we have the conjunction:

$$\bigwedge_{S \cap \Sigma_1 \neq \emptyset \text{ and } S \cap \Sigma_2 = \emptyset} z_S = 0$$

We claim that for every data word w, $w \models \mathcal{C}$ if and only if $\varphi_{\mathcal{C}}(\mathsf{Parikh}(\mathsf{Proj}(w)))$ holds.

Let w be a data word such that $w \models \mathcal{C}$. We need to show that $\varphi_{\mathcal{C}}(\mathsf{Parikh}(\mathsf{Proj}(w)))$ holds. As witnesses for z_S, for each $S \subseteq \Sigma$, we pick $z_S = |[S]_w|$. Now we need to show that all the conjuctions P1–P3 above are satisfied. P1 is definitely satisfied, as for each $a \in \Sigma$, $\sum_{S \ni a} z_S = |V_w(a)| \leq \#_w(a)$. P2 and P3 follow from Proposition 1.

- If $w \models V(\Sigma') \mapsto \Sigma'$, then $\#_w(a) = |V_w(a)|$ for each $a \in \Sigma$ and $[S]_w = \emptyset$, whenever $|S \cap \Sigma'| \geq 2$. So, P2 is automatically satisfied.
- If $w \models V(\Sigma_1) \subset V(\Sigma_2)$, then $[S]_w = \emptyset$, for all S such that $S \cap \Sigma_1 \neq \emptyset$ and $S \cap \Sigma_2 = \emptyset$. Obviously then P3 is satisfied.

Now suppose that v is a word such that $\varphi_{\mathcal{C}}(\mathsf{Parikh}(v))$ holds. We can assign data values to v such that the resulting data word w satisfies every constraints in $\mathcal{C}$. Let $z_S = m_S$ be some witnesses of that $\varphi_{\mathcal{C}}(\mathsf{Parikh}(v))$ holds. Let $K = \sum_S m_S$. We are going to assign the data values $\{1, \ldots, K\}$ to v as follows. Define a function

$$\xi : \{1, \ldots, K\} \rightarrow 2^{\Sigma} - \{\emptyset\},$$

such that $|\xi^{-1}(S)| = m_S$. We then assign the a-positions in v with the data values $\bigcup_{a \in S} \xi^{-1}(S)$, for each $a \in \Sigma$, resulting in a data word w. Such assignment is possible since $\sum_{a \in S} |\xi^{-1}(S)| = \sum_{a \in S} m_S \leq \#_v(a)$. By definition of the function ξ, we obtain that $[S]_w = \xi^{-1}(S)$. That $w \models \mathcal{C}$ follows immediately from Proposition 1. □

Lemma 2 immediately implies the decidability of a slightly simpler version of SAT-PROFILE. Consider the following problem:

PROBLEM:	SAT-AUTOMATON
INPUT:	a finite state automaton $\mathcal{A}$ and a collection $\mathcal{C}$ of disjunctive constraints
QUESTION:	is there a data word w such that $\mathsf{Proj}(w) \in \mathcal{L}(\mathcal{A})$ and $w \models \mathcal{C}$?

By Lemma 2, we can construct in exponential time a Presburger formula $\varphi_{\mathcal{C}}$ of exponential size such that for all data words w we have, $w \models \mathcal{C}$ if and only if $\varphi_{\mathcal{C}}(\mathsf{Parikh}(\mathsf{Proj}(w)))$. Combining it with Theorem 2, we immediately obtain the decidability of the above problem:

Corollary 1. SAT-AUTOMATON *is decidable with elementary complexity.*

The following lemma is crucial in our proof of Theorem 3.

Lemma 3. *Let v be a word over Σ. Suppose that for each $a \in \Sigma$, we are given a set V_a of data values such that*

- *if $V_a = \emptyset$, then $\#_v(a) = 0$; and*
- *$\#_v(a) \geq |V_a| \geq |\Sigma| + 3$ otherwise.*

Then we can assign a data value to each position in v such that the resulting data word w is locally different and for each $a \in \Sigma$, $V_a = V_w(a)$.

Proof. Let $v = a_1 \cdots a_n$. First we assign data values in the following manner: *Let $a \in \Sigma$. Assign each of the data values from V_a in $|V_a|$ number of a-positions in v. One position gets one data value.* Since $\#_a(v) \geq |V_a|$, such assignment is possible, and moreover, if $\#_a(v) > |V_a|$, then some a-positions are without data values. We do this for each $a \in \Sigma$.

Let $w = \binom{a_1}{d_1} \cdots \binom{a_n}{d_n}$ be the resulting data word, where we write $d_i = \sharp$ to denote that position i is still without data value. In the data word w, for each $a \in \Sigma$, we already have $V_w(a) = V_a$.

However, by assigning data values just like that, the data word w may not be locally different. There may exist $i \in \{1, \ldots, n-1\}$ such that $d_i = d_{i+1}$ and $d_i, d_{i+1} \neq \sharp$. We call such a position a *conflict position*. Now, we show that we can always rearrange the data values in w such that the resulting data word has no conflict positions. Suppose position i is a conflict position labeled a. Since there are only $|\Sigma|$ symbols, the data value d_i can only occur at most $|\Sigma|$ times in w. Since $|V_a| \geq |\Sigma| + 3 > |\Sigma|$, there exists a position j such that

- $a_j = a$ and $d_j \neq \sharp$;
- $d_{j-1}, d_{j+1} \neq d_i$.

Now there are $\geq |\Sigma| + 3 - |\Sigma| = 3$ such positions. From all such positions, pick one position j whose data value $d_j \neq d_{i-1}, d_{i+1}$. We can then swap the data values d_i and d_j, resulting in less number of conflict positions inside w. We can repeat this process until there is no more conflict positions inside w.

The final step is to assign data values for the positions in w which do not have data value. This is easy. Since for each $a \in \Sigma$, $|V_a| \geq |\Sigma| + 3 \geq 3$, if the data value $d_i = \sharp$, then we can choose one data value from V_{a_i} which is different from its left- and right-neighbors. This still ensures that we get a locally different data word at the end. This completes the proof. □

5 Proof of Theorem 3

For the sake presentation, we divide it into a few subsections. In Subsection 5.1, we present our algorithm for deciding SAT-PROFILE over locally different data words. Then, we explain how our algorithm can be extended to the general case in Subsection 5.2.

5.1 Satisfiability over Locally Different Data Words

In this subsection we give elementary algorithm to decide the problem SAT-LOCALLY-DIFFERENT defined below. This problem is still a more restricted version of SAT-PROFILE, but more general than SAT-AUTOMATON.

PROBLEM:	SAT-LOCALLY-DIFFERENT
INPUT:	a finite state automaton $\mathcal{A}$ and a collection $\mathcal{C}$ of disjunctive constraints
QUESTION:	is there a locally different data word w such that $\mathsf{Proj}(w) \in \mathcal{L}(\mathcal{A})$ and $w \models \mathcal{C}$?

We further divide the proof for satisfiability SAT-LOCALLY-DIFFERENT into two cases:

- First, we show how to decide SAT-LOCALLY-DIFFERENT over data words with "many" data values.
- Second, we settle SAT-LOCALLY-DIFFERENT in the general case.

We say that a data word w has *"many" data values* if for all $S \subseteq \Sigma$, the cardinality $|[S]_w|$ is either 0 or $\geq |\Sigma| + 3$. Notice that if a data word w has many data values, then either $|V_w(a)| = 0$ or $|V_w(a)| \geq |\Sigma| + 3$ for all $a \in \Sigma$.

The case of data words with many data values. By Lemma 2, we can construct a Presburger formula $\varphi_\mathcal{C}$ such that for every data word w,

$$w \models \mathcal{C} \text{ if and only if } \varphi_\mathcal{C}(\mathsf{Parikh}(\mathsf{Proj}(w))) \text{ holds.}$$

So, for every data word w, $w \in \mathcal{L}(\mathcal{A}, \mathcal{C})$ if and only if $\mathsf{Proj}(w) \in \mathcal{L}(\mathcal{A}, \varphi_\mathcal{C})$. Recall that the formula $\varphi_\mathcal{C}$ is of the form: $\exists z_{S_1} \cdots \exists z_{S_m} \psi_\mathcal{C}$, where $S_1, \ldots, S_m$ is the enumeration of non-empty subsets of Σ and the intention of each z_{S_i} is to represent $|[S_i]_w|$ for data words w for which $\varphi_\mathcal{C}(\mathsf{Parikh}(\mathsf{Proj}(w)))$ holds.

The idea is as follows: given a set $\mathcal{F} \subseteq 2^\Sigma - \{\emptyset\}$, we can decide the existence of a locally different data word $w \in \mathcal{L}(\mathcal{A}, \mathcal{C})$ such that $|[S]_w| = 0$, if $S \in \mathcal{F}$ and $|[S]_w| \geq |\Sigma| + 3$, if $S \notin \mathcal{F}$.

Now, to decide the existence of a locally different data word with many data values in $\mathcal{L}(\mathcal{A}, \mathcal{C})$, we do the following.

1. Guess a set $\mathcal{F} \subseteq 2^\Sigma - \{\emptyset\}$.
2. Construct the formula $\varphi_\mathcal{C}$ from $\mathcal{C}$ according to Lemma 2. Let $\varphi_\mathcal{C}$ be in the form of $\exists z_{S_1} \cdots \exists z_{S_m} \psi_\mathcal{C}$.
3. Define the formula $\varphi_{\mathcal{C},\mathcal{F}}$ as:

$$\exists z_{S_1} \cdots \exists z_{S_m} \Big(\psi_\mathcal{C} \wedge \bigwedge_{S_i \in \mathcal{F}} z_{S_i} = 0 \wedge \bigwedge_{S_i \notin \mathcal{F}} z_{S_i} \geq |\Sigma| + 3\Big)$$

4. Test the emptiness of $\mathcal{L}(\mathcal{A}, \varphi_{\mathcal{C},\mathcal{F}})$.

To show that such algorithm is correct, we claim the following.

Claim 4. *For every word $v \in \Sigma^*$, $v \in \mathcal{L}(\mathcal{A}, \varphi_{\mathcal{C},\mathcal{F}})$ for some $\mathcal{F} \subseteq 2^\Sigma$ if and only if there exists a locally different data word $w \in \mathcal{L}(\mathcal{A}, \mathcal{C})$ with many data values such that* $\mathsf{Proj}(w) = v$.

Proof. If $v \in \mathcal{L}(\mathcal{A}, \varphi_{\mathcal{C},\mathcal{F}})$ for some $\mathcal{F}$, then there exist witnesses $z_{S_i} = m_{S_i}$ such that $\varphi_{\mathcal{C},\mathcal{F}}(\mathsf{Parikh}(v))$ holds. By the construction of $\varphi_{\mathcal{C},\mathcal{F}}$, we have $m_{S_i} = 0$, if $S_i \in \mathcal{F}$ and $m_{S_i} \geq |\Sigma|+3$, if $S_i \notin \mathcal{F}$. As in the proof of Lemma 2, we can assign data values to each position of v, resulting in a data word w such that for each $S \subseteq \Sigma$, $|[S]_w| = m_S$ which is either $\geq |\Sigma| + 3$ or 0. This means that $|V_w(a)|$ is either $\geq |\Sigma| + 3$ or 0. (If $|V_w(a)| = 0$, it means that the symbol a does not appear in v.) By Lemma 3, we can rearrange the data values in w to obtain a locally different data word. This data word is in $\mathcal{L}(\mathcal{A}, \mathcal{C})$.

The converse is straightforward. if $w \in \mathcal{L}(\mathcal{A}, \mathcal{C})$ has many data values, then $v = \mathsf{Proj}(w)$ immediately satisfies $\varphi_{\mathcal{C},\mathcal{F}}$, where $\mathcal{F} = \{S_i \mid |[S_i]_w| = 0\}$. Thus, $v \in \mathcal{L}(\mathcal{A}, \varphi_{\mathcal{C},\mathcal{F}})$. □

The general case of SAT-LOCALLY-DIFFERENT. The algorithm is more or less the same as above. The only extra care needed is to consider the case if there exists a locally different data word $w \in \mathcal{L}(\mathcal{A}, \mathcal{C})$ such that $|[S]_w| \leq |\Sigma| + 2$, for some $S \subseteq \Sigma$.

As before, the idea is to decide, given a set $\mathcal{F} \subseteq 2^\Sigma - \{\emptyset\}$, whether there exists a locally different data word $w \in \mathcal{L}(\mathcal{A}, \mathcal{C})$ such that $|[S]_w| \leq |\Sigma| + 2$, if $S \in \mathcal{F}$ and $\geq |\Sigma| + 3$, otherwise. Again, we reduce the problem to the emptiness of a Presburger automaton.

The main difference is the way to deal with the $S \in \mathcal{F}$, as $S \in \mathcal{F}$ does not always imply that $[S]_w$ is empty but only that its cardinality is bounded by the constant $|\Sigma|+2$. For all these $S \in \mathcal{F}$, we can assume that the data $[S]_w$ consists of constant symbols, since $|[S]_w| \leq |\Sigma| + 2$. We denote such sets of constant symbols by Γ_S, for all $S \in \mathcal{F}$. Then we embed those constant symbols into the finite alphabet Σ and extend the automaton $\mathcal{A}$ to handle the constraints on them.

The details of the algorithm are as follows. It consists of four main steps.

1. **The guessing of the set $\mathcal{F}$ and the constants Γ_S's.**
   a) Guess a set $\mathcal{F} \subseteq 2^\Sigma - \{\emptyset\}$.
   b) For each $S \in \mathcal{F}$, guess an integer $m_S \leq |\Sigma|+2$ according to the following rule.
      - If $V(\Sigma') \mapsto \Sigma' \in \mathcal{C}$, then $m_S = 0$, if $|S \cap \Sigma'| \geq 2$.
      - If $V(\Sigma_1) \subseteq V(\Sigma_2) \in \mathcal{C}$, then $m_S = 0$, if $S \cap \Sigma_1 \neq \emptyset$ and $S \cap \Sigma_2 = \emptyset$.
   c) For each $S \in \mathcal{F}$, fix a set $\Gamma_S = \{\alpha_1^S, \ldots, \alpha_{m_S}^S\}$ of constants such that Γ_S's are disjoint, and $\Gamma_S \cap \mathbb{N} = \emptyset$. Let $\Gamma_\mathcal{F} = \bigcup_{S \in \mathcal{F}} \Gamma_S$.
2. **Embedding the constants of Γ_S's into $\mathcal{A}$.**
   Construct a finite state automaton $\mathcal{A}'$ (from the automaton $\mathcal{A}$) over the alphabet $\Sigma \cup \Sigma \times \Gamma_\mathcal{F}$ as follows. $\mathcal{A}'$ accepts the word $v = b_1 \cdots b_n$ over $\Sigma \cup \Sigma \times \Gamma_\mathcal{F}$ if and only if the following holds.

- A symbol $(a,d) \in \Sigma \times \Gamma_{\mathcal{F}}$ can appear in v if and only if $a \in S$ and $d \in \Gamma_S$.
- Let $u = a_1 \cdots a_n$ be a word over Σ such that

$$a_i = \begin{cases} b_i & \text{if } b_i \in \Sigma, \\ c & \text{if } b_i = (c,d) \in \Sigma \times \Gamma_{\mathcal{F}} \end{cases}$$

  Then, $u \in \mathcal{L}(\mathcal{A})$.
- For $i = 1, \ldots, n-1$, if $b_i = (a_i, d_i) \in \Sigma \times \Gamma_{\mathcal{F}}$ and $b_{i+1} = (a_{i+1}, d_{i+1}) \in \Gamma_{\mathcal{F}}$, then $d_i \neq d_{i+1}$.
- If $V(\Sigma') \mapsto \Sigma'$ is in $\mathcal{C}$, then for each $a \in \Sigma'$ and $\alpha \in \Gamma_S$, where $a \in S$, the symbol (a, α^S) appears exactly once in v.

Note that $\mathcal{A}'$ is defined from $\mathcal{A}$ with the parameters: $\mathcal{F}$ and $\{\Gamma_S \mid S \in \mathcal{F}\}$. The construction is straightforward and can be found in Appendix in [1].

3. Constructing the Presburger formula for $\mathcal{C}$.

a) Construct the formula $\varphi_{\mathcal{C}}$ from $\mathcal{C}$ according to Lemma 2. Let $\varphi_{\mathcal{C}}$ be in the form of $\exists z_{S_1} \cdots \exists z_{S_m}\, \psi_{\mathcal{C}}$.

b) Denote by $\varphi_{\mathcal{C},\mathcal{F}}$ the formula:

$$\exists z_{S_1} \cdots \exists z_{S_m} \Big(\psi_{\mathcal{C}} \wedge \bigwedge_{S_i \in \mathcal{F}} z_{S_i} = 0 \wedge \bigwedge_{S_i \notin \mathcal{F}} z_{S_i} \geq |\Sigma| + 3 \Big)$$

4. The decision step. Test the emptiness of $\mathcal{L}(\mathcal{A}', \varphi_{\mathcal{C},\mathcal{F}})$.

The correctness of the algorithm follows from Claim 5 below.

Claim 5. *There exists a locally different data word $w \in \mathcal{L}(\mathcal{A}, \mathcal{C})$ if and only if there exist a set $\mathcal{F} \subseteq 2^{\Sigma}$ and $\{\Gamma_S \mid S \in \mathcal{F}$ and $|\Gamma_S| \leq |\Sigma| + 2\}$ such that $\mathcal{L}(\mathcal{A}', \varphi_{\mathcal{C},\mathcal{F}}) \neq \emptyset$, where $\mathcal{A}'$ and $\varphi_{\mathcal{C},\mathcal{F}}$ are as defined in our algorithm and the constants Γ_S's respect Step 1.b) above.*

Proof. We prove "only if" part first. Let $w \in \mathcal{L}(\mathcal{A}, \mathcal{C})$ be a locally different data word. The set $\mathcal{F}$ is defined as follows.

- $S \in \mathcal{F}$, if the cardinality $|[S]_w| \leq |\Sigma| + 2$.
- $S \notin \mathcal{F}$, if the cardinality $|[S]_w| \geq |\Sigma| + 3$.

Without loss of generality, we assume that $[S]_w = \Gamma_S$, for $S \in \mathcal{F}$. Let $w = \binom{a_1}{d_1} \cdots \binom{a_n}{d_n}$. We construct the word $v = b_1 \cdots b_n$ as follows. For each $i = 1, \ldots, n$, $b_i = (a_i, d_i)$, if d_i is in some Γ_S, otherwise $b_i = a_i$.

The rest of data values are in $[S]_w$, for some $S \notin \mathcal{F}$. So, $z_S = |[S]_w| \geq |\Sigma| + 3$ serves as witnesses for $S \notin \mathcal{F}$, and $z_S = 0$, for $S \in \mathcal{F}$. Thus, $v \in \mathcal{L}(\mathcal{A}', \varphi_{\mathcal{C},\mathcal{F}})$.

Now we prove the "if" part. Suppose there exist some Γ_S's and a word v over the alphabet $\Sigma \cup (\Sigma \times \bigcup_{S \in \mathcal{S}} \Gamma_S)$ such that $v \in \mathcal{L}(\mathcal{A}', \varphi_{\mathcal{C},\mathcal{F}})$.

Let $v = b_1 \cdots b_n$. If $b_i = (a, \alpha) \in \Sigma \times \Gamma_S$, then we simply view α as the data value in that position. For the other positions, where $b_i = a \in \Sigma$, we assign the data values as before in Lemma 2.

Let $z_S = m_S$ be the witnesses that $v \in \mathcal{L}(\mathcal{A}', \varphi_{\mathcal{C},\mathcal{F}})$ holds. Let $K = \sum_S m_S$. Define the following function:

$$\xi : \{1, \ldots, K\} \rightarrow 2^{\Sigma} - \{\emptyset\},$$

where $|\xi^{-1}(S)| = m_S$.

For each $a \in \Sigma$, we assign the a-positions in v with the data values from $\bigcup_{a \in S} \xi^{-1}(S)$. If necessary, we can apply Lemma 3 to obtain a locally different data word. The data values from Γ_S does not prevent us from applying Lemma 3, since $\Gamma_{\mathcal{F}} \cap \{1, \ldots, K\} = \emptyset$. □

5.2 Satisfiability over General Data Words

Now we extend our idea above to prove Theorem 3. For that we need some auxiliary terms. Let $w = \binom{a_1}{d_1} \cdots \binom{a_n}{d_n}$ be a data word over Σ. A *zone* is a maximal interval $[i, j]$ with the same data values, i.e. $d_i = d_{i+1} = \cdots = d_j$ and $d_{i-1} \neq d_i$ (if $i > 1$) and $d_j \neq d_{j+1}$ (if $j < n$). Obviously each two consecutive zones have different data values. The zone $[i, j]$ is called an S-zone, if S is the set of labels occuring in the zone.

The *zonal partition* of w is a sequence $(k_1, \ldots, k_l)$, where $1 \leq k_1 < k_2 < \cdots < k_l \leq n$ such that $[1, k_1], [k_1 + 1, k_2], \ldots, [k_l + 1, n]$ are the zones in w. Let the zone $[1, k_1]$ be an S_1-zone, $[k_1 + 1, k_2]$ an S_2-zone, $[k_2 + 1..k_3]$ an S_3-zone, and so on. The *zonal word* of w is a data word over $\Sigma \cup 2^{\Sigma}$ defined as follows.

$$\mathsf{Zonal}(w) = a_1 \cdots a_{k_1} \binom{S_1}{d_{k_1}} a_{k_1+1} \cdots a_{k_2} \binom{S_2}{d_{k_2}} \cdots a_{k_l+1} \cdots a_n \binom{S_l}{d_n}.$$

That is, the zonal word of a data word is a word in which each zone is succeeded by a label $S \in 2^{\Sigma}$, if the zone is an S-zone.

Moreover, it is sufficient to assume that only the positions labeled with symbols from 2^{Σ} carry data values, i.e., data values of their respective zones. Since two consecutive zones have different data values, two consecutive positions (in $\mathsf{Zonal}(w)$) labeled with symbols from 2^{Σ} also have different data values.

Furthermore, if w is a data word over Σ, then for each $a \in \Sigma$,

$$V_w(a) = \bigcup_{a \in S} V_{\mathsf{Zonal}(w)}(S).$$

Proposition 2 below shows that disjunctive constraints for data words over the alphabet Σ can be converted into disjunctive constraints for the zonal data words over the alphabet $\Sigma \cup 2^{\Sigma}$.

Proposition 2. *For every data word w over Σ, the following holds.*

- *For $\Sigma' \subseteq \Sigma$, $w \models V(\Sigma') \mapsto \Sigma'$ if and only if*
  K1. $\mathsf{Zonal}(w) \models V(\mathcal{Q}) \mapsto \mathcal{Q}$, *where* $\mathcal{Q} = \{S \mid S \cap \Sigma' \neq \emptyset\}$;
  K2. in $\mathsf{Zonal}(w)$ *every zone contains at most one symbol from Σ'.*
  (By a zone in $\mathsf{Zonal}(w)$*, we mean a maximal interval in which every positions are labeled with symbols from Σ.)*
- *For $\Sigma_1, \Sigma_2 \subseteq \Sigma$, $w \models V(\Sigma_1) \subseteq V(\Sigma_2)$ if and only if* $\mathsf{Zonal}(w) \models V(\mathcal{Q}_1) \subseteq V(\mathcal{Q}_2)$*, where $\mathcal{Q}_1 = \{S \mid S \cap \Sigma_1 \neq \emptyset\}$ and $\mathcal{Q}_2 = \{S \mid S \cap \Sigma_2 \neq \emptyset\}$.*

Now, given a profile automaton $\mathcal{A}$ over the alphabet Σ, we can construct effectively an automaton $\mathcal{A}^{\text{ZONAL}}$ such that for all data word w,

$$\mathsf{Profile}(w) \in \mathcal{L}(\mathcal{A}) \text{ if and only if } \mathsf{Proj}(\mathsf{Zonal}(w)) \in \mathcal{L}(\mathcal{A}^{\text{ZONAL}}).$$

Such an automaton $\mathcal{A}^{\text{ZONAL}}$ is called a *zonal automaton* of $\mathcal{A}$. Moreover, if the dk $V(\Sigma') \mapsto \Sigma' \in \mathcal{C}$, we can impose the condition $K2$ in Proposition 2 inside the automaton $\mathcal{A}^{\text{ZONAL}}$.

This together with Proposition 2 imply that the instance $(\mathcal{A}, \mathcal{C})$ of SAT-PROFILE can be reduced to an instance of the following problem.

PROBLEM:	SAT-LOCALLY-DIFFERENT-FOR-ZONAL-WORDS
INPUT:	• a zonal automaton $\mathcal{A}^{\text{ZONAL}}$ • a collection $\mathcal{C}^{\text{ZONAL}}$ of disjunctive constraints over the alphabet 2^{Σ}
QUESTION:	is there a zonal word w such that • $\mathsf{Proj}(w) \in \mathcal{L}(\mathcal{A}^{\text{ZONAL}})$ and $w \models \mathcal{C}^{\text{ZONAL}}$ and • in which two consecutive positions labeled with symbols from 2^{Σ} have different data values?

The proof in the previous subsection can then be easily adapted to SAT-LOCALLY-DIFFERENT-FOR-ZONAL-WORDS. The details can be found in the Appendix in [1].

6 Analysis of the Complexity

As a conclusion, we provide the complexity of our algorithms.

SAT-AUTOMATON	: NEXPTIME NP(if the alphabet Σ is fixed)
SAT-LOCALLY-DIFFERENT	: NEXPTIME NP(if the alphabet Σ is fixed)
SAT-PROFILE	: 2-NEXPTIME NP(if the alphabet Σ is fixed)

In our algorithms, all three problems are reduced to the emptiness problem for Presburger automata which is decidable in NP(Theorem 2).

In SAT-AUTOMATON the exponential blow-up occurs when reducing the dk's and dic's in $\mathcal{C}$ to the existential Presburger formula $\varphi_{\mathcal{C}}$ (Lemma 2). This formula $\varphi_{\mathcal{C}}$ has exponentially many variables z_S, for every $S \subseteq \Sigma$. Of course, if the alphabet Σ is fixed, then the reduction is polynomial, hence, the NP-membership for SAT-AUTOMATON. It is the same complexity for SAT-LOCALLY-DIFFERENT.

For SAT-PROFILE the additional exponential blow-up occurs when translating the dk's and dic's over the alphabet Σ to the dk's and dic's over the alphabet 2^{Σ}. Now combining this with Lemma 1, we obtain the 4-NEXPTIME upper bound for the satisfaction of $\exists\text{MSO}^2(\sim, +1)$.

Acknowledgement. We acknowledge the financial support of the Future and Emerging Technologies (FET) programme within the Seventh Framework Programme for Research of the European Commission, under the FET-Open grant agreement FOX, number FP7- ICT-233599.

References

1. `http://homepages.inf.ed.ac.uk/ttan/publications/2010/sdw-lpar10.pdf`
2. Abiteboul, S., Hull, R., Vianu, V.: Foundations of Databases. Addison-Wesley, Reading (1995)
3. Björklund, H., Bojanczyk, M.: Bounded depth data trees. In: Arge, L., Cachin, C., Jurdziński, T., Tarlecki, A. (eds.) ICALP 2007. LNCS, vol. 4596, pp. 862–874. Springer, Heidelberg (2007)
4. Boasson, L.: Some applications of CFL's over infinte alphabets. In: Deussen, P. (ed.) GI-TCS 1981. LNCS, vol. 104, pp. 146–151. Springer, Heidelberg (1981)
5. Bojanczyk, M., Muscholl, A., Schwentick, T., Segoufin, L.: Two-variable logic on data trees and XML reasoning. J. ACM 56(3) (2009)
6. Bojanczyk, M., David, C., Muscholl, A., Schwentick, T., Segoufin, L.: Two-variable logic on words with data. In: LICS 2006, pp. 7–16 (2006)
7. Bouyer, P., Petit, A., Thérien, D.: An algebraic characterization of data and timed languages. In: Larsen, K.G., Nielsen, M. (eds.) CONCUR 2001. LNCS, vol. 2154, pp. 248–261. Springer, Heidelberg (2001)
8. Dal-Zilio, S., Lugiez, D., Meyssonnier, C.: A logic you can count on. In: POPL 2004, pp. 135–146 (2004)
9. Demri, S., Lazic, R.: LTL with the freeze quantifier and register automata. ACM TOCL 10(3) (2009)
10. Fan, W., Libkin, L.: On XML integrity constraints in the presence of DTDs. J. ACM 49(3), 368–406 (2002)
11. Figueira, D.: Satisfiability of downward XPath with data equality tests. In: PODS 2009, pp. 197–206 (2009)
12. Ginsburg, S., Spanier, E.H.: Semigroups, Presburger formulas, and languages. Pacific J. Math. 16, 285–296 (1966)
13. Grädel, E., Kolaitis, P., Vardi, M.: On the decision problem for two-variable first-order logic. BSL 3(1), 53–69 (1997)
14. Jurdzinski, M., Lazic, R.: Alternation-free modal mu-calculus for data trees. In: LICS 2007, pp. 131–140 (2007)
15. Kaminski, M., Tan, T.: Tree automata over infinite alphabets. In: Avron, A., Dershowitz, N., Rabinovich, A. (eds.) Pillars of Computer Science. LNCS, vol. 4800, pp. 386–423. Springer, Heidelberg (2008)
16. Libkin, L.: Logics for unranked trees: an overview. In: Caires, L., Italiano, G.F., Monteiro, L., Palamidessi, C., Yung, M. (eds.) ICALP 2005. LNCS, vol. 3580, pp. 35–50. Springer, Heidelberg (2005)
17. Neven, F.: Automata, logic, and XML. In: Bradfield, J.C. (ed.) CSL 2002 and EACSL 2002. LNCS, vol. 2471, pp. 2–26. Springer, Heidelberg (2002)
18. Neven, F., Schwentick, T., Vianu, V.: Finite state machines for strings over infinite alphabets. ACM TOCL 5(3), 403–435 (2004)
19. Otto, M.: Two variable first-order logic over ordered domains. J. Symb. Log. 66(2), 685–702 (2001)

20. Papadimitriou, C.: On the complexity of integer programming. J. ACM 28(4), 765–768 (1981)
21. Parikh, R.: On context-free languages. J. ACM 13(4), 570–581 (1966)
22. Schwentick, T.: Automata for XML – a survey. JCSS 73, 289–315 (2007)
23. Seidl, H., Schwentick, T., Muscholl, A.: Numerical document queries. In: PODS 2003, pp. 155–166 (2003)
24. Seidl, H., Schwentick, T., Muscholl, A., Habermehl, P.: Counting in trees for free. In: Díaz, J., Karhumäki, J., Lepistö, A., Sannella, D. (eds.) ICALP 2004. LNCS, vol. 3142, pp. 1136–1149. Springer, Heidelberg (2004)
25. Tan, T.: Graph reachability and pebble automata over infinite alphabets. In: LICS 2009, pp. 157–166 (2009)
26. Tan, T.: On pebble automata for data languages with decidable emptiness problem. In: Královič, R., Niwiński, D. (eds.) MFCS 2009. LNCS, vol. 5734, pp. 712–723. Springer, Heidelberg (2009)
27. Thomas, W.: Languages, automata, and logic. In: Handbook of Formal Languages, vol. 3, pp. 389–455. Springer, Heidelberg (1997)
28. Vianu, V.: A web Odyssey: from Codd to XML. In: PODS 2001, pp. 1–15 (2001)

Generic Methods for Formalising Sequent Calculi Applied to Provability Logic

Jeremy E. Dawson and Rajeev Goré

Logic and Computation Group, School of Computer Science
The Australian National University, Canberra ACT 0200, Australia
`http://users.rsise.anu.edu.au/~jeremy/`,
`http://users.rsise.anu.edu.au/~rpg/`

Abstract. We describe generic methods for reasoning about multiset-based sequent calculi which allow us to combine shallow and deep embeddings as desired. Our methods are modular, permit explicit structural rules, and are widely applicable to many sequent systems, even to other styles of calculi like natural deduction and term rewriting systems. We describe new axiomatic type classes which enable simplification of multiset or sequent expressions using existing algebraic manipulation facilities. We demonstrate the benefits of our combined approach by formalising in Isabelle/HOL a variant of a recent, non-trivial, pen-and-paper proof of cut-admissibility for the provability logic **GL**, where we abstract a large part of the proof in a way which is immediately applicable to other calculi. Our work also provides a machine-checked proof to settle the controversy surrounding the proof of cut-admissibility for **GL**.

Keywords: provability logic, cut admissibility, interactive theorem proving, proof theory.

1 Introduction

Sequent calculi provide a rigorous basis for meta-theoretic studies of various logics. The central theorem is cut-elimination/admissibility, which states that detours through lemmata can be avoided, since it can help to show many important logical properties like consistency, interpolation, and Beth definability. Cut-free sequent calculi are also used for automated deduction, for nonclassical extensions of logic programming, and for studying the connection between normalising lambda calculi and functional programming. Sequent calculi, and their extensions, therefore play an important role in logic and computation.

Meta-theoretic reasoning about sequent calculi is error-prone because it involves checking many combinatorial cases, some being very difficult, but many being similar. Invariably, authors resort to expressions like "the other cases are similar", or "we omit details". The literature contains many examples of meta-theoretic proofs containing serious and subtle errors in the original pencil-and-paper proofs. For example, the cut-elimination theorem for the modal "provability logic" **GL**, where $\Box\varphi$ can be read as "φ is provable in Peano Arithmetic", has a long and chequered history which has only recently been resolved [5].

C. Fermüller and A. Voronkov (Eds.): LPAR-17, LNCS 6397, pp. 263–277, 2010.

When reasoning about sequent calculi using proof assistants, we have to represent proof-theoretical concepts like "sequents", "derivations" and "derivability" in the meta-logic of the given proof assistant. The granularity of the representation plays a critical role in determining the versatility of the representation. At one extreme, we have "deep" embeddings in which a sequent and a derivation are represented explicitly as terms of the meta-logic, as espoused in our previous work on display calculi [2]. The advantage of this approach is that it allows us to encode fine-grained notions like "each structure variable appears at most once in the conclusion of a rule". The disadvantage of this approach is that it requires a lot of ancillary low-level work to capture essential notions like "rule instance". At the other extreme, we have "shallow" embeddings like the one in the Isabelle/Sequents package, which allows us to derive sequents, but does not allow us to reason about the derivations or derivability. Most practitioners [8,9,3] choose an approach somewhere between these extremes, which then limits their ability to generalise their work to other calculi or to handle arbitrary structural rules for example.

Here, we describe general methods for reasoning in Isabelle/HOL about the proof-theory of traditional, propositional, multiset-based sequent calculi. Our methods are modular in allowing an arbitrary set of rules, permit explicit structural rules, and are widely applicable to many sequent systems, even to other styles of calculi like natural deduction and term rewriting systems. They advance the "state of the art" in that they allow us to "mix and match" shallow and deep embeddings where appropriate, which, as far as we know, has not been done before. We then show how we used them to formalise a highly non-trivial proof of cut-admissibility for **GL** based on, but different from, that of [5].

In Section 2, we briefly describe traditional sequent calculi, discuss the need for multisets, and describe the controversy surrounding the cut-elimination theorem for the set-based sequent system GLS for provability logic **GL** . In Section 3 we describe general deep and shallow techniques and functions we have defined for reasoning about derivations and derivability, independently of the rules of a particular sequent system. We give very general induction principles which are useful beyond the application to GLS. We show how we formalise formulae, sequents and rules, and then show some of the **GL** sequent rules as examples. In Section 4 we describe an Isabelle axiomatic type class which we developed to facilitate reasoning about multisets of formulae, and sequents based on them. This development explores the interaction between lattice ($\wedge$, $\vee$, $\leq$) and "arithmetic" ($+$, $-$, 0, $\leq$) operations. In Section 5 we discuss how we made our Isabelle proofs as general as possible, and how they are useful for proving cut-elimination and other results in arbitrary sequent calculi which meet the associated preconditions. In Section 6 we describe the cut-admissibility proof for GLS.

We assume the reader is familiar with basic proof-theory, ML and Isabelle/HOL. In the paper we show some Isabelle code, edited to use mathematical symbols. The Appendix gives the actual Isabelle text of many definitions and theorems. Our Isabelle code can be found at `http://users.rsise.anu.edu.au/~jeremy/isabelle/200x/seqms/`. Some of this work was reported informally in [4].

2 Sequents, Multisets, Sets and Provability Logic

Proof-theorists typically work with sequents $\Gamma \vdash \Delta$ where Γ and Δ are "collections" of formulae. The "collections" found in the literature increase in complexity from simple sets for classical logic, to multisets for linear logic, to ordered lists for substructural logics, to complex tree structures for display logics. A sequent rule typically has a rule name, a (finite) number of premises, a side-condition and a conclusion. Rules are read top-down as "if all the premises hold then the conclusion holds". A derivation of the judgement $\Gamma \vdash \Delta$ is typically a finite tree of judgements with root $\Gamma \vdash \Delta$ where parents are obtained from children by "applying a rule". We use "derivation" to refer to a proof *within* a calculus, reserving "proof" for a meta-theoretic proof of a theorem *about* the calculus.

Provability logic **GL** is obtained by adding Löb's axiom $\Box(\Box A \to A) \to \Box A$ to propositional normal modal logic K. Its Kripke semantics is based on rooted transitive Kripke frames without infinite forward chains. It rose to prominence when Solovay showed that $\Box A$ could be interpreted as "A is provable in Peano Arithmetic" [10]. An initial proof-theoretic account was given by Leivant in 1981 when he "proved" cut-elimination for a set-based sequent calculus for **GL** [6]. But Valentini in 1983 found a simple counter-example and gave a new cut-elimination proof [11]. In 2001, Moen [7] claimed that Valentini's transformations don't terminate if the sequents $\Gamma \vdash \Delta$ are based on multisets. There is of course no *a priori* reason why a proof based on sets should not carry over with some modification to a proof based on multisets. The issue was recently resolved by Goré and Ramanayake [5] who gave a pen-and-paper proof that Moen is incorrect, and that Valentini's proof using multisets is *mostly* okay.

The sequent system GLS for the logic **GL** as given by Goré and Ramanayake in [5], like Valentini's, contains explicit weakening and contraction rules and, modulo these, a typical (additive) set of rules for the classical logical connectives $\neg, \wedge, \vee, \to$. The axiom $A \vdash A$ does not require atomic A. Since GLS admits axiom extension, it could have been formulated using $p \vdash p$, for p atomic. In fact the general result Theorem 2 doesn't depend on the axiom or on axiom extension.

The one additional rule *GLR* which characterises **GL** is shown below:

$$\frac{\Box X, X, \Box B \vdash B}{\Box X \vdash \Box B}\ GLR \text{ or } \ GLR(B) \text{ or } \ GLR(X, B)$$

The rule is unusual since the principal formula $\Box B$ changes polarity from conclusion to premise. To identify the principal formula involved, or all the formulae, we refer to it as $GLR(B)$, or $GLR(X, B)$. The full set of rules of GLS is shown in [5], but note that our formalisation does not regard the cut or multicut rules shown below as being part of the system.

We show a context-sharing cut rule and a context-splitting multicut rule. Given the contraction and weakening rules, the context-sharing and context-splitting versions are equivalent; our formal proofs show the admissibility of a context-splitting multicut rule where A is not contained in Γ'' or Δ''.

$$(\text{cut})\ \frac{\Gamma \vdash A, \Delta \qquad \Gamma, A \vdash \Delta}{\Gamma \vdash \Delta} \qquad (\text{multicut})\ \frac{\Gamma' \vdash A^n, \Delta' \qquad \Gamma'', A^m \vdash \Delta''}{\Gamma', \Gamma'' \vdash \Delta', \Delta''}$$

Thus our results will be lemmata of the form: if $\Gamma \vdash A, \Delta$ and $\Gamma, A \vdash \Delta$ are derivable then $\Gamma \vdash \Delta$ is derivable, where "derivable" means without using (cut).

3 Reasoning about Derivations and Derivability

3.1 Deep and Shallow Embeddings

In [2] we proved cut admissibility for **δRA**, the display calculus for relation algebras. The proof was based on a proof of Belnap, which applied generally to display calculi whose inference rules satisfied certain properties. In that paper we described the formalisation as a "deep embedding". We now believe that to describe a particular formalisation as either a "deep embedding" or a "shallow embedding" over-simplifies the issue as we now discuss.

In [2], we modelled an explicit derivation tree in HOL as a recursive structure which consists of a root sequent (which should be the conclusion of some rule), and an associated list of (sub)trees (each of which should derive a premise of that rule). This is expressed in the following recursive Isabelle datatype declaration:

```
datatype 'a dertree = Der 'a ('a dertree list)
    | Unf 'a (* unfinished leaf which remains unproved *)
```

We then had to express the property of such a tree, that it is in fact correctly based on the given rules, and so represents a valid derivation. We modelled a sequent rule as an object in HOL consisting of a list of premises and a conclusion, each of which was a sequent in the language of the logic (of relation algebras). Notably, our language of formulae included "variables" which could be instantiated with formulae, so we defined functions for such substitutions. This was necessary because we had to express conditions on the rules such as that a variable appearing in the premises also appears in the conclusion. It is much more common to let the variables in a rule be the variables of the theorem prover, and for the theorem prover to do the substitution. Thus it is more accurate to say that in [2], we used a deep embedding for *derivations*, *rules* and *variables*, since we modelled each of these features of the proof-theory explicitly rather than identifying them with analogous features of Isabelle.

In alternative ("shallow derivations") approaches to work of this type, the set of derivable sequents can be modelled as an inductively defined set, and there is no term representing the derivation tree as such, although the steps used in proving that a specific sequent is derivable could be written in the form of a derivation tree. That is, derivability in the sequent calculus studied equates to derivability in Isabelle, giving a shallow embedding of *derivations*.

We now briefly describe the functions we used to describe derivability. More details are in Appendix A.1, and a more expository account is given in [4].

```
types 'a psc = "'a list * 'a"        (* single step inference *)
consts
  derl, adm :: "'a psc set => 'a psc set"
  derrec    :: "'a psc set => 'a set => 'a set"
```

An inference rule of type `'a psc` is a list of premises and a conclusion. Then `derl rls` is the set of rules derivable from the rule set `rls`, `adm rls` is the set of admissible rules of the rule set `rls`, and `derrec rls prems` is the set of sequents derivable using rules `rls` from the set `prems` of premises. These were defined separately using Isabelle's package for inductively defined sets as below. Thus, using shallow derivations, the rules of the sequent calculus can either be encoded explicitly as in `derrec` or they can be encoded in the clauses for the inductive definition of the set of derivable sequents as in `ders`.

Shallow Embedding of Derivations and Deep Embedding of Rules:

$(\{\Gamma \vdash P,\ \ \Gamma \vdash Q\},\ \Gamma \vdash P \wedge Q) \in \texttt{rules}$ (etc for other rules)

$c \in \texttt{prems} \Longrightarrow c \in \texttt{derrec rules prems}$
$[|\ (ps, c) \in \texttt{rules}\ ;\ ps \subseteq \texttt{derrec rules prems}\ |] \Longrightarrow c \in \texttt{derrec rules prems}$

Shallow Embedding of Derivations and Shallow Embedding of Rules:

$c \in \texttt{prems} \Longrightarrow c \in \texttt{ders prems}$
$[|\ \Gamma \vdash P \in \texttt{ders prems}\ ;\ \Gamma \vdash Q \in \texttt{ders prems}\ |] \Longrightarrow \Gamma \vdash P \wedge Q \in \texttt{ders prems}$

The first clause for `derrec` says that each premise c in `prems` is derivable from `prems`, and the second says that a sequent c "obtained" from a set of derivable sequents ps by a rule (ps, c) is itself derivable. The set of rules `rules` is a parameter. The first clause for `ders` also says that each premise c in `prems` is derivable from `prems`. The rules however are no longer a parameter but are hard-coded as clauses in the definition of `ders` itself.

Thus, with a shallow embedding of derivations, we have a choice of either a deep or a shallow embedding of *rules*. It would also be possible to combine our deep embedding of derivations (`dertree`) with a shallow embedding of rules by encoding the rules in the function which checks whether a derivation tree is valid. Note however, that when we use a deep embedding of derivations in Lemma 3, our definition of validity is parameterised over the set of rules.

Our framework is generic in that a rule merely consists of "premises" and a "conclusion", and is independent of whether the things derived are formulae, sequents, or other constructs, but we will refer to them as sequents.

Our experience is that shallow embeddings generally permit easier proofs, but sometimes they are inadequate to express a desired concept. For example, with a deep embedding of rules it is easy to express that one set of rules is a subset of another set, but with a shallow embedding this is not possible. With a deep embedding of derivation trees it is easy to express that one property of derivation trees is the conjunction of two other properties, or that a derivation tree has a particular height, since each such tree has an explicit representation as a term, whereas to express such things using `ders` or `derrec` (as above), one would have to redefine these predicates incorporating the particular properties of interest. Indeed, in this work (see §6) we discuss how we found a shallow embedding of derivability inadequate, and we describe there how we "mix and match" the various styles as required.

3.2 Properties of Our Generic Derivability Predicates

We obtained the expected results linking derl and derrec, and a number of results expressing transitivity of derivation and the results of derivation using derived rules, of which the most elegant are:

```
derl_deriv_eq : "derl (derl ?rls) = derl ?rls" derrec_trans_eq :
"derrec ?rls (derrec ?rls ?prems)
                   = derrec ?rls ?prems"
```

derl_deriv_eq states that derivability using derived rules implies derivability using the original rules

derrec_trans_eq states that derivability from derivable sequents implies derivability from the original premises.

A simplified version of the induction principle generated by the definition of the inductive set derrec is as follows:

$$\frac{x \in \mathit{derrec\ rls\ prems} \quad \forall c \in \mathit{prems}.P\ c \quad \forall (ps, c) \in \mathit{rls}.(\forall p\ \mathit{in}\ ps.P\ p) \Rightarrow P\ c}{P\ x}$$

The principle says that if each rule preserves the property P from its premises to its conclusion, then so does the whole derivation, even though there is no explicit derivation as such. We contrast this principle with induction on the height of derivations where it is possible, and sometimes necessary, to transform a sub-tree in some height-preserving (or height-reducing) way, and assume that the transformed tree has property P. Such transformations are not available when using the induction principle above.

Where we have a property of two derivations, such as cut-admissibility, we need a more complex induction principle **Ind** which we derived, though, again, there are no explicit representations of derivation trees:

$$\frac{\begin{array}{l} \qquad cl \in \mathit{derrec\ rlsl}\ \{\} \qquad cr \in \mathit{derrec\ rlsr}\ \{\} \\ \forall (lps, lc) \in \mathit{rlsl}.\forall (rps, rc) \in \mathit{rlsr}. \\ \qquad (\forall lp \in lps.P\ lp\ rc) \wedge (\forall rp \in rps.P\ lc\ rp) \Rightarrow P\ lc\ rc \end{array}}{P\ cl\ cr}$$

Ind: Suppose cl and cr are the conclusions of the left and right subderivations. Assume that for every rule pair (lps, lc) and (rps, rc), if each premise lp in lps satisfies $P\ lp\ rc$, and each premise rp in rps satisfies $P\ lc\ rp$, then $P\ lc\ rc$ holds. Then we can conclude that $P\ cl\ cr$ holds.

Finally, (ps, c) is an admissible rule iff: if all premises in ps are derivable, then c is too: $(ps, c) \in \texttt{adm rls} \iff (ps \subseteq \texttt{derrec rls}\ \{\} \Rightarrow c \in \texttt{derrec rls}\ \{\})$.

We obtained the following four results, which were surprisingly tricky because adm is not monotonic (since any rule with a premise is in adm $\{\}$). For example, the last of these says that a derived rule, derived from the admissible rules, is itself admissible.

```
"derl ?rls <= adm ?rls"              "adm (adm ?rls) = adm ?rls"
"adm (derl ?rls) = adm ?rls"         "derl (adm ?rls) = adm ?rls"
```

3.3 Sequents, Formulae and the GLS Rules

We define a language of formula connectives, formula variables and primitive (atomic) propositions:

```
datatype formula = FC string (formula list) (* formula connective *)
                 | FV string                 (* formula variable *)
                 | PP string              (* primitive proposition *)
```

Although the formula connectives are fixed for each logic, the datatype is more general, using a single constructor `FC` for all formula connectives. We then define (for example) $P \wedge Q$ as `FC ''Btimes'' [P, Q]`. A sequent is a pair of multisets of formulae, written $\Gamma \vdash \Delta$.

Given a rule such as $(\vdash \wedge)$ in the two forms below,

$$\mathcal{C}_s = \frac{\vdash A \quad \vdash B}{\vdash A \wedge B} \qquad\qquad \mathcal{C}_e = \frac{X \vdash Y, A \quad X \vdash Y, B}{X \vdash Y, A \wedge B}$$

we call $\mathcal{C}_e$ an *extension* of $\mathcal{C}_s$, and we define functions `pscmap` and `extend`, where `pscmap` f applies f to premises and conclusion, so, using $+$ for multiset union,

$$\texttt{extend}\ (X \vdash Y)\ (U \vdash V) = (X + U) \vdash (Y + V)$$
$$\mathcal{C}_e = \texttt{pscmap}\ (\texttt{extend}\ (X \vdash Y))\ \mathcal{C}_s$$

Then we define `glss`, the set of rules of GLS by defining:

`glil` and `glir`: the unextended left and right introduction rules, like $\mathcal{C}_s$ above;
`wkrls` and `ctrrls` A: the unextended weakening and contraction (on A) rules;
`glne`: all of the above;
`glr` B: the *GLR*(B) rule;
`glss`: the axiom $A \vdash A$ (not requiring A to be atomic), the *GLR*(B) rule for all B, and all extensions of all rules in `glne`.

The Isabelle definitions are given in Appendix A.2. Note that in the *GLR* rule, X is a multiset, and $\Box X$ is informal notation for applying $\Box$ to each member of X; this is formalised as `mset_map`, used in the formalised *GLR* rule. Using a similar notation we write $\Box B^k$ for $(\Box B)^k$, the multiset containing n copies of $\Box B$. Development of `mset_map` and relevant lemmas is in the source files `Multiset_no_le.{thy,ML}`. Our results there also show multisets form a monad, see Appendix A.3 for details.

Our treatment of sequents and formulae amounts to a deep embedding of sequents and formulae which is independent of the set of rules. The implementation in [8] is a shallow embedding of sequents, which automatically implies the admissiblity of certain structural rules like contraction and weakening.

4 An Axiomatic Type Class for Multisets and Sequents

Isabelle provides a theory of finite multisets with an ordering which we did not use; we defined a different ordering $\leq$ analogous to $\subseteq$ for sets: $N \leq M$ if, for all x, N contains no more occurrences of x than does M.

An axiomatic type class in Isabelle is characterised by a number of axioms, which hold for all members of a type in the type class. The multiset operators $\leq$, $+$, $-$ and 0 have several useful properties, which are described by the axiomatic type classes pm0 and pm_ge0. For any type in class pm0, the operations $+$ and 0 form a commutative monoid and the following two properties hold.

$$A + B - A = B \qquad\qquad A - B - C = A - (B + C)$$

We then define a class pm_ge0 which also has an $\leq$ operator and a smallest element 0, in which the axioms of pm0 and the following hold.

$$0 \leq A \qquad\qquad B \leq A \Rightarrow B + (A - B) = A$$
$$m \leq n \Leftrightarrow m - n = 0 \qquad x < y \Leftrightarrow x \leq y \wedge x \neq y \qquad a \sqsubseteq b \Leftrightarrow a \leq b$$

The last three axioms could be given as definitions, except for a type where $\leq$, $<$ or $\sqsubseteq$ are already defined. We define $\sqsubseteq$ as a synonym for $\leq$, because Isabelle's lattice type class uses $\sqsubseteq$ as the order operator.

Lemma 1. *Multisets are in pm0 and pm_ge0 using our definition of $\leq$, and, if Γ and Δ are of any type in the classes pm0 or pm_ge0, then so is sequent $\Gamma \vdash \Delta$.*

Isabelle has "simplification procedures", which will (for example) simplify $a - b + c + b$ to $a + c$ for integers, or $a + b + c - b$ to $a + c$ for integers *or* naturals. The naturals obey the axioms above. We have been able to apply the simplification procedures for naturals, other than those involving the successor function Suc, to types of the classes pm0 and pm_ge0. This was a very great help in doing the proofs discussed in §6, especially since $X \vdash Y$ can be derived from $X' \vdash Y'$ by weakening if and only if $X \vdash Y \leq X' \vdash Y'$.

It is easy to show that, in the obvious way, multisets form a lattice. In fact we found the interesting result that the axioms of pm_ge0 are sufficient to give a lattice (with $\sqsubseteq$ as the order operator, defined as $a \sqsubseteq b$ iff $a \leq b$), so we have:

Lemma 2. *Any type of class pm_ge0 forms a lattice, using the definitions*

$$c \wedge d = c - (c - d) \qquad\qquad c \vee d = c + (d - c)$$

From these definitions it is possible (at some length) to prove the axioms for a lattice and so any type in the class pm_ge0 is also in Isabelle's class lattice. The source files for this development are pmg*.{thy,ML}.

5 Capturing the Core of Cut-Admissibility Proofs

Many cut-elimination proofs proceed via two main phases. The first phase transforms the given derivations using several "parametric" steps until the cut-formula is the principal formula of the final rule in the resulting sub-derivations above the cut. (In the diagram for $\mathcal{C}_e$ above, for example, a parametric formula in the rule application is one within the X or Y, but $A \wedge B$ is principal; a parametric step is used when the cut-formula is parametric in the bottom rule application of a sub-derivation above the cut). The "principal cut" is then "reduced" into cuts which are "smaller" in some well-founded ordering such as size of cut-formula. We describe how we captured this two-phase structure of cut-elimination proofs, and present a widely applicable result that a parametric step is possible under certain conditions.

In §3.2 we mentioned the induction principle **Ind** used for deriving cut-admissibility, or indeed any property P of pairs of subtrees. In the diagram below, to prove $P(\mathcal{C}_l, \mathcal{C}_r)$, the induction hypothesis is that $P(\mathcal{P}_{li}, \mathcal{C}_r)$ and $P(\mathcal{C}_l, \mathcal{P}_{rj})$ hold for all i and j:

$$\dfrac{\dfrac{\mathcal{P}_{l1} \ldots \mathcal{P}_{ln}}{\mathcal{C}_l}\,\rho_l \qquad \dfrac{\mathcal{P}_{r1} \ldots \mathcal{P}_{rm}}{\mathcal{C}_r}\,\rho_r}{?}\;(cut\ ?)$$

A proof of $P(\mathcal{C}_l, \mathcal{C}_r)$ using this induction hypothesis inevitably proceeds by cases on the actual rules ρ_l and ρ_r, and for a cut-formula A, on whether it is principal in either or both of ρ_l and ρ_r. But we also use induction on the size of the cut-formula, or, more generally, on some well-founded relation on formulae. So we actually consider a property P of a (cut) formula A and (left and right subtree conclusion) sequents $(\mathcal{C}_l, \mathcal{C}_r)$. In proving $P\ A\ (\mathcal{C}_l, \mathcal{C}_r)$, in addition to the inductive hypothesis above, we assume that $P\ A'\ (\mathcal{D}_l, \mathcal{D}_r)$ holds generally for A' smaller than A and all "`rls`-derivable" sequents $\mathcal{D}_l$ and $\mathcal{D}_r$: *i.e.* derivable from the empty set of premises using rules from rls. These intuitions give the following definition `gen_step2ssr` of a condition which permits one step of the inductive proof. See Appendix A.5 for reference to related more complex predicates and theorems.

Definition 1 (`gen_step2ssr`). *For a formula A, a property P, a subformula relation* `sub`*, a set of rules* `rls`*, inference rule instances $\mathcal{R}_l = (\mathcal{P}_{l1} \ldots \mathcal{P}_{ln}, \mathcal{C}_l)$ and $\mathcal{R}_r = (\mathcal{P}_{r1} \ldots \mathcal{P}_{rm}, \mathcal{C}_r)$,* `gen_step2ssr` *$P\ A$* `sub rls` *$(\mathcal{R}_l, \mathcal{R}_r)$ means:*

if *forall A' such that $(A', A) \in$* `sub` *and all* `rls`*-derivable sequents $\mathcal{D}_l$ and $\mathcal{D}_r$,*
$P\ A'\ (\mathcal{D}_l, \mathcal{D}_r)$ holds
and for each $\mathcal{P}_{li}$ in $\mathcal{P}_{l1} \ldots \mathcal{P}_{ln}$, $P\ A\ (\mathcal{P}_{li}, \mathcal{C}_r)$ holds
and for each $\mathcal{P}_{rj}$ in $\mathcal{P}_{r1} \ldots \mathcal{P}_{rm}$, $P\ A\ (\mathcal{C}_l, \mathcal{P}_{rj})$ holds
then *$P\ A\ (\mathcal{C}_l, \mathcal{C}_r)$ holds.*

The main theorem `gen_step2ssr_lem` below for proving an arbitrary property P states that if the step of the inductive proof is possible for all cases of final rule instances $\mathcal{R}_l$ and $\mathcal{R}_r$ on each side, then P holds in all cases.

Theorem 1 (`gen_step2ssr_lem`). *If*

- *A is in the well-founded part of the subformula relation* `sub`*,*
- *sequents $\mathcal{S}_l$ and $\mathcal{S}_r$ are* `rls`*-derivable, and*
- *for all formulae A', and all rules $\mathcal{R}_l$ and $\mathcal{R}_r$, our induction step condition* `gen_step2ssr` *$P\ A'$* `sub rls` *$(\mathcal{R}_l, \mathcal{R}_r)$ holds*

then $P\ A\ (\mathcal{S}_l, \mathcal{S}_r)$ holds.

$$\cfrac{\mu\left\{\cfrac{\Pi_l}{\Box X, X, \Box B \vdash B}\right.}{\Box X \vdash \Box B}\,GLR(B) \qquad \cfrac{\Pi_r}{\Box B^k, Y \vdash Z}\,\rho$$
$$\cdots\cdots\cdots\cdots\cdots\cdots\cdots\cdots\cdots\cdots \; (multicut\ ?)$$
$$\Box X, Y \vdash Z$$

Fig. 1. A multicut on cut formula $\Box B$ where $\Box B$ is left-principal via *GLR*

This enables us to split up an inductive proof, by showing, separately, that `gen_step2ssr` holds for particular cases of the final rules $(\mathcal{P}_l, \mathcal{C}_l)$ and $(\mathcal{P}_r, \mathcal{C}_r)$ on each side. For example, the inductive step for the case where the cut-formula A is parametric, not principal, on the left is encapsulated in the following theorem where `prop2 mar erls` A $(\mathcal{C}_l, \mathcal{C}_r)$ means that the conclusion of a multicut on `A` whose premises are $\mathcal{C}_l$ and $\mathcal{C}_r$ is derivable using rules `erls`.

Theorem 2 (`lmg_gen_steps`). *For any relation `sub` and any rule set `rls`, given an instance of multicut with left and right subtrees ending with rules $\mathcal{R}_l$ and $\mathcal{R}_r$:*

if *weakening is admissible for the rule set `erls`,*
and all extensions of some rule $(\mathcal{P}, X \vdash Y)$ are in the rule set `erls`,
and $\mathcal{R}_l$ is an extension of $(\mathcal{P}, X \vdash Y)$,
and the cut-formula A is not in Y (meaning that A is parametric on the left)
then *`gen_step2ssr (prop2 mar erls)` A `sub rls` $(\mathcal{R}_l, \mathcal{R}_r)$ holds.*

Theorem 2 codifies multi-cut elimination for parametric cut-formulae, and applies generally to many different calculi since it holds independently of the values of `sub` and `rls`. Of course, for a system with explicit weakening rules, such as GLS, weakening is *a fortiori* admissible. As we note later, the proof for GLS involves one really difficult case and a lot of fairly routine cases. In dealing with the routine cases, automated theorem proving has the benefit of ensuring that no detail is overlooked. Moreover, as in this example, we often have more general theorems that apply directly to a set of rules such as GLS.

Notice that all of this section has used a shallow embedding of derivations since no explicit derivation trees were required.

6 The Proof of Cut-Admissibility for GLS

Valentini's proof of cut-admissibility for GLS uses a triple induction on the size of the cut-formula, the heights of the derivations of the left and right premises of cut, and a third parameter which he called the "width". Roughly speaking, the width of a cut-instance is the number of *GLR* rule instances above that cut which contain a parametric ancestor of the cut-formula in their conclusion. The Goré and Ramanayake [5] pen-and-paper proof follows Valentini but gives a constructive way to calculate the width of a cut by inspecting the branches of the left and right sub-derivations of a cut rule instance.

As usual, the proof of cut-admissibility for GLS proceeds by considering whether the cut-formula is principal in the left or right premise of the cut, or principal in both. The crux of the proof is a "reduction" when the cut-formula is of the form $\Box B$ and is principal in both the left and right premises of the cut. The solution is to replace this cut on $\Box B$ by cuts which are "smaller" either because their cut-formula is smaller, or because their width is smaller. In reality, most of the work involves a cut instance which is only left-principal as shown in Figure 1, and most of this section is devoted to show how we utilised our general methods to formalise these "reductions" as given by Goré and Ramanayake [5]. But there are some important differences which we now explain.

As explained in §3.2, our general methods do not model derivation trees explicitly, since we use a shallow embedding. So our proof uses induction on the size of the cut-formula and on the fact of derivation, rather than on the size of the cut-formula and the height of derivation trees. Also, we actually proved the admissibility of "multicut": that is, if $\Gamma' \vdash A^n, \Delta'$ and $\Gamma'', A^m \vdash \Delta''$ are both cut-free derivable, then so is $\Gamma', \Gamma'' \vdash \Delta', \Delta''$. This avoids problems in the cases where these sequents are derived using contraction on A.

In all other aspects, our proof of cut-admissibility for GLS is based on that given by Goré and Ramanayake [5]. In particular, although we do not actually require [5, Lemma 19], we use the construction in that lemma, which is fundamental to overcoming the difficulties of adapting standard proofs to GLS, as we explain shortly. Consequently, our proof uses the idea of induction on the *width* as defined in [5], although as we shall see, our proof is expressed in terms of `del0`, which approximates to the ∂^0 of [5], not width *per se*.

To cater for width/∂^0, we could have altered our shallow embedding, `derrec`, but that destroys the modularity of our approach. Instead, we defined our `del0` by using the datatype `dertree` from §3.1 to represent explicit derivation tree objects. These trees, and the general lemmas about them, are similar to the trees of [2]. Thus we "mix and match" a deep embedding of derivation trees with a shallow embedding of inductively defined sets of derivable sequents.

To ensure the correctness of our "mixing and matching" we needed the following relationship between our definitions of derivability according to the two embeddings. A *valid* tree is one whose inferences are in the set of rules and which as a whole has no premises.

Lemma 3. *Sequent $X \vdash Y$ is derivable, shallowly, from the empty set of premises using rules `rls` (ie, is in `derrec rls` $\{\}$) iff some explicit derivation tree `dt` is valid wrt. `rls` and has a conclusion $X \vdash Y$.*

```
"(?a : derrec ?rls {}) = (EX dt. valid ?rls dt & conclDT dt = ?a)"
```

We now define a function `del0` which is closely related to ∂^0 and the width of a cut of [5], although we can avoid using the annotated derivations of [5].

Definition 2 (`del0`). *For derivation tree `dt` and formula B, define `del0` B `dt`:*

- *if the bottom rule of `dt` is GLR(Y, A) (for* any *Y, A), then `del0` B `dt` is 1 (0) if $\Box B$ is (is not) in the antecedent of the conclusion of `dt`*
- *if the bottom rule of `dt` is not GLR, then `del0` B `dt` is obtained by summing `del0` B `dt'` over all premise subtrees `dt'` of `dt`.*

Thus, the calculation of `del0` traces up each branch of an explicit derivation tree until an instance of the *GLR* rule is found: it then counts 1 if $\Box B$ is in the antecedent, meaning that B is in the X of the statement of *GLR*. Where the derivation tree branches below any *GLR* rule, the value is summed over the branches. (When we use `del0`, its argument will be the sub-tree μ of Figure 1.)

We now give a sequence of lemmata which eventually give the "reduction" for left-and-right *GLR*-principal occurrences of a cut-formula of the form $\Box B$.

Lemma 4 (`gr19e`). *If μ is a valid derivation tree with conclusion $\Box X, X, \Box B \vdash B$, and `del0` B $\mu = 0$, then $\Box X, X \vdash B$ is derivable.*

Proof. By applying the *GLR* rule to the conclusion, we can derive $\Box X \vdash \Box B$. Tracing $\Box B$ upwards in μ, it is parametric in each inference, except possibly weakening, contraction or the axiom $\Box B \vdash \Box B$. That is, since `del0` B $\mu = 0$, when we meet a *GLR* inference as we trace upwards, $\Box B$ must have already disappeared (through weakening). So, tracing upwards, we can change each instance of $\Box B$ to $\Box X$ in the usual way. The axiom $\Box B \vdash \Box B$ is changed to $\Box X \vdash \Box B$, which is derivable. Contraction is not problematic since we use, as the inductive hypothesis, that *all* occurrences of $\Box B$ can be replaced by $\Box X$. ⊣

To abbreviate the statement of several lemmas, we define a function `muxbn`, based on Figure 1, which is from [5]. It concerns a multicut on a cut-formula $\Box B$ which is left-principal because the bottom rule on the left is $GLR(B)$.

Definition 3 (`muxbn`). *`muxbn` B n holds iff: for all instances of Figure 1 (for fixed B) such that `del0` B $\mu \leq n$, the multicut in Figure 1 is admissible.*

The next lemma says that multicut admissibility on B implies `muxbn` B 0.

Lemma 5 (`del0_ca'`, `caB_muxbn'`). *If μ is a valid derivation tree with conclusion $\Box X, X, \Box B \vdash B$, and `del0` B $\mu = 0$, and multicut on B is admissible, and $\Box B^k, Y \vdash Z$ is derivable, then $\Box X, Y \vdash Z$ is derivable.*

That is, if multicut on B is admissible, then `muxbn` B 0 holds.

Proof. $\Box X \vdash \Box B$ is derivable from $\Box X, X, \Box B \vdash B$ via $GLR(X, B)$. By Lemma 4, $\Box X, X \vdash B$ is derivable. The rest of the proof is by induction on the derivation of $\Box B^k, Y \vdash Z$, in effect, by tracing relevant occurrences of $\Box B$ up that derivation. Weakening and contraction involving $\Box B$ are not problematic, and the axiom $\Box B \vdash \Box B$ is changed to $\Box X \vdash \Box B$, which is derivable. Suppose an inference $GLR(Y, C)$ is encountered, where B is in Y. This inference, allowing for multiple copies of B, is as shown below left where Z is Y with B deleted:

$$\dfrac{\Box B^k, B^k, \Box Z, Z, \Box C \vdash C}{\Box B^k, \Box Z \vdash \Box C}\, GLR(Y, C) \qquad \dfrac{\dfrac{\dfrac{\dfrac{\text{Lemma 4}}{\Box X, X \vdash B} \quad \Box X, B^k, \Box Z, Z, \Box C \vdash C}{\Box X, \Box X, X, \Box Z, Z, \Box C \vdash C}\, mcut(B)}{\Box X, X, \Box Z, Z, \Box C \vdash C}\, ctr}{\Box X, \Box Z \vdash \Box C}\, GLR(C)$$

By induction, we have $\Box X, B^k, \Box Z, Z, \Box C \vdash C$ is derivable. From there we have the derivation shown above right. As the machine-checking process showed us, additional weakening steps are necessary if $\Box B$ is in Z or if B is in $\Box Z$. $\dashv$

This construction is like that of case 2(a)(ii) in the proof of Theorem 20 of [5]. Having shown, in Lemma 5, that `muxbn` B 0 holds, we now use the construction of [5, Lemma 19] to show that `muxbn` $B\ n$ holds for all n: except that our inductive assumptions and results involve admissibility of multicut, not cut. Again we use induction: we assume that `muxbn` $B\ n$, and show that `muxbn` $B\ (n+1)$ holds.

So suppose a derivation tree $\mu/\Box X \vdash \Box B$ has a bottom inference $GLR(X, B)$, as shown in Figure 1, and `del0` $B\ \mu = n + 1$. We follow the construction of [5, Lemma 19] to obtain a derivation μ' of $\Box X, X, \Box B \vdash B$, where `del0` $B\ \mu' \leq n$.

Since `del0` $B\ \mu > 0$, the tree $\mu/\Box X \vdash \Box B$ is as shown below left (with other branches not shown). We first delete the topmost application of $GLR(A)$ leaving a tree μ^-. Then adjoin $\Box A$ to each antecedent of μ^- obtaining the tree on the right (call it $\mu^A/\Box A, \Box X \vdash \Box B$), whose topmost sequent is now a weakened axiom, and which requires us to weaken in an occurrence of A just above the final GLR-rule instance:

$$\dfrac{\dfrac{\dfrac{\dfrac{\Box G, G, \Box B^k, B^k, \Box A \vdash A}{\Box G, \Box B^k \vdash \Box A}\,GLR(A)}{\vdots}}{\Box X, X, \Box B \vdash B}}{\Box X \vdash \Box B}\,GLR(X, B) \qquad \dfrac{\dfrac{\dfrac{\dfrac{\Box A, \Box G, \Box B^k \vdash \Box A}{\vdots}}{\Box A, \Box X, X, \Box B \vdash B}}{\Box A, A, \Box X, X, \Box B \vdash B}\,(weakening)}{\Box A, \Box X \vdash \Box B}\,GLR(B)$$

Now `del0` $B\ \mu >$ `del0` $B\ \mu^A$, and so $\mu^A/\Box A, \Box X \vdash \Box B$ can be used as the left branch of an admissible (i.e. "smaller") multicut. We do this twice, the right branches being derivations of $\Box X, X, \Box B \vdash B$ and $\Box G, G, \Box B^k, B^k, \Box A \vdash A$ respectively; which after contractions, give derivations of $\Box A, \Box X, X \vdash B$ and $\Box G, G, \Box X, B^k, \Box A \vdash A$. These two are cuts 1 and 2 of the description in [5, Lemma 19], producing derivations which are cut-free equivalents of Λ_{11} and Λ_{12} from [5, Lemma 19]. The result `gr19a` in the Isabelle code gives the existence of these two derivations; it uses the result `add_Box_ant` which permits adding $\Box A$ to the antecedent of each sequent of a derivation tree.

We combine these derivations of $\Box A, \Box X, X \vdash B$ and $\Box G, G, \Box X, B^k, \Box A \vdash A$ using an admissible ("smaller") multicut on B, and then use contraction to obtain $\Box G, G, \Box A, \Box X, X \vdash A$. This is cut 3 of [5, Lemma 19]. Then the *GLR* rule gives $\Box G, \Box X \vdash \Box A$. This is derivation Λ_2 of [5, Lemma 19]. Because of this *GLR* rule at this point, we do not need to worry about the `del0` B values of any of the subtrees mentioned above, whose existence is given by the inductive assumptions of multicut-admissibility. We now weaken the conclusion of this tree to $\Box X, \Box G, \Box B^k \vdash \Box A$, giving (a counterpart of) the derivation Λ_3 of [5, Lemma 19].

Returning to μ^-, as below left, we this time adjoin $\Box X$ in the antecedent, giving the tree below right, but we can now use Λ_3 as a derivation for its leaf:

That is, we have replaced a given derivation μ of $\Box X, X, \Box B \vdash B$ where `del0` B $\mu = n+1$, with a derivation μ' of $\Box X, X, \Box B \vdash B$ where `del0` B $\mu' = n$.

$$\dfrac{\dfrac{\dfrac{\Box G, \Box B^k \vdash \Box A}{\vdots}}{\Box X, X, \Box B \vdash B}}{\Box X \vdash \Box B}\ GLR(\text{X,B}) \qquad \dfrac{\dfrac{\dfrac{\dfrac{\dfrac{\Lambda_3}{\Box X, \Box G, \Box B^k \vdash \Box A}}{\vdots}}{\Box X, \Box X, X, \Box B \vdash B}\ (contraction)}{\Box X, X, \Box B \vdash B}\ GLR}{\Box X \vdash \Box B}$$

We record this as the result as Lemma 6(a) (`gr19b`) below, however, we do not use this result directly. Instead, we obtain Lemma 6(b) (`gr19c'`) below by referring to Figure 1 and noting that we have replaced μ by μ'.

Lemma 6 (`gr19b, gr19c'`). *Assume that multicut-admissibility holds for cut-formula B, and that* ***muxbn*** *B n holds.*

(a) If μ is a derivation of $\Box X, X, \Box B \vdash B$, where ***del0*** *$B$ $\mu = n+1$, then there exists another derivation μ' of $\Box X, X, \Box B \vdash B$ with* ***del0*** *B $\mu' \leq n$.*
(b) ***muxbn*** *B $(n+1)$ holds.*

Proof. The proof of the first part is the construction described above. For the second part, we are given an instance of Figure 1, where μ has `del0` B $\mu = n+1$. Using the first part, we can transform μ to μ', with `del0` B $\mu' = n$. Since `muxbn` B n holds, the multicut on $\Box B$ where the left premise derivation is $\mu'/\Box X \vdash \Box B$ is admissible. Hence the conclusion $\Box X, Y \vdash Z$ of Figure 1 is derivable. ⊣

The next result, which we do not use directly, approximates to [5, Lemma 19].

Lemma 7 (`gr19d`). *If multicut-admissibility holds for cut-formula B,* ***muxbn*** *B 0 holds, and $\Box X, X, \Box B \vdash B$ is derivable, then $\Box X, X \vdash B$ is derivable.*

Proof. By using Lemma 6(b) repeatedly, `muxbn` B n holds for any n. ⊣

Lemma 8 (`caB_muxbn, cut_glr`). *If multicut-admissibility holds for cut-formula B, then it holds for cut-formula $\Box B$ for the case where the left premise derivation ends with a GLR(B) rule. That is,* ***muxbn*** *B n holds for any n.*

Proof. By combining Lemma 5 with repeated use of Lemma 6(b). ⊣

We now have the admissibility of principal multicuts on $\Box B$, which we indicated was the crux of the cut-admissibility for **GL**. For the other cases, the usual proofs hold. Although there is no particular difficulty in showing this, many details need to be checked: this takes almost 3 pages of [5], even with "omitting details", and citing "standard transformations". The value of automated theorem proving at this point is simply to ensure that all the necessary details have been checked. The proof uses techniques described in §5, which means that a relatively small amount of the proofs remaining for this theorem are peculiar to the GLS calculus. Consequently, we get:

Theorem 3 (`glss_ca`). *Multicut is admissible in GLS.*

7 Conclusions

We have described a formalised proof in the Isabelle theorem prover of cut admissibility for the sequent calculus GLS for the provability logic **GL**. The proof is based on the one from [5], particularly the construction in [5, Lemma 19], though we use it in a slightly different way. The Isabelle proof moves to and fro between our deep embedding of explicit trees (`dertree`) and our shallow embedding using `derrec`, so our proof has demonstrated the technique of combining use of a shallow embedding where adequate with a deep embedding where necessary. The work in §5, while complex, succeeds in extracting those parts of the cut elimination proof which follow a common pattern, and expressing them in a way which will be useful beyond the particular sequent system GLS.

We have made considerable use of definitions and theorems which are useful beyond this particular sequent system, or, indeed, beyond proofs about sequent systems. We have developed axiomatic type classes based on properties of $+$, $-$, 0 and $\leq$ for multisets, and shown how a rather small set of axioms about these operators is sufficient for defining a lattice. Multiset sequents (pairs of multisets) also belong to this type class. We have applied relevant simplification procedures to this type class, which was useful in our proofs. We have described extensive definitions and theorems relating to abstract derivability, which we have used in several different metalogical theories and proofs, and we have discussed the issue of deep versus shallow embeddings in the light of this and previous work.

References

1. Dawson, J.E., Goré, R.: Embedding display calculi into logical frameworks: Comparing Twelf and Isabelle. ENTCS, vol. 42, pp. 89–103
2. Dawson, J.E., Goré, R.: Formalised Cut Admissibility for Display Logic. In: Carreño, V.A., Muñoz, C.A., Tahar, S. (eds.) TPHOLs 2002. LNCS, vol. 2410, pp. 131–147. Springer, Heidelberg (2002)
3. Gacek, A.: The Abella interactive theorem prover (system description). In: Armando, A., Baumgartner, P., Dowek, G. (eds.) IJCAR 2008. LNCS (LNAI), vol. 5195, pp. 154–161. Springer, Heidelberg (2008)
4. Goré, R.: Machine Checking Proof Theory: An Application of Logic to Logic. In: Invited talk, Third Indian Conference on Logic and Applications, Chennai (January 2009)
5. Goré, R., Ramanayake, R.: Valentini's Cut-elimination for Provability Logic Resolved. In: Proc. AiML 2008, pp. 67–86. College Publications (2008), `http://users.rsise.anu.edu.au/~rpg/publications.html`
6. Leivant, D.: On the Proof Theory of the Modal Logic for Arithmetic Provability. Journal of Symbolic Logic 46, 531–538 (1981)
7. Moen, A.: The proposed algorithms for eliminating cuts in the provability calculus GLS do not terminate. In: NWPT 2001, Norwegian Computing Center (2001-12-10), `http://publ.nr.no/3411`
8. Pfenning, F.: Structural cut elimination. In: Proc. LICS 1994 (1994)
9. Pfenning, F., Schürmann, C.: System description: Twelf a meta-logical framework for deductive systems. In: Ganzinger, H. (ed.) CADE 1999. LNCS (LNAI), vol. 1632, pp. 202–206. Springer, Heidelberg (1999)
10. Solovay, R.M.: Provability Interpretations of Modal Logic. Israel Journal of Mathematics 25, 287–304 (1976)
11. Valentini, S.: The Modal Logic of Provability: Cut-elimination. Journal of Philosophical Logic 12, 471–476 (1983)

Characterising Probabilistic Processes Logically
(Extended Abstract)

Yuxin Deng[1,2,*] and Rob van Glabbeek[3,4]

[1]Dept. Comp. Sci. & Eng. and MOE-Microsoft Key Lab for Intell. Comp. & Syst., Shanghai Jiao Tong University, China
[2] State Key Lab of Comp. Sci., Inst. of Software, Chinese Academy of Sciences
[3] NICTA, Australia
[4] University of New South Wales, Australia

Abstract. In this paper we work on (bi)simulation semantics of processes that exhibit both nondeterministic and probabilistic behaviour. We propose a probabilistic extension of the modal mu-calculus and show how to derive characteristic formulae for various simulation-like preorders over finite-state processes without divergence. In addition, we show that even without the fixpoint operators this probabilistic mu-calculus can be used to characterise these behavioural relations in the sense that two states are equivalent if and only if they satisfy the same set of formulae.

1 Introduction

In concurrency theory, behavioural relations such as equivalences and refinement preorders form a basis for establishing system correctness. Usually both specifications and implementations are expressed as processes within the same framework, in which a specification describes some high-level behaviour and an implementation gives the technical details for achieving the behaviour. Then one chooses an equivalence or preorder to verify that the implementation realises the behaviour required by the specification.

A great many behavioural relations are defined on top of labelled transition systems, which offer an operational model of systems. For finitary (i.e. finite-state and finitely branching) systems, these behavioural relations can be computed in a mechanical way, and thus may be incorporated into automatic verification tools. In recent years, probabilistic constructs have been proven useful for giving quantitative specifications of system behaviour. The first papers on probabilistic concurrency theory [12,2,20] proceed by *replacing* nondeterministic with probabilistic constructs. The reconciliation of nondeterministic and probabilistic constructs starts with [13] and has received a lot of attention in the literature [35,31,21,30,16,22,1,18,25,3,34,23,9,7,4]. We shall also work in a framework that features the co-existence of probability and nondeterminism.

* Deng was supported by the National Natural Science Foundation of China (60703033).

C. Fermüller and A. Voronkov (Eds.): LPAR-17, LNCS 6397, pp. 278–293, 2010.

Among the behavioural relations that have proven useful in probabilistic concurrency theory are various types of *simulation* and *bisimulation* relations. Axiomatisations for bisimulations have been investigated in [1,10]. Logical characterisations of bisimulations and simulations have been studied in [31,27]. For example, in [31] the probabilistic computation tree logic (PCTL) [14] is used and it turns out that two states are bisimilar if and only if they satisfy the same set of PCTL formulae.

In the nonprobabilistic setting, there is a line of research on characteristic formulae. The goal is to seek a particular formula φ_s for a given state s such that a necessary and sufficient condition for any state t being bisimilar to s is to satisfy φ_s [32]. This is a very strong property in the sense that to check if t is bisimilar to s it suffices to consider the single formula φ_s and see if it can be satisfied by t. It offers a convenient method for equivalence or preorder checking.

In this paper we partially extend the results of [32] to a probabilistic setting that admits both probabilistic and nondeterministic choice; to make the main ideas neat we do not consider divergence. We present a probabilistic extension of the modal mu-calculus [19] (pMu), where a formula is interpreted as the set of probability distributions satisfying it. This is in contrast to the probabilistic semantics of the mu-calculus as studied in [16,22,23] where formulae denote lower bounds of probabilistic evidence of properties, and the semantics of the generalised probabilistic logic of [3] where a mu-calculus formula is interpreted as a set of deterministic trees that satisfy it.

We shall provide characteristic formulae for strong and weak probabilistic (bi)simulation as introduced in [31,30], as well as forward simulation [30] and failure simulation [7]. The results are obtained in two phases, which we illustrate by taking strong probabilistic bisimilarity $\sim$ as an example. Given a finite-state probabilistic labelled transition system with state space $\{s_1, ..., s_n\}$, we first construct an equation system E of modal formulae in pMu.

$$\begin{aligned} E : X_{s_1} &= \varphi_{s_1} \\ &\vdots \\ X_{s_n} &= \varphi_{s_n} \end{aligned}$$

A solution of the equation system is a function ρ that assigns to each variable X_{s_i} a set of distributions $\rho(X_{s_i})$. The greatest solution of the equation system, denoted by ν_E, has the property that $s_i \sim s_j$ if and only if the point distribution $\overline{s_j}$ is an element of $\nu_E(X_{s_i})$. In the second phase, we apply three transformation rules upon E in order to obtain a pMu formula $\varphi^{\sim}_{s_i}$ whose meaning $[\![\varphi^{\sim}_{s_i}]\!]$ is exactly captured by $\nu_E(X_{s_i})$. As a consequence, we derive a characteristic formula for s_i such that $s_i \sim s_j$ if and only if $\overline{s_j} \in [\![\varphi^{\sim}_{s_i}]\!]$.

Without the fixpoint operators pMu gives rise to a probabilistic extension of the Hennessy-Milner logic [15]. In analogy to the nonprobabilistic setting, it characterises (bi)simulations in the sense that $s \sim t$ if and only if the two states s, t satisfy the same set of formulae.

The paper is organised as follows. In Section 2 we recall the definitions of several (bi)simulations defined over probabilistic labelled transition systems. In Section 3 we introduce the syntax and semantics of pMu. In Section 4 we build characteristic equation systems and derive from them characteristic formulae for all our (bi)simulations. In Section 5 we consider the fixpoint-free fragment of pMu which characterises a state by the class of formulae it satisfies.

In this extended abstract many proofs are omitted; they can be found in [6].

2 Probabilistic (Bi)simulations

In this section we recall several probabilistic extensions of simulation and bisimulation [24] that appeared in the literature.

We begin with some notation concerning probability distributions. A *(discrete) probability distribution* over a set S is a function $\Delta : S \rightarrow [0,1]$ with $\sum_{s\in S}\Delta(s) = 1$; the *support* of Δ is given by $\lceil\Delta\rceil = \{s \in S \mid \Delta(s) > 0\}$. We write $\mathcal{D}(S)$, ranged over by Δ, Θ, for the set of all distributions over S. We also write $\overline{s}$ to denote the point distribution assigning probability 1 to s and 0 to all others, so that $\lceil\overline{s}\rceil = \{s\}$. If $p_i \geq 0$ and Δ_i is a distribution for each i in some index set I, and $\sum_{i\in I} p_i = 1$, then the probability distribution $\sum_{i\in I} p_i \cdot \Delta_i \in \mathcal{D}(S)$ is given by $(\sum_{i\in I} p_i \cdot \Delta_i)(s) = \sum_{i\in I} p_i \cdot \Delta_i(s)$; we will sometimes write it as $p_1 \cdot \Delta_1 + \ldots + p_n \cdot \Delta_n$ when $I = \{1,\ldots,n\}$.

Definition 1. A *finite state probabilistic labelled transition system* (pLTS) is a triple $\langle S, \mathsf{Act}_\tau, \rightarrow\rangle$, where

1. S is a finite set of states
2. Act_τ is a set of external actions Act augmented with an internal action $\tau \notin \mathsf{Act}$
3. $\rightarrow\ \subseteq S \times \mathsf{Act}_\tau \times \mathcal{D}(S)$.

We usually write $s \xrightarrow{a} \Delta$ for $(s,a,\Delta) \in \rightarrow$, $s \xrightarrow{a}$ for $\exists\Delta : s \xrightarrow{a} \Delta$, and $s \stackrel{a}{\not\rightarrow}$ for the negation of $s \xrightarrow{a}$. We write $s \stackrel{A}{\not\rightarrow}$ with $A \subseteq \mathsf{Act}$ when $\forall a \in A \cup \{\tau\} : s \stackrel{a}{\not\rightarrow}$, and $\Delta \stackrel{A}{\not\rightarrow}$ when $\forall s \in \lceil\Delta\rceil : s \stackrel{A}{\not\rightarrow}$. A pLTS is *finitely branching* if, for each state s, the set $\{(a,\Delta) \mid s \xrightarrow{a} \Delta\}$ is finite. A pLTS is *finitary* if it is finite-state and finitely branching.

To define probabilistic (bi)simulations, it is often necessary to lift a relation over states to one over distributions.

Definition 2. Given two sets S and T and a relation $\mathcal{R} \subseteq S \times T$. We lift $\mathcal{R}$ to a relation $\mathcal{R}^\dagger \subseteq \mathcal{D}(S) \times \mathcal{D}(T)$ by letting $\Delta\ \mathcal{R}^\dagger\ \Theta$ whenever

1. $\Delta = \sum_{i\in I} p_i \cdot \overline{s_i}$, where I is a countable index set and $\sum_{i\in I} p_i = 1$
2. for each $i \in I$ there is a state t_i such that $s_i\ \mathcal{R}\ t_i$
3. $\Theta = \sum_{i\in I} p_i \cdot \overline{t_i}$.

Note that in the decomposition of Δ, the states s_i are not necessarily distinct: that is, the decomposition is not in general unique, and similarly for the decomposition of Θ. For example, if $\mathcal{R} = \{(s_1,t_1),(s_1,t_2),(s_2,t_3),(s_3,t_3)\}$, $\Delta = \frac{1}{2}\overline{s_1} + \frac{1}{4}\overline{s_2} + \frac{1}{4}\overline{s_3}$, and $\Theta = \frac{1}{3}\overline{t_1} + \frac{1}{6}\overline{t_2} + \frac{1}{2}\overline{t_3}$, then $\Delta\ \mathcal{R}^\dagger\ \Theta$ holds because of the decompositions $\Delta = \frac{1}{3}\overline{s_1} + \frac{1}{6}\overline{s_1} + \frac{1}{4}\overline{s_2} + \frac{1}{4}\overline{s_3}$ and $\Theta = \frac{1}{3}\overline{t_1} + \frac{1}{6}\overline{t_2} + \frac{1}{4}\overline{t_3} + \frac{1}{4}\overline{t_3}$.

From the above definition, the next two properties follow [5]. In fact, they are sometimes used as alternative methods of lifting relations (see e.g. [31,20]).

Proposition 1. 1. Let Δ and Θ be distributions over S and T, respectively. Then $\Delta\ \mathcal{R}^\dagger\ \Theta$ iff there exists a weight function $w : S \times T \to [0, 1]$ such that
(a) $\forall s \in S : \sum_{t\in T} w(s, t) = \Delta(s)$
(b) $\forall t \in T : \sum_{s\in S} w(s, t) = \Theta(t)$
(c) $\forall (s, t) \in S \times T : w(s, t) > 0 \Rightarrow s\ \mathcal{R}\ t$.
2. Let Δ, Θ be distributions over S and $\mathcal{R}$ be an equivalence relation. Then $\Delta\ \mathcal{R}^\dagger\ \Theta$ iff $\Delta(C) = \Theta(C)$ for all equivalence classes $C \in S/\mathcal{R}$, where $\Delta(C)$ stands for the accumulated probability $\sum_{s\in C} \Delta(s)$. □

In a similar way, following [9], we can lift a relation $\mathcal{R} \subseteq S \times \mathcal{D}(T)$ to a relation $\mathcal{R}^\dagger \subseteq \mathcal{D}(S) \times \mathcal{D}(T)$, by letting $\Delta\ \mathcal{R}^\dagger\ \Theta$ whenever

1. $\Delta = \sum_{i\in I} p_i \cdot \overline{s_i}$, where I is a countable index set and $\sum_{i\in I} p_i = 1$
2. for each $i \in I$ there is a distribution Θ_i such that $s_i\ \mathcal{R}\ \Theta_i$
3. $\Theta = \sum_{i\in I} p_i \cdot \Theta_i$.

The above lifting constructions satisfy the following two useful properties.

Proposition 2. Suppose $\mathcal{R} \subseteq S \times S$ or $S \times \mathcal{D}(S)$ and $\sum_{i\in I} p_i = 1$. Then

1. $\Delta_i\ \mathcal{R}^\dagger\ \Theta_i$ for all $i \in I$ implies $(\sum_{i\in I} p_i \cdot \Delta_i)\ \mathcal{R}^\dagger\ (\sum_{i\in I} p_i \cdot \Theta_i)$.
2. If $(\sum_{i\in I} p_i \cdot \Delta_i)\ \mathcal{R}^\dagger\ \Theta$ then $\Theta = \sum_{i\in I} p_i \cdot \Theta_i$ for some set of distributions Θ_i such that $\Delta_i\ \mathcal{R}^\dagger\ \Theta_i$ for all $i \in I$. □

We write $s \xrightarrow{\hat{\tau}} \Delta$ if either $s \xrightarrow{\tau} \Delta$ or $\Delta = \overline{s}$, and $s \xrightarrow{\hat{a}} \Delta$ iff $s \xrightarrow{a} \Delta$ for $a \in \mathsf{Act}$. For any $a \in \mathsf{Act}_\tau$, we know that $\xrightarrow{\hat{a}} \subseteq S \times \mathcal{D}(S)$, so we can lift it to be a transition relation between distributions. With a slight abuse of notation we simply write $\Delta \xrightarrow{\hat{a}} \Theta$ for $\Delta\ (\xrightarrow{\hat{a}})^\dagger\ \Theta$. Then we define weak transitions $\stackrel{\hat{a}}{\Longrightarrow}$ by letting $\stackrel{\hat{\tau}}{\Longrightarrow}$ be the reflexive and transitive closure of $\xrightarrow{\hat{\tau}}$ and writing $\Delta \stackrel{\hat{a}}{\Longrightarrow} \Theta$ for $a \in \mathsf{Act}$ whenever $\Delta \stackrel{\hat{\tau}}{\Longrightarrow}\xrightarrow{\hat{a}}\stackrel{\hat{\tau}}{\Longrightarrow} \Theta$.

Definition 3. A *divergence* is a sequence of states s_i and distributions Δ_i with $s_i \xrightarrow{\tau} \Delta_i$ and $s_{i+1} \in \lceil \Delta_i \rceil$ for $i \geq 0$.

The above definition of $\stackrel{\hat{a}}{\Longrightarrow}$ is sensible only in the absence of divergence. In general, one would need a more complicated notion of $\stackrel{\hat{a}}{\Longrightarrow}$, such as proposed in [8]. Therefore, from here on we restrict attention to divergence-free pLTSs.

Definition 4. A relation $\mathcal{R} \subseteq S \times S$ is a *strong probabilistic simulation* if $s\ \mathcal{R}\ t$ and $a \in \mathsf{Act}_\tau$ implies

– if $s \xrightarrow{a} \Delta$ then there exists some Θ such that $\overline{t} \xrightarrow{a} \Theta$ and $\Delta\ \mathcal{R}^\dagger\ \Theta$

If both $\mathcal{R}$ and $\mathcal{R}^{-1}$ are strong probabilistic simulations, then $\mathcal{R}$ is a *strong probabilistic bisimulation*. A state s is related to another state t via *strong probabilistic similarity* (resp. *bisimilarity*), denoted $s \prec t$ (resp. $s \sim t$), if there exists a strong probabilistic simulation (resp. bisimulation) $\mathcal{R}$ such that $s\ \mathcal{R}\ t$. *Weak probabilistic similarity* ($\precsim$) and *weak probabilistic bisimilarity* ($\approx$) are defined in the same manner just by using $\overline{t} \stackrel{\hat{a}}{\Longrightarrow} \Theta$ in place of $\overline{t} \xrightarrow{a} \Theta$.

All four (bi)simulations above stem from [31,30]. There they were proposed as improvements over the strong bisimulation of [13] and the strong simulation of [17], both of which can be defined as the strong *probabilistic* (bi)simulation above, but using $t \xrightarrow{a} \Theta$ in place of $\overline{t} \xrightarrow{a} \Theta$. Logical characterisations for strong (bi)simulations are similar to those contributed here for strong probabilistic (bi)simulations, but require a state-based interpretation of the modalities $\langle a \rangle$ and $[a]$; see [6] for details. Other definitions of simulation have also appeared in the literature. Here we consider two typical ones: forward simulation [30] and failure simulation [7].

Definition 5. A relation $\mathcal{R} \subseteq S \times \mathcal{D}(S)$ is a *failure simulation* if $s \,\mathcal{R}\, \Theta$ implies

1. if $s \xrightarrow{a} \Delta$ with $a \in \mathsf{Act}_\tau$ then $\exists \Theta'$ such that $\Theta \stackrel{\hat{a}}{\Longrightarrow} \Theta'$ and $\Delta \,\mathcal{R}^\dagger\, \Theta'$;
2. if $s \stackrel{A}{\not\longrightarrow}$ with $A \subseteq \mathsf{Act}$ then $\exists \Theta'$ such that $\Theta \stackrel{\hat{\tau}}{\Longrightarrow} \Theta'$ and $\Theta' \stackrel{A}{\not\longrightarrow}$.

We write $s \lhd_{FS} \Theta$ if there is some failure simulation $\mathcal{R}$ such that $s \,\mathcal{R}\, \Theta$.

Similarly, we define a forward simulation and $s \lhd_S \Theta$ by dropping the second clause in Definition 5.

3 The Probabilistic Modal mu-Calculus

Let Var be a countable set of variables. We define a class $\mathcal{L}^{\mathrm{raw}}$ of modal formulae by the following grammar:

$$\varphi := \bigwedge_{i\in I} \varphi_i \mid \bigvee_{i\in I} \varphi_i \mid \neg\varphi \mid \langle a \rangle\varphi \mid [a]\varphi \mid \bigoplus_{i\in I} \varphi_i \mid \bigoplus_{i\in I} p_i \cdot \varphi_i \mid {\downarrow}\varphi \mid X \mid \mu X.\varphi \mid \nu X.\varphi$$

where I is an index set, $a \in \mathsf{Act}_\tau$ and $\sum_{i\in I} p_i = 1$. The *probabilistic modal mu-calculus* (pMu) is given by the subclass $\mathcal{L}$, obtained by imposing the syntactic condition that in $\mu X.\varphi$ and $\nu X.\varphi$ the variable X may occur in φ only within the scope of an even number of negations. The above syntax is obtained by adding a variant of the probabilistic construct $\bigoplus_{i\in I} p_i \cdot \varphi_i$, introduced in [7] in the context of a less expressive logic without fixpoint operators, as well as the novel modalities $\bigoplus_{i\in I} \varphi_i$ and ${\downarrow}\varphi$, to the syntax of the non-probabilistic mu-calculus [19]. As usual, one has $\bigwedge_{i\in\emptyset} \varphi_i = \mathtt{true}$ and $\bigvee_{i\in\emptyset} \varphi_i = \mathtt{false}$.

The two fixpoint operators μX and νX bind the respective variable X. We apply the usual terminology of free and bound variables in a formula and write $fv(\varphi)$ for the set of free variables in φ. A formula φ is *closed* if $fv(\varphi) = \emptyset$.

For any set Ω, write $\mathcal{P}(\Omega)$ for the power set of Ω. We use *environments*, which bind free variables to sets of distributions, in order to give semantics to formulae. Let

$$\mathsf{Env} = \{\, \rho \mid \rho : \mathsf{Var} \to \mathcal{P}(\mathcal{D}(S)) \,\}$$

be the set of all environments and ranged over by ρ. For a set $V \subseteq \mathcal{D}(S)$ and a variable $X \in \mathsf{Var}$, we write $\rho[X \mapsto V]$ for the environment that maps X to V and Y to $\rho(Y)$ for all $Y \neq X$.

The semantics of a formula φ in an environment ρ is given as the set of distributions $[\![\varphi]\!]_\rho$ satisfying it. This leads to a semantic functional $[\![\ ]\!] : \mathcal{L} \to$

Table 1. Strong and weak semantics of the probabilistic modal mu-calculus

$$
\begin{array}{|rcl|}
\hline
\llbracket \bigwedge_{i\in I}\varphi_i \rrbracket_\rho & = & \bigcap_{i\in I}\llbracket\varphi_i\rrbracket_\rho \qquad \text{so} \qquad \llbracket \texttt{true} \rrbracket_\rho = \mathcal{D}(S) \\
\llbracket \bigvee_{i\in I}\varphi_i \rrbracket_\rho & = & \bigcup_{i\in I}\llbracket\varphi_i\rrbracket_\rho \qquad \text{so} \qquad \llbracket \texttt{false} \rrbracket_\rho = \emptyset \\
\llbracket \neg\varphi \rrbracket_\rho & = & \mathcal{D}(S) \setminus \llbracket\varphi\rrbracket_\rho \\
\llbracket \langle a\rangle\varphi \rrbracket_\rho & = & \{\, \Delta \in \mathcal{D}(S) \mid \exists \Delta' : \Delta \xrightarrow{a} \Delta' \ \wedge\ \Delta' \in \llbracket\varphi\rrbracket_\rho \,\} \\
\llbracket [a]\varphi \rrbracket_\rho & = & \{\, \Delta \in \mathcal{D}(S) \mid \forall \Delta' : \Delta \xrightarrow{a} \Delta' \ \Rightarrow\ \Delta' \in \llbracket\varphi\rrbracket_\rho \,\} \\
\llbracket \bigoplus_{i\in I}\varphi_i \rrbracket_\rho & = & \{\, \Delta \in \mathcal{D}(S) \mid \Delta = \sum_{i\in I} p_i\cdot\Delta_i \text{ for some } p_i \text{ with } \sum_{I\in I} p_i = 1 \\
 & & \qquad \wedge\ \forall i\in I:\ \Delta_i \in \llbracket\varphi_i\rrbracket_\rho \,\} \\
\llbracket \bigoplus_{i\in I} p_i\cdot\varphi_i \rrbracket_\rho & = & \{\, \Delta \in \mathcal{D}(S) \mid \Delta = \sum_{i\in I} p_i\cdot\Delta_i \ \wedge\ \forall i\in I:\ \Delta_i \in \llbracket\varphi_i\rrbracket_\rho \,\} \\
\llbracket {\downarrow}\varphi \rrbracket_\rho & = & \{\, \Delta \in \mathcal{D}(S) \mid \forall s \in \lceil\Delta\rceil : \overline{s} \in \llbracket\varphi\rrbracket_\rho \,\} \\
\llbracket X \rrbracket_\rho & = & \rho(X) \\
\llbracket \mu X.\varphi \rrbracket_\rho & = & \bigcap\{\, V \subseteq \mathcal{D}(S) \mid \llbracket\varphi\rrbracket_{\rho[X\mapsto V]} \subseteq V \,\} \\
\llbracket \nu X.\varphi \rrbracket_\rho & = & \bigcup\{\, V \subseteq \mathcal{D}(S) \mid \llbracket\varphi\rrbracket_{\rho[X\mapsto V]} \supseteq V \,\} \\
\hline
\llbracket \langle a\rangle\varphi \rrbracket_\rho & = & \{\, \Delta \in \mathcal{D}(S) \mid \exists \Delta' : \Delta \stackrel{\hat{a}}{\Longrightarrow} \Delta' \ \wedge\ \Delta' \in \llbracket\varphi\rrbracket_\rho \,\} \\
\llbracket [a]\varphi \rrbracket_\rho & = & \{\, \Delta \in \mathcal{D}(S) \mid \forall \Delta' : \Delta \stackrel{\hat{a}}{\Longrightarrow} \Delta' \ \Rightarrow\ \Delta' \in \llbracket\varphi\rrbracket_\rho \,\} \\
\hline
\end{array}
$$

$\mathsf{Env} \to \mathcal{P}(\mathcal{D}(S))$ defined inductively in Table 1. As the meaning of a closed formula φ does not depend on the environment, one writes $\llbracket\varphi\rrbracket$ for $\llbracket\varphi\rrbracket_\rho$ where ρ is an arbitrary environment. In that case one also writes $\Delta \models \varphi$ for $\Delta \in \llbracket\varphi\rrbracket$.

Following [19,29] we give a *strong* and a *weak* semantics of the probabilistic modal mu-calculus. Both are the same as those of the modal mu-calculus [19,29] except that distributions of states are taking the roles of states. The power set of $\mathcal{D}(S)$, $\mathcal{P}(\mathcal{D}(S))$, may be viewed as the complete lattice $(\mathcal{P}(\mathcal{D}(S)), \mathcal{D}(S), \emptyset, \subseteq, \cup, \cap)$. Intuitively, we identify a formula with the set of distributions that make it true. For example, `true` holds for all distributions and dually `false` holds for no distribution. Conjunction and disjunction are interpreted by intersection and union of sets, and negation by complement. The formula $\langle a\rangle\varphi$ holds for a distribution Δ if there is a distribution Δ' that can be reached after an a-transition and that satisfies φ. Dually, $[a]\varphi$ holds for Δ if all distributions reachable from Δ by an a-transition satisfy φ. The formulas $\bigoplus_{i\in I}\varphi_i$ and $\bigoplus_{i\in I} p_i\cdot\varphi_i$ hold for Δ if the distribution can be decomposed into a convex combination of some distributions Δ_i and each of them satisfies the corresponding sub-formula φ_i; the first of these modalities allows *any* convex combination, whereas the second one specifies a particular one. The formula ${\downarrow}\varphi$ holds for Δ if all states in its support satisfy φ. The characterisation of the *least fixpoint formula* $\mu X.\varphi$ and the *greatest fixpoint formula* $\nu X.\varphi$ follows from the well-known Knaster-Tarski fixpoint theorem [33].

The weak semantics reflects the unobservable nature of internal actions; it differs from the strong semantics only in the use of the relations $\stackrel{\hat{a}}{\Longrightarrow}$ instead of $\xrightarrow{a}$ in the interpretation of the modalities $\langle a\rangle$ and $[a]$.

Note that there is some redundancy in the syntax of pMu: each of the constructs $\bigwedge_{i\in I}$, $\langle a\rangle$ and μ can be expressed in terms of its dual $\bigvee_{i\in I}$, $[a]$ and ν with the aid of negation. However, negation may not be redundant, as the dual of $\bigoplus_{i\in I} p_i\cdot\varphi_i$ does not appear to be expressible without using negation; moreover this dual lacks the intuitive appeal for introducing it as a new primitive.

We shall consider (closed) *equation systems* of formulae of the form

$$
\begin{aligned}
E : X_1 &= \varphi_1 \\
&\vdots \\
X_n &= \varphi_n
\end{aligned}
$$

where $X_1, ..., X_n$ are mutually distinct variables and $\varphi_1, ..., \varphi_n$ are formulae having at most $X_1, ..., X_n$ as free variables.

Table 2. Transformation rules

- Rule 1: $E \to F$
- Rule 2: $E \to G$
- Rule 3: $E \to H$ if $X_n \notin fv(\varphi_1, ..., \varphi_n)$

$$
\begin{array}{llll}
E: \; X_1 = \varphi_1 & F: \; X_1 = \varphi_1 & G: \; X_1 = \varphi_1[\varphi_n/X_n] & H: \; X_1 = \varphi_1 \\
\quad \vdots & \quad \vdots & \quad \vdots & \quad \vdots \\
X_{n-1} = \varphi_{n-1} & X_{n-1} = \varphi_{n-1} & X_{n-1} = \varphi_{n-1}[\varphi_n/X_n] & X_{n-1} = \varphi_{n-1} \\
X_n = \varphi_n & X_n = \nu X_n.\varphi_n & X_n = \varphi_n &
\end{array}
$$

Here E can be viewed as a function $E : \mathsf{Var} \to \mathcal{L}$ defined by $E(X_i) = \varphi_i$ for $i = 1, ..., n$ and $E(Y) = Y$ for other variables $Y \in \mathsf{Var}$.

An environment ρ is a *solution* of an equation system E if its assignment to X_i coincides with the interpretation of φ_i in the environment, that is,

$$\forall i : \rho(X_i) = [\![\varphi_i]\!]_\rho.$$

The existence of solutions for an equation system can be seen from the following arguments. The set Env, which includes all candidates for solutions, together with the partial order $\sqsubseteq$ defined by

$$\rho \sqsubseteq \rho' \text{ iff } \forall X \in \mathsf{Var} : \rho(X) \subseteq \rho'(X)$$

forms a complete lattice. The *equation functional* $\mathcal{F}_E : \mathsf{Env} \to \mathsf{Env}$ given in the notation of the λ-calculus by

$$\mathcal{F}_E := \lambda\rho.\lambda X.[\![E(X)]\!]_\rho$$

is monotonic, which can be shown by induction on the structure of $E(X)$. Thus, the Knaster-Tarski fixpoint theorem guarantees existence of solutions, and the greatest solution

$$\nu_E := \bigsqcup \{ \rho \mid \rho \sqsubseteq \mathcal{F}_E(\rho) \} \tag{1}$$

is the supremum of the set of all post-fixpoints of $\mathcal{F}_E$.

An expression $\nu_E(X)$, with X one of the variables used in E, denotes a set of distributions. Below we will use such expressions as if they were valid syntax in our probabilistic mu-calculus, with $[\![\nu_E(X)]\!]_\rho := \nu_E(X)$. This amounts to extending the greatest fixpoint operator ν to apply to finite sets of fixpoint equations, instead of single equations; the expression $\nu X.\varphi$ amounts to the special case $\nu_E(X)$ in which E consists of the single equation $X = \varphi$.

The use of expressions $\nu_E(X)$ is justified because they can be seen as syntactic sugar for authentic pMu expressions. As explained in [26], the three transformation rules in Table 2 can be used to obtain from an equation system E a pMu formula whose interpretation coincides with the interpretation of X_1 in the greatest solution of E.

Theorem 1. *Given a finite equation system E that uses the variable X, there is a pMu formula φ such that $\nu_E(X) = [\![\varphi]\!]$.* □

4 Characteristic Equation Systems

Following [32], the behaviour of a finite-state process can be characterised by an equation system of modal formulae. In the current section we show that this idea also applies in the probabilistic setting. For each behavioural relation $\mathcal{R}$ over a finite state space, ranging over the various simulation preorders and bisimulation equivalences reviewed in Section 2, we establish an equation system E of modal formulae in pMu.

$$\begin{aligned} E : X_{s_1} &= \varphi_{s_1} \\ &\vdots \\ X_{s_n} &= \varphi_{s_n} \end{aligned}$$

There is exactly one such equation for each state s_i, and the formulae φ_{s_i} do not contain fixpoint operators. This equation system is guaranteed to have a greatest solution ν_E which has the nice property that, for any states s, t in the state space in question, s is related to t via $\mathcal{R}$ if and only if the point distribution $\overline{t}$ belongs to the set of distributions assigned to the variable X_s by ν_E. Thus $\nu_E(X_s)$ is a *characteristic formula* for s w.r.t. $\mathcal{R}$ in the sense that $s \mathrel{\mathcal{R}} t$ iff $\overline{t}$ satisfies $\nu_E(X_s)$.

Strong probabilistic bisimulation. The key ingredient for the modal characterisation of strong probabilistic bisimulation is to construct an equation system that captures all the transitions of a pLTS. For each state s we build an equation $X_s = \varphi_s$, where X_s is a variable and φ_s is of the form $\varphi'_s \wedge \varphi''_s$ with φ'_s a formula describing the actions enabled by s and φ''_s a formula describing the consequences of performing these actions. Intuitively, if state s is related to state t in a bisimulation game, then φ'_s expresses the transitions that should be matched up by t and φ''_s expresses the capability of s to match up the transitions initiated by t. More specifically, the equation system is given by the following definition.

Definition 6. Given a pLTS, its *characteristic equation system* for strong probabilistic bisimulation consists of one equation $X_s = \varphi_s$ for each state $s \in S$, where

$$\varphi_s := (\bigwedge_{s \xrightarrow{a} \Delta} \langle a \rangle X_\Delta) \wedge (\bigwedge_{a \in \mathsf{Act}_\tau} [a] \bigoplus_{s \xrightarrow{a} \Delta} X_\Delta)^{1} \tag{2}$$

with $X_\Delta := \bigoplus_{s \in \lceil \Delta \rceil} \Delta(s) \cdot \downarrow X_s$.

The equation system thus constructed, interpreted according to the strong semantics of pMu, has the required property, as stated by the theorem below.

Theorem 2. *Let E be the characteristic equation system for strong probabilistic bisimulation on a given pLTS. Then, for all states s and t,*

1. *$s \mathcal{R} t$ for some strong probabilistic bisimulation $\mathcal{R}$ if and only if $\overline{t} \in \rho(X_s)$ for some post-fixpoint ρ of $\mathcal{F}_E$.*
2. *In particular, $s \sim t$ if and only if $\overline{t} \in [\![\nu_E(X_s)]\!]$, i.e., $\nu_E(X_s)$ is a characteristic formula for s w.r.t. strong probabilistic bisimilarity.*

Proof. Let E be the characteristic equation system for strong probabilistic bisimulation on a given pLTS. We only consider the first statement, from which the second statement follow immediately.

($\Leftarrow$) For this direction, assuming a post-fixpoint ρ of $\mathcal{F}_E$, we construct a probabilistic bisimulation relation that includes all state pairs (s,t) satisfying $\overline{t} \in \rho(X_s)$. Let $\mathcal{R} = \{\, (s,t) \mid \overline{t} \in \rho(X_s) \,\}$. We first show that

$$\Theta \in [\![X_\Delta]\!]_\rho \text{ implies } \Delta \, \mathcal{R}^\dagger \, \Theta. \tag{3}$$

Let $X_\Delta = \bigoplus_{i\in I} p_i \cdot {\downarrow} X_{s_i}$, so that $\Delta = \sum_{i\in I} p_i \cdot \overline{s_i}$. Suppose $\Theta \in [\![X_\Delta]\!]_\rho$. We have that $\Theta = \sum_{i\in I} p_i \cdot \Theta_i$ and, for all $i \in I$ and all $t \in \lceil \Theta_i \rceil$, that $\overline{t} \in [\![X_{s_i}]\!]_\rho$, i.e. $s_i \mathcal{R} t$. It follows that $\overline{s_i} \, \mathcal{R}^\dagger \, \Theta_i$ and thus $\Delta \, \mathcal{R}^\dagger \, \Theta$, using Proposition 2(1).

Now we show that $\mathcal{R}$ is a probabilistic bisimulation.

1. Suppose $s \mathcal{R} t$ and $s \xrightarrow{a} \Delta$. Then $\overline{t} \in \rho(X_s) \subseteq [\![\varphi_s]\!]_\rho$. It follows from (2) that $\overline{t} \in [\![\langle a \rangle X_\Delta]\!]_\rho$. So there exists some Θ such that $\overline{t} \xrightarrow{a} \Theta$ and $\Theta \in [\![X_\Delta]\!]_\rho$. Now we apply (3).
2. Suppose $s \mathcal{R} t$ and $t \xrightarrow{a} \Theta$. Then $\overline{t} \in \rho(X_s) \subseteq [\![\varphi_s]\!]_\rho$. It follows from (2) that $\overline{t} \in [\![[a] \bigvee_{\overline{s} \xrightarrow{a} \Delta} X_\Delta]\!]$. Notice that it must be the case that $\overline{s} \xrightarrow{a}$, otherwise, $\overline{t} \in [\![[a]\mathtt{false}]\!]_\rho$ and thus $t \not\xrightarrow{a}$, in contradiction with the assumption $t \xrightarrow{a} \Theta$. Therefore, $\Theta \in [\![\bigvee_{\overline{s} \xrightarrow{a} \Delta} X_\Delta]\!]_\rho$, which implies $\Theta \in [\![X_\Delta]\!]_\rho$ for some Δ with $\overline{s} \xrightarrow{a} \Delta$. Now we apply (3).

($\Rightarrow$) Given a strong probabilistic bisimulation $\mathcal{R}$, we construct a post-fixpoint of $\mathcal{F}_E$ such that whenever $s \mathcal{R} t$ then $\overline{t}$ falls into the set of distributions assigned to X_s by that post-fixpoint. We define the environment $\rho_\mathcal{R}$ by

$$\rho_\mathcal{R}(X_s) := \{ \overline{t} \mid s \mathcal{R} t \}$$

and show that $\rho_\mathcal{R}$ is a post-fixpoint of $\mathcal{F}_E$, i.e.

$$\rho_\mathcal{R} \sqsubseteq \mathcal{F}_E(\rho_\mathcal{R}). \tag{4}$$

[1] The subformula $\bigoplus_{s \xrightarrow{a} \Delta} X_\Delta$ is equivalent to $\bigvee_{\overline{s} \xrightarrow{a} \Delta} X_\Delta$, and this is the form that we use to prove Theorem 2. If the given pLTS has nondeterministic choices among different transitions labelled with the same action, this disjunction is infinite. For example, if $s \xrightarrow{a} \overline{s_i}$ for $i = 1, 2$, then $\overline{s} \xrightarrow{a} \Delta_p$, where $\Delta_p = p \cdot \overline{s_1} + (1-p) \cdot \overline{s_2}$, for any $p \in [0,1]$. The set $\{\Delta_p \mid p \in [0,1]\}$ is uncountable, though it is finitely generable, as the convex closure of the two-element set $\{\Delta_0, \Delta_1\}$. The formula $\bigoplus_{s \xrightarrow{a} \Delta} X_\Delta$ exploits that fact to bypass the infinite disjunction; this formula is finite if the underlying pLTS is finitary.

We first show that

$$\Delta\ \mathcal{R}^\dagger\ \Theta \text{ implies } \Theta \in [\![X_\Delta]\!]_{\rho_\mathcal{R}}. \tag{5}$$

Suppose $\Delta\ \mathcal{R}^\dagger\ \Theta$, we have that (i) $\Delta = \sum_{i\in I} p_i \cdot \overline{s_i}$, (ii) $\Theta = \sum_{i\in I} p_i \cdot \overline{t_i}$, (iii) $s_i\ \mathcal{R}\ t_i$ for all $i \in I$. We know from (iii) that $\overline{t_i} \in [\![X_{s_i}]\!]_{\rho_\mathcal{R}}$ and thus $\overline{t_i} \in [\![\downarrow X_{s_i}]\!]_{\rho_\mathcal{R}}$. Using (ii) we have that $\Theta \in [\![\bigoplus_{i\in I} p_i \cdot \downarrow X_{s_i}]\!]_{\rho_\mathcal{R}}$. Using (i) we obtain $\Theta \in [\![X_\Delta]\!]_{\rho_\mathcal{R}}$.

Now we are in a position to show (4). Suppose $\overline{t} \in \rho_\mathcal{R}(X_s)$. We must prove that $\overline{t} \in [\![\varphi_s]\!]_{\rho_\mathcal{R}}$, i.e.

$$\overline{t} \in \Big(\bigcap_{s \xrightarrow{a} \Delta} [\![\langle a\rangle X_\Delta]\!]_{\rho_\mathcal{R}} \Big) \cap \Big(\bigcap_{a\in \mathsf{Act}_\tau} [\![[a] \bigvee_{\overline{s} \xrightarrow{a} \Delta} X_\Delta]\!]_{\rho_\mathcal{R}} \Big)$$

by (2). This can be done by showing that $\overline{t}$ belongs to each of the two parts of the outermost intersection.

1. Assume that $s \xrightarrow{a} \Delta$ for some $a \in \mathsf{Act}_\tau$ and $\Delta \in \mathcal{D}(S)$. Since $s\ \mathcal{R}\ t$, there exists some Θ such that $\overline{t} \xrightarrow{a} \Theta$ and $\Delta\ \mathcal{R}^\dagger\ \Theta$. By (5), we get $\Theta \in [\![X_\Delta]\!]_{\rho_\mathcal{R}}$. It follows that $\overline{t} \in [\![\langle a\rangle X_\Delta]\!]_{\rho_\mathcal{R}}$.
2. Let $a \in Act_\tau$. Whenever $\overline{t} \xrightarrow{a} \Theta$, then by $s\ \mathcal{R}\ t$ there must be some Δ such that $\overline{s} \xrightarrow{a} \Delta$ and $\Delta\ \mathcal{R}^\dagger\ \Theta$. By (5), we get $\Theta \in [\![X_\Delta]\!]_{\rho_\mathcal{R}}$ and thus $\Theta \in [\![\bigvee_{\overline{s} \xrightarrow{a} \Delta} X_\Delta]\!]_{\rho_\mathcal{R}}$. As a consequence, $\overline{t} \in [\![[a] \bigvee_{\overline{s} \xrightarrow{a} \Delta} X_\Delta]\!]_{\rho_\mathcal{R}}$. □

Strong probabilistic simulation. In a simulation game, if state s is related to state t, we only need to check that all transitions initiated by s should be matched up by transitions from t, and we do not care about the inverse direction: the capability of s to simulate t. Therefore, it is not surprising that characteristic equation systems for strong probabilistic simulation are defined as in Definition 6 except that we drop the second part of the conjunction in (2), so φ_s takes the form

$$\varphi_s := \bigwedge_{s \xrightarrow{a} \Delta} \langle a\rangle X_\Delta \tag{6}$$

With this modification, we have the expected property for strong probabilistic simulation, which can be shown by using the ideas in the proof of Theorem 2, but with fewer cases to analyse.

Weak probabilistic bisimulation. Characteristic equation systems for weak probabilistic bisimulation are defined as in Definition 6 except that the weak semantics of pMu is employed and φ_s takes the form

$$\varphi_s := \Big(\bigwedge_{s \xrightarrow{a} \Delta} \langle a\rangle X_\Delta \Big) \wedge \Big(\bigwedge_{a\in \mathsf{Act}_\tau} [a] \bigvee_{\overline{s} \overset{\hat{a}}{\Longrightarrow} \Delta} X_\Delta \Big)\ [2] \tag{7}$$

[2] Using results from Markov Decision Processes [28], in a finitary pLTS also this infinite disjunction can be expressed as finite convex combination; however, we will not elaborate this here.

Weak probabilistic simulation. Characteristic equation systems for weak probabilistic simulation are in exactly the same form as characteristic equation systems for strong probabilistic simulation (cf. (6)), but using the weak semantics of pMu.

Forward simulation. Characteristic equation systems for forward simulation are in the same form as characteristic equation systems for weak probabilistic simulation, but with $X_\Delta := \bigoplus_{s\in\lceil\Delta\rceil} \Delta(s)\cdot X_s$, i.e. dropping the $\downarrow$.

Failure simulation. To give a modal characterisations for failure simulation we need to add modal formulae of the form $\mathbf{ref}(A)$ with $A \subseteq \mathsf{Act}$, first introduced in [7], to pMu, with the meaning given by

$$[\![\mathbf{ref}(A)]\!]_\rho = \{\, \Delta \in \mathcal{D}(S) \mid \exists \Delta' : \Delta \stackrel{\hat{\tau}}{\Longrightarrow} \Delta' \wedge \Delta' \stackrel{A}{\not\longrightarrow} \}$$

The formula $\mathbf{ref}(A)$ holds for Δ if by doing internal actions only Δ can evolve into a distribution such that no state in its support can perform an action from $A \cup \{\tau\}$. This time φ_s takes the form

$$\varphi_s := \begin{cases} \bigwedge_{s \xrightarrow{a} \Delta} \langle a\rangle X_\Delta & \text{if } s \xrightarrow{\tau} \\ (\bigwedge_{s \xrightarrow{a} \Delta} \langle a\rangle X_\Delta) \wedge \mathbf{ref}(\{\, a \mid s \stackrel{a}{\not\longrightarrow} \}) & \text{otherwise} \end{cases} \tag{8}$$

with $X_\Delta := \bigoplus_{s\in\lceil\Delta\rceil} \Delta(s)\cdot X_s$. Inspired by [7], here we distinguish two cases, depending on the possibility of making an internal transition from s.

With the above modifications, we have the counterpart of Theorem 2, with a similar proof.

Theorem 3. *Let $E_\prec$ be the characteristic equation system for strong probabilistic simulation on a given pLTS. Let $E_\approx$ ($E_{\precsim}, E_{\lhd_S}, E_{\lhd_{FS}}$, respectively) be the characteristic equation system for weak probabilistic bisimulation (weak probabilistic simulation, forward simulation, failure simulation, respectively) on a given divergence-free pLTS. Then, for all states s, t and distributions Θ,*

1. *$s\ \mathcal{R}\ t$ for some strong probabilistic simulation (weak probabilistic bisimulation, weak probabilistic simulation, respectively) $\mathcal{R}$ if and only if $\overline{t} \in \rho(X_s)$ for some post-fixpoint ρ of $\mathcal{F}_{E_\prec}$ ($\mathcal{F}_{E_\approx}$, $\mathcal{F}_{E_\precsim}$, respectively).*
2. *$s\ \mathcal{R}\ \Theta$ for some forward simulation (failure simulation) $\mathcal{R}$ if and only if $\Theta \in \rho(X_s)$ for some post-fixpoint ρ of $\mathcal{F}_{E_{\lhd_S}}$ ($\mathcal{F}_{E_{\lhd_{FS}}}$).*
3. *In particular,*
   (a) $s \prec t$ if and only if $\overline{t} \in [\![\nu_{E_\prec}(X_s)]\!]$.
   (b) $s \approx t$ if and only if $\overline{t} \in [\![\nu_{E_\approx}(X_s)]\!]$.
   (c) $s \precsim t$ if and only if $\overline{t} \in [\![\nu_{E_\precsim}(X_s)]\!]$.
   (d) $s \lhd_{FS} \Theta$ if and only if $\Theta \in [\![\nu_{E_{\lhd_S}}(X_s)]\!]$.
   (e) $s \lhd_{FS} \Theta$ if and only if $\Theta \in [\![\nu_{E_{\lhd_{FS}}}(X_s)]\!]$. □

We can also consider the strong case for $\lhd_S$ and $\lhd_{FS}$ by treating τ as an external action, and give characteristic equation systems. In the strong case for $\lhd_{FS}$ only the "otherwise" in (8) applies, with $\mathbf{ref}(A)$ represented as $\bigwedge_{a\in A}[a]\mathtt{false}$.

5 Modal Characterisations

In the previous sections we have pursued logical characterisations for various behavioural relations by characteristic formulae. A weaker form of characterisation, which is commonly called a modal characterisation of a behavioural relation, consists of isolating a class of formulae with the property that two states are equivalent if and only if they satisfy the same formulae from that class.

Definition 7. Let $\mathcal{L}^{\mu}_{\sim}$ be simply the class $\mathcal{L}$ of modal formulae defined in Section 3, equipped with the strong semantics of Table 1. With $\mathcal{L}^{\mu}_{\prec}$ we denote the fragment of this class obtained by skipping the modalities $\neg$ and $[a]$. The classes $\mathcal{L}^{\mu}_{\approx}$ and $\mathcal{L}^{\mu}_{\precsim}$ are defined likewise, but equipped with the weak semantics. Moreover, $\mathcal{L}^{\mu}_{\lhd_S}$ is the fragment of $\mathcal{L}^{\mu}_{\precsim}$ obtained by skipping $\downarrow$, and $\mathcal{L}^{\mu}_{\lhd_{FS}}$ is obtained from $\mathcal{L}^{\mu}_{\lhd_S}$ by addition of the modality $\mathbf{ref}(A)$.

In all cases, dropping the superscript μ denotes the subclass obtained by dropping the variables and fixpoint operators.

For $\mathcal{R}\in\{\sim,\prec,\approx,\precsim,\lhd_S,\lhd_{FS}\}$ we write $\Delta \sqsubseteq^{\mu}_{\mathcal{R}} \Theta$ just when $\Delta\in[\![\varphi]\!] \Rightarrow \Theta\in[\![\varphi]\!]$ for all closed $\varphi \in \mathcal{L}^{\mu}_{\mathcal{R}}$, and $\Delta \sqsubseteq_{\mathcal{R}} \Theta$ just when $\Delta\in[\![\varphi]\!] \Rightarrow \Theta\in[\![\varphi]\!]$ for all $\varphi \in \mathcal{L}_{\mathcal{R}}$.

Note that the relations $\sqsubseteq^{\mu}_{\sim}$, $\sqsubseteq^{\mu}_{\approx}$, $\sqsubseteq_{\sim}$ and $\sqsubseteq_{\approx}$ are symmetric. For this reason we will employ the symbol $\equiv$ instead of $\sqsubseteq$ when referring to them.

We have the following modal characterisation for strong probabilistic bisimilarity, strong probabilistic similarity, weak probabilistic bisimilarity, weak probabilistic similarity, forward similarity, and failure similarity.

Theorem 4 (Modal characterisation)
Let s and t be states in a divergence-free pLTS.
1. $s \sim t$ iff $\overline{s} \equiv^{\mu}_{\sim} \overline{t}$ iff $\overline{s} \equiv_{\sim} \overline{t}$.
2. $s \prec t$ iff $\overline{s} \sqsubseteq^{\mu}_{\prec} \overline{t}$ iff $\overline{s} \sqsubseteq_{\prec} \overline{t}$.
3. $s \approx t$ iff $\overline{s} \equiv^{\mu}_{\approx} \overline{t}$ iff $\overline{s} \equiv_{\approx} \overline{t}$.
4. $s \precsim t$ iff $\overline{s} \sqsubseteq^{\mu}_{\precsim} \overline{t}$ iff $\overline{s} \sqsubseteq_{\precsim} \overline{t}$.
5. $s \lhd_S \Theta$ iff $\overline{s} \sqsubseteq^{\mu}_{\lhd_S} \Theta$ iff $\overline{s} \sqsubseteq_{\lhd_S} \Theta$.
6. $s \lhd_{FS} \Theta$ iff $\overline{s} \sqsubseteq^{\mu}_{\lhd_{FS}} \Theta$ iff $\overline{s} \sqsubseteq_{\lhd_{FS}} \Theta$.

Note that $\overline{s} \equiv^{\mu}_{\sim} \overline{t} \Rightarrow s \sim t$ is an immediate consequence of Theorem 2: From $s \sim s$ we obtain $\overline{s} \in [\![\nu_E(X_s)]\!]$. Together with $\overline{s} \equiv^{\mu}_{\sim} \overline{t}$ this yields $\overline{t} \in [\![\nu_E(X_s)]\!]$, hence $s \sim t$.

Proof. We only prove the first statement; the others can be shown analogously. In fact we establish the more general result that

$$\Delta \sim^{\dagger} \Theta \qquad \Leftrightarrow \qquad \Delta \equiv^{\mu}_{\sim} \Theta \qquad \Leftrightarrow \qquad \Delta \equiv_{\sim} \Theta$$

from which statement 1 of Theorem 4 follows immediately. The implication $\Delta \sim^{\dagger} \Theta \Rightarrow \Delta \equiv^{\mu}_{\sim} \Theta$ expresses the *soundness* of the logic $\mathcal{L}^{\mu}_{\sim}$ w.r.t. the relation $\sim^{\dagger}$, whereas the implication $\Delta \equiv_{\sim} \Theta \Rightarrow \Delta \sim^{\dagger} \Theta$ expresses the *completeness* of $\mathcal{L}_{\sim}$ w.r.t. $\sim^{\dagger}$. The implication $\Delta \equiv^{\mu}_{\sim} \Theta \Rightarrow \Delta \equiv_{\sim} \Theta$ is trivial.

(Soundness) An environment $\rho : \mathsf{Var} \rightarrow \mathcal{P}(\mathcal{D}(S))$ is called *compatible with* $\sim^\dagger$ if for all $X \in \mathsf{Var}$ we have that

$$\Delta \sim^\dagger \Theta \Rightarrow (\Delta \in \rho(X) \Rightarrow \Theta \in \rho(X)).$$

We will show by structural induction on φ that

$$\Delta \sim^\dagger \Theta \Rightarrow (\Delta \in [\![\varphi]\!]_\rho \Rightarrow \Theta \in [\![\varphi]\!]_\rho)$$

for any environment ρ that is compatible with $\sim^\dagger$. By restricting attention to closed φ this implies the soundness of $\mathcal{L}^\mu_\sim$ w.r.t. $\sim^\dagger$. We consider a few interesting cases.

- Let $\Delta \sim^\dagger \Theta$ and $\Delta \in [\![\langle a \rangle \varphi]\!]_\rho$. Then $\Delta \xrightarrow{a} \Delta'$ and $\Delta' \in [\![\varphi]\!]_\rho$ for some Δ'. It follows that there is some Θ' with $\Theta \xrightarrow{a} \Theta'$ and $\Delta' \sim^\dagger \Theta'$. By induction we have $\Theta' \in [\![\varphi]\!]_\rho$, thus $\Theta \models \langle a \rangle \varphi$.
- Let $\Delta \sim^\dagger \Theta$ and $\Delta \in [\![[a]\varphi]\!]_\rho$. Suppose $\Theta \xrightarrow{a} \Theta'$. It can be seen that there is a Δ' with $\Delta \xrightarrow{a} \Delta'$ and $\Delta' \sim^\dagger \Theta'$. As $\Delta \in [\![[a]\varphi]\!]_\rho$ it must be that $\Delta' \in [\![\varphi]\!]_\rho$, and by induction we have $\Theta' \in [\![\varphi]\!]_\rho$. Thus $\Theta \in [\![[a]\varphi]\!]_\rho$.
- Let $\Delta \sim^\dagger \Theta$ and $\Delta \in [\![\bigoplus_{i \in I} p_i \cdot \varphi_i]\!]_\rho$. So $\Delta = \sum_{i \in i} p_i \cdot \Delta_i$ and for all $i \in I$ we have $\Delta_i \in [\![\varphi_i]\!]_\rho$. Since $\Delta \sim^\dagger \Theta$, by Proposition 2(2) we have $\Theta = \sum_{i \in I} p_i \cdot \Theta_i$ and $\Delta_i \sim^\dagger \Theta_i$. So by induction we have $\Theta_i \in [\![\varphi_i]\!]_\rho$ for all $i \in I$. Therefore, $\Theta \in [\![\bigoplus_{i \in I} p_i \cdot \varphi_i]\!]_\rho$. The case $\Delta \in [\![\bigoplus_{i \in I} \varphi_i]\!]_\rho$ goes likewise.
- Let $\Delta \sim^\dagger \Theta$ and $\Delta \in [\![\downarrow \varphi]\!]_\rho$. So for all $s \in \lceil \Delta \rceil$ we have $\overline{s} \in [\![\varphi]\!]_\rho$. From $\Delta \sim^\dagger \Theta$ it follows that for each $t \in \lceil \Theta \rceil$ there is an $s \in \lceil \Delta \rceil$ with $s \sim t$, thus $\overline{s} \sim^\dagger \overline{t}$. So by induction we have $\overline{t} \in [\![\varphi]\!]_\rho$ for all $t \in \lceil \Theta \rceil$. Therefore, $\Theta \in [\![\downarrow \varphi]\!]_\rho$.
- Suppose $\Delta \sim^\dagger \Theta$ and $\Theta \notin [\![\mu X.\varphi]\!]_\rho$. Then $\exists V \subseteq \mathcal{D}(S)$ with $\Theta \notin V$ and $[\![\varphi]\!]_{\rho[X \mapsto V]} \subseteq V$. Let $V' := \{\Delta' \mid \forall \Theta'.(\Delta' \sim^\dagger \Theta' \Rightarrow \Theta' \in V)\}$. Then $\Delta \notin V'$. It remains to show that $[\![\varphi]\!]_{\rho[X \mapsto V']} \subseteq V'$, because this implies $\Delta \notin [\![\mu X.\varphi]\!]_\rho$, which has to be shown.

  So let $\Delta' \in [\![\varphi]\!]_{\rho[X \mapsto V']}$. Take any Θ' with $\Delta' \sim^\dagger \Theta'$. By construction of V', the environment $\rho[X \mapsto V']$ is compatible with $\sim^\dagger$. Therefore, the induction hypothesis yields $\Theta' \in [\![\varphi]\!]_{\rho[X \mapsto V']}$. We have $V' \subseteq V$, and as $[\![\ ]\!]$ is monotonic we obtain $\Theta' \in [\![\varphi]\!]_{\rho[X \mapsto V']} \subseteq [\![\varphi]\!]_{\rho[X \mapsto V]} \subseteq V$. It follows that $\Delta' \in V'$.
- Suppose $\Delta \sim^\dagger \Theta$ and $\Delta \in [\![\nu X.\varphi]\!]_\rho$. Then $\exists V \subseteq \mathcal{D}(S)$ with $\Delta \in V$ and $[\![\varphi]\!]_{\rho[X \mapsto V]} \supseteq V$. Let $V' := \{\Theta' \mid \exists \Delta' \in V.\ \Delta' \sim^\dagger \Theta'\}$. Then $\Theta \in V'$. It remains to show that $[\![\varphi]\!]_{\rho[X \mapsto V']} \supseteq V'$, because this implies $\Theta \in [\![\nu X.\varphi]\!]_\rho$, which has to be shown.

  So let $\Theta' \notin [\![\varphi]\!]_{\rho[X \mapsto V']}$. Take any Δ' with $\Delta' \sim^\dagger \Theta'$. By construction of V', the environment $\rho[X \mapsto V']$ is compatible with $\sim^\dagger$. Therefore, the induction hypothesis yields $\Delta' \notin [\![\varphi]\!]_{\rho[X \mapsto V']}$. We have $V' \supseteq V$, and as $[\![\ ]\!]$ is monotonic we obtain $\Delta' \notin [\![\varphi]\!]_{\rho[X \mapsto V']} \supseteq [\![\varphi]\!]_{\rho[X \mapsto V]} \supseteq V$. It follows that $\Theta' \notin V'$.

(Completeness) Let $\mathcal{R} = \{(s,t) \mid \overline{s} \equiv_\sim \overline{t}\}$. We show that $\mathcal{R}$ is a strong probabilistic bisimulation. Suppose $s\ \mathcal{R}\ t$ and $s \xrightarrow{a} \Delta$. We have to show that there is some Θ with $\overline{t} \xrightarrow{a} \Theta$ and $\Delta\ \mathcal{R}^\dagger\ \Theta$. Consider the set

$$T := \{\Theta \mid \overline{t} \xrightarrow{a} \Theta \wedge \Theta = \sum_{s' \in \lceil \Delta \rceil} \Delta(s') \cdot \Theta_{s'} \wedge \exists s' \in \lceil \Delta \rceil, \exists t' \in \lceil \Theta_{s'} \rceil : \overline{s'} \not\equiv_\sim \overline{t'}\}$$

For each $\Theta \in T$ there must be some $s'_\Theta \in \lceil\Delta\rceil$ and $t'_\Theta \in \lceil\Theta_{s'_\Theta}\rceil$ and a formula φ_Θ with $\overline{s'_\Theta} \models \varphi_\Theta$ but $\overline{t'_\Theta} \not\models \varphi_\Theta$. So $\overline{s'} \models \bigwedge_{\{\Theta\in T|s'_\Theta=s'\}} \varphi_\Theta$ for each $s' \in \lceil\Delta\rceil$, and for each $\Theta \in T$ with $s'_\Theta = s'$ there is some $t'_\Theta \in \lceil\Theta_{s'}\rceil$ with $\overline{t'_\Theta} \not\models \bigwedge_{\{\Theta\in T|s'_\Theta=s'\}} \varphi_\Theta$. Let

$$\varphi := \langle a\rangle \bigoplus_{s'\in\lceil\Delta\rceil} \Delta(s') \cdot \downarrow \bigwedge_{\{\Theta\in T|s'_\Theta=s'\}} \varphi_\Theta.$$

It is clear that $\overline{s} \models \varphi$, hence $\overline{t} \models \varphi$ by $s\mathcal{R}t$. It follows that there must be a Θ^* with $\overline{t} \xrightarrow{a} \Theta^*$, $\Theta^* = \sum_{s'\in\lceil\Delta\rceil} \Delta(s') \cdot \Theta^*_{s'}$ and for each $s' \in\lceil\Delta\rceil$, $t' \in\lceil\Theta^*_{s'}\rceil$ we have $\overline{t'} \models \bigwedge_{\{\Theta\in T|s'_\Theta=s'\}} \varphi_\Theta$. This means that $\Theta^* \not\in T$ and hence for each $s' \in\lceil\Delta\rceil$, $t' \in\lceil\Theta^*_{s'}\rceil$ we have $\overline{s'} \equiv_\sim \overline{t'}$, i.e. $s'\mathcal{R}t'$. Consequently, we obtain $\Delta\ \mathcal{R}^\dagger\ \Theta^*$. By symmetry all transitions of t can be matched up by transitions of s. □

Modal characterisation of strong and weak probabilistic bisimulation has been studied in [27]. It is also based on a probabilistic extension of the Hennessy-Milner logic. Instead of our modalities $\bigoplus$ and $\downarrow$ they use a modality $[\cdot]_p$. Intuitively, a distribution Δ satisfies the formula $[\varphi]_p$ when the set of states satisfying φ is measured by Δ with probability at least p. So the formula $[\varphi]_p$ can be expressed by our logics in terms of the probabilistic choice $\bigoplus_{i\in I} p_i \cdot \varphi_i$ by setting $I = \{1, 2\}$, $p_1 = p$, $p_2 = 1-p$, $\varphi_1 = \downarrow\varphi$, and $\varphi_2 = \texttt{true}$. Furthermore, instead of our modality $\langle a\rangle$, they use a modality $\Diamond a$ that can be expressed in our logic by $\Diamond a\varphi = \langle a\rangle\downarrow\varphi$. We conjecture that our modalities $\langle a\rangle$ and $\bigoplus$ cannot be expressed in terms of the logic of [27], and that a logic of that type is unsuitable for characterising forward simulation or failure simulation.

When restricted to deterministic pLTSs (i.e., for each state and for each action, there exists at most one outgoing transition), probabilistic bisimulations can be characterised by simpler forms of logics, as observed in [20,11,27].

References

1. Bandini, E., Segala, R.: Axiomatizations for Probabilistic Bisimulation. In: Orejas, F., Spirakis, P.G., van Leeuwen, J. (eds.) ICALP 2001. LNCS, vol. 2076, pp. 370–381. Springer, Heidelberg (2001)
2. Christoff, I.: Testing equivalences and fully abstract models for probabilistic processes. In: Baeten, J.C.M., Klop, J.W. (eds.) CONCUR 1990. LNCS, vol. 458, pp. 126–140. Springer, Heidelberg (1990)
3. Cleaveland, R., Purushothaman Iyer, S., Narasimha, M.: Probabilistic temporal logics via the modal mu-calculus. Theoretical Computer Science 342(2-3), 316–350 (2005)
4. D'Argenio, P.R., Wolovick, N., Terraf, P.S., Celayes, P.: Nondeterministic Labeled Markov Processes: Bisimulations and Logical Characterization. In: Proc. QEST 2009, pp. 11–20. IEEE Computer Society, Los Alamitos (2009)
5. Deng, Y., Du, W.: A Local Algorithm for Checking Probabilistic Bisimilarity. In: Proc. FCST 2009, pp. 401–407. IEEE Computer Society, Los Alamitos (2009)
6. Deng, Y., van Glabbeek, R.J.: Characterising Probabilistic Processes Logically, `http://arxiv.org/abs/1007.5188`, Full version of this paper

7. Deng, Y., van Glabbeek, R.J., Hennessy, M., Morgan, C.C.: Characterising Testing Preorders for Finite Probabilistic Processes. Logical Methods in Computer Science 4(4), 4 (2008)
8. Deng, Y., van Glabbeek, R.J., Hennessy, M., Morgan, C.C.: Testing Finitary Probabilistic Processes. In: Bravetti, M., Zavattaro, G. (eds.) CONCUR 2009 - Concurrency Theory. LNCS, vol. 5710, pp. 274–288. Springer, Heidelberg (2009)
9. Deng, Y., van Glabbeek, R.J., Hennessy, M., Morgan, C.C., Zhang, C.: Remarks on Testing Probabilistic Processes. ENTCS 172, 359–397 (2007)
10. Deng, Y., Palamidessi, C.: Axiomatizations for probabilistic finite-state behaviors. Theoretical Computer Science 373(1-2), 92–114 (2007)
11. Desharnais, J., Edalat, A., Panangaden, P.: A logical characterization of bisimulation for labelled Markov processes. In: Proc. LICS 1998, pp. 478–489. IEEE Computer Society, Los Alamitos (1998)
12. Giacalone, A., Jou, C.-C., Smolka, S.A.: Algebraic reasoning for probabilistic concurrent systems. In: Proc. IFIP TC 2 Working Conference on Programming Concepts and Methods, pp. 443–458 (1990)
13. Hansson, H., Jonsson, B.: A Calculus for Communicating Systems with Time and Probabilities. In: Proc. RTSS 1990, pp. 278–287. IEEE Computer Society, Los Alamitos (1990)
14. Hansson, H., Jonsson, B.: A Logic for Reasoning about Time and Reliability. Formal Aspects of Computing 6(5), 512–535 (1994)
15. Hennessy, M., Milner, R.: Algebraic laws for nondeterminism and concurrency. Journal of the ACM 32(1), 137–161 (1985)
16. Huth, M., Kwiatkowska, M.: Quantitative analysis and model checking. In: Proc. LICS 1997, pp. 111–122. IEEE Computer Society, Los Alamitos (1997)
17. Jonsson, B., Larsen, K.G.: Specification and refinement of probabilistic processes. In: Proc. LICS 1991, pp. 266–277. Computer Society Press (1991)
18. Jonsson, B., Wang, Y.: Testing preorders for probabilistic processes can be characterized by simulations. Theoretical Computer Science 282(1), 33–51 (2002)
19. Kozen, D.: Results on the propositional mu-calculus. Theoretical Computer Science 27, 333–354 (1983)
20. Larsen, K.G., Skou, A.: Bisimulation through probabilistic testing. Information and Computation 94(1), 1–28 (1991)
21. Lowe, G.: Probabilistic and Prioritized Models of Timed CSP. Theoretical Computer Science 138, 315–352 (1995)
22. McIver, A.K., Morgan, C.C.: An expectation-based model for probabilistic temporal logic. Technical Report PRG-TR-13-97, Oxford University Computing Laboratory (1997)
23. McIver, A.K., Morgan, C.C.: Results on the Quantitative Mu-Calculus. ACM Transactions on Computational Logic 8(1) (2007)
24. Milner, R.: Communication and Concurrency. Prentice-Hall, Englewood Cliffs (1989)
25. Mislove, M.W., Ouaknine, J., Worrell, J.: Axioms for Probability and Nondeterminism. ENTCS 96, 7–28 (2004)
26. Müller-Olm, M.: Derivation of Characteristic Formulae. ENTCS 18, 159–170 (1998)
27. Parma, A., Segala, R.: Logical Characterizations of Bisimulations for Discrete Probabilistic Systems. In: Seidl, H. (ed.) FOSSACS 2007. LNCS, vol. 4423, pp. 287–301. Springer, Heidelberg (2007)
28. Puterman, M.L.: Markov Decision Processes. Wiley, Chichester (1994)

29. Ramakrishna, Y.S., Smolka, S.A.: Partial-order reduction in the weak modal mu-calculus. In: Mazurkiewicz, A., Winkowski, J. (eds.) LFCS 1997. LNCS, vol. 1234, pp. 5–24. Springer, Heidelberg (1997)
30. Segala, R.: Modeling and Verification of Randomized Distributed Real-Time Systems. Technical Report MIT/LCS/TR-676, PhD thesis, MIT, Dept. of EECS (1995)
31. Segala, R., Lynch, N.A.: Probabilistic Simulations for Probabilistic Processes. In: Jonsson, B., Parrow, J. (eds.) CONCUR 1994. LNCS, vol. 836, pp. 481–496. Springer, Heidelberg (1994)
32. Steffen, B., Ingólfsdóttir, A.: Characteristic Formulae for Processes with Divergence. Information and Computation 110, 149–163 (1994)
33. Tarski, A.: A lattice-theoretical fixpoint theorem and its application. Pacific Journal of Mathematics 5(2), 285–309 (1955)
34. Tix, R., Keimel, K., Plotkin, G.D.: Semantic Domains for Combining Probability and Non-Determinism. ENTCS 129, 1–104 (2005)
35. Wang, Y., Larsen, K.G.: Testing Probabilistic and Nondeterministic Processes. In: Proc. IFIP TC6/WG6.1 PSTV'92, C-8, North-Holland, pp. 47–61 (1992)

FCUBE: An Efficient Prover for Intuitionistic Propositional Logic

Mauro Ferrari[1], Camillo Fiorentini[2], and Guido Fiorino[3]

[1] DICOM, Univ. degli Studi dell'Insubria, Via Mazzini 5, 21100, Varese, Italy
[2] DSI, Univ. degli Studi di Milano, Via Comelico, 39, 20135 Milano, Italy
[3] DIMEQUANT, Univ. degli Studi di Milano-Bicocca
P.zza dell'Ateneo Nuovo 1, 20126 Milano, Italy

Abstract. We present FCUBE, a theorem prover for Intuitionistic propositional logic based on a tableau calculus. The main novelty of FCUBE is that it implements several optimization techniques that allow to prune the search space acting on different aspects of proof-search. We tested the efficiency of our techniques by comparing FCUBE with other theorem provers. We found that our prover outperforms the other provers on several interesting families of formulas.

1 Introduction

FCUBE[1] is a theorem prover for Intuitionistic propositional logic based on a tableau calculus. The main topic of this paper is the description of the strategy and the main optimizations on which FCUBE relies. Here, speaking of optimization we mean a family of techniques that allow us to reduce the search space acting on different aspects of proof search. In particular FCUBE implements *simplification* techniques, which reduce the size of the formulas treated by the prover so to avoid inessential branching and backtracking.

Unlike what happened for classical logic, where optimization techniques of the above kind have been investigated from the very beginning (see, e.g., [3,6]), in the case of tableau calculi for Intuitionistic and non classical logics very little work has been done in this direction. As far as we know, the only works that address these issues in the context of tableau calculi are [5,7] that essentially refer to classical and modal logics, and [4] which addresses the case of Intuitionistic tableau calculi. The optimization rules implemented in FCUBE are those presented in [4]. We remark that FCUBE is a prototype Prolog implementation of the above techniques and we did very little work to "optimize the implementation"; e.g., FCUBE is based on a very rough implementation of the relevant data structures. In spite of this, as discussed in Section 5, FCUBE outperforms other provers on several interesting families of formulas. The above considerations suggest that the study of optimization techniques is a promising line of research to improve the performances of Intuitionistic theorem provers.

[1] Available at `http://web-nuovo.dimequant.unimib.it/~guidofiorino/fcube.jsp`

C. Fermüller and A. Voronkov (Eds.): LPAR-17, LNCS 6397, pp. 294–301, 2010.

2 Preliminaries and Tableau Calculus

We consider the language $\mathcal{L}$ based on a denumerable set of propositional variables $\mathcal{PV}$, the logical connectives $\neg$, $\wedge$, $\vee$, $\rightarrow$ and the logical constants $\top$ and $\bot$.

We recall the main definitions about Kripke semantics (see, e.g., [2] for more details). A *Kripke model* for $\mathcal{L}$ is a structure $\underline{K} = \langle P, \leq, \rho, V\rangle$, where $\langle P, \leq, \rho\rangle$ is a poset with minimum ρ and V is a monotone function (the *valuation function*) mapping every $\alpha \in P$ to a subset of $\mathcal{PV}$. The forcing relation $\Vdash \subseteq P \times \mathcal{L}$ is defined as follows:

- $\alpha \Vdash \top$, $\alpha \nVdash \bot$ and, for $p \in \mathcal{PV}$, $\alpha \Vdash p$ iff $p \in V(\alpha)$;
- $\alpha \Vdash A \wedge B$ iff $\alpha \Vdash A$ and $\alpha \Vdash B$;
- $\alpha \Vdash A \vee B$ iff $\alpha \Vdash A$ or $\alpha \Vdash B$;
- $\alpha \Vdash A \rightarrow B$ iff, for every $\beta \in P$ such that $\alpha \leq \beta$, $\beta \Vdash A$ implies $\beta \Vdash B$;
- $\alpha \Vdash \neg A$ iff, for every $\alpha \leq \beta$, $\beta \nVdash A$ (i.e., $\beta \Vdash A$ does not hold).

Monotonicity property holds for arbitrary formulas, i.e., $\alpha \Vdash A$ and $\alpha \leq \beta$ imply $\beta \Vdash A$. A formula A *is valid in* $\underline{K}$ iff $\rho \Vdash A$. Intuitionistic propositional logic **Int** coincides with the set of formulas valid in all Kripke models [2].

The calculus implemented in FCUBE treats *signed formulas* of the kind $\mathbf{T}A$ or $\mathbf{F}A$, where $A \in \mathcal{L}$ The semantics of formulas extends to signed formulas as follows. Given a Kripke model $\underline{K} = \langle P, \leq, \rho, V\rangle$, $\alpha \in P$ and a signed formula H, α *realizes* H *in* $\underline{K}$ ($\underline{K}, \alpha \rhd H$) iff:

- $H \equiv \mathbf{T}A$ and $\alpha \Vdash A$;
- $H \equiv \mathbf{F}A$ and $\alpha \nVdash A$.

We say that $\underline{K}$ realizes H ($\underline{K} \rhd H$) iff $\underline{K}, \rho \rhd H$; H is *realizable* iff $\underline{K} \rhd H$ for some Kripke model $\underline{K}$. The above definitions extend in the obvious way to sets Δ of signed formulas; for instance, $\underline{K}, \alpha \rhd \Delta$ means that $\underline{K}, \alpha \rhd H$, for every $H \in \Delta$. By definition, $A \in$ **Int** iff $\mathbf{F}A$ is not realizable. We remark that, by the monotonicity property, **T**-signed formulas are upward persistent ($\underline{K}, \alpha \rhd \mathbf{T}A$ and $\alpha \leq \beta$ imply $\underline{K}, \beta \rhd \mathbf{T}A$), while **F**-signed formulas are downward persistent ($\underline{K}, \alpha \rhd \mathbf{F}A$ and $\beta \leq \alpha$ imply $\underline{K}, \beta \rhd \mathbf{F}A$).

FCUBE is based on the tableau calculus **Tab** of Fig.1[2]. In the formulation of the rules we use the notation Δ, H as a shorthand for $\Delta \cup \{H\}$. In the premise of a rule, writing Δ, H we assume that $H \notin \Delta$. Every rule applies to a set of signed formulas, but only acts on the signed formula H explicitly indicated in the premise; we call H the *major premise* of the rule, whereas we call all the other signed formulas *minor premises* of the rule. A rule r is *invertible* iff r is sound and, for every set Δ in the consequent, the realizability of Δ implies the realizability of the premise. A set Δ is *contradictory* iff either $\mathbf{T}\bot \in \Delta$ or $\mathbf{F}\top \in \Delta$ or, for some $A \in \mathcal{L}$, $\{\mathbf{F}A, \mathbf{T}A\} \subseteq \Delta$. A *proof-table* τ for Δ is defined as usual; when all the leaves of τ are contradictory, we say that τ is *closed* and Δ is provable.

As proved in [1], **Tab** is a complete for **Int**, that is $A \in$ **Int** iff $\mathbf{F}A$ is provable in **Tab**. The decision procedure described in Section 4 is inspired by [1].

[2] **Tab** essentially corresponds to the calculus of [1], the only difference is the absence of the sign $\mathbf{F_c}$. Here $\mathbf{F_c}A$ is replaced by the equivalent signed formula $\mathbf{T}\neg A$.

$$\frac{\Delta, \mathbf{T}(A \wedge B)}{\Delta, \mathbf{T}A, \mathbf{T}B}\,\mathbf{T}\wedge \qquad \frac{\Delta, \mathbf{F}(A \wedge B)}{\Delta, \mathbf{F}A \mid \Delta, \mathbf{F}B}\,\mathbf{F}\wedge \qquad \frac{\Delta, \mathbf{T}\neg(A \wedge B)}{\Delta_{\mathbf{T}}, \mathbf{T}\neg A \mid \Delta_{\mathbf{T}}, \mathbf{T}\neg B}\,\mathbf{T}\neg\wedge$$

$$\frac{\Delta, \mathbf{T}(A \vee B)}{\Delta, \mathbf{T}A \mid \Delta, \mathbf{T}B}\,\mathbf{T}\vee \qquad \frac{\Delta, \mathbf{F}(A \vee B)}{\Delta, \mathbf{F}A, \mathbf{F}B}\,\mathbf{F}\vee \qquad \frac{\Delta, \mathbf{T}\neg(A \vee B)}{\Delta, \mathbf{T}\neg A, \mathbf{T}\neg B}\,\mathbf{T}\neg\vee$$

$$\frac{\Delta, \mathbf{T}A, \mathbf{T}(A \to B)}{\Delta, \mathbf{T}A, \mathbf{T}B}\,MP \qquad \frac{\Delta_{\mathbf{T}}, \mathbf{T}(A \to B)}{\Delta_{\mathbf{T}}, \mathbf{T}\neg A \mid \Delta_{\mathbf{T}}, \mathbf{T}B}\,\mathbf{T}\to\text{-special}$$

$$\frac{\Delta, \mathbf{F}(A \to B)}{\Delta_{\mathbf{T}}, \mathbf{T}A, \mathbf{F}B}\,\mathbf{F}\to \qquad \frac{\Delta, \mathbf{T}\neg(A \to B)}{\Delta_{\mathbf{T}}, \mathbf{T}A, \mathbf{T}\neg B}\,\mathbf{T}\neg\to \qquad \frac{\Delta, \mathbf{F}\neg A}{\Delta_{\mathbf{T}}, \mathbf{T}A}\,\mathbf{F}\neg \qquad \frac{\Delta, \mathbf{T}\neg\neg A}{\Delta_{\mathbf{T}}, \mathbf{T}A}\,\mathbf{T}\neg\neg$$

$$\frac{\Delta, \mathbf{T}((A \wedge B) \to C)}{\Delta, \mathbf{T}(A \to (B \to C))}\,\mathbf{T}\to\wedge \qquad \frac{\Delta, \mathbf{T}(\neg A \to B)}{\Delta_{\mathbf{T}}, \mathbf{T}A \mid \Delta, \mathbf{T}B}\,\mathbf{T}\to\neg$$

$$\frac{\Delta, \mathbf{T}((A \vee B) \to C)}{\Delta, \mathbf{T}(A \to p), \mathbf{T}(B \to p), \mathbf{T}(p \to C)}\,\mathbf{T}\to\vee \quad \text{with } p \text{ a new atom}$$

$$\frac{\Delta, \mathbf{T}((A \to B) \to C)}{\Delta_{\mathbf{T}}, \mathbf{T}A, \mathbf{F}p, \mathbf{T}(p \to C), \mathbf{T}(B \to p) \mid \Delta, \mathbf{T}C}\,\mathbf{T}\to\to \quad \text{with } p \text{ a new atom}$$

$$\text{where } \Delta_{\mathbf{T}} = \{\mathbf{T}A \mid \mathbf{T}A \in \Delta\}$$

Fig. 1. The **Tab** calculus

3 Simplification Rules

In this section we describe the *simplification rules* implemented in FCUBE. The aim of these rules is to reduce the size of the formulas to be analyzed as much as possible before applying a rule of Fig. 1.

The first kind of simplification implemented in FCUBE exploits the well-known *boolean simplification rules* [4,7]. These rules simplify formulas containing the constants $\top$ and $\bot$ using Intuitionistic equivalences; e.g., $(A \vee \top) \wedge B$ simplifies to B, by the equivalences $A \vee \top \equiv \top$ and $B \wedge \top \equiv B$.

The other simplification rules used by FCUBE have been introduced in [4] and are described in Fig. 2. Given a signed formula H, $H[B/A]$ denotes the signed formula obtained by replacing every occurrence of A with B in H. Now, let Z, A and B be formulas; $Z\{B/A\}$ denotes the *partial substitution* of A with B in Z defined as follows: if $Z = A$ then $Z\{B/A\} = B$; if $Z = (X \odot Y)$ and $\odot \in \{\wedge, \vee\}$ then $Z\{B/A\} = X\{B/A\} \odot Y\{B/A\}$; if $Z = X \to Y$, $Z = \neg X$ or $Z \in \mathcal{PV}$ and $Z \neq A$, then $Z\{B/A\} = Z$. Note that partial substitutions do not act on subformulas under the scope of $\to$ or $\neg$. Given a signed formula $H = \mathcal{S}Z$, $H\{B/A\} = \mathcal{S}(Z\{B/A\})$. For a set of signed formulas Δ, $\Delta[B/A]$ (resp. $\Delta\{B/A\}$) is the set of signed formulas $H[B/A]$ (resp. $H\{B/A\}$) such that

$$\frac{\Delta, \mathbf{T}A}{\Delta[\top/A], \mathbf{T}A}\text{Replace-}\mathbf{T} \qquad \frac{\Delta, \mathbf{T}\neg A}{\Delta[\bot/A], \mathbf{T}\neg A}\text{Replace-}\mathbf{T}\neg \qquad \frac{\Delta, \mathbf{F}A}{\Delta\{\bot/A\}, \mathbf{F}A}\text{Replace-}\mathbf{F}$$

$$\frac{\Delta}{\Delta[\top/p]}\ \mathbf{T}\text{-perm if } p\preceq^{+}\Delta \qquad \frac{\Delta}{\Delta[\bot/p]}\ \mathbf{T}\neg\text{-perm if } p\preceq^{-}\Delta \qquad \frac{\Delta}{\Delta\{\bot/p\}}\ \mathbf{F}\text{-perm if } p\preceq^{-}_{w}\Delta$$

- $p\preceq^{-}\mathbf{F}p$ and $p\preceq^{+}\mathbf{T}p$
- $p\preceq^{l}\mathcal{S}\top$ and $p\preceq^{l}\mathcal{S}\bot$
- $p\preceq^{l}\mathcal{S}q$, where $q\in\mathcal{PV}$ and $q\neq p$
- $p\preceq^{l}\mathcal{S}(A\odot B)$ iff $p\preceq^{l}\mathcal{S}A$ and $p\preceq^{l}\mathcal{S}B$, where $\odot\in\{\wedge,\vee\}$
- $p\preceq^{l}\mathbf{F}(A\to B)$ iff $p\preceq^{l}\mathbf{T}A$ and $p\preceq^{l}\mathbf{F}B$
- $p\preceq^{l}\mathbf{T}(A\to B)$ iff $p\preceq^{l}\mathbf{F}A$ and $p\preceq^{l}\mathbf{T}B$
- $p\preceq^{l}\mathbf{F}\neg A$ iff $p\preceq^{l}\mathbf{T}A$
- $p\preceq^{l}\mathbf{T}\neg A$ iff $p\preceq^{l}\mathbf{F}A$.

- $p\preceq^{-}_{w}\mathcal{S}\top$ and $p\preceq^{-}_{w}\mathcal{S}\bot$
- $p\preceq^{-}_{w}\mathbf{F}A$ and $p\preceq^{-}_{w}\mathbf{T}\neg A$ for every A
- $p\preceq^{-}_{w}\mathbf{T}q$, where $q\in\mathcal{PV}$ and $q\neq p$
- $p\preceq^{-}_{w}\mathbf{T}(A\odot B)$ iff $p\preceq^{-}_{w}\mathbf{T}A$ and $p\preceq^{-}_{w}\mathbf{T}B$, where $\odot\in\{\wedge,\vee\}$
- $p\preceq^{-}_{w}\mathbf{T}(A\to B)$ iff $p\preceq^{-}_{w}\mathbf{T}B$.

where $\mathcal{S}\in\{\mathbf{T},\mathbf{F}\}$ and $l\in\{+,-\}$

Given a set of signed formulas Δ and $\preceq\in\{\preceq^{+},\preceq^{-},\preceq^{-}_{w}\}$, $p\preceq\Delta$ iff, for every $H\in\Delta$, $p\preceq H$.

Fig. 2. Simplification rules and polarities

$H\in\Delta$. The rules in the second line of Fig. 2 enable the substitution of $p\in\mathcal{PV}$ occurring with constant *polarity* in a set Δ (see the definition of $p\preceq^{+}H$, $p\preceq^{-}H$ and $p\preceq^{-}_{w}H$) with $\top$ or $\bot$. In [4] it is proved that:

Theorem 1. *The rules of Fig.2 are invertible.* □

Thus, simplification rules do not require backtracking.

4 FCUBE Strategy

Here we describe the main function F of FCUBE which implements the proof-search strategy (see Fig. 3). Let Δ be a set of signed formulas; $\mathrm{F}(\Delta)$ returns either a proof for Δ or a countermodel $\underline{K}$ for Δ, namely a Kripke model $\underline{K}$ such that $\underline{K}\rhd\Delta$. We introduce some notations. Given $H\in\Delta$, $\mathcal{R}_H(\Delta)$ is the instance of the rule of **Tab** having H as major premise and $\Delta\setminus\{H\}$ as minor premises. By $\Delta_{\mathbf{F}}$ we denote the set of $\mathbf{F}$-signed formulas of Δ. A *local formula* is a signed formula $\mathbf{F}L$ such that:

$$L ::= p \mid L\vee L \mid L\wedge A \mid A\wedge L \quad \text{where } p\in\mathcal{PV} \text{ and } A \text{ is any formula}$$

$\mathcal{LF}$ is the set of local formulas. An important property of $\mathcal{LF}$ is stated by the following theorem:

Theorem 2. *Let* $\underline{K}=\langle P,\leq,\rho,V\rangle$ *be a Kripke model,* $\alpha\in P$ *and* $\mathbf{F}L\in\mathcal{LF}$. *If* $\alpha\nVdash p$ *for every* p *occurring in* L, *then* $\alpha\nVdash L$. □

Function $\textsc{f}(\Delta)$

1. Apply to Δ the rules of Fig. 2 and boolean simplification rules as long as possible.
2. If Δ is a contradictory set, then return the proof $\pi = \Delta$.
3. If there exists $H \in \Delta$ such that $H \notin \mathcal{LF}$ and one of the rules $\mathbf{T}\wedge$, $\mathbf{T}\neg\neg$, MP, $\mathbf{T}\to\wedge$, $\mathbf{T}\to\vee$ and $\mathbf{F}\vee$ applies to H, let $\mathcal{R}_H(\Delta) = \frac{\Delta}{\Delta'}r$ and $\pi' = \textsc{f}(\Delta')$.
   If π' is a proof, then return the proof $\frac{\Delta}{\pi'}r$, else return the model π'.
4. If there exists $H \in \Delta$ such that $H \notin \mathcal{LF}$ and one of the rules $\mathbf{T}\vee$, $\mathbf{F}\wedge$, $\mathbf{T}\to-special$ applies to H, let $\mathcal{R}_H(\Delta) = \frac{\Delta}{\Delta' \mid \Delta''}r$, $\pi' = \textsc{f}(\Delta')$ and $\pi'' = \textsc{f}(\Delta'')$.
   If there is a model $\tau \in \{\pi', \pi''\}$ then return τ, else return the proof $\frac{\Delta}{\pi' | \pi''}r$.
5. Let $\Gamma_1 = \{ H \in \Delta \mid H = \mathbf{F}(A \to B) \text{ or } H = \mathbf{F}\neg A \}$.
   Let $\Gamma_2 = \{ K \in \Delta \mid K = \mathbf{T}((A \to B) \to C) \text{ or } K = \mathbf{T}(\neg A \to B) \}$.
   If $\Gamma_1 \cup \Gamma_2 \neq \emptyset$ then
   Let $\mathcal{M} = \emptyset$ ($\mathcal{M}$ is a set of Kripke models)
   For each $H \in \Gamma_1$ do
   Let $\mathcal{R}_H(\Delta) = \frac{\Delta}{\Delta'}r$ and $\pi' = \textsc{f}(\Delta')$.
   If π' is a proof then return the proof $\frac{\Delta}{\pi'}r$
   else if $\textsc{Real}(\pi', \Delta_{\mathbf{F}})$ then return π' else $\mathcal{M} = \mathcal{M} \cup \{\pi'\}$.
   For each $K \in \Gamma_2$ do
   Let $\mathcal{R}_K(\Delta) = \frac{\Delta}{\Delta' \mid \Delta''}r$, $\pi' = \textsc{f}(\Delta')$ and $\pi'' = \textsc{f}(\Delta'')$.
   If π'' is a model then return π''
   else if both π' and π'' are proofs, then return the proof $\frac{\Delta}{\pi' | \pi''}r$
   else if $\textsc{Real}(\pi', \Delta_{\mathbf{F}})$ then return π', else $\mathcal{M} = \mathcal{M} \cup \{\pi'\}$.
   Return the model $\textsc{Cm}(\Delta, \mathcal{M})$.
6. If there exists $H \in \Delta$ such that one of the rules $\mathbf{T}\neg\to$, $\mathbf{T}\neg\neg$ applies to H, let $\mathcal{R}_H(\Delta) = \frac{\Delta}{\Delta'}r$ and $\pi' = \textsc{f}(\Delta')$.
   If π' is a proof then return the proof $\frac{\Delta}{\pi'}r$, else return $\textsc{Cm}(\Delta, \{\pi\})$.
7. If $H = \mathbf{T}\neg(A \wedge B) \in \Delta$, let $\mathcal{R}_H(\Delta) = \frac{\Delta}{\Delta' \mid \Delta''}\mathbf{T}\neg\wedge$, $\pi' = \textsc{f}(\Delta')$ and $\pi'' = \textsc{f}(\Delta'')$.
   If there is a model $\tau \in \{\pi', \pi''\}$ then return $\textsc{Cm}(\Delta, \{\tau\})$, else return $\frac{\Delta}{\pi' | \pi''}\mathbf{T}\neg\wedge$.
8. Return $\textsc{Cm}(\Delta, \emptyset)$.

Function $\textsc{Cm}(\Delta, \mathcal{M})$
Let $\mathcal{M} = \{\underline{K}_1, \ldots, \underline{K}_n\}$, with $\underline{K}_i = \langle P_i, \leq_i, \rho_i, V_i \rangle$.
Let $\rho \notin \bigcup_{1 \leq i \leq n} P_i$.
Return $\underline{K} = \langle P, \leq, \rho, V \rangle$ where:
$P = \{\rho\} \cup \bigcup_{1 \leq i \leq n} P_i$
$\leq = \{(\rho, \alpha) \mid \alpha \in P\} \cup \bigcup_{1 \leq i \leq n} \leq_i$
$V = \{(\rho, p) \mid \mathbf{T}p \in \Delta\} \cup \bigcup_{1 \leq i \leq n} V_i$

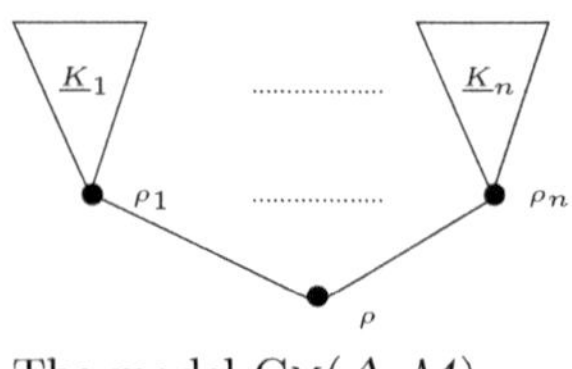

The model $\textsc{Cm}(\Delta, \mathcal{M})$

Fig. 3. The functions $\textsc{f}(\Delta)$ and $\textsc{Cm}(\Delta, \mathcal{M})$

We also exploit the functions CM and REAL defined as follows:

- The function CM (see Fig. 3) takes as input a set of signed formulas Δ and a (possibly empty) set of Kripke models $\mathcal{M}$ and builds a countermodel $\underline{K}$ for Δ using a standard technique to glue the models in $\mathcal{M}$ (see, e.g,. [2]).
- The function REAL takes as input a Kripke model $\underline{K} = \langle P, \leq, \rho, V\rangle$ and a set of signed formulas Δ and returns true *only if* ρ realizes Δ, i.e. if $\underline{K}, \rho \rhd \Delta$. In our strategy REAL is applied when the realizability of Δ can be decided only considering the valuation $V(\rho)$ (that is, without considering elements $\alpha > \rho$). In this case the test requires time linear in the size of Δ.

A high-level definition of F is given in Fig. 3. In the computation of F(Δ), we firstly try to reduce Δ by applying the simplification rules described in Section 3. Note that this step can reduce the search space; for instance in Step 4, if the set $\Delta \cup \{\mathbf{T}(A \vee B)\}$ simplifies to $\Delta \cup \{\mathbf{T}B\}$, we avoid the call F($\Delta \cup \{\mathbf{T}A\}$). Applying **Tab** rules, F gives precedence to invertible rules and, among them, single-conclusion rules are applied first. We point out that $\mathcal{LF}$-formulas are treated as atomic formulas since they are never decomposed by the **Tab** rules (they can be treated only by simplification rules), and this avoids useless computation. Finally, we remark that if one of the tests REAL($\pi', \Delta_{\mathbf{F}}$) in Step 5 successes, the iteration terminates and F returns the model π'.

We briefly account on the correctness of F. It is easy to check, by induction on Δ, that whenever F(Δ) returns a proof π, π is actually a proof of Δ. Let us assume that F(Δ) returns a Kripke model $\underline{K} = \langle P, \leq, \rho, V\rangle$; we have to prove that (*) $\underline{K}, \rho \rhd \Delta$. If $\underline{K}$ is returned in Step 3 or 4, (*) immediately follows. Let us consider Step 5. Suppose that $\underline{K} = \pi'$ is returned inside one of the for-each loops. By induction hypothesis $\underline{K}, \rho \rhd \Delta'$, which implies $\underline{K}, \rho \rhd \Delta_{\mathbf{T}}$. Moreover, being REAL($\underline{K}', \Delta_{\mathbf{F}}$) true, we also have $\underline{K}, \rho \rhd \Delta_{\mathbf{F}}$, hence (*) holds. Suppose now that $\underline{K}$ = CM($\Delta, \mathcal{M}$). Then, (*) follows by construction of $\underline{K}$ and the induction hypothesis. We only show that $\underline{K}, \rho \rhd \mathbf{F}A$, for every $\mathbf{F}A \in \Delta$. Let $\mathbf{F}A = \mathbf{F}(B \to C)$. Since $\mathbf{F}A \in \Gamma_1$, there is $\underline{K}' = \langle P', \leq', \rho', V'\rangle \in \mathcal{M}$ such that $\underline{K}', \rho' \rhd \mathbf{T}B$ and $\underline{K}', \rho' \rhd \mathbf{F}C$. Since $\rho < \rho'$ in $\underline{K}$, we have $\underline{K}, \rho \rhd \mathbf{F}(B \to C)$. If $A \in \mathcal{PV}$, then $\mathbf{T}A \notin \Delta$ (Step 2 guarantees that Δ is not contradictory), hence $\underline{K}, \rho \rhd \mathbf{F}A$. It only remains to consider the case $\mathbf{F}A \in \mathcal{LF}$. Note that in Step 1 all the $p \in \mathcal{PV}$ such that $\mathbf{T}p \in \Delta$ have been replaced by $\top$, hence for every p occurring in A, we have $\underline{K}, \rho \rhd \mathbf{F}p$. By Theorem 2 we get $\underline{K}, \rho \rhd \mathbf{F}A$. This concludes the proof of (*). The discussion about steps 6–8 is similar. Note that in Step 8 the set Δ only contains formulas of the kind $\mathbf{T}\top$, $\mathbf{F}\bot$, $\mathbf{T}p$, $\mathbf{F}p$, with $p \in \mathcal{PV}$, $\mathbf{T}(p \to A)$, with $\mathbf{T}p \notin \Delta$, and $\mathcal{LF}$-formulas; in this case the returned model CM($\Delta, \emptyset$) is a classical model for Δ.

The termination of F follows from the fact that at each recursive call the size of Δ strictly decreases.

5 Evaluation and Conclusions

We have performed some experiments to compare FCUBE to Imogen [8], which is the fastest among the provers tested on the formulas of the ILTP Library [9], and

Formula	Imogen	FCUBE	Basic	+BackT	+Branch
SYJ201+1.018	11.32	14.46	timeout	timeout	16.16
SYJ201+1.019	16.28	17.84	timeout	timeout	20.72
SYJ201+1.020	17.00	22.34	timeout	timeout	26.00
SYJ202+1.006	timeout	6.18	timeout	timeout	7.08
SYJ202+1.007	timeout	52.98	timeout	timeout	61.18
SYJ202+1.008	timeout	529.36	timeout	timeout	570.88
SYJ206+1.018	2.26	0.00	0.00	0.00	0.00
SYJ206+1.019	2.12	0.00	0.00	0.00	0.01
SYJ206+1.020	2.14	0.00	0.01	0.01	0.01
SYJ207+1.018	77.02	4.72	timeout	5.53	timeout
SYJ207+1.019	104.38	6.08	timeout	7.15	timeout
SYJ207+1.020	143.32	7.44	timeout	8.94	timeout
SYJ208+1.015	timeout	174.22	220.71	209.98	187.78
SYJ208+1.016	timeout	286.56	351.73	349.72	312.99
SYJ208+1.017	timeout	472.07	570.48	569.66	541.81
SYJ209+1.018	0.20	0.08	timeout	0.07	timeout
SYJ209+1.019	0.024	0.09	timeout	0.09	timeout
SYJ209+1.020	0.028	0.09	timeout	0.10	timeout
Nishimura.011	8.2	0.02	0.02	0.02	0.02
Nishimura.012	132	0.04	0.03	0.04	0.04
Nishimura.013	timeout	0.07	0.06	0.07	0.07

Fig. 4. Timings on ILTP library

to check how our optimizations affect the performances of FCUBE itself. In the experiments we considered formulas of the ILTP Library and some axiom-formulas characterizing intermediate logics. In Fig. 4, the second and third column describe the timings of Imogen and FCUBE, respectively. Times are expressed in seconds and the timeout is 600s[3]. We notice that FCUBE outperforms Imogen on the families SYJ202, SYJ206, SYJ207, SYJ208 and Nishimura. Imogen is slightly faster than FCUBE on the families SYJ201 and SYJ209. As regards the performances of FCUBE on the SYJ201 family, we emphasize that FCUBE strategy relies on PITP strategy [1] and PITP decides the formula SYJ201.20 in 0.01s. In this case the timings of FCUBE essentially depend on its rough data structures that do not handle efficiently multiple occurrences of the same formula. This highly affects the performances on formulas like SYJ201.20 $((\wedge_{i=0}^{40}(p_i \equiv p_{(i+1) \bmod 41} \rightarrow \wedge_{j=0}^{40} p_j)) \rightarrow \wedge_{j=0}^{40} p_j)$ where $\wedge_{j=0}^{40} p_j$ occurs 42-times. Indeed rewriting SYJ201.20 as $((q \equiv \wedge_{j=0}^{40} p_j \;\wedge\; \wedge_{i=0}^{40} (p_i \equiv p_{(i+1) \bmod 41} \rightarrow q)) \rightarrow q)$ FCUBE solves it in 2.23s while Imogen requires 33s. We also remark that the proof table for the latter formula contains 250 nodes, whereas the proof table for the original formula contains 246 nodes. This is a further clue that the lack of advanced data structures penalizes the strategy. According to these considerations we expect that the above techniques can highly improve the performances of provers using advanced data structures.

3 Experiments performed on a Intel(R) Xeon(TM) CPU 3.00GHz, Linux OS.

The last three columns of Fig. 4 analyze how the various optimizations affect FCUBE performances. Here we denote with Basic the version of FCUBE in which the only optimizations applied are those performed in Step 1; hence in steps 3 and 4 $\mathcal{LF}$-formulas are decomposed according to tableau rules and in Step 5 the test REAL is omitted. +Branch is Basic with the special treatment of $\mathcal{LF}$ formulas and +BackT is Basic with the REAL test. Note that the decomposition of $\mathcal{LF}$-formulas according to tableau rules increase the branch degree of a proof and the lack of the REAL-test increases the backtrack degree of proof-search. The timings show that Basic cannot decide the families SYJ201, SYJ202, SYJ207, SYJ209. +Branch decides the families SYJ201, SYJ202. +BackT decides the families SYJ207, SYJ209. The simplification rules of Fig. 2 also have a deep impact on the proof strategy as we showed in [4].

To conclude, FCUBE is a Prolog theorem prover for Intuitionistic propositional logic implementing some optimization techniques. In this paper we have briefly discussed the optimization techniques and we have shown how such optimizations can highly improve the performances of a tableau-based prover for Intuitionistic propositional logic. As a future work we aim to study further optimization techniques, their application to modal logics and the extension to the first-order case.

References

1. Avellone, A., Fiorino, G., Moscato, U.: Optimization techniques for propositional intuitionistic logic and their implementation. Theoretical Computer Science 409(1), 41–58 (2008)
2. Chagrov, A., Zakharyaschev, M.: Modal Logic. Oxford University Press, Oxford (1997)
3. Davis, M., Logemann, G., Loveland, D.: A machine program for theorem-proving. Communications of the ACM 5, 394–397 (1962)
4. Ferrari, M., Fiorentini, C., Fiorino, G.: Towards the use of simplification rules in intuitionistic tableaux. In: Gavanelli, M., Riguzzi, F. (eds.) CILC 2009: 24-esimo Convegno Italiano di Logica Computazionale (2009)
5. Hustadt, U., Schmidt, R.A.: Simplification and backjumping in modal tableau. In: de Swart, H. (ed.) TABLEAUX 1998. LNCS (LNAI), vol. 1397, pp. 187–201. Springer, Heidelberg (1998)
6. Davis, M., Putnam, H.: A computing procedure for quantification theory. Journal of the ACM 7, 201–215 (1960)
7. Massacci, F.: Simplification: A general constraint propagation technique for propositional and modal tableaux. In: de Swart, H. (ed.) TABLEAUX 1998. LNCS (LNAI), vol. 1397, pp. 217–231. Springer, Heidelberg (1998)
8. McLaughlin, S., Pfenning, F.: Imogen: Focusing the polarized inverse method for intuitionistic propositional logic. In: Cervesato, I., Veith, H., Voronkov, A. (eds.) LPAR 2008. LNCS (LNAI), vol. 5330, pp. 174–181. Springer, Heidelberg (2008)
9. Raths, T., Otten, J., Kreitz, C.: The ILTP problem library for intuitionistic logic. Journal of Automated Reasoning 31, 261–271 (2007)

Superposition-Based Analysis of First-Order Probabilistic Timed Automata*

Arnaud Fietzke[1,2], Holger Hermanns[2,3], and Christoph Weidenbach[1,2]

[1]Max-Planck-Institut für Informatik, Saarbrücken, Germany
[2] Saarland University – Computer Science, Saarbrücken, Germany
[3] INRIA Grenoble – Rhône-Alpes, France

Abstract. This paper discusses the analysis of first-order probabilistic timed automata (FPTA) by a combination of hierarchic first-order superposition-based theorem proving and probabilistic model checking. We develop the overall semantics of FPTAs and prove soundness and completeness of our method for reachability properties. Basically, we decompose FPTAs into their time plus first-order logic aspects on the one hand, and their probabilistic aspects on the other hand. Then we exploit the time plus first-order behavior by hierarchic superposition over linear arithmetic. The result of this analysis is the basis for the construction of a reachability equivalent (to the original FPTA) probabilistic timed automaton to which probabilistic model checking is finally applied. The hierarchic superposition calculus required for the analysis is sound and complete on the first-order formulas generated from FPTAs. It even works well in practice. We illustrate the potential behind it with a real-life DHCP protocol example, which we analyze by means of tool chain support.

1 Introduction

Probabilistic timed automata (PTA) [15] combine discrete probabilistic choice, real time and nondeterminism. They arise as the natural orthogonal combination of probabilistic [18] and timed [2] automata. This paper explores another dimension of expressiveness, apart from time and probability. In addition to time and probability, when developing more realistic models of systems, their behavior on (complex) data needs to be considered as well. For example, for systems in the context of real-life concurrent networking, one faces sophisticated protocol features such as dynamic message routing, message loss recovery mechanisms, message splitting and merging, different base-modulations, carrier sensing and collision avoidance mechanisms. All this is common practice in DHCP, WLAN, Bluetooth, or ZigBee, as well as in higher level protocols such as Pastry or skype.

However, such intricate protocol features can barely be analyzed in the formal PTA setting, as the most expressive logic available together with PTA is currently propositional logic [15,14,12].

* This work has been partly supported by the German Transregional Collaborative Research Center SFB/TR 14 AVACS.

C. Fermüller and A. Voronkov (Eds.): LPAR-17, LNCS 6397, pp. 302–316, 2010.

In this paper, we enrich the PTA model with a first-order logic background theory and first-order state variables and transition guards, as a powerful formalism to model complex data of real world systems. This allows us to express all the above features directly. It leads to the model of *First-Order Probabilistic Timed Automata* (FPTA), a proper generalization of PTA, of first-order logic, and of linear arithmetic. This paper provides the theoretical basis of FPTA (Section 3), including a notion of parallel composition, and a relevant example of its automatic analysis (Section 5).

Technically, we base the analysis on the hierarchical extension [3] of linear arithmetic with first-order logic, called FOL(LA), and the implementation of the corresponding superposition calculus SUP(LA) in SPASS(LA) [1]. While first-order logic theorem-hood is semi-decidable, theorem-hood in FOL(LA) is not even recursively enumerable, in general. Nevertheless, in the past we have already shown the combination to be complete for a number of cases [1] and also terminating on relevant examples. For FOL(LA) theories generated from FPTAs this is the case as well: the hierarchic superposition calculus is complete for this class (Theorem 1) and the DHCP example we present enjoys termination of the superposition calculus and is therefore amenable to automatic analysis.

The basic analysis idea is as follows. We first build the symbolic composition of a set of concurrent interacting FPTA. The resulting model is then translated into a labelled version of first-order logic over linear arithmetic, where probabilistic branching is replaced by labelled non-determinism and the control and structural aspects of the FPTA are encoded using special predicates. The advance of time is represented using linear arithmetic. Then we use first-order saturation-based theorem proving to obtain finite representations of the reachable states of the encoding. The underlying calculus is a labelled extension of the hierarchic calculus SUP(LA). In case a proof attempt yields a result after a finite period of time, it can be analyzed and the probabilistic aspects can be effectively regained via the introduced labels. By enumerating all proofs, a PTA can be reconstructed that is reachability-equivalent to the original FPTA. We submit this PTA to the tool MCPTA [8], which in turn uses the PRISM model checker [11] to compute timed reachability properties.

For FPTA, reachability properties are not decidable, and of course, this means that the tool chain we provide is not effective in general: proof attempts may fail, enumeration of proofs may not terminate, the input model might be too large, and so on. Nevertheless, we present a reasoning pipeline for proofs over FPTA, already with tool support, that can automatically prove (not model check) non-trivial properties of FPTA for interesting cases, including (infinite families of) infinite state systems. We exemplify the pipeline on aspects of a real-life DHCP protocol run taking care of message loss. For the given DHCP example we are able to calculate that, e.g., the probability of successfully obtaining a DHCP lease is 0.996, assuming a message loss probability of 0.1, and maximum two retransmissions per involved communication.

In summary, our contributions are (i) a new notion of First-Order PTA, properly generalizing PTA, including parallel composition, (ii) a sound and complete reasoning approach for the analysis of reachability properties of FPTA involving hierarchic superposition and model checking, (iii) a first tool chain supporting the approach, and (iv) a non-trivial DHCP protocol analysis example showing its potential. One of the most challenging parts of our work is the development of a label discipline for the LSUP(LA) calculus (Section 4.2) that, on the one hand, still enables termination of superposition for interesting classes of examples and, on the other hand, yields proofs covering every relevant path through the FPTA to some set of target states (Theorem 2).

The paper is organized as follows: in Section 2, we review basic notions of first-order logic and hierarchic superposition over linear arithmetic, and give the main definitions related to probabilistic timed automata and their semantics. Section 3 introduces FPTAs, their parallel composition and semantics. In Section 4, we define the encoding of FPTA reachability into labelled first-order clauses, we introduce the labelled superposition calculus LSUP(LA), and we show how to construct a reachability-equivalent VPTA from an FPTA and a set of labelled reachability proofs. The application of our method to the DHCP protocol example is discussed in Section 5. The paper ends with discussion of the achieved results and an overview of future directions of research (Section 6). A detailed account of the DHCP example and proofs of the theorems given in this paper can be found in a technical report [6].

2 Preliminaries

2.1 First-Order Logic, Hierarchic Superposition, SUP(LA)

We base our treatment of first-order reasoning on the framework of hierarchic superposition introduced in [3], and in particular on the case of a linear arithmetic base specification [1]: a *signature* is a pair $(\mathcal{S}, \mathcal{F})$ where $\mathcal{S}$ is a set of *sorts* and $\mathcal{F}$ is a set of *operator symbols*. An $\mathcal{F}$*-algebra* $\mathcal{A}$ consists of an $\mathcal{S}$-sorted family of non-empty carrier sets $\{S_\mathcal{A}\}_{S\in\mathcal{S}}$, and of a function $f_\mathcal{A} : (S_1)_\mathcal{A} \times \cdots \times (S_n)_\mathcal{A} \to S_\mathcal{A}$ for every $f : S_1 \ldots S_n \to S$ in $\mathcal{F}$. An algebra $\mathcal{A}$ is called *term-generated* if every element of any $S_\mathcal{A}$ is the interpretation of some ground term of sort S. A *specification* is a triple $Sp = (\mathcal{S}, \mathcal{F}, \mathcal{C})$ where $\mathcal{C}$ is a class of term-generated $\mathcal{F}$-algebras, called *models* of the specification. If $\mathcal{C}$ is the set of all $\mathcal{F}$-models of a certain set of $\mathcal{F}$-axioms Ax, then we write $(\mathcal{S}, \mathcal{F}, Ax)$ instead of $(\mathcal{S}, \mathcal{F}, \mathcal{C})$. A *hierarchic specification* is a pair (Sp, Sp') of specifications, where $Sp = (\mathcal{S}, \mathcal{F}, \mathcal{C})$ is called the *base specification* and $Sp' = (\mathcal{S}', \mathcal{F}', Ax')$ with $\mathcal{S}' \subseteq \mathcal{S}$ and $\mathcal{F}' \subseteq \mathcal{F}$. The operator symbols in $\mathcal{F}' \setminus \mathcal{F}$ and the axioms Ax' are called the *enrichment*.

The base specification we are interested in has the rationals $\mathbb{Q}$ as the only sort, the operator symbols $+, , \leq, <, \approx, >, \geq$ together with numerals to represent fractions (which we will just write as decimal numbers), and their standard interpretation over $\mathbb{Q}$ as model (actually, $\mathcal{C}$ is the set of all algebras isomorphic to the standard model). For our purposes, a *first-order theory* $\mathcal{T}$ over a signature $(\mathcal{S}, \mathcal{F})$ will be a set of $\mathcal{F}$-formulas, to be understood as an enrichment of the base specification. The *models* of $\mathcal{T}$ are those models of the formulas of $\mathcal{T}$ that extend the standard model.

In [1], an instantiation of the hierarchical superposition calculus to the linear arithmetic case, called SUP(LA), is presented, together with effective redundancy criteria. In SUP(LA), clauses appear in purified form $\Lambda \,\|\, \Gamma \rightarrow \Delta$, where Λ is a sequence of base specification (i.e. linear arithmetic) literals, called the *clause constraint.* The sequences Γ, Δ of first-order atoms only contain signature symbols from the free first-order theory, and all parts share universally quantified variables. A constrained empty clause $\Lambda \,\|\, \Box$ represents a contradiction if the constraint Λ is satisfiable in the theory of linear arithmetic.

Finally, we introduce the following notation: for a formula φ and a set of variables Y, $\mathrm{vars}_Y(\varphi) = \mathrm{vars}(\varphi) \cap Y$. For a first-order formula φ, we denote by $[\![\varphi]\!]_{\mathcal{T}}$ the set of vars(φ)-valuations satisfying φ in $\mathcal{T}$, omitting the subscript if it is clear from the context. Similarly, for a linear arithmetic expression C, we write $[\![C]\!]$ for the set of vars(C)-valuations satisfying C.

2.2 Probabilistic Timed Automata

Distributions. A *discrete probability distribution* over a countable set Q is a function $\mu : Q \rightarrow [0,1]$ such that $\sum_{q \in Q} \mu(q) = 1$. By Dist($Q$) we denote the set of discrete probability distributions over Q. The *support of a distribution* μ, written support(μ), is the largest set $Q' \subseteq Q$ such that $\mu(q) > 0$ for all $q \in Q'$. We call $\mu \in \mathit{Dist}(Q)$ *finite* if support(μ) is finite. If its support is a singleton set, i.e., support(μ) $= \{q\}$, μ is the point distribution for q, denoted by $\mathcal{D}(q)$.

Probabilistic Timed Automata with Discrete Variables. We follow the notation in [13,8]. Let $\mathbb{T}$ denote the *time domain* (in our case $\mathbb{Q}$). The set CF(X) of *constraint formulas* over a set of variables X is the smallest set closed under negation and disjunction and contains $\top$ (truth), $\bot$ (falsity) as well as all terms of the form $x \leq t$, $t \leq x$, $x_1 - x_2 \leq t$, $t \leq x_1 - x_2$, where $x, x_1, x_2 \in X$ and $t \in \mathbb{T}$. In timed automata [2] and all formalisms stemming from them, the passage of time is modeled by *clocks*, which are variables whose value, taken from $\mathbb{T}$, increases at a fixed rate. We assume a finite set $\mathcal{S}$ of *sorts*, where each variable x has an associated sort $S_x \in \mathcal{S}$ which is at the same time the domain, i.e. x takes values from S_x. The sort of all clock variables is $\mathbb{T}$. We will refer to all non-clock variables as *discrete variables.* A *ground valuation* v is a total function on variables such that $v(x) \in S_x$. We denote by Val_g the set of all ground valuations. A *ground assignment* A is a partial function on variables such that $A(x) \in S_x$, and $A(x) = 0$ whenever x is a clock variable for which $A(x)$ is defined. Given a ground valuation v, we denote by $v + t$ the ground valuation that agrees with v on all discrete variables, and assigns $v(x) + t$ to any clock variable x. For ground valuation v and ground assignment A, we denote by vA the composition of v and A, i.e. $vA(x) = A(x)$ if $x \in \mathrm{dom}(A)$, $vA(x) = v(x)$ otherwise. A *probabilistic timed automaton with discrete variables (VPTA)* is a tuple $(\mathcal{L}, L_0, X, \Sigma, \mathrm{inv}, \mathrm{prob})$ with $\mathcal{L}$ a finite set of *locations*, including the *initial location* L_0, X a finite set of *state variables*, partitioned into subsets X_C of clock variables and $X_D = X \setminus X_C$ of discrete variables, and Σ finite set of *actions.* The function $\mathrm{inv} : \mathcal{L} \rightarrow \mathrm{CF}(X)$ assigns *invariants* to all locations. The automaton may stay in a given location as long as the state variables satisfy the location's invariant. Finally prob $\subseteq^{fin} \mathcal{L} \times \mathrm{CF}(X) \times \Sigma \times \mathrm{Dist}(\mathrm{Asgn}_g \times \mathcal{L})$ is the *probabilistic edge relation.* A transition $(l, g, a, \nu) \in$ prob consists of an originating location l, a *guard* g that determines whether the transition is *enabled*, an *action label* a and a *target distribution* giving the probability to move to some other location while applying the assignment. A VPTA can be transformed into a standard probabilistic timed automaton (PTA) [13] by encoding the values of the non-clock variables in the locations. The PTA corresponding to a VPTA P is finite iff P is finite and S_x is finite for all $x \in X_D$.

Timed Probabilistic Update Systems. The formal semantics of VPTA is given in terms of a *timed probabilistic system (TPS)* [13], which is an unfolding of the VPTA starting in the initial location, with some initial valuation assigning zero to all clock variables. This semantics, however, is too coarse for our purposes. We therefore introduce the notion of a timed probabilistic *update* system, following an approach similar to [9]. A *timed probabilistic update system (TPUS)* is a tuple $(S, s_0, Act, U, \rightarrow)$ where S is a set of *states* with *initial state* $s_0 \in S$, Act is a set of *actions* and U is a set of *update labels.* The *probabilistic transition relation* is $\rightarrow \subseteq S \times (Act \cup \mathbb{T}) \times \mathrm{Dist}((U \uplus \{\mathsf{time}\}) \times S)$. For every $(s, a, \mu) \in \rightarrow$, if $a \in \mathbb{T}$, then $\mu = \mathcal{D}(\mathsf{time}, s')$, where s' is obtained from s by letting time pass; if $a \in Act$, then for all $(u, s') \in \mathrm{support}(\mu)$: $u \in U$. A probabilistic transition is made from a state $s \in S$ by first nondeterministically selecting an action-distribution or duration-distribution pair (a, μ) such that $(s, a, \mu) \in \rightarrow$, and second by making a probabilistic choice of update label u and target state s' according to the distribution μ, such that $\mu(u, s') > 0$. In the case of a duration-distribution pair, the update label is time and the target state is obtained from s by letting the given time pass. A finite *path* of a TPUS is a sequence $(s_0, a_0, u_0, \mu_0)(s_1, a_1, u_1, \mu_1) \ldots s_n$ of *steps*, such that $(s_i, a_i, \mu_i) \in \rightarrow$, and $(u_i, s_{i+1}) \in \mathrm{support}(\mu_i)$ for all $i = 0, \ldots, n-1$. An infinite path is a sequence $(s_0, a_0, u_0, \mu_0)(s_1, a_1, u_1, \mu_1) \ldots s_n$ with $(s_i, a_i, \mu_i) \in \rightarrow$, and $(u_i, s_{i+1}) \in \mathrm{support}(\mu_i)$ for all $i \geq 0$. Step i is a *discrete step* if $a_i \in Act$, a *time step* if $a_i \in \mathbb{T}$. Dropping the update labels induces a standard TPS (see [9]). Quantitative properties (see [13] for an overview) of TPS can be lifted to TPUS in a straightforward way: for instance, the maximum reachability probability of some state in a TPUS is the maximum reachability probability of that state in the induced TPS.

Semantics of VPTA. The semantics of a VPTA $P = (\mathcal{L}, L_0, X, \Sigma, \mathrm{inv}, \mathrm{prob})$ is the TPUS $[\![P]\!]$ with states $S = \{(L, v) \in \mathcal{L} \times \mathrm{Val}_g \mid v \models \mathrm{inv}(L)\}$, $s_0 = (L_0, v_0)$, $U = \mathrm{Asgn}_g$, and $\rightarrow$ being the smallest relation satisfying

$$\mathsf{time}\frac{s = (L, v) \quad v + t' \models \mathrm{inv}(L) \text{ for all } 0 \leq t' \leq t \quad s' = (L, v + t)}{(s, t, \mathcal{D}((\mathsf{time}, s'))) \in \rightarrow}$$

$$\mathsf{act}\frac{s = (L, v) \quad (L, g, a, \nu) \in \mathrm{prob} \quad v \models g}{(s, a, \mu) \in \rightarrow}$$

where $\mu(A,(L',v')) = \begin{cases} \nu(A,L') & \text{if } v' = vA \\ 0 & \text{otherwise.} \end{cases}$

Generalized VPTA. Finally, we introduce the concept of *generalized VPTA (GenVPTA)*, which will provide the semantics for the first-order PTA introduced in the next section. A generalized VPTA is a tuple $(\mathcal{L}, L_0, X, \Sigma, \mathrm{inv}, \mathrm{prob})$, different from a VPTA only in the fourth and last components: Σ is not restricted to be finite, and $\mathrm{prob} \subseteq \mathcal{L} \times \mathcal{P}(\mathrm{Val}_g(X)) \times \Sigma \times \mathrm{Dist}(\mathrm{Asgn}(X) \times \mathcal{L})$. The semantics of GenVPTA is defined analogously to that of VPTA, except that rule act is changed to

$$\mathsf{act}\frac{s = (L,v) \quad p = (L,\mathcal{V},a,\nu) \in \mathrm{prob} \quad v \in \mathcal{V}}{(s,a,\mu) \in \rightarrow}$$

Clearly, a generalized VPTA is equivalent to a finite VPTA (and can thus be encoded into finite PTA) if (i) Σ is finite, (ii) prob is finite, and (iii) for every $(L,\mathcal{V},a,\nu) \in \mathrm{prob}$, there exists $C \in \mathrm{CF}(X)$ that characterizes $\mathcal{V}$. By a *path* of a (generalized) VPTA, we mean a path of the underlying TPUS.

3 First-Order Probabilistic Timed Automata

Let $(\mathcal{S},\mathcal{F})$ be a signature. For a set X of variables, $T(X)$ denotes the set of $\mathcal{F}$-terms over X, $\mathcal{G}(X)$ denotes the set of $\mathcal{F}$-formulas of positive polarity over X, and the set $\mathrm{CCF}(X)$ of *convex constraint formulas* over X is the convex subset of $\mathrm{CF}(X)$. Furthermore, we assume a denumerable set $\mathcal{X}$ of $\mathcal{S}$-sorted variables with a subset Z of *auxiliary variables*. The set Asgn of *assignments* consists of all substitutions $\mathcal{X} \to T(\mathcal{X})$, such that clock variables are mapped to either themselves or to zero.

Definition 1 (FPTA). *A First-Order Probabilistic Timed Automaton (FPTA) is a tuple $P = (\mathcal{T}, \mathcal{L}, L_0, X, \Sigma, \mathrm{inv}, \mathrm{prob})$ with*

- $\mathcal{T}$ *a consistent, sorted first-order Horn theory, sufficiently complete extension of* $\mathbb{Q}$,
- $\mathcal{L}$ *finite set of* locations, *including the initial location* L_0,
- $X \subset (\mathcal{X} \setminus Z)$ *finite set of* state variables, *partitioned into subsets* X_C *of* clock variables *and* $X_D = X \setminus X_C$ *of* discrete variables,
- Σ *finite set of* actions,
- $\mathrm{inv} : \mathcal{L} \to \mathrm{CCF}(X)$ *are* location invariants,
- $\mathrm{prob} \subseteq^{fin} \mathcal{L} \times \mathcal{G}(\mathcal{X}) \times \Sigma \times \mathrm{Dist}(\mathrm{Asgn} \times \mathcal{L})$

If, for every $(L,\varphi,a,\nu) \in \mathrm{prob}$, it holds that $\mathrm{vars}(\varphi) \subseteq X \cup Z$, and for every $(A,L') \in \mathrm{support}(\nu)$, it holds that $\mathrm{vars}(\mathrm{cdom}(A)) \setminus X \subseteq \mathrm{vars}(\varphi)$, then we call P *variable-closed.* We call the elements of prob *branches*, and the tuples (p,A,L) with $p \in \mathrm{prob}$, $(A,L) \in \mathrm{support}(\nu_p)$ *edges* of the FPTA. Given $p = (L,\varphi,a,\nu)$, we write φ_p for φ etc. Edge (p,A,L) is *associated* with branch p. Given $e = (p,A,L)$, we also write p_e, A_e and L_e for p, A and L, respectively.

We restrict ourselves to convex invariants to keep the encoding of time-reachability (Section 4.1) sufficiently complete: without the assumption of convexity, an additional quantifier would be required on the left hand side of the implication (for all t' such that $0 \leq t' \leq t$). Transforming such a formula into clause normal form introduces Skolem functions ranging into the arithmetic sort.

Example 1. The purpose of auxiliary variables in guards is to allow binding: assume an FPTA with a single (discrete) state variable x, and let cons be an operator symbol representing a list constructor. A transition with guard $x \approx \mathrm{cons}(z, z')$ with $z, z' \in Z$, followed by an assignment $x \mapsto z'$, describes the operation of removing the head from list x, and storing the tail in x.

We define parallel composition for FPTAs via synchronization on shared actions [10], allowing automata to communicate by reading each other's state variables (in the style of [11]):

Definition 2 (Parallel composition of FPTA). *Let P_1, P_2 be two FPTAs with $X_1 \cap X_2 = \emptyset$, and such that $\mathcal{T}_1 \cup \mathcal{T}_2$ is a consistent, sufficiently complete extension of $\mathbb{Q}$. Furthermore, assume that for any two guards φ_1, φ_2 of P_1, P_2 (respectively) $\mathrm{vars}_Z(\varphi_1) \cap \mathrm{vars}_Z(\varphi_2) = \emptyset$. Then we define the parallel composition of P_1 and P_2 as*

$$P_1 \mid P_2 = (\mathcal{T}_1 \cup \mathcal{T}_2, \mathcal{L}_1 \times \mathcal{L}_2, (L_0^1, L_0^2), X_1 \cup X_2, \Sigma_1 \cup \Sigma_2, \mathrm{inv}, \mathrm{prob})$$

where $\mathrm{inv}(L_1, L_2) = \mathrm{inv}_1(L_1) \wedge \mathrm{inv}_2(L_2)$ and $((L_1, L_2), \varphi, a, \nu) \in \mathrm{prob}$ iff one of the following conditions holds:

- *$a \in \Sigma_1 \setminus \Sigma_2$ and there is $(L_1, \varphi, a, \nu_1) \in \mathrm{prob}_1$ such that $\nu = \nu_1 \cdot \mathcal{D}(\mathrm{Id}, L_2)$;*
- *$a \in \Sigma_2 \setminus \Sigma_1$ and there is $(L_2, \varphi, a, \nu_2) \in \mathrm{prob}_2$ such that $\nu = \mathcal{D}(\mathrm{Id}, L_1) \cdot \nu_2$;*
- *$a \in \Sigma_2 \cap \Sigma_1$ and there is $(L_1, \varphi_1, a, \nu_1) \in \mathrm{prob}_1$ and $(L_2, \varphi_2, a, \nu_2) \in \mathrm{prob}_2$ such that $\varphi = \varphi_1 \wedge \varphi_2$ and $\nu = \nu_1 \cdot \nu_2$,*

where $\cdot$ is the product operation on probability distributions [13,8].

Note that $P_1 \mid P_2$ can be variable-closed even if P_1, P_2 are not, in case the unbound variables in guards and assignments of P_1 are state variables of P_2 (and vice versa).

Example 2. Figure 1 shows an FPTA which models a simple DHCP server process. In Section 5, we will apply our analysis techniques to the parallel composition of the server process with FPTAs modelling a DHCP client, faulty networks and resend mechanisms. The server automaton has only nondeterministic branching. It synchronizes with the other automata via the actions csend and smsg. It has state variables *vsmsg* which is used for communication, being read by the other automata; *vsloip* and *vslomac* which store the IP- and MAC-address for which a DHCP offer has been sent; *svlaip* and *vslamac* which store the IP- and MAC-address for which a DHCP acknowledgement has been sent. The variable *vsmsg* is used both for sending and receiving messages: when the

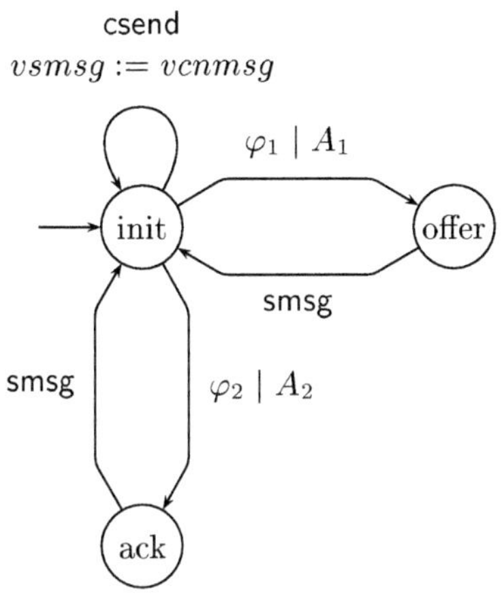

φ_1 :
$vsmsg \approx \text{ippacket}(vtime, \dots,$
$\text{dhcpdata}(\dots, \text{networkip}, \dots, vcmac,$
$\text{dhcpoptions}(\text{DHCPdiscover}, \dots))))$
$\wedge\ \text{Leasefree}(\text{leasfreetuple}(vscip, vcmac))$

$A_1 = \{$
$vsmsg := \text{ippacket}(vtime, \dots,$
$\text{dhcpdata}(\dots, vscip, \dots, vcmac,$
$\text{dhcpoptions}(\text{DHCPoffer}, \dots)))),$
$vsloip := vscip,$
$vslomac := vcmac\}$

φ_2 :
$vsmsg \approx \text{ippacket}(vtime, \dots,$
$\text{dhcpdata}(\dots, \text{networkip}, \dots, vslomac,$
$\text{dhcpoptions}(\text{DHCPrequest}, vsloip, \dots))))$

$A_2 = \{$
$vsmsg := \text{ippacket}(vtime, \dots,$
$\text{dhcpdata}(\dots, vslomac,$
$\text{dhcpoptions}(\text{DHCPack}, \dots)))),$
$vslaip := vsloip,$
$vslamac := vslomac\}$

Fig. 1. An FPTA modelling a DHCP server process

action csend is initiated by the client's network, the server copies the message from the client network (variable *vcnmsg*) into *vsmsg*. The guard φ_1 checks whether the received message is a DHCP discover message, and whether the IP address *vscip* (an auxiliary variable) is free for lease. If it is, the associated assignment A_1 creates the DHCP offer message, containing, among other things, the free IP address.

3.1 Semantics of FPTA

A *valuation* over X maps every $x \in X$ to a ground $\mathcal{F}$-term of sort S_x. We denote the set of all valuations over X by $\text{Val}(X)$. Note that any ground term of sort $\mathbb{Q}$ corresponds to a rational number, and any rational number is representable as a ground term. Hence we can talk about the value of a variable of sort $\mathbb{Q}$ under a valuation v, and we can perform arithmetic operations on valuations. For an assignment A and a valuation v, we denote by Av the assignment such that $Av(x)$ is the instantiation of $A(x)$ by v if $x \in \text{dom}(A)$, and $v(x)$ otherwise. For $v \in \text{Val}(X)$ and $Y \subseteq X$, we write $v|_Y$ for the valuation in $\text{Val}(Y)$ that agrees with v on Y. We write $v \sim_Y v'$ iff $v|_Y = v'|_Y$, and we denote by $\mathcal{V}|_Y$ the set $\{ v|_Y \mid v \in \mathcal{V} \}$, for $\mathcal{V} \subseteq \text{Val}(X)$.

Let $P = (\mathcal{T}, \mathcal{L}, L_0, X, \Sigma, \text{inv}, \text{prob})$ be an FPTA. The semantics of P is the generalized VPTA $G(P) = (\mathcal{L}, L_0, X, \Sigma_G, \text{inv}, \text{prob}_G)$ where $\Sigma_G = \{a_v \mid a \in \Sigma,$

$v \in \mathrm{Val}(Z)\}$, and for every $p = (L, \varphi, a, \nu) \in \mathrm{prob}$, for every $\sim_Z$-equivalence class $\mathcal{V}$ of $[\![\varphi]\!]$, there is $p_v \in \mathrm{prob}_G$ with

$$p_v = (L, \mathcal{V}|_X, a_v, \nu_v)$$
$$\nu_v(Av, L) = \nu(A, L)$$

where $v \in \mathrm{Val}(\mathrm{vars}_Z(\varphi_p))$ is the common Z-part of all valuations in $\mathcal{V}$, i.e., $\mathcal{V}|_Z = \{v\}$. The instantiation of the FPTA branches according to $\sim_Z$-equivalence classes is is necessary because auxiliary variables occurring in guards can also occur in edge assignments (see Example 1), hence a unique valuation of auxiliary variables has to be fixed for each branch. This means that auxiliary variables introduce additional nondeterminism (implicit in P, explicit in $G(P)$): different target states will be reachable depending on the choice of instantiation for the auxiliary variables in the guard. The definition of Σ_G ensures that $G(P)$ is action-deterministic if P is, which makes $(p, v) \mapsto p_v$ injective. This is just to make the proofs nicer, but not essential for correctness. Furthermore, we introduce a dummy variable $x_A \notin X$ and assume that FPTA assignments are in $\mathrm{Asgn}(X \uplus \{x_A\})$ such that $A(x_A) \neq A'(x_A)$ for any $A \neq A'$ in the support of an FPTA branch. This ensures that assignments are not collapsed when going from FPTA to (generalized) VPTA, hence the definition $\nu_v(Av, L) = \nu(A, L)$ above is welldefined, i.e., $A \mapsto Av$ is injective. By a *path* of an FPTA, we mean a path of the underlying TPUS.

4 Reachability Analysis in FOL

When analyzing timed probabilistic systems, one is typically interested in quantitative properties such as probabilistic and expected-time reachability [13]. *Probabilistic reachability* refers to the probability of reaching a set of states. Since FPTAs are nondeterministic, there is a minimum and a maximum reachability probability, depending on how the nondeterminism is resolved. *Expected-time reachability* refers to the expected time needed to reach a set of states. To compute these measures, the set of all paths reaching the set of target states has to be known. For VPTAs, effective algorithms are known and implemented [8,12]. Our goal is therefore to construct a VPTA that has the same probabilistic and expected-time reachability properties as the original FPTA, with respect to some set of target states. To this end, we represent the reachability relation of P as a first-order theory over linear arithmetic, treating probabilistic choice in the same way as nondeterministic choice. In order to cover all paths, the derivation of logical consequences from the theory must be combined with the aggregation of path information. To achieve this, clauses will be augmented with a label carrying structural information. The label will be a set of special atoms sharing variables with the clause. We translate FPTAs to FOL(LA) theories preserving the path property, i.e., paths in the FPTA correspond to reachability proofs of the SUP(LA) calculus extended by labels (see Section 4.2) in the generated (see Section 4.1) FOL(LA) theories (Theorem 2).

For the rest of the paper, let $P = (\mathcal{T}, \mathcal{L}, L_0, X, \Sigma, \mathrm{inv}, \mathrm{prob})$ be an arbitrary, fixed FPTA, and F a set of target states of P.

4.1 From FPTA to FOL(LA)

We encode reachability into FOL(LA) in the style of [17] and [19]. We introduce the following predicate symbols, distinct from any symbols of $\mathcal{T}$: for every $L \in \mathcal{L}$, a symbol L of arity $|X|$, using L to refer both to the location name and the associated predicate; for every edge e of P, we also use e as a predicate symbol of arity $|X| + |\operatorname{vars}_Z(\varphi_e)|$.

The *reachability theory* $\mathcal{R}_P$ is given by the following labelled clauses (all variables are universally quantified):

1. for every $L \in \mathcal{L}$:

$$\emptyset : L(\vec{x}) \wedge t \geq 0 \wedge \operatorname{inv}(L)[\vec{x} + t/\vec{x}] \rightarrow L(\vec{x} + t)$$

2. for every edge e of P:

$$\{\, e(\vec{x}, \vec{z})\,\} : L(\vec{x}) \wedge \varphi_e[\vec{x}, \vec{z}] \wedge \operatorname{inv}(L')[A_e(\vec{x})/\vec{x}] \rightarrow L'(A_e(\vec{x}))$$

3. for the initial state:

$$\emptyset : \quad \rightarrow L_0(\vec{v_0})$$

We write $\mathcal{R}_{P,F}$ for the theory obtained from $\mathcal{R}_P$ by also adding

4. for every $L(\vec{v}) \in F$:

$$\emptyset : L(\vec{v}) \rightarrow$$

4.2 Extending SUP(LA) with Labels

Any clausal resolution calculus can be extended to operate on labelled clauses (see for instance [16,7]). An inference rule with premises $C_1 \ldots C_n$ and conclusion $C\sigma$ is extended to a labelled rule:

$$\mathcal{I}\frac{\alpha_1 : C_1 \quad \ldots \quad \alpha_n : C_n}{(\alpha_1 \cup \cdots \cup \alpha_n : C)\sigma}$$

We extend the hierarchic SUP(LA) calculus [1] which combines first-order superposition with linear arithmetic.

Redundancy. Redundancy elimination, which removes logically redundant clauses from the search space, is a key ingredient to efficient theorem proving and also makes termination of saturation possible in many cases [20]. In our case, redundancy elimination has to be relaxed to make sure that clauses are not removed if they are required for path coverage.

Redundancy of labelled clauses is defined as follows (we consider here only the case of subsumption): for clause C, let $\operatorname{Loc}(C)$ denote the location literals and $\operatorname{Nloc}(C)$ the non-location literals of C. Then $\alpha : C$ is subsumed by $\beta : D$ if there exists a substitution σ such that

1. $\alpha = \beta\sigma$, and
2. $\text{Loc}(C) = \text{Loc}(D)\sigma$, and
3. $\text{Nloc}(D)\sigma \subseteq \text{Nloc}(C)$.

Note that this definition of subsumption is a proper generalization of the usual definition, since the only additional requirements we impose concern labels and location atoms. Furthermore, we assume a search strategy where all non-location literals are selected [21]. We call the resulting calculus LSUP(LA).

Theorem 1. *Let P be an FPTA, $\mathcal{R}_P$ its reachability theory and $\mathcal{T}$ its first-order background theory. Then LSUP(LA) is sound and complete on $\mathcal{T} \cup \mathcal{R}_P$.*

Proof. The theorem holds by construction: the added label discipline in LSUP(LA) has no effect on the semantics and on the inference rules of the SUP(LA) calculus. Only the redundancy notion in LSUP(LA) is more restrictive as it imposes further restrictions on the involved labels. So LSUP(LA) is complete on a set of clauses iff SUP(LA) is. The reachability theory $\mathcal{R}_P$ is sufficiently complete because it does not introduce any new function symbols. The background theory $\mathcal{T}$ is assumed to be sufficiently complete (Definition 1), hence the union of $\mathcal{T}$ and $\mathcal{R}_P$ is sufficiently complete as well.

4.3 From FOL(LA) to VPTA

An edge constraint is a tuple (e, Con), where e is an edge and Con a linear arithmetic constraint. We say that (e, Con) is *associated* with branch p if e is. From a labelled constrained clause

$$\alpha : \Lambda \parallel C$$

with $\alpha = \{ e_1(\ldots), \ldots, e_n(\ldots) \}$, we obtain set of edge constraints

$$\text{Con}(\alpha, \Lambda) = \{ (e_1, \text{Con}_1), \ldots, (e_n, \text{Con}_n) \}$$

where Con_i is the constraint corresponding to Λ and $e_i(\ldots)$:
for $e_i(s_1, \ldots, s_k, t_1, \ldots, t_m)$, $\text{Con}_i = \Lambda \cup \{x_i \approx s_i \mid s_i \neq x_i\} \cup \{z_i \approx t_i \mid t_i \neq z_i\}$. Let $\mathcal{E}$ be the set of edge constraints of all labelled empty clauses in the saturation of $\mathcal{T} \cup \mathcal{R}_{P,F}$ with LSUP(LA), and assume that $\mathcal{E}$ is finite. We denote by $\mathcal{E}_p$ the set of edge constraints in $\mathcal{E}$ associated with branch p. For every $p \in \text{prob}$ and $v \in \text{Val}(\text{vars}_Z(\varphi_p))$, let

$$\text{Con}_{p,v} \quad = \bigvee_{\substack{(e,\,\text{Con}) \in \mathcal{E}_p,\\ \text{Con}(v) \text{ satisfiable}}} \text{Con}(v)$$

where $\text{Con}(v)$ denotes the instantiation of Con by v.

Definition 3. *The VPTA* $\text{Sup}(P, F)$ *is* $(\mathcal{L}, L_0, X, \Sigma_G, \text{inv}, \text{prob}_{\mathcal{E}})$*, where for every* $\text{Con}_{p,v} \neq \bot$*,* $\text{prob}_{\mathcal{E}}$ *contains* $p_v^{\mathcal{E}}$ *with*

$$p_v^{\mathcal{E}} = (L, \text{Con}_{p,v}, a, \nu_v^{\mathcal{E}})$$
$$\nu_v^{\mathcal{E}}(Av, L) = \nu(A, L).$$

The idea of the construction is to partition the constraints in $\mathcal{E}_p$ into equivalence classes based on the values they assign to the auxiliary variables, as in the FPTA semantics (Section 3.1). The VPTA $\mathrm{Sup}(P, F)$ contains an instance $p_v^{\mathcal{E}}$ of the FPTA branch p for every equivalence class, as represented by v. In general, there may be infinitely many such equivalence classes for a given constraint. We therefore limit our approach to cases where auxiliary variables appear only in equations of the form $z \approx t$, where t is a ground term. In this case, there is one equivalence class for each equation. The restriction can be relaxed to handle inequalities over auxiliary variables, for instance if they are of integer sort and the inequalities describe a finite interval.

Path coverage. Given a path $(s_0, a_0, u_0, \mu_0)(s_1, a_1, u_1, \mu_1)\ldots$ of P, we say that an edge constraint (e, Con) *covers* step i if there exists $v \in \mathrm{Val}(\mathrm{vars}_Z(\varphi_e))$ such that $\mathrm{Con}(v)$ is satisfiable, and

1. $a_i = a_v$
2. $u_i = A_e(v)$ and
3. $v_i \models \mathrm{Con}(v)$

where v_i is valuation of state s_i, and a is the action associated with edge e. A set $\mathcal{E}$ of edge constraints covers path ω if every discrete step of ω is covered by some edge constraint in $\mathcal{E}$.

Theorem 2. *Let P be an FPTA, and F be a set of states of P, such that $\mathcal{T} \cup \mathcal{R}_{P,F}$ can be finitely saturated by LSUP(LA). Then the set of paths of P reaching F is identical to the set of paths of* $\mathrm{Sup}(P, F)$ *reaching F.*

Proof (Sketch). By Theorem 1, SUP(LA) is complete for $\mathcal{T} \cup \mathcal{R}_{P,F}$. The relaxed definition of redundancy ensures that also LSUP(LA) is complete with respect to path coverage: the saturation of $\mathcal{T} \cup \mathcal{R}_{P,F}$ with LSUP(LA) contains labelled empty clauses whose constraints together cover all possible paths of P that reach F. By construction of $\mathrm{Sup}(P, F)$, (i) any path of $\mathrm{Sup}(P, F)$ is a path of P, and (ii) any path of P covered by edge constraints from the saturation of $\mathcal{T} \cup \mathcal{R}_{P,F}$ is a path of $\mathrm{Sup}(P, F)$.

Corollary 1. *The FPTA P and the VPTA* $\mathrm{Sup}(P, F)$ *have the same minimum and maximum reachability probability and the same expected-time reachability with respect to F.*

5 Analyzing DHCP

We exemplify our results and tool chain on a simple model of a DHCP [5] dialog between a client and a server over a faulty network. The first-order structures of the FPTA represent messages as terms starting from the IP-layer. We omit detailed modeling of IP-addresses and the needed masking operations in order to keep the model small and to focus on timing and probability aspects. Our model could be extended that way (see the first-order LAN model available at http://www.spass-prover.org/prototypes/). Nevertheless, the term structure enables a reasonably detailed model of the network stack. The IP-address lease data base of the server is modeled in form of first-order atoms. For each participant (client, server) the model contains three layers – in the form of FPTA: the DHCP protocol layer, a resend mechanism, and the respective connected faulty networks. The networks have a fixed latency and message loss probability. A detailed description of the model can be found in [6].

The FPTA on the protocol layer closely follow the steps of the DHCP protocol from the *init* state to a *bound* state on the client side and the respective steps on the server side. The resend and network automata are identical for both server and client. The resend automaton tries two resends with a time out of 0.3 time units to the network before it gives up. The network forwards a message with probability 0.9 and causes a latency delay of 0.1 time units.

The composition of FPTAs (Definition 2), the translation from FPTA to FOL(LA) (Section 4.1) and the construction of the final VPTA (Section 4.3) have been produced manually. We are currently working on an extension to SPASS(LA) that will perform all these steps fully automatically. The saturation of the FOL(LA) translation and the probabilistic analysis were performed automatically by the SPASS(LA) theorem prover and the MCPTA model checker, respectively. The corresponding input files are available from the SPASS homepage (`http://www.spass-prover.org/prototypes/`). Note that the computationally most involved, crucial part is the actual reasoning on the FOL(LA) translation where proving reachability is undecidable, in general. All other parts of the analysis are decidable.

For the concrete example, we computed the probability of a successful client acquisition of a DHCP lease. SPASS(LA) takes about 1 hour (on recent Linux driven Xeon X5460 hardware) to saturate the translated FPTA composition, i.e., find all proofs of a *bound* state of the client. To this end SPASS(LA) generated about 10k clauses. From the proofs we manually built the VPTA. It involves 4 active clocks and 22 locations. We manually translated this into Modest [4], the input of the MCPTA model checker for probabilistic timed automata [8]. This checker applies an integral time semantics, and then uses the probabilistic model checker PRISM [11] as a back-end, which finally needs to build and analyze a (probabilistic automata) model comprising 255 states. As an example quantities, we are able to calculate that the probability of successfully obtaining a DHCP lease within 0.4 time units (meaning no message is lost) is 0.656, and the probability of obtaining one after 3.6 time units (allowing for message loss at every stage of the protocol) is 0.996.

6 Conclusion

This paper has presented an extension of probabilistic timed automata with first order formulas, and it has laid out the algorithmic foundation for analyzing reachability properties. The model is rich enough to express – apart from real time and probability – intricate protocol features such as message routing, message splitting and merging, different base-modulations, carrier sensing and collision avoidance mechanisms. We illustrated the potential behind it with a DHCP example, which we analyze by means of tool support. It involves SPASS(LA) for the time plus first-order analysis eventually yielding a VPTA that is then analyzed by the model checker MCPTA [8], using PRISM [11] as a backend.

Our tool chain has the following property: given an FPTA P and reachability problem F where the FOL(LA) translation for P ensures finite saturation with respect to finitely many FOL ground instances, we can effectively construct a finite VPTA $\mathrm{Sup}(P, F)$ that captures precisely the reachability probabilities of P with respect to F and hence enables effective computation of those via PTA model checkers.

This work offers more research potential. Although the FOL(LA) reachability part is undecidable in general, the SUP(LA) calculus is strong enough to generate proofs corresponding to infinite discrete-state VPTA. The question arises whether there is an extension of VPTA that can represent this infinity but still offers decidable reachability probability computation. Another dimension would be the inclusion of parameters. In our example, message latency, the number of resends and the waiting time were modeled by arithmetic constants. On the SUP(LA) side we know how this can be replaced by arithmetic parameters. An open question is the respective extension of the resulting VPTA theory.

Moreover, we are working on a formalization of message passing that will allow a more compositional approach to both the translation to FOL(LA) and the VPTA construction. The goal is to avoid the explicit construction of the parallel composition on the FPTA level, and to obtain component VPTAs corresponding to the initial component FPTAs.

Finally, we want to go beyond reachability: the superposition framework with its powerful redundancy elimination mechanisms often yields finite saturations even for infinite models. Based on a finite saturation of the reachability theory $\mathcal{R}_P$, more complex properties of the FPTA could be computed, such as nested PCTL formulas.

References

1. Althaus, E., Kruglov, E., Weidenbach, C.: Superposition modulo linear arithmetic SUP(LA). In: Ghilardi, S., Sebastiani, R. (eds.) FroCoS 2009. LNCS, vol. 5749, pp. 84–99. Springer, Heidelberg (2009)
2. Alur, R., Dill, D.L.: A theory of timed automata. Theoretical Computer Science 126(2), 183–235 (1994)
3. Bachmair, L., Ganzinger, H., Waldmann, U.: Refutational theorem proving for hierarchic first-order theories. Applicable Algebra in Engineering, Communication and Computing, AAECC 5(3/4), 193–212 (1994)
4. Bohnenkamp, H.C., D'Argenio, P.R., Hermanns, H., Katoen, J.-P.: MoDeST: A compositional modeling formalism for hard and softly timed systems. IEEE Transactions on Software Engineering 32(10), 812–830 (2006)

5. Droms, R.: Rfc 2131: Dynamic host configuration protocol. In: The Internet Engineering Task Force, IETF (1997), Obsoletes RFC 1541. Status: DRAFT STANDARD
6. Fietzke, A., Hermanns, H., Weidenbach, C.: Superposition-based analysis of first-order probabilistic timed automata. Reports of SFB/TR 14 AVACS 59, SFB/TR 14 AVACS (2010)
7. Fietzke, A., Weidenbach, C.: Labelled splitting. Ann. Math. Artif. Intell. 55(1-2), 3–34 (2009)
8. Hartmanns, A., Hermanns, H.: A modest approach to checking probabilistic timed automata. In: QEST, pp. 187–196. IEEE Computer Society, Los Alamitos (2009)
9. Hermanns, H., Wachter, B., Zhang, L.: Probabilistic CEGAR. In: Gupta, A., Malik, S. (eds.) CAV 2008. LNCS, vol. 5123, pp. 162–175. Springer, Heidelberg (2008)
10. Hoare, C.A.R.: Communicating sequential processes. Commun. ACM 21(8), 666–677 (1978)
11. Kwiatkowska, M., Norman, G., Parker, D.: Probabilistic Symbolic Model Checking with PRISM: A Hybrid Approach. International Journal on Software Tools for Technology Transfer (STTT) 6(2), 128–142 (2004)
12. Kwiatkowska, M., Norman, G., Parker, D.: Stochastic games for verification of probabilistic timed automata. In: Ouaknine, J., Vaandrager, F.W. (eds.) FORMATS 2009. LNCS, vol. 5813, pp. 212–227. Springer, Heidelberg (2009)
13. Kwiatkowska, M., Norman, G., Parker, D., Sproston, J.: Performance analysis of probabilistic timed automata using digital clocks. Formal Methods in System Design 29(1), 33–78 (2006)
14. Kwiatkowska, M., Norman, G., Sproston, J.: Probabilistic model checking of deadline properties in the IEEE 1934 FireWire root contention protocol. Formal Aspects of Computing 14(3), 295–318 (2003)
15. Kwiatkowska, M.Z., Norman, G., Sproston, J., Wang, F.: Symbolic model checking for probabilistic timed automata. Information and Computation 205(7), 1027–1077 (2007)
16. Lev-Ami, T., Weidenbach, C., Reps, T.W., Sagiv, M.: Labelled clauses. In: Pfenning, F. (ed.) CADE 2007. LNCS (LNAI), vol. 4603, pp. 311–327. Springer, Heidelberg (2007)
17. Nonnengart, A.: Hybrid systems verification by location elimination. In: Lynch, N.A., Krogh, B.H. (eds.) HSCC 2000. LNCS, vol. 1790, pp. 352–365. Springer, Heidelberg (2000)
18. Segala, R.: Modeling and Verification of Randomized Distributed Real-Time Systems. PhD thesis, University of Birmingham (2002)
19. Weidenbach, C.: Towards an automatic analysis of security protocols in first-order logic. In: Ganzinger, H. (ed.) CADE 1999. LNCS (LNAI), vol. 1632, pp. 314–328. Springer, Heidelberg (1999)
20. Weidenbach, C.: Combining superposition, sorts and splitting. In: Robinson, A., Voronkov, A. (eds.) Handbook of Automated Reasoning, ch. 27, vol. 2, pp. 1965–2012. Elsevier, Amsterdam (2001)
21. Weidenbach, C., Dimova, D., Fietzke, A., Kumar, R., Suda, M., Wischnewski, P.: Spass version 3.5. In: Schmidt, R.A. (ed.) Automated Deduction – CADE-22. LNCS, vol. 5663, pp. 140–145. Springer, Heidelberg (2009)

A Nonmonotonic Extension of KLM Preferential Logic P

Laura Giordano[1], Valentina Gliozzi[2], Nicola Olivetti[3], and Gian Luca Pozzato[2]

[1]Dip. di Informatica - U. Piemonte O. - Alessandria - Italy
laura@mfn.unipmn.it
[2] Dip. Informatica - Univ. di Torino - Italy
{gliozzi,pozzato}@di.unito.it
[3] LSIS-UMR CNRS 6168 - Marseille - France
nicola.olivetti@univ-cezanne.fr

Abstract. In this paper, we propose the logic $\mathbf{P}_{min}$, which is a nonmonotonic extension of Preferential logic **P** defined by Kraus, Lehmann and Magidor (KLM). In order to perform nonmonotonic inferences, we define a "minimal model" semantics. Given a modal interpretation of a minimal A-world as $A \land \Box\neg A$, the intuition is that preferred, or minimal models are those that minimize the number of worlds where $\neg\Box\neg A$ holds, that is of A-worlds which are not minimal. We also present a tableau calculus for deciding entailment in $\mathbf{P}_{min}$.

1 Introduction

In the early 90s [1] Kraus, Lehmann and Magidor (from now on KLM) proposed a formalization of nonmonotonic reasoning that was early recognized as a landmark. Their work led to a classification of nonmonotonic consequence relations, determining a hierarchy of stronger and stronger systems. The so called *KLM properties* have been widely accepted as the "conservative core" of default reasoning: they are properties that any concrete reasoning mechanism should satisfy. In KLM framework, defeasible knowledge is represented by a (finite) set of nonmonotonic conditionals or assertions of the form $A \mid\sim B$, whose reading is - depending on the context - *typically, As are Bs* or *normally, if A is true, also B is true*. By using a conditional, we can therefore express sentences as *artists are typically not rich* or *normally, if students work, they pass the exams*. The operator "$\mid\sim$" is nonmonotonic, in the sense that $A \mid\sim B$ does not imply $A \land C \mid\sim B$. By using the operator $\mid\sim$, one can consistently represent information that would be inconsistent, if interpreted in classical terms. For instance, a knowledge base Γ may consistently contain the conditionals: $artist \mid\sim \neg rich$, $artist \land successful \mid\sim rich$, expressing the fact that typically artists are not rich, except if they are successful, in which case they are rich. Observe that if $\mid\sim$ were interpreted as classical (or intuitionistic) implication, the knowledge base would be consistent only in case successful artists did not exist, which is clearly an unwanted condition.

In KLM framework, one can derive new conditional assertions from the knowledge base by means of a set of inference rules. The set of adopted rules defines

C. Fermüller and A. Voronkov (Eds.): LPAR-17, LNCS 6397, pp. 317–332, 2010.

some fundamental types of inference systems. The two systems that had the biggest echo in the literature are Preferential **P** and Rational **R** ([2,3,4,5,6,7], for a broader bibliography see [8]). Halpern and Friedman [9] have shown that **P** and **R** are natural and general systems: **P** (likewise **R**) is complete with respect to a wide spectrum of semantics, from ranked models, to parametrized probabilistic structures, ϵ-semantics and possibilistic structures. As an example of inference, from the knowledge base Γ above, in **P** one would derive that $artist \mid\sim \neg successful$, i.e. typically artists are not successful (successful artists being an exception).

From a semantic point of view, to each logic corresponds a kind of models, namely a class of possible-world structures equipped with a preference relation among worlds. More precisely, for **P** we have models with a preference relation $<$ (an irreflexive and transitive relation) on worlds. For the stronger **R** the preference relation is further assumed to be *modular*. In both cases, the meaning of a conditional assertion $A \mid\sim B$ is that B holds in the *most preferred* (or *minimal* or *typical*) worlds where A holds.

The main weakness of KLM systems is that they are *monotonic*: what can be inferred from a set of conditional assertions Γ can still be inferred from any set of assertions Γ' that includes Γ. In contrast, nonmonotonic inferences allow to draw a conclusion from a knowledge base Γ *in the absence of information to the contrary*, and to possibly withdraw the conclusion on the basis of more complete information. In the example above, if we knew that typically art students are artists, and indeed non successful artists, a nonmonotonic mechanism would allow us to conclude that they are not rich, similarly to typical artists. And it would allow us to make this conclusion in a nonmonotonic way, thus leaving us the freedom to withdraw our conclusion in case we learned that art students are atypical artists and are indeed rich. In order to make this kind of inference, the core set of KLM properties must be enriched with *nonmonotonic* inference mechanisms. This is the purpose of this paper.

Here, we take Preferential logic **P** as the underlying monotonic system in KLM framework. The choice of considering **P** rather than the stronger **R** is motivated by the exigence of avoiding some counterintuitive inferences supported by **R** as highlighted in [10]. This choice is also one of the main differences between our approach and existing nonmonotonic extensions of KLM systems, such as rational closure [4] and 1-entailment [3] that are based on the system **R**.

In this paper, we present the logic $\mathbf{P}_{min}$ that results from the addition to the system **P** of a nonmonotonic inference mechanism. $\mathbf{P}_{min}$ is based on a *minimal model approach*, based on the idea of restricting one's attention to models that contain as little as possible of non typical (or non minimal) worlds. The minimal models associated with a given knowledge base Γ being independent from the minimal models associated to Γ' for $\Gamma \subseteq \Gamma'$, $\mathbf{P}_{min}$ allows for nonmonotonic inferences. In the example above, in $\mathbf{P}_{min}$, we would derive that typically, art students are not rich ($art\_students \mid\sim \neg rich$). Moreover, we would no longer make the inference, should we discover that indeed $art\_students \mid\sim rich$.

We provide a decision procedure for checking satisfiability and validity in $\mathbf{P}_{min}$. Our decision procedure has the form of a tableaux calculus, with a two-step construction: the idea is that the top level construction generates open branches that are candidates to represent models, whereas the auxiliary construction checks whether a candidate branch represents a minimal model. Our procedure can be used to determine constructively an upper bound of the complexity of $\mathbf{P}_{min}$. Namely, we obtain that checking entailment for $\mathbf{P}_{min}$ is in Π_2, thus it has the same complexity as standard nonmonotonic (skeptical) mechanisms.

2 KLM Preferential Logic P

In this section, we recall the axiomatizations and semantics of the KLM logic **P**. For a complete picture of KLM systems, see [1,4]. The language of KLM logics consists just of conditional assertions $A \mid\sim B$. We consider here a richer language allowing boolean combinations of assertions and propositional formulas. As a consequence, we can have in our knowledge base negated conditionals, and we can handle more complex inferences than what can be done within the original KLM framework. Our language $\mathcal{L}$ is defined from a set of propositional variables ATM, the boolean connectives and the conditional operator $\mid\sim$. We use $A, B, C, ...$ to denote propositional formulas (that do not contain conditional formulas), whereas $F, G, ...$ are used to denote all formulas (including conditionals); $\Gamma, \Delta, ...$ represent sets of formulas. The formulas of $\mathcal{L}$ are defined as follows: if A is a propositional formula, $A \in \mathcal{L}$; if A and B are propositional formulas, $A \mid\sim B \in \mathcal{L}$; if F is a boolean combination of formulas of $\mathcal{L}$, $F \in \mathcal{L}$.

The axiomatization of **P** consists of all axioms and rules of propositional calculus together with the following axioms and rules. We use $\vdash_{PC}$ to denote provability in the propositional calculus, and $\vdash$ to denote provability in **P**:

- REF. $A \mid\sim A$ (reflexivity)
- LLE. If $\vdash_{PC} A \leftrightarrow B$, then $\vdash (A \mid\sim C) \rightarrow (B \mid\sim C)$ (left logical equivalence)
- RW. If $\vdash_{PC} A \rightarrow B$, then $\vdash (C \mid\sim A) \rightarrow (C \mid\sim B)$ (right weakening)
- CM. $((A \mid\sim B) \wedge (A \mid\sim C)) \rightarrow (A \wedge B \mid\sim C)$ (cautious monotonicity)
- AND. $((A \mid\sim B) \wedge (A \mid\sim C)) \rightarrow (A \mid\sim B \wedge C)$
- OR. $((A \mid\sim C) \wedge (B \mid\sim C)) \rightarrow (A \vee B \mid\sim C)$

REF states that A is always a default conclusion of A. LLE states that the syntactic form of the antecedent of a conditional formula is irrelevant. RW describes a similar property of the consequent. This allows to combine default and logical reasoning [9]. CM states that if B and C are two default conclusions of A, then adding one of the two conclusions to A will not cause the retraction of the other conclusion. AND states that it is possible to combine two default conclusions. OR states that it is allowed to reason by cases: if C is the default conclusion of two premises A and B, then it is also the default conclusion of their disjunction.

The semantics of **P** is defined by considering possible world structures with a *preference relation* $w < w'$ among worlds, whose meaning is that w is preferred to (or more typical than) w'. $A \mid\sim B$ holds in a model $\mathcal{M}$ if B holds in all *minimal worlds* (with respect to the relation $<$) where A holds.

Definition 1 (Preferential models). *A* preferential *model is a triple* $\mathcal{M} = \langle \mathcal{W}, <, V \rangle$*, where* $\mathcal{W}$ *is a non-empty set of items that we call worlds or individuals, according to the kind of knowledge we want to model,* $<$ *is an irreflexive and transitive relation on* $\mathcal{W}$*, and* V *is a function* $V : \mathcal{W} \longmapsto 2^{ATM}$*, which assigns to every world* w *the set of atoms holding in that world.*

Starting from V*, we define the evaluation function* $\models_{\mathbf{P}}$ *for all formulas.* $\models_{\mathbf{P}}$ *is defined in the standard way for boolean combinations of formulas. Furthermore, for* A *propositional, we define* $Min_<(A) = \{w \in \mathcal{W} \mid \mathcal{M}, w \models_{\mathbf{P}} A$ *and* $\forall w'$*,* $w' < w$ *implies* $\mathcal{M}, w' \not\models_{\mathbf{P}} A\}$*. We define:* $\mathcal{M}, w \models_{\mathbf{P}} A \mid\sim B$ *if for all* w'*, if* $w' \in Min_<(A)$ *then* $\mathcal{M}, w' \models_{\mathbf{P}} B$*.*

The relation $<$ *is assumed to satisfy the* smoothness condition*: if* $\mathcal{M}, w \models_{\mathbf{P}} A$*, then* $w \in Min_<(A)$ *or* $\exists w' \in Min_<(A)$ *s.t.* $w' < w$*.*

A formula is valid in a model $\mathcal{M}$ *(*$\mathcal{M} \models_{\mathbf{P}} F$*) if it is satisfied by all worlds in* $\mathcal{M}$*, and it is simply* valid *if it is valid in every model. A formula is* satisfiable *if its negation is not valid.* $\mathcal{M}$ *is a model of a set of formulas* Γ *(*$\mathcal{M} \models_{\mathbf{P}} \Gamma$*) if all formulas in* Γ *are valid in* $\mathcal{M}$*.*

Observe that the above definition of preferential model extends the definition by KLM in order to cope with boolean combinations of formulas. Notice also that the truth conditions for conditional formulas are given with respect to individual possible worlds for uniformity sake. Since the truth value of a conditional only depends on global properties of $\mathcal{M}$, we have that: $\mathcal{M}, w \models_{\mathbf{P}} A \mid\sim B$ iff $\mathcal{M} \models_{\mathbf{P}} A \mid\sim B$. Moreover, by the smoothness condition, we have that $Min_<(A) = \emptyset$ implies that no world in $\mathcal{M}$ satisfy A. Thus the logic can represent genuine S5-existential and universal modalities, given respectively by $\neg(A \mid\sim \bot)$ and $\neg A \mid\sim \bot$. Finally:

Definition 2 (Entailment in P). *A formula* F *is entailed in* **P** *by* Γ *(*$\Gamma \models_{\mathbf{P}} F$*) if it is valid in all models of* Γ*.*

In this paper, we consider a special kind of preferential models, based on multi-linear frames, that is to say structures where worlds are ordered in several linear chains. As shown in [8], the restriction to this kind of special models is fully legitimate, as they validate the same formulas as general models as defined in Definition 1 above. This restriction is partially motivated by algorithmic and efficiency considerations, as our tableaux calculus is based on them.

Definition 3 (Preferential multi-linear model). *A finite preferential model* $\mathcal{M} = (\mathcal{W}, <, V)$ *is multi-linear if the set of worlds* $\mathcal{W}$ *can be partitioned into a set of components* $\mathcal{W}_i$ *for* $i = 1, \ldots, n$*, that is* $\mathcal{W} = \mathcal{W}_1 \cup \ldots \cup \mathcal{W}_n$ *and 1) the relation* $<$ *is a total order on each* $\mathcal{W}_i$*; 2) elements in two different components* $\mathcal{W}_i$ *and* $\mathcal{W}_j$ *are incomparable w.r.t.* $<$*.*

Theorem 1 (Theorem 2.5 in [8]). *Let* Γ *be a set of formulas, if* Γ *is satisfiable with respect to the logic* **P***, then it has a multi-linear model.*

From now on, we shall refer to this definition of preferential model **P**.

For the purpose of the calculus, we consider an extension $\mathcal{L}^{\mathbf{P}}$ of the language $\mathcal{L}$ by formulas of the form $\Box A$, where A is propositional, whose intuitive meaning is that $\Box A$ holds in a world w if A holds in all the worlds preferred to w (i.e. in all w' such that $w' < w$). This language corresponds to the language of the tableaux calculus for KLM logics introduced in [8]. We extend the notion of preferential model to provide an evaluation of boxed formulas as follows:

Definition 4 (Truth condition of modality $\Box$). *$\mathcal{M}, w \models_{\mathbf{P}} \Box A$ if, for every $w' \in \mathcal{W}$, if $w' < w$ then $\mathcal{M}, w' \models_{\mathbf{P}} A$.*

From definition of $Min_<(A)$, it follows that for any formula A, we have that $w \in Min_<(A)$ iff $\mathcal{M}, w \models_{\mathbf{P}} A \wedge \Box\neg A$.

3 The Logic $\mathbf{P}_{min}$

$\mathbf{P}_{min}$ is a nonmonotonic extension of $\mathbf{P}$, based on the idea of considering only $\mathbf{P}$ models that, roughly speaking, minimize the non-typical objects (or the non typical worlds). Given a set of formulas Γ, we consider a finite set $\mathcal{L}_\Box$ of formulas: these are the formulas whose non typical instances we want to minimize, when considering which inferences we can draw from Γ. We assume that the set $\mathcal{L}_\Box$ contains at least all formulas A such that the conditional $A \mid\!\sim B$ occurs in Γ. We have seen that, in a model $\mathcal{M}$, w is a minimal (typical) A-world, i.e. $w \in Min_<(A)$, when w is an $A-$world (i.e., $\mathcal{M}, w \models_{\mathbf{P}} A$) and it is minimal (typical), i.e., $\mathcal{M}, w \models_{\mathbf{P}} \Box\neg A$. Minimizing non typical (non minimal) worlds w.r.t. $\mathcal{L}_\Box$ therefore amounts to minimizing worlds satisfying $\neg\Box\neg A$ for $A \in \mathcal{L}_\Box$. We define the set $\mathcal{M}^{\Box^-}_{\mathcal{L}_\Box}$ of negated boxed formulas holding in a model, relative to the formulas in $\mathcal{L}_\Box$. Given a model $\mathcal{M} = \langle \mathcal{W}, <, V \rangle$, we let: $\mathcal{M}^{\Box^-}_{\mathcal{L}_\Box} = \{(w, \neg\Box\neg A) \mid \mathcal{M}, w \models_{\mathbf{P}} \neg\Box\neg A,$ with $w \in \mathcal{W}, A \in \mathcal{L}_\Box\}$.

Definition 5 (Preferred and minimal models). *Given a model $\mathcal{M} = \langle \mathcal{W}_\mathcal{M}, <_\mathcal{M}, V_\mathcal{M} \rangle$ of a given set of formulas Γ and a model $\mathcal{N} = \langle \mathcal{W}_\mathcal{N}, <_\mathcal{N}, V_\mathcal{N} \rangle$ of Γ, we say that $\mathcal{M}$ is preferred to $\mathcal{N}$ with respect to $\mathcal{L}_\Box$, and we write $\mathcal{M} <_{\mathcal{L}_\Box} \mathcal{N}$, if: $\mathcal{W}_\mathcal{M} = \mathcal{W}_\mathcal{N}$, and $\mathcal{M}^{\Box^-}_{\mathcal{L}_\Box} \subset \mathcal{N}^{\Box^-}_{\mathcal{L}_\Box}$.*

A model $\mathcal{M}$ is a minimal model *for Γ (with respect to $\mathcal{L}_\Box$) if it is a model of Γ and there is no a model $\mathcal{M}'$ of Γ such that $\mathcal{M}' <_{\mathcal{L}_\Box} \mathcal{M}$.*

We can now define entailment in $\mathbf{P}_{min}$ as follows:

Definition 6 (Minimal Entailment in $\mathbf{P}_{min}$). *A formula F is minimally entailed in $\mathbf{P}_{min}$ by a set of formulas Γ with respect to $\mathcal{L}_\Box$ if it is valid in all models satisfying Γ that are minimal with respect to $\mathcal{L}_\Box$. We write $\Gamma \models^{\mathcal{L}_\Box}_{min} F$.*

It can be easily verified that this notion of entailment is nonmonotonic, as opposed to entailment in $\mathbf{P}$ that was monotonic. Indeed, in $\mathbf{P}_{min}$ the formulas minimally entailed by Γ might no longer be entailed by Γ': $\Gamma \subset \Gamma'$. Some significant properties of $\mathbf{P}_{min}$ are expressed in the next propositions. In the following, $\models_{PC}$ is entailment in classical logic.

Proposition 1. *Take a set of formulas Γ and a formula F. (i) If Γ has a model, then Γ has a minimal model with respect to any $\mathcal{L}_\Box$. (ii) Let us replace all formulas of the form $A \mid\sim B$ in Γ with $A \rightarrow B$, and call Γ' the resulting set of formulas. Similarly let F' be obtained from F by replacing conditional $\mid\sim$ by classical implication $\rightarrow$. If $\Gamma \models_{min}^{\mathcal{L}_\Box} F$ then $\Gamma' \models_{PC} F'$.*

Proof. (i) immediately follows from the finite model property of the logic P: given a finite model $\mathcal{M}$ of Γ the set of models $\mathcal{M}' <_{\mathcal{L}_\Box} \mathcal{M}$ is finite thus there exists a minimal model. Concerning (ii) let v be a classical model of Γ' (a propositional evaluation), define the trivial multi-linear model $\mathcal{M} = \langle \mathcal{W}_\mathcal{M}, <_\mathcal{M}, V_\mathcal{M} \rangle$, where $\mathcal{W}_\mathcal{M} = \{x_v\}$, $<_\mathcal{M} = \emptyset$, $V_\mathcal{M}(x_v) = \{P | v(P) = 1\}$. Observe that for every propositional formula G, $Min_<(G) = \{x_v\}$ if $v(G) = 1$ and $Min_<(G) = \emptyset$ otherwise. For every $A \mid\sim B \in \Gamma$, we know that $v(A \rightarrow B) = 1$; thus trivially for all $w' \in Min_<(A)$, $\mathcal{M}, w' \models_\mathbf{P} B$, that is $\mathcal{M}, x_v \models_\mathbf{P} A \mid\sim B$. Moreover, $\mathcal{M}_{\mathcal{L}_\Box}^{\Box^-} = \emptyset$. Thus $\mathcal{M}$ is a P-minimal model of Γ. Now we just apply the hypothesis and we obtain that $\mathcal{M}, x_v \models_\mathbf{P} F$, whence $v(F) = 1$. ■

The proposition (ii) states a kind of coherence with respect to classical logic: the inferences we make according to $\mathbf{P}_{min}$ are always a subset of inferences that we would make classically by interpreting $\mid\sim$ as classical implication. Obviously, the converse of (ii) is generally false. However, when Γ is just a set of positive conditionals, and F is a positive conditional, the converse of (ii) also holds.

Proposition 2. *Let Γ be a set of positive conditionals and let us denote by Γ' its classical counterpart as in the previous proposition. (i) if Γ' is inconsistent then also Γ is inconsistent. (ii) if $\Gamma' \models_{PC} A \rightarrow B$ then $\Gamma \models_{min}^{\mathcal{L}_\Box} A \mid\sim B$.*

Proof. (i) We proceed by contrapositive. Suppose Γ has a $\mathbf{P}$ model $\mathcal{M} = \langle \mathcal{W}_\mathcal{M}, <_\mathcal{M}, V_\mathcal{M} \rangle$. Take any world $x \in \mathcal{W}$ that is minimal wrt. $<$ (thus it has no predecessors); for every formula C we have $\mathcal{M}, x \models_\mathbf{P} \Box\neg C$. Thus for every formula C, $x \in Min_<(C)$ iff $\mathcal{M}, x \models_\mathbf{P} C$. Since $\mathcal{M} \models_\mathbf{P} \Gamma$, for every $C \mid\sim D \in \Gamma$, for every $w \in \mathcal{W}$, if $w \in Min_<(C)$ then $\mathcal{M}, w \models_\mathbf{P} D$. Therefore, if $\mathcal{M}, x \models_\mathbf{P} C$, since $x \in Min_<(C)$, we obtain $\mathcal{M}, x \models_\mathbf{P} D$, that is $\mathcal{M}, x \models_\mathbf{P} C \rightarrow D$. Thus x (as a propositional evaluation) satisfies every implication in Γ', and Γ' is consistent.

(ii) Suppose $\Gamma' \models_{PC} A \rightarrow B$. By (i) we can assume that Γ' is consistent, otherwise by (i) also Γ is inconsistent, and the result trivially follows. Therefore let v_0 be a propositional evaluation that satisfies Γ'. Let now $\mathcal{M} = \langle \mathcal{W}_\mathcal{M}, <_\mathcal{M}, V_\mathcal{M} \rangle$ be any $\mathbf{P}_{min}$-minimal model of Γ. Define $\mathcal{M}' = \langle \mathcal{W}_\mathcal{M}, <', V' \rangle$, where $<'$ is the empty relation and for all $w \in \mathcal{W}_\mathcal{M}$, $V'(w) = \{P \mid v_0(P) = 1\}$. We have that for all $w \in \mathcal{W}_\mathcal{M}$ and for every $C \rightarrow D \in \Gamma'$, $\mathcal{M}', w \models_\mathbf{P} C \rightarrow D$. Thus every implication of Γ' is valid in $\mathcal{M}'$. But, for every formula C $\mathcal{M}', w \models_\mathbf{P} \Box\neg C$, so that $w \in Min_<^{\mathcal{M}'}(C)$ iff $\mathcal{M}', w \models_\mathbf{P} C$. We can conclude that $\mathcal{M}' \models_\mathbf{P} \Gamma$. Furthermore, by minimality of $\mathcal{M}$ we cannot have $\mathcal{M}' <_{\mathcal{L}_\Box} \mathcal{M}$. Thus for every formula C, we have also $\mathcal{M}, w \models_\mathbf{P} \Box\neg C$. By reasoning as above, we infer that $w \in Min_<^{\mathcal{M}}(C)$ iff $\mathcal{M}, w \models_\mathbf{P} C$. Since $\mathcal{M} \models_\mathbf{P} \Gamma$, this entails that $\mathcal{M} \models_\mathbf{P} \Gamma'$. From this, we conclude that $\mathcal{M} \models_\mathbf{P} A \rightarrow B$, so that finally $\mathcal{M} \models_\mathbf{P} A \mid\sim B$. ■

The above properties entail that $\mathbf{P}_{min}$ behaves essentially as classical logic (and in particular $\mid\!\sim$ collapses to classical implication) for knowledge bases that are just a set of *positive conditionals*. As a consequence, $\mathbf{P}_{min}$ behaves monotonically for this restricted kind of knowledge bases, with respect to the *addition of positive conditionals*. Of course this is a very special case.

For all these reasons, the logic $\mathbf{P}_{min}$ turns out to be quite strong. If we consider the knowledge base of the Introduction, namely: $\Gamma = \{artist \mid\!\sim \neg rich, artist \wedge successful \mid\!\sim rich\}$, $\mathbf{P}_{min}$ would entail that $(artist \wedge successful) \mid\!\sim \bot$: typically, successful artists do not exist. This inference is meaningful if we consider that $\mathbf{P}_{min}$ minimizes the existence of non-typical elements of a model, and successful artists are non typical artists. As a difference with respect to classical logic, though, this is a nonmonotonic inference, since we can consistently add to the knowledge base the information that indeed successful artists exist. Observe that this fact would be expressed by a *negative conditional*.

In any case, it is true that in the meaning of a sentence like "typically, successful artists are rich", it is somewhat entailed that successful artists exist. For this reason, from now on we restrict our attentions to knowledge bases that explicitly include the information that there are typical As for all As such that the sentence "typically As are Bs" ($A \mid\!\sim B$) is in the knowledge base. This leads us to propose the following working definition:

Definition 7. *A well-behaved knowledge base* Γ *has the form* $\{A_i \mid\!\sim B_i, \neg(A_i \mid\!\sim \bot) \mid i = 1, \ldots, n\}$.

Therefore, the above knowledge base is transformed into the following one: $\Gamma' = \{artist \mid\!\sim \neg rich, artist \wedge successful \mid\!\sim rich, \neg(artist \mid\!\sim \bot), \neg(artist \wedge successful \mid\!\sim \bot)\}$. In the following, we we will consider well-behaved knowledge bases, although in principle one is free to use a knowledge base as Γ above (and to make the kind of strong inferences we mentioned). Obviously, a knowledge base may contain any formula of $\mathcal{L}$. In particular, it may contain negative conditionals, such as $\neg(artist \mid\!\sim french)$, saying that it is not true that typically artists are French. In the next section, we shall see that if we have these formulas, the choice of **P** rather than **R** as starting system makes a significant difference.

Example 1. Consider the example of art students mentioned in the Introduction. If we add to the previous knowledge base the information that typically, art students are non successful artists (and they do exist), we obtain the following knowledge base: $\Gamma'' = \Gamma' \cup \{art\_student \mid\!\sim artist \wedge \neg successful, \neg(art\_student \mid\!\sim \bot)\}$. It can be seen that $art\_student \mid\!\sim \neg rich$ is minimally entailed by Γ''.

3.1 Relations between $\mathbf{P}_{min}$ and 1-Entailment and Rational Closure

This is not the first nonmonotonic extension of KLM systems with a nonmonotonic inference mechanism. Lehmann and Magidor [4] propose the well-known rational closure that is a nonmonotonic mechanism built over the KLM system **R**.

Pearl in [3] proposes 1-entailment that is equivalent to rational closure. The first difference between our work and both 1-entailment and rational closure is that we start from KLM system **P** (and add a nonmonotonic mechanism to it), whereas they start from the stronger system **R**.

P versus R as the starting KLM system. Our choice of starting from **P** rather than from **R** is motivated by the fact that **R** is controversial, and enforces counterintuitive inferences, as outlined in [10]. To give some evidence, consider the example above of typical artists not being rich. If we knew that there is a typical American who is an artist but who is rich, and is therefore not a typical artist (i.e. if we added $\neg(american \mid\!\sim (\neg artist \vee \neg rich))$ to the knowledge base), if we adopt system **R**, we are forced to conclude that $artist \mid\!\sim \neg american$, saying that there are no typical artists who are American. The problem here is that in **R** we conclude something about all typical artists from what we know about a single (non typical) artist. What is most important is that in system **R**, we are forced to make this conclusion in a monotonic way: the addition of $\neg(artist \mid\!\sim \neg american)$, saying that indeed there are typical artists who are American, would lead to an inconsistent knowledge base.

Expressive power and strength of $\mathbf{P}_{min}$, compared to 1-entailment and rational closure. Further differences between our approach and both rational closure and 1-entailment lie both in expressivity, that is the kind of assertions that can be handled, and in the inferences' strength. First of all, it is not clear how 1-entailment can deal with negated conditionals, whence how it can represent assertions of the type "*not* all typical Americans have a given feature". In contrast, we have seen that negated conditionals are part of the language of $\mathbf{P}_{min}$. Secondly, the inferences that can be done in $\mathbf{P}_{min}$ and in 1-entailment are quite different. For instance, take the classical example of penguins, also considered by Pearl in [3]. In $\mathbf{P}_{min}$, from $penguin \mid\!\sim bird, bird \mid\!\sim fly, penguin \mid\!\sim \neg fly, penguin \mid\!\sim arctic$ (typically, penguins are birds, birds fly but penguins do not fly and penguins live in the arctic), we would nonmonotonically derive that $(penguin \wedge \neg arctic) \mid\!\sim \bot$: in the absence of information to the contrary, there are no penguins that do not live in the arctic. The inference holds both if we start from the given knowledge base, and if we consider its well-behaved extension. On the contrary, the inference does not hold in 1-entailment, nor in rational closure: in neither of the two one can derive a conditional of the form $A \mid\!\sim \bot$ from a consistent knowledge base. On the other hand, in 1-entailment (and rational closure) from the above knowledge base one derives that $bird \wedge white \mid\!\sim fly$, whereas this is not derivable in $\mathbf{P}_{min}$ in case we consider the well-behaved extension of the knowledge base (whereas it holds if we consider the knowledge base as it is). Therefore, $\mathbf{P}_{min}$ is significantly different from 1-entailment and rational closure as it can handle a richer language, and support different (sometime stronger) inferences. Indeed, we can prove that:

Proposition 3. *Let Γ be a set of positive conditionals.(i) $\mathbf{P}_{min}$ is strictly stronger than 1-entailment (for inferring positive conditionals); (ii) let Γ' be* *the well-behaved extension of Γ. $\mathbf{P}_{min}$ and 1-entailment inferences from Γ' are incomparable (for inferring positive conditionals).*

Notice that these differences would remain even if we chose **R** as the underlying monotonic system: the obtained logic would still be different from 1-entailment and rational closure.

4 A Tableaux Calculus for $\mathbf{P}_{min}$

In this section we present a tableau calculus for deciding whether a formula F is minimally entailed by a given set of formulas Γ. We introduce a labelled tableau calculus called $\mathcal{TAB}^{\mathbf{P}}_{min}$, which allows to reason about minimal models. $\mathcal{TAB}^{\mathbf{P}}_{min}$ performs a two-phase computation in order to check whether $\Gamma \models^{\mathcal{L}_T}_{min} F$. In particular, the procedure tries to build an open branch representing a minimal model satisfying $\Gamma \cup \{\neg F\}$. In the first phase, a tableau calculus, called $\mathcal{TAB}^{\mathbf{P}}_{PH1}$, simply verifies whether $\Gamma \cup \{\neg F\}$ is satisfiable in a **P** model, building candidate models. In the second phase another tableau calculus, called $\mathcal{TAB}^{\mathbf{P}}_{PH2}$, checks whether the candidate models found in the first phase are *minimal* models of Γ, i.e. for each open branch of the first phase, $\mathcal{TAB}^{\mathbf{P}}_{PH2}$ tries to build a "smaller" model of Γ, i.e. a model whose individuals satisfy less formulas $\neg\Box\neg A$ than the corresponding candidate model. Therefore, F is minimally entailed by Γ if there is no open branch in the tableau built by $\mathcal{TAB}^{\mathbf{P}}_{PH1}$ (therefore, there are no Preferential models satisfying Γ and $\neg F$) or for each open branch built by $\mathcal{TAB}^{\mathbf{P}}_{PH1}$, there is an open branch built by $\mathcal{TAB}^{\mathbf{P}}_{PH2}$ (therefore, the model corresponding to the branch of $\mathcal{TAB}^{\mathbf{P}}_{PH1}$ is not minimal, and there is a more preferred one corresponding to the open branch by $\mathcal{TAB}^{\mathbf{P}}_{PH2}$). The whole procedure $\mathcal{TAB}^{\mathbf{P}}_{min}$ is described at the end of this section (Definition 10).

The calculus $\mathcal{TAB}^{\mathbf{P}}_{min}$ makes use of labels to represent worlds. We consider a language $\mathcal{L}^{\mathbf{P}}$ and a denumerable alphabet of labels $\mathcal{A}$, whose elements are denoted by x, y, z, ...

4.1 Phase 1: The Calculus $\mathcal{TAB}^{\mathbf{P}}_{PH1}$

A tableau of $\mathcal{TAB}^{\mathbf{P}}_{PH1}$ is a tree whose nodes are sets of *labelled* formulas of the form $x : A$ or $x : A \mid\!\sim B^L$. L is a list of labels used in order to ensure the termination of the calculus. A branch is a sequence of nodes $\Gamma_1, \Gamma_2, \ldots, \Gamma_n$, where each node Γ_i is obtained from its immediate predecessor Γ_{i-1} by applying a rule of $\mathcal{TAB}^{\mathbf{P}}_{PH1}$, having Γ_{i-1} as the premise and Γ_i as one of its conclusions. A branch is closed if one of its nodes is an instance of (**AX**), otherwise it is open. A tableau is closed if all its branches are closed.

Definition 8 (Truth conditions of labelled formulas of $\mathcal{TAB}^{\mathbf{P}}_{PH1}$). *Given a model $\mathcal{M} = \langle \mathcal{W}, <, V \rangle$ and a label alphabet $\mathcal{A}$, we consider a mapping $I : \mathcal{A} \mapsto \mathcal{W}$. Given a formula α of the calculus $\mathcal{TAB}^{\mathbf{P}}_{min}$, we define $\mathcal{M} \models_{\mathbf{P}_I} x : F$ iff $\mathcal{M}, I(x) \models_{\mathbf{P}} F$. We say that a set of labelled formulas Γ is satisfiable if, for all $\alpha \in \Gamma$, we have that $\mathcal{M} \models_{\mathbf{P}_I} \alpha$, for some model $\mathcal{M}$ and some mapping I.*

$$(\mathbf{AX})\ \Gamma, x : P, x : \neg P \quad \text{with } P \in ATM \qquad (\wedge^+)\ \frac{\Gamma, x : F \wedge G}{\Gamma, x : F, x : G} \qquad (\wedge^-)\ \frac{\Gamma, x : \neg(F \wedge G)}{\Gamma, x : \neg F \qquad \Gamma, x : \neg G} \qquad (\neg)\ \frac{\Gamma, x : \neg\neg F}{\Gamma, x : F}$$

$$(cut)\ \frac{\Gamma}{\Gamma, x : \Box\neg A \qquad \Gamma, x : \neg\Box\neg A} \quad x \text{ occurs in } \Gamma,\ A \in \mathcal{L}_\Box$$

$$(\mid\!\sim^+)\ \frac{\Gamma, u : A \mid\!\sim B^L}{\Gamma, u : A \mid\!\sim B^{L,x}, x : \neg A \qquad \Gamma, u : A \mid\!\sim B^{L,x}, x : \neg\Box\neg A \qquad \Gamma, u : A \mid\!\sim B^{L,x}, x : B} \quad x \text{ occurs in } \Gamma,\ x \notin L$$

$$(\mid\!\sim^-)\ \frac{\Gamma, u : \neg(A \mid\!\sim B)}{\Gamma, x : A, x : \Box\neg A, x : \neg B \qquad \Gamma, y_1 : A, y_1 : \Box\neg A, y_1 : \neg B \qquad \Gamma, y_2 : A, y_2 : \Box\neg A, y_2 : \neg B \quad \cdots \quad \Gamma, y_n : A, y_n : \Box\neg A, y_n : \neg B} \quad \begin{array}{r} x \text{ new} \\ \text{for each } y_i \text{ occurring in } \Gamma \end{array}$$

$$(\Box^-)\ \frac{\Gamma, u : \neg\Box\neg A}{\Gamma, \Gamma^M_{u \to x}, x : A, x : \Box\neg A \qquad \Gamma, \Gamma^M_{u \to y_1}, y_1 : A, y_1 : \Box\neg A \qquad \Gamma, \Gamma^M_{u \to y_2}, y_2 : A, y_2 : \Box\neg A \quad \cdots \quad \Gamma, \Gamma^M_{u \to y_n}, y_n : A, y_n : \Box\neg A} \quad \begin{array}{r} x \text{ new} \\ \text{for each } y_i \text{ occurring in } \Gamma\ , u \neq y_i \end{array}$$

Fig. 1. The calculus $\mathcal{TAB}^{\mathbf{P}}_{PH1}$. To save space, we omit the standard rules for $\vee$ and $\rightarrow$.

In order to verify that a set of formulas Γ is unsatisfiable, we label all the formulas in Γ with a new label x, and verify that the resulting set of labelled formulas has a closed tableau. To this purpose, the rules of the calculus $\mathcal{TAB}^{\mathbf{P}}_{PH1}$ are applied until either a contradiction is generated (**AX**) or a model satisfying Γ can be obtained from the resulting open branch. For each conditional formulas $A \mid\!\sim B \in \Gamma$, we consider $x : A \mid\!\sim B^{\emptyset}$.

The rules of $\mathcal{TAB}^{\mathbf{P}}_{PH1}$ are shown in Figure 1. We define $\Gamma^M_{u \to x} = \{x : \neg A, x : \Box\neg A \mid u : \Box\neg A \in \Gamma\}$. Rules $(\mid\!\sim^-)$ and $(\Box^-)$ are called *dynamic* since they introduce a new variable in their conclusions. The other rules are called *static*. We do not need any extra rule for the positive occurrences of the $\Box$ operator, since these are taken into account by the computation of $\Gamma^M_{u \to x}$. The (cut) rule ensures that, given any formula $A \in \mathcal{L}_\Box$, an open branch built by $\mathcal{TAB}^{\mathbf{P}}_{PH1}$ contains either $x : \Box\neg A$ or $x : \neg\Box\neg A$ for each label x: this is needed in order to allow $\mathcal{TAB}^{\mathbf{P}}_{PH2}$ to check the minimality of the model corresponding to the open branch, as we will discuss later.

The calculus $\mathcal{TAB}^{\mathbf{P}}_{PH1}$ adopts the following standard strategy: the application of the $(\Box^-)$ rule is postponed to the application of all propositional rules and to the test of whether Γ is an instance of (**AX**) or not. The calculus so obtained is sound and complete with respect to the semantics in Definition 3.

Theorem 2 (Soundness and Completeness of $\mathcal{TAB}^{\mathbf{P}}_{PH1}$). *Given a set of formulas Γ, it is unsatisfiable iff it has a closed tableau in $\mathcal{TAB}^{\mathbf{P}}_{PH1}$.*

We can show that the calculus $\mathcal{TAB}^{\mathbf{P}}_{PH1}$ always terminates, i.e. every tableau built by $\mathcal{TAB}^{\mathbf{P}}_{PH1}$ is finite. Similarly to the calculus for **R** introduced in [8], it is easy to observe that it is useless to apply the rule $(\mid\!\sim^+)$ on the same conditional formula more than once in the same world, i.e. by using the same label x. We prevent redundant applications of $(\mid\!\sim^+)$ by keeping track of labels in which a conditional $u : A \mid\!\sim B$ has already been applied in the current branch. To this purpose, we add to each positive conditional the above mentioned list of *used* labels L; we then restrict the application of $(\mid\!\sim^+)$ only to labels not occurring in the corresponding list L. Moreover, the rule $(\mid\!\sim^-)$ can be applied only once for each negated conditional Γ. By virtue of the properties of $\Box$, no other additional machinery is required to ensure termination. The generation of infinite branches due to the interplay between rules ($\mid\!\sim^+$) and ($\Box^-$) cannot occur. Indeed, each application of ($\Box^-$) to a formula $x : \neg\Box\neg A$ (introduced by ($\mid\!\sim^+$)) adds the formula $y : \Box\neg A$ to the conclusion, so that ($\mid\!\sim^+$) can no longer consistently introduce $y : \neg\Box\neg A$. This is due to the properties of $\Box$ (no infinite descending chains of $<$ are allowed). Finally, the (cut) rule does not affect termination, since it is applied only to the finitely many formulas belonging to $\mathcal{L}_\Box$.

Theorem 3 (Termination of $\mathcal{TAB}^{\mathbf{P}}_{PH1}$). *Let Γ be a set of labelled formulas, then any tableau generated by $\mathcal{TAB}^{\mathbf{P}}_{PH1}$ for Γ is finite.*

Let us now conclude this section by refining the calculus $\mathcal{TAB}^{\mathbf{P}}_{PH1}$ in order to obtain a systematic procedure that allows the satisfiability problem of a set of formulas Γ to be decided in nondeterministic polynomial time. Let n be the size of the starting set Γ of which we want to verify the satisfiability. The number of applications of the rules is proportional to the number of labels introduced in the tableau. In turn, this is $O(2^n)$ due to the interplay between the rules ($\mid\!\sim^+$) and ($\Box^-$). Hence, the complexity of $\mathcal{TAB}^{\mathbf{P}}_{PH1}$ is exponential in n.

Similarly to what done in [8], in order to obtain an **NP** procedure we take advantage of the following facts:

1. Negated conditionals do not interact among themselves, thus they can be handled separately and eliminated always as a first step;
2. We can replace the ($\Box^-$) by a stronger rule $(\Box^-)_s$ which allows to build *mutlilinear* models, as defined in Definition 3.

Regarding (2), we can adopt the following strengthened version of ($\Box^-$). We use $\Gamma^{-i\Box}_{u\rightarrow x}$ to denote $\{x : \neg\Box\neg A_j \vee A_j \mid u : \neg\Box\neg A_j \in \Gamma \wedge j \neq i\}$.

$$\frac{\Gamma, u : \neg\Box\neg A_1, u : \neg\Box\neg A_2, \ldots, u : \neg\Box\neg A_m}{\Gamma, x : A_k, x : \Box\neg A_k, \Gamma^M_{u\rightarrow x}, \Gamma^{-k\Box}_{u\rightarrow x} \quad \ldots \quad \Gamma, y_i : A_k, y_i : \Box\neg A_k, \Gamma^M_{u\rightarrow y_i}, \Gamma^{-k\Box}_{u\rightarrow y_k}}\ (\Box^-_s)$$

where x is a new label, for each y_i occuring in Γ and for all $k = 1, 2, \ldots, m$. Rule $(\Box^-_s)$ contains: - m branches, one for each $u : \neg\Box\neg A_k$ in Γ, where a new minimal world x is created for A_k (i.e. $x : A_k$ and $x : \Box\neg A_k$ are added), and for all other $u : \neg\Box\neg A_j$, either $x : A_j$ holds in that world or the formula $x : \neg\Box\neg A_j$ is recorded; - other $m \times l$ branches, where l is the number of labels occurring in Γ, one for each label y_i and for each $u : \neg\Box\neg A_k$ in Γ; in these branches, a given y_i is chosen as a minimal world for A_k, that is to say $y_i : A_k$ and $y_i : \Box\neg A_k$ are added, and for all other $u : \neg\Box\neg A_j$, either $y_i : A_j$ holds in that world or the formula $y_i : \neg\Box\neg A_j$ is recorded.

The rule $(\Box^-_s)$ is sound with respect to multilinear models. The advantage of this rule over the original ($\Box^-$) rule is that all the negated box formulas labelled by u are treated in one step, introducing only a new label x in (some of) the conclusions, at the price of building an exponential number of branches. Instead, the original rule ($\Box^-$), introduces one new world *for each* $u : \neg\Box\neg A_k$ and, applied m times on all of them, m new worlds are introduced in each branch.

In the following, we describe a rule application's strategy that allows us to decide the satisfiability of a set of formulas Γ in non-deterministic polynomial time. As a first step, the strategy applies the boolean rules as long as possible. In case of branching rules, this operation nondeterministically selects (guesses) one of the conclusions of the rules. For each negated conditional, the strategy applies the rule $(\mid\!\sim^-)$ to it, generating a set Γ' that does not contain any negated conditional. On this node, the strategy applies the static rules as far as possible, then it iterates the following steps until either the current node contains an axiom or it does not contain negated boxed formulas $u : \neg\Box\neg A$: 1. apply the $(\Box_s^-)$ rule by guessing a branch; 2. apply the static rules as far as possible to the obtained node. If the final node does not contain an axiom, then we conclude that Γ' is satisfiable.

The overall complexity of the strategy can be estimated as follows. Consider that $n = \mid \Gamma \mid$. There are at most $O(n)$ negated conditionals, therefore the initial application of $(\mid\!\sim^-)$ introduces $O(n)$ labels in the obtained node Γ'. The number of different negated box formulas is at most $O(n)$, too. The strategy builds a tableau branch for Γ' by alternating applications of $(\Box_s^-)$ and of static rules (to saturate the obtained nodes). In case of branching rules, this saturation nondeterministically selects (guesses) one of the conclusions of the rules. Consider $\{u : \neg\Box\neg A_1, u : \neg\Box\neg A_2, \ldots, u : \neg\Box\neg A_m\} \subseteq \Gamma'$, and consider a branch generated by the application of the $(\Box_s^-)$ rule. In the worst case, a new label x_1 is introduced. Suppose also that the branch under consideration is the one containing $x_1 : A_1$ and $x_1 : \Box\neg A_1$. The $(\Box_s^-)$ rule can then be applied to formulas $x_1 : \neg\Box\neg A_k$, introducing also a further new label x_2. However, by the presence of $x_1 : \Box\neg A_1$, the rule $(\Box_s^-)$ can no longer consistently introduce $x_2 : \neg\Box\neg A_1$, since $x_2 : \Box\neg A_1 \in \Gamma^M_{x_1 \rightarrow x_2}$. Therefore, if $(\Box_s^-)$ can be applied (at most) n times in x_1 (one for each different negated boxed formula), then the rule can be applied (at most) $n - 1$ times in x_2, and so on. Therefore, at most $O(n)$ new labels are introduced by $(\Box_s^-)$ in each branch.

As the number of different subformulas of Γ is at most $O(n)$, in all steps involving the application of static rules, there are at most $O(n)$ applications of these rules. Therefore, the length of the tableau branch built by the strategy is $O(n^2)$. Finally, we observe that all the nodes of the tableau contain a number of formulas which is polynomial in n, therefore to test that a node contains an axiom has at most complexity polynomial in n. The above strategy allows to prove that:

Theorem 4 (Complexity of Phase 1). *The problem of deciding the satisfiability of a set of formulas Γ is in* NP.

Notice that the above strategy is able to build branches of polynomial length thanks to the presence of the rule (*cut*). Indeed, the key point is that, when the rule $(\Box_s^-)$ building multilinear models is applied to a given label u, *all negated boxed formulas* $u : \neg\Box\neg A_k$ belong to current set of formulas. It could be the case that, after an application of $(\Box_s^-)$ by using u, the same label u is used in one of the conclusions of another application of $(\Box_s^-)$, say to some x_i. Therefore, the application of static rules could introduce $u : \neg\Box\neg A$, and a further application

$$(\mathbf{AX})\ \langle \Gamma, x : P, x : \neg P \mid K \rangle \quad P \in ATM$$

$$(\mathbf{AX}_{\Box^-})\ \langle \Gamma, u : \neg\Box\neg P \mid K \rangle \quad u : \neg\Box\neg A \notin K$$

$$(\mathbf{AX}_{\emptyset})\ \langle \Gamma \mid \emptyset \rangle$$

$$(\neg)\ \frac{\langle \Gamma, x : \neg\neg F \mid K \rangle}{\langle \Gamma, x : F \mid K \rangle}$$

$$(\wedge^+)\ \frac{\langle \Gamma, x : F \wedge G \mid K \rangle}{\langle \Gamma, x : F, x : G \mid K \rangle}$$

$$(\wedge^-)\ \frac{\langle \Gamma, x : \neg(F \wedge G) \mid K \rangle}{\langle \Gamma, x : \neg F \mid K \rangle \qquad \langle \Gamma, x : \neg G \mid K \rangle}$$

$$(cut)\ \frac{\langle \Gamma \mid K \rangle}{\langle \Gamma, x : \Box\neg A \mid K \rangle \qquad \langle \Gamma, x : \neg\Box\neg A \mid K \rangle} \quad \text{if } x : \neg\Box\neg A \notin \Gamma \text{ and } x : \Box\neg A \notin \Gamma,\ x \in \mathcal{D}(\mathbf{B}), A \in \mathcal{L}_{\Box}$$

$$(\mid\!\sim^+)\ \frac{\langle \Gamma, u : A \mid\!\sim B^{L} \mid K \rangle}{\langle \Gamma, u : A \mid\!\sim B^{L,x}, x : \neg A \mid K \rangle \qquad \langle \Gamma, u : A \mid\!\sim B^{L,x}, x : \neg\Box\neg A \mid K \rangle \qquad \langle \Gamma, u : A \mid\!\sim B^{L,x}, x : B \mid K \rangle} \quad x \in \mathcal{D}(\mathbf{B}) \text{ and } x \notin L$$

$$(\mid\!\sim^-)\ \frac{\langle \Gamma, u : \neg(A \mid\!\sim B) \mid K \rangle}{\langle \Gamma, y_1 : A, y_1 : \Box\neg A, y_1 : \neg B \mid K \rangle \qquad \langle \Gamma, y_2 : A, y_2 : \Box\neg A, y_2 : \neg B \mid K \rangle \quad \cdots \quad \langle \Gamma, y_n : A, y_n : \Box\neg A, y_n : \neg B \mid K \rangle} \quad \text{for all } y_i \in \mathcal{D}(\mathbf{B})$$

$$(\Box_s^-)\ \frac{\langle \Gamma, u : \neg\Box\neg A_1, u : \neg\Box\neg A_2, \ldots, u : \neg\Box\neg A_m \mid K, u : \neg\Box\neg A_1, u : \neg\Box\neg A_2, \ldots, u : \neg\Box\neg A_m \rangle}{\langle \Gamma, \Gamma^{M}_{u \to y_i}, y_i : A_1, y_i : \Box\neg A_1, \Gamma^{-1^{\Box}}_{u \to y_i} \mid K \rangle \quad \langle \Gamma, \Gamma^{M}_{u \to y_i}, y_i : A_2, y_i : \Box\neg A_2, \Gamma^{-2^{\Box}}_{u \to y_i} \mid K \rangle \cdots \langle \Gamma, \Gamma^{M}_{u \to y_i}, y_i : A_m, y_i : \Box\neg A_m, \Gamma^{-m^{\Box}}_{u \to y_i} \mid K \rangle} \quad \text{for all } y_i \in \mathcal{D}(\mathbf{B}),\ u \neq y_i$$

Fig. 2. The calculus $\mathcal{TAB}^{\mathbf{P}}_{PH2}$

of $(\Box_s^-)$ could be needed. However, since (cut) is a static rule, and since $A \in \mathcal{L}_{\Box}$ because A is the antecedent of (at least) the conditional formula $A \mid\!\sim B$ generating $\neg\Box\neg A$, either $u : \neg\Box\neg A$ or $u : \Box\neg A$ have already been introduced in the branch *before* the second application of $(\Box_s^-)$, which is a dynamic rule.

4.2 Phase 2: The Calculus $\mathcal{TAB}^{\mathbf{P}}_{PH2}$

Let us now describe the calculus $\mathcal{TAB}^{\mathbf{P}}_{PH2}$ which, for each open branch $\mathbf{B}$ built by $\mathcal{TAB}^{\mathbf{P}}_{PH1}$, verifies if it is a minimal model of the initial set of formulas Γ.

Definition 9. *Given an open branch* $\mathbf{B}$ *of a tableau built from* $\mathcal{TAB}^{\mathbf{P}}_{PH1}$*, we define: (i)* $\mathcal{D}(\mathbf{B})$ *as the set of labels occurring on* $\mathbf{B}$*; (ii)* $\mathbf{B}^{\Box^-} = \{x : \neg\Box\neg A \mid x : \neg\Box\neg A$ *occurs in* $\mathbf{B}\}$.

A tableau of $\mathcal{TAB}^{\mathbf{P}}_{PH2}$ is a tree whose nodes are pairs of the form $\langle \Gamma \mid K \rangle$, where Γ is a set of labelled formulas of $\mathcal{L}^{\mathbf{P}}$, whereas Γ contains formulas of the form $x : \neg\Box\neg A$, with $A \in \mathcal{L}_{\Box}$.

The basic idea of $\mathcal{TAB}^{\mathbf{P}}_{PH2}$ is as follows. Given an open branch $\mathbf{B}$ built by $\mathcal{TAB}^{\mathbf{P}}_{PH1}$ and corresponding to a model $\mathcal{M}^{\mathbf{B}}$ of $\Gamma \cup \{\neg F\}$, $\mathcal{TAB}^{\mathbf{P}}_{PH2}$ checks whether $\mathcal{M}^{\mathbf{B}}$ is a minimal model of Γ by trying to build a model of Γ which is preferred to $\mathcal{M}^{\mathbf{B}}$. Obviously, since the calculus $\mathcal{TAB}^{\mathbf{P}}_{PH1}$ and the strategy on its application build *multilinear* models, the calculus $\mathcal{TAB}^{\mathbf{P}}_{PH2}$ also adopts the same strategy on the order of application of the rules and the refined rule $(\Box_s^-)$ in order to build only such multilinear models.

Checking (un)satisfiability of $\langle \Gamma \mid \mathbf{B}^{\Box^-} \rangle$ allows to verify whether the candidate model $\mathcal{M}^{\mathbf{B}}$ is minimal. More in detail, $\mathcal{TAB}^{\mathbf{P}}_{PH2}$ tries to build an open branch containing all the objects appearing on $\mathbf{B}$, i.e. those in $\mathcal{D}(\mathbf{B})$. To this aim, the dynamic rules use labels in $\mathcal{D}(\mathbf{B})$ instead of introducing new ones in their conclusions. The additional set Γ of a tableau node, initialized with $\mathbf{B}^{\Box^-}$, is used in order to ensure that any branch **B'** built by $\mathcal{TAB}^{\mathbf{P}}_{PH2}$ is preferred to **B**, that is **B'** only contains negated boxed formulas occurring in **B** and there exists at least one $x : \neg\Box\neg A$ that occurs in **B** and *does not occur* in **B'**. The rules of $\mathcal{TAB}^{\mathbf{P}}_{PH2}$ are shown in Figure 2.

More in detail, the rule $(\mid\!\sim^-)$ is applied to a set of formulas containing a formula $u : \neg(A \mid\!\sim B)$; it introduces $y : A, y : \Box\neg A$ and $y : \neg B$, where $y \in \mathcal{D}(\mathbf{B})$, instead of y being a new label. The choice of the label y introduces a branching in the tableau construction. The rule $(\mid\!\sim^+)$ is applied in the same way as in $\mathcal{TAB}^{\mathbf{P}}_{PH1}$ to *all the labels of* $\mathcal{D}(\mathbf{B})$ (and not only to those appearing in the branch). The rule $(\Box^-_s)$ is applied to a node $\langle \Gamma, u : \neg\Box\neg A_1, u : \neg\Box\neg A_2, \ldots, u : \neg\Box\neg A_m \mid K\rangle$, when $\{u : \neg\Box\neg A_1, u : \neg\Box\neg A_2, \ldots, u : \neg\Box\neg A_m\} \subseteq K$, i.e. when all the formulas $u : \neg\Box\neg A_1, u : \neg\Box\neg A_2, \ldots, u : \neg\Box\neg A_m$ also belong to the open branch **B**. In this case, the rule introduces a branch on the choice of the individual $y_i \in \mathcal{D}(\mathbf{B})$ which is preferred to u and is such that A_k and $\Box\neg A_k$ hold in y_i, recording, for all the other formulas $\neg\Box\neg A_j$, that either $y_i : A_j$ or $y_i : \neg\Box\neg A_j$ holds. Notice that, as a difference with the rule $(\Box^-_s)$ reformulated for $\mathcal{TAB}^{\mathbf{P}}_{PH1}$ in Phase 1, here the branches generating a new label x for each negated boxed formula $u : \neg\Box\neg A_k$ are no longer introduced.

In case a tableau node has the form $\langle \Gamma, u : \neg\Box\neg A \mid K\rangle$, and $u : \neg\Box\neg A \notin K$, then $\mathcal{TAB}^{\mathbf{P}}_{PH2}$ detects an inconsistency, called $(\mathbf{AX})_{\Box^-}$: this corresponds to the situation in which $u : \neg\Box\neg A$ does not belong to **B**, while $\Gamma, u : \neg\Box\neg A$ is satisfiable in a model $\mathcal{M}$ only if $\mathcal{M}$ contains $u : \neg\Box\neg A$, and hence only if $\mathcal{M}$ is *not* preferred to the model represented by **B**.

The calculus $\mathcal{TAB}^{\mathbf{P}}_{PH2}$ also contains the closing condition $(\mathbf{AX})_{\emptyset}$. Since each application of $(\Box^-_s)$ removes the principal formula $u : \neg\Box\neg A$ from the set Γ, when Γ is empty all the negated boxed formulas occurring in **B** also belong to the current branch. In this case, the model built by $\mathcal{TAB}^{\mathbf{P}}_{PH2}$ satisfies the same set of negated boxed formulas (for all labels) as **B** and, thus, it is not preferred to the one represented by **B**.

Theorem 5 (Soundness and completeness of $\mathcal{TAB}^{\mathbf{P}}_{PH2}$). *Given a set of labelled formulas Γ and a formula F, an open branch* **B** *built by $\mathcal{TAB}^{\mathbf{P}}_{PH1}$ for $\Gamma \cup \{\neg F\}$ is satisfiable by an injective mapping in a minimal model of Γ iff the tableau in $\mathcal{TAB}^{\mathbf{P}}_{PH2}$ for $\langle \Gamma \mid \mathbf{B}^{\Box^-}\rangle$ is closed.*

$\mathcal{TAB}^{\mathbf{P}}_{PH2}$ always terminates. Indeed, only a finite number of labels can occur on the branch (only those in $\mathcal{D}(\mathbf{B})$ which is finite). Moreover, the side conditions on the application of the rules copying their principal formulas in their conclusion(s) prevent the uncontrolled application of the same rules.

The overall procedure $\mathcal{TAB}^{\mathbf{P}}_{min}$ is defined as follows:

Definition 10. *Given a set of formulas Γ and a formula F, the calculus $\mathcal{TAB}^{\mathbf{P}}_{min}$ checks whether $\Gamma \models^{\mathcal{L}\Box}_{min} F$ by means of the following procedure:* (phase 1) *the calculus $\mathcal{TAB}^{\mathbf{P}}_{PH1}$ is applied to $\Gamma \cup \{\neg F\}$; if, for each branch* **B** *built by $\mathcal{TAB}^{\mathbf{P}}_{PH1}$, either (i)* **B** *is closed or (ii)* (phase 2) *the tableau built by the calculus $\mathcal{TAB}^{\mathbf{P}}_{PH2}$ for $\langle \Gamma \mid \mathbf{B}^{\Box^-}\rangle$ is open, then $\Gamma \models^{\mathcal{L}\Box}_{min} F$, otherwise $\Gamma \not\models^{\mathcal{L}\Box}_{min} F$.*

$\mathcal{TAB}^{\mathbf{P}}_{min}$ is a sound and complete decision procedure for verifying if a formula F can be minimally entailed from a set of formulas Γ. It can be shown that:

Theorem 6 (Complexity of Phase 2). *The problem of verifying that a branch* $\mathbf{B}$ *represents a minimal model for* Γ *in* $\mathcal{TAB}^{\mathbf{P}}_{PH2}$ *is in* NP *in the size of* $\mathbf{B}$.

By Theorems 4 and 6, we can prove that:

Theorem 7 (Complexity of $\mathcal{TAB}^{\mathbf{P}}_{min}$). *The problem of deciding whether* $\Gamma \models^{\mathcal{L}_\Box}_{min} F$ *is in* Π_2.

Example 2. As an example, let $\Gamma = \{artist \mid\!\sim \neg rich, \neg(artist \mid\!\sim \bot)\}$. We show that $\Gamma \models^{\mathcal{L}_\Box}_{min} artist \wedge blond \mid\!\sim \neg rich$ by means of the calculus $\mathcal{TAB}^{\mathbf{P}}_{min}$. To save space, we write A for *artist*, R for *rich* and B for *blond*. We consider $\mathcal{L}_\Box = \{A, A \wedge B\}$. The tableau $\mathcal{TAB}^{\mathbf{P}}_{PH1}$ starts by two applications of $(\mid\!\sim^-)$ on the initial set $\Gamma \cup \{\neg(A \wedge B \mid\!\sim \neg R)\}$, obtaining the node $\{x : A, x : \Box\neg A, x : \neg\bot, y : A \wedge B, y : \Box\neg(A \wedge B), y : \neg\neg R\}$. We apply $(\mid\!\sim^+)$, $(\neg)$, $(\wedge^+)$, and (cut). Disregarding the nodes that are instances of $(\mathbf{AX})$, the only left branch contains $\Gamma = \{x : A, x : \Box\neg A, x : \neg\bot, x : \neg R, x : \Box\neg(A\wedge B), y : A, y : B, y : \Box\neg(A\wedge B), y : R, y : \neg\Box\neg A\}$. Now we can apply the rule $(\Box^-_s)$, obtaining two conclusions. The first one adds to Γ the formulas $z : A, z : \Box\neg A, z : \neg(A \wedge B), z : \Box\neg(A \wedge B)$ where z is a new label, the other one intoduces the same formulas labelled by x itself. We then apply the rules $(\mid\!\sim^+)$ and $(\wedge^-)$. Disregarding branches containing axioms, the only two open branches, say $\mathbf{B_1}$ and $\mathbf{B_2}$, contain $\Gamma_1 = \Gamma \cup \{z : A, z : \Box\neg A, z : \neg(A \wedge B), z : \Box\neg(A \wedge B), z : \neg B, z : \neg R\}$ and $\Gamma_2 = \Gamma \cup \{x : \neg(A \wedge B), x : \Box\neg(A \wedge B), x : \neg B\}$, respectively, and their nodes cannot be further expanded. We now apply the calculus $\mathcal{TAB}^{\mathbf{P}}_{PH2}$ to both $\mathbf{B_1}$ and $\mathbf{B_2}$. Let us start with the latter one. The tableau starts with $\langle A \mid\!\sim \neg R, \neg(A \mid\!\sim \bot) \mid y : \neg\Box\neg A\rangle$. Applications of $(\mid\!\sim^-)$, $(\mid\!\sim^+)$ and (cut) lead to an open branch containing $x : A, x : \Box\neg A, x : \neg R, x : \Box\neg(A \wedge B), y : \neg A, y : \Box\neg A, y : \Box\neg(A \wedge B), z : \neg A, z : \Box\neg A, z : \Box\neg(A \wedge B)$. Similarly for $\mathbf{B_1}$. Since the tableaux in $\mathcal{TAB}^{\mathbf{P}}_{PH2}$ for $\mathbf{B_1}$ and $\mathbf{B_2}$ are open, these two branches are closed. Thus the whole procedure $\mathcal{TAB}^{\mathbf{P}}_{min}$ verifies that $\Gamma \models^{\mathcal{L}_\Box}_{min} A \wedge B \mid\!\sim \neg R$.

5 Conclusion

In this paper, we have proposed the logic $\mathbf{P}_{min}$, which is a nonmonotonic extension of the KLM system **P**. Our choice of starting from **P** rather than from the stronger **R** is that **P** avoids the unwanted inferences that **R** entails, and that are outlined in [10]. The system $\mathbf{P}_{min}$ turns out to be both more expressive and stronger, when compared to both 1-entailment and rational closure. We have also provided a two-phase tableau calculus for checking entailment in $\mathbf{P}_{min}$. Our procedure can be used to determine constructively an upper bound of the complexity of $\mathbf{P}_{min}$, namely that checking entailment is in Π_2.

Acknowledgements. The work has been supported by Project "MIUR PRIN08 LoDeN: Logiche Descrittive Nonmonotone: Complessità e implementazioni".

References

1. Kraus, S., Lehmann, D., Magidor, M.: Nonmonotonic reasoning, preferential models and cumulative logics. Artificial Intelligence 44(1-2), 167–207 (1990)
2. Benferhat, S., Dubois, D., Prade, H.: Nonmonotonic reasoning, conditional objects and possibility theory. Artificial Intelligence 92(1-2), 259–276 (1997)
3. Pearl, J.: System Z: A natural ordering of defaults with tractable applications to nonmonotonic reasoning. In: Proceedings of TARK, pp. 121–135 (1990)
4. Lehmann, D., Magidor, M.: What does a conditional knowledge base entail? Artificial Intelligence 55(1), 1–60 (1992)
5. Arieli, O., Avron, A.: General patterns for nonmonotonic reasoning: From basic entailments to plausible relations. Logic Journal of the IGPL 8(2), 119–148 (2000)
6. Dubois, D., Fargier, H., Perny, P.: Qualitative decision theory with preference relations and comparative uncertainty: An axiomatic approach. Artificial Intelligence 148(1-2), 219–260 (2003)
7. Giordano, L., Gliozzi, V., Olivetti, N., Pozzato, G.L.: Reasoning About Typicality in Preferential Description Logics. In: Hölldobler, S., Lutz, C., Wansing, H. (eds.) JELIA 2008. LNCS (LNAI), vol. 5293, pp. 192–205. Springer, Heidelberg (2008)
8. Giordano, L., Gliozzi, V., Olivetti, N., Pozzato, G.L.: Analytic Tableaux Calculi for KLM Logics of Nonmonotonic Reasoning. ACM ToCL 10(3) (2009)
9. Friedman, N., Halpern, J.Y.: Plausibility measures and default reasoning. Journal of the ACM 48(4), 648–685 (2001)
10. Giordano, L., Gliozzi, V., Olivetti, N., Pozzato, G.L.: Preferential vs Rational Description Logics: which one for Reasoning About Typicality?. To appear in Proceedings of ECAI 2010 (2010)

On Strong Normalization of the Calculus of Constructions with Type-Based Termination

Benjamin Grégoire and Jorge Luis Sacchini

INRIA Sophia Antipolis - Méditerranée, France
{Benjamin.Gregoire,Jorge-Luis.Sacchini}@inria.fr

Abstract. Termination of recursive functions is an important property in proof assistants based on dependent type theories; it implies consistency and decidability of type checking. Type-based termination is a mechanism for ensuring termination that uses types annotated with size information to check that recursive calls are performed on smaller arguments. Our long-term goal is to extend the Calculus of Inductive Constructions with a type-based termination mechanism and prove its logical consistency. In this paper, we present an extension of the Calculus of Constructions (including universes and impredicativity) with sized natural numbers, and prove strong normalization and logical consistency. Moreover, the proof can be easily adapted to include other inductive types.

1 Introduction

Termination of recursive functions is an important property in proof assistants based on dependent type theory; it implies consistency of the logic, and decidability of type checking. In current implementations, it is common to use syntactic criteria (called guard predicates) to ensure termination. Guard predicates are applied to the body of recursive functions to check that recursive calls are performed on structurally smaller arguments. However, these criteria are often difficult to understand and implement.

An alternative approach is *type-based termination*. The basic idea is the use of sized types, i.e., types decorated with size information. Termination is ensured by typing constraints, restricting recursive calls to smaller arguments. Compared to guard predicates, type-based termination provides a simple yet expressive mechanism for ensuring termination.

In previous work by the first author [4], the Calculus of Inductive Constructions (CIC) was extended with a type-based termination mechanism. The obtained system, called $\mathrm{CIC}\widehat{\ }$, has many desirable metatheoretical properties, including complete size inference. However, the logical consistency of $\mathrm{CIC}\widehat{\ }$ is derived from a conjecture stating strong normalization of well-typed terms.

Our long-term goal is to define a type-based termination mechanism for CIC that is proved consistent. This paper is a step in that direction. We present a simplified version of $\mathrm{CIC}\widehat{\ }$, called $\mathrm{CIC}\widehat{\ }_{-}$ (Sect. 3).

C. Fermüller and A. Voronkov (Eds.): LPAR-17, LNCS 6397, pp. 333–347, 2010.

Our main contribution is a proof of strong normalization (SN) and logical consistency for $\mathrm{CIC}\widehat{\_}$ restricted to one inductive type, namely natural numbers (Sect. 4). The interpretation of natural numbers is done in a generic way, and can be extended to other inductive types.

For lack of space, most of the proofs are omitted. The interested reader can find them in the long version of this paper [7].

2 A Primer on Type-Based Termination

Before giving the details of $\mathrm{CIC}\widehat{\_}$, this section introduces briefly the main ideas of sized types and type-based termination. Consider the type of natural numbers, defined by

$$\mathsf{nat} : \mathsf{Type} := \mathsf{O} : \mathsf{nat} \mid \mathsf{S} : \mathsf{nat} \to \mathsf{nat} \ .$$

With sized types, this defines a family of types of the form nat^s, where s is a size (or stage) expression. Size information is used to type recursive functions, as shown in the following (simplified) typing rule for fixpoint construction:

$$\frac{\Gamma(f : \mathsf{nat}^\imath \to U) \vdash M : \mathsf{nat}^{\widehat{\imath}} \to U\,[\imath := \widehat{\imath}]}{\Gamma \vdash (\mathsf{fix}\ f : \mathsf{nat} \to U := M) : \mathsf{nat}^s \to U\,[\imath := s]}$$

where $\imath$ is a stage variable, and $\widehat{\cdot}$ is the successor function on stages. Intuitively, $\mathsf{nat}^\imath$ and $\mathsf{nat}^{\widehat{\imath}}$ denote the type of natural numbers whose size is smaller than $\imath$ and $\imath + 1$, respectively. This intuition is reflected in the subtyping rule, stating that $\mathsf{nat}^\imath \leq \mathsf{nat}^{\widehat{\imath}} \leq \mathsf{nat}^\infty$, where nat^∞ denotes the usual type of natural numbers.

In the typing rule above, the body of the fixpoint, M, is a function that takes an argument of type $\mathsf{nat}^{\widehat{\imath}}$. The recursive calls to f in M are only allowed on terms of type $\mathsf{nat}^\imath$, that is, smaller than the size of the argument. This ensures that recursion terminates. Note that the variable $\imath$ can appear (positively) in U, which allows to write size-preserving functions. A typical example is the subtraction of natural numbers, which has type $\mathsf{nat}^s \to \mathsf{nat}^\infty \to \mathsf{nat}^s$, for any s. We can then write the division of natural numbers as[1]:

$$\begin{array}{l}
\mathsf{fix\ div} : \mathsf{nat} \to \mathsf{nat} \to \mathsf{nat} := \\
\quad \lambda\, m\ n : \mathsf{nat}.\ \mathsf{case}\ m_{\mathsf{nat}(\widehat{\imath})}\ \mathsf{of} \\
\qquad\qquad\qquad \mid \mathsf{O} \Rightarrow \mathsf{O}_{\mathsf{nat}(\widehat{\imath})} \\
\qquad\qquad\qquad \mid \mathsf{S}\ m'_{\mathsf{nat}(\imath)} \Rightarrow S\ (\mathsf{div}\ (\mathsf{minus}\ m'\ n)_{\mathsf{nat}(\imath)}\ n)_{\mathsf{nat}(\imath)}
\end{array}$$

The type annotations are given for clarification only, and are not written in the actual syntax. Since minus has type $\mathsf{nat}^s \to \mathsf{nat}^\infty \to \mathsf{nat}^s$, the recursive call in div is well-typed. The function div also has type $\mathsf{nat}^s \to \mathsf{nat}^\infty \to \mathsf{nat}^s$.

Note in the case expression that m has type $\mathsf{nat}^{\widehat{\imath}}$, while the recursive argument m' has a smaller type $\mathsf{nat}^\imath$. This mechanism ensures that we can make recursive calls on the recursive arguments of an inductive type. However, it is more powerful than guard predicates, thanks to the possibility of typing size-preserving

[1] div $m\ n$ computes $\left\lceil \frac{m}{n+1} \right\rceil$.

functions. For example, extending the system with sized lists, typical functions can be given more precise types:

$$\mathsf{map} : \Pi(A\ B : \mathsf{Type}).(A \to B) \to \mathsf{list}^{\imath}\ A \to \mathsf{list}^{\imath}\ B$$
$$\mathsf{filter} : \Pi(A : \mathsf{Type}).(A \to \mathsf{bool}) \to \mathsf{list}^{\imath}\ A \to \mathsf{list}^{\imath}\ A \times \mathsf{list}^{\imath}\ A$$

These functions allow to type programs that are not structurally recursive such as quicksort:

$$\begin{array}{l} \mathsf{fix}\ \mathsf{qsort} : \mathsf{list}\, A \to \mathsf{list}\, A := \\ \lambda l : \mathsf{list}\, A.\ \mathsf{case}\ l_{\mathsf{list}(\widehat{\imath})}\ \text{of} \\ \qquad\qquad \mid \mathsf{nil} \Rightarrow \mathsf{nil} \\ \qquad\qquad \mid \mathsf{cons}\ h\ t_{\mathsf{list}(\imath)} \Rightarrow \mathsf{let}\ (s, g) = \mathsf{filter}\ (<h)\ t_{\mathsf{list}(\imath)}\ \mathsf{in} \\ \qquad\qquad\qquad\qquad\qquad \mathsf{append}\ (\mathsf{qsort}\ s_{\mathsf{list}(\imath)})\ (\mathsf{cons}\ h\ (\mathsf{qsort}\ g_{\mathsf{list}(\imath)})) \end{array}$$

Note that the precise typing of filter allows the recursive calls in the above definition. However, in this case, qsort has type $\mathsf{list}^{\infty} A \to \mathsf{list}^{\infty} A$. For further examples and references, we refer the reader to [4].

3 System $\mathrm{CIC}\widehat{_{-}}$

$\mathrm{CIC}\widehat{_{-}}$ is an extension of CIC with a type-based termination mechanism. In this section we introduce the syntax and typing rules.

In order to treat impredicativity in the proof of SN, terms carry more type annotations in the case of abstraction and application [2,11]. However, the system we intend to use has a more traditional presentation. In the traditional presentation, abstractions have the form $\lambda x : T^{\circ}.M$ and applications have the form $M\,N$. We give here the annotated presentation we use in the proof of SN. The reduction rules and typing rules are adapted to the traditional presentation in the obvious way. Note that as a consequence of SN, we can prove the equivalence between both presentations [7].

Syntax. We consider a predicative hierarchy of sorts Type_i, for $i \in \mathbb{N}$, and an impredicative sort Prop. The set of sorts is denoted $\mathcal{U}$. We assume a denumerable set $\mathcal{X}$ of term variables. We use u to denote sorts, and f, x, y to denote term variables. Inductive types are annotated with stage expressions.

Definition 1 (Stages). *The syntax of stages is given by the following grammar, where $\mathcal{X}_{\mathcal{S}}$ denotes a denumerable set of stage variables.*

$$\mathcal{S} ::= \mathcal{X}_{\mathcal{S}} \mid \widehat{\mathcal{S}} \mid \infty$$

We use $\imath$, $\jmath$ to denote stage variables, and s, r to denote stages. The base of a stage expression is defined by $\lfloor \imath \rfloor = \imath$ and $\lfloor \widehat{s} \rfloor = \lfloor s \rfloor$ (the base of a stage containing ∞ is not defined).

The syntax features three classes of terms, whose difference lies in the type of annotations that inductive types carry. (This helps to ensure subject reduction and efficient type inference [4].) Bare terms carry no annotation. Position terms carry either no annotation, or a $\star$, which is used to indicate recursive positions in fixpoint functions. Finally, sized terms carry a stage expression.

Definition 2 (Terms). *The generic set of terms over the set a is defined by the grammar:*

$$\begin{array}{rl} \mathcal{T}[a] ::= & \mathcal{X} \mid \mathcal{U} \mid \lambda_{\mathcal{X}:\mathcal{T}^\circ.\mathcal{T}^\circ}\mathcal{T}[a] \mid \mathsf{app}_{\mathcal{X}:\mathcal{T}^\circ.\mathcal{T}^\circ}(\mathcal{T}[a],\mathcal{T}[a]) \mid \Pi\mathcal{X}:\mathcal{T}[a].\mathcal{T}[a] \\ & \mid \mathsf{nat}^a \mid \mathsf{O} \mid \mathsf{S}(\mathcal{T}[a]) \\ & \mathsf{case}_{\mathcal{T}^\circ}\ \mathcal{X} := \mathcal{T}[a] \text{ of } \mathcal{T}[a],\mathcal{T}[a] \mid \mathsf{fix}\ \mathcal{X}(\mathcal{X} : \mathsf{nat}^\star) : \mathcal{T}^\star := \mathcal{T}[a] \end{array}$$

The set of bare terms, position terms and sized terms are defined by $\mathcal{T}^\circ ::= \mathcal{T}[\epsilon]$, $\mathcal{T}^\star ::= \mathcal{T}[\{\epsilon,\star\}]$, and $\mathcal{T} ::= \mathcal{T}[\mathcal{S}]$, respectively. We use C, F, M, N, P, T, U to denote terms. Bare terms are usually denoted with a superscript $\circ$ and position terms with a superscript $\star$, as in M° and $M^\star$.

To deal with the different classes of terms, we use two erasure functions: the function $|.| : \mathcal{T}^\star \cup \mathcal{T} \to \mathcal{T}^\circ$ removes all annotations from a term; the function $|.|^\imath : \mathcal{T} \to \mathcal{T}^\star$ replaces all stage annotations s with $\star$ if $\lfloor s \rfloor = \imath$, or by ϵ otherwise. Given a term M, we write M^∞ to denote the term M where all size annotations are replaced with ∞, and $\mathrm{SV}(M)$ to denote the set of *stage variables* appearing in M.

Definition 3. *Reduction $\to$ is defined as the compatible closure of β-reduction, ι-reduction and μ-reduction:*

$$\begin{array}{rl} \mathsf{app}_{x:T^\circ.U^\circ}(\lambda_{x:T^\circ.U^\circ}M, N) & \to_\beta M\,[x := N] \\ \mathsf{case}_{T^\circ}\ x := \mathsf{O} \text{ of } N_0, N_1 & \to_\iota N_0 \\ \mathsf{case}_{T^\circ}\ x := \mathsf{S}(M) \text{ of } N_0, N_1 & \to_\iota \mathsf{app}_{y:\mathsf{nat}.T^\circ[x:=S(y)]}(N_1, M) \\ \mathsf{app}_{x:\mathsf{nat}.|U^\star|}(F, C) & \to_\mu \mathsf{app}_{x:\mathsf{nat}.|U^\star|}(M\,[f := F], C) \end{array}$$

where $F \equiv \mathsf{fix}\ f(x : \mathsf{nat}^\star) : U^\star := M$ and C is a term in constructor form (i.e., O or $\mathsf{S}(M)$ for some term M). We write $\leftarrow$, $\to^*$, $\approx$ and $\downarrow$ for the inverse relation, the reflexive transitive closure, the equivalence closure and the associated joinability relation of $\to$, respectively. ($M \downarrow N$ if $M \to^* P$ and $N \to^* P$ for some P.)

The reduction relation defined above, usually called *tight reduction*, is *not* confluent (on pseudoterms). However, is it confluent for well-typed terms (this is a consequence of SN). (Note that the reduction in the traditional presentation is confluent.)

Subtyping. We consider a subtyping relation derived from a partial order on stages.

Definition 4 (Substage). *The* substage relation, $\sqsubseteq\ \subseteq \mathcal{S} \times \mathcal{S}$, *is defined as the reflexive transitive closure of the relation containing $s \sqsubseteq \widehat{s}$ and $s \sqsubseteq \infty$, for all $s \in \mathcal{S}$.*

Definition 5 (Subtyping). *The* subtyping relation, $\leq \subseteq \mathcal{T} \times \mathcal{T}$, *is defined by following rules:*

$$\frac{T \downarrow U}{T \leq U} \qquad \frac{T \to^* \mathsf{nat}^s \quad U \to^* \mathsf{nat}^r \quad s \sqsubseteq r}{T \leq U}$$

$$\frac{T \to^* \Pi x : T_1.T_2 \quad U \to^* \Pi x : U_1.U_2 \quad U_1 \leq T_1 \quad T_2 \leq U_2}{T \leq U}$$

We define a notion of positivity with respect to a stage variable. It is used in the typing rules to restrict the types valid for recursion.

Definition 6. *We say that* $\imath$ is positive in T, *written* $\imath$ pos T, *if for every pair of stages* s, r, *such that* $s \sqsubseteq r$, $T[\imath := s] \leq T[\imath := r]$.

Remark: In the traditional presentation, the subtyping relation is defined in a more standard way, as the reflexive transitive closure of the following rules:

$$\frac{T \approx U}{T \leq U} \qquad \frac{U_1 \leq T_1 \quad T_2 \leq U_2}{\Pi x : T_1.T_2 \leq \Pi x : U_1.U_2} \qquad \frac{s \sqsubseteq r}{\mathsf{nat}^s \leq \mathsf{nat}^r}$$

We cannot use this definition in the annotated presentation, since reduction is not confluent.

Typing. In the typing rules, we restrict the use of size variables appearing in types. Intuitively, we only allow types that reduce to a term of the form

$$\Pi x_1 : T_1.\Pi x_2 : T_2. \ldots \Pi x_n : T_n.T_{n+1}, \qquad (*)$$

where each T_i is of the form (*), or is of the form nat^s, or satisfies $\mathrm{SV}(T_i) = \emptyset$. We call these types "simple". Formally, we define a predicate simple with the following clauses:

$$\frac{\mathrm{SV}(T) = \emptyset}{\mathsf{simple}(T)} \qquad \frac{}{\mathsf{simple}(\mathsf{nat}^s)} \qquad \frac{\mathsf{simple}(T_1) \quad \mathsf{simple}(T_2)}{\mathsf{simple}(\Pi x : T_1.T_2)}$$

Contexts and judgments. A context is a sequence of the form $(x_1 : T_1)(x_2 : T_2) \ldots (x_n : T_n)$, where $x_1, x_2, \ldots, x_n$ are distinct variables and $T_1, T_2, \ldots, T_n$ are sized terms. We use Γ, Δ, Θ to denote contexts and [] to denote the empty context.

We define two typing judgments: $\mathsf{WF}(\Gamma)$ means that context Γ is well formed; $\Gamma \vdash M : T$ means that the term M has type T in Γ. The typing rules are given in Fig. 1. The side conditions in some of the rules ensure that we restrict to simple types. If we remove these side conditions, the resulting system is that of CIC$\widehat{}$. In rule (fix) the condition $\imath \notin \mathrm{SV}(\Gamma, M)$ is therefore redundant, but we keep it to emphasize the difference with CIC$\widehat{}$.

Most of the rules are similar to that of CIC$\widehat{}$, with exception of the added type annotations. Note in rules (zero) and (succ) that constructors have a successor stage as type. In rule (case), as we mentioned in Sect. 2, the argument has type nat with a successor stage, allowing the recursive arguments to have smaller size. Note that, because of subtyping, any term of type nat can be given a successor size. In rule (fix) we introduce a fresh size variable for recursion. Not every type is valid for recursion, since it might lead to inconsistencies [1]. In our case, we require the size variable used for recursion to appear positively in the return type. The body, M, has a product type (function) with domain $\mathsf{nat}^{\hat{\imath}}$, while recursive calls to f can only be performed on terms of type $\mathsf{nat}^{\imath}$.

Simple metatheory. Usual metatheoretic results such as weakening, substitution and subject reduction can be proved for $\mathrm{CIC}\hat{}_{-}$ in the same way as for $\mathrm{CIC}\hat{}$. These properties are stated in Fig. 2.

4 Strong Normalization

In this section we prove the main results of the paper: strong normalization of $\mathrm{CIC}\hat{}_{-}$, and logical consistency (Theorem 1). The proof is based on Λ-sets as introduced by Altenkirch in his PhD thesis [2], and later used by Melliès and Werner [11] to prove strong normalization for Pure Type Systems.

A Λ-set X is a pair $(X_\circ, \models)$, where $X_\circ$ is a set, and $\models \subseteq \mathrm{SN} \times X_\circ$ is a realizability relation[2] (SN denotes the set of strongly normalizing terms). Intuitively, we define a set-theoretical interpretation (products are interpreted by function spaces, abstractions by functions and applications by function application), denoted $[\cdot]$, corresponding to the set part of a Λ-set.

We prove that the interpretation is sound: if $\Gamma \vdash M : T$, then $[M] \in [T]$ (Lemma 4). We can then prove that every term realizes its interpretation (Lemma 5), i.e. $M \models [M]$. Strong normalization (Corollary 1) follows from the fact that every realizers is strongly normalizing by definition.

In the case of $\mathrm{CIC}\hat{}_{-}$, the interpretation given above does not take size information into account. We therefore define a second (relational) interpretation to show that terms respect the size information given in the type (Sect. 4.3).

4.1 Preliminary Definitions

In this section we give the concepts necessary to define the interpretation of terms. Namely, saturated sets, Λ-sets, and inaccessible cardinals.

Saturated sets. We define saturated sets in terms of elimination contexts:

$$\begin{aligned} E[] ::= {} & [] \mid \mathsf{app}_{\mathcal{X}:\mathcal{T}^\circ.\mathcal{T}^\circ}(E[], \mathcal{T}) \mid \mathsf{case}_{\mathcal{T}^\circ}\ \mathcal{X} := E[]\ \mathsf{of}\ \mathcal{T}, \mathcal{T} \\ & \mid \mathsf{app}_{\mathcal{X}:\mathcal{T}^\circ.\mathcal{T}^\circ}(\mathsf{fix}\ \mathcal{X}(\mathcal{X} : \mathsf{nat}^\star) : \mathcal{T}^\star := \mathcal{T}, E[]) \end{aligned}$$

A term is *atomic* if it is of the form $E[x]$. We denote the set of atomic terms with AT, and the set of strongly normalizing terms with SN. Weak-head reduction is defined as $E[M] \rightarrow_{\mathrm{wh}} E[N]$ iff $M \rightarrow_{\beta\iota\mu} N$.

[2] Actually, for technical reasons, our definition is slightly different.

$$\text{(empty)}\quad \frac{}{\mathsf{WF}([])} \qquad \text{(cons)}\quad \frac{\mathsf{WF}(\Gamma) \qquad \Gamma \vdash T : u}{\mathsf{WF}(\Gamma(x:T))}\ \mathsf{simple}(T)$$

$$\text{(var)}\quad \frac{\mathsf{WF}(\Gamma) \qquad \Gamma(x) = T}{\Gamma \vdash x : T}$$

$$\text{(type)}\quad \frac{\mathsf{WF}(\Gamma)}{\Gamma \vdash \mathsf{Type}_i : \mathsf{Type}_{i+1}} \qquad \text{(prop)}\quad \frac{\mathsf{WF}(\Gamma)}{\Gamma \vdash \mathsf{Prop} : \mathsf{Type}_0}$$

$$(\Pi\text{-type})\quad \frac{\Gamma \vdash T : u \qquad \Gamma(x:T) \vdash U : \mathsf{Type}_j}{\Gamma \vdash \Pi x : T.U : \max(u, \mathsf{Type}_j)}$$

$$(\Pi\text{-prop})\quad \frac{\Gamma \vdash T : u \qquad \Gamma(x:T) \vdash U : \mathsf{Prop}}{\Gamma \vdash \Pi x : T.U : \mathsf{Prop}}$$

$$\text{(abs)}\quad \frac{\Gamma(x:T) \vdash M : U}{\Gamma \vdash \lambda_{x:|T|.|U|} M : \Pi x : T.U}\ \mathrm{SV}(M) = \emptyset$$

$$\text{(app)}\quad \frac{\Gamma \vdash M : \Pi x : T.U \qquad \Gamma \vdash N : T}{\Gamma \vdash \mathsf{app}_{x:|T|.|U|}(M, N) : U\,[x := N]}\ \mathrm{SV}(N) = \emptyset$$

$$\text{(nat)}\quad \frac{\mathsf{WF}(\Gamma)}{\Gamma \vdash \mathsf{nat}^s : \mathsf{Type}_0} \qquad \text{(zero)}\quad \frac{\mathsf{WF}(\Gamma)}{\Gamma \vdash \mathsf{O} : \mathsf{nat}^{\widehat{s}}} \qquad \text{(succ)}\quad \frac{\Gamma \vdash M : \mathsf{nat}^s}{\Gamma \vdash \mathsf{S}(M) : \mathsf{nat}^{\widehat{s}}}$$

$$\text{(case)}\quad \frac{\begin{array}{cc}\Gamma \vdash M : \mathsf{nat}^{\widehat{s}} & \Gamma(x : \mathsf{nat}^{\widehat{s}}) \vdash P : u \\ \Gamma \vdash N_0 : P\,[x := \mathsf{O}] & \Gamma \vdash N_1 : \Pi y : \mathsf{nat}^s.P\,[x := \mathsf{S}(y)]\end{array}}{\Gamma \vdash \mathsf{case}_{|P|}\ x := M\ \mathsf{of}\ N_0, N_1 : P\,[x := M]}\ \mathrm{SV}(M) = \emptyset$$

$$\text{(fix)}\quad \frac{\begin{array}{ccc}T \equiv \Pi(x : \mathsf{nat}^{\imath}).U & \imath\ \mathsf{pos}\ U & \imath \notin \mathrm{SV}(\Gamma, M) \\ \Gamma \vdash T : u & \Gamma(f : T) \vdash M : T\,[\imath := \widehat{\imath}] & \end{array}}{\Gamma \vdash \mathsf{fix}\ f(x : \mathsf{nat}^{\star}) : |U|^{\imath} := M : T\,[\imath := s]}\ \mathrm{SV}(M) = \emptyset$$

$$\text{(conv)}\quad \frac{\Gamma \vdash M : T \qquad \Gamma \vdash U : u \qquad T \leq U}{\Gamma \vdash M : U}\ \mathsf{simple}(U)$$

Fig. 1. Typing rules of $\mathrm{CIC}^{\widehat{}}_{-}$

Weakening: $\Gamma \vdash M : T \wedge \mathsf{WF}(\Gamma\Delta) \Rightarrow \Gamma\Delta \vdash M : T$

Substitution: $\left.\begin{array}{r}\Gamma(x:T)\Delta \vdash M : U \\ \Gamma \vdash N : T \\ \mathrm{SV}(N) = \emptyset\end{array}\right\} \Rightarrow \Gamma\Delta\,[x := N] \vdash M\,[x := N] : U\,[x := N]$

Stage Substitution: $\Gamma \vdash M : T \Rightarrow \Gamma\,[\imath := s] \vdash M\,[\imath := s] : T\,[\imath := s]$

Subject Reduction: $\Gamma \vdash M : T \wedge M \to M' \Rightarrow \Gamma \vdash M' : T$

Type validity: $\Gamma \vdash M : T \Rightarrow \Gamma \vdash T : u \wedge \mathsf{simple}(\mathrm{T})$

Fig. 2. Simple metatheory of $\mathrm{CIC}^{\widehat{}}_{-}$

Definition 7 (Saturated set). *A set of terms $X \subseteq \mathrm{SN}$ is saturated iff it satisfies the following conditions:*

(S1) $\mathrm{AT} \cap \mathrm{SN} \subseteq X$*;*
(S2) if $M \in \mathrm{SN}$ and $M \to_{\mathrm{wh}} M'$ and $M' \in X$, then $M \in X$.

Λ-sets. As mentioned above, we use Λ-sets [2,11] in the proof. However, our definition is slightly different, as explained below.

Definition 8 (Λ-set). *A Λ-set is a triple $X = (X_\circ, \models_X, \bot_X)$ where $X_\circ$ is a non-empty set, witnessed by $\bot_X \in X_\circ$, and $\models_X \subseteq \mathcal{T} \times X_\circ$.*

$X_\circ$ is the *carrier-set* and the elements of $X_\circ$ are called the *carriers* of X. The terms M such that $M \models_X \alpha$ for some $\alpha \in X_\circ$ are called the *realizers* of α. The element $\bot_X$ is called the *atomic element* of X. We write $\alpha \in X$ for $\alpha \in X_\circ$. A Λ-set X is included in a Λ-set Y, written $X \subseteq Y$, if $X_\circ \subseteq Y_\circ$, $\models_X \subseteq \models_Y$, and $\bot_X = \bot_Y$.

Definition 9 (Saturated Λ-set). *A Λ-set X is said to be* saturated *if*

1. *every realizer is strongly normalizable;*
2. *the atomic element $\bot_X$ is realized by any atomic strongly normalizable term;*
3. *for every $\alpha \in X_\circ$, if $N \models_X \alpha$, and $M \to_{\mathrm{wh}} N$ with $M \in \mathrm{SN}$, then $M \models_X \alpha$ (i.e., the set of realizers is closed under weak-head expansion).*

The difference between the definition in [2,11] and ours is that the atomic element of a Λ-set is explicit in the definition. The use of the atomic element will be evident in the definition of the interpretation of terms. However, the difference in the definition is not essential in our proof.

We define some operations on Λ-sets.

Definition 10 (Product). *Let X be a Λ-set and $\{Y_\alpha\}_{\alpha \in X_\circ}$ a $X_\circ$-indexed family of Λ-sets. We define the Λ-set $\Pi(X,Y)$ by:*

- $\Pi(X,Y)_\circ = \{f \in X_\circ \to \bigcup_{\alpha \in X_\circ} (Y_\alpha)_\circ : \forall \alpha \in X_\circ . f(\alpha) \in (Y_\alpha)_\circ\}$;
- $M \models_{\Pi(X,Y)} f \iff \forall \alpha \in X_\circ.\ T^\circ, U^\circ \in \mathrm{SN}.$
  $N \models_X \alpha \Rightarrow \mathsf{app}_{x:T^\circ.U^\circ}(M,N) \models_{Y_\alpha} f(\alpha)$;
- $\bot_{\Pi(X,Y)} = \alpha \in X_\circ \mapsto \bot_{Y_\alpha}$.

Lemma 1. *If X and every $\{Y_\alpha\}_{\alpha \in X_\circ}$ are saturated Λ-sets, so is $\Pi(X,Y)$.*

Definition 11 (Cartesian product). *Let X, Y be Λ-sets. We define the Λ-set $X \times Y$ by: $(X \times Y)_\circ = X_\circ \times Y_\circ$; $M \models_{X \times Y} (\alpha, \beta) \iff M \models_X \alpha \wedge M \models_Y \beta$; and $\bot_{X \times Y} = (\bot_X, \bot_Y)$.*

We write X^2 for $X \times X$.

Lemma 2. *If X and Y are saturated Λ-sets, so is $X \times Y$.*

Definition 12 (Λ-iso). *Let X and Y be Λ-sets. A Λ-iso f from X to Y is a one-to-one function $f : X_\circ \to Y_\circ$ such that $M \models_X \alpha \iff M \models_Y f(\alpha)$, and $f(\bot_X) = \bot_Y$.*

Inaccessible cardinals. We assume an increasing sequence of inaccessible cardinals $\{\lambda_i\}_{i \in \mathbb{N}}$. Let V_α be the cumulative hierarchy of sets. We define $\mathcal{U}_i$ to be the set of saturated Λ-set whose carrier-set are in V_{λ_i}. The set $\mathcal{U}_i$ can be viewed as a Λ-set $(\mathcal{U}_i, \mathrm{SN} \times \mathcal{U}_i, \{\emptyset\})$[3]. Following [10], we interpret the predicative sorts using large universes.

4.2 The Interpretation

Stages. Stages are interpreted by ordinals. We use $\mathfrak{a}$, $\mathfrak{b}$, ... to denote ordinals. Since we have only natural numbers as a sized type, we can safely interpret stages with the smallest infinite ordinal, ω. If we include higher-order sized types (such as well-founded trees), we need to interpret stages using higher ordinals.

Definition 13 (Stage interpretation). *A stage assignment π is a function from $\mathcal{X}_\mathcal{S}$ to ω. Given a stage assignment π, the interpretation of a stage s under π, written $(\!|s|\!)_\pi$, is defined by:*

$$(\!|\imath|\!)_\pi = \pi(\imath), \qquad (\!|\infty|\!)_\pi = \omega, \qquad (\!|\hat{s}|\!)_\pi = (\!|s|\!)_\pi \mathbin{\hat{+}} 1$$

where $\mathfrak{a} \mathbin{\hat{+}} 1 = \mathfrak{a} + 1$ if $\mathfrak{a} < \omega$, and $\omega \mathbin{\hat{+}} 1 = \omega$.

We use ∞ to denote the stage assignment such that $\infty(\imath) = \omega$ for all $\imath$.

Inductive types. Inductive types are interpreted as the least fixed point of a monotone operator. For our case, we define a function $\mathcal{F}_\mathcal{N}$, such that if X is a Λ-set, $\mathcal{F}_\mathcal{N}(X)$ is also a Λ-set defined by:

- $\mathcal{F}_\mathcal{N}(X)_\circ = \{\emptyset\} \cup \{(0, \emptyset)\} \cup \{(1, \alpha) : \alpha \in X_\circ\}$;
- $M \models_{\mathcal{F}_\mathcal{N}(X)} \alpha$, with $M \in \mathrm{SN}$, iff one the following conditions holds:
  - $\alpha = \emptyset$ and $M \to_{\mathrm{wh}}{}^* N \in \mathrm{AT}$;
  - $\alpha = (0, \emptyset)$ and $M \to_{\mathrm{wh}}{}^* \mathsf{O}$; or
  - $\alpha = (1, \alpha')$ and $M \to_{\mathrm{wh}}{}^* \mathsf{S}(M')$ with $M' \models_X \alpha'$.
- $\bot_{\mathcal{F}_\mathcal{N}(X)} = \emptyset$,

It is clear that if X is a saturated Λ-set, then $\mathcal{F}_\mathcal{N}(X)$ is also a saturated Λ-set. Note that $\mathcal{F}_\mathcal{N}$ is monotone, in the sense that if $X \subseteq Y$, then $\mathcal{F}_\mathcal{N}(X) \subseteq \mathcal{F}_\mathcal{N}(Y)$. We write $\mathcal{F}_\mathcal{N}^k$ to mean function $\mathcal{F}_\mathcal{N}$ iterated k times.

Consider the Λ-set $\bot = (\{\emptyset\}, \mathrm{SN} \cap \mathrm{AT} \times \{\emptyset\}, \emptyset)$. A fixpoint of $\mathcal{F}_\mathcal{N}(X)$ is reached by iterating ω times, starting from $\bot$. Let $\mathcal{N} = \mathcal{F}_\mathcal{N}^\omega(\bot)$.

Impredicativity. Following [11], we interpret the impredicative universe as the set of degenerated Λ-sets.

Definition 14. *A Λ-set X is* degenerated, *if the carrier-set $X_\circ$ is a singleton $\{A\}$, where A is a saturated set, $M \models_X A$ iff $M \in A$, and $\bot_X = A$.*

We write $\overline{A}$ for the degenerated Λ-set corresponding to a saturated set A.

---

3 We choose $\{\emptyset\}$ as atomic element, but any element of $\mathcal{U}_i$ will do.

A proposition, i.e. a term T of type Prop, is represented by a degenerated Λ-set, whose only carrier represents a (possible) canonical proof.

Given a Λ-set X and a function Y such that for each $\alpha \in X_\circ$, Y_α is a degenerated Λ-set (with carrier y_α), the carrier-set of $\Pi(X,Y)$ is a singleton (the only element being $\alpha \in X_\circ \mapsto y_\alpha$). The canonical representation of $\Pi(X,Y)$ is given by the degenerated Λ-set corresponding to the saturated set

$$\downarrow(X,Y) = \{M \in \mathrm{SN} : N \models_X \alpha \Rightarrow \mathsf{app}_{x:T^\circ.U^\circ}(M,N) \models_{Y_\alpha} y_\alpha\} \ .$$

Note that there is a Λ-iso $p(X,Y) : \Pi(X,Y) \to \overline{\downarrow(X,Y)}$.

In the interpretation, we need to convert between the interpretation of a proof term as an element of $\Pi(X,Y)$ (if it needs to be applied), or as the canonical proof $\downarrow(X,Y)$. For this, we use the isomorphism $p(X,Y)$.

We define the functions $\Pi_{\Gamma\vdash T}$, $\downarrow_{\Gamma\vdash T}$, $\uparrow_{\Gamma\vdash T}$ that give the interpretation of products, abstractions, and applications (respectively), depending if the type T is a proposition or not. In the case of proposition, these functions convert between $\Pi(X,Y)$ and the canonical representation $\downarrow(X,Y)$. Otherwise, there is no conversion needed. Their definition is given by:

- if $\Gamma^\infty \vdash T^\infty : \mathsf{Prop}$, then $\Pi_{\Gamma\vdash T}(X,Y) = \overline{\downarrow(X,Y)}$, $\downarrow_{\Gamma\vdash T} (X,Y) = p(X,Y)$, and $\uparrow_{\Gamma\vdash T} (X,Y) = p^{-1}(X,Y)$;
- otherwise, $\Pi_{\Gamma\vdash T}(X,Y) = \Pi(X,Y)$, $\downarrow_{\Gamma\vdash T} (X,Y) = \mathrm{id}_{\Pi(X,Y)}$, and $\uparrow_{\Gamma\vdash T} (X,Y) = \mathrm{id}_{\Pi(X,Y)}$.

Terms and contexts. The interpretation of an erased context Γ is denoted $[\Gamma]$ (an erased context is a context formed by erased terms). Assume a stage assignment π. Given an erased context Γ, a term M and a sequence of values γ, the interpretation of M under Γ is denoted $[\Gamma \vdash M]^\pi_\gamma$.

We define the interpretation by induction on the structure of terms and contexts. In the case of fixpoint construction we use Hilbert's choice operator.

Definition 15 (Interpretation of terms and contexts)

$$
\begin{aligned}
[[]] &= \{\emptyset\}\\
[\Gamma(x:T)] &= \{(\gamma,\alpha) : \gamma \in [\Gamma] \wedge \alpha \in [\Gamma \vdash T^\infty]^\infty_\gamma\}\\
[\Gamma \vdash \mathsf{Type}_i]^\pi_\gamma &= \mathcal{U}_i\\
[\Gamma \vdash \mathsf{Prop}]^\pi_\gamma &= \{X : X \textit{ is a degenerated } \Lambda\textit{-set}\}\\
[\Gamma \vdash x]^\pi_\gamma &= \gamma(x)\\
[\Gamma \vdash \Pi x : T.U]^\pi_\gamma &= \Pi_{\Gamma\vdash \Pi x:T.U}([\Gamma \vdash T]^\pi_\gamma, [\Gamma(x:T) \vdash U]^\pi_{\gamma,\_})\\
[\Gamma \vdash \lambda_{x:T^\circ.U^\circ} M]^\pi_\gamma &= \downarrow_{\Gamma\vdash \Pi x:T^\circ.U^\circ}([\Gamma(x:T^\infty) \vdash M]^\pi_{\gamma,\_})\\
[\Gamma \vdash \mathsf{app}_{x:T^\circ.U^\circ}(M,N)]^\pi_\gamma &= \uparrow_{\Gamma\vdash \Pi x:T^\circ.U^\circ}([\Gamma \vdash M]^\pi_\gamma)([\Gamma \vdash N]^\pi_\gamma)\\
[\Gamma \vdash \mathsf{nat}^s]^\pi_\gamma &= \mathcal{F}_{\mathcal{N}}^{(\!|s|\!)_\pi}(\bot)\\
[\Gamma \vdash \mathsf{O}]^\pi_\gamma &= (0,\emptyset)\\
[\Gamma \vdash \mathsf{S}(N)]^\pi_\gamma &= (1,[\Gamma \vdash N]^\pi_\gamma)
\end{aligned}
$$

$$[\Gamma \vdash \mathsf{case}_{P^\circ}\ x := M \ \mathsf{of}\ N_0, N_1]^\pi_\gamma = \begin{cases} \bot_{[\Gamma(x\,:\,\mathsf{nat})\,\vdash\, P^\infty]^\pi_{\gamma,\bot}} & \textit{if } [\Gamma \vdash M]^\pi_\gamma = \emptyset; \\ [\Gamma \vdash N_0]^\pi_\gamma & \textit{if } [\Gamma \vdash M]^\pi_\gamma = (0,\emptyset); \\ \uparrow_{\Gamma \vdash T}([\Gamma \vdash N_1]^\pi_\gamma)(\alpha) & \textit{if } [\Gamma \vdash M]^\pi_\gamma = (1,\alpha) \end{cases}$$

$$\textit{where } T \equiv \Pi y : \mathsf{nat}.P^\circ\,[x := S(y)]$$

$$[\Gamma \vdash \mathsf{fix}\ f(x : \mathsf{nat}^\star) : U^\star := M]^\pi_\gamma = \epsilon(F, P)$$

where $F \in [\Gamma \vdash \Pi x : \mathsf{nat}^\infty.U^\infty]^\pi_\gamma$*,* P *is the conjunction of the following properties:*

$$\uparrow(F)\emptyset = \bot_{[\Gamma(x\,:\,\mathsf{nat})\,\vdash\, U^\infty]^\pi_{\gamma,\emptyset}}; \tag{1}$$

$$\uparrow(F)(0,\emptyset) = \uparrow([\Gamma(f : |T|) \vdash M]^\pi_{\gamma,F})(0,\emptyset); \tag{2}$$

$$\uparrow(F)(1,\alpha) = \uparrow([\Gamma(f : |T|) \vdash M]^\pi_{\gamma,F})(1,\alpha), \textit{for all } (1,\alpha) \in \mathcal{N} \tag{3}$$

and we write $|T|$ *for* $\Pi x : \mathsf{nat}.|U|$ *and* $\uparrow$ *for* $\uparrow_{\Gamma \vdash |T|}$.

We write $[\Gamma(x : T) \vdash M]^\pi_{\gamma,\_}$ *as a short hand for*

$$\alpha \in [\Gamma \vdash T]^\pi_\gamma \mapsto [\Gamma(x : |T|) \vdash M]^\pi_{\gamma,\alpha}\ .$$

The conditions imposed on the interpretation of fixpoint construction ensure the stability under μ-reductions. In the main soundness theorem, we prove that the typing rules for fixpoint ensure the existence of a unique function F satisfying the above conditions.

4.3 Interpretation of Simple Types

We define a second (relational) interpretation for simple types. The intention of this second interpretation is to cope with the lack of size annotations in types. Consider the following derivation:

$$\frac{\Gamma(x : \mathsf{nat}^s) \vdash M : \mathsf{nat}^r}{\Gamma \vdash \lambda x : \mathsf{nat}.M : \mathsf{nat}^s \to \mathsf{nat}^r}$$

Note that s and r above could be any size expression. But this size information is not present in the term $\lambda x : \mathsf{nat}.M$. The interpretation of this term is a function in the set $\mathbb{N} \to \mathbb{N}$, specifically $\alpha \in \mathbb{N} \mapsto [M]_\alpha$. To show that the term respects the sizes s and r, we use the relational interpretation of the type. In the case of $\mathsf{nat}^s \to \mathsf{nat}^r$, the relational interpretation, denoted $[\![\cdot]\!]$, is

$$[\![\mathsf{nat}^s \to \mathsf{nat}^r]\!] = \{(f_1, f_2) \in \mathbb{N} \to \mathbb{N} : \alpha < [s] \Rightarrow f_1\alpha = f_2\alpha < [r]\}$$

Then, the interpretation satisfies $([\lambda x : \mathsf{nat}.M], [\lambda x : \mathsf{nat}.M]) \in [\![\mathsf{nat}^s \to \mathsf{nat}^r]\!]$. The relational interpretation can be extended to simple types. Intuitively, the soundness judgment says that if $\Gamma \vdash M : T$, then $([M], [M]) \in [\![T]\!]$.

The relational interpretation also satisfies the contravariance rule. Consider a stage $s' \sqsubseteq s$; the relational interpretation of $\mathsf{nat}^{s'} \to \mathsf{nat}^r$ gives

$$[\![\mathsf{nat}^{s'} \to \mathsf{nat}^r]\!] = \{(f_1, f_2) \in \mathbb{N} \to \mathbb{N} : \alpha < [s'] \Rightarrow f_1\alpha = f_2\alpha < [r]\}$$

Since $[s'] \leq [s]$, we have $[\![\mathsf{nat}^s \to \mathsf{nat}^r]\!] \subseteq [\![\mathsf{nat}^{s'} \to \mathsf{nat}^r]\!]$.

Definition. Let T be a simple type such that $[\Gamma \vdash T^\infty]^\pi_{\gamma_1}$, $[\Gamma \vdash T^\infty]^\pi_{\gamma_2}$, $[\Gamma \vdash T]^\pi_{\gamma_1}$, and $[\Gamma \vdash T]^\pi_{\gamma_2}$ are Λ-sets and that $[\Gamma \vdash T]^\pi_{\gamma_1} = [\Gamma \vdash T]^\pi_{\gamma_2}$. The relational interpretation of T, denoted $[\![\Gamma \vdash T]\!]^\pi_{\gamma_1,\gamma_2}$, is a Λ-set with a carrier-set included in

$$[\Gamma \vdash T^\infty]^\pi_{\gamma_1} \times [\Gamma \vdash T^\infty]^\pi_{\gamma_2} \ .$$

It is defined as follows: if $\Gamma^\infty \vdash T^\infty : \mathsf{Prop}$, then

$$[\![\Gamma \vdash T]\!]^\pi_{\gamma_1,\gamma_2} = [\Gamma \vdash T]^\pi_{\gamma_1} \times [\Gamma \vdash T]^\pi_{\gamma_2};$$

otherwise, it is defined by induction on the structure of T:

- if $T \equiv \Pi x : T_1.T_2$ and $\mathsf{simple}(T_1)$ and $\mathsf{simple}(T_2)$. Assume $[\![\Gamma \vdash T_1]\!]^\pi_{\gamma_1,\gamma_2}$ is a defined Λ-set (denoted by $[\![T_1]\!]$), and for every $(\alpha_1,\alpha_2) \in [\![T_1]\!]$, $[\![\Gamma(x : |T_1|) \vdash T_2]\!]^\pi_{(\gamma_1,\alpha_1),(\gamma_2,\alpha_2)}$ is a defined Λ-set (denoted by $[\![T_2]\!](\alpha_1,\alpha_2)$).
  We define $[\![\Gamma \vdash T]\!]^\pi_{\gamma_1,\gamma_2} = (X, \models, \bot)$, where

$$\begin{aligned} X = \{(f_1,f_2) \in [\Gamma \vdash T^\infty]^\pi_{\gamma_1} \times [\Gamma \vdash T^\infty]^\pi_{\gamma_2} :& \\ (\alpha_1,\alpha_2) \in [\![T_1]\!] \Rightarrow (f_1(\alpha_1), f_2(\alpha_2)) \in [\![T_2]\!](\alpha_1,\alpha_2)\};& \end{aligned} \tag{4}$$

$$\begin{aligned} M \models (f_1,f_2) \iff & N \models_{[\![T_1]\!]} (\alpha_1,\alpha_2) \Rightarrow \\ & \mathsf{app}_{x:T^\circ.U^\circ}(M,N) \models_{[\![T_2]\!](\alpha_1,\alpha_2)} (f_1(\alpha_1), f_2(\alpha_2)) \end{aligned} \tag{5}$$

$$\bot = (\bot_{[\Gamma \vdash T^\infty]^\pi_{\gamma_1}}, \bot_{[\Gamma \vdash T^\infty]^\pi_{\gamma_2}}); \tag{6}$$

- if $T \equiv \mathsf{nat}^s$, we define $[\![\Gamma \vdash \mathsf{nat}^s]\!]^\pi_{\gamma_1,\gamma_2} = ([\Gamma \vdash \mathsf{nat}^s]^\pi_{\gamma_1})^2$;
- otherwise, $\mathrm{SV}(T) = \emptyset$ and we define $[\![\Gamma \vdash T]\!]^\pi_{\gamma_1,\gamma_2} = ([\Gamma \vdash T]^\pi_{\gamma_1})^2$.

Note that, intuitively, α_1 and α_2 are related in $[\![\mathsf{nat}^s]\!]^\pi$ if they are equal, and the "height" of α_1 is less than $(\!|s|\!)_\pi$.

Given a simple type T, such that $\mathrm{SV}(T) = \emptyset$, there might be more than one clause of the above definition that applies. The following lemma states that the definition does not depend on which clause we use.

Lemma 3. *Let T be a term such that $\mathsf{simple}(T)$ and $\mathrm{SV}(T) = \emptyset$. If $[\![\Gamma \vdash T]\!]^\pi_{\gamma_1,\gamma_2}$ is defined, then $[\![\Gamma \vdash T]\!]^\pi_{\gamma_1,\gamma_2} = ([\Gamma \vdash T]^\pi_{\gamma_1})^2$.*

Figure 3 sums up some properties of the interpretation: stability under weakening, substitution (of stages and terms), and reduction, monotonicity of stage substitution, and soundness of subtyping. We use $\doteq$ to denote Kleene equality: $a \doteq b$ iff a and b are both defined and equal, or if both are undefined.

4.4 Soundness

We extend the relational interpretation of types to contexts in the following way:

$$\begin{aligned} [\![[]]\!]^\pi &= \{(\emptyset,\emptyset)\} \\ [\![\Gamma(x:T)]\!]^\pi &= \{((\gamma_1,\alpha_1),(\gamma_2,\alpha_2)) : (\gamma_1,\gamma_2) \in [\![\Gamma]\!]^\pi \wedge (\alpha_1,\alpha_2) \in [\![\Gamma \vdash T]\!]^\pi_{\gamma_1,\gamma_2}\} \end{aligned}$$

Below is the main soundness theorem. In the following, we write $[\Gamma \vdash M]^\pi_{\gamma_1,\gamma_2}$ to mean $([\Gamma \vdash M]^\pi_{\gamma_1}, [\Gamma \vdash M]^\pi_{\gamma_2})$.

Term interpretation

Weakening: $[\Gamma\Delta \vdash M]^{\pi}_{\gamma,\delta} \doteq [\Gamma(z:T)\Delta \vdash M]^{\pi}_{\gamma,\alpha,\delta}$

Substitution: $[\Gamma \vdash M\,[\imath := s]]^{\pi}_{\gamma} \doteq [\Gamma \vdash M]^{\pi(\imath:=(\!|s|\!)_{\pi})}_{\gamma}$

$$[\Gamma, \Delta\,[x := N] \vdash M\,[x := N]]^{\pi}_{\gamma,\delta} \doteq [\Gamma(x:T)\Delta \vdash M]^{\pi}_{\gamma,[\Gamma\,\vdash\,N]^{\pi}_{\gamma},\delta}$$

Reduction: $M \to N \Rightarrow [\Gamma \vdash M]^{\pi}_{\gamma} \doteq [\Gamma \vdash N]^{\pi}_{\gamma}$

Relational interpretation

Weakening: $[\![\Gamma\Delta \vdash U]\!]^{\pi}_{(\gamma_1,\delta_1),(\gamma_2,\delta_2)} \doteq [\![\Gamma(z:T)\Delta \vdash U]\!]^{\pi}_{(\gamma_1,\alpha_1,\delta_1),(\gamma_2,\alpha_2,\delta_2)}$

Substitution: $[\![\Gamma \vdash T\,[\imath := s]]\!]^{\pi}_{\gamma_1,\gamma_2} \doteq [\![\Gamma \vdash T]\!]^{\pi(\imath:=(\!|s|\!)_{\pi})}_{\gamma_1,\gamma_2}$

$$[\![\Gamma\Delta\,[x := N] \vdash T\,[x := N]]\!]^{\pi}_{(\gamma_1,\delta_1),(\gamma_2,\delta_2)} \doteq [\![\Gamma(x:U)\Delta \vdash T]\!]^{\pi}_{(\gamma_1,\nu_1,\delta_1),(\gamma_2,\nu_2,\delta_2)}$$

where $\nu_1 \equiv [\Gamma \vdash N]^{\pi}_{\gamma_1}$
$\nu_2 \equiv [\Gamma \vdash N]^{\pi}_{\gamma_2}$

Monotony: $s \sqsubseteq r \wedge \imath \;\mathsf{pos}\; T \Rightarrow [\![\Gamma \vdash T]\!]^{\pi(\imath:=s)}_{\gamma_1,\gamma_2} \subseteq [\![\Gamma \vdash T]\!]^{\pi(\imath:=r)}_{\gamma_1,\gamma_2}$

Subtyping: $T \leq U \Rightarrow [\![\Gamma \vdash T]\!]^{\pi}_{\gamma_1,\gamma_2} \subseteq [\![\Gamma \vdash U]\!]^{\pi}_{\gamma_1,\gamma_2}$

Fig. 3. Properties of the interpretation

Lemma 4 (Soundness)

1. *If $\Gamma \vdash M : T$ and $(\gamma_1, \gamma_2) \in [\![\Gamma]\!]^{\pi}$, then $[\Gamma \vdash M]^{\pi}_{\gamma_1,\gamma_2}$, $[\![\Gamma \vdash T]\!]^{\pi}_{\gamma_1,\gamma_2}$ are defined and*
$$[\Gamma \vdash M]^{\pi}_{\gamma_1,\gamma_2} \in [\![\Gamma \vdash T]\!]^{\pi}_{\gamma_1,\gamma_2}\ .$$
2. *If $\Gamma \vdash T : u$, $\mathsf{simple}(T)$, and $(\gamma_1, \gamma_2) \in [\![\Gamma]\!]^{\pi}$, then $[\![\Gamma \vdash T]\!]^{\pi}_{\gamma_1,\gamma_2}$ is a defined Λ-set.*
3. *If $\mathsf{WF}(\Gamma)$ and $(\gamma_1, \gamma_2) \in [\![\Gamma]\!]^{\pi}$, then $(\gamma_1, \gamma_1) \in [\![\Gamma]\!]^{\pi}$ and $(\gamma_1, \gamma_1) \in [\![\Gamma]\!]^{\infty}$.*

4.5 Strong Normalization

In this section we prove our main result: strong normalization of $\mathrm{CIC}^{\widehat{}}_{-}$.

A substitution is a mapping θ from variables to terms, such that $\theta(x) \neq x$ for a finite number of variables x. We use θ to denote substitutions, and ε to denote the identity substitution. We write $\theta(x \mapsto M)$ for the substitution that gives M when applied to x and $\theta(y)$ when applied to $y \neq x$. We write $M\theta$ for the capture-avoiding substitution of the free variables of M with θ.

Definition 16. *Let $(\gamma_1, \gamma_2) \in [\![\Gamma]\!]^{\pi}$. We define $\theta \models^{\Gamma}_{\pi} (\gamma_1, \gamma_2)$ by the following clauses:*

$$\frac{}{\varepsilon \models^{\Gamma}_{\pi} []} \qquad \frac{\theta \models^{\Gamma}_{\pi} (\gamma_1, \gamma_2) \qquad M \models_{[\![\Gamma \vdash T]\!]^{\pi}_{\gamma_1,\gamma_2}} (\alpha_1, \alpha_2)}{\theta(x \mapsto M) \models^{\Gamma(x:T)}_{\pi} (\gamma_1, \alpha_1), (\gamma_2, \alpha_2)}$$

Lemma 5. *If $\Gamma \vdash M : T$ and $(\gamma_1, \gamma_2) \in [\![\Gamma]\!]^{\pi}$ and $\theta \models^{\Gamma}_{\pi} (\gamma_1, \gamma_2)$, then*

$$M\theta \models_{[\![\Gamma \vdash T]\!]^{\pi}_{\gamma_1,\gamma_2}} [\Gamma \vdash M]^{\pi}_{\gamma_1,\gamma_2}$$

Corollary 1. *If $\Gamma \vdash M : T$ then M is strongly normalizing.*

Proof. It is not difficult to see that $\varepsilon \models_{\pi}^{\Gamma} \bot_{\Gamma}$, where $\bot_{\Gamma}$ is the sequence of atomic elements of relational interpretation the types of Γ. The result follows from the previous lemma, and the fact that realizers are strongly normalizing. □

As a consequence of soundness and strong normalization, we can easily derive logical consistency.

Theorem 1. *There is no term M such that $\vdash M : \Pi x : \mathsf{Prop}.x$.*

5 Related Work

The idea of using sized types to ensure termination and productivity was initiated by Hughes, Pareto and Sabry [8]. Abel [1] extended system F^{ω} with sized (co-)inductive types. In turn, $\mathrm{CIC}\widehat{\_}$ is derived from $\mathrm{CIC}\widehat{\ }$ [4]. We refer to these papers for further information and examples, and focus on work related to strong normalization.

Our proof of strong normalization closely follows the work of Melliès and Werner [11]. The authors use Λ-sets to develop a generic proof of strong normalization for Pure Type Systems. They avoid the use of inaccessible cardinals, but it is unlikely that the same can be achieved in the presence of inductive types.

Λ-sets were introduced by Altenkirch in [2]. He develops a generic model for the Calculus of Constructions (CC), that can be instantiated with Λ-sets to obtain a proof of strong normalization. He also extends the proof to include one inductive type (trees) at the impredicative level.

There are in the literature several proofs of strong normalization for (non-dependent) typed lambda calculi extended with sized types. We refer the reader to [1,4] for further references.

On dependent types, an extension with type-based termination was first considered by Giménez [6]. However, stages are not explicitly represented, which complicates the definition of mutually recursive functions.

Barras [3] has formalized in Coq a proof of consistency $\mathrm{CC}\omega$ extended with natural numbers. Termination of recursive functions is ensured by a restricted form of sized types, inspired by the work of Giménez. However, it is not possible to express size-preserving functions, which prevents the typing of quicksort.

Blanqui [5] uses sized types to ensure termination of CC extended with higher-order rewrite rules. In our case, we use just fix/case instead of rewrite rules. However, he makes some assumptions on the confluence and subject reduction of the combination of rewriting and β-reduction. Nevertheless, it is of interest to see if these techniques can be extended to $\mathrm{CIC}\widehat{\_}$.

Finally, let us mention the work of Wahlstedt [12]. He proves weak normalization of a predicative type theory in the style of Martin-Löf type theory. Termination is ensured using the size-change principle [9]. While this principle is very powerful, his system cannot express size-preserving functions.

6 Conclusions

We presented $\mathrm{CIC}^{\widehat{~}}_{-}$, an extension of CIC with a type-based termination mechanism. We have restricted to one inductive type, namely natural numbers, and we have proved that the system is strongly normalizing and logically consistent. The interpretation can be extended to other (positive) inductive types (in the predicative universes). This is a intermediate result towards our goal of proving logical consistency of an extension of CIC with a type-based termination mechanism.

There are some issues related with $\mathrm{CIC}^{\widehat{~}}$ that are present in $\mathrm{CIC}^{\widehat{~}}_{-}$ and have not been addressed in this work, namely, global definitions and mutually recursive functions. We have preliminary results in this direction.

Acknowledgments. The authors would like to thank Bruno Barras, Hugo Herbelin, and Benjamin Werner for many discussions on strong normalization and type-based termination.

References

1. Abel, A.: A Polymorphic Lambda-Calculus with Sized Higher-Order Types. PhD thesis, Ludwig-Maximilians-Universität München (2006)
2. Altenkirch, T.: Constructions, Inductive Types and Strong Normalization. PhD thesis, University of Edinburgh (November 1993)
3. Barras, B.: Sets in coq, coq in sets. In: 1st Coq Workshop (August 2009)
4. Barthe, G., Grégoire, B., Pastawski, F.: $\mathrm{CIC}^{\widehat{~}}$: Type-based termination of recursive definitions in the Calculus of Inductive Constructions. In: Hermann, M., Voronkov, A. (eds.) LPAR 2006. LNCS (LNAI), vol. 4246, pp. 257–271. Springer, Heidelberg (2006)
5. Blanqui, F.: A type-based termination criterion for dependently-typed higher-order rewrite systems. In: van Oostrom, V. (ed.) RTA 2004. LNCS, vol. 3091, pp. 24–39. Springer, Heidelberg (2004)
6. Giménez, E.: Structural recursive definitions in type theory. In: Larsen, K.G., Skyum, S., Winskel, G. (eds.) ICALP 1998. LNCS, vol. 1443, pp. 397–408. Springer, Heidelberg (1998)
7. Grgoire, B., Sacchini, J.L.: On strong normalization of the Calculus of Constructions with type-based termination (2010), `http://www-sop.inria.fr/members/Jorge-Luis.Sacchini/papers/sn.pdf`
8. Hughes, J., Pareto, L., Sabry, A.: Proving the correctness of reactive systems using sized types. In: POPL, pp. 410–423 (1996)
9. Lee, C.S., Jones, N.D., Ben-Amram, A.M.: The size-change principle for program termination. In: POPL, pp. 81–92 (2001)
10. Luo, Z.: Computation and reasoning: a type theory for computer science. Oxford University Press, Inc., New York (1994)
11. Melliès, P.-A., Werner, B.: A generic normalisation proof for pure type systems. In: Giménez, E. (ed.) TYPES 1996. LNCS, vol. 1512, pp. 254–276. Springer, Heidelberg (1998)
12. Wahlstedt, D.: Dependent Type Theory with Parameterized First-Order Data Types and Well-Founded Recursion. PhD thesis, Chalmers University of Technology (2007) ISBN 978-91-7291-979-2

Aligators for Arrays*
(Tool Paper)

Thomas A. Henzinger[1], Thibaud Hottelier[2],
Laura Kovács[3], and Andrey Rybalchenko[4]

[1] IST Austria
[2] UC Berkeley
[3] TU Vienna
[4] TUM

Abstract. This paper presents Aligators, a tool for the generation of universally quantified array invariants. Aligators leverages recurrence solving and algebraic techniques to carry out inductive reasoning over array content. The Aligators' loop extraction module allows treatment of multi-path loops by exploiting their commutativity and serializability properties. Our experience in applying Aligators on a collection of loops from open source software projects indicates the applicability of recurrence and algebraic solving techniques for reasoning about arrays.

1 Introduction

Loop invariants build a basis for reasoning about programs and their automatic discovery is a major challenge. Construction of invariant equalities over numeric scalar variables can be efficiently automated using recurrence solving and computer algebra techniques [15]. A combination of quantifier elimination techniques together with a program instrumentation using an auxiliary loop counter variable generalizes the method of [15] to the construction of invariant inequalities [12]. While the methods of [15,12] are restricted to reasoning over scalars, recurrence solving and algebraic techniques can provide a basis for computing invariants over vector data types, e.g., arrays. For a restricted class of loops that do not contain any branching statements and under non-deterministic treatment of the loop condition, we can compute universally quantified array invariants by using recurrence solving over the loop body [13].

In this paper we eliminate the restrictions of [15,12,13], and present the Aligators tool for generating quantified array invariants for loops containing conditional statements that takes loop conditions into account. Quantified loop invariants are inferred by Aligators based on recurrence solving over array indexes. The obtained invariants are derived without using pre- and post conditions; the specification of the loop can be subsequently used further. The invariant inference engine of Aligators relies on two steps (Section 3.2): (i) it applies full power of inductive reasoning provided by recurrence solving over scalar variables and derives the most precise inductive content over

* This research was partly supported by the Swiss NSF. The third author is supported by an FWF Hertha Firnberg Research grant (T425-N23).

C. Fermüller and A. Voronkov (Eds.): LPAR-17, LNCS 6397, pp. 348–356, 2010.

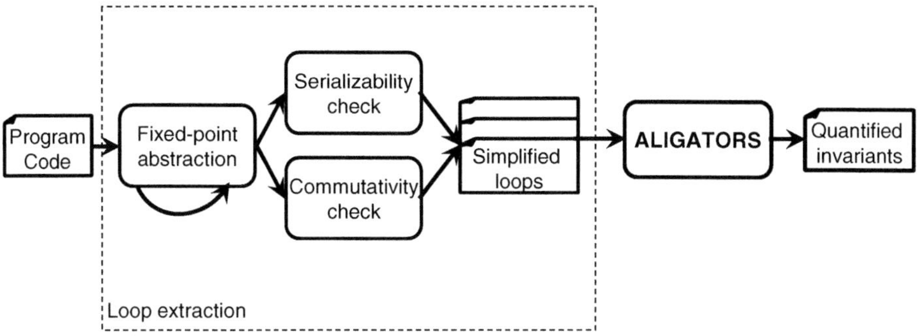

Fig. 1. The overall workflow of Aligators

scalars, (ii) it combines recurrence solving and algebraic techniques with the theory of uninterpreted functions to derive invariant properties over arrays. Due to the exact computations of the algebraic techniques, Aligators only supports loops with restricted branching control-flow (Section 3.1).

To make Aligators amenable for practical software verification, we built and interfaced Aligators with a loop extraction module (Section 4.1). This module takes as input a large code, and applies path analysis heuristics to turn loops into the format required by Aligators.

The overall workflow of Aligators is illustrated in Figure 1.

Implementation and Experiments. Aligators is implemented in Mathematica 5.2 [19], whereas the loop extraction module interfaced with Aligators is written in OCaml [5]. Aligators can be downloaded from

`http://mtc.epfl.ch/software-tools/Aligators/`

We have successfully applied Aligators on interesting examples involving arithmetic and array reasoning (Section 4), as well as on a large number of loops extracted from the Netlib repository (`www.netlib.org`). The invariants returned by Aligators were generated in essentially no time, on a machine with a 2.0GHz CPU and 2GB of RAM.

Related Work. Universally quantified invariants are crucial in the verification process of programs with unbounded data structures – see e.g. [7,14,9,18,10,16].

In [14,9,18] quantified invariants are inferred by deploying predicate abstraction over a set of a priori defined predicates. Alternatively, in [10] quantified invariants are derived by using constraint solving over the unknown coefficients of an a priori fixed invariant template. Unlike these works, Aligators requires no user guidance in providing predicates or templates, but it can be applied to loops with a restricted control-flow.

Based on interval-based abstract interpretation, in [7,11] quantified invariants are also generated with no user guidance. Unlike these approaches, we do not use abstract interpretation, and apply simple path analysis to translate multi-path loops into simple ones. In [16] invariants with quantifier alternations are obtained using a first-order theorem prover. Contrarily to [16], we combine uninterpreted functions with recurrence solving over array indexes, but can only infer universally quantified invariants.

Table 1. Aligators results on benchmarks from [7,14,9]

Benchmark	Program	Quantified invariant
Copy [7]	i:=0; **while** ($i < N$) **do** $B[i]$:=$A[i]$; i:=$i+1$ **end do**	$\forall k.\ 0 \leq k<i \Longrightarrow (B[k] = A[k] \wedge k < N)$
Copy_Prop [14]	i:=0; **while** ($i < N$) **do** $A[i]$:=0; i:=$i+1$ **end do**; i:=0; **while** ($i < N$) **do** $B[i]$:=$A[i]$; i:=$i+1$ **end do**	$(\forall k.\ 0 \leq k<i \Longrightarrow (A[k] = 0 \wedge k < N))$ $\wedge$ $(\forall k.\ 0 \leq k<N \Longrightarrow (B[k] = A[k] \wedge k < N))$
Init [14]	i:=0; **while** ($i < N$) **do** $A[i]$:=0; i:=$i+1$ **end do**	$\forall k.\ 0 \leq k<i \Longrightarrow (A[k] = 0 \wedge k < N)$
Partition [9]	i:=0; j_1:=0; j_2:=0; **while** ($i < N$) **do** **if** ($A[i] \geq 0$) **then** $C[j_1]$:=$A[i]$; j_1:=j_1+1 **else** $B[j_2]$:=$A[i]$; j_2:=j_2+1 **end if**; i:=$i+1$ **end do**	$(\forall k.\ 0 \leq k<j_1 \Longrightarrow (k < N \wedge C[k] \geq 0))$ $\wedge$ $(\forall k.\ 0 \leq k<j_2 \Longrightarrow (k < N \wedge B[k] < 0))$
Part_Init1 [14]	i:=0; j:=0; **while** ($i < N$) **do** **if** ($A[i] \geq 0$) **then** $B[j]$:=i; j:=$j+1$ **end if**; i:=$i+1$ **end do**	$\forall k.\ 0 \leq k<j \Longrightarrow (B[k] < N \wedge A[B[k]] \geq 0)$
Part_Init2 [7]	i:=0; j:=0; **while** ($i < N$) **do** **if** ($A[i] = B[i]$) **then** $C[j]$:=i; j:=$j+1$ **end if**; i:=$i+1$ **end do**	$\forall k.\ 0 \leq k<j \Longrightarrow (C[k] < N \wedge A[C[k]]=B[C[k]])$
Permutation	i:=0; **while** ($i < N$) **do** $B[\sigma(i)]$:=$A[i]$;; i:=$i+1$ **end do**	$\forall k.\ 0 \leq k<i \Longrightarrow (B[\sigma(k)] = A[k] \wedge k < N)$
Vararg [14]	i:=0; **while** ($A[i] \neq 0$) **do** i:=$i+1$; **end do**	$\forall k.\ 0 \leq k<i \Longrightarrow (A[k] < 0 \vee A[k] > 0)$

2 Aligators in Action

To invoke Aligators, one uses the following command.

Command 2.1 : `Aligators[Loop, IniVal → list of assignments]`

Input: Loop[1] and, *optionally*, a list of assignments specifying initial values of scalars
Output: Loop invariant $\phi_{Var} \wedge \phi_{Arrs}$, where ϕ_{Var} is a scalar invariant and ϕ_{Arrs} is a quantified invariant over arrays

EXAMPLE 2.1: Consider the Partition program [9] given in Table 1. The loop copies the non-negative (resp. negative) elements of an array A into an array B (resp. into an array C). The invariant returned by Aligators is listed below.

[1] Inputs to Aligators are `while`-loops as in (1).

$$\begin{array}{ll}\texttt{Input:} & \text{Aligators}[\underline{\textbf{while}}\ (i < N)\ \underline{\textbf{do}} \\ & \quad \underline{\textbf{if}}\ (A[i] \geq 0)\ \underline{\textbf{then}}\ C[j_1] := A[i];\ j_1 := j_1 + 1 \\ & \quad \underline{\textbf{else}}\ B[j_2] := A[i];\ j_2 := j_2 + 1\ \underline{\textbf{end if}}; \\ & \quad i := i + 1\ \underline{\textbf{end do}}, \\ & \quad \texttt{IniVal} \rightarrow \{i := 0;\ j_1 := 0;\ j_2 := 0\}]\end{array}$$

$$\begin{array}{ll}\texttt{Output:} & (i = j_1 + j_2) \wedge (N > 0 \implies i \leq N) \wedge \\ & (\forall k) \big(0 \leq k < j_1 \implies (k < N \wedge C[k] \geq 0)\big) \wedge \\ & (\forall k) \big(0 \leq k < j_2 \implies (k < N \wedge B[k] < 0)\big)\end{array}$$

The above invariant is composed of (i) two quantifier-free linear properties over the scalars i, j_1, and j_2, and (ii) two quantified properties over the arrays B and C. Let us note that the scalar invariant generation method of [15,12] would fail deriving such a complex invariant, as first-order reasoning over the arrays B and C would be required. Moreover, due to the presence of conditional statements in the loop body, the technique of [13] could not be either applied for quantified invariant generation.

3 Invariant Generation with Aligators

Aligators offers software support for automated invariant generation by algebraic techniques over the rationals and *arrays*.

3.1 Programming Model

Notations. In what follows, $\mathbb{K}$ denotes the domain of values of scalar variables (e.g. integers $\mathbb{Z}$). Throughout this paper, the set of scalar and array variables will respectively be denoted by Var and $Arrs$, where $Arrs = RArrs \cup WArrs$ is a disjoint union of the sets $RArrs$ of *read-only* and $WArrs$ of *write-only* array variables.

Expressions. The language of expressions of Aligators' input contains constants from $\mathbb{K}$, variables from $Var \cup Arrs$, logical variables, and some function and predicate symbols. We only consider the arithmetical function symbols $+$, $-$, and $\cdot$ as interpreted, all other function symbols are uninterpreted. Similarly, only the arithmetical predicate symbols $=$, $\neq$, $\leq$, $\geq$, $<$ and $>$ are interpreted, all other predicate symbols are treated as uninterpreted. For an array variable A and expression e, we will write $A[e]$ to mean the element of A at position e.

Inputs to Aligators. The syntax of Aligators inputs is given below.

$$\begin{array}{l}\underline{\textbf{while}}\ (b_0)\ \underline{\textbf{do}} \\ \quad \underline{\textbf{if}}\ (b_1)\ \underline{\textbf{then}}\ \alpha_{11}; \ldots; \alpha_{1s_1} \\ \quad \underline{\textbf{else}}\ \ldots\ \underline{\textbf{else}}\ \underline{\textbf{if}}\ (b_d)\ \alpha_{d1}; \ldots; \alpha_{ds_d}\ \underline{\textbf{end if}} \\ \underline{\textbf{end do}}\end{array} \tag{1}$$

where $b_0, \ldots, b_d$ are boolean expressions, and α_{kl} are assignment statements over $Var \cup Arrs$. For simplicity, we represent (1) by an equivalent collection of *guarded assignments* [3], as given below.

$$\begin{array}{l}G_1 \rightarrow \alpha_{11}; \ldots; \alpha_{1s_1} \\ \quad \ldots \\ G_d \rightarrow \alpha_{d1}; \ldots; \alpha_{ds_d}\end{array}, \tag{2}$$

where formulas G_k are called the *guards* of the guarded assignments. The loop (2) is a *multi-path loop* if $d > 1$. If $d = 1$, the loop (2) is called a *simple-loop*.

Similarly to [13], the following conditions on (2) are imposed:

1. For all $k, l \in \{1, \ldots, d\}$, if $k \neq l$ then the formula $G_k \wedge G_l$ is unsatisfiable.
2. If some α_{ku} updates an array variable $A_u \in WArrs$, and some α_{kv} for $u \neq v$ in the *same guarded assignment* updates an array variable $A_v \in WArrs$, then A_u and A_v are different arrays.
3. The assignments α_{ku}'s have one of the following forms:

   (a) Array assignments: $A[e] := f(Var \cup RArrs)$, (3)

   where $A \in WArrs$, e is an expression over Var, and $f(Var \cup RArrs)$ is an arbitrary expression over $Var \cup RArrs$, but contains no write-arrays.

   (b) Scalar assignments: $x := poly(Var)$, (4)

   where $x \in Var$, and $poly(Var)$ is a polynomial expression in $\mathbb{K}[Var]$ over Var such that the total degree of any monomial in x from $poly(Var)$ is exactly 1.
4. If some α_{ku} updates a variable $v \in Var \cup Arrs$, and some α_{lv} with $l \neq k$ updates the same variable v, then α_{ku} is syntactically the same as α_{lv}. That is, variable v is modified in the same way in the kth and lth guarded assignments.

In what follows, a variable $v \in Var \cup Arrs$ satisfying condition 4 above will be called a *commutable* variable. Note that a *commutable* variable is modified in the same way in all guarded assignments of (2). That is, updates to a commutable variable are described by *only one* polynomial expression as given in (4). Reasoning over commutable variables requires thus no case distinctions between various behaviors on different guarded assignments of (2). The guarded assignments[2] of (2) are called *commutable* if their common variables are commutable.

3.2 Invariant Inference with Aligators

Invariant Generation over Scalars. Invariant properties over scalars variables are inferred as presented in [15,12]. Namely, (i) assignments over scalars are modeled by recurrence equations over *the loop counter* n; (ii) closed forms of variables as functions of n are derived by recurrence solving; (iii) (all) scalar invariant equalities are inferred by eliminating n from the closed forms of variables; and (iv) scalar invariant inequalities over commutable variable are obtained using quantifier elimination over n.

Invariant Generation over Arrays. In our process of quantified invariant generation, (i) we first rewrite (1) into (2), (ii) generate quantified invariants over non-commutable array variables for each simple-loop given by a guarded assignment of (2), and (iii) take conjunction of the quantified invariants to obtain a quantified invariant of (1).

(i) Input loops (1) to Aligators satisfy[3] the restrictions 1-4 given on page 352. Hence, guards are disjoint, and branches are commutable. Internally, Aligators rewrites an input

[2] Respectively, conditional branches of (1).

[3] Aligators checks whether an input loop satisfies the restrictions of Section 3.1. If this is not the case, Aligators returns an error messages about the violated restriction.

loop (1) into (2) (as illustrated in Example 3.2), and proceeds with generating invariants for the simple-loops of (2).
(ii) Aligators next infers quantified invariants for the following simple-loop of (2):

$$G \rightarrow \alpha_1; \ldots; \alpha_s. \tag{5}$$

W.l.o.g., we assume that (5) contains only one array update, as below:

$$A[i] := f(\mathit{Var} \cup \mathit{RArrs}), \text{ where } i \in \mathit{Var} \text{ and } A \in \mathit{WArrs} \text{ are non-commutable.} \tag{6}$$

Based on the programming model given on page 352, since variables i and A are non-commutable, changes to i and A can only happen on the guarded assignment (5). Recurrence solving thus can be applied to derive exact closed form representation of i and A.

Let us denote by $n \geq 0$ the loop counter. We write $x^{(n)}$ to mean the value of $x \in \mathit{Var}$ at iteration n. As array updates satisfy the restrictions of Section 3.1, we write $A[x^{(n)}]$ instead of $A^{(n)}[x^{(n)}]$ to speak about the value of the xth element of A at iteration n of the loop.

Based on (5) and (6), at iteration n of (5) the following property holds:

$$G^{(n)} \wedge A[i^{(n+1)}] = f(\mathit{Var}^{(n+1)} \cup \mathit{RArrs}), \tag{7}$$

where $\mathit{Var}^{(n+1)} = \{x^{(n+1)} \mid x \in \mathit{Var}\}$, and $G^{(n)}$ is the formula obtained by substituting variables x with $x^{(n)}$ in G. Formula (7) holds at any iteration k upto n. Hence:

$$(\forall k) 0 \leq k \leq n \implies G^{(k)} \wedge A[i^{(k+1)}] = f(\mathit{Var}^{(k+1)} \cup \mathit{RArrs}) \tag{8}$$

We further eliminate n from (8), as follows. (i) If the closed forms of loop variables is a linear system in n, linear algebra methods are used to express n as a linear function $p(Var) \in \mathbb{K}[Var]$. (ii) Otherwise, Gröbner basis computation [1] is used to compute n as a polynomial function $p(Var) \in \mathbb{K}[Var]$. We thus obtain the quantified invariant:

$$(\forall k) 0 \leq k \leq p(\mathit{Var}) \implies G^{(k)} \wedge A[i^{(k+1)}] = f(\mathit{Var}^{(k+1)} \cup \mathit{RArrs}) \tag{9}$$

EXAMPLE 3.1: Consider $i < N \wedge A[i] > 0 \rightarrow C[j_1] := A[i]; j_1 := j_1 + 1; i := i + 1$. Let $n \geq 0$ denote its loop counter. Following (8), we have:

$$i^{(n)} < N \wedge A[i^{(n)}] > 0 \ \wedge \ C[j_1^{(n+1)} - 1] = A[i^{(n+1)} - 1],$$

where $j_1^{(n+1)} = j_1^{(n)} + 1$ and $i^{(n+1)} = i^{(n)} + 1$. Using recurrence solving and replacing the (final) value $j_1^{(n+1)}$ by j_1, we obtain $n = j_1 - 1 - j_1^{(0)}$. It thus follows:

$$(\forall k) 0 \leq k \leq j_1 - 1 - j_1^{(0)} \implies k < N \wedge A[k] > 0 \ \wedge \ C[k] = A[k].$$

(iii) To turn (9) into a quantified invariant of (2), we finally make sure that:
- when eliminating n from (8), n is computed as a polynomial function over only *non-commutable scalar variables*;
- formula (9) is simplified to contain only *non-commutable scalar and array variables*.

The quantified invariant of (1) is given by the conjunction of the quantified invariants without commutable variables of each simple-loop of (2).

EXAMPLE 3.2: The main steps for quantified invariant generations with Aligators are illustrated on the Partition program of Table 1. The initial values of both i and j_1 are 0.

(i) Guarded assignments:	(ii) Quantified invariants with commutable variables:	without commutable variables:
$i < N \wedge A[i] \geq 0$ $\rightarrow C[j_1]:=A[i];$ $j_1:=j_1+1; i:=i+1$	$(\forall k)0 \leq k < j_1 \implies$ $k < N \wedge A[k] \geq 0 \wedge A[k] = C[k]$	$(\forall k)0 \leq k < j_1 \implies$ $k < N \wedge C[k] \geq 0$
$i < N \wedge A[i] < 0$ $\rightarrow B[j_2]:=A[i];$ $j_2:=j_2+1; i:=i+1$	$(\forall k)0 \leq k < j_2 \implies$ $k < N \wedge A[k] < 0 \wedge B[k] = A[k]$	$(\forall k)0 \leq k < j_2 \implies$ $k < N \wedge B[k] < 0$

The final invariant of the Partition program is given in Example 2.1.

4 Experimental Results

We report on our experimental results with Aligators, obtained on a machine with 2.0GHz CPU and 2GB of RAM.

Aligators on benchmark examples. We ran Aligators on a collection of benchmark examples taken from [7,14,9]. Our results are summarized in Table 1.

4.1 Loop Extraction for Aligators

Aligators supports modular reasoning by analyzing one loop at a time. To run Aligators on large programs with more than one loop, we built and interfaced Aligators with a loop extraction module written in OCaml [5]. This module extracts and translates loops from large C programs into the shape of (1). For doing so, the loop extraction module takes one complex C program as input, and outputs one or more loops that can be further fed into Aligators. To this end, three main techniques[4] are applied: (i) *fixed point abstraction*, (ii) *serializability check*, and (iii) *commutativity check*.

Fixed Point Abstraction. Given a loop, the goal of this step is to find the largest sequence of loop assignments satisfying the restrictions given in Section 3.1. To this end, we abstract away all loop assignments that either violate the input requirements of Aligators, or depend on variables whose assignments do not satisfy Section 3.1. For abstracting assignment away, we check if the assignment is side-effect free. If yes, the assignment can be soundly approximated by an uninterpreted function. We recursively repeat the previous steps, until a fixed point is reached. As a result, we either obtain an empty loop body which means that the loop does not fit into our programming model, or a sequence of assignments that is a sound approximation of the original loop.

Serializability check. Let us denote by ρ_i the guarded assignment $G_i \rightarrow \alpha_{i1}; \ldots; \alpha_{is_i}$ from (2). The role of the serialization check is to turn, if possible, a multi-path loop (2) into an equivalent collection of simple-loops.

[4] The loop extraction module performs other small steps as well – e.g. for-loops are rewritten in their while-loop format.

Table 2. The first column is the name of the program analyzed. The second and third columns give respectively the lines of code and the total number of loops. The fourth column contains the number of loops that fall into our programming model. The fifth column presents the number of loops for which invariants were inferred by Aligators, whereas the last column gives the number of those invariants which describe one or more array content.

Program	LoC	Loops	Analyzable Loops	Invariants	Array Invariants
Gzip	8607	201	100	62	39
Bzip2	6698	260	106	75	35
OggEnc	58413	680	464	185	11

Using regular expression-like notation, we check whether the set of all possible loop executions is included in the set $\mathcal{L} = \{\rho_{i_1}^*; \ldots; \rho_{i_d}^* | \, (\rho_{i_1}, \ldots, \rho_{i_d})$ is a permutation of $(\rho_1, \ldots, \rho_d)\}$. Solving this query involves reasoning in the combined quantifier-free theory of integers, arrays, and uninterpreted functions, which can be efficiently solved using SMT solvers. To this end, we make use of the SMT solver Z3 [2].

Note that the serializability check requires the construction of all permutations of length d over $(\rho_1, \ldots, \rho_d)$. Our experimental results show that the number d of loop paths in practice is small. For the programs we analyzed, more than 80% of the loops have less than 3 branches, and 5% of the loops have been simplified with the serializability check.

EXAMPLE 4.1: Consider the loop given below.

i :=1;
<u>**for**</u>(i :=1; $i \leq n$; i++) <u>**do**</u>
 <u>**if**</u> ($i \leq a$) <u>**then**</u> $A[i]$:=$B[i]$ <u>**else**</u> $A[i]$:=0 <u>**end if**</u>
<u>**end do**</u>

The result of serializability check on the above loop is a collection of two simple-loops, as follows.

$i := 1$
<u>**while**</u>($i \leq a$) <u>**do**</u>
 $A[i]$:=$B[i]$; $i := i + 1$
<u>**end do**</u>

i :=$a + 1$
<u>**while**</u>($i \leq n$) <u>**do**</u>
$A[i]$:=0; $i := i + 1$
<u>**end do**</u>

Commutativity check. The goal of this step is to collapse multi-path loops (2) with only commutable variables into a simple-loop. To this end, we check whether the assignments of variables are syntactically the same in all branches.

Aligator on large programs. We ran Aligators on two file-compression tools, Gzip [6] and Bzip2 [17], and on the MP3 encoder OggEnc [4]. The results are presented in Table 2. The array invariants inferred by Aligators express copy/permutation/shift/ initialization relations between two arrays. Our results suggests that Aligators generated invariants for over 25% of the extracted loops. The second column of Table 2 shows that roughly half of the loops fits into our programming model. The obtained invariants were generated by Aligators in essentially no time; Aligators can analyze and reason about 50 loops per second.

5 Conclusion

We describe Aligators, an automated tool for quantified invariant generation for programs over arrays. Our tool requires no user guidance, it applies recurrence solving to arrays, and has been successfully applied to generate invariants for loops extracted from large, non-trivial programs. Further work includes integrating control-flow refinement techniques, such as [8], into Aligators, and using our tool in conjunction with other approaches, such as [10,16], to invariant generation.

References

1. Buchberger, B.: An Algorithm for Finding the Basis Elements of the Residue Class Ring of a Zero Dimensional Polynomial Ideal. J. of Symbolic Computation 41(3-4), 475–511 (2006)
2. de Moura, L., Bjørner, N.: Z3: An Efficient SMT Solver. In: Ramakrishnan, C.R., Rehof, J. (eds.) TACAS 2008. LNCS, vol. 4963, pp. 337–340. Springer, Heidelberg (2008)
3. Dijkstra, E.W.: A Discipline of Programming. Prentice-Hall, Englewood Cliffs (1976)
4. Smith, M., et al.: The OggEnc Home Page (1994), `http://www.xiph.org/`
5. Leroy, X., et al.: The Objective Caml system - release 3.11. INRIA (2008)
6. Gailly, J., Adler, M.: The Gzip Home Page (1991), `http://www.gzip.org/`
7. Gopan, D., Reps, T.W., Sagiv, S.: A Framework for Numeric Analysis of Array Operations. In: Proc. of POPL, pp. 338–350 (2005)
8. Gulwani, S., Jain, S., Koskinen, E.: Control-flow Refinement and Progress Invariants for Bound Analysis. In: Proc. of PLDI, pp. 375–385 (2009)
9. Gulwani, S., Tiwari, A.: Combining Abstract Interpreters. In: Proc. of PLDI, pp. 376–386 (2006)
10. Gupta, A., Rybalchenko, A.: InvGen: An Efficient Invariant Generator. In: Bouajjani, A., Maler, O. (eds.) Computer Aided Verification. LNCS, vol. 5643, pp. 634–640. Springer, Heidelberg (2009)
11. Halbwachs, N., Péron, M.: Discovering Properties about Arrays in Simple Programs. In: Proc. of PLDI, pp. 339–348 (2008)
12. Henzinger, T.A., Hottelier, T., Kovács, L.: Valigator: A Verification Tool with Bound and Invariant Generation. In: Cervesato, I., Veith, H., Voronkov, A. (eds.) LPAR 2008. LNCS (LNAI), vol. 5330, pp. 333–342. Springer, Heidelberg (2008)
13. Henzinger, T.A., Hottelier, T., Kovács, L., Voronkov, A.: Invariant and Type Inference for Matrices. In: Barthe, G., Hermenegildo, M. (eds.) VMCAI 2010. LNCS, vol. 5944, pp. 163–179. Springer, Heidelberg (2010)
14. Jhala, R., McMillan, K.L.: Array Abstractions from Proofs. In: Damm, W., Hermanns, H. (eds.) CAV 2007. LNCS, vol. 4590, pp. 193–206. Springer, Heidelberg (2007)
15. Kovács, L.: Reasoning Algebraically About P-Solvable Loops. In: Ramakrishnan, C.R., Rehof, J. (eds.) TACAS 2008. LNCS, vol. 4963, pp. 249–264. Springer, Heidelberg (2008)
16. Kovács, L., Voronkov, A.: Finding Loop Invariants for Programs over Arrays Using a Theorem Prover. In: Chechik, M., Wirsing, M. (eds.) FASE 2009. LNCS, vol. 5503, pp. 470–485. Springer, Heidelberg (2009)
17. Seward, J.: The Bzip2 Home Page (1996), `http://www.bzip.org/`
18. Srivastava, S., Gulwani, S.: Program Verification using Templates over Predicate Abstraction. In: Proc. of PLDI, pp. 223–234 (2009)
19. Wolfram, S.: The Mathematica Book. Version 5.0. Wolfram Media (2003)

Clause Elimination Procedures for CNF Formulas*

Marijn Heule[1], Matti Järvisalo[2], and Armin Biere[3]

[1] Department of Software Technology, Delft University of Technology, The Netherlands
[2] Department of Computer Science, University of Helsinki, Finland
[3] Institute for Formal Models and Verification, Johannes Kepler University Linz, Austria

Abstract. We develop and analyze clause elimination procedures, a specific family of simplification techniques for conjunctive normal form (CNF) formulas. Extending known procedures such as tautology, subsumption, and blocked clause elimination, we introduce novel elimination procedures based on *hidden* and *asymmetric* variants of these techniques. We analyze the resulting nine (including five new) clause elimination procedures from various perspectives: *size reduction*, *BCP-preservance*, *confluence*, and *logical equivalence*. For the variants not preserving logical equivalence, we show how to reconstruct solutions to original CNFs from satisfying assignments to simplified CNFs. We also identify a clause elimination procedure that does a transitive reduction of the binary implication graph underlying any CNF formula purely on the CNF level.

1 Introduction

Simplification techniques applied both before (i.e., in preprocessing) and during search have proven integral in enabling efficient conjunctive normal form (CNF) level Boolean satisfiability (SAT) solving for real-world application domains. Indeed, there is a large body of work on preprocessing CNF formulas (see [1–11] for examples), based on e.g. variable elimination and equivalence reasoning. Further, while many SAT solvers rely mainly on Boolean constraint propagation (i.e., unit propagation) during search, it is possible to improve solving efficiency by applying additional simplification techniques also during search, as witnessed e.g. by PrecoSAT (`http://fmv.jku.at/precosat`)—one of the most successful SAT solvers in the 2009 SAT Competition. Noticeably, when scheduling *combinations* of simplification techniques during search, even quite simply ideas, such as removal of subsumed clauses, can bring additional gains by enabling further simplifications by other techniques.

This work is motivated on one hand by the possibilities of lifting SAT solving efficiency further by integrating additional simplification techniques to the solving process before and/or during search, and on the other by understanding the relationships between different simplification techniques. In this paper, we concentrate on developing and analyzing clause elimination procedures, a specific family of simplification techniques for CNF formulas. Prior examples of such procedures are (explicit) tautology elimination (removing all tautologies from a CNF), subsumption elimination [7] (removing all subsumed clauses), and blocked clause elimination [11] (removing *blocked*

* The first author is supported by Dutch Organization for Scientific Research under grant 617.023.611, and the second author by Academy of Finland under grant #132812.

C. Fermüller and A. Voronkov (Eds.): LPAR-17, LNCS 6397, pp. 357–371, 2010.

clauses [12]). As extensions of these procedures we introduce novel elimination procedures based on *hidden* and *asymmetric* variants of the techniques.

We analyze the resulting nine clause elimination procedures from various perspectives. One property is *effectiveness* (or *size reduction*), i.e., the ability to remove clauses and thus reduce the size of the CNF formula. Another orthogonal and practically relevant property is *BCP-preservance*, i.e, the ability to preserve all possible Boolean constraint propagations (i.e., unit propagations) that can also be done on the original CNF. The third property, *confluence*, implies that a procedure has a unique fixpoint. The fourth is *logical equivalence* w.r.t. the original CNF, i.e. preserving the set of satisfying assignments. For the variants that do not preserve logical equivalence, we show how to efficiently reconstruct solutions to original CNFs from satisfying assignments to simplified CNFs; this is important since in many application scenarios one needs to extract a satisfying assignment (witness) to the original SAT instances. Furthermore, we develop an extension of hidden tautology elimination that does a *transitive reduction* [13] (a structural property) of the binary implication graph underlying any CNF formula purely on the CNF level. We also evaluate the practical effectiveness of selected procedures, investigating both the CNF size reduction and resulting solving times.

This paper is organized as follows. After preliminaries (Sect. 2), we present an overview of the results on the properties of clause elimination procedures (Sect. 3). Then detailed analysis is presented (Sect. 4–6), followed by a section on solution reconstruction (Sect. 7). Then, before concluding, experimental results are presented (Sect. 8).

2 Preliminaries

CNF. For a Boolean variable x, there are two *literals*, the positive literal, denoted by x, and the negative literal, denoted by $\bar{x}$. A *clause* is a disjunction of literals and a CNF formula a conjunction of clauses. A clause can be seen as a finite set of literals and a CNF formula as a finite set of clauses. A *unit clause* contains exactly one literal. A clause is a *tautology* if it contains both x and $\bar{x}$ for some x. A truth assignment for a CNF formula F is a function τ that maps variables in F to $\{\mathbf{t}, \mathbf{f}\}$. If $\tau(x) = v$, then $\tau(\bar{x}) = \neg v$, where $\neg\mathbf{t} = \mathbf{f}$ and $\neg\mathbf{f} = \mathbf{t}$. A clause C is satisfied by τ if $\tau(l) = \mathbf{t}$ for some $l \in C$. An assignment τ satisfies F if it satisfies every clause in F. The set of literals occurring in a CNF formula F is denoted by $\mathsf{lits}(F)$. Formulas are *logically equivalent* if they have the same set of satisfying assignments over the common variables.

BCP and Failed Literals. For a CNF formula F, *Boolean constraint propagation* (BCP) (or *unit propagation*) propagates all unit clauses, i.e. repeats the following until fixpoint: if there is a unit clause $(l) \in F$, remove from $F \setminus \{(l)\}$ all clauses that contain the literal l, and remove the literal $\bar{l}$ from all clauses in F. The resulting formula is referred to as $\mathrm{BCP}(F)$. If $(l) \in \mathrm{BCP}(F)$ for some unit clause $(l) \notin F$, we say that BCP assigns the literal l to $\mathbf{t}$ (and the literal $\bar{l}$ to $\mathbf{f}$). If $(l), (\bar{l}) \in \mathrm{BCP}(F)$ for some literal $l \notin F$ (or, equivalently, $\emptyset \in \mathrm{BCP}(F)$), we say that BCP derives a conflict.

For a partial assignment τ over the variables in F, let $\mathrm{BCP}(F, \tau) := \mathrm{BCP}(F \cup T_\tau \cup F_\tau)$, where $T_\tau = \{(x) \mid \tau(x) = \mathbf{t}\}$ and $F_\tau = \{(\bar{x}) \mid \tau(x) = \mathbf{f}\}$. It is easy to see that BCP has a unique fixpoint for any CNF formula, i.e., BCP is *confluent*.

A literal l is a *failed literal* if $\text{BCP}(F \cup \{(l)\})$ contains the empty clause $\emptyset$, implying that F is logically equivalent to $\text{BCP}(F \cup \{(\bar{l})\})$. For a formula F, *failed literal elimination* [1–3] (FLE) repeats the following until fixpoint: if there is a failed literal l in F, let $F := \text{BCP}(F \cup \{(\bar{l})\})$. We denote the formula resulting from applying failed literal elimination on F by $\text{FLE}(F)$. Since BCP is confluent, so is FLE, too.

Binary Implication Graphs and Equivalent Literal Substitution. Given a CNF formula F, we denote in the following by F_2 the set of binary clauses contained in F. For any F, one can associate with F_2 a unique directed *binary implication graph* (or simply $\mathsf{BIG}(F)$) with the node set $\mathsf{lits}(F_2)$ and edge relation $\{\langle \bar{l}, l' \rangle, \langle \bar{l}', l \rangle \mid (l \vee l') \in F_2\}$. In other words, for each binary clause $(l \vee l')$ in F, the two implications $\bar{l} \rightarrow l'$ and $\bar{l}' \rightarrow l$, represented by the binary clause, occur as edges in $\mathsf{BIG}(F)$. The strongly connected components (SCCs) of $\mathsf{BIG}(F)$ describe equivalent classes of literals (or simply equivalent literals) in F_2. *Equivalent literal substitution* (ELS) refers to substituting in F, for each SCC G of $\mathsf{BIG}(F)$, all occurrences of the literals occurring in G with the representative literal of G. Similar definitions occur in [8]. Notice that ELS is confluent modulo variable renaming.

3 Overview of Contributions

Before more detailed analysis, we now give an overview of the main results of this paper. We focus on nine different clause elimination procedures that are based on three variants (*explicit*, *hidden*, and *asymmetric*) of clause elimination techniques that remove *tautological*, *subsumed*, and *blocked* clauses. For (explicit) *tautology elimination* (TE), we have the variants *hidden tautology elimination* (HTE) and *asymmetric tautology elimination* (ATE). For (explicit) *subsumption elimination* (SE), we introduce the *hidden* and *asymmetric* variant HSE and ASE, respectively, and for (explicit) *blocked clause elimination* (BCE), the *hidden* and *asymmetric* variants HBCE and ABCE, resp.

A relevant aspect of simplification techniques is the question of how much a specific technique reduces the size of CNF formulas. In this paper we analyze the *relative effectiveness* of the considered clause elimination procedures based on the clauses removed by the procedures. For this we apply the following natural definition of effectiveness.

Definition 1. *Assume two clause elimination procedures S_1 and S_2 that take as input an arbitrary CNF formula F and each outputs a CNF formula that consists of a subset of F that is satisfiability-equivalent to F. Procedure S_1 is* at least as effective as *S_2 if, for any F and any output $S_1(F)$ and $S_2(F)$ of S_1 and S_2 on input F, respectively, we have that $S_1(F) \subseteq S_2(F)$; S_2 is* not as effective as *S_1 if there is an F for which there are outputs $S_1(F)$ and $S_2(F)$ of S_1 and S_2, respectively, such that $S_1(F) \subset S_2(F)$; and S_1 is* more effective than *S_2 if (i) S_1 is at least as effective as S_2, and (ii) S_2 is not as effective as S_1.*

Our definition of relative effectiveness takes into account *non-confluent* elimination procedures, i.e., procedures that do not generally have a unique fixpoint and that may thus have more than one possible output for a given input. The result of a non-confluent simplification procedure can be very unpredictable due to the non-uniqueness of results.

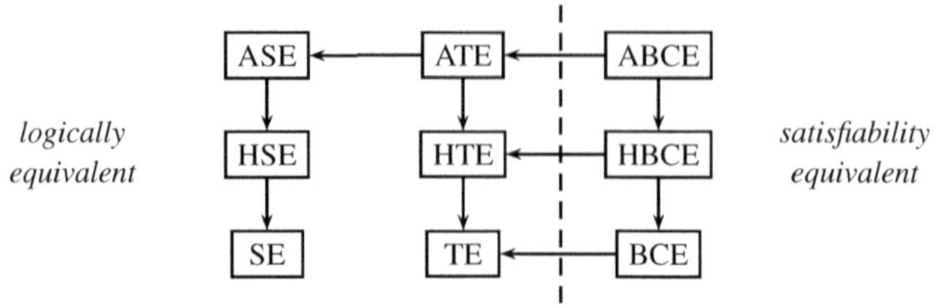

Fig. 1. Relative effectiveness hierarchy of clause elimination procedures. An edge from X to Y means that X is more effective than Y. A missing edge from X to Y means that X is not as effective as Y. However, notice that transitive edges are missing from the figure for clarity.

Our analysis on relative effectiveness results in an effectiveness hierarchy (Fig. 1) for the considered elimination procedures. For example, we show that for each of the known *explicit* techniques, the *hidden* and *asymmetric* variants are more effective, the latter of which being the most effective one of the three. In this sense, the novel variants are proper generalizations of the known explicit techniques. It also turns out that the most effective technique is the asymmetric variant of blocked clause elimination.

The further analysis presented in this paper considers the properties listed in Table 1. While each of the techniques preserves satisfiability (and are thus sound), it turns out that the variants of blocked clause elimination do not preserve logical equivalence; this is the motivation for demonstrating in Sect. 7 how one can efficiently reconstruct original solutions based on satisfying assignments for CNFs simplified using these variants. A further property of simplification techniques is BCP-preservance, which implies that relevant unit propagation (restricted to the remaining variables in the simplified CNF formula) possible in the original CNF is also possible in the simplified CNF under any partial assignment. This property is solver-related and very much practically relevant, since BCP is an integral part of a vast majority of SAT solvers today.

Definition 2. *For a formula F, a preprocessing procedure S* preserves BCP on F *if under any partial assignment τ over the variables in F and for any formula $S(F)$ resulting from applying S on F, we have that (i) for any literal l occurring in $S(F)$, $(l) \in \text{BCP}(F, \tau)$ implies $(l) \in \text{BCP}(S(F), \tau)$, and (ii) $\emptyset \in \text{BCP}(F, \tau)$ implies $\emptyset \in \text{BCP}(S(F), \tau)$ (the empty clause is obtained, i.e.,* BCP *derives a conflict). S is* BCP-preserving *if S preserves* BCP *on every CNF formula.*

Notice that our definition is similar to *deductive power* as defined in [10]. Also notice that BCP-preservance implies that logical equivalence is also preserved.

Interestingly, in turns out that BCP-preservance is quite a strict property, as only the basic SE and TE have it. However, by naturally combining HTE with a restricted version of FLE and ELS, we identify *extended hidden tautology elimination* (eHTE) which is *both* BCP-preserving *and* confluent (denoted in Table 1 with $*$), using conditions under which HTE does a *transitive reduction* [13] on the binary implication graphs underlying CNF formulas.

We proceed by giving detailed analysis of each of the variants of tautology, subsumption, and blocked clause based elimination procedures.

Table 1. Properties of clause elimination procedures

	SE	HSE	ASE	TE	HTE	ATE	BCE	HBCE	ABCE
satisfiability-equivalent	yes	yes	yes	yes	yes	yes	yes	yes	yes
logically equivalent	yes	yes	yes	yes	yes	yes	no	no	no
BCP-preserving	yes	no	no	yes	no / yes*	no	no	no	no
confluent	yes	no	no	yes	no / yes*	no	yes	no	no

4 Tautology-Based Clause Elimination Procedures

We begin by considering tautology elimination, introducing its hidden and asymmetric variants, and analyzing these procedures in more detail. For a given formula F, *tautology elimination* (TE) repeats the following until fixpoint: if there is a tautological clause $C \in F$, let $F := F \setminus \{C\}$. We refer to the reduced formula after applying tautology elimination on F as $\mathrm{TE}(F)$. It is easy to see that TE is confluent and BCP-preserving, and also that for any CNF formula F, $\mathrm{TE}(F)$ is logically equivalent to F.

4.1 Hidden Tautology Elimination

For a given clause C and a CNF formula F, we denote by (*hidden literal addition*) $\mathrm{HLA}(F, C)$ the *unique* clause resulting from repeating the following clause extension steps until fixpoint: if there is a literal $l_0 \in C$ such that there is a clause $(l_0 \vee l) \in F_2 \setminus \{C\}$ for some literal l, let $C := C \cup \{\bar{l}\}$. Notice that $\mathrm{HLA}(F, C) = \mathrm{HLA}(F_2, C)$. Furthermore, notice that for any $l \in \mathrm{HLA}(F, C) \setminus C$, there is for some $l_0 \in C$ a chain of binary clauses $(l_0 \vee \bar{l}_1), (l_1 \vee \bar{l}_2), \ldots, (l_{k-1} \vee \bar{l}_k)$ with $l = l_k$, equivalent to the implication chains $\bar{l}_0 \rightarrow \bar{l}_1, \bar{l}_1 \rightarrow \bar{l}_2, \ldots, \bar{l}_{k-1} \rightarrow \bar{l}_k$ and $l_k \rightarrow l_{k-1}, l_{k-1} \rightarrow l_{k-2}, \ldots, l_1 \rightarrow l_0$, in F_2 (equivalently, paths in $\mathsf{BIG}(F)$).

Lemma 1. *For any CNF formula F and clause $C \in F$, $(F \setminus \{C\}) \cup \{\mathrm{HLA}(F, C)\}$ is logically equivalent to F.*

Proof. For any literal $l \in \mathrm{HLA}(F, C) \setminus C$, by the definition of $\mathrm{HLA}(F, C)$, there is a $i \geq 0$ such that $l \rightarrow l_i, \ldots, l_1 \rightarrow l_0$ with $l_0 \in C$. Hence $(l_0) \in \mathrm{BCP}((F \setminus \{C\}) \cup \{(l)\})$, which implies that for any satisfying assignment τ for $(F \setminus \{C\})$ and $\mathrm{HLA}(F, C)$, if $\tau(l) = \mathbf{t}$ then $\tau(l_0) = \mathbf{t}$. Thus τ satisfies C and therefore also F. □

Alternatively, observe that each extension step in computing HLA is an application of self-subsuming resolution [7] in reverse order.

For a given CNF formula F, a clause $C \in F$ is a *hidden tautology* if and only if $\mathrm{HLA}(F, C)$ is a tautology. *Hidden tautology elimination* repeats the following until fixpoint: if there is a clause C such that $\mathrm{HLA}(F, C)$ is a tautology, let $F := F \setminus \{C\}$. A formula resulting from this procedure is denoted by $\mathrm{HTE}(F)$.

Lemma 2. HTE *is more effective than* TE.

Proof. HTE is at least as effective as TE due to $C \subseteq \mathrm{HLA}(F, C)$: if C is a tautology, so is $\mathrm{HLA}(F, C)$. Moreover, let $F = (a \vee b) \wedge (\bar{b} \vee c) \wedge (a \vee c)$. Since $\mathrm{HLA}(F, (a \vee c)) = (a \vee \bar{a} \vee b \vee \bar{b} \vee c \vee \bar{c})$, HTE can remove $(a \vee c)$ from F, in contrast to TE. □

Proposition 1. HTE *is not confluent.*

Proof. Consider the formula $F = (\bar{a} \vee b) \wedge (\bar{a} \vee c) \wedge (a \vee \bar{c}) \wedge (\bar{b} \vee c) \wedge (b \vee \bar{c})$. Now, $\text{HLA}(F, (\bar{a} \vee b)) = \text{HLA}(F, (\bar{a} \vee c)) = \text{HLA}(F, (b \vee \bar{c})) = (a \vee \bar{a} \vee b \vee \bar{b} \vee c \vee \bar{c})$. HTE can remove either $(\bar{a} \vee b)$ or both $(\bar{a} \vee c), (b \vee \bar{c})$. □

Proposition 2. *For any CNF formula F, any* $\text{HTE}(F)$ *is logically equivalent to F.*

Proof. Follows from the fact that TE preserves logical equivalence and Lemma 1. □

Proposition 3. HTE *is not* BCP*-preserving.*

Proof. Consider the formula $F = (a \vee b) \wedge (b \vee c) \wedge (b \vee \bar{c})$. HTE can remove clause $(a \vee b)$. Consider the assignment τ which assigns $\tau(a) = \mathbf{f}$. We have $(b) \in \text{BCP}(F, \tau)$. However, $(b) \notin \text{BCP}(F \setminus \{(a \vee b)\}, \tau)$. □

Although HTE is not confluent and does not preserve BCP in general, we identify eHTE, a natural variant of HTE which is both BCP-preserving and confluent.

For some intuition, consider again the formula $F = (a \vee b) \wedge (b \vee c) \wedge (b \vee \bar{c})$. Notice that $\bar{b} \in \text{HLA}(F, (b)) = (\bar{a} \vee b \vee \bar{b} \vee c \vee \bar{c})$. Recall that HTE can only remove $(a \vee b)$ from F. However, since $\bar{b} \in \text{HLA}(F, (b))$, $\bar{b}$ is a failed literal. Consequently, we can remove (*all*) clauses containing the literal b from F and add a unit clause (b). In general, we have the following.

Lemma 3. *Given a CNF formula F, for any literal l it holds that l is a failed literal in F_2 if and only if $\bar{l} \in \text{HLA}(F_2, (l))$.*

Proof. There is a path from l to $\bar{l}$ in $\mathsf{BIG}(F)$ if and only if $\bar{l} \in \text{HLA}(F_2, (l))$. □

Based on this observation, given a CNF formula F, binary-clause restricted failed literal elimination FLE_2 repeats the following until fixpoint: if there is a literal $l \in \mathsf{lits}(F_2)$ with $\bar{l} \in \text{HLA}(F_2, (l))$, let $F := \text{BCP}(F \cup \{(l)\})$. Since FLE is confluent, so is FLE_2. Refer to [8] for algorithmic aspects in computing FLE_2.

It turns out that for any CNF formula it holds that after applying FLE_2, HTE does the equivalent of a *transitive reduction*[1] of the binary implication graph $\mathsf{BIG}(\text{FLE}_2(F))$.

Lemma 4. *Given a CNF formula F, let $F' :=$* $\text{FLE}_2(F)$. *Let F'_{HTE} stand for any formula resulting from applying* HTE *on F'. It then holds that* $\mathsf{BIG}(F'_{\text{HTE}})$ *is a transitive reduction of* $\mathsf{BIG}(F')$.

Proof. Since $\mathsf{BIG}(F')$ is only influenced by F'_2, we focus on binary clauses removed from F' by HTE. For such a binary clause $C = (l \vee l')$, there are the edges $\bar{l} \to l'$ and $\bar{l}' \to l$ in $\mathsf{BIG}(F')$. Since neither l nor l' is a failed literal in F', there are also two paths $\bar{l} \to \ldots \to c$ and $\bar{l}' \to \ldots \to \bar{c}$ in $\mathsf{BIG}(F' \setminus C)$ such that $c, \bar{c} \in \text{HLA}(F', C)$. Hence there are also the paths $\bar{l} \to \ldots \to c \to \ldots \to l'$ and $\bar{l}' \to \ldots \to \bar{c} \to \ldots \to l$, and hence both $\bar{l} \to l'$ and $\bar{l}' \to l$ are transitive edges in $\mathsf{BIG}(F')$. This shows that HTE only removes transitive edges of $\mathsf{BIG}(F')$. Applying HTE until fixpoint, all such transitive edges are removed from $\mathsf{BIG}(F')$, since any such $C = (l \vee l')$, such that there are the paths $\bar{l} \to \ldots \to c \to \ldots \to l'$ and $\bar{l}' \to \ldots \to \bar{c} \to \ldots \to l$, is a hidden tautology. □

[1] A directed graph G' is a transitive reduction [13] of the directed graph G provided that (i) G' has a directed path from node u to node v if and only if G has a directed path from node u to node v, and (ii) there is no graph with fewer edges than G' satisfying condition (i).

Notice that for every formula F such that $\mathsf{BIG}(F)$ is acyclic, it holds that $\mathsf{BIG}(F)$ has a unique transitive reduction, since the transitive reduction of any directed acyclic graph is unique [13]. In this case, there are no non-trivial SCCs in $\mathsf{BIG}(F)$. Furthermore, even for directed graph with cycles, the transitive reduction is unique modulo node equivalence classes [13]. This implies that applying the *combination* of $\mathrm{FLE}_2(F)$ and ELS before HTE, i.e., additionally substituting equivalent literals with the representatives of the literal equivalence classes (non-trivial strongly connected components) in $\mathsf{BIG}(\mathrm{FLE}_2(F))$, a unique transitive reduction (module variable renaming) is obtained.

With this intuition, for a formula F, extended hidden tautology elimination (eHTE) does the following two steps:

1. Repeat until fixpoint: (1a) Let $F := \mathrm{FLE}_2(F)$. (1b) Let $F := \mathrm{ELS}(F)$.
2. Apply HTE on F.

By the discussion above, eHTE is confluent.

Theorem 1. eHTE *is confluent.*

Furthermore, it turns out that by applying HTE on $\mathrm{FLE}_2(F)$, BCP is preserved in general; that is, even without applying equivalent literal substitution (Step 1b), we have a BCP-preserving variant of HTE.

Lemma 5. *For any CNF formula F,* HTE *preserves* BCP *on* $\mathrm{FLE}_2(F)$ *w.r.t.* F.

Proof. Consider an arbitrary CNF formula F, and let $F := \mathrm{FLE}_2(F)$. Assume that HTE removes a clause $C = (l_1 \vee \cdots \vee l_k) \in F$ from F; hence C is a hidden tautology in F, i.e., $\mathrm{HLA}(F, C)$ is a tautology.

Due to first applying FLE_2, C can not be a unit clause (l_1): otherwise, (l_1) would be a failed literal in F. The only way for BCP on all clauses of F to use C is that we have an assignment τ with $\tau(l_1) = \cdots = \tau(l_{k-1}) = \mathbf{f}$, in which case BCP on F can derive the unit clause (l_k), i.e., assign l_k to $\mathbf{t}$; hence the case that C is a tautology is trivial. If C is a binary clause $(l_1 \vee l_2)$, then by Lemma 4 the implications representing C are transitive edges in $\mathsf{BIG}(F \setminus \{C\})$, and hence there are alternative implication chains between l_1^{i+1} and l_2^{i+1} in F which preserve BCP over C.

Now assume that C contains at least three literals and $\mathrm{HLA}(F, C)$ contains the opposite literals l and $\bar{l}$. Due to FLE_2, by assigning only a single l_i for some $i \in \{1, \ldots, k-1\}$ to $\mathbf{f}$, BCP on binary clauses F_2 only, can not derive a conflict, and hence can not derive the unit clauses (l) and $(\bar{l})$. Otherwise $\bar{l}_i$ would be a failed literal. Therefore there are two distinct literals $l', l'' \in C$, based on which $\bar{l}$ and l are included in $\mathrm{HLA}(F, C)$, and $\mathsf{BIG}(F)$ contains two implication chains $\bar{l}' \rightarrow \bar{l}'_1, \bar{l}'_1 \rightarrow \bar{l}'_2, \ldots, \bar{l}'_{k'} \rightarrow l$ and $\bar{l}'' \rightarrow \bar{l}''_1, \bar{l}''_1 \rightarrow \bar{l}''_2, \ldots, \bar{l}''_{k''} \rightarrow \bar{l}$. Now there are two cases:

1. $l', l'' \in C \setminus \{l_k\}$. Since $\tau(l') = \tau(l'') = \mathbf{f}$, it follows that $(l), (\bar{l}) \in \mathrm{BCP}(F \setminus \{C\}, \tau)$, i.e., BCP derives a conflict without using C.
2. $l' \in C \setminus \{l_k\}$ and $l'' = l_k$. Then $\tau(l') = \mathbf{f}$, and it follows that $(l) \in \mathrm{BCP}(F \setminus \{C\}, \tau)$. Hence l is assigned to $\mathbf{t}$ by BCP under τ. Furthermore, since $l'' = l_k$ and the implication chain $\bar{l}_k \rightarrow \bar{l}''_1, \bar{l}''_1 \rightarrow \bar{l}''_2, \ldots, \bar{l}''_{k''} \rightarrow \bar{l}$ can be seen in the reversed order as $l \rightarrow l''_{k''}, l''_{k''} \rightarrow l''_{k''-1}, \ldots, l''_1 \rightarrow l_k$, after assigning l to $\mathbf{t}$ it follows that $(l_k) \in \mathrm{BCP}(F \setminus \{C\}, \tau)$. Hence BCP assigns l_k to $\mathbf{t}$ without using C. □

Furthermore, since ELS only does variable renaming by substituting equivalent literals, it can not interfere with BCP, and we have the following.

Theorem 2. *e*HTE *is* BCP-*preserving.*

Moreover, the following lemma follows the intuition on failed literals in HLA.

Lemma 6. *e*HTE *is more effective than* HTE.

In fact, here Step 1b of *e*HTE can again be omitted without affecting this result.

4.2 Asymmetric Tautology Elimination

For a clause C and a CNF formula F, (*asymmetric literal addition*) $\mathrm{ALA}(F, C)$ denotes the *unique* clause resulting from repeating the following until fixpoint: if $l_1, \ldots, l_k \in C$ and there is a clause $(l_1 \vee \ldots \vee l_k \vee l) \in F \setminus \{C\}$ for some literal l, let $C := C \cup \{\bar{l}\}$. A clause C is called an *asymmetric tautology* if and only if $\mathrm{ALA}(F, C)$ is a tautology.

Given a formula F, *asymmetric tautology elimination* (ATE) repeats the following until fixpoint: if there is an asymmetric tautological clause $C \in F$, let $F := F \setminus \{C\}$.

Lemma 7. $\mathrm{ALA}(F, C)$ *is a tautology if and only if* BCP *on* $(F \setminus \{C\}) \cup \bigcup_{l \in C}\{(\bar{l})\})$ *derives a conflict.*

As can be seen from Lemma 7, ATE performs what could be called *asymmetric branching* on clauses, which is used, e.g., in the technique of *clause distillation* [9].

The example in the proof of Proposition 1 implies the following.

Proposition 4. ATE *is not confluent.*

Proposition 5. *For any CNF formula* F*,* $\mathrm{ATE}(F)$ *is logically equivalent to* F*.*

Proof. For any clause C removed by ATE, $(F \setminus \{C\}) \cup \bigcup_{l \in C}\{(\bar{l})\}$ is unsatisfiable. This implies that $F \setminus \{C\} \models C$, i.e., $F \setminus \{C\}$ logically entails C. □

Proposition 6. ATE *is not* BCP-*preserving.*

Proof. Consider the following translation of x = If-Then-Else(c, t, e) into CNF:

$$(\bar{x} \vee \bar{c} \vee t) \wedge (x \vee \bar{c} \vee \bar{t}) \wedge (\bar{x} \vee c \vee e) \wedge (x \vee c \vee \bar{e}) \wedge (x \vee \bar{e} \vee \bar{t}) \wedge (\bar{x} \vee e \vee t)$$

Notice that ATE can remove $(x \vee \bar{e} \vee \bar{t})$ and $(\bar{x} \vee e \vee t)$. However, after removal, for truth assignment $\tau(e) = \tau(t) = \mathbf{f}$, BCP will no longer assign x to $\mathbf{t}$. Also, for truth assignment $\tau(e) = \tau(t) = \mathbf{t}$, BCP will no longer assign x to $\mathbf{f}$. □

The fact that $\mathrm{HLA}(F, C) = \mathrm{ALA}(F_2, C)$ implies the following.

Lemma 8. *For any CNF formula* F *and clause* $C \in F$*,* $\mathrm{HLA}(F, C) \subseteq \mathrm{ALA}(F, C)$.

Lemma 9. ATE *is more effective than* HTE.

Proof. ATE is at least as effective as HTE due to $\mathrm{HLA}(F, C) \subseteq \mathrm{ALA}(F, C)$: if $\mathrm{HLA}(F, C)$ is a tautology, then $\mathrm{ALA}(F, C)$ is a tautology. Moreover, consider the formula $F = (a \vee b \vee c) \wedge (a \vee b \vee d) \wedge (a \vee c \vee \bar{d})$. ATE will remove $(a \vee b \vee c)$ from F, while HTE removes none of the clauses. □

5 Subsumption-Based Clause Elimination Procedures

We now turn to the explicit, hidden, and asymmetric variants of the procedures that eliminate subsumed clauses. Given a CNF formula F, a clause $C_1 \in F$ *subsumes* (another) clause $C_2 \in F$ in F if and only if $C_1 \subset C_2$, and then C_2 is *subsumed by* C_1. Any assignment that satisfies C_1 will also satisfy C_2. For a given formula F, *subsumption elimination* (SE) repeats the following until fixpoint: if there is a subsumed clause $C \in F$, let $F := F \setminus \{C\}$. We refer to the reduced formula after applying subsumption elimination on F as $\text{SE}(F)$. It is easy to see that SE is confluent and BCP-preserving, and that for any CNF formula F, $\text{SE}(F)$ is logically equivalent to F.

5.1 Hidden Subsumption Elimination

For a given formula F, *hidden subsumption elimination* (HSE) repeats the following until fixpoint: if there is a clause $C \in F$ for which $\text{HLA}(F, C)$ is subsumed in F, let $F := F \setminus \{C\}$.

By replacing HTE with HSE in the proof of Proposition 1 we have the following.

Proposition 7. HSE *is not confluent.*

Lemma 10. *For any CNF formula F,* $\text{HSE}(F)$ *is logically equivalent to F.*

Proof. Follows from Lemma 1 and the fact that SE preserves logical equivalence. □

Proposition 8. HSE *is not* BCP*-preserving.*

Proof. Let $F = (a \vee b \vee c) \wedge (a \vee b \vee d) \wedge (b \vee \bar{c})$. HSE can remove $(a \vee b \vee d)$, because $\text{HLA}(F, (a \vee b \vee d)) = (a \vee b \vee c \vee d)$ is subsumed by $(a \vee b \vee c)$. Consider the assignment τ which assigns $\tau(a) = \tau(d) = \mathbf{f}$. We have $(b) \in \text{BCP}(F, \tau)$. However, $(b) \notin \text{BCP}(F \setminus \{(a \vee b \vee d)\}, \tau)$. □

Notice that the above proof also holds after F is simplified by FLE.

Lemma 11. HSE *is more effective than* SE.

Proof. HSE is at least as effective as SE since for any CNF formula F, (i) for every clause $C \in F$, $C \subseteq \text{HLA}(F, C)$, and (ii) if C is subsumed then any clause $C' \supseteq C$ is subsumed. Moreover, let $F = (a \vee b \vee c) \wedge (a \vee b \vee d) \wedge (b \vee \bar{c}) \wedge (\bar{a} \vee d \vee \bar{d})$. HSE can remove $(a \vee b \vee d)$ because $\text{HLA}(F, (a \vee b \vee d)) = (a \vee b \vee c \vee d)$, in contrast to SE. □

Also notice that, given two identical clauses C_1 and C_2 (i.e., $C_1 \subseteq C_2$ and $C_2 \subseteq C_1$), HSE can remove either C_1 or C_2, while SE cannot.

Lemma 12. *It holds that (i)* HSE *is not as effective as* HTE, *and that (ii)* HTE *is not as effective as* HSE.

Proof. Consider the formula F_{HSE}. HTE can remove the tautology $(\bar{a} \vee d \vee \bar{d})$, but no other clauses. HSE can remove $(a \vee b \vee d)$, but no other clauses. □

5.2 Asymmetric Subsumption Elimination

For a given formula F, *asymmetric subsumption elimination* (ASE) repeats the following until fixpoint: if there is a clause $C \in F$ for which $\text{ALA}(F, C)$ is subsumed in F, let $F := F \setminus \{C\}$.

By replacing ATE with ASE in the proof of Lemma 6 we have the following.

Proposition 9. ASE *is not* BCP*-preserving.*

Lemma 13. ASE *is more effective than* HSE.

Proof. ASE is at least as effective as HSE since (i) for every clause $C \in F$ we have $\text{HLA}(F, C) \subseteq \text{ALA}(F, C)$ (Lemma 8), and (ii) if C is subsumed then any clause $C' \supseteq C$ is subsumed. Moreover, consider the formula $F = (a \vee b \vee c) \wedge (a \vee b \vee d) \wedge (a \vee c \vee \bar{d})$. ASE will remove $(a \vee b \vee c)$ from F, while HSE removes no clauses from F. □

Lemma 14. ATE *is more effective than* ASE.

Proof. To see that ATE is at least as effective as ASE, consider the following. If there is a clause $C \in F$ for which $\text{ALA}(F, C)$ is subsumed by $C' \in F \setminus \{C\}$, then $\text{ALA}(F, C)$ is a tautology: say $\text{ALA}(F, C)$ is subsumed by $C' = (l_1 \vee \ldots \vee l_k)$. Due to the update rule of ALA, $\bar{l}_1, \ldots, \bar{l}_k \in \text{ALA}(F, C)$. Moreover, consider the formula $F = (a \vee \bar{a})$. ASE will not remove this tautology, in contrast to ATE. □

6 Clause Elimination Procedures Based on Blocked Clauses

As the final family of clause elimination procedures considered in this paper, we now introduce and analyze procedures that eliminate blocked clauses [12].

The resolution rule states that, given two clauses $C_1 = \{l, a_1, \ldots, a_n\}$ and $C_2 = \{\bar{l}, b_2, \ldots, b_m\}$, the implied clause $C = \{a_1, \ldots, a_n, b_1, \ldots, b_m\}$, called the *resolvent* of C_1 and C_2, can be inferred by *resolving* on the literal l, and write $C = C_1 \otimes_l C_2$.

Given a CNF formula F, a clause C and a literal $l \in C$, the literal l *blocks* C w.r.t. F if (i) for each clause $C' \in F$ with $\bar{l} \in C'$, $C \otimes_l C'$ is a tautology, or (ii) $\bar{l} \in C$, i.e., C is itself a tautology[2]. Given a CNF formula F, a clause C is *blocked* w.r.t. F if there is a literal that blocks C w.r.t. F. Removal of blocked clauses preserves satisfiability [12].

For a CNF formula F, *blocked clause elimination* (BCE) repeats the following until fixpoint: if there is a blocked clause $C \in F$ w.r.t. F, let $F := F \setminus \{C\}$. The CNF formula resulting from applying BCE on F is denoted by $\text{BCE}(F)$.

Proposition 10. *For some CNF formula F,* $\text{BCE}(F)$ *is not logically equivalent to F.*

Proof. Consider the following CNF formula, having a structure that is often observed in CNF encodings of graph coloring problems.

$$F_{\text{BCE}} = (a \vee b \vee c) \wedge (d \vee e \vee f) \wedge (\bar{a} \vee \bar{d}) \wedge (\bar{b} \vee \bar{e}) \wedge (\bar{c} \vee \bar{f}) \wedge \\ (\bar{a} \vee \bar{b}) \wedge (\bar{a} \vee \bar{c}) \wedge (\bar{b} \vee \bar{c}) \wedge (\bar{d} \vee \bar{e}) \wedge (\bar{d} \vee \bar{f}) \wedge (\bar{e} \vee \bar{f}).$$

---

[2] Here $\bar{l} \in C$ is included in order to handle the special case that for any tautological *binary* clause $(l \vee \bar{l})$, both l and $\bar{l}$ block the clause. Notice that, even without this addition, every *non-binary* tautological clause contains at least one literal that blocks the clause.

BCE can remove the last six binary clauses (the second row) in F_{BCE}. Consider the truth assignment τ with $\tau(a) = \tau(b) = \tau(f) = \mathbf{t}$ and $\tau(c) = \tau(d) = \tau(e) = \mathbf{f}$. Although τ satisfies $\text{BCE}(F_{\text{BCE}})$, the clause $(\bar{a} \vee \bar{b})$ in F_{BCE} is falsified by τ. □

6.1 Hidden Blocked Clause Elimination

For a given CNF formula F, a clause $C \in F$ is called *hidden blocked* if $\text{HLA}(F, C)$ is blocked w.r.t. F. *Hidden blocked clause elimination* (HBCE) repeats the following until fixpoint: if there is a hidden blocked clause $C \in F$, remove C from F.

Lemma 15. *Removal of an arbitrary hidden blocked clause preserves satisfiability.*

Proof. Follows from the facts that F is logically equivalent to $(F \setminus \{C\}) \cup \{\text{HLA}(F, C)\}$ and that BCE preserves satisfiability. □

Proposition 11. HBCE *is not confluent.*

Proof. Let $F = (\bar{a} \vee b) \wedge (\bar{a} \vee c) \wedge (a \vee \bar{d}) \wedge (\bar{b} \vee d) \wedge (\bar{c} \vee d)$. F contains four hidden blocked clauses: $\text{HLA}(F, (\bar{a} \vee b)) = (\bar{a} \vee b \vee \bar{c} \vee \bar{d})$ with blocking literal b, $\text{HLA}(F, (\bar{a} \vee c)) = (\bar{a} \vee \bar{b} \vee c \vee \bar{d})$ with blocking literal c, $\text{HLA}(F, (\bar{b} \vee d)) = (a \vee \bar{b} \vee c \vee d)$ with blocking literal $\bar{b}$, and $\text{HLA}(F, (\bar{c} \vee d)) = (a \vee b \vee \bar{c} \vee d)$ with blocking literal $\bar{c}$. HBCE removes either $(\bar{a} \vee b)$ and $(\bar{b} \vee d)$, or $(\bar{a} \vee c)$ and $(\bar{c} \vee d)$. □

Replacing BCE with HBCE in the proof of Proposition 10, we have the following.

Proposition 12. *For some CNF formula F,* $\text{HBCE}(F)$ *is not logically equivalent to F.*

Lemma 16. HBCE *is more effective than* BCE *and* HTE.

Proof. HBCE is at least as effective as BCE due to $C \subseteq \text{HLA}(F, C)$ and that each blocking literal $l \in C$ is also blocking $\text{HLA}(F, C)$. HBCE is at least as effective as HTE since tautologies are blocked clauses. Moreover, let $F = (a \vee c) \wedge (\bar{a} \vee d) \wedge (\bar{b} \vee c) \wedge (b \vee d) \wedge (\bar{c} \vee \bar{d})$. Now $\text{HLA}(F, (a \vee c)) = (a \vee b \vee c \vee \bar{d})$ with blocking literal a, and $\text{HLA}(F, (\bar{a} \vee d)) = (\bar{a} \vee \bar{b} \vee \bar{c} \vee d)$ with blocking literal $\bar{a}$. Hence HBCE removes both $(a \vee c)$ and $(\bar{a} \vee d)$, while neither BCE nor HTE can remove any clause of F. □

6.2 Asymmetric Blocked Clause Elimination

For a given CNF formula F, a clause $C \in F$ is called asymmetric blocked if $\text{ALA}(F, C)$ is blocked w.r.t. F. *Asymmetric blocked clause elimination* (ABCE) repeats the following until fixpoint: if there is an asymmetric blocked clause $C \in F$, let $F := F \setminus \{C\}$.

Lemma 17. *Removal of an asymmetric blocked clause preserves satisfiability.*

Proof. Follows from the facts that F is logically equivalent to $(F \setminus \{C\}) \cup \{\text{ALA}(F, C)\}$ and that BCE preserves satisfiability. □

Proposition 13. ABCE *is not confluent.*

Proof. Let $F = (\bar{a} \vee b) \wedge (\bar{a} \vee c) \wedge (a \vee \bar{d}) \wedge (\bar{b} \vee d) \wedge (\bar{c} \vee d)$. F contains four asymmetric blocked clauses: $\text{ALA}(F, (\bar{a} \vee b)) = (\bar{a} \vee b \vee \bar{c} \vee \bar{d})$ with blocking literal b,

$\text{ALA}(F, (\bar{a} \vee c)) = (\bar{a} \vee \bar{b} \vee c \vee \bar{d})$ with blocking literal c, $\text{ALA}(F, (\bar{b} \vee d)) = (a \vee \bar{b} \vee c \vee d)$ with blocking literal $\bar{b}$, and $\text{ALA}(F, (\bar{c} \vee d)) = (a \vee b \vee \bar{c} \vee d)$ with blocking literal $\bar{c}$. ABCE removes either $(\bar{a} \vee b)$ and $(\bar{b} \vee d)$, or $(\bar{a} \vee c)$ or $(\bar{c} \vee d)$ from F. □

Replacing BCE with ABCE in the proof of Proposition 10, we have the following.

Proposition 14. *For some CNF formula F,* ABCE(F) *is not logically equivalent to F.*

Lemma 18. ABCE *is more effective than* HBCE *and* ATE.

Proof. ABCE is at least as effective as HBCE due to $\text{HLA}(F, C) \subseteq \text{ALA}(F, C)$ (recall Lemma 8): if $\text{HLA}(F, C)$ is a tautology, then $\text{ALA}(F, C)$ is a tautology. ABCE is at least as effective as ATE since tautologies are blocked clauses. Moreover, consider the formula $F_{\text{ABCE}} = (\bar{a} \vee b \vee c) \wedge (b \vee c \vee \bar{d}) \wedge (a \vee d) \wedge (\bar{b} \vee \bar{d}) \wedge (\bar{c} \vee \bar{d})$. Now $\text{ALA}(F_{\text{ABCE}}, (\bar{a} \vee b \vee c)) = (\bar{a} \vee b \vee c \vee d)$ in which b and c are blocking literals. Hence ABCE can remove $(\bar{a} \vee b \vee c)$ (and in fact all clauses in F_{ABCE}). Neither HBCE nor ATE can remove any clause from F_{ABCE}. □

7 Reconstructing Solutions After HBCE and ABCE

Since the elimination procedures based on blocked clauses do not preserve logical equivalence, a truth assignment τ satisfying BCE(F) may not satisfy F. However, a satisfying assignment for F can be constructed based on τ as follows [14]. Add the clauses $C \in F \setminus \text{BCE}(F)$ back in the opposite order of their elimination. In case C is satisfied by τ, do nothing. Otherwise, assuming that $l \in C$ is blocking C, flip the truth value of l in τ to **t**. After all clauses have been added, the modified τ satisfies F.

We now show that this procedure can be used to reconstruct solutions for formulas simplified using HBCE or ABCE. The lemmas will focus on ALA, but because HLA is a restricted version of ALA, all lemmas also hold when ALA is replaced by HLA.

Lemma 19. *Given a clause $C \in F$, if* $\text{ALA}(F, C)$ *is blocked and not a tautology, then there is a literal $l \in C$ blocking it.*

Proof. By construction, for each literal $l \in \text{ALA}(F, C) \setminus C$, here is a clause $C' \in F$ that contains $\bar{l}$ and $C' \setminus \{\bar{l}\} \subseteq \text{ALA}(F, C)$. Therefore, because $\text{ALA}(F, C)$ is not a tautology, $C' \otimes_l \text{ALA}(F, C) = \text{ALA}(F, C) \setminus \{l\}$ is not a tautology either. Hence l is not blocking $\text{ALA}(F, C)$. □

Lemma 20. *Given a CNF formula F and a truth assignment τ satisfying F, if $C \notin F$ is falsified by τ, then* $\text{ALA}(F, C)$ *is falsified by τ.*

Proof. From Lemma 7 follows that $F \cup \{\text{ALA}(F, C)\}$ is logically equivalent to $F \cup \{C\}$. Therefore, $\text{ALA}(F, C)$ is satisfied by τ if and only if τ satisfies C. □

Lemma 21. *Given a CNF formula F and a truth assignment τ satisfying F, if $C \notin F$ is falsified by τ and* $\text{ALA}(F, C)$ *is blocked w.r.t. F with blocking literal $l \in C$, then τ satisfies at least two literals in each clause $C' \in F$ with $\bar{l} \in C'$.*

Proof. First, such $C' \in F$ contain a literal $\bar{l}$ which is satisfied by τ. Second, because l is blocking, each clause C' must contain one more literal $l' \neq \bar{l}$ such that $\bar{l'} \in \text{ALA}(F, C)$. Since all literals in $\text{ALA}(F, C)$ are falsified by τ, l' must be satisfied by τ. □

Combining these three lemmas, we can reconstruct a solution for F if we have a satisfying assignment τ for any ABCE(F) (and also any HBCE(F)). The clauses $C \in F \setminus$ ABCE(F) are added back in reverse order of elimination to ensure that ALA(F, C) is blocked. If C is satisfied by F do nothing. Otherwise, we know that there is a literal $l \in C$ blocking ALA(F, C); recall Lemma 19. Furthermore, all literals in ALA(F, C) are falsified; recall Lemma 20. However, any $C' \in F$ containing $\bar{l}$ has two satisfied literals; recall Lemma 21. Therefore, by flipping the truth assignment for l to **t**, C becomes satisfied, while no such C' becomes falsified.

Theorem 3. *The following holds for an arbitrary CNF formula F and truth assignment τ satisfying F. For any clause $C \notin F$ for which C,* HLA(F, C)*, or* ALA(F, C) *is blocked w.r.t. F with blocking literal l, either (i) τ satisfies $F \cup \{C\}$, or (ii) τ', which is a copy of τ except for $\tau'(l) =$* **t**, *satisfies $F \cup \{C\}$.*

The reconstruction proof provides several useful elements that can be used to implement HBCE and ABCE more efficiently. First, since only original literals $l \in C$ can be blocking HLA(F, C) or ALA(F, C), we can avoid a blocking literal check for all literals $l \in$ HLA(F, C) $\setminus C$ or $l \in$ ALA(F, C) $\setminus C$. Second, it is enough to save each removed *original* clause C. None of the additional literals in the *extended* clause HLA(F, C) (or ALA(F, C), resp.) not occurring in C have to be flipped.

8 Experimental Evaluation

We shortly present initial experiments results on the effectiveness of selected clause elimination procedures, focusing on the current implementations of HTE and HBCE. The benchmarks set used consists of the 2009 SAT Competition application instances (292 in total), with each instance processed beforehand with BCP. A comparison of the effectiveness of BCE, HTE, and HBCE (all until fixpoint) is shown on the left in Fig. 2, illustrating the percentage of clauses remaining after applying the individual techniques (with original number of clauses 100%). Here data for each plot is sorted according to the reduction percentage, with the percentages of clauses remaining on the y-axis. We include BCE due to recent encouraging results presented in [11]. In line with our analysis (recall Fig. 1), HBCE is clearly the most effective technique. There is not that clear a winner between BCE and HTE, although HTE does prevail in the end.

The hidden clause elimination procedures are probably the most interesting novel techniques in practice, because they can be implemented efficiently. In particular, eHTE is expected to be useful, since it also preserves BCP. Since we have no efficient implementation of FLE_2 and ELS at this time, the experiments on practical use focus on HTE instead.

As can be seen on the right in Fig. 2 (time as a function of number of instances solved), HTE gives gains w.r.t. solution times for MiniSAT 2.0. Here we used the version of MiniSAT without the built-in preprocessor to see the effect of HTE on its own. Notice that we also conducted an additional experiment in which we first preprocessed all instances using SatELite [7]; this resulted in similar performance gains.

For most benchmarks in the SAT 2009 application suit, the cost of applying HTE is less then a second. However, on instances in which BIG(F) contains large SCCs, the

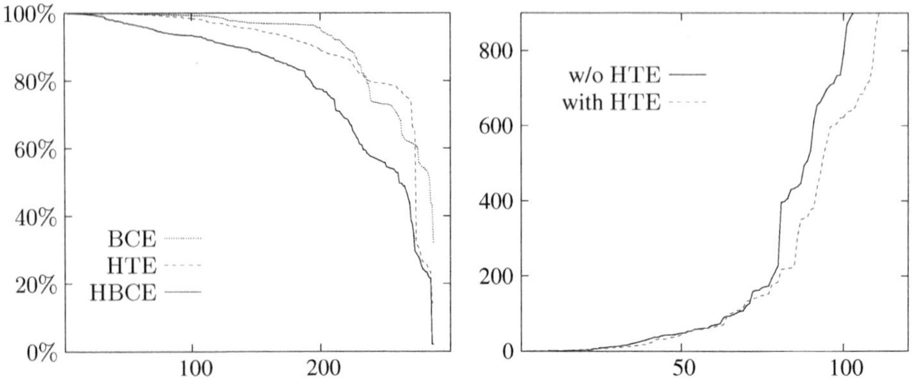

Fig. 2. Comparison of the effectiveness of various clause elimination procedures on the size of SAT 2009 benchmark instances (left). Also, the number of instances solved in less than t seconds by MiniSAT 2.0 without and with HTE as preprocessing step (right).

computational cost is on average 60 seconds. We expect that by combining HTE with ELS, as in eHTE, HTE will be quite efficient also for these instances.

Applying any of the asymmetric clause elimination procedures until fixpoint will hardly be useful in practice. The most important reason is that all these procedures are very costly. Also, because they do not preserve BCP, for several instances they can decrease performance even in case these costs are neglected. However, the asymmetric procedures will probably be of practical use when they are restricted. For instance, by only applying them on long clauses or for a short time (i.e., not until fixpoint).

Our implementation of HTE does not explicitly compute $\text{HLA}(F, C)$ for each $C \in F$. Instead, for each literal $l \in \mathsf{lits}(F)$, we compute $\text{HLA}(F, (l))$. Elimination of clauses is realized as follows: First, mark each literal l' for which $\bar{l}' \in \text{HLA}(F, (l))$ with label l. Second, for all clauses C with $l \in C$ we check whether there is a literal $l'' \in C$ marked with label l. If there is, then C is a hidden tautology. In order to make this procedure sound, we need to add a unit clause (l) in case $\bar{l} \in \text{HLA}(F, (l))$. Notice that this 'trick' cannot be used for HBCE. So, $\text{HLA}(F, C)$ needs to be explicitly computed to check whether $\text{HLA}(F, C)$ is a hidden blocked clause. This makes our current implementation of HBCE much more costly (compared to HTE). Also, while performing HBCE, some clauses can become hidden blocked clauses. Therefore, when run until fixpoint, multiple loops through the clauses are required (in contrast to HTE). As a result of this, our current implementation of HBCE is on average ten times as slow as the implementation of HTE, making HBCE at the moment impractical. However, as stated above, the cost of HTE and HBCE can be reduced by first applying ELS.

9 Conclusions

We introduced novel clause elimination procedures as hidden and asymmetric variants of the known techniques of tautology, subsumption, and blocked clause elimination. We analyzed all of the variants from various perspectives—relative effectiveness,

BCP-preservance, confluence, logical equivalence—highlighting intricate differences between the procedures. This also resulted in a relative effectiveness hierarchy, in which the asymmetric variant of blocked clause elimination dominates all other procedures.

As one of the most interesting results, we developed eHTE, a variant of hidden tautology elimination, that is both BCP-preserving and confluent, and at the same time more effective than the other procedures (tautology and subsumption elimination) that have both of these properties. In fact, eHTE does a transitive reduction (a structural property) of the binary implication graph underlying any CNF formula purely on the CNF level. Furthermore, we showed how to reconstruct solutions for the procedures, and presented experimental results on the practical effectiveness of selected procedures.

Efficient implementations of the introduced procedures and integration of the most practical ones with other simplification techniques remains as important further work.

References

1. Freeman, J.: Improvements to propositional satisfiability search algorithms. PhD thesis, University of Pennsylvania (1995)
2. Le Berre, D.: Exploiting the real power of unit propagation lookahead. Electronic Notes in Discrete Mathematics 9, 59–80 (2001)
3. Lynce, I., Marques-Silva, J.: The interaction between simplification and search in propositional satisfiability. In: CP 2001 Workshop on Modeling and Problem Formulation (2001)
4. Bacchus, F.: Enhancing Davis Putnam with extended binary clause reasoning. In: Proc. AAAI, pp. 613–619. AAAI Press, Menlo Park (2002)
5. Subbarayan, S., Pradhan, D.K.: NiVER: Non-increasing variable elimination resolution for preprocessing SAT instances. In: Hoos, H.H., Mitchell, D.G. (eds.) SAT 2004. LNCS, vol. 3542, pp. 276–291. Springer, Heidelberg (2005)
6. Gershman, R., Strichman, O.: Cost-effective hyper-resolution for preprocessing CNF formulas. In: Bacchus, F., Walsh, T. (eds.) SAT 2005. LNCS, vol. 3569, pp. 423–429. Springer, Heidelberg (2005)
7. Eén, N., Biere, A.: Effective preprocessing in SAT through variable and clause elimination. In: Bacchus, F., Walsh, T. (eds.) SAT 2005. LNCS, vol. 3569, pp. 61–75. Springer, Heidelberg (2005)
8. Gelder, A.V.: Toward leaner binary-clause reasoning in a satisfiability solver. Annals of Mathematics and Artificial Intelligence 43(1), 239–253 (2005)
9. Jin, H., Somenzi, F.: An incremental algorithm to check satisfiability for bounded model checking. Electronic Notes in Theoretical Computer Science 119(2), 51–65 (2005)
10. Han, H., Somenzi, F.: Alembic: An efficient algorithm for CNF preprocessing. In: Proc. DAC, pp. 582–587. IEEE, Los Alamitos (2007)
11. Järvisalo, M., Biere, A., Heule, M.: Blocked clause elimination. In: Esparza, J., Majumdar, R. (eds.) TACAS 2010. LNCS, vol. 6015, pp. 129–144. Springer, Heidelberg (2010)
12. Kullmann, O.: On a generalization of extended resolution. Discrete Applied Mathematics 96–97, 149–176 (1999)
13. Aho, A., Garey, M., Ullman, J.: The transitive reduction of a directed graph. SIAM Journal on Computing 1(2), 131–137 (1972)
14. Järvisalo, M., Biere, A.: Reconstructing solutions after blocked clause elimination. In: Strichman, O., Szeider, S. (eds.) Theory and Applications of Satisfiability Testing – SAT 2010. LNCS, vol. 6175, pp. 340–345. Springer, Heidelberg (2010)

Partitioning SAT Instances for Distributed Solving

Antti E. J. Hyvärinen, Tommi Junttila, and Ilkka Niemelä

Aalto University
Department of Information and Computer Science
P.O. Box 15400, FI-00076 AALTO, Finland
{Antti.Hyvarinen,Tommi.Junttila,Ilkka.Niemela}@tkk.fi

Abstract. In this paper we study the problem of solving hard propositional satisfiability problem (SAT) instances in a computing grid or cloud, where run times and communication between parallel running computations are limited. We study analytically an approach where the instance is partitioned iteratively into a tree of subproblems and each node in the tree is solved in parallel. We present new methods for constructing partitions which combine clause learning and lookahead. The methods are incorporated into the iterative approach and its performance is demonstrated with an extensive comparison against the best sequential solvers in the SAT competition 2009 as well as against two efficient parallel solvers.

1 Introduction

This paper[1] develops novel techniques for solving hard instances of the propositional satisfiability (SAT) problem in widely distributed computing environments such as computing grids or clouds. An example of this kind of an environment is NorduGrid (`http://www.nordugrid.org/`) that we use in some of the experiments of this paper. NorduGrid provides a high number of readily available, high-end, heterogeneous computing facilities cost-efficiently, suggesting that this type of computing is an interesting target for applications such as SAT solving. The distributed environments in this work differ in some significant aspects from some other common distributed computing environments, such as multi-core workstations, and even local parallel environments, such as computing clusters: once a computation or a job is submitted to a grid or a cloud, the execution of the job is not immediate, as it is delayed by an amount of time depending on the availability of the computing resources; the executing jobs have limited communication capabilities restricted by the site security policies; and the jobs are only allowed to use a predetermined amount of CPU time and memory during their execution.

The goal of this work is to develop distributed SAT solving for such environments using the best available SAT solvers as black-box subroutines with minimal modifications. The goal can be straightforwardly achieved by exploiting the randomized nature of current state-of-the-art SAT solvers with the *simple distribution* (SD) approach, where one just runs a randomized solver a number of times independently. This leads to surprisingly good speed-ups even in a grid environment with substantial communication and other delays [1]. The approach could be extended by applying particular restart

[1] A full version of the paper is available via `http://users.ics.tkk.fi/aehyvari/`.

C. Fermüller and A. Voronkov (Eds.): LPAR-17, LNCS 6397, pp. 372–386, 2010.

strategies [2,3] or employing an algorithm portfolio scheme [4,5]. Another key feature in modern SAT solvers is the use of conflict driven clause learning techniques. Extending the simple distribution approach with this feature leads to a powerful SAT solving technique [6,7].

While the SD approach has led to surprisingly good performance, it provides no mechanism for splitting the search into more manageable portions which can be treated in parallel. A *partition function* maps a SAT instance to a set of *derived* instances by constraining the instance so that the original instance is satisfiable if and only if at least one of the derived instances is. We call *plain partitioning* an approach where a partition function is used once and each resulting instance is solved in parallel. A typical approach to splitting the search space is to use guiding path or semantic decomposition based techniques [8,9,10,11,12,13]. However, these techniques impose constraints on the underlying solver technology and are not ideal for grids and clouds since they require relatively frequent communication between jobs. Furthermore, an improper partition function can produce derived instances as difficult to solve as the original instance. In such cases plain partitioning leads to a detrimental speed-up anomaly, where an increase in parallelism results in an increase in expected run time even if the delays in the environment are ignored [14]. In an environment with run time limitations this results in a decrease of the probability of solving the instance.

This work differs from solvers based on partitioning (e.g., [13]) and simple distribution (e.g., [7]) by studying an approach for distributed SAT solving with *partition trees* [15]. The approach can be seen as a generalization of *nagging* [16]. The partition tree approach aims at combining the strengths of partitioning and simple distribution, has modest communication requirements and can use any SAT solver as a black-box subroutine. The basic idea in the partition tree approach is straightforward: jobs consisting of a solver and a SAT instance run in the distributed environment. A partition function is used to construct the SAT instances, which are organized as a tree. The first job, consisting of the original instance, will be the root of the tree; the subsequent child jobs are constructed by applying the partition function to the original instance, and later recursively to the derived instances. The resulting tree is expanded until a solution can be determined or all available parallel resources are in use. In the latter case, the resource limits guarantee that jobs will eventually terminate and more constrained, hopefully easier to solve, jobs can be submitted to the environment. The contributions of this work include the following:

- We study analytically the performance of the partition tree approach, extending the results in [14].
- We present two new partition functions which use unit propagation lookahead, and develop a novel method for exploiting a clause learning conflict analysis technique in lookahead computation. We also improve the partition function presented in [15].
- We perform an exhaustive experimental analysis on application instances unsolved in SAT competition 2009 by comparing the partition tree approach against state-of-the-art parallel and sequential SAT solvers.

To the best of our knowledge, this work is the first to show that the combination of partitioning and simple distribution is in practice able to solve many instances that could not be solved with the current state-of-the-art SAT solvers.

2 Preliminaries

A literal l is a propositional variable x or its negation $\neg x$; as usual, we define that $\neg\neg x = x$. A clause is a disjunction of literals and a (CNF) formula is a conjunction of clauses. A clause is unit if it only contains one literal. Whenever convenient, we may interpret a formula as a set of clauses and a clause as a set of literals. For instance, the formula $\phi = (x) \wedge (\neg x \vee \neg y) \wedge (y \vee \neg x \vee z) \wedge (x \vee y)$ can be represented as a set $\{\{x\}, \{\neg x, \neg y\}, \{y, \neg x, z\}, \{x, y\}\}$. Let $\text{vars}(\phi)$ denote the set of variables occurring in ϕ and $\text{lits}(\phi) = \{x, \neg x \mid x \in \text{vars}(\phi)\}$. A truth assignment τ for a formula ϕ is a subset of $\text{lits}(\phi)$; τ is (i) inconsistent if both $x \in \tau$ and $\neg x \in \tau$ for some variable x, (ii) consistent if it is not inconsistent, and (iii) complete for ϕ if either $x \in \tau$ or $\neg x \in \tau$ for each $x \in \text{vars}(\phi)$. A literal l is assigned to true by τ if $l \in \tau$ and to false if $\neg l \in \tau$; if it is assigned to either, it is called assigned by τ. For any truth assignment or other set of literals τ, we write $\phi \wedge \tau$ to denote the formula $\phi \wedge \bigwedge_{l \in \tau}(l)$. A consistent truth assignment satisfies the formula ϕ if it includes at least one literal of each clause in ϕ; if such a satisfying assignment exists, ϕ is satisfiable and unsatisfiable otherwise.

Given a formula ϕ and a truth assignment τ for it, we use $\text{up}(\phi, \tau)$ to denote the set of literals implied by *unit propagation* on ϕ under τ; formally, $\text{up}(\phi, \tau)$ is the smallest set U of literals satisfying (i) $\tau \subseteq U$, and (ii) if a clause $(l_1 \vee ... \vee l_n)$ is in ϕ and $\{\neg l_1, ..., \neg l_{i-1}, \neg l_{i+1}, ..., \neg l_n\} \subseteq U$, then $l_i \in U$. Note that if ϕ contains a unit clause (l), then $l \in \text{up}(\phi, \tau)$ for all truth assignments τ. Obviously, if $\text{up}(\phi, \tau)$ is inconsistent, then the formula $\phi \wedge \tau$ is unsatisfiable.

3 Approaches to Distributed Solving

This section reviews and studies three approaches to distributed solving: the simple distribution, the plain partitioning (also studied in, e.g., [1,14]), and the partition tree approach originally presented in [15]. In the analysis we first ignore the run time limitations typically imposed by a grid on the individual executions of jobs, and then use an example to illustrate how they affect the results. The central assumption in the discussion is that given a SAT instance and a solver, the run time of the solver obeys a random distribution. The assumption is especially realistic for SAT solving, since most modern sequential solvers already employ some form of randomization, for example taking as input a seed used to initialize the pseudo random number generator of the solver.

Simple Distribution. In simple distribution SAT solvers are run in parallel and the solution is obtained from the first solver that finishes and finds the instance either satisfiable or unsatisfiable. This approach has an obvious drawback, since minimum run time of the instance limits the obtainable speed-up.

Plain Partitioning. The simple distribution approach can be strengthened by forcing constraints on the overlap of the work of independent SAT solvers. The constraints result in smaller search spaces for the solvers and, hopefully, executions which can be finished in shorter time than the original execution. In this work, we use *partition functions* to constrain the overlap. A *partition function* $\mathcal{P}$ maps a SAT instance

ϕ and an integer $n \geq 2$ to a set $\mathcal{P}(\phi, n) = \{\phi_1, \ldots, \phi_n\}$ of *derived instances* such that (i) $\phi \equiv (\phi_1 \vee \ldots \vee \phi_n)$, and (ii) $\phi_i \wedge \phi_j$ is unsatisfiable for $i \neq j$. From (i) it follows that the instance ϕ is satisfiable if and only if at least one derived instance is satisfiable.

The plain partitioning works by applying a partition function $\mathcal{P}$ to an instance ϕ and solving the derived instances $\phi_1, \ldots, \phi_n$ in parallel. The plain partitioning approach bears close resemblance to the guiding path approach [10,17], and, provided that the derived instances always have lower run time than the original instance, the plain partitioning approach can solve arbitrarily difficult problems given a sufficiently large n [14]. However, the plain partitioning has some fundamental problems which prevent it from being a practical solving method in distributed environments as such. Firstly, it is, of course, problematic to determine the value for n. Secondly, a more subtle problem is that if no guarantees can be given on the run times of the derived instances and the instance to be solved is unsatisfiable, increasing n arbitrarily may in fact increase the expected run time. We call a badly working partition function, which results in derived instances with run times equal to that of the original instance, a *void partition function*[2]. Void partition functions are especially harmful for proving unsatisfiability, since it is not possible to obtain any speedup with a void partition function in the plain partitioning [14]:

Proposition 1. *Let ϕ be an unsatisfiable instance and $\mathcal{P}$ a void partition function. Then the expected run time of the plain partitioning approach is at least as large when using the partition function $\mathcal{P}(\phi, n)$ as when using $\mathcal{P}(\phi, n-1)$.*

The Partition Tree Approach. To overcome these difficulties, we can instead use $\mathcal{P}$ to construct a *partition tree* and attempt the solving of the nodes in the tree in parallel. A partition tree of a formula ϕ is a tree rooted at ϕ, where nodes are propositional formulas, all except the leaves having n children constructed with a partition function. A SAT instance can be shown satisfiable by showing any node of the partition tree satisfiable, and unsatisfiable by solving at least one instance on every path from the root to the leaves. See Fig. 1(b) for an example of a partition tree and such a set of instances (illustrated by the shaded area). This approach has the advantage over the plain partitioning that the expected run time of the approach cannot be higher than that of solving ϕ with a sequential SAT solver: since ϕ is in the root of the partition tree, showing it unsatisfiable suffices to prove unsatisfiability. We prove the following stronger claim for the partition tree approach, which intuitively states that if more parallel resources are used, the expected time required to solve the instance ϕ will not increase. We formalize this assuming that all leaves of the tree have the same amount k of ancestors (i.e., the *height* of the tree is k), and all instances in the tree are executed simultaneously with no delay.

Proposition 2. *Let ϕ be an unsatisfiable instance, T_k and T_m be two partition trees of height k and m, respectively, constructed with a void partition function, and $k < m$. Then the expected run time of the partition tree approach is at most as large when using T_m as when using T_k.*

[2] A partition function can be void, for example, when the SAT instance consists of an unsatisfiable and a satisfiable part sharing no variables, the partitioning constrains only the satisfiable part but a solver searches on the unsatisfiable part.

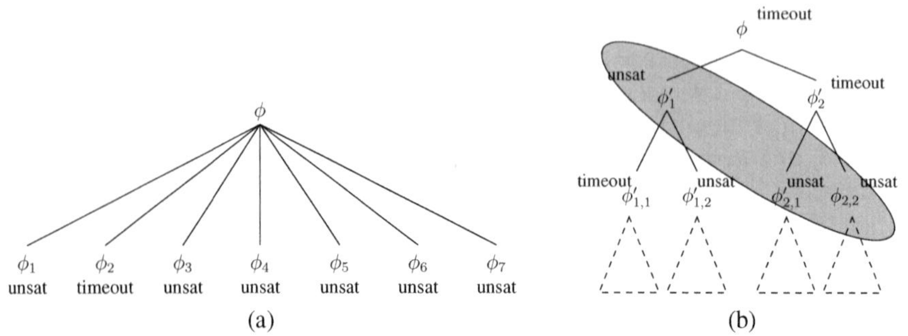

Fig. 1. An example of solving an unsatisfiable SAT instance ϕ with (a) the plain partitioning to seven derived instances, and (b) the partition tree approach.

The comparison between the plain partitioning and the partition tree approach is similar when the environment limits the run times of individual executions of the nodes, but in this case it is also possible that the instance cannot be solved. Figure 1 shows an example where an instance ϕ is solved using a randomized SAT solver in a distributed environment with (a) the plain partitioning and (b) the partition tree approach. Since the run time of the solver on an instance obeys a random distribution, solving the instance depends on the "luck" of the solver. Let the partition function be void, meaning that all the derived instances are as difficult as the original instance. Suppose that the plain partitioning approach uses 7 CPUs to run the instances $\phi_1, \phi_2, \ldots, \phi_7$ in parallel. The plain partitioning approach is "unlucky" and fails to find a solution since the instance ϕ_2 is terminated unsuccessfully when the run time limit of the corresponding execution is exceeded. On the other hand, suppose that the partition tree approach uses 7 CPUs to run the instances $\phi, \phi'_1, \phi'_2, \phi'_{1,1}, \phi'_{1,2}, \phi'_{2,1}, \phi'_{2,2}$ in parallel and is even more unlucky, failing to find solutions for the three instances ϕ, $\phi'_{1,1}$ and ϕ'_2. In the partition tree approach, however, the instance ϕ'_1 is solved and therefore the subtree rooted at ϕ'_1 can be determined unsatisfiable even though $\phi'_{1,1}$ times out. And the subtree rooted at ϕ'_2 is determined unsatisfiable even though ϕ'_2 times out since $\phi'_{2,1}$ and $\phi'_{2,2}$ are solved. Thus, the original instance ϕ is also determined unsatisfiable in the partition tree approach. Note that the same scenario is possible even if the partition function is not void.

In practice the computing environment (grid or cloud) places some limitations on the partition tree approach. Most notably, the number of obtainable parallel computing resources is limited and therefore only a subset of the instances in an arbitrary partition tree can be executed simultaneously. Since the executions times of the solvers running in parallel and trying to solve these instances are also bounded, the resources will always become available again. Therefore the partition tree can be constructed iteratively on-the-fly. In our experiments, we construct the partition tree in breadth first order. That is, the original instance ϕ is first submitted for solving and, while it is being solved, the partition function is applied to it locally to produce its children in the tree; the children are then in turn submitted for solving whenever resources are available and iteratively repartitioned. Once a subtree is shown unsatisfiable, it is no longer expanded, and therefore it is not necessary to determine the height of the tree in advance.

4 DPLL-Based Partitioning with Lookahead

Our first new partition function utilizes and extends the ideas applied in traditional, chronologically backtracking and non-learning, DPLL-based SAT solvers employing unit propagation lookahead (see e.g. [18]) such as SATZ [19] and MARCH_EQ [20]. Given a formula ϕ, such solvers basically try to iteratively build a satisfying truth assignment τ by heuristically selecting a currently unassigned literal l and then considering two branches: one for the truth assignment $\text{up}(\phi, \tau \cup \{\neg l\})$ and one for $\text{up}(\phi, \tau \cup \{l\})$. If the considered truth assignment is inconsistent, the branch is closed and the solver backtracks chronologically. In order to prune the resulting *search tree*, these solvers also apply the so-called *one-step unit propagation lookahead* (or simply lookahead) to extend truth assignments in a satisfiability preserving way and, thus, also to detect inconsistencies and close unsuccessful branches earlier. As the truth assignments in the search tree nodes k steps below the root are mutually exclusive and cover all satisfying truth assignments, our core idea here is to use these assignments as partitioning constraints when we want to partition a formula into 2^k derived formulas.

We next review the lookahead procedure (Sect. 4.1) and formally describe the partition function (Sect. 4.2). In addition, we give a novel technique for speeding up the computation of lookahead (Sect. 4.3) and, for the sake of analyzing the results in forthcoming sections, evaluate the efficiency of the lookahead procedure when applied as a preprocessing technique for formula simplification (Sect. 4.4).

4.1 One-Step Unit Propagation Lookahead

The lookahead is based on the so-called failed literal rule. Given a formula ϕ and a truth assignment τ for it, a literal $l \in \text{lits}(\phi)$ is a *failed literal* under $\phi \wedge \tau$ if $\text{up}(\phi, \tau \cup \{l\})$ is inconsistent. As a consequence, if l is a failed literal under $\phi \wedge \tau$, then $\phi \wedge (\tau \cup \{l\})$ is unsatisfiable, implying that $\phi \wedge \tau$ is satisfiable iff $\phi \wedge (\tau \cup \{\neg l\})$ is. The *failed literal rule* states that if l is a failed literal under $\phi \wedge \tau$, then one can extend τ with $\neg l$ when searching for the satisfying truth assignments for $\phi \wedge \tau$. As an example, assume a formula $\phi = (\neg x_4 \vee \neg x_7 \vee x_{15}) \wedge (\neg x_{15} \vee \neg x_3 \vee x_{21}) \wedge (\neg x_{21} \vee x_5 \vee x_{17}) \wedge (\neg x_{17} \vee \neg x_{60} \vee x_{89}) \wedge (\neg x_{17} \vee \neg x_{89}) \wedge \ldots$ and a truth assignment $\tau = \{x_7, x_3, \neg x_5, x_{60}\}$. Now x_4 is a failed literal under $\phi \wedge \tau$ as $\text{up}(\phi, \tau \cup \{x_4\})$ is inconsistent: x_4 and x_7 imply x_{15}, x_{15} and x_3 imply x_{21}, x_{21} and $\neg x_5$ imply x_{17}, x_{17} and x_{60} imply x_{89} and x_{17} implies $\neg x_{89}$. Thus $\phi \wedge \tau$ is satisfiable iff $\phi \wedge (\tau \cup \{\neg x_4\})$ is.

The lookahead procedure then applies the failed literal rule until there are no more failed literals unassigned by the truth assignment τ. Formally, the result of applying lookahead on a formula ϕ and truth assignment τ, denoted by $\text{lookahead}(\phi, \tau)$, is the smallest set U of literals including τ and closed under the failed literal rule: if a literal $l \in \text{lits}(\phi)$ is a failed literal under $\phi \wedge U$, then $\neg l \in U$. Observe that (i) if $\text{lookahead}(\phi, \tau)$ is inconsistent, then $\phi \wedge \tau$ is unsatisfiable, and (ii) $\phi \wedge \tau$ is satisfiable iff $\phi \wedge \text{lookahead}(\phi, \tau)$ is.

Note that computing the lookahead can very time consuming: the best currently known techniques require in the worst case at least cubic time in the number of variables in the formula. Thus, solvers such as SATZ and MARCH_EQ do not usually compute the full lookahead but only try to apply the failed literal rule to a subset of the unassigned variables. Naturally, many heuristics have been developed to speedup lookahead computation (see e.g. [18] for existing ones and Sect. 4.3 below for a new one). In addition to the failed literal rule, there are also other search tree pruning rules such as the "necessary assignments" and "double lookahead" rules (see e.g. [18,21]); evaluation of the efficiency of these rules in the context of partitioning is left for future work.

4.2 The Partition Function

As mentioned above, the proposed partition function uses the (up to) 2^k nodes at depth k in the search tree of a non-learning, DPLL-based lookahead SAT solver to partition the formula ϕ. The pseudo-code for the function is shown in Fig. 4(a); to obtain a partitioning, it is invoked with *dpll-la-partition*$(\phi, \emptyset, 0, k)$.

In the pseudo-code, the function *lookahead*(ϕ, τ') computes both the lookahead set $\tau'' = \text{lookahead}(\phi, \tau')$ and a *variable selection heuristic* function h associating a value to each variable x not assigned by τ''. In our experiments, we use the following *lookahead balancing heuristics* function (adopted from the SMODELS stable models solver [22]) that tries to estimate the worst case search tree size after selecting x. As x is not assigned by τ'', we define the "remaining search tree size estimates" $h^-_{\phi,\tau}(x) = 2^{|\text{vars}(\phi)|-|\text{up}(\phi,\tau\cup\{\neg x\})|}$ and $h^+_{\phi,\tau}(x) = 2^{|\text{vars}(\phi)|-|\text{up}(\phi,\tau\cup\{x\})|}$, i.e. the numbers of unassigned variables after branching on $\neg x$ and x, respectively, and performing unit propagation. To estimate the remaining search tree size on both branches, we define the heuristic function h to be

$$h_{\phi,\tau}(x) = \max\left\{h^-_{\phi,\tau}(x), h^+_{\phi,\tau}(x)\right\}$$

and select a variable that minimizes the function (ties are broken, e.g., randomly). Observe that this heuristic function is obtained practically as a side product when computing the lookahead. The computation of the lookahead and the heuristic function h is very important for obtaining small search trees (and, thus, good partitionings); therefore, whenever a time limit is imposed on the partition function, we try to divide the available time evenly between the lookahead functions in the search tree nodes.

4.3 Exploiting Unique Implication Points

We now show how to apply the conflict analysis technique [23,24] used in modern clause learning SAT solvers to enhance the failed literal rule in a way that allows it sometimes to detect multiple failed literals at the same time.

Assume a formula ϕ, a consistent truth assignment τ for ϕ that is closed under unit propagation (meaning that $\text{up}(\phi, \tau) = \tau$), and a literal $l_\star \in \text{lits}(\phi)$ that is not assigned by τ. We now want to check whether $l_\star$ is a failed literal under $\phi \wedge \tau$, i.e. whether $\text{up}(\phi, \tau \cup \{l_\star\})$ is inconsistent. To do this, we start from the assignment $\tau \cup \{l_\star\}$ and apply unit propagation until no new literals can be deduced or an inconsistency is found. We now assume that $\text{up}(\phi, \tau \cup \{l_\star\})$ is inconsistent. Assuming that the computation of $\text{up}(\phi, \tau \cup \{l_\star\})$ is terminated as soon as an inconsistency is detected, it can be characterized by the corresponding *conflict graph*, which is a directed acyclic graph $\mathcal{G}_{\phi,\tau,l_\star} = \langle \mathcal{V}, \mathcal{E} \rangle$ with a vertex set $\mathcal{V} \subseteq \text{lits}(\phi) \cup \{\lambda\}$ for a special symbol $\lambda \notin \text{vars}(\phi)$ and fulfilling the following conditions:

1. If $l \in \mathcal{V}$, $l \neq \lambda$, and $l \in \tau \cup \{l_\star\}$, then l does not have any incoming edges.
2. If $l \in \mathcal{V}$, $l \neq \lambda$, and $l \notin \tau \cup \{l_\star\}$, then l has a non-empty set of incoming edges originating from the vertices $l_1,...,l_k$ and the clause $(\neg l_1 \vee ... \vee \neg l_k \vee l)$ is in ϕ.
3. There is exactly one variable $x \in \mathrm{vars}(\phi)$ such that both $x, \neg x \in \mathcal{V}$. The special symbol λ is a vertex that has incoming edges from these vertices x and $\neg x$ only.

A vertex $l' \neq \lambda$ such that $\neg l' \notin \tau$ is a *unique implication point* in the conflict graph if all the paths from the vertex $l_\star$ to the vertex λ go through l' (observe that, by definition, the vertex $l_\star$ is a unique implication point). As the edges incoming to a vertex describe one application of the unit propagation rule, we have the following result. Take any unique implication point l' and the sub-graph of $\mathcal{G}_{\phi,\tau,l_\star}$ induced by the vertex set consisting the vertex l' and the vertices having a path to λ not visiting l'. Now this sub-graph is the conflict graph corresponding to a computation of $\mathrm{up}(\phi, \tau \cup \{l'\})$ and, thus, $\mathrm{up}(\phi, \tau \cup \{l'\})$ is inconsistent and l' is a failed literal under $\phi \wedge \tau$.

As an example, assume a formula $\phi = (\neg x_4 \vee \neg x_7 \vee x_{15}) \wedge (\neg x_{15} \vee \neg x_3 \vee x_{21}) \wedge (\neg x_{21} \vee x_5 \vee x_{17}) \wedge (\neg x_{17} \vee \neg x_{60} \vee x_{89}) \wedge (\neg x_{17} \vee \neg x_{89}) \wedge ...$ and a truth assignment $\tau = \{x_7, x_3, \neg x_5, x_{60}\}$ closed under unit propagation. Now x_4 is a failed literal under $\phi \wedge \tau$ as $\mathrm{up}(\phi, \tau \cup \{x_4\})$ is conflicting; the conflict graph corresponding to a sequence of unit propagation rule applications is shown in Fig. 2. Now the nodes x_4, x_{15}, x_{21} and x_{17} are all unique implication points and, thus, the literals x_4, x_{15}, x_{21} and x_{17} are all failed literals under $\phi \wedge \tau$. Observe that $\neg x_{15}$, $\neg x_{21}$ and $\neg x_{17}$ do not necessarily belong to the set $\mathrm{up}(\phi, \tau \cup \{\neg x_4\})$ and, thus, this unique implication point exploitation method is able to derive truly additional failed literals.

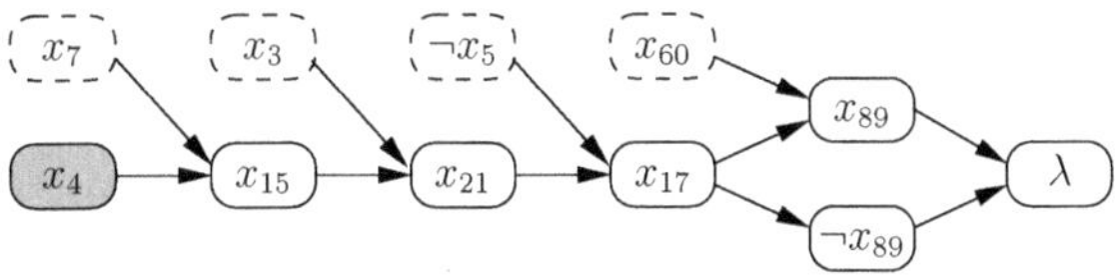

Fig. 2. A conflict graph

We have experimentally evaluated the efficiency of this technique by implementing a lookahead procedure including it on top of the MiniSat solver [25] (version 1.14) and computing the lookahead set $\mathrm{lookahead}(\phi, \emptyset)$ for all the 887 formulas ϕ in the "crafted", "industrial", and "random" categories of the SAT-COMP 2007 solver competition benchmark set (see `http://www.satcompetition.org/`). The lookahead computation time was limited to 300 seconds: of the 887 formulas, the lookahead computation finished within 300 seconds on 853/855 formulas (without/with unique implication point exploitation) while for the others possibly only a subset of $\mathrm{lookahead}(\phi, \emptyset)$ was computed. The computation time results in Fig. 3(a) show that on a number of problems it is definitely worthwhile to find and use the unique implication points as a 2–4 times speedup can be obtained. Furthermore, the results also show that the computation of unique implication points is not computationally too expensive when compared to the rest of the lookahead computation; thus when the unique implication point technique does not help, it does not significantly slow down the lookahead computation, either.

4.4 Lookahead as a Preprocessing Technique

One may now think that applying lookahead as a preprocessing step might make the formula significantly easier to solve. That is, given a formula ϕ, if we compute the

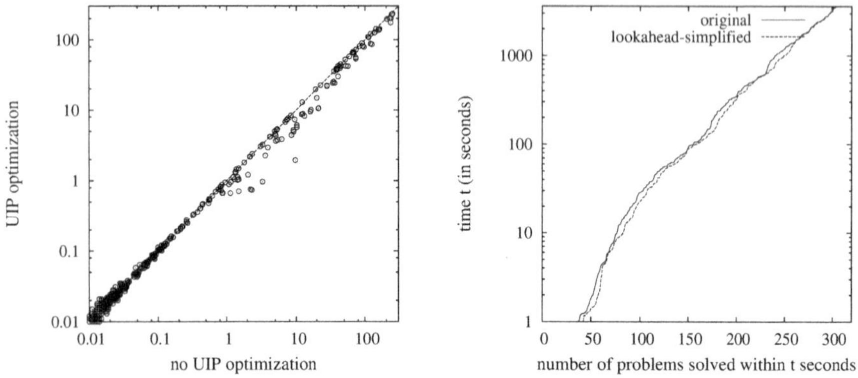

(a) comparing lookahead computation times (in seconds)

(b) the effect of applying lookahead as a preprocessing technique

Fig. 3. Some experimental results on computing and applying lookahead

lookahead $\text{lookahead}(\phi, \emptyset)$ and add the unit clauses found to ϕ, then the resulting formula $\phi \wedge \text{lookahead}(\phi, \emptyset)$ would be much easier to solve than ϕ. Unfortunately, this is not the case, at least when considering the 573 formulas in the "crafted" and "application" categories of the SAT-COMP 2009 solver competition (see `http://www.satcompetition.org/`). Figure 3(b) shows a digest of the run times of MINISAT on the original 573 formulas as well as on the corresponding lookahead-simplified formulas. The lookahead computation time, which was limited to 300 seconds, is not included in the "lookahead-simplified" plot; of the 573 formulas, the lookahead computation finished within 300 seconds on 516 formulas. The results clearly show that performing lookahead-based formula simplification does not give substantial run time benefits on these instances. And if the lookahead computation time was included in the "lookahead-simplified" plot, the result be would slightly worse than the "original" plot.

We have included this negative result as it shows that the positive results we obtain later in this paper, when applying lookahead for partitioning SAT formulas, are not caused by the fact that simply applying lookahead to the original formula would have produced as good results.

5 Partitioning with Scattering

The partition function presented in Sect. 4 can be contrasted to the *scattering* approach presented in [15]. The approach is a generalization of DPLL-based partitioning, in a sense that not only literals but also longer clauses are conjoined with the original instance. More formally, given an input formula ϕ, the derived instances are of the form

$$\phi_i = \begin{cases} \phi \wedge c_1 & \text{when } i = 1, \\ \phi \wedge \neg c_1 \wedge \ldots \wedge \neg c_{i-1} \wedge c_i & \text{when } 1 < i < n, \text{ and} \\ \phi \wedge \neg c_1 \wedge \ldots \wedge \neg c_{n-1} & \text{when } i = n, \end{cases}$$

where $c_i = x_1 \wedge \ldots \wedge x_{d_i}$ conjoins literals and $\neg c_i = \neg x_1 \vee \ldots \vee \neg x_{d_i}$ is a clause.

```
dpll-la-partition(φ,τ,i,k):
let τ' := up(φ, τ)
let ⟨τ'', h⟩ := lookahead(φ, τ')
if τ'' is inconsistent
   return
if τ'' satisfies φ or i = k
   Output the derived formula φ ∧ τ''
   return
let x be h-best and unassigned by τ''
call dpll-la-partition(φ,τ'' ∪ {x},i+1,k)
call dpll-la-partition(φ,τ'' ∪ {¬x},i+1,k)
```

(a) DPLL-based partitioning with lookahead

```
cdcl-partition(φ, d_1, ..., d_n):
1  let τ := ∅, dl := 0, and i := 1
2  while true
3     let τ' := up(φ, τ)
4     let ⟨τ'', h⟩ := lookahead(φ, τ')
5     if τ'' is inconsistent
6        let dl := analyze()
7        if dl = −1 return done
8        else backtrack(dl)
9     else if dl = d_i
10       Output the derived formula φ ∧ τ''
11       if i = n return done
12       let φ := φ ∧ (¬x_1 ∨ ... ∨ ¬x_{d_i})
13       let i := i + 1
14       backtrack(0)
15    else
16       let dl := dl + 1
17       let x_dl be h-best and unassigned by τ''
18       if x_dl = None return sat
19       let τ := τ ∪ τ'' ∪ {x_dl}
```

(b) Scattering-based lookahead partitioning

Fig. 4. Algorithms for partitioning

Fig. 4(b) presents the *cdcl-partition* algorithm for scattering. The algorithm takes as input an instance ϕ and an integral sequence $d_1, \ldots, d_n$ determining the number of literals in the constraints $c_1, \ldots, c_{n-1}$ such that the derived instances have search spaces of roughly equal size. The algorithm is based on the conflict-driven clause learning (CDCL) solver search, altered so that once a sufficient amount of decision literals is chosen, the literals are used to produce a partition, the solver backtracks to the topmost decision level, inserts a clause consisting of the negation of the decision literals, and continues the partitioning on the altered instance on lines 10–14.

We extend the algorithm described in [15] by a lookahead-type call similar to the one described in Sect. 4 by computing not only the unit propagation $\text{up}(\phi, \tau)$ but also $\text{lookahead}(\phi, \tau)$, effectively implementing a CDCL solver with lookahead. In contrast to the *dpll-la-partition*() algorithm in Fig. 4(a), we use the first unique implication point (1-UIP), as in most CDCL solvers, to guide the backtracking.

The algorithm proves an instance unsatisfiable on line 7, if it has not altered the instance on line 12. Hence, the algorithm can be used for sequential SAT solving by disabling the partition construction on lines 10–14. We implemented the algorithm on top of MINISAT version 1.14, and compared its performance against the unaltered MINISAT v1.14 implementation on a randomly selected set of instances consisting of approximately half of the crafted and applications categories of the SAT-COMP 2009 solver competition. The lookahead-implementation could solve less than half of the instances solved by MINISAT; similar results are independently obtained in [26]. However, lookahead turns out to be a useful approach to producing partitions, as shown below.

6 Benchmarking Partition Functions

The experiments in this section demonstrate differences between the following partition functions, also used in the main experiments presented in the next section:

- DPLL-based partitioning with lookahead, described in Sect. 4,
- Scattering-based partitioning with lookahead, described in Sect. 5, and
- Scattering-based partitioning with the VSIDS heuristic. This function is originally described in [15], but is completely re-implemented for this work and performs search not only initially but also between every derived instances.

To compare the performances of the partition functions, we used all three partition functions to partition an instance once and then solved the derived instances using MINISAT. As benchmarks we chose all the 573 instances in the *crafted* and *application* categories of the 2009 SAT competition.

The results are reported in Fig. 5. Each instance was partitioned into eight derived instances using scattering-based partitioning with lookahead (*LA scatter*) and VSIDS heuristic (*VSIDS scatter*), and the DPLL-based partitioning with lookahead function (*LA DPLL*). The time-out for each partition function was 300 seconds, and the derived instances were solved using a standard SAT solver (MINISAT v1.14) and 3600 s time-out. The figure shows the run time of the plain partitioning approach, that is, the shortest run time of the satisfiable derived instances for a satisfiable instance, and the longest run time of the derived instances of an unsatisfiable instance. For comparison, the figure also provides the run time of the standard SAT solver on the original instances with no partitioning (*minisat*). The figure reports zero solving time for some instances for the scattering-based partitioning with VSIDS heuristic, as some instances were solved with this method already in the partition phase.

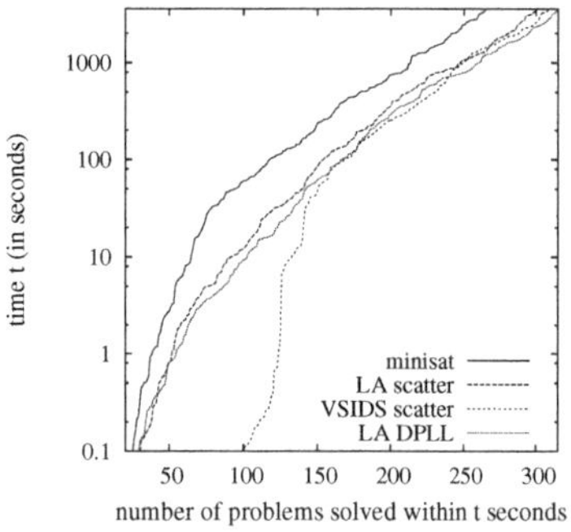

Fig. 5. Comparing plain MINISAT, VSIDS scattering, lookahead scattering and DPLL-based lookahead partitioning

The DPLL-based partitioning with lookahead solves most instances from the benchmark set. This is a surprising result, since in principle, the greater freedom of the scattering approach in choosing the literals should increase the solving performance. More confirmation for this conclusion will be given in the next section, where the DPLL-based lookahead partitioning is especially efficient in instances that are relatively easy to solve. The scattering-based partition function with VSIDS heuristic also slightly outperforms the scattering-based partition function with lookahead heuristic.

7 Experiments on the Partition Tree Approach

The main experiments of the work, presented in this section, concentrate on solving challenging SAT instances, mainly those that were either solved by no solver in the SAT competition 2009, or whose solving consumed much time.

Table 1. Wall-clock solving times in seconds for instances from the *applications* category not solved in SAT competition 2009

Name	Type	LA DPLL	LA scatter	VSIDS scatter	SD 64	MANYSAT	PLINGELING
9dlx_vliw_at_b_iq8	UNSAT	—	—	—	—	—	**3256.41**
9dlx_vliw_at_b_iq9	UNSAT	—	—	—	—	—	**5164.00**
AProVE07-25	UNSAT	**8992.60**	9176.91	11347.42	—	—	—
dated-5-19-u	UNSAT	16557.82	20155.96	**4124.62**	—	—	4465.00
eq.atree.braun.12.unsat	UNSAT	3157.19	**2357.55**	3006.19	20797.60	15338.00	—
eq.atree.braun.13.unsat	UNSAT	**7117.39**	8504.50	8158.85	—	—	—
gss-24-s100	SAT	1977.19	3449.55	2271.24	**968.23**	13190.00	2929.92
gss-26-s100	SAT	10844.22	—	**6057.80**	—	—	18173.00
gss-32-s100	SAT	—	**16412.40**	—	—	—	—
gus-md5-14	UNSAT	**14779.03**	16264.37	16098.04	—	—	—
ndhf_xits_09_UNSAT	UNSAT	—	—	**14793.78**	—	—	—
rpoc_xits_09_UNSAT	UNSAT	—	—	**12388.32**	—	—	—
sortnet-8-ipc5-h19-sat	SAT	—	—	—	—	—	**2699.62**
total-10-17-u	UNSAT	4431.21	7198.23	5099.73	—	10216.00	**3672.00**

The partition trees were constructed in breadth-first order, and the approach was allowed to simultaneously use 64 CPUs from the NorduGrid computing grid[3]. Three time outs were used in the solving process: the time outs for the partition functions, for the computing in the nodes, and for the full approach. Each partition function invocation was allowed to run for at most 5 minutes, after which it had to produce the derived instances. Solving of each tree node was attempted until a time out ranging from 60 to 90 minutes was reached[4] or the node was solved. The solving was allowed to use at most 1 gigabyte of memory. Finally, the partition tree approach was terminated if it did not succeed in solving the instance in its own time out of 6 hours wall clock time. Hence the maximum CPU time consumed in the grid while solving any instance was $6 \times 64 = 384$ hours, or 16 days.

The partition tree approach was used first on solving all 63 instances of the application category solved in the SAT competition 2009 by no solver. The approach solved 11 such instances, shown in Table 1. The wall clock times for DPLL-based lookahead, scattering-based lookahead and scattering-based VSIDS partition functions are shown in columns LA DPLL, LA scatter, and VSIDS scatter, respectively. The times include all communication delays. While the result is good as such, it can be argued that comparing the solver against only the SAT competition results is unfair for at least three reasons. The time-out in the SAT competition was 10000 seconds, which is approximately only three hours, the computers used in the competition might be dramatically different from those we have available, and only sequential solvers are compared. To compensate this, we tried three alternate parallel solvers again on all the 63 instances, one based on running the original MINISAT v1.14 in parallel using different random seeds as in the simple distribution approach (column SD 64), one using the publicly available version 1.0 of the MANYSAT parallel SAT solver [7] (column MANYSAT), and one using the PLINGELING version 276 parallel SAT solver [27] (column PLINGELING). The simple

[3] `http://www.nordugrid.org/`

[4] The time limit is not constant to avoid a decrease in performance caused by simultaneous finishing of a large number of jobs.

distribution approach memory limit was again one gigabyte per solver, and each solver had a time limit of 6 hours, whereas MANYSAT and PLINGELING had the same time limit and a 32 gigabytes memory limit. The solvers were run with 12 threads and cores.

The results show that the partition tree approach performs best when used with the scattering-based partition function with VSIDS heuristic, solving 10 unsolved instances. The DPLL-based partition function, on the other hand, seems to solve many of the easier instances faster than the other two functions.

In all the instances of the benchmark set, with the exception of one satisfiable instance, the partition tree approach performs better than the simple distribution approach, even though the delays in the partition tree approach are significantly higher. In particular, the simple distribution approach and did not solve any of the 52 instances the partition tree approach did not solve.

Since the instances in the benchmark set provide little evidence on the scalability of the partition tree approach, we also attempted to solve all 15 instances from the *crafted* and *applications* categories of SAT competition 2009 that were solved by at least one solver but the best run time was over 1 hour. The results are reported in Table 2. For comparison the table reports the best sequential competition result in column COMP.

In these easier instances, it seems that the DPLL-based partition function with lookahead (column LA DPLL) produces usually the best results in the partition tree approach. In two cases the SD 64 approach is better than either the scattering-based VSIDS or lookahead approach. The average run time of MINISAT seems to be for both instances much higher than the minimum reported in the *SD 64* column.

The table also reports a number of instances where the result of at least one solver in SAT competition 2009 was better than any of the partition tree results. In these cases also the MINISAT solver could not find a solution before the timeout. We could

Table 2. Wall-clock times in seconds for the partition tree approaches, simple distribution and MANYSAT as well as the SAT-COMP results

Name	Type	LA DPLL	LA scatter	VSIDS scatter	SD 64	COMP	MANYSAT	PLINGELING
9dlx_vliw_at_b_iq7	UNSAT	—	—	—	—	6836.20	7665.00	**1576.08**
AProVE07-01	UNSAT	1465.22	**1322.04**	2451.36	20230.30	6816.94	13219.00	21144.00
dated-5-13-u	UNSAT	3881.60	4745.52	4563.15	—	8005.27	15818.00	**2524.05**
gss-22-s100	SAT	**830.77**	1151.13	4246.25	2280.82	4326.83	—	1136.39
gss-27-s100	SAT	—	—	9156.71	—	**7132.69**	—	18013.00
gus-md5-11	UNSAT	**1190.28**	2077.99	2092.54	5057.39	4518.06	20184.00	—
maxor128	UNSAT	—	—	—	—	7131.52	—	**2227.07**
maxxor064	UNSAT	—	—	—	—	5162.75	**2837.28**	9346.00
minandmaxor128	UNSAT	—	—	—	—	5143.44	4228.00	**3737.00**
mod4block_3vars_7gates	UNSAT	**1740.17**	1755.47	2326.02	—	4109.89	—	5048.00
new-difficult-26-243-24-70	SAT	3260.86	8887.61	5087.98	3311.62	4440.72	13343.00	**0.17**
rbcl_xits_08_UNSAT	UNSAT	4557.86	**2390.50**	3695.97	—	3892.92	10136.00	4783.00
sgen1-unsat-109-100	UNSAT	**1363.14**	3000.48	4196.36	14675.60	4045.49	—	—
UR-20-10p1	SAT	4463.24	—	—	—	8766.23	8164.00	**3598.17**
UTI-20-10p1	SAT	—	7097.74	—	—	6289.06	**750.76**	892.84
Challenge instances for MINISAT								
countbitsarray02_32	UNSAT	1746.29	3003.50	997.84	2504.93	834.519	969.67	**258.60**
simon-s02b-k2f-gr-rcs-w8	UNSAT	3816.20	3106.70	14756.10	—	6.40	153.59	**5.01**
vange-col-abb313GPIA-9-c	SAT	—	—	—	—	**445.09**	—	520.95
velev-pipe-uns-1.0-8	UNSAT	—	—	—	—	307.48	337.94	**202.54**
vmpc_34	SAT	12452.59	1350.17	1479.62	2796.19	**35.347**	490.71	4064.00

experimentally find some more instances which turned out to be relatively easy for some SAT solver in the competition but extremely challenging for our approach which is based on MINISAT. These instances are presented in the bottom part of Table 2.

The partition tree approach solves several instances which were not solved in the SAT-COMP 2009 solver competition. While we could find other instances that were solved in the competition and we failed to solve, our results suggest that also the simple distribution approach fails to solve these instances. We conclude that the partition tree approach genuinely improves the efficiency of MINISAT, and similar results cannot be achieved simply by running randomized MINISAT in parallel. The results raise an interesting future question on how other solvers would benefit from the approach.

8 Conclusions

This work studies approaches to distributed solving of propositional satisfiability problem (SAT) instances. We justify analytically that the partition tree approach, first described in [15], can perform well in situations where two commonly used approaches, simple distribution and plain partitioning [14], perform badly. We develop two novel *partition functions* which use unit propagation lookahead, and benchmark their efficiency against an improved version of a previously presented partition function. Finally, we study the efficiency of the partition tree approach together with the three partition functions in practice by attempting the solving of all unsolved application instances of the SAT competition 2009.

The results show that the partition tree approach is much more powerful than the initial results in [15] suggest. The approach could solve many of the unsolved instances which could not be solved even in our extensive experiments with two well-performing parallel solvers.

Acknowledgments. The authors are grateful for the financial support of the Academy of Finland (project 122399), Helsinki Graduate School in Computer Science and Engineering, Jenny and Antti Wihuri Foundation, Finnish Foundation for Technology Promotion, Emil Aaltosen Säätiö, the Nokia Foundation, and Technology Industries of Finland Centennial Foundation.

References

1. Hyvärinen, A.E.J., Junttila, T., Niemelä, I.: Strategies for solving SAT in Grids by randomized search. In: Autexier, S., Campbell, J., Rubio, J., Sorge, V., Suzuki, M., Wiedijk, F. (eds.) AISC 2008, Calculemus 2008, and MKM 2008. LNCS (LNAI), vol. 5144, pp. 125–140. Springer, Heidelberg (2008)
2. Luby, M., Sinclair, A., Zuckerman, D.: Optimal speedup of Las Vegas algorithms. Information Processing Letters 47(4), 173–180 (1993)
3. Luby, M., Ertel, W.: Optimal parallelization of Las Vegas algorithms. In: Enjalbert, P., Mayr, E.W., Wagner, K.W. (eds.) STACS 1994. LNCS, vol. 775, pp. 463–474. Springer, Heidelberg (1994)
4. Huberman, B.A., Lukose, R.M., Hogg, T.: An economics approach to hard computational problems. Science 275(5296), 51–54 (1997)
5. Gomes, C.P., Selman, B.: Algorithm portfolios. Artificial Intelligence 126(1–2), 43–62 (2001)

6. Hyvärinen, A.E.J., Junttila, T., Niemelä, I.: Incorporating clause learning in grid-based randomized SAT solving. Journal on Satisfiability, Boolean Modeling and Computation 6, 223–244 (2009)
7. Hamadi, Y., Jabbour, S., Saïs, L.: ManySAT: a parallel SAT solver. Journal on Satisfiability, Boolean Modeling and Computation 6, 245–262 (2009)
8. Speckenmeyer, E., Monien, B., Vornberger, O.: Superlinear speedup for parallel backtracking. In: Houstis, E.N., Polychronopoulos, C.D., Papatheodorou, T.S. (eds.) ICS 1987. LNCS, vol. 297, pp. 985–993. Springer, Heidelberg (1988)
9. Böhm, M., Speckenmeyer, E.: A fast parallel SAT-solver: Efficient workload balancing. Annals of Mathematics and Artificial Intelligence 17(4–3), 381–400 (1996)
10. Zhang, H., Bonacina, M., Hsiang, J.: PSATO: A distributed propositional prover and its application to quasigroup problems. Journal of Symbolic Computation 21(4), 543–560 (1996)
11. Jurkowiak, B., Li, C., Utard, G.: A parallelization scheme based on work stealing for a class of SAT solvers. Journal of Automated Reasoning 34(1), 73–101 (2005)
12. Michel, L., See, A., van Hentenryck, P.: Parallelizing constraint programs transparently. In: Bessière, C. (ed.) CP 2007. LNCS, vol. 4741, pp. 514–528. Springer, Heidelberg (2007)
13. Chrabakh, W., Wolski, R.: GridSAT: a system for solving satisfiability problems using a computational grid. Parallel Computing 32(9), 660–687
14. Hyvärinen, A.E.J., Junttila, T., Niemelä, I.: Partitioning the search space of a randomized search. In: Serra, R. (ed.) AI*IA 2009. LNCS (LNAI), vol. 5883, pp. 243–252. Springer, Heidelberg (2009)
15. Hyvärinen, A.E.J., Junttila, T., Niemelä, I.: A distribution method for solving SAT in grids. In: Biere, A., Gomes, C.P. (eds.) SAT 2006. LNCS, vol. 4121, pp. 430–435. Springer, Heidelberg (2006)
16. Segre, A.M., Forman, S.L., Resta, G., Wildenberg, A.: Nagging: A scalable fault-tolerant paradigm for distributed search. Artificial Intelligence 140(1/2), 71–106 (2002)
17. Blochinger, W., Sinz, C., Küchlin, W.: Parallel propositional satisfiability checking with distributed dynamic learning. Parallel Computing 29(7), 969–994 (2003)
18. Heule, M., van Maaren, H.: Look-ahead based SAT solvers. In: Handbook of Satisfiability. Frontiers in Artificial Intelligence and Applications, vol. 185, pp. 155–184. IOS Press, Amsterdam (2009)
19. Li, C.M., Anbulagan: Look-ahead versus look-back for satisfiability problems. In: Smolka, G. (ed.) CP 1997. LNCS, vol. 1330, pp. 341–355. Springer, Heidelberg (1997)
20. Heule, M., Dufour, M., van Zwieten, J., van Maaren, H.: March_eq: Implementing additional reasoning into an efficient look-ahead SAT solver. In: Hoos, H.H., Mitchell, D.G. (eds.) SAT 2004. LNCS, vol. 3542, pp. 345–359. Springer, Heidelberg (2005)
21. Le Berre, D.: Exploiting the real power of unit propagation lookahead. In: Proc. SAT 2001. Electronic Notes in Discrete Mathematics, vol. 9, pp. 59–80. Elsevier, Amsterdam (2001)
22. Simons, P., Niemelä, I., Soininen, T.: Extending and implementing the stable model semantics. Artificial Intelligence 138(1-2), 181–234 (2002)
23. Marques-Silva, J.P., Sakallah, K.A.: GRASP: A search algorithm for propositional satisfiability. IEEE Transactions on Computers 48(5), 506–521 (1999)
24. Zhang, L., Madigan, C.F., Moskewicz, M.W., Malik, S.: Efficient conflict driven learning in boolean satisfiability solver. In: Proc. ICCAD 2001, pp. 279–285. ACM, New York (2001)
25. Eén, N., Sörensson, N.: An extensible SAT-solver. In: Giunchiglia, E., Tacchella, A. (eds.) SAT 2003. LNCS, vol. 2919, pp. 502–518. Springer, Heidelberg (2004)
26. Giunchiglia, E., Maratea, M., Tacchella, A.: (In)Effectiveness of look-ahead techniques in a modern SAT solver. In: Rossi, F. (ed.) CP 2003. LNCS, vol. 2833, pp. 842–846. Springer, Heidelberg (2003)
27. Biere, A.: Lingeling, Plingeling, PicoSAT and PrecoSAT at SAT race 2010. Technical Report 10/1, Institute for Formal Models and Verification, Johannes Kepler University (2010)

Infinite Families of Finite String Rewriting Systems and Their Confluence

Jean-Pierre Jouannaud and Benjamin Monate

INRIA-LIAMA and Tsinghua University
CEA, LIST

Abstract. We introduce *parameterized rewrite systems* for describing *infinite families of finite string rewrite systems* depending upon non-negative integer parameters, as well as ways to reason *uniformly* over these families. Unlike previous work, the vocabulary on which a rewrite system in the family is built depends itself on the integer parameters. Rewriting makes use of a toolkit for *parameterized words* which allows to describe a rewrite step made independently by all systems in an infinite family by a single, effective parameterized rewrite step. The main result is a confluence test for all systems in a family at once, based on a critical pair lemma classically based on computing finitely many overlaps between left-hand sides of parameterized rules and then checking for their joinability (which decidability is not garanteed).

1 Introduction

Consider a family of groups $\{S_N\}_{N \in \mathbb{N}}$ with generators $a_1, \ldots, a_N$ satisfying:

$$a_i^2 = \epsilon \mid 1 \leq i \leq N, \qquad a_i a_j = a_j a_i \mid i > j+1 \wedge 1 \leq i, j \leq N$$

This axiomatization depends upon the *parameter* $N \in \mathbb{N}$ in four essential ways: there is one finite set of axioms for each value of the parameter N; and in each set, the number of equations depends on N; the vocabulary depends on N; words in the equations depend on N via integer variables i, j satisfying arithmetic constraints in which N occurs.

The methodology for proving properties of S_N for a given N by machine is well-known: it requires the computation of a complete (confluent and terminating) string rewriting system for S_N. This can be achieved for each given $N \in \mathbb{N}$ by using Knuth-Bendix completion or one of its variants. The study by machine of various finite groups has been carried out in the non-parameterized case, in particular by Le Chenadec [7,8].

Much apparatus has later been developed to describe and reason about infinite languages of terms by using tailored unification algorithms [2,10,5,9]. Such languages arise for example in Knuth-Bendix completion when the process diverges.

However, all formalisms we know of, *whether mentioned or not*, allow one to represent terms on a *given fixed vocabulary* and specify and reason about a *single algebraic structure*, which does not fit at all our purpose here.

In this paper we show how to deal *at once* with the *infinite family* $\{S_N\}_{N \in \mathbb{N}}$, *without instantiating the parameter* N. To achieve this goal, we define an extension of the notions of (families of) words, equations and rewrite rules in case the alphabet itself depends on the parameter N. We then show how to mechanize termination proofs and

C. Fermüller and A. Voronkov (Eds.): LPAR-17, LNCS 6397, pp. 387–401, 2010.

reduce local confluence of such systems to the joinability of finitely many critical pairs. As a result, the above infinite family $\mathcal{S}_N$ can be directly presented as the complete parameterized string rewriting system:

$$a_i^2 \to \epsilon \mid 1 \leq i \leq N, \qquad a_i a_j \to a_j a_i \mid i > j+1 \wedge 1 \leq i, j \leq N$$

We stress that our ultimate goal is *not* the study of parameterized groups, which should be seen as an example illustrating techniques which we believe to be of general interest. In this respect, the framework we develop, and the methodology used to lift results from plain rewriting to parameterized rewriting is more important to us than the actual technical results, whatever difficult they indeed are.

We define parameterized words in Section 3, show how to decide equality and factor out parameterized words in Section 4, and introduce parameterized rewriting in Section 5 before we investigate termination and confluence in this setting. An application to dihedral groups is carried out in Section 5 with the rewriting toolkit C*i*ME2 [3], implemented in part by the second author for his PhD thesis, which results are generalized in the present work.

2 Preliminaries

We assume given an infinite alphabet of constant symbols $\mathcal{A} = \{a_i\}_{i \in \mathcal{N}}$ called *generators* or *letters*.

Our formalism relies heavily on the existential fragment of Presburger Arithmetic (PrA) using $0, s, +$ as operations for defining terms, $=, >, <, \geq, \leq$ as predicates for defining formulas, and two disjoint sets of *arithmetic variables*: a set $\mathcal{P}$ of *parameters* denoted by capital letters, and a set I of *dependent variables* denoted by lower-case letters. Values of variables in I depend upon values of parameters via a Presburger constraint, hence their name. We call *solution* of φ an assignment which satisfies φ. We use $\psi \models_{PrA} \varphi$ for *entailment* in PrA, meaning that any solution of ψ is a solution of φ. We use $\top, \bot$ for the logical constants $true$ and $false$ respectively, $\mathcal{V}ar(e)$ for the set of free variables of an expression e of any kind, $\mathcal{V}arI(e)$ for $\mathcal{V}ar(e) \cap I$ and $\mathcal{V}ar\mathcal{P}(e)$ for $\mathcal{V}ar(e) \cap \mathcal{P}$. We refer to [4,1,6] for missing notations and definitions.

3 Parameterized Words

3.1 Syntax

Definition 1. Parameterized words *are pairs written $w \mid \psi$ made of:*
– *a* word-expression w *defined by the following grammar of axiom W:*

$$\begin{array}{rcl} W & := & \epsilon \mid a_f W \mid (F)^e W \\ F & := & a_f \mid a_f F \end{array} \quad \left\{ \begin{array}{l} \text{where } e, f \textit{ denote arithmetic} \\ \textit{variables or constants in } \mathbb{N}. \end{array} \right.$$

– *a quantifier-free formula ψ of* PrA *s.t.* $\mathcal{V}ar\mathcal{P}(\psi) = \{N_i\}_{i \in [1..n]}$, $\mathcal{V}ar(w) \subseteq \mathcal{V}ar(\psi)$, *and* $\forall k_1 \ldots k_n \in \mathbb{N}^n$, *the formula* $\psi \wedge \bigwedge_{i \in [1..n]} N_i = k_i$ *has finitely many solutions.*

A word-expression is: reduced *if all exponents are variables;* constant *if* $\mathcal{V}ar(w) = \emptyset$; flat *if it has no exponent; a* word *if it is constant and flat. In* $(w)^e$, w *is a non-empty flat word-expression with* exponent e. *In* a_f, f *is the* index *of the* letter a.

Limitations: the grammar forbids nesting of exponents: a^{i^j} is not a parameterized word. This restriction is also compulsory for terms with integer exponents as defined in [2]: nesting allows for easy encodings of Peano arithmetic. All variables are arithmetic: variables standing for words are out of scope of this paper. There is no theoretical reason for restricting PrA to its existential fragment, apart from its lower complexity. All other syntactic restrictions are for convenience.

Lexicography: we use φ, ψ, θ for Presburger constraints, s, t, u, v, w for arbitrary word-expressions, x, y, z for flat ones, a for the letter a_1 and b for a_2 in examples, and write n for $s^n(0)$ and $n + u$ for $s^n(u)$.

We use bold letters $\mathbf{p}, \mathbf{q}$ to stress constant exponents in word-expressions like $(x)^{\mathbf{p}}$.

Conventions: we sometimes write a^i instead of $(a)^i$ and , $x^{\mathbf{p}}$ instead of $(x)^{\mathbf{p}}$; word-expressions can be easily expanded into reduced ones; we also identify constant word-expressions with words; for convenience, we allow us to write $\mathbf{p} * n$ for the sum $\mathbf{p}$-times of n when $\mathbf{p}$ is a constant in $\mathbb{N}$.

3.2 Semantics

Terms with integer exponents [2], or of a primal grammar [5] denote sets of terms. Because we distinguish *local* dependent variables constrained by a formula of PrA from *global* parameters which can take arbitrary values in $\mathbb{N}$, a parameterized word $w \mid \varphi$ denotes an $\mathbb{N}^{|\mathcal{P}|}$-indexed family of sets of words, and words in each set are obtained by replacing in w the variables in I by the natural numbers satisfying the constraint φ for the considered value of the parameters in $\mathcal{P}$. An *arithmetic valuation* is an application from $\mathcal{P} \cup I$ to $\mathbb{N}^{|\mathcal{P} \cup I|}$ which we split into two, ν for the parameters, and μ for the dependent variables. Given an expression e, we write $\nu(e)$ (resp. $\mu(e)$) for the expression obtained by replacing the variables in $\mathcal{P}$ (resp. I) by their value and possibly eliminating constant exponents. Note that $\mu(\nu(w))$ is a constant word-expression if $w \mid \varphi$ is a parameterized word, and that $\mu(\nu(\varphi))$ is a formula without arithmetic variable, hence evaluates to $\top$ or $\bot$ in PrA. We call *instance* of $w \mid \varphi$ a word $\mu(\nu(w))$ such that $\mu\nu$ satisfies φ. We use a bracketed notation for the semantics of expressions of any kind.

Definition 2. *We define successively the interpretation of a parameterized word $u \mid \psi$ and of a constant word-expression:*

$$[u \mid \psi] = \{[u \mid \psi]_\nu\}_{\nu \in \mathcal{P} \mapsto \mathbb{N}^{|\mathcal{P}|}}$$

$$[u \mid \psi]_\nu = \{[\mu(\nu(u))] \mid \mu \in I \mapsto \mathbb{N}^{|I|} \text{ such that } \mu \models_{PrA} \nu(\psi)\}$$

$$[\epsilon] = \epsilon \qquad [a_n x] = a_n\, [x] \qquad [(x)^n y] = \underbrace{x \cdots x}_{n\ times}\, [y]$$

Consider for example the parameterized word $(a_i^N \mid 0 < i < N)$. Then,
- $\left[a_i^N \mid 0 < i < N\right]_{N=0} = \emptyset$ since the formula $0 < i < 0$ is unsatisfiable;
- $\left[a_i^N \mid 0 < i < N\right]_{N=1} = \emptyset$ since the formula $0 < i < 1$ is unsatisfiable;
- $\left[a_i^N \mid 0 < i < N\right]_{N=2} = \{a_1 a_1\}$, since $0 < i < 2$ implies $i = 1$;
- $\left[a_i^N \mid 0 < i < N\right]_{N=3} = \{a_1 a_1 a_1, a_2 a_2 a_2\}$, since $0 < i < 3$ implies $i \in \{1, 2\}$.

Therefore, $\left[(a_i^N \mid 0 < i < N)\right] = \{\{\}, \{\}, \{a_1 a_1\}, \{a_1 a_1 a_1, a_2 a_2 a_2\}, \ldots\}$. We see that separating arithmetic variables in two sets is used in the semantics to stratify the interpretation of a parameterized word into an infinite family of finite sets of words.

It is *convenient* to consider *conjunctive parameterized words* $(u \mid \varphi) \wedge (v \mid \psi)$ and *disjunctive parameterized words* $(u \mid \varphi) \vee (v \mid \psi)$, interpreting conjunction and disjunction as set intersection and set union at the set level of interpretation. Conjunctive and disjunctive words do *not* allow for any more expressivity: we shall give an algorithm replacing conjunctive words by disjunctive ones (**Intersection**, page 8), and can always move disjunctions from words to PrA formulas by systematizing the following trick: $\{a^ib \mid i \leq N\} \vee \{b^ia \mid i \leq N\} = \{a^ib^j \mid i \leq N \wedge j = 1\} \vee \{b^ka^l \mid k \leq N \wedge l = 1\} = \{a^ib^jb^ka^l \mid (i \leq N \wedge j = 1 \wedge k = l = 0) \vee (k \leq N \wedge l = 1 \wedge i = j = 0)\}$.

4 The Rewriting Toolkit for Parameterized Words

To rewrite a parameterized word, we need to factor it out via a lefthand side of rule. To test for confluence, we need to check equality of parameterized words, which shall require computing their intersection. To compute critical pairs, we need to compute overlaps of parameterized words. Verifying equality, computing factors and overlaps are the main algorithmic difficulties of this framework. We choose to present the rewriting toolkit first, before to introduce parameterized rewriting itself. For lack of space, we treat in details factorization, and then sketch how intersection, equality and overlaps can be derived. Examples are shown for factorization and equality. These algorithms have a non-polynomial complexity, but in our practice rules have usually a small size.

4.1 Auxiliary Algorithms

All our algorithms, factorization, equality checking and computing overlaps, use as basic building blocks two auxiliary algorithms, for computing common divisors and non-empty common repeated prefixes of two terms. We start with these two algorithms, taking advantage of their relative simplicity to sketch their description.

gcd takes two non-empty flat word-expressions x, y and returns a possibly empty finite set of *solutions* $\{(z_i, \mathbf{k}_i, \mathbf{l}_i \mid \theta_i)\}_i$ with $z_i \in \mathcal{A}^+; \mathbf{k}_i, \mathbf{l}_i \in \mathbb{N}^+; \theta_i \not\models_{\mathrm{PrA}} \bot$ satisfying:
(i) soundness: $\forall \mu\nu$ such that $\mu\nu \models_{\mathrm{PrA}} \theta_i,\ \ \mu\nu(x) = \mu\nu(z_i^{\mathbf{k}_i})$ and $\mu\nu(y) = \mu\nu(z_i^{\mathbf{l}_i})$;
(ii) completeness: $\forall \mu\nu$ such that $\mu\nu(x) = \mu\nu(z^{\mathbf{k}})$ and $\mu\nu(y) = \mu\nu(z^{\mathbf{l}})$ for some triple $(z, \mathbf{k}, \mathbf{l})$, there exists $(z_i, \mathbf{k}_i, \mathbf{l}_i \mid \theta_i)$ such that $\mu\nu \models_{\mathrm{PrA}} \theta_i$.

Consider for example $x = a_k a_l, y = a_i a_j a_i a_j$. Then $\{(a_k a_l, 1, 2 \mid k = i \wedge l = j)\}$ is a solution of $\mathbf{gcd}(x, y)$. The solution $(a_k, 2, 4 \mid i = j = k = l)$ is indeed an *instance* of the previous one, since $i = j = k = l \models_{\mathrm{PrA}} k = i \wedge l = j$.

Let now $x = a_i a_j a_k a_l a_m a_n$ and $y = a_i a_j a_k a_l a_m a_n a_i a_j a_k a_l a_m a_n$. There are two incomparable solutions, $(a_i a_j, 3, 6 \mid i = k = m \wedge j = l = n)$ and $(a_i a_j a_k, 2, 4 \mid i = l \wedge j = m \wedge k = n)$ which must both be returned by **gcd** for sake of completeness. An initial constraint φ can be accomodated by returning $\{(z_i \neq \epsilon, \mathbf{k}_i, \mathbf{l}_i \mid \varphi \wedge \theta_i)\}_i$.

There is an easy *guess and check* algorithm for **gcd**, in which the only needed guesses are the triples of natural numbers p, k, l such that $|x| = p \times k$ and $|y| = p \times l$. The constraint θ under which $x = z^k$ and $y = z^l$ is then obtained by equating the respective indices of all flat word-expressions to be equated. An initial constraint φ is accomodated by returning $\{(z_i \neq \epsilon, \mathbf{k}_i, \mathbf{l}_i \mid \varphi \wedge \theta_i)\}_i$. One may of course be willing to pay the price for filtering out redundant guesses. The answer set is empty iff factoring is impossible.

gpref takes two non-empty flat word-expressions x, y with $|x| < |y|$ and returns a (possibly empty) finite complete set of triples written $\{(\mathbf{p}_i \neq 0, t_i \neq \epsilon \mid \theta_i)\}_i$ such that:
(i) soundness: $\forall \mu\nu.\mu\nu \models_{PrA} \theta_i$, $\mu\nu(y) = \mu\nu((x)^{\mathbf{p}_i} t_i)$ and $\mu\nu(x)$ is not prefix of $\mu\nu(t_i)$;
(ii) completeness: $\forall \mu\nu$ such that $\mu\nu(y) = (\mu\nu(x))^{\mathbf{p}} \mu\nu(t)$ for some pair $(\mathbf{p}, t)$, there exists $(\mathbf{p}_i, t_i \mid \theta_i)$ such that $\mu\nu \models_{PrA} \theta_i$.

Let for example $x = a_i a_j$ and $y = a_i a_j a_k a_l a_j a_i$. Then $\mathbf{gpref}(x, y) = \{(a_i a_j, 1, 1, a_k a_l a_j a_i \mid i \neq k \vee j \neq l), (a_i a_j, 1, 2, a_j a_i \mid i = k \ \wedge \ j = l \ \wedge \ i \neq j)\}$, which can be obtained by a *guess and check* algorithm as before.

4.2 Factoring

We address now the problem of factoring a parameterized word into one or several quadruples made of a prefix, a given *non-empty* factor, a suffix and a constraint characterizing under which additional condition this decomposition holds. Traditionally, factors are associated with positions. Here, the notion of position is not at all clear: in $a^N b a^N$ the position $N + 1$ of b depends on the parameter, but the first position of a to the right of b is $N + 2$ if $N > 0$ and is not defined if $N = 0$. This makes it difficult to reduce factoring to equality by first non-deterministically guessing a prefix and a suffix position and then checking the delimited factor for equality.

Let us first look whether the word aba is a factor of the parameterized word $a^N b a^N \mid N > 0$. There is a unique possibility to decompose $a^N b a^N$ so as to obtain the factor aba, namely : $a^N b a^N = a^{N-1} abab^{N-1}$. We can therefore write informally that $(a^N b a^N \mid N > 0) = (a^{N-1}, aba, b^{N-1} \mid N > 0)$.

Consider now whether $(ba)^j b \mid j < N$ is a factor of $(ab)^i \mid i \leq N$. This time, we can write $(ab)^i \mid i \leq N = ((ab)^l a, (ba)^j b, \epsilon \mid i \leq N \wedge j < N \wedge i = l{+}j{+}k{+}1) \vee ((ab)^i \mid i \leq N \ \wedge \ j < N \ \wedge \ i \neq l + j + k + 1)$. Factoring here is partial, the constraint of the factorized term being strengthened.

Let us finally check if $a^N b a^N$ is a factor in aba, obtaining this time a disjunction of two possible decompositions: $aba = (\epsilon, a^N b a^N, \epsilon \mid N = 1) \vee (a, a^N b a^N, a \mid N = 0)$, that do not cover all possible values of N: factoring is again partial, the constraint of the factoring term being strengthened this time.

Factoring requires searching where a given factor starts in a given parameterized word. To answer this need, our algorithm is organized in two steps. First, the search for a prefix, from which point on an equality check can start. This search is exhaustive, we then need to check equality of the factor with a prefix of the other parameterized word in the second phase. The suffix is of course obtained at the end of this second phase when successful.

Consider the factorization of the parameterized word $w_0 \mid \varphi$ by the parameterized word $s_0 \mid \psi$. We aim at a *representation* of all solutions as a parameterized factorization. To this end, our rules operate on quintuples (u, v, w, s, φ), written as $(u, v, w, s \mid \varphi)$, by maintaining two invariants: $uvw = w_0$ and $vs = s_0$. The word-expression v is therefore both a factor of w_0 and a prefix of s_0. To control the enumeration of all potential prefixes u, we use a special symbol "_" to block the rules checking for a factor until it is replaced by ϵ from which point on the prefix u is frozen. A factorization is obtained when $s = \epsilon$ and $v = s_0$, the word-expression w being then the suffix of that factorization.

[Factorization.] Input: two parameterized words $w_0 \neq \epsilon \mid \varphi$ and $s_0 \mid \psi$; **Output:** a factorization $\vee_i(u_i, v_i, w_i \mid \psi_i)$ such that $\psi_i \not\models_{\mathrm{PrA}} \bot$

$$\text{(Start)}\ \frac{w_0 \mid \varphi,\ s_0 \mid \psi}{\epsilon, \_, w_0, s_0 \mid \varphi \wedge \psi} \quad \text{(Elim)}\ \frac{(u,v,w,s \mid \varphi) \vee P}{P} \quad \text{(Out)}\ \frac{\bigvee_i (u_i, v_i, w_i, \epsilon \mid \varphi_i)}{\bigvee_i (u_i, v_i, w_i \mid \varphi_i)}$$

$$\textbf{if} \quad \varphi \models_{\mathrm{PrA}} \bot$$

$$\text{FindPref: (1)}\ \frac{u, \_, \epsilon, s \mid \varphi}{u, \epsilon, \epsilon, s \mid \varphi} \qquad (2)\ \frac{u, \_, a_i w, s \mid \varphi}{(u, \epsilon, a_i w, s \mid \varphi) \vee (u a_i, \_, w, s \mid \varphi)}$$

$$(3)\ \frac{u, \_, (x)^n w, s \mid \varphi}{(\bigvee_{x=yz} u(x)^i y, \epsilon, z(x)^j w, s \mid \varphi \wedge n = i+j+1) \vee (u(x)^n, \_, w, s)}$$

$$\text{Finish: (1)}\ \frac{u, \epsilon, \epsilon, a_i s \mid \varphi}{\bot} \qquad (2)\ \frac{u, \epsilon, \epsilon, (x)^n s \mid \varphi}{u, \epsilon, \epsilon, s \mid \varphi \wedge n = 0}$$

$$\text{CheckFactor:} \qquad (1)\ \frac{u, v, a_i w, a_j s \mid \varphi}{u, v a_i, w, s \mid \varphi \wedge i = j}$$

$$(2)\ \frac{u, v, a_i w, (a_j y)^n s \mid \varphi}{(u, v, a_i w, s \mid \varphi \wedge n = 0) \vee (u, v a_i, w, (y a_j)^k y s \mid \varphi \wedge n = k+1 \wedge i = j)}$$

$$(3)\ \frac{u, v, (a_i x)^m w, a_j s \mid \varphi}{(u, v, w, a_j s \mid \varphi \wedge m = 0) \vee (u, v a_i, (x a_j)^k x w, s \mid \varphi \wedge m = k+1 \wedge i = j)}$$

$$(4)\ \frac{u, v, (x)^m w, (y)^n s \mid \varphi}{\begin{array}{l} [u, v, (x)^m w, s \mid \varphi \wedge n = 0] \vee [u, v, w, (y)^n s \mid \varphi \wedge m = 0] \\ \vee \bigvee_{(z,\mathbf{p},\mathbf{q} \mid \theta) \in \mathbf{gcd}(x,y)} \\ {[u, v(z)^j, (z)^i w, s \mid \varphi \wedge \theta \wedge j = \mathbf{q} * n \wedge i + j = \mathbf{p} * m \wedge i \geq 0 \wedge n \neq 0] \vee} \\ {[u, v(z)^i, w, (z)^j s \mid \varphi \wedge \theta \wedge i = \mathbf{p} * m \wedge j + i = \mathbf{q} * n \wedge j > 0 \wedge m \neq 0]} \\ \vee \bigvee_{(\mathbf{p}, z \mid \theta) \in \mathbf{gpref}(x,y)} \bigvee_{\mathbf{q} \in [1..\mathbf{p}]} [u, v x^{\mathbf{q}}, w, x^{\mathbf{p}-\mathbf{q}} z(y)^l s \mid \varphi \wedge \theta \wedge n = l+1] \\ \vee \bigvee_{(\mathbf{p}, z \mid \theta) \in \mathbf{gpref}(y,x)} \bigvee_{\mathbf{q} \in [1..\mathbf{p}]} [u, v x^{\mathbf{q}}, x^{\mathbf{p}-\mathbf{q}} z(x)^l w, s \mid \varphi \wedge \theta \wedge m = l+1] \end{array}}$$

FindPref (3) is slightly redundant to maintain a one line formulation. In **CheckFactor** (4), the word-expressions w, s are maintained in reduced form: $x^{\mathbf{q}}$ and $x^{\mathbf{p}-\mathbf{q}}$ stand for (expanded) words. Note that $j = \mathbf{q}*n \wedge i+j = \mathbf{p}*m \wedge i \geq 0 \wedge n \neq 0$ implies $m \neq 0$. Fresh dependent variables appear in conclusions, making termination non-trivial.

We now illustrate **Factoring** with the simple example of the word-expression $w = a^N b a^N$ with the word $s = aba$. We describe the transformations in a rewriting style, starting with the search for a prefix. The arrow rewriting symbol may use a shortened rule name in index and a disjunct number in exponent to ease the reading. Non-modified disjuncts are replaced by dots:

$$(a^N ba^N, aba) \Rightarrow_{Start} (\epsilon, \_, a^N ba^N, aba) \Rightarrow_{FP(3)}$$
$$(a^i, \epsilon, aa^j ba^N, aba \mid N = i+j+1) \vee (a^i a, \epsilon, a^j ba^N, aba \mid N = i+j+1) \vee$$
$$(a^N, \_, ba^N, aba) \Rightarrow^3_{FP(2)}$$
$$\ldots (a^N, \epsilon, ba^N, aba) \vee (a^N b, \_, a^N, aba) \Rightarrow^4_{FP(3)}$$
$$\ldots (a^N ba^i, \epsilon, aa^j, aba \mid N = i+j+1) \vee (a^N ba^i a, \epsilon, a^j, aba \mid N = i+j+1) \vee$$
$$(a^N ba^N, \_, \epsilon, aba) \Rightarrow^6_{FP(1)}$$
$$\ldots (a^N ba^N, \epsilon, \epsilon, aba) \Rightarrow^6_{Finish(1)}$$
$$(a^i, \epsilon, aa^j ba^N, aba \mid N = i+j+1) \vee (a^i a, \epsilon, a^j ba^N, aba \mid N = i+j+1) \vee$$
$$(a^N, \epsilon, ba^N, aba) \vee$$
$$(a^N ba^i, \epsilon, aa^j, aba \mid N = i+j+1) \vee (a^N ba^i a, \epsilon, a^j, aba \mid N = i+j+1) \Rightarrow^3_{CF(1)}$$
$$(a^i, \epsilon, aa^j ba^N, aba \mid N = i+j+1) \vee (a^i a, \epsilon, a^j ba^N, aba \mid N = i+j+1) \vee$$
$$(a^N ba^i, \epsilon, aa^j, aba \mid N = i+j+1) \vee (a^N ba^i a, \epsilon, a^j, aba \mid N = i+j+1)$$

The last two disjuncts fail quickly. We proceed with the successful first two. Disjuncts resulting in immediate failure are abbreviated by dots and eliminated on the fly:

$$(a^i, \epsilon, aa^j ba^N, aba \mid N = i+j+1) \Rightarrow_{CF(1)} (a^i, a, a^j ba^N, ba, \mid N = i+j+1)$$
$$\Rightarrow_{CF(3)} (a^i, a, ba^N, ba \mid N = i+j+1 \ \wedge \ j = 0) \vee (\ldots \mid \bot) \Rightarrow^2_{Elim} \Rightarrow_{CF(1)}$$
$$(a^i, ab, a^N, a \mid N = i+j+1 \ \wedge \ j = 0) \Rightarrow_{CF(3)}$$
$$(a^i, aba, \epsilon, a \mid \bot) \vee (a^i, aba, a^i, \epsilon \mid N = i+j+1 \ \wedge \ j = 0 \ \wedge \ N = i+1)$$
$$\Rightarrow^1_{Elim} \Rightarrow_O (a^i, aba, a^i \mid N = i+1)$$

$$(a^i a, \epsilon, a^j ba^N, aba \mid N = i+j+1) \Rightarrow_{CF(3)}$$
$$(a^i a, \epsilon, ba^N, aba \mid N = i+j+1 \ \wedge \ j = 0) \vee$$
$$(a^i a, a, a^k ba^N, ba \mid N = i+j+1 \ \wedge \ j = k+1) \Rightarrow^1_{CF(1)} \Rightarrow^1_{Elim}$$
$$(a^i a, a, a^k ba^N, ba \mid N = i+j+1 \ \wedge \ j = k+1) \Rightarrow_{CF(3)}$$
$$(\ldots \mid \bot) \vee (a^i a, a, ba^N, ba \mid N = i+j+1 \ \wedge \ j = k+1 \ \wedge \ k = 0) \Rightarrow^1_{Elim} \Rightarrow_{CF(1)}$$
$$(a^i a, ab, a^N, a \mid N = i+j+1 \ \wedge \ j = k+1 \ \wedge \ k = 0) \Rightarrow_{CF(3)}$$
$$(\ldots \mid \bot) \vee (a^i a, aba, a^l, \epsilon \mid N = i+j+1 \ \wedge \ j = k+1 \ \wedge \ k = 0 \ \wedge \ N = l+1)$$
$$\Rightarrow^1_{Elim} \Rightarrow_O (a^i a, aba, a^l \mid N = i+2 \ \wedge \ N = l+1)$$

The final result is therefore the redundant factorization
$(a^i, aba, a^i \mid N = i+1) \vee (a^i a, aba, a^l \mid N = i+2 \ \wedge \ N = l+1)$
This redundancy originates in our formulation of **FindPref** (3), which can be fixed.

We are left indeed showing that our algorithm factors out parameterized words.

Definition 3. *A triple of words (u, v, w) is a* solution *of the factorization problem of a parameterized word $s \mid \psi$ by a parameterized word $t \mid \varphi$ such that $\mathcal{V}arI(\varphi) \cap \mathcal{V}arI(\psi) = \emptyset$, if there exist a valuation $\mu\nu$ of the arithmetic variables such that $\mu\nu \models_{\mathrm{PrA}} \varphi \wedge \psi$, $\mu\nu(v) = \mu\nu(t)$ and $\mu\nu(uvw) = \mu\nu(s)$.*

Definition 4. *Given two parameterized words $s \mid \varphi$ and $v \mid \psi$ such that $\mathcal{V}arI(\varphi) \cap \mathcal{V}arI(\psi) = \emptyset$, $\bigvee_i (u_i, v_i, w_i \mid \theta_i)$ is a* complete factorization *of $s \mid \varphi$ by $v \mid \psi$ (each disjunct being one particular factorization) iff*

(i)[soundness] for each valuation $\mu\nu$ such that $\mu\nu \models_{\mathrm{PrA}} \theta_i$, the triple $(\mu\nu(u_i, v_i, w_i))$ is a solution of the factorization problem of $s \mid \varphi$ by $v \mid \psi$;

(ii)[completeness] For each valuation $\mu\nu$ such that $\mu\nu \models_{\mathrm{PrA}} (\varphi \ \wedge \ \psi)$, either $\exists i$ such that $\mu\nu \models_{\mathrm{PrA}} \theta_i$, or $\mu\nu(v)$ is not a factor of $\mu\nu(s)$.

Theorem 1. *Given two parameterized words $v \mid \psi$ and $s \mid \varphi$ in this order,* Factorization *returns a finite (possibly empty), complete factorization of $s \mid \varphi$ by $v \mid \psi$.*

Proof. (sketch) Termination; we interpret a disjunction of factorization formulas by the multiset of the interpretations of its disjuncts. The interpretation of a disjunct $(u, v, w, s \mid \varphi)$, where w, s are assumed w.l.o.g. to be reduced word-expressions, is defined as the pair $(k+l, m+n)$ of natural numbers, compared lexicographically, in which: k, l are the number of factors of the form $(x)^i$, with i a dependent variable, in w, s respectively, while m, n are the lengths of the longuest flat word prefix of w, s respectively. It is easy to see that **Finish** and **CheckFactor** (4,5) decrease $k+l$, **Check-Factor** (1,2,3) maintain $k+l$ and decrease $m+n$, while other rules can be easily taken care of separately. This shows termination, hence finiteness of the set of answers.

Soundness: it is implied by the two invariants maintained by the rules.

Completeness: first, there is one rule for each possible kind of word-expression for w and s. We justify **CheckFactor** (4), which is the most difficult rule. The first disjunct assumes $m = 0$ or $n = 0$, so we can then assume both $m \neq 0$ and $n \neq 0$. We reason of course (implicitely) on the instances of $(u, v, (x)^m w, (y)^n s \mid \varphi)$, since the algorithms **gcd** and **grpef** will compute them for us. By assumption, $|x| \leq |y|$, hence x is a prefix of y. There are then two cases: either x and y share a common "divisor" z (yielding two possibilities for eliminating one of them), or x "divides" y (**p** times with a non-empty reminder t), in which case it is only possible to eliminate x. □

Note that the factorizations rules do not treat parameters differently from dependent variables. So far, the difference between both is only in the semantics. This suggests that the framework should scale to trees using existing toolboxes or variants.

4.3 Intersection, Equality and Left-Overlaps

All these operations can be derived from the previous algorithm.

Intersection. Intersection is a stepping stone for deciding equality. The problem is to compute a description of the words which are common instances of two given parameterized words $u \mid \varphi$ and $v \mid \psi$. The difference with factorization is that the prefix and the suffix must be both empty. It therefore suffices to modify the **Start** rule, which conclusion should be $(\epsilon, \epsilon, w_0, s_0 \mid \varphi \wedge \psi)$ (therefore eliminating the need for the **FindPref** rules, the **Finish (2)** rule which should output $\perp$ as **Finish (1)**, and the **Out** rule in which u_i and v_i should be ϵ, and the conclusion the disjunction $\bigvee_i \varphi_i$. It is then immediate to see that we can simplify the format of formulas in this case, keeping only a triple $(w, s \mid \varphi)$, which we can of course write as $(w = s \mid \varphi)$.

Equality. We need to decide whether two disjunctive parameterized words $u_0 \mid \varphi_0 \vee \ldots u_m \mid \varphi_m$ and $v_0 \mid \varphi_0 \vee \ldots v_n \mid \varphi_n$ have *exactly* the same set of instances. We assume wlog that for all pairs (i, j), $u_i \mid \varphi_i$ and $v_i \mid \varphi_j$ have different sets of dependent variables. In the case of two parameterized words, we can apply **Intersection** to $(u_0 \mid \varphi_0)$ and $(v_0 \mid \psi_0)$, and check the equivalence in PrA of the obtained formula with the starting one $\varphi_0 \wedge \psi_0$. In the case of a disjunction of parameterized words, we can apply **Intersection** to the $(n+1) \times (m+1)$ equality problems $u_i \mid \varphi_i, v_j \mid \psi_j$, resulting in $(m+1) \times (n+1)$ constraints $\theta_{i,j}$, and then check that $\bigwedge_{i,j} \varphi_i \ \wedge \ \psi_j$ is equivalent in PrA to $\bigwedge_i (\bigvee_j \theta_{(i,j)}) \ \wedge \ \bigwedge_j (\bigvee_i \theta_{(i,j)})$.

Consider the two words $a(ba)^i \mid i \leq N$ and $(ab)^j a \mid j \leq N$. We explain the use of the rules in words, and in cases of disjunctions, treat the disjuncts in turn.

- Initial formula: $a(ba)^i = (ab)^j a \mid i \leq N \ \wedge \ j \leq N$;
- We split on $j = 0$, using **CheckFactor** (2); in the branch $j > 0$, we simplify the head occurrence of a and permute the word under exponent, yielding the result: $(a(ba)^i = a \mid j = 0 \ \wedge \ i \leq N \ \wedge \ j \leq N) \vee ((ba)^i = (ba)^{j-1} ba \mid j > 0 \ \wedge \ \ldots)$;
- Second, we simplify a in the obtained first disjunct, and get: $((ba)^i = \epsilon \mid j = 0 \ \wedge \ i \leq N \ \wedge \ j \leq N) \vee ((ba)^i = (ba)^{j-1} ba \mid j > 0 \ \wedge \ \ldots$;
- Applied to the first disjunct, the rule **Finish** (2) forces the value $i = 0$, yielding:
  $(\epsilon = \epsilon \mid i = 0 \ \wedge \ j = 0 \ \wedge \ i \leq N \ \wedge \ j \leq N)$
  $\vee \ ((ba)^i = (ba)^{j-1} ba \mid j > 0 \ \wedge \ i \leq N \ \wedge \ j \leq N$;
- We now apply the rule **CheckFactor** (4) to the second disjunct (using **gcd**):
  $(\epsilon = \epsilon \mid i = 0 \ \wedge \ j = 0 \ \wedge \ i \leq N \ \wedge \ j \leq N)$
  $\vee \ \epsilon = (ba)^{j-1-i} ba \mid j - 1 - i \geq 0 \ \wedge \ j > 0 \ \wedge \ i \leq N \ \wedge \ j \leq N$
  $\vee \ (ba)^{i-j+1} = ba \mid i - j + 1 \geq 0 \ \wedge \ j > 0 \ \wedge \ i \leq N \ \wedge \ j \leq N$;
- The second disjunct now simplifies away by using **Finish** (1), then **Elim**, yielding:
  $(\epsilon = \epsilon \mid i = 0 \ \wedge \ j = 0 \ \wedge \ i \leq N \ \wedge \ j \leq N)$
  $\vee \ (ba)^{i-j+1} = ba \mid i - j + 1 \geq 0 \ \wedge \ j > 0 \ \wedge \ i \leq N \ \wedge \ j \leq N$;
- **CheckFactor** (3) now applies, hence we get:
  $(\epsilon = \epsilon \mid i = 0 \ \wedge \ j = 0 \ \wedge \ i \leq N \ \wedge \ j \leq N)$
  $\vee \ \epsilon = ba \mid i - j + 1 = 0 \ \wedge \ i - j + 1 \geq 0 \ \wedge \ j > 0 \ \wedge \ i \leq N \ \wedge \ j \leq N$
  $\vee \ (ab)^{i-j} a = a \mid i - j \geq 0 \ \wedge \ i - j + 1 \geq 0 \ \wedge \ j > 0 \ \wedge \ i \leq N \ \wedge \ j \leq N$;
- Using now **Finish** (2), this simplifies to:
  $(\epsilon = \epsilon \mid i = 0 \ \wedge \ j = 0 \ \wedge \ i \leq N \ \wedge \ j \leq N)$
  $\vee \ (ab)^{i-j} a = a \mid i - j \geq 0 \ \wedge \ i - j + 1 \geq 0 \ \wedge \ j > 0 \ \wedge \ i \leq N \ \wedge \ j \leq N$;
- **CheckFactor** (3) now applies again resulting in:
  $(\epsilon = \epsilon \mid i = 0 \ \wedge \ j = 0 \ \wedge \ i \leq N \ \wedge \ j \leq N)$
  $\vee \ a = a \mid i = j \ \wedge \ i - j \geq 0 \ \wedge \ i - j + 1 \geq 0 \ \wedge \ j > 0 \ \wedge \ i \leq N \ \wedge \ j \leq N$
  $\vee \ (ba)^{i-j-1} ba = \epsilon \mid i - j \geq 0 \ \wedge \ i - j + 1 \geq 0 \ \wedge \ j > 0 \ \wedge \ i \leq N \ \wedge \ j \leq N$;
- The third disjunct now simplifies away by using **Finish** (1), then **Elim**, yielding:
  $(\epsilon = \epsilon \mid i = 0 \ \wedge \ j = 0 \ \wedge \ i \leq N \ \wedge \ j \leq N)$
  $\vee \ a = a \mid i = j \ \wedge \ i - j \geq 0 \ \wedge \ i - j + 1 \geq 0 \ \wedge \ j > 0 \ \wedge \ i \leq N \ \wedge \ j \leq N$;
- Using **CheckFactor** (1), we finally get:
  $(\epsilon = \epsilon \mid i = 0 \ \wedge \ j = 0 \ \wedge \ i \leq N \ \wedge \ j \leq N)$
  $\vee \ \epsilon = \epsilon \mid i = j \ \wedge \ i - j \geq 0 \ \wedge \ i - j + 1 \geq 0 \ \wedge \ j > 0 \ \wedge \ i \leq N \ \wedge \ j \leq N$;
- which yields the result by using **Output**:
  $(i = 0 \ \wedge \ j = 0 \ \wedge \ i \leq N \ \wedge \ j \leq N)$
  $\vee \ i = j \ \wedge \ i - j \geq 0 \ \wedge \ i - j + 1 \geq 0 \ \wedge \ j > 0 \ \wedge \ i \leq N \ \wedge \ j \leq N$.

The above formula is equivalent to $i = j \ \wedge \ j \leq N \ \wedge \ i \leq N$ in PrA, which expresses the *precise relationship* between the instances of the equal parameterized words.

Left-overlaps. A *left-overlap* of the word s over the word t is any triple (u, v, w) such that $s = uv$ and $t = vw$. Complete sets of overlaps are then disjunctions of quadruples $(u_i, v_i, w_i \mid \theta_i)$ satisfying an induced soundness and completeness condition as before.

The algorithm for computing a *complete set of left-overlaps* of $w_0 \mid \varphi$ over $s_0 \mid \psi$ is very similar to the one for computing a complete factorization, using the same quadruples (u, v, w, s), the same initialization phase, the same search for a prefix u of w_0 before to start the comparison between the obtained suffix w of w_0 and s_0, the same rules for computing the common part v, and maintaining the same invariants $s_0 = uvw$ and $vs = w_0$. The only difference is that the "suffix" w must be empty in the end. The corresponding modifications of the **Finish** rules is left to the reader.

5 Parameterized Rewriting

We are now ready for investigating properties of parameterized rewrite systems.

Definition 1. *A* parameterized rewrite rule *is a triple $l \rightarrow r \mid \varphi$ made of a lefthand side word-expression l, a righthand side word-expression r and a constraint φ such that $l \mid \varphi$ and $r \mid \varphi$ are parameterized words and $\mathcal{V}ar(l, r) \subseteq \mathcal{V}ar(\varphi)$.*

A parameterized rewrite system *is a set of parameterized rewrite rules $\{l_i \rightarrow r_i \mid \varphi_i\}_i$.*

We shall assume w.l.o.g. that for all $i \in [1..n]$, $\mathcal{V}ar\mathcal{P}(\varphi_i) = \mathcal{P}$.

A parameterized rewrite system R denotes an infinite family of finite word rewrite systems $\{[R_\nu]\}_{\nu \in \mathcal{P} \rightarrow \mathbb{N}^{|\mathcal{P}|}}$ defined as follows:

$$\begin{aligned}
[R] &= \{[R_\nu] \mid \nu \in \mathcal{P} \rightarrow \mathbb{N}^{|\mathcal{P}|}\} \\
R_\nu &= \{(\nu(l) \rightarrow \nu(r) \mid \nu(\varphi)) \mid l \rightarrow r \mid \varphi \in R\} \\
[R_\nu] &= \{\mu(\nu(l)) \rightarrow \mu(\nu(r)) \mid l \rightarrow r \mid \varphi \in R, \text{ and } \mu \in I \rightarrow \mathbb{N}^{|I|} \text{ s.t. } \mu \models_{\mathrm{PrA}} \nu(\varphi)\}
\end{aligned}$$

The rewrite system $[R_\nu]$ is called an *instance* of R.

Consider the parameterized rewrite systems $R = \{a_i^i \rightarrow a_j \mid 0 \leq i < j \leq N\}$ and $R' = \{(u_i u_j)^N \rightarrow u_j u_i \mid i - j \geq 2 \wedge i, j < N\}$. We have:

$$R_{N=2} = \{a_i^i \rightarrow a_j \mid 0 \leq i < j \leq 2\} \quad [R_{N=2}] = \{\epsilon \rightarrow a_1; \epsilon \rightarrow a_2; a_1 \rightarrow a_2\}$$

$$R'_{N=5} = \{(u_i u_j)^5 \rightarrow u_j u_i \mid i - j \geq 2 \wedge i, j < 5\}$$

$$[R'_{N=5}] = \left\{ \begin{array}{ll} u_3 u_1 u_3 u_1 u_3 u_1 u_3 u_1 u_3 u_1 & \rightarrow u_1 u_3, \\ u_4 u_1 u_4 u_1 u_4 u_1 u_4 u_1 u_4 u_1 & \rightarrow u_1 u_4, \\ u_4 u_2 u_4 u_2 u_4 u_2 u_4 u_2 u_4 u_2 & \rightarrow u_2 u_4 \end{array} \right\}$$

There are three ways to understand R: as a set of parameterized rewrite rules operating on parameterized words ; and for each value ν of the parameters, either as a set of parameterized rules R_ν with dependent variables only depending on integer *values*, or as a set $[R_\nu]$ of rules on words. Rewriting can then be defined at several levels: on words with rules (both having possibly exponents), on parameterized words with rules, on words with parameterized rules, etc. These definitions need be consistent at all levels, that is, be related by commutation lemmas in order to capture families of critical pairs in $[R_\nu]$ and their joinability by critical pairs in R_ν and their joinability, and the latter by critical pairs in R and their joinability. This requires a careful definition of parameterized rewriting, as shown by the coming example.

Consider the parameterized rewrite system $R = \{a^iba^i \rightarrow a^ib^i \mid i \leq N, aba \rightarrow \epsilon\}$. The parameterized word $a^iba^i \mid i \leq N$ can be seen as the disjunction $(b \mid i = 0) \vee (a^{i-1}abaa^{i-1} \mid i > 0 \ \wedge \ i \leq N)$, and therefore aba is a factor of $a^iba^i \mid i \leq N$ subjected to the additional constraint $i > 0$: we can rewrite the word a^iba^i with the rule $aba \rightarrow \epsilon$ if $i > 0$, but we cannot if $i = 0$. The parameterized word $a^iba^i \mid i \leq N$ can therefore be rewritten with the rule $aba \rightarrow \epsilon$ into the disjunctive parameterized word $(a^iba^i \mid i \leq N \ \wedge \ i = 0) \vee (a^{i-1}a^{i-1} \mid i \leq N \ \wedge \ i > 0)$, that is $(b \mid i = 0) \vee (a^ia^i \mid 0 < i \leq N)$, hence capturing both cases at once.

Definition 5. *Given a parameterized word $s \mid \varphi$ and a parameterized rewrite rule $l \rightarrow r \mid \psi$ such that (i) $\mathcal{V}ar\mathcal{P}(\psi) \subseteq \mathcal{V}ar\mathcal{P}(\varphi)$ and (ii) $\vee_i(u_i, v_i, w_i \mid \theta_i)$ is a complete, non-empty factorization of $s \mid \varphi$ by $l \mid \psi$, then $s \mid \varphi$* rewrites *with $l \rightarrow r \mid \psi$ to the parameterized disjunctive word $\bigvee_i(u_irw_i \mid \theta_i) \vee (s \mid \varphi \ \wedge \ \bigwedge_i(\neg\theta_i))$, written $s \mid \varphi \longrightarrow_{l \rightarrow r \mid \psi} (\ \bigvee_i(u_irw_i \mid \theta_i) \vee (s \mid \varphi \ \wedge \ \bigwedge_i(\neg\theta_i))$.*

The formulas $\bigvee_i(u_irw_i \mid \theta_i)$ and $\bigwedge_i(\neg\theta_i)$ characterize respectively the positive *and* negative *parts of the rewrite.*

A rewriting step is called uniform *if the righthand side is a (single) parameterized word, i.e., the factorization of $s \mid \varphi$ by $l \mid \psi$ has the form $(u, l, w \mid \theta)$ with $\varphi \models_{\mathrm{PrA}} \theta$.*

Rewriting by a set of parameterized rules is defined as expected.

Note that we do not allow rewriting with an empty factorization, which would result in a trivial rewrite step. In general, the result of rewriting a parameterized word by a parameterized rule is a disjunction of parameterized words by definition of factorization: first, l does not appear exponentiated in the factorization of $s \mid \varphi$ by $l \mid \psi$; second, the finite number of possible interpretations for the dependent variables, given a value of the parameter variables, is of course maintained as a result of the factorization process.

Further, by definition of a factorization, $\theta_i \not\models_{\mathrm{PrA}} \perp$ and therefore the word $u_irw_i \mid \theta_i$ has a non-empty interpretation. On the other hand, it is quite possible that θ and φ are equivalent in Presburger arithmetic in case of a uniform rewrite step, in which case the rewriting result is the single parameterized word $urw \mid \theta$.

We now relate parameterized rewriting with R operating on a parameterized word $u \mid \varphi$ with rewriting the corresponding instances of $u \mid \varphi$ with $[R_\nu]$. We therefore skip the intermediate level of rewriting with R_ν. This relationship is expressed by the following key lemma, which will be a main tool in our study of parameterized rewriting:

Lemma 1 (Lifting). *Let $s \mid \varphi$ be a parameterized word. Then, $\mu(\nu(s)) \longrightarrow_{[R_\nu]} t$ for some rule instance $\mu(\nu(l)) \rightarrow \mu(\nu(r))$ of $l \rightarrow r \mid \psi \in R$ iff $(\ \bigvee_i u_i, l, w_i \mid \theta_i)$ is a complete factorization of $s \mid \varphi$ by $l \mid \psi$, $\mu\nu \models_{\mathrm{PrA}} \theta_i$ for some i, and $t = \mu(\nu(u_irw_i))$.*

Proof. Follows easily from Definitions 4 and 5: □

Lifting takes care of positive rewrites. A negative rewrite is nothing but an artefact which reduces the set of instances of a parameterized word without changing the word itself. Negative rewrites play a central role for *derivations*, since they allow us to capture at once all possible derivations on words by derivations on parameterized words.

We write $t \mid \varphi \longrightarrow^*_R s \mid \psi$ for the reflexive, transitive closure of $\longrightarrow_R$, called a *derivation*, and $t \mid \varphi \longleftrightarrow^*_R s \mid \psi$ for its reflexive, symmetric transitive closure, called a *conversion*, for which R is as usual interpreted as a set of equations.

5.1 Termination of Parameterized Rewriting

Unfortunately, termination of parameterized rewriting does not characterize termination of its instances, as shown by the coming example of a (plain) rewrite system which terminates trivially on words, but does not on parameterized words. Let $R = \{ab \rightarrow \epsilon\}$. We have:

$(ab)^i \mid i \leq N \longrightarrow_{ab \rightarrow \epsilon} (ab)^k(ab)^l \mid i > 0 \wedge i = k + l + 1 \wedge i \leq N = (ab)^j \mid i > 0 \wedge i = j+1 \wedge i \leq N \longrightarrow_{ab \rightarrow \epsilon} (ab)^m(ab)^n \mid i > 0 \wedge j > 0 \wedge j = m+n+1 \wedge i > 0 \wedge i = j+1 \wedge i \leq N \longrightarrow_{ab \rightarrow \epsilon} \cdots$

We cannot therefore expect a parameterized system to be terminating on parameterized words in general (actually in most cases), but we are indeed only interested in the termination of its instances on words. In the above case, we can trivially show that $ab \rightarrow \epsilon$ terminates on words. Yet, it may be difficult for parameterized rules. A simple remark shows however that automation is at reach. Consider the two rewrite systems $R = \{a^i \rightarrow \epsilon \mid i \leq n\}$ and $S = \{a^i \rightarrow \epsilon \mid 1 \leq i \leq n\}$ which describe the same set of instances on words except for the non-terminating instance $\epsilon \rightarrow \epsilon$ of R which is not an instance of S. As long as the parameterized rule $a^i \rightarrow \epsilon$ does not degenerate (here, into the rule $\epsilon \rightarrow \epsilon$), it can be seen as a terminating rule over word-expressions built from the alphabet, concatenation, and exponentiation. The degenerated cases can easily be computed by solving equations of the form $(x)^i = \epsilon$ for x a non-empty word, therefore adding $i = 0$ to the constraint of the considered rule. In the previous two examples, we get the parameterized rule instances $\{\epsilon \rightarrow \epsilon \mid i \leq n \wedge i = 0\}$ and $\{\epsilon \rightarrow \epsilon \mid 1 \leq i \leq n \wedge i = 0\}$, but the second disappears. More generally,

Theorem 2. *Let R a parameterized rewriting system and $C(R)$ be obtained as follows:*

$C(R \cup \{l \rightarrow r \mid \theta\}) = C(R) \cup C(l \rightarrow r \mid \theta)$

$C(l = x_1(y_1)^{i_1} \ldots (y_n)^{i_n} x_{n+1} \rightarrow r \mid \theta) = \{(l\!\downarrow \rightarrow r \mid \theta \wedge \bigwedge_{j \in J} i_j \neq 0 \mid J \subseteq [1:n]\}$

where $l\!\downarrow$ is obtained from l by replacing i_k by 0 in l for $k \in [1..n] \setminus J$, then $(y_k)^0$ by ϵ and finally eliminating superflous ϵ's.

Then, all instances of R terminate on words if there exists a well-founded rewrite ordering $\succ$ on word-expressions such that:

(i) $s \succ t$ implies $\mu\nu(usv) \succ \mu\nu(utv)$ for all word-expressions u, v and valuations $\mu\nu$;

(ii) $x \succ y$ implies $\mu\nu((x)^i) \succ \mu\nu((y)^i)$ for all valuations $\mu\nu$ such that $\mu\nu \models_{\mathrm{PrA}} i \neq 0$;

(iii) $l \succ r$ for all rules $(l \rightarrow r \mid \theta) \in C(R)$ for which $\theta \not\models_{\mathrm{PrA}} \bot$.

Proof. (sketch). First, an arbitrary derivation on words with some rewrite system $[R_\nu]$ is also a derivation with $[C(R)_\nu]$, which can be seen as a parameterized derivation with $C(R)$ by using the Lifting Lemma. Condition (iii) then allows us to make it an ordered sequence on parameterized-words. Conditions (i,ii) allow finally to move the ordering on parameterized-words back to the original sequence of words. □

Existing techniques apply directly provided they satisfy conditions (i,ii), which is normally the case since exponents cannot be instantiated by 0 in a rule of $C(R)$. The use of exponential interpretations would be a natural choice by allowing to interpret exponentiation on words by arithmetic exponentiation. Polynomial interpretations also do.

In the previous two examples, we ended up checking the pairs $a^i \succ \epsilon, \epsilon \succ \epsilon$ which fails for any interpretation, and $a^i \succ \epsilon$ which succeeds, using for example as interpretation the number of letters in a parameterized-word.

5.2 Confluence of Parameterized Rewriting

Confluence raises other difficulties. For an example, let $R = \{ac \rightarrow \epsilon, def \rightarrow \epsilon\}$. R is confluent on words, since it is terminating and has no critical pairs. But positive rewriting (stressed by using $\Longrightarrow$) with R is not confluent on parameterized-words:
$ab^icde^if \mid i \leq N \Longrightarrow_{ac\rightarrow\epsilon} df \mid i = 0 \wedge i \leq N$ and
$ab^icde^if \mid i \leq N \Longrightarrow_{def\rightarrow\epsilon} abc \mid i = 1 \wedge i \leq N$, two words which cannot be joined. Observe however that the factorization constraints $i = 0$ and $i = 1$ are incompatible: the word ab^icde^if does not have instances rewritable by both rules. And indeed, the problem disappears when positive and negative rewriting are carried along together:
$ab^icde^if \mid i \leq N \longrightarrow_{ac\rightarrow\epsilon} (df \mid i = 0 \wedge i \leq N) \vee (ab^icde^if \mid i \neq 0 \wedge i \leq N)$, and
$ab^icde^if \mid i \leq N \longrightarrow_{def\rightarrow\epsilon} (abc \mid i = 1 \wedge i \leq N) \vee (ab^icde^if \mid i \neq 1 \wedge i \leq N)$,
and since these rewrites are sort of orthogonal, they both rewrite to a word equal to
$(df \mid i{=}0 \wedge i \leq N) \vee (abc \mid i{=}1 \wedge i \leq N)$
$\vee\, (ab^icde^if \mid i \neq 0 \wedge i \neq 1 \wedge i \leq N)$.

Theorem 3. *The instances of a parameterized rewrite system R are confluent (resp. locally confluent) on words iff parameterized rewriting with R is confluent (resp. locally confluent) on parameterized words.*

Proof. Follows from the lifting Lemma 1. □

We now turn our attention to a critical pair analysis of local confluence. Consider the parameterized rewrite system $R = \{a^iba^i \rightarrow a^ib^i \mid i \leq N, aba \rightarrow \epsilon\}$. Since aba is a factor of $a^iba^i \rightarrow a^ib^i \mid i \leq N$ under the additional constraint $i > 0$, the lefthand side of the first rule can be rewritten by the second rule. And since $a^iba^i \rightarrow a^ib^i \mid i \leq N$ is a factor of aba under the additional constraint $i = 0$, the lefthand side of the second can be rewritten by the first. We can indeed describe all critical pairs of each rewrite system $[R]_\nu$ by computing factorizations and left-overlaps.

Consider the parameterized system $R = \{a_Na_i \rightarrow a_N \mid 0 < i < N\}$, which all instances are critical pair-free. Let $a_Na_i \rightarrow a_N \mid 0 < i < N$ and $a_Na_j \rightarrow a_N \mid 0 < j < N$ be two arbitrary rules in R. Their instances belong to the same system $[R_n]$ provided they share the same parameter N, while the dependent variable is renamed (otherwise, we would have the same rule). It is easy to see that a_Na_i and a_Na_j cannot overlap unless $i = j$, in which case we have a trivial critical pair. On the other hand, rules of different systems $[R_n]$ and $[R_m]$ do overlap and yield non-joinable critical pairs. This example shows the practical need of the two kinds of variables in our model.

Definition 2. *Let $l \rightarrow r \mid \varphi$ and $g \rightarrow d \mid \psi$ be two rules of a parameterized rewriting system R such that $\mathcal{V}arI(\varphi) \cap \mathcal{V}arI(\psi) = \emptyset$.*

(i) Let $\vee_i(u_i, g_i, v_i \mid \theta_i)$ be a complete factorization of $l \mid \varphi$ by $g \mid \psi$. The pair $(r \mid \bigvee_i \theta_i, \bigvee_i u_idv_i \mid \theta_i)$ is called a critical pair *of $g \rightarrow d \mid \psi$ on $l \rightarrow r \mid \varphi$;*

(ii) Let $(\bigvee_i(u_i, v_i, w_i \mid \theta_i)$ be a complete left-overlap of $l \mid \varphi$ on $g \mid \psi$. The pair $(\bigvee_i u_ir \mid \theta_i, \bigvee_i dw_i \mid \theta_i)$ is called a critical overlapping pair *of $l \rightarrow r \mid \varphi$ on $g \rightarrow d \mid \psi$.*

Lemma 2. *For each valuation ν, the set of critical pairs in $[R_\nu]$ is the set of corresponding instances of the critical and overlapping pairs in R.*

Proof. Follows again from the lifting Lemma 1. □

Lemma 3. *Parameterized rewriting with R is locally confluent iff all critical and overlapping pairs of R are joinable by parameterized rewriting.*

Proof. (sketch). The only if direction is straightforward, but the converse is more subtle. Let $s \mid \varphi \longrightarrow (u \mid \theta) \vee (s \mid \varphi \wedge \neg\theta)$, and $s \mid \varphi \longrightarrow (v \mid \gamma) \vee (s \mid \varphi \wedge \neg\gamma)$. Then,
$(u \mid \theta) \vee (s \mid \varphi \wedge \neg\theta) =$
$(u \mid \theta \wedge \gamma) \vee (u \mid \theta \wedge \neg\gamma) \vee (s \mid \varphi \wedge \neg\theta \wedge \gamma) \vee (s \mid \varphi \wedge \neg\theta \wedge \neg\gamma) =$
$(u \mid \theta \wedge \gamma) \vee (u \mid \theta \wedge \neg\gamma) \vee (s \mid \neg\theta \wedge \gamma) \vee (s \mid \varphi \wedge \neg\theta \wedge \neg\gamma)$.
Similarly (but we change the order of disjuncts), $(v \mid \gamma) \vee (s \mid \varphi \wedge \neg\gamma) =$
$(v \mid \theta \wedge \gamma) \vee (s \mid \theta \wedge \neg\gamma) \vee (v \mid \neg\theta \wedge \gamma) \vee (s \mid \varphi \wedge \neg\theta \wedge \neg\gamma)$.

We see that the first disjuncts of both expressions are joinable by a critical pair analysis; the second disjuncts are joinable by a rewrite step with $g \to d \mid \psi$; the third disjuncts are joinable by a rewrite step with $l \to r \mid \varphi$; and the fourth disjuncts are equal. □

Using Lemmas 2, 3 and Newman's lemma, we get the main practical result of this work:

Theorem 4. *Assume the rewrite systems $[\![R_\nu]\!]$ on words are terminating. Then, they are confluent iff all critical and overlapping pairs of R are joinable.*

Unfortunately, this does not imply the decidability of confluence or local-confluence even under our termination assumption since parameterized rewriting may be non-terminating, and therefore the usual joinability check may not terminate for some pairs. We don't know, however, whether joinability is decidable or undecidable in our model of parameterized rewriting. This problem is left open.

5.3 Implementation and Example

As an example, consider the presentation of dihedral groups of order $N > 1$ by $R_N = \{s^2 \to \epsilon; sr \to r^{N-1}; r^N \to \epsilon\}$, which we input to the tool C*i*ME2[3] in the format:

```
let N = parameters "N";
let S = pword_signature N "s | {N>=2}; r | {N>=2}" ;
let R = psrs S "s s -> | {N>=2};
                s r -> r^{N-1} s | {N>=2} ;
                r^{N} -> | {N>=2};"

        ;
let Rnorm = psrs S "s r^{k} -> r^{N-k} s |{N>=2 /\
                                          1<=k<=N-1 };";

pconfluent_ext R Rnorm;
```

The procedure `Rnorm` iterates the second rule, allowing us to overcome some limitations of the current implementation to uniform rewrite proofs introduced in definition 5. C*i*ME2 computes 13 overlapping pairs joinable immediately while 4 others need a few (uniform) rewrite steps. In case $N = 1$, the lefthand side sr of the second rule becomes reducible by the third rule $r^2 \to \epsilon$, while this is not the case if $N > 1$: the restriction $N > 1$ present in the C*i*ME2 specification allows one to comply with the restriction to uniform rewrite proofs: C*i*ME2 is not able to show the joinability of all critical pairs if $N > 1$ is changed to $N > 0$.

6 Conclusion

We have defined a framework of parameterized rewrite systems operating on parameterized words for describing infinite families of rewriting systems on words and mechanize their study, using a sophisticated rewriting toolkit for parameterized words.

We have given a method for showing termination of all instances of a parameterized system R by using an adequate ordering for checking the rules of a transformed system $C(R)$, therefore allowing to reuse existing tools.

We have reduced confluence of all instances of a parameterized rewriting system to the joinability of its finitely many critical or overlapping pairs under termination of the instances. Whether joinability can be decided in this context merits further investigations.

We could have made the choice of a more abstract framework based on parameterized structures for representing infinite families of rewriting systems on that structure, assuming the necessary toolkit for the parameterized structure, and then apply the abstract results to parameterized words as described here or parameterized trees as described in [2,5]. We indeed conjecture (but have not checked) that our approach scales up, opening up interesting applications for example to multicore hardware modelisations.

Formalisms for representing families of terms, equations or rules fall in two categories: tree automata and term schematizations. Our formalism of parameterized words belongs to the second but its strong closure properties suggest to blend it with automata in the line of [9], a recent bridge between both kinds of worlds.

Acknowledgments. To Evelyne Contejean and Claude Marché for discussions with the second author and to the several anonymous referees who helped shaping this paper.

References

1. Book, R.V., Otto, F.: String Rewriting Systems. In: Text and monographs in Computer Science. Springer, Berlin (1993)
2. Comon, H.: On unification of terms with integer exponents. Math. Systems Theory 28, 67–88 (1995)
3. Contejean, E., Marché, C., Monate, B., Urbain, X.: Cime version 2. Technical report, Université Paris-Sud (2000)
4. Dershowitz, N., Jouannaud, J.-P.: Rewrite systems. In: van Leeuwen, J. (ed.) Handbook of Theoretical Computer Science, vol. B, pp. 243–309. North-Holland, Amsterdam (1990)
5. Hermann, M., Galbavý, R.: Unification of infinite sets of terms schematized by primal grammars. Theoretical Computer Science 176(1–2), 111–158 (1997)
6. Klop, J.W., et al.: Term rewriting systems. In: Cambridge Tracts in Theoretical Computer Science, vol. 55. Cambridge University Press, Cambridge (2003)
7. Le Chenadec, P.: Canonical forms in finitely presented algebras. Pitman, London (1986)
8. Le Chenadec, P.: Analysis of dehn's algorithm by critical pairs. Theoretical Computer Science 51(1-2), 27–52 (1987)
9. Peltier, N.: A unified view of tree automata and term schematisations. In: Ausiello, G., Karhumäki, J., Mauri, G., Luke Ong, C.-H. (eds.) IFIP TCS. IFIP, vol. 273, pp. 491–505. Springer, Heidelberg (2008)
10. Salzer, G.: On unification of infinite sets of terms and its applications. In: Voronkov, A. (ed.) LPAR 1992. LNCS, vol. 624, pp. 409–421. Springer, Heidelberg (1992)

Polite Theories Revisited*

Dejan Jovanović and Clark Barrett

New York University
{dejan,barrett}@cs.nyu.edu

Abstract. The classic method of Nelson and Oppen for combining decision procedures requires the theories to be stably-infinite. Unfortunately, some important theories do not fall into this category (e.g. the theory of bit-vectors). To remedy this problem, previous work introduced the notion of *polite* theories. Polite theories can be combined with any other theory using an extension of the Nelson-Oppen approach. In this paper we revisit the notion of polite theories, fixing a subtle flaw in the original definition. We give a new combination theorem which specifies the degree to which politeness is preserved when combining polite theories. We also give conditions under which politeness is preserved when instantiating theories by identifying two sorts. These results lead to a more general variant of the theorem for combining multiple polite theories.

1 Introduction

The seminal paper of Nelson and Oppen [5] introduced a general combination framework that allows the creation of a decision procedure for the combination of two first-order theories in a *modular* fashion. Using the Nelson-Oppen framework, decision procedures for two individual theories can be used as black boxes to create a decision procedure for the combined theory.

Although very general and widely-used in practice, the Nelson-Oppen approach is not applicable to all theories encountered in practical applications. A significant restriction of Nelson-Oppen is the requirement that theories be *stably-infinite*. While many important theories are stably-infinite, some are not, including those with inherently finite domains such as the theory of bit-vectors. As bit-precise reasoning about both programs and hardware is becoming more important and more feasible, it is desirable to find ways of overcoming this restriction.

As a possible remedy for this problem, the notion of *shiny theories* and an appropriate combination algorithm was introduced in [13]. The requirements on a shiny theory are stronger than just stable-infiniteness, but this allows it to be combined with an arbitrary other (possibly non-stably-infinite) theory. The main drawback to this approach is the requirement that a shiny theory T has to be equipped with a function $mincard_T$. This function, given a set of constraints, must be able to compute the minimal cardinality of a T-interpretation that satisfies the constraints.

* This work was funded in part by SRC contract 2008-TJ-1850.

C. Fermüller and A. Voronkov (Eds.): LPAR-17, LNCS 6397, pp. 402–416, 2010.

A related approach for combining theories is presented in [4]. The authors start from a framework of parametrically polymorphic logics to devise a Nelson-Oppen-style combination procedure for theories that are *flexible*. Flexibility is a property similar to the ability to move to a bigger or a smaller (infinite) model via the Löwenheim-Skolem theorem in first-order logic. Most commonly-used theories can be represented in this framework and are shown to be flexible. Reasoning about cardinality also plays a major role in this approach–a solver for a parametric theory (called a strong solver) is required to process not only the formula being checked, but also a set of cardinality constraints over the domain sizes. Although this direction is promising, particularly because of the advantages of parametricity, the approach as developed thus far would be cumbersome to implement in a practical system. In particular, while reasoning about cardinalities is possible for a wide class of important theories, it can be computationally expensive, and theory decision procedures are typically not designed with this additional requirement in mind.

An alternative approach uses the notion of *polite theories* introduced in [8]. Polite theories can also be combined with an arbitrary other theory. However, this approach does not require the computation of the *mincard* function. Instead, a decision procedure for a polite theory must be able to generate explicitly a *witness* formula that enumerates any required domain elements using additional variables. The authors show that many commonly-used theories are polite (including theories of lists, arrays, sets, and multi-sets). This approach seems more practical than those that require reasoning about cardinalities explicitly. And, while proving that a theory is polite can be difficult and needs to be done on a per-theory basis, once this is done, the combination method can be easily implemented.

In this paper, we revisit and extend the results on polite theories from [8]. Section 2 gives definitions and background on many-sorted logic and theory combination. Section 3 begins by introducing polite theories, making a small but needed modification to the definition of finite witnessability (one of the two properties that make up politeness), and then goes on to show that when combining polite theories, the resulting theory is also polite (with respect to a possibly reduced set of sorts). Section 4 addresses *theory instantiation*, the construction of a new theory by identifying two sorts in an existing theory; we prove that instantiation preserves politeness. Finally, Section 3.4 discusses the combination of multiple polite theories, culminating in a combination result that is more general than the ones presented in [8].

Due to space limitations, proofs of the results in this paper are omitted. The full paper with proofs is available from the authors as a technical report [3].

2 Preliminaries

2.1 Many-Sorted First-Order Logic

We start with a brief overview of the syntax and semantics of many-sorted first-order logic. For a more detailed exposition, we refer the reader to [2,11].

Syntax. A *signature* Σ is a triple (S, F, P) where S is a set of *sorts*, F is a set of *function symbols*, and P is a set of *predicate symbols.* For a signature $\Sigma = (S, F, P)$, we write $\Sigma^{\mathbb{S}}$ for the set S of sorts, $\Sigma^{\mathbb{F}}$ for the set F of function symbols, and $\Sigma^{\mathbb{P}}$ for the set P of predicates. Each predicate and function symbol is associated with an *arity*, a tuple constructed from the sorts in S. We write $\Sigma_1 \cup \Sigma_2 = (S_1 \cup S_2, F_1 \cup F_2, P_1 \cup P_2)$ for the union[1] of signatures $\Sigma_1 = (S_1, F_1, P_1)$ and $\Sigma_2 = (S_2, F_2, P_2)$. Additionally, we write $\Sigma_1 \subseteq \Sigma_2$ if $S_1 \subseteq S_2$, $F_1 \subseteq F_2$, $P_1 \subseteq P_2$, and the symbols of Σ_1 have the same arity as those in Σ_2.

For a signature Σ, we assume the logic (but not the signature) includes an equality symbol $=_\sigma$, for each sort $\sigma \in \Sigma^{\mathbb{S}}$. We will frequently omit the subscript on equality when the sort of the equation is not relevant to the discussion. We assume the standard notions of a Σ*-term*, Σ*-literal*, and Σ*-formula.* In the following, we assume that all formulas are quantifier-free, if not explicitly stated otherwise. A literal is called *flat* if it is of the form $x = y$, $x \neq y$, $x = f(y_1, \ldots, y_n)$, $p(y_1, \ldots, y_n)$, or $\neg p(y_1, \ldots, y_n)$, where $x, y, y_1, \ldots, y_n$ are variables, f is a function symbol, and p is a predicate symbol.

If ϕ is a term or a formula, we will denote by $vars_\sigma(\phi)$ the set of variables of sort σ that occur (free) in ϕ. We overload this function in the usual way, $vars_S(\phi)$ denoting variables in ϕ of the sorts in S, and $vars(\phi)$ denoting all variables in ϕ. We also sometimes refer to a set Φ of formulas as if it were a single formula, in which case the intended meaning is the conjunction $\bigwedge \Phi$ of the formulas in the set.

Semantics. Let Σ be a signature, and let X be a set of variables whose sorts are in $\Sigma^{\mathbb{S}}$. A Σ*-interpretation* $\mathcal{A}$ over X is a map that interprets: each sort $\sigma \in \Sigma^{\mathbb{S}}$ as a non-empty domain A_σ,[2] each variable $x \in X$ of sort σ as an element $x^{\mathcal{A}} \in A_\sigma$, each function symbol $f \in \Sigma^{\mathbb{F}}$ of arity $\sigma_1 \times \cdots \times \sigma_n \times \tau$ as a function $f^{\mathcal{A}} : A_{\sigma_1} \times \cdots \times A_{\sigma_n} \to A_\tau$, each predicate symbol $p \in \Sigma^{\mathbb{P}}$ of arity $\sigma_1 \times \cdots \times \sigma_n$ as a subset $p^{\mathcal{A}}$ of $A_{\sigma_1} \times \cdots \times A_{\sigma_n}$. A Σ*-structure* is a Σ-interpretation over an empty set of variables. As usual, the interpretations of terms and formulas in an interpretation $\mathcal{A}$ are defined inductively over their structure (with equality, Boolean operations, and quantifiers interpreted as usual). For a term t, we denote with $t^{\mathcal{A}}$ the evaluation of t under the interpretation $\mathcal{A}$. Likewise, for a formula ϕ, we denote with $\phi^{\mathcal{A}}$ the truth-value (true or false) of ϕ under interpretation $\mathcal{A}$. A Σ-formula ϕ is *satisfiable* iff it evaluates to true in some Σ-interpretation over $vars(\phi)$.

Given a Σ-interpretation $\mathcal{A}$, a vector of variables $\overrightarrow{x}$, and a vector of domain elements of $\mathcal{A}$, $\overrightarrow{a}$, we denote by $\mathcal{A}\{\overrightarrow{x} \leftarrow \overrightarrow{a}\}$ the Σ-interpretation with the same domains as $\mathcal{A}$ that interprets each variable in $\overrightarrow{x}$ as the corresponding element

[1] In this paper, when combining two signatures, we always assume that function and predicate symbols from the signatures do not overlap, so that the union operation is well-defined. On the other hand, the signatures are allowed to have non-disjoint sets of sorts.

[2] In the rest of the paper we will use the calligraphic letters $\mathcal{A}$, $\mathcal{B}$, ... to denote interpretations, and the corresponding subscripted Roman letters A_σ, B_σ, ... to denote the domains of the interpretations.

in $\overrightarrow{a}$ and all other symbols as in $\mathcal{A}$ (note that to be well-defined, we require that for each corresponding pair (x_i, a_i) in $\overrightarrow{x}$ and $\overrightarrow{a}$, we must have $a_i \in A_{\sigma_i}$ where σ_i is the sort of x_i).

Let $\mathcal{A}$ be an Ω-interpretation over some set V of variables. For a signature $\Sigma \subseteq \Omega$, and a set of variables $U \subseteq V$, we denote with $\mathcal{A}^{\Sigma,U}$ the interpretation obtained from $\mathcal{A}$ by restricting it to interpret only the symbols in Σ and the variables in U.

Theories. We will use the definition of theories as classes of structures, rather than sets of sentences. We define a theory formally as follows (see e.g. [12] and Definition 2 in [8]).

Definition 1 (Theory). *Given a set of Σ-sentences* $\mathbf{Ax}$ *a Σ-theory $T_{\mathbf{Ax}}$ is a pair $(\Sigma, \mathbf{A})$ where Σ is a signature and $\mathbf{A}$ is the class of Σ-structures that satisfy* $\mathbf{Ax}$.

Given a theory $T = (\Sigma, \mathbf{A})$, a T*-interpretation* is a Σ-interpretation $\mathcal{A}$ such that $\mathcal{A}^{\Sigma,\emptyset} \in \mathbf{A}$. A Σ-formula ϕ is T-satisfiable iff it is satisfiable in some T-interpretation $\mathcal{A}$. This is denoted as $\mathcal{A} \vDash_T \phi$, or just $\mathcal{A} \vDash \phi$ if the theory is clear from the context. Given a Σ-theory T, two Σ-formulas ϕ and ψ are T-equivalent if they evaluate to the same truth value in every T-interpretation.

2.2 Combination of Theories

As theories in our formalism are represented by classes of structures, a combination of two theories is represented by those structures that can interpret both theories (Definition 3 in [8]).

Definition 2 (Combination). *Let $T_1 = (\Sigma_1, \mathbf{A}_1)$ and $T_2 = (\Sigma_2, \mathbf{A}_2)$ be two theories. The* combination *of T_1 and T_2 is the theory $T_1 \oplus T_2 = (\Sigma, \mathbf{A})$ where $\Sigma = \Sigma_1 \cup \Sigma_2$ and $\mathbf{A} = \{\Sigma$-structures $\mathcal{A} \mid \mathcal{A}^{\Sigma_1,\emptyset} \in \mathbf{A_1}$ and $\mathcal{A}^{\Sigma_2,\emptyset} \in \mathbf{A_2}\}$.*

The set of Σ-structures resulting from the combination of two theories is indeed a theory in the sense of Definition 1. If $\mathbf{Ax}_1$ is the set of sentences defining theory T_1, and $\mathbf{Ax}_2$ is the set of sentences defining theory T_2, then $\mathbf{A}$ is the set of Σ-structures that satisfy the set $\mathbf{Ax} = \mathbf{Ax}_1 \cup \mathbf{Ax}_2$ (see Proposition 4 in [8]).

Given decision procedures for the satisfiability of formulas in theories T_1 and T_2, we are interested in constructing a decision procedure for satisfiability in $T_1 \oplus T_2$ using as black boxes the known procedures for T_1 and T_2. The Nelson-Oppen combination method [5,10,11] gives a general mechanism for doing this. Given a formula ϕ over the combined signature $\Sigma_1 \cup \Sigma_2$, the first step is to *purify* ϕ by constructing an equisatisfiable set of formulas $\phi_1 \cup \phi_2$ such that each ϕ_i consists of only Σ_i-formulas. This can easily be done by finding a pure (i.e. Σ_i-for some i) subterm t, replacing it with a new variable v, adding the equation $v = t$, and then repeating this process until all formulas are pure. The next step is to force the decision procedures for the individual theories to agree on whether variables appearing in both ϕ_1 and ϕ_2 (called *shared* variables) are equal. This is done by introducing an *arrangement* over the shared variables [8,10].

Definition 3 (Arrangement). *Given a set of variables V over a set of sorts S, with $V_\sigma = vars_\sigma(V)$ so that $V = \bigcup_{\sigma \in S} V_\sigma$, we call a formula δ_V an* arrangement *of V if there exists a family of equivalence relations $E = \{ E_\sigma \subseteq V_\sigma \times V_\sigma \mid \sigma \in S \}$, such that the equivalence relations induce δ_V, i.e. $\delta_V = \bigwedge_{\sigma \in S} \delta_\sigma$, where each δ_σ is determined by E_σ as follows:*

$$\delta_\sigma = \bigwedge_{(x,y) \in E_\sigma} (x = y) \wedge \bigwedge_{(x,y) \in \overline{E}_\sigma} (x \neq y) \ .$$

In the above definition, $\overline{E}_\sigma$ denotes the complement of the equivalence relation E_σ, i.e. $V_\sigma \times V_\sigma \setminus E_\sigma$. When the family of equivalence relations is not clear from the context, we will denote the arrangement as $\delta_V(E)$.

The Nelson-Oppen method is only complete when the theories satisfy certain conditions. Sufficient conditions for completeness are signature-disjointness and *stable-infiniteness.* Stable-infiniteness was originally introduced in a single-sorted setting [6]. In the many-sorted setting, stable-infiniteness is defined with respect to a subset of the signature sorts (Definition 6 from [11]).

Definition 4 (Stable-Infiniteness). *Let Σ be a signature, let $S \subseteq \Sigma^{\mathbb{S}}$ be a set of sorts, and let T be a Σ-theory. We say that T is* stably-infinite *with respect to S if for every T-satisfiable quantifier-free Σ-formula ϕ, there exists a T-interpretation $\mathcal{A}$ satisfying ϕ, such that A_σ is infinite for each sort $\sigma \in S$.*

The Nelson-Oppen combination theorem states that, given two theories T_1 and T_2, stably-infinite over (at least) the set of common sorts $\Sigma_1^{\mathbb{S}} \cap \Sigma_2^{\mathbb{S}}$, and whose signatures are otherwise disjoint, ϕ is satisfiable in $T_1 \oplus T_2$ iff there exists an arrangement δ_V of the shared variables $V = vars(\phi_1) \cap vars(\phi_2)$ such that $\phi_i \cup \delta_V$ is satisfiable in T_i, for $i = 1, 2$.

It is interesting to note that stable-infiniteness is preserved when combining theories, a fact that follows easily from known results.

Proposition 1. *Let Σ_1 and Σ_2 be signatures. If*

- *T_1 is a Σ_1-theory stably-infinite with respect to $S_1 \subseteq \Sigma_1^{\mathbb{S}}$,*
- *T_2 is a Σ_2-theory stably-infinite with respect to $S_2 \subseteq \Sigma_2^{\mathbb{S}}$,*
- *$\Sigma_1^{\mathbb{S}} \cap \Sigma_2^{\mathbb{S}} = S_1 \cap S_2$,*

then $T_1 \oplus T_2$ is a $(\Sigma_1 \cup \Sigma_2)$-theory and is stably-infinite with respect to $S_1 \cup S_2$.

Although many interesting theories are stably-infinite, some important theories are not. For example, the theory of fixed-size bit-vectors contains sorts whose domains are all finite. Hence, this theory cannot be stably-infinite. The Nelson-Oppen method may be incomplete for combinations involving this theory as shown by the following example.

Example 1. Consider the theory of arrays T_{array} where both indices and elements are of the same sort bv, so that the sorts of T_{array} are $\{\mathsf{array}, \mathsf{bv}\}$, and a theory T_{bv} that requires the sort bv to be interpreted as bit-vectors of size 1. Both theories are decidable and we would like to decide the combination theory in a Nelson-Oppen-like framework. Let $a_1, \ldots, a_5$ be array variables and consider the following constraints:

$$a_i \neq a_j, \text{ for } 1 \leq i < j \leq 5 \ .$$

These constraints are entirely within the language of T_{array} (i.e. no purification is necessary), there are no shared variables, and there are no constraints over bit-vectors. Thus, the array theory decision procedure is given all of the constraints and the bit-vector decision procedure is given an empty set of constraints. Any decision procedure for the theory of arrays will tell us that these constraints are satisfiable. But, there are only four possible different arrays with elements and indices over bit-vectors of size 1, so this set of constraints is unsatisfiable.

The notion of politeness, which we define in the following section allows us to overcome this problem.

3 Polite Theories

Polite theories were introduced in [8] to extend the Nelson-Oppen method to allow combinations with non-stably-infinite theories. A theory can be combined with any other theory (with no common function or predicate symbols) if it is *polite* with respect to the set of shared sorts. The notion of politeness depends on two other important properties: *smoothness* and *finite witnessability.* In this section, we define these terms, noting that our definition of finite witnessability differs slightly from that given in [8] in order to fix a correctness problem in that paper (as we explain below). We then give a new theorem showing that the combination of two theories preserves politeness with respect to some of the sorts.

3.1 Definitions

First we define the smoothness property of a theory (Definition 7 from [8]).

Definition 5 (Smoothness). *Let Σ be a signature, let $S \subseteq \Sigma^{\mathbb{S}}$ be a set of sorts, and let T be a Σ-theory. We say that T is* smooth *with respect to S if:*

- *for every T-satisfiable quantifier-free Σ-formula ϕ,*
- *for every T-interpretation $\mathcal{A}$ satisfying ϕ,*
- *for all choices of cardinal numbers κ_σ, such that $\kappa_\sigma \geq |A_\sigma|$ for all $\sigma \in S$,*

there exists a T-interpretation $\mathcal{B}$ satisfying ϕ such that $|B_\sigma| = \kappa_\sigma$, for all $\sigma \in S$.

Recall that when a theory T is stably-infinite with respect to a sort σ and a T-interpretation exists, we can always find another T-interpretation in which the domain of σ is infinite. On the other hand, if T is smooth with respect to σ and we have a T-interpretation, then there exist interpretations in which the domain of σ can be chosen to be any larger size. Hence every theory that is smooth with respect to a set of sorts S is also stably-infinite with respect to S.

Being able to combine two interpretations from different theories mainly depends on the ability to bring the domains of the shared sorts to the same size. This is where stable-infiniteness helps in the Nelson-Oppen framework: it ensures that the domains of the shared sorts can have the same infinite cardinalities. Since we are interested in combining theories that may require finite domains, we need more flexibility than that afforded by stable-infiniteness. Smoothness gives us more flexibility in resizing structures upwards. This is not quite enough as we also need to ensure that the structures are small enough. Rather than attempting to resize structures downwards, we rely on the notion of *finite witnessability* which allows us to find a kind of "minimal" structure for a theory.

Definition 6 (Finite Witnessability). *Let Σ be a signature, let $S \subseteq \Sigma^{\mathbb{S}}$ be a set of sorts, and let T be a Σ-theory. We say that T is* finitely witnessable *with respect to S if there exists a computable function, witness, which, for every quantifier-free Σ-formula ϕ, returns a quantifier-free Σ-formula $\psi = witness(\phi)$ such that*

- *ϕ and $(\exists \overrightarrow{w})\psi$ are T-equivalent, where $\overrightarrow{w} = vars(\psi) \setminus vars(\phi)$ are fresh variables;*
- *if $\psi \wedge \delta_V$ is T-satisfiable, for an arrangement δ_V, where V is a set of variables of sorts in S, then there exists a T-interpretation $\mathcal{A}$ satisfying $\psi \wedge \delta_V$ such that $A_\sigma = [vars_\sigma(\psi \wedge \delta_V)]^{\mathcal{A}}$, for all $\sigma \in S$,*

where the notation $[U]^{\mathcal{A}}$ indicates the set $\{ v^{\mathcal{A}} \mid v \in U \}$.

Both of the definitions above use an arbitrary quantifier-free formula ϕ in the definition. As shown by Proposition 11 and Proposition 12 in [7], it is enough to restrict ourselves to conjunctions of flat literals in the definitions. This follows in a straightforward fashion from the fact that we can always construct an equisatisfiable formula in disjunctive normal form over flat literals.

It is important to note that our definition of finite witnessability differs from the definition given in [8]. Their definition is equivalent to ours except that there is no mention of an arrangement (i.e. the formula ψ appears alone everywhere $\psi \wedge \delta_V$ appears in the definition above). The reason for this is explained and illustrated in Section 3.2 below.

Finally, a theory that is both smooth and finitely witnessable is *polite* (Definition 9 in [8]).

Definition 7 (Politeness). *Let Σ be a signature, let $S \subseteq \Sigma^{\mathbb{S}}$ be a set of sorts, and let T be a Σ-theory. We say that T is* polite *with respect to S if it is both smooth and finitely witnessable with respect to S.*

Note that any theory is polite (stably-infinite, smooth, finitely witnessable) with respect to an empty set of sorts.

Example 2. The extensional theory of arrays T_{array} has a signature Σ_{array} that contains a sort elem for elements, a sort index for indices, and a sort array for arrays, as well as the two function symbols $\mathsf{read} : \mathsf{array} \times \mathsf{index} \mapsto \mathsf{elem}$ and

$\mathsf{write} : \mathsf{array} \times \mathsf{index} \times \mathsf{elem} \mapsto \mathsf{array}$. Semantics of the array function symbols can be axiomatized as usual, and we refer the reader to [9] for more detail.

It is not hard to see that T_{array} is smooth with respect to the sorts $\{\mathsf{index}, \mathsf{elem}\}$ – any interpretation satisfying a quantifier-free formula ϕ can be extended to arbitrary cardinalities over indices and elements by adding as many additional indices and elements as we need while keeping the satisfiability of ϕ.

As for finite witnessability, it is enough to use a witness transformation that works over conjunctions of flat literals and replaces each array disequality $a \neq b$ with the conjunction of literals $e_1 = \mathsf{read}(a, i) \wedge e_2 = \mathsf{read}(b, i) \wedge e_1 \neq e_2$, where i is a fresh variable of sort index and e_1, e_2 are fresh variables of sort elem. The witness function creates a fresh witness index i, to witness the position where a and b are different, and names those different elements e_1 and e_2. For the detailed proof of politeness for the theory T_{array} we refer the reader to [8].

3.2 Finite Witnessability Revisited

A main result of [8] is a combination method for two theories, one of which is polite over the shared sorts.

Proposition 2 (Proposition 12 of [8]). *Let T_i be a Σ_i-theory for $i = 1, 2$ such that the two theories have no function or predicate symbols in common. Assume that T_2 is polite with respect to $S = \Sigma_1^{\mathbb{S}} \cap \Sigma_2^{\mathbb{S}}$. Also, let Γ_i be a set of Σ_i literals for $i = 1, 2$, and let $\psi_2 = witness_{T_2}(\Gamma_2)$. Finally, let $V_\sigma = vars_\sigma(\psi_2)$, for each $\sigma \in S$, and let $V = \bigcup_{\sigma \in S} V_\sigma$. Then the following are equivalent:*

1. *$\Gamma_1 \cup \Gamma_2$ is $(T_1 \oplus T_2)$-satisfiable;*
2. *There exists an arrangement δ_V such that $\Gamma_1 \cup \delta_V$ is T_1-satisfiable and $\{\psi_2\} \cup \delta_V$ is T_2-satisfiable.*

Proposition 2 differs from the standard Nelson-Oppen theorem in its application of the witness function to Γ_2 and in that the arrangement is over *all* the variables with shared sorts in ψ_2 rather than just over the shared variables.

As mentioned above, our definition of finite witnessability (Definition 6 above) differs from the definition given in [8]. Without the change, Proposition 2 does not hold, as demonstrated by the following example.

Example 3. Let Σ be a signature containing no function or predicate symbols and a single sort σ. Let T_1 be a Σ-theory containing all structures such that the domain of σ has exactly one element (i.e. the structures of T_1 are those satisfying $\forall\, x\, y.\, x = y$). Similarly, let T_2 be a Σ-theory over the same sort σ containing all structures such that the domain of σ has at least two elements (i.e. axiomatized by $\exists\, x\, y.\, x \neq y$). Note that the combination of these two theories contains no structures, and hence no formula is satisfiable in $T_1 \oplus T_2$.

Theory T_2 is clearly smooth with respect to σ. To be polite, T_2 must also be finitely witnessable with respect to σ. Consider the following candidate witness function:

$$witness(\phi) \triangleq \phi \wedge w_1 = w_1 \wedge w_2 = w_2 \ ,$$

where w_1 and w_2 are fresh variables of sort σ not appearing in ϕ.

Let ϕ be a conjunction of flat Σ-literals, let $\psi = \mathit{witness}(\phi)$, and let $V = \mathit{vars}(\psi)$. It is easy to see that the first condition for finite witnessability holds: ϕ is satisfied in a T_2 model iff $\exists\, w_1 w_2.\ \psi$ is. Now, consider the second condition according to [8] (i.e. without the arrangement). We must show that if ψ is T_2-satisfiable (in interpretation $\mathcal{B}$, say), then there exists a T_2-interpretation $\mathcal{A}$ satisfying ψ such that $A_\sigma = [V]^{\mathcal{A}}$. The obvious candidate for $\mathcal{A}$ is obtained by setting $A_\sigma = [V]^{\mathcal{B}}$ and by letting $\mathcal{A}$ interpret only those variables in V (interpreting them as in $\mathcal{B}$). Clearly $\mathcal{A}$ satisfies ψ. However, if $[V]^{\mathcal{B}}$ contains only one element, then $\mathcal{A}$ is not a T_2-interpretation. But in this case, we can always first modify the way variables are interpreted in $\mathcal{B}$ to ensure that $w_2^{\mathcal{B}}$ is different from $w_1^{\mathcal{B}}$ ($\mathcal{B}$ is a T_2-interpretation, so B_σ must contain at least two different elements). Since w_2 does not appear in ϕ, this change cannot affect the satisfiability of ψ in $\mathcal{B}$. After making this change, $[V]^{\mathcal{B}}$ is guaranteed to contain at least two elements, so we can always construct $\mathcal{A}$ as described above. Thus, the second condition for finite witnessability is satisfied and the candidate witness function is indeed a witness function according to [8].

As we will see below, however, this witness function leads to problems. Notice that according to the definition of finite witnessability in this paper, the candidate witness function is not acceptable. To see why, consider again the second condition. Let δ_V be an arrangement of V. According to our definition, we must show that if $\psi \wedge \delta_V$ is satisfied by T_2-interpretation $\mathcal{B}$, then there exists a T_2-interpretation $\mathcal{A}$ satisfying $\psi \wedge \delta_V$ such that $A_\sigma = [V]^{\mathcal{A}}$. We can consider the same construction as above, but this time, the case when $[V]^{\mathcal{B}}$ contains only one element cannot be handled as before. This is because δ_V requires $\mathcal{A}$ to preserve equalities and disequalities in V. In particular, δ_V may include $w_1 = w_2$. In this case, there is no way to construct an appropriate interpretation $\mathcal{A}$.

Now, we show what happens if the candidate witness function given above is allowed. Consider using Proposition 2 to check the satisfiability of $x = x$ (where x is a variable of sort σ). Although this is trivially satisfiable in any theory that has at least one structure, it is not satisfiable in $T_1 \oplus T_2$ since there are no structures to satisfy it. To apply the proposition we let $\Gamma_1 = \emptyset$, $\Gamma_2 = \{x = x\}$,

$$\psi_2 = \mathit{witness}(\Gamma_2) = (x = x \wedge w_1 = w_1 \wedge w_2 = w_2)\ ,$$

and $V = \mathit{vars}(\psi_2) = \{x, w_1, w_2\}$. Proposition 2 allows us to choose an arrangement over the variables of V. Let $\delta_V = \{x = w_1, x = w_2, w_1 = w_2\}$ be an arrangement over the variables in V. It is easy to see that $\Gamma_1 \cup \delta_V$ is satisfiable in a T_1-interpretation $\mathcal{A}$ and $\psi_2 \cup \delta_V$ is satisfiable in a T_2-interpretation $\mathcal{B}$, where $\mathcal{A}$ and $\mathcal{B}$ interpret the domains and variables as follows:

$$\sigma^{\mathcal{A}} = \{a_1\}, \sigma^{\mathcal{B}} = \{b_1, b_2\}, x^{\mathcal{A}} = w_1^{\mathcal{A}} = w_2^{\mathcal{A}} = a_1, x^{\mathcal{B}} = w_1^{\mathcal{B}} = w_2^{\mathcal{B}} = b_1\ .$$

Thus, according to Proposition 2, $\Gamma_1 \cup \Gamma_2$ should be $T_1 \oplus T_2$-satisfiable, but we know that this is impossible. Finally, consider what happens if we use a witness function for T_2 that is acceptable according to our new definition:

$$\mathit{witness}(\phi) \triangleq \phi \wedge w_1 \neq w_2\ .$$

If we look at the same example using this witness function, we can verify that for every arrangement δ_V, either $w_1 \neq w_2 \in \delta_V$, in which case $\Gamma_1 \cup \delta_V$ is not T_1-satisfiable, or else $w_1 = w_2 \in \delta_V$, in which case $witness(\Gamma_2) \cup \delta_V$ is not T_2-satisfiable.

As shown by the example above, the definition of finite witnessability in [8] is not strong enough. It allows witness functions that can falsify Proposition 2. The changes in Definition 6 remedy the problem.

In the same paper, the authors also prove that a number of theories are polite. We are confident that the proofs of politeness for the theories of equality, arrays, sets, and multi-sets are still correct, given the new definition. Other results in the paper (in particular the proof of politeness for the theory of lists and the proof that shiny theories are polite) have some problems in their current form. We hope to address these in future work.

3.3 A New Combination Theorem for Polite Theories

Proposition 2 shows how to combine two theories, one of which is polite. However, the theorem tells us nothing about the politeness of the resulting (combined) theory. In particular, if we want to combine more than two theories by iterating the combination method, we cannot assume that the result of applying Proposition 2 is a theory that is polite with respect to any (non-empty) set of sorts.

In this section, we show that the combination described in Proposition 2 does preserve politeness over some of the sorts. This lays the foundation for the more general combination theorem described in Section 3.4.

Theorem 1. *Let Σ_1 and Σ_2 be signatures and let $S = \Sigma_1^{\mathbb{S}} \cap \Sigma_2^{\mathbb{S}}$. If*

1. *T_1 is a Σ_1-theory polite with respect to $S_1 \subseteq \Sigma_1^{\mathbb{S}}$,*
2. *T_2 is a Σ_2-theory polite with respect to $S_2 \subseteq \Sigma_2^{\mathbb{S}}$,*
3. *$S \subseteq S_2$,*

then $T_1 \oplus T_2$ is polite with respect to $S^* = S_1 \cup \left(S_2 \setminus \Sigma_1^{\mathbb{S}}\right)$.

We illustrate the application of the theorem with an example using two theories of arrays.

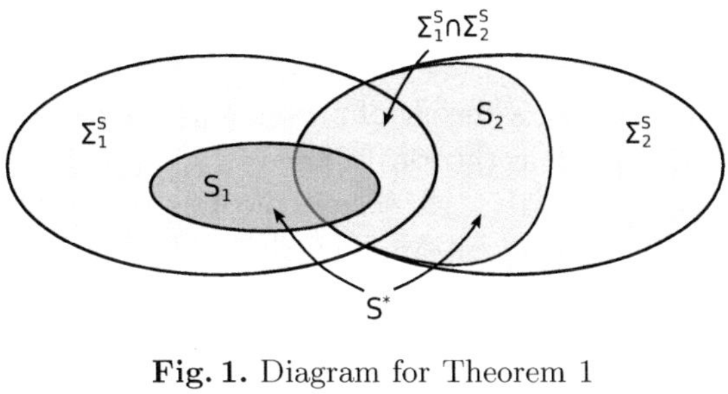

Fig. 1. Diagram for Theorem 1

Example 4. Let $T_{\mathsf{array},1}$ and $T_{\mathsf{array},2}$ be two theories of arrays over the sets of sorts $S_1 = \{\mathsf{array}_1, \mathsf{index}_1, \mathsf{elem}_1\}$ and $S_2 = \{\mathsf{array}_2, \mathsf{index}_2, \mathsf{array}_1\}$ respectively. These two theories together model two-dimensional arrays with indices in index_1 and index_2, and elements in elem_1.

We know that the theory $T_{\mathsf{array},1}$ is polite with respect to $S_1^* = \{\mathsf{index}_1, \mathsf{elem}_1\}$, and the theory $T_{\mathsf{array},2}$ is polite with respect to $S_2^* = \{\mathsf{index}_2, \mathsf{array}_1\}$. Using Theorem 1, we know that we can combine them into a theory T_{array} that is polite with respect to the set $S_1^* \cup (S_2^* \setminus \{\mathsf{array}_1\}) = \{\mathsf{index}_1, \mathsf{index}_2, \mathsf{elem}_1\}$. This means that we can combine the theory of two-dimensional arrays with any other theories that operate over the elements and indices, even if they are not stably-infinite (such as bit-vectors for example).

An interesting corollary of Theorem 1 is that, if both theories are polite with respect to the shared sorts then, analogously to Proposition 1, we get a theory that is polite with respect to the union of the sorts.

Corollary 1. *Let Σ_1 and Σ_2 be signatures. If*

- *T_1 is a Σ_1-theory polite with respect to $S_1 \subseteq \Sigma_1^{\mathbb{S}}$,*
- *T_2 is a Σ_2-theory polite with respect to $S_2 \subseteq \Sigma_2^{\mathbb{S}}$,*
- *$\Sigma_1^{\mathbb{S}} \cap \Sigma_2^{\mathbb{S}} = S_1 \cap S_2$,*

then $T_1 \oplus T_2$ is polite with respect to $S_1 \cup S_2$.

3.4 Combining Multiple Polite Theories

Now we give a general theorem for combining multiple theories in a sequential manner.

Theorem 2. *Let T_i be a Σ_i-theory, for $1 \leq i \leq n$. Assume that*

- *theories T_i have no function or predicate symbols in common;*
- *the quantifier-free satisfiability problem of T_i is decidable, for $1 \leq i \leq n$;*
- *T_i is polite with respect to S_i, for $1 \leq i \leq n$;*
- *$\Sigma_i^{\mathbb{S}} \cap \Sigma_j^{\mathbb{S}} \subseteq S_j$, for $1 \leq i < j \leq n$.*

Then the quantifier-free satisfiability problem for $T = T_1 \oplus \cdots \oplus T_n$ is decidable. Moreover, the resulting theory T is polite with respect to the set of sorts $S = \cup_{j=1}^{n}(S_j \setminus (\cup_{i<j} \Sigma_i^{\mathbb{S}}))$.

Example 5. Assume we have a theory of arrays $T_{\mathsf{array},1}$ over the sorts $\Sigma_{\mathsf{array},1}^{\mathbb{S}} = \{\mathsf{array}_1, \mathsf{index}_1, \mathsf{elem}\}$, as well as theories of arrays $T_{\mathsf{array},k}$ over the sorts $\Sigma_{\mathsf{array},k}^{\mathbb{S}} = \{\mathsf{array}_k, \mathsf{index}_k, \mathsf{array}_{k-1}\}$, for $k \geq 2$. These theories represent different layers in the theory of n-dimensional arrays. The theories satisfy the assumption of Theorem 2 and thus we can combine them into the full theory $T_{\mathsf{array}} = T_{\mathsf{array},1} \oplus \cdots \oplus T_{\mathsf{array},n}$. This theory is polite with respect to the union of all indices and elements $S = \{\mathsf{index}_1, \mathsf{index}_2, \ldots, \mathsf{index}_n, \mathsf{elem}\}$.

Note that, although we are combining theories in a straightforward fashion, we could not have used Theorem 14 from [7] to achieve this combination, since the common intersection of the polite sets of sorts is empty, and the pairwise intersection of sorts is not. More importantly, we are able to easily deduce the politeness of the resulting theory. We finish this section with a theorem that gives an easy complete method for checking whether we can combine a set of theories in the framework of multiple polite theories.

Theorem 3. *Let $T_1, T_2, \ldots, T_n$ be pairwise signature-disjoint theories such that individual quantifier-free T_i-satisfiability problems are decidable. The quantifier-free satisfiability problem of $T = T_1 \oplus \cdots \oplus T_n$ is decidable by iterating the polite combination method for two theories if and only if there is a reordering of the theories T_i that satisfies the conditions of Theorem 2.*

4 Theory Instantiations

The way theories are defined in Definition 1 is meant to be general, i.e. the sorts can be interpreted in any domain. But, sometimes we are interested in a variant of a theory obtained by identifying some of the sorts. For example, consider a theory of arrays with elements and indices, i.e. $\Sigma^{\mathbb{S}}_{\mathsf{array}} = \{\mathsf{array}, \mathsf{elem}, \mathsf{index}\}$. In practice, we often deal with a closely related theory of arrays in which the indices and the elements are from the same sort. Note that these two theories are indeed different – in the general theory of arrays, the well-sortedness prevents us from comparing indices with elements (the term $\mathsf{read}(a, i) \neq i$ is not well-sorted, for example). We will call this merging of sorts *theory instantiation by sort equality.*

Definition 8 (Signature Instantiation). *Let $\Sigma = (S, F, P)$ be a signature. We call $\Sigma_s^{\sigma_1=\sigma_2} = (S', F', P')$ a signature instantiation by sort equality $\sigma_1 = \sigma_2$, for sorts $\sigma_1, \sigma_2 \in S$ and $s \notin S$, if the following holds:*

- *$S' = (S \setminus \{\sigma_1, \sigma_2\}) \cup \{s\}$;*
- *F' contains the same function symbols as F except that we replace σ_1 and σ_2 with s in every arity;*
- *P' contains the same predicate symbols as P except that we replace σ_1 and σ_2 with s in every arity.*

To enable the translation of formulas from the instantiated signature to the original signature and vice versa, we will use the satisfiability-preserving syntactic formula transformation α that maps conjunctions of flat $\Sigma_s^{\sigma_1=\sigma_2}$-literals into formulas from the signature Σ. Given such a conjunction $\phi = \bigwedge_{1 \leq k \leq m} l_k$, with $vars_s(\phi) = \{v_1, v_2, \ldots, v_n\}$, we first introduce fresh variables $v_i^{\sigma_1}$ of sort σ_1, and $v_i^{\sigma_2}$ of sort σ_2, for $i = 1, \ldots, n$. The function α transforms the formula ϕ into

$$\alpha(\phi) \triangleq \bigwedge_{1 \leq k \leq m} \alpha_l(l_k) \wedge \bigwedge_{1 \leq i < j \leq n} \left(v_i^{\sigma_1} =_{\sigma_1} v_j^{\sigma_1} \leftrightarrow v_i^{\sigma_2} =_{\sigma_2} v_j^{\sigma_2}\right) ,$$

The transformation α_l acts on the individual literals as follows:

- Literals of the form $x =_\sigma y$ and $x \neq_\sigma y$, where $\sigma \neq s$, are left unchanged.
- Literals of the form $x =_s y$ and $x \neq_s y$ are transformed into $x^{\sigma_1} =_{\sigma_1} y^{\sigma_1}$ and $x^{\sigma_1} \neq_{\sigma_1} y^{\sigma_1}$ respectively.[3]
- Literals of the form $x =_\sigma f(y_1, \dots, y_n)$, where $\sigma \neq s$, are transformed into $x =_\sigma f(y_1^*, \dots, y_n^*)$. The variables y_i^* are taken to comply with the original arity of f in Σ, i.e.

$$y_i^* = \begin{cases} y_i^{\sigma_1} & \text{if } y_i \text{ should be of sort } \sigma_1 \text{ in the arity of } f \text{ in } \Sigma, \\ y_i^{\sigma_2} & \text{if } y_i \text{ should be of sort } \sigma_2 \text{ in the arity of } f \text{ in } \Sigma, \\ y_i & \text{otherwise.} \end{cases}$$

- Literals of the form $x =_s f(y_1, \dots, y_n)$ are transformed into either $x^{\sigma_1} =_{\sigma_1} f(y_1^*, \dots, y_n^*)$ or $x^{\sigma_2} =_{\sigma_2} f(y_1^*, \dots, y_n^*)$, depending on the sort of the co-domain of f in Σ.
- Literals of the form $p(y_1, \dots, y_n)$ and $\neg p(y_1, \dots, y_n)$ are transformed in a similar manner.

In the other direction, we define a transformation γ_V, where V is a set of variables of sort s, from Σ-formulas to $\Sigma_s^{\sigma_1=\sigma_2}$-formulas, as follows

$$\gamma_V(\phi) = \phi \wedge \bigwedge_{v \in V} (v^{\sigma_1} = v \wedge v^{\sigma_2} = v) \ .$$

In the new formula variables formerly of sort σ_1 or σ_2 are now of sort s.

Definition 9 (Theory Instantiation). *Let Σ be a signature and $T = (\Sigma, \mathbf{A})$ be a Σ-theory. We call a theory $T_s^{\sigma_1=\sigma_2} = (\Sigma_s^{\sigma_1=\sigma_2}, \mathbf{B})$ the theory instantiated by sort equality $\sigma_1 = \sigma_2$, for sorts $\sigma_1, \sigma_2 \in \Sigma^{\mathbb{S}}$ and $s \notin \Sigma^{\mathbb{S}}$, when $\mathcal{B} \in \mathbf{B}$ iff*

- *there exists an $\mathcal{A} \in \mathbf{A}$ such that $B_s = A_{\sigma_1} = A_{\sigma_2}$, and $B_\sigma = A_\sigma$ for $\sigma \neq s$; and*
- *all the predicate and function symbols in $\Sigma_s^{\sigma_1=\sigma_2}$ are interpreted in $\mathcal{B}$ exactly the same as they are interpreted in $\mathcal{A}$.*

The above definition simply restricts the original theory structures to those in which the sorts σ_1 and σ_2 are interpreted by the same domain. The lemma below shows that the result, $T_s^{\sigma_1=\sigma_2}$, is indeed a theory.

Lemma 1. *Let T and $\mathbf{B}$ be as in Definition 9, and let $\mathbf{Ax}$ be the set of closed Σ-formulas that defines T. The class $\mathbf{B}$ is exactly the set of $\Sigma_s^{\sigma_1=\sigma_2}$-structures that satisfies the set of formulas $\gamma_\emptyset(\mathbf{Ax}) = \{\gamma_\emptyset(\phi) \mid \phi \in \mathbf{Ax}\}$.*

[3] The choice of σ_1 over σ_2 is arbitrary, as the right part of $\alpha(\phi)$ will force the same on the dual variables.

Our motivating example is the theory of arrays where we restrict the sorts elem and index to be equal to each other and to bv, i.e. we are interested in the theory $T_{\mathsf{array}}^{\mathsf{bv}} = (T_{\mathsf{array}})_{\mathsf{bv}}^{\mathsf{elem}=\mathsf{index}}$. We know that T_{array} is polite with respect to the sorts elem and index. We want to know whether it is also the case that $T_{\mathsf{array}}^{\mathsf{bv}}$ is polite with respect to the sort bv.

The main result of this section is to show that by merging two sorts σ_1 and σ_2 in a theory, we preserve the politeness of the theory: the new theory will be polite with respect to the same set of sorts as the original theory, modulo renaming of the instantiated sorts σ_1 and σ_2.

Theorem 4. *Let Σ be a signature, $\sigma_1, \sigma_2 \in \Sigma^{\mathbb{S}}$, and $s \notin \Sigma^{\mathbb{S}}$. If Σ-theory T is polite with respect to S, where $\sigma_1, \sigma_2 \in S$ and $s \notin S$, then $T_s^{\sigma_1=\sigma_2}$ is polite with respect to $S' = S \setminus \{\sigma_1, \sigma_2\} \cup \{s\}$. Furthermore, if witness is a witness function for theory T, then an acceptable witness function for $T_s^{\sigma_1=\sigma_2}$ is*

$$witness_s^{\sigma_1=\sigma_2}(\phi) = (\gamma_{vars_s(\phi)} \circ witness \circ \alpha)(\phi) \ .$$

Example 6. Consider again example 5, i.e. we have a theory of arrays T_{array} that operates over the sorts $\Sigma^{\mathbb{S}} = \{\mathsf{array}_1, \ldots, \mathsf{array}_n, \mathsf{index}_1, \ldots \mathsf{index}_n, \mathsf{elem}_1\}$ and is polite with respect to the index and element sorts $\Sigma^{\mathbb{S}} = \{\mathsf{index}_1, \ldots \mathsf{index}_n, \mathsf{elem}_1\}$. Using Theorem 4, we can now safely replace the sorts index_1, index_2 and elem_1 with the sort of bit-vectors bv, obtaining a theory $T_{\mathsf{array(bv)}}$ of n-dimensional arrays where the elements and the indices are of the same bit-vector sort. This theory $T_{\mathsf{array(bv)}}$ of arrays over bit-vectors is polite with respect to the sort bv, and therefore we can safely combine it with the theory of bit-vectors T_{bv}.

Using the combination method for polite theories, we can therefore get a *sound and complete decision procedure for deciding the theory of n-dimensional arrays over bit-vectors*, given a decision procedure and witness function for the theory of arrays T_{array} and a decision procedure for the theory of bit-vectors T_{bv}.

5 Conclusion

One of the crucial issues in the development of verification systems is the problem of combining decision procedures. Nelson and Oppen laid the foundation for the most commonly used framework, but their approach is limited by the requirement that the theories involved be stably-infinite. In this paper we revisited the problem of modular combination of non-stably-infinite theories in a many-sorted setting, using the previously introduced [8] notion of polite theories. We corrected the definition of polite theories that made the combination method incomplete. Then we gave several new results that can be used to construct new polite theories from existing ones. These results led to a general combination result for multiple polite theories. Our result is not only applicable to a broader class of theories, but also precisely describes the politeness of the resulting theory. In future work, we plan to investigate the politeness of other common theories including general theories of inductive data-types [1]. We also are interested in finding efficient witness functions that minimize the number of variables that need to be considered in the arrangement shared by all theories.

Acknowledgments. We would like to thank the anonymous reviewers as well as Cesare Tinelli who provided valuable feedback on this work.

References

1. Barrett, C., Shikanian, I., Tinelli, C.: An abstract decision procedure for a theory of inductive data types. Journal on Satisfiability, Boolean Modeling and Computation 3, 21–46 (2007)
2. Enderton, H.B.: A mathematical introduction to logic. Academic Press, New York (1972)
3. Jovanović, D., Barrett, C.: Polite theories revisited. Technical Report TR2010-922, Department of Computer Science, New York University (January 2010)
4. Krstić, S., Goel, A., Grundy, J., Tinelli, C.: Combined Satisfiability Modulo Parametric Theories. In: Grumberg, O., Huth, M. (eds.) TACAS 2007. LNCS, vol. 4424, pp. 602–617. Springer, Heidelberg (2007)
5. Nelson, G., Oppen, D.C.: Simplification by cooperating decision procedures. ACM Transactions on Programming Languages and Systems 1(2), 245–257 (1979)
6. Oppen, D.C.: Complexity, convexity and combinations of theories. Theoretical Computer Science 12(3), 291–302 (1980)
7. Ranise, S., Ringeissen, C., Zarba, C.: Combining Data Structures with Nonstably Infinite Theories using Many-Sorted Logic. Research Report RR-5678, INRIA (2005)
8. Ranise, S., Ringeissen, C., Zarba, C.G.: Combining Data Structures with Nonstably Infinite Theories Using Many-Sorted Logic. In: Gramlich, B. (ed.) FroCos 2005. LNCS (LNAI), vol. 3717, pp. 48–64. Springer, Heidelberg (2005)
9. Stump, A., Dill, D.L., Barrett, C.W., Levitt, J.: A decision procedure for an extensional theory of arrays. In: Proceedings of the 16th IEEE Symposium on Logic in Computer Science (LICS 2001), June 2001, pp. 29–37. IEEE Computer Society, Boston (June 2001)
10. Tinelli, C., Harandi, M.T.: A new correctness proof of the Nelson–Oppen combination procedure. In: Frontiers of Combining Systems. Applied Logic, pp. 103–120. Kluwer Academic Publishers, Dordrecht (1996)
11. Tinelli, C., Zarba, C.: Combining decision procedures for sorted theories. In: Alferes, J.J., Leite, J. (eds.) JELIA 2004. LNCS (LNAI), vol. 3229, pp. 641–653. Springer, Heidelberg (2004)
12. Tinelli, C., Zarba, C.: Combining decision procedures for theories in sorted logics. Technical Report 04-01, Department of Computer Science, The University of Iowa (February 2004)
13. Tinelli, C., Zarba, C.G.: Combining nonstably infinite theories. Journal of Automated Reasoning 34(3), 209–238 (2005)

Clausal Graph Tableaux for Hybrid Logic with Eventualities and Difference

Mark Kaminski and Gert Smolka

Saarland University, Saarbrücken, Germany

Abstract. We introduce the method of clausal graph tableaux at the example of hybrid logic with difference and star modalities. Clausal graph tableaux are prefix-free and terminate by construction. They provide an abstract method of establishing the small model property of modal logics. In contrast to the filtration method, clausal graph tableaux result in goal-directed decision procedures. Until now no goal-directed decision procedure for the logic considered in this paper was known. There is the promise that clausal graph tableaux lead to a new class of effective decision procedures.

1 Introduction

For modal logic there exist two basic kinds of tableau decision procedures. The more traditional kind, dating back to Kripke [21] and further developed by Fitting [9], Massacci [24] and others, sees tableaux as rooted trees labeled with formulas and, sometimes, auxiliary meta-level information. The formulas on an individual tableau branch are interpreted conjunctively while the different branches are interpreted disjunctively. Tableau calculi are designed so that the set of all branches of a tableau represents an exhaustive enumeration of ways to satisfy the formula at the root of the tableau. A typical decision procedure for satisfiability based on tree tableaux will explore the tableau branch by branch until it finds an evident branch. An evident branch is a satisfiable branch that syntactically describes a model of all of its formulas, in particular of the root formula. Most modern tree tableau calculi model possible worlds and the accessibility relation between them by prefixes (either at the meta level [24] or at the object level [3]). Prefixed tableaux usually allow for straightforward completeness arguments but often require complicated blocking mechanisms [21,16] for termination.

An alternative view of tableaux was developed by Pratt [27] and elaborated by Goré et al. [12,14] for PDL. There, tableaux are seen as possibly cyclic graphs. Given a graph tableau, a corresponding (typically infinite) tree tableau can be obtained by a tree unfolding of the graph. A decision procedure based on graph tableaux conceptually consists of two stages. First, given an input formula s, the procedure constructs the tableau (graph) for s. Then, the procedure checks if the constructed graph contains an evident subtableau that contains s. While being presented as two successive steps in [27], the two stages are interleaved in [12,14]

C. Fermüller and A. Voronkov (Eds.): LPAR-17, LNCS 6397, pp. 417–431, 2010.

for performance reasons. For temporal logics, the graph tableau approach is adopted by Manna and Wolper [23] and by Kesten et al. [20] (there also exist decision procedures for alternation-free μ-calculi based on graph tableaux [30] that are, however, not incremental in the sense of [20]). Graph tableaux are usually set up in a way that makes termination obvious, often allowing to obtain worst-case optimal decision procedures for expressive logics [27,12,14].

In this paper we propose a uniform treatment of a family of modal and hybrid logics by graph tableaux. To abstract away from propositional reasoning, we employ a clausal form developed for tree tableaux in our previous work [19] (note that our clausal form is different from the normal form by the same name used in [25,13]). Our present investigations focus on graph tableaux as a way of establishing the small model property and decidability of modal logics, a role that has traditionally been filled by filtration. Filtration [5] was invented by Lemmon and Scott [22] and further developed by Segerberg [29] and, in a somewhat different form, by Gabbay [10]. Fischer and Ladner [8] were the first to apply filtration to a logic with eventualities. While being similarly elegant to filtration, graph tableaux offer an important advantage. Rather than just providing an upper bound on the size of a minimal model of a satisfiable formula, they provide a way of constructing such a model in a goal-directed way.

We demonstrate clausal graph tableaux on H^*_D, which is modal logic extended with nominals, eventualities and the difference operator. Nominals are formulas of the form x that hold exactly for the state x. Eventualities are formulas of the form $\Diamond^* s$ that hold for a state if it can reach in $n \geq 0$ steps a state satisfying the formula s. A difference formula $\mathsf{D}s$ holds for a state if there is a different state satisfying s. Nominals and the difference operator D equip modal logic with equality, a characteristic feature of hybrid logic [5,2]. Eventualities extend modal logic with reflexive transitive closure and are an essential feature of PDL [8,15] and temporal logics [26,6,7]. One can see H^*_D either as hybrid logic extended with eventualities or as stripped-down PDL extended with nominals and D. Due to the inductive nature of eventualities, H^*_D is not compact (consider $\Diamond^* \neg p$, p, $\Box p$, $\Box\Box p$, ...). The EXPTIME-hardness of H^*_D follows from Fischer and Ladner's proof for PDL [8] (see Blackburn et al. [5], Theorem 6.52). The method in this paper yields a NEXPTIME upper bound for H^*_D. This seems to be the first upper bound established for H^*_D.

In [19], we develop a clausal tree tableau calculus for H^* (modal logic with nominals and eventualities). While it is easy to give clausal tree tableaux for hybrid logic with D, we found it difficult to give an elegant clausal treatment of logics containing both eventualities and difference (such as H^*_D and $HPDL_D$) using tree tableaux. Moreover, the graph tableau approach has not been applied so far to logics with nominals. By adapting the clausal approach and the solutions developed for nominals in [19] to graph tableaux, we are able to give a satisfactory treatment of both eventualities and D within a single framework. Unlike the approach in [19], which works on a single branch of a tree tableau at a time, the present approach is fully deterministic, representing all possible choices within a single graph tableau. This allows us to share the computational costs necessary to deal with D across the tableau instead of paying them on every branch. Another advantage of graph tableaux over the approach in [19] is a significantly simpler soundness argument. The soundness of the calculus in [19] relies on an invariant of tableau branches, called straightness. To maintain the invariant, a technique reminiscent of blocking is used. The present approach does not rely on any such invariants for soundness. We believe that following the ideas in [18] the present approach scales to HPDL_{D} (PDL extended with nominals and D).

We see the main contribution of the present paper in extending the graph tableau approach to hybrid logic with eventualities and difference, while at the same time giving the first goal-directed decision procedure for this logic. The use of a clausal form allows for an elegant presentation and simple, modular correctness arguments.

The paper is organized as follows. First, we introduce the approach on the basic modal logic with eventualities. Then we show how graph tableaux adapt to basic hybrid logic and hybrid logic with difference. Finally, we combine the treatment of eventualities with that of nominals and the difference operator.

Due to lack of space, many proofs are omitted. For full proofs, we refer to [17].

2 Hybrid Logic with Eventualities and Difference

We define the syntax and semantics of the basic hybrid logic with eventualities and difference. We assume that two kind of names, called *nominals* and *predicates*, are given. Nominals (written x, y) denote states and predicates (written p, q) denote sets of states. *Formulas* are defined as follows:

$$s ::= x \mid p \mid \neg s \mid s \wedge s \mid \Diamond s \mid \Diamond^* s \mid \mathsf{D} s$$

For simplicity we employ only a single transition relation. The extension of the approach to multimodal logic is straightforward. Formulas prefixed with the *diamond operators* $\Diamond$ and $\Diamond^*$ are called *diamond formulas* and formulas prefixed with the *difference operator* D are called *difference formulas*.

An *interpretation* $\mathcal{I}$ consists of the following components:

- A nonempty set $|\mathcal{I}|$ of *states*.
- A *transition relation* $\rightarrow_{\mathcal{I}} \subseteq |\mathcal{I}| \times |\mathcal{I}|$.
- A state $\mathcal{I}x \in |\mathcal{I}|$ for every nominal x.
- A set $\mathcal{I}p \subseteq |\mathcal{I}|$ for every predicate p.

The *satisfaction relation* $\mathcal{I}, X \models s$ between interpretations $\mathcal{I}$, states $X \in |\mathcal{I}|$, and formulas s is defined by induction on s:

$$\begin{aligned}
\mathcal{I}, X \models x &\iff X = \mathcal{I}x & \mathcal{I}, X \models s \wedge t &\iff \mathcal{I}, X \models s \text{ and } \mathcal{I}, X \models t \\
\mathcal{I}, X \models p &\iff X \in \mathcal{I}p & \mathcal{I}, X \models \Diamond s &\iff \exists Y\colon\ X \rightarrow_{\mathcal{I}} Y \text{ and } \mathcal{I}, Y \models s \\
\mathcal{I}, X \models \neg s &\iff \text{not } \mathcal{I}, X \models s & \mathcal{I}, X \models \Diamond^* s &\iff \exists Y\colon\ X \rightarrow_{\mathcal{I}}^* Y \text{ and } \mathcal{I}, Y \models s \\
& & \mathcal{I}, X \models \mathsf{D} s &\iff \exists Y\colon\ X \neq Y \text{ and } \mathcal{I}, Y \models s
\end{aligned}$$

$\rightarrow_{\mathcal{I}}^*$ denotes the reflexive transitive closure of $\rightarrow_{\mathcal{I}}$

Given a set A of formulas, we write $\mathcal{I}, X \models A$ if $\mathcal{I}, X \models s$ for all formulas $s \in A$. An interpretation $\mathcal{I}$ *satisfies* (or is a *model* of) a formula s or a set A of formulas if there is a state $X \in |\mathcal{I}|$ such that $\mathcal{I}, X \models s$ or, respectively, $\mathcal{I}, X \models A$. A formula s (a set A) is *satisfiable* if s (A) has a model.

The *complement* $\sim$ of a formula s is t if $s = \neg t$ and $\neg s$ otherwise. Note that $\sim\sim s = s$ if s is not a double negation. We use the notations $s \vee t := \neg(\sim s \wedge \sim t)$, $\Box s := \neg\Diamond\sim s$, $\Box^* s := \neg\Diamond^*\sim s$, and $\bar{\mathsf{D}} s := \neg\mathsf{D}\sim s$. Note that $\sim\Diamond p = \Box\neg p$ and $\sim\Diamond\neg p = \Box p$. Moreover, we define $\Diamond^+ s := \Diamond\Diamond^* s$ and $\Box^+ s := \Box\Box^* s$ (note that $\Box^+ s = \Box\Box^* s = \neg\Diamond\sim\neg\Diamond^*\sim s = \neg\Diamond\Diamond^*\sim s = \neg\Diamond^+\sim s$). An *eventuality* is a formula of the form $\Diamond^* s$ or $\Diamond^+ s$. All other diamond formulas are called *simple*.

We write $\mathrm{H}^*_{\mathsf{D}}$ for the full logic and define several sublogics:

K	$p \mid \neg s \mid s \wedge s \mid \Diamond s$
K^*	K extended with $\Diamond^* s$
H	K extended with x
H_{D}	H extended with $\mathsf{D}s$
H^*	H extended with $\Diamond^* s$ (or K^* extended with x)
$\mathrm{H}^*_{\mathsf{D}}$	H_{D} extended with $\Diamond^* s$ (or H^* extended with $\mathsf{D}s$)

3 Clausal Form

We define a clausal form for our logic. The clausal form allows us to abstract from propositional reasoning and to focus on modal reasoning. Rather than committing to a particular clausal form, we make explicit the abstract properties of the clausal form that we need for our results. This makes our results more widely applicable since the abstract properties are general enough to allow for different clausal forms, in particular for clausal forms compatible with propositional optimizations like semantic branching [31]. A naive computable clausal form is then suggested in the proof of Proposition 3.3.

A *basic formula* is a formula of the form x, p, $\Diamond s$, or $\mathsf{D}s$. A *literal* is a basic formula or the complement of a basic formula. A *clause* (denoted by C, D) is a finite set of literals that contains no complementary pair. Note that since clauses contain no complementary literals, for every finite set A of basic formulas there are $3^{|A|}$ clauses C such that $C \subseteq A \cup \{\, \neg s \mid s \in A \,\}$. Clauses are interpreted conjunctively. *Satisfaction of clauses* (i.e., $\mathcal{I}, X \models C$) is a special case of satisfaction of sets of formulas (i.e., $\mathcal{I}, X \models A$), which was defined in §2. For instance, the clause $\{\Diamond p,\ \Box(\neg p \wedge q)\}$ is unsatisfiable. Note that every clause not containing literals of the form $\Diamond s$ or $\mathsf{D}s$ is satisfiable.

To deal with the difference operator, our approach assumes an injective function that assigns to every literal $\mathsf{D}s$ a nominal $x_{\mathsf{D}s}$. Intuitively, a nominal $x_{\mathsf{D}s}$ is supposed to denote a state that satisfies s, provided such a state exists. If it does, all states that are different from the one denoted by $x_{\mathsf{D}s}$ satisfy $\mathsf{D}s$. A *base* is a set A of basic formulas such that:

1. If $s \in A$ and t is a basic subformula of s, then $t \in A$.
2. If $s \in A$ and $\Diamond^* t$ is a subformula of s, then $\Diamond^+ t \in A$.
3. If $\mathsf{D}s \in A$, then $x_{\mathsf{D}s} \in A$.

While conditions (1) and (2) are required for all extensions of K*, (3) is only needed for the difference operator. A set A is called a *base of a formula* s if A is a base, contains every basic subformula of s and, additionally, $\Diamond^+ t \in A$ whenever $\Diamond^* t$ is a subformula of s. Note that in particular we have that every base of a formula $\Box^* s$ (i.e., $\neg\Diamond^* {\sim} s$) is also a base of $\Box^+ s$ (i.e., $\neg\Diamond^+ {\sim} s$). Intuitively, a base of a formula s contains all basic formulas that need to be evaluated (not necessarily all at the same state) to determine the truth value of s. A set A is a *base of a set of formulas* B if A is a base of every $s \in B$. Let A be a set of formulas. We write $\mathcal{B}A$ for the least base of A. It can be shown that $\mathcal{B}A$ is finite if A is finite, and that the size of $\mathcal{B}A$ is linear in the size of A, i.e., the sum of the sizes of the formulas occurring as elements of A (except for the nominals $x_{\mathrm{D}s}$, $\mathcal{B}s$ is a subset of the Fischer-Ladner closure of s; cf. [8,15]).

The *support relation* $C \rhd s$ between clauses C and formulas s is defined by induction on s:

$$
\begin{aligned}
C \rhd s &\iff s \in C \quad \text{if } s \text{ is a literal} & C \rhd \neg\neg s &\iff C \rhd s \\
C \rhd s \wedge t &\iff C \rhd s \text{ and } C \rhd t & C \rhd s \vee t &\iff C \rhd s \text{ or } C \rhd t \\
C \rhd \Diamond^* s &\iff C \rhd s \text{ or } C \rhd \Diamond^+ s & C \rhd \Box^* s &\iff C \rhd s \text{ and } C \rhd \Box^+ s
\end{aligned}
$$

We say C *supports* s if $C \rhd s$. We write $C \rhd A$ and say C *supports* A if $C \rhd s$ for every $s \in A$. Note that $C \rhd D \iff D \subseteq C$ if C and D are clauses.

Proposition 3.1. *If $C \rhd A$ and $C \subseteq D$ and $B \subseteq A$, then $D \rhd B$.*

Proposition 3.2. *If $\mathcal{I}, X \models C$ and $C \rhd A$, then $\mathcal{I}, X \models A$.*

A *DNF* (disjunctive normal form) is a function $\mathcal{D}$ that maps every finite set A of formulas to a finite set of clauses such that:

1. $\mathcal{I}, X \models A \iff \exists D \in \mathcal{D}A\colon\ \mathcal{I}, X \models D$.
2. $C \rhd A \iff \exists D \in \mathcal{D}A\colon\ D \subseteq C$.
3. If $C \in \mathcal{D}A$, then $C \subseteq \mathcal{B}A \cup \{\, \neg s \mid s \in \mathcal{B}A \,\}$.

Note that the third property of DNFs may equivalently be stated as follows: If $C \in \mathcal{D}A$, then $\mathcal{B}C \subseteq \mathcal{B}A$. Note further that, restricted to propositional logic, our notion of a DNF reduces to the common notion of a propositional DNF. Consider, for instance, a function $\mathcal{D}$ such that $\mathcal{D}\{p_1 \wedge (\neg p_2 \vee p_3)\} = \{\{p_1, \neg p_2\}, \{p_1, p_3\}\}$. Clearly, $\mathcal{D}$ is a DNF according to the above definition. By interpreting $\{\{p_1, \neg p_2\}, \{p_1, p_3\}\}$ as $(p_1 \wedge \neg p_2) \vee (p_1 \wedge p_3)$ we see that $\mathcal{D}$ indeed computes a DNF of $p_1 \wedge (\neg p_2 \vee p_3)$.

Proposition 3.3. *There is a computable DNF.*

Proof. The definition of the support relation can be seen as a tableau-style decomposition procedure for formulas. The clauses of a DNF can be obtained with the literals the decomposition produces. The direction "$\Leftarrow$" of property (1) of DNFs follows with Proposition 3.2. Properties (2) and (3) of DNFs easily follow, respectively, from the definitions of the support relation and the base of a formula. $\Box$

For the rest of the paper, we fix some computable DNF $\mathcal{D}$. In our examples, in particular in Examples 4.1 and 5.1, we assume that $\mathcal{D}$ is defined as suggested in the proof of Proposition 3.3. In particular, we assume that $\mathcal{D}C = \{C\}$ for all clauses C, and $\mathcal{D}\{s \wedge t\} = \{\{s, t\}\}$ for every two non-complementary literals s, t.

The *request of a clause* C is $\mathcal{R}C := \{\, t \mid \Box t \in C \,\}$.

Proposition 3.4. *If* $\mathcal{I}, X \models C$ *and* $X \to_{\mathcal{I}} Y$*, then* $\mathcal{I}, Y \models \mathcal{R}C$.

4 Tableaux for K*

To demonstrate the basic ideas of the graph tableau approach, we begin with a tableau system for K*, the basic modal logic with eventualities. Hence, for the rest of the section, we restrict formulas to be of the form:

$$s ::= p \mid \neg s \mid s \wedge s \mid \Diamond s \mid \Diamond^* s$$

Basic formulas, literals and clauses are restricted accordingly.

A *claim* is a pair $C^{\Diamond s}$ such that $\Diamond s \in C$. Given a formula s and a set A, we write $A\,;s$ for the set $A \cup \{s\}$. A *link* is a triple $C^{\Diamond s}D$ such that $C^{\Diamond s}$ is a claim and either

1. $\Diamond s$ is not an eventuality and $D \in \mathcal{D}(\mathcal{R}C\,; s)$, or
2. $s = \Diamond^* t$ and $D \in \mathcal{D}(\mathcal{R}C\,; t) \cup \mathcal{D}(\mathcal{R}C\,; \Diamond s)$.

A *tableau* is a finite non-empty set T of clauses and links such that $C, D \in T$ whenever $C^s D \in T$. A tableau T is *complete* if $C^{\Diamond s}D \in T$ whenever $\Diamond s \in C \in T$ and $C^{\Diamond s}D$ is a link. Given a tableau T, we define $\mathcal{B}T$ as the least set A that is a base of all $C \in T$. It is easily seen that $\mathcal{B}T = \bigcup \{\, \mathcal{B}C \mid C \in T \,\}$.

The architecture of a decision procedure based on graph tableaux is as follows. Given a clause C, we construct a tableau T that contains C and satisfies certain completeness criteria. The size of T will be exponentially bounded in the size of the base of C. If C is satisfiable, T will contain a subtableau that syntactically describes a model of C. We call such subtableaux evident. The existence of evident subtableaux is decidable since T is finite. Given the decision procedure for clauses, a procedure for formulas is immediate by property (1) of DNFs.

Proposition 4.1. *If* $C^s D$ *is a link, then* $\mathcal{B}D \subseteq \mathcal{B}C$.

For every clause C, we can construct a complete tableau T containing C by closing the initial tableau $\{C\}$ under the following *completion rule*:

$$\frac{D}{E,\ D^{\Diamond s}E} \quad \Diamond s \in D,\ \ D^{\Diamond s}E \text{ link}$$

The closure is finite since for all clauses D added by the construction we have $\mathcal{B}D \subseteq \mathcal{B}C$ (follows by Proposition 4.1). Hence, the number of clauses in T is bounded by $3^{|\mathcal{B}C|}$. The number of links in T is then bounded by $|\mathcal{B}C| \cdot 9^{|\mathcal{B}C|}$. Clearly, $C \in T$ and $\mathcal{B}T = \mathcal{B}C$.

Proposition 4.2. *For every clause C there is a complete tableau T such that $C \in T$, $\mathcal{B}T = \mathcal{B}C$, and $|T| = 3^{|\mathcal{B}C|} + |\mathcal{B}C| \cdot 9^{|\mathcal{B}C|}$.*

A *run for $C^{\Diamond^+ s}$ in T* is a sequence of clauses $C_1 \dots C_n$ such that:

1. $C_1 = C$.
2. $\forall i \in [1, n-1]\colon\ C_i{}^{\Diamond^+ s} C_{i+1} \in T$.
3. $C_n \rhd s$.

We call a tableau evident if every claim has an outgoing link and every claim of the form $C^{\Diamond^+ s}$ has a run. More precisely: A tableau T is *evident* if:

1. $\forall \Diamond s \in C \in T\ \exists D\colon\ C^{\Diamond s} D \in T$.
2. T has a run for $C^{\Diamond^+ s}$ whenever $\Diamond^+ s \in C \in T$.

An interpretation *satisfies* (or is a *model* of) a tableau if it satisfies all of its clauses.

Example 4.1. Consider the complete tableau T for the clause $C_0 = \{\Diamond^+ p,\ \Diamond\Diamond p,\ \Box\neg p,\ \neg p\}$ obtained with the above completion rule.

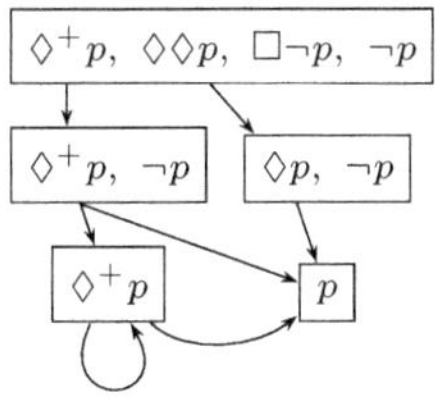

Links of the form $C^s D$ are represented graphically by arrows going from the formula s in the clause C to the clause D. Consider the claim $C_0{}^{\Diamond^+ p}$. Since $\Diamond^+ p$ is an eventuality and $\mathcal{R}C_0 = \{\neg p\}$, a triple $C_0{}^{\Diamond^+ p} D$ is a link if and only if $D \in \mathcal{D}\{p, \neg p\} \cup \mathcal{D}\{\Diamond^+ p, \neg p\} = \emptyset \cup \{\{\Diamond^+ p, \neg p\}\} = \{\{\Diamond^+ p, \neg p\}\}$. Hence, $\{\Diamond^+ p, \neg p\}$ is the only clause and $C_0{}^{\Diamond^+ p}\{\Diamond^+ p, \neg p\}$ the only link that is added by the completion rule for the claim $C_0{}^{\Diamond^+ p}$. Note that T is evident since every claim has at least one outgoing link and the clause $\{p\}$ is reachable from every diamond $\Diamond^+ p$. In particular, $\{\Diamond^+ p, \neg p\}\{\Diamond^+ p\}\{p\}$ is a run for $\{\Diamond^+ p, \neg p\}^{\Diamond^+ p}$ in T.

Theorem 4.1 (Model Existence). *Evident tableaux have finite models.*

Proof. Let T be an evident tableau. We choose an interpretation $\mathcal{I}$ such that:

- $|\mathcal{I}| = \{\, C \mid C \in T \,\}$
- $C \to_{\mathcal{I}} D \iff \exists s\colon\ C^{\Diamond s} D \in T$
- $C \in \mathcal{I}p \iff p \in C$

Clearly, $|\mathcal{I}|$ is finite since T is finite.

We show $\forall s\ \forall C \in T\colon\ C \rhd s \implies \mathcal{I}, C \models s$ by induction on s. Let $C \in T$ and $C \rhd s$. We show $\mathcal{I}, C \models s$ by case analysis. The argument is straightforward except possibly for the cases $s = \Diamond^* t$ and $s = \Box^* t$.

Let $s = \Diamond^* t$. Since $C \triangleright s$, we have either $C \triangleright t$ or $C \triangleright \Diamond^+ t$. If $C \triangleright t$, then $\mathcal{I}, C \models t$ by the inductive hypothesis, and the claim follows. Otherwise, let $C \triangleright \Diamond^+ t$. Then $\Diamond^+ t \in C \in T$. By the second evidence condition we know that there is a run for $C^{\Diamond^+ t}$ in T. Thus $C \to^*_{\mathcal{I}} D$ and $D \triangleright t$ for some clause $D \in \Gamma$. Hence $\mathcal{I}, D \models t$ by the inductive hypothesis. The claim follows.

Let $s = \Box^* t$. Let $C = C_1 \to_{\mathcal{I}} \ldots \to_{\mathcal{I}} C_n$. We show $\mathcal{I}, C_n \models t$ by induction on n. If $n = 1$, we have $C_n \models s$ by assumption. Hence $C_n \models t$ and the claim follows by the outer inductive hypothesis. If $n > 1$, we have $s \in \mathcal{R}C_1$ since $\Box s \in C_1$ since $C_1 \triangleright \Box s$ since $C_1 \triangleright s$. Thus $C_2 \triangleright s$ and the claim follows by the inner inductive hypothesis. □

A tableau T' is a *subtableau* of a tableau T if $T' \subseteq T$.

Theorem 4.2 (Evidence). *Let T be a complete tableau and $C \in T$. If C is satisfiable, then there is an evident subtableau of T containing C.*

Proof (Sketch). Let T and C be as required, and let $\mathcal{I}$ be a model of C. We define U to consist of the clauses of T that are satisfied by $\mathcal{I}$, and the edges $D^s E \in T$ such that $\{D, E\} \subseteq U$. It is easily seen that U is a subtableau of T and that $C \in U$, so it remains to show that U is evident. Showing evidence condition (1) is straightforward. As for condition (2), observe that whenever we have $\mathcal{I}, X_0 \models \Diamond^+ s$, this means that there is a sequence of states $X_1 \ldots X_n$ ($n \geq 1$) such that, for all $i \in [1, n]$, $X_{i-1} \to_{\mathcal{I}} X_i$, and $\mathcal{I}, X_n \models s$. Now, to show condition (2), we show that, given a claim $C_0{}^{\Diamond^+ s}$ and assuming $\mathcal{I}, X_0 \models C_0$, the sequence $X_1 \ldots X_n$ can be "projected" onto clauses $C_1 \ldots C_n$ of U such that, for all $i \in [1, n]$, we have (a) $\mathcal{I}, X_i \models C_i$, (b) $X_{i-1} \to_{\mathcal{I}} X_i$ implies $C_{i-1}{}^{\Diamond^+ s} C_i \in U$, and (c) $C_n \triangleright s$. Clearly, this implies that $C_0 C_1 \ldots C_n$ is a run for $C_0{}^{\Diamond^+ s}$, which suffices for the claim. □

5 Tableaux for $\mathsf{H_D}$

Before we proceed to the full logic, let us develop graph tableaux for $\mathsf{H_D}$. This will allow us to introduce the machinery needed for nominals without the complications that are added by eventualities. To account for nominals, we will allow links to clauses that are larger than those given by the DNF of the diamond formula and the request of the source clause. To reduce redundancy in complete graph tableaux, we will introduce the notion of a link closure and require a complete tableau to contain an evident subtableau in its link closure. We will point out which parts of the construction are needed for hybrid logic in general and which are there specifically to account for the difference operator. The formulas of $\mathsf{H_D}$ look as follows:

$$s ::= x \mid p \mid \neg s \mid s \wedge s \mid \Diamond s \mid \mathsf{D}s$$

To deal with nominals, we need to adapt the definition of links. A *link* is a triple $C^{\Diamond s} D$ such that $C^{\Diamond s}$ is a claim and $D \triangleright \mathcal{R}C \,;\, s$. A link $C^{\Diamond s} D$ is called *minimal* if $D \in \mathcal{D}(\mathcal{R}C \,;\, s)$ (i.e., minimal links are precisely the special kind of links used in § 4). Proposition 4.1 adapts as follows:

Proposition 5.1. *If $C^s D$ is a minimal link, then $\mathcal{B}D \subseteq \mathcal{B}C$.*

Given the new definition of links, tableaux are defined as before. A tableau T is *complete* if:

1. If $\Diamond s \in C \in T$ and $C^{\Diamond s}D$ is a minimal link, then $C^{\Diamond s}D \in T$.
2. If $C \in T$ and $x \in \mathcal{B}C$, then $\{x\} \in T$.
3. If $C, D \in T$, $x \in C \cap D$, and $C \cup D$ is a clause, then $C \cup D \in T$.
4. If $\mathsf{D}s \in C \in T$, $x_{\mathsf{D}s} \notin C$, and $D \in \mathcal{D}\{x_{\mathsf{D}s},\ s\}$, then $D \in T$.
5. If $\mathsf{D}s \in C \in T$, $x_{\mathsf{D}s} \in C$, and $D \in \mathcal{D}\{\neg x_{\mathsf{D}s},\ s\}$, then $D \in T$.
6. If $\bar{\mathsf{D}}s \in C \in T$, $D \in T$, $D \not\triangleright s$, and $C \cup D$ is a clause, then $C \cup D \in T$.
7. If $\bar{\mathsf{D}}s \in C \in T$, $D \in T$, $D \not\triangleright s$, and $E \in \mathcal{D}(D\,; s)$, then $E \in T$.

Note that to obtain a complete system for H, only the first three of the completeness criteria are needed. The last four criteria are there exclusively to deal with D and its dual. Recall that the idea behind the completion rules is to generate enough clauses so that we can select an evident subset. Criterion (1) is the obvious adaptation of the completeness criterion from § 4. Criteria (2) and (3) are motivated by the semantics of nominals. Every nominal x has to denote some state that, obviously, satisfies $\{x\}$. Moreover, if two clauses are satisfied by the same model and have a nominal in common, then they hold in the same state of the model, and hence their union is also satisfiable. For (4) and (5), recall that a nominal $x_{\mathsf{D}s}$ is assumed to denote a state that satisfies s (provided such a state exists). So, if $\mathsf{D}s$ is satisfiable anywhere in a model, then $\{x_{\mathsf{D}s},\ s\}$ is satisfiable, and if $\{\mathsf{D}s,\ x_{\mathsf{D}s}\}$ is satisfiable, then so is $\{\neg x_{\mathsf{D}s},\ s\}$. Criteria (6) and (7) are motivated as follows. If $\bar{\mathsf{D}}s$ holds in a state X, then every state that is distinct from X satisfies s. So, every given state Y must either be equal to X (cf. (6)) or satisfy s (cf. (7)).

Note that, analogously to the above tableau construction rule in § 4, the above completeness criteria can be interpreted as tableau rules (called *completion rules*). So, for instance, criterion (1) and (3) translate to, respectively:

$$1)\ \frac{D}{E,\ D^{\Diamond s}E}\ \Diamond s \in D,\ D^{\Diamond s}E \text{ minimal link} \qquad 3)\ \frac{D,\ E}{C \cup E}\ D \cup E \text{ clause, } \exists x\colon x \in D \cap E$$

Analogously to the argument in § 4, we obtain:

Proposition 5.2. *For every clause C there is a complete tableau T such that $C \in T$, $\mathcal{B}T = \mathcal{B}C$, and $|T| = 3^{|\mathcal{B}C|} + |\mathcal{B}C| \cdot 9^{|\mathcal{B}C|}$.*

We define $A^T := A \cup \{\, s \mid \exists x \in A\ \exists C \in T\colon\ x \in C \text{ and } s \in C\,\}$. A tableau T is *evident* if:

1. $\forall \Diamond s \in C \in T\ \exists D\colon\ C^{\Diamond s}D \in T$.
2. If $C \in T$ and $x \in \mathcal{B}C$, then there is some $D \in T$ such that $x \in D$.
3. If $C \in T$, then $C = C^T$.
4. If $\mathsf{D}s \in C \in T$, then there is some $D \in T$ such that $D \neq C$ and $D \triangleright s$.
5. If $\bar{\mathsf{D}}s \in C \in T$, then, for all $D \in T$ such that $D \neq C$, we have $D \triangleright s$.

Again, for hybrid logic without D we only need the first three conditions.

In the presence of nominals and D, clauses introduced by the rule for criterion (1) may be too small to be included in the evident tableau (because of evidence condition (3) or (5)). While criteria (3), (6) and (7) will ensure that the complete tableau contains the larger clauses that are needed, they will add no links to the new clauses. Instead, we add the required links in a uniform way by defining the *link closure* $\hat{T}$ of a tableau T as $\hat{T} := T \cup \{ C^s D \mid \exists E\colon\ E \subseteq D \text{ and } C^s E \in T \}$.

Example 5.1. Consider the following complete tableau T for the unsatisfiable clause $\{\Diamond(y \wedge \mathsf{D}y)\}$.

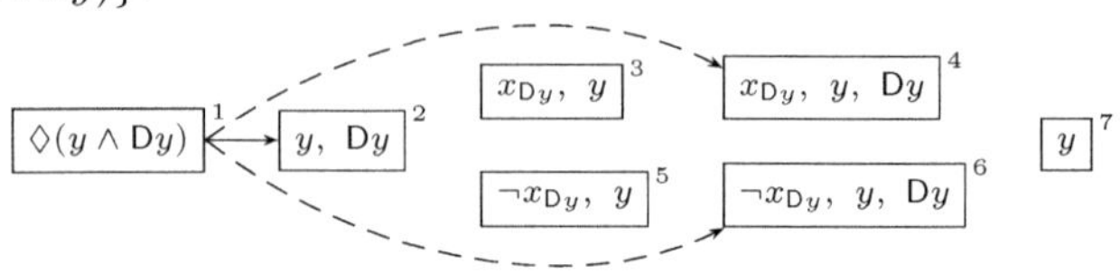

The numbers indicate in which order the clauses are introduced by the completion rules. So, clause (2) is derived from (1) by the rule corresponding to completeness criterion (1), clause (3) follows from (2) by the rule for criterion (4), clause (4) follows from (2) and (3) by the rule for criterion (3), clause (5) follows from (4) by the rule for criterion (5), clause (6) follows from (2) and (5) by the rule for criterion (3), and clause (7) follows by the rule for criterion (2) applied to any of the preceding clauses. Note that the rule for criterion (3) does not apply to clauses (4) and (5) since their union is not a clause. The dashed arrows stand for the additional links in the link closure $\hat{T}$.

The tableau $\hat{T}$ contains no evident subtableau that contains $\{\Diamond(y \wedge \mathsf{D}y)\}$ (i.e., clause (1)). By evidence condition (1), an evident subtableau of $\hat{T}$ containing clause (1) would also have to contain either (2), (4) or (6), all of which contain the nominal y and the formula $\mathsf{D}y$. Then, by evidence condition (4), the subtableau would have to contain a second clause containing y. However, having two distinct clauses that contain the same nominal contradicts evidence condition (3).

As before for K*, one of our goals will be showing that complete tableaux for satisfiable clauses have evident subtableaux (now modulo link closure). This also explains why we introduce nominals $x_{\mathsf{D}s}$. We need them to ensure that subtableaux of a complete tableau satisfy evidence condition (4). Assume we simplified completeness criteria (4) and (5) to:

$$\text{If } \mathsf{D}s \in C \in T \text{ and } D \in \mathcal{D}\{s\}, \text{ then } D \in T.$$

Then $T := \{\{\bar{\mathsf{D}}\mathsf{D}p,\ \mathsf{D}p,\ \neg p\},\ \{\mathsf{D}p,\ p\},\ \{p\}\}$ would be a complete tableau. Moreover, $\hat{T} = T$. Although all clauses of T are satisfiable, T contains no evident subtableau containing $\{\bar{\mathsf{D}}\mathsf{D}p,\ \mathsf{D}p,\ \neg p\}$.

Theorem 5.1 (Model Existence). *Evident tableaux have finite models.*

Proof. Let T be an evident tableau. By evidence conditions (2) and (3), for every $x \in \mathcal{B}T$ we have a unique clause $C \in T$ such that $x \in C$. We choose an interpretation $\mathcal{I}$ as in the proof of Theorem 4.1 such that additionally, for all $x \in \mathcal{B}T$, $\mathcal{I}x = C \iff x \in C$. Again, $|\mathcal{I}|$ is finite as so is T. We show $\forall s\ \forall C \in T\colon\ C \rhd s \implies \mathcal{I}, C \models s$ by induction on s. The verification of the individual cases is straightforward. $\square$

Theorem 5.2 (Evidence). *Let T be a complete tableau and let $C \in T$ be such that, for all $t \in C$ and $\mathsf{D}s \in \mathcal{B}T$, $x_{\mathsf{D}s}$ does not occur in t. If C is satisfiable, then there is an evident subtableau U of $\hat{T}$ and a clause $D \in U$ such that $C \subseteq D$.*

Proof (Sketch). Let T and C be as required, and let $\mathcal{I}$ be a model of C (with some additional constraints). We define U to consist of the maximal clauses among all clauses of T that are satisfied by $\mathcal{I}$. As the edges of U we take all $D^sE \in \hat{T}$ such that $\{D,\ E\} \subseteq U$. One can show that U has the desired properties. $\square$

6 Tableaux for H^* and $\mathrm{H}^*_{\mathsf{D}}$

Now that we know how graph tableaux look for eventualities and nominals in isolation, let us approach their combinations, H^* and $\mathrm{H}^*_{\mathsf{D}}$. The addition of D to H turns out to be particularly straightforward since the cases for D in the proofs of evidence and model existence for H_{D} can be treated orthogonally from the rest of the respective arguments. For H^*, this is no longer the case. While model existence is still straightforward, given a meaningful definition of an evident tableau, D significantly complicates the evidence proof when combined with eventualities.

Links and minimal links are now defined as follows. A *link* is a triple $C^{\Diamond s}D$ such that $C^{\Diamond s}$ is a claim and either

1. $\Diamond s$ is not an eventuality and $D \rhd \mathcal{R}C\,;s$, or
2. $s = \Diamond^* t$ and $D \rhd \mathcal{R}C\,;t$ or $D \rhd \mathcal{R}C\,;\Diamond s$.

A link $C^{\Diamond s}D$ is called *minimal* if

1. $\Diamond s$ is not an eventuality and $D \in \mathcal{D}(\mathcal{R}C\,;s)$, or
2. $s = \Diamond^* t$ and $D \in \mathcal{D}(\mathcal{R}C\,;t) \cup \mathcal{D}(\mathcal{R}C\,;\Diamond s)$.

Given the new definitions, tableaux are defined as in § 4. The completeness criteria, completion rules and the link closure for $\mathrm{H}^*_{\mathsf{D}}$ (resp., H^*) look exactly the same as for H_{D} (resp., H). Also, Propositions 5.1 and 5.2 are easy to re-prove for the new definitions.

As it turns out, taking maximal clauses to obtain evidence in the presence of nominals, as it is done in the proof of Theorem 5.2, may destroy runs that are necessary for evidence in the presence of eventualities. Consider the following tableau (a):

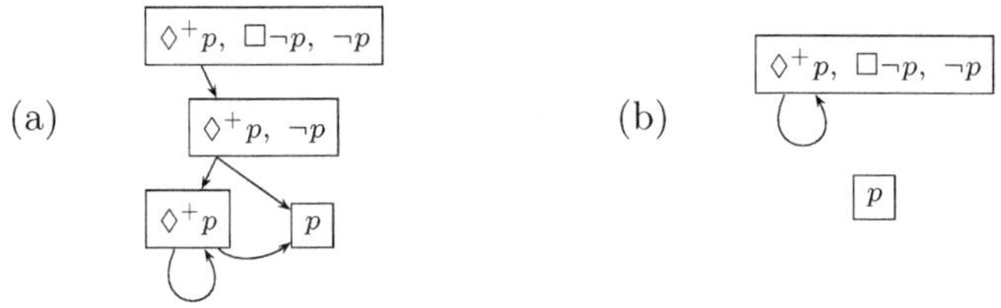

The tableau (a) is complete and satisfies the evidence conditions for K*. All clauses of (a) are satisfiable. However, the maximal clauses construction in the proof of Theorem 5.2 produces the tableau (b), which does not satisfy evidence condition (2) for K*. In the absence of D we can solve the problem by adapting the construction from [19] to graph tableaux. To cope with D, however, the approach needs considerable refinement.

The evidence conditions for H^*_{D} are obtained by taking the union of the conditions for K* and H_{D}. A tableau T is *evident* if:

1. $\forall \Diamond s \in C \in T\ \exists D\colon\ C^{\Diamond s} D \in T$.
2. T has a run for $C^{\Diamond^+ s}$ whenever $\Diamond^+ s \in C \in T$.
3. If $C \in T$ and $x \in \mathcal{B}C$, then there is some $D \in T$ such that $x \in D$.
4. If $C \in T$, then $C = C^T$.
5. If $\mathsf{D}s \in C \in T$, then there is some $D \in T$ such that $D \neq C$ and $D \rhd s$.
6. If $\bar{\mathsf{D}}s \in C \in T$, then, for all $D \in T$ such that $D \neq C$, we have $D \rhd s$.

Theorem 6.1 (Model Existence). *Evident tableaux have finite models.*

Proof. Let T be an evident tableau. We choose $\mathcal{I}$ as in the proof of Theorem 5.1 and show $\forall s\ \forall C \in T\colon\ C \rhd s \implies \mathcal{I}, C \models s$ by induction on s. The case distinction on the shape of s proceeds as in the proofs of Theorems 4.1 and 5.1. All cases but $s = \Diamond^* t$ and $s = \Box^* t$ proceed exactly as in the proof of Theorem 5.1. The cases $s = \Diamond^* t$ and $s = \Box^* t$ that are not covered by the proof of Theorem 5.1 proceed as in the proof of Theorem 4.1. □

As for evidence, let us begin with with an outline of the proof for H*.

Theorem 6.2 (Evidence for H*). *Let T be a complete tableau for* H* *and let $C \in T$. If C is satisfiable, then there is an evident subtableau U of $\hat{T}$ and a clause $D \in U$ such that $C \subseteq D$.*

Proof. Let T and C be as required, and let $\mathcal{I}$ be a model of C. Let $T' := \{\, E \in T \mid \mathcal{I} \text{ satisfies } E \,\}$. We define U such that:

1. $D \in U \ :\Longleftrightarrow\ D \in T'$ and $D = D^{T'}$.
2. $D^{\Diamond s} E \in U \ :\Longleftrightarrow\ D^{\Diamond s} E \in \hat{T}$ and $\{D,\ E\} \subseteq U$.

It is straightforward to verify that U is an evident subtableau of $\hat{T}$ that contains a superclause of C. □

Unfortunately, the construction in the proof of Theorem 6.2 for selecting an evident subtableau does not work in the presence of D. The problem is caused by the evidence condition for formulas $\bar{\mathsf{D}}s$ (condition (6)). Consider the complete tableau $T := \{\{\bar{\mathsf{D}}p\},\ \{p\},\ \{\bar{\mathsf{D}}p,\ p\}\}$. Let $\mathcal{I}$ be an interpretation such that $|\mathcal{I}| = \mathcal{I}p = \{X\}$. Clearly, $\mathcal{I}$ satisfies all clauses of T. Since T contains no nominals, the construction in the proof of Theorem 6.2 for $\mathcal{I}$ yields $U = T$. However, T does not satisfy evidence condition (6) since $\bar{\mathsf{D}}p \in \{\bar{\mathsf{D}}p,\ p\} \in T$ but also $\{\bar{\mathsf{D}}p\} \in T$ (clearly, $\{\bar{\mathsf{D}}p\} \not\rhd p$). Note that although U is not evident, it still contains evident subtableaux ($\{\{\bar{\mathsf{D}}p\}\}$, $\{\{\bar{\mathsf{D}}p,\ p\}\}$ and $\{\{p\},\ \{\bar{\mathsf{D}}p,\ p\}\}$). As we noted in the beginning of the section, it is now not possible to take the maximal clauses of U since this will in general destroy the evidence of eventualities (condition (2)). In the following, we will demonstrate how we can select an evident subtableau of U while preserving condition (2).

A key observation is that for every formula $\bar{\mathsf{D}}s$ that holds in some state $X \in |\mathcal{I}|$, we either have that s holds everywhere in $\mathcal{I}$, or that X is the unique state satisfying $\bar{\mathsf{D}}s$ and all other states satisfy s. Hence, for every formula $\bar{\mathsf{D}}s$ for which evidence condition (6) is violated (in a tableau T satisfied by $\mathcal{I}$), we can establish (6) by removing all clauses that do not support s (if s holds everywhere) or all such clauses except one (otherwise). In the latter case, we can select the remaining clause to be the largest clause containing $\bar{\mathsf{D}}s$. Since $\mathcal{I}$ satisfies T and X is the unique state in $\mathcal{I}$ satisfying $\bar{\mathsf{D}}s$, none of the clauses supporting s will contain $\bar{\mathsf{D}}s$, which guarantees that (6) is satisfied in the resulting tableau.

Lemma 6.1. *Let T be a complete tableau and $\mathcal{I}$ an interpretation. Let*

$$T' := \{\, C \in T \mid \mathcal{I} \text{ satisfies } C \,\}$$

Let $\bar{\mathsf{D}}s_1 \dots \bar{\mathsf{D}}s_n$ be an injective enumeration of the set $\{\, \bar{\mathsf{D}}s \mid \bar{\mathsf{D}}s \in C \in T' \,\}$. Let $T'_0 := \{\, C \in T' \mid C = C^{T'} \,\}$. For all $i \in [1,n]$ we construct a set T'_i from T'_{i-1} as follows:

- *If $\forall X \in |\mathcal{I}|\colon\ \mathcal{I}, X \models s_i$, then $T'_i := \{\, C \in T'_{i-1} \mid C \rhd s_i \,\}$.*
- *Otherwise, $T'_i := \{\, C \in T'_{i-1} \mid C \rhd s_i \,\} ; \bigcup \{\, C \in T'_{i-1} \mid \bar{\mathsf{D}}s_i \in C \,\}$.*

Then, for all $i \in [1,n]$:

1. *If $C \in T'_{i-1} \cap T'_i$, $D \in T'_{i-1}$, and $C \subseteq D$, then $D \in T'_i$.*
2. *If $C \in T'_{i-1}$ and $\mathcal{I}, X \models C$, then $C \subseteq D$ for some $D \in T'_i$ such that $\mathcal{I}, X \models D$.*
3. *$T'_i \subseteq T'_{i-1}$.*
4. *If $C \in T'_i$, then $C = C^{T'_i}$ (i.e., T'_i satisfies evidence condition (4)).*
5. *Let $j \in [1,i]$, $\bar{\mathsf{D}}s_j \in C \in T'_i$, and $D \in T'_i$ such that $D \neq C$. Then $D \rhd s_j$ (i.e., T'_i satisfies evidence condition (6) restricted to $\bar{\mathsf{D}}s_1, \dots, \bar{\mathsf{D}}s_i$).*

Theorem 6.3 (Evidence). *Let T be a complete tableau and let $C \in T$ be such that, for all $t \in C$ and $\mathsf{D}s \in \mathcal{B}T$, $x_{\mathsf{D}s}$ does not occur in t. If C is satisfiable, then there is an evident subtableau U of $\hat{T}$ and a clause $D \in U$ such that $C \subseteq D$.*

Proof (Sketch). Let T and C be as required, and let $\mathcal{I}$ be a model of C (with some additional constraints). Let T', $\mathsf{D}s_1 \dots \mathsf{D}s_n$, $T'_1, \dots, T'_n$ be defined from T and $\mathcal{I}$ as in Lemma 6.1. We define $U := T'_n \cup \{\, D^s E \in \hat{T} \mid \{D,\ E\} \subseteq T'_n \,\}$. Evidence conditions (4) and (6) hold by Lemma 6.1 (4,5). To show condition (2), we use the same basic technique as for K* (see the proof of Theorem 4.2). The argument is now more complex since not every clause from T that is satisfied by some state in $\mathcal{I}$ is still there in U. To show that we can still match every "witness sequence" $X_0 \dots X_n$ by a run $C_0 \dots C_n$, Lemma 6.1 (2) plays a crucial role. Lemma 6.1 (2) implies that for every satisfiable clause C in T there exists a superclause D in U that holds in the same state as C. Together with Lemma 6.1 (3), asserting that U is a subset of T with respect to clauses, Lemma 6.1 (2) is also central for showing evidence conditions (1), (3) and (5). □

7 Conclusion

The paper presents the first goal-directed decision procedure for hybrid logic with eventualities and difference. A naive two-phase implementation of the procedure seems straightforward. Given an input clause C, we first compute a complete tableau containing C. This step takes at most deterministic exponential time in the size of the input (more precisely, in the size of the base of the input). To determine whether C is satisfiable, it then remains to check for the existence of an evident subtableau containing C. Naively, this can be done by repeatedly guessing candidate subtableaux and then checking their evidence. While the non-deterministic running time for the second phase is polynomial in the size of the complete tableau, because of the guessing, the deterministic algorithm is exponential. Hence, the combined procedure is in NEXPTIME, allowing for implementations with doubly exponential complexity. Based on results for related logics [1,28], we conjecture H^*_D to be EXPTIME-complete. To reduce the complexity of our procedure to EXPTIME, provided this is possible at all, more work is needed. A promising direction is developing a polynomial algorithm for the second phase of the procedure, possibly following the ideas of [27]. The main complication here is that the procedure in [27] relies on the assumption that for every satisfiable formula s there exists a unique largest evident subtableau containing s. In our case, this assumption does not hold. In the presence of nominals, a complete tableau may contain several evident subtableaux whose union is not evident. Following [12,14], one could also interleave the first and the second phase of the procedure so as to allow early pruning of unsatisfiable clauses. Compared to interleaved procedures for nominal-free logics [12,14], such a procedure would have to deal with an additional difficulty, namely the link closure, which can contain considerably more links than the complete tableau.

References

1. Areces, C., Blackburn, P., Marx, M.: The computational complexity of hybrid temporal logics. L. J. IGPL 8(5), 653–679 (2000)
2. Areces, C., ten Cate, B.: Hybrid logics. In: Blackburn, et al. (eds.) [4], pp. 821–868
3. Blackburn, P.: Internalizing labelled deduction. J. Log. Comput. 10(1), 137–168 (2000)
4. Blackburn, P., van Benthem, J., Wolter, F. (eds.): Handbook of Modal Logic, Studies in Logic and Practical Reasoning, vol. 3. Elsevier, Amsterdam (2007)
5. Blackburn, P., de Rijke, M., Venema, Y.: Modal Logic. Cambridge University Press, Cambridge (2001)
6. Emerson, E.A., Clarke, E.M.: Using branching time temporal logic to synthesize synchronization skeletons. Sci. Comput. Programming 2(3), 241–266 (1982)
7. Emerson, E.A., Halpern, J.Y.: "Sometimes" and "not never" revisited: On branching versus linear time temporal logic. J. ACM 33(1), 151–178 (1986)
8. Fischer, M.J., Ladner, R.E.: Propositional dynamic logic of regular programs. J. Comput. System Sci. 194–211 (1979)
9. Fitting, M.: Proof Methods for Modal and Intuitionistic Logics. Reidel, Dordrecht (1983)
10. Gabbay, D.M.: Selective filtration in modal logic, Part A. Semantic tableaux method. Theoria 36(3), 323–330 (1970)

11. Giesl, J., Hähnle, R. (eds.): IJCAR 2010. LNCS(LNAI), vol. 6173. Springer, Heidelberg (2010)
12. Goré, R., Nguyen, L.A.: EXPTIME tableaux with global caching for description logics with transitive roles, inverse roles and role hierarchies. In: Olivetti, N. (ed.) TABLEAUX 2007. LNCS (LNAI), vol. 4548, pp. 133–148. Springer, Heidelberg (2007)
13. Goré, R., Nguyen, L.A.: Clausal tableaux for multimodal logics of belief. Fund. Inform. 94(1), 21–40 (2009)
14. Goré, R., Widmann, F.: Optimal tableaux for propositional dynamic logic with converse. In: Giesl, Hähnle (eds.) [11], pp. 225–239
15. Harel, D., Kozen, D., Tiuryn, J.: Dynamic Logic. The MIT Press, Cambridge (2000)
16. Horrocks, I., Hustadt, U., Sattler, U., Schmidt, R.: Computational modal logic. In: Blackburn, et al. (eds.) [4], pp. 181–245
17. Kaminski, M., Smolka, G.: Clausal graph tableaux for hybrid logic with eventualities and difference. Technical report, Saarland University (2010), `http://www.ps.uni-saarland.de/Publications/details/KaminskiSmolka:2010:ClausalGraph.html`
18. Kaminski, M., Smolka, G.: Clausal tableaux for hybrid PDL. Technical report, Saarland University (2010), `http://www.ps.uni-saarland.de/Publications/details/KaminskiSmolka:2010:HPDL.html`
19. Kaminski, M., Smolka, G.: Terminating tableaux for hybrid logic with eventualities. In: Giesl, Hähnle (eds.) [11], pp. 240–254
20. Kesten, Y., Manna, Z., McGuire, H., Pnueli, A.: A decision algorithm for full propositional temporal logic. In: Courcoubetis, C. (ed.) CAV 1993. LNCS, vol. 697, pp. 97–109. Springer, Heidelberg (1993)
21. Kripke, S.A.: Semantical analysis of modal logic I: Normal modal propositional calculi. Z. Math. Logik Grundlagen Math. 9, 67–96 (1963)
22. Lemmon, E.J., Scott, D.: The 'Lemmon Notes': An Introduction to Modal Logic. Blackwell, Malden (1977)
23. Manna, Z., Wolper, P.: Synthesis of communicating processes from temporal logic specifications. ACM TOPLAS 6(1), 68–93 (1984)
24. Massacci, F.: Single step tableaux for modal logics. J. Autom. Reasoning 24(3), 319–364 (2000)
25. Nguyen, L.A.: A new space bound for the modal logics K4, KD4 and S4. In: Kutyłowski, M., Wierzbicki, T., Pacholski, L. (eds.) MFCS 1999. LNCS, vol. 1672, pp. 321–331. Springer, Heidelberg (1999)
26. Pnueli, A.: The temporal logic of programs. In: Proc. 18th Annual Symp. on Foundations of Computer Science (FOCS 1977), pp. 46–57. IEEE Computer Society Press, Los Alamitos (1977)
27. Pratt, V.R.: A near-optimal method for reasoning about action. J. Comput. System Sci. 20(2), 231–254 (1980)
28. Sattler, U., Vardi, M.Y.: The hybrid μ-calculus. In: Goré, R.P., Leitsch, A., Nipkow, T. (eds.) IJCAR 2001. LNCS (LNAI), vol. 2083, pp. 76–91. Springer, Heidelberg (2001)
29. Segerberg, K.: An Essay in Classical Modal Logic. No. 13 in Filosofiska Studier. University of Uppsala (1971)
30. Tanabe, Y., Takahashi, K., Hagiya, M.: A decision procedure for alternation-free modal μ-calculi. In: Areces, C., Goldblatt, R. (eds.) Advances in Modal Logic, vol. 7, pp. 341–362. College Publications (2008)
31. Tsarkov, D., Horrocks, I., Patel-Schneider, P.F.: Optimizing terminological reasoning for expressive description logics. J. Autom. Reasoning 39(3), 277–316 (2007)

The Consistency of the CADIAG-2 Knowledge Base: A Probabilistic Approach

Pavel Klinov[1], Bijan Parsia[1], and David Picado-Muiño[2]

[1] University of Manchester
Oxford Road, Manchester M13 9PL, UK
{pklinov,bparsia}@cs.man.ac.uk
[2] Institut für Diskrete Mathematik und Geometrie
Wiedner Hauptstrasse 8 / 104. A-1040 Vienna, Austria
picado@logic.at

Abstract. The paper presents the methodology and the results of checking consistency of the knowledge base of CADIAG-2, a large-scale medical expert system. Such knowledge base consists of a large collection of rules representing knowledge about various medical entities (symptoms, signs, diseases...) and relationships between them. The major portion of the rules are uncertain, i.e., they specify *to what degree* a medical entity is *confirmed* by another medical entity or a combination of them. Given the size of the system and the uncertainty it has been challenging to validate its consistency. Recent attempts to partially formalise CADIAG-2's knowledge base into decidable Gödel logics have shown that, on that formalisation, CADIAG-2 is inconsistent. In this paper we verify this result with an alternative, more expressive formalisation of CADIAG-2 as a set of probabilistic conditional statements and apply a state-of-the-art probabilistic logic solver to determine *satisfiability* of the knowledge base and to extract conflicting sets of rules. As CADIAG-2 is too large to be handled out of the box we describe an approach to split the knowledge base into fragments that can be tested independently and prove that such methodology is complete (i.e., is guaranteed to find all conflicts). With this approach we are able to determine that CADIAG-2 contains numerous sets of conflicting rules and compute all of them for a slightly relaxed version of the knowledge base.

1 Introduction

CADIAG-2 (Computer Assisted DIAGnosis) is a well-known rule-based expert system aimed at providing support in diagnostic decision making in the field of internal medicine. Its design and construction was initiated in the early 80's at the Medical University of Vienna by K.P. Adlassnig – see [1], [2], [3] or [4] for more on the origins and design of CADIAG-2.

CADIAG-2 consists of two fundamental pieces: the inference engine and the knowledge base. The inference engine — see [5] or [6] for alternative formalisations and analyses of CADIAG-2's inference — is based on methods of approximate reasoning in fuzzy set theory, in the sense of [7] and [8]. In fact CADIAG-2

C. Fermüller and A. Voronkov (Eds.): LPAR-17, LNCS 6397, pp. 432–446, 2010.

is presented in some monographs as an example of a fuzzy expert system — see [9], [10]. The knowledge base consists of a set of *IF-THEN* rules — known in the literature as *production* rules — intended to represent relationships between distinct medical entities: symptoms, findings, signs and test results on the one hand and diseases and therapies on the other. The vast majority of them are binary (i.e., they relate single medical entities) and only such rules are considered in this paper. The one that follows is an example of a binary rule of CADIAG-2 (taken from [3]):

```
IF suspicion of liver metastases by liver palpation
THEN pancreatic cancer
with degree of confirmation 0.3
```

The *degree of confirmation* refers, intuitively, to the degree to which the antecedent (i.e., '*suspicion of liver metastases by liver palpation*' in the example above) confirms the consequent (i.e., '*pancreatic cancer*' above).

In this paper we present a formalisation of a coded version of the binary fragment of CADIAG-2's knowledge base (i.e., that contains only codes for the identification of the distinct medical entities) as a probabilistic logic theory. We then check the satisfiability of that formalisation with *Pronto*, our probabilistic Description Logic (DL) reasoner, which we briefly introduce. We find that CADIAG-2 is highly unsatisfiable (confirming the results of an alternative, weaker formalisation, [11]) and analyse the sources of unsatisfiability.

To our knowledge, the probabilistic version of CADIAG-2 is the largest PSAT (Probabilistic SATisfiability) problem to be solved by an automated reasoner and is certainly the largest non-artificial one. This is, perhaps, a bit misleading as it is comparatively easy to detect unsatisfiability by first heuristically detecting small but likely unsatisfiable fragments, and then performing a satisfiability check on each fragment. While this might suffice to validate that the knowledge base is unsatisfiable it is not sufficient, without further qualification, to detect all conflicting sets of rules, nor can it ensure that a satisfiable fragment is so in the context of the entire knowledge base. As CADIAG-2 is too large (the number of rules in the binary fragment we are concerned with is over 18000) we describe an approach to split the knowledge base into comparatively large fragments that can be tested independently and prove that such methodology is complete (i.e., is guaranteed to find all conflict sets). With this methodology we are able to determine that CADIAG-2 contains numerous sets of conflicting rules and compute all of them for a slightly relaxed interpretation of the knowledge base.

2 Notation and Preliminary Definitions

Throughout we will be working with a finite set $\mathcal{L} = S \cup D = \{P_1, ..., P_n\}$ of unary predicates in a first-order language, for some $n \in \mathbb{N}$. $\mathcal{L}$ is intended to represent the set of medical entities occurring in the inference rules of the expert system CADIAG-2, with S the set of symptoms, findings, signs and test results (to which we will commonly refer as *symptoms*) and D the set of therapies and diseases (to which we will commonly refer as *diseases*).

Definition 1. *An interpretation $\mathcal{I}$ of $\mathcal{L}$ is a pair $(D^{\mathcal{I}}, V^{\mathcal{I}})$, where $D^{\mathcal{I}}$ is a finite, non-empty set and $V^{\mathcal{I}}$ is a map from $\mathcal{L} \times D^{\mathcal{I}}$ to $[0,1]$.*

An interpretation $\mathcal{I}$ is said to be *classical* if $V^{\mathcal{I}}(P,a) \in \{0,1\}$ for all $(P,a) \in \mathcal{L} \times D^{\mathcal{I}}$. It is said to be *rational* if $V^{\mathcal{I}}(P,a) \in [0,1] \cap \mathbb{Q}$ for all $(P,a) \in \mathcal{L} \times D^{\mathcal{I}}$.

Given an interpretation $\mathcal{I}$ of $\mathcal{L}$, we will refer to the elements in $D^{\mathcal{I}}$ by latin characters $a, b, c...$ and to the elements in $\mathcal{L}$ by uppercase latin characters $P, Q...$ (possibly with suffices).

Let $L = \{p_1, ..., p_n\}$ be a finite propositional language, for $n \in \mathbb{N}$, and SL its closure under boolean connectives.

Definition 2. *Let $w : SL \longrightarrow [0,1]$. We say that w is a probability function on L if the following two conditions hold, for all $\theta, \phi \in SL$:*

- *If $\models \theta$ then $w(\theta) = 1$.*
- *If $\models \neg(\theta \wedge \phi)$ then $w(\theta \vee \phi) = w(\theta) + w(\phi)$.*[1]

We can restrict probability functions on L to values in $[0,1] \cap \mathbb{Q}$. We will call such probability functions *rational*.

A probability distribution w on L can be characterized by the values it assigns to the expressions of the form $\pm p_1 \wedge ... \wedge \pm p_n$, which we call *states* or *worlds*, where $+p$ and $-p$ stand for p and $\neg p$ respectively. We denote the set of states in L by W and define, for $\phi \in SL$, W_ϕ as follows:

$$W_\phi = \{s \in W \mid s \models \phi\}.$$

We define conditional probability from the notion of unconditional probability on conditional statements in L in the conventional way.

3 The Knowledge Base in CADIAG-2

We can classify CADIAG-2's binary rules (Φ_{CB}) into three different types: rules in which both antecedent and consequent are medical entities in S (*symptom-symptom*, $\Phi_{S|S}$), rules in which both antecedent and consequent are medical entities in D (*disease-disease*, $\Phi_{D|D}$) and those in which the antecedent is a medical entity in S and the consequent an entity in D (*symptom-disease*, $\Phi_{D|S}$).[2] The degree of confirmation in a rule of the first two types is a value in the set $\{0,1\}$ and it is in this sense that we say that rules of these types are *classical.*

Let $\langle P, Q, \eta \rangle \in \Phi_{CB}$ be a rule in CADIAG-2's binary knowledge base, with $P, Q \in \mathcal{L}$ and $\eta \in [0,1] \cap \mathbb{Q}$. The value η is intended to quantify the *degree* to which P (the antecedent) *confirms* Q (the consequent) and claimed in most of

[1] Here (and throughout) $\models$ is classical entailment.

[2] CADIAG-2's knowledge base formally contains values for conditional relations with a medical entity in D as the antecedent and a medical entity in S as the consequent. However, such rules are not used by CADIAG-2's inference mechanism and therefore are not taken into account in this paper.

the literature on CADIAG-2 (see, for example, [2] or [3]) to have been calculated from a certain database or interpretation $\mathcal{I}$ as follows:[3]

$$\frac{\sum_{a\in D^{\mathcal{I}}} min\{V^{\mathcal{I}}(P,a), V^{\mathcal{I}}(Q,a)\}}{\sum_{a\in D^{\mathcal{I}}} V^{\mathcal{I}}(P,a)} = \eta \tag{1}$$

Notice that this expression generalises the concept of *conditional probability* or *frequency* that one gets when restricting the model to classical interpretations. Under such a restriction η becomes a probability (in the sense of frequency) and its meaning is intuitive and formally well understood. However, when allowing in (1) valuations other than classical the intuitive meaning of η is lost. Certainly, (1) would benefit from a serious attempt to clarify its meaning when allowing valuations other than classical but it is not the purpose of this paper to do so. As we will see later, whether the interpretation of (1) is assumed in terms of any valuations or in terms of only classical valuations (i.e., a probabilistic interpretation) will be indifferent to our satisfiability-checking purposes.

Throughout we will use the expression $Q/_{\mathcal{I}}P = \eta$ to abbreviate (1). Sometimes, in order to generalise results, we will be considering an interval, say $\Omega \subseteq [0,1]$, instead of a single value (i.e., η in (1)) and we will be using the expression $Q/_{\mathcal{I}}P \in \Omega$ to abbreviate the corresponding modification of (1). Such modification is motivated by the possibility of alternative, suitable interpretations of the rules in Φ_{CB} that one could consider interesting in the view of some theoretical or practical aspects. Among these alternative interpretations we consider replacing η in equation (1) by the interval $[\eta, 1]$ (i.e., consider η a lower bound for the degrees of confirmation instead of a precise one) or replacing η whenever $\eta \in (0,1)$ by an interval of the form $[\eta - \epsilon, \eta + \epsilon]$, for ϵ small (i.e., a slightly relaxed interpretation of Φ_{CB}).

We will denote the collection of real intervals in $[0,1]$ by $\mathfrak{I}$. We will normally refer to intervals of the form $[\eta, \eta] \in \mathfrak{I}$ by η itself.

For the next definition and proposition let $\mathcal{I}$ be an interpretation of $\mathcal{L}$ and $\Phi \subseteq \mathcal{R}_{\mathcal{L}}$, for

$$\mathcal{R}_{\mathcal{L}} = \{\langle P, Q, \Omega\rangle \mid P, Q \in \mathcal{L},\ \Omega \in \mathfrak{I}\}.$$

Definition 3. *We say that $\mathcal{I}$ is a model of Φ (denoted $\models_{\mathcal{I}} \Phi$) if $Q/_{\mathcal{I}}P \in \Omega$ for all $\langle P, Q, \Omega\rangle \in \Phi$.*

Proposition 1. *Φ has a classical model if and only if it has a rational model.*

Proof. The right implication follows trivially from the fact that every classical interpretation is also rational. In order to prove the left implication let us assume that $\mathcal{I} = (D^{\mathcal{I}}, V^{\mathcal{I}})$ is a rational interpretation such that $\models_{\mathcal{I}} \Phi$.

Let C be the set given by the values $V^{\mathcal{I}}(P,a)$, for $(P,a) \in \mathcal{L} \times D^{\mathcal{I}}$. It is assumed that all the values in C are rational. Let us consider the minimum

[3] We say in *most* of the literature. There are some references in which the interpretation suggested for η in $\langle P, Q, \eta\rangle$ is different. For example in [1] it is claimed that η can be interpreted as a frequency and thus $\langle P, Q, \eta\rangle$ as a probabilistic conditional statement.

common multiple of the denominators of all the elements of C, say $q \in \mathbb{N}$. We next construct a new interpretation $\mathcal{J}$ from $\mathcal{I}$ such that $\models_{\mathcal{J}} \Phi$.[4]

We first define $D^{\mathcal{J}}$ from $D^{\mathcal{I}}$. For each element $a \in D^{\mathcal{I}}$ we set q elements in the domain $D^{\mathcal{J}}$, labelled as follows: $\{a_1, ..., a_q\}$. Let us consider now $P \in \mathcal{L}$ and $a \in D^{\mathcal{I}}$ and assume that $V^{\mathcal{I}}(P, a) = \frac{p}{q}$. We define $V^{\mathcal{J}}$ on $\mathcal{L} \times D^{\mathcal{J}}$ from $V^{\mathcal{I}}$ as follows, for $i \in \{1, ..., q\}$:

$$V^{\mathcal{J}}(P, a_i) = \begin{cases} 1 \; if \;\; i \leq p \\ 0 \; otherwise \end{cases}$$

It is easy to see that $\mathcal{J}$ thus defined is such that $\models_{\mathcal{J}} \Phi$.

For what follows we will be considering the collection of intervals $\mathfrak{I}^*$ in the set $[0, 1]$. $\mathfrak{I}^*$ differs from $\mathfrak{I}$ in that an interval $\Omega \in \mathfrak{I}^*$ needs to have its maximum and/or minimum in $\mathbb{Q}$, provided it has a maximum and/or a minimum.

We define

$$R^*_{\mathcal{L}} = \{\langle P, Q, \Omega \rangle \mid P, Q \in \mathcal{L}, \; \Omega \in \mathfrak{I}^*\}$$

and consider $\Phi \subseteq R^*_{\mathcal{L}}$ for the next proposition.

Proposition 2. *If Φ has a model then it has a rational model.*

Proof. Let $\mathcal{I}$ be an interpretation such that $\models_{\mathcal{I}} \Phi$. We then have that, for all $\langle P, Q, \Omega \rangle$ in Φ, $Q/_{\mathcal{I}}P \in \Omega$.

For each $Q/_{\mathcal{I}}P \in \Omega$ we consider the inequalities

$$\sum_{a \in D^{\mathcal{I}}} \eta_1 \, V^{\mathcal{I}}(P, a) < \sum_{a \in D^{\mathcal{I}}} min\{V^{\mathcal{I}}(P, a), V^{\mathcal{I}}(Q, a)\} < \sum_{a \in D^{\mathcal{I}}} \eta_2 \, V^{\mathcal{I}}(P, a),$$

where Ω is assumed to be of the form $(\eta_1, \eta_2) \in \mathfrak{I}^*$ (for $\Omega \in \mathfrak{I}^*$ of any other form we replace '$<$' in the inequalities above by '$\leq$' as required) and with

$$\min\{V^{\mathcal{I}}(P, a), V^{\mathcal{I}}(Q, a)\}$$

replaced by $V^{\mathcal{I}}(P, a)$ or $V^{\mathcal{I}}(Q, a)$ accordingly.

Let us also consider, for each $Q/_{\mathcal{I}}P \in \Omega$, the inequalities

$$0 \leq V^{\mathcal{I}}(P, a), V^{\mathcal{I}}(Q, a) \leq 1,$$

$$\sum_{a \in D^{\mathcal{I}}} V^{\mathcal{I}}(P, a) > 0$$

and, for $V^{\mathcal{I}}(P, a)$ greater than $V^{\mathcal{I}}(Q, a)$, the inequality $V^{\mathcal{I}}(Q, a) \leq V^{\mathcal{I}}(P, a)$ (the inequality $V^{\mathcal{I}}(Q, a) \geq V^{\mathcal{I}}(P, a)$ otherwise).

The solution set of the linear system above with unknown values $V^{\mathcal{I}}(P, a)$, $V^{\mathcal{I}}(Q, a)$ is not empty ($\mathcal{I}$ is assumed to be a solution of the system) and needs to contain rational solutions (due to the form of the intervals in $\mathfrak{I}^*$). Therefore, there has to exist a rational interpretation of $\mathcal{L}$ that models Φ.

---

[4] It is worth stressing here again that the predicates in $\mathcal{L}$, and thus the predicates involved in (1), are atomic predicates.

Corollary 1. *Φ has a model if and only if it has a classical model.*

By Corollary 1 we have that Φ_{CB} will have a model if and only if it has a classical model.

For the next definition let w be a probability function on $\mathcal{L}$, where $\mathcal{L}$ here is regarded as a propositional language, and $\langle P, Q, \Omega \rangle$ a triple in $\mathcal{R}_{\mathcal{L}}$, with $P, Q \in \mathcal{L}$ and $\Omega \in \mathfrak{I}$.

Definition 4. *We say that the probability function w on $\mathcal{L}$ satisfies $\langle P, Q, \Omega \rangle$ (denoted $\models_w \langle P, Q, \Omega \rangle$) if $w(P) > 0$ and*

$$\frac{w(P \wedge Q)}{w(P)} \in \Omega.$$

In that sense we say that $\langle P, Q, \Omega \rangle$ is *satisfiable* (or consistent)[5] if there exists a probability function w on L that satisfies $\langle P, Q, \Omega \rangle$. We extend the notion of satisfiability for sets of rules in $\mathcal{R}_{\mathcal{L}}$ in the trivial way.

For the next proposition let $\Phi \subseteq \mathcal{R}^*_{\mathcal{L}}$.

Proposition 3. *Φ is satisfiable if and only if it has a model.*

Proof. That Φ has a model if and only if it is satisfied by a rational probability function is clear. On the other hand, one can prove that if a probability function satisfies Φ then there exists a rational probability function that satisfies Φ by an argument similar to that of the proof of Proposition 2 by considering the corresponding system of linear inequalities with variables the *worlds* in $\mathcal{L}$.

Proposition 3 implies that Φ_{CB} can be regarded, for consistency-checking purposes, as a knowledge base formalised in propositional probabilistic logic (or *PPL*).

For the last definition of this section let $\Phi \subseteq \mathcal{R}_{\mathcal{L}}$.

Definition 5. *We say that Φ is a minimal unsatisfiable set (or minimal inconsistent set) if it is not satisfiable and, for all $\Phi^* \subset \Phi$, Φ^* is satisfiable.*

4 Checking Satisfiability of CADIAG-2

Our main goals are to solve the PSAT problem (Probabilistic SATisfiability) for Φ_{CB} and, provided Φ_{CB} is unsatisfiable (which turns out to be the case), to figure out the minimal sets of conflicting rules (see Definition 5). Despite the fact that Φ_{CB} is formalised as a propositional knowledge base and that there exist several propositional PSAT solvers, we use *Pronto* (see [12]), our probabilistic Description Logic reasoner, for several reasons.

The first reason is that, unlike propositional solvers, it treats classical (i.e., certain) and probabilistic knowledge separately and scales perfectly with respect to the amount of the former. Φ_{CB} contains many classical formulas (for example,

[5] We use both terms indistinctively throughout.

the number of rules in $\Phi_{D|D}$ is over 200) and so, given the scalability limits of PPL solvers (about 1000 formulas), they are likely to be unable to handle a sufficient number of uncertain *symptom-disease* rules in addition to $\Phi_{D|D}$ and (a fragment of) $\Phi_{S|S}$.

The second reason is that *Pronto* has *pinpointing* capabilities for finding all minimal sets of conflicting formulas in an unsatisfiable knowledge base. This feature is critical in the context of this work given the size of CADIAG-2 and, as we will see shortly, the number of potentially overlapping inconsistencies. It must be noted that finding all minimal inconsistencies is by no means a trivial extension of the PSAT algorithm (for example, its naive implementation using a PSAT solver as a black-box reasoner is not practical due to the hardness of PSAT). Even with our implementation, the number of conflicts in most fragments results in a significant slowdown of reasoning.

Finally, we are interested in evaluating our algorithms (see the next section) on a large and naturally occurring knowledge base such as Φ_{CB}.

4.1 Algorithms

In this section we briefly sketch the PSAT and conflict-finding algorithms implemented in *Pronto* within the frame of classical propositional logic (since for Φ_{CB} a formalisation in terms of the probabilistic DL language is not necessary).

Probabilistic satisfiability algorithm. For the sake of clarity and brevity we will consider the case of PSAT for sets of probabilistic conditional statements of the form $\langle \top, \phi, \eta \rangle$ on L (a finite propositional language), with $\phi \in SL$, where '$\top$' abbreviates 'always true' (a tautology in SL) and η represents the probability assigned to it (i.e., all probabilistic statements considered are unconditional and assigned point-valued probabilities. It is straightforward, but technically awkward and space consuming, to generalise the procedure to handle conditional interval statements, see [12]).

We say that a collection of probabilistic conditional statements of such form, say Φ, is satisfiable if and only if the objective value of the following linear program is equal to 1:

$$\begin{aligned} & max \sum_{s \in W} x_s \\ & s.t. \sum_{s \in W_\phi} x_s = \eta \times \sum_{s \in W} x_s, \text{ for each } \langle \top, \phi, \eta \rangle \in \Phi \\ & \sum_{s \in W} x_s \leq 1 \text{ and all } x_s \geq 0 \end{aligned} \tag{2}$$

where x_s is the assignment to the possible world $s \in W$.

Let A denote the matrix of linear coefficients in (2). At every step of the simplex algorithm, A is represented as a combination (B, N) where B and N are the submatrices of the *basic* and *non-basic* variables, respectively. Values of non-basic variables are fixed to zero and the solver proceeds by replacing one basic variable (i.e., column in A) by a non-basic one until the optimal solution is found. As the size of A is exponential in the size of our language L, one should determine the entering column without representing A explicitly. This is done using the column generation technique in which entering columns are computed by optimizing a subproblem (sometimes referred to as the *pricing-out problem*). Observe that the above system of linear inequalities always admits a solution, e.g. all $x_s = 0$ even if Φ is unsatisfiable, which facilitates the column generation process. Note, however, that the actual linear programs solved in Pronto are considerably more involved, in particular, they include stabilization variables to improve convergence.

The critical step is to formulate linear constraints for the pricing-out problem such that every solution (a column) corresponds to a possible world in W. In the propositional case this can be done by employing a well-known formulation of SAT as a mixed-integer linear program [13]. In the case of an expressive language, such as Description Logic [14], there appears to be no easy way of determining a set of constraints H for the pricing-out problem such that its set of solutions is in one-to-one correspondence with W. *Pronto* implements a novel *hybrid* procedure to compute H iteratively via interaction with a DL reasoner.

The main idea of the algorithm is that every column produced as a solution to the pricing-out problem is converted to a DL concept expression which is then checked for satisfiability by the DL reasoner. If the expression is satisfiable, it means that the column corresponds to a possible world (W in our context) and can be added to (2). Otherwise, the justifications of unsatisfiability (see [15]) are converted into linear constraints and added to the pricing-out problem, which is then re-optimized. Finally, either an entering column is found or the pricing-out problem becomes infeasible, which implies that the system (2) is optimal.

A detailed description of the PSAT algorithm is beyond the scope of this paper and is left as the core of a future paper.

Conflict finding algorithm. A satisfiability algorithm is not sufficient for a comprehensive analysis of an inconsistent knowledge base. Typically users need to identify those fragments of the knowledge base which cause the inconsistency in order to repair them. Such fragments are also required to be minimal so that the user can choose a repair strategy with minimal impact on the rest of the knowledge base.

We are interested in determining the minimal unsatisfiable subsets of a certain collection of probabilistic conditional statements in L, say Φ.

We apply the classical approach to finding minimal unsatisfiable sets based on hitting sets which dates back to Reiter (see [16]). Reiter's hitting set tree (HST) algorithm requires, as a subroutine, a satisfiability procedure which can extract one minimal unsatisfiable set from the knowledge base. It then systematically removes each axiom from that minimal unsatisfiable set and applies the satisfiability procedure again to generate a new minimal unsatisfiable set. By being systematic in the "repairs", the procedure finds all minimal unsatisfiable sets in the knowledge base. We reduce the problem of finding a single minimal unsatisfiable subset of Φ to the problem of finding a minimal infeasible subset of inequalities in the corresponding linear system of the form (2) above. Such subsets are known as *irreducible infeasible systems*(IIS) in the LP literature [17]. However, given that the system (2) is never represented in its full version the application of the Ryan and Parker's algorithm is far from straightforward.[6] If the optimal value of the system (2) is less than 1 then some inequalities have non-zero dual values. Such inequalities correspond to conflicting constraints in Φ but are not guaranteed to be minimal (though is typically quite small and close to the minimal set). We then do a brute force trial and error search to remove all superfluous constraints.

4.2 Decomposition of CADIAG-2

To our knowledge, none of the existing probabilistic solvers can solve PSAT for Φ_{CB} taken as a whole within reasonable amount of time (see Table 1 for a precise account of the size of Φ_{CB}). However, Φ_{CB} has a certain structure that allows splitting it into fragments that can be examined independently. A crucial property of our probabilistic formalisation of CADIAG-2 is that Φ_{CB} is satisfiable if and only if all of the fragments are individually satisfiable, as we show below.

Table 1. Characteristics of CADIAG-2

Number of distinct symptoms	1761
Number of distinct disease	341
Number of symptom-symptom rules (size of $\Phi_{S\|S}$)	720
Number of disease-disease rules (size of $\Phi_{D\|D}$)	218
Number of symptom-disease rules (size of $\Phi_{D\|S}$)	17573

We can regard Φ_{CB} as a directed graph where the nodes are the medical entities in $\mathcal{L}$ and the edges are given by the rules in Φ_{CB} (i.e., a rule of the form $\langle P, Q, \eta\rangle$ in Φ_{CB} would correspond to an edge directed from P to Q).

Let $P \in \mathcal{L}$. We denote by $\Phi_P \subseteq \Phi_{CB}$ the set of rules that yield a directed edge in a path from P to any other medical entity in $\mathcal{L}$ or a directed edge in a path from any medical entity in $\mathcal{L}$ to P.

For the next two results let us consider two medical entities $P_1, P_2 \in S$ and assume that there is no path from P_1 to P_2 in Φ_{CB} or vice versa and that there is no medical entity $P \in \mathcal{L}$ from which there exists a path both to P_1 and P_2.

Proposition 4. *If Φ_{P_1} and Φ_{P_2} are satisfiable then $\Phi_{P_1} \cup \Phi_{P_2}$ is satisfiable.*

[6] We leave it for future research to investigate how multiple irreducible infeasible systems can be generated at once when the linear system is constructed through column generation.

Proof. Let $\mathcal{I}_1$ and $\mathcal{I}_2$ be interpretations that satisfy Φ_{P_1} and Φ_{P_2} respectively. We can assume without loss of generality that $D^{\mathcal{I}_1} \cap D^{\mathcal{I}_2} = \emptyset$. We can construct an interpretation $\mathcal{I}$ from $\mathcal{I}_1$ and $\mathcal{I}_2$ that satisfies $\Phi_{P_1} \cup \Phi_{P_2}$ in a pretty trivial way by setting $D^{\mathcal{I}} = D^{\mathcal{I}_1} \cup D^{\mathcal{I}_2}$ and $V^{\mathcal{I}}(P,a) = 1$ if and only if $V^{\mathcal{I}_1}(P,a) = 1$ or $V^{\mathcal{I}_2}(P,a) = 1$ and 0 otherwise, for all $(P,a) \in \mathcal{L} \times D^{\mathcal{I}}$. In can be easily seen that $\mathcal{I}$ thus defined satisfies $\Phi_{P_1} \cup \Phi_{P_2}$.

Corollary 2. *If Φ is a minimal unsatisfiable set of rules in $\Phi_{P_1} \cup \Phi_{P_2}$ then Φ needs to be contained in Φ_{P_1} or Φ_{P_2}.*

Proof. It follows trivially from Proposition 4. Notice that if Φ were a minimal inconsistent set in $\Phi_{P_1} \cup \Phi_{P_2}$ and that it were neither contained in Φ_{P_1} nor in Φ_{P_2} then we could define satisfiable subsets from Φ_{P_1} and Φ_{P_2} of the same structure (possibly by removing rules from other minimal inconsistent subsets of Φ_{P_1} and Φ_{P_2}, but none from Φ).

Although trivial, it is worth mentioning that the previous propositions also hold for any alternative interpretation of the rules in terms of probabilistic intervals (i.e., by taking certain real intervals in place of precise probabilities).

Φ_{CB} has the following properties which will enable us to decompose it into a set of fragments:

P1. All formulas contain only atomic medical entities (i.e., entities in $\mathcal{L}$).
P2. All probabilistic formulas in $\Phi_{D|S}$ condition only on symptoms (uncertain rules are unidirectional).
P3. The graph of $\Phi_{S|S}$ contains many disconnected subgraphs.

We split Φ_{CB} into a set of fragments of the form Φ_P, where $P \in S$ is a symptom such that there is no rule in Φ_{CB} of the form $\langle Q, P, \eta \rangle$. For simplicity we include the entire $\Phi_{D|D}$ in each fragment since it is decomposable to a much less extent than $\Phi_{S|S}$. The largest fragments have around 200 probabilistic formulas that normally relate two or three connected symptoms to diseases.

Corollary 2 guarantees that all minimal unsatisfiable sets of formulas in Φ_{CB} can be found by computing such sets for each fragment. Thus, our methodology is simply a systematic analysis of the fragments of the form Φ_P, which involves a PSAT test and, if the fragment is unsatisfiable, the computation of all minimal unsatisfiable sets in it (see the algorithms in the two previous subsections).

5 Results

We present here results concerning the consistency check of Φ_{CB} when considering a slightly relaxed interpretation of Φ_{CB} by replacing each rule of type *symptom-disease* of the form $\langle P, Q, \eta \rangle \in \Phi_{CB}$, for some $P, Q \in \mathcal{L}$ and $\eta \in (0,1) \cap \mathbb{Q}$, by $\langle P, Q, \Omega_\eta \rangle$, with

$$\Omega_\eta = [\eta - 0.01, \eta + 0.01] = [\eta^-, \eta^+].^7$$

[7] The degrees of confirmation of the rules in Φ_{CB} are all of the form $\frac{k}{100}$, for some $k \in \{0, 1, ..., 100\} \subset \mathbb{Z}$. Thus Ω_η is well defined.

We have opted for checking consistency of this slightly relaxed interpretation of the rules in Φ_{CB} against a precise interpretation (i.e., the standard interpretation with precise values) because of time constraints. The implementation of our algorithms for the relaxed interpretation of Φ_{CB} completes the task of finding all minimal unsatisfiable subsets in a reasonable amount of time (around one hour). It is a well-known fact in model-diagnosis theory that computing *all* minimal unsatisfiable subsets of a certain knowledge base requires a number of satisfiability tests (in our case, PSAT tests) that is exponential in the number of unsatisfiable subsets. Our relaxed interpretation of Φ_{CB} already contains a high number of unsatisfiable sets (as we will just see) and a precise interpretation adds up more. Furthermore, some of the unsatisfiable sets that are present in the precise interpretation and not in our relaxed one are relatively large (some contain 7 rules) and do not overlap with other unsatisfiable sets. Such facts bring the algorithm's running time closer to its worst case.

An example of a type of minimal unsatisfiable set detected under a precise interpretation of the rules but not under our relaxed version is the one that follows:

$$\langle P_1, Q_1, \eta_1 \rangle,\ \ \langle P_1, Q_2, \eta_2 \rangle\ \langle P_2, Q_1, \eta_3 \rangle\ \langle P_2, Q_3, \eta_4 \rangle,$$
$$\langle Q_1, Q_3, 1 \rangle\ \langle Q_2, Q_3, 1 \rangle\ \langle P_1, P_2, 1 \rangle,$$

for $P_1, P_2 \in S$, $Q_1, Q_2, Q_3 \in D$, $\eta_1, \eta_2, \eta_3, \eta_4 \in [0,1]$, with $\eta_3 = \eta_4$ and $\eta_1 < \eta_2$. Notice that the rules $\langle P_2, Q_1, \eta_3 \rangle$ and $\langle P_2, Q_3, \eta_4 \rangle$ along with $\langle Q_1, Q_3, 1 \rangle$ intuitively claim that the set of patients with symptom P_2 and disease Q_2 coincides with the set of patients with symptom P_2 and disease Q_3 when assuming $\eta_3 = \eta_4$. Under such an assumption the rules $\langle P_1, Q_1, \eta_1 \rangle$ and $\langle P_1, Q_2, \eta_2 \rangle$ along with the remaining classical rules generate an inconsistency whenever $\eta_1 < \eta_2$. Notice also that, for example, for $\eta_3 < \eta_4$ the set would not be unsatisfiable and thus our relaxed interval intepretation would yield this set consistent (assuming $\eta_3, \eta_4 < 1$).

For the sake of simplicity we will adopt the same notation for the rules of type *symptom-disease* of the form $\langle P, Q, \eta \rangle$, with $\eta \in \{0, 1\}$. We will write $\langle P, Q, \Omega_\eta \rangle$, with $\Omega_\eta = [\eta, \eta] = [\eta^-, \eta^+]$.

We list the different types of minimal unsatisfiable sets encountered in Φ_{CB} under this relaxed interpretation of the rules:

Type 1. Our first type of minimal unsatisfiable set in Φ_{CB} is given by a collection of rules of the form

$$\langle P, Q_1, \Omega_\eta \rangle,\ \ \langle P, Q_2, \Omega_\zeta \rangle,\ \ \langle Q_1, Q_2, 1 \rangle,$$

for $P \in S$, $Q_1, Q_2 \in D$, $\eta, \zeta \in [0,1]$ and $\zeta^+ < \eta^-$.

By $\zeta^+ < \eta^-$ we are intuitively assuming that the number of patients that have both symptom P and disease Q_1 is greater than the number of patients with both symptom P and disease Q_2, which contradicts $\langle Q_1, Q_2, 1 \rangle$ (i.e., the assumption that all patients that have disease Q_1 have also disease Q_2).

Type 2. Our second type of minimal unsatisfiable set in Φ_{CB} is given by a set of rules of the form

$$\langle P, Q_1, \Omega_\eta \rangle,\ \ \langle P, Q_2, \Omega_\zeta \rangle,\ \ \langle Q_1, Q_2, 0 \rangle,$$

for $P \in S$, $Q_1, Q_2 \in D$, $\eta, \zeta \in [0,1]$ and $\eta^- + \zeta^- > 1$.

Notice that the rule $\langle Q_1, Q_2, 0\rangle$ assumes *disjointness* between Q_1 and Q_2 (intuitively, there cannot be a patient with both disease Q_1 and Q_2), which rules out the possibility of consistency whenever $\eta^- + \zeta^- > 1$.

Type 3. The third type of minimal conflict set in Φ_{CB} is given by a set of the form

$$\langle P_1, Q, \Omega_\eta\rangle, \ \langle P_2, Q, \Omega_1\rangle, \ \langle P_1, P_2, 1\rangle,$$

for $P_1, P_2 \in S$, $Q \in D$, $\eta \in [0,1]$ and $\eta^+ < 1$.

Intuitively, the rule $\langle P_1, P_2, 1\rangle$ says that all patients with symptom P_1 also have symptom P_2. The rule $\langle P_2, Q, \Omega_1\rangle$ intuitively says that all patients with symptom P_2 have disease Q. These two facts together imply that patients with symptom P_1 should all have disease Q (i.e., $\eta^+ = 1$).

Type 4. The fourth and last type of minimal unsatisfiable set is given by a collection of rules of the form

$$\langle P, Q_1, \Omega_\eta\rangle, \ \langle P, Q_2, \Omega_\zeta\rangle, \ \langle P, Q_3, \Omega_\lambda\rangle \ \langle Q_1, Q_3, 1\rangle, \ \langle Q_2, Q_3, 1\rangle, \ \langle Q_1, Q_2, 0\rangle,$$

with $P \in S$, $Q_1, Q_2, Q_3 \in D$, $\eta, \zeta, \lambda \in [0,1]$, $\lambda^+ < \eta^- + \zeta^- \leq 1$ and $\zeta^-, \eta^- \leq \lambda^+$ (to guarantee minimality).

Intuitively, assuming $\langle P, Q_1, \Omega_\eta\rangle$, $\langle P, Q_2, \Omega_\zeta\rangle$ and $\langle Q_1, Q_2, 0\rangle$, the proportion of patients that, having symptom P, have either disease Q_1 or Q_2 is at least $\eta^- + \zeta^-$. On the other hand, assuming $\langle Q_1, Q_3, 1\rangle$ and $\langle Q_2, Q_3, 1\rangle$, we have that all patients with disease either Q_1 or Q_2 have also disease Q_3. Thus, under such assumptions, satisfiability requires that $\lambda^+ \geq \eta^- + \zeta^-$.

A thorough analysis of these types of inconsistencies in connection with the whole knowledge base and with possible repair strategies and in relation to other sets of inconsistencies obtained under alternative interpretations of Φ_{CB} (as briefly pointed above, under the standard interpretation of the rules or when regarding η in $\langle P, Q, \eta\rangle \in \Phi_{CB}$ as a lower-bound threshold) is being done at present.

Table 2. Number of minimal unsatisfiable sets in Φ_{CB} and size (relaxed interpretation)

Type of minimal unsatisfiable set	Amount	Number of rules involved
Type 1	420	3
Type 2	5	3
Type 3	1	3
Type 4	269	6

6 Related Work

Consistency-checking methods and algorithms for large-scale databases have long been of relevance in scientific computational research. In relation to expert systems and in particular to CADIAG-2 it is worth referring to [18] as an example of research of this nature. In this paper, a classical first-order logic theorem prover was used to analyze the predecessor of CADIAG-2 (CADIAG-1), which did not contain any uncertain rules, and that helped to detect some inconsistent sets of rules. Consistency-checking in CADIAG-2 by means of formal methods is harder mostly because one has to use an appropriate formalism for representing degrees of confirmation in rules (in particular in *symptom-disease* rules). Very recently the first such attempt (see [11]) was made using a specific fragment of monadic infinite-valued Gödel logic G (denoted by $G^{\sim}$) extended with classical, involutive negation.

In [11] a sentence in $G^{\sim}$ is associated to each rule of the form $\langle P, Q, \eta\rangle$ in Φ_{CB}. It is proved that, for $\langle P, Q, \eta\rangle \in \Phi_{CB}$ and θ the sentence in $G^{\sim}$ associated to it, the following holds:

- If $\eta \in (0,1)$ then θ is satisfied by a certain interpretation $\mathcal{I}$ of $\mathcal{L}$ if and only if $Q/_{\mathcal{I}}P \in (0,1)$.
- If $\eta \in \{0,1\}$ then θ is satisfied by a certain interpretation $\mathcal{I}$ of $\mathcal{L}$ if and only if $Q/_{\mathcal{I}}P = \eta$.

In [11] the problem of checking satisfiability of the set of sentences in $G^{\sim}$ associated to the rules in Φ_{CB} is proved to be equivalent to the problem of satisfiability in classical first-order logic for such sentences (i.e., equivalent to determining whether there is a classical interpretation of $\mathcal{L}$ that satisfies the sentences associated to the rules).

The relation between our approach and that in [11] is clear in the light of the results stated in Section 3. We will have that a certain collection of rules $\Phi \subseteq \Phi_{CB}$ will be found to be inconsistent according to the approach defined in [11] if and only if there is no probability function w on $\mathcal{L}$ such that $\models_w \Phi^*$, where Φ^* is defined from Φ by replacing η in each rule $\langle P, Q, \eta\rangle \in \Phi$ by the interval $(0,1)$.

Unlike the approach in [11], our probabilistic formalisation is equisatisfiable with Φ_{CB} (see Proposition 3) and ensures finding all minimal unsatisfiable sets of rules. In [11] the fragment of compound rules in CADIAG-2 is also considered in addition to the binary fragment (at the expense of a further weakening in the information expressed by the formulas in $G^{\sim}$ representing these rules). As mentioned earlier, we do not consider CADIAG-2's compound rules in this paper. Certainly, we would require additional efforts to ensure (if possible at all) equisatisfiability and completeness of our decomposition procedure (as given by Proposition 4 for Φ_{CB}) if we consider CADIAG-2's compound rules, although the former would not be necessary if we assumed a probabilistic interpretation of the rules from the outset.

7 Conclusion

While CADIAG-2's knowledge base is, when formalised as a probabilistic logic theory, *highly* unsatisfiable it is unclear what action this calls for. Inconsistency in a knowledge base may capture critical information and maintaining it may be critical to the integrity of the represented knowledge (see [19] for a more comprehensive discussion). An ongoing research challenge is to study and *measure* the inconsistencies in CADIAG-2 in order to understand them better and to determine suitable repair strategies.

Regardless of one's preferred strategy for resolving the conflicts, it is clear that detecting them is critical to a complete understanding of the knowledge base which is challenging when we reach CADIAG-2's size. Even with our (fortuitous) decomposition, the extraction of all conflicts under the standard interpretation of the rules in CADIAG-2 is unfeasible for everyday knowledge base development (we estimate that it will take weeks to extract all conflicts. Of course, if the modellers decide that producing and maintaining a satisfiable version is the right course of action then even several weeks would not be unreasonable as a one-time cost). Subsequent satisfiability checks would go much faster, especially as one can check only the relevant fragment a modeller is working on. This is similar to various proposals from the description logic community for modular ontology development (see [20,21,22]). As part of our future work we intend to integrate more general modular analysis into our reasoner as an optimization. We intend to investigate whether it is necessary to do this decomposition outside of the solver (that is, by decomposing the input knowledge base before even starting to solve PSAT) in the rather crude manner we currently do, or whether modular analysis can be more tightly integrated with the reasoning process.

We have, as yet, to attempt entailment from CADIAG-2 or any of its fragments. It is not clear yet the extent to which one could generate interesting queries for CADIAG-2's knowledge base (or, more generally, for CADIAG-2 like knowledge bases) once it has been repaired and possibly modified for inferential purposes (see [6]).

We hope that CADIAG-2, or CADIAG-2 like problems, will be taken up by the PSAT solving community. CADIAG-2 is interestingly different in kind, not only in size, from traditional generated problems while its size sets a new base line for scalable PSAT.

References

1. Adlassnig, K., Kolarz, G., Scheithauer, W., Grabner, H.: Approach to a hospital-based application of a medical expert system. Informatics for Health and Social Care 11(3), 205–223 (1986)
2. Adlassnig, K., Kolarz, G., Effenberger, W., Grabner, H.: Cadiag: Approaches to computer-assisted medical diagnosis. Computers in Biology and Medicine 15, 315–335 (1985)
3. Adlassnig, K.: Fuzzy set theory in medical diagnosis. IEEE Transactions on Systems, Man and Cybernetics 16(2), 260–265 (1986)
4. Leitich, H., Adlassnig, K., Kolarz, G.: Evaluation of two different models of semi-automatic knowledge acquisition for the medical consultant system CADIAG-2/RHEUMA. Artificial Intelligence in Medicine 25, 215–225 (2002)
5. Ciabattoni, A., Vetterlein, T.: On the fuzzy (logical) content of Cadiag2. Fuzzy Sets and Systems (2009) (to appear shortly)

6. Picado Muiño, D.: The (probabilistic) logical content of cadiag2. In: Proceedings of ICAART 2010, pp. 28–35 (2010)
7. Zadeh, L.: Fuzzy sets. Information and Control 8, 338–353 (1965)
8. Zadeh, L.: Fuzzy logic and approximate reasoning. Synthese 30, 407–428 (1975)
9. Klir, G., Folger, T.: Fuzzy Sets, Uncertainty and Information. Prentice-Hall International, Englewood Cliffs (1988)
10. Zimmermann, H.: Fuzzy Set Theory and its Applications. Kluwer Academic Publisher, Dordrecht (1991)
11. Ciabattoni, A., Rusnok, P.: On the classical content of monadic $G^{\sim}$ and its applications to a fuzzy medical expert system. In: Proceedings of the 12th International Conference on the Principles of Knowledge Representation and Reasoning (2010)
12. Klinov, P., Parsia, B.: Pronto: A practical probabilistic description logic reasoner. In: International Workshop on Uncertainty in Description Logics (2010)
13. Hooker, J.N.: Quantitative approach to logical reasoning. Decision Support Systems 4, 45–69 (1988)
14. Baader, F., Calvanese, D., McGuiness, D., Nardi, D., Patel-Schneider, P.F.: Description Logic Handbook. Cambridge University Press, Cambridge (2003)
15. Horridge, M., Parsia, B., Sattler, U.: Laconic and precise justifications in OWL. In: Sheth, A.P., Staab, S., Dean, M., Paolucci, M., Maynard, D., Finin, T., Thirunarayan, K. (eds.) ISWC 2008. LNCS, vol. 5318, pp. 323–338. Springer, Heidelberg (2008)
16. Reiter, R.: A theory of diagnosis from first principles. Artificial Intelligence 32, 57–95 (1987)
17. Parker, M., Ryan, J.: Finding the minimum weight IIS cover of an infeasible system of linear inequalities. Ann. Math. Artif. Intell. 17(1-2), 107–126 (1996)
18. Moser, W., Adlassnig, K.: Consistency checking of binary categorical relationships in a medical knowledge bases. Artificial Intelligence in Medicine 8, 389–407 (1992)
19. Gabbay, D.M., Hunter, A.: Making inconsistency respectable: a logical framework for inconsistency in reasoning. In: Jorrand, P., Kelemen, J. (eds.) FAIR 1991. LNCS, vol. 535, pp. 19–32. Springer, Heidelberg (1991)
20. Sattler, U., Schneider, T., Zakharyaschev, M.: Which kind of module should I extract? In: Grau, B.C., Horrocks, I., Motik, B., Sattler, U. (eds.) Description Logics. CEUR Workshop Proceedings, CEUR-WS.org, vol. 477 (2009)
21. Cuenca Grau, B., Horrocks, I., Kazakov, Y., Sattler, U.: Extracting modules from ontologies: A logic-based approach. In: Stuckenschmidt, H., Parent, C., Spaccapietra, S. (eds.) Modular Ontologies. LNCS, vol. 5445, pp. 159–186. Springer, Heidelberg (2009)
22. Cuenca Grau, B., Parsia, B., Sirin, E.: Ontology integration using ϵ-connections. In: Stuckenschmidt, H., Parent, C., Spaccapietra, S. (eds.) Modular Ontologies. LNCS, vol. 5445, pp. 293–320. Springer, Heidelberg (2009)

On the Complexity of Model Expansion*

Antonina Kolokolova, Yongmei Liu, David Mitchell, and Eugenia Ternovska

[1] Memorial University of Newfoundland, Canada
[2] Sun Yat-sen University, China
[3] Simon Fraser University, Canada
kol@cs.mun.ca, ymliu@mail.sysu.edu.cn, mitchell@cs.sfu.ca, ter@cs.sfu.ca

Abstract. We study the complexity of model expansion (MX), which is the problem of expanding a given finite structure with additional relations to produce a finite model of a given formula. This is the logical task underlying many practical constraint languages and systems for representing and solving search problems, and our work is motivated by the need to provide theoretical foundations for these. We present results on both data and combined complexity of MX for several fragments and extensions of FO that are relevant for this purpose, in particular the guarded fragment GF_k of FO and extensions of FO and GF_k with inductive definitions. We present these in the context of the two closely related, but more studied, problems of model checking and finite satisfiability. To obtain results on FO(ID), the extension of FO with inductive definitions, we provide translations between FO(ID) with FO(LFP), which are of independent interest.

1 Introduction

Fagin's theorem, which states that existential second order logic ($\exists$SO) exactly captures the complexity class NP [6], initiated the area of descriptive complexity theory [14], the study of the relationship between logics and complexity classes. Descriptive complexity results can be seen as providing a way to view logics as "declarative programming languages" for problems in the corresponding classes. In [19], the third and fourth authors proposed explicitly taking this idea as the formal basis on which to build practical tools for representing and solving search problems. On this view, a problem specification is a formula ϕ in some suitable logic $\mathcal{L}$, a problem instance is a finite structure $\mathcal{A}$ for some part of the vocabulary of ϕ (the "instance vocabulary"). $\mathcal{A}$ is a model of $\exists\bar{S}\phi$, where $\bar{S}$ is the remaining ("expansion") vocabulary of ϕ, and a solution for $\mathcal{A}$ is a witness for the second order existential quantifiers. Thus, problem solving entails expanding a given structure to satisfy a given formula. It is not too hard to see that this is the formal task underlying a wide variety of actual constraint languages and systems.

The major emphasis of most practical systems is on NP search problems. Fagin's theorem tell us FO has the right expressive power for a specification language for NP, and the effectiveness of modern SAT solvers provides an easy way to build a solver

* Earlier versions of this work were presented at LCC 2006 and LaSh 2006. The work presented here was carried out while the first two authors were PIMS post-doctoral fellows at Simon Fraser University.

C. Fermüller and A. Voronkov (Eds.): LPAR-17, LNCS 6397, pp. 447–458, 2010.

Table 1. Complexity of model checking, model expansion and satisfiability problems, for FO and related logics on finite structures. $\equiv_C$K denotes capturing of complexity class K on class C of finite structures; K-c denotes completeness for class K. New results are presented in bold; other results are provided with references or are easy corollaries.

Logic	Model checking		Model expansion		Satisfiability
	Combined	Data	Combined	Data	
FO	PSPACE-c [21]	$\equiv_{BIT}$ AC^0 [2]	NEXP-c [25,19]	$\equiv$NP [6]	Undecidable [24]
FO(LFP)	EXP-c [25]	$\equiv_s$P [13,25,18]	NEXP-c	$\equiv$NP	Undecidable
FO(ID)	**EXP-c**	$\equiv_{\mathbf{s}}$**P**	**NEXP-c**	$\equiv$NP	Undecidable
FO^k	P-c [26,11]	$\in AC^0$	NP-c [26]	NP-c, $\not\equiv$NP	$k \geq 3$: Undecidable $k=2$: NEXP-c [10] $k=1$: EXP-c
GF_k	P-c [11,7]	$\in AC^0$	**NEXP-c**	$k \geq 2$: $\equiv$**NP** $k=1$: NP-c	$k \geq 2$:Undecidable $k=1$:2EXP-c [9]
RGF_k	na	na	**NP-c**	**NP-c,** $\not\equiv$**NP**	na
μGF	UP$\cap$co-UP [15]	$\in$ P	NEXP-c	NP-c	2EXP-c [12]
GF_k(ID)	$\in$EXP	$\in$P	NEXP-c	$k \geq 2$: $\equiv$NP	$k \geq 2$:Undecidable

via grounding to SAT. However, practical specification languages require a variety of convenience features, so we are interested model expansion for logics which would provide a natural formal basis for such features. The main purpose of this paper is to summarize what is known about model expansion for the restriction of FO to guarded fragments (to support types and efficient grounding), the extension of FO with induction as in FO(ID) [4] and FO(LFP), and the combination of the two, filling in gaps as needed.

Table 1 presents the summary, placing facts about model expansion in the context of the two related, but more familiar, tasks of model checking and satisfiability in the finite. In the table, new results are presented in bold. We use K-c to denote completeness for complexity class K, and $\equiv_C$K to denote capturing of complexity class K on a class C of finite structures (see Definition 2).

2 Definitions

For each logic $\mathcal{L}$, we consider three tasks: satisfiability, model checking, and model expansion, all for finite structures. For model checking and model expansion, we consider two notions of complexity, so-called data complexity and combined complexity. In this section we present definitions for these. We denote by $vocab(\phi)$ the vocabulary of formula ϕ.

Definition 1. *For a given logic $\mathcal{L}$, we consider complexity of three problems.*

1. Model Checking*: given $(\mathcal{A}, \phi)$, where ϕ is a sentence of $\mathcal{L}$ and $\mathcal{A}$ is a finite structure for $vocab(\phi)$, does $\mathcal{A} \models \phi$?*

2. Model Expansion *(MX): given* $(\mathcal{A}, \phi)$, *where* ϕ *is a sentence in* L, $\mathcal{A}$ *is a finite* σ*-structure where* $\sigma \subset vocab(\phi)$, *is there an expansion* $\mathcal{A}'$ *of* $\mathcal{A}$ *to* $vocab(\phi)$ *such that* $\mathcal{A}' \models \phi$*?*
3. Finite Satisfiability*: given a sentence* ϕ *in* L, *is there a finite* $\mathcal{A}$ *for* $vocab(\phi)$ *such that* $\mathcal{A} \models \phi$*?*

The first and the last of these problems have been studied for a long time. Our focus is on model expansion.

Example 1. Let $\mathcal{A}$ be a graph $G = (V; E)$, and let ϕ be

$$\forall x \forall y \, [(Clique(x) \land Clique(y)) \supset (x = y \lor E(x, y))].$$

If $\mathcal{B}$ is an expansion of $\mathcal{A}$ to $vocab(\phi)$, then $\mathcal{B} \models \phi$ iff $Clique^{\mathcal{B}}$ is a set of vertices that forms a clique in $\mathcal{B}$.

For model checking and model expansion we consider two notions of complexity. These were introduced by [25]; here we follow the presentation of [16]. Let $enc()$ denote some standard encoding of structures and formulas as binary strings.

Definition 2. *Let K be a complexity class and* $\mathcal{L}$ *a logic. Let P be the problem of model checking or model expansion.*

1. *The* data complexity *of P for* $\mathcal{L}$ *is K if for every sentence* ϕ *of* $\mathcal{L}$ *the language* $\{enc(\mathcal{A}) | (\mathcal{A}, \phi) \in P\}$ *belongs to K. The* data complexity *of P for* $\mathcal{L}$ *is K-hard if for some sentence* ϕ *of* $\mathcal{L}$ *the language* $\{enc(\mathcal{A}) | (\mathcal{A}, \phi) \in P\}$ *is K-hard. The* combined complexity *of* $\mathcal{L}$ *is K (resp. K-hard) if the language* $\{(enc(\mathcal{A}), enc(\phi)) \mid (\mathcal{A}, \phi) \in P\}$ *belongs to K (resp. is K-hard).*
2. *Let C be a class of finite structures. P for* $\mathcal{L}$ captures *K on C if the data complexity of P for* $\mathcal{L}$ *is K and for every property Q of structures from C that is in K there is a sentence* ϕ_Q *of* $\mathcal{L}$ *such that* $\mathcal{A} \models \phi_Q$ *iff* $\mathcal{A}$ *has property Q, for every* $\mathcal{A} \in C$.

Clearly, the complexity of MX lies between complexities of model checking and satisfiability, since in that case, a part of the input structure is given. E.g. in the case of FO, we avoid undecidability by fixing the universe.

3 Complexity of MX for First-Order Logic

Complexities of model checking and satisfiability for first-order logic were determined decades ago. The combined complexity of model checking for FO is PSPACE-complete by reduction to QBF [21]. The data complexity of FO AC^0; moreover, FO captures AC^0 over structures with the BIT predicate (or arithmetic structures) [2].

MX for a logic $\mathcal{L}$ is equivalent to model checking for $\exists$SO($\mathcal{L}$). That is, there exists an expansion of a structure $\mathcal{A}$ that satisfies a formula ϕ iff $\mathcal{A}$ satisfies ϕ preceded by existential quantifiers for all expansion predicates. Many complexity properties for MX follow from this observation and well-known results on model checking.

Theorem 1. *The combined complexity of MX for FO is NEXP-complete; MX for FO captures* NP.

Proof. The first part is implicit in the proof of expression complexity of $\exists$SO in [25] (a different proof is presented in [19].) The second part is just Fagin's theorem [6].

It follows that MX for Π_i formulas captures level Σ_{i+1} of the polynomial hierarchy.

Remark 1. In some cases, the only information about the model that is given as an instance for the model expansion is the size of the model (i.e., the instance vocabulary σ is empty). In that case, it is reasonable to give the size of a model as a number in binary notation. This leads to an exponential increase in complexity (since the structure itself is exponential in the size of the input).

Although data complexity of model expansion for full first-order logic is NP-complete, there are fragments of FO for which model expansion is tractable. In particular, the results of [8] translate into the following.

Definition 3. *A* universal Horn formula *is a first-order formula consisting of a conjunction of Horn clauses, preceded by universal first-order quantifiers. Here, a clause is Horn if it contains at most one positive occurrence of an expansion predicate. A* universal Krom formula *is defined similarly, except that the restriction is at most two occurrences of expansion predicates per clause.*

Theorem 2. *The data complexity of the MX problem for universal Horn and Krom formulae is, respectively, P-complete and NL-complete. Moreover, MX for universal Horn and Krom captures P and NL, respectively, over successor structures.*

4 Complexity of MX for Guarded Fragments of FO

The guarded fragment GF of FO was introduced by Andréka *et al.* [1], and has recently received considerable attention. Here any existentially quantified subformula ϕ must be conjoined with a guard, i.e., an atomic formula over all free variables of ϕ. Gottlob *et al.* [7] extended GF to the k-guarded fragment GF$_k$, where the conjunction of up to k atoms may act as a guard.

The combined complexity of model checking for GF$_k$ is P-complete [11,7]. In particular, model checking for GF$_k$ can be done in time $O(ln^k)$, where l is the size of the formula, and n is the size of the structure [17]. The finite satisfiability problem for GF is 2EXP-complete [9].

In this section, we discuss complexity of MX for GF$_k$: we show that the combined complexity of MX for GF$_k$, $k \geq 1$, is the same as that for FO, and MX for GF$_k$, $k \geq 2$, captures NP just as MX for FO does. We also identify a fragment of GF$_k$, which we denote by RGF$_k$, such that the combined complexity of MX for RGF$_k$ is NP-complete. Although the data complexity of MX for RGF$_k$ is NP-complete, we show that it does not capture NP. As a corollary of our main results, we show that finite satisfiability for GF$_k$, $k \geq 2$ is undecidable.

Definition 4. *The* k-guarded fragment *GF_k of FO is the smallest set of formulas that*
1. Contains all atomic formulas;
2. Is closed under Boolean operations;
3. Contains $\exists \bar{x}(G_1 \wedge \ldots \wedge G_m \wedge \phi)$, if the G_i are atomic, $m \leq k$, $\phi \in GF_k$, and every free variable of ϕ appears in some G_i. Here $G_1 \wedge \ldots \wedge G_m$ is called the guard *of ϕ.*

A fragment of GF_k that is of particular interest in application of model expansion is RGF_k, which we use to denote sentences from GF_k in which all guards are given by the instance structure (i.e., no expansion predicates appear in guards). Let FO^k denote FO formulas that use at most k distinct variables. Then it is easy to see that any FO^k formula can be rewritten in linear time into an equivalent one in RGF_k, by using atoms of the form $x = x$ as parts of the guards when necessary. For example, the formula $\exists x \exists y[R(x) \wedge E(x, y)]$ can be rewritten to $\exists x \exists y[R(x) \wedge y = y \wedge E(x, y)]$, where R is an instance predicate, and E is an expansion predicate.

Lemma 1. *There is a polynomial-time algorithm that, given an arbitrary ∃SO sentence, constructs an equivalent ∃SO sentence whose first-order part is in* GF_2.

Proof. Suppose ϕ is a ∃SO sentence $\exists X_1 \ldots \exists X_m\, \varphi$, where φ is FO. Let l be the size of ϕ, and let k be the width of φ, that is, the maximum number of free variables in any subformula of φ. We introduce k new predicates $U_1, \ldots, U_k$ such that the arity of U_i is i, $1 \le i \le k$. Let φ' be the formula obtained from φ by replacing any subformula $\exists \bar{x}\, \psi(\bar{x})$ with $\exists \bar{x}(U_i(\bar{x}) \wedge \psi(\bar{x}))$ and any subformula $\forall \bar{x}\, \psi(\bar{x})$ with $\forall \bar{x}(U_i(\bar{x}) \supset \psi(\bar{x}))$, where i is the length of $\bar{x}$. Let η be the formula

$$\bigwedge_{i=0}^{k-1} \forall x_1 \ldots \forall x_{i+1}(x_1 = x_1 \wedge U_i(x_2 \ldots x_{i+1}) \supset U_{i+1}(x_1 \ldots x_{i+1})).$$

It is easy to see that any model of η interprets U_i as the i-ary universal relation, $1 \le i \le k$. Now let ϕ' be the ∃SO sentence $\exists X_1 \ldots \exists X_m \exists U_1 \ldots \exists U_k\ (\varphi' \wedge \eta)$. Clearly, $\varphi' \wedge \eta \in GF_2$, and ϕ' is equivalent to ϕ. Also, both φ' and η are of size $O(l^2)$, and hence ϕ' is of size $O(l^2)$.

Lemma 2. *There exists a polynomial-time algorithm that, given a structure $\mathcal{M}$ and an ∃SO sentence ϕ, constructs a structure $\mathcal{M}'$and an ∃SO sentence $\phi_{\mathcal{M}}$ such that the first-order part of $\phi_{\mathcal{M}}$ is in GF_1, and $\mathcal{M} \models \phi$ iff $\mathcal{M}' \models \phi_{\mathcal{M}}$.*

Proof. Suppose $\mathcal{M}$ is a structure, and ϕ is an ∃SO sentence. Let n be the size of $\mathcal{M}$, and let l be the size of ϕ. For each domain element a of $\mathcal{M}$, we introduce a new constant symbol c_a. Let $\mathcal{M}'$be the structure that expands $\mathcal{M}$ by interpreting c_a as a. Let ϕ' be the ∃SO sentence constructed from ϕ as in the proof of Lemma 1. Now let $\phi_{\mathcal{M}}$ be the sentence obtained from ϕ' by replacing each subformula $\forall x_1 \ldots \forall x_{i+1}(x_1 = x_1 \wedge U_i(x_2 \ldots x_{i+1}) \supset U_{i+1}(x_1 \ldots x_{i+1}))$ with

$$\bigwedge_{a \in dom(M)} \forall x_2 \ldots \forall x_{i+1}(U_i(x_2 \ldots x_{i+1}) \supset U_{i+1}(c_a x_2 \ldots x_{i+1})).$$

Clearly, the first-order part of $\phi_{\mathcal{M}}$ is in GF_1, $\mathcal{M} \models \phi$ iff $\mathcal{M}' \models \phi_{\mathcal{M}}$, and the size of $\phi_{\mathcal{M}}$ is $O(l^2 n)$.

Theorem 3. *1. The combined complexity of MX for GF_k, $k \ge 1$ is NEXP-complete;*
2. MX for GF_k, $k \ge 2$, captures NP;
3. The finite satisfiability problem for GF_k, $k \ge 2$, is undecidable.

Proof. 1. follows from Lemma 2 and the fact that the combined complexity of MX for FO is in NEXP;
2. follows from Lemma 1 and the fact that MX for FO captures NP;
3. By the proof of Lemma 1, finite satisfiability for FO can be reduced to that for GF_2.

Lemma 3 ([19]). *3-SAT can be reduced to MX for a formula $\phi \in RGF_1$.*

Proof. Suppose $\Gamma = \{C_1, \ldots, C_m\}$ is a set of 3-clauses. Let $\mathcal{A}$ be the structure with universe $\{a, \neg a \mid a \in atoms(\Gamma)\}$ such that $\mathcal{A}$ interprets $Clause$ as the set of clauses in Γ and interprets $Complements$ as the set of complementary literals. Let ϕ be

$$\forall x \forall y \forall z (Clause(x, y, z) \supset True(x) \vee True(y) \vee True(z))$$
$$\wedge \forall x \forall y (Complements(x, y) \supset (True(x) \equiv \neg True(y))).$$

Clearly, $\phi \in \text{RGF}_1$, and Γ is satisfiable iff $\mathcal{A}$ can be expanded to a model of ϕ.

We quote the following result concerning polynomial-time grounding of RGF_k sentences:

Lemma 4 ([20]). *There is an algorithm that, given a structure $\mathcal{A}$ and a RGF_k sentence ϕ, constructs in $O(l^2 n^k)$ time a propositional formula ψ such that $\mathcal{A}$ can be expanded to a model of ϕ iff ψ is satisfiable, where l is the size of ϕ, and n the size of $\mathcal{A}$.*

Theorem 4. *(1) The combined complexity of MX for RGF_k is NP-complete. (2) The data complexity of MX for GF_1 and RGF_k is NP-complete. (3) MX for RGF_k and hence also FO^k does not capture NP.*

Proof. (1) follows from Lemmas 4 and 3. (2) follows from Lemma 3 and that the data complexity of MX for FO is in NP. (3): Since SAT can be decided in nondeterministic $O(n^2)$ time, by Lemma 4, MX for RGF_k can be decided in nondeterministic $O(n^{2k})$ time. By Cook's NTIME hierarchy theorem [3], for any $i > 2k$, there is a problem that can be solved in nondeterministic $O(n^i)$ time but not nondeterministic $O(n^{i-1})$ time. Thus there are infinitely many problems in NP that cannot be expressed by MX for RGF_k.

5 Complexity of ID-Logic

One limitation of first-order logic as a practical language is its lack of mechanism to describe recursion or induction. Therefore, a natural way to extend first-order logic is by adding inductive definitions. One such approach, called ID-logic, is presented in [4]. ID-logic is an extention of classical logic in which (non-monotone) definitions can appear as atomic formulae. FO(ID) is the extension of FO with such definitions.

Definition 5. *An* inductive definition *Δ is a set of rules of the form $\forall \bar{x}(X(\bar{t}) \leftarrow \phi)$ where X is a predicate symbol of arity r, $\bar{x}$ is a tuple of object variables, $\bar{t}$ a tuple of object variables of length r, ϕ is an arbitrary first-order formula.*

The semantics of the logic is defined by the standard satisfaction recursion of classical logic, augmented with one additional rule saying that a valuation I satifies a definition D if it is the 2-valued well-founded model of this definition. While the well-founded semantics can be defined in several ways, we use a definition where one constructs a sequence $(I^{\xi}, J^{\xi})_{\xi \geq o}$ of approximations (under- and over-estimates) of the intended model of the definition Δ extending I_o, which is a structure providing interpretations to open (i.e., those not appearing in the heads of the rules) symbols of Δ (see [4] for details). Each new element I^{ξ} is obtained by what we call a "double step" in the proof below, i.e., the square of the so-called stable operator ST_{Δ}. This operator is in tern is equivalent to a least fixpoint, as will be seen in the proof. The sequence $(I^{\xi}, J^{\xi})_{\xi \geq o}$ has a limit (I, J), where I and J are the least (respectively, the greatest) fixpoints of ST^2_{Δ}. A good (total) definition is such that $I = J$, otherwise the entire theory does not have a model. Here, we introduce a formula $CONS_{\Delta}$ which expresses this consistency (totality) criterion, but using least fixpoints only.

Example 2. Consider formula $\Delta_{even} \wedge \forall x(E(x) \vee E(s(x)))$, where

$$\Delta_{even} \equiv \left\{ \begin{array}{c} E(x) \leftarrow x = 0 \\ E(s(s(x))) \leftarrow E(x) \wedge \neg E(s(x)) \end{array} \right\}.$$

This formula states that every number is either even or odd. Definition Δ_{even} is one of possible definitions of even numbers, which is total on natural numbers, but not on integers.

5.1 Equivalence between FO(ID) and FO(LFP)

In this section, we study a FO fragment of ID-logic, FO(ID). We show that the expressive power of FO(ID) is equivalent, over finite structures, to that of FO(LFP). This result allows us to transfer known complexity results for FO(LFP) to FO(ID).

Lemma 5. *FO(ID) $\subseteq$ FO(LFP).*

Proof. We start by showing how to evaluate a single definition Δ (which can have multiple defined predicates). If a definition is not total on I_0, we need to ensure that there is no model for the whole theory. Then we can use evaluated definitions to construct a $FO(LFP)$ formula corresponding to the original FO(ID) formula.

A definition Δ for a given initialization of open predicates from I_0 is evaluated as follows.

Replace in Δ all negative occurrences of X_i by X_i' for new variables X_i'. For example, a rule $\forall \bar{x}(X_i(\bar{t}(\bar{x})) \leftarrow \neg X_j(\bar{t}'(\bar{x})))$ becomes replaced with $\forall \bar{x}(X_i(\bar{t}(\bar{x})) \leftarrow \neg X_j'(\bar{t}'(\bar{x})))$ Let ϕ be a formula encoding Δ after this substitution.

Computing one (double) step of the evaluation (a step corresponding to evaluating ϕ with I and then J giving the values for negated literals) becomes

$$\psi \equiv LFP_{\bar{x},\bar{X}} \phi([LFP_{\bar{x},\bar{X}} \phi]^j / X_j'), \tag{*}$$

by semantics of FO(ID). Here fixpoints are simultaneous on all X_i and the notation $[LFP_{\bar{x},\bar{X}}\phi]^j/X'_j$ means replacing the occurrences of X'_j in ϕ with the fixpoint of X_j in the simultaneous least fixed point of ϕ over all $\bar{X}$.

To simplify the presentation assume, using the fact that simultaneous LFP is equivalent to LFP, that a variable X encodes all variables X_i. Then, the simultaneous LFPs from ψ become just LFPs.

Let Y be a variable encoding the fixpoint of X after the double step $(*)$. This variable is used to initialize X'_i before the next double step. Since after each step ψ the variable Y contains the partial truth assignments on structure I after the ith (double) step of the evaluation procedure, Y is monotone. Therefore, there exists a fixpoint of Y defined by ψ, and it is the least fixed point. Therefore, the formula

$$\Psi_\Delta(\bar{u}) \equiv [LFP_{\bar{y},Y}\psi(Y)]\bar{u}$$

computes the values of the defined predicates in ϕ whenever the fixpoint exists. This is also true when Y is treated as a list of predicates $X_1 \dots X_k$ being defined in Δ, in which case LFP in Ψ_Δ is a simultaneous fixed point.

It is possible, though, that the value computed using the upper bound estimation (the innermost LFP of the double step $(*)$) is different from the outer LFP in the double step. If this is the case, then the following formula is false:

$$CONS_\Delta \equiv \forall \bar{z}([LFP_{\bar{y},Y}\psi(Y)]\bar{z} \leftrightarrow LFP_{\bar{x},\bar{X}}\psi(\bar{x}, LFP_{\bar{y},Y}\psi(Y)/X'_i))[\bar{z}]$$

Suppose now that the FO(ID) theory is defined by a formula with multiple definitions. Let ϕ' be a first-order formula with occurrences of definitions $\Delta_1 \dots \Delta_m$ for some m. To simplify the presentation, view each definition as defining one predicate P_i. If the fixpoint of Δ_i exists, then $\forall \bar{x} P_i(\bar{x}) \leftrightarrow \Psi_{\Delta_i}(\bar{x})$, so occurrences of P_i in ϕ' can be treated as occurrences of Ψ_{Δ_i}. From the point of view of evaluation, it is more efficient to compute $P_i \equiv \Psi_{\Delta_i}$ and then refer just to P_i.

Finally, ϕ' is converted to a formula

$$\Phi \equiv \bigwedge_{i=1}^{m} CONS_{\Delta_i} \wedge \phi'((\forall \bar{x}(P_i(\bar{x}) \leftrightarrow \Psi_{\Delta_i}(\bar{x})))/\Delta_i)$$

That is, Φ is a conjunction of two parts: the conjunction of consistency formulas ensures that all definitions were total, and ϕ' remains the same except all definitions are replaced by the FO(LFP) formulas computing them.

The resulting formula is in FO(LFP).

Example 3. Recall the formula from Example 2 stating that every number is either even or odd. The following describes a construction of an equivalent FO(LFP) formula.

A formula corresponding to Δ_{even} becomes, after replacing $\neg E$ with $\neg E'$,

$$(\phi_E(x, E, E') \equiv (\exists y(x = y \wedge y = 0)) \vee (\exists y(x = s(s(y)) \wedge E(y) \wedge \neg E'(s(y)))).$$

Define $\psi_E(z, E') \equiv [LFP_{x,E}\phi_E(x, E, LFP_{E,x}\phi_E(x, E, E')))]z$. This computes one iteration of the stable operator ST^2_Δ.

Now, $\Psi_\Delta \equiv LFP_{z,E'}\psi_E(z, E')$. Consistency is checked by $\forall u \Psi_\Delta(u) \leftrightarrow [LFP_{x,E}\psi_E(x, E, \Psi_\Delta)]u$. Now, the final formula becomes

$$(\forall u \Psi_\Delta(u) \leftrightarrow [LFP_{x,E}\psi_E(x, E, \Psi_\Delta)]u) \wedge (\forall x(P(x) \leftrightarrow \Psi_\Delta(x)) \wedge (P(x) \vee P(s(X))).$$

Here, the first conjunct checks that the definition "makes sense", otherwise the formula does not have a model, the second part defines a particular variable $P(x)$ to represent the defined E, and the last part uses P outside of the definition Δ_E.

Lemma 6. *FO(LFP) $\subseteq$ FO(ID)*

Proof. By Theorem 9.4.2 of [5], every FO(LFP) formula is equivalent to one of the form $\forall u[LFP_{\bar{z},Z}\psi]\tilde{u}$, where $\psi \in \Delta_2$, which can be written as an FO(ID) formula $\{Z(\bar{z}) \leftarrow \psi\}$.

Therefore, the following holds:

Theorem 5. *The complexity of model checking for ID-logic and FO(LFP) coincide over finite structures.*

Corollary 1. *The combined complexity of the model checking for FO(ID) is complete for EXP; the expression complexity for FO(ID) is complete for P; $FO(ID)$ captures P over successor structures.*

5.2 Complexity of MX for FO(ID)

Intuitively, adding polynomial-time computable predicates to an NP predicate should not add expressive power, suggesting that both combined and data complexities of MX for FO(ID) (or, equivalently, FO(LFP)) should coincide with the those for FO without inductive definitions or least fixed points.

Theorem 6. *The combined complexity of MX for FO(ID) is NEXP-complete; The data complexity for MX of FO(ID) is NP-complete, and NP is captured by existential second-order with inductive definitions $\exists$SO(ID).*

Proof. We know from Theorem 1 that data complexity for MX problem is hard for NP and combined complexity hard for NEXP. Therefore, it is sufficient to show membership of MX in these classes.

The evaluation algorithm proceeds as follows. Use non-determinism to guess the expansion predicates. Now the problem is reduced to evaluating the FO(ID) formula on an expanded structure. This can be done in polynomial time of the size of the structure when formula is fixed (by [13,25,18]) and in exponential time when the formula is a part of the input by [25]. In the second case, the size of the expansion predicates can be exponential in the size of the structure (since their arity is not constant), but in NEXP we can guess exponential-size certificates.

Fragments of FO(ID) with Polytime MX. Recall that MX for universal Horn formulae was P-complete. We would like to add inductive definitions to such formulae so that the complexity of the resulting logic is still in P. The following example shows that allowing unrestricted use of expansion predicates in the inductive definitions makes it possible to encode NP-complete problems.

Example 4. The classical example of 3-colourability is representable as a formula with three expansion predicates R, B, G, encoding colours:

$$\forall v, w(R(v) \vee B(v) \vee G(v)) \wedge \bigwedge_{Q \in R,G,B} (\neg Q(v) \vee \neg Q(w) \vee \neg E(v,w)).$$

The only part of this formula which is not Horn is the first disjunction. It can be replaced by the inductive definition with a rule $X(i) \leftarrow Q(i)$ for every colour Q. Now, the first disjunction is equivalent to $\forall v X(v)$. Note that the definition of FO(ID) requires that such X be minimal, therefore, this does not introduce spurious positives.

However, if we disallow any occurrences of the expansion predicates in inductive definitions, P-completeness is preserved.

Lemma 7. *Adding inductive definitions to universal Horn formulae defined on page 450 preserves data complexity of MX to be P-complete, when expansion predicates do not occur in inductive definitions.*

Proof. By theorem 2, data complexity of MX for universal Horn formulae is P-complete. Therefore, a polytime algorithm for MX of universal Horn formulae can first evaluate all inductive definitions, and then run Grädel's algorithm for evaluating existential second-order Horn formulae replacing all defined predicates by their computed values.

We can also add expansion predicates in a restricted fashion. First, all expansion predicates occurring in definitions have to be defined (i.e, occur in a head of a rule of some definition). Second, such predicates cannot be defined in terms of each other unless they are in the same definition. Third, the definitions can only occur as conjunction to the rest of the formula. Intuitively, in this case, if expansion predicates in the body of a definition are either given values already, or are being defined in that definition, then the definition can be evaluated. The intuition here is similar to the intuition of RGF_k.

Definition 6. *Let $\{\bar{X}_1, \ldots, \bar{X}_k\}$ be all expansion predicates occurring in a first-order formula ϕ. Then ϕ is in* RFO(ID) *if (1) for each $\bar{X}_i$ there is a definition Δ_i defining all predicates in $\bar{X}_i$, and Δ_i is conjuncted with the rest of the formula. (2) The only expansion predicates allowed in the body of Δ_i are among $\bar{X}_1, \ldots, \bar{X}_{i-1}$; the body of Δ_1 contains no expansion predicates.*

More generally, ϕ is in RuHorn(ID) if there are also expansion predicates $\bar{P}$ which do not occur in the definitions and with all definitions removed, ϕ is universal Horn with respect to $\bar{P}$.

Theorem 7. *MX for RFO(ID) is P-complete.*

Corollary 2. *MX for RuHorn(ID) is P-complete.*

6 Conclusion

We presented complexity results for model expansion for a number of logics closely related to FO. For providing a foundation for practical constraint languages, future work needs to consider similar problems in the presence of arithmetic and other interpreted function symbols. For some steps in this direction, see [23,22].

We know that GF(ID) (guarded logic with inductive definitions) coincides with μGF on total structures; however, the question is still open whether they coincide everywhere, as FO(ID) and FO(LFP) do. The problem lies in a different treatment of inductive definitions that are not total.

Acknowledgments

The authors are grateful to the Natural Sciences and Engineering Council of Canada and to the Pacific Institute for Mathematical Sciences for financial support.

References

1. Andréka, H., van Benthem, J., Németi, I.: Modal languages and bounded fragments of predicate logic. Journal of Philosophical Logic 49(3), 217–274 (1998)
2. Barrington, D.M., Immerman, N., Straubing, H.: On uniformity within NC^1. Journal of Computer and System Sciences 41(3), 274–306 (1990)
3. Cook, S.A.: A hierarchy for nondeterministic time complexity. Journal of Computer and System Sciences 7(4), 343–353 (1973)
4. Denecker, M., Ternovska, E.: A logic of non-monotone inductive definitions. ACM transactions on computational logic (TOCL) 9(2), 1–52 (2008)
5. Ebbinghaus, H.D., Flum, J.: Finite model theory. Springer, Heidelberg (1995)
6. Fagin, R.: Generalized first-order spectra and polynomial-time recognizable sets. In: Complexity of computation, SIAM-AMC, vol. 7, pp. 43–73 (1974)
7. Gottlob, G., Leone, N., Scarcello, F.: Robbers, marshals, and guards: game theoretic and logical characterizations of hypertree width. In: Twentieth ACM SIGMOD-SIGACT-SIGART Symposium on Principles of Database Systems (PODS 2001), pp. 195–206 (2001)
8. Grädel, E.: Capturing Complexity Classes by Fragments of Second Order Logic. Theoretical Computer Science 101, 35–57 (1992)
9. Grädel, E.: On the restraining power of guards. Journal of Symbolic Logic 64, 1719–1742 (1999)
10. Grädel, E., Kolaitis, P.G., Vardi, M.Y.: On the decision problem for two-variable first-order logic. Bulletin of Symbolic Logic 3, 53–69 (1997)
11. Grädel, E., Otto, M.: On logics with two variables. Theoretical Computer Science 224, 73–113 (1999)
12. Grädel, E., Walukiewicz, I.: Guarded fixed point logic. In: Fourteenth Annual IEEE Symposium on Logic in Computer Science (LICS 1999), pp. 45–55 (1999)
13. Immerman, N.: Relational queries computable in polytime. In: Fourteenth Annual ACM Symposium on Theory of Computing (STOC 1982), pp. 147–152 (1982)
14. Immerman, N.: Descriptive complexity. Springer, New York (1999)
15. Jurdzinski, M.: Deciding the winner in parity games is in UP $\cap$ co-UP. Information Processing Letters 69, 119–124 (1998)

16. Libkin, L.: Elements of Finite Model Theory. Springer, Heidelberg (2004)
17. Liu, Y., Levesque, H.J.: A tractability result for reasoning with incomplete first-order knowledge bases. In: 18th Int. Joint Conf. on Artif. Intell. (IJCAI 2003), pp. 83–88 (2003)
18. Livchak, A.: Languages for polynomial-time queries. In: Computer-based modeling and optimization of heat-power and electrochemical objects, p. 41 (1982)
19. Mitchell, D., Ternovska, E.: A framework for representing and solving NP search problems. In: 20th National Conf. on Artif. Intell. (AAAI), pp. 430–435 (2005)
20. Patterson, M., Liu, Y., Ternovska, E., Gupta, A.: Grounding for model expansion in k-guarded formulas with inductive definitions. In: 22nd International Joint Conference on Artificial Intelligence, IJCAI 2007 (2007)
21. Stockmeyer, L.: The Complexity of Decision Problems in Automata Theory. Ph.D. thesis, MIT (1974)
22. Tasharrofi, S., Ternovska, E.: Capturing NP for search problems with built-in arithmetic. In: Fermüller, C., Voronkov, A. (eds.) LPAR-17. LNCS, vol. 6397, Springer, Heidelberg (2010)
23. Ternovska, E., Mitchell, D.: Declarative programming of search problems with built-in arithmetic. In: 21st International Joint Conference on Artificial Intelligence, IJCAI 2009 (2009)
24. Trahtenbrot, B.: The impossibility of an algorithm for the decision problem for finite domains. Doklady Academii Nauk SSSR 70, 569–572 (1950) (in Russian)
25. Vardi, M.Y.: The complexity of relational query languages. In: Fourteenth Annual ACM Symposium on Theory of Computing (STOC 1982), pp. 137–146 (1982)
26. Vardi, M.Y.: On the complexity of bounded-variable queries. In: Fourteenth ACM SIGACT-SIGMOD-SIGART Symposium on Principles of Database Systems (PODS 1995), pp. 266–276 (1995)

Labelled Unit Superposition Calculi for Instantiation-Based Reasoning

Konstantin Korovin* and Christoph Sticksel

School of Computer Science
The University of Manchester
{korovin,sticksel}@cs.man.ac.uk

Abstract. The Inst-Gen-Eq method is an instantiation-based calculus which is complete for first-order clause logic modulo equality. Its distinctive feature is that it combines first-order reasoning with efficient ground satisfiability checking which is delegated in a modular way to any state-of-the-art ground SMT solver. The first-order reasoning modulo equality employs a superposition-style calculus which generates the instances needed by the ground solver to refine a model of a ground abstraction or to witness unsatisfiability.

In this paper we present and compare different labelling mechanisms in the unit superposition calculus that facilitates finding the necessary instances. We demonstrate and evaluate how different label structures such as sets, AND/OR trees and OBDDs affect the interplay between the proof procedure and blocking mechanisms for redundancy elimination.

1 Introduction

Instantiation-based methods (IMs) are a class of calculi for first-order clausal logic. The common idea is to instantiate clauses in a smart way and to employ efficient propositional or more general ground reasoning methods in order to prove unsatisfiability or to find a model. There is considerable current interest in instantiation-based methods (see [1,9,6]), motivated by their attractive features, some of which are complementary to other contemporary methods. Among other important properties, all known IMs naturally decide the first-order logic fragment of effectively propositional logic (EPR), also called Bernays-Schönfinkel class, which has applications in areas as diverse as bounded model checking ([11]), logic programming ([3]) and knowledge representation ([5]).

In many applications efficient equational reasoning is indispensable. While theoretical foundations of equational reasoning in several instantiation-based methods have been laid already some time ago ([8,4,2]), due to a number of challenging issues only now practical implementations of the calculi appear.

In this paper we take up equational reasoning in the Inst-Gen-Eq calculus as presented in [4]. One of the distinctive features of the Inst-Gen method is a modular combination of ground reasoning based on any off-the-shelf SMT solver with superposition style first-order reasoning. A major practical challenge in this approach is efficient extraction of relevant substitutions from superposition proofs, which are used for instance

* Supported by the Royal Society.

C. Fermüller and A. Voronkov (Eds.): LPAR-17, LNCS 6397, pp. 459–473, 2010.

generation. Here we need to explore potentially all non-redundant superposition proofs of the contradiction, extract relevant substitutions and efficiently propagate redundancy elimination from instantiation into superposition derivations.

In this paper we address this challenge by introducing a labelled unit superposition calculus. Labels are used to collect relevant substitutions during superposition derivations and facilitate efficient instance generation. Non-trivial issues arise when we merge several superposition derivations which is done by a new merging rule. Merging allows to share several derivations of the same literal which avoids repeated work and can be used to strengthen redundancy elimination.

We introduce and investigate different label structures based on sets, AND/OR trees and OBDDs and highlight how the label structure can be exploited for redundancy elimination. Finally we have implemented these approaches and compared their performance on the TPTP library.

2 The Inst-Gen Method Modulo Equality

We consider first-order clausal logic with equality. Given a set of first-order clauses S we first form its ground abstraction $S\bot$ by mapping all variables to the same ground term, conventionally denoted $\bot$. Overloading the notation, we use $\bot$ also for the substitution that maps all variables to the ground term $\bot$. If the ground abstraction $S\bot$ is unsatisfiable (modulo equality), the original set S is also unsatisfiable and the procedure can terminate. Otherwise, there is a model $I_\bot$ of the ground abstraction $S\bot$ and the first-order instantiation process is guided by means of a selection function sel based on $I_\bot$. The selection function assigns to each first-order clause C in S exactly one literal $\mathrm{sel}(C) = L$ from C such that $I_\bot \models L\bot$. At least one such literal always exists as the ground abstraction of the clause is true in the model $I_\bot$.

If the set of selected (not necessarily ground) literals, seen as unit clauses, is satisfiable in first-order logic with equality, a model for the clause set S exists and it has thus been proved satisfiable. Otherwise, there is a subset of the selected literals which is inconsistent. We instantiate the clauses these literals are selected in such that the inconsistency can already be witnessed in the ground abstraction. Thus the ground model has to be refined in order to resolve the inconsistency. For non-equational literals it suffices to search for unifiable complementary literal pairs. In the presence of equations, we apply the unit superposition calculus in order to find inconsistent literals and to obtain instantiating substitutions.

Definition 1 (Unit Superposition)

$$\frac{l \simeq r \qquad s[l'] \simeq t}{(s[r] \simeq t)\sigma}\,(\sigma) \qquad\qquad \frac{l \simeq r \qquad s[l'] \not\simeq t}{(s[r] \not\simeq t)\sigma}\,(\sigma) \qquad\qquad \frac{l \not\simeq r}{\square}\,(\sigma)$$

(i) $\sigma = \mathrm{mgu}(l, l')$, *(ii)* l' *is not a variable, (iii)* $l\sigma\rho \succ r\sigma\rho$ *and (iv)* $s[l']\sigma\rho \succ t\sigma\rho$ *for some grounding substitution* ρ $\qquad \sigma = \mathrm{mgu}(l, r)$

The unit superposition calculus is similar to the standard superposition calculus, see, e.g., [10]. For simplicity and without loss of generality we assume pure equational logic where all atoms are equations. Different literals are made variable-disjoint and as we only have literals, i.e. unit clauses, we reduce the inference rules to the ones above.

A *proof* of the contradiction, denoted $\square$, is a tree where each leaf is a selected literal in a clause, inner nodes are obtained by applying inference rules to the parent nodes and the root is the contradiction $\square$. Every proof of a contradiction shows that the literals at the leaves are inconsistent in first-order and the clauses these literals are selected in have to be instantiated in a way that the ground solver can witness the inconsistency. Then the model of the ground abstraction has to be refined, possibly leading to further conflicts or making the ground abstraction unsatisfiable. If no contradiction can be proved from the set of selected literals, the first-order clause set is satisfiable. Let us note that unlike in standard superposition where one proof of the contradiction suffices, we need to explore all non-redundant proofs by unit superposition. Different proofs generate different clause instances and potentially all of them are necessary to witness unsatisfiability of the given set of clauses.

If in the unit superposition calculus the premises $l \simeq r$ and $s[l'] \simeq t$ can be inferred to $(s[r] \simeq t)\sigma$, then the ground abstraction $(s[r] \simeq t)\sigma\bot$ of the conclusion follows (modulo equality) from the ground abstractions of the premises instantiated with the mgu σ, namely $(l \simeq r)\sigma\bot$ and $(s[l'] \simeq t)\sigma\bot$. The same argument holds for the disequation $s[l'] \not\simeq t$. Further, if $l \not\simeq r$ can be inferred to the contradiction $\square$ using σ, then the ground abstraction $(l \not\simeq r)\sigma\bot$ is also contradictory. By induction over the inferences in a proof of the contradiction we can show that there are *relevant substitutions* to the leaf literals such that the ground abstractions of the instantiated literals are contradictory.

The following extraction of relevant instances from proofs of the contradiction has been described and proved complete in [4]. For each leaf literal in a proof its relevant substitution is obtained by composing the substitutions from inferences along the branch. The set of *relevant instances* of a unit superposition proof is $\{C_1\theta_1, \ldots, C_n\theta_n\}$ where $\theta_1, \ldots, \theta_n$ are the relevant substitutions to the leaf literals and $C_1, \ldots, C_n$ are clauses the leaf literals are selected in. In order to witness the inconsistency in the ground abstraction and to force a refinement of the ground model, we add the relevant instances to the original clause set and form their ground abstractions.

However, in practice this approach of extracting substitutions has some shortcomings that we will discuss in this paper along with more robust mechanisms to obtain relevant instances. Let us demonstrate the Inst-Gen-Eq method by way of an example and point out the problems that we will address in the following sections.

Example 1. Consider the following unsatisfiable set of clauses.

$f(x, y) \simeq f(y, x)$	(1)	$f(a, b) \simeq g(c)$	(3)
$f(u, v) \not\simeq g(z) \vee u \simeq z$	(2)	$a \not\simeq b$	(4)

The ground abstractions of clauses (1) and (2) are $f(\bot, \bot) \simeq f(\bot, \bot)$ and $f(\bot, \bot) \not\simeq g(\bot) \vee \bot \simeq \bot$, respectively. Clauses (3) and (4) are ground and therefore identical to their ground abstractions. The ground abstractions of the first literals in each clause are satisfiable and can therefore be selected. With the following unit superposition proof we find the selected literals in clauses (2) and (3) to be inconsistent in first order.

$$\cfrac{\cfrac{\overset{(3)}{f(a,b) \simeq g(c)} \qquad \overset{(2)}{f(u,v) \not\simeq g(z)}}{g(c) \not\simeq g(z)}\ [a/u, b/v]}{\square}\ [c/z] \tag{$*$}$$

In order to make the inconsistency visible in the ground abstraction, we add an instance of clause (2) with the substitution $[a/u, b/v, c/z]$ obtained by composing the two substitutions in the proof. No substitution is applied to (3) because it is already ground.

$$f(a,b) \not\simeq g(c) \ \vee \ a \simeq c \tag{5}$$

We can prove another inconsistency in the set of selected literals.

$$\cfrac{\cfrac{\overset{(3)}{f(a,b) \simeq g(c)} \qquad \cfrac{\overset{(1)}{f(x,y) \simeq f(y,x)} \qquad \overset{(2)}{f(u,v) \not\simeq g(z)}}{f(v,u) \not\simeq g(z)}\ [u/x, v/y]}{g(c) \not\simeq g(z)}\ [a/v, b/u]}{\square}\ [c/z] \tag{$\dagger$}$$

After instantiating clauses (1) and (2) at the leaves of the proof with respective substitutions of $[b/x, a/y]$ and $[b/u, a/v, c/z]$ the ground abstraction consisting of clauses (3)-(7) becomes unsatisfiable. Again, the ground clause (3) cannot be instantiated.

$$f(b,a) \simeq f(a,b) \tag{6}$$

$$f(b,a) \not\simeq g(c) \ \vee \ b \simeq c \tag{7}$$

The main challenge we face in a practical implementation of the unit superposition calculus is the treatment of literal variants. Obviously, it is desirable to identify all literal variants in order to make the calculus less prolific and to avoid trivial non-termination. If all literal variants were treated separately, a commutativity axiom like $f(x,y) \simeq f(y,x)$ could infer an infinite number of variants of the literal $f(u,v) \not\simeq g(z)$ since we consider all literals to be variable disjoint.

On the other hand, the literal $f(u,v) \not\simeq g(z)$ occurs twice in the same branch of the second proof tree ($\dagger$) in Example 1 above. Linking both occurrences of the literal in the proof would collapse the proof tree into a graph with a cycle which is highly inconvenient in an implementation of the calculus. When composing substitutions on a branch of the proof tree, we would need to compose the substitution with itself an unbounded number of times. While in Example 1 the composition of the substitution $[u/x, v/y]$ with itself can only generate a finite number of instances, this is not the case for a substitution like $[f(x)/x]$.

To overcome these problems, we introduce labels for literals in unit superposition where we accumulate composed substitutions from inferences. The relevant instances can then be read off the label of the contradiction, thus obsoleting the need to trace a proof tree. Further, the labels will allow us to treat literal variants initially as disjoint while merging of literals is done in an explicit step that keeps track of literal variants merged in the label. This allows to uniformly treat literal variants in an implementation of the calculus and to include them in the usual heuristics in a given clause algorithm.

3 Set Labelled Unit Superposition

To each literal we attach a label and we consider literals with different labels to be distinct and also distinguish between variants of a literal. However, our calculus provides an explicit inference step to merge two variants of a literal into one with a label that joins both their labels. The labels of conclusions accumulate substitutions from their inferences, in this way eagerly extracting substitutions in a proof. The merging step combines the two proofs of a literal and its variant. Further inference steps are then simultaneously applied to both proofs.

The basic element of any literal label is a *closure* which is a pair of a clause C and a substitution θ, written as $C \cdot \theta$. In the first and simplest structure for labelling literals, a *label* $\mathcal{L}$ is a set of closures $\{C_1 \cdot \theta_1, \ldots, C_n \cdot \theta_n\}$. Given a substitution σ, the *σ-instance* of the label $\mathcal{L}$ is the label $\mathcal{L}\sigma = \{C_1 \cdot \theta_1\sigma, \ldots, C_n \cdot \theta_n\sigma\}$.

Initially, we create for each clause C, where L is the selected literal in C, a labelled literal $\{C \cdot []\}\colon L$ from the clause C and the empty substitution $[]$. We therefore distinguish between literals from different clauses in the beginning.

We modify the inference rules of the unit superposition calculus from Definition 1 to work on set labelled literals and add a merging rule for literals which are variants of each other. Note that the labels are only a mechanism for bookkeeping, they do not occur in the side conditions of the inferences.

Definition 2 (Set Labelled Unit Superposition)

Merging

$$\frac{\mathcal{L}\colon l \simeq r \qquad \mathcal{L}'\colon l' \simeq r'}{\mathcal{L} \cup \mathcal{L}'\sigma\colon l \simeq r}\ (\sigma) \qquad \frac{\mathcal{L}\colon l \not\simeq r \qquad \mathcal{L}'\colon l' \not\simeq r'}{\mathcal{L} \cup \mathcal{L}'\sigma\colon l \not\simeq r}\ (\sigma)$$

where σ is a renaming such that $l'\sigma = l$ and $r'\sigma = r$. The conclusion replaces the two premises.

Superposition

$$\frac{\mathcal{L}\colon l \simeq r \qquad \mathcal{L}'\colon s[l'] \simeq t}{\mathcal{L}\sigma \cup \mathcal{L}'\sigma\colon (s[r] \simeq t)\sigma}\ (\sigma) \qquad \frac{\mathcal{L}\colon l \simeq r \qquad \mathcal{L}'\colon s[l'] \not\simeq t}{\mathcal{L}\sigma \cup \mathcal{L}'\sigma\colon (s[r] \not\simeq t)\sigma}\ (\sigma)$$

where (i) $\sigma = \mathrm{mgu}(l, l')$, (ii) l' is not a variable, (iii) $l\sigma\rho \succ r\sigma\rho$ and (iv) $s[l']\sigma\rho \succ t\rho$ for some grounding substitution ρ.

Equality Resolution

$$\frac{\mathcal{L}\colon (l \not\simeq r)}{\mathcal{L}\sigma\colon \square}\ (\sigma)$$

where $\sigma = \mathrm{mgu}(l, r)$.

Having derived a labelled contradiction, we now do not need to trace a proof tree to obtain the relevant instances. Instead, we can read the clauses to be instantiated and their respective relevant substitutions off the label: the set of *relevant instances* of a set labelled literal $\{C_1 \cdot \theta_1, \ldots, C_n \cdot \theta_n\}$: L is the set $\{C_1\theta_1, \ldots, C_n\theta_n\}$.

Replacing extraction of substitutions from proofs with the labelling approach above preserves completeness of the instantiation procedure if *Inst-fairness* as in Lemma 6 in [4] is upheld. This requires unit superposition (i) to derive the contradiction from certain non-redundant selected literals and (ii) to generate instances such that the conflict on selected literal becomes redundant. We will show that our labelled calculus satisfies these two properties by a simulation argument.[1]

Unlabelled and labelled unit superposition in Definition 1 and Definition 2, respectively, have the same side conditions and the same premises lead to the same conclusion. We can therefore state the following lemma from which (i) follows.

Lemma 1. *Any unlabelled unit superposition derivation can be stepwise simulated by set labelled unit superposition using only superposition and equality resolution.*

The required instances in (ii) are provided by the relevant instances extracted from a proof of the contradiction. We show that the relevant instances of an unlabelled proof of a literal are contained in the relevant instances of a label of the literal in every corresponding labelled proof. We first consider labelled unit superposition without merging and in a second step show that inserting merging inferences is compatible.

Lemma 2. *Let the literal L be derived by unlabelled unit superposition and let the relevant instances extracted from the proof of L be $C_1\theta_1, \ldots, C_n\theta_n$. The stepwise simulation by set labelled unit superposition yields the labelled literal $\mathcal{L}$: L where $\mathcal{L}$ contains the set of closures $\{C_1 \cdot \theta_1, \ldots, C_n \cdot \theta_n\}$.*

To finish the argument we have to include merging inferences which can occur at any step of a labelled unit superposition derivation. The conclusion of a merging inference replaces its premises and renames the literals to make them identical. We therefore must ensure that after merging literals the relevant instances that were in the label of a premise remain in the label of the conclusion.

Lemma 3. *Let L be a literal and let the relevant instances extracted from its proof be $C_1\theta_1, \ldots, C_n\theta_n$. After a merging inference with the labelled literal $\mathcal{L}$: L as the left premise (the right premise, respectively) the label of the conclusion contains the closures $C_1 \cdot \theta_1, \ldots, C_n \cdot \theta_n$ (respectively $C_1 \cdot \theta_1\sigma, \ldots, C_n \cdot \theta_n\sigma$).*

Finally if unit superposition is applied in a fair way, that is every non-redundant inference is drawn eventually, we can state the completeness theorem which is based on results from [4].

Corollary 1. *A fair labelled unit superposition process with instantiation of relevant instances from contradictions yields an Inst-fair saturation process.*

Let us resume our running example, demonstrating the merging inference rule before we point out some disadvantages of set labels and move on to different label structures in the next sections.

[1] For proofs see `http://www.cs.man.ac.uk/~sticksec/LPAR2010-Full.pdf`

Example 2. We draw an inference which corresponds to the first inference in proof (†) in Example 1 from the selected literals in clauses (1) and (2).

$$\frac{\overset{(1)}{\{(1)\cdot[]\}\colon f(x,y)\simeq f(y,x)} \qquad \overset{(2)}{\{(2)\cdot[]\}\colon f(u,v)\not\simeq g(z)}}{\{(1)\cdot[u/x,v/y],(2)\cdot[]\}\colon f(v,u)\not\simeq g(z)}\,[u/x,v/y] \qquad (\dagger')$$

We note that applying the substitution $[u/x, v/y]$ to the closure $(2) \cdot []$ results in the same closure as the variables x and y in the domain of the substitution do not occur in the closure. The conclusion $f(v, u) \not\simeq g(z)$ is a variant of the right premise and we can merge the two literal variants into one which replaces the distinct variants.

$$\frac{\overset{(2)}{\{(2)\cdot[]\}\colon f(u,v)\not\simeq g(z)} \qquad \overset{(\dagger')}{\{(1)\cdot[u/x,v/y],(2)\cdot[]\}\colon f(v,u)\not\simeq g(z)}}{\{(2)\cdot[],(1)\cdot[v/x,u/y],(2)\cdot[v/u,u/v]\}\colon f(u,v)\not\simeq g(z)}\,[v/u,u/v] \qquad (\ddagger)$$

With superposition and equality resolution which are the last steps in both proofs (∗) and (†) in Example 1, we derive the contradiction.

$$\frac{\dfrac{\overset{(3)}{\{(3)\cdot[]\}\colon f(a,b)\simeq g(c)} \qquad \overset{(\ddagger)}{\{(2)\cdot[],(1)\cdot[v/x,u/y],(2)\cdot[v/u,u/v]\}\colon f(u,v)\not\simeq g(z)}}{\{(3)\cdot[],(2)\cdot[a/u,b/v],(1)\cdot[b/x,a/y],(2)\cdot[b/u,a/v]\}\colon g(c)\not\simeq g(z)}\,[a/u,b/v]}{\{(3)\cdot[],(2)\cdot[a/u,b/v,c/z],(1)\cdot[b/x,a/y],(2)\cdot[b/u,a/v,c/z]\}\colon \square}\,[c/z] \qquad (*')$$

The instances of the clauses in the label of the contradiction with their respective substitutions are exactly the instances (5)-(7) in Example 1 and unsatisfiability can be shown on the ground abstraction of clauses (1)-(7).

We can exploit the observation that set labels can become saturated to prove that set labelled unit superposition is a decision procedure for the Bernays-Schönfinkel fragment of first-order clause logic with equality. We first need to introduce some terminology motivated by the usual idea in theorem proving that clauses are equal modulo renaming. We extend this notion to closures and labelled literals in the following ways.

Two closures $C \cdot \theta$ and $C' \cdot \theta'$ are *equivalent up to renaming away* from a set of variables $\mathcal{V}$ if there exists a renaming μ where $\mathrm{rng}(\mu) \cap \mathcal{V} = \emptyset$ such that $C \cdot \theta = C'\mu \cdot \mu^{-1}\theta'\mu$. Intuitively we want the closures to be equal if C and C' as well as $C\theta$ and $C'\theta'$ are equal up to renaming, therefore we have to "pull out" the renaming μ from the substitution θ'. Further, we want to make the clauses variable-disjoint from $\mathcal{V}$, which becomes obvious in the next step.

For a labelled literal $\mathcal{L}\colon L$ we do not distinguish closures in $\mathcal{L}$ equivalent up to renaming away from $\mathrm{var}(L)$. Clauses in the label $\mathcal{L}$ are made variable-disjoint from L and without loss of generality we assume that for a closure $C \cdot \theta$ it is $\mathrm{dom}(\theta) \subseteq \mathrm{var}(C)$.

We say that a set of closures $\mathcal{S}$ is *equivalent up to renaming away* from a set of variables $\mathcal{V}$ to a set of closures $\mathcal{S}'$ if for every closure in $\mathcal{S}$ there is a closure equivalent up to renaming away from $\mathcal{V}$ in $\mathcal{S}'$ and vice versa.

Finally, two labelled literals $\mathcal{L}\colon L$ and $\mathcal{L}'\colon L'$ are *equivalent up to renaming* if there is a renaming ρ such that $L = L'\rho$ and $\mathcal{L}$ is equivalent to $\mathcal{L}'\rho$ up to renaming away from $\mathrm{var}(L)$. We then do not distinguish between labelled literals equivalent up to renaming.

Theorem 1. *Inst-Gen-Eq with set labelled unit superposition is a decision procedure for the Bernays-Schönfinkel fragment of first-order logic with equality.*

Proof. There is only a finite number of labelled literals that are not equivalent up to renaming and thus only a finite number of relevant instances from labels of contradictions. The set labelled unit superposition calculus can therefore derive only a finite number of distinct set labelled literals.

As discussed, set labels make available the relevant instances directly, thus obsoleting the need to trace a proof tree. The proof of a literal cannot be reconstructed from its label as the union of labels in merging and superposition inferences loses the proof structure. However, the relevant instances are all that is needed to witness the inconsistency of the selection in the ground abstraction. Further, the merging inference can combine several proofs with their common parts factored out in the union of the labels.

4 Redundancy Elimination and Selection Changes

Although set labels are a concise and powerful enough mechanism in many practical cases, they show a weakness when we consider redundancy that occurs in the incremental process of instantiation. Set labels collect clauses at the leaves of proofs and accumulate respective relevant substitutions. Merging inferences combine superposition proofs and the conclusion contains closures from several proofs. When a leaf clause becomes redundant with the accumulated relevant substitution, every proof with the clause at a leaf is redundant and all leaf clauses in this proof can be eliminated. However, in a set label we cannot separate out all closures corresponding to the redundant proof from a set label since the structure is lost when two proofs are merged.

Example 3. Let us assume that the unlabelled unit superposition proof (†) in Example 1 becomes redundant due to the accumulated substitution applied to (2).[2] Let us further assume proof $(*)$ is not redundant. In the labelled unit superposition calculus in Example 2, both proofs were merged and we had $\{(3) \cdot [], (2) \cdot [a/u, b/v, c/z], (1) \cdot [b/x, a/y], (2) \cdot [b/u, a/v, c/z]\}$ as the label of the contradiction.

We would obtain the set label $\{(2) \cdot [b/u, a/v, c/z], (1) \cdot [b/x, a/y], (3) \cdot []\}$ from the redundant proof (†) and we want to eliminate these redundant closures from the set label of the merged proofs. However, the set label from the non-redundant proof $(*)$ is $\{(3) \cdot [], (2) \cdot [a/u, b/v, c/z]\}$ and we have to retain these closures.

As the information about the proof structure cannot be recovered from a set label, we cannot eliminate all closures from the a set label. In particular, we would need to know that the proofs overlap on closure $(3) \cdot []$ and not on $(1) \cdot [b/x, a/y]$.

A similar problem arises from changes in the selection function. The model of the ground abstraction may change in a way that a different literal has to be selected in a clause than before. In that case, all proofs with the previously selected literal at a leaf should be eliminated. Again, we want to remove a subset of the clauses in the label of a literal and it is not possible to determine if a clause has to be kept in the label as it may well be from the label of a non-redundant proof that was merged.

---

[2] See `http://www.cs.man.ac.uk/~sticksec/LPAR2010-Full.pdf` for an extended example with concrete redundancy.

The cause of the problem is that we use the set union for combining labels in both the merging inference and in the superposition inference. In the next section we will present a different label structure that preserves the shape of proofs by using two different operations in merging and superposition.

Let us finally note that set labels are still a useful sound and complete mechanism. Unit superposition with set labels merely generates more instances of clauses than strictly necessary while adding these instances does not harm soundness nor completeness. An instance of a clause is a sound consequence of the clause. Although we cannot determine the full subset to be eliminated from a label, we can safely remove each clause from a label which has become redundant with its substitution or where the selection has changed. In Section 7 we will evaluate an implementation of set labels with this restricted elimination against the more powerful elimination in the next section.

5 Tree Labelled Unit Superposition

In order to eliminate redundancy in a labelled unit superposition calculus as described above, we need to preserve a certain Boolean structure in the label. To this end we can regard a closure $C \cdot \theta$ as a propositional variable. A merging inference corresponds to a disjunction and a superposition to a conjunction of labels. Eliminating parts of a label then means assigning false to propositional variables in the tree where the corresponding closures have become redundant and simplifying the Boolean structure.

Let us write the disjunction of two labels as $\mathcal{T}_1 \sqcup \mathcal{T}_2$ and the conjunction of two labels as $\mathcal{T}_1 \sqcap \mathcal{T}_2$. A tree label is then either a closure $C \cdot \theta$, a conjunction $\bigsqcap_{i=1}^{n} \mathcal{T}_i$ or a disjunction $\bigsqcup_{i=1}^{n} \mathcal{T}_i$ of n tree labels $\mathcal{T}_1, \ldots, \mathcal{T}_n$. This structure is isomorphic to an AND/OR tree where all non-leaf nodes are either labelled as AND nodes or OR nodes. AND and OR nodes alternate on each level of the tree such that AND nodes only have OR nodes as successors and vice versa for OR nodes. We call this label a tree label.

Definition 3. *A* tree label *is an AND/OR tree where each leaf is a closure $C \cdot \theta$. The* σ-instance *of a tree label $\mathcal{T}$ is the AND/OR tree $\mathcal{T}$ with the substitution σ applied at each leaf such that $C \cdot \theta$ becomes $C \cdot \theta\sigma$.*

In order to eliminate from a tree label a closure that has become redundant, we assign false to the propositional variable and simplify the tree with Boolean operations.

Definition 4. *The $C \cdot \theta$*-restriction *$\mathcal{T}|_{C \cdot \theta}$ of an AND/OR tree $\mathcal{T}$ is the tree obtained by replacing every occurrence of $C \cdot \theta$ in $\mathcal{T}$ with the constant* false *and recursively simplifying the tree using the rules (i)* false $\sqcup\, \mathcal{U} \rightarrow \mathcal{U}$ *and (ii)* false $\sqcap\, \mathcal{U} \rightarrow$ false.

The strength of tree labels when compared to set labels is the precise elimination of redundancy by restriction. If the closure $C \cdot \theta$ has become redundant, then we can simplify the tree label $C \cdot \theta \sqcup \mathcal{T}$ to $\mathcal{T}$ and the label $C \cdot \theta \sqcap \mathcal{T}$ to the empty label. Literals with the latter label are redundant and can be discarded.

We now define a unit superposition calculus with different operators to combine labels in the merging and the superposition inference, namely $\sqcup$ and $\sqcap$, respectively.

Definition 5 (Tree Labelled Unit Superposition)

Restriction

$$\frac{\mathcal{T} : L}{\mathcal{T}|_{C \cdot \theta} : L}$$

where $C \cdot \theta$ is redundant. The label of the literal is replaced with its restriction.

Merging

$$\frac{\mathcal{T} : l \simeq r \qquad \mathcal{T}' : l' \simeq r'}{\mathcal{T} \sqcup \mathcal{T}'\sigma : l \simeq r}\ (\sigma) \qquad \frac{\mathcal{T} : l \not\simeq r \qquad \mathcal{T}' : l' \not\simeq r'}{\mathcal{T} \sqcup \mathcal{T}'\sigma : l \not\simeq r}\ (\sigma)$$

where σ is a renaming such that $l'\sigma = l$ and $r'\sigma = r$. The conclusion replaces the two premises.

Superposition

$$\frac{\mathcal{T} : l \simeq r \qquad \mathcal{T}' : s[l'] \simeq t}{(\mathcal{T} \sqcap \mathcal{T}')\sigma : (s[r] \simeq t)\sigma}\ (\sigma) \qquad \frac{\mathcal{T} : l \simeq r \qquad \mathcal{T}' : s[l'] \not\simeq t}{(\mathcal{T} \sqcap \mathcal{T}')\sigma : (s[r] \not\simeq t)\sigma}\ (\sigma)$$

where (i) $\sigma = \mathrm{mgu}(l, l')$, (ii) l' is not a variable, (iii) $l\sigma\rho \succ r\sigma\rho$ and (iv) $s[l']\sigma\rho \succ t\rho$ for some grounding substitution ρ.

Equality Resolution

$$\frac{\mathcal{T} : (l \not\simeq r)}{\mathcal{T}\sigma : \square}\ (\sigma)$$

where $\sigma = \mathrm{mgu}(l, r)$.

As in the set labelled unit superposition calculus, we start with the selected literals which are labelled with the respective clauses they are selected in. Upon finding the contradiction we generate the instances of all clauses at the leaves of the tree. The set of *relevant instances* of a tree label is the set of closures occurring at leaves of the AND/OR tree.

In order to show that tree labelled unit superposition can replace set labelled unit superposition and in turn unlabelled unit superposition with extraction of relevant instances from proofs, we need to extend the simulation argument from Section 3.

Tree labelled unit superposition can stepwise simulate set labelled unit superposition using only superposition, merging and equality resolution inferences and the relevant instances in set labels are identical to the relevant instances in the tree label. Therefore Lemmas 1, 2 and 3 apply for tree labels as well, but we additionally have to deal with the restriction inference and show that it preserves completeness using the following lemma.

Lemma 4. *A restriction inference on $C \cdot \theta$ eliminates exactly those closures from the tree label which occur in corresponding unlabelled proofs, redundant due to $C \cdot \theta$.*

The lemma follows by induction over the proof structure the tree labelled literal was derived from. Let us give an example to illustrate elimination by restriction and the subsequent simplification of the AND/OR tree.

Example 4. The contradiction in the set labelled unit superposition proof $(*')$ from Example 2 has the set label

$$\Big\{(3)\cdot[], (2)\cdot[a/u, b/v, c/z], (1)\cdot[b/x, a/y], (2)\cdot[b/u, a/v, c/z]\Big\}.$$

In a tree labelled unit superposition proof, we obtain the label

$$(3)\cdot[] \sqcap \Big((2)\cdot[a/u, b/v, c/z] \sqcup \Big((1)\cdot[b/x, a/y] \sqcap (2)\cdot[b/u, a/v, c/z]\Big)\Big)$$

which preserves the structure of the two proofs that were merged.

If we were to eliminate $(2)\cdot[b/u, a/v, c/z]$ which corresponds to the leaf literal $f(u,v) \not\simeq g(z)$ in proof (†) in Example 1, the tree label becomes

$$(3)\cdot[] \sqcap \Big((2)\cdot[a/u, b/v, c/z] \sqcup \Big((1)\cdot[b/x, a/y] \sqcap \mathsf{false}\Big)\Big) = \\ (3)\cdot[] \sqcap (2)\cdot[a/u, b/v, c/z].$$

Eliminating $(2)\cdot[a/u, b/v, c/z]$ which corresponds to $f(u,v) \not\simeq g(z)$ in proof $(*)$ in Example 1 leaves us with

$$(3)\cdot[] \sqcap \Big(\mathsf{false} \sqcup \Big((1)\cdot[b/x, a/y] \sqcap (2)\cdot[b/u, a/v, c/z]\Big)\Big) = \\ (3)\cdot[] \sqcap (1)\cdot[b/x, a/y] \sqcap (2)\cdot[b/u, a/v, c/z].$$

Both tree labels then lead to exactly the instances that were generated from the separate proofs in Example 1.

6 OBDD Labelled Unit Superposition

Two labelled literals $\mathcal{L}_1 : L$ and $\mathcal{L}_2 : L$ are identical if their labels are. Moreover, since labels encode proofs and certain proofs are isomorphic, we can generalise the notion of identity on labelled literals to equivalence based on logical equivalence of Boolean formulae. Exploiting equivalence of labels in a labelled unit superposition procedure is not only an important simplification step, in some cases it is essential for termination as we will show on our running example.

Equivalence of two set labels can easily be checked: if their sets are equal, their relevant instances are equal and the literals do not need to be distinguished. Here, the property that sets are unordered collections of elements leads to a natural normal form where equivalence of labels can be checked efficiently. However, the situation is not so easy for tree labels since they are not produced in a normal form. The sequence of merging and superposition inferences determines the shape of the tree which makes comparing tree labels by their shape unusable except in simple cases.

Standard normal forms of Boolean formulae are the disjunctive and conjunctive normal forms (DNF and CNF) which are unfortunately frequently exponential in the size of the original formula. However, approaches like the definitional transformation, which introduces new variables for subterms of the original formula, do not produce a unique normal form, which makes checking equivalence of labels more difficult.

In this section we propose tree labels based on ordered binary decision diagrams (OBDDs) which offer particularly promising features, above all unique normal forms and checking of equivalence in constant time. An OBDD is a graph with common subtrees shared, it provides a compact and well-understood normal form of Boolean formulae. OBDDs are used in similar contexts to encode Boolean structures, e.g. [9].

Definition 6. *An* OBDD label $\mathcal{B}$ *is an OBDD where each node is a closure* $C \cdot \theta$*. The* σ-instance *of an OBDD label* $\mathcal{B}$ *is the OBDD* $\mathcal{B}\sigma$ *where each closure* $C \cdot \theta$ *is replaced with* $C \cdot \theta\sigma$*.*

We remark that σ-instantiation of an OBDD may require changing the variable ordering in the OBDD and thus a reordering of the OBDD.

Definition 7. *The* $C \cdot \theta$-restriction $\mathcal{B}|_{C \cdot \theta}$ *of an OBDD label is obtained by replacing each node* $C \cdot \theta$ *in* $\mathcal{B}$ *with* false *and reducing the OBDD.*

The inference rules of OBDD labelled unit superposition are in straightforward analogy to tree labelled unit superposition in Definition 5 where tree labels are replaced with OBDDs. We obtain relevant instances from an OBDD label in the obvious way: the set of *relevant instances* of an OBDD label $\mathcal{B}$ is the set of all nodes $C \cdot \theta$ in $\mathcal{B}$.

Let us further discuss our running example where keeping the Boolean structure of a tree label in an OBDD normal form prevents non-termination in the case of not normalised tree labels.

Example 5. We notice that the equation $f(x, y) \simeq f(y, x)$ is not orientable in any simplification ordering and must therefore be applied in both directions. Let $\mathcal{T}_1$ and $\mathcal{T}_2$ be the labels of $f(x, y) \simeq f(y, x)$ and $f(u, v) \not\simeq g(z)$, respectively.

We draw a first superposition inference between the literals with the equation in the given orientation

$$\frac{\overset{(1)}{\mathcal{T}_1 \colon f(x,y) \simeq f(y,x)} \qquad \overset{(2)}{\mathcal{T}_2 \colon f(u,v) \not\simeq g(z)}}{\mathcal{T}_1[u/x, v/y] \sqcap \mathcal{T}_2[] \colon f(v,u) \not\simeq g(z)}\ [u/x, v/y] \qquad (i)$$

and merge the conclusion with the premise

$$\frac{\overset{(2)}{\mathcal{T}_2[] \colon f(u,v) \not\simeq g(z)} \qquad \overset{(i)}{\mathcal{T}_1[u/x, v/y] \sqcap \mathcal{T}_2[] \colon f(v,u) \not\simeq g(z)}}{\mathcal{T}_2[] \sqcup \Big(\mathcal{T}_1[v/x, u/y] \sqcap \mathcal{T}_2[v/u, u/v]\Big) \colon f(u,v) \not\simeq g(z)}\ [v/u, u/v] \qquad (ii)$$

A second superposition with the equation reversed

$$\frac{\overset{(1)}{\mathcal{T}_1 \colon f(y,x) \simeq f(x,y)} \qquad \overset{(2)}{\mathcal{T}_2 \colon f(u,v) \not\simeq g(z)}}{\mathcal{T}_1[v/x, u/y] \sqcap \mathcal{T}_2[] \colon f(v,u) \not\simeq g(z)}\ [v/x, u/y] \qquad (iii)$$

results in the same conclusion with a different label. We merge it again

$$\frac{\overset{(2)}{\mathcal{T}_2[] \colon f(u,v) \not\simeq g(z)} \qquad \overset{(iii)}{\mathcal{T}_1[v/x, u/y] \sqcap \mathcal{T}_2[] \colon f(v,u) \not\simeq g(z)}}{\mathcal{T}_2[] \sqcup \Big(\mathcal{T}_1[u/x, v/y] \sqcap \mathcal{T}_2[v/u, u/v]\Big) \colon f(u,v) \not\simeq g(z)}\ [v/u, u/v] \qquad (iv)$$

and obtain the following tree label from (ii) and (iv)

$$\mathcal{T}_2[] \sqcup \left(\mathcal{T}_1[v/x, u/y] \sqcap \mathcal{T}_2[v/u, u/v]\right) \sqcup \left(\mathcal{T}_1[u/x, v/y] \sqcap \mathcal{T}_2[v/u, u/v]\right).$$

Let us abbreviate this label to

$$\mathcal{T}_2^1 \sqcup \left(\mathcal{T}_1^{-1} \sqcap \mathcal{T}_2^{-1}\right) \sqcup \left(\mathcal{T}_1^1 \sqcap \mathcal{T}_2^{-1}\right) \quad \text{(a)}$$

using the superscript ^{1} to denote the substitutions $[]$ and $[u/x, v/y]$ as well as $^{-1}$ for $[v/x, u/y]$ and $[v/u, u/v]$. The corresponding set label is

$$\left\{\mathcal{T}_2^1, \mathcal{T}_2^{-1}, \mathcal{T}_1^1, \mathcal{T}_1^{-1}\right\}.$$

It is now necessary to repeat inferences (i) and (iii) for $f(v,u) \not\simeq g(z)$ with the label $\mathcal{T}_2$ being (a). We note that for the substitutions applied to $\mathcal{T}_2$ in the merging, we have $\mathcal{T}_1^{-1}[v/u, u/v] = \mathcal{T}_1^1$, $\mathcal{T}_1^1[v/u, u/v] = \mathcal{T}_1^{-1}$, $\mathcal{T}_2^{-1}[v/u, u/v] = \mathcal{T}_2^1$ and $\mathcal{T}_2^1[v/u, u/v] = \mathcal{T}_2^{-1}$.

The label of the conclusion has the structure of (a) where $\mathcal{T}_2^1$ is substituted by (a) and $\mathcal{T}_2^{-1}$ by (a) with the substitution $[v/u, u/v]$ applied.

$$\begin{aligned}\mathcal{T}_2^1 \sqcup \left(\mathcal{T}_1^{-1} \sqcap \mathcal{T}_2^{-1}\right) \sqcup \left(\mathcal{T}_1^1 \sqcap \mathcal{T}_2^{-1}\right) \sqcup &\\ \left(\mathcal{T}_1^{-1} \sqcap \left(\mathcal{T}_2^{-1} \sqcup \left(\mathcal{T}_1^1 \sqcap \mathcal{T}_2^1\right) \sqcup \left(\mathcal{T}_1^{-1} \sqcap \mathcal{T}_2^1\right)\right)\right) \sqcup &\\ \left(\mathcal{T}_1^1 \sqcap \left(\mathcal{T}_2^{-1} \sqcup \left(\mathcal{T}_1^1 \sqcap \mathcal{T}_2^1\right) \sqcup \left(\mathcal{T}_1^{-1} \sqcap \mathcal{T}_2^1\right)\right)\right) & \quad \text{(b)}\end{aligned}$$

The set label does not change as no new leaves are added in the tree label. Literals with identical labels are identical and therefore no further inferences are necessary.

As the tree labels (a) and (b) have a different structure from the way they were built up during the inferences, they are distinct and we would continue with inferences, obtaining ever-growing labels in the conclusion.

If we, however, transform both labels to an OBDD using the same ordering, we obtain the relatively simple OBDD shown to the right. Just as for set labels we do not need to generate further inferences from here.

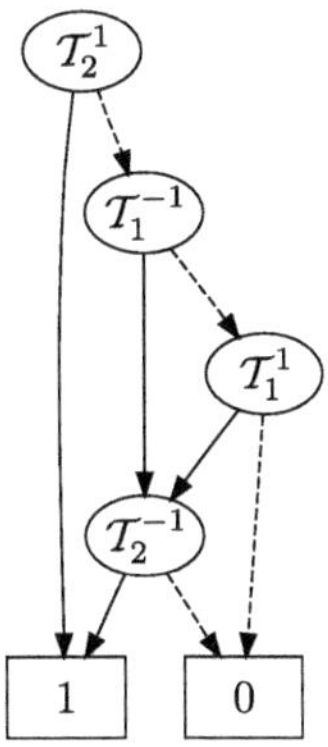

OBDD labels are in a normal form as set labels are, therefore we can state a variant of Theorem 1.

Theorem 2. *Inst-Gen-Eq with OBDD labelled unit superposition is a decision procedure for the Bernays-Schönfinkel fragment of first-order logic with equality.*

Proof. There is only a finite number of distinct closures and therefore only a finite number of OBDDs built from these closures. Therefore there is only a finite number of distinct OBDD labelled literals and the OBDD labelled unit superposition calculus will therefore terminate after a finite number of inference steps.

7 Implementation and Evaluation

We have implemented set, tree and OBDD labels in our iProver-Eq system (see [7]) and evaluated it with the TPTP benchmark library v4.0.1. We have used a cluster of Intel Xeon Quad Core machines with 2.33GHz and 2GB of memory limit and ran each of the 13783 problems for at most 120 seconds. In total, 4848 problems were solved by at least one label implementation and 3970 problems were solved by all three implementations.

As expected, the performance on non-equational problems was equal in all three label implementations, therefore we only focus on the 9054 problems with at least one equation, see Figure 1.

The results show that set and tree labels exhibit a comparable performance on both the overall number of solved problems and the number of problems that were solved fastest in the implementation. The number of problems solved only with set and tree labels (193 and 216) are significant, as well as the number of problems solved with other labels but not with the respective implementation (259 and 282). In a direct comparison, there are 195 problems where tree labels are more than twice as fast as set labels, whereas vice versa set labels are twice as fast on only 70 problems.

Despite the fact that OBDD labels provide a normal form, efficient checking for label equivalence and precise elimination of redundancy, in practice they remain considerably weaker than trees and sets. Their performance is mainly hit by the effort spent building OBDD labels which can become rather large. In the problems that were solved, OBDDs were well-behaved so that the number of nodes in OBDDs was in most cases much less than quadratic in the number of variables, i.e. closures in labels. Problems that were not solved in the time limit mostly had either a large number of closures (up to 50,000) or the Boolean structure had to be represented with a large number of nodes (many with several millions). Nevertheless, there are 119 problems solved with OBDD labels which are not solved with both of the other label implementations. Further, on 93 problems OBDD labels are faster than both the other labels, which include 9 problems with a runtime greater than one second where OBDD labels are significantly faster.

Problems	solved	not solved	fastest
set	2006	259	601
tree	1983	282	699
OBDD	1512	753	93

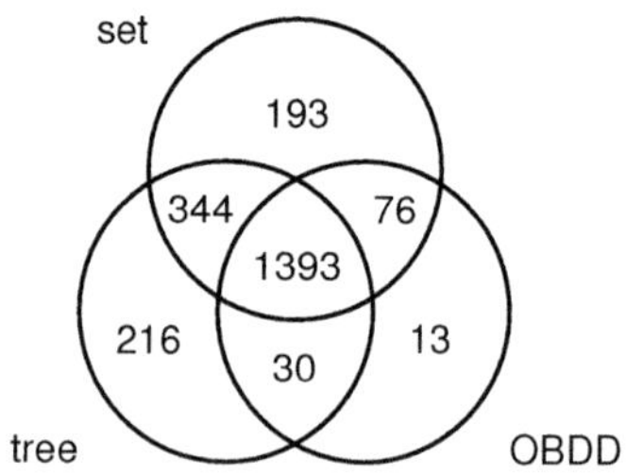

Fig. 1. Comparing labels on the number of solved equational problems out of 9054 in total: set labels solved 2006 problems and were fastest on 601 problems, while 259 problems were only solved with other labels. 193 problems could be solved with set labels and not with tree or OBDD labels, 30 problems were not solved with set labels but both with tree and OBDD labels and 1393 problems were solved with all three labels.

The results make hybrid approaches, such as a combination of tree and set labels, look promising. We will also further investigate how to improve OBDD labels with techniques exploiting the specific structure of labels.

8 Conclusion

In this paper we introduced a labelled superposition calculus for efficient instance generation for equational reasoning in the Inst-Gen framework. We investigated and evaluated several label structures based on sets, AND/OR trees and OBDDs. Our implementation and experimental results show that our labelled approach has a promising potential. We observe that different label structures are complementary in performance on many problems which indicates further investigation is needed regarding possible combinations of these techniques. In further work we will also explore possibilities to make use of the information in labels in other calculi and applications, for example for query answering.

References

1. Baumgartner, P.: Logical Engineering with Instance-Based Methods. In: Pfenning, F. (ed.) CADE 2007. LNCS (LNAI), vol. 4603, pp. 404–409. Springer, Heidelberg (2007)
2. Baumgartner, P., Tinelli, C.: The Model Evolution Calculus with Equality. In: Nieuwenhuis, R. (ed.) CADE 2005. LNCS (LNAI), vol. 3632, pp. 392–408. Springer, Heidelberg (2005)
3. Eiter, T., Faber, W., Traxler, P.: Testing Strong Equivalence of Datalog Programs - Implementation and Examples. In: Baral, C., Greco, G., Leone, N., Terracina, G. (eds.) LPNMR 2005. LNCS (LNAI), vol. 3662, pp. 437–441. Springer, Heidelberg (2005)
4. Ganzinger, H., Korovin, K.: Integrating Equational Reasoning into Instantiation-Based Theorem Proving. In: Marcinkowski, J., Tarlecki, A. (eds.) CSL 2004. LNCS, vol. 3210, pp. 71–84. Springer, Heidelberg (2004)
5. Hustadt, U., Motik, B., Sattler, U.: Reducing SHIQ- Description Logic to Disjunctive Datalog Programs. In: KR 2004, pp. 152–162. AAAI Press, Menlo Park (2004)
6. Korovin, K.: Instantiation-Based Automated Reasoning: From Theory to Practice. In: Schmidt, R.A. (ed.) CADE 2009. LNCS, vol. 5663, pp. 163–166. Springer, Heidelberg (2009)
7. Korovin, K., Sticksel, C.: iProver-Eq – An Instantiation-based Theorem Prover with Equality. In: Giesl, J., Hähnle, R. (eds.) IJCAR 2010. LNCS, vol. 6173, pp. 196–202. Springer, Heidelberg (2010)
8. Letz, R., Stenz, G.: Integration of Equality Reasoning into the Disconnection Calculus. In: Egly, U., Fermüller, C. (eds.) TABLEAUX 2002. LNCS (LNAI), vol. 2381, pp. 176–190. Springer, Heidelberg (2002)
9. de Moura, L., Bjørner, N.: Deciding Effectively Propositional Logic Using DPLL and Substitution Sets. In: Armando, A., Baumgartner, P., Dowek, G. (eds.) IJCAR 2008. LNCS (LNAI), vol. 5195, pp. 410–425. Springer, Heidelberg (2008)
10. Nieuwenhuis, R., Rubio, A.: Paramodulation-based theorem proving. In: Robinson, A., Voronkov, A. (eds.) Handbook of Automated Reasoning. Elsevier, Amsterdam (1999)
11. Pérez, J.A.N., Voronkov, A.: Encodings of Bounded LTL Model Checking in Effectively Propositional Logic. In: Pfenning, F. (ed.) CADE 2007. LNCS (LNAI), vol. 4603, pp. 346–361. Springer, Heidelberg (2007)

Boosting Local Search Thanks to CDCL

Gilles Audemard, Jean-Marie Lagniez, Bertrand Mazure, and Lakhdar Saïs

Université Lille-Nord de France
CRIL - CNRS UMR 8188
Artois, F-62307 Lens
{audemard,lagniez,mazure,sais}@cril.fr

Abstract. In this paper, a novel hybrid and complete approach for propositional satisfiability, called SATHYS (*Sat Hybrid Solver*), is introduced. It efficiently combines the strength of both local search and CDCL based SAT solvers. Considering the consistent partial assignment under construction by the CDCL SAT solver, local search is used to extend it to a model of the Boolean formula, while the CDCL component is used by the local search one as a strategy to escape from a local minimum. Additionally, both solvers heavily cooperate thanks to relevant information gathered during search. Experimentations on SAT instances taken from the last competitions demonstrate the efficiency and the robustness of our hybrid solver with respect to the state-of-the-art CDCL based, local search and hybrid SAT solvers.

1 Introduction

The SAT problem, namely the issue of checking whether a Boolean formula in Conjunctive Normal Form (CNF) is satisfiable or not, is a central issue in many artificial intelligence and computer science domains, including hardware and software verification, planning, cryptography and bioinformatics. These last two decades, many approaches have been proposed to solve large application SAT instances, based on logically complete or incomplete methods. Both stochastic local search (SLS) techniques [34,33,20] and elaborate variants of the DPLL procedure [7], commonly named modern SAT solvers [30,9], can now solve many families of hard SAT instances. Based on different paradigms, these two kinds of approaches admit complementary behavior in terms of performances. Modern SAT or CDCL (Conflict Driven Clause Learning) solvers are particularly efficient on application benchmarks while local search performs better on random SAT instances. Stochastic Local search (Algorithm 2) and modern SAT solvers (Algorithm 1) are recognized as two important search paradigms. Their differences arise in the way the search space is explored. In SLS, the algorithm explores the search space in a non systematic way starting from a complete assignment and moving to another complete assignment by inverting the truth value of a chosen variable (this is a flip). After a fixed number of flips, another complete assignment is generated, and the process is repeated. Modern SAT solvers explore the search space in a systematic way by developing a search tree, where at each node the current partial assignment is extended by assigning a selected variable and propagating unit literals. In SLS, the search process can lead to a local minimum, in this case several strategies are designed to escape from

C. Fermüller and A. Voronkov (Eds.): LPAR-17, LNCS 6397, pp. 474–488, 2010.

such minimum. In modern SAT solvers, the process can lead to a conflict and in this case several learning strategies are designed for resolving such a conflict [38].

Combining stochastic local search and conflict driven clause learning solvers is clearly a challenging issue as stated by Selman *et al.* [35] in 1997 (challenge 7) and in 2003 [24]. Such a combination might exploit the strength of both approaches and might result in a new but more efficient hybrid SAT solver. Several attempts have been made these last years [4] and different hybrid solvers have been designed leading to real progress towards the resolution of this challenging issue (see section 5). However, the challenge remains open as the performance of these proposed hybrid solvers is far from those of the CDCL based solvers particularly on application instances. Our goal in this paper is to design a hybrid SLS/CDCL solver that outperforms the local search techniques, while significantly reducing the gap with CDCL based solvers particularly on application category.

In this paper, we propose a new hybridization of local search and modern SAT solver, named SATHYS (*Sat Hybrid Solver*). In our approach, both components heavily cooperate through relevant information gathered during search. More precisely, our hybrid solver alternatively performs the search process using local search and CDCL based SAT solvers. On the one hand, at each node of the search tree, the local search component is used to extend to the model, the current (consistent) partial assignment built by the CDCL based component. On the other hand, the CDCL part is conditionally invoked by the local search component when a local minimum is encountered. Each solver benefits from the other in several ways. First, each time a local minimum is reached, the local search technique updates the activity of the boundary variables [14]. The idea is to direct the CDCL search towards boundary points proven to be important by Goldberg in [14]. Secondly, the polarities of the literals involved in the best complete assignment found during local search are exploited by the CDCL component. From the other side, the CDCL solver shares with local search the current partial assignment together with the learnt clauses. The originality of our proposed hybrid SAT solver arises in alternating search of both components while exchanging relevant information.

The rest of the paper is organized as follows. Section 2 introduces some definitions and notations. Then, we present CDCL and SLS solvers in a unified way. Section 3 describes our new hybrid solver. In Section 4 we provide some experimental comparison with different SAT solvers including the CDCL solver MINISAT and several well known SLS and hybrid solvers. Before concluding, section 5 discusses the related works.

2 Technical Background

2.1 Preliminary Definitions and Notations

Let $\mathcal{V} = \{x_1, ..., x_n\}$ be a set of propositional variables, a *literal* ℓ is either a positive x_i or a negative variable $\overline{x_i}$. The two literals x and $\overline{x}$ are said *complementary*. We denote by $\overline{\ell}$ the complementary literal of ℓ. A *clause* $c_i = (\ell_1 \vee \ldots \vee \ell_{n_i})$ is a disjunction of literals. A *unit clause* is a clause with only one literal, called *unit literal*. A formula $\Sigma = (c_1 \wedge \ldots \wedge c_m)$ is in conjunctive normal form (CNF) as it is a conjunction of clauses. The set of variables involved in Σ will be noted $\mathcal{V}_\Sigma$. An *interpretation* $\mathcal{I}$ of a Boolean formula Σ associates a truth value $\mathcal{I}(x) \in \{false, true\}$ to some variables $x \in \mathcal{V}_\Sigma$. $\mathcal{I}$

is *complete* if it assigns a truth value to every $x \in \mathcal{V}_\Sigma$, and *partial* otherwise. A complete (resp. partial) interpretation will be noted $\mathcal{I}_c$ (resp. $\mathcal{I}_p$). A clause, a CNF formula and an interpretation can be represented using sets.

It should say that a *clause* β *is falsified (resp. satisfied) by* $\mathcal{I}$ if $\forall \ell \in \beta$ (resp. $\exists \ell \in \beta$), β is falsified (resp. satisfied) by ℓ under $\mathcal{I}$. $\Sigma_{|\ell}$ denotes the formula simplified by the assignment of the literal ℓ to $true$, that is $\Sigma_{|\ell} = \{\alpha \setminus \{\bar{\ell}\}$ such that $\alpha \in \Sigma$ and $\ell \notin \alpha\}$. This notation can be extended to an interpretation. Let $\mathcal{I} = \{\ell_1, ..., \ell_n\}$ be an interpretation, $\Sigma_{|\mathcal{I}} = (...(\Sigma|_{\ell_1})...|_{\ell_n})$.

A *model* of a formula Σ, noted $\mathcal{I} \models \Sigma$, is an interpretation $\mathcal{I}$ such that $\forall c \in \Sigma$, c is satisfied by $\mathcal{I}$. On the contrary, an interpretation $\mathcal{I}$ is called a *nogood* of Σ, noted $\mathcal{I} \not\models \Sigma$, if $\exists c \in \beta$ such that c is falsified by $\mathcal{I}$.

SAT is the problem of checking whether a CNF formula admits a model or not. If the answer is positive, then the formula is called *satisfiable*, else it is called *unsatisfiable*.

2.2 CDCL Solvers

CDCL based SAT solvers (Algorithm 1), generally referred as modern SAT solvers [30], are based on classical unit propagation (lines 2, 14 and 15) efficiently combined through incremental data structures, restart policies (line 15) [15], activity-based variable selection heuristics (VSIDS-like) (line 12) [30], and clause learning (line 6) [36].

A CDCL based SAT solver is a sophisticated variant of the well known DPLL [7] procedure. At each node of the search tree, the assigned literals (the decision literal and the propagated ones) are labeled with the same *decision level* starting from 1 and increased at each decision (or branching step). After backtracking, some variables are unassigned and the current decision level is decreased accordingly. At level m, the current partial interpretation $\mathcal{I}_p$ can be represented as an ordered sequence of decision-propagation steps made at the different levels. We note $\mathcal{I}_p^i$ where $i \leq m$, the partial interpretation $\mathcal{I}_p$ restricted to the first i sequences of decision-propagation. An *asserting level* associated to a falsified clause $\alpha = (x \vee \beta)$ under an interpretation $\mathcal{I}_p$ (in short $level(\alpha, \mathcal{I}_p)$) is defined as the level j such that $\alpha|_{\mathcal{I}_p^j} = x$ and x represents the *asserting literal* of α under $\mathcal{I}_p$.

Algorithm 1 describes the general skeleton of a CDCL based SAT solver. Let us briefly explain its main components. A more detailed description of modern SAT solvers can be found in [6]. The algorithm initializes the learnt database Γ as the empty set (line 1), then unit propagation is applied on the original formula Σ (line 2). The function $BCP(\Sigma)$ returns the set of propagated literals. The main loop contains several cases. First, if all variables are assigned then the formula is empty and $\mathcal{I}$ is a model of Σ (line 4). If the partial assignment $\mathcal{I}_p$ is consistent, then a new decision variable is chosen and unit propagation is performed (lines 12, 13 and 14). Otherwise, a conflict is reached and a nogood (or a learnt clause) α is computed (line 6). If α is the empty clause, then the instance is proven unsatisfiable (line 8). Otherwise, $\alpha = (x \vee \beta)$ and j the asserting level of α w.r.t. $\mathcal{I}_p$. After that, the clause α is added to the learnt database (line 9) and the algorithm backtracks to level j by computing a new partial interpretation $\mathcal{I}_p^j$ (line 10). At level j the asserting literal $x \in \alpha$ is propagated (line 14). Finally, the algorithm restarts if the cutoff value in terms of the number of conflicts is reached (line 15).

Algorithm 1. CDCL solver

Input: a CNF formula Σ
Output: SAT or UNSAT

$\Gamma \leftarrow \emptyset$;
$\mathcal{I}_p \leftarrow BCP(\Sigma)$;
while *(true)* **do**
  if $(\Sigma_{|\mathcal{I}_p} = \emptyset)$ **then return** SAT;
  if $(\emptyset \in \Sigma_{|\mathcal{I}_p})$ **then**
    $\alpha{=}(x \vee \beta) \leftarrow analyzeConflict(\Sigma \cup \Gamma, \mathcal{I}_p)$;
    $j \leftarrow level(\alpha, \mathcal{I}_p)$;
    if $(\alpha = \emptyset)$ **then return** UNSAT;
    $\Gamma \leftarrow \Gamma \cup \{\alpha\}$;
    $\mathcal{I}_p \leftarrow \mathcal{I}_p^j$;
  else
    $x \leftarrow chooseDecisionLiteral(\Sigma_{|\mathcal{I}_p})$;
    $\mathcal{I}_p \leftarrow \mathcal{I}_p \cup \{x\}$;
  $\mathcal{I}_p \leftarrow \mathcal{I}_p \cup BCP((\Sigma \cup \Gamma)_{|\mathcal{I}_p})$;
  if $(restart())$ **then** $\mathcal{I}_p \leftarrow BCP(\Sigma \cup \Gamma)$;

2.3 Local Search Solvers

Algorithm 2 gives the general scheme of a local search solver. It uses a stochastic walk over complete interpretations of Σ. At each *step* (or *flip*), it tries to reduce the number of falsified clauses (this step is usually called a *descent*). The next complete interpretation is chosen among the neighbors (interpretations that differ only by the truth value of one variable) of the current one (line 7). A local minimum is reached when no descent is possible. In such a case, a strategy is used in order to escape from this minimum (line 5). Like in CDCL solvers, sometimes a restart (called a try in SLS) is performed and a new complete interpretation is generated. However restarts in CDCL and SLS solvers have not exactly the same role. In the CDCL case, it is now well admitted that restarts are used to reorder variables, directing the solver to the same part of the search space using a different branch. On the other hand, restarts in SLS solvers are used in order to diversify the search by generating a new complete interpretation.

3 SatHys: A Novel Hybrid Approach

In this section, we present SatHys, our hybrid solver for SAT which is available at `http://www.cril.fr/~lagniez/sathys`. Before giving its formal description, we provide some intuitions and motivations behind the design of SatHys.

3.1 Motivations

Recently, several works have shown that local search techniques provide relevant information for locating unsatisfiable cores [16,17]. Motivated by these results, we propose

Algorithm 2. Local Search solver

```
Input: a CNF formula Σ
Output: SAT
I_c ← completeInterpretation(Σ) ;
while (true) do
    if (Σ|I_c = ∅) then return SAT;
    if a local minimum is reached then
        x ← chooseLitteralToEscapeMinima(Σ, I_c);
    else
        x ← chooseLitteralToFlip(Σ, I_c);
    flip(I_c, x);
    if (restart()) then I_c ← completeInterpretation(Σ);
```

a new hybridization scheme of SLS and CDCL solvers. In our hybrid approach, the two methods heavily interact and play complementary roles:

1. SLS directs the CDCL search towards the proof of unsatisfiability ;
2. CDCL directs the SLS search towards a model if it exists.

Let us briefly summarize these bidirectional interactions.

SLS → CDCL. The SLS affects the CDCL solver at two different levels known to be important for the efficiency of satisfiability solvers. First, the activity of the variables usually maintained by CDCL are dynamically refined by the SLS component. This local search refinement of the activity-based heuristic (VSIDS) is achieved using the notion of boundary points introduced recently by E. Goldberg in [14]. A boundary point is a complete interpretation (point) $\mathcal{I}$ such that there exists at least one literal ℓ belonging to all clauses falsified by $\mathcal{I}$. In [14], it was shown that focusing resolution on such kind of literals ℓ improves the proof quality by reducing the length of the refutation. From the recent work by Grégoire *et al.* [17], we can also deduce that if the boundary point corresponds to a local minimum, then the literal ℓ belongs to at least one unsatisfiable core. Considering these two interesting features of boundary points, we exploit this notion to refine the activity of the clauses. When a local minimum is reached, updating the activity of the variables associated to literals appearing in all the falsified clauses by the boundary point might guide CDCL towards the most important part of the search space. Indeed, favoring the assignment of such literals aims to direct the search to unsatisfiable cores and might reduce the length of the resolution proof.

The second interaction level where SLS influences with CDCL is on the assignment polarity ($false$, $true$) of the chosen variable. More precisely, when the next variable to assign is chosen by CDCL, its polarity is taken from the best complete interpretation (in terms of the number of satisfied clauses) found by the SLS solver. Usually, in CDCL solvers such as Rsat [32], the assignment polarity (or phase) follows a progress saving scheme. Each time a variable is assigned, its truth value is saved, and used as the polarity of the variable when such a variable is selected again.

CDCL $\longrightarrow$ SLS. From CDCL to SLS, the current CDCL branch made of the set of decisions and propagations is provided to SLS. Using such a partial interpretation, the SLS solver tries to extend it into a model by focusing search on the remaining unassigned variables. In this way, local search exploits variable dependencies provided by the decisions and propagations of the CDCL solver. Let us recall that exploiting variable dependencies is identified as an important issue for the efficiency of local search based techniques [35,24,31]. On the other hand, as the CDCL solver is called when SLS reaches a local minimum, the new partial interpretation revised by CDCL contains several flipped variables. Consequently, from the local search side CDCL can be seen as a strategy that helps local search to escape from local minima.

3.2 Formal Description

Even if the main core of the SATHYS hybrid solver is a local search based algorithm, the integration of the CDCL part leads to a complete hybrid solver able to prove both satisfiability and unsatisfiability. In this section, we give a detailed description of our approach as depicted by the Algorithm 3.

First of all, the algorithm starts with an empty set of learnt clauses (Γ) and a complete interpretation $\mathcal{I}_c$ built by randomly extending the current partial interpretation $\mathcal{I}_p$ obtained by propagating unit literals on the original formula (lines 2–3). Note that function BCP (Boolean Constraint Propagation) returns the set of propagated unit literals. After this initialization step local search process is performed. If there exists a neighboring interpretation (an interpretation that differs from $\mathcal{I}_c$ by only the truth value of one variable x), that reduces the number of falsified clauses (descent phase), then the variable x is flipped, i.e. its truth value is reversed (lines 22-23). It is important to note that only variables out of $\mathcal{I}_p$ can be flipped. Indeed, the variables involved in $\mathcal{I}_p$ are considered tabu during the local search step. This partial interpretation evolves during the search and is modified in the CDCL part of the algorithm (lines 11–19). However at each iteration of the loop (line 4), we have $\mathcal{I}_p \subseteq \mathcal{I}_c$.

When a local minimum is reached (line 6), we select one of the two following strategies : (1) call the CDCL component of the solver (lines 11–19) or (2) apply any other repair strategy, like novelty [29] or rsaps [22], to escape from such local minima (lines 8–9). The selection between the two strategies is done using a condition based on the search progress `SLSprogress` that will be explained later.

Each time the CDCL part of the solver is called (lines 11-20), a decision literal ℓ is chosen (line 11). Then unit propagation is performed (line 12). If it leads to a contradiction (line 13), a classical analysis is performed, the learnt clause γ is added to the learnt database Γ before back-jumping to the level j. If the learnt clause is empty, then the the formula is proven unsatisfiable (line 16). As long as the current partial interpretation $\mathcal{I}_p$ is not consistent, the process continues (see the loop line 13). At the end of this process, the consistent partial interpretation $\mathcal{I}_p$ is extended to a complete one $\mathcal{I}_c$ (line 20) and the local search component continues the search process. After each CDCL part, the partial interpretation $\mathcal{I}_p$ is modified (line 19). Consequently, the fixed part of the complete interpretation $\mathcal{I}_c$ is also modified. In this way, we derive a new strategy based on CDCL to escape from local minima.

Algorithm 3. SATHYS

Input: a CNF formula Σ

Output: SAT or UNSAT

1 $\Gamma \leftarrow \emptyset$;
2 $\mathcal{I}_p \leftarrow BCP(\Sigma)$;
3 $\mathcal{I}_c \leftarrow \mathcal{I}_p \cup completeInterpretation(\Sigma_{|\mathcal{I}_p})$;
4 **while** *(true)* **do**
5   **if** $(\Sigma_{|\mathcal{I}_c} = \emptyset)$ **then return** SAT;
6   **if** *a local minimum is reached* **then**
7   **if** (`SLSprogress` > 0) **then**
8       $\ell \leftarrow chooseLitteralToEscapeLocalMinima(\Sigma_{|\mathcal{I}_p}, \mathcal{I}_c)$;
9       $flip(\mathcal{I}_c, \ell)$;
10   **else**
11       $\mathcal{I}_p \leftarrow \mathcal{I}_p \cup \{\ell\}$ with $\ell \notin \mathcal{I}_p$;
12       $\mathcal{I}_p \leftarrow \mathcal{I}_p \cup BCP((\Sigma \cup \Gamma)_{|\mathcal{I}_p})$;
13   **while** $(\emptyset \in (\Sigma \cup \Gamma)_{|\mathcal{I}_p})$ **do**
14         $\gamma = (\ell \vee \beta) \leftarrow analyzeConflict(\Sigma \cup \Gamma, \mathcal{I}_p)$;
15         $j \leftarrow level(\gamma, \mathcal{I}_p)$;
16   **if** $(\gamma = \emptyset)$ **then return** UNSAT;
17         $\Gamma \leftarrow \Gamma \cup \{\gamma\}$;
18         $\mathcal{I}_p \leftarrow \mathcal{I}_p^j$;
19         $\mathcal{I}_p \leftarrow \mathcal{I}_p \cup BCP((\Sigma \cup \Gamma)_{|\mathcal{I}_p})$;
20       $\mathcal{I}_c \leftarrow \mathcal{I}_p \cup (\mathcal{I}_c \setminus \mathcal{I}_p)$;
21   **else**
22     $x \leftarrow chooseLitteralToFlip(\Sigma_{|\mathcal{I}_p}, \mathcal{I}_c)$;
23     $flip(\mathcal{I}_c, \ell)$;
24   **if** *(restart())* **then**
25     $\mathcal{I}_p \leftarrow BCP(\Sigma \cup \Gamma)$;
26     $\mathcal{I}_c \leftarrow \mathcal{I}_p \cup completeInterpretation(\Sigma_{|\mathcal{I}_p})$;

This process is repeated until the next restart (line 24). As long as a model is not found or the unsatisfiability of the formula is not proven the solver restarts the previous process with a new initial complete interpretation (lines 25-26).

In the following, we introduce some improvements embedded in our solver SATHYS.

Calling the CDCL oracle. The behavior of our hybrid method heavily depends on the value of the variable `SLSprogress` (see Algorithm 3, line 7). We use a similar mechanism as it is done in [21]. When the local search engine reduces the MAXSAT value found in the current restart, this variable `SLSprogress` is increased. Our reasoning is that as long as SLS allows improvements i.e. increases the number of satisfied clauses, the execution of SLS is favored. Each time a local minimum is reached, the value of `SLSprogress` is decreased. By getting frequently stuck in local minima, it seems that the local search engine has a real difficulty to improve the current interpretation. In this case, we need to call the CDCL engine in order to escape from these local minima.

Activity based heuristic for CDCL. The heuristic used in the CDCL part of the Algorithm 3 is a slightly modified version of VSIDS [30]. Indeed, as usual, all weights of the variables are increased during the conflict analysis. Furthermore, when a local minimum is reached, we look for a boundary point and we increase the activity of the variable with one of its literals appearing in all the falsified clauses. In this way, and as explained above, our aim is to generate shorter resolution proofs.

Polarity of the decision literals. The polarity of the decision variable is known to be very important for the efficiency of SAT solvers. We propose here to use both engines in order to choose the best polarity for a given variable. At each restart, we store the interpretation associated to the current MAXSAT value and we modify it using progress saving [32]. Then when a given decision variable is chosen by CDCL, its polarity is taken from the last memorized complete interpretation with the best MAXSAT value. Indeed, we focus the search near the MAXSAT value, so near a solution by taking into account dependencies between variables.

4 Experimental Validation

In this section, we provide an experimental validation of our hybrid solver SATHYS. Like most other solvers, we use SatElite in a preprocessing step [8]. Instances from the SAT'09 competition are used as a test set. They are divided into three different categories: crafted (281 instances), application (292) and random (570).

Let us note that these instances are carefully selected for the SAT competition because of their relevance. From the results of the last SAT competitions, one can have in mind that most of the state-of-the-art SAT solvers present very close performance in terms of the number of solved instances. For example, PRECOSAT [3] and GLUCOSE [1] were ex-aequo in terms of the number of solved instances in the application category SAT +UNSAT).

The experimentation has been conducted on the same cluster as for last SAT 2009 competition (Intel Xeon 3GHz under Linux with a RAM memory size of 2GB). The time limit (time-out) has been set to 1200 CPU seconds.

4.1 Effectiveness of the Collaboration

First of all, our goal is to highlight that our hybrid scheme is really relevant. To measure the relevance of the different improvements introduced to SATHYS (described in the previous sections), we compared SATHYS with the following variants:

- SATHYS$_{nb}$: the VSIDS heuristic is not updated when a boundary point is discovered.
- SATHYS$_{cdclAtEachLM}$: instead of using the variable `SLSprogress` we call the CDCL solver at each local minimum.
- SATHYS$_{noPolarity}$: Literal polarity are not updated with the MAXSAT interpretation.

Table 1. Comparison of different versions of the SATHYS solver. For each category, we provide the number of solved instances. The total number of solved instances on all categories is also given.

solver	Crafted	Application	Random	total
SATHYS	104	**148**	189	**441**
SATHYS_{nb}	103	144	**191**	438
$\text{SATHYS}_{cdclAtEachLM}$	101	141	8	250
$\text{SATHYS}_{noPolarity}$	**106**	142	188	436

The Table 1 summarizes the results obtained by the four versions of SATHYS solver.

Not surprisingly, we can note that SATHYS_{nb} is the best one on random instances. Indeed, random instances are globally unsatisfiable i.e. the unsatisfiable core tends to include all the clauses of the original formula. As the role of the activities (VSIDS) is to focus the search on the most important part of formula, this is clearly not relevant in case of random instances. Also, the boundary points are useless for this kind of instances.

Concerning $\text{SATHYS}_{cdclAtEachLM}$, this version is the worst one. Indeed, too many calls of CDCL consumes clearly too much time. Moreover, as CDCL approaches are not well suited for random instances, calling CDCL penalizes SATHYS. We can note that the number of calls to the CDCL engine has an important impact on the performances of SATHYS. Consequently, fine-tuning the local search progress (`SLSprogress`) is crucial for the efficiency of our hybrid approach.

Concerning $\text{SATHYS}_{noPolarity}$, this version obtains good performance on the crafted category. However, literals polarity seems to be a relevant criteria for application instances considered as the most important category by the SAT community.

In summary, the cooperation scheme designed in SATHYS and described in the previous section improves the robustness and the efficiency of our hybrid solver.

4.2 Comparison

In this section, we compare our solver against some of the well known SAT solvers. Many of them are considered as the state-of-the-art SAT solvers in at least one category of instances. We can note that four solvers considered in our comparative experiments have obtained a gold medal at the SAT competition in 2009 in different categories.

- Two SLS methods: WSAT [34] with rnovelty strategy and ADAPTG2 [27].
- Two hybrid approaches: HYBRIDGM [2] and HINOTOS[26].
- Five complete approaches: MINISAT [9], GLUCOSE [1], PRECOSAT [3], RSAT [32], and CLASP [13].
- A portfolio solver : SATZILLA_I [37].

Table 2 summarizes the obtained results. Let us start this comparison with local search solvers. We can note that they perform better than SATHYS only in the random category of instances. This is not surprising since they are particularly suited to this kind of instances. On the other categories of instances, local search based techniques obtain bad results. As underlined during the SAT'09 competition, the main weak point of local

Table 2. SATHYS vs. some other SAT solvers. For each category and each solver, the number of solved instances is provided.

	Crafted			Application			Random			
	total	(sat	unsat)	total	(sat	unsat)	total	(sat	unsat)	total
ADAPTG2	68	(68	0)	8	(8	0)	**294**	(**294**	0)	375
GNOVELTY+	54	(54	0)	7	(7	0)	281	(281	0)	342
SATHYS	104	(71	33)	148	(63	85)	189	(189	0)	**441**
HYBRIDGM	51	(51	5)	0	(5	0)	294	(294	0)	350
HINOTOS	105	(69	36)	107	(39	68)	77	(65	11)	288
MINISAT	99	(72	27)	152	(59	93)	3	(3	0)	254
GLUCOSE	114	(75	39)	152	(54	98)	17	(17	0)	266
PRECOSAT	122	(81	41)	**164**	(**65**	**99**)	2	(2	0)	288
RSAT	105	(71	34)	143	(53	90)	5	(5	0)	253
CLASP	**131**	(78	**53**)	138	(53	85)	84	(66	18)	353
SATZILLA_I	128	(**86**	42)	142	(60	82)	145	(90	**55**)	415

search based solvers resides in their inefficiency on the application category. Improving local search based techniques on application category remains a very challenging issue. As the skeleton of our solver is an SLS technique, where the CDCL component can be considered as a strategy for escaping from local minima, the good performances of our hybrid solver provides real advances on this important issue.

Comparatively with other hybrid solvers, SATHYS is the best one w.r.t. in the application category. HYBRIDGM seems to be tuned for random instances whereas HINOTOS and SATHYS are comparable on crafted category. The results show clearly that our hybrid solver outperforms all the hybrid approaches.

SATHYS is very competitive with respect to the sate-of-the-art CDCL solvers in both crafted and application categories. To our best knowledge, it is the first time that an hybrid solver is able to obtain such promising results. On random instances, classical CDCL solvers present a very bad behavior. On this last category, clause learning and back-jumping are useless.

Interestingly enough, SATHYS is also very competitive with respect to the portfolio based solver SATZILLA. This portfolio uses CDCL, local search and lookahead solvers. In this approach, the different solvers are called independently.

To summarize, SATHYS is the first competitive solver on all the three categories of SAT instances (crafted, application and random). It is also the most robust one: it obtains the best overall results in terms of the total number of solved instances and it is often close to the first rank on each category.

The previous table provides information about the number of solved instances in the considered time limit. Also, we present the classical scatter plot in order to compare SATHYS with one of the best known hybrid solver HINOTOS, PRECOSAT (the state-of-the-art solver on application category), CLASP (the best solver on crafted category) and SATZILLA (it obtains the second best overall results behind SATHYS). In these curves, the y-axis represents the time (in log scale) of SATHYS and the x-axis the time of the other solver. So, a dot below the diagonal represents an instance where SATHYS is faster than the other solver. This is shown in Figure 1.

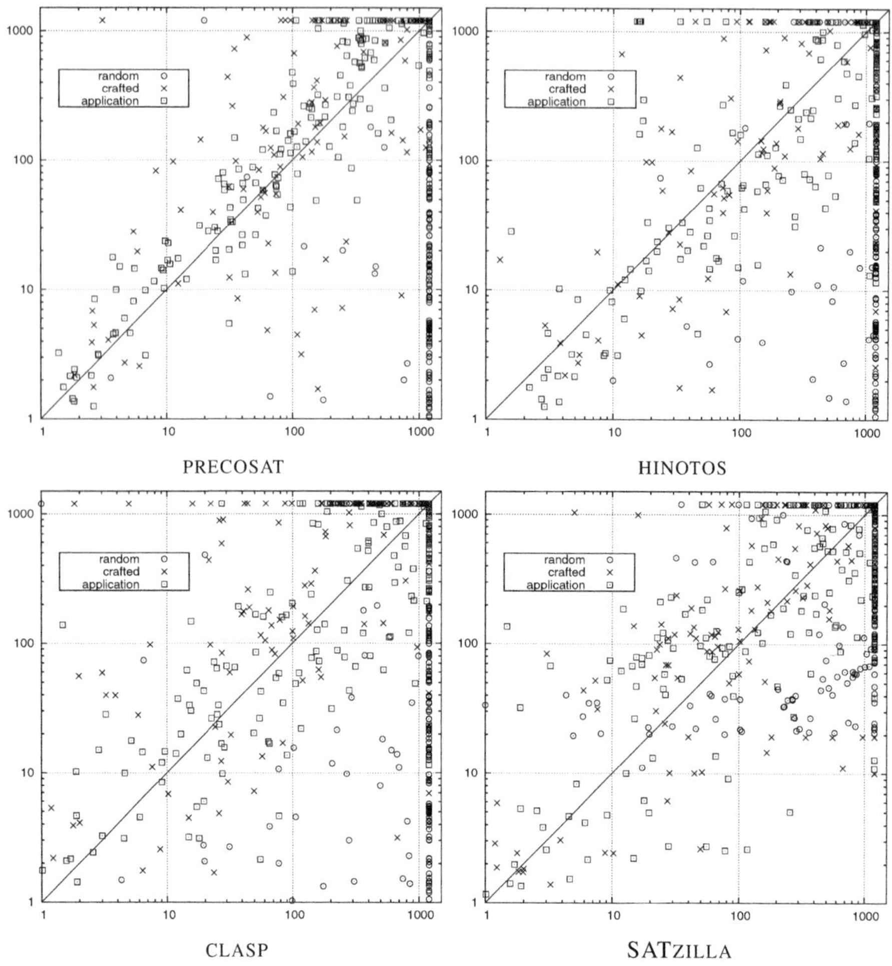

Fig. 1. Scatter plot: SATHYS vs. {PRECOSAT,HINOTOS,CLASP,SATZILLA}

Analyzing these figures, we can conclude that SATHYS outperforms HINOTOS. However our approach is slightly slower than PRECOSAT, which is one of the best CDCL solvers. However, SATHYS solves more instances than PRECOSAT. Comparatively with CLASP, we can observe that our method obtains similar performance on application and crafted instances, but SATHYS is better on random instances. Finally, it is impossible to differentiate SATZILLA and SATHYS in terms of CPU time.

Finally, we also want to hightlight that our solver is competitive on difficult hard SAT and UNSAT instances from crafted and application categories. Table 3 provides results on a selection of instances. Because of lack of space we do not report the results for each solver. However, to be as fair as possible, we also report the best result obtained in the competition over the 50 submitted solvers (BEST column). SATHYS is efficient on SAT as well as UNSAT instances.

Table 3. Highlight results on a selection of instances. Results are reported in seconds.

	SAT	BEST	SATHYS	HINOTOS	GLUCOSE	PRECOSAT	CLASP	SATZILLA
q_query_3_L100_coli	N	183	677	–	577	**414**	780	–
post-c32s-col400-16	N	66	247	380	714	141	**66**	125
countbitsarray02_32	N	926	1100	–	**926**	–	–	–
maxxororand032	N	579	**768**	–	–	–	–	–
minand128	N	16	71	219	26	26	**23**	212
rpoc_xits_08_UNSAT	N	154	1036	1115	398	**159**	–	589
gt-ordering-unsat-gt-060	N	15	171	–	–	**149**	–	–
9dlx_vliw_at_b_iq3	N	430	1137	–	–	–	1095	**430**
gss-19-s100	Y	38	641	–	611	–	–	**38**
UCG-20-5p1	Y	413	835	–	–	**537**	–	–
UTI-15-10p1	Y	392	935	–	**392**	–	–	1140
gt-ordering-sat-gt-040	Y	15	**6**	–	–	149	–	–
em_9_3_5_exp	Y	18	288	209	**51**	181	140	276
ndhf_xits_20	Y	1.6	180	–	–	249	–	75
partial-10-15-s	Y	228	**1092**	–	–	–	–	–
vmpc_30	Y	18	825	–	–	292	**159**	551
velev-pipe-sat-1.0-b7	Y	14	294	–	–	343	–	**87**
new-difficult-21-168-19-90	Y	0.1	**141**	–	–	–	370	416
mod3block_3vars_9gates...	Y	5.7	**4.8**	–	126	63	26	24
rbsat-v945c61409g10	Y	21	362	–	898	**147**	150	933
instance_n8_i9_pp	Y	41	**115**	454	1117	800	–	421

In conclusion of this experimental comparison, SATHYS is a very efficient solver in three categories (crafted, application and random) and consequently, it is the most robust solver. From the above results, we can consider SATHYS as the first hybrid solver that brings real advances to three of the ten challenges proposed in [35,24]:

- Challenge 5: *Design a practical stochastic local search procedure for proving unsatisfiability*;
- Challenge 6: *Improve stochastic local search on structured problems by efficiently handling variable dependencies*;
- Challenge 7: *Demonstrate the successful combination of stochastic search and systematic search techniques, by the creation of a new algorithm that outperforms the best previous examples of both approaches.*

5 Related Work

We presents here the most noticeable approaches combining local search and DPLL based ones. They can be classified in three different categories depending on which of the two solvers is considered as the main core of the hybrid solver.

The first category includes those using DPLL as the main solver and SLS as an oracle. In [5], SLS is used in a preprocessing step to derive a static variable ordering for DPLL. Weights representing the number of times each clause is falsified during the local search pretreatment is computed. The variable occurring most often in clauses with higher weights is selected first. The approach proposed in [28] extends the previous one, while invoking SLS at each node of the search tree. The SLS oracle is used to both extend the current partial assignment to a model or to select the next variable to assign according to similar clause weighting process. Similarly to [28], in [11], the authors introduce some conditions to reduce the number of calls to SLS. The variables are dynamically ordered according to local-search statistics. In [19], an hybrid constraint solving schema which retains some systematicity of constructive search while incorporating the heuristic guidance and lack of commitment to variable assignment of local search. The proposed method backtracks through a space of complete but possibly inconsistent solutions while supporting the freedom to move arbitrarily under heuristic guidance. hybridGM is an incomplete SAT solver proposed in [2] focusses the DPLL-search around local minima with only one unsatisfied clause.

If a formula is satisfiable, chances are to find a satisfying assignment around such minima. hybridGM's DPLL component then completely checks these areas of the search space. SATUN [12] an extension of hybridGM performs local search as it is done by hybridGM, but for a limited amount of time. The limit is set in a way that gives local search a reasonable chance to find a satisfying assignment. In case the formula is satisfiable, this will result in a performance competitive with the hybrid's SLS component. As soon as the limit is reached, the formula is expected to be unsatisfiable. SATUN's DPLL component will then perform a search on the complete search space of the formula to confirm that assumption.

The second category considers SLS as the main core of the hybrid solver. Among these approaches, we can cite the approach proposed in [18], where DPLL is used to derive implications between literals. These implications are used to both simplify the formula and to compute dependency relations between literals used during the local search phase.

In [23] the algorithm starts with a partial or complete interpretation. At each step constraint propagation is applied. In case of conflict, a nogood is learnt and local search is applied to repair the current partial interpretation. Otherwise, the current consistent interpretation is extended in a classical way. In [25], the authors propose an hybrid strategy based on shared memory, ideally suited for multi-core processor architectures. They particularly show that DPLL can provide highly effective guidance for a local search style solver for the MAXSAT problem. More precisely, DPLL shares its current partial assignment with SLS and a flip is not allowed if the variable is assigned with the same polarity by DPLL. The two solvers are run simultaneously on two different cores.

Finally, the last category contains hybrid solvers where both engines play an equal role. The hybrid solver HBISAT [10] and its extended and improved version hinotos [26] belong to this category. In both approaches, a local search is used to identify a subset of clauses to be passed to a DPLL SAT solver through an incremental interface. In other words, the guided local search identifies incremental sets of clauses that are hard, and these clauses are subsequently added to the clause database of the DPLL-based solver. In addition, the solution obtained by the DPLL solver on the subset of clauses is fed back to the local search solver to jump over any locally optimal points.

6 Conclusion

In this paper a novel integration of SLS and CDCL based SAT solvers is introduced. This hybrid solver represents an original combination of both engines. The two components heavily cooperate towards proving the satisfiability or unsatisfiability of the SAT formula. Such strong cooperation lies in the exploitation of SLS for directing CDCL search towards unsatisfiability proof; and CDCL for escaping from SLS local minima. SATHYS, the resulting method, obtains very good results on a wide range of instances taken from the last competitions. These results show important performance improvements of the state-of-the-art SLS and hybrid SLS solvers particularly on crafted and application category. More interestingly, SATHYS significantly reduces the performance gap between SLS and CDCL solvers while becoming extremely competitive with most of the state-of-the arts CDCL solvers on application instances. Consequently, SATHYS can be considered as the first successful hybrid SAT solver. A future work, we first plan to investigate how conflict driven clause learning can be adapted to local search based techniques. Secondly, as the cooperation scheme between the two solvers integrated in SATHYS is proven to be efficient, we plan to design a new parallel version of SATHYS in order to benefit from the computational resources of multicore based architectures.

References

1. Audemard, G., Simon, L.: Predicting learnt clauses quality in modern SAT solvers. In: Proceedings of International Joint Conference on Artificial Intelligence, pp. 399–404 (2009)
2. Balint, A., Henn, M., Gableske, O.: A novel approach to combine a SLS- and DPLL-solver for the satisfiability problem. In: Kullmann, O. (ed.) SAT 2009. LNCS, vol. 5584, pp. 284–297. Springer, Heidelberg (2009)
3. Biere, A.: PicoSAT essentials. Journal on Satisfiability 4, 75–97 (2008)
4. Biere, A., Heule, M., van Maaren, H., Walsh, T. (eds.): *Handbook of Satisfiability*, February 2009. Frontiers in Artificial Intelligence and Applications, vol. 185. IOS Press, Amsterdam (2009)
5. Crawford, J.: Solving satisfiability problems using a combination of systematic and local search. In: Second Challenge on Satisfiability Testing organized by Center for Discrete Mathematics and Computer Science of Rutgers University (1996)
6. Darwiche, A., Pipatsrisawat, K.: Complete Algorithms, ch. 3, pp. 99–130. IOS Press, Amsterdam (2009)
7. Davis, M., Logemann, G., Loveland, D.: A machine program for theorem-proving. Communication of ACM 5(7), 394–397 (1962)
8. Eén, N., Biere, A.: Effective preprocessing in SAT through variable and clause elimination. In: Bacchus, F., Walsh, T. (eds.) SAT 2005. LNCS, vol. 3569, pp. 61–75. Springer, Heidelberg (2005)
9. Een, N., Sörensson, N.: An extensible SAT-solver. In: Giunchiglia, E., Tacchella, A. (eds.) SAT 2003. LNCS, vol. 2919, pp. 502–518. Springer, Heidelberg (2004)
10. Fang, L., Hsiao, M.: A new hybrid solution to boost SAT solver performance. In: Proceedings of DATE, pp. 1307–1313 (2007)
11. Ferris, B., Fröhlich, J.: Walksat as an informed heuristic to DPLL in SAT solving. Technical report, CSE 573: Artificial Intelligence (2004)
12. Gableske, O., Rüth, J.: Satun: A complete hybrid sat solver. SAT2010 paper draft (2010)
13. Gebser, M., Kaufmann, B., Neumann, A., Schaub, T.: Conflict-driven answer set solving. In: Proceedings IJCAI 2007, pp. 386–392 (2007)
14. Goldberg, E.: Boundary points and resolution. In: Kullmann, O. (ed.) SAT 2009. LNCS, vol. 5584, pp. 147–160. Springer, Heidelberg (2009)
15. Gomes, C., Selman, B., Kautz, H.: Boosting combinatorial search through randomization. In: AAAI/IAAI, pp. 431–437 (1998)

16. Gregoire, E., Mazure, B., Piette, C.: Extracting MUSes. In: proceedings of ECAI, pp. 387–391 (2006)
17. Gregoire, E., Mazure, B., Piette, C.: Local-search extraction of muses. Constraints 12(3), 325–344 (2007)
18. Habet, D., Li, C.M., Devendeville, L., Vasquez, M.: A hybrid approach for sat. In: Van Hentenryck, P. (ed.) CP 2002. LNCS, vol. 2470, pp. 172–184. Springer, Heidelberg (2002)
19. Havens, W., Dilkina, B.: A hybrid schema for systematic local search. In: Canadian Conference on AI, pp. 248–260 (2004)
20. Hirsch, E., Kojevnikov, A.: Unitwalk: A new SAT solver that uses local search guided by unit clause elimination. Annals of Mathematical and Artificial Intelligence 43(1), 91–111 (2005)
21. Hoos, H.: An adaptive noise mechanism for walksat. In: proceedings of AAAI, pp. 655–660 (2002)
22. Hutter, F., Tompkins, D.A.D., Hoos, H.H.: Scaling and probabilistic smoothing: Efficient dynamic local search for SAT. In: Van Hentenryck, P. (ed.) CP 2002. LNCS, vol. 2470, pp. 233–248. Springer, Heidelberg (2002)
23. Jussien, N., Lhomme, O.: Local search with constraint propagation and conflict-based heuristics. In: AAAI/IAAI, pp. 169–174 (2000)
24. Kautz, H., Selman, B.: Ten challenges redux: Recent progress in propositional reasoning and search. In: Rossi, F. (ed.) CP 2003. LNCS, vol. 2833, pp. 1–18. Springer, Heidelberg (2003)
25. Kroc, L., Sabharwal, A., Gomes, C.P., Selman, B.: Integrating systematic and local search paradigms: A new strategy for maxsat. In: IJCAI, pp. 544–551 (2009)
26. Letombe, F., Marques-Silva, J.: Improvements to hybrid incremental sat algorithms. In: Kleine Büning, H., Zhao, X. (eds.) SAT 2008. LNCS, vol. 4996, pp. 168–181. Springer, Heidelberg (2008)
27. Li, C.M., Wei, W., Zhang, H.: Combining adaptive noise and look-ahead in local search for sat. In: Marques-Silva, J., Sakallah, K.A. (eds.) SAT 2007. LNCS, vol. 4501, pp. 121–133. Springer, Heidelberg (2007)
28. Mazure, B., Saïs, L., Grégoire, E.: Boosting complete techniques thanks to local search methods. Ann. Math. Artif. Intell. 22(3-4), 319–331 (1998)
29. McAllester, D., Selman, B., Kautz, H.: Evidence for invariants in local search. In: Proceedings of AAAI, pp. 321–326 (1997)
30. Moskewicz, M., Madigan, C., Zhao, Y., Zhang, L., Malik, S.: Chaff: Engineering an efficient SAT solver. In: Proceedings of DAC, pp. 530–535 (2001)
31. Pham, D.N., Thornton, J., Sattar, A.: Building structure into local search for sat. In: proceedings of IJCAI, pp. 2359–2364 (2007)
32. Pipatsrisawat, K., Darwiche, A.: A lightweight component caching scheme for satisfiability solvers. In: Marques-Silva, J., Sakallah, K.A. (eds.) SAT 2007. LNCS, vol. 4501, pp. 294–299. Springer, Heidelberg (2007)
33. Selman, B., Kautz, H.: An empirical study of greedy local search for satisfiability testing. In: Proceedings of AAAI, pp. 46–51 (1993)
34. Selman, B., Kautz, H., Cohen, B.: Noise strategies for improving local search. In: proceedings of AAAI, pp. 337–343 (1994)
35. Selman, B., Kautz, H., McAllester, D.: Ten challenges in propositional reasoning and search. In: Proceedings of IJCAI, pp. 50–54 (1997)
36. Marques Silva, J., Sakallah, K.: Grasp - a new search algorithm for satisfiability. In: ICCAD, pp. 220–227 (1996)
37. Xu, L., Hutter, F., Hoos, H.: K Leyton-Brown. Satzilla: Portfolio-based algorithm selection for sat. Journal of Artificial Intelligence Research 32, 565–606 (2008)
38. Zhang, L., Madigan, C., Moskewicz, M., Malik, S.: Efficient conflict driven learning in boolean satisfiability solver. In: proceedings of ICCAD, pp. 279–285 (2001)

Interpolating Quantifier-Free Presburger Arithmetic

Daniel Kroening[1], Jérôme Leroux[2], and Philipp Rümmer[1]

[1] Oxford University Computing Laboratory, United Kingdom
[2] Laboratoire Bordelais de Recherche en Informatique, France

Abstract. Craig interpolation has become a key ingredient in many symbolic model checkers, serving as an approximative replacement for expensive quantifier elimination. In this paper, we focus on an interpolating decision procedure for the full quantifier-free fragment of *Presburger Arithmetic*, i.e., linear arithmetic over the integers, a theory which is a good fit for the analysis of software systems. In contrast to earlier procedures based on quantifier elimination and the Omega test, our approach uses integer linear programming techniques: relaxation of interpolation problems to the rationals, and a complete branch-and-bound rule tailored to efficient interpolation. Equations are handled via a dedicated polynomial-time sub-procedure. We have fully implemented our procedure on top of the SMT-solver OpenSMT and present an extensive experimental evaluation.

1 Introduction

Craig interpolation has become a key ingredient in many symbolic model checkers, serving as an approximative replacement for expensive quantifier elimination [10]. The application of Craig interpolants in lieu of quantifier elimination relies on the availability of an effective *interpolating decision procedure*. In this paper, we focus on an interpolating decision procedure for the *quantifier-free fragment of Presburger Arithmetic (QFPA for short)*, that is linear arithmetic over the integers, a theory which is a good fit for the analysis of software systems. An interpolant ψ for a pair (ϕ_A, ϕ_B) of Presburger formulas is a Presburger formula such that free variables in ψ occur both in ϕ_A and ϕ_B, and such that ϕ_A entails ψ and ϕ_B entails $\neg\psi$.

Interpolating decision procedures typically derive the interpolant from a proof of inconsistency of ϕ_A and ϕ_B, which in turn is computed by a decision procedure for the underlying logic. Decision problems arising in software analysis are often large, and call for a scalable algorithm. The most efficient decision procedures for the quantifier-free fragment of the Presburger arithmetic known today use the Simplex algorithm in combination with a variant of the *branch-and-bound technique*. The Simplex algorithm is used to solve the *relaxed problem*, in which the variables are permitted to take fractional values. In case a variable x obtains the fractional value r, branch-and-bound will consider the two sub-problems in which $x \leq \lfloor r \rfloor$ or $x \geq \lceil r \rceil$, respectively. The original problem has an integer solution iff one of the two sub-problems has a solution. Branch-and-bound is incomplete by itself, and usually augmented by a *cutting-plane* technique, e.g., *Gomory's cutting planes*. An instance of an efficient implementation of these techniques is the SMT-solver Z3 [6].

In principle, any cut-based decision procedure for Presburger can be used for the computation of interpolants. The primary problem is computational cost: for the most

C. Fermüller and A. Voronkov (Eds.): LPAR-17, LNCS 6397, pp. 489–503, 2010.

common cut rules (in particular for Gomory's cutting planes) it is possible to construct cases where the derivation of interpolants from proofs has exponential complexity. This high complexity is caused by *mixed cuts*, which involve rounding (rational) constant terms of inequalities that are derived from both ϕ_A and ϕ_B. Intuitively, interpolating calculi rely on identifying which parts of ϕ_A and ϕ_B are contributing to an intermediate argument; additional effort is required when rounding intermediate arguments derived from both ϕ_A and ϕ_B.

The contribution of this paper is a novel interpolating decision procedure for the full QFPA fragment. Our algorithm computes in polynomial time interpolants for two classes of constraints (i) conjunctions of inequality constraints unsatisfiable over the rationals, and (ii) conjunctions of equality and divisibility constraints unsatisfiable over the integers. For the full QFPA fragment, the algorithm is exponential in the worst case. This complexity is proved tight since we exhibit formulas such that every interpolant is exponentially large. Moreover the algorithm improves the doubly exponential upper bound complexity known for the computation of interpolants based on the elimination of blocks of quantifiers [17]. Our general procedure integrates efficient reasoning and interpolation for equalities by means of a transformation of matrices into Smith Normal Form, which resembles a known procedure for interpolating linear diophantine equations [7]. For reasoning about inequalities, our procedure uses a complete version of the branch-and-cut principle that avoids mixed cuts and therefore allows interpolant extraction from proofs in polynomial time. Since the proof size is exponentially large in the worst case, we deduce an exponential upper bound for the runtime of the algorithm.

Related Work. Interpolation procedures have been proposed for various fragments of linear integer arithmetic. McMillan considers the logic of difference-bound constraints [12]. This logic, a fragment of QFPA, is decidable by reduction to rational arithmetic. As an extension, Cimatti et al. [5] present an interpolation procedure for the unit two variable per inequality (UTVPI) fragment of linear integer arithmetic. Both fragments allow efficient reasoning and interpolation, but are not sufficient to express many typical program constructs, such as integer division. In [7], interpolation procedures for QFPA restricted to conjunctions of integer linear (dis)equalities, and for QFPA restricted to conjunctions of divisibility constraints are given. The combination of both fragments with integer linear inequalities is not supported, however. Our work closes this gap, as it permits predicates involving all types of constraints.

Lynch et al. [9] define an interpolation procedure for linear rational arithmetic, and extend it to integer arithmetic by means of Gomory cuts. For integer arithmetic, however, interpolation in [9] can produce formulas that violate the vocabulary condition (i.e., can contain variables that are not common to ϕ_A and ϕ_B), and are therefore not true interpolants. The problem is that Gomory cuts used in [9] do not prevent mixed cuts, for which no efficient interpolation is possible in QFPA.

Brillout et al. [2] define a complete interpolating sequent calculus for QFPA. The calculus contains a rule strengthen that is general enough to simulate arbitrary (possibly mixed) Gomory cuts, but in general causes exponential complexity of interpolant extraction from proofs. In contrast, our cut rule (which is embedded in an effective decision procedure) enables extraction with polynomial complexity.

The recent SMT-solver *SmtInterpol* decides and interpolates problems in linear integer arithmetic, apparently using an architecture similar to the one in [11]. To the best of our knowledge, the precise design and calculus of *SmtInterpol* has not been documented in publications yet (see Sect. 9 for an empirical comparison with our approach).

Interpolation for rational arithmetic is a well-explored field. McMillan presents an interpolating theorem prover for linear rational arithmetic and uninterpreted functions [11]; an interpolating SMT-solver for the same logic has been developed by Beyer et al. [1]. Rybalchenko et al. introduce an algorithm for interpolating rational arithmetic with uninterpreted functions without the need for explicit proofs [15].

2 Interpolation for Quantifier-Free Presburger Formulas

Naturally, if there exists an interpolant ψ for (ϕ_A, ϕ_B) then $\phi_A \wedge \phi_B$ is unsatisfiable. Conversely, if $\phi_A \wedge \phi_B$ is unsatisfiable, interpolants for (ϕ_A, ϕ_B) can be obtained by introducing the sets X_A, X_B of free variables of respectively ϕ_A and ϕ_B, and the following Presburger formulas:

$$\begin{array}{lcrl} \psi_\bot & = & (\exists x)_{x \in X_A \setminus X_B} & \phi_A \\ \psi_\top & = & \neg\,(\exists x)_{x \in X_B \setminus X_A} & \phi_B \end{array}$$

Since $\phi_A \wedge \phi_B$ is unsatisfiable we observe that $\psi_\bot$ and $\psi_\top$ are two interpolants for (ϕ_A, ϕ_B). The formulas $\psi_\bot$ and $\psi_\top$ are respectively called the *strongest interpolant* and the *weakest interpolant* since $\psi_\bot$ entails ψ and ψ entails $\psi_\top$ for any interpolant ψ.

We are interested in computing quantifier-free Presburger interpolants for pairs of quantifier-free Presburger formulas. Formulas in this logic are defined by fixing a countable set X of variables. Quantifier-free Presburger formulas are formulas in the following grammar where $x \in X$, $\alpha \in \mathbb{Z}$, $\beta \in \mathbb{Z}$ and $m \in \mathbb{N}_{\geq 2}$:

$$\begin{array}{lcl} \phi & ::= & p \mid \neg\phi \mid \phi \wedge \phi \mid \phi \vee \phi \\ p & ::= & l \neq \beta \mid l = \beta \mid l \leq \beta \mid l \in \beta + m\mathbb{Z} \\ l & ::= & 0 \mid \alpha x \mid l + l \end{array}$$

The category l denotes *linear terms*. The category p denotes *predicates of linear arithmetic*. For simplicity reason, we only allow constants β as right-hand side of the predicates. Predicates $l \neq \beta$, $l = \beta$ and $l \leq \beta$ are respectively *disequality predicates*, *equality predicates*, and *inequality predicates*. Predicates $l \in \beta + m\mathbb{Z}$ are *divisibility predicates*, which are short-hand notation for $\exists x\ l - mx = \beta$. These predicates are included to allow quantifier-free interpolation. In fact, let us consider the pair $(x - 2y = 0,\ x - 2z = 1)$ of quantifier-free Presburger formulas. Note that x is the unique free variable that occurs in both formulas. The even divisibility predicate $x \in 2\mathbb{Z}$ is an interpolant; any interpolant requires at least one divisibility predicate.

The semantics of Presburger formulas is defined as is common over the domain $\mathbb{Z}$ of integers. We write $\phi \models \psi$ to express that ϕ *entails* ψ, i.e., ψ holds whenever ϕ holds.

Since Presburger formulas are effectively equivalent to quantifier-free Presburger formulas, we can compute two quantifier-free Presburger formulas $\psi'_\bot$ and $\psi'_\top$ equivalent to $\psi_\bot$ and $\psi_\top$ respectively. In particular if $\phi_A \wedge \phi_B$ is unsatisfiable, we deduce that $\psi'_\bot$ and $\psi'_\top$ are two quantifier-free interpolants for (ϕ_A, ϕ_B). However, the computation of $\psi'_\bot$ or $\psi'_\top$ requires a lot of useless computational efforts. For instance if ϕ_A is a formula of the form $(x = 0) \wedge \phi'_A$ and ϕ_B is a formula of the form $(x = 1) \wedge \phi'_B$ where ϕ'_A and ϕ'_B are very complex Presburger formulas, it is sufficient to consider $\psi = (x = 0)$ to obtain an interpolant for (ϕ_A, ϕ_B); eliminating variables for computing $\psi'_\bot$ and $\psi'_\top$ can be very difficult. From a theoretical point of view, up to our knowledge the best known upper-bound complexity for eliminating blocks of existential quantifiers is double-exponential [17].

In this paper we provide an algorithm computing interpolants for the QFPA fragment in exponential time in the worst case. We first show that this result is tight. For this purpose, consider the following families of formulas (where $n \in \mathbb{N}_{>1}$):

$$\phi_A^n \;=\; -n < y + 2nx \leq 0, \qquad \phi_B^n \;=\; 0 < y + 2nz \leq n\,.$$

We can observe that ϕ_A^n and ϕ_B^n are inconsistent, and that the only interpolant for the interpolation problem (ϕ_A^n, ϕ_B^n) is the following formula ψ (up to equivalence):

$$\psi \;=\; \Big(y \in -n + 1 + 2n\mathbb{N}\Big) \vee \Big(y \in -n + 2 + 2n\mathbb{N}\Big) \vee \cdots \vee \Big(y \in 2n\mathbb{N}\Big)$$

The size of ψ is linear in n, and therefore exponential in the size of (ϕ_A^n, ϕ_B^n); the same holds for all equivalent quantifier-free formulas in Presburger arithmetic.

Using a SAT approach [11] we reduce the interpolation computation problem to conjunctions of *literals* (predicates or negation of predicates) extracted from ϕ_A and ϕ_B. In particular, w.l.o.g. we can assume that ϕ_A, ϕ_B are conjunctions of *literals*. By introducing fresh variables, we can assume that explicit divisibility predicates do not appear. In fact, let us consider the formulas ϕ'_A and ϕ'_B obtained from ϕ_A and ϕ_B by replacing $l \in \beta + m\mathbb{Z}$ and $\neg(l \in \beta + m\mathbb{Z})$ by respectively $l - mx = \beta$ and $l - mx - y = \beta \wedge -y \leq -1 \wedge y \leq m - 1$ where x, y are two fresh variables distinct for each replaced predicate. Since introduced variables are local to either ϕ'_A or ϕ'_B we deduce that any formula is an interpolant for (ϕ_A, ϕ_B) if and only if it is an interpolant for (ϕ'_A, ϕ'_B). Thus, we can assume without loss of generality that ϕ_A and ϕ_B do not contain divisibility predicates.

Finally, since the negations of the predicates $l \neq \beta$, $l = \beta$, $l \leq \beta$ are equivalent to the predicates $l = \beta$, $l \neq \beta$, $-l \leq -\beta - 1$, we can assume that the literals of ϕ_A and ϕ_B are predicates (without negation). We have reduced our problem to the computation of interpolants for formulas ϕ_A, ϕ_B that are conjunctions of disequality, equality and inequality predicates.

3 Overview of the Interpolation Procedure

We assume the vocabulary $X = \{x_1, \ldots, x_n\}$, using an arbitrary but fixed enumeration of the variables, and denote the vector of all variables by $x = (x_1, \ldots, x_n)^t$. We identify a linear term l with the matrix product $l = u^t x$ where $u = (\alpha_1, \ldots, \alpha_n)^t \in \mathbb{Z}^n$ denotes coefficients of x in l, i.e. $l = \alpha_1 x_1 + \cdots + \alpha_n x_n$. We associate to a predicate p the vector $u_p \in \mathbb{Z}^n$, the relation $\#_p \in \{\neq, =, \leq\}$, and the integer $\beta_p \in \mathbb{Z}$ such that p is denoted by $u_p^t x \#_p \beta_p$. *Valuations* of X are identified with vectors $v = (v_1, \ldots, v_n)^t \in \mathbb{Z}^n$ such that v *satisfies* a predicate p if $u_p^t v \#_p \beta_p$ holds. We introduce the *ith elementary vector* $e_{i,n}$ *of* $\mathbb{Z}^n$ (simply denoted by e_i when n is unambiguous) defined by:

$$e_{i,n} = (\underbrace{0,\ldots,0}_{i-1 \text{ zeroes}},1,0,\ldots,0)^t \in \mathbb{Z}^n$$

Predicates are strengthened with *interval* labels. The ordered set $(\mathbb{Z},\leq)$ is extended into $(\mathbb{Z}_\infty,\leq)$ where $\mathbb{Z}_\infty = \mathbb{Z}\cup\{-\infty,\infty\}$ and $\leq$ satisfies $-\infty \leq \delta \leq \infty$ for every $\delta \in \mathbb{Z}_\infty$. An *(integral) interval* is a a set of the form $[\![\delta_-,\delta_+]\!] = \{\delta \in \mathbb{Z} \mid \delta_- \leq \delta \leq \delta_+\}$ where $\delta_-,\delta_+ \in \mathbb{Z}_\infty$. The interval $[\![\delta,\delta]\!]$ where $\delta \in \mathbb{Z}$ is simply denoted by $\{\delta\}$. In the sequel, a predicate p labelled with an interval I is denoted by $(p)_I$. Semantically, a labelled predicate $(p)_I$ is satisfied by a valuation v if v satisfies p and $u_p^t v \in I$. In order to simplify the presentation, we assume that $I \subseteq \{\beta_p\}$ if p is an equality and $I \subseteq [\![-\infty,\beta_p]\!]$ if p is an inequality. The label of a disequality can be any interval. Observe that any unlabeled formula ϕ is equivalent to a labelled one satisfying the previous labeling conventions. Given a conjunction ϕ of labelled predicates, we denote by $\bar{\phi}$ the formula obtained from ϕ by unlabeling the predicates.

We first show on the following example how the unsatisfiability of a conjunction $\phi = \phi_A \wedge \phi_B$ can be discovered by analyzing *systems of inequalities over the rational numbers* and *systems of equalities over the integers*. We consider the following formulas:

$$\phi_A = (x-2y \leq 0)_{[\![-\infty,0]\!]} \wedge (2y-x \leq 0)_{[\![-\infty,0]\!]} \qquad \phi_B = (x-2z \leq 1)_{[\![-\infty,1]\!]} \wedge (2z-x \leq -1)_{[\![-\infty,-1]\!]}$$

The label of $(2z-x \leq -1)_{[\![-\infty,-1]\!]}$ is first partitioned into $J_1 \cup J_2$ where $J_1 = [\![-\infty,-2]\!]$ and $J_2 = \{-1\}$. We observe that ϕ is unsatisfiable if and only if both the formulas $\phi_1 = \phi_{A,1} \wedge \phi_{B,1}$ and $\phi_2 = \phi_{A,2} \wedge \phi_{B,2}$ are unsatisfiable, where $\phi_{A,1} = \phi_A, \phi_{A,2} = \phi_A$, and:

$$\phi_{B,1} = (x-2z \leq 1)_{[\![-\infty,1]\!]} \wedge (2z-x \leq -1)_{J_1} \qquad \phi_{B,2} = (x-2z \leq 1)_{[\![-\infty,1]\!]} \wedge (2z-x \leq -1)_{J_2}$$

We introduce the system of *interval predicates* extracted from ϕ_1 labels, i.e. $-\infty \leq x-2y \leq 0 \wedge -\infty \leq 2y-x \leq 0 \wedge -\infty \leq x-2z \leq 1 \wedge -\infty \leq 2z-x \leq -2$. An LP-solver decides in polynomial time its unsatisfiability over the rational numbers. In particular we deduce that ϕ_1 is unsatisfiable over the integers. The unsatisfiability of ϕ_2 is obtained by partitioning the label of $(x-2y \leq 0)_{[\![-\infty,0]\!]}$ into $J_3 \cup J_4$ where $J_3 = [\![-\infty,-1]\!]$ and $J_4 = \{0\}$. We observe that ϕ_2 is unsatisfiable if and only if both the following formulas $\phi_3 = \phi_{A,3} \wedge \phi_{B,3}$ and $\phi_4 = \phi_{A,4} \wedge \phi_{B,4}$ are unsatisfiable, where $\phi_{B,3} = \phi_{B,2}, \phi_{B,4} = \phi_{B,2}$, and:

$$\phi_{A,3} = (x-2y \leq 0)_{J_3} \wedge (2y-x \leq 0)_{[\![-\infty,0]\!]} \qquad \phi_{A,4} = (x-2y \leq 0)_{J_4} \wedge (2y-x \leq 0)_{[\![-\infty,0]\!]}$$

From the system of interval predicates extracted from ϕ_3 labels, an LP-solver shows that ϕ_3 is unsatisfiable. Finally, let us consider the system of equalities extracted from the ϕ_4 labels, i.e. $x-2y = 0 \wedge 2z-x = -1$. Since this system is unsatisfiable over the integers, we deduce that ϕ_4 is unsatisfiable. We have proved that ϕ is unsatisfiable by strengthening predicates until either a system of inequalities becomes unsatisfiable over the rational numbers, or a system of equalities becomes unsatisfiable over the integers.

Now, we exhibit a way for computing an interpolant ψ for (ϕ_A, ϕ_B). From the system of inequalities proving that ϕ_1 is unsatisfiable over the rational numbers, we deduce in Sect. 5 that $\psi_1 = (true)$ is an interpolant for $(\phi_{A,1}, \phi_{B,1})$. The same approach shows that $\psi_3 = (\mathit{false})$ is an interpolant for $(\phi_{A,3}, \phi_{B,3})$. From the system of equalities proving that ϕ_4 is unsatisfiable, we deduce in Sect. 4 that $\psi_4 = (x \in 2\mathbb{Z})$ is an interpolant for $(\phi_{A,4}, \phi_{B,4})$. Finally, we show in Sect. 7 that an interpolant for (ϕ_A, ϕ_B) can be obtained from ψ_1, ψ_3 and ψ_4 by considering the following tree where the leaves ϕ_1, ϕ_3 and ϕ_4 are respectively labelled by the interpolants ψ_1, ψ_3 and ψ_4, where the node ϕ is labelled by $\wedge$ since the partitioned label of ϕ comes from its B part, and where the node ϕ_2 is labelled by $\vee$ since the partitioned label of ϕ_2 comes from its A part. This tree provides the interpolant $\psi = \mathit{true} \wedge (\mathit{false} \vee x \in 2\mathbb{Z})$ for (ϕ_A, ϕ_B):

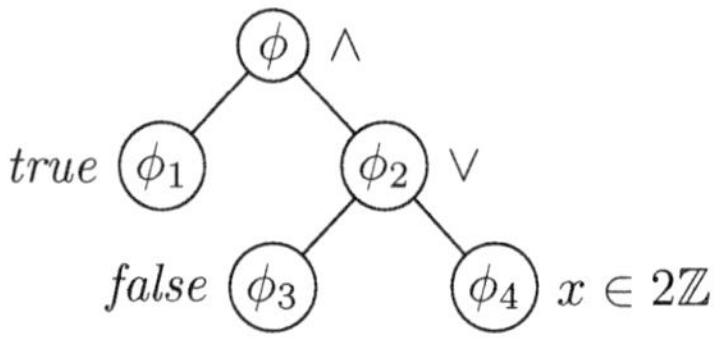

Our general algorithm follows this approach. Now, let us assume that ϕ_A and ϕ_B are any conjunctions of labelled predicates. Interpolants for (ϕ_A, ϕ_B) or valuations w satisfying $\bar{\phi}_A \wedge \bar{\phi}_B$ are computed using algorithm interpolant(ϕ_A , ϕ_B).

```
interpolant( φA , φB )
  if check_equality( φA , φB ) returns a formula ψ return ψ
  if check_inequality( φA , φB ) returns a formula ψ return ψ
  if check_unsatpred( φA , φB ) returns a formula ψ return ψ
  return strengthening( φA , φB )
```

This algorithm first executes three sub-algorithms check_equality, check_inequality and check_unsatpred respectively presented in Sect. 4, Sect. 5 and Sect. 6:

- check_equality returns in polynomial time an interpolant if a system of equalities extracted from ϕ_A and ϕ_B labels is unsatisfiable over the integers.
- check_inequality returns in polynomial time an interpolant if a system of inequalities extracted from ϕ_A and ϕ_B labels is unsatisfiable over the rational numbers.
- check_unsatpred returns in linear time an interpolant if an unsatisfiable labelled predicate occurs in ϕ_A or ϕ_B. This sub-algorithm is required for the termination when disequalities occur in ϕ_A or ϕ_B.

When these sub-algorithms fail in computing an interpolant, the sub-algorithm strengthening is executed. It tries to compute a valuation satisfying $\bar{\phi}_A \wedge \bar{\phi}_B$. If it fails, the label of a predicate is partitioned and algorithm interpolant is recursively called on each element of the partition. This last sub-algorithm is presented in Sect. 7.

4 Unsatisfiable Equalities over the Integers

This section describes interpolation in the case that the inconsistency of $\phi_A \wedge \phi_B$ is caused by equations. To this end, we extract a system $U_A x = d_A$ of equations from ϕ_A, where $U_A \in \mathbb{Z}^{m \times n}$ is an integer matrix and $d_A \in \mathbb{Z}^m$ is an integer vector. The system $U_A x = d_A$ consists of all equations $u_p^t x = \delta$ such that ϕ_A contains a predicate p labelled with a singleton $J = \{\delta\}$. The same is done for ϕ_B by introducing $U_B \in \mathbb{Z}^{l \times n}$ and $d_B \in \mathbb{Z}^l$. We also introduce the formulas ϕ'_A and ϕ'_B obtained from ϕ_A and ϕ_B by keeping the other labelled predicates $(p)_I$ with I not reduced to a singleton. The conjunctions ϕ_A, ϕ_B can then be represented in the form

$$\phi_A \;=\; U_A x = d_A \wedge \phi'_A, \qquad \phi_B \;=\; U_B x = d_B \wedge \phi'_B$$

In order to examine the satisfiability of the two systems $U_A x = d_A$, $U_B x = d_B$ of equations, we combine them to

$$Ux = d, \qquad U = \begin{pmatrix} U_A \\ U_B \end{pmatrix} \in \mathbb{Z}^{(l+m)\times n},\; d = \begin{pmatrix} d_A \\ d_B \end{pmatrix} \in \mathbb{Z}^{l+m}$$

and solve them by transforming the matrix U into *Smith Normal Form* (SNF):

Lemma 4.1 (Smith Normal Form of integer matrices). *Suppose $U \in \mathbb{Z}^{k \times n}$ is an integer matrix. U can be represented as $U = LSR$, such that $L \in \mathbb{Z}^{k \times k}$ and $R \in \mathbb{Z}^{n \times n}$ are invertible (in the respective rings of integer matrices), and $S \in \mathbb{Z}^{k \times n}$ is in* Smith Normal Form*:*

$$S = \begin{pmatrix} \alpha_1 & 0 & \cdots & & & \cdots & 0 \\ 0 & \alpha_2 & \ddots & & & & \vdots \\ \vdots & \ddots & \ddots & \ddots & & & \\ & & \ddots & \alpha_r & 0 & & \\ \vdots & & & 0 & 0 & & \vdots \\ 0 & \cdots & & & & \cdots & 0 \end{pmatrix}$$

where $r \leq \min\{k, n\}$ and $\alpha_1, \ldots, \alpha_r$ are positive integers such that $\alpha_{i+1} \in \alpha_i \mathbb{Z}$ for all $i \in \{1, \ldots, r-1\}$. The matrices L, S, R can effectively be computed from U in polynomial time [8].

Given the decomposition $U = LSR$, the satisfiability of the system $Ux = d \Leftrightarrow SRx = L^{-1}d$ can directly be determined: a solution to the equations exists if and only if (i) each element α_i of S divides the ith component of $L^{-1}d$, and (ii) for each $r < i \leq k$ the ith component of $L^{-1}d$ is zero.

We first consider the case that the system $Ux = d$ is unsatisfiable (satisfiable systems are discussed in Sect. 7). In this case, an interpolant can be computed from the equations without involving the inequalities or disequalities in ϕ'_A, ϕ'_B. An interpolation procedure for equations has been described in [7] (using transformation of matrices to Hermite Normal Form) and can easily be carried over to our context of matrices in SNF.

If $Ux = d$ is unsatisfiable, then the equivalent system $S(Rx) = L^{-1}d$ contains an unsatisfiable equation

$$e_i^t S(Rx) = e_i^t L^{-1} d$$

such that the right-hand side $e_i^t L^{-1} d$ cannot be represented as an integral linear combination of the left-hand side coefficients $e_i^t S$. This equation can be obtained as a linear combination of the equations in $Ux = d$ by left-multiplying with the row vector $s^t = e_i^t L^{-1}$. Restricting this linear combination to the equations from ϕ_A and eliminating variables that only occur in ϕ_A (the variables $X_A \backslash X_B$) yields an interpolant:

$$\psi = (\exists x_j)_{x_j \in X_A \backslash X_B}\ s^t \begin{pmatrix} U_A \\ 0 \end{pmatrix} x = s^t \begin{pmatrix} d_A \\ 0 \end{pmatrix}$$

Note that a quantifier-free interpolant can trivially be obtained by rewriting the existential quantifiers to a divisibility constraint: a formula like $\exists y_1, \ldots, y_u.\ \beta_1 y_1 + \cdots + \beta_u y_u + l = \beta$ is equivalent to the constraint $l \in \beta + \gcd(\beta_1, \ldots, \beta_u)\mathbb{Z}$.

To see that ψ is indeed an interpolant for (ϕ_A, ϕ_B), we can first observe that the following entailments hold:

$$\phi_A \models U_A x = d_A \models s^t \begin{pmatrix} U_A \\ 0 \end{pmatrix} x = s^t \begin{pmatrix} d_A \\ 0 \end{pmatrix} \models \psi$$

Vice versa, because $s^t U x = s^t d$ is unsatisfiable and the variables $X_A \backslash X_B$ do not occur in ϕ_B, it is also the case that ϕ_B and ψ are inconsistent:

$$\phi_B \models s^t \begin{pmatrix} 0 \\ U_B \end{pmatrix} x = s^t \begin{pmatrix} 0 \\ d_B \end{pmatrix} \models \neg\psi$$

The following algorithm summarizes the equality interpolation procedure:

```
check_equality( φ_A , φ_B )
  extract equality systems U_A x = d_A and U_B x = d_B from φ_A and φ_B
  let L, S, R be the Smith Normal Form decomposition of U
  if there exists i such that e_i^t S R x = e_i^t L^{-1} d is unsatisfiable
   let s^t = e_i^t L^{-1}
    return a divisibility predicate equivalent to:
      (∃x)_{x ∈ X_A \ X_B} s^t (U_A; 0) x = s^t (d_A; 0)
```

Proposition 4.2. *Algorithm* check_equality(ϕ_A , ϕ_B) *returns in polynomial time an interpolant for* (ϕ_A, ϕ_B) *if the system of equalities* $Ux = d$ *is not satisfiable over the integers.*

5 Unsatisfiable Inequalities over the Rationals

Interpolation procedures for linear inequalities over the rationals have been described in [13, 11], and are in the following paragraphs adapted to our setting. In order to examine the satisfiability of $\phi_A \wedge \phi_B$ over the rationals, we extract systems of inequalities $C_A x \leq c_A$ and $C_B x \leq c_B$ (with $C_A \in \mathbb{Z}^{m' \times n}$, $C_B \in \mathbb{Z}^{l' \times n}$, $c_A \in \mathbb{Z}^{m'}$, and $c_B \in \mathbb{Z}^{l'}$) from the labelled predicates in ϕ_A, ϕ_B. More precisely, whenever ϕ_A contains a predicate $(p)_I$ such that $I = [\![\delta_-, \delta_+]\!]$ then $C_A x \leq c_A$ contains the inequalities $-u_p^t x \leq -\delta_-$ and

$u_p^t x \leq \delta_+$ if $\delta_-, \delta_+ \in \mathbb{Z}$. Predicates labelled with an interval I such that $\delta_- = -\infty$ or $\delta_+ = \infty$ are in the same way translated to single inequalities.

The system $C_B x \leq c_B$ is constructed in the same manner from ϕ_B. As in Sect. 4, we then combine both systems into one:

$$Cx \leq c, \qquad C = \begin{pmatrix} C_A \\ C_B \end{pmatrix} \in \mathbb{Z}^{(l'+m')\times n}, \; c = \begin{pmatrix} c_A \\ c_B \end{pmatrix} \in \mathbb{Z}^{l'+m'}$$

A complete criterion for the solvability of $Cx \leq c$ is given by *Farkas' lemma* [16]:

Lemma 5.1 (Farkas). *Suppose $C \in \mathbb{Q}^{k\times n}$ is a rational matrix and $c \in \mathbb{Q}^k$ is a vector. Exactly one of the following statements is true:*

- *The system $Cx \leq c$ is satisfiable: there is a vector $v \in \mathbb{Q}^n$ such that $Cv \leq c$.*
- *There is a non-negative vector $w \in \mathbb{Q}^k$ such that $w^t C = 0$ and $w^t c < 0$.*

We can decide in polynomial time which case holds, and simultaneously compute the corresponding vector v or w.

For the rest of this section, let us assume that the second case holds, and that we have computed a non-negative vector $w \in \mathbb{Q}^{l'+m'}$ as in the lemma (the first case is discussed in the next section). Without loss of generality, we assume that w is integral, because w can be multiplied with any possibly occurring denominators. The following inequality is an interpolant for (ϕ_A, ϕ_B):

$$\psi = w^t \begin{pmatrix} C_A \\ 0 \end{pmatrix} x \leq w^t \begin{pmatrix} c_A \\ 0 \end{pmatrix}$$

To see that ψ is an interpolant, first recall that $w^t C = 0$, which implies that the term $w^t \binom{C_A}{0} x$ only contains variables that also occur in $w^t \binom{0}{C_B} x$. This means that all free variables in ψ occur both in ϕ_A and ϕ_B.

Furthermore, the entailment $\phi_A \models \psi$ holds:

$$\phi_A \models C_A x \leq c_A \models \begin{pmatrix} C_A \\ 0 \end{pmatrix} x \leq \begin{pmatrix} c_A \\ 0 \end{pmatrix} \models \psi$$

We can, vice versa, derive a formula from ϕ_B that contradicts ψ, because the combined inequality $w^t C x \leq w^t c$ is unsatisfiable by construction:

$$\phi_B \models C_B x \leq c_B \models \begin{pmatrix} 0 \\ C_B \end{pmatrix} x \leq \begin{pmatrix} 0 \\ c_B \end{pmatrix} \models w^t \begin{pmatrix} 0 \\ C_B \end{pmatrix} x \leq w^t \begin{pmatrix} 0 \\ c_B \end{pmatrix} \models \neg\psi$$

Altogether, we have proved that ψ is an interpolant for (ϕ_A, ϕ_B). The following algorithm summarizes the inequality interpolation procedure:

```
check_inequality( φ_A , φ_B )
  extract inequality systems C_A x ≤ c_A and C_B x ≤ c_B from φ_A and φ_B
  if there exists w ∈ Z^k such that w^t C = 0 and w^t c < 0
    return the inequality predicate:
      w^t (C_A; 0) x ≤ w^t (c_A; 0)
```

Proposition 5.2. *Algorithm* check_inequality(ϕ_A , ϕ_B) *returns in polynomial time an interpolant for (ϕ_A, ϕ_B) if the system of inequalities $Cx \leq c$ is not satisfiable over the rationals.*

6 Unsatisfiable Predicates

We observe that *false* or *true* are trivial interpolants for (ϕ_A, ϕ_B) if an unsatisfiable predicate $(p)_I$ occurs in ϕ_A or ϕ_B. Algorithm check_unsatpred implements this idea. This algorithm is important for the termination of algorithm interpolant. In fact, an alternative version of algorithm interpolant without check_unsatpred never terminates on (ϕ_A, ϕ_B) with $\phi_A = (x = 0)_{\{0\}}$ and $\phi_B = (x \neq 0)_{\mathbb{Z}}$.

```
check_unsatpred( φA , φB )
  if an unsatisfiable predicate (p)I occurs in φA return false
  if an unsatisfiable predicate (p)I occurs in φB return true
```

Proposition 6.1. *Algorithm* check_unsatpred(ϕ_A , ϕ_B) *returns in linear time an interpolant for* (ϕ_A, ϕ_B) *if an unsatisfiable predicate* $(p)_I$ *occurs in* ϕ_A *or* ϕ_B.

7 When Strengthening Is Necessary

We assume that (i) the system of equalities $Ux = d$ introduced in Sect. 4 admits an integral solution, and (ii) the system of inequalities $Cx \leq c$ introduced in Sect. 5 admits a rational solution.

Farkas' lemma provides in polynomial time a vector $v \in \mathbb{Q}^n$ such that $Cv \leq c$. This vector is rounded up to a vector $w \in \mathbb{Z}^n$ satisfying the system of equalities $Ux = d$ by using the Smith Normal Form decomposition LSR of U (see Sect. 4):

$$w = R^{-1}[Rv]$$

where $[Rv]$ is the *integral part* of Rv, i.e. the unique vector in $\mathbb{Z}^n$ such that there exists a vector $\epsilon \in \mathbb{Q}^n$ satisfying $Rv = [Rv] + \epsilon$ and $-\frac{1}{2} < \epsilon_i \leq \frac{1}{2}$ for every i.

Lemma 7.1. *Vector w satisfies the system of equalities $Ux = d$.*

Intuitively w is "not so far" from v since $v = w + R^{-1}\epsilon$, and since v satisfies the system of inequalities $Cx \leq c$ it is quite possible that w also satisfies this system. Hence this vector is a good candidate for a valuation satisfying $\phi_A \wedge \phi_B$. Note that if w does not satisfy this conjunction but it satisfies the more relaxed formula $\bar{\phi}_A \wedge \bar{\phi}_B$ obtained from $\phi_A \wedge \phi_B$ by removing the labels, we have discovered a solution to our original problem (labels are just used to prove the unsatisfiability). So let us assume that w is not a solution of $\bar{\phi}_A \wedge \bar{\phi}_B$. In this case, there exists a labelled predicate $(p)_I$ that occurs in $\phi_A \wedge \phi_B$ such that w does not satisfy p. We introduce the *pivot value* $\mu = u_p^t v$ for partitioning I into the following three disjoint intervals $I_\mu^<$, $I_\mu^=$, and $I_\mu^>$ where $I_\mu^\# = \{\delta \in I \mid \delta \# \mu\}$. We select the rational value μ for partitioning I since $\mu \in I$ (recall that v satisfies the system $Cx \leq c$). Note that the integral value $u_p^t w$ is not a good choice for partitioning I since in general this value is not in I. In particular w is just used to select a predicate p and its value is no longer used in the sequel.

The decomposition of I into $(I_\mu^<, I_\mu^=, I_\mu^>)$ should not be replaced by the partitions $(I_\mu^<, I_\mu^\geq)$ or $(I_\mu^\leq, I_\mu^>)$ since the termination of the algorithm is no longer guaranteed with these partitions. In fact the partition $(I_\mu^<, I_\mu^\geq)$ degenerates to $(\emptyset, I)$ if μ is the lower bound of I and the partition $(I_\mu^\leq, I_\mu^>)$ degenerates to $(I, \emptyset)$ if μ is the upper bound of I. Intuitively in these two cases the predicate $(p)_I$ is not really strengthened.

An interpolant ψ for (ϕ_A, ϕ_B) is deduced from interpolants $\psi^\#$ of $(\phi_A^\#, \phi_B^\#)$ for each $\# \in \{<, =, >\}$ by introducing the following formula:

$$\psi = \begin{cases} \psi^< \vee \psi^= \vee \psi^> & \text{if } (p)_I \text{ occurs in } \phi_A \\ \psi^< \wedge \psi^= \wedge \psi^> & \text{if } (p)_I \text{ occurs in } \phi_B \end{cases}$$

---

strengthening(ϕ_A , ϕ_B)
  `let` $v \in \mathbb{Q}^n$ such that $Cv \leq c$
  `let` $w = R^{-1}[Rv]$
  `if` w satisfies $\bar{\phi}_A \wedge \bar{\phi}_B$ `return` w
  `let` $(p)_I$ be a labelled predicate of $\phi_A \wedge \phi_B$ such that w does not satisfy p
  `let` $\mu = u_p^t v$
  `foreach` $\# \in \{<, =, >\}$
    `let` $(\phi_A^\#, \phi_B^\#)$ obtained from (ϕ_A, ϕ_B) by replacing I by $I_\mu^\#$
    `let` $\psi^\#$=interpolant($\phi_A^\#$, $\phi_B^\#$)
    `if` the previous function returns a valuation w `return` w
  `return` $\begin{cases} \psi^< \vee \psi^= \vee \psi^> & \texttt{if } (p)_I \text{ occurs in } \phi_A \\ \psi^< \wedge \psi^= \wedge \psi^> & \texttt{if } (p)_I \text{ occurs in } \phi_B \end{cases}$

Proposition 7.2. *When algorithm* interpolant(ϕ_A , ϕ_B) *terminates, it returns either an interpolant for* (ϕ_A, ϕ_B) *or a valuation* $w \in \mathbb{Z}^n$ *satisfying* $\bar{\phi}_A \wedge \bar{\phi}_B$.

8 Termination and Complexity

The exponential worst case execution time of interpolant is proved using a rooted tree that logs the algorithm execution. As expected a node N denotes a recursive sub-call of interpolant with input (ϕ_A^N, ϕ_B^N). Internal nodes N have three children denoted by $N_\#$ with $\# \in \{<, =, >\}$.

We first examine sub-algorithm strengthening(ϕ_A , ϕ_B) when the computed vector $v \in \mathbb{Q}^n$ is rounded up into an integer vector $w \in \mathbb{Z}^n$ that is not a solution of $\bar{\phi}_A \wedge \bar{\phi}_B$. We denote by $(p)_I$ a labelled predicate that occurs in ϕ_A or ϕ_B such that w does not satisfy p.

Lemma 8.1. *The set I contains at least two distinct integers.*

Recall that p is a predicate of the form $u_p^t x \#_p \beta_p$. The *distance* of the pivot value μ to β_p is bounded by the following lemma where $||z||_1 = |z_1| + \cdots + |z_n|$ for any vector $z = (z_1, \ldots, z_n)^t \in \mathbb{Z}^n$.

Lemma 8.2. *We have* $|\mu - \beta_p| \leq \frac{1}{2} \left|\left|u_p^t R^{-1}\right|\right|_1$.

We introduce an integer s denoting the size of the input problem, i.e. the number of bits to denote (ϕ_A, ϕ_B) with integral coefficients encoded in binary. Since the lines of the computed matrices U are vectors u_p for some predicates p, we deduce that the size of the matrix U is bounded by s. As the Smith Normal Form of a matrix U is obtained with a polynomial time algorithm, we deduce that there exists a polynomial P such that $\frac{1}{2}\left|\left|u_p^t R^{-1}\right|\right|_1 < 2^{P(s)}$ at any step of the computation. From the previous Lemma 8.2 we deduce that every pivot value μ satisfies $|\mu - \beta_p| < 2^{P(s)}$. Let us recall that the pivot value μ is used by sub-algorithm strengthening to partition I into three intervals $I_\mu^<$, $I_\mu^=$ and $I_\mu^>$. An immediate induction shows that every predicate p is labelled by an interval with integral bounds in $[\![\beta_p - 2^{P(s)}, \beta_p + 2^{P(s)}]\!]$. In particular the number of possible intervals I that label a predicate p is bounded by $(2 + 2^{P(s)+1})^2$. Let k denote the number of predicates. We have proved that the number of possible labelings is bounded by $(2 + 2^{P(s)+1})^{2k}$.

Lemma 8.3. *Intervals $I_\mu^<$, $I_\mu^=$ and $I_\mu^>$ are strictly included in I.*

Lemma 8.4. *Two distinct internal nodes have distinct labels.*

From the previous lemma we deduce that the number of internal nodes N is bounded by $(2 + 2^{P(s)+1})^{2k}$. As an internal node has at most three leaf children, we deduce that the number of nodes is bounded by $4(2 + 2^{P(s)+1})^{2k} = O(4^{Q(s)})$ where Q is the polynomial $Q(s) = 2s(P(s) + 1)$. We have proved the following theorem.

Theorem 8.5. *In exponential time in the worst case, algorithm* interpolant(ϕ_A , ϕ_B) *returns either a valuation satisfying $\bar{\phi}_A \wedge \bar{\phi}_B$ or an interpolant for (ϕ_A, ϕ_B).*

9 Experimental Evaluation

We have created a prototypical implementation of our interpolating decision procedure and integrated it as a theory solver into the SMT-solver OpenSMT [3], with the long-term goal of creating an interpolating SMT-solver to be used in model checkers. The prototype was developed on top of a recent development version of OpenSMT that already provided an interpolation procedure for propositional logic. In order to implement the algorithm check_inequality, we internally invoke the LP solver present in OpenSMT, which realizes the algorithm from [6].

To the best of our knowledge, the following tools and algorithms are the only ones available for comparison (also see Sect. 1):

- the theorem prover *iPrincess* [2], which implements an interpolating decision procedure for QFPA based on a sequent calculus,
- the SMT-solver *SmtInterpol*,[1] a recently released interpolating decision procedure for linear integer arithmetic that uses an architecture similar to the one in *Foci* [11],
- *quantifier elimination (QE) procedures*, which can be used to generate interpolants as illustrated in Sect. 2; for our experiments, we use the implementation of the Omega test [14] available in *iPrincess*.

[1] `http://swt.informatik.uni-freiburg.de/research/tools/smtinterpol`

Table 1. Results of applying the four compared tools to SMT-LIB benchmarks (times in seconds). Experiments were done on an Intel Xeon X5667 4-core machine with 3.07GHz, heap-space limited to 12GB, running Linux, with a timeout of 900s.

		OpenSMT	**SmtInterpol**	**iPrincess**	**Omega QE**
Averest	10/9	10/1/31.75/ 90/221	8/4/97.02/ 72/149	0/0/–/ –/–	–/–/203.89/ 8/132639
CIRC/multiplier	16/1	5/1/48.94/ 45/2357	5/1/24.40/ 45/48827	6/1/130.46/ 35/12764	–/–/108.71/ 125/15392
CIRC/simplebitadder	17/0	7/0/102.81/ 63/23362	5/0/8.58/ 45/41077	6/0/412.82/ 49/47218	–/–/97.83/ 129/93181
check	4/1	4/1/0.77/ 36/1.7	2/1/0.17/ 18/2.3	4/1/36.65/ 33/485	–/–/0.26/ 30/0.67
nec-smt/small	17/18	1/0/251.95/ 9/36	7/0/259.86/ 63/1728	0/0/–/ –/–	–/–/134.88/ 66/15867
mathsat	100/21	74/15/52.96/ 666/2020	65/13/45.74/ 585/126705	11/11/61.78/ 99/13745	–/–/168.81/ 612/101088
rings	294/0	9/0/59.93/ 81/4611	0/0/–/ –/–	54/0/108.01/ 62/3470	–/–/227.25/ 1474/55307
wisa	2/3	0/0/–/ –/–	1/2/394.22/ 9/1039	0/0/–/ –/–	–/–/67.01/ 14/23709
	unsat/sat	*unsat / sat / average time / #interpolants / average int. size*			

The benchmarks for our experiments are derived from different families of the SMT-LIB category QF-LIA. Some of the selected families (e.g., *rings*) are specifically designed to test integer reasoning capabilities, and contain problems satisfiable over rationals. Because SMT-LIB benchmarks are usually conjunctions at the outermost level, we partitioned them into $A \wedge B$ by choosing the first $\frac{k}{10} \cdot n$ of the benchmark conjuncts as A, the rest as B (where n is the total number of conjuncts, and $k \in \{1, \ldots, 9\}$). This yields 9 interpolation problems for each SMT-LIB benchmark.

Our experimental results are summarized in Table 1:[2]

- the number unsatisfiable/satisfiable problems tested, and the number of unsat/sat results that the tools were able to derive; in the remaining cases, either a timeout or a memory-out occurred. No figures are given for QE, which does not decide satisfiability of interpolation problems.
- the average time (in seconds) required to solve each benchmark, including the time for computing the 9 interpolants for a benchmarks. For QE, this is simply the average time to compute 9 interpolants.
- the total number of interpolants that could be computed. For OpenSMT and SmtInterpol, which compute interpolants on-the-fly while solving a problem, this is always $9\times$ the number of unsat results. iPrincess first constructs a proof for a problem, and afterwards extracts interpolants, which means that sometimes fewer than 9 interpolants can be computed (interpolant extraction has exponential complexity).

[2] http://www.philipp.ruemmer.org/interpolating-opensmt.shtml

- the average size of generated interpolants, in terms of the number of equations, inequalities, and occurrences of propositional variables in the interpolant.[3]

Discussion. The experimental results show that our implementation in OpenSMT is competitive with all compared interpolation procedures: in 4 of the 8 families, it is able to prove the largest of problems unsatisfiable (and to compute interpolants for them); in all families but *CIRC/simplebitadder*, the runtime is smaller or comparable with the other tools; in 4 families, the generated interpolants are significantly smaller (on average) than the interpolants computed by the other tools.

QE is able to generate a large number of interpolants in the families *CIRC/multiplier*, *CIRC/simplebitadder*, and *rings*, albeit the generation is slow (on average) and the interpolants are large. It can be observed that our construction of interpolation problems by choosing arbitrary partitionings of SMT-LIB problems tends to generate many trivial interpolation problems, in the sense that the partition ϕ_A does not contain any local variables (or only few). On such interpolation problems, QE naturally performs very well; with an increasing number of local symbols, the performance of QE quickly degrades (also see [2] for a discussion of this phenomenon).

The complexity of interpolant extraction in iPrincess (which can be exponential due to mixed cuts) becomes visible in *rings*, where the prover can solve many more problems than the other systems, but can only produce a small number of interpolants.

Conclusion. We have presented an algorithm computing interpolants in the quantifier-free fragment of Presburger arithmetic in exponential time in the worst case. This algorithm combines the one presented in [7] that computes interpolants in polynomial time for systems of equalities over the integers and the one presented in [11] that computes interpolant in polynomial time for systems of inequalities over the rational numbers, without any overhead. In fact, sub-algorithm strengthening is called only if sub-algorithms check_equality and check_inequality fail in computing an interpolant.

Even though we limit the presentation to conjunctions of literals, following [11] the algorithm can be applied to any formula of the QFPA fragment. In the worst case this extended algorithm calls the presented algorithm for each conjunction of literals extracted from ϕ_A and ϕ_B. In particular the worst case complexity is still exponential (we call an exponential number of times an exponential algorithm and $2^n 2^n = 4^n$). In particular our algorithm matches the exponential lower bound complexity.

We have created a prototypical implementation of our interpolating decision procedure. The experimental results show that our implementation is competitive with all compared interpolation procedures; work on further optimizations and further benchmarks is in progress. We are interested in applying interpolation to the verification of *safety properties* for *counter-systems*, a class of automata equipped with a finite set of counters (applications of these automata are given in [4]). More precisely, we plan to implement the combination of the *lazy-interpolation framework* [12] with the *acceleration framework* presented in [4] that requires an efficient interpolator for QFPA.

[3] OpenSMT generates interpolants that use the SMT-LIB `flet` operator to achieve a more compact representation, as a result of how propositional interpolants are computed. Eliminating `flet`s can sometimes significantly increase the size of interpolants, but is practically not necessary for further processing, which is why `flet`s have been kept for our comparison.

Acknowledgements. We would like to thank the OpenSMT team and Gérald Point for help with the implementation, Thomas Wahl for discussions, and the anonymous referees for helpful comments.

References

[1] Beyer, D., Zufferey, D., Majumdar, R.: CSIsat: Interpolation for LA+EUF. In: Gupta, A., Malik, S. (eds.) CAV 2008. LNCS, vol. 5123, pp. 304–308. Springer, Heidelberg (2008)

[2] Brillout, A., Kroening, D., Rümmer, P., Wahl, T.: An interpolating sequent calculus for quantifier-free Presburger arithmetic. In: Giesl, J., Hähnle, R. (eds.) Automated Reasoning. LNCS, vol. 6173, pp. 384–399. Springer, Heidelberg (2010)

[3] Bruttomesso, R., Pek, E., Sharygina, N., Tsitovich, A.: The OpenSMT solver. In: Esparza, J., Majumdar, R. (eds.) TACAS 2010. LNCS, vol. 6015, pp. 150–153. Springer, Heidelberg (2010)

[4] Caniart, N., Fleury, E., Leroux, J., Zeitoun, M.: Accelerating interpolation-based model-checking. In: Ramakrishnan, C.R., Rehof, J. (eds.) TACAS 2008. LNCS, vol. 4963, pp. 428–442. Springer, Heidelberg (2008)

[5] Cimatti, A., Griggio, A., Sebastiani, R.: Interpolant generation for UTVPI. In: Schmidt, R.A. (ed.) CADE 2009. LNCS, vol. 5663, pp. 167–182. Springer, Heidelberg (2009)

[6] Dutertre, B., de Moura, L.M.: A fast linear-arithmetic solver for DPLL(T). In: Ball, T., Jones, R.B. (eds.) CAV 2006. LNCS, vol. 4144, pp. 81–94. Springer, Heidelberg (2006)

[7] Jain, H., Clarke, E.M., Grumberg, O.: Efficient Craig interpolation for linear diophantine (dis)equations and linear modular equations. In: Gupta, A., Malik, S. (eds.) CAV 2008. LNCS, vol. 5123, pp. 254–267. Springer, Heidelberg (2008)

[8] Kannan, R., Bachem, A.: Polynomial algorithms for computing the Smith and Hermite normal forms of an integer matrix. SIAM J. Comput. 8(4), 499–507 (1979)

[9] Lynch, C., Tang, Y.: Interpolants for linear arithmetic in SMT. In: Cha, S(S.), Choi, J.-Y., Kim, M., Lee, I., Viswanathan, M. (eds.) ATVA 2008. LNCS, vol. 5311, pp. 156–170. Springer, Heidelberg (2008)

[10] McMillan, K.L.: Applications of Craig interpolants in model checking. In: Halbwachs, N., Zuck, L.D. (eds.) TACAS 2005. LNCS, vol. 3440, pp. 1–12. Springer, Heidelberg (2005)

[11] McMillan, K.L.: An interpolating theorem prover. Theor. Comput. Sci. 345(1) (2005)

[12] McMillan, K.L.: Lazy abstraction with interpolants. In: Ball, T., Jones, R.B. (eds.) CAV 2006. LNCS, vol. 4144, pp. 123–136. Springer, Heidelberg (2006)

[13] Pudlák, P.: Lower bounds for resolution and cutting plane proofs and monotone computations. J. Symb. Log. 62(3), 981–998 (1997)

[14] Pugh, W.: The Omega test: a fast and practical integer programming algorithm for dependence analysis. Communications of the ACM 8, 102–114 (1992)

[15] Rybalchenko, A., Sofronie-Stokkermans, V.: Constraint solving for interpolation. In: Cook, B., Podelski, A. (eds.) VMCAI 2007. LNCS, vol. 4349, pp. 346–362. Springer, Heidelberg (2007)

[16] Schrijver, A.: Theory of Linear and Integer Programming. Wiley, Chichester (1986)

[17] Weispfenning, V.: Complexity and uniformity of elimination in Presburger arithmetic. In: ISSAC, pp. 48–53 (1997)

Variable Compression in ProbLog

Theofrastos Mantadelis and Gerda Janssens

Departement Computerwetenschappen, K.U. Leuven
Celestijnenlaan 200A - bus 2402, B-3001 Heverlee, Belgium
firstname.lastname@cs.kuleuven.be

Abstract. In order to compute the probability of a query, ProbLog represents the proofs of the query as disjunctions of conjunctions, for which a Reduced Ordered Binary Decision Diagram (ROBDD) is computed. The paper identifies patterns of Boolean variables that occur in Boolean formulae, namely AND-clusters and OR-clusters. Our method compresses the variables in these clusters and thus reduces the size of ROBDDs without affecting the probability.

We give a polynomial algorithm that detects AND-clusters in disjunctive normal form (DNF) Boolean formulae, or OR-clusters in conjunctive normal form (CNF) Boolean formulae.

We do an experimental evaluation of the effects of AND-cluster compression for a real application of ProbLog. With our prototype implementation we have a significant improvement in performance (up to 87%) for the generation of ROBDDs. Moreover, compressing AND-clusters of Boolean variables in the DNFs makes it feasible to deal with ProbLog queries that give rise to larger DNFs.

Keywords: ProbLog, Statistical Relation Learning, Probabilistic Logic Programming, Variable Compression, Binary Decision Diagrams.

1 Introduction

ProbLog [1,2] is a probabilistic framework that extends Prolog with probabilistic facts. ProbLog computes the probability of a query in two main steps. First, ProbLog collects the probabilistic facts for each SLD proof of the query. Each probabilistic fact is represented by a Boolean variable, each proof by the conjunction of probabilistic facts used in the proof, and the set of all proofs by a disjunction of conjunctions (a DNF). In the second step, ProbLog uses ROBDDs [3,4] to calculate the success probability of the query. Note that assessing the probability of a DNF Boolean formula is a #P-complete problem [5] and using ROBBDs is a state-of-the-art approach [6].

For typical ProbLog applications, generating a ROBDD can become one of the limiting factors. The size of the constructed ROBDD depends heavily on the variable ordering. There has been a lot of research on finding efficient variable orderings by using static [7,8] and dynamic heuristics [9,10]. In this paper we present variable compression as a complementary approach to construct smaller ROBDDs. We observed patterns (AND-clusters, OR-clusters) in the ROBDDs

C. Fermüller and A. Voronkov (Eds.): LPAR-17, LNCS 6397, pp. 504–518, 2010.

that make it possible to replace a set of Boolean variables with a single new one without affecting the final probability. To benefit from the variable compression, the clusters should be discovered before the actual ROBDD generation.

The paper has two main contributions. The first contribution is the definition of the AND-clusters and OR-clusters, their usage in assessing the probability of a DNF Boolean formula, and their usage for compressing ROBDDs. The second contribution is the Book Marking algorithm that detects AND-clusters in ProbLog set of proofs.

We also evaluate experimentally the effects of the AND-clusters in a typical ProbLog application [1,11]. Our experiments show the impact of the AND-cluster compression: the number of variables in the ROBDD is on average reduced by 28% and the time performance of the generation of the ROBDDs improves on average by 41%. The AND-cluster compression also allowed us to compute queries that caused timeouts. In our benchmarks AND-cluster compression is beneficial for larger DNFs where the cost of executing the bookmarking algorithm is lower than the time gain we have during ROBDD generation.

We briefly introduce ProbLog in Section 2 and explain how ROBDDs are used. In Section 3 we define AND-clusters, OR-clusters and present their use in a probabilistic context. The Book Marking algorithm for AND-clusters is in Section 4. The experiments follow in Section 5 and the complexity analysis is in Section 6. Finally, Section 7 concludes.

2 ProbLog and Its Use of ROBDDs

2.1 The ProbLog Language

A ProbLog program T [2] consists of a set of labelled ground facts $p_i :: pf_i$ together with a set of definite clauses. Each such fact pf_i is true with probability p_i, that is, these facts correspond to random variables, which are assumed to be mutually independent. Together, they thus define a distribution over subsets of $L_T = \{pf_1, \ldots, pf_n\}$. The definite clauses add arbitrary *background knowledge* (BK) to those sets of *logical* facts. Given the one-to-one mapping between ground definite clause programs and Herbrand interpretations, a ProbLog program also defines a distribution over its Herbrand interpretations.

ProbLog inference calculates the *success probability* $P_s(q|T)$ of a query q in a ProbLog program T, that is, the probability that the query q is *provable* in a logic program that combines BK with a randomly sampled subset of L_T.

Figure 1 shows a small ProbLog program encoding a probabilistic graph and the graph that is represented by the probabilistic facts `edge/2`. The success probability of `path(1,3)` corresponds to the probability that a randomly sampled subgraph contains at least one of the four possible paths from node `1` to node `3`.

2.2 Program Execution in ProbLog

ProbLog programs are executed in two steps. Given a ProbLog program T and a query q, the first step, *SLD-resolution*, collects all proofs for query q in $BK \cup L_T$.

```
0.5::edge(1, 2). % x0   0.4::edge(1, 4). % x1   0.7::edge(2, 3). % x2
0.8::edge(2, 6). % x3   0.9::edge(4, 5). % x4   0.7::edge(5, 2). % x5
0.6::edge(5, 7). % x6   0.4::edge(6, 3). % x7   0.3::edge(6, 7). % x8
path(X, Y):- path(X, Y, [X]).
path(X, Y, _):- edge(X, Y).
path(X, Y, A):- edge(X, Z), \+ member(Z, A), path(Z, Y, [Z|A]).
% Query: problog_exact(path(1, 3), Probability)
```

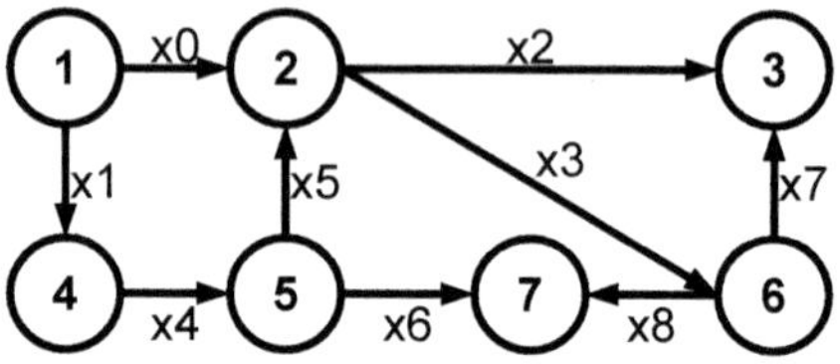

Fig. 1. Example ProbLog program path/2 and its graph

Proofs are stored as lists of probabilistic facts in a *trie data structure*. This trie represents the proofs of the query q in a compact way as it exploits prefix sharing between proofs. The usage of tries is not important for this paper.

In our example, SLD resolution finds four proofs for the query `path(1,3)` which are represented by the following lists of probabilistic `edge/2` facts:

```
edge(1,2),edge(2,3)
edge(1,2),edge(2,6),edge(6,3)
edge(1,4),edge(4,5),edge(5,2),edge(2,3)
edge(1,4),edge(4,5),edge(5,2),edge(2,6),edge(6,3)
```

In general these lists of probabilistic facts express the Boolean formula:

$$\bigvee_{pr_j \in proofs} \left(\bigwedge_{pf_i \in pr_j} pf_i \right) \tag{1}$$

where the pf_i represent the probabilistic facts used in proof pr_j. Using the x_i to represent the `edge/2` facts as indicated in the ProbLog program, the DNF for the `path(1,3)` query is the formula $(x_0 \wedge x_2) \vee (x_0 \wedge x_3 \wedge x_7) \vee (x_1 \wedge x_4 \wedge x_5 \wedge x_2) \vee (x_1 \wedge x_4 \wedge x_5 \wedge x_3 \wedge x_7)$. In order to compute the correct probability for (1), ProbLog faces the disjoint sum problem [6]. ProbLog solves this in its second step, namely by the transformation of the disjunction of conjunctions into mutually disjoint conjunctions by constructing a ROBDD for (1).

A ROBDD for the `path(1,3)` example of Figure 1 is given in Figure 2a. The topmost circular node in the ROBDD corresponds to the probabilistic fact x_0 and is called a variable node. A variable node has two successors pointed to by the **high** edge and the **low** edge. Edges are implicitly directed: they point downwards. The ROBDD that is rooted at the low successor represents the Boolean expression that is yielded by substituting "false" for the variable. The high successor represents the Boolean expression that is yielded by substituting "true". The "true" node 1 and the "false" node 0 represent whether the binary

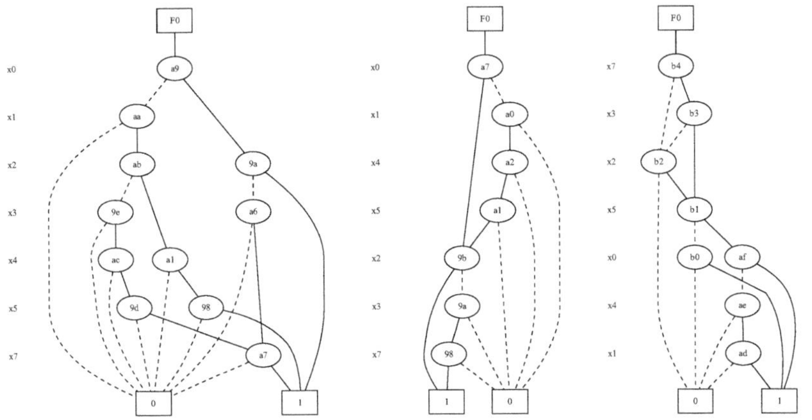

(a) Bad ordering. x0-x1-x2-x3-x4-x5-x7 (b) Good ordering. x0-x1-x4-x5-x2-x3-x7 (c) ProbLog ordering. x7-x3-x2-x5-x0-x4-x1

Fig. 2. ROBDD for the query `path(1,3)`

formula is satisfied or not. The paths from the root to node 1 give the disjoint sum as a disjunction of disjoint conjunctions.

The computation of the probability is bottom up and linear in the size of the ROBDD. Details are in [2]. ProbLog computes that 0.498296 is the exact probability that a path from node 1 to node 3 exists.

Note that in general a variable can have multiple nodes in a ROBDD. For example, in Figure 2a the variables x2, x3, x4, x5 have two nodes each. A ROBDD imposes an order on the Boolean variables and the different variables appear in that order in all the paths of the ROBDD. ROBDDs are reduced which means that two nodes never have the same successors if they are nodes of the same variable and that no node has the same high and low successor. These reductions do not perform the variable compression we are aiming at.

3 Variable Compression

3.1 Motivation

ProbLog uses ROBDDs to compute the success probability of a query. While the complexity of the calculation of the probability is linear in terms of the size of the ROBDD, the generation of the ROBDD is NP-hard.

It is well-known that the variable ordering used to construct the ROBDD for a Boolean formula has an impact on the size of the ROBDD. For our `path(1,3)` example, Figure 2a until 2c use different variable orderings. The orderings that give rise to smaller ROBDDs are called good orderings: constructing smaller ROBDDs takes less time and space and also the computation of the probability is faster. State-of-the-art ROBDD tools use heuristics to decide about the variable ordering, whose search space is exponential.

We reduce the search space for the variable ordering by decreasing the number of variables in the Boolean formula, namely by replacing subsets of variables by new representative variables. We call this **variable compression**. We can only do variable compression if we do not affect the probability.

We discovered sets of variables in the ROBDDs for which we can compute the contribution of such a set of variables to the probability of the ROBDD independently from the rest of the ROBBD. For example, the set of variables x1, x4 and x5 in Figure 2b. This implies that we can replace those three variables by a new representative variable, whose probability is computed from the probabilities of x1, x4 and x5. Later in this section we define this set as an AND-cluster.

In order to do variable compression before ROBDD generation, we need to detect these patterns in the Boolean formulae, or in the case of ProbLog at the level of the DNF (1). It turns out that in the proofs of `path(1,3)` either the probabilistic facts corresponding to x1, x4 and x5 appear all three together in a proof, or none of them occurs. The AND-clusters are determined for particular DNFs and as such they are query-dependent. For path(1,7), x1, x4 and x5 no longer form an AND-cluster as we also have a proof `edge(1,4),edge(4,5),edge(5,7)` that does not contain x5. Now only x1 and x4 form an AND-cluster.

As the AND-clusters are query-dependent, they do not appear in the ProbLog source program itself. Although one could be tempted to replace the facts `edge(1,4),edge(4,5)` by a single one, this is not a good idea because path/2 queries could have 4 as a starting node.

3.2 Cluster Definitions

We define two kinds of clusters and proof that their compression does not effect the final probability. We define the clusters in terms of the ROBDDs because the patterns can also be valuable for other application areas that use ROBDDs.

Definition 1. *Let F be a Boolean formula with variables $v_1, \ldots, v_l$. The variables $\{x_1, \ldots, x_k\} \subseteq \{v_1, \ldots, v_l\}, k > 1$, form an **AND-cluster** if there exists a variable ordering such that the ROBDD R of F*

1. *has only one node n_i for variable $x_i, 1 \leq i \leq k$,*
2. *node n_j has as only incoming edge the high edge of node $n_{j-1}, 2 \leq j \leq k$,*
3. *and the low edges of the nodes $\{n_1, ..., n_k\}$ connect to the same node in R.*

Definition 2. *Let F be a Boolean formula with variables $v_1, \ldots, v_l$. The variables $\{x_1, \ldots, x_k\} \subseteq \{v_1, \ldots, v_l\}, k > 1$, form an **OR-cluster** if there exists a variable ordering such that the ROBDD R of F*

1. *has only one node n_i for variable $x_i, 1 \leq i \leq k$,*
2. *node n_j has as only incoming edge the low edge of node $n_{j-1}, 2 \leq j \leq k$,*
3. *and the high edges of the nodes $\{n_1, ..., n_k\}$ connect to the same node in R.*

In a probabilistic framework like ProbLog that uses ROBDDs to calculate probabilities, each ROBDD variable has an assigned probability. To be able to compress the clusters of variables to new representative variables, we need to compute the probabilities of the representative variables such that the probabilty we compute for the ROBDD as a whole does not change.

Theorem 1 (Probability of AND-cluster). *To replace an AND-cluster* $\{x_1, \ldots, x_n\}$ *by a representative variable* V *with probability* $P_V = P_{AND}(\{x_1, \ldots, x_n\}) = \prod_{i=1}^{n} P(x_i)$ *does not change the probability of the ROBBD as a whole.*

Proof. First consider the simple case of a ROBDD that consist of exactly one AND-cluster, $\{x_1, \ldots, x_n\}$. The probability of this ROBDD is $P(x_1) \cdot ... \cdot P(x_i) \cdot ... \cdot P(x_n) \cdot 1 + (1 - P(x_1) \cdot ... \cdot P(x_i) \cdot ... \cdot P(x_n)) \cdot 0 = \prod_{i=1}^{n} P(x_i)$. But in general, an AND-cluster has an outgoing high edge to a part T with P_T and its low edges connect to a part F with P_F. The probability of the ROBDD part that includes the AND-cluster can be generalised as $P = P(x_1) \cdot ... \cdot P(x_i) \cdot ... \cdot P(x_n) \cdot P_T + (1 - P(x_1) \cdot ... \cdot P(x_i) \cdot ... \cdot P(x_n)) \cdot P_F = P_T \cdot \prod_{i=1}^{n} P(x_i) + P_F - P_F \cdot \prod_{i=1}^{n} P(x_i) = (P_T - P_F) \cdot \prod_{i=1}^{n} P(x_i) + P_F$. If we replace the AND-cluster with a new representative variable V with P_V and calculate the probability, we get $P = P_V \cdot P_T + (1 - P_V) \cdot P_F = P_V \cdot P_T + P_F - P_V \cdot P_F = (P_T - P_F) \cdot P_V + P_F$. Therefore $P_V = P_{AND}(\{x_1, \ldots, x_n\}) = \prod_{i=1}^{n} P(x_i)$.

Theorem 2 (Probability of an OR-cluster). *To replace an OR-cluster* $\{x_1, \ldots, x_n\}$ *to the representative variable* V *with probability* $P_V = P_{OR}(\{x_1, \ldots, x_n\}) = P(x_1) + (1 - P(x_1)) \cdot P_{OR}(\{x_2, \ldots, x_n\})$ *and* $P_{OR}(\{x_n\}) = P(x_n)$ *does not change the probability of the ROBBD as a whole.*

Proof. First consider the simple case of a ROBDD that consist of exactly one OR-cluster, $\{x_1, \ldots, x_n\}$. The probability of this ROBDD is $P(x_1) \cdot 1 + (1 - P(x_1)) \cdot (P(x_2) \cdot 1 + (1 - P(x_2)) \cdot \ldots \cdot (P(x_i) \cdot 1 + (1 - P(x_i)) \cdot \ldots \cdot (P(x_n) \cdot 1 + (1 - P(x_n)) \cdot 0)) \ldots) = P(x_1) + (1 - P(x_1)) \cdot P_{OR}(\{x_2, \ldots, x_n\})$. But in general an OR-cluster has its high edges to a part T with P_T and an outgoing low edge to a part F with P_F. The probability can be generalised as $P = P(x_1) \cdot P_T + (1 - P(x_1)) \cdot (P(x_2) \cdot P_T + (1 - P(x_2)) \cdot \ldots \cdot (P(x_i) \cdot P_T + (1 - P(x_i)) \cdot \ldots \cdot (P(x_n) \cdot P_T + (1 - P(x_n)) \cdot P_F)) \ldots) = (P(x_1) + (1 - P(x_1)) \cdot P(x_2) + \ldots + (1 - P(x_1)) \cdot \ldots \cdot (1 - P(x_{i-1})) \cdot P(x_i) + \ldots + (1 - P(x_1)) \cdot \ldots \cdot (1 - P(x_{n-1})) \cdot P(x_n)) \cdot P_T + (1 - P(x_1)) \cdot \ldots \cdot (1 - P(x_n)) \cdot (P_F / P_T)$. If we replace the OR-cluster with a new representative variable V with P_V and calculate the probability, we get $P = P_V \cdot P_T + (1 - P_V) \cdot P_F$ if we replace $P_V = P(x_1) + (1 - P(x_1)) \cdot P(x_2) + \ldots + (1 - P(x_1)) \cdot \ldots \cdot (1 - P(x_{i-1})) \cdot P(x_i) + \ldots + (1 - P(x_1)) \cdot \ldots \cdot (1 - P(x_{n-1})) \cdot P(x_n)$ then we need to prove that $1 - P_V = (1 - P(x_1)) \cdot \ldots \cdot (1 - P(x_n)) \Rightarrow 1 - (P(x_1) + (1 - P(x_1)) \cdot P(x_2) + \ldots + (1 - P(x_1)) \cdot \ldots \cdot (1 - P(x_{i-1})) \cdot P(x_i) + \ldots + (1 - P(x_1)) \cdot \ldots \cdot (1 - P(x_{n-1})) \cdot P(x_n)) = (1 - P(x_1)) \cdot \ldots \cdot (1 - P(x_n))$. Finally by using the distribution rule we see that the previous formula is a tautology. Therefore $P_V = P_{OR}(\{x_1, \ldots, x_n\}) = P(x_1) + (1 - P(x_1)) \cdot P_{OR}(\{x_2, \ldots, x_n\})$.

3.3 Using the Clusters for Variable Compression

We illustrate the variable compression with our `path(1,3)` example. In Figure 3a we have two AND-clusters, $\{x1, x4, x5\}$ and $\{x3, x7\}$. After compression we obtain the ROBDD in Figure 3b with two new Boolean variables $x1, 4, 5$, $x3, 7$ and their associated probabilities $P(x1, 4, 5)$[1], $P(x3, 7)$[2]. After AND-compression we now have two OR-clusters, $\{x0, x1, 4, 5\}$ and $\{x3, 7, x2\}$ as shown in Figure 3b; by further compressing them we get the ROBDD in Figure 3c with two new Boolean variables $x0, 1, 4, 5$, $x3, 7, 2$ and their probabilities $P(x0, 1, 4, 5)$[3], $P(x3, 7, 2)$[4]. Finally, by compressing the single AND-cluster $\{x0, 1, 4, 5, x3, 7, 2\}$ of the ROBDD in Figure 3c we end up with the ROBDD in Figure 3d that has a single Boolean variable $x0, 1, 4, 5, 3, 7, 2$ and probability $P(x0, 1, 4, 5, 3, 7, 2)$[5].

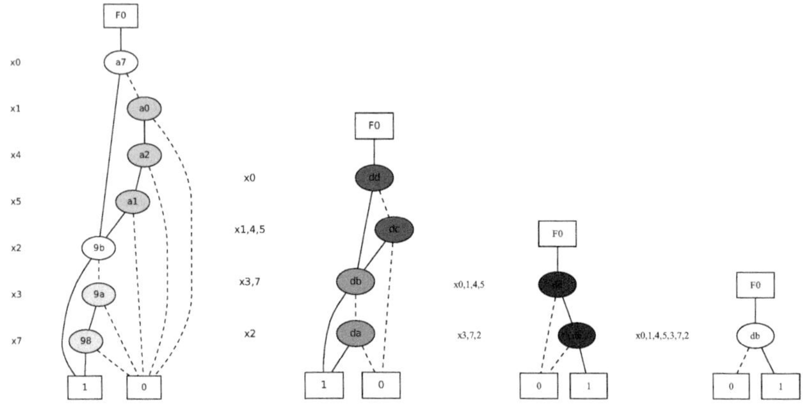

(a) AND-clusters. (b) OR-clusters. (c) AND-cluster. (d) Compressed.

Fig. 3. Compressing ROBDD of `path(1,3)`. Notation: coloured nodes represent clusters

Not all ROBDDs can be compressed to a single variable, iterating AND/OR-cluster based variable compression can lead to an easier to construct ROBDD. We want to use variable compression to be able to deal with queries that caused timeouts. So, we are willing to pay a certain cost to detect the clusters. In order to use our variable compression in practise, we first have to detect AND-clusters in DNFs. In the rest of this paper we focus on AND-clusters and we already obtain promising results with AND-cluster variable compression. The detection of OR-clusters in the DNFs is part of future work.

---

[1] $P(x1, 4, 5) = P_{AND}(\{x1, x4, x5\}) = 0.4 \cdot 0.9 \cdot 0.7 = 0.252$

[2] $P(x3, 7) = P_{AND}(\{x3, x7\}) = 0.8 \cdot 0.4 = 0.32$

[3] $P(x0, 1, 4, 5) = P_{OR}(\{x0, x1, 4, 5\}) = 0.5 + (1 - 0.5) \cdot 0.252 = 0.626$

[4] $P(x3, 7, 2) = P_{OR}(\{x3, 7, x2\}) = 0.32 + (1 - 0.32) \cdot 0.7 = 0.796$

[5] $P(x0, 1, 4, 5, 3, 7, 2) = P_{AND}(\{x0, 1, 4, 5, x3, 7, 2\}) = 0.626 \cdot 0.796 = 0.498296$

4 Discovering AND-clusters

To be able to benefit from AND-cluster compression, we need to identify them before the ROBDD generation. Fortunately, AND-clusters also appear in the DNF representing the proofs: either all the probabilistic facts of an AND-cluster appear in a proof, or none of them. A naive approach to detect AND-clusters is to find longest common subsequences (LCS) in conjunctions of the DNF, however this is an NP-hard problem [12]. As our problem is a special case of the LCS we can do better.

Lemma 1. *Every set of probabilistic facts* $\{pf_1, ..., pf_n\}$ *in a set of proofs* $\{pr_1, \ldots, pr_m\}$ *satisfying* $\forall pf_i \in \{pf_1, ..., pf_n\}$ $occur(pf_i) = (\bigcap_{pf_i \in pr_j} pr_j) \cap (\bigcap_{pf_i \notin pr_j} \overline{pr_j}) = \{pf_1, ..., pf_n\}$ *forms an AND-cluster.*

The first part of $occur(pf_i)$ is the set of probabilistic facts that occur in each proof in which pf_i occurs. The second part is the set of probabilistic facts that do not occur in proofs that do not contain pf. We use $\overline{pr_j}$ to denote the complement of the set pr_j with respect to the set of the probabilistic facts in all proofs. The first set is a possible AND-cluster for pf_i but it might also contain probabilistic facts that occur in proofs that do not contain pf_i. In order to exclude the latter ones, the possible AND-cluster has to be restricted to probabilistic facts that only occur in proofs containing pf_i.

4.1 The Book Marking Algorithm

Based on Lemma 1, the Book Marking algorithm in Table 1 deals with all the proofs one by one and ensures that for all probabilistic facts pf_i seen by the algorithm so far $occur(pf_i)$ is computed. The algorithm encodes a proof by a bit string. We order the probabilistic facts by their chronological appearance in the proofs. The ith probabilistic fact is denoted by $pf(i)$. The ith bit encodes whether the probabilistic fact $pf(i)$ is used in the proof. We refer to the bitstring as the **occurrence number** (ON) of the proof.

We use a two dimensional matrix (MA) of bits to represent the AND-clusters. Row k corresponds to the probabilistic fact $pf(k)$ and represents $occur(pf(k))$. Column l represents the probabilistic fact $pf(l)$. The element l of a row k indicates whether $pf(l)$ forms an AND-cluster with $pf(k)$. This matrix grows incrementally as we deal with the proofs one by one and the size of each dimension is equal to the number of different, already seen probabilistic facts.

Dealing with a new proof involves computing ON and then computing its impact on the AND-clusters already in MA according to Lemma 1 using the following three operations:

1. for each previously seen probabilistic fact i which appears in this proof, we compute $MA[i] = MA[i] \wedge ON$,
2. for each previously seen probabilistic fact i that does not occur in this proof, we compute $MA[i] = MA[i] \wedge \neg ON$,
3. we grow MA to include AND-clusters for the probabilistic facts that were not seen before.

Table 1. The Book Marking algorithm

```
bookmarking(DNF) {
  for each Proof in DNF {
    ON = bit_encode(Proof)
    for (i = 0; i < MatrixSize; i++) {
      if (2 ^ i & ON) > 0 then
      \\ Old row of pf in ON - operation 1
      MA[i] = MA[i] & ON
      else
      \\ Old row of pf not in ON - operation 2
      MA[i] = MA[i] & neg(ON)
    }
    for (i = MatrixSize; i < ListLength; i++) {
      \\ Add a new row - operation 3
      MA[i] = neg(2 ^ MatrixSize - 1) & ON
    }
    MatrixSize = ListLength
  }
}
```

After all proofs of the DNF have been dealt with, all the rows in MA with more than one active bit (i.e. set to 1) represent an AND-cluster.

4.2 An Example of the Book Marking Algorithm

As an example for the Book Marking algorithm we use the proofs of `path(1,3)`: {x0, x2}, {x0, x3, x7}, {x1, x4, x5, x2}, {x1, x4, x5, x3, x7}. Each row of Table 2 corresponds to a single proof (PR), and has the probabilistic fact order (OL), the occurrence number (ON) and the matrix (MA).

For the first proof the algorithm uses the order $x0 < x2$ to compute 11 as the occurrence number of the proof. As initially the matrix MA is empty, operation 3 uses the ON to construct a MA with two rows and two columns with all bits activated.

For the second proof the algorithm adds $x3$ and $x7$ to the order which becomes $x0 < x2 < x3 < x7$. The algorithm computes $ON = 1101$; note that we are reading the bitstrings from right to left. Operation 1 computes the conjunction of 1101 with the row of $x0$: $11 \wedge 1101 = 0011 \wedge 1101 = 0001$. This operation sets the bit corresponding to $x2$ to 0 as $x0$ and $x2$ are no longer an AND-cluster. For the row of $x2$, operation 2 computes $11 \wedge neg(1101) = 0011 \wedge 0010 = 0010$ and sets the bit for the probabilistic fact $x0$ to 0. Finally, the algorithm extends MA by two new rows and columns for the probabilistic facts $x3$ and $x7$ with as values of the rows $neg(11) \wedge 1101 = 1100 \wedge 1101 = 1100$. Note that also the existing rows are expanded with new columns set to 0.

When all proofs are dealt with, the Book Marking Algorithm has found two different AND-clusters, namely $\{x1, x4, x5\}$ and $\{x3, x7\}$. Without variable compression, ProbLog generates the ROBDD of Figure 2c, which has a

Table 2. Book Marking algorithm example

<table>
<tr><td>Proof(PR) = x0, x2
Order List(OL) = [x0, x2]
Occurrence Number (ON) = 11 = 3
Matrix(MA) = [3, 3]</td><td>$\begin{array}{cc|c} 1 & 1 & x2 \\ 1 & 1 & x0 \\ \hline x2 & x0 & \end{array}$</td></tr>
<tr><td>PR = x0, x3, x7
OL = [x0, x2, x3, x7]
ON = 1101 = 13
MA = [3 $\land$ 13, 3 $\land$ neg(13), neg(3) $\land$ 13, neg(3) $\land$ 13]
MA = [1, 2, 12, 12]</td><td>$\begin{array}{cccc|c} 1 & 1 & 0 & 0 & x7 \\ 1 & 1 & 0 & 0 & x3 \\ 0 & 0 & 1 & 0 & x2 \\ 0 & 0 & 0 & 1 & x0 \\ \hline x7 & x3 & x2 & x0 & \end{array}$</td></tr>
<tr><td>PR = x1, x4, x5, x2
OL = [x0, x2, x3, x7, x1, x4, x5]
ON = 1110010 = 114
MA = [1 $\land$ neg(114), 2 $\land$ 114, 12 $\land$ neg(114),
12 $\land$ neg(114), neg(15) $\land$ 114,
neg(15) $\land$ 114, neg(15) $\land$ 114]
MA = [1, 2, 12, 12, 112, 112, 112]</td><td>$\begin{array}{ccccccc|c} 1 & 1 & 1 & 0 & 0 & 0 & 0 & x5 \\ 1 & 1 & 1 & 0 & 0 & 0 & 0 & x4 \\ 1 & 1 & 1 & 0 & 0 & 0 & 0 & x1 \\ 0 & 0 & 0 & 1 & 1 & 0 & 0 & x7 \\ 0 & 0 & 0 & 1 & 1 & 0 & 0 & x3 \\ 0 & 0 & 0 & 0 & 0 & 1 & 0 & x2 \\ 0 & 0 & 0 & 0 & 0 & 0 & 1 & x0 \\ \hline x5 & x4 & x1 & x7 & x3 & x2 & x0 & \end{array}$</td></tr>
<tr><td>PR = x1, x4, x5, x3, x7
OL = [x0, x2, x3, x7, x1, x4, x5]
ON = 1111100 = 124
MA = [1 $\land$ neg(124), 2 $\land$ neg(124), 12 $\land$ 124,
12 $\land$ 124, 112 $\land$ 124, 112 $\land$ 124, 112 $\land$ 124]
MA = [1, 2, 12, 12, 112, 112, 112]</td><td>$\begin{array}{ccccccc|c} 1 & 1 & 1 & 0 & 0 & 0 & 0 & x5 \\ 1 & 1 & 1 & 0 & 0 & 0 & 0 & x4 \\ 1 & 1 & 1 & 0 & 0 & 0 & 0 & x1 \\ 0 & 0 & 0 & 1 & 1 & 0 & 0 & x7 \\ 0 & 0 & 0 & 1 & 1 & 0 & 0 & x3 \\ 0 & 0 & 0 & 0 & 0 & 1 & 0 & x2 \\ 0 & 0 & 0 & 0 & 0 & 0 & 1 & x0 \\ \hline x5 & x4 & x1 & x7 & x3 & x2 & x0 & \end{array}$</td></tr>
</table>

size in between the sizes of the other two ROBDDs in Figure 2. After compressing the variables of the AND-clusters to a representative variable $x1, 4, 5$ with $P(x1, 4, 5) = 0.252$ and $x3, 7$ with $P(x3, 7) = 0.32$, we get the compressed proofs: {x0, x2}, {x0, x3,7}, {x1,4,5, x2}, {x1,4,5, x3,7}. For the compressed proofs, ProbLog generates the ROBBD of Figure 3b.

The algorithm as presented here only tackles proofs that contains either positive or negative occurrences of each probabilistic fact and not both. If in one proof a probabilistic fact is positive and in an other is negative, this probabilistic fact does not form an AND-cluster.

5 Experiments for AND-clusters

We implemented the variable compression method using only AND-clusters within ProbLog. To judge the practicality and the impact we use ProbLog benchmarks that discover links in real biological networks [11]. Graphs model probabilistic links between concepts such as genes, proteins, etc.. The first benchmark consists of a graph of concepts related to the Alzheimer disease that has 23060 edges; because of the size, inference for this graph soon becomes intractable. We query for the existence of a path between two given nodes, to control the problem size we limit the maximum path length. For the second benchmark, we take the experiments (the same data sets and the same queries) from [1]. All the graphs are fragments of the same network [11]. The experiments should give answers to the following questions:

1. What is the compression ratio in a real life data set?
2. How does compression improve the performance of generating a ROBDD?
3. In which cases is the variable compression beneficial?

The default setting of ProbLog is to use CUDD's [13] group sifting [14] dynamic reordering during ROBDD generation. CUDD uses the following memory-time trade-off. It starts by consuming memory without reordering the variables, once the memory usage passes a threshold, it starts reordering the variables and as a consequence it consumes time. While CUDD is implemented in C, our Book Marking algorithm is implemented in Yap Prolog [15].

When we increase the problem size for the first benchmark, we see that the ROBDD generation time is the limiting factor. We executed three different queries with a timeout of 1 hour for the ROBDD generation. Each query was executed 5 times and we present the averaged times for the ROBDD generation. Table 3 presents the comparison of executing the queries with four different settings. The first and second column use the dynamic reordering strategy; the third and the fourth use the order in which probabilistic facts appear in the proofs as a static ordering; the first and third column use variable compression of AND-clusters. Our experiments confirm that for big ProbLog problems dynamic reordering performs better than static ordering. Variable compression improves the ROBDD generation times and has the expected effect both for dynamic and static orderings.

The second part of Table 3 presents the compression statistics which are independent of the reordering method: the time to do variable compression, the number of AND-clusters found, the number of variables before compression (ovars), the number of variables after compression (cvars), and finally the variable compression ratio[6]. We note that the time cost for doing the variable compression is by far less than the time gained during ROBDD generation. More importantly, the time for finding the AND-clusters is polynomial (as shown in the next section), while that for ROBDD generation is exponential. Because our constant costs are relatively high, we notice that in small problems variable compression needs more time than we gain during ROBDD generation, but those problems are solved very fast either way. The benefit of variable compressing is far more significant for larger problem sizes.

In order to confirm the positive results for the compression ratio and the better performance of the ROBDD generation, we use the larger set of experiments of our second benchmark. We study the impact of variable compression in combination with dynamic reordering as it was confirmed to be the better option for ProbLog. In this benchmark, all the queries can be computed without variable compression. The behaviour of queries is diverse, as some spent most of the

[6] Ratio = (ovars - cvars) / ovars

Table 3. First benchmark results. The reported times are in milliseconds. Longer path lengths timeout. A - indicates a timeout and * that the system runs out of memory.

	Path Length	Reordering Compressed	Reordering only	Static Compressed	Static	Compression statistics time	clusters	ovars	cvars	ratio
(a)	8	4	4	5	5	7	11	34	23	32%
	9	51	97	7	9	22	17	91	71	22%
	10	153	297	10	12	32	25	137	110	20%
	11	24,830	90,529	*	*	336	76	337	254	25%
	12	3,083,750	-	-	-	835	92	479	378	21%
(b)	8	5	4	4	5	5	7	26	17	35%
	9	282	417	24,904	47,000	72	49	170	119	30%
	10	1,035	1970	*	*	91	53	226	169	25%
	11	1,019,588	-	-	-	966	104	528	410	22%
(c)	4	4	4	4	4	0	3	13	10	23%
	5	95	246	18	23	64	42	135	91	33%
	6	224	497	74	122	33	45	180	131	27%
	7	58,917	2,488,793	*	*	385	92	455	350	23%

Table 4. Averaged results and standard deviation. Where Comp. Ratio = (number of variables before compression - number of variables after compression) / number of variables before compression, ROBDD Gen. Time Gain = (ROBDD time without compression - ROBDD time with compression) / ROBDD time without compression and Compression Time Ratio= (SLD time with book marking algorithm - SLD time without) / SLD time without.

Query Group	ROBDD Comp. Ratio	ROBDD Gen. Time Gain	Compression Time Ratio
Small	$(28 \pm 11)\%$	$(40 \pm 36)\%$	$(26 \pm 41)\%$
Big	$(27 \pm 5)\%$	$(47 \pm 23)\%$	$(69 \pm 107)\%$
All	$(28 \pm 10)\%$	$(41 \pm 36)\%$	$(32 \pm 53)\%$

time in the ROBDD generation and others in SLD-resolution. Among the 360 queries of [1], 100 queries do not use any probabilistic facts. We divided the other 260 queries in 3 groups: the first group contains 92 queries that generate tiny ROBDDs with less than 20 variables; the second group contains 152 queries that generate small ROBDDs with 20 or more variables but less than 100; and finally the third group contains the queries that generated relatively big ROBDDs with more than 100 variables.

For the 'Tiny' group we obtain an average compression ratio of 42%. Their ROBDD generation times and the variable compression times are too small to draw any conclusions. For the other two groups, we compute averages for each group and for both groups together. The results are in Table 4. We give the variable compression ratio, the time gain realised for the ROBDD generation, and the variable compression time relative to the SLD resolution time.

While the results might be specific for the application, they confirm the actual presence of AND-clusters in real world datasets. In this real dataset we encounter a compression ratio that ranges from 7% to 61% with an average of 28%. The compression ratio results are similar to the ones of the first benchmark.

In the 'Small query' group 44% of the queries have a small number of variables and they do not need variable reordering neither before nor after compression: their time gain is near 0. Most of the other queries in the 'Small query' group need reordering before and no reordering after compression, so they have a huge time gain up to 87%. On average we end up with a gain of 40%.

For the 'Big query' group the average gain is larger namely 47%, but the variation is less as all the queries need reordering before and after compression. Here the gain comes from having less variables that have to be dealt with during the reordering by the state-of-the-art tool.

Comparing the variable compression time with the SLD-resolution time shows that the former is smaller than the latter, but its cost is relatively higher for the 'Big' queries.

Our experiments[7] yield promising results, answering our initial questions by showing that there is in real life ProbLog applications a role for variable compression as it improves significantly the performance of the ROBDD generation.

6 Complexity Analysis

The Book Marking algorithm in Table 1 has a worst case complexity of $O(M \cdot N^2)$ where M is the number of proofs seen and N is the number of different probabilistic facts; usually for ProbLog applications $M >> N$. For all M proofs, we do a bitwise encoding, and then we modify the matrix MA.

By using an indexed table, the encoding of a proof is done in $O(N)$ time and requires $O(N)$ space to remember the index for each probabilistic fact encountered. Each proof needs to modify MA which is an NxN bit table. Activating or deactivating a bit in the table is done in constant time, but in the worst case all bits needs to be processed resulting in $O(N^2)$ operations. So, the total time complexity is $O(M \cdot (N + N^2)) = O(M \cdot N^2)$ and the total space complexity $O(N + N^2) = O(N^2)$.

One can take advantage of the symmetry and other properties of the NxN bit matrix MA to avoid some computations. These optimisations reduce the constant times rather than the complexity. One such optimisation is that we use arbitrary precision integers to represent each row of MA.

7 Related Work and Conclusions

We exploit regularities, AND-clusters and OR-clusters, observed in ROBDDs to improve the generation of ROBDDs for DNFs in ProbLog. Variable compression based on these clusters reduces the number of variables in the DNFs. This results in smaller ROBDDs, whose generation uses less time and memory, and as such

[7] For our experiments we used an Intel^R Core^{TM}2 Duo CPU at 3.00GHz with 2GB of RAM memory running Ubuntu 8.04.2 Linux.

we can deal with ProbLog queries that used to cause timeouts. Our method is a pre-processing step that detects clusters of Boolean variables. Taking into account the probabilistic setting, variable compression is feasible and can be followed by any other variable ordering heuristic. For other applications, one might be able to find different meaningful compressions or one might just use our clusters as input to existing variable ordering heuristics.

Variable ordering heuristics also exploit structural properties of the problem modelled by the ROBDD such as connected variables [16,14]. Heuristics designed for one application area might perform poorly in another context [17]. We are not aware of variable ordering heuristics to be used in a probabilistic context.

Hintsanen [18] argues that structural properties are important for finding the most reliable subgraph. He calculates the probability of subgraphs connecting two nodes and search for the subgraph with the maximum probability. The paper identifies as a special case the series-parallel subgraphs for which they can compute the probability polynomially. These series-parallel subgraphs have similarities with our AND/OR-clusters.

We have presented a polynomial algorithm for detecting the AND-clusters and we have obtained promising results for an application using a real database. For ProbLog the best results are obtained by combining AND-cluster variable compression with the group sifting dynamic variable ordering of CUDD. By using variable compression we managed to answer more queries. We showed that AND-cluster based variable compression is beneficial for more complex ROBDD.

For a future implementation of the Book Marking algorithm, C would be a better choice than Prolog both for time efficiency as for space. This would reduce many hidden constant costs of Prolog and would also save Prolog garbage collector executions. It is worth noting that the AND-clusters could be computed in parallel with the SLD-resolution.

In addition to the technical improvements, a challenging task is to investigate how we can take advantage of OR-clusters and compress the ROBDDs even more. Finally, the goal would be to generalise the method and to be able to compress repeated structures in the ROBDD. The size of the ROBDDs is one of the limits that is currently reached when executing ProbLog programs. We think that an approach based on variable compression can push this limit.

Acknowledgements

We want to thank Bart Demoen and Angelika Kimmig for the valuable discussions and comments. This research is supported by: GOA/08/008 "Probabilistic Logic Learning".

References

1. De Raedt, L., Kimmig, A., Toivonen, H.: ProbLog: A probabilistic prolog and its application in link discovery. In: Proceedings of IJCAI, pp. 2462–2467 (2007)
2. Kimmig, A., Santos Costa, V., Rocha, R., Demoen, B., De Raedt, L.: On the efficient execution of ProbLog programs. In: Garcia de la Banda, M., Pontelli, E. (eds.) ICLP 2008. LNCS, vol. 5366, pp. 175–189. Springer, Heidelberg (2008)

3. Akers, S.B.: Binary decision diagrams. IEEE Trans. Computers 27(6), 509–516 (1978)
4. Bryant, R.E.: Graph-based algorithms for boolean function manipulation. IEEE Trans. Computers 35(8), 677–691 (1986)
5. Valiant, L.G.: The complexity of enumeration and reliability problems. SIAM Journal on Computing 8(3), 410–421 (1979)
6. Rauzy, A., Châtelet, E., Dutuit, Y., Bérenguer, C.: A practical comparison of methods to assess sum-of-products. Reliab. Eng. Syst. Safe 79(1), 33–42 (2003)
7. Fujita, M., Fujisawa, H., Kawato, M.: Evaluation and improvements of boolean comparison method based on binary decision diagrams. In: Proceedings of ICCAD, pp. 2–5 (1988)
8. Malik, S., Wang, A., Brayton, R., Sangionvanni-Vincentelli, A.: Logic verification using binary decision diagrams in a logic synthesis environment. In: Proceedings of ICCAD, pp. 6–9 (1988)
9. Rudell, R.: Dynamic variable ordering for ordered binary decision diagrams. In: Proceedings of ICCAD, pp. 42–47 (1993)
10. Somenzi, F.: Efficient manipulation of decision diagrams. STTT 3(2), 171–181 (2001)
11. Sevon, P., Eronen, L., Hintsanen, P., Kulovesi, K., Toivonen, H.: Link discovery in graphs derived from biological databases. In: Leser, U., Naumann, F., Eckman, B. (eds.) DILS 2006. LNCS (LNBI), vol. 4075, pp. 35–49. Springer, Heidelberg (2006)
12. Maier, D.: The complexity of some problems on subsequences and supersequences. ACM 25(2), 322–336 (1978)
13. Somenzi, F.: CUDD: Colorado university decision diagram package release 2.4.1 (2005), http://vlsi.colorado.edu/~fabio/CUDD/
14. Panda, S., Somenzi, F.: Who are the variables in your neighborhood. In: Proceedings of ICCAD, pp. 74–77 (1995)
15. Santos Costa, V., Damas, L., Reis, R., Azevedo, R.: YAP User's Manual (2002), http://www.ncc.up.pt/~vsc/Yap
16. Aloul, F.A., Markov, I.L., Sakallah, K.A.: Faster SAT and smaller BDDs via common function structure. In: Proceedings of ICCAD, pp. 443–448 (2001)
17. Narodytska, N., Walsh, T.: Constraint and variable ordering heuristics for compiling configuration problems. In: Proceedings of IJCAI, pp. 149–154 (2007)
18. Hintsanen, P.: The most reliable subgraph problem. In: Kok, J.N., Koronacki, J., Lopez de Mantaras, R., Matwin, S., Mladenič, D., Skowron, A. (eds.) PKDD 2007. LNCS (LNAI), vol. 4702, pp. 471–478. Springer, Heidelberg (2007)

Improving Resource-Unaware SAT Solvers

Steffen Hölldobler, Norbert Manthey*, and Ari Saptawijaya

ICCL – International Center for Computational Logic
Technische Universität Dresden, 01062 Dresden, Germany
{sh,norbert,ari}@janeway.inf.tu-dresden.de

Abstract. The paper discusses cache utilization in state-of-the-art SAT solvers. The aim of the study is to show how a resource-unaware SAT solver can be improved by utilizing the cache sensibly. The analysis is performed on a CDCL-based SAT solver using a subset of the industrial SAT Competition 2009 benchmark. For the analysis, the total cycles, the resource stall cycles, the L2 cache hits and the L2 cache misses are traced using sample based profiling. Based on the analysis, several techniques – some of which have not been used in SAT solvers so far – are proposed resulting in a combined speedup up to 83% without affecting the search path of the solver. The average speedup on the benchmark is 60%. The *new* techniques are also applied to *MiniSAT2.0* improving its runtime by 20% on average.

1 Introduction

The satisfiability problem (SAT) is one of the most intensely studied problems in Computer Science with numerous applications within Computer Science itself and beyond. SAT has not only triggered important developments within Theoretical Computer Science (see e.g. [8]), but the active development of SAT solvers in recent years has turned SAT solvers into powerful tools to solve SAT encoded problems in various fields, from group theory over hardware and software verification, planning, scheduling, termination analysis, configuration and security to bioinformatics (see e.g. [5,12,14,15]).

Encoding real world problems often results in large SAT instances with millions of variables and clauses. The quest to solve such problems pushes computers to their limits and requires advanced methods and techniques on all levels from the logic and calculus level over heuristics, data structures, software and systems level to the hardware or computing resources level.

The recent success of SAT solvers is based on various developments including advances on the calculus level like conflict-directed clause learning (CDCL), advanced heuristics including restarts, improved data structures like the two-watched-literal schema, and advanced low-level processes like intelligent cache utilization. Whereas the improvements on the calculus level, the heuristics and the data structures are usually well-documented (see e.g. [9,18,19,21]), we found

* Supported by the European Master's Program in Computational Logic (EMCL).

C. Fermüller and A. Voronkov (Eds.): LPAR-17, LNCS 6397, pp. 519–534, 2010.

that in most of the cases the techniques and methods applied in low-level processes can only be understood by studying the sometimes quite intertwined code of the SAT solvers; declarative descriptions were missing with the exception of [7,25]. On the other hand, state-of-the-art SAT solvers must be aware and must make clever use of low-level processes and the underlying hardware in order to compete on the highest level in SAT competitions and SAT races and, more importantly, in order to solve real world problems.

In this paper we study how computing resources are utilized by a SAT solver while solving industrial problems. In particular, we observe and analyze the use of caches in solving SAT instances. We aim at a clever use of caches as caches allow faster data access compared to main memory access.

Our study uses mainly the CDCL-based SAT solver *riss* [16], which was developed at the ICCL as a student project, but we apply our analysis and findings also to *MiniSAT2.0*. The industrial problems in the study are taken from a subset of the benchmark set used in the SAT competition 2009. The measurements are conducted using the HPCToolkit [1] via sample-based profiling. At each sample point, the performance counter is accessed using the PAPI library [3]. Using these measurement tools, we observe the following processor events: total cycles, resource stall cycles, L2 cache hits and L2 cache misses. Additionally, the numbers of clause read-accesses and write-accesses are collected.

Based on the runtime analysis from the measurements we suggest several improvements. The first suggestion is to use a *slab allocator* [6]. A slab allocator reserves one huge amount of memory and partitions it into slabs of a fixed size, the so-called *slab size*. The single slabs can be allocated and freed by the application. Consequently, the application controls the use of memory and the system memory overhead per allocation is saved. Using appropriate *clause representation schemes* and the slab allocator leads to a speedup of the runtime performance of 23%. The second suggestion is to use *propagation prefetching schemes*, which lead to a speedup of 12%. On the other hand, applying prefetching during conflict analysis turned out to be ineffective.

Based on the implementation analysis, we also carry out some experiments to improve memory access. These concern the *reuse of vectors*, the *compression of data structures* needed for the representation of literals and partial assignments, and the *combination of information* about decision level and reason clause per variable [20]. We also suggest to maintain the watcher list lazily in that a gap in the list due to the removal of a clause is not closed immediately but is only closed once the propagation has terminated. The *lazy maintenance of the watcher list* leads to a speedup of 23%.

The most encouraging result is obtained when several improvements are combined. In our experiments we obtain a combined speedup of up to 83% and 60% on average. One should observe that the improvements considered herein do not change the search-path in finding a solution.

Besides our solver *riss*, we also measure and evaluate the cache performance of *MiniSAT2.0* [10]. After applying some of the above mentioned improvements we observe a speedup of 20% on average.

The paper is organized as follows. The description of the solver is given in Section 2. In Sections 3 and 4 the measurements are described and analyzed. The improvements are suggested in Section 5. Finally, in Section 6 related and future work are discussed.

2 Description of the Solver

The solver *riss* (available at [2]) is based on the CDCL procedure. Customized from the solver *HydraSAT* [4], *riss* is implemented in C++. It is compiled to a 64-bit binary using the GNU Compiler version 4.1.2 with the highest optimization level `-O3`.

A literal is implemented using a 32-bit unsigned integer. A clause is implemented by storing its activity (32-bit floating point), its size (32-bit unsigned integer) and a pointer to the literals of the clause. In case a clause is used in several solver components, no copy of this clause is made. Instead, only the address of the clause is shared among the components. Finally, a formula is implemented as a vector of pointers to clauses it contains. Auxiliary data structures used in the solver are vectors, stacks, double-ended queues and priority queues. The first three are adopted from the C++ Standard Template Library. The priority queue is implemented using a binary heap. The used data structures are chosen as simple as possible to analyze the effect of existing and new improvements. The SAT solver *riss* has the following components:

- *Unit Propagation.* The two watched-literal scheme [19] is used. As usual, this scheme is realized by maintaining watcher lists. The solver *riss* handles binary clauses separately. Unit propagation is performed firstly on binary clauses and then on longer clauses. Due to the special treatment for binary clauses, watcher lists for literals occurring in binary clauses are introduced. For binary clauses, the watcher list of a literal does not only store the pointer to the clauses, but it stores also the other literal of the clause.
- *Conflict Analysis.* The first UIP scheme [18] is used. Additionally, the learnt clause obtained from the conflict analysis is further minimized using self-subsumption [11].
- *Decision Heuristics.* The decision heuristic follows the basic principle of VSIDS [19]. Each variable is assigned an activity and the variable with the highest activity is picked as a decision variable. Every 1000 decisions an attempt to pick a decision variable randomly takes place (up to ten attempts). If these attempts fail, a deterministic decision is made using the activity-based heuristic. Decision variables are assigned negative polarity.
- *Restart Heuristics.* A restart is triggered when the number of conflicts has reached a certain value. These values come from a geometric sequence with increase factor and base set to 1.5 and 100, respectively.
- *Removal Heuristics.* Learnt clauses are removed immediately after a restart. Our heuristic removes learnt clauses with more than six literals and the oldest 55% of the remaining learnt clauses with more than two literals.

3 Measurement

The measurement is conducted using the HPCToolkit [1] via sample-based profiling. The solver is run and halted at a specified processor event and the method currently running is analyzed. Such an event is triggered when a performance counter reaches the maximum of its period. When the program is halted, the performance counters are read using the PAPI Library [3]. The precision of the measurement is assured due to the long run of the solver.

In the measurement, four processor events are traced simultaneously: total cycles, resource stall cycles, L2 cache hits and L2 cache misses. The sample rate for the total cycles is 10^6, whereas the sample rate for the other three events are set to 10^5. In addition to tracing processor events, the numbers of clause read-accesses and write-accesses are observed. Analyzing the behavior of literal read-accesses and write-accesses in clauses allows us to learn which among the two accesses is more frequent and which positions of the clauses are accessed most frequently. Hence, the more frequent accesses can be treated specially.

For the measurement, 40 problem instances of the industrial benchmark from the SAT competition 2009 are used. These instances are all the instances that can be solved within 45 minutes timeout using the basic version of *riss*, i.e. without any improvement which will be discussed subsequently. Appendix A shows the selected instances together with their solving time and memory usage. The total runtime for the benchmark is 9.5 hours. The measurement is performed on a hardware with AMD Opteron 285 2.66 GHz processor, 1024 KB Level 2 Cache, 2 GB main memory, 64-byte cache line size. In the subsequent sections, the computation of *runtime*, *wait rate*, *L2 cache access*, *L2 cache miss rate* and *work cycles* is as usual:

- runtime = total cycles × CPU frequency,
- wait rate = stall cycles / total cycles,
- L2 cache access = L2 cache misses + L2 cache hits,
- L2 cache miss rate = L2 cache misses / L2 cache access,
- work cycles = total cycles − stall cycles.

Because L1 cache is not analyzed, *memory access* refers to L2 cache and main memory access in the sequel.

4 Results and Analysis

Based on the measurement results, a runtime and an implementation analysis is performed. Whereas the former involves the analysis on the processor events and data structure accesses, the latter is concerned with the improvement of the implementation.

4.1 Runtime Analysis

It is important to know which part of the data is accessed most frequently. This information cannot be obtained using the HPCToolkit. Thus, additional runs for

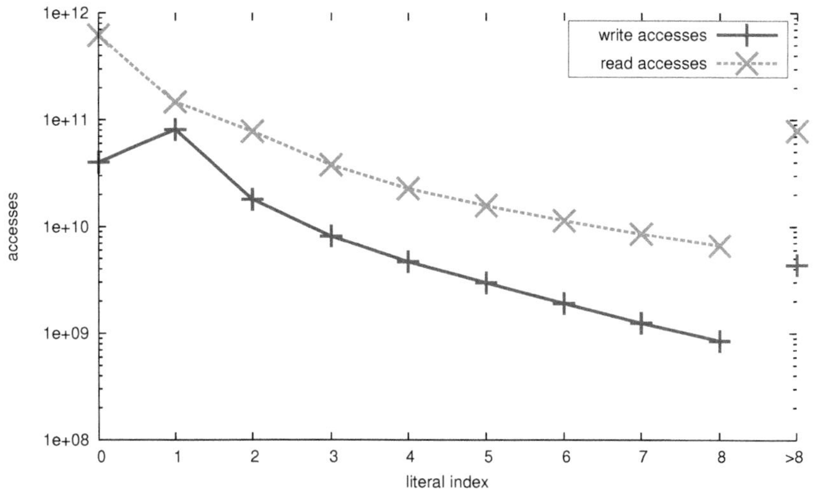

Fig. 1. Literal accesses in clauses. Literal index denotes the position of the literal stored in the clause and > 8 refers to all accessed indexes greater than 8. Note that the Y-axis of the diagram uses a log scale to show more clearly that the number of accesses is decreasing exponentially.

measurement have to be performed. Fig. 1 depicts the literal accesses in clauses. The most frequently accessed literals are the literal at index 0 (60% read access, 25% write access) and at index 1 (15% read access, 50% write access) of the literal array. The total number of write accesses is only 17% of read accesses. Note that literals are only accessed by the unit propagation and in the conflict analysis components. The very frequent access of the first two literals is caused by the implementation of the unit propagation where the first two literals are always the watched ones.

Table 1 shows the distribution of each processor event amongst the solver components. It can be seen that most of the runtime is spent by the unit propagation. The conflict analysis component consumes only about 6% of the runtime, whereas the remaining components share only 2% of the runtime. Most of the L2 cache misses and hits are produced in the unit propagation as well. Hence, this component needs to be optimized in order to obtain a high impact for the solver's performance.

Based on the measurement result, the wait rate of the solver is 82%. This value indicates that the solver does not use the provided resources well. Computing the L2 cache miss rate, we obtain the value of 40% for our solver.

Analyzing the unit propagation further, we obtain the distribution of each processor event for the propagation on binary clauses and on longer clauses as shown in Table 2. The result indicates that the unit propagation component spends most of its runtime in propagating units on clauses with more than two literals, with most of the time spent in literal read accesses (45.8%) and maintaining the watcher lists (24.26%).

Table 1. Distribution of processor events in solver

Component	Total Cycles	Stall Cycles	L2 Misses	L2 Accesses
Decision Heuristics	1.77%	1.59%	3.13%	2.95%
Removal Heuristics	0.31%	0.21%	0.09%	0.21%
Conflict Analysis	5.74%	5.42%	6.27%	7.27%
Restart Event Heuristics	0.00%	1.33%	0.00%	0.00%
Unit Propagation	91.65%	92.62%	90.08%	88.94%

Table 2. Distribution of processor events for Unit Propagation

	Total Cycles	Stall Cycles	L2 Misses	L2 Accesses
Propagate on binary clauses	5.71%	5.55%	7.95%	5.64%
Propagate on longer clauses	83.86%	85.30%	78.17%	79.78%
Literal read access	45.8%	54.49%	24.07%	12.57%
Maintain watcher list	24.26%	18.59%	2.19%	36.64%

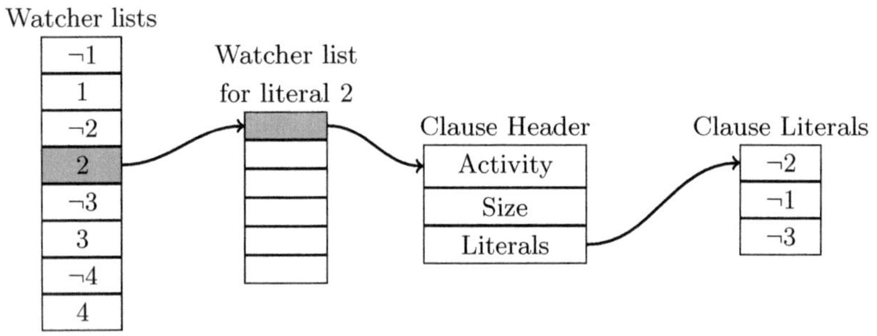

Fig. 2. Accessing the first literal of a clause using the two watched-literal scheme

Following the two watched-literal scheme, the watcher list of the literal to propagate is accessed and all clauses occurring in this list are processed sequentially. Visiting these clauses results in two cache misses if the other watched literal is not satisfied. This scheme is considered expensive, because some part of the penalty of the cache misses can be reduced as explained in Section 5.1. The memory scheme of accessing the first literal of a clause in a watcher list during propagation is shown in Fig. 2. The first cache miss occurs when the clause header is visited. The second one results from visiting the first literal afterwards. Note that the cache misses in looking up the truth value of a literal are negligible (less than 2%). The cache miss due to the extraction of the watcher list of a literal occurs only once (while propagating this literal); it is referred to as 0th *cache miss* in the sequel.

4.2 Implementation Analysis

The amount of memory accessed during solving instances can be reduced by compressing data, especially boolean arrays and the truth-value assignment of the solver. Applying the assignment compression [7] saves 75% compared to the original size, because four ternary truth values (positive, negative, undefined) can be stored in a byte. A similar approach can be applied to boolean arrays, which saves about 88% of its original size. Nevertheless, the compression of boolean arrays has a cost as it requires additional instructions that are executed every time the array is accessed. The consequences of either choice are discussed in Section 5.2.

To enable the phase-saving heuristic in choosing the polarity of a decision variable [21], the truth-value assignment also stores the backup polarity (i.e. the polarity previously assigned but erased due to backtracking) for every variable. This polarity is stored next to the current polarity. Thus, reading only an assignment loads every second byte (that stores the backup polarity) unnecessarily into the cache. In fact, this byte that stores the backup polarity is used only when the variable is assigned undefined or a polarity should be chosen.

Memory accesses can be avoided in the implementation by reusing data structures. A newly created vector without specifying a size results in a vector with no allocated storage capacity. Enlarging a vector allocates a new piece of memory and copies the content of the old piece of memory to the new one. Afterwards, the old piece of memory is freed. On the other hand, clearing a vector keeps its allocated capacity. Thus, copying memory can be avoided by clearing and reusing a vector, instead of deleting the vector and creating a new one.

Furthermore, memory accesses can be reduced by storing data that is likely to be accessed at the same time close together. For example, the decision level and the clause that implies a certain variable assignment (*reason clause*) per variable can be stored in a single array instead of two separate arrays [20].

5 Improvements

The analysis from Section 4 suggests some improvements with the goal to reduce cache misses and improving data locality. The main reason for cache misses is the separation of the clause header and the clause literals. We discuss and evaluate several improvements in this section.

5.1 Clause Access Improvements

Cache clause. The first idea is to move literals from the clause literals to the clause header. This improvement is called *cache clause*. By moving four literals (see next paragraph for explanation), we obtain 19%[1] of runtime speedup. This result is similar to clause packing improvement in [7]. The number of L2 cache misses is reduced by 32%. Choosing to access the locally stored literals or the clause literals increases the work cycles by 3%.

Slab allocator. With the cache clause improvement, the size of the clause header becomes 32-byte, so that two clause headers fit exactly on one cache line. Because

[1] In the sequel, all percent values are average values on the benchmark in Appendix A, if not specified otherwise.

all clauses are allocated using the memory allocator `malloc`, 8-byte additional storage (for system information) is added to *every* allocation. This storage prevents the system to place two clause headers compactly on a single cache line. Using the *slab allocator* this additional storage can be avoided [6], because it stores the 8-byte system information only *once* before its 4 KBytes page-aligned blocks (allocated using the `valloc()` function), allowing the clause headers to be stored compactly. The slab allocator alone does not affect the runtime and main memory accesses, but combining it with the cache clause leads to a better improvement. Combining the two improvements results in 23% speedup of the runtime and the number of L2 cache misses is reduced by 26% compared to the basic version of *riss*.

Flattened clause. Another approach is to store the clause in an array[2] and to combine the clause header and literals [10]. With this scheme, accessing the size and the activity of a clause is less flexible, because these accesses cannot be done via accessing a class member. The literal access remains a simple array access because it is executed most frequently. No additional instructions are needed to determine whether to access the locally stored literals or the clause literals. Accessing the size or the activity has to be done using a negative index. Fig. 3 shows the implementation and the memory scheme of the flattened clause improvement.[3] Together with the `malloc` allocator, this scheme yields 21% runtime speedup. The L2 cache miss rate is decreased by 20% and 24% of the L2 cache accesses in the basic version of the solver are caught by the L1 cache. Combining the flattened clause with the slab allocator improves the runtime by 22%. In order to handle clauses with variable sizes, one needs a separate allocator for each size (due to the fixed slab size). Multiple slab allocators of different sizes are then combined in a wrapper. Allocating a clause uses the allocator for the corresponding size (of the clause), which is chosen from the wrapper.

Blocking literal. The improvements in clause implementation avoid the second cache miss occurring in visiting the clauses in a watcher list as discussed in Section 4.1. In [7], some literals of the clauses in a watcher list are stored directly in the watcher list itself in order to avoid the first cache miss. Unfortunately the search path may change using this improvement. This approach is known as *blocking literal* scheme [23].

Prefetching schemes. The first cache miss can also be avoided if the prefetch unit is used to store the clauses of a watcher list in the cache. The GNU Compiler provides an instruction `__builtin_prefetch(void*)` that tells the prefetch unit of the CPU the address to fetch into the cache. Because the watcher list is traversed linearly, clauses can be prefetched. To avoid 0th cache miss, the

[2] We prefer a flat array over a structure as we like to store the pointer to the very first literal and not to a struct, where the first two elements are size and activity.

[3] The function `activity()` could be implemented more simple. As long as the clause header contains only 32 bit values, one could also use `((float*)literals)[-2]` to access the activity of the clause. The long version is preferred because the elements of the clause header can be seen explicitly.

```
typedef literal_t* cls;
cls literals;

literal_t literal(cls literals,uint32_t index) {
   return literals[index];
}
uint32_t size(cls literals) {
   return ((uint32_t*)literals)[-1];
}
float activity(cls literals) {
   return ((float*)(&(((uint32_t*)literals)[-1])))[-1];
}
```

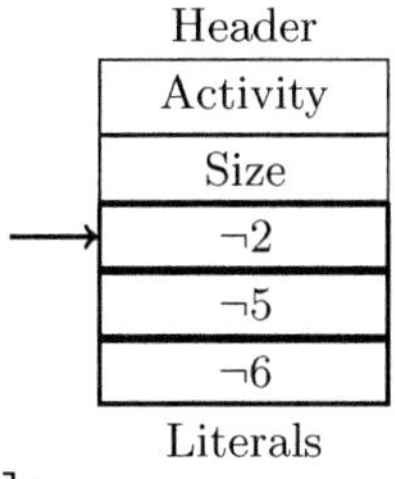

Fig. 3. The implementation and the memory scheme of the flattened clause

corresponding watcher list is prefetched as soon as another literal is added to the propagation queue. Prefetching the clauses (effectively the clause headers) can be done in two ways: either all clauses in the currently visited watcher list are prefetched (*first prefetching scheme*) or the clauses from the watcher lists of the first d literals in the propagation queue are prefetched (*second prefetching scheme*). Note that d is a parameter and it refers to the number of consecutive literals in the propagation queue.

The following results are obtained without improving the implementation of clause. The first prefetching scheme delivers 12% speedup and the stall cycles are reduced to 84%. The results of the second prefetching scheme depend on the parameter d. For $d = 10$, we gain 4% speedup of the runtime. This parameter can be tuned further, but this is not considered in the current work. In both schemes the number of work cycles, cache hits and cache misses increase because unnecessary clauses are prefetched due to a conflict which stops the unit propagation. The cache miss penalty of misses that occurred during prefetching do not have any negative impact on the runtime, because memory is prefetched by the prefetch unit in parallel to the execution of the algorithm in the CPU.

5.2 Reducing Memory Accesses

As shown in Table 2, the maintenance of the watcher lists, i.e. removing elements from the watcher list, needs almost 25% of runtime. Removing a clause from a watcher list pushes all subsequent clauses one position forward. As a result, lots of memory accesses are performed. Using a linked-list instead of a vector for a watcher list reduces the memory accesses by 13%, but increases the runtime by 20%. The negative impact is caused by the high miss rate of L2 cache, i.e. 71%, which results from the non-linear read access of the list elements.

Lazy maintenance. In the maintenance of a watcher list there is no need to push all subsequent clauses immediately to fill in the "gaps" which occur due to the removal of clauses. The watcher list can be maintained lazily. This can be illustrated as follows. Suppose that the first clause is removed from the list, the pointer of this clause is kept, marked as a gap, and subsequent clauses are not pushed immediately forward. Suppose that the second clause has also to be removed, then we leave a wider gap (of two clauses) in the list. If the third clause is not removed from the list then this clause can be pushed forward to the top of the list, making the gap in the list smaller. Note that only this clause is pushed forward as the following clauses could be potentially removed as well leaving a new gap. In the end, when the propagation stops (e.g. due to a conflict) then all the gaps can be removed at once from the watcher list. This lazy maintenance of watcher list results in 23% speedup of the solver's runtime, decreases the memory accesses by 35% and, thus, increases the L2 miss rate by 54%. This scheme also decreases the work cycles by 52%. These results indicate that the process of maintaining a watcher list is buffered completely in the L2 cache. The complexity of the maintenance is improved from quadratic to linear.

Compressed assignment and boolean arrays. Data structure compression may reduce memory accesses further. This compression includes the compression of the truth-value assignment and boolean arrays. These improvements are called *compressed assignment* and *compressed boolean arrays.* Our experiment shows that both compressions do not lead to any impact on the runtime performance. Some speedup gained from less L2 cache hits and misses has to compensate the execution of compression and decompression operations.

Negative index assignment. The assignment can be stored more compactly by storing the backup polarities from the currently used ones separately, rather than storing both polarities next to each other (cf. Section 4.2). The assignment is partitioned in two halves, albeit stored in a single array.[4] The half partition of backup polarities is identified by indexing the assignment with the negative variable. The number of memory accesses is reduced by 1% using this scheme and the runtime is slightly better than the runtime with respect to the compressed assignment and boolean arrays.

Combining decision level and reason clause. In order to analyze conflict, the decision level and the clause that implies a certain variable assignment (reason clause) need to be stored. If a variable is assigned or when backtracking is performed, both the decision level and the reason clause of the variable are updated. Thus, instead of storing the two information in separate arrays, they can be combined and stored in a single array [20]. The runtime of our solver is not affected by this improvement.

Compression of literals. Compressing the literals as done in *siege* [22] is also analyzed. The compression is able to store three literals in a 64-bit integer and reduces the storage needed by 33% in the best case. The maximum number of variables in the formula is reduced to 2^{20}, because the representation of one compressed literal is stored in 21-bit. The number of L2 cache misses reduces by 3%, but the number of work cycles increases by 17%. As a result, the runtime does not change. The number of memory accesses decreased by almost 1%.

[4] It can alternatively be realized using two separate arrays.

Vector reuse. The implementation of the conflict analysis needs three vectors. The first one stores the literals of the learnt clause. The second vector stores a backup of the first one during minimizing the learnt clause. The last vector stores temporary literals that have to be processed. Clearing and reusing these vectors lead to 4% runtime improvement and the number of memory accesses decreases by 3%.

Prefetching of reason clauses. Conflict analysis performs resolution and thus needs to read many clauses. The order of these clauses depends on the order of the literals on the trail and the information whether the current literal on the trail is contained in the current intermediate resolvent. To improve the clause read accesses, prefetching is applied to some of the reason clauses of the current conflict clause. The first n reason clauses are prefetched. Again, n is a new parameter that can be tuned for the benchmark. Prefetching the first three, six or ten reason clauses does not affect the runtime of the solver significantly.

5.3 Applying Improvements to MiniSAT2.0

The solver *riss* uses similar data structures as *MiniSAT2.0*. This leads to similar behavior as well. The analysis can only be done on 39 out of 40 problem instances because *MiniSAT2.0* fails to solve one instance within the timeout. *MiniSAT2.0* needs only 80% of the memory accesses compared to our solver. Due to a similar number of L2 cache misses, the L2 cache miss rate of *MiniSAT2.0* is 50%. The wait rate of *MiniSAT2.0* is equal to our solver. Because the two solvers implement different search algorithms, their runtime cannot be compared. However the similar number of work cycles indicates that the two solvers are suited for the benchmark equally well.

MiniSAT2.0 is more resource-aware than the original version of *riss*. Some of the improvements discussed herein are already implemented, namely the flattened clause approach and the lazy removal. Thus, only the slab allocator and prefetching can be applied. Adding only the slab allocator to *MiniSAT2.0* does not change the runtime. Applying prefetching in unit propagation results in 20% improvement (available at [2]). Adding both approaches does not speed up the solver further. The improved version of *MiniSAT2.0* solved all benchmark instances.

5.4 Combination of Improvements

Most of the improvements described previously can be combined. Table 3 gives the results of the six combinations with respect to the total cycles, L2 accesses, L2 miss rate and wait rate. Note that the values for total cycles and L2 accesses of each combination are relative to those of the basic version, whereas the values for the L2 miss rate and wait rate are absolute. The following acronyms are used: CC, slab, VR, P1, NA, CBA, CA and LM refer to the cache clause (with four local literals), slab allocator, vector reuse, the first prefetching scheme, the negative index assignment, the compressed boolean arrays, the compressed assignment and the lazy maintenance improvement, respectively.

Table 3. Results of improvement combinations. In this table, Basic refers to the basic version of the solver, Comb1 = CC + slab + VR + P1 + LM, Comb2 = FC + slab + VR + P1 + LM, Comb3 = Comb1 + NA, Comb4 = Comb2 + NA, Com5 = Comb3 + CBA and Comb6 = Comb1 + CA + CBA

Configuration	Total Cycles	L2 Accesses	L2 Miss Rate	Wait rate
Basic	100.0%	100.0%	40.94%	81.12%
Comb1	40.93%	56.3%	47.68%	75.56%
Comb2	39.91%	56.72%	48.7%	75.88%
Comb3	41.01%	56.01%	48.05%	75.82%
Comb4	40.9%	56.51%	48.86%	76.14%
Comb5	40.69%	54.56%	48.25%	74.86%
Comb6	39.7%	51.71%	49.3%	72.21%

Table 4. Comparing cycles distribution of basic version and combined improvements

	Total Cycles	Improvement total cycles	Work Cycles	Improvement work cycles
Comb6	100%	60.31%	100%	42.62%
Decision Heuristic	4.28%	0.07%	4.52%	-0.02%
Removal Heuristic	0.68%	0.04%	2.33%	-0.58%
Conflict Analysis	13%	0.58%	15.97%	-1.99%
Restart Event Heuristic	0%	1.33%	0.01%	1.33%
Unit Propagation	80.87%	59.55%	74.48%	44.56%
Propagate on binary clauses	14.42%	-0.01%	13.07%	-1.08%
Propagate on longer clauses	61.47%	59.46%	54.14%	46.32%
Literal read access	9.17%	16.04%	8.34%	-3.87%
Maintain watched list	0.22%	24.18%	0.34%	49.51%
Prefetch memory	23.14%	-9.18%	3.46%	-1.98%

All combinations result in a runtime improvement of almost 60% on average. Combinations with slab, VR, P1, LM together with a clause improvement (CC or FC), as in Comb1 and Comb2, serve as the core of optimizations. The performance drops significantly when only slab, VR, P1 and LM are considered (without any clause improvement), where we obtain 64.49% total cycles, 73.92% L2 accesses, 55.42% L2 miss rate and 84.45% wait rate. The gained improvement does not interfere with compressing data structures much. We only further analyze the combination with the best runtime improvement, viz. Comb6. Appendix A gives the runtime and used amount of memory per instance. Adding further improvements to this combination does not lead to significant changes in runtime. Table 4 shows the distribution of the runtime and the work cycles for Comb6. It also lists the amount of improvement obtained by comparing its absolute runtime (and work cycles) to the runtime (and work cycles, respectively) of the basic version. Compared to the basic version of the solver (Table 1), the distribution of the total cycles moves from the unit propagation to other components. The conflict analysis now needs 13% of the runtime. The work cycles change mainly for the unit propagation. The major improvement is achieved in propagating longer clauses. The runtime improvement of this part is caused by the improvement of the literal read access (16%) and the lazy maintenance of the watcher list (24%). The newly introduced prefetching scheme consumes about 9% of this improvement.

The unit propagation still remains at the heart of the solver and is the part where further improvements concerning the resource usage should be applied. The usage of the prefetch function seems to offer some space for the optimization of the solver, because it requires only about 4% of the work cycles but consumes about 23% of the total runtime.

6 Conclusion and Future Work

In this paper we present a study on the utilization of computing resources in state-of-the-art SAT solvers. The aim is to improve the resource usage in SAT solving and, consequently, the overall performance of SAT solvers. We analyze the cache performance of the SAT solver *riss* via sample-based profiling on a subset of the industrial benchmark set from the SAT competition 2009. The analysis leads to several improvements including the efficient representation of clauses as well as the use of slab allocators and clause-prefetching schemes in two watched-literal propagation. Additionally, compression schemes of several data structures and lazy maintenance of watcher list are suggested. By combining several improvements a speedup of up to 83%, and 60% on average, can be obtained. In addition to the findings reported in a preliminary version of this paper [17] we also analyze the compact storage of the information about decision level and reason clause as well as prefetching during conflict analysis. Moreover, the suggestions of using a slab allocator and prefetching are also applied to *MiniSAT2.0* resulting in a speedup of 20% on average.

The idea of cache clause improvement and compressed assignment is also considered in [7] to improve *MiniSAT*. *MiniSAT* also enjoys lazy maintenance of watcher lists similar to what we describe here. There is also some similarity between the idea of the flattened clause and the clause representation described in [24], where the clause head and body are combined and stored in an array. Compared to [24], the additional clause offsets array is not needed because we do not store the whole clause database in a single array. We also record in our clause representation the activity of clause instead of the number of watched literals. The combined storage of the variables level and reason clause information is also implemented in *RSat* [20].

Cache performance of SAT solvers has also been studied in [25]. Compared to [25], we do not study the cache performance on various unit propagation schemes. Instead, we consider only the two watched-literal propagation, which is commonly used in recent solvers, and study some further improvements including the use of a slab allocator and clause prefetching schemes. We also examine the cache performance of *MiniSAT2.0* (and *riss*) using measurement tools different from [25]. In order to better validate the analysis, our measurements are conducted on more SAT instances taken from a recent benchmark used at the SAT competition 2009.

We also considered *MiniSAT2.1*. It turned out that *MiniSAT2.1* is difficult to compare to *MiniSAT2.0* and *riss* with respect to the utilization of computing resources for various reasons: *MiniSAT2.1* implements a blocking literal approach to avoid the first cache miss which interferes with the prefetching approach proposed herein, it uses a different allocator, and implements a different search algorithm.

The approach presented in this paper is limited. We should consider additional SAT instances; we should consider additional metrics like cycles per instruction, L2 miss rate per instruction, or L2 demand miss rate; we should consider additional unit propagation schemes; we should consider other hardware; and we should consider simulation based profiling. In general, we would like to have an environment which allows us to configure, test and evaluate SAT solvers with respect to all kinds of SAT instances and metrics. Ideally, the environment should also support formal correctness proofs for the SAT solvers.

As future work we would like to study translation lookaside buffers [13]. A preliminary study involving *riss* has shown that using a page size of 2 MBytes (instead of 4 KBytes) leads to a speedup of 10%. For this result, the benchmark was run on an Intel Core i7 860 CPU with 8 MBytes L2 cache and a clock frequency of 2.80 GHz. Using a page size of 2 MBytes has decreased the runtime of both, the basic and the improved version of the solver.

Another interesting direction is the effect of branch miss-prediction and the related cache behavior. The implemented solvers of the ICCL are usually component-based and support a large number of runtime parameters. Running the chosen configuration implies that lots of if-statements have to be processed and, thus, the code contains lots of conditional branch instructions. At the moment we are measuring the prediction rate of our solver and try to study its influence to the caches afterwards.

We would also like to study improvements that affect the search path including the blocking literal approach. In this line of work, a metric has to be defined in order to compare different search paths.

Acknowledgment. The authors would like to thank Julian Stecklina and Hermann Härtig as well as all members of the SAT project group at the ICCL for many fruitful discussions, hints, and suggestions.

References

1. HPCToolkit, `http://hpctoolkit.org/`
2. ICCL SAT project group, `http://www.wv.inf.tu-dresden.de/Research/SATSolving/`
3. PAPI library, `http://icl.cs.utk.edu/papi/`
4. Baldow, C., Gräter, F., Hölldobler, S., Manthey, N., Seelemann, M., Steinke, P., Wernhard, C., Winkler, K., Zenker, E.: HydraSAT 2009.3 solver description. SAT 2009 Competitive Event Booklet, `http://www.cril.univ-artois.fr/SAT09/solvers/booklet.pdf`

5. Béjar, R., Manyà, F.: Solving the round robin problem using propositional logic. In: Procs. 17th National Conf. on Artificial Intelligence and 12th Conf. on Innovative Applications of Artificial Intelligence (2000)
6. Bonwick, J.: The slab allocator: an object-caching kernel memory allocator. In: Proceedings of the USENIX Summer 1994 Technical Conference (1994)
7. Chu, G., Harwood, A., Stuckey, P.J.: Cache conscious data structures for boolean satisfiability solvers. JSAT 6, 99–120 (2009)
8. Cook, S.A.: The complexity of theorem-proving procedures. In: Procs. 3rd Annual ACM Symposium on Theory of Computing (1971)
9. Davis, M., Logemann, G., Loveland, D.: A machine program for theorem proving. Communications of the ACM 5(7), 394–397 (1962)
10. Eén, N., Sörensson, N.: An extensible SAT-solver. In: Giunchiglia, E., Tacchella, A. (eds.) SAT 2003. LNCS, vol. 2919, Springer, Heidelberg (2004)
11. Eén, N., Sörensson, N.: MiniSAT - a SAT solver with conflict-clause minimization. In: Poster - 8th SAT (2005)
12. Fuhs, C., Giesl, J., Middeldorp, A., Schneider-Kamp, P., Thiemann, R., Zankl, H.: SAT solving for termination analysis with polynomial interpretations. In: Marques-Silva, J., Sakallah, K.A. (eds.) SAT 2007. LNCS, vol. 4501, Springer, Heidelberg (2007)
13. Hennessy, J., Patterson, D.: Computer Architecture - A Quantitative Approach. Morgan Kaufmann, San Francisco (1996)
14. Kautz, H., Selman, B.: Planning as satisfiability. In: Procs. 10th European Conference on Artificial Intelligence (1992)
15. Lynce, I., Marques-Silva, J.: SAT in bioinformatics: making the case with haplotype inference. In: Biere, A., Gomes, C.P. (eds.) SAT 2006. LNCS, vol. 4121, Springer, Heidelberg (2006)
16. Manthey, N.: riss 2010 solver description. SAT Race (2010) (submitted to), `http://www.ki.inf.tu-dresden.de/~norbert/webdata/data/riss-short.pdf`
17. Manthey, N., Saptawijaya, A.: Towards improving the resource usage of SAT-solvers. In: Pragmatics of SAT Workshop (2010) (to appear)
18. Marques-Silva, J.P., Sakallah, K.A.: GRASP: A new search algorithm for satisfiability. In: Alur, R., Henzinger, T.A. (eds.) CAV 1996. LNCS, vol. 1102. Springer, Heidelberg (1996)
19. Moskewicz, M., Madigan, C., Zhao, Y., Zhang, L., Malik, S.: Chaff: Engineering an efficient SAT solver. In: Design Automation Conference, pp. 530–535 (2001)
20. Pipatsrisawat, K., Darwiche, A.: RSat solver description for SAT competition, SAT, Competitive Event Booklet (2009), `http://www.cril.univ-artois.fr/SAT09/solvers/booklet.pdf`
21. Pipatsrisawat, K., Darwiche, A.: A lightweight component caching scheme for satisfiability solvers. In: Marques-Silva, J., Sakallah, K.A. (eds.) SAT 2007. LNCS, vol. 4501. Springer, Heidelberg (2007)
22. Ryan, L.O.: Efficient algorithms for clause learning SAT solvers. Master's thesis, Simon Fraser University, Canada (2004)
23. Sörensson, N., Eén, N.: MiniSAT 2.1 and MiniSAT++ 1.0 - SAT race, editions. SAT, Competitive Event Booklet (2008), `http://www.cril.univ-artois.fr/SAT09/solvers/booklet.pdf`
24. van Gelder, A.: Generalizations of watched literals for backtracking search. In: Seventh International Symposium on AI and Mathematics (2002)
25. Zhang, L., Malik, S.: Cache performance of SAT solvers: a case study for efficient implementation of algorithms. In: Giunchiglia, E., Tacchella, A. (eds.) SAT 2003. LNCS, vol. 2919, pp. 287–298. Springer, Heidelberg (2004)

A Problem Instances Used in the Measurement

Instances	Solving Time (seconds)	Memory Usage (KB)	Satisfiable?	Comb6 Solving Time (seconds)	Comb6 Memory Usage (KB)
ACG-10-5p0.cnf	169.062565	170968	no	136.284517	157404
AProVE09-20.cnf	1756.697786	203888	yes	690.167132	189568
UCG-15-5p0.cnf	476.773796	321968	no	354.950183	299132
UCG-20-5p1.cnf	1226.080625	474164	yes	864.186008	438676
UR-15-5p0.cnf	574.231887	338256	no	424.722543	314796
UTI-10-10p0.cnf	607.533968	388956	no	391.532469	368260
UTI-15-10p0.cnf	1027.736229	601984	no	674.366145	569592
blocks-4-ipc5-h22-unknown.cnf	570.543656	269496	no	387.100192	228484
cmu-bmc-longmult15.cnf	130.956184	26744	no	41.038564	21940
countbitswegner064.cnf	2585.413578	266988	no	710.664413	251164
eq.atree.braun.8.unsat.cnf	256.244014	30292	no	67.508219	26544
gss-16-s100.cnf	243.911243	38484	yes	186.859678	31492
gss-17-s100.cnf	357.822362	40828	yes	265.224575	33632
gss-20-s100.cnf	705.240074	51040	yes	446.959933	43296
gus-md5-07.cnf	121.45559	98880	no	80.96906	84092
gus-md5-09.cnf	820.299265	102548	no	517.428337	86196
manol-pipe-c10nidw_s.cnf	820.53928	625660	no	363.090691	544076
manol-pipe-c6bidw_i.cnf	257.124069	175516	no	109.158822	151748
manol-pipe-c6nidw_i.cnf	273.521094	181600	no	112.223013	157352
manol-pipe-g10id.cnf	812.70279	339084	no	169.682604	302568
manol-pipe-g10nid.cnf	2334.201878	570644	no	561.383084	514792
mizh-md5-47-3.cnf	814.090877	275084	yes	396.752795	254432
mizh-md5-47-4.cnf	668.657788	246784	yes	326.028375	225876
mizh-sha0-35-3.cnf	219.293705	153244	yes	104.942558	138980
ndhf_xits_20_SAT.cnf	393.776609	252364	yes	200.740545	232580
post-c32s-gcdm16-22.cnf	998.362393	257068	yes	354.654164	224016
q_query_3_L60_coli.sat.cnf	336.085004	240176	yes	128.248015	210628
q_query_3_L70_coli.sat.cnf	561.367083	285092	yes	215.357459	248620
q_query_3_l44_lambda.cnf	2024.402517	135872	no	479.485966	120156
q_query_3_l45_lambda.cnf	1767.374454	133816	no	488.114505	118532
q_query_3_l48_lambda.cnf	2068.153251	136716	no	524.03275	120612
rbcl_xits_06_UNSAT.cnf	415.165946	32620	no	58.451653	29076
schup-l2s-abp4-1-k31.cnf	448.384022	69608	no	158.749921	61040
schup-l2s-guid-1-k56.cnf	2439.468457	306456	no	1035.388707	280568
schup-l2s-motst-2-k315.cnf	344.433525	561832	yes	267.844739	486528
simon-s02b-dp11u10.cnf	1189.330328	80564	no	324.756296	71560
uts-l05-ipc5-h27-unknown.cnf	353.102067	163212	no	168.186511	139832
uts-l06-ipc5-h31-unknown.cnf	1186.990182	284108	no	486.886428	244824
vmpc_24.cnf	659.017186	73148	yes	184.459528	68824
vmpc_26.cnf	539.513717	84628	yes	174.962934	79120

Expansion Nets: Proof-Nets for Propositional Classical Logic

Richard McKinley

Theoretische Informatik und Logik, Institut für Informatik und Angewandete Mathematik, Üniversität Bern

Abstract. We give a calculus of proof-nets for classical propositional logic. These nets improve on a proposal due to Robinson by validating the associativity and commutativity of contraction, and provide canonical representants for classical sequent proofs modulo natural equivalences. We present the relationship between sequent proofs and proof-nets as an annotated sequent calculus, deriving formulae decorated with *expansion/deletion trees*. We then show a subcalculus, *expansion nets*, which in addition to these good properties has a polynomial-time correctness criterion.

1 Introduction

In contrast to the well-developed theory of proof-identity for intuitionistic natural deduction (given by interpretation of proofs in a cartesian-closed category), the theory of identity for proofs in classical logic is very poorly understood. Investigations by several researchers over the last ten years [16,7,12,13,2,11] have only served to underline the difficulty of the problem. Many of these difficulties concern proofs with cuts; here the problem is that proof-identity must account for the nonconfluence of cut-elimination. Yet even for cut-free proofs, opinions on the "right notion" of proof-identity differ. A reasonable minimal requirement is that proofs differing by *commuting conversions* of noninterfering sequent rules should be equal. Proof-nets [9] are a tool for providing canonical representants of such equivalence classes of proofs. A proposal by Robinson [16] gives proof-nets for propositional classical logic, but fails to provide canonical representants for sequent proofs because it contains explicit weakening attachments. The proof-identities induced by Robinson's nets do not include, among other desirable proof-identities, commutativity/associativity of contraction, a key assumption in the development of abstract models of proofs. In Führmann and Pym's work [7], a categorical model of proofs is built from equivalence classes of Robinson's nets, ensuring that the structure interpreting the structural rule in the resulting category forms a commutative monoid, and that those monoids are constructed pointwise.

In this paper we take Robinson's nets as a starting point for developing a more abstract notion of proof-net for classical logic. Our nets are concrete representatives of the equivalence classes used in [7]. We then go on to identify a

C. Fermüller and A. Voronkov (Eds.): LPAR-17, LNCS 6397, pp. 535–549, 2010.

$$\frac{}{p,\ \bar{p}}\,Ax \qquad\qquad \frac{}{\top}\,Ax_{\top}$$

$$\frac{\Gamma, |A, B}{\Gamma, A \vee B}\,\vee \qquad \frac{\Gamma, A \qquad \Delta, B}{\Gamma, \Delta,\ A \wedge B}\,\wedge$$

$$\frac{\Gamma,\ A, A}{\Gamma, A}\,C \qquad\qquad \frac{\Gamma}{\Gamma, B}\,W$$

Fig. 1. Cut-free multiplicative **LK** (one-sided)

subcalculus of these nets which has a polynomial-time correctness criterion, and therefore forms a propositional proof system [3].

1.1 Preliminaries

We assume familiarity with proof-nets for unit free multiplicative linear logic $\mathbf{MLL}^-$ with Mix. In particular, we assume knowledge of the *switching graph* condition for multiplicative proof structures, and how it leads to a proof of sequentialization for $\mathbf{MLL}^-$ + Mix proof nets [5,6]. We will also assume, without proof, the existence of a *polynomial time* correctness criterion equivalent to the switching criterion; such a criterion is given by attempting to sequentialize by searching for *splitting pars*, a technique first described in [6], and available in English translation in the Linear Logic Primer [4].

2 Proof Nets with Contraction and Weakening

Robinson's proof-nets for classical logic [16] are based very closely on Girard's proof-nets for **MLL** with units [9]. The basic idea comes from [8]: correctness is given by treating the conjunctions and axioms of classical logic in the same way as the linear logic axiom and tensor, and treating both contraction and disjunction in the same way as the linear logic "par" connective. However, unlike Girard's nets, Robinson's nets are presented in a two-sided form, with multiple premises and multiple conclusions, deriving formulae with an explicit negation connective. We will consider a small variant of this calculus: one-sided nets, over formulae of classical logic in *negation normal form.* A cut-free sequent calculus deriving multisets of such formulae, with explicit structural rules and multiplicatively formulated logical rules, is given in Figure 1. Considering one-sided nets allows us to give a more compact presentation of our systems: the one-sidedness is not necessary for the approach, however, and the results of the subsequent sections carry over easily to a two-sided setting. A more important departure from Robinson's setting is the treatment of weakening, as will be explained below.

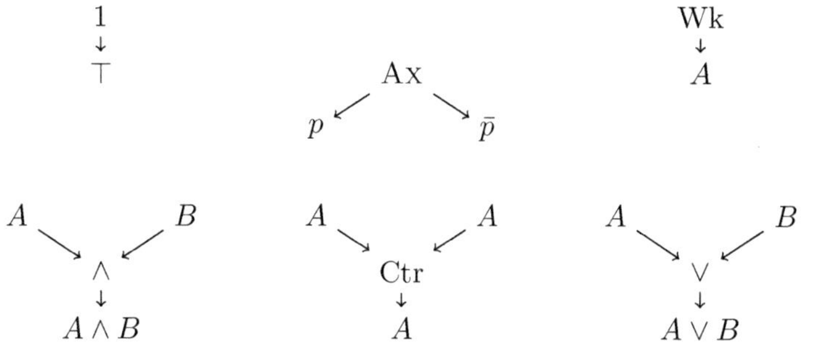

Fig. 2. Proof nets for classical logic with unrestricted contraction and weakening

The definition of these nets begins with a notion of *proof structure*: an object which locally has the structure of a proof-net:

Definition 1. *A* Robinson proof-structure *is a directed graph built from the subgraphs in Figure 2 having no incoming edges.*

We refer to the vertices of a Robinson structure labelled with formulae of propositional logic as *formula-nodes*. The other vertices are referred to as *rule-nodes*.

To obtain a correctness criterion, it is necessary to anchor each weakening to some other node of the proof. In [16] this anchoring is part of the structure of the weakening node: we instead use the more usual notion of an *attachment*.

Definition 2. *An* attachment f *for a Robinson proof-structure F is a function mapping each rule node labelled with Wk to some other rule-node of the proof-structure. By an attached proof structure, we mean a pair (F, f) of a proof structure F and an attachment f for F.*

Example 1. Below we see two different attachments of the same proof structure, represented by the grey arrows:

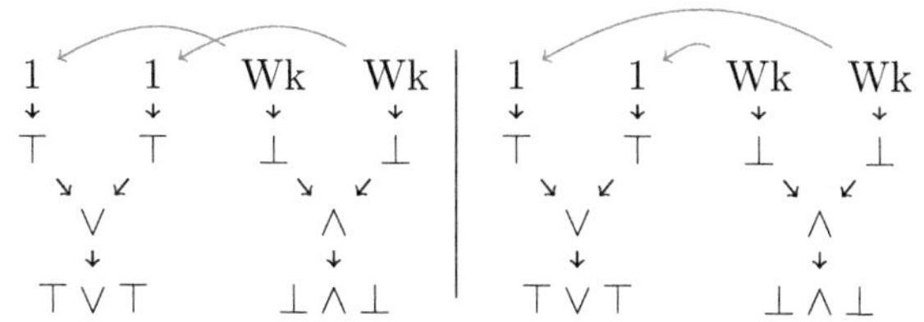

(1)

A proof in LK can be seen as a recipe for building an attached proof structure: each rule of the calculus corresponding to a rule node. This procedure is sometimes referred to as desequentialization, and is described in detail in [16].

One chooses the attachment for a weakening from one of the formulae present in the context of the weakening rule; this arbitrary choice means that attached proof-nets themselves cannot be the canonical proof objects we seek. For **MLL**, the right notion of canonical proof object is a *quotient* of attached proof-nets by so-called *Trimble rewiring* [17], whereby two proof-nets are equivalent if just one of the attachments of a unit is changed. According to Trimble rewiring, the two attached nets in (1) are different; this is important, as the corresponding morphisms are distinguished in some $*$-autonomous categories. We know of no natural model of *classical* proofs (whatever the formulation) where such proofs are distinguished, and so are happy to take *unattached* nets as proof-objects in their own right.

The standard problem in the theory of proof-nets is to give a global *correctness criterion* for identifying, among the proof-structures, those which can be obtained from desequentializing a sequent proof. This then leads to a *sequentialization theorem*, allowing one to reconstruct a sequent proof out of a correct proof-net. As Robinson nets ae so closely modelled on **MLL** nets, we may adapt any of the many equivalent formulations of correctness for **MLL** nets. For example, the following is the switching graph criterion, suitably altered for our setting:

Definition 3. *Let F be a Robinson proof-structure.*

(a) A rule-node of F is switched *if it is a Ctr or $\vee$ node. A* switching *of a Robinson proof-structure is a choice, for each switched node, of one of its successors.*
(b) Given an attachment f for F, and a switching σ for F, the switching graph *$\sigma(F, f)$ is the graph obtained by deleting from F all edges from a switched node to its successor not chosen by σ, forgetting directedness of edges, and adding an edge from each Wk node to its image under f.*
(c) (F, f) is ACC-correct *if, for each switching σ, $\sigma(F, f)$ is acyclic and connected.*
(d) F is a Robinson net *if, for some f, (F, f) is ACC-correct.*

Correctness for (unattached) Robinson nets is in **NP**, since it is necessary to guess an attachment before testing the switching criterion.

Theorem 1 (Robinson).

*(a) Every proof-structure arising from an **LK** proof is a Robinson-net.*
*(b) Every Robinson-net can be obtained by desequentializing an **LK** proof.*

Using the techniques developed in [6,4], we can capture reasoning the in presence of the Mix rule:

$$\frac{\vdash \Gamma \qquad \vdash \Delta}{\vdash \Gamma, \Delta}\ \textsc{Mix}$$

Definition 4. *Let F be a Robinson proof-structure, and f an attachment for F*

(a) (F, f) *is* AC-correct *if, for each switching σ, $\sigma(F, f)$ is acyclic.*
(b) F *is a* MIX-net *if there is an attachment f such that (F, f) is AC-correct.*

Theorem 2. *(a) Every proof-structure arising from a sequent proof in the system in Figure 1 plus* MIX *is a* MIX*-net.*
(b) Every MIX*-net can be obtained by desequentializing a sequent proof with* MIX.

The mix rule does not allow us to prove more theorems, but it extends the space of proofs available to us. It will be important later; in its presence, we can give a complete class of proof nets with polynomial-time correctness.

3 Expansion/Deletion Nets

As a way of presenting proofs, unattached Robinson-style proof-nets are a substantial improvement over **LK** proofs. Two sequent derivations differing by a simple permutation of rule occurrences desequentialize to the same proof-net. However proof identity in classical logic is more complicated than it is, for example, in $\mathbf{MLL}^-$; simple rule permutations are not the only source of non-canonicity in proofs. In the following section we consider sources of non-canonicity arising from the contraction rule, which Robinson's nets suffer from as acutely as the sequent calculus. We will then give a new formulation of proof nets (expansion/deletion nets) which do not exhibit these problems.

3.1 Problems with Contraction

Contraction is not associative. Given three copies of the conclusion A, there are two ways we can contract them, which should be equivalent.

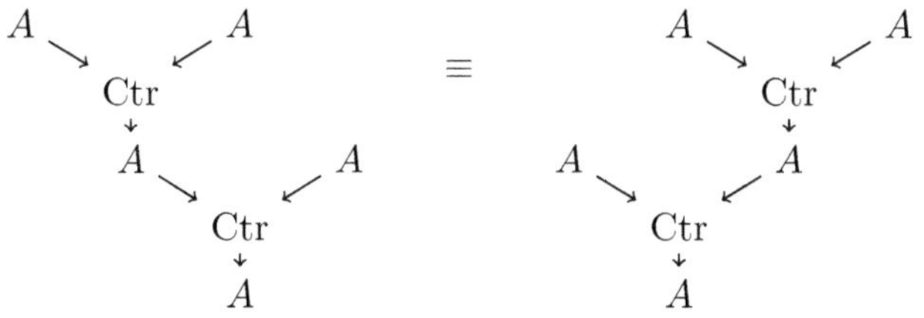

Girard suggests an obvious fix in [8]: n-ary contraction nodes. In addition, we should require that the conclusion of the link is not in turn the premise of another contraction link. We will call contractions of this special kind *expansions.*

Weakening is not a unit for contraction. Given a proof-net deriving a formula A, we can weaken to form another copy of A and then immediately apply contraction, to again obtain a proof of A. We would prefer that weakening be a unit to contraction; that these two proofs of A be identified.

Contraction on disjunctions is not pointwise. The following two figures contain the same essential information, and two proofs differing by them are essentially the same:

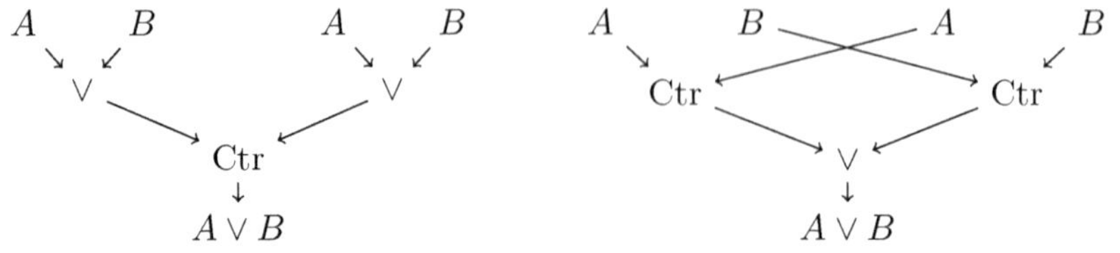

We can ensure that only one of these figures may appear in our nets by forbidding the contraction node to act on disjunctions, this is natural, since the sequent rule introducing disjunction is *invertible.*

3.2 Expansion/Deletion Trees

In our view a proof net is best seen as a forest together with a relation on the nodes of the forest (representing the axiom links of a proof net as usually presented). For $\mathbf{MLL}^-$ (with or without mix) the forest is built from formula trees, but for classical logic the trees must contain additional structure, to account for contraction and weakening. Our proof nets will be built from typed *expansion/deletion trees* or ed-trees; these can be seen as formula trees where, at a node typed $p, \bar{p}$ or $A \wedge B$, we can *expand* (corresponding to a single n-ary contraction) or *delete* (corresponding to weakening).

Definition 5 (Expansion/deletion trees). *Let $\mathcal{X} = \mathsf{x}, \mathsf{y}, \ldots$ be a countable set – the* axiom variables. *An expansion/deletion tree (or ed-tree) over $\mathcal{X}$ is of the form t below:*

$$t ::= 1 \mid * \mid (w + \cdots + w) \mid (t \vee t) \qquad w ::= \mathsf{x} \mid \bar{\mathsf{x}} \mid t \otimes t$$

where $(w + \cdots + w)$ denotes a nonempty finite formal sum, and $*$ denotes the empty formal sum. We call the empty sum a deletion, *and a nonempty sum an* expansion. *We call the members of the grammar w "witnesses".*

The advantage of using formal sums of witnesses to keep track of contractions is that formal sums are associative and commutative: that $*$ is the unit for the formal sum means that weakening will be the unit for contraction.

Types for ed-trees and witnesses are as follows:

Definition 6. *A* type *is either*

(a) A formula of classical propositional logic;
(b) A witness type *of one of the two following forms:*
- *A* positive witness type, *written $[p]$, where p is a positive atom;*
- *A* negative witness type, *written $[\bar{p}]$, where $\bar{p}$ is a negative atom; or*
- *A conjunctive witness type, written $A \otimes B$, where A and B are formulae of propositional classical logic.*

$$\frac{}{\bar{\mathsf{x}} : [\bar{p}]} \qquad \frac{}{1 : \top} \qquad \frac{}{* : A} \qquad \frac{}{\mathsf{x} : [p]}$$

$$\frac{t : A \quad s : B}{t \vee s : A \vee B} \qquad \frac{t : A \quad s : B}{t \otimes s : A \otimes B}$$

$$\frac{w_1 : [p] \;\cdots\; w_n : [p]}{(w_1 + \cdots + w_n) : p} \qquad \frac{w_1 : [\bar{p}] \;\cdots\; w_n : [\bar{p}]}{(w_1 + \cdots + w_n) : \bar{p}} \qquad \frac{w_1 : A \otimes B \;\cdots\; w_n : A \otimes B}{(w_1 + \cdots + w_n) : A \wedge B}$$

Fig. 3. Typing derivations for terms

Definition 7. *A typed term is a pair $t : A$ of a term t and a type A, derivable in the typing system given in Figure 3.*

The typing rules in Figure 3 ensure that the conclusion of an expansion is never the premise of another expansion.

Having found the right notion of tree, a proof-structure is just a forest of those trees. We will refer to these forests as *annotated sequents*, since we will later give sequent calculi deriving them.

Definition 8. *An* annotated sequent *is a forest F of typed ed-trees in which axiom variables occur in dual pairs: that is*

(a) each axiom variable x, and each negated variable $\bar{\mathsf{y}}$, occurs at most once in F, and
(b) there is an occurrence of $\bar{\mathsf{x}}$ in F if and only if there is an occurrence of x.

The type of an annotated sequent F is the ordinary sequent comprising the multiset of types of the the ed-trees making up F.

To see an annotated sequent as a proof structure in the more usual sense we can consider its graph, in which we add axiom links to the forest:

Definition 9. *The* graph *of an annotated sequent F is a directed graph with vertices given by instances of subtrees of F; we call these the* nodes *of F. The edges of the graph are given by the forest structure (with edges directed toward the root), plus an edge from x to $\bar{\mathsf{x}}$ for each variable x appearing in F. The edges above a $\otimes$ or $\vee$ node are ordered; edges above expansion nodes are unordered.*

Example 2. The following annotated sequent is a proof of Pierce's law

$$(((\bar{\mathsf{x}}) \vee *) \otimes (\bar{\mathsf{y}})) : (\bar{p} \vee q) \wedge \bar{p}, \quad (\mathsf{x} + \mathsf{y}) : p \tag{2}$$

The graph of this annotated sequent is

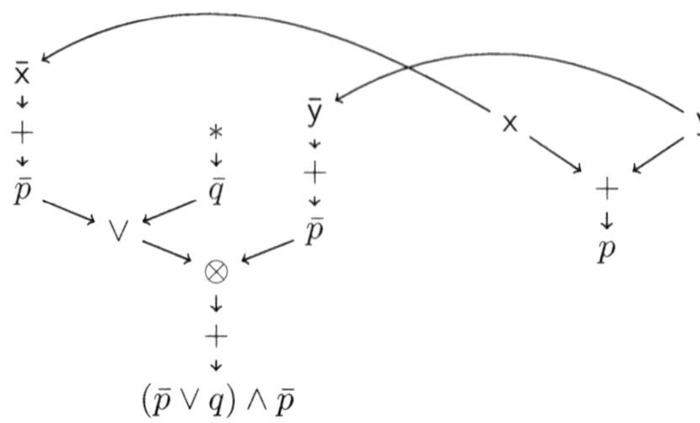

(3)

Correctness for annotated sequents is analogous to that for Robinson structures:

Definition 10. *Let F be an annotated sequent. An attachment for F is a function assigning, to each deletion $*$ of F, some other subterm of F. An attached annotated sequent is a pair (F, f) of an annotated sequent F and an attachment f for F.*

Definition 11. *Let (F, f) be an attached annotated sequent.*

(a) A switching σ for (F, f) is a choice of successor for each expansion node and each $\vee$ node.
(b) The switching graph $\sigma(F, f)$ is obtained from the graph of F by
  1: deleting all incoming edges to each expansion and $\vee$ node, other than those coming from the nodes chosen by the switching,
  2: forgetting the directedness of edges,
  3: adding an edge between each deletion and its image under the attachment f.
(c) (F, f) is an ed-net if, for every switching σ of F, $\sigma(F, f)$ is acyclic.

3.3 Expansion Nets

We consider now a subclass of ed-nets, *expansion nets*, which are interesting because they have a *default attachment*; this allows a polynomial time correctness criterion.

Definition 12. *(a) An expansion/deletion tree t is an* expansion tree *if every deletion $*$ in t occurs as the left or right disjunct of a disjunctive subterm of t.*
(b) An ed-net F is an expansion net *if every term appearing in F is an expansion tree.*

Definition 13. *Let F be a forest of typed expansion trees. The* default attachment *of F is a function assigning to each subterm of the form $*$, the subterm t with which it forms $t \vee *$ or $* \vee t$.*

$$\frac{}{\vdash 1 : \top}\,\mathrm{Ax}_\top \qquad \frac{}{(\bar{\mathsf{x}}) : \bar{p},\ (\mathsf{x}) : p}\,\mathrm{Ax}$$

$$\frac{F,\ t : A,\ s : B}{F,\ t \vee s : A \vee B}\,\vee \qquad \frac{F,\ t : A \qquad G,\ s : B}{F, G,\ (t \otimes s) : A \wedge B}\,\wedge$$

$$\frac{F}{F,\ * : A}\,\mathrm{W} \qquad \frac{F \quad G}{F,\ G}\,\mathrm{Mix}$$

$$\frac{F,\ t : A \wedge B,\ s : A \wedge B}{F,\ t + s : A \wedge B}\,\mathrm{C}_\wedge \qquad \frac{F,\ s : p,\ t : p}{F,\ s + t : p}\,\mathrm{C}_p \qquad \frac{F,\ s : \bar{p},\ t : \bar{p}}{F,\ s + t : \bar{p}}\,\mathrm{C}_{\bar{p}}$$

Fig. 4. $\mathbf{LK}_{ed}$

This default attachment can then be used to check correctness:

Proposition 1. *A forest of typed expansion trees F is an expansion-net if and only if, for every switching σ, $\sigma(F, f)$ is acyclic, where f is the default attachment.*

Since the acyclicity of the switching graphs can be decided polynomially, correctness for expansion-nets is polynomial time.

Remark 1. Let $\mathbf{MLL}^*$ be the subset of binary **MLL** formulae (in which each atom occurs at most once) having no subformula of the form $(\bot \otimes A)$ or $(A \otimes \bot)$. A similar argument to the one above shows that provability for this fragment of **MLL** is decidable in polynomial time: the formula itself defines a proof-net with a default attachment for each $\bot$. By replacing switched nodes with par and unswitched nodes with tensor, an expansion net gives rise to a binary **MLL** formula; this formula belongs to $\mathbf{MLL}^*$, and so its provability can be checked in polynomial time.

What remains to prove is that we have not lost any theorems of propositional logic by restricting contraction and weakening: that the system of expansion nets is *complete*. To see this, we consider the relationship between sequent proofs and expansion nets. Specifically, we give an *annotated* sequent calculus deriving annotated sequents. We first give a sequent calculus deriving ed-nets, and then give a restricted system deriving expansion nets.

4 Decorating Sequent Derivations with Terms

In Figure 4 we give a sequent-style calculus for deriving annotated sequents. One should think of this calculus in the same way as a lambda-term-annotated

$$\frac{F,\ t:A,\ s:B}{F,\ \ t\vee s:A\vee B}\vee \qquad \frac{F,\ t:A}{F,\ t\vee *:A\vee B}\vee_L \qquad \frac{F,\ s:B}{F,\ *\vee s:A\vee B}\vee_R$$

Fig. 5. The three disjunction rules of $\mathbf{LK}_e$

sequent system for intuitionisitic logic; the annotated sequents themselves are proof objects, with the sequent proof giving their inductive buildup. The annotated system plays, for $\mathbf{LK}_{ed}$, the role of desequentialization.

Example 3. The following annotated sequent proof illustrates how contractions at the level of sequent proofs are interpreted by expansions at the level of the annotated sequents.

$$\dfrac{\dfrac{\dfrac{\dfrac{}{(\bar{\mathsf{x}}):\bar{a},\ (\mathsf{x}):a}\text{Ax} \quad \dfrac{}{(\bar{\mathsf{y}}):\bar{a},\ (\mathsf{y}):a}\text{Ax}}{(\bar{\mathsf{x}}):\bar{a},\ (\bar{\mathsf{y}}):\bar{a},(\mathsf{x}\otimes\mathsf{y}):a\wedge a}\wedge \quad \dfrac{}{(\bar{\mathsf{z}}):\bar{a},\ (\mathsf{z}):a}\text{Ax}}{(\bar{\mathsf{x}}):\bar{a},\ (\bar{\mathsf{y}}):\bar{a},\ \bar{\mathsf{z}}:\bar{a},\ ((\mathsf{x}\otimes\mathsf{y})\otimes\mathsf{z}):(a\wedge a)\wedge a}\wedge}{(\bar{\mathsf{x}}):\bar{a},\ (\bar{\mathsf{y}}+\bar{\mathsf{z}}):\bar{a},\ ((\mathsf{x}\otimes\mathsf{y})\otimes\mathsf{z}):(a\wedge a)\wedge a}\text{C}}{(\bar{\mathsf{x}}+\bar{\mathsf{y}}+\bar{\mathsf{z}}):\bar{a},\ ((\mathsf{x}\otimes\mathsf{y})\otimes\mathsf{z}):(a\wedge a)\wedge a}\text{C} \tag{4}$$

The particular way in which the contractions are carried out does not affect the annotated endsequent: any commutation or association of the contractions gives rise to the same term assignment.

Applying the standard sequentialization techniches to ed-nets, we obtain the following statement of the surjectivity of desequentialization:

Proposition 2. *An annotated sequent F is an ed-net if and only if it can be derived in $\boldsymbol{LK}_{ed}$.*

Given a proof in $\mathbf{LK}_{ed}$, we can recover an ordinary sequent proof by forgetting the annotations: this yields a proof in **LK**. This forgetful projection of $\mathbf{LK}_{ed}$ is a *subcalculus* of **LK**, since it only has contractions for conjunctions and atoms. If we can show all the missing contractions admissible in $\mathbf{LK}_{ed}$, then we have shown that $\mathbf{LK}_{ed}$ (and, by extension, expansion/deletion nets) are complete. In fact, we will show an even more restricted calculus, $\mathbf{LK}_e$, complete: this calculus derives expansion nets. Completeness of $\mathbf{LK}_{ed}$ will then follow as a corollary.

4.1 A Calculus Deriving Expansion Nets

Let $\mathbf{LK}_e$ be derived from $\mathbf{LK}_{ed}$ as follows; $\mathbf{LK}_e$ consists of all the rules of $\mathbf{LK}_{ed}$ except W, and has in addition the two rules $\vee_L$ and $\vee_R$ shown in Figure 5. In $\mathbf{LK}_e$, the subterm $*$ is never introduced except by these disjunction rules, and so the conclusion of an $\mathbf{LK}_e$ derivation consists of expansion trees.

We show now that $\mathbf{LK}_e$ and $\mathbf{LK}_{ed}$ are equivalent with respect to provability – that is, they prove the same theorems. The easier direction is the following:

Proposition 3. *If* $\boldsymbol{LK}_e \vdash t : A$*, then* $\boldsymbol{LK}_{ed} \vdash t : A$.

Proof. By induction on the length of proofs. The property clearly holds for the axioms. For every rule in $\mathbf{LK}_e$ other than $\vee_L$ and $\vee_R$, there is a corresponding rule in $\mathbf{LK}_{ed}$, and the proof is easy. We need only show the admissibility of $\vee_L$ and $\vee_R$. But these can be easily simulated by one application of weakening followed by one of the $\mathbf{LK}_{ed}$ $\vee$ rule.

For the opposite direction, we will need the following easy lemma:

Lemma 1. *(a) If* $\boldsymbol{LK}_e \vdash F, t \vee s : A \vee B$*, and* $s, t \neq *$*, then* $\boldsymbol{LK}_e \vdash t : A, s : B$.
(b) If $\boldsymbol{LK}_e \vdash F,\ t \vee * : A \vee B$ *or* $\boldsymbol{LK}_e \vdash F,\ * \vee t : B \vee A$*, then* $\boldsymbol{LK}_e \vdash F,\ t : A$.

Since $\mathbf{LK}_e$ is not complete for sequents, but only for (annotated) formulae, we cannot directly prove that if $\mathbf{LK}_{ed}$ proves a sequent of type Γ, so does $\mathbf{LK}_e$. Instead, we prove that, if $\mathbf{LK}_{ed}$ proves a sequent of type Γ, there is a term t such that $\mathbf{LK}_e$ proves $t : \bigvee \Gamma$. We first observe that re-association of disjunctions is admissible in $\mathbf{LK}_e$.

Lemma 2. *Let* $t : A$ *and* $s : B$ *be expansion tree differing by association of disjunctions in some subterm. Then* $\boldsymbol{LK}_e \vdash t : A$ *if and only if* $\boldsymbol{LK}_e \vdash s : B$.

Proposition 4. *If* F *has type* $\Gamma = A_1, \ldots, A_n$*, and* $\boldsymbol{LK}_{ed} \vdash F$*, then there are terms* $t_i : A_i$ *such that, if* $t = (((t_1 \vee t_2) \vee \ldots t_{n-1}) \vee t_n)$*, then* $\boldsymbol{LK}_e \vdash t : (((A_1 \vee A_2) \vee \ldots A_{n-1}) \vee A_n)$.

Proof. For any proof in $\mathbf{LK}_{ed}$ of an annotated sequent $s_1 : A_1, \ldots s_n : A_n$, we give a sequence $t_1 : A_1, \ldots t_n : A_n$ such that $t = (((t_1 \vee t_2) \vee \ldots t_{n-1}) \vee t_n) : \bigvee \Gamma$ is provable in $\mathbf{LK}_e$, by induction on the height of a proof in $\mathbf{LK}_{ed}$.

For the axioms of $\mathbf{LK}_{ed}$, the claim is clearly true. For the inductive step, we proceed by case analysis on the last rule ρ of the $\mathbf{LK}_{ed}$ proof. In each case, we assume that the proposition holds for the premisses of ρ, and that A_n is the active formula of ρ.

- $\rho = \mathrm{W}$ By the induction hypothesis, we have terms $t_1 : A_1 \ldots t_{n-1} : A_{n-1}$ with $\mathbf{LK}_e \vdash ((t_1 \vee t_2) \vee \ldots t_{n-1}) : ((A_1 \vee A_2) \vee \cdots \vee A_{n-1})$ apply the rule $\vee_L$ in $\mathbf{LK}_e$, to add a new disjunct of type A_n to the conclusion.
- $\rho = \vee$ In the case of the $\vee$ rule, applied to an annotated sequent $F, s_{n-1} : A, s_n : B$, consider the subterms $t_{n-1} : A$ and $t_n : B$ of t. If $t = (((t_1 \vee t_2) \vee *) \cdots *)$ then apply Lemma 1 twice, followed by $\vee_L$, to obtain a proof of the correct form. Otherwise, there is a reassociation of t which has the correct form.
- $\rho = \mathrm{C}$ Similar to the treatment of disjunction.

$\rho =$ Mix Suppose that $\mathbf{LK}_{ed} \vdash F$ and $\mathbf{LK}_{ed} \vdash G$, where F has type $A_1, \ldots, A_n$ and G has type $B_1, \ldots B_m$, and that we have corresponding $\mathbf{LK}_e$-provable terms t and s. The result of applying the $\mathbf{LK}_e$ Mix-rule can be reassociated to have the correct form.

$\rho = \wedge$ Given annotated sequents $F_1, s_1 : A_1$ and $F_2, s_2 : A_2$, with corresponding $\mathbf{LK}_e$-provable terms t and t', let t_{A_1} and t_{A_2} be the disjuncts of t and t' corresponding to s_1 and s_2:

- If neither t_{A_1} nor t_{A_2} is $*$, then we may apply Lemma 1 twice, followed by $\wedge$ and then $\vee$, to obtain a proof of the correct shape.
- If both $t_{A_1} = *$ and $t_{A_2} = *$ are $*$ then apply Lemma 1 to remove the deletions. By applying the $\mathbf{LK}_e$ Mix-rule and then $\vee_L$, we obtain a provable term of the required shape.
- The final case is where exactly one $t_{A_i} = *$; without loss of generality, let it be t_{A_1}. We treat this much like a cut against weakening in **LK**. We know that $\mathbf{LK}_e \vdash (((t_1 \vee t_2) \vee \ldots t_m) \vee *)$. By Lemma 1, $\mathbf{LK}_e \vdash (((t_1 \vee t_2) \vee \ldots t_m)$. Now "weaken" the conclusion once for $A \wedge B$ and once for each member of F_2: that is, apply $\vee_L$ once for each of those formulae. The result is an $\mathbf{LK}_e$ provable term $((((t_1 \vee t_2) \vee \ldots t_m) \vee *) \vee \cdots \vee *)$ of the correct type.

The content of the above result is that, at the theorem level, the rules of conjunction, disjunction, weakening and Mixare admissible in $\mathbf{LK}_e$; the contraction rule is also admissible when restricted to atoms and conjunctions. In the following section we demonstrate the general admissibility of contraction in $\mathbf{LK}_e$, which is enough to see that it is a complete calculus for classical propositional logic.

4.2 Cut-Free Completeness of $\mathbf{LK}_e$

By cut-free completeness of $\mathbf{LK}_e$, we mean the following:

Theorem 3. *For every formula A of classical propositional logic such that $\vdash A$ in **LK**, there is an expansion tree t such that $\mathbf{LK}_e \vdash t : A$.*

To show this, we need only show that the contraction rule of **LK** is admissible for theorems of $\mathbf{LK}_e$, in the sense that, if $t : B \vee (A \vee A)$ is provable, then there is a term t' so that $t' : B \vee A$ is provable ; the remaining cases to check are disjunctions and the unit $\top$. The following lemma will be essential:

Lemma 3. *(a) If $\mathbf{LK}_e \vdash F, 1 : \top$, then $\mathbf{LK}_e \vdash F$.*
(b) If $\mathbf{LK}_e \vdash t \vee 1 : A \vee \top$, then either $t = *$ or $\mathbf{LK}_e \vdash t : A$.

Proof. By induction on the length of proofs. For example, in case the last rule proving $F,\ 1 : \top$ is a conjunction

$$\frac{\vdash G_1,\ t : A,\ 1 : \top \qquad G_2,\ s : B}{\vdash G_1,\ G_2,\ (t \otimes s) : A \wedge B,\ 1 : \top} \wedge$$

$G_1,\ t : A$ is is provable, and so we may prove $G_1, G_2,\ (t \otimes s) : A \wedge B$ □

Lemma 4. *If* $\boldsymbol{LK}_e \vdash t \vee (s_1 \vee s_2) : B \vee (A \vee A)$*, then there is a term* s *such that* $\boldsymbol{LK}_e \vdash t \vee s : B \vee A$.

Proof. If either one or both s_i is $*$, this can be easily shown using Lemma 1. Similarly, if A is a conjunction or atom, we can use Lemma 1 and the relevant contraction rule of $\mathbf{LK}_e$. If A is the unit $\top$, then s_1 and s_2 are equal to 1, and by Lemma 3, $\mathbf{LK}_e \vdash t \vee 1 : B \vee \top$. Finally, suppose that the claim holds for all formulae of size n, and let $A = B_1 \vee B_2$ of size $n+1$. Apply Lemma 1 four times to obtain a proof of

$$t : B,\ t_a : B_1,\ t_b : B_2,\ t_c : B_1,\ t_d : B_2$$

using $\vee$ and the induction hypothesis, we obtain a proof of $(t \vee u) \vee v : (B \vee B_1) \vee B_2$ and by reassociating the disjunctions we obtain a proof of $t \vee (u \vee v) : B \vee (B_1 \vee B_2)$ □

Corollary 1. *If* A *is provable in* $\boldsymbol{LK}$*, then there is an expansion/deletion tree* t *such that* $\boldsymbol{LK}_e \vdash t : A$.

5 Conclusions and Further Work

We have given a calculus of proof-nets which identifies more sequent proofs than Robinson's proposal, while maintaining a connection with the sequent calculus. Other researchers have given abstract notions of proof-net for classical logic; these make the identifications we wish to make but lack a strong connection to the sequent calculus. Lamarche and Strassburger [12] give two notions of proof-net, both of which validate more identities than Robinson. The $\mathbb{B}$-nets are nothing more than binary linkings on a sequent forest: they possess sequentialization into an additive sequent calculus, but checking correctness of such a net is no more efficient than checking the truth-table of the conclusion. The same paper introduces $\mathbb{N}$-nets, which give a better account of proof-identity, but for which no correctness criterion/sequentialization theorem is known. Hughes's combinatorial proofs [10,11] also make more identifications than Robinson's nets, and have a polynomial-time correctness criterion. However, the mapping from sequent proofs to combinatorial proofs is not surjective; there are correct combinatorial proofs which do not correspond to a sequent-calculus proof. Moreover, Hughes's approach does not deal directly with the units $\top$ and $\bot$. Hughes's system can be seen as a kind of "Herbrand's theorem for propositional logic", reducing provability in unit-free propositional logic (coNP) to provability in the binary fragment of unit free **MLL** + Mix (P-time). Seen in this light, our result extends this connection to the classical units; we reduce provability in propositional logic to provability in a (polytime decidable) fragment of **MLL** + Mix (with units).

In both of the cases above, there is a mismatch between sequent calculus and the proposed proof nets: the nets we present here are, we believe, the first sufficiently abstract nets to maintain a good correspondence to sequent calculus proofs.

We mention now some further work.

Garbage collection. Given a subterm of the form $s = *\otimes t$ or $s = t\otimes *$ in an ed-net, we can view the subproof introducing t as *garbage*; garbage collection would be an algorithm taking a net with garbage and returning a garbage free net: i.e. an expansion net. For similar situations in MAL+MIX nets [1] and combinatorial proofs, there is a confluent garbage collection algorithm; unfortunately, attempts to apply those methods to ed-nets yield annotated sequents which fail to satisfy correctness. This opens up two directions for further research: to find a garbage collection procedure which stays within correct proof nets, or to find a good generalization of correctness so that the existing algorithms work.

Cut-elimination. We can easily add cuts to ed-nets by adding a new constructor $\bowtie$ for terms, with typing rule

$$\frac{t : A \qquad s : \bar{A}}{t \bowtie s : \textsc{Cut}}$$

It is then possible to define a weakly normalizing cut-elimination procedure based on Gentzen's original procedure; the definition of the reductions requires the notion of *subnet*, which for ed-nets is rather tricky to define. Since cut-elimination depends on the calculation of subnets (either kingdoms or empires) it is not local; this is somewhat alien to the spirit of proof nets, but it is not clear if a cut-reduction theory for such proof-nets can be local and retain a close correspondence to the sequent calculus. One way to improve the cut-reduction theory of the nets is to *asymmetrize* all the cuts, by insisting that, for each dual pair A and $\bar{A}$, contraction is admissible for one of the pair. This is only a challenge for the atoms, where we need contraction on both p and $\bar{p}$ for completeness. Nevertheless, this is possible, by treating the atoms in the same way as universal/existential quantifiers, leading to a calculus in which the contraction/contraction and weakening/weakening critical pairs cannot be formed.

Classical quantifiers. The terminology *expansion/deletion* recalls Miller [15], whose *expansion tree proofs* can be seen as a prototype notion of proof-net for classical logic. The paper [14] makes this connection explicit in the case of first-order prenex formulae; the paper introduces a notion of *Herbrand net*, in which provability at the propositional level is treated as trivial — propositional axioms are replaced by arbitrary propositional tautologies. We foresee no major obstacles in combining Herbrand nets with the results of the current paper to capture nets for first- or higher-order classical quantifiers.

Nets for additively formulated classical logic. The correctness/sequentialization results for our nets are heavily tied to the multiplicatively formulated sequent calculus. It is, of course, possible to extract an ed-net from a proof in an additively formulated calculus, but there are natural identities in those calculi which are not validated by our nets. Taking the view that the additive and multiplicative classical connectives are essentially different operations (that happen to coincide at the level of provability), we look for natural notions of proof net for additively formulated classical logic.

Acknowledgements. Thanks to Kai Brünnler, Lutz Strassburger and Willem Heijltjes for useful discussions while working on this paper. This work was supported by the ANR grant "INFER" and an SNF Ambizione fellowship.

References

1. Bellin, G.: Two paradigms of logical computation in affine logic? In: Logic for concurrency and synchronisation, pp. 111–144 (2003)
2. Bellin, G., Hyland, M., Robinson, E., Urban, C.: Categorical proof theory of classical propositional calculus. Theor. Comput. Sci. 364(2), 146–165 (2006)
3. Cook, S.A., Reckhow, R.A.: The relative efficiency of propositional proof systems. J. Symb. Logic 44(1), 36–50 (1979)
4. Danos, V., Di Cosmo, R.: The linear logic primer. lecture notes, `http://www.dicosmo.org/CourseNotes/LinLog/`
5. Danos, V., Regnier, L.: The structure of multiplicatives. Archive for Mathematical Logic 28, 181–203 (1989)
6. Danos, V.: La Logique Linéaire Appliquée l'étude de Divers Processus de Normalisation. PhD thesis, University of Paris VII (1990)
7. Führmann, C., Pym, D.: Order-enriched categorical models of the classical sequent calculus. Journal of Pure and Applied Algebra 204(1), 21–78 (2006)
8. Girard, J.-Y.: A new constructive logic: Classical logic. Mathematical Structures in Computer Science 1(3), 255–296 (1991)
9. Girard, J.-Y.: Proof-nets: The parallel syntax for proof-theory. In: Logic and Algebra, pp. 97–124. Marcel Dekker, New York (1996)
10. Hughes, D.J.D.: Towards Hilbert's 24th problem: Combinatorial proof invariants. Electron. Notes Theor. Comput. Sci. 165, 37–63 (2006)
11. Hughes, D.J.D.: Proofs Without Syntax. Annals of Mathematics 143(3), 1065–1076 (2006)
12. Lamarche, F., Strassburger, L.: Naming proofs in classical logic. In: Urzyczyn, P. (ed.) TLCA 2005. LNCS, vol. 3461, pp. 246–261. Springer, Heidelberg (2005)
13. Lamarche, F., Strassburger, L.: Constructing free boolean categories. In: LICS 2005: Proceedings of the 20th Annual IEEE Symposium on Logic in Computer Science, Washington, DC, USA, pp. 209–218. IEEE Computer Society, Los Alamitos (2005)
14. McKinley, R.: Proof nets for Herbrand's theorem (Preprint), `http://arxiv.org/abs/1005.3986v1`
15. Miller, D.: A compact representation of proofs. Studia Logica 46(4), 347–370 (1987)
16. Robinson, E.: Proof nets for classical logic. Journal of Logic and Computation 13(5), 777–797 (2003)
17. Trimble, T.H.: Linear logic, bimodules, and full coherence for autonomous categories. PhD thesis, Rutgers University (1994)

Revisiting Matrix Interpretations for Polynomial Derivational Complexity of Term Rewriting*

Friedrich Neurauter, Harald Zankl, and Aart Middeldorp

Institute of Computer Science, University of Innsbruck, Austria

Abstract. Matrix interpretations can be used to bound the derivational complexity of term rewrite systems. In particular, triangular matrix interpretations over the natural numbers are known to induce polynomial upper bounds on the derivational complexity of (compatible) rewrite systems. Using techniques from linear algebra, we show how one can generalize the method to matrices that are not necessarily triangular but nevertheless polynomially bounded. Moreover, we show that our approach also applies to matrix interpretations over the real (algebraic) numbers. In particular, it allows triangular matrix interpretations to infer tighter bounds than the original approach.

Keywords: Derivational complexity, polynomial matrix interpretations.

1 Introduction

Many powerful techniques for establishing termination of term rewrite systems have been developed in the course of time, most of which have been automated successfully, as is evident in the results of the (annual) international competition for termination and complexity tools.[1] Moreover, Hofbauer and Lautemann observe in [9] that "proving termination with one of these specific techniques in general proves more than just the absence of infinite derivations. It turns out that in many cases such a proof implies an upper bound on the maximal length of derivations", which they consider as a natural measure for the complexity of (terminating) term rewrite systems. More precisely, the resulting notion of *derivational complexity* relates the length of a longest derivation to the size of its initial term. For example, polynomial interpretations imply a double-exponential upper bound on the derivational complexity [9]. However, since term rewriting is a model of computation and algorithms of polynomial complexity are widely accepted as *feasible*, one is especially interested in polynomial derivational complexity. But currently only few techniques for establishing feasible upper complexity bounds are known. Commonly, they are stripped-down variants of existing termination techniques. For example, if a term rewrite system can be shown terminating by a matrix interpretation (over the natural numbers) [5, 10] that orients all rewrite rules strictly, then its derivational complexity is

* This research is supported by FWF (Austrian Science Fund) project P22467.

[1] `http://termcomp.uibk.ac.at`

C. Fermüller and A. Voronkov (Eds.): LPAR-17, LNCS 6397, pp. 550–564, 2010.

at most exponential. However, by restricting the shape of the matrices to upper triangular form, one obtains a method for establishing polynomial derivational complexity [13], where the degree of the polynomial depends on the dimension of the matrices. Using match-bounds [7] or arctic matrix interpretations [12], linear derivational complexity can be inferred.

In this paper we investigate the method of (triangular) matrix interpretations that is widely used in current automated termination and complexity tools. Using techniques from linear algebra, we show how one can generalize the method of triangular matrix interpretations, as introduced in [13], to matrix interpretations that are not necessarily triangular but nevertheless induce polynomial upper bounds on the derivational complexity of compatible term rewrite systems. Moreover, we show that our approach also applies to matrix interpretations over the real (algebraic) numbers. In particular, we also show how one can infer tighter bounds from triangular matrix interpretations by examining the diagonal structure of upper triangular (complexity) matrices.

The remainder of this paper is organized as follows. Section 2 introduces basic notions of term rewriting and some mathematical prerequisites. In Section 3, we review matrix interpretations in the context of complexity analysis of term rewriting, before presenting our main result in Section 4. In Section 5, we give details on implementation-specific issues. Finally, we provide experimental results in Section 6, before concluding in Section 7.

2 Preliminaries

We assume familiarity with the basics of term rewriting [2, 17]. Let $\mathcal{V}$ denote a countably infinite set of variables and $\mathcal{F}$ a fixed-arity signature. The set of *terms* over $\mathcal{F}$ and $\mathcal{V}$ is denoted by $\mathcal{T}(\mathcal{F},\mathcal{V})$. The *size* $|t|$ of a term t is defined as the number of symbols occurring in it and the *depth* of t is defined as follows: if t is a variable or a constant, then $\text{depth}(t) := 0$, otherwise $\text{depth}(f(t_1,\dots,t_n)) := 1 + \max\{\text{depth}(t_i) \mid 1 \leqslant i \leqslant n\}$. A *rewrite rule* is a pair of terms written as $l \to r$, such that l is not a variable and all variables in r are contained in l. A *term rewrite system* $\mathcal{R}$ (TRS for short) over $\mathcal{T}(\mathcal{F},\mathcal{V})$ is a set of rewrite rules. For complexity analysis we assume TRSs to be finite. The rewrite relation induced by $\to$ is denoted by $\to_{\mathcal{R}}$. As usual, $\to_{\mathcal{R}}^*$ denotes the reflexive transitive closure of $\to_{\mathcal{R}}$ and $\to_{\mathcal{R}}^n$ its n-th iterate. A term $s \in \mathcal{T}(\mathcal{F},\mathcal{V})$ is called a *normal form* if there is no term t such that $s \to_{\mathcal{R}} t$.

The *derivation height* of a term t with respect to a TRS $\mathcal{R}$ is defined as follows: $\mathsf{dh}(t, \to_{\mathcal{R}}) := \max\{n \mid \exists u\ t \to_{\mathcal{R}}^n u\}$. The *derivational complexity* function of a terminating TRS $\mathcal{R}$ computes the maximal derivation height of all terms up to a given size, i.e., $\mathsf{dc}_{\mathcal{R}} \colon \mathbb{N} \setminus \{0\} \to \mathbb{N}, k \mapsto \max\{\mathsf{dh}(t, \to_{\mathcal{R}}) \mid |t| \leqslant k\}$. Sometimes we say that $\mathcal{R}$ has linear, quadratic, etc. derivational complexity if $\mathsf{dc}_{\mathcal{R}}(k)$ can be bounded by a linear, quadratic, etc. polynomial in k.

An important concept for establishing termination of TRSs is the notion of well-founded monotone algebras. An *$\mathcal{F}$-algebra* $\mathcal{A}$ consists of a non-empty carrier A and interpretation functions $f_{\mathcal{A}} \colon A^n \to A$ for every n-ary $f \in \mathcal{F}$. By

$[\alpha]_{\mathcal{A}}(\cdot)\colon \mathcal{T}(\mathcal{F},\mathcal{V}) \to A$ we denote the usual evaluation function of $\mathcal{A}$ with respect to a variable assignment $\alpha\colon \mathcal{V} \to A$. A *well-founded monotone $\mathcal{F}$-algebra* is a pair $(\mathcal{A}, >_A)$, where $\mathcal{A}$ is an $\mathcal{F}$-algebra and $>_A$ is a well-founded order on A such that every $f_{\mathcal{A}}$ is strictly monotone in all arguments (with respect to $>_A$). A well-founded monotone algebra naturally induces an order $\succ_{\mathcal{A}}$ on terms: $s \succ_{\mathcal{A}} t$ if $[\alpha]_{\mathcal{A}}(s) >_A [\alpha]_{\mathcal{A}}(t)$ for all assignments α of elements of A to the variables in s and t. Finally, it is well-known that a TRS $\mathcal{R}$ is terminating if and only if it is *compatible* with a well-founded monotone algebra $(\mathcal{A}, >_A)$, where compatibility means that $l \succ_{\mathcal{A}} r$ for every rewrite rule $l \to r \in \mathcal{R}$.

Linear Algebra. As usual, we denote by $\mathbb{N}$, $\mathbb{Z}$, $\mathbb{Q}$ and $\mathbb{R}$ the sets of natural, integer, rational and real numbers. Given some $D \in \{\mathbb{N}, \mathbb{Z}, \mathbb{Q}, \mathbb{R}\}$ and $m \in D$, $>_D$ denotes the natural order of the respective domain and $D_m := \{x \in D \mid x \geqslant m\}$; e.g., $\mathbb{R}_0$ refers to the set of all non-negative real numbers. For any ring R (e.g., $\mathbb{Z}$, $\mathbb{Q}$, $\mathbb{R}$), we denote the ring of all n-dimensional square matrices over R by $R^{n\times n}$, and $R[x_1,\dots,x_n]$ denotes the associated *polynomial ring* in n *indeterminates* $x_1,\dots,x_n$. In the special case $n = 1$, a polynomial $P \in R[x]$ can be written as follows: $P(x) = \sum_{k=0}^{d} a_k x^k$ ($d \in \mathbb{N}$). For the largest k such that $a_k \neq 0$, we call $a_k x^k$ the *leading term* of P, a_k its *leading coefficient* and k its *degree*. P is said to be *monic* if its leading coefficient is one. Moreover, it is said to be *linear*, *quadratic*, *cubic* etc. if its degree is one, two, three etc.

We say that a matrix is *non-negative* if all its entries are non-negative. Abusing notation, we denote the set of all non-negative n-dimensional square matrices of $\mathbb{Z}^{n\times n}$ by $\mathbb{N}^{n\times n}$. An *upper triangular* matrix is a matrix, where all entries below the main diagonal are zero. An *upper triangular complexity* matrix is a non-negative upper triangular matrix whose diagonal entries are at most one and whose top-left entry is exactly one. As usual, we denote the *transpose* of a matrix (vector) A by A^T. The *characteristic polynomial* of a square matrix $A \in R^{n\times n}$ is defined as $\chi_A(\lambda) := \det(\lambda I_n - A)$, where I_n denotes the n-dimensional identity matrix and det the determinant of a matrix. It is monic and its degree is n. The equation $\chi_A(\lambda) = 0$ is called the *characteristic equation* of A. The *eigenvalues* of A are precisely the solutions of its characteristic equation, and the *spectral radius* $\rho(A)$ of A is the maximum of the absolute values of all eigenvalues. By m_λ we denote the *multiplicity* of the eigenvalue λ. A non-zero vector x is an *eigenvector* of A if $Ax = \lambda x$ for some eigenvalue λ of A. The Cayley-Hamilton theorem [15] states that every matrix satisfies its own characteristic equation, that is, $\chi_A(A) = 0$, and it holds for square matrices over commutative rings.

Recurrence Relations. Informally, a recurrence relation is an equation that recursively defines a sequence; each element of the sequence is defined as a function of the preceding elements. For example, the Fibonacci numbers are defined by $F_n = F_{n-1} + F_{n-2}$ with $F_0 = 0$ and $F_1 = 1$. Solving a recurrence relation means obtaining a closed-form solution; in this example, a non-recursive function of n.

A *linear homogeneous recurrence relation with constant coefficients* is an equation of the form $a_n = c_1 a_{n-1} + c_2 a_{n-2} + \cdots + c_d a_{n-d}$, where the $d \geqslant 1$ *coefficients* $c_1,\dots,c_d$ are constants with $c_d \neq 0$. The same coefficients yield the *characteristic polynomial* $\chi(\lambda) := \lambda^d - c_1\lambda^{d-1} - c_2\lambda^{d-2} - \cdots - c_d$ whose d roots play a key role in the solution of a recurrence relation (cf. [3, 4]). To be precise, if $\lambda_1, \lambda_2, \ldots, \lambda_r$ $(1 \leqslant r \leqslant d)$ are the distinct (possibly complex) roots of the characteristic polynomial such that λ_i is of multiplicity m_i $(i = 1, 2, \ldots, r)$, then the general solution of the recurrence relation is given by

$$a_n = \sum_{i=1}^{r}(c_{i1} + c_{i2}n + \cdots + c_{im_i}n^{m_i-1})\lambda_i^n$$

where the c_{ik}'s are (complex) constants. Any real solution is of this form as well, with the imaginary part zero. Moreover, if the coefficients of $\chi(\lambda)$ are real numbers, its non-real roots always come in conjugate pairs; i.e., if $\lambda_j := r_j(\cos(\phi_j) + i\sin(\phi_j))$ is a root of $\chi(\lambda)$, then so is its complex conjugate $\lambda_j^* := r_j(\cos(\phi_j) - i\sin(\phi_j))$. In this case, avoiding the use of complex numbers, the most general real solution can be written as

$$\begin{aligned}a_n = &\sum_i (c_{i1} + c_{i2}n + \cdots + c_{im_i}n^{m_i-1})\lambda_i^n\\ &+ \sum_j (d_{j1} + d_{j2}n + \cdots + d_{jm_j}n^{m_j-1})r_j^n\cos(n\phi_j)\\ &+ \sum_j (d'_{j1} + d'_{j2}n + \cdots + d'_{jm_j}n^{m_j-1})r_j^n\sin(n\phi_j)\end{aligned}$$

where the c_{ik}'s, d_{jk}'s and d'_{jk}'s are real constants, the λ_i's the distinct real roots of $\chi(\lambda)$ and the λ_j's, $\lambda_j := r_j(\cos(\phi_j) + i\sin(\phi_j))$, the distinct complex roots (modulo conjugates).

3 Matrix Interpretations and Derivational Complexity

Next we review the method of matrix interpretations in the context of complexity analysis of term rewriting. Matrix interpretations [10,5] were originally introduced over the natural numbers. Later on they were lifted to the reals [1, 21, 6] using the same technique that was already used to lift polynomial interpretations from $\mathbb{N}$ to $\mathbb{R}$ (cf. [8]). Similarly, the first results relating matrix interpretations and derivational complexity of TRSs (cf. [13], triangular matrix interpretations) are based on matrix interpretations over the natural numbers. But these results have never been lifted to the reals. In the next section we shall see, however, how this follows from a more general result that holds for matrix interpretations over both $\mathbb{N}$ and $\mathbb{R}$, the foundations of which are laid in the present chapter.

Let $\mathcal{F}$ denote a signature. A *matrix interpretation* $\mathcal{M}$ over $\mathbb{N}$ is a well-founded monotone algebra, where the carrier M is the set $\mathbb{N}^n$ for some fixed dimension $n \in \mathbb{N} \setminus \{0\}$. The well-founded order $>_M$ on M is defined as follows:

$$(x_1, x_2, \ldots, x_n)^T >_M (y_1, y_2, \ldots, y_n)^T :\Longleftrightarrow x_1 >_{\mathbb{N}} y_1 \wedge x_2 \geqslant_{\mathbb{N}} y_2 \wedge \cdots \wedge x_n \geqslant_{\mathbb{N}} y_n$$

For each k-ary function symbol $f \in \mathcal{F}$, we choose an interpretation function

$$f_{\mathcal{M}} \colon (\mathbb{N}^n)^k \to \mathbb{N}^n, (\boldsymbol{x_1}, \dots, \boldsymbol{x_k}) \mapsto F_1\boldsymbol{x_1} + \cdots + F_k\boldsymbol{x_k} + \boldsymbol{f}$$

where $\boldsymbol{f} \in \mathbb{N}^n$ and $F_1, \dots, F_k \in \mathbb{N}^{n\times n}$. In addition, we require $(F_i)_{1,1} \geqslant_{\mathbb{N}} 1$ for all $i = 1, \dots, k$ to achieve strict monotonicity of $f_{\mathcal{M}}$ in all arguments. Finally, a *triangular matrix interpretation* over $\mathbb{N}$ is a matrix interpretation over $\mathbb{N}$, where all matrices are upper triangular complexity matrices.

When extending matrix interpretations from $\mathbb{N}$ to $\mathbb{R}$, the main problem is the non-well-foundedness of $>_{\mathbb{R}}$. This problem is overcome by $>_{\mathbb{R},\delta}$, which is defined as follows: given some fixed positive real number δ, $x >_{\mathbb{R},\delta} y$ if and only if $x - y \geqslant_{\mathbb{R}} \delta$ for all $x, y \in \mathbb{R}$. Thus $>_{\mathbb{R},\delta}$ is well-founded on subsets of $\mathbb{R}$ that are bounded from below. Then a *matrix interpretation* $\mathcal{M}$ over $\mathbb{R}$ is a well-founded monotone algebra, where the carrier M is the set $\mathbb{R}_0^n$ for some fixed dimension $n \in \mathbb{N} \setminus \{0\}$. The well-founded order $>_M$ on M is defined as follows:

$$(x_1, x_2, \dots, x_n)^T >_M (y_1, y_2, \dots, y_n)^T :\Longleftrightarrow x_1 >_{\mathbb{R},\delta} y_1 \wedge x_2 \geqslant_{\mathbb{R}} y_2 \wedge \cdots \wedge x_n \geqslant_{\mathbb{R}} y_n$$

For each k-ary function symbol f, we choose an interpretation function

$$f_{\mathcal{M}} \colon (\mathbb{R}_0^n)^k \to \mathbb{R}_0^n, (\boldsymbol{x_1}, \dots, \boldsymbol{x_k}) \mapsto F_1\boldsymbol{x_1} + \ldots + F_k\boldsymbol{x_k} + \boldsymbol{f}$$

where $\boldsymbol{f} \in \mathbb{R}_0^n$ and $F_1, \dots, F_k$ are non-negative matrices in $\mathbb{R}^{n\times n}$ with $(F_i)_{1,1} \geqslant_{\mathbb{R}} 1$ for all $i = 1, \dots, k$ in order to achieve strict monotonicity of $f_{\mathcal{M}}$ in all arguments. Again, a *triangular matrix interpretation* over $\mathbb{R}$ is a matrix interpretation over $\mathbb{R}$, where all matrices are upper triangular complexity matrices.

Remark 1. Concerning polynomial interpretations, it was recently shown in [14] that it suffices to consider the set $\mathbb{R}_{\mathsf{alg}}$ of real *algebraic*[2] numbers instead of the entire set $\mathbb{R}$ of real numbers. To be precise, it was shown that polynomial termination over $\mathbb{R}$ is equivalent to polynomial termination over $\mathbb{R}_{\mathsf{alg}}$. Observing that the technique of [14] readily applies to matrix interpretations as well, we may draw the conclusion that matrix interpretations over $\mathbb{R}$ are equivalent to matrix interpretations over $\mathbb{R}_{\mathsf{alg}}$ with respect to proving termination of TRSs.

Matrix interpretations over $\mathbb{R}$ can be used to bound the derivational complexity of compatible TRSs.[3] Let $\mathcal{M}$ be a matrix interpretation over $\mathbb{R}$ that is compatible with some TRS $\mathcal{R}$. Then any rewrite sequence

$$t = t_0 \to_{\mathcal{R}} t_1 \to_{\mathcal{R}} t_2 \to_{\mathcal{R}} t_3 \to_{\mathcal{R}} t_4 \to_{\mathcal{R}} \cdots$$

gives rise to a strictly decreasing sequence of vectors of non-negative real numbers

$$[\alpha]_{\mathcal{M}}(t) >_M [\alpha]_{\mathcal{M}}(t_1) >_M [\alpha]_{\mathcal{M}}(t_2) >_M [\alpha]_{\mathcal{M}}(t_3) >_M [\alpha]_{\mathcal{M}}(t_4) >_M \cdots$$

[2] A real number is said to be algebraic if it is a root of a non-zero polynomial in one variable with integer coefficients.

[3] The reasoning presented in the sequel readily includes matrix interpretations over $\mathbb{N}$ as a special case (by letting $\delta = 1$ and observing that $x >_{\mathbb{N}} y$ if and only if $x \geqslant_{\mathbb{N}} y+1$).

for all variable assignments α. In particular, by definition of $>_M$, the first components of these vectors form a sequence of non-negative real numbers that is strictly decreasing with respect to the order $>_{\mathbb{R},\delta}$, and every rewrite step causes a decrease of at least δ. Hence, the first component of the vector $\frac{1}{\delta} \cdot [\alpha]_{\mathcal{M}}(t)$ gives an upper bound on $\mathsf{dh}(t, \rightarrow_{\mathcal{R}})$. So if we manage to bound (the first component of) this vector for all terms t up to a given (but arbitrary) size k, then we have actually established an upper bound on the derivational complexity of $\mathcal{R}$. Moreover, as we are only interested in the asymptotic growth of $\frac{1}{\delta} \cdot [\alpha]_{\mathcal{M}}(t)$ with respect to the size of t, we may neglect the multiplicative factor $\frac{1}{\delta}$ because δ is a constant. As already observed in [13], this problem essentially reduces to bounding the entries of finite matrix products of the form $M_1 \cdot M_2 \cdot \ldots \cdot M_k$, $M_i \in \mathcal{M}$. Such products arise naturally when evaluating terms in a matrix interpretation; e.g., if $t := \mathsf{f}(\mathsf{g}(\mathsf{a}, \mathsf{b}), \mathsf{c})$ then $[\alpha]_{\mathcal{M}}(t) = F_1 G_1 \boldsymbol{a} + F_1 G_2 \boldsymbol{b} + F_1 \boldsymbol{g} + F_2 \boldsymbol{c} + \boldsymbol{f}$. As in [13], we reduce this problem to the analysis of the growth of the powers of a single matrix. To this end, we note that for all $1 \leqslant i, j \leqslant n$, $(M_1 \cdot M_2 \cdot \ldots \cdot M_k)_{i,j} \leqslant (A^k)_{i,j}$, where the matrix A is the component-wise maximum of all matrices occurring in $\mathcal{M}$; i.e., $A_{i,j} := \max\{B_{i,j} \mid B \in \mathcal{M}\}$ for all $1 \leqslant i, j \leqslant n$. If $|t| \leqslant k$ then the length of each product is at most $\operatorname{depth}(t)$ ($\leqslant k$) and the number of products equals the number of subterms of t, which is also bounded by k. Thus any lemma stating that the entries of the matrix A^k are polynomially bounded in k of degree $d - 1$ can readily be used as the basis of a corresponding theorem that establishes a polynomial upper bound of degree d on the derivational complexity of all TRSs that are compatible with the matrix interpretation $\mathcal{M}$. In [13], for example, this is achieved by restricting the shape of the matrices to upper triangular form.

Lemma 2 ([13, Lemma 5]). *Let $A \in \mathbb{N}^{n \times n}$ be an upper triangular complexity matrix and $k \in \mathbb{N}$. Then $(A^k)_{i,j} \in O(k^{n-1})$ for all $1 \leqslant i, j \leqslant n$.*

Theorem 3 ([13, Theorem 6]). *If a TRS $\mathcal{R}$ is compatible with a triangular matrix interpretation of dimension n, then $\mathsf{dc}_{\mathcal{R}}(k) \in O(k^n)$.*

However, we claim that Lemma 2 only gives a rough estimate of the growth of the entries of the matrix A^k, i.e., the degree of the polynomial bound can be lowered in many cases. To this end, we provide a more concise analysis of the growth of A^k in the next section, obtaining a replacement for Lemma 2, which allows us to tighten the bounds established by Theorem 3. In particular, our refinement holds for matrix interpretations over both $\mathbb{N}$ and $\mathbb{R}$. Moreover, we remark that the restriction of the shape of the matrices is another source for improvement. Clearly, there are also non-triangular matrices that exhibit polynomial growth, but in general non-triangular matrix interpretations do not induce polynomial (but rather exponential) upper bounds on the derivational complexity of compatible TRSs. So in order to be useful in (automated) complexity analysis of term rewriting, a characterization of polynomially bounded matrices is required such that, when searching for a compatible matrix interpretation for a given TRS, it is guaranteed beforehand that the search process only considers such matrices. This is the main goal of the following sections.

4 Main Result

In this section we elaborate on how to lift the restriction to upper triangular matrices. To this end, we leverage the Cayley-Hamilton theorem and the theory of linear homogeneous recurrence relations to completely characterize the growth of the powers of real square matrices (independently of the shape of the matrices). In particular, we show that the key point with respect to polynomial boundedness of such matrices is the nature of their eigenvalues. According to the discussion in Section 3, our results apply to matrix interpretations over $\mathbb{N}$ and $\mathbb{R}$ alike.

Lemma 4. *Let $A \in \mathbb{R}_0^{n \times n}$. Then $\rho(A) \leqslant 1$ if and only if all entries of A^k ($k \in \mathbb{N}$) are asymptotically bounded by a polynomial in k of degree d, where $d := \max_\lambda(0, m_\lambda - 1)$ and λ are the eigenvalues with absolute value exactly one.*

Proof. First, let us assume that $\rho(A) > 1$, i.e., A has an eigenvalue λ of absolute value strictly greater than one. For any eigenvector x associated to λ, we have $Ax = \lambda x$ and hence $A^k x = \lambda^k x$. Since x is non-zero by definition and $|\lambda| > 1$, there is at least one component of $\lambda^k x$ whose absolute value grows exponentially in k. But this can only be the case if at least one entry of A^k grows exponentially in k as well. Conversely, if $\rho(A) \leqslant 1$, we have to show that the entries of A^k are polynomially bounded. Since A is a real $n \times n$ matrix, its characteristic polynomial $\chi_A(\lambda)$ is a monic polynomial of degree n with real coefficients. Without loss of generality, it can be written as $\chi_A(\lambda) = \lambda^t \cdot p(\lambda)$, $0 \leqslant t \leqslant n$, where t is maximal and p is a monic polynomial of degree $n - t$. By the Cayley-Hamilton theorem, A satisfies its own characteristic equation, that is, $\chi_A(A) = 0$. Clearly, if $t = n$ then $A^k = 0$ for all $k \geqslant n$ and $d = 0$, such that the claim follows trivially. If $t < n$ we rearrange the equation $\chi_A(A) = 0$ into the form $A^n = c_1 A^{n-1} + c_2 A^{n-2} + \cdots + c_{n-t} A^t$ with coefficients $c_1, \ldots, c_{n-t}$, readily obtaining a recursive equation for the powers of A, namely, for all $k \geqslant n \in \mathbb{N}$ $A^k = c_1 A^{k-1} + c_2 A^{k-2} + \cdots + c_{n-t} A^{k-(n-t)}$. Thus we establish the following recurrence relation

$$A_k = c_1 A_{k-1} + c_2 A_{k-2} + \cdots + c_{n-t} A_{k-(n-t)} \tag{1}$$

and note that the sequence $(A_j)_{j \geqslant t}$ where $A_j := A^j$ satisfies it by construction. This is a linear homogeneous recurrence relation with constant coefficients and characteristic polynomial $\chi(\lambda) = p(\lambda)$. Since the coefficients of $\chi(\lambda)$ are real numbers, the non-real roots (eigenvalues) always come in conjugate pairs; i.e., if $\lambda_j := r_j(\cos(\phi_j) + i \sin(\phi_j))$ is a root of $\chi(\lambda)$, then so is its complex conjugate $\lambda_j^* := r_j(\cos(\phi_j) - i \sin(\phi_j))$. Thus the general solution of (1) can be written as

$$\begin{aligned} A_k = {} & \sum_i (C_{i,0} + C_{i,1} k + \cdots + C_{i,m_i-1} k^{m_i-1}) \lambda_i^k \\ & + \sum_j (D_{j,0} + D_{j,1} k + \cdots + D_{j,m_j-1} k^{m_j-1}) r_j^k \cos(k\phi_j) \\ & + \sum_j (D'_{j,0} + D'_{j,1} k + \cdots + D'_{j,m_j-1} k^{m_j-1}) r_j^k \sin(k\phi_j) \end{aligned} \tag{2}$$

where the λ_i's are the distinct real roots of $\chi(\lambda)$, each having multiplicity m_i, and the λ_j's, $\lambda_j := r_j(\cos(\phi_j) + i\sin(\phi_j))$, the distinct complex roots (modulo conjugates), each having multiplicity m_j. By assumption, the absolute values of all eigenvalues are at most one; hence, $|\lambda_i| \leqslant 1$ and $r_j \leqslant 1$ in (2), such that the asymptotic growth of the entries of the matrix A^k is polynomial rather than exponential. In particular, the degree d of the polynomial bound is at most $m-1$, where m is the largest of the multiplicities of the eigenvalues with absolute value exactly one. If there are no such eigenvalues, then $\rho(A) < 1$ and $\lim_{k\to\infty} A^k = 0$, such that $d = 0$. □

Example 5. Consider the 4×4 matrix $A := (A_{i,j})_{1\leqslant i,j\leqslant 4}$ with all entries zero except $A_{1,1} = A_{2,4} = A_{3,2} = A_{4,3} = 1$. It has one real eigenvalue $\lambda_1 = 1$ of multiplicity two and a pair of complex conjugate eigenvalues $\lambda_2 = \frac{1}{2}(-1 + i\sqrt{3})$ and $\lambda_2^* = \frac{1}{2}(-1 - i\sqrt{3})$ of multiplicity one, all of which have absolute value exactly one. Hence, the spectral radius $\rho(A)$ of A is also one. According to Lemma 4, the entries of the matrix A^k, $k \in \mathbb{N}$, are bounded by a linear polynomial in k. The actual bound, however, is even lower since $A^4 = A$, such that the powers of A are trivially bounded by a constant, and we can use the method outlined in the proof of Lemma 4 to show this. To this end, we note that the characteristic polynomial of A is $\chi_A(\lambda) = \lambda^4 - \lambda^3 - \lambda + 1$. Thus, by the Cayley-Hamilton theorem, we obtain the recursive equation $A^k = A^{k-1} + A^{k-3} - A^{k-4}$ for all $k \geqslant 4 \in \mathbb{N}$, the general solution of which can be written as

$$A^k = (C_0 + C_1 k)\lambda_1^k + D\, r^k \cos(k\phi) + D'\, r^k \sin(k\phi) \tag{3}$$

where $r(\cos(\phi) + i\sin(\phi)) = \lambda_2$, that is, $r = 1$ and $\phi = \frac{2\pi}{3}$. In the next step, the exact values of the four constants C_0, C_1, D and D' can be determined, for example, by letting $k = 4, 5, 6, 7$ in (3) and solving the resulting systems of linear equations. In doing so, one learns that C_1 is zero, which means that the linear summand in (3) vanishes. Further, we obtain $A^k = C_0 + D\cos(k\phi) + D'\sin(k\phi)$,

$$C_0 := \begin{pmatrix} 1 & 0 & 0 & 0 \\ 0 & \frac{1}{3} & \frac{1}{3} & \frac{1}{3} \\ 0 & \frac{1}{3} & \frac{1}{3} & \frac{1}{3} \\ 0 & \frac{1}{3} & \frac{1}{3} & \frac{1}{3} \end{pmatrix} \quad D := \begin{pmatrix} 0 & 0 & 0 & 0 \\ 0 & \frac{2}{3} & -\frac{1}{3} & -\frac{1}{3} \\ 0 & -\frac{1}{3} & \frac{2}{3} & -\frac{1}{3} \\ 0 & -\frac{1}{3} & -\frac{1}{3} & \frac{2}{3} \end{pmatrix} \quad D' := \begin{pmatrix} 0 & 0 & 0 & 0 \\ 0 & 0 & -\frac{\sqrt{3}}{3} & \frac{\sqrt{3}}{3} \\ 0 & \frac{\sqrt{3}}{3} & 0 & -\frac{\sqrt{3}}{3} \\ 0 & -\frac{\sqrt{3}}{3} & \frac{\sqrt{3}}{3} & 0 \end{pmatrix}$$

which explains why the powers of A are bounded by a constant. In particular, the periodic nature of the sequence $(A^k)_{k\in\mathbb{N}}$ becomes evident.

On the basis of Lemma 4, we now establish the following theorem concerning complexity analysis of TRSs that holds for matrix interpretations over $\mathbb{N}$ and $\mathbb{R}$.

Theorem 6. *Let $\mathcal{R}$ be a TRS and $\mathcal{M}$ a compatible matrix interpretation of dimension n. Further, let A denote the component-wise maximum of all matrices occurring in $\mathcal{M}$. If the spectral radius of A is at most one, then $\mathsf{dc}_{\mathcal{R}}(k) \in O(k^{d+1})$, where $d := \max_\lambda(0, m_\lambda - 1)$ and λ are the eigenvalues of A with absolute value exactly one.*

Remark 7. Actually the d in Theorem 6 can be strengthened to $\max_\lambda(0, m_\lambda) - 1$ because the pathological case $\rho(A) < 1$ implies $\mathsf{dc}_\mathcal{R}(k) \in O(k^0)$.

The next example shows why triangular matrices may fail. Similar (but larger) systems are contained in TPDB [18], e.g., TRS/Cime_04/dpqs.xml.

Example 8. Consider the TRS $\mathcal{R} = \{\mathsf{f}(\mathsf{f}(x)) \to \mathsf{f}(\mathsf{c}(\mathsf{f}(x))), \mathsf{c}(\mathsf{c}(x)) \to x\}$ which is compatible with the matrix interpretation

$$\mathsf{f}_\mathcal{M}(\boldsymbol{x}) = \begin{pmatrix} 1\,1\,0 \\ 0\,0\,0 \\ 0\,0\,0 \end{pmatrix} \boldsymbol{x} + \begin{pmatrix} 0 \\ 1 \\ 0 \end{pmatrix} \qquad \mathsf{c}_\mathcal{M}(\boldsymbol{x}) = \begin{pmatrix} 1\,0\,2 \\ 0\,0\,1 \\ 0\,1\,0 \end{pmatrix} \boldsymbol{x}$$

The eigenvalues of the component-wise maximum matrix are -1, 1 and 1; hence, Theorem 6 deduces a quadratic upper bound on the derivational complexity of $\mathcal{R}$. There cannot exist a *triangular* matrix interpretation compatible with $\mathcal{R}$ since the second rule demands that all diagonal entries in $\mathsf{c}_\mathcal{M}$ are non-zero, but then the first rule can no longer be oriented.

Next we specialize Theorem 6 to triangular matrix interpretations. In such interpretations all matrices are upper triangular complexity matrices whose diagonal entries are restricted to the closed interval $[0, 1]$ and whose top-left entry is always one. Hence, this is also true for the component-wise maximum matrix A. Since the diagonal entries of a triangular matrix give the multiset of its eigenvalues, the matrix A is therefore guaranteed to have spectral radius one.

Theorem 9. *Let $\mathcal{R}$ be a TRS and $\mathcal{M}$ a compatible triangular matrix interpretation over $\mathbb{N}$ or $\mathbb{R}$ of dimension n. Further, let A denote the component-wise maximum of all matrices occurring in $\mathcal{M}$, and let d denote the number of ones occurring along the diagonal of A. Then $\mathsf{dc}_\mathcal{R}(k) \in O(k^d)$.*[4]

Note that the bound established by Theorem 9 for matrix interpretations over $\mathbb{N}$ is at least as tight as the one of Theorem 3 since $d \leqslant n$.

Example 10. The TRS $\mathcal{R} = \{\mathsf{a}(\mathsf{b}(\mathsf{a}(x))) \to \mathsf{a}(\mathsf{b}(\mathsf{b}(\mathsf{a}(x)))), \mathsf{b}(\mathsf{b}(\mathsf{b}(x))) \to \mathsf{b}(\mathsf{b}(x))\}$[5] is compatible with the triangular matrix interpretation

$$\mathsf{a}_\mathcal{M}(\boldsymbol{x}) = \begin{pmatrix} 1\,2\,1 \\ 0\,0\,1 \\ 0\,0\,0 \end{pmatrix} \boldsymbol{x} + \begin{pmatrix} 0 \\ 1 \\ 1 \end{pmatrix} \qquad \mathsf{b}_\mathcal{M}(\boldsymbol{x}) = \begin{pmatrix} 1\,0\,2 \\ 0\,0\,1 \\ 0\,0\,0 \end{pmatrix} \boldsymbol{x} + \begin{pmatrix} 1 \\ 0 \\ 0 \end{pmatrix}$$

The diagonal of the component-wise maximum of the two matrices has the shape $(1, 0, 0)$. Hence, $\mathcal{R}$ has (at most) linear derivational complexity by Theorem 9, whereas the bound established by Theorem 3 is cubic. Incidentally, the bound inferred from Theorem 9 is even optimal since it is easy to see that the derivational complexity of $\mathcal{R}$ is at least linear. It is easy to show that there are no triangular matrix interpretations of dimension one and two compatible with $\mathcal{R}$.

The final example shows the benefit of matrix interpretations over $\mathbb{R}$.

---

[4] Independently in [19, Proposition 7.6] the same result has been established for $\mathbb{N}$.

[5] TPDB problem TRS/Zantema_04/z126.xml

Example 11. Consider the TRS $\mathcal{R}$.[6] There exists a matrix interpretation (see website in Footnote 8) compatible with $\mathcal{R}$ such that the diagonal of the component-wise maximum matrix has the shape $(1, \frac{1}{2}, 0)$. Due to Theorem 9, the derivational complexity of $\mathcal{R}$ is at most linear. Our implementation could find a triangular matrix interpretation of the same dimension over $\mathbb{N}$ compatible with $\mathcal{R}$ establishing a quadratic but not a linear bound.

5 Implementation Issues

In Theorem 6, we consider some TRS together with a compatible matrix interpretation and demand that the component-wise maximum matrix A has spectral radius at most one. So we have to make sure that the absolute values of all its eigenvalues (real and complex ones) are at most one. However, since A is a non-negative real square matrix, we only have to ensure this condition for all (non-negative) real eigenvalues of A. This follows directly from the Perron-Frobenius theorem ([16], weak form), which states that the spectral radius of a non-negative real square matrix is an eigenvalue of the matrix; i.e., there exists a non-negative real eigenvalue that dominates in absolute value all eigenvalues.

Concerning the automation of Theorem 6, the main problem that has to be dealt with is the following. Given some square matrix A with unknown entries, all of which are supposed to be non-negative real (or integer) numbers, we need a set of constraints, expressed in terms of the unknown entries, that enforce $\rho(A) \leqslant 1$; e.g., for which non-negative values of a, b, c and d has the matrix

$$A := \begin{pmatrix} a & b \\ c & d \end{pmatrix}$$

spectral radius at most one? In the sequel, we present three different approaches.

(A) The first approach is based on the explicit calculation of the eigenvalues of A, i.e., the explicit calculation of the roots of the characteristic polynomial $\chi_A(\lambda)$. For the two-dimensional case, we have $\chi_A(\lambda) = \lambda^2 - (a + d)\lambda + ad - bc$, and by the quadratic formula we obtain the roots $\lambda_{1,2} = \frac{a+d}{2} \pm \frac{\sqrt{(a-d)^2+4bc}}{2}$, both of which are real because all matrix entries are non-negative. In particular, λ_2 ($\geqslant \lambda_1$) is non-negative, such that it suffices to require $\lambda_2 \leqslant 1$ according to the Perron-Frobenius theorem. Simplifying this condition as much as possible, we infer that the matrix A has spectral radius at most one if and only if $a+d \leqslant 2$ and $a + d \leqslant ad - bc + 1$. This explicit approach also applies to matrices of dimension three and four since there exist formulas for the solution of arbitrary cubic and quartic polynomial equations with symbolic coefficients (though the respective calculations are tedious). However, for equations of degree five or higher, there are no formulas that express the solutions of such equations in terms of their coefficients using only the four basic arithmetic operations and radicals (n-th roots, for some integer n).

[6] TPDB problem TRS/Secret_05_SRS/matchbox2.xml

(B) Next we present an alternative and simpler approach for three-dimensional matrices. To this end, let A be some arbitrary three-dimensional non-negative real square matrix with entries $a, b, \ldots, i$ and characteristic polynomial $\chi_A(\lambda)$

$$\lambda^3 - (a+e+i)\lambda^2 + (ei - fh + ai - cg + ae - bd)\lambda - (aei + bfg + cdh - ceg - bdi - afh)$$

which we abbreviate by $\lambda^3 + p\lambda^2 + q\lambda + r$. By the Perron-Frobenius theorem, it suffices to constrain the real roots of $\chi_A(\lambda)$ to the closed interval $[-1, 1]$. To this end, we make use of the well-known fact that a cubic polynomial like $\chi_A(\lambda)$ either has only one real root (and two complex conjugate roots) if its *discriminant* $D := p^2q^2 - 4q^3 - 4p^3r - 27r^2 + 18pqr$ is negative or three (not necessarily distinct) real roots if $D \geqslant 0$. Visualizing the geometric shape of $\chi_A(\lambda)$, it is not hard to see that in the latter case all three roots are in $[-1, 1]$ if and only if $\chi_A(-1) \leqslant 0$, $\chi_A(1) \geqslant 0$ and $\chi'_A(\lambda) \geqslant 0$ for all $\lambda \in \mathbb{R}$ with $|\lambda| \geqslant 1$ (here χ'_A denotes the first derivative of χ_A). Thus we conclude that the matrix A has spectral radius at most one if and only if

$$\begin{aligned} &(D < 0 \wedge \chi_A(-1) \leqslant 0 \wedge \chi_A(1) \geqslant 0) \vee \\ &(\chi_A(-1) \leqslant 0 \wedge \chi_A(1) \geqslant 0 \wedge \chi'_A(\lambda) \geqslant 0 \text{ for all } |\lambda| \geqslant 1) \end{aligned}$$

These are polynomial constraints in the entries of A. In particular, the constraint $\chi'_A(\lambda) = 3\lambda^2 + 2p\lambda + q \geqslant 0$ for all $|\lambda| \geqslant 1$ can be shown to be equivalent to

$$(p^2 - 3q \leqslant 0) \vee (-3 \leqslant p \leqslant 3 \wedge -(q+3) \leqslant 2p \leqslant q+3)$$

by means of the quadratic formula. Here the term $p^2 - 3q$ is essentially the discriminant of $\chi'_A(\lambda)$; if it is negative, then $\chi'_A(\lambda)$ has no real root, such that the constraint holds trivially, otherwise it has two real roots λ_1 and λ_2. In case $\lambda_1 = \lambda_2$, the constraint also holds because then $\chi'_A(\lambda) = 3 \cdot (\lambda - \lambda_1)^2$. Finally, if $\lambda_1 \neq \lambda_2$, then both must necessarily lie in the closed interval $[-1, 1]$ for the constraint to hold, which is ensured by the second disjunct in the above formula.

(C) Last but not least, we present a generic method that works for matrices with unknown entries of any dimension. To this end, let A be an n-dimensional square matrix whose entries are supposed to be real numbers (not necessarily non-negative). Its characteristic polynomial is a monic polynomial of degree n, which can be written as $\chi_A(\lambda) = \lambda^n + \sum_{i=0}^{n-1} c_i\lambda^i$, where the coefficients c_i, $0 \leqslant i \leqslant n-1$, are polynomial expressions in the entries of A. Since all coefficients are supposed to be real numbers, $\chi_A(\lambda)$ can always be factored as

$$\chi_A(\lambda) = (\lambda - r)^b \cdot \prod_j (\lambda^2 + p_j\lambda + q_j)^{m_j} \tag{4}$$

where $b = 0$ if n is even, $b = 1$ otherwise, $m_j \geqslant 1$ ($m_j \in \mathbb{N}$) is the multiplicity of the quadratic factor $\lambda^2 + p_j\lambda + q_j$, and $r, p_j, q_j \in \mathbb{R}$. Thus the absolute values of all roots (real and complex ones) of $\chi_A(\lambda)$ are at most one if and only if $|r| \leqslant 1$ (in case $b = 1$) and the absolute values of the roots of all quadratic factors are at most one. So when does the latter condition hold for a given quadratic factor $\lambda^2 + p_j\lambda + q_j$? By the quadratic formula, we obtain the roots $\lambda_{1,2} := -\frac{p_j}{2} \pm \frac{\sqrt{p_j^2-4q_j}}{2}$. If the discriminant $p_j^2 - 4q_j$ is negative, both roots are complex, i.e., $\lambda_{1,2} := -\frac{p_j}{2} \pm i\frac{\sqrt{4q_j-p_j^2}}{2}$ and have absolute value $|\lambda_1| = |\lambda_2| = \sqrt{q_j}$. Hence, we demand $\sqrt{q_j} \leqslant 1$, or equivalently, $q_j \leqslant 1$. In the other case, if $p_j^2 - 4q_j \geqslant 0$, both roots are real, and the constraints $|\lambda_1| \leqslant 1$ and $|\lambda_2| \leqslant 1$ simplify to

$$-2 \leqslant p_j \leqslant 2 \text{ and } -(q_j+1) \leqslant p_j \leqslant q_j + 1$$

As a consequence, the matrix $A \in \mathbb{R}^{n\times n}$ with characteristic polynomial (4) has spectral radius at most one if and only if $b = 1$ implies $-1 \leqslant r \leqslant 1$ and for all quadratic factors $\lambda^2 + p_j\lambda + q_j$ in (4),

$$(p_j^2 - 4q_j < 0 \wedge q_j \leqslant 1) \vee (p_j^2 - 4q_j \geqslant 0 \wedge -2 \leqslant p_j \leqslant 2 \wedge -(q_j+1) \leqslant p_j \leqslant q_j+1)$$

Non-negative Integer Matrices. If all matrix entries are non-negative integers, one can also apply a totally different approach. It is based on graph theory and the following lemma, which is an immediate consequence of [11, Corollary 1].[7]

Lemma 12. *Let $A \in \mathbb{N}^{n\times n}$. Then $\rho(A) > 1$ if and only if $(A^k)_{i,i} > 1$ for some $k \in \mathbb{N}$ and $i \in \{1,\dots,n\}$.*

Viewing $A \in \mathbb{N}^{n\times n}$ as the adjacency matrix of a directed weighted graph G_A of n vertices numbered from 1 to n, such that for every positive entry $A_{i,j}$ there is an edge from vertex i to vertex j of weight $A_{i,j}$, the condition $(A^k)_{i,i} > 1$ for some $i \in \{1,\dots,n\}$ mentioned in the previous lemma holds if and only if

1. there is a cycle in G_A containing at least one edge of weight $w > 1$, or
2. there are (at least) two different paths (cycles) from some vertex to itself.

This is due to the well-known fact that the entry $(A^k)_{i,j}$ equals the sum of the weights of all distinct paths in G_A of length k from vertex i to vertex j, where the weight w of a path is the product of the weights of its edges (in particular, $w \geqslant 1$). Hence, we have $\rho(A) \leqslant 1$ if and only if neither of the two conditions holds. Since every cycle of G_A is composed of simple cycles, that is, cycles with no repeated vertices (aside from the necessary repetition of the start and end vertex), we may restrict to simple cycles for both conditions.

Next we make two important observations. First, for $A \in \mathbb{N}^{n\times n}$, G_A cannot have a simple cycle containing an edge of weight greater than one if every matrix in the set $\{A, A^2, \dots, A^n\}$ has diagonal entries less than or equal to one. Concerning the second condition, let us assume that there are two different simple cycles C_1 and C_2 of length l_1 and l_2, $1 \leqslant l_1, l_2 \leqslant n$, from some vertex i to itself. Considering all paths of length $\mathsf{lcm}(l_1, l_2)$, the least common multiple of l_1 and l_2, we clearly have $(A^{\mathsf{lcm}(l_1,l_2)})_{i,i} > 1$. In addition, we also have $(A^{l_1+l_2})_{i,i} > 1$ because there are two different cycles, each of weight at least one, from vertex i to itself of length $l_1 + l_2$, namely, the concatenation of C_1 and C_2 as well as the

[7] The joint spectral radius of a singleton set $\{A\}$ of matrices coincides with $\rho(A)$.

concatenation of C_2 and C_1. Hence, we can detect the existence of the cycles C_1 and C_2 by examining the diagonal entries of all matrices in the set $\{A, A^2, \dots, A^m\}$, where $m := \min(l_1+l_2, \mathsf{lcm}(l_1, l_2))$. More generally, we can detect any pair of cycles satisfying condition 2 by examining the diagonal entries of the matrices in the set $\{A, A^2, \dots, A^{p(n)}\}$, where $p(n) := \max\{\min(l_1 + l_2, \mathsf{lcm}(l_1, l_2)) \mid 1 \leqslant l_1, l_2 \leqslant n\}$. The left part of the table below shows the values of $p(n)$ for various values of n.

n	1	2	3	4	5	6
$p(n)$	1	2	5	7	9	11

n	1	2	3	4	5	6
$q(n)$	1	2	3	5	7	9

In particular, we observe that $p(n) \geqslant n$ for $n \geqslant 1$, and we draw the following conclusion. If every matrix in the set $\{A, A^2, \dots, A^{p(n)}\}$ has diagonal entries less than or equal to one, then neither condition 1 nor condition 2 can hold, which implies $\rho(A) \leqslant 1$. The converse is obvious.

Now let us apply this result to matrix interpretations. By definition, all matrices of a matrix interpretation $\mathcal{M}$ must have a top-left entry of at least one. Hence, this is also true for the maximum matrix A of $\mathcal{M}$. In other words, in G_A, vertex 1 has a loop (of length one) to itself. This corresponds to a dimension reduction by one for precluding all instances of condition 2. More precisely, we do not have to consider the cases $l_1 = n$ or $l_2 = n$ because then not only C_1 and C_2 but also C_1 (C_2) and the loop of vertex 1 satisfy condition 2 (for $n > 1$), and we can detect this by examining the diagonal entries of the matrix A^n, which has to be considered anyway for precluding all instances of condition 1. Therefore, if $A_{1,1} > 0$, we have $\rho(A) \leqslant 1$ if and only if every matrix in the set $\{A, A^2, \dots, A^{q(n)}\}$ has diagonal entries less than or equal to one, where $q(n) := \max(n, p(n-1))$ for $n > 1$ and $q(1) := 1$. Some values for $q(n)$ are displayed in the right part of the above table.

6 Experimental Results

The criteria proposed in this paper have been implemented in the complexity tool CaT [20] and the 1172 non-duplicating TRSs in TPDB 7.0.2 have been considered. All tests have been performed on a server equipped with 64 GB of main memory and eight dual-core AMD Opteron® 885 processors running at a clock rate of 2.6 GHz with a time limit of 60 seconds per system.[8]

We searched for matrix interpretations of dimension $d \in \{1, \dots, 5\}$ by encoding the constraints as an SMT problem (quantifier-free non-linear arithmetic), which is solved by bit-blasting. We used $\max(2, 6 - d)$ $(7 - d)$ bits to represent coefficients (intermediate results). The numerators of rational numbers are represented with the bit-width mentioned above while all denominators are 2. CaT found compatible matrix interpretations (not necessarily polynomially bounded) for 287 TRSs, giving an upper bound on the number of systems our results can apply to (if used stand-alone).

Table 1 indicates the number of systems where the labeled approach yields polynomial upper bounds on the derivational complexity. The first row shows

[8] For full details see `http://cl-informatik.uibk.ac.at/software/cat/polymatrix`.

Table 1. Polynomial bounds for 1172 systems

	$O(k)$	$O(k^2)$	$O(k^3)$	$O(k^n)$
Theorem 3|$9_{\mathbb{N}}$|$9_{\mathbb{R}}$	46| 85| 88	158|184|185	177|202|196	203|205|199
A|B|C|Lemma 12	61|68| 80| 64	158|176|185|175	–|182|191|180	–|–|193|190
row 1|row 2|row 1+2	88| 80| 88	191|185|200	205|191|209	208|196|212
CaT(2009)|CaT(2010)	208|214	299|309	310|321	328|329

that the theorems proposed in this paper allow to infer tighter upper bounds from triangular matrices than [13]; e.g., the number of linear (quadratic) upper bounds increases by 84% (16%) if one compares Theorems 3 and $9_{\mathbb{N}}$. The results for (possibly) non-triangular matrix interpretations are reported in the second row. The generic method based on factoring the characteristic polynomial (C) is implemented by comparing the coefficients from the characteristic polynomial with the coefficients of equation (4). Note that only this non-triangular approach allows to add upper bounds on the multiplicity of eigenvalues to the matrix encoding, which explains the high score for linear bounds. Since encoding A (B) is becoming harder for larger dimensions, we implemented it for dimensions one and two (and three) only (explaining the – in the table). Row three relates the approaches based on triangular and non-triangular matrices. Here row 1 corresponds to the accumulated power of Theorems 3 and 9 and row 2 to A, B, C, and Lemma 12, respectively. The impact of the methods proposed in this paper when integrated into the 2009 competition version of CaT is shown in row four. CaT was the strongest (derivational) complexity prover in 2008, 2009, and 2010. Since most parts of this paper aim at tightening bounds, it is not surprising that the total number of polynomial bounds did not increase significantly.

7 Conclusion, Related and Future Work

We have presented a characterization of matrix interpretations that induce polynomial upper bounds on the derivational complexity of compatible TRSs. Contrary to previous approaches, our method applies to matrix interpretations over $\mathbb{N}$ and $\mathbb{R}$ alike and does not restrict the shape of the matrices. At the core of our method is the analysis of the growth of finite products of matrices. In particular, we estimate the growth of a product of the form $M_1 \cdot M_2 \cdot \ldots \cdot M_k$ by the growth of a (suitably chosen) matrix A^k, which is determined by its spectral radius. For future work, the investigation of joint spectral radius theory [11] looks promising since the joint spectral radius is a measure of the maximal growth of products of matrices taken from a set and has been the subject of intense research.

Concerning related work, very recently (and independently) Waldmann [19] provides a characterization of polynomially bounded matrix interpretations over $\mathbb{N}$, which extends triangular matrix interpretations. In [19] matrices are viewed as weighted (word) automata and the derivational complexity of TRSs is bounded by the growth of the weight function computed by such automata. We believe that the method is at least as powerful as our approach for matrix interpretations over $\mathbb{N}$. In contrast to our approach, it can handle the TRS in [19, Example 7.5], probably because it is not based on the maximum matrix. In practice, the method based on automata is much harder to implement (cf. [19, Section 8]). Unlike our approach, it only applies to matrix interpretations over $\mathbb{N}$; the extension to $\mathbb{R}$ ($\mathbb{Q}$) raises non-trivial issues (cf. [19, Section 10]).

References

1. Alarcón, B., Lucas, S., Navarro-Marset, R.: Proving termination with matrix interpretations over the reals. In: WST 2009, pp. 12–15 (2009)
2. Baader, F., Nipkow, T.: Term Rewriting and All That. Cambridge University Press, Cambridge (1998)
3. Charalambides, C.A.: Enumerative Combinatorics. Chapman & Hall/CRC, Boca Raton (2002)
4. Chuan-Chong, C., Khee-Meng, K.: Principles and Techniques in Combinatorics. World Scientific Publishing Company, Singapore (1992)
5. Endrullis, J., Waldmann, J., Zantema, H.: Matrix interpretations for proving termination of term rewriting. JAR 40(2–3), 195–220 (2008)
6. Gebhardt, A., Hofbauer, D., Waldmann, J.: Matrix evolutions. In: WST 2007, pp. 4–8 (2007)
7. Geser, A., Hofbauer, D., Waldmann, J., Zantema, H.: On tree automata that certify termination of left-linear term rewriting systems. I&C 205(4), 512–534 (2007)
8. Hofbauer, D.: Termination proofs by context-dependent interpretations. In: Middeldorp, A. (ed.) RTA 2001. LNCS, vol. 2051, pp. 108–121. Springer, Heidelberg (2001)
9. Hofbauer, D., Lautemann, C.: Termination proofs and the length of derivations (preliminary version). In: Dershowitz, N. (ed.) RTA 1989. LNCS, vol. 355, pp. 167–177. Springer, Heidelberg (1989)
10. Hofbauer, D., Waldmann, J.: Termination of string rewriting with matrix interpretations. In: Pfenning, F. (ed.) RTA 2006. LNCS, vol. 4098, pp. 328–342. Springer, Heidelberg (2006)
11. Jungers, R.M., Protasov, V., Blondel, V.D.: Efficient algorithms for deciding the type of growth of products of integer matrices. LAA 428(10), 2296–2311 (2008)
12. Koprowski, A., Waldmann, J.: Arctic termination ... below zero. In: Voronkov, A. (ed.) RTA 2008. LNCS, vol. 5117, pp. 202–216. Springer, Heidelberg (2008)
13. Moser, G., Schnabl, A., Waldmann, J.: Complexity analysis of term rewriting based on matrix and context dependent interpretations. In: FSTTCS 2008. LIPIcs, vol. 2, pp. 304–315 (2008)
14. Neurauter, F., Middeldorp, A.: Polynomial interpretations over the reals do not subsume polynomial interpretations over the integers. In: RTA 2010. LIPIcs, vol. 6, pp. 243–258 (2010)
15. Rose, H.E.: Linear Algebra: A Pure Mathematical Approach. Birkhäuser, Basel (2002)
16. Serre, D.: Matrices: Theory and Applications. Springer, Heidelberg (2002)
17. Terese: Term Rewriting Systems. Cambridge Tracts in Theoretical Computer Science, vol. 55. Cambridge University Press, Cambridge (2003)
18. Termination problem data base, version 7.0.2. (2010), `http://termcomp.uibk.ac.at/status/downloads/tpdb-7.0.2.tar.gz`
19. Waldmann, J.: Polynomially bounded matrix interpretations. In: RTA 2010. LIPIcs, vol. 6, pp. 357–372 (2010)
20. Zankl, H., Korp, M.: Modular complexity analysis via relative complexity. In: RTA 2010. LIPIcs, vol. 6, pp. 385–400 (2010)
21. Zankl, H., Middeldorp, A.: Satisfiability of non-linear (ir)rational arithmetic. In: LPAR-16. LNCS, vol. 6355. Springer, Heidelberg (to appear, 2010)

An Isabelle-Like Procedural Mode for HOL Light

Petros Papapanagiotou and Jacques Fleuriot

University of Edinburgh
School of Informatics
Informatics Forum, 10 Crichton Street
Edinburgh EH8 9AB, UK
P.Papapanagiotou@sms.ed.ac.uk, jdf@inf.ed.ac.uk

Abstract. HOL Light is a modern theorem proving system characterised by its powerful, low level interface that allows for flexibility and programmability. However, considerable effort is required to become accustomed to the system and to reach a point where one can comfortably achieve simple natural deduction proofs. Isabelle is another powerful and widely used theorem prover that provides useful features for natural deduction proofs, including its meta-logic and its four main natural deduction tactics. In this paper we describe our efforts to emulate some of these features of Isabelle in HOL Light. One of our aims is to decrease the learning curve of HOL Light and make it more accessible and usable by a range of users, while preserving its programmability.

1 Introduction

In recent years, research in automated reasoning has resulted in powerful theorem proving systems (proof assistants), which are capable of proving a huge variety of theorems in any formally specified subset of higher-order logic, either automatically or interactively. A lot of automated tactics have been implemented, for instance based on decision procedures [1] and model elimination [2]. Most importantly, many of these systems are implemented in such a way so as to ensure the soundness and correctness of the formalization, for example by using the LCF approach [3] and allowing only conservative extensions of theories.

Proof assistants are generally characterised by a steep learning curve: they require from a few weeks to several months for the average beginner to become accustomed to their functionality and comfortable enough to use them effectively. Although they are generally complicated systems, the difficulty of usage varies from system to system. HOL Light, the proof assistant at the focus of this paper, is a powerful system that allows interaction at a low level, resulting in much flexibility and programmability. As a low-level theorem proving system, HOL Light is often considered to be more difficult to harness than many other proof assistants. Isabelle, for its part, is another powerful and widely used proof assistant, which, although still complicated, is considered a more user-friendly system. This is attributed to its small set of basic tactics as well as its powerful automated tools.

C. Fermüller and A. Voronkov (Eds.): LPAR-17, LNCS 6397, pp. 565–580, 2010.

In this work, by taking advantage of the flexible and highly programmable environment of HOL Light, we emulate the basic Isabelle tactics in an effort to create a more user-friendly interface for natural deduction [4] proofs in HOL Light. Natural deduction is a proof calculus that relies mainly on the use of introduction and elimination inference rules for forward and backward reasoning respectively. For instance, in Figure 1 we show two simple natural deduction proof trees of the following two statements:

$$nd\_lemma: \ (P \rightarrow Q \wedge R) \longrightarrow ((P \rightarrow Q) \wedge (P \rightarrow R))$$

and

$$nd\_lemma2: \ (\forall x.\ (P\ x \rightarrow Q\ x)) \rightarrow \neg(\exists x.\ P\ x \wedge \neg Q\ x)$$

In this figure, each step of the proofs is annotated with the corresponding natural deduction rule being used. The annotation consists of the symbol of the logical connective corresponding to the rule and an i for introduction rules or an e for elimination rules. Rules that produce new assumptions are also tagged with a unique number, eg. $\rightarrow i_3$. The new assumptions are then surrounded by square brackets [ ] and tagged with the same number so as to be easily associated with the rule that produced them.

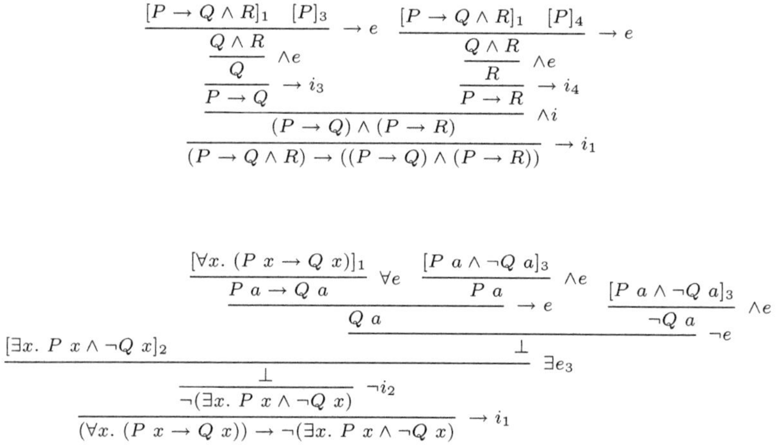

Fig. 1. Two examples of simple natural deduction proof trees

In this paper, while avoiding to delve too deeply into the implementation details, we give an idea of the functionality of our tactics and how these allow natural deduction style proofs in HOL Light. In Section 2, we describe HOL Light in more detail and explain the tradeoff between flexibility and user-friendliness and why the system has a steeper learning curve compared to other theorem proving systems. In Section 3, we decribe Isabelle and its procedural proof style and demonstrate why it is considered relatively user-friendly. We analyse our efforts towards emulating some of the features that result from Isabelle's meta-logic and its basic rule tactics in Section 4, whereas in Section 5, we discuss the limitations of our implementation as well as our plans for further development.

2 HOL Light

HOL Light [5] is a member of the HOL family of theorem provers. It was initially built as an attempt to overcome certain disadvantages of its predecessors. The system, written in OCaml, is lightweight and flexible and allows for interaction at multiple levels. We describe a few of its more salient features next.

2.1 Overview

The system has equality as the only primitive concept and a few primitive inference rules. These form the basis for other, more complex, inference rules for forward reasoning and for tactics for backwards reasoning. Built on top of these, HOL Light has its own automated methods for proofs such as the model elimination procedure MESON [6]. Additionally, it has an array of *conversion* methods that allow for efficient and fine-grained manipulation (such as rewriting or numerical reduction) of formulas. Theories ranging from Peano arithmetic to multivariable real analysis have already been formalised and are available for use within the system.

Implementation-wise, HOL Light is based on the LCF approach, which guarantees that any proved theorem is a logical consequence of the primitive axioms [3]. In practice, this is achieved using the OCaml type "*thm*" whose instances are theorems that are only derivable through the use of inference rules. The logical consequence symbol "$\vdash$" is only used in such HOL Light *thm*s. So, for instance, $x = y \vdash y = x$ is an example of a HOL Light theorem. The LCF approach, combined with the close interaction between the logic level and OCaml, allow for a smooth implementation and integration of techniques and tools that can seamlessly interact with the internals and methods of HOL Light. For example, it is possible to create arbitrarily complex tactics for manipulating the goal state of a proof, as long as the validity of the result can be verified using either the available or custom, derived inference rules.

In a nutshell, HOL Light is a flexible, highly programmable system that offers capabilities for fine, low-level control of both automated and interactive proofs. As mentioned by Harrison, it was designed to be "the Linux of Theorem Provers"[1]. As one might expect, though, there is a tradeoff between this flexibility and the complexity and user-friendliness of the system. This is discussed in the next section.

2.2 Proof Construction in HOL Light

In HOL Light, interactive proofs are constructed following a procedural proof style. The conjecture, given as a HOL Light term, may be set as a goal using the

[1] `http://www.math.kobe-u.ac.jp/icms2006/icms2006-video/video/v103.html`

command "*g*". Other commands known as tactics are used to refine it. A tactic can be applied using the "*e*" command (see Figure 4) and can either eliminate the goal by producing its proof or result in any number of new subgoals. It is worth noting that most tactics in HOL Light aim to affect only the conclusion of the goal with limited interaction with the assumptions. If an assumption is required in more complicated proof steps, it is usually *undischarged*, moving it to the conclusion (ie. it becomes an antecedent to the current conclusion), and manipulated there. The proof is complete when all subgoals have been proven. The command top_thm can then be used to return the proven theorem as an instance of the *thm* type.

Packaging the proofs. A complete proof in HOL Light is most commonly packaged within a prove statement (see Figure 2). All the tactics that prove the goal are thus packaged into a single composite tactic using the various available *tacticals*, with THEN and THENL being the most commonly used ones (the latter being used for the application of different tactics to different subgoals). All the currently available theories in HOL Light contain theorems packaged in such prove statements. Although HOL Light offers this as a concise and programmatically efficient way to package the finished proofs, it limits the readability and replayability of the proofs drastically. Especially when a goal is split into multiple subgoals, it becomes difficult for the user to follow the proof during replay and to have a clear image of the sequence of steps and the effects of each step.

Variety of tactics and tacticals. Further difficulties in the user interaction with HOL Light are due to its large variety of tactics. Available tactics range from simple applications of natural deduction rules to complex ones with multiple arguments. Moreover, each natural deduction rule is represented by a different tactic which results in a very large number of commands even for simple proofs. This can be constrasted to Isabelle, where only four natural deduction tactics are needed for natural deduction proofs (see Section 3). Examples of HOL Light tactics and their complexity are discussed in Section 4.1.

The situation is worsened for the novice user by the existence of complex *theorem tactics*. For example, CONJUNCTS_THEN must be given another tactic as an argument that will then be applied to each of the conjuncts in an existing assumption (see Figure 2). There are multiple types of tactics and tacticals, involving terms, theorems, lists of theorems or other tactics as arguments. Although this variety of commands provides a flexible environment for the expert user and system developer, it requires considerable effort on behalf of the novice user to become acquainted with their usage and generally adjust to HOL Light's particular style of procedural proofs.

Examples. In Figure 1, the natural deduction proof trees of the two examples *nd_lemma* and *nd_lemma2* (as introduced in Section 1) are shown. The corresponding proofs in HOL Light (without making use of the available automated tactics such as TAUT) are shown in Figure 2. The proofs divert considerably from the original natural deduction trees, since not all natural deduction inference rules are directly available as HOL Light tactics. We analyse these examples further in Section 4.1.

```
let nd_lemma = prove ( `(P ==> (Q ∧ R)) ==> ((P==>Q) ∧ (P==>R))`,
  DISCH_TAC THEN CONJ_TAC
  THEN DISCH_TAC THEN UNDISCH_TAC `P ==> Q ∧ R`
  THEN ANTS_TAC THENL
   [ FIRST_ASSUM ACCEPT_TAC ; DISCH_THEN (ACCEPT_TAC o CONJUNCT1);
     FIRST_ASSUM ACCEPT_TAC ; DISCH_THEN (ACCEPT_TAC o CONJUNCT2)]);;

let nd_lemma2 = prove (`(!x. P x ==> Q x) ==> ~ (?x. P x ∧ ~ Q x)`,
  DISCH_TAC THEN DISCH_THEN (CHOOSE_THEN ASSUME_TAC) THEN
  FIRST_X_ASSUM (CONJUNCTS_THEN ASSUME_TAC) THEN
  FIRST_X_ASSUM (ANTE_RES_THEN MP_TAC) THEN
  FIRST_ASSUM (ACCEPT_TAC o NOT_ELIM));;
```

Fig. 2. Two examples of simple proofs in HOL Light. Note that $\sim$ denotes negation ($\neg$), ! denotes universal quantification ($\forall$), and ? denotes existential quantification ($\exists$).

As a final remark here, we note that there is a desire on the part of Harrison to make HOL Light more user-friendly. This is expressed within his "future wishes" list [7] and our current effort can be viewed as a step in that direction. In particular, one of our immediate audience will be experienced Isabelle users, although more generally, through the new small suite of tactics, we hope to cut down on the time required for anyone to become familiar with the system.

3 Isabelle

Isabelle [8] is a well known and widely used Higher Order Logic theorem prover written in Standard ML. We give a brief overview of some of its main features in the next few Sections.

3.1 Overview

Isabelle is by nature an interactive theorem prover, but also includes a number of automated tactics and decision procedures such as its simplifier and its auto and blast [9] methods. Overall, it is generally viewed as a sound system, widely accepted by the theorem proving community. The system provides a formal, convenient meta-logic [8] for the formalisation of theorems and inference rules in particular logics such as higher-order logic (HOL) and ZF set theory. In this work, we are concerned with the higher-order logic version of the system known as Isabelle/HOL. Of particular interest, are the uses of metavariables, meta-level implication and meta-level quantification. We give a brief, relatively informal overview of some of these features next:

- At the user level, metavariables (or schematic variables, are usually distinguished from other free variables by a preceding "?". Their characteristic is that they can be instantiated to any other term during a proof. Thus the reflexive property of equality is formalised as the theorem $?a = ?a$ which allows the metavariable $?a$ to be arbitrarily instantiated.
- Meta-level implication is used to represent logical consequence from a list of assumptions to a conclusion. In Isabelle/HOL, this is distinguished from

normal implication through the use of a double arrow ($\Longrightarrow$) instead of the single arrow ($\longrightarrow$) of normal logical implication. For example, $p \Longrightarrow q$ can be interpreted as "assuming p we can prove q" while $[\![p;\ q]\!] \Longrightarrow r$ (which stands for $p \Longrightarrow (q \Longrightarrow r)$) means that "having p and q as assumptions we can prove r".

- Meta-level quantification involves the use of "$\bigwedge$-bound" variables [10]. The "$\bigwedge$" symbol denotes a meta-level universal quantifier which bounds a variable to a particular subgoal. This is particularly useful in the formalisation of the universal introduction rule. We describe its use further in Section 5.

3.2 Isabelle's Procedural Proof Style

Natural Deduction plays a central role in Isabelle's procedural proofs, whereby inference rules can be broadly distinguished into three categories: *introduction*, *elimination*, and *destruction* rules. This categorization resembles the normal distinction between introdution and elimination rules in natural deduction, with the main difference being in the further distinction of elimination rules into Isabelle-style elimination (a notion slightly different from the one in natural deduction) and destruction rules. Each rule is described with the help of the meta-logic and follows the following general form:

$$[\![P_1;\ P_2; ...\ P_n]\!] \Longrightarrow Q$$

Each premise P_i can consist of a meta-level implication as in the example of the Isabelle disjunction elimination rule:

$$disjE : [\![?P \vee ?Q;\ ?P \Longrightarrow ?R; ?Q \Longrightarrow ?R]\!] \Longrightarrow ?R$$

Normal object-level implication can also be represented, as in the example of the implication introduction rule:

$$impI : [\![?P \Longrightarrow ?Q]\!] \Longrightarrow ?P \longrightarrow ?Q$$

Paying attention to the distinction between meta-level and object-level implication, this rule can be interpreted in a forward direction as "if given $?P$ we can prove $?Q$ then we can deduce that $?P$ implies $?Q$" or in a backward direction as "in order to prove that $?P$ implies $?Q$, we have to prove Q with P as an assumption". These rules are better described using natural deduction proof trees as shown in Figure 3 [10].

The four tactics. Basic rule application occurs through one of four tactics (or methods): rule, erule, drule and frule. We briefly describe the application of each of the four tactics with any given rule $[\![P_1;\ P_2; ...\ P_n]\!] \Longrightarrow Q$:

- The rule tactic unifies Q with the current subgoal. Each P_i is then instantiated and added as a new subgoal for a total of n new subgoals. Note that each P_i may consist of meta-level implication so that the new subgoal may have its own assumptions added to the assumptions of the current subgoal. The rule tactic is appropriate for backward reasoning using introduction rules.

$[\![?P\vee ?Q;\ ?P \Longrightarrow ?R; ?Q \Longrightarrow ?R]\!] \Longrightarrow ?R$	$[\![?P \Longrightarrow ?Q]\!] \Longrightarrow ?P \longrightarrow ?Q$	$[\![?P; ?Q]\!] \Longrightarrow ?P\wedge ?Q$
$\dfrac{?P\vee ?Q \quad \begin{matrix}?P\\ \vdots\\ ?R\end{matrix} \quad \begin{matrix}?Q\\ \vdots\\ ?R\end{matrix}}{?R}\ disjE$	$\dfrac{\begin{matrix}?P\\ \vdots\\ ?Q\end{matrix}}{?P \longrightarrow ?Q}\ impI$	$\dfrac{?P \quad ?Q}{?P\wedge ?Q}\ conjI$

Fig. 3. Isabelle's disjE, impI and conjI rules

- The erule tactic behaves similarly to rule but also unifies P_1 (*major premise*) with one of the assumptions in the current subgoal. The matching assumption is deleted (eliminated) from the current subgoal and $n-1$ new subgoals are introduced. The erule tactic is appropriate for elimination rules. In the example of disjE, the erule tactic would eliminate an assumption matching $?P\vee ?Q$ and produce two new subgoals $?P \Longrightarrow ?R$ and $?Q \Longrightarrow ?R$ instantiated appropriately.
- The drule tactic is appropriate for forward reasoning with destruction rules. It unifies the major premise P_1 with one of the assumptions of the current subgoal which is then deleted (destroyed) and $n-1$ new subgoals are introduced. The current subgoal with Q added as an assumption forms the nth subgoal.
- The frule tactic is identical to the drule tactic, but does not delete the matching assumption, allowing for it to be reused in the proof if need be.

Extensions of the four tactics. It is often the case that there are several possible matches when one of the four tactics is applied. For example, drule may be able to match the major premise of an inference rule with more than one assumptions. If we consider $[\![a \wedge b;\ c \wedge d]\!] \Longrightarrow d$ as our current goal, and the conjunction elimination rule *conjunct*2 : $[\![?P\wedge ?Q]\!] \Longrightarrow ?Q$, the major premise $?P\wedge ?Q$ can be unified with both $a\wedge b$ and $c\wedge d$. However, in this particular case we would rather match it to $c \wedge d$ so that we can obtain d. Isabelle will only try to unify the first matching assumption, so we have to guide it into matching $c \wedge d$. This can be accomplished using a variant of drule called drule_tac. This tactic allows us to provide a partial instantiation for the metavariables of the inference rule. In our example, instead of using apply (drule conjunct2) we would use apply (drule_tac P=c in conjunct2). This would instantiate $?P$ to c therefore forcing the major premise to match the desired $c\wedge d$. There are "_tac" extended tactics for all four methods described above. We note also that Isabelle provides alternative ways of instantiating variables in rules to be applied but these will not be covered here.

More tactics. There are several other tactics available in Isabelle, such as subgoal_tac that introduces a new subgoal, case_tac that uses a case split over a variable and cut_tac that introduces a new assumption. Moreover, the simplification tactic simp is often used for rewriting both the goal and the assumptions. Finally, as mentioned before, there is a variety of automated tactics that simplify or try to prove the goal such as clarify, auto, blast etc.

Examples. Following our examples from Section 1, the natural deduction proofs of *nd_lemma* and *nd_lemma2* (as defined in Section 1) in Isabelle are shown on the left in Figure 4. Compared to the HOL Light proofs from Figure 2, these proofs are more readable and much closer to the natural deduction proof trees as shown in Figure 1. There is a clear sequence of steps and the proof can be easily replayed so as to monitor the effect of every rule application. The breaking up of the subgoals is still unclear, but every rule is only applied to one subgoal at a time so that a relatively easy to follow proof replay is possible.

```
lemma nd_lemma:
"(P ⟶ Q ∧ R) ⟶ ((P ⟶ Q) ∧ (P ⟶ R))"
apply (rule impI)
apply (erule conjE)
apply (rule impI)
apply (rule conjI)
apply (drule mp)
apply assumption
apply assumption
apply (drule_tac Q=R in mp)
apply assumption
apply assumption
done
```

```
g `(P==>(Q ∧ R))==>((P==>Q) ∧ (P==>R))`;;
e (rule impI);;
e (erule conjE);;
e (rule impI);;
e (rule conjI);;
e (drule mp);;
e assumption;;
e assumption;;
e (drule_tac [`Q`,`R`] mp);;
e assumption;;
e assumption;;
let nd_lemma = top_thm();;
```

```
lemma nd_lemma2:
"(∀x. (P x ⟶ Q x)) ⟶ ¬(∃x. P x ∧ ¬Q x)"
apply (rule impI)
apply (rule notI)
apply (erule exE)
apply (erule conjE)
apply (erule notE)
apply (erule allE)
apply (drule mp)
apply assumption
apply assumption
done
```

```
g `(!x:A. P x ==> Q x) ==> ~(?x. P x ∧ ~Q x)`;;
e (rule impI);;
e (rule notI);;
e (exE `a:A`);;
e (erule conjE);;
e (erule notE);;
e (erule allE);;
e (drule mp);;
e (meta_assumption [`(a':A)`]);;
e (meta_assumption [`(a':A)`]);;
let nd_lemma2 = top_thm();;
```

Fig. 4. Two examples of simple natural deduction proofs in Isabelle (left) and in HOL Light using the Isabelle-like tactics (right)

Overall, Isabelle's interface at the user level is relatively simple, with a small set of commands that can make use of any proven theorem. There is still a learning curve until the user can be comfortable with the syntax and with using the available tactics, but having only four major tactics for natural deduction proofs makes for a more user-friendly environment, especially for a beginner, compared to the plethora of available tactics in HOL Light.

4 "Isabelle Light"

Our efforts have been towards emulating some of the main aspects of Isabelle's procedural proof style within HOL Light. The powerful, low-level, programmable environment of HOL Light allows for a transparent emulation where Isabelle-like tactics are integrated in the system as normal HOL Light tactics. We describe the results and the most challenging parts of our implementation next.

4.1 Overview

A list of Isabelle tactics and their implemented counterparts in HOL Light is shown in Figure 5. Our implementation includes the emulation of the four Isabelle style natural deduction tactics and their extensions. These tactics can be used with most of the natural deduction inference rules. The two Isabelle natural deduction rules exE ($\exists e$) and allI ($\forall i$) are the only rules that are being treated differently due to the limitations of our system (see Section 5).

Isabelle syntax	'Isabelle Light'
rule th	rule th
rule_tac p=a, q=b in th	rule_tac [('p','a');('q','b')] th
erule exE	exE 'x:A'
rule allI	allI
case_tac "tm"	case_tac 'tm'
subgoal_tac "tm"	subgoal_tac 'tm'
simp	simp[ ]
simp add: th1 th2	simp[th1;th2]
assumption	assumption
assumption	meta_assumption ['p:A';'q:B']

Fig. 5. Isabelle tactics and their HOL Light counterparts

Examples. The 'Isabelle Light' proofs of *nd_lemma* and *nd_lemma2* (see Section 1) are shown in Figure 4. In contrast to the original HOL Light proofs, shown in Figure 2, they are noticeably similar to the corresponding Isabelle proofs. In the former, there is no clear sequence of natural deduction steps and an attempt to replay the proof step by step may prove non-trivial. For example, the DISCH_THEN (ACCEPT_TAC o CONJUNCT1) statement in the first proof combines the application of three natural deduction proof steps, namely implication introduction (DISCH_THEN), conjunction elimination (CONJUNCT1), and assumption matching (ACCEPT_TAC), in a single step[2]. In the new proof, these three steps are distinct and thus easier to follow and replay.

Moreover, in the original HOL Light proofs we note the use of UNDISCH_TAC to undischarge an assumption, move it to the conclusion of the goal and use it there. This is a purely HOL Light specific step that is unrelated to the natural deduction proof and which our new mechanism makes redundant.

These examples also demonstrate how there is a different tactic in HOL Light for each natural deduction inference rule. For example, the application of the implication introduction rule (impI in Isabelle) requires the use of the DISCH_TAC tactic (or its more complicated variant, DISCH_THEN). Furthermore, conjunction elimination is achieved through the use of the CONJUNCTS_THEN theorem tactic in combination with another theorem tactic (eg. ASSUME_TAC). This increases the complexity of the system in terms of both learning and remembering the usage of each tactic. The usage of each logical rule can only be seen through

[2] Note that the o operator corresponds to functional composition.

the *effects* of the respective tactic on the goal, whereas representing the rules as theorems, as in Isabelle, provides better inspectability.

In comparison, the Isabelle-style proofs in Figure 4 are simpler to understand, given that only one of the four natural deduction tactics combined with an inference rule is used in each step. Additionally, the names of the inference rules being used relate to the original natural deduction inference rules better, making them easier to remember. We have therefore drawn from the advantages of the Isabelle proof style, including better readability, replayability and similarity to the actual natural deduction proof (see Figure 1).

Beyond natural deduction. Although natural deduction is the main focus here, our implemented tactics go beyond that. In particular, we have provided the counterparts of the subgoal_tac and case_tac Isabelle tactics and have attempted to reconstruct a version of Isabelle's simp tactic. As we discussed in Section 2.2, assumptions in HOL Light are rarely manipulated beyond a few simple inference steps. As a result, even though HOL Light includes its own powerful rewriting tactic, it is designed to leave the assumptions unaffected. Our implemented simp tactic follows the behaviour of Isabelle's simp tactic which enables rewriting of the assumptions prior to rewritting the conclusion of the goal. Moreover, we provide a meson shortcut for HOL Light's model elimination based tactic ASM_MESON_TAC[ ], which allows the automated proof of many theorems that can also be proven by Isabelle's tableau-tactic blast.

Compatibility. It is worth noting that our Isabelle-like tactics are implemented transparently, at the same level as the original HOL Light tactics. Effectively, this provides the user with an enhanced user interface where either HOL Light or Isabelle Light tactics or even their combinations (eg. through THEN or THENL) can be used in the same proof. Therefore, a user already familiar with HOL Light needs not convert to a new user interface, but simply become accustomed to the new tactics should they wish to use them.

In Figure 6, we include a slightly more complicated proof of a theorem about multiplicative functions included in the HOL Light distribution. An alternative proof using our implemented Isabelle-like tactics is also given. In the original proof there is a variety of tactics being used, such as the ones described for the other two examples, but also more obscure ones such as the STRIP_TAC. The use of MP_TAC to add assumptions as antecedents to the conclusion of the goal is also evident. Moreover, one may notice the necessity of using a lambda abstraction to properly manipulate an antecedent. In contrast, the Isabelle-like proof only uses a limited set of tactics and natural deduction rules. Assumptions are manipulated transparently as part of tactic applications, without any need for explicit intermediate commands. We also demonstrate the smooth interaction of our implemented tactics with the HOL Light tacticals such as THEN and REPEAT. Finally, our tactics render the use of both the lambda abstraction and the intermediate lemma MONO_FORALL unnecessary.

In the remaining few sections, we proceed to describe some of the design and implementation details underlying the current work.

```
let MULTIPLICATIVE_IGNOREZERO =
 prove (`!f g. (!n. ~(n = 0) ==> g(n) = f(n)) /\ multiplicative f ==> multiplicative g`,
  REPEAT GEN_TAC THEN SIMP_TAC[MULTIPLICATIVE; ARITH_EQ] THEN
  REPEAT(DISCH_THEN(CONJUNCTS_THEN2 ASSUME_TAC MP_TAC)) THEN
  REPEAT(MATCH_MP_TAC MONO_FORALL THEN GEN_TAC) THEN
  DISCH_THEN(fun th -> STRIP_TAC THEN MP_TAC th) THEN
  ASM_REWRITE_TAC[] THEN ASM_MESON_TAC[MULT_EQ_0]);;

g `!f g. (!n. ~(n = 0) ==> g(n) = f(n)) /\ multiplicative f ==> multiplicative g`;;
e (REPEAT allI);;
e (simp[MULTIPLICATIVE; ARITH_EQ]);;
e (rule impI);;
e (REPEAT(erule conjE));;
e (REPEAT allI);;
e (rule impI);;
e (REPEAT(erule conjE));;
e (erule_tac [`a`,`m`] allE);;
e (erule_tac [`a`,`n`] allE);;
e (REPEAT(drule mp));;
e (REPEAT(rule conjI) THEN assumption);;
e (meson[MULT_EQ_0]);;
let MULTIPLICATIVE_IGNOREZERO = top_thm();;
```

Fig. 6. A more complicated example of a proof as originally found in HOL Light (within "Examples/multiplicative.ml") and using the new Isabelle-like tactics

4.2 The Meta-level

The primary challenge of our work was to emulate features that are provided by Isabelle's meta-logic within HOL Light. HOL Light does not use a meta-logic as part of the formalisation of the goals and theorems, but it relies on the OCaml toplevel. A goal is described as an OCaml *pair* of a list of labelled theorems (assumptions) and a term (conclusion). There is, notably, no meta-level implication available as part of the logic. Each of the available tactics in HOL Light refines the first goal in the current goalstate and returns a new goalstate that may include any number of subgoals.

Meta-theorems. In order to emulate the Isabelle behaviour, a user should expect to be able to use any HOL Light theorem as an inference rule with the new tactics. We, therefore, have a need for both describing and proving Isabelle-like natural deduction inference rules as HOL Light theorems. In order to achieve this, we emulate 'meta-level' implication at the syntactic level. We define a meta-level implication symbol ===> (as opposed to the shorter ==> of normal HOL Light implication) which, in effect, is just syntactic sugar for the normal HOL Light implication. However, it captures the idea of derivation as an inference rule, thereby allowing the user to distinguish the assumptions from the conclusion of the rule and to read it in a similar way to that described in Section 3.2 for the Isabelle rules. We call HOL Light theorems that include this meta-level implication *meta-theorems*. Using this syntax for meta-level implication we can describe all natural deduction inference rules as meta-theorems, except from those involving meta-level quantification (see Section 5).

In order to obtain and prove such meta-theorems, we implemented a mechanism to introduce conjectures as new goals involving our meta-level implication. We also introduced an MTAUT tactic that uses HOL Light's TAUT tautology prover to prove trivial propositional meta-theorems. Given the above, and following the example from Section 3.2, Isabelle's disjE rule is initially derived in our system as a HOL Light meta-theorem as follows:

```
let disjE = MTAUT `P ∨ Q===>(P===>R)===>(Q===>R)===>R`;;
```

Meta-rules. It is worth noting at this point that, even though meta-theorems are straightforward to specify and use at the user-level, a more flexible and thus complicated specification of the corresponding inference rules is required at the implementation level. We call such specifications *meta-rules*. These have a particular structure, which facilitates the implementation of the natural deduction tactics (see Section 4.3). We will not cover the implementation of this specification in detail in this paper, but we provide the internal representations of our Isabelle-like *disjE* and *conjI* as examples in Figure 7. As shown in this figure, meta-rules are implemented using an OCaml triplet that includes the following elements:

1. The conclusion of the rule as a HOL Light term.
2. The list of the meta-assumptions of the rule. Each of these meta-assumptions is represented using a pair that matches the HOL Light subgoal type and consists of a list of labelled (in this case not explicitly but merely with an empty string) theorems/assumptions and a conclusion.
3. A HOL Light theorem (thm) that can be used for the justification of the rule. We provide a few more details on the justification theorem in the following section.

The relatively complicated syntax of meta-rules makes them hard to use at the user level. For that reason, we provide an automated method which seemlessly converts HOL Light meta-theorems to the underlying meta-rules, thereby allowing users to apply the tactics directly on the more user-friendly meta-theorems. Thus, the novice user, for instance, never needs to be aware or use the meta-rules.

4.3 Implementing the Isabelle-Like Tactics

Having established a sufficient emulation for meta-theorems, the implementation of the tactics corresponding to Isabelle's rule methods was then relatively straightforward. HOL Light provides tools for term to term and term to theorem matching as well as instantiation tools. Moreover, it is flexible enough to allow arbitrarily complex tactics as long as their effects on the current goal can be justified using the available HOL Light inference rules.

Justification of the four tactics. Formally justifying the behaviour of the four natural deduction tactics is an important step for compliance with the LCF approach followed by HOL Light. As explained in Section 2.2, the application of a tactic to a goal in HOL Light may result in any number of new subgoals. If the proof is completed successfully, this means that each of the newly created subgoals was eventually proven, with their proofs resulting in a HOL Light theorem (thm). Each tactic must, therefore, provide a justification which allows the proof of the initial goal from the proven subgoals.

```
('r',                                       Conclusion
  [
    ([            ], 'p ∨ q');            ⎫
    ([("", 'p ⊢ p')], 'r');               ⎬ Meta-assumptions
    ([("", 'q ⊢ q')], 'r')                ⎭
  ],
  'p ∨ q, p ==> r, q ==> r ⊢ r'           Justification theorem
)
```

```
('p ∧ q',                                   Conclusion
  [
    ([            ], 'p');                ⎫ Meta-assumptions
    ([            ], 'q');                ⎭
  ],
  'p, q ⊢ p ∧ q'                           Justification theorem
)
```

Fig. 7. Isabelle-like disjunction elimination (disjE) and conjunction introduction (conjI) rules as implementation-level meta-rules in HOL Light

In order to justify the behaviour of the four tactics, we use the justification theorem included in the meta-rule structure of the inference rule being applied. In particular, we attempt to use each of the proven subgoals to eliminate the assumptions of this justification theorem. So, for instance, in Figure 7, the justification theorem for conjI is $p,\ q \vdash p \wedge q$. Thus, when using it with the rule tactic, the two subgoals produced, once proven, will satisfy each of the two assumptions p and q of the justification theorem. This then leads to the proof of the conclusion $p \wedge q$ which has been matched to the original goal. Variations of this approach are used for the other three tactics as well.

Instantiation lists. Another challenging part of our implementation was the introduction of instantiations, or what we described in Section 3.2 as the "_tac" extensions to the tactics. We decided to represent such instantiation choices at the user level using lists of pairs that we simply call *instantiation lists.*

As a result, our Isabelle drule_tac example in Section 3.2 apply (drule_tac P=c in conjunct2) is converted to e (drule_tac [('P','c')] conjunct2) in HOL Light. An example of the usage of drule_tac in an actual proof both in Isabelle and HOL Light is demonstrated in the first example proof in Figure 4.

5 Limitations and Future Work

The primary limitations of the current version of our system reside in the use of metavariables and the lack of meta-level quantification. These are reviewed next.

5.1 Limitations of Meta-variables

Although metavariables exist in HOL Light, their usage is limited. The single HOL Light tactic that allows the unification of the goal with one of the assumptions with metavariable instantiation (this is analogous to Isabelle's assumption tactic) uses limited term unification (First Order unification without type instantiation). These limitations are propagated to our system for now. Moreover, HOL Light does not allow our assumption tactic direct access to the introduced metavariables and so, in order to function properly, the user must provide the list of meta-variables manually. We have, therefore, introduced a meta_assumption tactic which must be used as an alternative to assumption when metavariables are involved in the goal and which must be given the list of metavariables in the goalstate as an argument (see Figure 5).

5.2 Meta-level Quantification

So far, we have not considered any solutions for the emulation of meta-level quantification. Due to this limitation, out of all the rules of natural deduction for First Order logic, we are unable to express the universal introduction and existential elimination rules as meta-theorems in HOL Light at this stage. We have therefore implemented these rules as separate tactics allI and exE respectively. These tactics are shortcuts to using HOL Light's GEN_TAC and X_CHOOSE_TAC respectively. Another side-effect of the lack of meta-level quantification is the fact that some incorrect meta-variable instantiations may be allowed during the proofs. This occurs when a meta-variable bound by an already introduced variable is instantiated without taking into immediate account that the instantiation for that meta-variable should be fresh. At the end of the proof, HOL Light will fail to reconstruct the proven theorem if an incorrect instantiation occurred, thereby maintaining soundness, but only after the user has been lead to believe that the proof was successful.

5.3 Future Work

Plans for further improvements include steps towards reconstructing tactics with behaviours similar to Isabelle's automated tactics, focusing on the commonly used clarify and auto tactics. In particular, clarify is a non-aggressive version of auto that does not carry out any simplification [10].

Furthermore, our future work will focus on an extensive evaluation of the system. The evaluation will be based on reconstruction of some Isabelle theories in HOL Light using our system. Moreover, we will invite various users, from novices in the area of automated reasoning to experienced Isabelle users to try out the system and provide feedback. We aim to evaluate how easily new users can become accustomed to HOL Light and how comfortable expert users feel when porting their Isabelle proofs in HOL Light.

Finally, we hope to investigate potential emulations of features from other tactic languages, with the aim of making HOL Light friendlier for users beyond Isabelle. One possibility would be to emulate some of the features of *Ltac*, the tactic language available in the proof assistant Coq [11].

6 Conclusion

We have described our efforts to improve the user-level interaction with HOL Light so as to make it more user-friendly for novice users as well as users familiar with Isabelle.

Our initial focus has been on the emulation of features that result from Isabelle's meta-logic, including meta-level implication and the usage of metavariables in HOL Light. We have also created representations for Isabelle styled natural deduction rules both at a user-level and at an implementation-level. Using these, we reconstructed the four basic natural deduction tactics of Isabelle and their extended variations as HOL Light tactics. We consider the sample proofs that we translated from Isabelle to HOL Light relatively close to the syntax and style of Isabelle. Moreover, our implemented tactics seemlessly embed into HOL Light, offering extra functionality and maintaining compatibility with the existing proof style. We believe this is a first step to a more user-friendly HOL Light within the standards of the procedural proof style of Isabelle.

Acknowledgments. We thank the referees for their helpful comments. This research is funded by an EPSRC studentship and by EPSRC grant EP/E005713/1.

References

1. McLaughlin, S., Harrison, J.: A proof-producing decision procedure for real arithmetic. In: Nieuwenhuis, R. (ed.) CADE 2005. LNCS (LNAI), vol. 3632, pp. 295–314. Springer, Heidelberg (2005)
2. Loveland, D.: Mechanical Theorem-Proving by Model Elimination. Journal of the ACM (JACM) 15, 236–251 (1968)
3. Paulson, L.: Logic and computation: interactive proof with Cambridge LCF. Cambridge Univ. Pr., Cambridge (1990)
4. Prawitz, D.: Natural deduction: A proof-theoretical study. Almqvist & Wiksell Stockholm (1965)
5. Harrison, J.: HOL Light: A tutorial introduction. In: Srivas, M., Camilleri, A. (eds.) FMCAD 1996. LNCS, vol. 1166, pp. 265–269. Springer, Heidelberg (1996)
6. Harrison, J.: Optimizing proof search in model elimination. In: McRobbie, M.A., Slaney, J.K. (eds.) CADE 1996. LNCS, vol. 1104, pp. 313–327. Springer, Heidelberg (1996)
7. Harrison, J.: HOL Light: future wishes. In: Talk at Workshop on Interactive Theorem Proving, Cambridge (2009), `http://www.cl.cam.ac.uk/~jrh13/slides/itp-25aug09/slides.pdf`
8. Paulson, L.: Isabelle.: Generic Theorem Prover. Springer, Heidelberg (1994)

9. Paulson, L.: A generic tableau prover and its integration with Isabelle. J. UCS 5, 73–87 (1999)
10. Nipkow, T., Paulson, L., Wenzel, M.: Isabelle/HOL: a proof assistant for higher-order logic. Springer, Heidelberg (2002)
11. Delahaye, D.: A tactic language for the system Coq. In: Parigot, M., Voronkov, A. (eds.) LPAR 2000. LNCS (LNAI), vol. 1955, pp. 377–440. Springer, Heidelberg (2000)

Bottom-Up Tree Automata with Term Constraints

Andreas Reuß and Helmut Seidl

Technische Universität München
Institut für Informatik I2
Boltzmannstraße 3
85748 Garching

Abstract. We introduce bottom-up tree automata with equality and disequality term constraints. These constraints are more expressive than the equality and disequality constraints between brothers introduced by Bogaert and Tison in 1992. Our new class of automata is still closed under Boolean operations. Moreover, we show that for tree automata with term constraints not only membership but also emptiness is decidable. This contrasts with the undecidability of emptiness for automata with arbitrary equality constraints between subterms identified by paths as shown in 1981 by Mongy.

1 Introduction

Finite tree automata have been widely used for the specification of tree languages. Such automata, however, are restricted to inspect their input only locally during a bottom-up traversal. Many efforts therefore have been made to enhance the expressiveness of such devices. A way to achieve this is to add constraints to the transitions of the automaton.

In [12], Mongy proposes automata which allow transitions to be constrained by equalities of subtrees which are identified by *paths*. Since the resulting class of languages is not closed under complementation, [5] generalizes these automata by additionally allowing disequality constraints between subtrees identified by paths. Let us call such constraints *path constraints* and the corresponding automata *path-constrained automata (PCA)*. For both classes, however, the emptiness problem is undecidable. In fact, Tommasi shows that already for automata with equality tests between *cousins* emptiness is not decidable [13].

For this reason, Bogaert and Tison consider automata where only equalities and disequalities between *direct* subterms, i.e., constraints on paths of length one, are allowed [2]. This class is known as the class of tree automata with constraints between *brothers*. The emptiness problem for this class is decidable. Later, Caron et al. observe that emptiness is also decidable for arbitrary path-constrained automata if only the number of equality constraints along each path of trees is bounded [3]. These results have been applied to derive a decision procedure for inductive reducibility of rewrite systems [7] and, more generally, for the first-order theory of encompassment [4]. In fact, automata with disequality path constraints only are sufficient for deciding inductive reducibility [6]. Another class of automata with certain equality constraints and disequality path constraints have recently been applied to solve the HOM problem for regular tree languages [10]. Another interesting class of tree automata with *global* equality

C. Fermüller and A. Voronkov (Eds.): LPAR-17, LNCS 6397, pp. 581–593, 2010.

and disequality constraints is considered by Godoy et al. in the context of MSO logic with isomorphism tests and unification with membership constraints [8,1]. Extensions of constraints between brothers in ranked trees to constraints between siblings in unranked trees are studied by Löding and Wong [11].

Here, we build on a formulation of tree automata by means of *Horn clauses* (see, e.g., [9]).

In this formalism, constraints between brothers can be expressed by means of equalities and disequalities between variables. We generalize this class of constraints to constraints between arbitrary *terms*. We show that the resulting class of term-constrained automata (TCA) is closed under Boolean operations. We also show that emptiness for TCA is still decidable.

The rest of the paper is organized as follows. After providing basic definitions and concepts in Section 2, we relate the expressiveness of TCA to tree automata with path constraints in section 3. Additionally we show that TCA are closed under Boolean operations. In Section 4, we then present an algorithm for deciding emptiness of a generalized form of TCA with disequality constraints only. In Section 5, we then show how to construct to each TCA a (generalized) TCA without equality constraints. By this construction, the emptiness test from Section 4 can be applied to decide emptiness also for arbitrary TCA.

2 Preliminaries

We consider ordered ranked trees made up of symbols from a ranked alphabet (Σ, ar) where Σ denotes a set of symbols and $ar : \Sigma \to \mathbb{N} \cup \{0\}$ is a function which specifies each symbol's arity. If the arities of symbols are understood, the ranked alphabet is denoted by Σ alone. For a ranked alphabet Σ, and a (countable) set $\mathbf{X} = \{\mathbf{x}_1, \mathbf{x}_2, \ldots\}$ of *variables* with $\Sigma \cap \mathbf{X} = \emptyset$, the set $\mathcal{T}_\Sigma(\mathbf{X})$ of (finite ordered) trees over Σ and $\mathbf{X}$ consists of all terms t given by the grammar:

$$t \quad ::= \quad \mathbf{x}_i \mid a \mid b(t_1, \ldots, t_k)$$

where $a, b \in \Sigma$, and a has arity 0, while b has arity $k > 0$. The tree t is called *ground* if t does not contain any variable $\mathbf{x}_i \in \mathbf{X}$. The set of ground terms is also denoted by $\mathcal{T}_\Sigma$.

Assume we are given a finite set $\mathcal{P}$ of unary predicates. Then a *literal* A is a term of the form $p(t)$ where $p \in \mathcal{P}$ and $t \in \mathcal{T}_\Sigma(\mathbf{X})$. A *term constraint* is a conjunction of atomic constraints where a constraint either is an equality $\mathbf{x}_i = s$ or a disequality $\mathbf{x}_j \neq t$ for variables $\mathbf{x}_i, \mathbf{x}_j$ and terms s, t. A substitution θ is a mapping $\theta : \mathbf{X} \to \mathcal{T}_\Sigma(\mathbf{X})$. We write $t\theta$ and $A\theta$ for the result of applying θ to the term t and the literal A, respectively. θ is called *ground* if $\mathbf{x}_i\theta$ is ground for all i. The substitution θ satisfies the term constraint ϕ (denoted by: $\theta \models \phi$) if it satisfies each constraint occurring in ϕ. The substitution θ satisfies the constraint $\mathbf{x}_i = s$ if $\mathbf{x}_i\theta = s\theta$. Likewise, the substitution θ satisfies the constraint $\mathbf{x}_i \neq t$ if $\mathbf{x}_i\theta \neq t\theta$.

A *constrained Horn clause* c is given by $B_0 \Leftarrow B_1, \ldots, B_m, \phi$ where $B_0, \ldots, B_m$ are literals and ϕ is a term constraint. The left-hand side B_0 is the *head* of the clause c while the sequence $B_1, \ldots, B_m, \phi$ denotes the *body* of c. The constraint ϕ imposes an additional restriction on the applicability of the clause. A constraint ϕ which is always true can be omitted. Assume that we are given a finite set $\mathcal{C}$ of constrained Horn clauses. Then the *least* model $\mathcal{M}_\mathcal{C}$ of $\mathcal{C}$ is the least set M of ground facts $p(t), t \in \mathcal{T}_\Sigma$, such that $\mathcal{M}_\mathcal{C} \supseteq \mathcal{T}_\mathcal{C}(\mathcal{M}_\mathcal{C})$. Here, the operator $\mathcal{T}_\mathcal{C}$ is defined as follows. Assume that M is any set of ground facts $p(t)$. Then $\mathcal{T}_\mathcal{C}(M)$ is the set of all ground facts $B_0\theta$ where θ is a ground substitution, $B_0 \Leftarrow B_1, \ldots, B_m, \phi$ is in $\mathcal{C}$, $B_1\theta, \ldots, B_m\theta \in M$, and $\theta \models \phi$. The set $\mathcal{M}_\mathcal{C}$ is therefore given by

$$\mathcal{M}_\mathcal{C} = \bigcup\{\mathcal{T}_\mathcal{C}^i(\emptyset) \mid i \geq 0\} \ .$$

The language $\{t \in \mathcal{T}_\Sigma \mid p(t) \in \mathcal{M}_\mathcal{C}\}$ of p is also denoted by $\mathcal{L}_\mathcal{C}(p)$. For convenience, we also consider the set $\mathcal{L}_\mathcal{C}^i(p) = \{t \in \mathcal{T}_\Sigma \mid p(t) \in \mathcal{T}_\mathcal{C}^i(\emptyset)\}$ which consists of all trees t where the fact $p(t)$ can be derived by at most i rounds of fixpoint iteration. Consider as an example the set $\mathcal{C}$ consisting of two (non-constrained) Horn clauses:

$$p(f(\mathbf{x}_1)) \Leftarrow p(\mathbf{x}_1), \qquad\qquad p(a) \Leftarrow$$

Here, we have $\mathcal{L}_\mathcal{C}^i(p) = \{f^j(a) \mid 0 \leq j \leq i-1\}$ where the number of elements in $\mathcal{L}_\mathcal{C}^i(p)$ is given by $|\mathcal{L}_\mathcal{C}^i(p)| = i$, and the language of p is

$$\mathcal{L}_\mathcal{C}(p) = \bigcup\{\mathcal{L}_\mathcal{C}^i(p) \mid i \geq 0\} = \{f^i(a) \mid i \geq 0\} = \{a, f(a), f(f(a)), ...\} \ .$$

In this paper, we consider tree automata as a particular restricted form of sets of (constrained) Horn clauses [9]. Here, unary predicates serve as states while clauses provide the transitions of the automaton. A constrained Horn clause c is an *automata clause* if it is of the form:

$$p(a) \Leftarrow \qquad \text{or} \qquad p(b(\mathbf{x}_1, \ldots, \mathbf{x}_k)) \Leftarrow p_1(\mathbf{x}_1), \ldots, p_k(\mathbf{x}_k), \phi$$

where $a, b \in \Sigma$, $p, p_1, \ldots, p_k \in \mathcal{P}$ are predicates, and ϕ may only mention variables from $\{\mathbf{x}_1, \ldots, \mathbf{x}_k\}$. A *finite tree automaton with term constraints* (TCA for short) then is a pair $A = (\mathcal{C}, F)$ where $\mathcal{C}$ is a finite set of automata clauses and $F \subseteq \mathcal{P}$ is a finite set of accepting predicates (or states). The language of A then is given by $\mathcal{L}(A) = \bigcup\{\mathcal{L}_\mathcal{C}(p) \mid p \in F\}$. Using dynamic programming, we obtain the following proposition:

Proposition 1. *Membership (of a ground term) is decidable in polynomial time for TCA.*

This also holds for automata with complex heads, i.e., heads of the form $p(t)$ where $p \in \mathcal{P}$, and t is a term which mentions all variables $\mathbf{x}_1, \ldots, \mathbf{x}_k$.

For a ground tree t', let $\mathsf{valid}_\mathcal{C}(t')$ denote the set of all predicates p with $t' \in \mathcal{L}_\mathcal{C}(p)$. The algorithm for testing membership of a tree t determines for all subtrees t' of t, the set $\mathsf{valid}_\mathcal{C}(t')$. Then $t' \in \mathcal{L}_\mathcal{C}(p)$ iff $p \in \mathsf{valid}_\mathcal{C}(t')$. The algorithm proceeds bottom-up over t. Assume that the algorithm has already determined the sets $\mathsf{valid}_\mathcal{C}(t')$ for all proper subtrees t' of a tree t_1. In order to determine $\mathsf{valid}_\mathcal{C}(t_1)$, the algorithm iterates over all clauses of the TCA. The set $\mathsf{valid}_\mathcal{C}(t_1)$ then consists of all predicates p for which there is a clause $p(s) \Leftarrow p_1(\mathbf{x}_1), \ldots, p_k(\mathbf{x}_k), \phi$ with $t_1 = s\theta$, $\theta = \{\mathbf{x}_1 \mapsto s_1, \ldots, \mathbf{x}_k \mapsto s_k\}$, such that for all $i = 1, \ldots, k$, $p_i \in \mathsf{valid}_\mathcal{C}(s_i)$ and $\theta \models \phi$. Thus, the set $\mathsf{valid}_\mathcal{C}(t_1)$ can be computed in time polynomial in the size of the TCA and t_1. Consequently, the set $\mathsf{valid}_\mathcal{C}(t')$ for all subtrees t' of t can also be determined in polynomial time. This completes the proof. □

3 Expressiveness and Closure Properties

Tree automata with constraints between brothers can be represented by TCA where all terms occurring in constraints are variables and vice versa. Let us call such automata *variable-constrained* automata (VCA). In addition to constraints on variables as in VCA, TCA in general allow also for comparisons like $\mathbf{x}_i \neq f(\mathbf{x}_j)$, which express relations between subtrees at different levels (depths) in the input trees. We have:

Theorem 2. *TCA are strictly more expressive than VCA.*

Proof. By definition, each VCA V can be considered as a TCA defining the same language. For the reverse direction, consider the TCA $A = (\mathcal{C}, F)$ with $F = \{p\}$, and $\mathcal{C} = \{c_1, c_2, c_3\}$, where:

$$\begin{aligned} c_1 &\equiv p(b(\mathbf{x}_1, \mathbf{x}_2)) \Leftarrow q(\mathbf{x}_1), q(\mathbf{x}_2), \mathbf{x}_1 = f(\mathbf{x}_2) \\ c_2 &\equiv q(f(\mathbf{x}_1)) \qquad \Leftarrow q(\mathbf{x}_1) \\ c_3 &\equiv q(a) \qquad\qquad \Leftarrow \end{aligned}$$

Here, $\mathcal{L}(A) = \mathcal{L}_\mathcal{C}(p) = \{b(f^{i+1}(a), f^i(a)) \mid i \geq 0\}$. We show by contradiction that no VCA $V = (\mathcal{C}', F')$ exists with $\mathcal{L}(V) = \mathcal{L}(A)$. From $|\mathcal{L}(V)| = |\mathcal{L}(A)| = |\mathcal{L}_\mathcal{C}(p)| = \infty$, it follows for some predicate $p' \in F'$ with $\mathcal{L}_{\mathcal{C}'}(p') \subseteq \mathcal{L}_\mathcal{C}(p)$, that $|\mathcal{L}_{\mathcal{C}'}(p')| = \infty$. Therefore, there exists a clause $c \equiv p'(b(\mathbf{x}_1, \mathbf{x}_2)) \Leftarrow q_1(\mathbf{x}_1), q_2(\mathbf{x}_2), \phi_c$ in $\mathcal{C}'$ such that c can produce infinitely many trees $t \in \mathcal{L}_\mathcal{C}(p) \cap \mathcal{L}_{\mathcal{C}'}(p')$. Let t_1, t_2 be two such trees with $t_1 = b(f^{i+1}(a), f^i(a))$ and $t_2 = b(f^{j+1}(a), f^j(a))$, $j > i \geq 0$. By construction, we have:

(1) $f^{j+1}(a) \in \mathcal{L}_{\mathcal{C}'}(q_1)$, $f^i(a) \in \mathcal{L}_{\mathcal{C}'}(q_2)$, but
(2) $b(f^{j+1}(a), f^i(a)) \notin \mathcal{L}_{\mathcal{C}'}(p') \subseteq \{b(f^{k+1}(a), f^k(a)) \mid k \geq 0\}$, and
(3) $t_1, t_2 \in \mathcal{L}_{\mathcal{C}'}(p')$ by application of c.

In the following we show that every combination of (dis)equality constraints between $\mathbf{x}_1, \mathbf{x}_2$ in ϕ_c leads to a contradiction:

(i) If either $\mathbf{x}_1 \neq \mathbf{x}_1$ or $\mathbf{x}_2 \neq \mathbf{x}_2$ in ϕ_c, then ϕ_c is unsatisfiable and therefore (3) cannot hold.
(ii) If either $\mathbf{x}_1 = \mathbf{x}_2$ or $\mathbf{x}_2 = \mathbf{x}_1$ in ϕ_c, neither t_1 nor t_2 can be generated by c contradicting again (3).
(iii) Both $\mathbf{x}_1 = \mathbf{x}_1$ in ϕ_c and $\mathbf{x}_2 = \mathbf{x}_2$ in ϕ_c are tautologies. Therefore now assume that ϕ_c is a tautology or equivalent to $\mathbf{x}_1 \neq \mathbf{x}_2$. Then $f^{j+1}(a) \neq f^i(a)$, and therefore $\theta \models \phi_c$ for $\theta(\mathbf{x}_1) = f^{j+1}(a)$, $\theta(\mathbf{x}_2) = f^i(a)$. We conclude that $b(f^{j+1}(a), f^i(a)) \in \mathcal{L}_{\mathcal{C}'}(p')$ contradicting (2). □

For path-constrained automata (PCA) the emptiness problem is not decidable [12]. Paths identify *subterms*. A path is represented as a sequence of integers. E.g., the constraint $1.2 = 2$ in the body of a clause $p(h(\mathbf{x}_1, \mathbf{x}_2)) \Leftarrow r(\mathbf{x}_1), s(\mathbf{x}_2), 1.2 = 2$ means that the second argument of $\mathbf{x}_1$ must exist and equal $\mathbf{x}_2$. Likewise, the constraint $1.2 \neq 2$ in the body of a clause $p(h(\mathbf{x}_1, \mathbf{x}_2)) \Leftarrow r(\mathbf{x}_1), s(\mathbf{x}_2), 1.2 \neq 2$ means that either at least one of the paths 1.2, 2 does not exist or both exist and the two corresponding subterms are different. It is not difficult to see that PCA can simulate TCA.

Proposition 3. *For every TCA A, a PCA A' can be constructed with $\mathcal{L}(A) = \mathcal{L}(A')$.* □

Assume that the maximal depth of a term occurring in a constraint of A is k. The idea of the construction is that A' records the topmost constructors up to depth k of the current argument within the predicate (or state) and then enforces the required equalities or disequalities by means of path constraints. The clause $p(h(\mathbf{x}_1, \mathbf{x}_2)) \Leftarrow r(\mathbf{x}_1), s(\mathbf{x}_2), \mathbf{x}_1 = f(\mathbf{x}_2, \mathbf{x}_2)$ then is simulated by the clauses $p_{h(\_,\_)}(h(\mathbf{x}_1, \mathbf{x}_2)) \Leftarrow r_{f(\_,\_)}(\mathbf{x}_1), s_t(\mathbf{x}_2), 2 = 1.1, 2 = 1.2$ for arbitrary patterns t of depth 1.

Likewise, path constraints can be expressed by term constraints — but only if we allow *extra* variables $\mathbf{y}_i$ which do not occur in the head. The constraint $1.2 = 2$, for example can be expressed by a disjunction $\bigvee \phi_f$ over all $f \in \Sigma$ with $ar(f) = r \geq 2$ where ϕ_f is given by $\mathbf{x}_1 = f(\mathbf{y}_1, \ldots, \mathbf{y}_r) \wedge \mathbf{x}_2 = \mathbf{y}_2$. By this reduction, we conclude:

Proposition 4. *Emptiness for the extension of TCA with term constraints which may use variables $\mathbf{y}_i$ not occurring in the respective heads, is undecidable.* □

PCA with disequality constraints only have been used in [6] to decide ground reducibility. They do not allow for equality tests. However, since path constraints for tree automata in general are more expressive than term constraints without auxiliary variables, we conjecture that PCA with disequalties only are incomparable to TCA.

In the following, we collect some extensions to the language of constraints used by TCA which do not increase expressiveness.

Arbitrary Boolean Formulas. Assume that the constraint ϕ of a clause c is an arbitrary Boolean formula over atomic constraints, i.e., equalities $\mathbf{x}_i = s$ and disequalities $\mathbf{x}_j \neq t$ between $\mathbf{x}_i, \mathbf{x}_j$ and terms s, t. Then we can construct a set of clauses $c_1, \ldots, c_r$ which are equivalent to c and whose constraints are conjunctions of atomic constraints. For this, we first transform ϕ to DNF (disjunctive normal form) $\phi \equiv \phi_1 \vee \ldots \vee \phi_r$. This step may introduce negations of the original atomic constraints, i.e. an equality $\mathbf{x}_j = t$ may result from a disequality $\mathbf{x}_j \neq t$ and vice versa. Second, we build for each of the conjunctions $\phi_1, \ldots, \phi_r$ in the DNF form of ϕ one extra clause c_i with term constraint ϕ_i.

Arbitrary Terms. Our definition of *term constraint* requires the left-hand sides of the equalities and disequalities to be single variables $\mathbf{x}_i \in \mathbf{X}$. Without increasing expressiveness, we as well may allow arbitrary terms on left-hand sides, since every constraint $s = t$ and $s \neq t$ can be split into equivalent conjunctions of equalities $\mathbf{x}_i = t_i$ and disjunctions of disequalities $\mathbf{x}_i \neq t_i$, respectively. The resulting positive Boolean combinations over constraints can then be transformed in each clause to DNF (disjunctive normal form) and used to build equivalent sets of automata clauses, as described above. E.g., the clause

$$H \Leftarrow p_1(\mathbf{x}_1), p_2(\mathbf{x}_2), p_3(\mathbf{x}_3),\ g(\mathbf{x}_1, a) = g(\mathbf{x}_3, \mathbf{x}_2) \wedge f(\mathbf{x}_1, \mathbf{x}_2) \neq f(\mathbf{x}_2, \mathbf{x}_3)$$

is equivalent to the clause

$$\begin{aligned} H \Leftarrow p_1(\mathbf{x}_1), p_2(\mathbf{x}_2), p_3(\mathbf{x}_3),\ &(\mathbf{x}_1 = \mathbf{x}_3 \wedge \mathbf{x}_2 = a \wedge \mathbf{x}_1 \neq \mathbf{x}_2) \\ &\vee (\mathbf{x}_1 = \mathbf{x}_3 \wedge \mathbf{x}_2 = a \wedge \mathbf{x}_2 \neq \mathbf{x}_3) \end{aligned}$$

which in turn is equivalent to the set

$$\{ H \Leftarrow p_1(\mathbf{x}_1), p_2(\mathbf{x}_2), p_3(\mathbf{x}_3),\ \mathbf{x}_1 = \mathbf{x}_3 \wedge \mathbf{x}_2 = a \wedge \mathbf{x}_1 \neq \mathbf{x}_2, \\ H \Leftarrow p_1(\mathbf{x}_1), p_2(\mathbf{x}_2), p_3(\mathbf{x}_3),\ \mathbf{x}_1 = \mathbf{x}_3 \wedge \mathbf{x}_2 = a \wedge \mathbf{x}_2 \neq \mathbf{x}_3\} \ .$$

Henceforth, we therefore allow ϕ to be an arbitrary Boolean formula over equality and disequality constraints between arbitrary terms (not mentioning additional variables), unless specified otherwise.

Deterministic TCA. Let $\mathcal{C}$ be a set of automata clauses over a fixed ranked alphabet Σ. Then $\mathcal{C}$ is *deterministic* if for each $t \in \mathcal{T}_\Sigma$, there is at most one $p \in \mathcal{P}$ such that $t \in \mathcal{L}_\mathcal{C}(p)$. $\mathcal{C}$ is *total deterministic* if for each $t \in \mathcal{T}_\Sigma$, there is exactly one $p \in \mathcal{P}$ such that $t \in \mathcal{L}_\mathcal{C}(p)$. A TCA $A = (\mathcal{C}, F)$ is (total) deterministic if $\mathcal{C}$ is (total) deterministic. For every TCA $A = (\mathcal{C}, F)$ an equivalent total deterministic automaton $A' = (\mathcal{C}', F')$ can be constructed with $\mathcal{L}(A') = \mathcal{L}(A)$ by means of the powerset construction. The powerset construction is a standard automata technique. A general construction for constrained automata can, e.g., be found in [5]. For TCA, the powerset automaton A' can be constructed as follows. The predicates $\mathcal{P}'$ of A' are taken from the powerset of the set of predicates $\mathcal{P}$ of A, and $F' = \{P \in \mathcal{P}' \mid P \cap F \neq \emptyset\}$. We define $P(a) \Leftarrow\ \in \mathcal{C}'$ if and only if $P = \{p \in \mathcal{P} \mid p(a) \Leftarrow\ \in \mathcal{C}\}$ and, similarly:

$$P(b(\mathbf{x}_1, \ldots, \mathbf{x}_k)) \Leftarrow P_1(\mathbf{x}_1), \ldots, P_k(\mathbf{x}_k), \phi' \in \mathcal{C}'$$

iff P is a subset of the set

$$\{p \in \mathcal{P} \mid p(b(\mathbf{x}_1, \ldots, \mathbf{x}_k)) \Leftarrow p_1(\mathbf{x}_1), \ldots, p_k(\mathbf{x}_k), \phi \in \mathcal{C}, p_1 \in P_1, \ldots, p_k \in P_k\}$$

and

$$\phi' = \bigwedge_{p \in P} \Big(\bigvee_{\substack{p(b(\mathbf{x}_1,\ldots,\mathbf{x}_k)) \Leftarrow p_1(\mathbf{x}_1),\ldots,p_k(\mathbf{x}_k),\phi'' \in \mathcal{C} \\ p_i \in P_i}} \phi'' \Big) \\ \wedge \bigwedge_{p \notin P} \Big(\bigwedge_{\substack{p(b(\mathbf{x}_1,\ldots,\mathbf{x}_k)) \Leftarrow p_1(\mathbf{x}_1),\ldots,p_k(\mathbf{x}_k),\phi'' \in \mathcal{C} \\ p_i \in P_i}} \neg\phi'' \Big) \ .$$

Note that in the construction of ϕ' an atomic constraint $\mathbf{x}_i = t$ may result from a constraint $\mathbf{x}_i \neq t$ and vice versa. We have:

Proposition 5. *For every TCA, an equivalent total deterministic TCA exists and can be constructed in exponential time.* □

In a total deterministic automaton, for each tree $t \in \mathcal{T}_\Sigma$ there is exactly one predicate p with $t \in \mathcal{L}_\mathcal{C}(p)$. This allows for complementation, yielding the same good closure properties for TCA as for non-constrained tree automata. Complementation $\overline{A}$ of a TCA A can be done in two steps. In the first step, a total deterministic TCA is constructed which is equivalent to A. Thus, the powerset construction for the set $\mathcal{C}$ consisting of the two clauses

$$p(f(\mathbf{x}_1)) \Leftarrow p(\mathbf{x}_1), \mathbf{x}_1 = a \qquad p(a) \Leftarrow$$

would result in the clauses:

$$\{p\}(f(\mathbf{x}_1)) \Leftarrow \{p\}(\mathbf{x}_1), \mathbf{x}_1 = a \qquad \{p\}(a) \Leftarrow \\ \emptyset(f(\mathbf{x}_1)) \Leftarrow \{p\}(\mathbf{x}_1), \mathbf{x}_1 \neq a \qquad \emptyset(f(\mathbf{x}_1)) \Leftarrow \emptyset(\mathbf{x}_1)$$

If Σ also contains a symbol b of arity 0, we additionally must add the clause $\emptyset(b) \Leftarrow$.

In the second step of complementation, the final states are exchanged with the non-final ones.

The union $A_1 \cup A_2$ of two TCA $A_1 = (\mathcal{C}_1, F_1)$ and $A_2 = (\mathcal{C}_2, F_2)$ is defined by $(\mathcal{C}_1 \cup \mathcal{C}_2, F_1 \cup F_2)$, assuming $\mathcal{C}_1 \cap \mathcal{C}_2 = F_1 \cap F_2 = \emptyset$. An automaton for the intersection of two tree automata A_1 and A_2 can be constructed as $\overline{\overline{A_1} \cup \overline{A_2}}$, or – more efficiently – by a direct construction which uses the Cartesian products of original states and transitions [5]. Thus, we obtain:

Proposition 6. *TCA are closed under union, intersection, and complementation.* □

4 Automata with Disequality Constraints Only

We now consider the class TCA$_{\neq}$ of automata with disequality constraints only. We additionally allow TCA$_{\neq}$ clauses to have *complex* heads, i.e., literals $p(t)$ where $p \in \mathcal{P}$, and t is an arbitrary term. So we consider clauses of the form:

$$p(t) \Leftarrow p_1(\mathbf{x}_1), \ldots, p_k(\mathbf{x}_k), \phi$$

where $p, p_1, \ldots, p_k \in \mathcal{P}$ are predicates, ϕ is a conjunction of disequalities $t_i \neq t_j$, and ϕ and t may only mention variables from $\{\mathbf{x}_1, \ldots, \mathbf{x}_k\}$ $(k \geq 0)$. The number of disequalities in a clause $c \in \mathcal{C}$ is denoted $dc(c)$.

Emptiness. A semi-algorithm for non-emptiness of TCA$_{\neq}$ computes for $i \geq 1$, the set $\mathcal{L}^i_{\mathcal{C}}(p)$ for all predicates p until an accepting state p' is found for which $\mathcal{L}^i_{\mathcal{C}}(p') \neq \emptyset$. Here, the set $\mathcal{L}^i_{\mathcal{C}}(p)$ can be computed from the sets $\mathcal{L}^{i-1}_{\mathcal{C}}(q)$, $q \in \mathcal{P}$, by applying the implications $c \in \mathcal{C}$ (starting with $\mathcal{L}^0_{\mathcal{C}}(p) = \emptyset$, $p \in \mathcal{P}$).

For non-constrained automata, each round $i \geq 1$ finds all recognized trees of *depth* i. Since each predicate p with $\mathcal{L}_{\mathcal{C}}(p) \neq \emptyset$ recognizes at least one tree of depth linear in $|\mathcal{P}|$, after a linear number of rounds (non-)emptiness is decided. Constraints, however, can delay the derivation process: if a term constraint ϕ of a clause $c \equiv p(t) \Leftarrow p_1(\mathbf{x}_1), \ldots, p_k(\mathbf{x}_k), \phi$ is false for every substitution θ with $\mathbf{x}_i\theta \in \mathcal{L}^j_{\mathcal{C}}(p_i), i \in \{1, \ldots, k\}$, then c cannot produce a tree in round $j+1$ even if $\mathcal{L}^j_{\mathcal{C}}(p_i) \neq \emptyset$ for all i. Still, c may later produce a tree for a suitable combination of trees $t_i \in \mathcal{L}^m_{\mathcal{C}}(p_i), m > j$.

We will establish an upper bound for the number of rounds which are needed in order to decide TCA$_{\neq}$-emptiness. By a counting argument, it suffices to increase the sets $\mathcal{L}^i_{\mathcal{C}}(p)$ only up to a fixed number of trees. We claim that for proving non-emptiness of a predicate q, at most $(\sum_{c \in \mathcal{C}} dc(c)) + 1$ trees for each predicate $p \neq q$ suffice. This claim follows from the next lemma which says that each term constraint ϕ of a clause c "filters out" at most $dc(c)$ trees:

Lemma 7. *Let $A = (\mathcal{C}, F)$ be a TCA$_{\neq}$ and $c \in \mathcal{C}$ be an automata clause with $c \equiv q(t) \Leftarrow p_1(\mathbf{x}_1), \ldots, p_k(\mathbf{x}_k), \phi$. Assume there is a number $d \geq 0$ such that $\exists\theta\ \forall i \in \{1, \ldots, k\}\ \mathbf{x}_i\theta \in \mathcal{L}^d_{\mathcal{C}}(p_i) \wedge \theta \models \phi$. Then $|\mathcal{L}^{d+1}_{\mathcal{C}}(q)| \geq \max_{1 \leq i \leq k} \{|\mathcal{L}^d_{\mathcal{C}}(p_i)| - dc(c)\}$.*

Proof. Let $p_j \in \{p_1, \ldots, p_k\}$ and $\phi \equiv C_1 \wedge \ldots \wedge C_m, m = dc(c)$. Reorder the C_i s. t. $\mathbf{x}_j$ is mentioned exactly in $C_1, \ldots, C_l, 0 \leq l \leq m$. Choose θ s.t. $\theta \models C_{l+1} \wedge \ldots \wedge C_m$ and $\mathbf{x}_i\theta \in \mathcal{L}_\mathcal{C}^d(p_i)$ for all $i \in \{1, \ldots, k\} \setminus \{j\}$. Making $C_1, \ldots, C_l$ true by choosing $\theta(\mathbf{x}_j)$ can be considered as an instance of the pigeonhole principle implying that there are at least $|\mathcal{L}_\mathcal{C}^d(p_j)| - l \geq |\mathcal{L}_\mathcal{C}^d(p_j)| - m$ different trees in $\mathcal{L}_\mathcal{C}^d(p_j)$ which satisfy all $C_i, 1 \leq i \leq l$. Each of them can be used in combination with the trees $\mathbf{x}_i\theta, i \neq j$, to produce one tree for $\mathcal{L}_\mathcal{C}^{d+1}(q)$. □

Theorem 8. *Let $A = (\mathcal{C}, F)$ be a TCA$_{\neq}$ with $n = |\mathcal{P}|$ predicates and $d = \sum_{c \in \mathcal{C}} dc(c)$ disequality constraints. Then for all $p \in \mathcal{P}$, it holds that $\mathcal{L}_\mathcal{C}(p) = \emptyset$ iff $\mathcal{L}_\mathcal{C}^{n(d+1)}(p) = \emptyset$.*

Proof. Direction "⇒" is trivial. For a proof of "⇐", consider the derivation process where we stop after round r iff $\forall p\ (|\mathcal{L}_\mathcal{C}^r(p)| \leq d \Rightarrow |\mathcal{L}_\mathcal{C}^{r+1}(p)| = |\mathcal{L}_\mathcal{C}^r(p)|)$. This process terminates after at most $n(d+1)$ rounds, i.e., $r \leq n(d+1)$, since in every round $i \leq r$ at least one set of cardinality $\leq d$ increases, which is only possible $\leq n(d+1)$ times. Assume for a contradiction that $\mathcal{L}_\mathcal{C}(p) \neq \emptyset$ but $\mathcal{L}_\mathcal{C}^r(p) = \emptyset$.

Let j be minimal such that $j > r$ and $\mathcal{L}_\mathcal{C}^j(p) \neq \emptyset$ but $\mathcal{L}_\mathcal{C}^{j-1}(p) = \emptyset$ for some predicate p by application of some clause c_j in round j. The derivations between rounds $r+1$ and $j-1$ only increase non-empty sets since j is minimal, and the stopping condition of the derivation process ensures that $j > r+1$ holds. We inductively define a chain of clauses $c_{r+1}, \ldots, c_j$ where the indexes correspond to rounds such that $\forall i \in \{r+1, \ldots, j-1\}$ $c_i \equiv q_i(t_i) \Leftarrow p_{i_1}(\mathbf{x}_{i_1}), \ldots, p_{i_k}(\mathbf{x}_{i_k}), \phi_i$ is chosen such that $\mathcal{L}_\mathcal{C}^i(q_i) \backslash \mathcal{L}_\mathcal{C}^{i-1}(q_i) \neq \emptyset$, and $q_i(\mathbf{x}_k)$ occurs in the body of c_{i+1} (for some $\mathbf{x}_k \in \mathbf{X}$). The chain exists because every derivation by some clause c_{i+1} in round $i+1 > 1$ would already occur in round i if $\mathcal{L}_\mathcal{C}^i(q) = \mathcal{L}_\mathcal{C}^{i-1}(q)$ for all $q \in \mathcal{P}$ in the body of c_{i+1}. Let $q_{r+1}, \ldots, q_j$ be the respective head predicates (especially, $q_j = p$) and $\mathcal{L}_\mathcal{C}^r(q_{r+1}), \ldots, \mathcal{L}_\mathcal{C}^{j-1}(q_j)$ the increased sets ($\mathcal{L}_\mathcal{C}^{i-1}(q_i)$is increased in round i, possibly by applying c_i.)

By Lemma 7, we have $|\mathcal{L}_\mathcal{C}^{i-1}(q_i)| \leq |\mathcal{L}_\mathcal{C}^i(q_{i+1})| + dc(c_{i+1})$ for $i = r+1, \ldots, j-1$. Since $\mathcal{L}_\mathcal{C}^{j-1}(q_j) = \mathcal{L}_\mathcal{C}^{j-1}(p) = \emptyset$, it follows that $|\mathcal{L}_\mathcal{C}^r(q_{r+1})| \leq \sum_{i=r+2}^{j} dc(c_i)$ for the set $\mathcal{L}_\mathcal{C}^r(q_{r+1})$ which is increased in round $r+1$.

If $q_i \neq q_k$ for all $r+1 \leq i < k \leq j$, then $\sum_{i=r+2}^{j} dc(c_i) \leq \sum_{c \in \mathcal{C}} dc(c) = d$, and we get a contradiction because $|\mathcal{L}_\mathcal{C}^r(q_{r+1})| \leq d$ and also $\mathcal{L}_\mathcal{C}^{r+1}(q_{r+1}) \setminus \mathcal{L}_\mathcal{C}^r(q_{r+1}) \neq \emptyset$, violating the assumption that $\forall p\ (|\mathcal{L}_\mathcal{C}^r(p)| \leq d \Rightarrow |\mathcal{L}_\mathcal{C}^{r+1}(p)| = |\mathcal{L}_\mathcal{C}^r(p)|)$.

If on the other hand $q_i = q_k$ for some $r+1 \leq i < k \leq j$, then $|\mathcal{L}_\mathcal{C}^r(q_{r+1})| \leq \sum_{c \in \mathcal{C}} dc(c)$ also holds: Let i, k be such a pair such that $k - i$ is maximal. Then we have $\mathcal{L}_\mathcal{C}^m(q_k) = \mathcal{L}_\mathcal{C}^m(q_i) \forall m$, and $\mathcal{L}_\mathcal{C}^{i-1}(q_i) \subseteq \mathcal{L}_\mathcal{C}^{k-1}(q_i)$, hence $|\mathcal{L}_\mathcal{C}^{i-1}(q_i)| \leq |\mathcal{L}_\mathcal{C}^{k-1}(q_k)|$. Both facts together yield $|\mathcal{L}_\mathcal{C}^r(q_{r+1})| \leq \sum_{m=r+2}^{i} dc(c_m) + \sum_{m=k+1}^{j} dc(c_m)$. From maximality of $k - i$, it follows that $q_{r+1}, \ldots, q_i$ are pairwise disjoint with $q_{k+1}, \ldots, q_j$, and so also $c_{r+1}, \ldots, c_i$ are pairwise disjoint with $c_{k+1}, \ldots, c_j$. Recursively removing multiple occurrences of clauses c_m in both sums over chain segments (with consecutive indexes) in the same way, together with the disjointness of these segments with respect to their members, finally proves that $|\mathcal{L}_\mathcal{C}^r(q_{r+1})| \leq \sum_{c \in \mathcal{C}} dc(c)$. □

5 General TCA

We now turn to automata with (arbitrary) term constraints (TCA). There, atomic constraints are either disequalities $s \neq t$ or equalities $s = t$ for terms s and t. So we consider clauses of these two forms:

$$p(a) \Leftarrow$$
$$p(b(\mathbf{x}_1, \ldots, \mathbf{x}_k)) \Leftarrow p_1(\mathbf{x}_1), \ldots, p_k(\mathbf{x}_k), \phi$$

where $a, b \in \Sigma$, $p, p_1, \ldots, p_k \in \mathcal{P}$ are predicates, and ϕ is a Boolean combination of equalities and disequalities which may only mention variables from $\{\mathbf{x}_1, \ldots, \mathbf{x}_k\}$. If ϕ is a conjunction of atomic constraints, we also write ϕ as a comma-separated sequence of these.

Normal Form for Term Constraints. A term constraint ϕ is in *normal form* if it is equal to $\bot$ (false) or is a conjunction of atomic constraints where all left-hand sides of equality constraints are variables $\mathbf{x}_i \in \mathbf{X}$, and the following holds:

(1) If $\mathbf{x}_i = \mathbf{x}_j$ occurs in ϕ, then $i < j$; and
(2) If an equality constraint $\mathbf{x}_i = t$ occurs in ϕ, then $\mathbf{x}_i$ does not occur in any other atomic constraint of ϕ.

The following fact is wellknown.

Proposition 9. *For every term constraint ϕ, a disjunction $\phi' \equiv \phi_1 \vee \ldots \vee \phi_r$ of term constraints ϕ_i can be constructed such that each ϕ_i is in normal form and ϕ is equivalent to ϕ', i.e., for all ground substitutions θ,*

$$\theta \models \phi \quad \textit{iff} \quad \theta \models \phi' \qquad \square$$

In order to construct ϕ', we first transform ϕ into disjunctive normal form $\phi'_1 \vee \ldots \vee \phi'_r$. Then we further proceed with each ϕ'_i separately. Let $\phi'_i \equiv \psi_1 \wedge \psi_2$ where ψ_1 and ψ_2 consist of all equality constraints and all disequality constraints of ϕ'_i, respectively. If ψ_1 is unsatisfiable, we return $\bot$ for ϕ_i, i.e., remove it from the disjunction. Otherwise, a most general unifier σ of ψ_1 can be constructed with the properties (1), (2). Assume that $\sigma = \{\mathbf{x}_{j_1} \mapsto t_1, \ldots, \mathbf{x}_{j_s} \mapsto t_s\}$. Then the corresponding conjunction ϕ_i is given by:

$$\mathbf{x}_{j_1} = t_1, \ldots, \mathbf{x}_{j_s} = t_s, \psi_2\sigma$$

Consider, e.g., $\phi \equiv \mathbf{x}_1 = \mathbf{x}_2, \mathbf{x}_1 = f(\mathbf{x}_4), \mathbf{x}_2 = f(\mathbf{x}_3)$. The normal form of this term constraint is $\phi' \equiv \mathbf{x}_1 = f(\mathbf{x}_4), \mathbf{x}_3 = \mathbf{x}_4, \mathbf{x}_2 = f(\mathbf{x}_4)$.

Saturating deterministic TCA. Let $A = (\mathcal{C}, F)$ denote a deterministic TCA (possibly with equality constraints). Our goal is to construct an equivalent deterministic TCA $A' = (\mathcal{C}', F)$ (with the same set of predicates and accepting predicates) which is *saturated*. This means that every clause c given by $H \Leftarrow p_1(\mathbf{x}_1), \ldots, p_k(\mathbf{x}_k), \phi$ has the following properties. Let X and Y denote the set of variables occurring in left-hand sides and right-hand sides of equality constraints in ϕ, respectively. Then

1. ϕ is in normal form;
2. for all ground substitutions $\theta : \mathbf{X} \to \mathcal{T}_\Sigma$ with $\theta \models \phi$ and $\mathbf{x}_i\theta \in \mathcal{L}_\mathcal{C}(p_i)$ for all $\mathbf{x}_i \in Y$, $\mathbf{x}_j\theta \in \mathcal{L}_\mathcal{C}(p_j)$ also for all $\mathbf{x}_j \in X$.

In this case, the literals $p_j(\mathbf{x}_j), \mathbf{x}_j \in X$, are redundant and therefore can be removed. Let $\phi \equiv \bigwedge_{\mathbf{x}_i \in X}(\mathbf{x}_i = t_i) \wedge \phi'$ where ϕ' contains disequality constraints only. Let $\tau : X \to \mathcal{T}_\Sigma(Y)$ denote the substitution $\tau = \{\mathbf{x}_i \mapsto t_i \mid \mathbf{x}_i \in X\}$. Let $\mathbf{x}_{j_1}, \ldots, \mathbf{x}_{j_r}$ be an enumeration of the variables of the clause which are not in X. Then the clause:

$$H\tau \Leftarrow p_{j_1}(\mathbf{x}_{j_1}), \ldots, p_{j_r}(\mathbf{x}_{j_r}), \phi'$$

has disequality constraints only and is equivalent to the clause c. Thus, we obtain:

Proposition 10. *For every saturated deterministic TCA A, a TCA$_{\neq}$ A' can be constructed such that $\mathcal{L}(A) = \mathcal{L}(A')$.* □

In particular, this means that emptiness for saturated deterministic TCA is decidable.

Example. Consider the deterministic set of clauses $\mathcal{C} = \{c_1, c_2, c_3, c_4\}$ with

$$\begin{array}{ll} c_1 \equiv p(h(\mathbf{x}_1, \mathbf{x}_2)) & \Leftarrow p_1(\mathbf{x}_1), p_2(\mathbf{x}_2),\ \mathbf{x}_1 = f(\mathbf{x}_2, \mathbf{x}_2), \mathbf{x}_1 \neq a \\ c_2 \equiv p_1(f(\mathbf{x}_1, \mathbf{x}_2)) & \Leftarrow p_2(\mathbf{x}_1), p_2(\mathbf{x}_2),\ \mathbf{x}_2 = a \\ c_3 \equiv p_2(g(\mathbf{x}_1)) & \Leftarrow p_2(\mathbf{x}_1) \\ c_4 \equiv p_2(a) & \Leftarrow \end{array}$$

over $\Sigma = \{a, h, f, g\}$ and $\mathcal{P} = \{p, p_1, p_2\}$. Here, clauses c_2, c_3 and c_4 are saturated, while clause c_1 is not. By adding the constraint $\mathbf{x}_2 = a$, we obtain from c_1 the clause:

$$p(h(\mathbf{x}_1, \mathbf{x}_2)) \Leftarrow p_1(\mathbf{x}_1), p_2(\mathbf{x}_2), \mathbf{x}_1 = f(\mathbf{x}_2, \mathbf{x}_2), \mathbf{x}_2 = a, \mathbf{x}_1 \neq a$$

or:

$$p(h(\mathbf{x}_1, \mathbf{x}_2)) \Leftarrow p_1(\mathbf{x}_1), p_2(\mathbf{x}_2), \mathbf{x}_1 = f(a, a), \mathbf{x}_2 = a, \mathbf{x}_1 \neq a$$

which is saturated and equivalent to c_1. The languages of the predicates are $\mathcal{L}_\mathcal{C}(p) = \{h(f(a, a), a)\}$, $\mathcal{L}_\mathcal{C}(p_1) = \{f(g^i(a), a) \mid i \geq 0\}$, $\mathcal{L}_\mathcal{C}(p_2) = \{g^i(a) \mid i \geq 0\}$. The set $\mathcal{C}'$ of an equivalent TCA$_{\neq}$ thus is given by $\mathcal{C}' = \{c_1', c_2', c_3, c_4\}$ with

$$\begin{array}{ll} c_1' \equiv p(h(f(a, a), a)) \Leftarrow & \\ c_2' \equiv p_1(f(\mathbf{x}_1, a)) & \Leftarrow p_2(\mathbf{x}_1) \end{array}$$

In the following, let $A = (\mathcal{C}, F)$ denote a fixed deterministic TCA. We observe:

Proposition 11. *Let $\mathbf{X}$ denote a set of variables. For every $\mathbf{x}_i \in \mathbf{X}$, let p_i denote a predicate. Then for every term $t \in \mathcal{T}_\Sigma(\mathbf{X})$ and predicate p, a constraint $\Psi_{t,p}$ can be constructed such that for all ground substitutions $\theta : \mathbf{X} \to \mathcal{T}_\Sigma$ with $\mathbf{x}_i\theta \in \mathcal{L}_\mathcal{C}(p_i)$ for all $\mathbf{x}_i \in \mathbf{X}$,*

$$t\theta \in \mathcal{L}_\mathcal{C}(p) \quad \textit{iff} \quad \theta \models \Psi_{t,p}$$

Proof. We proceed by induction on the structure of t, with the two base cases:

(1) if $t = \mathbf{x}_i$, $\mathbf{x}_i \in \mathbf{X}$ then $\Psi_{t,p}$ is $\top$ (true) if $p = p_i$, and $\bot$ otherwise;
(2) if $t = a$, $a \in \Sigma$ then $\Psi_{t,p}$ is $\top$ if $p(a) \Leftarrow \in \mathcal{C}$, and $\bot$ otherwise.

In both cases, the assertion of the proposition is satisfied.

For the induction step, let $t = f(t_1, \ldots, t_k)$. Let θ' denote the substitution with $\mathbf{x}_i\theta' = t_i$ for $i = 1, \ldots, k$. Then we define:

$$\Psi_{t,p} \equiv \bigvee\{\phi\theta' \wedge \Psi_{t_1,p_1} \wedge \ldots \wedge \Psi_{t_k,p_k} \mid p(f(\mathbf{x}_1, \ldots, \mathbf{x}_k)) \Leftarrow p_1(\mathbf{x}_1), \ldots, p_k(\mathbf{x}_k), \phi \in \mathcal{C}\}$$

Now assume that θ is a ground substitution such that $t\theta \in \mathcal{L}_{\mathcal{C}}(p)$. By definition, $t\theta = f(t_1\theta, \ldots, t_k\theta)$. Since A is deterministic, there exist predicates $p_1, \ldots, p_k$ and a clause $p(f(\mathbf{x}_1, \ldots, \mathbf{x}_k)) \Leftarrow p_1(\mathbf{x}_1), \ldots, p_k(\mathbf{x}_k), \phi$ such that the following holds:

1. $t_i\theta \in \mathcal{L}_{\mathcal{C}}(p_i)$ for all $i = 1, \ldots, k$;
2. $\theta'\theta \models \phi$ where $\mathbf{x}_i\theta'\theta = t_i\theta$.

By induction hypothesis, the first item implies that $\theta \models \Psi_{t_i,p_i}$ for all i. From the second item, we deduce that $\theta \models \phi\theta'$ as well, and therefore by definition $\theta \models \Psi_{t,p}$. For the reverse implication, assume that $\theta \models \Psi_{t,p}$. Then some clause $p(f(\mathbf{x}_1, \ldots, \mathbf{x}_k)) \Leftarrow p_1(\mathbf{x}_1), \ldots, p_k(\mathbf{x}_k), \phi$ exists such that

1. $\theta \models \Psi_{t_i,p_i}$ for all i, and
2. $\theta \models \phi\theta'$.

By induction hypothesis, we conclude from the first item that $t_i\theta \in \mathcal{L}_{\mathcal{C}}(p_i)$ for all i. By the second item, $\theta'\theta \models \phi$. Overall, we therefore can apply the clause to the t_i to produce t, i.e., $t \in \mathcal{L}_{\mathcal{C}}(p)$. □

Assume that $H \Leftarrow p_1(\mathbf{x}_1), \ldots, p_k(\mathbf{x}_k), \phi$ is an automata clause where the constraint ϕ is in normal form $(\bigwedge_{\mathbf{x}_i \in X} \mathbf{x}_i = t_i) \wedge \phi'$ where ϕ' consists of disequalities only. Let Ψ_{t_i,p_i} be the constraints as provided by Proposition 11 for the right-hand sides t_i of $\mathbf{x}_i \in X$ in ϕ. Let $\overline{\phi}$ denote the constraint:

$$\phi \wedge \bigwedge\{\Psi_{t_i,p_i} \mid \mathbf{x}_i \in X\}$$

Then the following holds:

Proposition 12. *For a ground substitution θ, the following statements are equivalent:*

1. $\theta \models \phi$ *and* $\mathbf{x}_i\theta \in \mathcal{L}_{\mathcal{C}}(p_i)$ *for all* i;
2. $\theta \models \overline{\phi}$ *and* $\mathbf{x}_i\theta \in \mathcal{L}_{\mathcal{C}}(p_i)$ *for all* $\mathbf{x}_i \notin X$. □

The constraint $\overline{\phi}$ need not be in normal form, but is equivalent to a (possibly empty) finite disjunction of constraints $\overline{\phi_1} \vee \ldots \vee \overline{\phi_s}$ where each $\overline{\phi_j}$ is in normal form. The clause $H \Leftarrow p_1(\mathbf{x}_1), \ldots, p_k(\mathbf{x}_k), \phi$ then is equivalent to the set of clauses $c_j, j = 1, \ldots, s$, given by

$$H \Leftarrow p_1(\mathbf{x}_1), \ldots, p_k(\mathbf{x}_k), \overline{\phi_j}$$

Let X_j denote the set of left-hand sides of equalities in $\overline{\phi_j}$. Then $X \subseteq X_j$ for all j. Whenever $X = X_j$, the clause c_j is saturated. Otherwise, we apply the same procedure to the clause c_j. Since $X \subset X_j$, i.e., the set of variables occurring on left-hand sides of equalities has become strictly larger, this refinement may occur at most at k levels. Overall, we therefore have proved the following theorem:

Theorem 13. *For every deterministic TCA $A = (\mathcal{C}, F)$, a saturated deterministic TCA $A' = (\mathcal{C}', F)$ with the same set of predicates can be constructed such that $\mathcal{L}(A) = \mathcal{L}(A')$.* □

By Proposition 5, for every TCA, an equivalent deterministic TCA can be constructed, which, by Theorem 13, can be saturated. By Proposition 10 we furthermore know, that every saturated deterministic TCA can be transformed into an equivalent $\text{TCA}_{\neq}$ — to which we can apply the emptiness test from Theorem 8. In summary, we therefore have obtained:

Theorem 14. *For every TCA A, it can be decided whether or not $\mathcal{L}(A) = \emptyset$.* □

6 Conclusion

In this paper, we have introduced a novel class of tree automata with equality and disequality term constraints (TCA). The languages accepted by our class of automata are closed under Boolean operations for tree languages, i.e., union, intersection, and complementation. We showed that TCA are strictly more expressive than tree automata with constraints between brothers of [2], but less expressive than tree automata with arbitrary path constraints [5]. While emptiness is undecidable for the latter class of automata, we showed that emptiness for TCA is decidable. Our algorithm relies on a determinization procedure for TCA together with a nontrivial transformation of deterministic TCA into a class of automata with disequality constraints only. It remains as an open problem to evaluate precise complexity bounds for the proposed algorithm and evaluate how it behaves on practical examples. It also would be interesting to clarify the expressiveness of our class in comparison with the classes of constrained automata used in [10,1].

Acknowledgements. We like to thank Andreas Gaiser, Sylvia Friese, Andrea Flexeder, and the LPAR reviewers for many helpful comments and hints.

References

1. Barguño, L., Creus, C., Godoy, G., Jacquemard, F., Vacher, C.: The emptiness problem for tree automata with global constraints. In: Proceedings of the 25th Annual IEEE Symposium on Logic in Computer Science (LICS 2010), Edinburgh, Scotland, UK, July 2010. IEEE Computer Society Press, Los Alamitos (2010), `http://www.lsv.ens-cachan.fr/Publis/PAPERS/PDF/BCGJV-lics10.pdf` (to appear)
2. Bogaert, B., Tison, S.: Equality and disequality constraints on direct subterms in tree automata. In: STACS 1992: Proceedings of the 9th Annual Symposium on Theoretical Aspects of Computer Science, London, UK, pp. 161–171. Springer, Heidelberg (1992) ISBN 3-540-55210-3
3. Caron, A.-C., Comon, H., Coquidé, J.-L., Dauchet, M., Jacquemard, F.: Pumping, cleaning and symbolic constraints solving. In: Shamir, E., Abiteboul, S. (eds.) ICALP 1994. LNCS, vol. 820, pp. 436–449. Springer, Heidelberg (1994), ISBN 3-540-58201-0

4. Caron, A.-C., Coquidé, J.-L., Dauchet, M.: Encompassment properties and automata with constraints. In: Kirchner, C. (ed.) RTA 1993. LNCS, vol. 690, pp. 328–342. Springer, Heidelberg (1993), ISBN 3-540-56868-9
5. Comon, H., Dauchet, M., Gilleron, R., Löding, C., Jacquemard, F., Lugiez, D., Tison, S., Tommasi, M.: Tree automata techniques and applications (2007), http://www.grappa.univ-lille3.fr/tata (release October 12, 2007)
6. Comon, H., Jacquemard, F.: Ground reducibility is exptime-complete. In: LICS 1997: Proceedings of the 12th Annual IEEE Symposium on Logic in Computer Science, Washington, DC, USA, p. 26. IEEE Computer Society, Los Alamitos (1997) ISBN 0-8186-7925-5
7. Comon, H., Jacquemard, F.: Ground reducibility and automata with disequality constraints. In: Enjalbert, P., Mayr, E.W., Wagner, K.W. (eds.) STACS 1994. LNCS, vol. 775, pp. 151–162. Springer, Heidelberg (1994), ISBN 3-540-57785-8
8. Filiot, E., Talbot, J.-M., Tison, S.: Tree automata with global constraints. In: Ito, M., Toyama, M. (eds.) DLT 2008. LNCS, vol. 5257, pp. 314–326. Springer, Heidelberg (2008), ISBN 978-3-540-85779-2, doi: http://dx.doi.org/10.1007/978-3-540-85780-8_25.
9. Frühwirth, T.W., Shapiro, E.Y., Vardi, M.Y., Yardeni, E.: Logic programs as types for logic programs. In: LICS, pp. 300–309 (1991)
10. Godoy, G., Giménez, O., Ramos, L., Àlvarez, C.: The hom problem is decidable. In: STOC, pp. 485–494 (2010)
11. Löding, C., Wong, K.: On nondeterministic unranked tree automata with sibling constraints. In: FSTTCS, pp. 311–322 (2009)
12. Mongy, J.: Transformation de noyaux reconnaissables d'arbres. PhD thesis, Laboratoire d'Informatique Fondamentale de Lille, Université des Sciences et Technologies de Lille, Villeneuve d'Ascq, France (1981)
13. Tommasi, M.: Automates d'arbres avec tests d'égalité entre cousins germains. Mémoire de DEA, Univ. Lille I (1992)

Constructors, Sufficient Completeness, and Deadlock Freedom of Rewrite Theories

Camilo Rocha and José Meseguer

University of Illinois at Urbana-Champaign
{hrochan2,meseguer}@cs.illinois.edu

Abstract. Sufficient completeness has been throughly studied for equational specifications, where function symbols are classified into *constructors* and *defined* symbols. But what should sufficient completeness mean for a rewrite theory $\mathcal{R} = (\Sigma, E, R)$ with equations E and non-equational rules R describing concurrent transitions in a system? This work argues that a rewrite theory naturally has *two* notions of constructor: the usual one for its equations E, and a different one for its rules R. The sufficient completeness of constructors for the rules R turns out to be intimately related with *deadlock freedom*, i.e., $\mathcal{R}$ has no deadlocks outside the constructors for R. The relation between these two notions is studied in the setting of unconditional order-sorted rewrite theories. Sufficient conditions are given allowing the automatic checking of sufficient completeness, deadlock freedom, and other related properties, by propositional tree automata modulo equational axioms such as associativity, commutativity, and identity. They are used to extend the Maude Sufficient Completeness Checker from the checking of equational theories to that of both equational and rewrite theories. Finally, the usefulness of the proposed notion of constructors in proving inductive theorems about the reachability rewrite relation $\rightarrow_{\mathcal{R}}$ associated to a rewrite theory $\mathcal{R}$ (and also about the joinability relation $\downarrow_{\mathcal{R}}$) is both characterized and illustrated with an example.

1 Introduction

Formal specification and declarative programming of concurrent systems can be naturally achieved with rewrite theories [29] of the form $\mathcal{R} = (\Sigma, E, R)$, where (Σ, E) is an equational theory axiomatizing the set of system *states* as elements of the initial algebra $\mathcal{T}_{\Sigma/E}$, and where the system's *concurrent transitions* are axiomatized by the rules R. *Equational deduction* with the theory (Σ, E) allows for proofs of equalities $t = u$ between Σ-terms, written $(\Sigma, E) \vdash t = u$, and *rewriting logic deduction* with the theory $\mathcal{R}$ (see [29]) allows for proofs of sequents of the form $t \rightarrow v$, intuitively meaning that state t can *reach* state v after a possibly complex combination of zero, one, or more transitions, written $\mathcal{R} \vdash t \rightarrow v$. This paper is concerned with the *sufficient completeness* and *deadlock freedom* of rewrite theories $\mathcal{R}$, with automatic proof methods for checking these properties, and with the closely related topic of *constructor-based inductive reasoning* for $\mathcal{R}$.

C. Fermüller and A. Voronkov (Eds.): LPAR-17, LNCS 6397, pp. 594–609, 2010.

A Running Example. Consider the following system comprising a sender of a list of numbers, a receiver of such a list, and a communication channel through which numbers are sent to the receiver, and acknowledgments are sent back to the sender. It can be specified (with essentially self-explanatory syntax) as the following rewrite theory CHANNEL=($\Sigma_{\texttt{CHANNEL}}$, $E_{\texttt{CHANNEL}}$, $R_{\texttt{CHANNEL}}$) in the Maude rewriting logic language [9].

```
mod CHANNEL is
  sorts Nat List NilList EmptyChannel Channel Terminal State .
  subsorts NilList < List . subsorts Nat EmptyChannel < Channel . subsorts Terminal < State .
  op 0 : -> Nat [ctor metadata "rctor"] .  op s_ : Nat -> Nat [ctor metadata "rctor"] .
  op nil : -> NilList [ctor metadata "rctor"] .
  op _;_ : Nat List -> List [ctor metadata "rctor"] . op _@_ : List List -> List .
  op mt : -> EmptyChannel [ctor metadata "rctor"] .
  op ack : -> Channel [ctor metadata "rctor"] .
  op <_:_:_> : List Channel List -> State [ctor] .
  op <_:_:_> : NilList EmptyChannel List -> Terminal [ctor metadata "rctor"] .
  vars M N : Nat .  vars L L' : List .
  eq [ap01] : nil @ L = L .       eq [ap02] : (N ; L) @ L' = N ; (L @ L') .
  rl [send] : < N ; L : mt : L' > => < L : N : L' > .
  rl [recv] : < L : N : L' > => < L : ack : L' @ (N ; nil) > .
  rl [ack]  : < L : ack : L' > => < L : mt : L' > .
endm
```

Note that the type structure is *order-sorted*, with sorts sometimes including smaller subsorts, and with operators sometimes overloaded in smaller subsorts. The signature $\Sigma_{\texttt{CHANNEL}}$ is here given by the `sorts`, `subsorts`, and operator (`op`) declarations, where the list of argument sorts is followed by the result sort. The *constructor* (`ctor`) and *rewrite-constructor* (`metadata "rctor"`) declarations are essential for the sufficient completeness and inductive reasoning concepts and methods discussed below. States of this systems are (ground) terms of sort `State`, that is, ground terms of the form $< l\ :\ c\ :\ l' >$, where l is the list of numbers still to be sent by the sender, c is the current contents of the channel, and l' is the list of numbers already received by the receiver. The contents c can be either a natural number built up with 0 and the successor operator s, or the empty contents `mt`, or an acknowledgment `ack`. Lists of natural numbers are defined with the function symbols `nil`, `_;_`, and `_@_`, with `_;_` a list "cons" operator, and `_@_` a list append operator. The equations $E_{\texttt{CHANNEL}}$ are labelled `[ap0]` and `[ap1]`, and are declared with the `eq` keyword; they define the append function in the usual way. The rules $R_{\texttt{CHANNEL}}$ specifying the system's transitions are labelled `[send]`,`[recv]`, and `[ack]`, and are declared with the `rl` keyword. Rule `[send]` puts the leftmost number of the sender's list in the channel if the channel is empty, rule `[recv]` appends the number in the channel to the receiver's list and sends back an `ack`, and rule `[ack]` consumes the `ack` message and clears the channel so that a new number can be sent. Note that the sort `Terminal` is the subsort of `State` determined by those states $< l\ :\ c\ :\ l' >$ such that $l =$ `nil` and $c =$ `mt`. The intention, of course, is to characterize the terminal or final states of the system, for which no more transitions are possible.

Sufficient Completeness and Deadlock Freedom. Sufficient completeness is proved relative to a subsignature of *constructor operators*. However, since a rewrite theory comprises deduction with both equations E and rules R, in this work we argue that there are *two different notions of constructors* for $\mathcal{R}$, and therefore two different notions of sufficient completeness with quite different meanings:

1. *equational constructors*, or *E-constructors*, are specified by a subsignature $\Omega \subseteq \Sigma$, and then *E-sufficient completeness* is the usual requirement that for each sort s and each ground term $t \in T_\Sigma$ of that sort there is a ground term $u \in T_\Omega$ of sort s such that $(\Sigma, E) \vdash t = u$, and
2. *rewrite constructors*, or *$\mathcal{R}$-constructors*, are specified by a subsignature $\Upsilon \subseteq \Sigma$, and then *$\mathcal{R}$-sufficient completeness* is the different requirement that for each sort s and each ground term $t \in T_\Sigma$ of that sort there is a ground term $v \in T_\Upsilon$ of sort s such that $\mathcal{R} \vdash t \to v$.

Intuitively, *E-sufficient completeness* means that the operators in $\Sigma - \Omega$ are *fully defined* by means of the equations E, so any ground term can be proved equal by E to one where only operators in Ω are used. The `ctor` keyword is used above for this purpose. Note that the only symbol not having the `ctor` declaration is the list append operator `_@_`. Therefore, $E_{\texttt{CHANNEL}}$-sufficient completeness is the claim that `_@_` is fully defined by the equations `[ap0]` and `[ap1]`.

How should $\mathcal{R}$-sufficient completeness be intuitively understood? First of all, note that, because of rewriting logic's equality rule (see [8]), whenever there is a proof of $(\Sigma, E) \vdash t = u$ there is also a (zero-step) proof of $\mathcal{R} \vdash t \to u$. That is, since the states of $\mathcal{R}$ are E-equivalence classes of terms $[t]_E$, there is already a representative term $u \in [t]_E$ with $u \in T_\Omega$, so that E-constructors are *trivially* $\mathcal{R}$-constructors. Therefore, for $\mathcal{R}$-constructors to have any teeth, a more restrictive subsignature $\Upsilon \subseteq \Omega$ is needed, so that each ground Σ-term of a given sort reaches *nontrivially* a ground Υ-term of the same sort. $\mathcal{R}$-sufficient completeness then provides an algebraic notion of *deadlock freedom*, that is, of *proper termination*. A concurrent system design often has an intended set P of *goal states* that any computation should ultimately reach. A system is then called *deadlock-free* outside P iff all *terminal* system states belong to P. Therefore, $\mathcal{R}$-sufficient completeness implies that $\mathcal{R}$ is *deadlock free outside* T_Υ. In the `CHANNEL` example, Υ is specified by the operators having the `metadata "rctor"` declaration. Since only terms of sort `State` can be rewritten by the rules $R_{\texttt{CHANNEL}}$, the key point is that only the subsort-smallest version of the operator

```
op <_:_:_> : NilList EmptyChannel List -> Terminal [ctor metadata "rctor"] .
```

has the `metadata "rctor"` declaration. This means that every state is expected to be rewritable with $R_{\texttt{CHANNEL}}$ to one of the form $<$ `nil` : `mt` : $l >$. It is easy to see by inspection of the rules in $R_{\texttt{CHANNEL}}$ that all such states are terminal states. Section 5 shows that, conversely, all terminal states are of that form.

Automatic Proof Methods. In this work we also investigate *automatic sufficient completeness proof methods* based on equational tree automata under appropriate left-linearity assumptions, and it reports on their implementation in an extension of Maude's Sufficient Completeness Checker (SCC) [17]. The need for equational tree automata, as opposed to just standard tree automata, comes from the fact that the equations E in many rewrite theories $\mathcal{R} = (\Sigma, E, R)$ naturally decompose as a disjoint union $E = G \cup A$, where A is a set of structural axioms such as associativity, and/or commutativity, and/or identity for some operators in Σ, and the equations G are (ground) confluent and terminating modulo A.

Inductive Reasoning. It is well-known that E-constructors are essential for *inductive equational reasoning*, i.e., reasoning about the theorems satisfied by the initial algebra $\mathcal{T}_{\Sigma/E}$. For instance, in the `CHANNEL` example the `ctor` declaration for `nil` and `_;_` can be used to prove by structural induction that append is associative, i.e., that $\mathcal{T}_{\Sigma_{\texttt{CHANNEL}}/E_{\texttt{CHANNEL}}} \models (\forall l, l', l'' : \texttt{List})\, l@(l'@l'') = (l@l')@l''$. This paper shows that $\mathcal{R}$-constructors (and also E-constructors) play a similarly crucial role in reasoning about *inductive reachability properties* of the initial model $\mathcal{T}_{\mathcal{R}}$ of the rewrite theory $\mathcal{R}$, which intuitively models the states and concurrent computations of the system defined by $\mathcal{R}$. For example, it presents a detailed proof of the fact that $\mathcal{T}_{\texttt{CHANNEL}}$ satisfies the inductive ground reachability property

$$\mathcal{T}_{\texttt{CHANNEL}} \models (\forall l, l' : \texttt{List}) < l : \texttt{mt} : \texttt{nil} > \to < \texttt{nil} : \texttt{mt} : l' > \implies l = l'$$

from which it is easy to show that: (i) all sequences of numbers in the sender are fully received in order by the receiver; and (ii) the protocol terminates with the sent list in the receiver, the sender with empty list, and the channel empty. The importance of $\mathcal{R}$-constructors for inductive reasoning about *ground joinability*, that is, about the relation $\_ \downarrow_{\mathcal{R}} \_$, is also studied in this work.

Proof for all the results in this paper, as well as formal verification experiments summarized here, can be found in [32].

2 Preliminaries

2.1 Rewrite Theories and the Initial Reachability Model $\mathcal{T}_{\mathcal{R}}$

Rewriting logic [29] is parametric on the underlying equational logic. Order-sorted equational logic is used as the the underlying equational logic throughout this paper. In an order-sorted signature $\Sigma = (S, F, \leq)$, the sorts S form a poset $(S, \leq)$ and the function symbols in $F = \{F_{w,s}\}_{(w,s)\in S^* \times S}$ can be subsort overloaded. The existence of a subset $K \subseteq S$ of *top sorts* is assumed, one per connected component of $(S, \leq)$, and each operator $f \in F_{s_1 \ldots s_n, s}$ is also assumed to be declared at the level of its top sorts $f \in F_{k_1 \ldots k_n, k}$. Given a S-sorted set $X = \{X_s\}_{s\in S}$ of disjoint sets of variables, $T_\Sigma(X) = \{T_\Sigma(X)_s\}_{s\in S}$ denotes the set of Σ-terms with variables in X, and T_Σ (resp., $T_{\Sigma,s}$), the set of *ground* Σ-terms (resp., of *ground* Σ-terms of sort s). It is also assumed that if $t \in T_\Sigma(X)_s$ and $s \leq s'$, then $t \in T_\Sigma(X)_{s'}$, for all sorts $s, s' \in S$.

Definition 1. *An* (unconditional) order-sorted rewrite theory *(RT) is a tuple* $\mathcal{R} = (\Sigma, E, R)$, *where* $\mathcal{E}_{\mathcal{R}} = (\Sigma, E)$ *is an (unconditional) order-sorted equational theory, and* R *is a set of universally quantified* (unconditional) rewrite rules *of the form* $l \to r$ *with* $l, r \in T_\Sigma(X)_k$ *for some top sort* $k \in K$.

Sentences in rewriting logic are *sequents* $(\forall X)\, t \to u$, with $t, u \in T_\Sigma(X)_k$ for $k \in K$. A RT $\mathcal{R}$ *entails* a sequent $(\forall X)\, t \to u$, written $\mathcal{R} \vdash (\forall X)\, t \to u$, iff $(\forall X)\, t \to u$ can be obtained by finite application of the deduction rules in [8]. For an equality $(\forall X)\, t = u$, $\mathcal{R} \vdash (\forall X)\, t = u$ iff $\mathcal{E}_\mathcal{R} \vdash (\forall X)\, t = u$.

Definition 2 ([8]). *Given an order-sorted equational signature Σ, a Σ-*reachability model *is a pair $\mathcal{A}_\to = (\mathcal{A}, \to_\mathcal{A})$ where $\mathcal{A} = (A, \iota_\mathcal{A})$ is an (order-sorted) Σ-algebra, and $\to_\mathcal{A} = \{\to_{\mathcal{A},k}\}_{k \in K}$ is a K-indexed family of binary relations, with $\to_{\mathcal{A},k} \subseteq A_k^2$ such that $\to_{\mathcal{A},k}$ is reflexive and transitive, and for each $f \in F_{k_1 \ldots k_n, k}$, whenever $a_1 \in \mathcal{A}_{k_1}, \ldots, a_n \in \mathcal{A}_{k_n}$, and $a_i \to_{\mathcal{A}_{k_i}} a_i'$ for $1 \leq i \leq n$, then $f_\mathcal{A}(a_1, \ldots, a_n) \to_{\mathcal{A},k} f_\mathcal{A}(a_1', \ldots, a_n')$. Given a RT $\mathcal{R} = (\Sigma, E, R)$, the* initial reachability model *of $\mathcal{R}$, denoted by $\mathcal{T}_\mathcal{R} = (\mathcal{T}_{\Sigma/E}, \to_\mathcal{R})$, has the initial (Σ, E)-algebra $\mathcal{T}_{\Sigma/E}$ for its states and satisfies $[t]_E \to_\mathcal{R} [u]_E$ iff $\mathcal{R} \vdash t \to u$, for $t, u \in T_\Sigma$.*

2.2 The Canonical Reachability Model $\mathcal{C}an_\mathcal{R}$

Rewriting logic's rules of deduction [8] allow for correct reasoning about a RT $\mathcal{R} = (\Sigma, E, R)$. But because they are based on the equational deduction relation $=_E$, which is in general undecidable, it may be undecidable whether just a *one-rewrite* inference step $[t]_E \xrightarrow{1}_\mathcal{R} [u]_E$ can be taken. Furthermore, even if deduction with E is decidable, there may be an infinite number of terms in E-equivalence classes; so, an infinite search may be needed to find a term $t' \in [t]_E$ that can be rewritten with the rules in R. Therefore, the most useful rewrite theories satisfy some *executability conditions* under which the relation $\to_\mathcal{R}$ can be reduced to simpler forms of rewriting.

First, it is reasonable to have a disjoint union $E \cup A$ of sets of equations in $\mathcal{R} = (\Sigma, E \cup A, R)$, with A a collection of axioms (such as associativity, and/or commutativity, and/or identity) for which there exists a *matching algorithm modulo* A producing a finite number of A-matching substitutions. The second condition is that E should be *ground sort-decreasing*, *ground confluent*, and *ground strongly-normalizing* modulo A. This means that in the rewrite theory $\mathcal{R}_E = (\Sigma, A, \overrightarrow{E})$, where $\overrightarrow{E} = \{(\forall X)\, l \to r \mid (\forall X)\, l = r \in E\}$, with simpler rewrite relation $\to_{\mathcal{R}_E}$: (i) for each $s \in S$ and $[t]_A \in T_{\Sigma/A,s}$, $[t]_A \to_{\mathcal{R}_E} [u]_A$ implies $[u]_A \in T_{\Sigma/A,s}$, and (ii) for each sort $s \in S$ and for each $[t]_A \in T_{\Sigma/A,s}$ all maximal $\xrightarrow{1}_{\mathcal{R}_E}$-sequences beginning with $[t]_A$ terminate in a *unique* A-equivalence class $[\mathrm{can}_{\Sigma,E/A}(t)]_A \in T_{\Sigma/A,s}$, called the *$E$-canonical form* of $[t]_A$. The third condition is that the rules R should be *ground coherent* relative to the equations E modulo A [33]. Ground coherence precisely means that, in the rewrite theories $\mathcal{R}_E = (\Sigma, A, \overrightarrow{E})$ and $\mathcal{R}_R = (\Sigma, A, R)$ (which have decidable rewrite relations $\to_{\mathcal{R}_E}$ and $\to_{\mathcal{R}_R}$ because of the assumptions on A), for each A-equivalence class $[t]_A$ such that $[t]_A \xrightarrow{1}_{\mathcal{R}_R} [u]_A$ there is a rewrite $[\mathrm{can}_{\Sigma,E/A}(t)]_A \xrightarrow{1}_{\mathcal{R}_R} [v]_A$ such that $[\mathrm{can}_{\Sigma,E/A}(u)]_A = [\mathrm{can}_{\Sigma,E/A}(v)]_A$. Ground coherence means that rewriting with R modulo $E \cup A$ can be achieved by adopting the strategy of first simplifying to canonical form with E modulo A, and then applying a rule in R modulo A.

Definition 3. *$\mathcal{R} = (\Sigma, E \cup A, R)$ is called* executable *iff it satisfies the three executability conditions above.*

Proposition 1 ([8]). *Let $\mathcal{R} = (\Sigma, E \cup A, R)$ be executable, with order-sorted signature $\Sigma = (S, F, \leq)$. The* canonical reachability model *of $\mathcal{R}$ is the Σ-reachability model $\mathcal{C}an_{\mathcal{R}} = (\mathcal{C}an_{\Sigma,E/A}, \rightarrow_{\mathcal{C}an_{\mathcal{R}}})$, where (1) $\mathcal{C}an_{\Sigma,E/A}$ is the* canonical term algebra *$\mathcal{C}an_{\Sigma,E/A} = (\{\mathrm{Can}_{\Sigma,E/A,s}\}_{s\in S}, \iota_{\mathcal{C}an_{\Sigma,E/A}})$ in which for each $s \in S$, $\mathrm{Can}_{\Sigma,E/A,s} = \{[\mathrm{can}_{\Sigma,E/A}(t)]_A \in T_{\Sigma/A} \mid t \in T_{\Sigma,s}\}$, and for each $f \in F$, the equality $f_{\mathcal{C}an_{\Sigma,E/A}}([t_1]_A, \ldots, [t_n]_A) = [\mathrm{can}_{\Sigma,E/A}(f(t_1, \ldots, t_n))]_A$ defines the Σ-algebra structure $\iota_{\mathcal{C}an_{\Sigma,E/A}}$, and (2) $\rightarrow_{\mathcal{C}an_{\mathcal{R}}} = \{([\mathrm{can}_{\Sigma,E/A}(t)]_A, [\mathrm{can}_{\Sigma,E/A}(u)]_A) \mid \mathcal{R} \vdash t \rightarrow u' \wedge u' \in [\mathrm{can}_{\Sigma,E/A}(u)]_A\}$. Then, the initial reachability model $\mathcal{T}_{\mathcal{R}}$ and the canonical reachability model $\mathcal{C}an_{\mathcal{R}}$ are isomorphic (written $\mathcal{T}_{\mathcal{R}} \cong \mathcal{C}an_{\mathcal{R}}$).*

3 Sufficient Completeness and Deadlock Freedom

In this section two different notions of constructors and of sufficient completeness are proposed for an RT $\mathcal{R}$, and $\mathcal{R}$-constructors are related to deadlock freedom.

Definition 4. *Let $\mathcal{R} = (\Sigma, E, R)$ be a RT. A* constructor signature pair *for $\mathcal{R}$ is a pair (Υ, Ω) of order-sorted subsignatures $\Upsilon = (S, F_\Upsilon, \leq) \subseteq \Omega = (S, F_\Omega, \leq) \subseteq \Sigma = (S, F, \leq)$. The S-sorted set $T_\Omega = \{T_{\Omega,s}\}_{s\in S}$ is called the* set of E-constructor terms, *and the S-sorted set $T_\Upsilon = \{T_{\Upsilon,s}\}_{s\in S}$ is called the* set of $\mathcal{R}$-constructor terms.

The intuition behind E-constructor terms is that any ground Σ-term should be *provably equal* to a term in T_Ω; for $\mathcal{R}$-constructor terms is that any Σ-term should be *rewritable in a finite number of steps* to a term in T_Υ.

The notion of *sufficient completeness* of a rewrite theory $\mathcal{R}$ relative to a constructor signature pair (Υ, Ω) is that Ω are the constructors for the equations and Υ the constructor for the rules, which includes the standard concept of constructor for equational specifications as a special case.

Definition 5. *Let $\mathcal{R} = (\Sigma, E, R)$ have signature $\Sigma = (S, F, \leq)$, and let (Υ, Ω) be a constructor signature pair. $\mathcal{R}$ is called:* E-sufficiently complete *relative to Ω iff (1) $(\forall s \in S)(\forall t \in T_{\Sigma,s})(\exists u \in T_{\Omega,s})\, \mathcal{E}_{\mathcal{R}} \vdash t = u$;* $\mathcal{R}$-sufficiently complete *relative to Υ iff (2) $(\forall s \in S)(\forall t \in T_{\Sigma,s})(\exists v \in T_{\Upsilon,s})\, \mathcal{R} \vdash t \rightarrow v$; and* sufficiently complete *relative to (Υ, Ω) iff (1) and (2) hold. The constructors Ω are called* E-constructors, *and the constructors Υ are called* $\mathcal{R}$-constructors.

Note that Definition 5 makes explicit use of sort information by requiring the witnesses u and v to have sort less or equal than s. This sort requirement can be crucial, for example, when inducting on a variable x_s of sort s.

Definition 5 does not yet make any use of the executability assumptions about $\mathcal{R}$. Under such assumptions, the notion of sufficient completeness for $\mathcal{R} = (\Sigma, E \cup A, R)$ can be further sharpened by relating it to two other fundamental concepts, namely those of the canonical term algebra $\mathcal{C}an_{\Sigma,E/A}$ for $(\Sigma, E \cup A)$ (see Proposition 1) and the set $\mathrm{Norm}_{\mathcal{R}/A}$ of $\mathcal{R}$-normal forms of $\mathcal{R}$.

Definition 6. *Let $\mathcal{R} = (\Sigma, E \cup A, R)$ be executable. The S-sorted family of sets* $\mathrm{Norm}_{\mathcal{R}/A} \subseteq \mathrm{Can}_{\Sigma,E/A}$, *called the family of $\mathcal{R}$-*terminal states *of $Can_{\mathcal{R}}$, is defined for each $s \in S$ by the condition $[t]_A \in \mathrm{Norm}_{\mathcal{R}/A,s}$ iff $[t]_A \in \mathrm{Can}_{\Sigma,E/A,s}$ and $(\nexists u \in T_\Sigma)\mathcal{R} \vdash t \xrightarrow{1} u$. Call $\mathcal{R}$* ground weakly-normalizing (modulo A) *iff $(\forall t \in T_\Sigma)(\exists [v]_A \in \mathrm{Norm}_{\mathcal{R}/A})\mathcal{R} \vdash t \to v$, and* ground sort-decreasing (modulo A) *iff $[t]_A \in T_{\Sigma/A,s}$ and $[t]_A \xrightarrow{1}_{\mathcal{R}_R} [u]_A$ imply $[u]_A \in T_{\Sigma/A,s}$.*

Theorem 1. *Let $\mathcal{R} = (\Sigma, E \cup A, R)$ be executable, ground weakly-normalizing and ground sort-decreasing, and let (Υ, Ω) be a constructor signature pair. If (1) $\mathrm{Can}_{\Sigma,E/A} \subseteq T_{\Omega/A}$ and (2) $\mathrm{Norm}_{\mathcal{R}/A} \subseteq T_{\Upsilon/A}$ hold, then $\mathcal{R}$ is sufficiently complete relative to (Υ, Ω).*

By definition (see Section 1), condition (2) in Theorem 1 exactly means that $\mathcal{R}$ is *deadlock free* outside $T_{\Upsilon/A}$. Therefore, if $\mathcal{R}$ is *canonically sufficiently complete* relative to (Υ, Ω), then it is deadlock free outside $T_{\Upsilon/A}$.

Definition 7. $\mathcal{R} = (\Sigma, E \cup A, R)$ *is called* canonically sufficiently complete *relative to (Υ, Ω) iff it is executable, ground weakly-normalizing, ground sort-decreasing, and satisfies conditions (1) and (2) in Theorem 1. Furthermore, Ω is called a* signature of E-free constructors modulo A *iff $\mathrm{Can}_{\Omega,E/A} = T_{\Omega/A}$, and Υ is called a* signature of $\mathcal{R}$-terminal constructors *iff $\mathrm{Norm}_{\mathcal{R}/A} = T_{\Upsilon/A}$.*

The sets $T_{\Omega/A}$ and $T_{\Upsilon/A}$ provide respective *envelopes* containing the key sets $\mathrm{Can}_{\Sigma,E/A}$ (the set of states of $Can_{\mathcal{R}}$) and $\mathrm{Norm}_{\mathcal{R}/A}$ (the set of terminal states of $Can_{\mathcal{R}}$). Furthermore, if Ω is a signature of E-free constructors modulo A, and Υ is a signature of $\mathcal{R}$-terminal constructors, these envelopes are *tight*, in the sense that $T_{\Omega/A}$ and $T_{\Upsilon/A}$ *exactly characterize* $\mathrm{Can}_{\Sigma,E/A}$ and $\mathrm{Norm}_{\mathcal{R}/A}$, respectively.

For purposes of checking canonical sufficient completeness, as well as checking signatures of E-constructors and $\mathcal{R}$-terminal constructors for $\mathcal{R} = (\Sigma, E \cup A, R)$, it is helpful to be in a situation in which the rewrite relations induced by $\mathcal{R}$ can be jointly captured by a simpler rewriting relations.

Definition 8. *For $\mathcal{R} = (\Sigma, E \cup A, R)$, define the RTs $\mathcal{R}_E = (\Sigma, A, \overrightarrow{E})$, and $\mathcal{R}_{R \cup E} = (\Sigma, A, R \cup \overrightarrow{E})$.*

Although $\mathcal{R}_E$ and $\mathcal{R}_{R\cup E}$ ignore the semantic distinction between the equations E and the rules R of $\mathcal{R}$, under suitable executability assumptions they respectively simulate each type of deduction with $\mathcal{R}$. In particular: (i) the sets $\mathrm{Can}_{\Sigma,E/A}$ and $\mathrm{Norm}_{\mathcal{R}_E/A}$ coincide, and (ii) the sets $\mathrm{Norm}_{\mathcal{R}_{R\cup E}/A}$ and $\mathrm{Norm}_{\mathcal{R}/A}$ also coincide, even though $\mathcal{R}_{R\cup E}$ has a simpler rewrite relation than $\mathcal{R}$.

Theorem 2. *Let $\mathcal{R} = (\Sigma, E \cup A, R)$ be executable and ground sort-decreasing. Then, (1) $\mathrm{Norm}_{\mathcal{R}_E/A} = \mathrm{Can}_{\Sigma,E/A}$, and (2) $\mathrm{Norm}_{\mathcal{R}_{R\cup E}/A} = \mathrm{Norm}_{\mathcal{R}/A}$.*

4 Checking the Properties with PTA

Tree automata techniques have been used to check the sufficient completeness of equational specifications, e.g., [12,19,17]. Given a constructor signature pair

(Υ, Ω) for $\mathcal{R} = (\Sigma, E \cup A, R)$, in this section we introduce sufficient conditions under which the problems of deciding whether $\mathcal{R}$ is canonically sufficiently complete relative to (Υ, Ω), Ω is a signature of E-free constructors, and Υ is signature of $\mathcal{R}$-terminal constructors, can all be reduced to emptiness checks of languages recognized by propositional tree automata. The treatment here generalizes that of [19,17], where such automata were used to check E-sufficient completeness.

4.1 Propositional Tree Automata

Propositional Tree Automata [20] (PTA) extend traditional equational tree automata by allowing inputs to range over a many-sorted signature instead of over an unsorted signature, recognition is done modulo axioms, and an input term is accepted if its set of reachable states satisfies a given proposition.

Definition 9. *A* propositional tree automaton *is a tuple* $\mathcal{A} = (K, F, Q, \Gamma, A, \Delta)$ *where* (K, F) *is a many-sorted signature, i.e., a set* K *of sorts and a* $K^* \times K$*-indexed set* F *of function symbols,* $Q = \{Q_k\}_{k \in K}$ *is a* K*-indexed set of pairwise disjoint sets of states such that* $Q_k \cap F_{\epsilon,k'} = \emptyset$ *for each* $k, k' \in K$, $\Gamma = \{\gamma_k\}_{k \in K}$ *is a* K*-indexed set of Boolean propositions where the atoms in each* γ_k *are among the states in* Q_k, A *is a set of unconditional* (K, F)*-equational axioms, and* Δ *is a set of* transition rules *of the form* $f(p_1, \ \ldots, p_n) \to q$, *or* $p \to q$, *for some* $k \in K$, $p, q \in Q_k$, $f \in F_{k_1 \ldots k_n, k}$, *and* $p_i \in Q_{k_i}$.

A PTA $\mathcal{A}$ can be regarded as a RT $\mathcal{R}_{\mathcal{A}}$, so that $L(\mathcal{A})$, the *language accepted* by $\mathcal{A}$, can be defined in terms of reachability in $\mathcal{R}_{\mathcal{A}}$.

Definition 10. *Let* $\mathcal{A} = (K, F, Q, \Gamma, A, \Delta)$ *be a PTA, and let* $\Sigma = (K, F \cup Q, \emptyset)$, *where each* $q \in Q_k$ *is viewed as a constant of sort* $k \in K$. *Then,* $\mathcal{R}_{\mathcal{A}} = (\Sigma, A, \Delta)$ *is the* associated RT *of* $\mathcal{A}$ *and the* move relation $\to_{\mathcal{A}}$ *is the binary relation defined by* $t \to_{\mathcal{A}} u$ *iff* $[t]_A \xrightarrow{1}_{\mathcal{R}_{\mathcal{A}}} [u]_A$, *for* $t, u \in T_\Sigma$. *Let* $\mathrm{Reach}_{\mathcal{A},k} : T_\Sigma \longrightarrow \mathcal{P}(Q_k)$ *be the map* $t \mapsto \{q \in Q_k \mid \mathcal{A} \vdash t \to q\}$, *for each* $k \in K$. *Then,* $L(\mathcal{A}) = \{L(\mathcal{A})_k\}_{k \in K}$, *where* $L(\mathcal{A})_k = \{t \in T_{\Sigma,k} \mid \mathrm{Reach}_{\mathcal{A},k}(t) \models \gamma_k\}$, *and where* $\models$ *denotes the satisfaction relation of propositional logic.*

When the emptiness problem for PTA is decidable, other typical decision problems, such as inclusion, universality and intersection-emptiness are all decidable due to the Boolean closure properties of PTAs. As shown in [20], when A is any combination of associativity, commutativity and identity axioms, but excluding the case in which there is an associative but not commutative symbol in A, the emptiness problem for PTA is decidable. In the special case in which there are associative but not commutative symbols in A, machine learning techniques can be applied to create a semi-decision procedure which can always show non-emptiness, and can show emptiness under certain regularity conditions [20].

Definition 11. $\mathcal{R} = (\Sigma, A, R)$ *is* PTA-checkable *iff* $\mathcal{R}$ *is ground weakly normalizing and ground sort-decreasing,* $S_k \cap F_{\epsilon,k} = \emptyset$ *for each* $k \in K$, *the axioms* A *are any combination of associativity, commutativity and identity axioms, except for the cases in which a symbol is associative but not commutative, and every rule in* R *is of the form* $f(t_1, \ldots, t_n) \to t$, *with* $f(t_1, \ldots, t_n)$ *linear.*

4.2 Checking Canonical Sufficient Completeness

$\mathcal{R} = (\Sigma, E \cup A, R)$, with $\Sigma = (S, F, \leq)$, is *not* canonically sufficiently complete relative to the constructor signature pair (Υ, Ω) iff there is a sort $s \in S$ and a term $t \in T_{\Sigma,s}$ such that either (i) $[t]_A \in \mathrm{Norm}_{\mathcal{R}_E/A,s} - T_{\Omega/A,s}$ or (ii) $[t]_A \in \mathrm{Norm}_{\mathcal{R}_{R\cup E}/A,s} - T_{\Upsilon/A,s}$. Under PTA-checkability, canonical sufficient completeness can be reduced to an emptiness problem of PTAs by constructing two automata that accept precisely those terms $t \in T_{\Sigma,s}$ such that $[t]_A$ satisfies (i) or (ii). Theorem 3 extends to RTs Theorem 5.4.2 in [17] for equational specifications.

Theorem 3. *Let $\mathcal{R} = (\Sigma, E \cup A, R)$ be executable, ground weakly-normalizing, and ground sort-decreasing, and let (Υ, Ω) be a constructor signature pair. If $\mathcal{R}_E$ and $\mathcal{R}_{R\cup E}$ are PTA-checkable, then there are PTAs $\mathcal{A}_E$ and $\mathcal{A}_{R\cup E}$ s.t. $\mathcal{R}$ is canonically sufficiently complete relative to (Ω, Υ) iff $L(\mathcal{A}_E) = L(\mathcal{A}_{R\cup E}) = \emptyset$.*

4.3 Checking Signatures of E-Free and $\mathcal{R}$-Terminal Constructors

Recall that if $\mathcal{R} = (\Sigma, E \cup A, R)$, with signature $\Sigma = (S, F, \leq)$, is canonically sufficiently complete relative to (Υ, Ω), then Ω is an E-free constructor signature iff $(\forall s \in S)\ T_{\Omega/A,s} - \mathrm{Norm}_{\mathcal{R}_E/A,s} = \emptyset$, and Υ is an $\mathcal{R}$-terminal constructor signature iff $(\forall s \in S)\ T_{\Upsilon/A,s} - \mathrm{Norm}_{\mathcal{R}/A,s} = \emptyset$.

Theorem 4. *Let $\mathcal{R} = (\Sigma, E \cup A, R)$ be canonically sufficiently complete relative to (Υ, Ω), and with $\mathcal{R}_E$ and $\mathcal{R}_{R\cup E}$ PTA-checkable. Then there are PTAs $\mathcal{B}_E$ and $\mathcal{B}_{R\cup E}$ such that Ω is a signature of E-free constructors modulo A iff $L(\mathcal{B}_E) = \emptyset$, and Υ is a signature of $\mathcal{R}$-terminal constructors iff $L(\mathcal{B}_{R\cup E}) = \emptyset$.*

4.4 The Extended Maude Sufficient Completeness Checker

The Maude Sufficient Completeness Checker [19] (SCC) has been extended in this work to construct the automata defined in the proofs of Theorems 3 and 4, so that sufficient completeness checks, and also checks for E-free constructors and $\mathcal{R}$-terminal constructors, can be automatically handled for such RTs.

Given an executable RT $\mathcal{R} = (\Sigma, E \cup A, R)$ annotated with constructor signature pair (Υ, Ω) in the syntax of Maude and satisfying the conditions in Theorem 3, the SCC's command `scc-df` builds the automata $\mathcal{A}_E$ and $\mathcal{A}_{R\cup E}$ and checks for their emptiness. For the running example, it works as expected:

```
Maude> (scc-df CHANNEL .)
Checking sufficient completeness and deadlock freeness of CHANNEL...
Success: The equational subtheory of CHANNEL is sufficiently complete under the assumption
that it is ground weakly-normalizing, ground confluent, and ground sort-decreasing.
Success: The rewrite theory CHANNEL is deadlock-free outside rctor-terms under the assumption
that it is ground weakly-normalizing, ground sort-decreasing, and ground coherent.
```

For $\mathcal{R}$ and (Υ, Ω) as above, and under the assumption of $\mathcal{R}$ being canonically sufficiently complete relative to (Υ, Ω), the SCC's commands `free-terminal` builds the automata $L(\mathcal{B}_E)$ and $L(\mathcal{B}_{R\cup E})$ and checks for their emptiness.

```
Maude> (free-terminal CHANNEL .)
Checking freeness of constructors of CHANNEL...
Success: The equational subtheory of CHANNEL has equational free constructors under the
assumption that it is sufficiently complete, ground weakly-normalizing, ground confluent,
and ground sort-decreasing.
Success: CHANNEL has terminal constructors under the assumption that it is deadlock-free
outside rctor-terms, ground weakly-normalizing, ground sort-decreasing, and ground coherent.
```

5 Constructor-Based Inductive Reasoning

In this section we discuss the crucial role that $\mathcal{R}$-constructors and E-constructors play in inductive proofs of ground reachability and ground joinability properties for a rewrite theory $\mathcal{R}$. Due to space limitations, the discussion does *not* cover in detail either the theoretical foundations for the soundness of the inductive arguments given in the examples, or the alternative proof techniques that could be used for these properties. The aim here is more modest, namely to characterize when it is sound to use constructors in such inductive proofs, and to illustrate with the running example the key role played by constructors in such proofs.

5.1 Ground Reachability

Ground reachability is an inductive property of RTs particularly important for establishing reachability properties of concurrent systems specified by RTs, for instance, when algorithmic model checking techniques are limited. In this section we clarify the role of constructors in ground reachability proofs.

Definition 12. *Let $\mathcal{R}$ be a RT with signature $\Sigma=(S,F,\leq)$, and let $t,u \in T_\Sigma(X)_s$ for some $s \in S$. Then u is* (deductively) $\mathcal{R}$-reachable *from t iff $\mathcal{R} \vdash (\forall X)\, t \to u$, and u is* ground $\mathcal{R}$-reachable *from t, written $\mathcal{R} \Vdash (\forall X)\, t \to u$, iff $\mathcal{R} \vdash t\theta \to u\theta$ for each* ground substitution *$\theta : X \longrightarrow T_\Sigma$ (i.e., mapping $\theta : X \longrightarrow T_\Sigma$ such that $\theta(x_s) \in T_{\Sigma,s}$ for every $x_s \in X_s$).*

Reasoning in $\mathcal{R}$ about an inductive property φ requires a deduction relation $\vdash_{\text{ind}}$ with inductive inference support such that $\mathcal{R} \Vdash \varphi$ (i.e., $\mathcal{T}_\mathcal{R} \models \varphi$) if $\mathcal{R} \vdash_{\text{ind}} \varphi$.

Inductive reasoning about ground reachability for a rewrite theory $\mathcal{R}$ is somewhat subtle, because there is the risk of the target term in the reachability goal becoming a "moving" target. The problem is that rewrite sequents are not symmetric and the proofs obtained by induction over $\mathcal{R}$-constructor terms cannot be "lifted" to proofs for Ω-terms in general. A solution for this problem is to require the E-equivalence class of the target term in the reachability goal to be invariant under the substitutions used in the proof, by constraining the variables occurring in the target term. Namely, for a constructor-based structural induction proof of ground reachability to be sound, it is mandatory to consider all E-constructor terms of sort s when the induction variable occurs in the target term of the reachability goal. However, for a variable outside the target term it is enough to consider $\mathcal{R}$-constructor terms.

Theorem 5. *Let $\mathcal{R}$ have signature $\Sigma = (S, F, \leq)$, let $t, u \in T_\Sigma(X)_s$ for some $s \in S$, and let $\theta : X \longrightarrow T_\Sigma$. If $\mathcal{R}$ is sufficiently complete relative to the constructor signature pair (Υ, Ω), then there exists a ground substitution $\eta : X \longrightarrow T_\Omega$*

such that (1) $\eta(x) \in T_{\Upsilon}$ *for each* $x \in \text{Vars}(t) - \text{Vars}(u)$*, and* $\mathcal{E}_{\mathcal{R}} \vdash \theta(x) = \eta(x)$ *for each* $x \in \text{Vars}(u)$*, and (2)* $\mathcal{R} \vdash t\theta \to t\eta$*. Furthermore,* $\mathcal{R} \Vdash (\forall X)\, t \to u$ *iff* $\mathcal{R} \vdash t\eta \to u\eta$ *for each* η *as above.*

Formal Properties of CHANNEL. Recall the CHANNEL specification from Section 1, with constructor signature pair $(\Upsilon_{\texttt{CHANNEL}}, \Omega_{\texttt{CHANNEL}})$. Two key properties of CHANNEL are of particular interest:

1. *In-order reception*: every (ground) *terminal* state reachable from an *initial* state of the form $< l : \texttt{mt} : \texttt{nil} >$ preserves the order of messages, i.e.,
   $\texttt{CHANNEL} \Vdash (\forall l, l' : \texttt{List})\ < l : \texttt{mt} : \texttt{nil} > \to < \texttt{nil} : \texttt{mt} : l' > \implies l = l'.$
2. *Proper termination*: the protocol terminates in a state of sort Terminal.

Observe that, if CHANNEL is strongly-normalizing and the constructor subsignature $\Upsilon_{\texttt{CHANNEL}}$ is a signature of terminal constructors, then (1) and (2) together ensure that the protocol always terminates with successful in-order communication. Note also that (1) cannot be checked by standard model-checking algorithms because the number of ground instances of l is countably infinite.

CHANNEL is executable (see [32]), and it is sufficiently complete relative to its constructor signature pair, as was shown in Section 4. This latter fact implies that the reachability condition in (1) is not void. Two complementary proofs are required for establishing (1), namely, a proof of the *existence* of a reachable terminal state preserving the order of messages for each initial state, and a proof of the *uniqueness* of such a terminal state. Property (2) follows directly from the strong-normalization of $\texttt{CHANNEL}_{R_{\texttt{CHANNEL}} \cup E_{\texttt{CHANNEL}}}$ (see [32]), plus the fact that $\Upsilon_{\texttt{CHANNEL}}$ is a signature of terminal constructors as verified in Section 4.4.

The existence claim is a logical consequence of the following inductive claim:
$\texttt{CHANNEL} \vdash_{\text{ind}} (\forall l, l' : \texttt{List})\ < l : \texttt{mt} : l' > \to < \texttt{nil} : \texttt{mt} : l' \,@\, l > .$

Using the sufficient completeness of CHANNEL relative to the constructor signature pair $(\Upsilon_{\texttt{CHANNEL}}, \Omega_{\texttt{CHANNEL}})$, the steps of the constructor-based inductive proof are a *base case* in which the property is proved for $l = \texttt{nil}$, and an *inductive case* in which the property is proved for $l = n; \texttt{l}$, assuming there is a proof for $l = \texttt{l}$, with l a fresh "constant" of sort List. The soundness of the proof follows from Theorem 5 and the soundness of structural induction.

– *Base case.* $\texttt{CHANNEL} \Vdash < \texttt{nil} : \texttt{mt} : l' > \xrightarrow{0} < \texttt{nil} : \texttt{mt} : l' \,@\, \texttt{nil} >$, because $(\forall l : \texttt{List})\, l \,@\, \texttt{nil} = l$ inductively holds in $\mathcal{E}_{\texttt{CHANNEL}}$ (see [32]).
– *Inductive case.* Assume the property holds for $l = \texttt{l}$, where l is a "fresh" constant of sort List. Let $l = n; \texttt{l}$ with n a variable of sort Nat:

$$
\begin{array}{ll}
& < n; \texttt{l} : \texttt{mt} : l' > \\
\xrightarrow{3} & \{\ \texttt{[send]},\ \texttt{[recv]},\ \text{and}\ \texttt{[ack]}\ \} \\
& < \texttt{l} : \texttt{mt} : l' \,@\, (n; \texttt{nil}) > \\
\to & \{\ \text{induction hypothesis}\ \} \\
& < \texttt{nil} : \texttt{mt} : (l' \,@\, (n; \texttt{nil})) \,@\, l > \\
= & \{\ \text{assoc. of @ is an inductive consequence of}\ \mathcal{E}_{\texttt{CHANNEL}}\ \} \\
& < \texttt{nil} : \texttt{mt} : l' \,@\, ((n; \texttt{nil}) \,@\, l) > \\
= & \{\ \texttt{[ap01]}\ \text{and}\ \texttt{[ap02]}\ \} \\
& < \texttt{nil} : \texttt{mt} : l' \,@\, (n; l) >
\end{array}
$$

The uniqueness proof requires a ground confluence argument about CHANNEL. A RT $\mathcal{R} = (\Sigma, E \cup A, R)$ is *ground confluent* iff $\mathcal{R} \vdash t \to u$ and $\mathcal{R} \vdash t \to v$ implies $\mathcal{R} \vdash u \downarrow v$, for $t, u, v \in T_\Sigma$ (see Definition 13 in Section 5.2). A ground confluence proof for $\mathcal{R}$ is not mechanizable in general because of the undecidability of equational deduction with $E \cup A$. However, if $\mathcal{R}$ is executable and the rewrite rules $R \cup \overrightarrow{E}$ are ground sort-decreasing, ground confluent, and ground weakly-normalizing modulo A, then $\mathcal{R}$ inherits the ground confluence from $\mathcal{R}_{R\cup E}$, for which automated methods have better chances of success because of the executability assumptions on A (see Section 2.2). The key observation is that for rewrite proofs $\mathcal{R} \vdash t \to u$ and $\mathcal{R} \vdash t \to v$, there are analogous rewrite proofs $\mathcal{R}_{R\cup E} \vdash t \to \mathrm{can}_{\Sigma,E/A}(u)$ and $\mathcal{R}_{R\cup E} \vdash t \to \mathrm{can}_{\Sigma,E/A}(v)$, and since $\mathcal{R}_{R\cup E}$ is ground confluent, the $\mathcal{R}_{R\cup E}$-joinability witness for $\mathrm{can}_{\Sigma,E/A}(u)$ and $\mathrm{can}_{\Sigma,E/A}(v)$ is also a witness for the $\mathcal{R}$-joinability of u and v.

$\mathtt{CHANNEL}_{R_{\mathtt{CHANNEL}} \cup E_{\mathtt{CHANNEL}}}$ is ground sort-decreasing, ground confluent, and ground strongly normalizing (see [32]), which establishes the uniqueness proof for (1). Therefore, as desired, the CHANNEL protocol always terminates in a state of sort Terminal with successful in-order communication.

5.2 Ground Joinability

The notion of ground joinability is of great importance in the field of term rewriting and also in theorem proving, see, e.g., [31,2,23,28,3,1,5]. In particular, it is a key technique for proving ground confluence. In this section we explain how $\mathcal{R}$-constructors can be used to prove ground joinability; the reader is referred to [32] for an illustrative example of these ideas.

Definition 13. *Let $\mathcal{R}$ be a RT with signature $\Sigma = (S, F, \leq)$, and let $t, u \in T_\Sigma(X)_s$ for some $s \in S$. The terms t and u are called* (deductively) $\mathcal{R}$-joinable, *written $\mathcal{R} \vdash (\forall X)\, t \downarrow u$, iff $\exists v \in T_\Sigma(X)_s$ such that $\mathcal{R} \vdash (\forall X)\, t \to v$ and $\mathcal{R} \vdash (\forall X)\, u \to v$, and* ground $\mathcal{R}$-joinable, *written $\mathcal{R} \Vdash (\forall X)\, t \downarrow u$, iff $\mathcal{R} \vdash t\theta \downarrow u\theta$ for all ground substitutions $\theta : X \longrightarrow T_\Sigma$.*

For inductive reasoning about ground joinability the situation is easier than for ground reachability, because the lack of symmetry of rewrite sequents does not play a crucial role in this case. As shown by Theorem 6, for the constructor-based inductive proof to be sound, it is sufficient to consider all $\mathcal{R}$-constructor terms of sort s when inducting on a variable x_s.

Theorem 6. *Let $\mathcal{R}$ be a RT with signature $\Sigma = (S, F, \leq)$, and let $t, u \in T_\Sigma(X)_s$ for some $s \in S$. If $\mathcal{R}$ is sufficiently complete relative to the constructor signature pair (Υ, Ω), then $\mathcal{R} \Vdash (\forall X)\, t \downarrow u$ iff $(\forall \eta : X \longrightarrow T_\Upsilon)\, \mathcal{R} \vdash t\eta \downarrow u\eta$.*

6 Related Work

Sufficient completeness was first defined in Guttag's thesis [15]; this property is in general undecidable, even for unconditional equational specifications [15,16].

Sufficient completeness of equational specifications has been widely studied, see, e.g., [21,30,10,22,4,6,5,27]. For a good review of the literature up to the 1980s and for important (un)decidability results see [25,24]. A closely connected concept is *ground reducibility*, see, e.g., [31,25,11,26,13]. Tree automata methods have been used since the late 1980s for both sufficient completeness and ground reducibility, see, e.g., [11,13,19,6], and Chapter 4 of [12] and references there. For order-sorted and membership equational logic specifications, sufficient completeness has been studied in, e.g., [7,18,5], and for order-sorted specifications modulo axioms, including the context-sensitive case, in [19,17].

The work presented here combines and generalizes two different research strands. On the one hand, it can be seen as a natural generalization from the case of equations E to that of both equations E and rules R, of the work in [19,17] on (propositional) equational tree automata methods for checking sufficient completeness of left-linear equations modulo axioms for order-sorted specifications. On the other hand, it also generalizes the work by I. Gnaedig and H. Kirchner [14] on constructors for non-terminating rewrite systems in the following precise sense: the notion of sufficient completeness proposed in [14] exactly corresponds to that of $\mathcal{R}$-sufficient completeness in this work for the special case of a rewrite theory $\mathcal{R} = (\Sigma, \emptyset, R)$, where Σ has a single sort and there are no equations. The treatment of the more general case of rewrite theories $\mathcal{R} = (\Sigma, E \cup A, R)$ clarifies the important distinction between constructors for equations and constructors for rules, extends the ideas to the more general order-sorted case modulo axioms, and provides new *automated* tree automata techniques complementing the narrowing-based techniques proposed in [14], and, to the best of the authors' knowledge, investigates for the first time the relationship between $\mathcal{R}$-constructors and deadlock freedom, and the use of $\mathcal{R}$-constructors (and E-constructors) for inductive proofs of ground reachability.

7 Concluding Remarks and Future Work

This work has proposed notions of constructors and of sufficient completeness for rewrite theories $\mathcal{R} = (\Sigma, E, R)$, making a crucial distinction between E-constructors and $\mathcal{R}$-constructors. It has motivated why they are useful both to check that specifications are "fully defined" in their equational part, and deadlock free in their non-equational transitions. It has developed the theoretical foundations of sufficient completeness in the setting of order-sorted rewrite theories of which equations and rules are applied modulo equational axioms such as associativity and/or commutativity and/or identity. It has also shown how, except for the case of associativity without commutativity, the property is decidable by propositional tree automata under reasonable linearity assumptions, and is supported by the extension of the Maude SCC tool reported here. Finally, it has shown how $\mathcal{R}$-constructors (and E-constructors) play a crucial role in inductive proofs of ground reachability and ground joinability. All the ideas presented here, as well as the SCC tool, have been extended in [32] to the case of *generalized rewrite theories* [8] $\mathcal{R} = (\Sigma, E \cup A, R, \phi)$, where ϕ is a *frozenness map* assigning to each n-argument function symbol f in Σ a subset $\phi(f) \subseteq \{1, \ldots, n\}$ of argument positions under which rewriting with R is forbidden. This generalizes to the level of non-equational rules the analogous treatment in [19,17] of sufficient completeness for equational specifications $(\Sigma, E \cup A)$ with a *context-sensitive* rewriting map μ, with $\mu(f) \subseteq \{1, \ldots, n\}$.

As usual, much work remains ahead. Since the goal in this work has been to obtain *automatic* techniques for checking the sufficient completeness of a rewrite theory, some restrictions have been imposed, such as treating only the order-sorted case (leaving out the case of membership equational theories), and also assuming that equations and rules are left-linear and unconditional. The notion of a sufficiently complete rewrite theory is equally meaningful and useful without these restrictions. Therefore, reasoning techniques that will allow such a property to be established for more general rewrite theories should be investigated, even if such techniques are no longer automatic. The related topic of constructor-based inductive techniques for ground reachability and ground joinability has only been sketched; it deserves a more comprehensive analysis in future work, in which a detailed comparison with alternative approaches to proving such properties should also be given.

Acknowledgements. The authors would like to thank Joe Hendrix for fruitful discussions on these ideas and the SCC tool, and the anonymous referees for comments that helped to improve the paper. This work has been partially supported by NSF grants CNS 07-16638 and CCF 09-05584.

References

1. Avenhaus, J., Hillenbrand, T., Löchner, B.: On using ground joinable equations in equational theorem proving. Journal of Symbolic Computation 36(1-2), 217–233 (2003)
2. Bachmair, L., Dershowitz, N., Plaisted, D.A.: Completion without failure. In: Kaci, A.H., Nivat, M. (eds.) Resolution of Equations in Algebraic Structures. Rewriting Techniques, vol. 2, pp. 1–30. Academic Press, New York (1989)
3. Becker, K.: Proving ground confluence and inductive validity in constructor based equational specifications. In: Gaudel, M.-C., Jouannaud, J.-P. (eds.) CAAP 1993, FASE 1993, and TAPSOFT 1993. LNCS, vol. 668, pp. 46–60. Springer, Heidelberg (1993) ISBN 3-540-56610-4
4. Bouhoula, A.: Using induction and rewriting to verify and complete parameterized specifications. Theoretical Computer Science 170(1-2), 245–276 (1996)
5. Bouhoula, A.: Simultaneous checking of completeness and ground confluence for algebraic specifications. ACM Transactions on Computational Logic 10(3) (2009)
6. Bouhoula, A., Jacquemard, F.: Automated induction with constrained tree automata. In: Armando, A., Baumgartner, P., Dowek, G. (eds.) IJCAR 2008. LNCS (LNAI), vol. 5195, pp. 539–554. Springer, Heidelberg (2008)
7. Bouhoula, A., Jouannaud, J.-P., Meseguer, J.: Specification and proof in membership equational logic. Theoretical Computer Science 236(1-2), 35–132 (2000)
8. Bruni, R., Meseguer, J.: Semantic foundations for generalized rewrite theories. Theoretical Computer Science 360(1-3), 386–414 (2006)

9. Clavel, M., Durán, F., Eker, S., Lincoln, P., Martí-Oliet, N., Meseguer, J., Quesada, J.: Maude: specification and programming in rewriting logic. Theoretical Computer Science 285, 187–243 (2002)
10. Comon, H.: Sufficient completness, term rewriting systems and "anti-unification". In: Siekmann, J.H. (ed.) CADE 1986. LNCS, vol. 230, pp. 3–540. Springer, Heidelberg (1986), ISBN 3-540-16780-3
11. Comon, H.: An effective method for handling initial algebras. In: Grabowski, J., Wechler, W., Lescanne, P. (eds.) ALP 1988. LNCS, vol. 343, pp. 108–118. Springer, Heidelberg (1989), ISBN 3-540-50667-5
12. Comon, H., Dauchet, M., Gilleron, R., Löding, C., Jacquemard, F., Lugiez, D., Tison, S., Tommasi, M.: Tree automata techniques and applications (2007)
13. Comon, H., Jacquemard, F.: Ground reducibility is EXPTIME-complete. Information and Computation 187(1), 123–153 (2003)
14. Gnaedig, I., Kirchner, H.: Computing constructor forms with non terminating rewrite programs. In: Bossi, A., Maher, M.J. (eds.) PPDP, pp. 121–132. ACM, New York (2006) ISBN 1-59593-388-3
15. Guttag, J.: The Specification and Application to Programming of Abstract Data Types. PhD thesis, University of Toronto, Computer Science Department (1975)
16. Guttag, J.V., Horning, J.J.: The algebraic specification of abstract data types. Acta Informatica 10, 27–52 (1978)
17. Hendrix, J.: Decision Procedures for Equationally Based Reasoning. PhD thesis, University of Illinois at Urbana-Champaign (April 2008)
18. Hendrix, J., Clavel, M., Meseguer, J.: A sufficient completeness reasoning tool for partial specifications. In: Giesl, J. (ed.) RTA 2005. LNCS, vol. 3467, pp. 165–174. Springer, Heidelberg (2005), ISBN 3-540-25596-6
19. Hendrix, J., Meseguer, J.: On the completeness of context-sensitive order-sorted specifications. In: Baader, F. (ed.) RTA 2007. LNCS, vol. 4533, pp. 229–245. Springer, Heidelberg (2007), ISBN 978-3-540-73447-5
20. Hendrix, J., Ohsaki, H., Viswanathan, M.: Propositional tree automata. In: Pfenning, F. (ed.) RTA 2006. LNCS, vol. 4098, pp. 50–65. Springer, Heidelberg (2006), ISBN 3-540-36834-5
21. Huet, G.P., Hullot, J.-M.: Proofs by induction in equational theories with constructors. In: FOCS, pp. 96–107. IEEE, Los Alamitos (1980)
22. Jouannaud, J.-P., Kounalis, E.: Automatic proofs by induction in theories without constructors. Information and Computation 82(1), 1–33 (1989)
23. Kapur, D., Narendran, P., Otto, F.: On ground-confluence of term rewriting systems. Information and Computation 86(1), 14–31 (1990)
24. Kapur, D., Narendran, P., Rosenkrantz, D.J., Zhang, H.: Sufficient-completeness, ground-reducibility and their complexity. Acta Informatica 28(4), 311–350 (1991)
25. Kapur, D., Narendran, P., Zhang, H.: On sufficient-completeness and related properties of term rewriting systems. Acta Informatica 24(4), 395–415 (1987)
26. Kounalis, E.: Testing for the ground (co-)reducibility property in term-rewriting systems. Theoretical Computer Science 106(1), 87–117 (1992)
27. Lazrek, A., Lescanne, P., Thiel, J.-J.: Tools for proving inductive equalities, relative completeness, and omega-completeness. Information and Computation 84(1), 47–70 (1990)
28. Martin, U., Nipkow, T.: Ordered rewriting and confluence. In: Stickel, M.E. (ed.) CADE 1990. LNCS, vol. 449, pp. 366–380. Springer, Heidelberg (1990), ISBN 3-540-52885-7
29. Meseguer, J.: Conditional rewriting logic as a unified model of concurrency. Theoretical Computer Science 96(1), 73–155 (1992)

30. Nipkow, T., Weikum, G.: A decidability result about sufficient-completeness of axiomatically specified abstract data types. In: Cremers, A.B., Kriegel, H.-P. (eds.) GI-TCS 1983. LNCS, vol. 145, pp. 257–268. Springer, Heidelberg (1982), ISBN 3-540-11973-6
31. Plaisted, D.: Semantic confluence tests and completion methods. Information and Control 65, 182–215 (1985)
32. Rocha, C., Meseguer, J.: Constructors, sufficient completeness and deadlock freedom of generalized rewrite theories. Technical report, University of Illinois at Urbana-Champaign (2010)
33. Viry, P.: Equational rules for rewriting logic. Theoretical Computer Science 285, 487–517 (2002)

PBINT, A Logic for Modelling Search Problems Involving Arithmetic

Shahab Tasharrofi and Eugenia Ternovska

Simon Fraser University, Canada
{sta44,ter}@cs.sfu.ca

Abstract. Motivated by computer science challenges, Grädel and Gurevich [13] suggested to extend the approach and methods of finite model theory beyond finite structures, an approach they called Metafinite Model Theory. We develop this direction further, in application to constraint specification/modelling languages. Following [27], we use a framework based on embedded model theory, but with a different background structure, the structure of arithmetic which contains at least $(\mathbb{N}; 0, 1, +, \times, <, || \; ||)$, where $||x||$ returns the size of the binary encoding of x. We prove that on these structures, we can *unconditionally* capture NP using a variant of a guarded logic. This improves the result of [27] (and thus indirectly [13]) by eliminating the small cost condition on input structures.

As a consequence, our logic (an idealized specification language) allows one to represent common arithmetical problems such as integer factorization or disjoint scheduling naturally, with built-in arithmetic, as opposed to using a binary encoding. Thus, this result gives a remedy to a problem with practical specification languages, namely that there are common arithmetical problems that can be decided in NP but cannot be axiomatized naturally in current modelling languages. We give some examples of such axiomatizations in PBINT and explain how our result applies to constraint specification/modelling languages.

1 Introduction

This paper shows an application of descriptive complexity [17,12] to developing foundations of constraint specification/modelling languages, a sub-area of AI. Such languages are developed in several communities, have associated solvers, and are intended as universal languages for search problems in some complexity classes, usually NP (e.g. scheduling, planning, etc.). Examples include languages and systems of Answer Set Programming [25,10], modelling languages from the CP community such as ESSENCE [9], or the language of the IDP system[1] [29]. These languages do not closely correspond to FO logic – they often contain inductive definitions and built-in arithmetic. Designers usually focus on the convenience of the language, and rarely pay attention to the expressiveness. For each language, several tasks can be studied – satisfiability and model checking are among them. Here, since we are interested in search problems, we focus on the task of *model expansion (MX)*, the logical task of expanding a given structure with new relations. The user axiomatizes their problem in some logic $\mathcal{L}$ (a specification/modelling language). The task of model expansion for $\mathcal{L}$ (abbreviated $\mathcal{L}$-MX), is:

[1] A language and system based on FO(ID), an extension of first-order logic with inductive definitions under well-founded semantics, see [7].

C. Fermüller and A. Voronkov (Eds.): LPAR-17, LNCS 6397, pp. 610–624, 2010.

Model Expansion for logic $\mathcal{L}$

Given: *1.* An $\mathcal{L}$-formula ϕ with vocabulary $\sigma \cup \varepsilon$
2. A structure $\mathcal{A}$ for σ
Find: an expansion of $\mathcal{A}$, to $\sigma \cup \varepsilon$, that satisfies ϕ.

Thus, we expand the structure $\mathcal{A}$ with relations and functions to interpret ε, obtaining a model $\mathcal{B}$ of ϕ. The complexity of this task obviously lies in-between that of model checking (the entire structure is given) and satisfiability (no part of a structure is given). In the *combined setting* an instance consists of a structure together with a formula. We focus here on *data complexity*, where the formula is fixed and the input consists of an instance structure only. We call σ, the vocabulary of $\mathcal{A}$, the *instance* vocabulary, and $\varepsilon := vocab(\phi) \setminus \sigma$ the *expansion* vocabulary.

Remark 1. Since FO MX can specify exactly the problems that $\exists$SO can, one might ask why we don't stick with the standard notion of $\exists$SO model checking. Primarily it is because we rarely use pure FO, and because for each language $\mathcal{L}$, MX is just one among several tasks of interest.

Descriptive complexity [17] and metafinite model theory [13,12] can find applications in constraint modelling languages. The authors of [21] emphasized the importance of the property of *capturing NP* and other complexity classes for such languages. The capturing property is of fundamental importance as it shows that, for a given language:
(a) *we can express all of NP* – giving the user an assurance of universality of the language for a given complexity class,
(b) *no more than NP can be expressed* – thus solving can be achieved by means of constructing a universal polytime reduction to an NP complete problem such as SAT or CSP. This reduction is called propositionalization or *grounding*.
The authors proposed to take the capturing property as a *fundamental guarding principle* in the development and study of declarative programming for search problems in this complexity class, and started careful development of foundations of modelling languages of search problems based on extensions and fragments of first-order (FO) logic. While the current focus is on the complexity class NP, by no means, do we suggest that the expressive power of the languages for search problems should be *limited* to NP. Our goal is to design languages for non-specialist users who may have no knowledge of complexity classes. The users will be given a simple syntax within which they are *safe*, and they would be encouraged to express their problems in that syntax.

The classic Fagin's theorem [8], relating $\exists$SO and NP, states that parameterized (formula is fixed) FO MX captures NP. However, FO lacks many features needed for practical specification languages such as a built-in support for arithmetic. Fagin's theorem allows one to represent all problems in NP, however, there is no direct way to deal with numbers and operations on them since in logic we have abstract domain elements. Therefore, problems involving numbers have to encode their inputs and outputs using elements of the domain. A usable logic for these problems would use standard arithmetic, as in all realistic modelling languages.

A solution, inspired by a previous proposal [13], was given in [27]. There, MX ideas were extended to *embedded MX* to provide mathematical foundation for dealing with infinite arithmetic structure with $\times, +, <$, etc., and aggregate functions (min, sum etc.), operations that are considered "built-in". The authors needed a method for handling operations with outputs outside of the input domain, as is common in practical languages. They also desired universal quantification over integers since it is convenient and is used in practice. Access to the arithmetical structure through weight terms as in [13] was not sufficient. They defined two new logics, GGF_k and DGGF_k. The former is an extension of the k-guarded fragment of FO (or FO(ID)), in which instance predicates are used as guards of quantifiers and expansion predicates (here, GG stands for double-guarded, not for [13]). DGGF_k, is an extension of GGF_k in which definable guards are allowed, provided they are polysize in the domain size. The extension allows for quantifying over variables whose values fall outside of the input domain. It was proven that, under a small-cost condition, NP is captured for both fragments. That is, (a) for every problem in NP (represented by a class of logical structures) there is a specification in the logic such that an instance (a structure) is in the class iff there is an expansion of that structure that satisfies the specification; and (b) for every specification in the logic, the task of MX is in NP. The small cost condition says that values of the input numbers cannot be bigger than $2^{poly(n)}$, where $poly(n)$ is some polynomial in the size n of the domain.

The two fragments provide natural axiomatizations (that do not involve binary encodings) but have two limitations:

(1) Poly-size guards are too limiting. Suppose we want to output the total weight of all items in a $Knapsack$ (an expansion predicate). A natural axiom would be: $\exists x\ (G(x) \land Output(x) \land x = \Sigma_y(\ Weight(y)\ :\ Knapsack(y))$. We cannot use a polysize guard G: there are up to 2^n distinct sums, where n is the size of the domain.
(2) Small cost condition cannot be satisfied in natural axiomatizations of some common problems in NP such as integer factorization or a quadratic programming problem: given m, a, c find x such that $x^2 = a \pmod{m} \land x > c$.

The values of the given integers, m and a, are, in general, unlimited in the size of the input domain, which is 3.

As we show in [26], several practical modelling languages, including the system languages of ASP and IDP, meet the same challenges regarding the small cost condition. Both these languages capture NP over small cost arithmetical structures and, also, none of these languages can axiomatize factorization or the quadratic residue problem (two prominent non-small cost problems) using their built-in arithmetic. Although we did not discuss it in [26], the same analysis applies to some other system languages such as NP-SPEC [3] to show that their built-in arithmetic has limited expressibility.

Here, we introduce a new logic, PBINT, which is suitable for modelling problems that involve arithmetic as it eliminates the small cost condition and captures NP for all problems involving arithmetic. The logic can be viewed as an idealized specification/modelling language. PBINT uses a different background structure than that of [27], namely the structure containing at least $(\mathbb{N}; 0, 1, +, \times, <, ||\ ||)$, among other polytime relations. PBINT eliminates the two drawbacks above while retaining three important features:

- **Natural logic.** All problems with arithmetical operations can be axiomatized naturally (without e.g. binary encodings and with quantifiers over numbers).
- **Capturing NP**. The result is due to a new kind of existential and upper guards, and a slightly different set of allowable arithmetic operations.
- **Polytime Grounding**. The grounding time is polynomial in the size of the binary encoding of the input structure (not necessarily in the domain size).

2 Background: MX with Arithmetic

Throughout the paper, we use $:=$ for "denotes", $\Rightarrow$ for material implication, and $\exists\bar{x}$ for $\exists x_1 \ldots \exists x_n$, similarly for $\forall\bar{x}$.

Embedded MX. Embedded finite model theory (see [19]), the study of finite structures whose domain is drawn from some infinite structure, was introduced to study databases that contain numbers and numerical constraints. Rather than think of a database as a finite structure, we take it to be a set of finite relations over an infinite domain.

Definition 1. *A structure $\mathcal{A}$ is* embedded *in an infinite* background *(or* secondary*) structure $\mathcal{M} = (U; \bar{M})$ if it is a structure $\mathcal{A} = (U; \bar{R})$ with a finite set $\bar{R}$ of finite relations and functions, where $\bar{M} \cap \bar{R} = \emptyset$. The set of elements of U that occur in some relation of $\mathcal{A}$ is the* active domain of $\mathcal{A}$, *denoted $adom_{\mathcal{A}}$.*

Example 1. Consider a company database with a table containing employee numbers, salaries and pension plans. This database is a finite structure embedded in the infinite background structure of the natural numbers with the standard arithmetic operations. Queries over embedded databases may use the database relations and the arithmetical operations whose interpretation is provided by the infinite background structure. E.g. the following query (a FO formula with free variable x) returns people whose total salary and pension plan contribution is above \$100,000: $\exists s \exists p\, (empl(x, s, p) \wedge s + p \geq \$100,000)$.

In database research, embedded structures are used with logics for expressing queries. Here, we use them similarly, with logics for MX specifications. Throughout, we use the following conventions: σ denotes the vocabulary of the embedded structure $\mathcal{A} = (\mathcal{U}; \bar{\mathcal{R}})$, which is the instance structure; ν denotes the vocabulary of an infinite background structure $\mathcal{M} = (U; \bar{M})$; ε is an expansion vocabulary; $\bar{R}$ and $\bar{M}$ always denote the interpretations of σ and ν, respectively. We treat $\bar{R}$ and $\bar{M}$ as tuples or as sets, depending on the context. A formula ϕ over $\sigma \cup \nu \cup \varepsilon$ constitutes an MX specification. The model expansion task remains the same: expand a (now embedded) σ-structure to satisfy ϕ.

A Logic for Embedded MX: Double-guarded logic. Just as [27], we use a guarded logic in an embedded setting, which allows us to quantify over elements of the background structure (unlike, e.g. [13]). Again, we use an adaptation of the guarded fragment GF_k of FO [11]. In formulas of GF_k, a conjunction of up to k atoms acts as a *guard* for each quantified variable.

Definition 2. *The* k-guarded fragment GF_k *of FO (with respect to* σ*) is the smallest set of formulas that:*

1. *contains all atomic formulas;*
2. *is closed under Boolean operations;*
3. *contains* $\exists \bar{x}\ (G_1 \wedge \ldots \wedge G_m \wedge \phi)$, *provided the* G_i *are atomic formulas of* σ, $m \leq k$, $\phi \in GF_k$, *and each free variable of* ϕ *appears in some* G_i.
4. *contains* $\forall \bar{x}\ (G_1 \wedge \ldots \wedge G_m \supset \phi)$ *provided the* G_i *are atomic formulas of* σ, $m \leq k$, $\phi \in GF_k$, *and each free variable of* ϕ *appears in some* G_i.
   For a formula $\psi := \exists \bar{x}\ (G_1 \wedge \ldots \wedge G_m \wedge \phi)$, *conjunction* $G_1 \wedge \ldots \wedge G_m$ *is called the* existential guard *of the tuple of quantifiers* $\exists \bar{x}$; universal guard *is defined similarly.*

Example 2. Let ε be $\{E_1, E_2\}$. The following formula is not guarded: $\forall x \forall y\ (E_1(x, y) \supset E_2(x, y))$. It is guarded when E_1 is replaced by P which is not in ε. The following formula is the standard encoding of the temporal formula $Until(P_1, P_2)$: $\exists v_2\ (R(v_1, v_2) \wedge P_2(v_2) \wedge \forall v_3\ (R(v_1, v_3) \wedge R(v_3, v_2) \supset P_1(v_3)))$. The formula is 2-guarded, i.e., is in GF_2, but it is not 1-guarded.

The guards of GF_k are used to restrict the range of quantifiers. We also use "upper guard" axioms, which restrict the elements in expansion relations to those occurring in the interpretation of guard atoms. To formalize this, we introduce the following restriction of FO, denoted $\mathrm{GGF}_k(\varepsilon)$.

Definition 3. *The double-guarded fragment* $\mathrm{GGF}_k(\varepsilon)$ *of FO, for a given vocabulary* ε, *is the set of formulas of the form* $\phi \wedge \psi$, *with* $\varepsilon \subset vocab(\phi \wedge \psi)$, *where* ϕ *is a formula of* GF_k, *and* ψ *is a conjunction of* upper guard axioms, *one for each symbol of* ε *occurring in* ψ, *of the form* $\forall \bar{x}\ (E(\bar{x}) \supset G_1(\bar{x}_1) \wedge \cdots \wedge G_m(\bar{x}_m))$, *where* $m \leq k$, *and the union of free variables in the* G_i *is precisely* $\bar{x}$.

We call the guards of GF_k, that restrict the range of quantifiers, *lower guards*, and the guards from Def. 3 *upper guards*. Upper guards on expansion functions are discussed later. In GGF_k, all upper and lower guards are from the instance vocabulary σ, so ranges of quantifiers and expansion predicates are explicitly limited to $adom_{\mathcal{A}}$. In DGGF_k, this restriction is relaxed, adding a mechanism for "user-defined" guard relations that may contain elements outside $adom_{\mathcal{A}}$. The authors assume that the instance vocabulary always contains the predicate symbol $adom_{\mathcal{A}}$, which always denotes the active domain. Then $adom_{\mathcal{A}}(x)$ can be used as a guard atom (upper or lower)[2]. Guards provide a logical formalization of some aspects of the type systems of some existing constraint modelling languages [22]. Lower guards correspond to declaring the types of variables, and upper guards to declaring the types of expansion predicates.

So far, we explained how *formulas* are constructed. To finish definition of the logic, we need to define well-formed terms. This definition depends in the vocabulary of the background structure. The authors of [27] used *arithmetical structures*, same as [13].

[2] The relation which corresponds to the active domain is definable with respect to each instance structure, but the defining FO formula requires disjunctions, thus cannot be used as a guard and the predicate symbol $adom_{\mathcal{A}}(x)$ is necessary.

Arithmetical Structure In addition to standard arithmetical operators, it has a collection of *multiset operations*, including max, min, sum and product.

Definition 4. *An* Arithmetical structure *is a structure $\mathcal{N}$ containing at least* $(\mathbb{N}; 0, 1, \chi, <, +, \cdot, min, max, \Sigma, \Pi)$, *with domain* $\mathbb{N}$, *the natural numbers, and where* min, max, Σ, *and* Π *are multiset operations and* $\chi[\phi](\bar{x})$ *is the characteristic function. Other functions, predicates, and multiset operations may be included, provided every function and relation of* $\mathcal{N}$ *is polytime computable.*

Well-formed terms are defined over $\nu \cup \sigma \cup \varepsilon$ by induction, as usual. The details are not important here. The authors of [27] proved that, using operations mentioned above, the MX task for logics GGF_k and DGGF_k and for structures embedded in arithmetical structures captures NP under small cost condition.

3 Logic PBINT

The first step towards eliminating the limitations of the previous logics is to use a different background structure.

Definition 5. *A* Compact Arithmetical structure *is a structure* $\mathcal{N}^c$ *containing at least* $(\mathbb{N}; 0, 1, +, \times, <, || \; ||)$ *with domain* $\mathbb{N}$, *the natural numbers, where* 0, 1, $+$, $\times$ *and* $<$ *have their usual meaning and* $||x||$ *returns the size of binary encoding of number* x, *i.e.,* $||x|| = 1 + \lfloor log_2(x+1) \rfloor$. *Other functions, predicates, and multi-set operations* (min, max *etc.) may be included, provided every function and relation of* $\mathcal{N}^c$ *is polytime computable.*

Our capturing results in Section 4 remain valid even when the background structure's domain changes from $\mathbb{N}$ to $\mathbb{Z}$ (although a more detailed proof would be needed).

Requirements on σ. As before, we consider embedded MX, but the embedding is into the compact arithmetical structure. We make some assumptions about the instance vocabulary σ. It contains predicate $adom_{\mathcal{A}}$ and a constant $SIZE$. The constant $SIZE$ is equal to $|adom_{\mathcal{A}}| \times S$ where $|adom_{\mathcal{A}}|$ is the number of elements in the active domain and S is the size of binary encoding of the maximum element of the active domain. In other words, $SIZE$ upper-bounds the number of bits needed to encode (in binary) the input structure $\mathcal{A}$ embedded in $\mathcal{N}^c$. We also need a constant $default$ denoting a particular default value needed in upper guards on functions. Its meaning is specified by the user.

Logic PBINT. We introduce a new logic, PBINT, standing for Polynomially Bounded Integers. This logic is a variant of the double-guarded logic except we use compact arithmetical structures and allow functions in σ and ε, or new kinds of guards, with more freedom in existential and upper guards on the outputs of expansion functions. The three forms of guards in PBINT are as follows:

1. **Instance Guards** are instance predicates (including $adom_{\mathcal{A}}$) interpreted by the instance structure $\mathcal{A}$. Note that, although we do not require it to be so, all specifications can be rewritten to only use $adom_{\mathcal{A}}$ as a guard.

2. **Polynomial Range Guards** are relations of the form $p(SIZE) \leq x \leq p'(SIZE)$ with p and p' two polynomials.
3. **PBINT Guards** are relations of the form $||x|| \leq poly(SIZE)$ where $poly(SIZE)$ is a polynomial depending only on the constant $SIZE$.

Instance guards and polynomial range guards define ranges of size at most polynomial in the binary encoding size of structure. However, PBINT guards can define ranges with exponentially many different integers. For example, condition $||x|| \leq SIZE$ is equivalent to $x \leq 2^{SIZE-1} - 1$, exponential the in value of $SIZE$. Also note that guards definable by stratifiable inductive definitions with (1), (2) as the base cases can be added without changing our results.

Definition 6 (logic PBINT). *We define our logic as follows.*
Background Structure: *the compact arithmetical structure.*
Terms *are constructed as usual over $\nu \cup \sigma \cup \varepsilon$.*
Formulas:

(a) **Upper Guards**
   i. *Expansion* relations *are upper-guarded by instance or polynomial range guards.*
   ii. *An expansion* function *f has an upper guard axiom of the form $\forall \bar{x} \forall y \; (f(\bar{x}) = y \Rightarrow (G(\bar{x}, y) \vee y = default))$ where $G(\bar{x}, y)$ is a conjunction of guards jointly guarding variables $\bar{x}$ and y so that $\bar{x}$ is upper-guarded by instance or polynomial range guards and y is upper-guarded by any of the three types of guards.*

(b) **Lower Guards**
   i. *Existential guards: any of the three types of guards.*
   ii. *Universal guards: instance or polynomial range guards.*

The upper guards on expansion functions need the $y = default$ disjunct to keep the upper guard meaningful. Otherwise, any expansion function would have its input restricted by a guard $G(\bar{x}, y)$ which is in contradiction to the totality of functions (therefore making the specification outright false).

A similar problem happens when instance functions are allowed: the usual definition of active domain becomes meaningless because a function is total and thus defined on all the integers making the active domain equal to $\mathbb{N}$. While it is possible to disallow the instance functions, it is certainly not desirable for any nice practical logic. Therefore, we choose to allow instance functions, but to require them to have upper guards and the "default" value for inputs outside of the intended range, just as for expansion functions. Active domain now contains all elements of the universe contained in all instance relations, together with all elements in the ranges of the instance functions. This trick also enables us to ensure that both instance and expansion functions have finite (also polynomial size) representation.

Example 3 (Disjoint Scheduling). Given a set of Tasks, $t_1, \cdots, t_n$ and a set of constraints, find a schedule that satisfies all the constraints. Each task t_i has an earliest starting time $EST(t_i)$, a latest ending time $LET(t_i)$ and a length $L(t_i)$. There are also two predicates $P(t_i, t_j)$, that says task t_i should end before task t_j starts, and $D(t_i, t_j)$, which means that the two tasks t_i and t_j cannot overlap. We are asked to find two functions $start(t_i)$ and $end(t_i)$ satisfying the given conditions.

In PBINT, we axiomatize this problem as follows: Instance vocabulary σ consists of symbols EST, LET, L, $Task$, P and D. Expansion vocabulary consists of two functions $start$ and end which are upper-guarded as follows:

$$\begin{aligned}&\forall t \forall s\, (start(t) = s \Rightarrow\\&\quad (Task(t) \wedge ||s|| \leq SIZE) \vee s = default),\\&\forall t \forall e\, (end(t) = e \Rightarrow\\&\quad (Task(t) \wedge ||e|| \leq SIZE) \vee e = default).\end{aligned}$$

The following sentences axiomatize the problem statement:

$$\begin{aligned}&\forall t_i\, (Task(t_i) \Rightarrow start(t_i) \geq EST(t_i)),\\&\forall t_i\, (Task(t_i) \Rightarrow end(t_i) \leq LET(t_i)),\\&\forall t_i\, (Task(t_i) \Rightarrow start(t_i) + L(t_i) = end(t_i)),\\&\forall t_i \forall t_j\, (P(t_i, t_j) \Rightarrow end(t_i) \leq start(t_j)),\\&\forall t_i \forall t_j\, (D(t_i, t_j) \Rightarrow\\&\quad end(t_i) \leq start(t_j) \vee end(t_j) \leq start(t_i)).\end{aligned}$$

In a practical language, usually upper and lower guards are defined by types and need not be given explicitly. For example, here, the predicate $Task$ is a type and functions $start$ and end are functions from the type $Task$ to integer type. So, predicate $Task$ disappears from the above sentences.

Now, let us compare how this problem is axiomatized under small cost condition. Note that this class of structures dissatisfies the small cost condition because values in a structure, e.g. $LET(t_i)$, are not related to the domain size, i.e., the number of tasks. So, another class of structures is needed here. One general choice would be to encode all numbers in binary. For example, instead of function EST, there will be predicate $EST'(t_i, j)$ for which, $EST(t) = n$ iff $n = \Sigma_k(2^k : EST'(t, k))$. To simplify, let us also assume that there is a unary relation B defining the set of bit indices, e.g. all values appearing in the second position of a tuple in EST' are in B. Also, assume that 0 is the minimum value in B and that if $p > 0$ is in B, so is $p - 1$. Now that we are no longer working on "built-in" numbers, numerical operations have to be axiomatized. For example, formula $start(t_i) \leq EST(t_i)$ is replaced by: (all quantified variables below are lower-guarded by B)

$$\begin{aligned}&E(0) \vee \exists k\, (\neg start'(t_i, k) \wedge EST'(t_i, k) \wedge E(k+1)),\\&E(k) := \forall k'\, (k' \geq k \Rightarrow (start'(t_i, k) \Leftrightarrow EST'(t_i, k))).\end{aligned}$$

Other inequalities in the above axioms are replaced by similar formulas. The addition operator in $start(t_i) + L(t_i) = end(t_i)$ is axiomatized as follows: (all quantifiers are lower-guarded by B and operator $\oplus$ stands for logical xor)

$$\begin{aligned}&\forall k\, (start(t_i, k) \oplus L(t_i, k) \oplus C(k) \Leftrightarrow end(t_i, k)),\\&C(k) :=\\&\quad \exists k'\, (L(t_i, k') \wedge start(t_i, k') \wedge k' < k \wedge CF(k, k')),\\&CF(k, k') :=\\&\quad \forall k''\, (k' < k < k'' \Rightarrow L(t_i, k'') \vee start(t_i, k'')).\end{aligned}$$

The first axiomatization is incomparably more natural.

Example 4 (Factorization). You are given a number n and asked to find some nontrivial factorization for n. Here, σ only has constant n and ϵ only has constants p and q which are upper-guarded as follows $||p|| \leq SIZE$ and $||q|| \leq SIZE$ where $||c|| \leq SIZE$ abbreviates $\forall m\ (c = m \Rightarrow ||m|| \leq SIZE)$ in case of zero-ary (constant) expansion functions. Now, the axiomatization is:

$$p > 1 \wedge p < n \wedge q > 1 \wedge q < n \wedge p \times q = n.$$

Example 5 (Quadratic Residues). You are given numbers r, n and c and asked to find a number x such that $x^2 \equiv r \pmod{n}$ and $x < c$. Here, instance vocabulary consists of constants n, r and c and expansion vocabulary only has constant x upper-guarded by sentence $||x|| \leq SIZE$. The axiomatization consists of two sentences $0 \leq x \wedge x \leq c \wedge x < n$ and $\exists q\ (||q|| \leq SIZE \wedge x \times x = q \times n + r)$.

Both Factorization and Quadratic Residue problems would have to be axiomatized in binary in the logics of [27].

4 Capturing NP

Theorem 1. *Let $\mathcal{K}$ be an isomorphism-closed class of compact arithmetical embedded structures over vocabulary σ. Then the following are equivalent:*

1. *$\mathcal{K} \in NP$,*
2. *there is a PBINT sentence ϕ of a vocabulary $\tau = \sigma \cup \nu \cup \varepsilon$, such that $\mathcal{A} \in \mathcal{K}$ iff there exists an expansion $\mathcal{B}$ of $\mathcal{A}$ with $\mathcal{B} \models \phi$.*

The proof for the two different directions of this theorem are given in separate subsections. But, first, we introduce a characterization for PTIME due to Bellantoni and Cook [1] which is needed for our proof of (1) $\Rightarrow$ (2).

4.1 Bellantoni-Cook Characterization of PTIME

We briefly describe a functional language introduced by Bellantoni and Cook [1] which captures polytime functions. It has originally been defined to work on strings in $\{0,1\}^*$. But, as such strings encode numbers, we have reformulated the operations in numerical terms.

Functions in Bellantoni-Cook form have two sets of parameters separated by a semi-colon. Parameters to the left of semicolon are called "normal" inputs and those to its right are "safe" inputs. This separation disables the possibility of introducing recursions whose depth depend on the result of other recursions. This property is essential to prove that such functions are poly-time computable. Here are the constructs:

1. Zero: $Z(;) = 0$.
2. Projections $\pi_j^{n,m}(x_1, \cdots, x_n; x_{n+1}, \cdots, x_{n+m}) = x_j$.
3. Successors $S_0(;a) = 2 \times a,\ S_1(;a) = 2 \times a + 1$.
4. Modulo 2: $M(;a) = a \bmod 2$.

5. Predecessor: $P(;a) = \lfloor \frac{a}{2} \rfloor$.
6. Conditional: $C(;a,b,c) =$ **if** $2|a$ **then** b **else** c.
7. Safe recursion that defines $n+1$-ary function f based on n-ary function g and the $n+2$-ary functions h_0 and h_1:

$$
\begin{aligned}
&f(0,\overline{x};\overline{y}) = g(\overline{x};\overline{y}),\\
&f(2a,\overline{x};\overline{y}) = h_0(a,\overline{x};\overline{y},f(a,\overline{x};\overline{y})),\\
&f(2a+1,\overline{x};\overline{y}) = h_1(a,\overline{x};\overline{y},f(a,\overline{x};\overline{y})).
\end{aligned}
$$

8. Safe composition that defines function f based on functions $r_0,\cdots,r_{k+k'}$:

$$
\begin{aligned}
&f(\bar{x};\bar{y}) =\\
&\quad r_0(r_1(\bar{x};),...,r_k(\bar{x};);r_{k+1}(\bar{x};\bar{y}),...,r_{k+k'}(\bar{x};\bar{y})).
\end{aligned}
$$

This language interests us as it is a purely syntactic characterization of PTIME which is based on numbers. Furthermore, the language is free of any unnatural functions for bounding growth of numbers.

Bellantoni-Cook's theorem says that any function defined in this form is PTIME and that for any PTIME computable function $f(\overline{a})$, there is a function $f'(w;\overline{a})$ such that $f(\overline{a}) = f'(w;\overline{a})$ for all a's and for all w's satisfying $||w|| \geq p_f(\overline{||a||})$ (where $||x||$ is the binary encoding size of x and p_f is a polynomial depending on f and constructible based on Bellantoni-Cook's proof).

4.2 NP $\subseteq$ PBINT MX

Proof. Let us first review our proof structure for (1) $\Rightarrow$ (2).

1. We know NP problems have PTIME verifiers.
2. By Bellantoni and Cook's theorem, every such polytime verifier can be given in their syntax.
3. So, it remains to show that, verifier V in Bellantoni-Cook form, can be turned into axiomatization ϕ in PBINT so that for σ-structure $\mathcal{A}$, ϕ is satisfiable by an expansion of $\mathcal{A}$ iff there is a polysize certificate for $\mathcal{A}$ accepted by V.

As this proof is so detailed, we only include the proof idea here. The full proof is in the Appendix.

The proof constructs PBINT specification ϕ based on verifier V. In ϕ, expansion vocabulary ε consists of:

1. $B : \mathbb{N} \times \mathbb{N}$ to map start times to functions, e.g., $B(5, c_f)$ means that, at time 5, function f has started running (c_f is a constant used to refer to function f).
2. $E : \mathbb{N} \times \mathbb{N}$ which, similarly, maps start times to end times, e.g., $E(5, 10)$ means that the function that had started running at time 5 ended running at time 10, and together with $B(5, c_f)$, it means that function f started at time 5 and ended at time 10.
3. $r : \mathbb{N} \rightarrow \mathbb{N}$ is used to store result of function executions. It is needed only when execution of a function terminates. For instance, continuing example above, having $r(10) = 2$ means that result of computing function f is 2 (because it was f that ended at time 10).

4. $arg : \mathbb{N} \times \mathbb{N} \rightarrow \mathbb{N}$ is used for storing function arguments. Semantically, $arg(n, m) = k$ means that the mth argument of function starting at time n is k. For example, having $arg(5, 1) = 7$ together with examples listed in items (1) to (3), means that function f started running and at time 5 on argument 7, and it finished at time 10 and gave result 2, so $f(7) = 2$.

This expansion vocabulary enables us to simulate the behavior of a program in Bellantoni-Cook form. We will have axioms saying what each function does. For example, for base function Z we have that it finishes immediately and gives zero as result. This is axiomatized as below:

$$\forall n\ (T(n) \wedge B(n, c_Z) \Rightarrow E(n, n+1)),$$
$$\forall n\ (T(n) \wedge B(n, c_Z) \Rightarrow r(n+1) = 0).$$

where $T(n)$ is a lower guard which bounds the time needed for simulating verifier V (a polynomial in the size of binary encoding of structure).

All other base functions have similarly simple axiomatizations. Functions defined in terms of other functions (using safe recursion or safe composition) need more complex (but still straightforward) axiomatizations. All these details can be found in the full proof.

There are some more subtle issues that have to be addressed in order to give a correct proof, e.g. encoding structures as numbers. All these subtleties are dealt with in the full proof given in the Appendix (which did not fit here, please see the online version).

4.3 PBINT MX$\subseteq$ NP

Proof. Here, the proof goes as follows:

1. We first show that, given an MX specification ϕ in PBINT, you can find equivalent ψ in ∃SO by using binary encodings of numbers.
2. Next, we show that structure $\mathcal{A}$ for ϕ is convertible to structure $\mathcal{A}'$ for ψ (in poly-time) so that satisfying expansion $\mathcal{B}$ of $\mathcal{A}$ exists iff satisfying expansion $\mathcal{B}'$ of $\mathcal{A}'$ exists.
3. Then, by Fagin's theorem, PBINT MX$\subseteq$NP.

To obtain ψ, we first create a specification in which all existentially quantified variables with PBINT guard G are replaced by skolemized PBINT functions upper-guarded by G. Then, this specification is converted to ψ by replacing PBINT functions with relations that encode value of the function in binary. For example, for PBINT function $f(x_1, \cdots, x_n)$, relation $Q_f(x_1, x_2, \cdots, x_n, k)$ is introduced with k being guarded by new relation R. The idea is that $Q_f(x_1, \cdots, x_n, k)$ holds iff the k-th bit of binary encoding of $f(x_1, \cdots, x_n)$ is one.

We know that all numbers in a PBINT specification are guarded. Hence, there is a polynomial $p(n)$ such that $2^{p(SIZE)}$ is greater than all numbers generated in ϕ. So, assuming that we have a relation R containing all numbers $0, \cdots, p(SIZE)$, describing operations of background structure is easy. For example, assuming that x, y and z are encoded by unary predicates Q_x, Q_y and Q_z, the relation $x = y + z$ can be axiomatized as follows:

$$\forall k\ (R(k) \Rightarrow$$
$$(Carry(k) \Leftrightarrow (Q_x(k) \Leftrightarrow (Q_y(k) \Leftrightarrow \neg Q_z(k))))),$$
$$Carry(k) :=$$
$$\exists k'\ (R(k') \wedge k' < k \wedge Q_y(k') \wedge Q_z(k') \wedge CF(k, k')),$$
$$CF(k, k') :=$$
$$\forall k''\ (R(k'') \wedge k' < k'' < k \Rightarrow Q_y(k'') \vee Q_z(k'')).$$

Although cumbersome, all other background operations can be similarly axiomatized.

Now, structure $\mathcal{A}'$ is obtained from $\mathcal{A}$ by adding unary relation R to $\mathcal{A}$ and converting all numbers in $\mathcal{A}$ to their binary representation. These tasks can be done in polytime and so obtaining $\mathcal{A}'$ from $\mathcal{A}$ is polytime achievable.

So, as ψ is in $\exists$SO, the task of model expansion for ψ is in NP. Also, as $\mathcal{A}$ is polytime convertible to $\mathcal{A}'$ and existence of a satisfying expansion for $\mathcal{A}$ is equivalent to existence of a satisfying expansion for $\mathcal{A}'$, model expansion for ϕ will also be in NP.

5 Related Work

Research in databases over infinite structures can be traced back to the seminal paper by Chandra and Harel [4]. There are several follow-up papers with developments in several directions including [28,24,13], and more recent [12]. Topor [28] studies the relative expressive power of several query languages in the presence of arithmetical operations. He also investigates domain independence and genericity in such frameworks.

Another line of database-motivated work over infinite background structures is embedded model theory (See [19,20]). Work in this area generally reduces questions on embedded finite models to questions on normal finite models. An important result in this area is the natural-domain-active-domain collapse for $\exists$SO for embedded finite models, as well as other deep expressiveness results. The work also describes a notion of safety (through e.g. range-restriction) to achieve safety with many background structures, and connections between safety and decidability. The active domain quantifiers are similar to our proposal of lower guards, however our goal was to reflect what is used in practical languages, namely the so-called domain predicates of Answer Set Programming and type information from other languages. We've done it through the use of upper and lower guards. In general, research in database theory is mostly focused around computability and the expressive power of query languages, while our interest, following [12] is in capturing complexity classes, but in connection with specification/modelling languages. We plan, however, to investigate the applicability of domain-independence, range-restrictedness and other notions from embedded model theory to practical modelling languages.

Grädel and Gurevich [13] studied logics over infinite background structures in a more general computer science context. They characterized NP for arithmetical structures under some small weight property, generalized to the small cost condition in [27] (see [27] for a more detailed discussion). While this condition corresponds to existing practical languages such as ASP and IDP system (see our paper [26] for more details), our work here gives an unconditional result for capturing NP in the presence of arithmetical structures, and thus is a step forward in the development of such languages. Instead of controlling access to the background structure through the use of weight terms [13], we rely on guarded fragments, which is much closer to practical specification languages.

The work we mentioned so far is the closest to our proposal, and was the most inspirational. The research on descriptive complexity in the embedded setting also includes the work of Grädel and Meer [15], as well as Grädel and Kreutzer [14]. Another line (Cook, Kolokolova and others [6]) establishes connections between bounded arithmetic and finite model theory, in particular by relying on Grädel's characterization of PTIME. While this work is less relevant here, we still plan to provide more detail in the journal version of the paper.

Another direction on capturing complexity classes is bounded arithmetic, including [2,23,1]. However, the characterization of complexity classes there is in terms of *provability* in systems with a limited collection of non-logical symbols, and is not applicable here.

There are many different characterizations of PTIME such as Leivant's [18], Immerman's [16], Cobham's [5] and Bellantoni-Cook characterization [1]. Leivant's characterization says that PTIME functions are exactly those that are provable in a logic called $L_2(QF^+)$. Immerman's logic is a fix-point logic with least fix-point operator and $\leq$ which works on structures with abstract domain elements. The two other characterizations of Cobham's and Bellantoni-Cook have the property of characterizing PTIME as a set of functions working on numbers and so better suited for our purpose of characterizing search problems over arithmetical structures. Also, the safe recursion and safe composition operators in the Cook-Bellantoni characterization give us a more natural way of guaranteeing that the result of the simulation we need in our proof falls within some bounds. Therefore, we choose the Bellantoni-Cook characterization [1] over Cobham's as the basis of our proof.

Built-in arithmetic is implemented in many modelling languages, e.g. the MX-based IDP system [29] and LPARSE [25]. However, as we showed in a parallel work in [26], such languages have limited expressiveness in the presence of arithmetic constraints. For example, we showed in [26] that the two problems of integer factorization and quadratic residues are not expressible in ASP and IDP systems using their built-in arithmetic. Also, in many cases, allowing arithmetic constraints without careful restrictions provides the language with very high expressiveness, as is shown for ESSENCE [22].

6 Conclusion

In modelling languages, you are frequently faced with the problem of having a framework to support both a natural specification of problems, and reasoning about those problems. In this paper, we took our measure of naturality to be being able to use "built-in" arithmetic, and our measure of reasoning to be being in NP. We showed some examples of problems of practical importance and argued that our fragment of logic is able to represent them naturally. We proved that embedded (in $\mathcal{N}^c$) MX for PBINT captures exactly NP. This result guarantees universality of our logic for this complexity class and also settles our reasoning abilities by showing that all PBINT axiomatizations can be efficiently (in polytime) grounded to any state of the art solver of NP problems.

Our work is a significant step forward from the previous proposal since it overcomes a number of limitations.

The language we proposed is natural because it is essentially FO logic, where guards can be made "invisible" through "hiding" them in a type system. Solving can be achieved through grounding to SAT, a work which is being performed in our group, but falls outside the scope of this paper.

In summary, our work has shown a new application of descriptive complexity and metafinite model theory, and contributed to those areas by improving a previous result of capturing NP for arithmetical structures. Future directions include (a) analysis of existing languages in connection with our results here, similar to what was done for ESSENCE with respect to the previous proposal [22]; (b) design of logics with different background structures, (c) extending the framework to deal with combination of languages, interacting in a modular system, (d) continue with our implementation development.

Acknowledgement. This work is generously funded by NSERC, MITACS and D-Wave. We also express our gratitude towards the anonymous referees for their useful comments.

References

1. Bellantoni, S., Cook, S.: A new recursion-theoretic characterization of the polytime functions (extended abstract). In: STOC 1992: Proceedings of the twenty-fourth annual ACM symposium on Theory of computing, pp. 283–293 (1992)
2. Buss, S.R.: Bounded arithmetic. PhD thesis, Princeton University (1985)
3. Cadoli, M., Palopoli, L., Schaerf, A., Vasile, D.: Np-spec: An executable specification language for solving all problems in np. In: Gupta, G. (ed.) PADL 1999. LNCS, vol. 1551, pp. 16–30. Springer, Heidelberg (1999)
4. Chandra, A., Harel, D.: Computable queries for relational databases. Journal of Computer and System Sciences 21, 156–178 (1980)
5. Cobham, A.: The intrinsic computational difficulty of functions. In: Bar-Hillel, Y. (ed.) Proc. of the 1964 International Congress for Logic, Methodology, and the Philosophy of Science, pp. 24–30 (1964)
6. Cook, S., Kolokolova, A.: A second-order system for polytime reasoning based on grädel's theorem. In: Proceedings of Sixteenth Annual IEEE Symposium on Logic in Computer Science (LICS 2001), pp. 177–186 (2001)
7. Denecker, M., Ternovska, E.: A logic of non-monotone inductive definitions. TOCL 9(2), 1–51 (2008)
8. Fagin, R.: Generalized first-order spectra and polynomial-time recognizable sets. In: Complexity of computation, SIAM-AMC proceedings, vol. 7, pp. 43–73 (1974)
9. Frisch, A.M., Grum, M., Jefferson, C., Hernandez, B.M., Miguel, I.: The essence of essence: A constraint language for specifying combinatorial problems. In: Proc. of the Fourth International Workshop on Modelling and Reformulating Constraint Satisfaction Problems, pp. 73–88 (2005)
10. Gebser, M., Schaub, T., Thiele, S.: Gringo: A new grounder for answer set programming. In: Baral, C., Brewka, G., Schlipf, J. (eds.) LPNMR 2007. LNCS (LNAI), vol. 4483, pp. 266–271. Springer, Heidelberg (2007)

11. Gottlob, G., Leone, N., Scarcello, F.: Robbers, marshals, and guards: game theoretic and logical characterizations of hypertree width. In: PODS 2001 (2001)
12. Grädel, E.: Finite Model Theory and Descriptive Complexity, pp. 125–230. Springer, Heidelberg (2007)
13. Grädel, E., Gurevich, Y.: Metafinite model theory. Inf. Comput. 140(1), 26–81 (1998)
14. Grädel, E., Kreutzer, S.: Descriptive complexity theory for constraint databases. In: Flum, J., Rodríguez-Artalejo, M. (eds.) CSL 1999. LNCS, vol. 1683, pp. 67–81. Springer, Heidelberg (1999)
15. Grädel, E., Meer, K.: Descriptive complexity theory over the real numbers. Mathematics of Numerical Analysis: Real Number Algorithms 32, 381–403 (1996)
16. Immerman, N.: Relational queries computable in polynomial time. In: STOC 1982: Proceedings of the 14th Annual ACM Symposium on Theory of Computing, pp. 147–152 (1982)
17. Immerman, N.: Descriptive complexity (1999)
18. Leivant, D.: A foundational delineation of computational feasibility. In: LICS 1991: Proceedings of the sixth Annual IEEE Symposium on Logic in Computer Science, pp. 2–11 (1991)
19. Libkin, L.: Elements of Finite Model Theory (2004)
20. Libkin, L.: Embedded Finite Models and Constraint Databases, pp. 257–338. Springer, Heidelberg (2007)
21. Mitchell, D.G., Ternovska, E.: A framework for representing and solving NP search problems. In: Proc. AAAI 2005 (2005)
22. Mitchell, D.G., Ternovska, E.: Expressiveness and abstraction in ESSENCE. Constraints 13(2), 343–384 (2008)
23. Skelley, A.: Theories and Proof Systems for PSPACE and the EXP-Time Hierarchy. PhD thesis, University of Toronto (2005)
24. Suciu, D.: Domain-independent queries on databases with external functions. Theor. Comput. Sci. 190(2), 279–315 (1998)
25. Syrjänen, T.: Lparse 1.0 User's Manual (2000), `http://www.tcs.hut.fi/Software/smodels/lparse.ps.gz`
26. Tasharrofi, S., Ternovska, E.: Built-in arithmetic in knowledge representation languages. In: Proc. of Logic and Search, LaSh 2010 (2010)
27. Ternovska, E., Mitchell, D.G.: Declarative programming of search problems with built-in arithmetic. In: Proc. of 21st International Joint Conference on Artificial Intelligence (IJCAI 2009), pp. 942–947 (2009)
28. Topor, R.: Safe database queries with arithmetic relations. In: Proc. 14th Australian Computer Science Conf., pp. 1–13 (1991)
29. Wittocx, J., Marien, M.: The IDP System, KU Leuven (June 2008), `www.cs.kuleuven.be/~dtai/krr/software/idpmanual.pdf`

Resolution for Stochastic Boolean Satisfiability*

Tino Teige and Martin Fränzle

Carl von Ossietzky Universität, Oldenburg, Germany
{teige,fraenzle}@informatik.uni-oldenburg.de

Abstract. The stochastic Boolean satisfiability (SSAT) problem was introduced by Papadimitriou in 1985 by adding a probabilistic model of uncertainty to propositional satisfiability through *randomized* quantification. SSAT has many applications, e.g., in probabilistic planning and, more recently by integrating arithmetic, in probabilistic model checking. In this paper, we first present a new result on the computational complexity of SSAT: SSAT remains PSPACE-complete even for its restriction to 2CNF. Second, we propose a sound and complete resolution calculus for SSAT complementing the classical backtracking search algorithms.

1 Introduction

In 1985, Papadimitriou proposed the idea of modeling uncertainty in propositional satisfiability (SAT) by introducing *randomized* quantification in addition to existential quantification. This gives the notion of *stochastic Boolean satisfiability* (SSAT) [1]. An SSAT formula consists of a quantifier prefix and of a propositional formula. The quantifier prefix is an alternating sequence of existentially quantified variables and variables bound by randomized quantifiers. The meaning of a randomized variable x is that x takes value `true` with a certain probability p and value `false` with the complementary probability $1 - p$. Due to the presence of such probabilistic assignments, the semantics of an SSAT formula Φ is no longer qualitative in the sense that Φ is true or false, as it is for existential and universal quantifiers, but rather *quantitative*. For SSAT formulae Φ, we ask for the *maximum probability of satisfaction*. Intuitively, a solution of Φ is a tree of assignments to the existential variables, depending on the probabilistically determined values of preceding randomized variables, that maximize the probability of satisfying the propositional formula.

In recent years, the SSAT framework became popular within the Artificial Intelligence (AI) community, as many problems from that area exhibiting uncertainty can be described as SSAT problems or even special cases of SSAT, in particular probabilistic planning problems [2,3,4]. Inspired by that work, other communities have started to exploit the idea of SSAT in their formalisms and methods. The Constraint Programming (CP) community is working on

* This work has been partially supported by the German Research Council (DFG) as part of the Transregional Collaborative Research Center "Automatic Verification and Analysis of Complex Systems" (SFB/TR 14 AVACS, www.avacs.org).

C. Fermüller and A. Voronkov (Eds.): LPAR-17, LNCS 6397, pp. 625–639, 2010.

$$\Phi = \exists x \,\reflectbox{R}^{0.3} y : (x \vee \neg y) \wedge (\neg x \vee y)$$

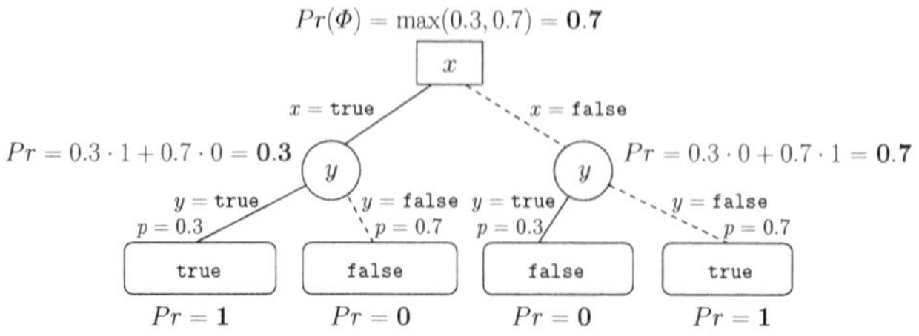

Fig. 1. Semantics of an SSAT formula depicted as a tree

stochastic constraint satisfaction problems [5,6,7] to address, e.g., multi-objective decision making under uncertainty [8]. Most recently, the Model Checking community suggested an approach based on stochastic satisfiability for the symbolic analysis of probabilistic (hybrid) systems. To do so, the authors of [9] extended SSAT wrt. arithmetic theories –as known from *satisfiability modulo theories* (SMT) [10]– which leads to the notion of *stochastic satisfiability modulo theories* (SSMT). By the expressive power of SSMT, bounded probabilistic reachability problems of uncertain hybrid systems can be phrased as SSMT formulae. Though the general SSAT problem is PSPACE-complete, the plethora of real-world applications calls for practically efficient algorithms. The first SSAT algorithm was suggested by Littman [11] and is an extension of the Davis-Putnam-Logemann-Loveland (DPLL) procedure [12,13] for SAT with appropriate quantifier handling and algorithmic optimizations like *unit propagation*, *purification*, and *thresholding*. Recently, Majercik further improved the DPLL-style SSAT algorithm by *non-chronological backtracking* [14]. The SSMT algorithm from [9,15] builds on the SSAT procedures but also integrates an underlying theory solver, and was successfully applied to a realistic case study [16].

In this paper, we make two contributions that shed a bit more light on the nature of SSAT. In Section 3, we investigate the computational complexity of the SSAT subclass where the propositional formula is in 2CNF. It turns out that even this special case, called S2SAT, is as hard as the general problem, i.e. PSPACE-complete. To the best of our knowledge the precise complexity of S2SAT was so far open. In Section 4, we propose a novel approach to solve SSAT problems. All existing SSAT algorithms implement a DPLL-based backtracking search explicitly traversing the tree given by the quantifier prefix. Following the idea of *resolution* for propositional and first-order formulae [17] and for QBF formulae [18], we develop a sound and complete resolution calculus for SSAT and theoretically compare it with the classical DPLL-SSAT approach.

2 Preliminaries

A *stochastic Boolean satisfiability* (SSAT) formula is given by $\Phi = \mathcal{Q} : \varphi$ with a prefix $\mathcal{Q} = Q_1 x_1 \dots Q_n x_n$ of quantified propositional variables x_i, where Q_i is either an existential quantifier $\exists$ or a randomized quantifier $\reflectbox{R}^{p_i}$ with a rational constant $0 < p_i < 1$, and a propositional formula φ s.t. $Var(\varphi) \subseteq \{x_1, \ldots, x_n\}$, where $Var(\varphi)$ denotes the set of all variables in φ. W.l.o.g., we may assume that φ is in *conjunctive normal form* (CNF), i.e. a conjunction of disjunctions of propositional literals. A literal ℓ is a propositional variable, i.e. $\ell = x_i$, or its negation, i.e. $\ell = \neg x_i$. The semantics of Φ, as illustrated in Fig. 1, is defined by the *maximum probability of satisfaction* $Pr(\Phi)$ as follows.

$$\begin{aligned}
Pr(\varepsilon : \varphi) &= \begin{cases} 0 & \text{if } \varphi \text{ is equivalent to } \texttt{false} \\ 1 & \text{if } \varphi \text{ is equivalent to } \texttt{true} \end{cases} \\
Pr(\exists x\ \mathcal{Q} : \varphi) &= \max(Pr(\mathcal{Q} : \varphi[\texttt{true}/x]), Pr(\mathcal{Q} : \varphi[\texttt{false}/x])) \\
Pr(\text{Я}^p x\ \mathcal{Q} : \varphi) &= p \cdot Pr(\mathcal{Q} : \varphi[\texttt{true}/x]) \ + \ (1-p) \cdot Pr(\mathcal{Q} : \varphi[\texttt{false}/x])
\end{aligned}$$

Note that the semantics is well-defined as Φ has no free variables s.t. all variables have been substituted by the constants `true` and `false` when reaching the quantifier-free base case. Given any SSAT formula Φ and any rational constant $0 \leq t \leq 1$, the SSAT decision problem (Φ, t) asks for whether $Pr(\Phi) \geq t$ holds.

All existing algorithms to solve SSAT are based on a DPLL-based backtracking search that mimics the semantics above. Fig. 2 shows the standard SSAT procedure presented in [19] (in a version without universal quantifiers). DPLL-SSAT$(\Phi, \theta_l, \theta_u)$ takes as inputs an SSAT formula Φ and two threshold values θ_l, θ_u with $0 \leq \theta_l \leq \theta_u \leq 1$. DPLL-SSAT then returns value $p = Pr(\Phi)$ if $\theta_l \leq Pr(\Phi) < \theta_u$. Otherwise, it returns a witness value $p < \theta_l$ iff $Pr(\Phi) < \theta_l$, and $p \geq \theta_u$ iff $Pr(\Phi) \geq \theta_u$. These thresholds are exploited during search to boost efficiency by skipping some recursive calls of DPLL-SSAT which is called *thresholding* (cf. Fig. 2). Two other algorithmic optimizations are *unit propagation* and *purification*. The first one detects *unit* literals and immediately propagates them. A literal in clause c is unit if it is undecided and all other literals in c are `false`. Similarly, purification propagates *pure* literals. A literal ℓ in an undecided clause is pure if no undecided clause contains the negation of ℓ. Purification is not possible for randomized variables as both branches have some contribution.

Before we state some properties of SSAT formulae that are essential for the resolution calculus introduced in Section 4, we formally define the assignment ff_c that falsifies a disjunctive clause c and that is unique wrt. c's variables. Let c be a non-tautological disjunction of propositional literals, i.e. $\not\models c$. Then, the mapping $\mathit{ff}_c : Var(c) \to \mathbb{B}$ is defined by $\forall x \in Var(c) : \mathit{ff}_c(x) = \begin{cases} \texttt{true} & ; \neg x \in c \\ \texttt{false} & ; \ x \in c \end{cases}$. That is, c evaluates to `false` under assignment ff_c. The following rather technical proposition comprises simple but important observations which the soundness of the proposed SSAT resolution relies on. Intuitively, property 1 states that under an assignment τ that falsifies a clause c in a propositional formula φ in CNF, the satisfaction probability of the SSAT formula $\mathcal{Q} : \varphi$ under τ is 0. Property 2 rephrases the semantics of quantifiers: from $Pr(\mathcal{Q} : \varphi[\texttt{true}/x]) = p_1$ and $Pr(\mathcal{Q} : \varphi[\texttt{false}/x]) = p_2$ it immediately follows that $Pr(\exists x\ \mathcal{Q} : \varphi) = \max(p_1, p_2)$ and $Pr(\text{Я}^p x\ \mathcal{Q} : \varphi) = p \cdot p_1 + (1-p) \cdot p_2$. Property 3 safely estimates the value of $Pr(\text{Я}^p x\ \mathcal{Q} : \varphi)$ if just one of the values $Pr(\mathcal{Q} : \varphi[\texttt{true}/x])$ or $Pr(\mathcal{Q} : \varphi[\texttt{false}/x])$ is known by taking the safe upper bound 1 for the other value.

DPLL-SSAT($\mathcal{Q} : \varphi, \theta_l, \theta_u$)
  if φ contains a clause equivalent to `false` **then return** 0.
  if all clauses in φ equivalent to `true` **then return** 1.
  // Unit propagation
  if φ contains a unit literal ℓ with $Var(\ell) = \{x\}$ **then**
    if $\mathcal{Q} = \mathcal{Q}_1 \exists x \mathcal{Q}_2$ **then return** DPLL-SSAT($\mathcal{Q}_1\mathcal{Q}_2 : \varphi[v(\ell)/x], \theta_l, \theta_u$).
    if $\mathcal{Q} = \mathcal{Q}_1 \text{Я}^p x \mathcal{Q}_2$ **then return** DPLL-SSAT($\mathcal{Q}_1\mathcal{Q}_2 : \varphi[v(\ell)/x], \theta_l/p(\ell), \theta_u/p(\ell)$) $\cdot\, p(\ell)$.
  // Purification
  if φ contains a pure literal ℓ with $Var(\ell) = \{x\}$ **then**
    if $\mathcal{Q} = \mathcal{Q}_1 \exists x \mathcal{Q}_2$ **then return** DPLL-SSAT($\mathcal{Q}_1\mathcal{Q}_2 : \varphi[v(\ell)/x], \theta_l, \theta_u$).
  // Branching and thresholding
  if $\mathcal{Q} = \exists x \mathcal{Q}'$ **then**
    p_1 = DPLL-SSAT($\mathcal{Q}' : \varphi[\texttt{true}/x], \theta_l, \theta_u$).
    if $p_1 \geq \theta_u$ **then return** p_1.
    p_2 = DPLL-SSAT($\mathcal{Q}' : \varphi[\texttt{false}/x], \max(\theta_l, p_1), \theta_u$).
    return $\max(p_1, p_2)$.
  if $\mathcal{Q} = \text{Я}^p x \mathcal{Q}'$ **then**
    p_1 = DPLL-SSAT($\mathcal{Q}' : \varphi[\texttt{true}/x], (\theta_l - (1-p))/p, \theta_u/p$).
    if $p_1 \cdot p + (1-p) < \theta_l$ **then return** $p_1 \cdot p$.
    if $p_1 \cdot p \geq \theta_u$ **then return** $p_1 \cdot p$.
    p_2 = DPLL-SSAT($\mathcal{Q}' : \varphi[\texttt{false}/x], (\theta_l - p_1 \cdot p)/(1-p), (\theta_u - p_1 \cdot p)/(1-p)$).
    return $p_1 \cdot p + p_2 \cdot (1-p)$.

Fig. 2. DPLL-based backtracking algorithm for SSAT from [19]. If literal ℓ is positive then $v(\ell) = \texttt{true}, p(\ell) = p$, otherwise $v(\ell) = \texttt{false}, p(\ell) = 1 - p$.

Proposition 1. *Let φ be some propositional formula with $Var(\varphi) = \{x_1, \ldots, x_n\}$, $\mathcal{Q} = Q_{i+1}x_{i+1} \ldots Q_n x_n$ be a quantifier prefix, and $Var(\varphi) \downarrow_j := \{x_1, \ldots, x_j\}$ for $j \leq n$. Then, the following properties hold.*

1. *If φ is in CNF and there is a non-tautological clause $c \in \varphi$ s.t. $Var(c) \subseteq Var(\varphi) \downarrow_i$ then for each $\tau : Var(\varphi) \downarrow_i \rightarrow \mathbb{B}$ with $\forall x \in Var(c) : \tau(x) = \mathit{ff}_c(x)$:*
$$Pr(\mathcal{Q} : \varphi[\tau(x_1)/x_1] \ldots [\tau(x_i)/x_i]) \;=\; 0.$$
2. *For $k \in \{1, 2\}$ let be $V_k \subseteq Var(\varphi) \downarrow_{(i-1)}$, and $\tau_k : V_k \rightarrow \mathbb{B}$ s.t. for each $\tau'_k : Var(\varphi) \downarrow_{(i-1)} \rightarrow \mathbb{B}$ with $\forall x \in V_k : \tau'_k(x) = \tau_k(x)$ it holds that*
$$Pr(\mathcal{Q} : \varphi[\tau'_1(x_1)/x_1] \ldots [\tau'_1(x_{i-1})/x_{i-1}][\texttt{true}/x_i]) \;\leq\; p_1,$$
$$Pr(\mathcal{Q} : \varphi[\tau'_2(x_1)/x_1] \ldots [\tau'_2(x_{i-1})/x_{i-1}][\texttt{false}/x_i]) \;\leq\; p_2.$$
If $\forall x \in V_1 \cap V_2 : \tau_1(x) = \tau_2(x)$ then for each $\tau : Var(\varphi) \downarrow_{(i-1)} \rightarrow \mathbb{B}$ with $\forall x \in V_1 : \tau(x) = \tau_1(x)$ and $\forall x \in V_2 : \tau(x) = \tau_2(x)$ it holds that
(a) $Pr(\exists x_i\ \mathcal{Q} : \varphi[\tau(x_1)/x_1] \ldots [\tau(x_{i-1})/x_{i-1}]) \;\leq\; \max(p_1, p_2)$ and
(b) $Pr(\text{Я}^p x_i\ \mathcal{Q} : \varphi[\tau(x_1)/x_1] \ldots [\tau(x_{i-1})/x_{i-1}]) \;\leq\; p \cdot p_1 + (1-p) \cdot p_2$.
3. *Let $V_1 \subseteq Var(\varphi) \downarrow_{(i-1)}$, and $\tau_1 : V_1 \rightarrow \mathbb{B}$ s.t. for each $\tau : Var(\varphi) \downarrow_{(i-1)} \rightarrow \mathbb{B}$ with $\forall x \in V_1 : \tau(x) = \tau_1(x)$ it holds that*
$$Pr(\mathcal{Q} : \varphi[\tau(x_1)/x_1] \ldots [\tau(x_{i-1})/x_{i-1}][v_{x_i}/x_i]) \;\leq\; p_1$$
where $v_{x_i} \in \mathbb{B}$. Then,
$$Pr(\text{Я}^p x_i\ \mathcal{Q} : \varphi[\tau(x_1)/x_1] \ldots [\tau(x_{i-1})/x_{i-1}]) \;\leq\; p' \cdot p_1 + (1-p')$$
where $p' = p$ if $v_{x_i} = \texttt{true}$, and $p' = 1 - p$ if $v_{x_i} = \texttt{false}$.

Proof. For property 1, by construction of τ and since clause c is non-tautological, it holds that $c[\tau(x_1)/x_1]\dots[\tau(x_i)/x_i] \equiv \texttt{false}$. Since φ is in CNF and $c \in \varphi$, it follows that formula $\varphi[\tau(x_1)/x_1]\dots[\tau(x_i)/x_i]$ with variables $x_{i+1},\dots,x_n$ is unsatisfiable. Immediately, $Pr(\mathcal{Q} : \varphi[\tau(x_1)/x_1]\dots[\tau(x_i)/x_i]) = 0$. Property 2 follows immediately from the definition of Pr. Property 3 is a direct consequence of property 2b since w.l.o.g. we may assume that $0 \leq p_2 \leq 1$ holds. □

3 Computational Complexity of SSAT

It is well-known that the general SSAT decision problem is PSPACE-complete. The hardness can be easily shown by a reduction from the *quantified Boolean formula* (QBF) problem: given a QBF instance $\mathcal{Q} : \varphi$ (where $\mathcal{Q}$ may contain existential and universal quantifiers), we construct the SSAT formula $\mathcal{Q}' : \varphi$ s.t. $\mathcal{Q}'$ arises from $\mathcal{Q}$ by replacing all universal quantifiers by randomized ones $Ʀ^p$ with some rational $0 < p < 1$. Then $\mathcal{Q} : \varphi$ is $\texttt{true}$ iff $Pr(\mathcal{Q}' : \varphi) \geq 1$. This reduction shows that QBF can be seen as a special case of SSAT, while both general problems share PSPACE-completeness. There is some extensive work on the complexity of SSAT and QBF subcases that gives a better insight into the relation of both problems. When restricting a QBF formula to just existential or to just universal variables, this results in the well-known NP-complete SAT problem and the co-NP-complete tautology (TAUT) problem, respectively. The subclass of SSAT that allows only randomized variables gives the PP-complete ("probabilistic polynomial time") MAJSAT problem. Recall that (co-)NP $\subseteq$ PP $\subseteq$ PSPACE holds. Thus, randomized quantifiers are in some sense computationally harder than just existential or just universal ones. In addition to restricting the quantifier prefix, it is of interest to consider special shapes of the propositional formula. A propositional formula is in kCNF iff it is in CNF and each of its clauses contains exactly k literals. The special cases of SAT, TAUT, QBF, MAJSAT, and SSAT for which the formulae are in 3CNF do not change the complexity results mentioned above. Restricting however a QBF formula to be in 2CNF, the resulting QBF subproblem can be solved in linear time [20], and thus also the corresponding subcases of SAT and TAUT. The same restriction of MAJSAT, called MAJ2SAT, however remains PP-complete [21]. This is an interesting result as alternating existential and universal quantifiers seem to be computationally harder than just randomized ones for formulae in kCNF with $k \geq 3$, but computationally weaker for formulae in 2CNF. In the following, we will investigate the complexity of the SSAT subclass for which the propositional formula is in 2CNF. We call this problem S2SAT. As MAJ2SAT is PP-complete, it immediately follows that S2SAT is PP-hard. The precise complexity of S2SAT, however, was so far open to the best of our knowledge.

We will show that S2SAT is as hard as the general SSAT problem, i.e. PSPACE-complete. PSPACE-membership immediately follows from the fact that S2SAT is a subcase of SSAT. We prove PSPACE-hardness by a linear-time many-one reduction from the PSPACE-complete decision problem 1-in-3 Q3SAT. A 1-in-3 Q3SAT formula $\mathcal{Q} : \varphi$ is simply a Q3SAT formula, i.e. a QBF formula with φ in 3CNF. While quantifier treatment remains unchanged, satisfaction of φ, however, differs from the standard definition: φ is *1-in-3 satisfied* under truth assignment τ iff each clause $c \in \varphi$ is *1-in-3 satisfied* under τ iff *exactly one* literal in each c is satisfied under τ. PSPACE-hardness can be shown by reduction from Q3SAT that relies on the reduction from 3SAT to 1-in-3 3SAT by Schaefer [22]. For an arbitrary Q3SAT instance $\mathcal{Q} : \varphi$ with $\varphi = cl_1 \wedge \ldots \wedge cl_m$ we construct the 1-in-3 Q3SAT instance $\mathcal{Q}' : \varphi'$ as follows. For each clause $cl_i = (\ell_1^i \vee \ell_2^i \vee \ell_3^i) \in \varphi$ we introduce five 1-in-3 Q3SAT clauses $\mathit{one\text{-}in\text{-}three}(cl_i) := (\ell_1^i \vee a_i \vee d_i) \wedge (\ell_2^i \vee b_i \vee d_i) \wedge (a_i \vee b_i \vee e_i) \wedge (c_i \vee d_i \vee f_i) \wedge (\ell_3^i \vee c_i \vee \texttt{false})$ with six fresh Boolean variables $a_i, b_i, c_i, d_i, e_i, f_i$ and the constant literal `false` that is never satisfied. It holds that cl_i is satisfied under τ iff $\exists a_i, b_i, c_i, d_i, e_i, f_i : \mathit{one\text{-}in\text{-}three}(cl_i)$ is 1-in-3 satisfied under τ. By setting $\mathcal{Q}' := \mathcal{Q}\ \exists a_1, b_1, \ldots, e_m, f_m$ and $\varphi' := \bigwedge_{i=1}^{m} \mathit{one\text{-}in\text{-}three}(cl_i)$, it follows that $\mathcal{Q} : \varphi$ is true iff $\mathcal{Q}' : \varphi'$ is 1-in-3 true, i.e. true under 1-in-3 satisfaction. Note that $\mathcal{Q}' : \varphi'$ is of size linear in $Q : \varphi$ ($6m$ new variables and $5m$ clauses).

Theorem 1. S2SAT *is* PSPACE*-complete.*

Proof. PSPACE-membership is obvious as SSAT lies in PSPACE. We prove PSPACE-hardness by a linear-time many-one reduction from 1-in-3 Q3SAT.

Let $\mathcal{Q} : \varphi$ be a 1-in-3 Q3SAT instance. We will construct an S2SAT instance (Φ, t) s.t. $\mathcal{Q} : \varphi$ is 1-in-3 true iff $Pr(\Phi) \geq t$. First observe that $\mathcal{Q} : \varphi$ is 1-in-3 true iff $Pr(\mathcal{Q}' : \varphi) \geq 1$ under 1-in-3 satisfaction where $\mathcal{Q}'$ arises from $\mathcal{Q}$ by replacing all universal quantifiers by randomized ones $\text{ꟼ}^{0.5}$. Let be $\varphi = \{(\ell_1^1 \vee \ell_2^1 \vee \ell_3^1), \ldots, (\ell_1^m \vee \ell_2^m \vee \ell_3^m)\}$. Now, we introduce $3m$ fresh randomized variables (three randomized variables per clause) all with the same probability $p = 0.9$ resulting in the prefix $\mathcal{Q}'' := \mathcal{Q}'\ \text{ꟼ}^{0.9} r_1^1, r_2^1, r_3^1, \ldots, r_1^m, r_2^m, r_3^m$ of Φ. The following propositional formula ψ of Φ ensures that *at most* one literal per clause in φ is `true`. To also enforce that *at least* one literal per clause is `true`, the probability threshold t will be set correspondingly by taking account of the probabilities of the randomized variables $\text{ꟼ}^{0.9} r_j^i$ to rule out non-solutions of φ.

$$\psi := \bigwedge_{i=1}^{m} \left(\overbrace{\left(\bigwedge_{j=1}^{3} (\ell_j^i \vee \neg r_j^i) \wedge (neg(\ell_j^i) \vee r_j^i) \right)}^{\text{identify value of literal } \ell_j^i \text{ with variable } r_j^i} \quad \overbrace{\begin{array}{l} \wedge(\neg r_1^i \vee \neg r_2^i) \\ \wedge(\neg r_1^i \vee \neg r_3^i) \\ \wedge(\neg r_2^i \vee \neg r_3^i) \end{array}}^{\text{at most one true literal per clause}} \right)$$

where $neg(\ell)$ returns the opposite literal of ℓ, i.e. it returns x if $\ell = \neg x$, and $\neg x$ otherwise. Note that ψ is in 2CNF and Φ is of size linear in $\mathcal{Q} : \varphi$ (Φ contains $3m$ new variables and $9m$ clauses).

We now show that $Pr(\mathcal{Q}' : \varphi) \geq 1$ under 1-in-3 satisfaction iff $Pr(\Phi) \geq 0.009^m$. Let be $\mathcal{Q}' = Q_1 x_1 \ldots Q_n x_n$. Note that under each assignment τ to the variables in $\mathcal{Q}'$ there exists a unique assignment τ' to the randomized variables r_1^i, r_2^i, r_3^i s.t. the combined assignment τ'' to all variables in $\mathcal{Q}''$ with $\tau''(x_i) = \tau(x_i)$ and $\tau''(r_j^i) = \tau'(r_j^i)$ satisfies $\bigwedge_{j=1}^{3} (\ell_j^i \vee \neg r_j^i) \wedge (neg(\ell_j^i) \vee r_j^i)$ in ψ for each $1 \leq i \leq m$, i.e. at least one of

$$Pr(\text{ꟼ}^{0.9} r_{k+1}, \ldots, r_{3m} : \psi[\tau(x_1)/x_1] \ldots [\tau'(r_1)/r_1] \ldots [\tau'(r_{k-1})/r_{k-1}][\texttt{true}/r_k]),$$
$$Pr(\text{ꟼ}^{0.9} r_{k+1}, \ldots, r_{3m} : \psi[\tau(x_1)/x_1] \ldots [\tau'(r_1)/r_1] \ldots [\tau'(r_{k-1})/r_{k-1}][\texttt{false}/r_k])$$

is 0 for each $1 \leq k \leq 3m$. Due to $(\neg r_1^i \vee \neg r_2^i) \wedge (\neg r_1^i \vee \neg r_3^i) \wedge (\neg r_2^i \vee \neg r_3^i) \in \psi$ and because of setting r_j^i to `true` with probability 0.9 and to `false` with 0.1, for each assignment τ to the variables in $\mathcal{Q}'$ it holds that $Pr(\text{Я}^{0.9} r_1^1, \ldots, r_3^m : \psi[\tau(x_1)/x_1] \ldots [\tau(x_n)/x_n]) \leq 0.009^m$.

Furthermore, for each assignment τ to the variables in $\mathcal{Q}'$ that 1-in-3 satisfies φ, i.e. $Pr(\varepsilon : \varphi[\tau(x_1)/x_1] \ldots [\tau(x_n)/x_n]) \geq 1$ under 1-in-3 satisfaction, the unique assignment τ' also satisfies $(\neg r_1^i \vee \neg r_2^i) \wedge (\neg r_1^i \vee \neg r_3^i) \wedge (\neg r_2^i \vee \neg r_3^i)$ for each $1 \leq i \leq m$, since each clause in φ has exactly one true literal under τ, and thus τ'' satisfies ψ. Therefore, for each $1 \leq i \leq m$ exactly one variable of r_1^i, r_2^i, r_3^i is set to `true` by τ', from which follows that $Pr(\text{Я}^{0.9} r_1^1, \ldots, r_3^m : \psi[\tau(x_1)/x_1] \ldots [\tau(x_n)/x_n]) = 0.009^m$. Vice versa, if for some assignment τ to the variables in $\mathcal{Q}'$ it holds that $Pr(\text{Я}^{0.9} r_1^1, \ldots, r_3^m : \psi[\tau(x_1)/x_1] \ldots [\tau(x_n)/x_n]) = 0.009^m$ then for each $1 \leq i \leq m$ exactly one variable of r_1^i, r_2^i, r_3^i is set to `true` by τ' due to $(\neg r_1^i \vee \neg r_2^i) \wedge (\neg r_1^i \vee \neg r_3^i) \wedge (\neg r_2^i \vee \neg r_3^i)$ and due to $\text{Я}^{0.9} r_j^i$. From $\bigwedge_{j=1}^{3} (\ell_j^i \vee \neg r_j^i) \wedge (\neg \ell_j^i \vee r_j^i)$, we conclude that each clause in φ has exactly one true literal under τ. Thus, $Pr(\varepsilon : \varphi[\tau(x_1)/x_1] \ldots [\tau(x_n)/x_n]) \geq 1$ under 1-in-3 satisfaction. Summarizing, $Pr(\varepsilon : \varphi[\tau(x_1)/x_1] \ldots [\tau(x_n)/x_n]) \geq 1$ under 1-in-3 satisfaction iff $Pr(\text{Я}^{0.9} r_1^1, \ldots, r_3^m : \psi[\tau(x_1)/x_1] \ldots [\tau(x_n)/x_n]) = 0.009^m$. From this fact and due to $Pr(\text{Я}^{0.9} r_1^1, \ldots, r_3^m : \psi[\tau(x_1)/x_1] \ldots [\tau(x_n)/x_n]) \leq 0.009^m$ for each τ, it immediately follows by definition that $Pr(\mathcal{Q}' : \varphi) \geq 1$ under 1-in-3 satisfaction iff $Pr(\Phi) = 0.009^m$ iff $Pr(\Phi) \geq 0.009^m$. To complete the reduction, we choose the rational constant $t := 0.009^m$.

The resulting S2SAT instance (Φ, t) contains $n + 3m$ variables and $9m$ clauses where n is the number of variables and m is the number of clauses in $\mathcal{Q} : \varphi$. The rational constant $t = 0.009^m$ can be represented by a decimal fraction of size $\mathcal{O}(m)$. Thus, (Φ, t) can be constructed in linear time. □

We remark that S2SAT with just *homogeneous* probabilities in randomized quantifiers, i.e. $\text{Я}^{0.5}$, is of the same complexity while the proof is slightly more complex. In brief, $3m$ more randomized variables are appended to $\mathcal{Q}''$ (on the right) and ψ is extended by $3m$ more clauses, i.e. $\text{Я}^{0.5} h_1^i, h_2^i, h_3^i$ and $(r_1^i \vee \neg h_1^i) \wedge (r_2^i \vee \neg h_2^i) \wedge (r_3^i \vee \neg h_3^i)$ per clause c_i. Then, if $r_j^i =$ `true` both assignments to h_j^i satisfy $(r_j^i \vee \neg h_j^i)$, and otherwise, i.e. $r_j^i =$ `false`, just $h_j^i =$ `false` does. Thus, for each i one of r_1^i, r_2^i, r_3^i is true iff the corresponding probability is 0.5^5, and all r_j^i are false iff the probability is 0.5^6. It remains to set $t := 0.5^{5m}$.

4 Resolution for SSAT

In this section, we propose a novel approach to solve SSAT problems. All existing SSAT algorithms implement a DPLL-based backtracking procedure as in Fig. 2, explicitly traversing the tree given by the quantifier prefix and computing the individual satisfaction probabilities for each subtree, as indicated by Fig. 1. Following the idea of *resolution* for propositional and first-order formulae [17] and for QBF formulae [18], we develop a sound and complete resolution calculus for SSAT. Recall that resolution for both SAT and QBF shows polynomial-time solvability on their restrictions to 2CNF as each resolution step yields clauses of size at most two, of which just quadratically many exist. Note that the same property cannot be expected for SSAT resolution due to PSPACE-completeness of S2SAT (Theorem 1). Therefore, a sound and complete resolution calculus for SSAT must involve some rule that destroys the above property.

In the sequel, let $\Phi = \mathcal{Q} : \varphi$ be an SSAT formula where φ is in CNF. W.l.o.g., φ does not contain tautological clauses[1], i.e. $\forall c \in \varphi : \not\models c$. Let $\mathcal{Q} = Q_1 x_1 \ldots Q_n x_n$ be some quantifier prefix and φ be some propositional formula with $Var(\varphi) \subseteq \{x_1, \ldots, x_n\}$. Then, the quantifier prefix $\mathcal{Q}(\varphi)$ is given by the smallest prefix of $\mathcal{Q}$ that contains all variables from φ, i.e. $\mathcal{Q}(\varphi) = Q_1 x_1 \ldots Q_i x_i$ where $x_i \in Var(\varphi)$ and for each $j > i : x_j \notin Var(\varphi)$.

Starting with clauses in φ, *S-resolution* is given by the consecutive application of rules R.1-R.5 to derive new clauses c^p that are annotated with some values $0 \leq p < 1$. It is important to remark that in contrast to classical resolution such clauses c^p are not necessarily semantic consequences of φ but are just entailed with some probability. Informally speaking, the derivation of a clause c^p means that under SSAT formula $\mathcal{Q} : \varphi$, the clause c is violated with a maximum probability at most p, i.e. the satisfaction probability of $\mathcal{Q} : (\varphi \wedge \neg c)$ is at most p. More intuitively, the minimum probability that clause c is implied by φ is at least $1-p$. This follows from the observation that $Pr(\mathcal{Q} : \psi) = 1 - Pr(\mathcal{Q}' : \neg\psi)$, where $\mathcal{Q}'$ arises from $\mathcal{Q}$ by replacing existential quantifiers by universal ones, where universal quantifiers call for *minimizing* the satisfaction probability. We thus have $Pr(\mathcal{Q}' : (\varphi \Rightarrow c)) \geq 1 - Pr(\mathcal{Q} : (\varphi \wedge \neg c))$. Once the empty clause $\emptyset^p$ is derived, it follows that the probability of the given SSAT formula is at most p, i.e. $Pr(\mathcal{Q} : (\varphi \wedge \neg \texttt{false})) = Pr(\mathcal{Q} : \varphi) \leq p$. The first rule R.1 is just of technical nature, and derives a clause c^0 from an original clause c in φ.

$$\text{(R.1)} \qquad \frac{c \in \varphi}{c^0}$$

The second rule R.2 derives a redundant clause by adding some literal ℓ to clause c^p. To keep soundness of this rule, the literal ℓ may not talk about a variable x that already occurs in c^p. Furthermore, the variable x must appear in the quantifier prefix $\mathcal{Q}(c)$ of clause c. Such an extension rule is redundant in classical resolution schemes for SAT and QBF. In the stochastic case, we need such rule to achieve completeness of S-resolution. Note that this rule impedes a potential polynomial-time solvability for SSAT formulae in 2CNF as sizes of derived clauses are no longer guaranteed to be at most two. Though completeness might be obtained in another way, the choice of extension rule R.2 seems to be justified by Theorem 1 (PSPACE-completeness of S2SAT), indicating that a polynomial time algorithm for S2SAT cannot be expected.

$$\text{(R.2)} \qquad \frac{c^p, Qx \in \mathcal{Q}(c), x \notin Var(c), \ell \in \{x, \neg x\}}{(c \vee \ell)^p}$$

[1] Tautological clauses c are redundant, i.e. $Pr(\mathcal{Q} : (\varphi \wedge c)) = Pr(\mathcal{Q} : \varphi)$.

Rules R.3 and R.4 constitute the actual resolution rules as known from the non-stochastic case. Depending on whether an existential (R.3) or a randomized variable (R.4) is resolved upon, the probability value of the resolvent clause is computed according to the semantics $Pr(\Phi)$.

$$\text{(R.3)}\quad \frac{(c_1 \vee \neg x)^{p_1}, (c_2 \vee x)^{p_2}, \exists x \in \mathcal{Q}, \exists x \notin \mathcal{Q}(c_1 \vee c_2), \not\models (c_1 \vee c_2)}{(c_1 \vee c_2)^{\max(p_1,p_2)}}$$

$$\text{(R.4)}\quad \frac{(c_1 \vee \neg x)^{p_1}, (c_2 \vee x)^{p_2}, \text{Я}^p x \in \mathcal{Q}, \text{Я}^p x \notin \mathcal{Q}(c_1 \vee c_2), \not\models (c_1 \vee c_2)}{(c_1 \vee c_2)^{p \cdot p_1 + (1-p)\cdot p_2}}$$

The final rule R.5 is similar in nature to rule (a) of the QBF resolution scheme in [18], where all universal literals not preceding any existential literal in a clause can be removed. In the stochastic case, we yet have to take care about the probability of the resulting clause. Therefore, we pessimistically resolve clause $(c \vee \ell)^{p_1}$ with the non-existing clause $(c \vee \neg\ell)^1$. The latter clause is annotated with the highest possible probability 1 that is always a safe upper bound. Thus, the resolvent clause $c^{p'\cdot p_1 + (1-p')}$ takes a valid upper bound probability.

$$\text{(R.5)}\quad \frac{(c \vee \ell)^{p_1}, \ell \in \{x, \neg x\}, \text{Я}^p x \in \mathcal{Q}, \text{Я}^p x \notin \mathcal{Q}(c), p' = \begin{cases} p \,;\, \ell = \neg x \\ 1-p \,;\, \ell = x \end{cases}}{c^{p'\cdot p_1 + (1-p')}}$$

Given the above rules R.1 to R.5, S-resolution is sound in the following sense.

Lemma 1. *Let clause c^p be derivable by S-resolution. Further, let be $\mathcal{Q}(c) = Q_1 x_1 \ldots Q_i x_i$. Then, for each $\tau : Var(\varphi) \downarrow_i \rightarrow \mathbb{B}$ with $\forall x \in Var(c) : \tau(x) = \mathit{ff}_c(x)$ it holds that*

$$Pr(Q_{i+1}x_{i+1} \ldots Q_n x_n : \varphi[\tau(x_1)/x_1] \ldots [\tau(x_i)/x_i]) \leq p.$$

Proof. We show the lemma by induction over the application of rules R.1-R.5. In the base case, we can just derive clauses $c^{p=0}$ by R.1 from clauses in φ. For this step, the assumption holds by property 1 of Proposition 1. Now assume that the assumption holds for all clauses in the premises of rules R.2-R.5. For rules R.3, R.4, and R.5, by Proposition 1, properties 2a, 2b, and 3, resp., it follows that for each $\tau' : Var(\varphi) \downarrow_{j-1} \rightarrow \mathbb{B}$ with $\forall x \in Var(c) : \tau'(x) = \mathit{ff}_c(x)$:

$$Pr(Q_j x_j \ldots Q_n x_n : \varphi[\tau'(x_1)/x_1] \ldots [\tau'(x_{j-1})/x_{j-1}]) \leq p,$$

where $x_j = x$ and $j \geq i+1$. Since variables $x_{i+1}, \ldots, x_{j-1}$ do not occur in the derived clause c^p, for $k = j-1$ to $i+1$ we successively conclude that

$$Pr(Q_{k+1}x_{k+1} \ldots Q_n x_n : \varphi[\tau'(x_1)/x_1] \ldots [\tau'(x_{k-1})/x_{k-1}][\mathtt{true}/x_k]) \leq p,$$
$$Pr(Q_{k+1}x_{k+1} \ldots Q_n x_n : \varphi[\tau'(x_1)/x_1] \ldots [\tau'(x_{k-1})/x_{k-1}][\mathtt{false}/x_k]) \leq p,$$

which finally leads to the desired result by choosing $\tau := \tau'$, i.e.

$$Pr(Q_{i+1}x_{i+1} \ldots Q_n x_n : \varphi[\tau(x_1)/x_1] \ldots [\tau(x_i)/x_i]) \leq p.$$

Soundness of rule R.2 is obvious: $x \notin Var(c)$ and thus there are at least two τ_1, τ_2 with $\tau_1(x) = \mathtt{true}$ and $\tau_2(x) = \mathtt{false}$ that satisfy the assumption for c^p. Hence, each such τ with $\tau(x) = \mathit{ff}_{(c\vee\ell)}(x)$ satisfies the assumption for $(c \vee l)^p$.□

Corollary 1 (Soundness of S-resolution). *If the empty clause $\emptyset^p$ is derivable by S-resolution from a given* SSAT *formula $\mathcal{Q} : \varphi$ then $Pr(\mathcal{Q} : \varphi) \leq p$.*

Corollary 1 follows directly from Lemma 1. Theorem 2 shows completeness.

Theorem 2 (Completeness of S-resolution). *If $Pr(\mathcal{Q} : \varphi) = p < 1$ for some* SSAT *formula $\mathcal{Q} : \varphi$ then the empty clause $\emptyset^p$ is derivable by S-resolution.*

Proof. If $\emptyset \in \varphi$, i.e. φ contains an empty clause, then $p = 0$ and the empty clause $\emptyset^0$ is derivable by rule R.1. In the remaining proof, we assume that $\emptyset \notin \varphi$. We prove the theorem by induction over the number of quantifiers in the quantifier prefix $\mathcal{Q}$. If $\mathcal{Q} = \exists x$ then $(\neg x), (x) \in \varphi$, hence $p = 0$, since otherwise $p = 1$. Then, $(\neg x)^0$ and $(x)^0$ are derivable from $(\neg x)$ and (x) by R.1, and R.3 finally yields $\emptyset^0$. If $\mathcal{Q} = \text{Я}^{p_x} x$ then $(\neg x) \in \varphi$ or $(x) \in \varphi$, since otherwise $p = 1$. If $(\neg x) \in \varphi$ and $(x) \notin \varphi$, i.e. $p = 1 - p_x$, the empty clause $\emptyset^{1-p_x=p}$ is derivable by R.1, yielding $(\neg x)^0$, and R.5, yielding $\emptyset^{p_x \cdot 0+(1-p_x)}$. Analogously, if $(\neg x) \notin \varphi$ and $(x) \in \varphi$, i.e. $p = p_x$, the empty clause $\emptyset^{p_x=p}$ is derivable. If $(\neg x) \in \varphi$ and $(x) \in \varphi$, i.e. $p = 0$, the empty clause $\emptyset^0$ is derivable by R.1, yielding $(\neg x)^0$ and $(x)^0$, and R.4, yielding $\emptyset^{p_x \cdot 0+(1-p_x) \cdot 0}$.

In the induction step, we will show that $\emptyset^{pr}$ is derivable for $Pr(Qx\, \mathcal{Q} : \varphi) = pr < 1$. Let $p_1 = Pr(\mathcal{Q} : \varphi[\texttt{true}/x])$ and $p_2 = Pr(\mathcal{Q} : \varphi[\texttt{false}/x])$. Induction hypothesis assumes that if $p_1 < 1$ (resp. $p_2 < 1$) then $\emptyset^{p_1}$ (resp. $\emptyset^{p_2}$) is derivable from $\mathcal{Q} : \varphi[\texttt{true}/x]$ (resp. $\mathcal{Q} : \varphi[\texttt{false}/x]$).

If $Q = \exists$ then $pr = \max(p_1, p_2)$, and since $pr < 1$ it follows that $p_1, p_2 < 1$. By induction hypothesis, the same resolution sequence as for $\mathcal{Q} : \varphi[\texttt{true}/x]$ derives one of the clauses $\emptyset^{p_1}$, $(\neg x)^{p_1}$ for $\exists x\ \mathcal{Q} : \varphi$. Analogously, one of the clauses $\emptyset^{p_2}$, $(x)^{p_2}$ is derivable by the same resolution sequence as for $\mathcal{Q} : \varphi[\texttt{false}/x]$. Let us consider any resolution sequence R for $\exists x\ \mathcal{Q} : \varphi$ deriving $\emptyset^{p_1}$ that is minimal in the sense that no application of any rule in R can be omitted in order to derive $\emptyset^{p_1}$. Observe that each clause c involved in R does not contain variable x, i.e. $x \notin Var(c)$: first, the positive literal x cannot be contained in c since R yields $\emptyset^{p_1}$ for $\mathcal{Q} : \varphi[\texttt{true}/x]$. Second, the negative literal $\neg x$ cannot be contained in c since R yields $\emptyset^{p_1}$ for $\exists x\ \mathcal{Q} : \varphi$ and R is minimal. Furthermore, $\emptyset^{p_1}$ cannot be derived directly from a clause $c \in \varphi$, since $\emptyset \notin \varphi$. Thus, one of the rules R.3, R.4, or R.5 must be applied in R. Let R' be the resolution sequence that works as R except for the following modifications: for one clause c^0 that occurs in R and is derived by R.1, rule R.2 is applied to obtain clause $(\neg x \vee c)^0$. For the latter application, note that $\exists x \in \mathcal{Q}(c)$. In the premise of each rule in R, c^0 is then replaced by $(\neg x \vee c)^0$. Since R is minimal, i.e. c^0 is a predecessor of $\emptyset^{p_1}$, and by the rules of S-resolution, it follows that R' derives $(\neg x)^{p_1}$ for $\exists x\ \mathcal{Q} : \varphi$. Hence, $(\neg x)^{p_1}$ is always derivable from $\exists x\ \mathcal{Q} : \varphi$. With the same argument, $(x)^{p_2}$ is derivable. R.3 finally yields $\emptyset^{\max(p_1,p_2)=pr}$.

If $Q = \text{Я}^{p_x}$ then $pr = p_x \cdot p_1 + (1 - p_x) \cdot p_2$. As $pr < 1$ holds, at least one of p_1, p_2 is less than 1. For case $p_1, p_2 < 1$, as shown above for $Q = \exists$, clauses $(\neg x)^{p_1}$ and $(x)^{p_2}$ are derivable from $\text{Я}^{p_x} x\ \mathcal{Q} : \varphi$. R.4 then gives $\emptyset^{p_x \cdot p_1+(1-p_x) \cdot p_2=pr}$. For case $p_1 < 1, p_2 = 1$, clause $(\neg x)^{p_1}$ is derivable, and R.5 yields $\emptyset^{p_x \cdot p_1+(1-p_x)=pr}$. Analogously for $p_1 = 1, p_2 < 1$, clause $\emptyset^{(1-p_x) \cdot p_2+p_x=pr}$ is derivable. □

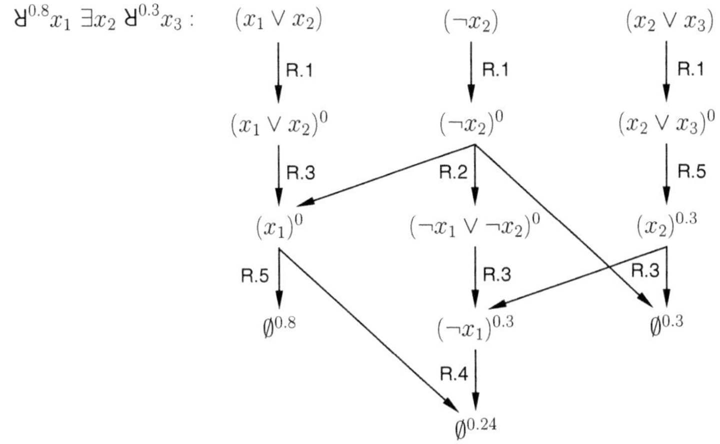

Fig. 3. Different derivations of the empty clause by S-resolution. Arrows denote applications of the corresponding resolution rules.

Example. Consider the SSAT formula $\Phi = \text{R}^{0.8}x_1 \; \exists x_2 \; \text{R}^{0.3}x_3 : (x_1 \vee x_2) \wedge (\neg x_2) \wedge (x_2 \vee x_3)$. There is just one satisfying assignment, namely $x_1 = \texttt{true}, x_2 = \texttt{false}, x_3 = \texttt{true}$, and the maximum probability of satisfaction thus is $Pr(\Phi) = 0.24$. In Fig. 3, three different derivations of empty clauses are depicted. Each empty clause proves an upper bound of $Pr(\Phi)$ according to Corollary 1, while only $\emptyset^{0.24}$ constitutes the exact probability of satisfaction. Such a derivation of $\emptyset^p$ with $p = Pr(\Phi)$ always exists due to Theorem 2.

Theoretical evaluation. For a theoretical assessment, we compare S-resolution with the standard SSAT procedure DPLL-SSAT from Fig. 2. As both approaches are sound and complete, we are interested in their *proof complexity*, i.e. the size of their proofs. We define the *size of a proof* that an SSAT instance (Φ, t) is true or false as the number of steps needed by a method to decide (Φ, t), i.e. the number of rule applications for S-resolution and the number of recursions for DPLL-SSAT. Both approaches may produce proofs of exponential size in worst case (examples are given below). We will thus compare their *smallest* proofs.

For a fair comparison we have to distinguish between true and false SSAT instances. The rationale is that S-resolution yields only upper bounds on satisfaction probabilities. To decide a true SSAT instance (Φ, t), i.e. $Pr(\Phi) \geq t$, S-resolution needs to derive all empty clauses $\emptyset^p$ (which implies to apply all rules until no new clause can be derived) to give a positive answer. Note that there can be exponentially many derivations of empty clauses. DPLL-SSAT with its algorithmic optimizations however potentially outputs the result much earlier. For instance, consider the family of SSAT formulae $\text{R}^{0.5}y_1 \ldots \text{R}^{0.5}y_n : (y_1) \wedge \ldots \wedge (y_n)$ and $t = 0.5^{n+1}$. Observe that the number of derivations of empty clauses $\emptyset^p$ is exponential in n and that for each $\emptyset^p$ it holds that $p > t$. DPLL-SSAT, however, solves the problem in n steps, e.g., just by unit propagation. Thus, DPLL-SSAT will never be worse, and potentially much more efficient, than S-resolution on true SSAT instances whenever exponentially many empty-clause derivations exist, which generally is the case.

Let us consider the case where the SSAT instance (Φ, t) is false, i.e. $Pr(\Phi) < t$. We will first show that on such instances, each DPLL-SSAT proof of size k can be easily transformed into an S-resolution proof of size $\mathcal{O}(k^2)$, i.e. with just a quadratic overhead. Thereafter, we present a family of SSAT instances for which the smallest S-resolution proof is of constant size while DPLL-SSAT needs in best case exponentially many computation steps.

Proposition 2. *For false* SSAT *instances each* DPLL-SSAT *proof of size k can be transformed into an S-resolution proof of size $\mathcal{O}(k^2)$.*

We sketch the proof of Proposition 2 by explaining how a derivation of an empty clause $\emptyset^p$ with $p < t$ can be constructed from a DPLL-SSAT(Φ, t, t) proof search. Foremost observe that due to assumption $Pr(\Phi) < t$, the upper threshold θ_u will never be exceeded by any intermediate probability result (cf. Fig. 2), as otherwise $Pr(\Phi) \geq t$ would hold. For our purpose, we slightly modify DPLL-SSAT. In order to keep track of the current partial variable assignment, DPLL-SSAT takes an additional input pa that is a set of literals representing the current partial assignment. To solve an SSAT problem, we call DPLL-SSAT(Φ, t, t, pa) with $pa = \emptyset$. Moreover, the return value of DPLL-SSAT now is a pair of the probability value p and a derived clause c^{pr} annotated with a probability value pr, as explained below. Note that the concrete implementation as shown in Fig. 2 must be adapted correspondingly. However, both changes do not influence the probability result p of DPLL-SSAT. For base case "`false`" of DPLL-SSAT, we return the pair $(0, c^0)$ where clause c consists of all negated literals in the set pa. This clause c^0 is derivable by one application of R.1 and at most $|pa| - 1$ applications of R.2. In case that all clauses are satisfied, i.e. base case "`true`", we cannot apply any rule. To indicate this "failure", we return $(1, \emptyset^1)$ with the non-derivable clause $\emptyset^1$. When branching for variable x we recursively call DPLL-SSAT on the extended assignment $pa \cup \{\ell\}$ where $\ell = x$ if x is substituted by `true` and $\ell = \neg x$ otherwise. Let $c_1^{pr_1}$ and $c_2^{pr_2}$ be the clauses returned by the recursive calls. We first consider the existential case. Recall again that $p_1 \geq \theta_u$ will never be satisfied. If both $pr_1, pr_2 < 1$, i.e. both clauses could be derived by S-resolution, we return the resolved clause $((c_1 \cup c_2) - \{x, \neg x\})^{\max(pr_1, pr_2)}$ by rule R.3. If $pr_1 = 1$ or $pr_2 = 1$ then no rule is applicable and we return clause $\emptyset^1$ to indicate this. For the randomized case, let first be $pr_1, pr_2 < 1$. If $p_1 \cdot p + (1 - p) < \theta_l$ holds then we return $(c_1 - \{\neg x\})^{pr_1 \cdot p + (1-p)}$ by R.5. Otherwise, the returned clause is $((c_1 \cup c_2) - \{x, \neg x\})^{pr_1 \cdot p + pr_2 \cdot (1-p))}$ by R.4. If $pr_1 < 1$ and $pr_2 = 1$ then we derive $(c_1 - \{\neg x\})^{pr_1 \cdot p + (1-p)}$ by R.5. Analogously for $pr_1 = 1$ and $pr_2 < 1$, $(c_2 - \{x\})^{p + pr_2 \cdot (1-p)}$. If $pr_1 = pr_2 = 1$ then no rule is applicable indicated by $\emptyset^1$.

Special attention must be devoted to unit propagation and purification. For purification observe that propagating a pure literal will never cause a clause violation by definition. Thus, we neglect this assignment and keep the set pa for the recursive call of DPLL-SSAT and just pass through clause c^{pr} returned by recursion. Note that unit propagation moves a quantifier in the prefix to the left, i.e. $\mathcal{Q}_1 Qx \mathcal{Q}_2 \leadsto Qx \mathcal{Q}_1 \mathcal{Q}_2$. This of course is not a valid operation in general. However, this is correct for unit literals, i.e. $Pr(\mathcal{Q}_1 Qx \mathcal{Q}_2 : \varphi \wedge \ell) = Pr(Qx \mathcal{Q}_1 \mathcal{Q}_2 : \varphi \wedge \ell)$ with $\ell \in \{x, \neg x\}$, as the value of x satisfying ℓ does not depend on $\mathcal{Q}_1$. This semantics-preserving quantifier reshuffling justifies the derivation of clause c^{pr} by recursive call DPLL-SSAT with updated assignment $pa \cup \{\ell\}$. Now observe that assignment $pa \cup \{\neg\ell\}$ violates some clause, as ℓ is unit. Clause $(c' \cup \{\ell\})^0$ is thus derivable by S-resolution, where c' consists of all negated literals in pa. If $pr < 1$, we return clause $((c \cup c') - \{\neg\ell\})^{pr}$ in the existential case by R.3, and $((c \cup c') - \{\neg\ell\})^{pr \cdot p(\ell)}$ in the randomized case by R.4. If $pr = 1$, we return $\emptyset^1$ and $(c')^{p(\ell)}$ for the existential and randomized case, respectively. For each returned pair (p, c^{pr}) it holds that $p \leq pr$. Furthermore, if $p < \theta_l$ then $pr < \theta_l$. This is given by the base case $p_1 \cdot p + (1-p) < \theta_l$ and by manipulating the thresholds for recursion (cf. Fig. 2). Thus, the initial call DPLL-SSAT$(\Phi, t, t, \emptyset)$ returns a pair $(p, \emptyset^{pr})$ with $pr < t$, i.e. the empty clause $\emptyset^{pr}$ is derivable by S-resolution, iff $Pr(\Phi) < t$. Observe that at most one clause is derived per DPLL-SSAT call, except for the base case "`false`". Let k be the DPLL-SSAT proof size and $f \leq k$ be the number of DPLL-SSAT calls that directly lead to the base case "`false`". Further, let a_i for $1 \leq i \leq f$ be the number of variables that are assigned values when reaching the i-th base case "`false`". Clearly, $a_i \geq |pa|$. Thus, for i-th base case "`false`", at most a_i new clauses are derived by R.1 and R.2. Hence, the S-resolution proof size k' is at most $k + \sum_{i=1}^{f} a_i$. Very conservatively, $a_i \leq k$ for each i. Immediately, $k' \leq k + f \cdot k \leq k + k^2 \in \mathcal{O}(k^2)$.

Proposition 3. *There is a family of false* SSAT *instances for which the smallest S-resolution proof is of constant size while the smallest* DPLL-SSAT *proof is of exponential size.*

To prove Proposition 3, consider the family of SSAT formulae $\Phi_{n \in \mathbb{N}_{>0}} =$

$$Q_{1,1}x_{1,1} \dots Q_{1,n}x_{1,n} Q_{2,n}x_{2,n} Q_{3,n}x_{3,n} \dots Q_{2,1}x_{2,1} Q_{3,1}x_{3,1} : \bigwedge_{i=1}^{n} all\_comb(x_{1,i}, x_{2,i}, x_{3,i})$$

where $all\_comb(x_{1,i}, x_{2,i}, x_{3,i}) = (x_{1,i} \vee x_{2,i} \vee x_{3,i}) \wedge (x_{1,i} \vee x_{2,i} \vee \neg x_{3,i}) \wedge \dots \wedge (\neg x_{1,i} \vee \neg x_{2,i} \vee \neg x_{3,i})$ is a predicate in 3CNF that gives all non-tautological clauses with the three variables $x_{1,i}, x_{2,i}, x_{3,i}$. Obviously, $all\_comb(x_{1,i}, x_{2,i}, x_{3,i})$ is unsatisfiable, and thus $Pr(\Phi_n) = 0$. Hence, for each $t > 0$ it holds that the SSAT instance (Φ_n, t) is false. S-resolution needs in best case only 7 resolution steps to derive the empty clause $\emptyset^0$, namely by resolving only clauses in $all\_comb(x_{1,i}, x_{2,i}, x_{3,i})$ for some i. DPLL-SSAT however needs exponentially many steps in n to solve the problem. The rationale is that a conflict, i.e. base case "`false`", is detected not before variables $x_{1,1} \dots x_{1,n} x_{2,n}$ are assigned. After setting $x_{2,n}$, the conflict in $all\_comb(x_{1,n}, x_{2,n}, x_{3,n})$ is revealed by unit propagation. However, after backtracking to some point where $x_{2,n}$ is unassigned, the conflict is no longer present and is only revisited after branching for $x_{2,n}$ again. Hence, DPLL-SSAT must traverse all 2^{n+1} assignments to the variables $x_{1,1} \dots x_{1,n} x_{2,n}$ until Φ_n is solved.

It is expected that *conflict-driven clause learning* [23] as employed in DPLL-based SAT solvers is beneficial to significantly improve DPLL-SSAT proof sizes on problems of such or similar structures. An interesting issue for future research thus is to investigate how S-resolution can be instrumental in developing a more general clause learning scheme to be integrated into DPLL-based SSAT algorithms: by Lemma 1, a derived clause $(c \vee \ell)^p$ means that under each assignment that falsifies $(c \vee \ell)$, the satisfaction probability of the remaining subproblem is at most p. The inductive argument in the proof of Theorem 2 suggests that there are also clauses $(c \vee \ell)^p$ for which the probability of the subproblem is *exactly* p. Thus, under a partial assignment that falsifies c one could directly propagate literal ℓ as the satisfaction probability of the other branch, for which the negation of ℓ holds, is already known, namely p.

5 Discussion and Future Work

In this paper, we have explained two contributions to the field of stochastic propositional satisfiability solving. First, we have shown that the restriction of SSAT to formulae in 2CNF is PSPACE-complete, i.e. as hard as the general problem. Second, we have introduced a sound and complete resolution calculus for SSAT that complements the work on classical DPLL-based SSAT algorithms. While each DPLL-SSAT proof for false SSAT instances can be transformed into an S-resolution proof with just a quadratic overhead, there is a family of SSAT instances for which the smallest S-resolution proof is of constant size and each DPLL-SSAT proof, however, is of exponential size.

Similar to *proofs of unsatisfiability* for SAT, S-resolution provides a theoretical framework to generate *proofs of satisfiability with insufficient probability*. Such proofs permit the subsequent validation of SSAT solver results as well as the extraction of small subformulae having the same satisfaction probabilities as the original formula. In future work, we will concentrate on two challenging issues. Motivated by the success of clause learning in SAT solving, we will investigate an SSAT clause learning scheme based on S-resolution to significantly improve performance of DPLL-based SSAT solvers. Another topic is the potential application of S-resolution for computing stochastic variants of Craig interpolants, expected to provide a technique enhancing applications of SSAT solving, among them the extension of SSAT-based bounded model checking of probabilistic systems like Markov Decision Processes to unbounded model checking.

References

1. Papadimitriou, C.H.: Games against nature. J. Comput. Syst. Sci. 31(2), 288–301 (1985)
2. Littman, M.L., Majercik, S.M., Pitassi, T.: Stochastic Boolean Satisfiability. Journal of Automated Reasoning 27(3), 251–296 (2001)
3. Majercik, S.M., Littman, M.L.: MAXPLAN: A New Approach to Probabilistic Planning. In: Artificial Intelligence Planning Systems, pp. 86–93 (1998)
4. Majercik, S.M., Littman, M.L.: Contingent Planning Under Uncertainty via Stochastic Satisfiability. Artificial Intelligence Special Issue on Planning With Uncertainty and Incomplete Information 147(1-2), 119–162 (2003)

5. Walsh, T.: Stochastic constraint programming. In: Proc. of the 15th European Conference on Artificial Intelligence (ECAI 2002), IOS Press, Amsterdam (2002)
6. Tarim, A., Manandhar, S., Walsh, T.: Stochastic constraint programming: A scenario-based approach. Constraints 11(1), 53–80 (2006)
7. Balafoutis, T., Stergiou, K.: Algorithms for Stochastic CSPs. In: Benhamou, F. (ed.) CP 2006. LNCS, vol. 4204, pp. 44–58. Springer, Heidelberg (2006)
8. Bordeaux, L., Samulowitz, H.: On the stochastic constraint satisfaction framework. In: SAC, pp. 316–320. ACM, New York (2007)
9. Fränzle, M., Hermanns, H., Teige, T.: Stochastic satisfiability modulo theory: A novel technique for the analysis of probabilistic hybrid systems. In: Egerstedt, M., Mishra, B. (eds.) HSCC 2008. LNCS, vol. 4981, pp. 172–186. Springer, Heidelberg (2008)
10. Barrett, C., Sebastiani, R., Seshia, S.A., Tinelli, C.: Satisfiability modulo theories. In: [24], ch. 26, pp. 825–885
11. Littman, M.L.: Initial Experiments in Stochastic Satisfiability. In: Proc. of the 16th National Conference on Artificial Intelligence, pp. 667–672 (1999)
12. Davis, M., Putnam, H.: A Computing Procedure for Quantification Theory. Journal of the ACM 7(3), 201–215 (1960)
13. Davis, M., Logemann, G., Loveland, D.: A Machine Program for Theorem Proving. Communications of the ACM 5, 394–397 (1962)
14. Majercik, S.M.: Nonchronological backtracking in stochastic Boolean satisfiability. In: ICTAI, pp. 498–507. IEEE Computer Society, Los Alamitos (2004)
15. Teige, T., Fränzle, M.: Stochastic satisfiability modulo theories for non-linear arithmetic. In: Perron, L., Trick, M.A. (eds.) CPAIOR 2008. LNCS, vol. 5015, pp. 248–262. Springer, Heidelberg (2008)
16. Teige, T., Eggers, A., Fränzle, M.: Constraint-based analysis of concurrent probabilistic hybrid systems: An application to networked automation systems. Nonlinear Analysis: Hybrid Systems (2010) (to appear)
17. Robinson, J.A.: A machine-oriented logic based on the resolution principle. J. ACM 12(1), 23–41 (1965)
18. Büning, H.K., Karpinski, M., Flögel, A.: Resolution for quantified Boolean formulas. Inf. Comput. 117(1), 12–18 (1995)
19. Majercik, S.M.: Stochastic Boolean satisfiability. In: [24], vol. 27, pp. 887–925
20. Aspvall, B., Plass, M.F., Tarjan, R.E.: A linear-time algorithm for testing the truth of certain quantified Boolean formulas. Inf. Process. Lett. 8(3), 121–123 (1979)
21. Goldsmith, J., Hagen, M., Mundhenk, M.: Complexity of DNF and isomorphism of monotone formulas. In: Jedrzejowicz, J., Szepietowski, A. (eds.) MFCS 2005. LNCS, vol. 3618, pp. 410–421. Springer, Heidelberg (2005)
22. Schaefer, T.J.: The complexity of satisfiability problems. In: Proc. of the Tenth Annual ACM Symposium on Theory of Computing, pp. 216–226. ACM, New York (1978)
23. Silva, J.P.M., Lynce, I., Malik, S.: Conflict-driven clause learning SAT solvers. In: [24], ch. 4, pp. 131–153
24. Biere, A., Heule, M.J.H., van Maaren, H., Walsh, T. (eds.): Handbook of Satisfiability. Frontiers in Artificial Intelligence and Applications, vol. 185. IOS Press, Amsterdam (February 2009)

Symbolic Automata Constraint Solving

Margus Veanes, Nikolaj Bjørner, and Leonardo de Moura

Microsoft Research Redmond, WA, USA
{margus,nbjorner,leonardo}@microsoft.com

Abstract. Constraints over regular and context-free languages are common in the context of string-manipulating programs. Efficient solving of such constraints, often in combination with arithmetic and other theories, has many useful applications in program analysis and testing. We introduce and evaluate a method for symbolically expressing and solving constraints over automata, including subset constraints. Our method uses techniques present in the state-of-the-art SMT solver Z3.

1 Introduction

Regular expressions are used in different applications to express validity constraints over strings. In our case, the original motivation for supporting regular expression constraints comes from two particular applications: program analysis [13], and database query analysis [19], where the application is to synthesize data-base tables from SQL queries. In the latter case, *like-patterns* are special kinds of regular expressions that are common in SQL queries, consider e.g.:

$$\texttt{SELECT} * \texttt{FROM}\ T\quad \texttt{WHERE}\ C\ \texttt{LIKE}\ r_1\ \texttt{AND NOT}\ C\ \texttt{LIKE}\ r_2\ \texttt{AND LEN}(C) < D + E \qquad (1)$$

that selects all rows from a table T having columns C, D and E, where the C-value matches the like-pattern r_1, does not match the like-pattern r_2 and whose length is less than the sum of D-value and E-value. The analysis discussed in [19] aims at generating tables that satisfy a test condition, e.g., that the result of (1) is nonempty. A core part of that analysis is to find solutions to select-conditions of the above form.

We introduce a technique that allows conditions such as SELECT of (1) to be expressed and analyzed using satisfiability modulo theories (SMT) solving in a way that is extensible with other constraints and theories. The central idea behind the technique is the notion of a *symbolic (language) acceptor* for a language (set of strings) L, as a binary predicate $Acc^L(w, k)$ that is true modulo a theory $Th(L)$ iff $w \in L$ and k is the length $|w|$ of w. For a regular expression r the symbolic acceptor for $L(r)$ is constructed from a symbolic finite automaton A_r that accepts $L(r)$; the symbolic acceptor is denoted by Acc^{A_r} and the theory is denoted by $Th(A_r)$. The automaton A_r is itself symbolic in the sense that its moves are labeled by formulas rather than individual characters, which provides a succinct way to represent automata.

In particular, solving the select condition in (1) corresponds to solving,

$$Acc^{A_{r_1}}(c, k) \wedge \neg Acc^{A_{r_2}}(c, k) \wedge k < d + e \qquad (2)$$

C. Fermüller and A. Voronkov (Eds.): LPAR-17, LNCS 6397, pp. 640–654, 2010.

modulo the theories $Th(A_{r_1})$, $Th(A_{r_2})$ and linear arithmetic. A *solution* of (2) is a mapping of particular values for c, k, d, and e which makes (2) true (modulo the given theories).

In applications such as [13,19], that build on the SMT technology, a fundamental aspect is that new theories can be added seamlessly and work in combination with existing theories.

The construction of $Th(A)$ builds on automata theory that offers a choice between various logically equivalent forms of axiomatization and composition techniques for performance considerations. For example, an encoding for (1) that is equivalent to the direct encoding (2) has the form

$$Acc^{A_{r_1} \times \overline{A_{r_2}}}(c, k) \wedge k < d + e \tag{3}$$

where $\overline{A}$ denotes the complement of A and $A \times B$ denotes the product of A and B. Since complementation may cause exponential blowup in the size of an automaton, it may be useful to use an encoding that combines product with complementation as *difference*:

$$Acc^{A_{r_1} \setminus A_{r_2}}(c, k) \wedge k < d + e \tag{4}$$

Note that if $L(r_1) \subseteq L(r_2)$ in (1), i.e., $L(r_1) \setminus L(r_2) = \emptyset$ then the query (1) is *infeasible*. In contrast to (2), the encoding in (4) provides some benefits for the integration with SMT solving, since it can detect emptiness during the incremental difference construction. Independently, difference checking provides a way to check *subset* constraints, that have other useful applications [9].

Combination of regular constraints on strings with quantifier free linear arithmetic and length constraints is known to be decidable [22,23]. One can effectively compute an upper bound on the length of all strings, see [17]. By using these bounds to restrict the maximum length of strings in solutions of acceptor formulas, one obtains a *complete* decision procedure for solving linear arithmetic with regular constraints and length constraints with the approach described in this paper. For context free languages the approach gives a complete semi-decision procedure.

We describe a specialized algorithm for constructing the difference $A \setminus B$ between a symbolic PDA A and a symbolic FA B. This algorithm is of interest independently from the main application context; one use of the algorithm is for checking subset constraints of the form $L_1 \subseteq L_2$ where L_1 is context free and L_2 is regular without the need to provide fixed length bounds for the words. We evaluate the performance of the different approaches we implemented in a prototype tool and provide a comparison with the HAMPI tool [11].

2 Preliminaries

In the following, we assume familiarity with classical automata theory [10], logic and model theory [8]. We are working in a fixed multi-sorted universe $\mathcal{U}$ of values. For each sort σ, $\mathcal{U}^\sigma$ is a separate sub-universe of $\mathcal{U}$. The basic sorts needed in this paper are the Boolean sort $\mathbb{B}$, $\mathcal{U}^{\mathbb{B}} = \{true, false\}$, and the sort of *n-bit-vectors*, for a given number $n \geq 1$; an n-bit-vector is essentially a vector of n Booleans. *Characters* are represented by n-bit-vectors of fixed length n, such that $n = 7$ (8) bits encode standard (extended) ASCII characters, and $n = 16$ encode Unicode characters. With n clear from the context, we write $\mathbb{C}$ for the character sort. The complete alphabet is $\mathcal{U}^{\mathbb{C}}$. Constant characters are for example written as `'a'`.

There is a *built-in* (predefined) *signature* of function symbols and a built-in theory (set of axioms) for those symbols. Each function symbol f of arity $n \geq 0$ has a given domain sort $\sigma_0 \times \cdots \times \sigma_{n-1}$, when $n > 0$, and a given range sort σ, $f : \sigma_0 \times \cdots \times \sigma_{n-1} \to \sigma$. For example, there is a built-in Boolean function $< : \mathbb{C} \times \mathbb{C} \to \mathbb{B}$ that provides a strict total order of all the characters. One can also declare *fresh* (new) *uninterpreted* function symbols f of arity $n \geq 0$, for a given domain sort and a given range sort. Using model theoretic terminology, these new symbols *expand* the signature. A *constant* is a nullary function symbol. Well-sorted *terms* and *formulas* (Boolean terms) are defined as usual. We write $FV(t)$ for the set of free variables in a term (or formula) t. A term or formula without free variables is *closed*. Let $\mathcal{F}_{\mathbb{C}}$ denote the set of all quantifier-free formulas with at most one fixed free variable of sort $\mathbb{C}$. *Throughout the paper, we denote that variable by* χ. Given $\varphi \in \mathcal{F}_{\mathbb{C}}$, and a character or term t of sort $\mathbb{C}$, we write $\varphi[t]$ for the formula where each occurrence of χ is replaced by t.

A *model* is a mapping from function symbols to their interpretations (values). The built-in function symbols have the same interpretation in all models, keeping that in mind, we may omit them from the model. A *model for a formula* φ provides an interpretation for all the uninterpreted symbols in φ. A model M for a closed formula φ *satisfies* φ, $M \models \varphi$, if the interpretations provided by M make φ true. A closed formula φ is *satisfiable* if it has a model. A formula φ with $FV(\varphi) = \bar{x}$ is *satisfiable* if its existential closure $\exists\bar{x}\varphi$ is satisfiable. We write $\models \varphi$, if φ is *valid* (true in all models for φ). For $\varphi \in \mathcal{F}_{\mathbb{C}}$, we write $[\![\varphi]\!]$ for the set of all $a \in \mathcal{U}^{\mathbb{C}}$ such that $\models \varphi[a]$.

For example, the character range set `[a-z\d]` in a regex is translated into the formula $\psi = (\texttt{'a'} \leq \chi \wedge \chi \leq \texttt{'z'}) \vee (\texttt{'0'} \leq \chi \wedge \chi \leq \texttt{'9'})$ with χ as the single free variable in ψ. The formula ψ is satisfiable; $\psi[\texttt{'b'}]$ is true; $\psi[\texttt{'A'}]$ is false. Note that `'a'`, `'z'`, `'0'` and `'9'` in ψ stand for terms that use only built-in function symbols and denote the bit-vector encodings of the corresponding characters and digits.

3 Symbolic Automata

We use a representation of automata where several transitions from a source state to a target state are combined into a single symbolic move. Symbolic moves are labeled by formulas from $\mathcal{F}_{\mathbb{C}}$ that represent *sets of characters* rather than individual characters. This representation has the advantage of being more succinct for symbolic analysis than an *explicit* representation. The following definition builds directly on the standard definition of PDAs.

Definition 1. A *Symbolic Push Down Automaton* or *SPDA* A is a tuple $(Q, \varphi_\Sigma, Z, \Delta, q_0, z_0, F)$, where Q is a finite set of *states*, φ_Σ is a formula in $\mathcal{F}_\mathbb{C}$ called *input predicate*, Z is a finite set of *stack symbols*, $q_0 \in Q$ is the *initial state*, $z_0 \in Z$ is the *initial stack symbol*, $F \subseteq Q$ is the set of *final states* and $\Delta : Q \times Z \times \mathcal{F}_\mathbb{C} \times Q \times Z^*$ is the *move relation*.

An SPDA A denotes the PDA $[\![A]\!]$ whose input alphabet is $[\![\varphi_\Sigma]\!]$ and $[\![A]\!]$ has a transition $(q, z, a, p, \boldsymbol{z})$ for each $(q, z, \varphi, p, \boldsymbol{z}) \in \Delta$ and $a \in [\![\varphi \wedge \varphi_\Sigma]\!]$. The remaining components map directly to the corresponding components of a PDA. When φ_Σ is *true*, i.e., when the input alphabet is $U^\mathbb{C}$, we omit φ_Σ from the definition.

An ϵSPDA A may in addition have moves where the condition is $\epsilon \notin \mathcal{F}_\mathbb{C}$, denoting the corresponding ϵ-move in $[\![A]\!]$. Let $\rho = (q, z, \alpha, p, \boldsymbol{z})$ be a move of an ϵSPDA A.We define $Src(\rho) \stackrel{\text{def}}{=} q$, $Tgt(\rho) \stackrel{\text{def}}{=} p$, $Cnd(\rho) \stackrel{\text{def}}{=} \alpha$, $Pop(\rho) \stackrel{\text{def}}{=} z$, and $Push(\rho) \stackrel{\text{def}}{=} \boldsymbol{z}$. We also use the following notations

$$\Delta_A(q) \stackrel{\text{def}}{=} \{\rho \mid \rho \in \Delta_A, Src(\rho) = q\}$$
$$\Delta_A(q, z) \stackrel{\text{def}}{=} \{\rho \mid \rho \in \Delta_A(q), Pop(\rho) = z\}$$

and furthermore will allow lifting functions to sets. For example, $\Delta_A(Q) \stackrel{\text{def}}{=} \cup\{\Delta_A(q) \mid q \in Q\}$. We write Δ_A^ϵ for the set of all epsilon moves in Δ_A and $\Delta_A^{\not\epsilon}$ for $\Delta_A \setminus \Delta_A^\epsilon$.

An ϵSPDA A is *clean* if all moves in $\Delta_A^{\not\epsilon}$ have satisfiable conditions, and *normalized* if there are no two moves in $\Delta_A^{\not\epsilon}$ that differ only with respect to their condition.

The language $L(A)$ accepted by A is the language $L([\![A]\!])$ accepted by the PDA $[\![A]\!]$.

It is clear that for any ϵSPDA A there is a normalized ϵSPDA A' such that $[\![A]\!] = [\![A']\!]$: just combine all nonepsilon moves that only differ with respect to their conditions into a single move by making a disjunction of their conditions.

Elimination of epsilon moves from an ϵSPDA corresponds to transforming the corresponding context free grammar into Greibach Normal Form (GNF), which can be done in polynomial time. Move conditions play no active role in the algorithm. (Terminals are in general treated as black boxes in normal form transformations of grammars.) In the prototype tool we use a variation of the Blum-Koch algorithm [3] for GNF transformation that has worst case time complexity $O(n^4)$.

Definition 2. An ϵSPDA A *represents a symbolic finite automaton with epsilon moves* or *ϵSFA* if for all $\rho \in \Delta_A$, $Pop(\rho) = Push(\rho) = z_{0A}$.

When considering an ϵSPDA A that represents an ϵSFA, we omit the stack symbols and denote A by the tuple $(Q_A, \varphi_{\Sigma A}, \Delta_A, q_{0A}, F_A)$. We use [14] as the concrete language definition of regular expressions or *regexes* in this paper. The translation from a regex to an ϵSFA follows very closely the standard algorithm, see e.g., [10, Section 2.5], for converting a standard regular expression into a

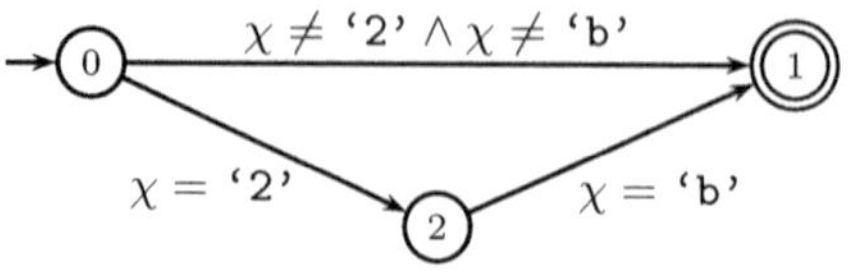

Fig. 1. Sample ϵSFA generated from the regex `^(2b|[^2b])$`

finite automaton with epsilon moves. A sample regex and corresponding ϵSFA are illustrated in Figure 1.

When we say SPDA or SFA we assume that epsilon moves are not present.

4 Symbolic Language Acceptors

To encode language acceptors, we use particular kinds of axioms, all of which are equations of the form

$$\forall \bar{x}(t_{\mathrm{lhs}} = t_{\mathrm{rhs}}) \tag{5}$$

where $FV(t_{\mathrm{lhs}}) = \bar{x}$ and $FV(t_{\mathrm{rhs}}) \subseteq \bar{x}$. When t_{lhs} and t_{rhs} are formulas, we often write '$\Leftrightarrow$' instead of '$=$'. The left-hand-side t_{lhs} of (5) is called the *head* of (5) and the right-hand-side t_{rhs} of (5) is called the *body* of (5)

Many SMT solvers support various kinds of patterns for triggering axioms. Yet in this paper, we use the convention that the pattern of an equational axiom is always its head.

The same convention is used in [19]. Axioms are asserted as equations that are expanded during proof search. Expanding the formula up front is problematic since the equational axioms introduced for automata are in general mutually recursive (as shown below) and a naive a priori exhaustive expansion would in most cases not terminate. Straight-forward depth-bounded expansions are also not practical as the size of the bounded expansion is easily exponential in the depth.

The overall idea behind the axioms introduced below is as follows. For a given ϵSPDA A we construct a theory $Th(A)$ that includes a particular axiom with head $Acc^A(w,k)$. The main property of $Th(A)$ is that it precisely characterizes the language accepted by A as the set of solutions w and k for $Th(A) \wedge Acc^A(w,k)$, where k is the length of w.

Lists. Lists are built-in algebraic data-types and are accompanied with standard constructors and accessors. For each sort σ, $\mathbb{L}\langle\sigma\rangle$ is the *list sort* with element sort σ. For a given element sort σ there is an empty list ε (of sort $\mathbb{L}\langle\sigma\rangle$) and if e is an element of sort σ and l is a list of sort $\mathbb{L}\langle\sigma\rangle$ then $[e|l]$ is a list of sort $\mathbb{L}\langle\sigma\rangle$. The accessors are, as usual, *hd* (head) and *tl* (tail). *Words* or *strings* are represented by lists of characters; we write $\mathbb{W}$ for the sort $\mathbb{L}\langle\mathbb{C}\rangle$. We adopt the common convention that $[a,b,c]$ stands for the list $[a|[b|[c|\varepsilon]]]$ and we use $l_1 \cdot l_2$ for concatenation of l_1 and l_2.

Construction of Th(A). Let A be a given ϵSPDA. Assume A is normalized. Let $\mathbb{N}$ be a built-in non-negative numeral sort such as a bit-vector or integer sort restricted to non-negative integers. We use $\mathbb{N}$ for representing the length $|l|$ of a list l, i.e., the number of elements in l. Let $\mathbb{Z}$ be a sort for representing Z_A and assume that $Z_A \subseteq \mathcal{U}^{\mathbb{Z}}$. By slight abuse of notation, we also use elements in $\mathcal{U}$ as terms. We may assume, without loss of generality that $\mathbb{Z}$ is a fixed numeral sort as well. We represent a *stack* as an element of sort $\mathbb{S} = \mathbb{L}\langle\mathbb{Z}\rangle$.

For all $q \in Q_A$, declare the predicate symbol

$$Acc_q^A : \mathbb{W} \times \mathbb{N} \times \mathbb{S} \to \mathbb{B}$$

Recall that an *ID* of $[\![A]\!]$ is a triple (q, w, s) where $q \in Q_{[\![A]\!]}$, w is a word and s is a stack [10]. For defining the axioms it is more convenient to use *acceptance by the empty stack* rather than final states, the language accepted by the empty stack is denoted by $N([\![A]\!])$ in [10, page 112]. The transformation of A to an equivalent ϵSPDA A' such that $L([\![A]\!]) = N([\![A']\!])$ is straightforward. We therefore assume below that $F_A = \emptyset$.

The idea behind the axioms defined below is that the formula $Acc_q^A(w, n, s)$ holds iff $|w| = n$ and $(q, w, s) \vdash_{[\![A]\!]}^* (p, \varepsilon, \varepsilon)$ for some $p \in Q_{[\![A]\!]}$, where $\vdash_{[\![A]\!]}$ is the step relation of $[\![A]\!]$ as defined in [10, page 112]. We write $\vdash_A$ for $\vdash_{[\![A]\!]}$. Declare also

$$Acc^A : \mathbb{W} \times \mathbb{N} \to \mathbb{B}$$

The intuition is that $Acc^A(w, n)$ holds iff $|w| = n$ and $w \in L(A)$.

Definition 3. Fix $q \in Q_A$ and $z \in Z_A$. Assume $\Delta_A(q, z)$ is

$$\{(q, z, \varphi_i, q_i, \boldsymbol{z}_i) \mid 1 \le i \le m\} \cup \{(q, z, \epsilon, q_i, \boldsymbol{z}_i) \mid m < i \le k\}.$$

Define

$$\begin{aligned}
ax^A &\stackrel{\text{def}}{=} \forall w\, n\, (Acc^A(w, n) \Leftrightarrow Acc_{q_{0A}}^A(w, n, [z_{0A}]))\\
ax_q^A &\stackrel{\text{def}}{=} \forall w\, n\, (Acc_q^A(w, n, \varepsilon) \Leftrightarrow (w = \varepsilon \wedge n = 0))\\
ax_{q,z}^A &\stackrel{\text{def}}{=} \forall w\, n\, s\, (Acc_q^A(w, n, [z|s]) \Leftrightarrow\\
&\qquad ((w \neq \varepsilon \wedge n > 0 \wedge (\bigvee_{i=1}^{m} (\varphi_i[hd(w)] \wedge Acc_{q_i}^A(tl(w), n{-}1, \boldsymbol{z}_i \cdot s))))\\
&\qquad \vee \bigvee_{j=m+1}^{k} Acc_{q_j}^A(w, n, \boldsymbol{z}_j \cdot s))) \qquad (6)\\
Th(A) &\stackrel{\text{def}}{=} \{ax^A\} \cup \{ax_q^A, ax_{q,z}^A \mid q \in Q_A, z \in Z_A\}.
\end{aligned}$$

Definition 4. An *ϵ-loop* of A is a derivation $(q, w, s) \vdash_A^+ (q, w, s')$ s.t. $|s| \le |s'|$.

Intuitively, an ϵ-loop is a derivation that does not consume any characters from the input word and starts and ends in the same state for some stacks that do not decrease in size. Note that an ϵ-loop can only involve ϵ-moves, since any nonepsilon move decreases the length of the input word by one. Define the binary relation $\vdash^{\epsilon}_{A}$: $((Q_A \times Z_A^*) \times (Q_A \times Z_A^*))$ called the *ϵ-step relation of A* as:

$$(q_1, s_1) \vdash^{\epsilon}_{A} (q_2, s_2) \stackrel{\text{def}}{=} (q_1, \varepsilon, s_1) \vdash_A (q_2, \varepsilon, s_2)$$

Lemma 1. *If A has no ϵ-loops then $\vdash^{\epsilon}_{A}$ is wellfounded.*

Proof. Assume A has no ϵ-loops and suppose, by contradiction, that there is an infinite chain $((q_i, s_i) \vdash^{\epsilon}_{A} (q_{i+1}, s_{i+1}))_{i<\omega}$. Since Q_A is finite, there is a fixed q and an infinite subset $I \subseteq \omega$ such that $q = q_i$ for $i \in I$ and $(q, \varepsilon, s_i) \vdash^{+}_{A} (q, \varepsilon, s_j)$ for $i, j \in I$ such that $i < j$. Since Z_A is finite and I is infinite, it follows that $|s_i| \leq |s_j|$ for some $i, j \in I$ where $i < j$, contradicting ϵ-loop-freeness of A. ⊠

Theorem 1. *Assume that $\vdash^{\epsilon}_{A}$ is wellfounded. For all $w \in \mathcal{U}^{\mathbb{W}}$ and $n \in \mathcal{U}^{\mathbb{N}}$:*

$$Th(A) \models Acc^A(w, n) \iff w \in L(A) \text{ and } |w| = n.$$

Proof. By using that $\vdash^{\epsilon}_{A}$ is wellfounded, define $(w_1, (q_1, s_1)) \succ (w_2, (q_2, s_2))$ as the *lexicographic order*: $|w_1| > |w_2|$ or, $|w_1| = |w_2|$ and $(q_1, s_1) \vdash^{\epsilon}_{A} (q_2, s_2)$.

For each axiom $ax_{q,z}$ in $Th(A)$ we show that each occurrence of Acc_p^A in the body of $ax_{q,z}$ is smaller wrt $\succ$ than the head of $ax_{q,z}$. For the cases when $w \neq \varepsilon$ we have that

$$(w, (q, [z|s])) \succ (tl(w), (q_i, \boldsymbol{z}_i \cdot s))$$

by using that $|w| > |tl(w)|$ according to the built-in theory of lists. For the case of the epsilon moves in (6) we have that

$$(w, (q, [z|s])) \succ (w, (q_j, \boldsymbol{z}_j \cdot s))$$

since $(q, \varepsilon, [z|s]) \vdash_A (q_j, \varepsilon, \boldsymbol{z}_j \cdot s)$ and thus $(q, [z|s]) \vdash^{\epsilon}_{A} (q_j, \boldsymbol{z}_j \cdot s)$.

It follows that the set of axioms is mathematically well-defined. We can now prove, by induction over the length of w that the following statement holds, which is also directly evident from the definitions. For all IDs (q, w, s) of $[\![A]\!]$:

$$\exists p \in Q_A((q, w, s) \vdash^{*}_{A} (p, \varepsilon, \varepsilon)) \iff Th(A) \models Acc_q^A(w, |w|, s).$$

Finally, let $q = q_{0A}$, $s = [z_{0A}]$ and use axiom ax^A. ⊠

In general, presence of ϵ-loops may imply that $\vdash^{\epsilon}_{A}$ is not wellfounded and the theorem fails, as illustrated by the following example. Moreover, for ϵSFAs, ϵ-loop-freeness is *equivalent* to $\vdash^{\epsilon}_{A}$ being wellfounded.

Example 1. Let $A = (\{q\}, \{z\}, q, z, \emptyset, \{(q, z, \epsilon, q, (z))\})$. For example $(q, \varepsilon, (z)) \vdash_A (q, \varepsilon, (z))$. The language accepted by A is empty. The theory $Th(A)$ for A includes the axiom $ax^A_{q,z}$: $\forall w\, n\, s\, (Acc_q^A(w, n, [z|s]) \Leftrightarrow Acc_q^A(w, n, [z|s]))$. This axiom is a useless tautology. Consider for example a model M with an interpretation for Acc_q^A such that $M \models Acc_q^A(\varepsilon, 0, (z))$ and expand M so that $M \models ax^A \wedge ax_q^A$. Then $M \models Acc^A(\varepsilon, 0)$ but $\varepsilon \notin L(A)$. ⊠

For ϵSFAs full epsilon elimination may cause quadratic increase in the number of moves, although the number of states may decrease. For ϵSPDAs the increase is even higher (although still polynomial) by using GNF transformation. For symbolic analysis this may create more complex axioms than needed and may reduce the performance considerably [18]. For ϵSFAs A we implemented *ϵ-loop-elimination* by using the following construction, that does not increse the number of moves. Recall the definition of *ϵ-closure*, denoted here by $\epsilon(q)$, as the closure of $\{q\}$ by ϵ-moves [10]. Similarly, define $\ni(q)$ as the closure of $\{q\}$ by ϵ-moves in reverse. Let $\widetilde{q} \stackrel{\text{def}}{=} \epsilon(q) \cap \ni(q)$ (note that $\{q\} \subseteq \widetilde{q}$) and let

$$\widetilde{A} \stackrel{\text{def}}{=} (\{\widetilde{q} \mid q \in Q_A\}, \varphi_{\Sigma A}, \{(\widetilde{q}, \varphi, \widetilde{p}) \mid (q, \varphi, p) \in \Delta_A\}, \widetilde{q_{0A}}, \{\widetilde{q} \mid q \in F_A\})$$

It is straightforward to show that $\widetilde{A}$ is ϵ-loop-free and equivalent to A. For ϵSPDAs we have not investigated specialized algorithms for ϵ-loop-elimination and resort to extended GNF (EGNF) transformation [3] that, translated into ϵSPDAs, allows some ϵ-moves but eliminates ϵ-loops.[1]

5 Difference Construction

We describe an algorithm that is used below for encoding difference constraints. The input to the algorithm consists of a clean SPDA A and a clean SFA B, and the output of the algorithm is a clean SPDA C that is equivalent to $A \times \overline{B}$, i.e., $L(C) = L(A) \setminus L(B)$. Thus, $L(C) = \emptyset$ iff $L(A) \subseteq L(B)$.

The general idea behind the algorithm is to incrementally determinize and complement B, and simultaneously compose it with A, while keeping the construction clean. During this process the SMT solver is used to generate all solutions to *cube* formulas that represent satisfiable combinations of move conditions for all moves from subsets of states of B that arise during determinization of B. Given a finite sequence of formulas $\boldsymbol{\varphi} = (\varphi_i)_{i<n}$ from $\mathcal{F}_{\mathbb{C}}$, and distinct Boolean constants $\boldsymbol{b} = (b_i)_{i<n}$ define

$$Cube(\boldsymbol{\varphi}, \boldsymbol{b}) \stackrel{\text{def}}{=} \bigwedge_{i<n} \varphi_i \Leftrightarrow b_i.$$

Recall that the variable χ is shared in all the φ_i. A *solution* of $Cube(\boldsymbol{\varphi}, \boldsymbol{b})$ is a model M such that $M \models \exists\chi\, Cube(\boldsymbol{\varphi}, \boldsymbol{b})$. In particular, M provides a truth assignment to all the b_i's. Given a set G of formulas we write $\bigvee G$ for the formula $\bigvee_{\varphi\in G} \varphi$, similarly for $\bigwedge G$. The following property follows by using basic model theory.

Proposition 1. *If M is a solution of $Cube(\boldsymbol{\varphi}, \boldsymbol{b})$ then $\bigwedge\{\varphi_i \mid i < n, M \models b_i\}$ is satisfiable.*

[1] Absence of ϵ-loops does not directly follow from the definition of EGNF that allows grammar productions of the form $A \to B$ where A and B are nonterminals, thus $A \to B$ and $B \to A$ would be allowed simultaneously. But the algorithm in [3] for converting a CFG to EGNF will not generate such circular productions.

Given a solution M of $\mathit{Cube}(\varphi, \boldsymbol{b})$, let φ_M denote the formula

$$\bigwedge(\{b_i \mid M \models b_i\} \cup \{\neg b_i \mid M \models \neg b_i\})$$

We use the following iterative model generation procedure to generate the set $\mathit{Solutions}(\mathit{Cube}(\varphi, \boldsymbol{b}))$ of all solutions of $\mathit{Cube}(\varphi, \boldsymbol{b})$.

1. Initially let $\mathbf{M} = \emptyset$.
2. Keep adding solutions of $\mathit{Cube}(\varphi, \boldsymbol{b})$ to $\mathbf{M}$ until $\mathit{Cube}(\varphi, \boldsymbol{b}) \wedge \bigwedge_{M \in \mathbf{M}} \neg\varphi_M$ is unsatisfiable.
3. Let $\mathit{Solutions}(\mathit{Cube}(\varphi, \boldsymbol{b})) = \mathbf{M}$.

The procedure is still exponential (in n) in the *worst case*, but seems to work well in practice. It is also better than creating all subsets of $\boldsymbol{\varphi}$ and filtering out all combinations that are unsatisfiable, which is *always* exponential.

The following property is used in the difference construction algorithm for generating all satisfiable subsets of move conditions for a given set of moves.

Proposition 2. *Let $\boldsymbol{\varphi}$ and $\boldsymbol{b}$ be as above. For all subsets G of $\boldsymbol{\varphi}$, $\bigwedge G$ is satisfiable if and only if there exists $M \in \mathit{Solutions}(\mathit{Cube}(\varphi, \boldsymbol{b}))$ such that $M \models b_i$ for all $\varphi_i \in G$.*

An SFA A is *total* if for all $q \in Q_A$, the formula $\forall\chi \bigvee\{\mathit{Cnd}(t) \mid t \in \Delta_A(q)\}$ is valid. In order to make an SFA that is not total into an equivalent total SFA, one can add a new *dead state* d to it with the move (d, true, d), and a new move (q, φ, d) from each state q where φ is satisfiable and $\varphi = \bigwedge\{\neg\mathit{Cnd}(t) \mid t \in \Delta(q)\}$. Clearly, determinism is preserved by this transformation. An SFA A is *determinisitic* if $[\![A]\!]$ is deterministic. Note that, it is easy to show that A is deterministic iff for all (p, φ_1, q_1) and (p, φ_2, q_2) in Δ_A, if $q_1 \neq q_2$ then $\varphi_1 \wedge \varphi_2$ is unsatisfiable. Given a total deterministic SFA A, the *complement* $\overline{A}$ of A is the deterministic SFA $(Q_A, q_{0A}, Q_A \setminus F_A, \Delta_A)$.

It is easy to see that for a total deterministic SFA A, $\overline{L(A)} = L(\overline{A})$. We use the following property of regular languages to speed up the difference construction in some cases, with a low initial overhead. For regular languages it is a well-known fact that reversing the language preserves regularity. Given an ϵSFA A with nonempty $L(A)$ and a state $q \notin Q_A$, the *reverse* A^r of A with initial state q is the ϵSFA

$$(Q_A \cup \{q\}, q, \{q_{0A}\}, \{(\mathit{Tgt}(t), \mathit{Cnd}(t), \mathit{Src}(t)) \mid t \in \Delta_A\} \cup \{(q, \epsilon, p) \mid p \in F_A\})$$

Given a word s let s^r denote the word that is s in reverse and let L^r denote the language $\{s^r \mid s \in L\}$. (Note that $L = (L^r)^r$.) It follows that $L(A^r) = L(A)^r$. We make use of the property $\overline{L(A)} = L(\overline{A^r})^r$.

The point of reversing is that complementation of an SFA A requires determinization that may cause exponential blowup in the size of the automaton, which can be avoided if A^r is deterministic. A classical example is the SFA A for the regex `[ab]*a[ab]{n}` where n is a positive integer. A has $n + 2$ states and the size of the minimum deterministic SFA for this regex has 2^{n+1} states, whereas A^r is deterministic.

We are now ready to describe the algorithm. Let A be an SPDA and B an SFA. Assume that A is clean and B is normalized, clean, and total.

Check the special cases first:

- If B is deterministic let $C = A \times \overline{B}$.
- Else, if A represents an SFA and B^r is deterministic let $C = (A^r \times \overline{B^r})^r$.

General case. We describe the algorithm as a depth-first-exploration algorithm using a stack S as a frontier, a set $V : (Q_A \times 2^{Q_B}) \times Z_A$ of visited elements, and a set T of moves. Initially, let $q_{0C} = \langle q_{0A}, \{q_{0B}\}\rangle$, $S = (\langle q_{0C}, z_{0A}\rangle)$, $V = \{\langle q_{0C}, z_{0A}\rangle\}$, and $T = \emptyset$.

(i) If S is empty go to (iv) else pop $\langle\langle p, \mathbf{q}\rangle, z\rangle$ from S.
(ii) Let $\Delta_A(p, z) = (p, z, \varphi_i, p_i, \boldsymbol{z}_i)_{i<m}$, $\Delta_B(\mathbf{q}) = (\_, \psi_i, q_i)_{i<n}$. Let $\boldsymbol{a} = (a_i)_{i<m}$ and $\boldsymbol{b} = (b_i)_{i<n}$ be fresh Boolean constants. Compute

$$\mathbf{M} = \mathit{Solutions}(\mathit{Cube}((\varphi_i)_{i<m} \cdot (\psi_i)_{i<n}, \boldsymbol{a} \cdot \boldsymbol{b}))$$

with the additional constraint that $\bigvee \boldsymbol{a}$ is true. For each move $(p, z, \varphi_i, p_i, \boldsymbol{z}_i)$ of A and for each solution M in $\mathbf{M}$ such that $M \models a_i$ do the following. Let

$$\gamma = \varphi_i \wedge \bigwedge(\{\psi_j \mid M \models b_j\} \cup \{\neg\psi_j \mid M \models \neg b_j\}), \quad \mathbf{q}' = \{q_j \mid M \models b_j\}.$$

Add the move $(\langle p, \mathbf{q}\rangle, z, \gamma, \langle p_i, \mathbf{q}'\rangle, \boldsymbol{z}_i)$ to T. For each $z' \in \boldsymbol{z}_i$ define $v = \langle\langle p_i, \mathbf{q}'\rangle, z'\rangle$, if $v \notin V$ then add v to V and if there exists $\rho \in \Delta_A$ such that $\mathit{Src}(\rho) = p'$ and $\mathit{Pop}(\rho) = z'$ then push v to S.
(iii) Go to (i).
(iv) Compute the set of final states $F = \{\langle p, \mathbf{q}\rangle \mid \langle p, \mathbf{q}\rangle \in \pi_1(V), p \in F_A, \mathbf{q} \cap F_B = \emptyset\}$. If $F = \emptyset$ let $C = (\{q_{0C}\}, \{z_{0A}\}, q_{0C}, z_{0A}, \emptyset, \emptyset)$, else let $C = (\pi_1(V), \pi_2(V), q_{0C}, z_{0A}, F, T)$.

The complementation of B in the algorithm is reflected in the computation of F where a state of C is final if its first component is a final A-state and its second component, that is a set of B-states, *includes no final B state.*

The totality of B is assumed in the computation of $\mathbf{M}$, where each solution will make at least one a_i and at least one b_j true. The totality assumption can be avoided by representing a "dead state" implicitly in the algorithm. The presentation of the algorithm gets technically more involved in this case.

To see that B is indeed incrementally determinized, consider any two moves

$$\rho_1 = (\mathbf{q}, \bigwedge_{M_1 \models b_j} \psi_j \wedge \bigwedge_{M_1 \models \neg b_j} \neg\psi_j, \{q_j \mid M_1 \models b_j\})$$

$$\rho_2 = (\mathbf{q}, \bigwedge_{M_2 \models b_j} \psi_j \wedge \bigwedge_{M_2 \models \neg b_j} \neg\psi_j, \{q_j \mid M_2 \models b_j\})$$

that are composed with moves of A and added to T in Step (ii), where $M_1, M_2 \in \mathbf{M}$. We need to show that if $\mathit{Tgt}(\rho_1) \neq \mathit{Tgt}(\rho_2)$ (i.e., for some b_j, $M_1 \models b_j$ and

$M_2 \models \neg b_j$), then $Cnd(\rho_1) \wedge Cnd(\rho_2)$ is unsatisfiable, which holds because there is at least one ψ_j such that ψ_j is a conjunct of $Cnd(\rho_1)$ and $\neg\psi_j$ is a conjunct of $Cnd(\rho_2)$.

The property that all possible satisfiable combinations of B-moves are considered in Step (ii) and that the composition with A-moves preserves satisfiability of the conditions of the moves added to T, follows from Proposition 2 and the added constraint that $\bigvee \boldsymbol{a}$ is true in the computation of $\mathbf{M}$.

Finally, note that if A represents an SFA then so does C.

5.1 Difference Checking

The difference algorithm has a more efficient version in the case when A above also represents an SFA and the purpose is to find a *single* witness in $L(A) \setminus L(B)$. In this case the explicit construction of $L(A) \setminus L(B)$ is not needed since $Th(L(A) \setminus L(B))$ is not needed. The checking of final states can be done when an element is popped from S and a "witness tree" can be incrementally updated (instead of T) that records links backwards from newly found target states to their source states. This algorithm has the same complexity as the full construction in the general case, but may finish sooner when $L(A) \setminus L(B)$ is nonempty.

6 Implementation

The algorithms and the axiom generation discussed above, have been implemented in a prototype tool for analyzing regular expressions and context free grammars. The SMT solver Z3 [6] is used for satisfiability checking and model generation. We use some features that are specific to Z3, including the integrated combination of decision procedures for algebraic data-types, integer linear arithmetic, bit-vectors and quantifier instantiation. We also make use of incremental features so that we can manipulate logical contexts while exploring different combinations of constraints. Use of algebraic data-types is central in the construction of the language acceptors, as was illustrated in Section 4. The definitions of the axioms match very closely with the implementation.

Working within a context enables *incremental* use of the solver. A context includes declarations for a set of symbols, assertions for a set of formulas, and the status of the last satisfiability check (if any). There is a *current context* and a backtrack stack of previous contexts. Contexts can be saved through *pushing* and restored through *popping*. The use of contexts is illustrated below

```
z3.Push(); //push a new context for collecting solutions
Term[] b = ...    //fresh Boolean constants for B-moves
Term[] a = ...    //fresh Boolean constants for A-moves
Term[] cube = ... //corresponding cube equations
z3.AssertCnstr(z3.MkAnd(cube)); //assert the cube formula
z3.AssertCnstr(z3.MkOr(a)); //at least one a[i] must hold
Model M;
while (z3.CheckAndGetModel(out M) != LBool.False) //get M
{
  AddToSolutions(M);                    //record M
  z3.AssertCnstr(Negate(M,a,b));        //exclude M
}
z3.Pop(); //return to the previous context
```

Table 1. Sample regexes

<table>
<tr><td>\w+([-+.]\w+)*@\w+([-.]\w+)*\.\w+([-.]\w+)*([,;]\s*\w+([-+.]\w+)*@\w+([-.]\w+)*\.\w+([-.]\w+)*)*</td></tr>
<tr><td>$?(\d{1,3},?(\d{3},?)*\d{3}(\.\d{0,2})?|\d{1,3}(\.\d{0,2})?|\.\d{1,2}?)</td></tr>
<tr><td>([A-Z]{2}|[a-z]{2} \d{2} [A-Z]{1,2}|[a-z]{1,2} \d{1,4})?([A-Z]{3}|[a-z]{3} \d{1,4})?</td></tr>
<tr><td>[A-Za-z0-9](([\.\-]?[a-zA-Z0-9]+)*)@([A-Za-z0-9]+)(([\.\-]?[a-zA-Z0-9]+)*)\. ([A-Za-z][A-Za-z]+)</td></tr>
<tr><td>(\w|-)+@((\w|-)+\.)+(\w|-)+</td></tr>
<tr><td>[+-]?([0-9]*\.?[0-9]+|[0-9]+\.?[0-9]*)([eE][+-]?[0-9]+)?</td></tr>
<tr><td>((\w|\d|\-|\.)+)@{1}(((\w|\d|\-){1,67})|((\w|\d|\-)+\.(\w|\d|\-){1,67}))\.((([a-z]|[A-Z]|\d){2,4})(\.([a-z] |[AZ]|\d){2})?)</td></tr>
<tr><td>(([A-Za-z0-9]+ +)|([A-Za-z0-9]+\-+)|([A-Za-z0-9]+\.+)|([A-Za-z0-9]+\++))*[A-Za-z0-9]+@((\w+\-+)|(\w+\.))*\w {1,63}\.[a-zA-Z]{2,6}</td></tr>
<tr><td>(([a-zA-Z0-9 \-\.]+)@([a-zA-Z0-9 \-\.]+)\.([a-zA-Z]{2,5}){1,25})+([;.](([a-zA-Z0-9 \-\.]+)@([a-zA-Z0-9 \-\.
]+)\.([a-zA-Z]{2,5}){1,25})+)*</td></tr>
<tr><td>((\w+([-+.]\w+)*@\w+([-.]\w+)*\.\w+([-.]\w+)*)\s*[,]{0,1}\s*)+</td></tr>
</table>

Table 2. Experiments. For $1 \leq i \leq 10$, A_i is a ϵSFA for the regex in row i in Table 1. *Time* is $\sum_{1 \leq i,j \leq 10, i \neq j} t_{i,j}$, where $t_{i,j}$ is the time to generate a member $x \in L(A_i) \backslash L(A_j)$ where $i \neq j$.

Experiment	*Time*	*Formulas checked by Z3*
direct encoding	15s	$Th(A_i) \wedge Th(A_j) \wedge Acc^{A_i}(x,k) \wedge \neg Acc^{A_j}(x,k)$
difference algorithm	60s	$Th(A_i \setminus A_j) \wedge Acc^{A_i \setminus A_j}(x,k)$
difference checking	10s	No axioms for the automata are asserted, but Z3 is used for solving cube formulas.

and shows a simplified code snippet from the tool responsible for computing *Solutions*(*Cube*($\varphi, \boldsymbol{b}$)) in the difference construction algorithm in Section 5, where the solutions are generated incrementally using a context, and the *model generation* feature is used to extract solutions from Z3.

7 Evaluation

We conducted several experiments where we evaluated the performance of the difference algorithm and the axiomatization approach.[2] The following experiments were run on a laptop with an Intel dual core T7500 2.2GHz processor. We used a collection of 10 complex regexes r_i extracted from a case study in [13] that are representative for various practical usages. Table 1 shows the samples. For several r_i the corresponding automaton A_i has thousands of states. In all cases, $A_i \setminus A_j$ for $i \neq j$ is nonempty. There are a total of 90 such combinations.

Experiments are shown in Table 2. The table does not reflect experiments where the set difference is empty (i.e. for the case $i = j$ but assuming that A_j is made slighltly different from A_i in $A_i \setminus A_j$ so that the theories are not identical but accept the same words): in this case the *direct* encoding diverges when A_i encodes an infinite language. In contrast, the *difference* constructions remain

[2] More details are available in [17].

robust, i.e., the construction of $A \setminus B$ terminates with the empty automaton when $A \setminus B$ is empty.

To our knowledge, a system that comes closest to the scope of ours is the open source string constraint solver Hampi [11]. We conducted a similar experiment using Hampi. Given the regexes r_i in Table 1, Hampi's input corresponding to the membership constraint $x \in L(r_i) \setminus L(r_j)$ is:

$$\texttt{var}\ x : l;\ \texttt{reg}\ a := R_i;\ \texttt{reg}\ b := R_2;\ \texttt{assert}\ x\ \texttt{in}\ a;\ \texttt{assert}\ x\ \texttt{not in}\ b;$$

where R_i is a Hampi representation of the regex r_i. The declaration $\texttt{var}\ x : l$ constrains the length of x to be l. Altough Hampi supports length ranges $\texttt{var}\ x : l_{lower} .. l_{upper}$ the range declaration caused segmentation faults in the underlying STP [7] solver, so we resorted to using the more restricted case. The experiment with using $l = 10$ took a toal of 2min to complete for the 90 cases. By setting $l = 15$, the experiment took 4min 30sec to complete. For values of $l < 10$, several of the membership constraints become unsatisfiable and fail to detect nonemptiness of $L(r_i) \setminus L(r_j)$. For example, for $l = 3$, the experiment took 1min and 30sec, but for most of the constraints the result was unsat.

8 Related Work

The work presented here is a nontrivial extension of the work started in [18] where different ϵSFA algorithms and their effect on language acceptors for ϵSFAs (including minimization and determinization) are studied. The experiments in [18] failed in determinization, which needed the idea of solving *cube* formulas. Moreover, the approach of language acceptors presented in [18] does not support precise length constraints, and the axioms were not studied for ϵSPDAs. Theorem 1 generalizes a similar statement for ϵSFAs in [18].

Although, an extension of FAs with predicates has been suggested earlier [21], we are not aware of similar results for PDAs that make the difference algorithm possible. We are also not aware of symbolic analysis with SMT being studied, based on such extensions.

The Hampi [11] tool, that is a string constraint solver, supports encoding of difference constraints $L(R_1) \setminus L(R_2)$ between regular expressions R_1 and R_2, where R_1 can be obtained as a finitization of a context free grammar. Unlike in our case, Hampi turns string constraints over fixed-size string variables into a query to STP [7]. STP is a solver for bit-vectors and arrays. The input size needs to be fixed, since STP does not support axioms or algebraic data types, and potential combination with other theories, e.g. linear arithmetic, is not in the scope of STP.

A decision procedure for subset constraints over regular language variables is introduced in [9] by reasoning over dependency graphs. In contrast, we showed how finite push-down automata can be generalized by making transitions symbolic, and how a decision procedure can be embedded into a background theory of an SMT solver.

Several decision problems related to CFGs are studied in [2] and depth-bounded versions thereof are mapped to SAT solving. In particular, an algorithm is provided for checking bounded version of ambiguity (whether a string has more than one parse tree in a given grammar) of CFGs, that provides an advantage over an algorithm in [15], by providing a *witness* in case of ambiguity. Using SMT and the approach presented here, an interesting direction for future work is to study extensions of symbolic acceptors based on *grammars* that capture *parse trees*, which is also related to symbolic acceptors for tree-automata. A parse tree can be represented with an algebraic data-type based on the productions of the grammar. Potentially, this approach can be used for ambiguity checking and in addition to providing a witness, avoids the need to provide a priori depth-bounds.

Several program analysis techniques for programs with strings [22,5,16,20] build on automata libraries [12,1] that efficiently handle transitions over sets of characters as either BDDs [4] or interval constraints. Most of those approaches suffer from the separation of the decision procedures that are not tightly coupled. Constraints over strings are decided by one solver, while constraints over other domains are decided by other solvers, but the solvers usually cannot be combined in an efficient, sound or complete fashion. SMT solvers directly address this problem by combining decision procedures for a variety of theories. Particular examples from applications involving strings are: symbolic analysis of SQL queries [19] and analysis of .NET programs [13].

9 Conclusion

We believe that the use of symbolic language acceptors as a purely logical description of formal languages and their mapping to state of the art SMT solving techniques opens up a new approach to analyzing and solving language theoretic problems in combination with automata theoretic techniques. We have demonstrated the scalability of the technique on solving extended regular constraints, that have direct applications in static analysis, testing, and database query analysis.

Acknowledgement. The Hampi comparison in Section 7 would not have been possible without the help of *Pieter Hooimeijer* who set up the whole environment for the experiment and provided scripts for converting the regexes in Table 1 to Hampi format.

References

1. BRICS finite state automata utilities, `http://www.brics.dk/automaton/`
2. Axelsson, R., Heljanko, K., Lange, M.: Analyzing context-free grammars using an incremental SAT solver. In: Aceto, L., Damgård, I., Goldberg, L.A., Halldórsson, M.M., Ingólfsdóttir, A., Walukiewicz, I. (eds.) ICALP 2008, Part II. LNCS, vol. 5126, pp. 410–422. Springer, Heidelberg (2008)

3. Blum, N., Koch, R.: Greibach Normal Form Transformation Revisited. Inf. Comput. 150(1), 112–118 (1999)
4. Brace, K.S., Rudell, R.L., Bryant, R.E.: Efficient implementation of a BDD package. In: DAC 1990, pp. 40–45. ACM, New York (1990)
5. Christensen, A.S., Møller, A., Schwartzbach, M.I.: Precise Analysis of String Expressions. In: Cousot, R. (ed.) SAS 2003. LNCS, vol. 2694, pp. 1–18. Springer, Heidelberg (2003)
6. de Moura, L., Bjørner, N.: Z3: An Efficient SMT Solver. In: Ramakrishnan, C.R., Rehof, J. (eds.) TACAS 2008. LNCS, vol. TACAS 2008, pp. 337–340. Springer, Heidelberg (2008)
7. Ganesh, V., Dill, D.L.: A Decision Procedure for Bit-Vectors and Arrays. In: Damm, W., Hermanns, H. (eds.) CAV 2007. LNCS, vol. 4590, pp. 519–531. Springer, Heidelberg (2007)
8. Hodges, W.: Model theory. Cambridge Univ. Press, Cambridge (1995)
9. Hooimeijer, P., Weimer, W.: A decision procedure for subset constraints over regular languages. In: PLDI, pp. 188–198 (2009)
10. Hopcroft, J.E., Ullman, J.D.: Introduction to Automata Theory, Languages, and Computation. Addison-Wesley, Reading (1979)
11. Kiezun, A., Ganesh, V., Guo, P.J., Hooimeijer, P., Ernst, M.D.: HAMPI: a solver for string constraints. In: ISSTA 2009, pp. 105–116. ACM, New York (2009)
12. Klarlund, N.: Mona & Fido: The Logic-Automaton Connection in Practice. In: Nielsen, M. (ed.) CSL 1997. LNCS, vol. 1414, pp. 311–326. Springer, Heidelberg (1998)
13. Li, N., Xie, T., Tillmann, N., de Halleux, P., Schulte, W.: Reggae: Automated test generation for programs using complex regular expressions. In: ASE 2009 (2009)
14. MSDN. .NET Framework Regular Expressions (2009), `http://msdn.microsoft.com/en-us/library/hs600312.aspx`
15. Schmitz, S.: Conservative ambiguity detection in context-free grammars. In: Arge, L., Cachin, C., Jurdziński, T., Tarlecki, A. (eds.) ICALP 2007. LNCS, vol. 4596, pp. 692–703. Springer, Heidelberg (2007)
16. Shannon, D., Hajra, S., Lee, A., Zhan, D., Khurshid, S.: Abstracting Symbolic Execution with String Analysis. In: MUTATION 2007, pp. 13–22. IEEE, Los Alamitos (2007)
17. Veanes, M., Bjørner, N., de Moura, L.: Solving extended regular constraints symbolically. Technical Report MSR-TR-2009-177, Microsoft Research (2009)
18. Veanes, M., de Halleux, P., Tillmann, N.: Rex: Symbolic Regular Expression Explorer. In: ICST 2010, IEEE, Los Alamitos (2010)
19. Veanes, M., Tillmann, N., de Halleux, J.: Qex: Symbolic SQL query explorer. In: LPAR-16. LNCS (LNAI). Springer, Heidelberg (2010)
20. Wassermann, G., Gould, C., Su, Z., Devanbu, P.: Static checking of dynamically generated queries in database applications. ACM TSEM 16(4), 14 (2007)
21. Watson, B.W.: chapter Implementing and using finite automata toolkits, pp. 19–36. Cambridge U. Press, Cambridge (1999)
22. Yu, F., Bultan, T., Cova, M., Ibarra, O.H.: Symbolic String Verification: An Automata-Based Approach. In: Havelund, K., Majumdar, R., Palsberg, J. (eds.) SPIN 2008. LNCS, vol. 5156, pp. 306–324. Springer, Heidelberg (2008)
23. Yu, F., Bultan, T., Ibarra, O.H.: Symbolic String Verification: Combining String Analysis and Size Analysis. In: Kowlaewski, S., Philippou, A. (eds.) TACAS 2009. LNCS, vol. 5505, pp. 322–336. Springer, Heidelberg (2009)

Author Index

GPSR Compliance

The European Union's (EU) General Product Safety Regulation (GPSR) is a set of rules that requires consumer products to be safe and our obligations to ensure this.

If you have any concerns about our products, you can contact us on ProductSafety@springernature.com

In case Publisher is established outside the EU, the EU authorized representative is:

Springer Nature Customer Service Center GmbH
Europaplatz 3
69115 Heidelberg, Germany

Batch number: 10704691

Printed by Printforce, the Netherlands